South India

THE ROUGH GUIDE

written and researched by

David Abram, Devdan Sen, Nick Edwards, Beth Wooldridge and Mike Ford

THE ROUGH GUIDES

THE ROUGH GUIDES

TRAVEL GUIDES • PHRASEBOOKS • MUSIC AND REFERENCE GUIDES

We set out to do something different when the first Rough Guide was published in 1982. Mark Ellingham, just out of university, was travelling in Greece. He brought along the popular guides of the day, but found they were all lacking in some way. They were either strong on ruins and museums but went on for pages without mentioning a beach or taverna. Or they were so conscious of the need to save money that they lost sight of Greece's cultural and historical significance. Also, none of the books told him anything about Greece's contemporary life – its politics, its culture, its people, and how they lived.

So with no job in prospect, Mark decided to write his own guidebook, one which aimed to provide practical information that was second to none, detailing the best beaches and the hottest clubs and restaurants, while also giving hard-hitting accounts of every sight, both famous and obscure, and providing up-to-the-minute information on contemporary culture. It was a guide that encouraged independent travellers to find the best of Greece, and was a great success, getting shortlisted for the Thomas Cook travel guide award, and encouraging Mark, along with three friends, to expand the series.

The Rough Guide list grew rapidly and the letters flooded in, indicating a much broader readership than had been anticipated, but one which uniformly appreciated the Rough Guide mix of practical detail and humour, irreverence and enthusiasm. Things haven't changed. The same four friends who began the series are still the caretakers of the Rough Guide mission today: to provide the most reliable, up-to-date and entertaining information to independent-minded travellers of all ages, on all budgets.

We now publish more than 150 titles and have offices in London and New York. The travel guides are written and researched by a dedicated team of more than 100 authors, based in Britain, Europe, the USA and Australia. We have also created a unique series of phrasebooks to accompany the travel series, along with an acclaimed series of music guides, and a best-selling pocket guide to the Internet and World Wide Web. We also publish comprehensive travel information on our Web site:

www.roughguides.com

HELP US UPDATE

We've gone to a lot of effort to ensure that the first edition of The Rough Guide to South India is accurate and up-to-date. However, things change – places get "discovered", opening hours are notoriously fickle, restaurants and rooms raise prices or lower standards. If you feel we've got it wrong or left something out, we'd like to know, and if you can remember the address, the price, the time, the phone number, so much the better.

We'll credit all contributions, and send a copy of the next edition (or any other Rough Guide if you prefer) for the best letters. Please mark letters: "Rough Guide South India Update" and send to:

Rough Guides, 62–70 Shorts Gardens, London WC2H 9AB, or
Rough Guides, 375 Hudson St, New York NY 10014.
Or send email to: mail@roughguides.co.uk
Online updates about this book can be found on Rough Guides' Web site at www.roughguides.com

THE AUTHORS

David Abram, born in Cardiff, Wales, first travelled to India in 1983 before going to the University of Warwick, where he read French and European Literature. Subsequent travels have taken him as an English teacher to various southern European countries, as an anthropologist to a Native American reservation in the US, and as a Rough Guide author to Goa, the Scottish Highlands, Corsica and England. These days, however, he finds himself equally content to stay at home in Barrow Gurney, near Bristol, playing clarinet to his Django Reinhardt CDs and performing with a local swing group.

Devdan Sen, born in West Bengal, travelled extensively in his own country and studied Indian classical music for several years before leaving to study at the School of Oriental and African Studies in London. He is now based in Surrey, England, though writing, climbing and photography give him plenty of excuses to get back to India as much as possible.

Nick Edwards was born in 1957 and grew up in South London before studying Classics and Modern Greek at Oxford. The Hellenic connection led to him spending most of the eighties teaching English in Athens. He now divides his time between EFL examining in Greece and London, Rough Guide trips to Greece and India and a new marital home with Maria in Pittsburgh. Other enduring loves are Spurs, alternative music and esoteric philosophy.

Beth Wooldridge grew up in Kenya, South Africa and London. She studied Anthropology and History at Swansea University, and since graduating has lived in India, travel writing and working at the UNHCR in Delhi. Currently studying for a Masters degree at the School of Oriental and African Studies in the UK, she returns home to India as often as possible.

Mike Ford has been meandering through Asia for seven years and first visited India in 1985. He has returned several times since, drawn by the madness, mayhem, *chai* stalls, and Himalayan heights, and considers India as his second home. He is a keen photographer and has staged several exhibitions in England. In the early 1990s he led a fundraising expedition across the Indian Himalaya to raise money for primary healthcare projects in India. In between travel assignments Mike teaches English as a Foreign Language and is a keen *tabla* student, playing classical Indian and fusion music from his base in Bristol.

ACKNOWLEDGEMENTS

David: Thanks to the office of the Deputy Director of Indian Airlines, New Delhi, for getting us out of Port Blair in a medical emergency; Catherine Lyons, for hotmailing those Kodaikanal trekking tips; and Juliette, Pretti, Manisha and Justin in Madurai. For friendship, hospitality and help, thank you to: Ajit Sukija (Goa); Shelly, Teresa and family (Goa); G Ramesh (Chennai); Nalini Chettur (Giggles Bookshop, Chennai); Raj and Pushpa in Coonoor, who fixed my mangled toe; and Thea Owen (Tiruvannamalai).

Devdan: Thanks to the Department of Tourism Government of India, the Department of Tourism Government of Karnataka, the Kerala Tourism Development Corporation, Jet Airways, Air India. I would specially like to thank: Pauleen, J.C. Mahtab and his entire family, Rajni Swaminadhan, Gracy Thomas, Sanjay Singh, Dr A. Jayathilak IAS, Mr Veerabhadrachari IAS, B. Shivananda Aradhya, Janaki Umesh Narayan, P.J. Varghese, S. Boregowda, K.S. Shivalingappa, P.G. Gautam, M. Srinagesh Hegde, S.G. Hegde and Mr Dharmapal.

Nick: Thanks to all the staff of the APTDC, Hyderabad. Special thanks for expert malaria treatment to Drs Dubey, Bhushan, Hajela and all the staff of the Hajela Hospital, Bhopal. Ta to Auntie Dos for constant support. Finally, a heart-felt thank you to Maria for constant inspiration and use of the Mac in a warm place.

Beth: Thanks to Mum, Dad, Zig and Soph, Annie, Louise and Martin; you were all stars with your support and advice, whatever the distance. Thank you also to Babuji and Meena, Lisa, Nigel, Kulpreet, and Simran – the Delhi *wallahs*. Sam, Adrian and Alex, your support was invaluable, as was the help of the MTDC (Mumbai and Aurangabad). For the kind assistance of Ramdut Tripathi, Mr Yadav (Aurangabad), Dr Bhoir (Mumbai), Mr Singh of the Government of India Tourist Board, Nomad's Travel Store (London) and Jet Airways, thank you.

Mike: Thanks to Mrs Roma Singh in Delhi and Mr Sharad Kirane in Mumbai. Thanks also to Thinley and Tashi, Mark and Helen, Robert, Deana and to many friends in Bristol and beyond. In memory of Mick Smart, a longtime travelling companion and friend. Om shanti.

CONTENTS

South India

THE ROUGH GUIDE

There are more than one hundred and fifty Rough Guide titles covering destinations from Amsterdam to Zimbabwe

Forthcoming titles include

Croatia • Cuba • Las Vegas • Rome • Switzerland

Rough Guide Reference Series

Classical Music • Drum 'n' Bass • European Football • House
The Internet • Jazz • Music USA • Opera • Reggae • Rock
World Music

Rough Guide Phrasebooks

Czech • Dutch • Egyptian Arabic • European • French • German • Greek
Hindi & Urdu • Hungarian • Indonesian • Italian • Japanese
Mandarin Chinese • Mexican Spanish • Polish • Portuguese • Russian
Spanish • Swahili • Thai • Turkish • Vietnamese

ROUGH GUIDE CREDITS

Text editors: Lisa Nellis, Martin Dunford
Series editor: Mark Ellingham
Editorial: Martin Dunford, Jonathan Buckley, Jo Mead, Kate Berens, Amanda Tomlin, Ann-Marie Shaw, Paul Gray, Helena Smith, Judith Bamber, Orla Duane, Olivia Eccleshall, Ruth Blackmore, Sophie Martin, Geoff Howard, Claire Saunders, Gavin Thomas, Alexander Mark Rogers, Polly Thomas, Joe Staines, Andrew Tomičić, Richard Lim, Claire Fogg (UK); Andrew Rosenberg, Mary Beth Maioli (US)
Cartography: Maxine Repath, Nichola Goodliffe, Ed Wright, Stratigraphics
Production: Susanne Hillen, Andy Hilliard, Link Hall, Helen Ostick, Julia Bovis, Michelle Draycott, Anna Wray, Katie Pringle, Robert Evers
Picture research: Louise Boulton, Catherine Marshall
Online editors: Kate Hands (UK); Kelly Cross (US)
Finance: John Fisher, Gary Singh, Ed Downey, Mark Hall
Marketing & Publicity: Richard Trillo, Niki Smith, David Wearn, Jemima Broadbridge (UK); Jean-Marie Kelly, Simon Carloss, Myra Campolo (US)
Administration: Tania Hummel, Charlotte Marriott, Demelza Dallow, Francisca Kellett

ACKNOWLEDGEMENTS

A collective thank you from all the authors to Jo Mead, who set this book up, and Lisa Nellis, who edited it with unflagging good humour through a hot summer. Thanks also to Robert Evers for patient typesetting; Maxine Repath, Ed Wright and Stratigraphics for clear-headed cartography and Jennifer Speake for eagle-eyed proofreading. Additional thanks to Susanne Hillen, Martin Dunford and Francisca Kellett. Significant sections of this title have been adapted from material written for previous editions of the Rough Guide to India by Gareth John Williams and Harriet Podger; without their enduringly valuable contributions our task would have been much harder.

For individual author acknowledgements, see p.v

PUBLISHING INFORMATION

This first edition published November 1999 by Rough Guides Ltd, 62–70 Shorts Gardens, London, WC2H 9AB.
Distributed by the Penguin Group:
Penguin Books Ltd, 27 Wrights Lane, London W8 5TZ
Penguin Books USA Inc., 375 Hudson Street, New York 10014, USA
Penguin Books Australia Ltd, 487 Maroondah Highway, PO Box 257, Ringwood, Victoria 3134, Australia
Penguin Books Canada Ltd, 10 Alcorn Avenue, Toronto, Ontario, Canada M4V 1E4
Penguin Books (NZ) Ltd, 182–190 Wairau Road, Auckland 10, New Zealand
Typeset in Linotron Univers and Century Old Style to an original design by Andrew Oliver.
Printed at Clays Ltd, St Ives PLC

656pp – Includes index
A catalogue record for this book is available from the British Library
ISBN 1-85828-469-4

• CHAPTER 3: KARNATAKA 179–273

• CHAPTER 4: KERALA 274–366

• CHAPTER 5: CHENNAI (MADRAS) 367–392

• CHAPTER 6: TAMIL NADU 393–498

• CHAPTER 7: ANDHRA PRADESH 499–520

• CHAPTER 8: THE ANDAMAN ISLANDS 521–541

PART THREE CONTEXTS 543

LIST OF MAPS

MAP SYMBOLS

REGIONAL MAPS

- Railway
- Main road
- Minor road
- Track or trail
- River
- Ferry
- International boundary
- State boundary
- Chapter division boundary
- Mountains
- Peak
- Pass
- Rocks
- Waterfall
- Viewpoint
- Mudflats
- Marshland
- Beach
- Church
- Place of interest
- Airport
- Lighthouse

STREET MAPS

- Railway
- Main road
- Secondary road
- Lane
- Track
- Path
- Steps
- River
- Wall
- Accommodation
- Restaurant
- Building
- Church
- Tourist office
- Post office
- Telephone
- Hospital
- Public transport stand
- Football pitch
- Parking

COMMON SYMBOLS

- Mosque or Muslim monument
- Hindu or Jain temple
- Ghat
- Park

INTRODUCTION

Though its borders are uncertain, there's no doubt that **South India**, the tapering tropical half of this mighty peninsula, differs radically from the landlocked north. Stepping off a winter flight from foggy Delhi into the glasshouse humidity of Chennai (Madras) or Thiruvanathapuram (Trivandrum), you enter a world far removed from the muted hues of Punjab and the great Indian river plains. In the south, the coconut groves seem a deeper green and the rice paddy positively luminescent, the faces darker brown and the vermilion caste marks smeared over them arrestingly red. The region's heavy rainfall means that lush wheatfields and palm plantations patchwork the sun-bleached volcanic soils during all but the hottest months. But under a sun whose rays feel concentrated by a giant magnifying glass, the ubiquitous colours of South India – of silk saris, shimmering classical dance costumes, roadside film posters and frangipani flowers – radiate with a life of their own. It is easy to see why Alexander Frater, faced with the shirt-drenching pre-monsoonal heat of southern Kerala, thought that at any moment "...with a whoosh and a muffled whump, the whole place must spontaneously ignite."

South India's three mightiest rivers – the Godavari, the Krishna and the Kaveri – and their countless tributaries, flow east across a low, fertile alluvial basin that has been inhabited as long as anywhere in the subcontinent. Separated from the prehistoric Indus valley civilizations of the northwest by tracts of barren hills, the earliest South Indian societies are thought to have evolved independently of their northern cousins. Periodic invasions – from the marauding Muslims whose descendants would later erect the Taj Mahal, to the evangelizing, pepper-hungry Portuguese and ineffectual French – left their marks on the territory referred to in some of India's oldest inscriptions as **Dravidadesa**, "Land of the Tamils". None, however, not even the ruthlessly efficient British, ever fully subjugated the south. As a result, traditions, languages and ways of life have endured intact here for more than two thousand years – a fact that lends to any journey into the region a unique resonance.

The persistence of a distinctly Dravidian culture in part accounts for the **regionalism** that has increasingly dominated the political and cultural life of the South since Independence in 1947. With the exception of Goa, a former Portuguese colony, and the Andaman and Nicobar Islands, the borders of the states covered in this book – Karnataka, Kerala, Tamil Nadu and Andhra Pradesh – were drawn along linguistic lines. Each boasts its own distinctive styles of music, dance, architecture and cuisine, not to mention religious cults, dress and mutually incomprehensible languages. Moreover, attempts by New Delhi to homogenize the country by imposing Hindi, the most widely spoken language in the North, as the medium of education and government, have consistently met with resistance, stimulating support for the regional parties whose larger-than-life leaders beam munificently from giant hoardings in every major town and city.

More pervasive even than the power of politics in South India is the influence of **religion**, which, despite the country's resolutely secular constitution, still permeates every aspect of life. Of the four major faiths, **Hinduism** is by far the most prevalent, practised by around eighty percent of the population. If the sacred peaks of the Himalaya are Hinduism's head, and the Ganges its main artery, then the temple complexes of the South are its spiritual heart and soul. Soaring high above every skyline, their colossal towers are emblematic of the awe with which the deities enshrined inside them have been held for centuries. Some, like the Shore temple at Tiruchendur in Tamil Nadu, are thought to be as old as human speech itself; others, such as the Sabarimala forest shrine in Kerala are less ancient, but attract greater numbers of pilgrims than even

PAKISTAN
HARYANA
Moradabad
TIBET
DELHI
NEPAL
Bikaner
UTTAR
PRADESH
Ganges
RAJASTHAN
Jaisalmer
Agra
KATHMANDU
Lucknow
Jaipur
Kanpur
Jodhpur
Patna
Jhansi
Yamuna
Varanasi
Allahabad
Udaipur
Gaya
BIHAR
GUJARAT
Ujjain
Ahmedabad
Bhopal
Indore
MADHYA PRADESH
Vadodara
Rajkot
Raipur
Surat
Nagpur
ORISSA
Bhusawal
Puri
Mumbai
(Bombay)
MAHARASHTRA
Pune
Warangal
Vishakapatnam
Hyderabad
BAY OF
BENGAL
ANDHRA
PRADESH
Badami
Vijayawada
Panjim
GOA
Vijayanagar
(Hampi)
ARABIAN
SEA
KARNATAKA
Tirupati
Halebid
Belur
Bangalore
Chennai
(Madras)
Mangalore
Kanchipuram
Mamallapuram
Mysore
Pondicherry
Port Blair
LAKSHADWEEP
TAMIL
NADU
Tiruchirapalli
KERALA
Thanjavur
Madurai
Andaman Islands
(950 km due east)
Kochi
N
Rameshwaram
Kollam
Thiruvananthapuram
Kovalam
Kanniyakumari
INDIAN
OCEAN
SRI
LANKA
COLOMBO
0
400 km
The international boundaries on this map are purported to be neither correct nor authoritative by Survey of India directives. Publisher.

Mecca. For foreign visitors, however, the most extraordinary of all have to be the colossal Chola shrines of Tamil Nadu. Joining the crowds that stream through Madurai's Meenakshi-Sundareshwar temple or Shri Ramalingeshwara in Rameshwaram, will take you to the very taproot of the world's last surviving classical culture, some of whose hymns, prayers and rites predate the Egyptian pyramids.

By comparison, **Islam**, South India's second religion, is a fledgling faith, first introduced by Arab traders along the coast. Later, offshoots of the Muslim dynasties that ruled the North carved out feudal kingdoms beyond the Godavari, establishing a band of Islamic culture across the middle of the Deccan plateau. Other elements in the great South Indian melting pot include a dozen or more denominations of **Christianity**, ranging from the ancient Syrian Orthodoxy believed to have been introduced by the apostle St Thomas, to the Roman Catholicism of Old Goa's Portuguese Jesuits. The region also harbours sites sacred to **Jains**, followers of the prophet Mahavira, a contemporary of Buddha, while in Kochi, Kerala, a vestigial population of elderly **Jews** is all that remains of a once thriving mercantile community.

Since Independence, these diverse groups have coexisted more or less peacefully, rarely succumbing to the waves of communal blood-letting that have often blighted life in the northern cities. Over the past five or six years, supposedly as a reaction to the rise of Hindu extremist parties, bombs and riots have erupted around the Muslim ghettos of Mumbai (Bombay) and Coimbatore (in western Tamil Nadu), but these are widely held as isolated flare-ups rather than a growing trend. The last decade has seen a dramatic rise in **caste violence**, however. The age-old hierarchy introduced by the Aryans more than three thousand years ago still forms the backbone of South Indian society, crossing all religious and ethnic divides. But recent political reforms have enabled members of disadvantaged minorities to claim a fairer share of government jobs and university places, as well as political posts (the current president of India is of low-caste South Indian origin), and this has generated widespread resentment, strengthening the very divisions positive discrimination was intended to dissolve.

South India, though, remains one of the most relaxed and congenial parts of Asia to explore. It is also among the easiest. In all but the remotest districts, **accommodation** is plentiful, clean and inexpensive by Western standards. Freshly cooked, nutritious **food** is nearly always available. **Getting around** is usually straightforward, although the sheer size and problematic geography of the South means journeys can be long. The region's extensive rail network is a miraculous feat, moving vast numbers of people at all times of the day and night, and if a train isn't heading where you want to go, a bus probably will be. Furthermore, the widespread use of English makes communication easy. South Indians are the most garrulous and inquisitive of travellers, and train rides are always enlivened by conversations that invariably begin with the refrain of "Coming from?" or "Your native place?"

The extent to which you enjoy travelling in South India will probably depend less on your luck with hotels, restaurants and transport than your reaction to the country itself. Many people expect some kind of exotic time warp, and are indignant to find a consumer culture that's as unashamedly materialistic as anywhere. It is a credit to the South Indians' legendary capacity for assimilating new ideas, however, that both the modern and traditional thrive side by side. Walking through downtown Bangalore, you could brush shoulders with a software programmer one moment and a saffron-clad ascetic the next, while bullock carts and stray cattle mingle with Japanese hatchbacks. There are, of course, the usual travel hassles: interminable queues, packed buses and constant encroachments on your personal space. Yet, just when your nerves feel stretched to breaking point, South India always offers something that makes the effort worthwhile: a glimpse of a wild elephant from a train window; a sumptuous vegetarian meal delicately arranged on a fresh banana leaf; or a hint of fragrant cardamom in your tea after an all-night Kathakali recital.

Where to go

South India's boundaries vary according to who you're talking to: while some regard the Krishna River, the upper limit of India's last Hindu empire, as the real North–South divide, others place the subcontinent's main cultural fault line at the Godavari River, or further north still, at the Vindhya Hills, the barrier of arid table-topped mountains bounding the Ganges Basin. In this guide we've started with **Mumbai (Bombay)**, a hot, congested and seedy city that is the arrival point for most international flights. Mumbai gets a pretty bad press, and most people pass straight through. But those who stay find themselves witness to the reality of modern-day India, from the deprivations of the city's slum-dwellings to the glitz and glamour of Bollywood movies.

The other principal gateway is **Chennai (Madras)**, capital of **Tamil Nadu**, in the deep south, which is a slightly less stressful point of entry. Although it's another major metropolis bursting at the seams, hidden under its congested surface are artful gems such as regular public performances of music and dance. With regular flights and ship departures to **Port Blair**, Chennai is also the principal springboard for the **Andaman Islands**, a remote archipelago ringed by coral reefs and crystal-clear seas, 1000km east of the mainland in the Bay of Bengal.

The majority of visitors' first stop after Chennai is **Mamallapuram**, an ancient port littered with weather-worn sculpture sites, including the famous Shore temple. To get right off the beaten track you only have to head inland to **Kanchipuram**, whose innumerable Hindu shrines span the golden age of the illustrious Chola kingdom, or to **Tiruvannamalai**, where one of the region's most massive temple complexes rises dramatically from the base of a sacred mountain, site of countless ashrams and meditation caves. Back on the coast, the former French colony of **Pondicherry** retains a distinctly Gallic feel, particularly in its restaurants, where you can order *coq au vin* and bottles of burgundy before a stroll along the promenade. The **Kaveri** (Cauvery) **Delta**, further south, harbours astonishing crops of monuments, some of the most impressive of which are around **Thanjavur (Tanjore)**, the Cholas' former capital, dominated by the awesome Brihadishwara temple. You could profitably spend days exploring the town's watery hinterland, hunting out bronze-casting villages, crumbling ruins and other forgotten sacred sites among the web of rivers and irrigation canals. Most travellers press on south to **Madurai**, the region's most atmospherically charged city, where the mighty Meenakshi-Sundareshwar temple presides over a quintessentially Tamil swirl of life.

The two other most compelling destinations in Tamil Nadu are the island of **Rameshwaram**, whose main temple features a vast enclosure of pillared corridors, and **Kannyakumari**, the auspicious southernmost tip of India, where the Bay of Bengal, Indian Ocean and Arabian Sea flow together. The dark shadows visible on the horizon from here mark the start of the **Western Ghats**, which stretch for more than 1000km in a virtually unbroken chain all the way to Mumbai, forming a sheer barrier between Tamil Nadu and neighbouring Kerala. Covered in immense forests and windswept grasslands, the mountains rise to the highest peaks in peninsular India, with sides sculpted by tea terraces, coffee plantations and cardamom groves. The hill stations of **Udhagamandalam** (or **Ooty**, as it's still better known) and **Kodaikanal**, established by India's former colonial rulers as retreats from the searing summer heat of the plains, attract hordes of Indian visitors in the run-up to the rains, but see plenty of foreign tourist traffic during the winter, too.

Neighbouring **Kerala**'s appeal lies less in its religious monuments, many of which remain off-limits to non-Hindus, than its infectiously easy-going, tropical ambience. Covering a long thin coastal strip backed by a steep wall of hills, this is the wettest and most densely populated state in the south. It is also the most distinctive, with a culture that sets it squarely apart. Its surreal form of ritualized theatre (Kathakali), faintly

Southeast Asian architecture and ubiquitous communist graffiti (Kerala was the first place in the world to gain a democratically elected communist government), are perhaps the most visual expressions of this difference. But spend a couple of days exploring the spicy backstreets of old **Kochi** (Cochin), the jungles of the Cardamom Hills around the **Periyar Wildlife Sanctuary** or the hidden aquatic world of the coastal **backwaters**, and you'll see why many travellers end up staying here a lot longer than they originally intended. If you're not pushed for time and find yourself crossing northern Kerala during the winter, set aside a few days to search for Teyyam, a spectacular masked dance form unique to the villages around **Kannur**.

A short ride across the mountains takes you to **Mysore**, in **Karnataka**, whose opulent maharaja's palace, colourful markets and comfortable California-like climate have made it among South India's most popular tourist destinations. Bangalore, the hectic modern capital, is not one of the highlights of the state, which are for the main part scattered over a vast area of rolling, granite-boulder-strewn uplands. Most, such as the richly carved Hoysala temples of **Belur** and **Halebid**, or the extraordinary Jain colossus at **Sravanabelgola**, are religious monuments. Amongst other extraordinary sights are the mausolea, mosques and Persian-style palaces of **Bijapur**, Karnataka, often dubbed the "Agra of the South". Almost unsurpassable, however, is the awesome scale and faded splendour of the Vijayangar ruins at **Hampi**, on the Tungabhadra River. Until it was ransacked by a confederacy of Muslim Sultanates in 1565, this was the magnificent capital of South India's last Hindu empire, encompassing most of the peninsula.

Only one day's journey to the west, the palm-fringed, white-sand beaches of **Goa** offer a change of scenery from the rocky terrain of the Deccan. Succumbing to the hedonistic pleasures of warm sea water, constant sunshine and cheap drinks, many travellers find it hard to tear themselves away from the coast. Further east, a string of smaller former dynastic capitals punctuate the journey across the heart of the Deccan plateau to **Hyderabad**, capital of **Andhra Pradesh**, whose principal landmarks are the Charminar and Golconda fort. Andhra's other attractions, by contrast, lie much further off the beaten track. Comparatively few Western visitors ever reach them, but **Puttaparthy**, the ashram of India's most famous living saint, Sai Baba, and **Tirupati**, whose temple receives more pilgrims than anywhere else on earth, are essential stops for South Indians.

When to go

The relentless tropical sun aside, the source of South India's irrepressible fecundity lies in its high **rainfall**. Unlike the north of the country, which sees only a single deluge in the summer, most of peninsular India receives two annual monsoons – one sucked in from the Arabian Sea in the southwest, and the other on stormy northwesterly winds off the Bay of Bengal. The heaviest rains are reserved for the Western Ghats, a chain of mountains running parallel with the southwest coast. Cloaked for the most part in dense forest, these form a curtain that impedes the path of the first summer monsoon, which breaks in June and lasts through October.

In a nutshell, you should, when planning a trip to South India, avoid the rainy seasons. The novelty of torrential downpours and the general mayhem that attend the annual deluges wears off very quickly. Road blockages, landslides and burst river banks can interrupt the best-laid travel plans, not to mention the discomfort of being wet through for days on end; the widespread flooding is also none too healthy, emptying the sewers and polluting reservoirs. Broadly speaking, rule out the period between **April** and **September**, when the southwest monsoon is in full swing across the whole peninsula. From **late October** until **April**, the weather is perfect in Karnataka and Goa, but less reliable in Kerala, where, by **November**, the "retreating", or northwest monsoon means constant grey skies and showers. Being on the eastern side of the mountains, Tamil

Nadu gets even heavier rains at this time. To enjoy the far south and the Andaman Islands at their best, come **between January and March**, before the heat starts to build up again. **Late April** and **May** are simply insufferable for anyone not accustomed to intense tropical heat.

AVERAGE TEMPERATURES AND RAINFALL

		Jan	Feb	Mar	Apr	May	June	July	Aug	Sept	Oct	Nov	Dec
Bangalore (Kar)	Av daily max (°C)	28	31	33	34	33	30	28	29	28	28	27	27
	Rainfall (mm)	13	22	30	50	135	263	320	318	253	134	29	4
Chennai (TN)	Av daily max (°C)	29	31	33	35	38	37	35	35	34	32	29	28
	Rainfall (mm)	24	7	15	25	52	53	83	124	118	267	309	139
Hyderabad (AP)	Av daily max (°C)	29	31	35	37	39	34	30	29	30	30	29	28
	Rainfall (mm)	2	1	3	1	5	7	89	86	14	1	5	2
Kochi (Ker)	Av daily max (°C)	31	31	31	31	31	29	28	28	28	29	30	30
	Rainfall (mm)	9	34	50	139	364	756	572	386	235	333	184	37
Madurai (TN)	Av daily max (°C)	30	32	35	36	37	37	36	35	35	33	31	30
	Rainfall (mm)	26	16	21	81	59	31	48	117	123	179	161	143
Mumbai (M)	Av daily max (°C)	31	32	33	33	33	32	30	29	30	32	33	32
	Rainfall (mm)	0	1	0	0	20	647	945	660	309	17	7	1
Panjim (Goa)	Av daily max (°C)	31	32	32	33	33	31	29	29	29	31	33	33
	Rainfall (mm)	2	0	4	17	18	580	892	341	277	122	20	37

PART ONE

THE BASICS

GETTING THERE FROM BRITAIN AND IRELAND

Most visitors to South India fly into the major international gateways of Mumbai and Chennai. Nonstop flights reach Mumbai in just 9 hours and Chennai in 10 hours. If cutting costs is a priority then consider an indirect flight – involving a change of plane and possibly a stopover en route; several indirect services travel via Europe or the Gulf. To satisfy the ever-increasing numbers of travellers and holidaymakers heading for Goa and Kerala, various package specialists operate seasonal charter flights. If you are covering a wider itinerary encompassing other areas of India, you may prefer to fly into Delhi – which can offer you further options and cheaper fares. However you go, though, be sure to shop around, as prices can vary wildly between agents.

SCHEDULED FLIGHTS

British Airways and Air India fly **nonstop** daily from **London to Mumbai**. Discounted return fares range from £450 in low season (roughly Jan–June & Nov) to upwards of £600 in high season (July, Aug & Dec). BA also flies nonstop from **London to Chennai** twice weekly (Tues & Sat), and flights cost from £600 low season and from £725 high season. Most days, around three non-stop flights leave **London for Delhi**: Air India, British Airways and Air Canada are some of the airlines who fly the route, and prices are much the same as those to Mumbai. Air Canada, which doesn't fly to India in the summer, tends to be the cheapest of the major airlines.

Apart from some charter flights mentioned below, there are no **direct** flights to India from **regional airports**. From Manchester, your best bet is to take an **indirect** flight with Emirates to Delhi or Mumbai via Dubai for £420–520, depending on season. KLM and KLM UK fly out of most regional airports in the UK to Amsterdam where you can connect with their flight to Mumbai. Similarly, Air France flies to Paris for connection on to Mumbai. In general, both KLM and Air France are cheaper than BA – by approximately £50–100 – with return tickets often discounted to as low as £420.

Of the many other indirect options which exist, you can fly to **Chennai** with Air India (changing at Mumbai) or with Air Lanka (changing at Colombo, Sri Lanka) for £550–600. Air Lanka also flies, via Sri Lanka, to Tiruchirapalli and Thiruvananthapuram (Trivandrum), **Kerala**. Air India fly twice-weekly from London to Thiruvananthapuram, changing at Mumbai. A quicker option, however, is to take one of several flights via the Gulf, including daily flights from London on Gulf Air or Emirates. Several airlines, including Indian Airlines, Air India and a handful of Middle Eastern airlines, also fly between the Gulf and Kerala and connect with **Thiruvananthapuram**, **Kochi/Ernakulam** and **Kozhikode**. A recent addition, Air India now fly, via Mumbai, to **Bangalore**, Karnataka. Extremely cheap fares on indirect flights to **Delhi** – down to as little as £300 return out of season – can usually be found if you're prepared to fly with airlines such as Aeroflot, Tarom, Air Uzbekistan or Syrian Arab Airlines. For a full run-down of airlines and their destinations in South India see box on p.4.

CHARTER FLIGHTS

Various package specialists, such as Inspirations, Manos and Somak (see below for a full list) operate winter (Oct–May) **charters to Goa and Kerala**, departing from London and regional airports. These deals are usually for stays of two weeks – though stays can be extended to four and in some cases six weeks. Surprisingly, they often work out cheaper than a standard scheduled deal to Mumbai. However, your fare must include some form of accommodation (even if it isn't advertised as such), which you can occupy

AIRLINES IN BRITAIN AND IRELAND

Air Canada 7–8 Conduit St, London W1 (☎0990/247226). Attractive fares but they don't fly to India in the summer.

Air France 10 Warwick St, 1st Floor, London W1R (☎0181/742 6600, *www.airfrance.fr)*. One of the best of the major airlines, flying via Paris where you will need to change planes before continuing on to Mumbai or Delhi.

Air India 55 Berkeley Square, London W1 (☎0171/495 7951 or ☎0181/560 9996, *www.airindia.com*). Daily nonstop flights from London to Delhi and Mumbai with direct connections to Chennai and indirect connections via Mumbai to Thiruvananthapuram and Bangalore as well as Calcutta and Ahmedabad.

Air Lanka 22 Regent St, London SW1 (☎0171/930 4688). Competitively priced airline with connections to Chennai and Thiruvananthapuram via Colombo – a change that may involve an overnight halt.

British Airways 156 Regent St, London W1 (☎0345/222111, *www.british-airways.com*). Daily nonstop flights from London to Delhi and Mumbai with direct connections to Chennai (2 weekly) and Calcutta (2 weekly).

Egypt Air 29 Piccadilly, London W1 (☎0171/734 2395). Flights into Mumbai with a change in Cairo, where for an extra £100 you can get a stopover. Their prices remain unchanged throughout the year and are especially attractive in high season.

Emirates 95 Cromwell Rd, London SW7 (☎0171/808 0808, *www.emirates.com*). Flights from London and Manchester to Mumbai via the Gulf, where you can also change onto a direct flight to Kerala.

Gulf Air 10 Albermarle St, London W1X (☎0171/408 1717, *www.gulfairco.com*). Flights from London and Manchester to Mumbai and Delhi via Abu Dhabi, Bahrain or Muscat in the Gulf; you can also fly to the Gulf and change onto a direct flight to Kerala.

KLM Ticket Office, Terminal 4, Heathrow, London (☎0990/750 900, *www.klm.nl*). Flights to Delhi and Mumbai, with a change at Amsterdam, on KLM or Northwest; also KLM Air UK, Stansted Airport, Essex CM24 (☎01990/074074).

Royal Jordanian 32 Brook St, London W1 (☎0171/878 6300). Competitively priced airline with flights via Amman to Delhi and Mumbai; connections to South Indian destinations via internal airlines work well. Overnight stop at Amman on the way back.

on arrival and then ditch when you're ready to move on. Charter tickets are generally sold through high-street travel agents, and ads in the travel pages of newspapers. Once in India, you may be offered the return leg of a charter flight for sale; this practice is particularly prevalent in Goa. Bear in mind, however, that under no circumstances is it possible to leave India on a charter flight if you entered on a scheduled flight or overland.

DISCOUNT AGENTS

For the best flight deals to South India you are generally advised to contact **discount agents**, who offer excess seats for airlines at rock-bottom prices; typical agents include STA, Usit CAMPUS, and Trailfinders (for a full list of reliable operators see box on p.5). Some of these specialize in **student travel** and **under-26s**, so check the restrictions on your ticket. Also worth consulting are ads in major regional newspapers or the national Sunday papers – the *Sunday Times* or the *Observer* – or listings in magazines such as *Time Out*. Smaller agents, or **bucket shops**, also known as "consolidators", generally offer unbeatable prices, but are not always reliable. It's best to use a company that's a member of ATOL, as ATOL membership guarantees the customer a refund if the company goes bust. At the very least, ensure you get a printed receipt with your full travel itinerary when you pay for your ticket.

At certain times (Christmas for one), the best-value flights can get booked up weeks, even months, in advance, so plan ahead.

PACKAGE HOLIDAYS

A large number of operators offer **package holidays** to South India, covering activities such as trekking and safaris, as well as sightseeing and sunbathing. Specialist minority-interest tours range from steam locomotives and war history, to

DISCOUNT FLIGHT AGENTS IN BRITAIN AND IRELAND

Arrowguide Ltd, 29 Dering St, London W1 (☎0171/629 9516). A long-established and reliable consolidator that specializes in cheap flights to Asia.

Bridge the World 47 Chalk Farm Rd, London NW1 (☎0171/911 0900). Specialists in round-the-world tickets, with good deals aimed at the backpacker market.

North South Travel Moulsham Mill Centre, Parkway, Chelmsford, Essex CM2 7PX (☎01245/492882). Friendly and competitive agency, offering discounted fares with profits used to support sustainable tourism and projects in the developing world.

STA Travel 86 Old Brompton Rd, London SW7 (☎0171/581 4132), 117 Euston Rd, London NW1 (☎0171/465 0484), 11 Goodge St, London W1 (☎0171/361 6262); 38 North St, Brighton (☎01273/728282); 25 Queen's Rd, Bristol (☎0117/929 4399); 38 Sidney St, Cambridge (☎01223/366966); 75 Deansgate, Manchester (☎0161/834 0668); 88 Vicar Lane, Leeds (☎0113/244 9212); 9 St Mary's Place, Newcastle-upon-Tyne (☎0191/233 2111); 36 George St, Oxford (☎01865/792800); 184 Byres Rd, Glasgow (☎0141/338 6000). Discount fares, with particularly good deals for students and young people.

Trailfinders 42–50 Earls Court Rd, London W8 (☎0171/938 33660); 194 Kensington High St, London W8 (☎0171/938 3939); 58 Deansgate, Manchester (☎0161/839 6969); 254-284 Sauchiehall St, Glasgow (☎0141/353 2224); 22–24 The Priory Queensway, Birmingham (☎0121/236 1234); 48 Corn St, Bristol (☎0117/929 9000). One of the best-informed and most efficient agents dealing with Asia; good for round-the-world tickets, too.

The Travel Bug 125 Gloucester Rd, London SW7 (☎0171/835 2000); 597 Cheetham Hill Rd, Manchester (☎0161/721 4000). Offers a large range of discounted tickets.

Travel Cuts 295 Regent St, London W1 (☎0171/255 2082). Specialists in budget, student and youth travel and round-the-world tickets.

Usit CAMPUS 52 Grosvenor Gardens, London SW1W (☎0171/730 8111); 541 Bristol Rd, Birmingham (☎0121/414 1848); 61 Ditchling Rd, Clifton, Brighton (☎01273/570226); 39 Queen's Rd, Clifton, Bristol (☎0117/929 2494); 5 Emmanuel St, Cambridge (☎01223/324283); 53 Forest Rd, Edinburgh (☎0131/225 6111); 122 George St, Glasgow (☎0141/553 1818); 166 Deansgate, Manchester (☎0161/833 2046); 105-106 St Aldates, Oxford (☎01865/242067). Student and youth travel specialists, with additional branches in YHA shops and on campuses all over Britain.

USIT Now 21 Aston Quay, O'Connell Bridge, Dublin 2, Ireland (☎01/602 1777). Student and youth specialists for flights and trains, with branches in Belfast, Cork, Galway, Limerick and Waterford.

Welcome Travel 58 Wells Street, London W1P 3RA (☎0171/436 3011). Agents for Air India offering discount fares.

religion and food. Even if you book a general sightseeing tour, most agents have a good range of options. Tours offered include primarily Bangalore, Hyderabad, Chennai, Kovalam and Kochi. Some also offer wildlife tours and combined tours taking in other regions of India. In addition, many companies will arrange **tailor-made tours**, and can help you plan your own itinerary.

Of course, any package holiday is a lot easier than going under your own steam, particularly if you only have a short time and don't want to use it up on making your own travel bookings. On the other hand, a typical sightseeing tour can rather isolate you from the country, shutting you off in air-conditioned hotels and buses. Specialist trips such as trekking and tailor-made tours will work out rather expensive, compared to what you'd pay if you organized everything yourself, but they do cut out a lot of hassle. However, Goa beach holidays and packages to Kovalam in Kerala – particularly with charter operators – can work out cheaper than the cost of a normal flight, and usually offer tour options as extras. One-week packages to Goa including flights and accommodation for example are available for around £450.

ROUND-THE-WORLD TICKETS

If you have time to spare, you could take in India as a stopover, while flying, for example, between

SPECIALIST OPERATORS

Abercrombie and Kent ☎0171/730 9600, *www.abercrombiekent.com* Upmarket sightseeing and tailor-made holidays, trekking and wildlife trips.
Bales ☎01306/740048 Well-established India tour operator with a range of sightseeing and wildlife trips.
Coromandel ☎01572/821330 Tailor-made, special-interest tours, including textile tours to village craft workshops.
Cox & Kings ☎0171/873 5000, *www.coxandkings.com* Tailor-made itineraries with operators established in the days of the Raj.
Discover India ☎0181/429 3300 Tailor-made trips including pilgrimages, cricket, golf and football tours.
Essential India ☎01225/868544, *www.essential-india.co.uk* Courses in a wide range of subjects, from writing, painting, and pottery and outdoor pursuits, for individuals or groups.
Hayes and Jarvis For catalogues ☎0181/748 5050 Offers a large choice of destinations in India, and can be booked through high-street travel agents.
Indian Encounters ☎01929/481421 Theme tours including golf, painting, textiles, plus camel safaris and tailor-made itineraries.
Inspirations ☎01293/822244 Specialists for Goa and Kerala packages.
Kambala ☎01803/732488 One of the few operators specializing in tours for the over-50s. General sightseeing and craft holidays.
Kerala Connections ☎01892/722440, fax 734 913, *www.keralaconnect.co.uk* Specializing in Kerala, good for a range of accommodation and useful for suggesting itineraries.
Kuoni Travel ☎01306/742888 One of the largest package and charter tour operators flying to numerous destinations in India.
Manos ☎0171/216 8070 Specializing in Goa and Kerala packages.
Munjeeta Travel ☎01483/773331 Home-stay holidays lodging with Indian families.
Mysteries of India ☎0181/574 2727 Imaginative, tailor-made and small group holidays, including home-stays along the backwaters and Keralan plantations.
Partnership Travel ☎0181/343 3446, *www.partnershiptravel.co.uk* New venture specializing in mid- and upmarket tailor-made itineraries in South India.
Pettitts India ☎01892/515966, *www.pettitts.co.uk* Tailor-made holidays off the beaten track.
The Romance of India by Rail ☎01232/329477 Set itineraries and tailor-made tours by train.
Somak Holidays ☎0181/423 3000, *www.somak.co.uk* Goa beach holidays with optional sightseeing and wildlife extensions.
Soul of India ☎01902/561485, *www.soulofindia.com* Guided tours, for individuals or groups, of sacred India, including the Christian South.
Trans Indus Travel ☎ 0181/566 2729 Fixed and competitively priced tailor-made tours; specialists in wildlife, fishing and trekking.
Western & Oriental ☎ 0171/313 6611, fax 313 6601, *www.westernoriental.com* Well organized independent tour operator with good South India itineraries.

Britain and Australia, or on a **round-the-world ticket**, which makes a lot of sense if you are planning a long trip with several stops in Asia. A typical one, say with Quantas and British Airways (£1000–1400), open for a year, would depart and return to London, taking in Mumbai, Singapore, Sydney, Honolulu and LA; variations could include doing overland legs between destinations.

FLIGHTS FROM IRELAND

There are no nonstop flights to India **from Ireland**, so you need to fly via another city. You can fly from **Dublin**, through to South India, with British Airways via London, KLM via Amsterdam, Air France via Paris and Swissair via Zurich. Of these, Swissair – which has one flight a week to Mumbai and charges around IR£600 at any time of the year – is the most competitive in high season. However, Royal Jordanian is the best deal with a flight out of **Shannon** – via Amman – in low season for IR£340 return (rising to IR£700 in high season). Aeroflot's daily flight from Shannon – via Moscow – at around IR£500 any time, is a reasonable alternative. Finally, flying KLM from **Belfast** to Delhi or Mumbai costs the same as from London.

GETTING THERE FROM NORTH AMERICA

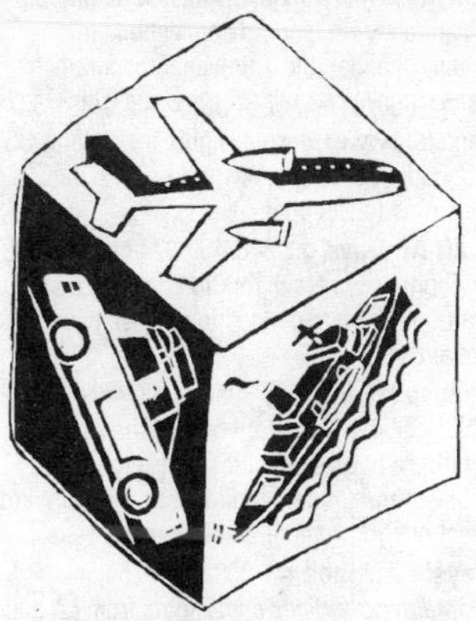

India is on the other side of the planet from North America. If you live on the East Coast it's somewhat shorter to go via Europe, and from the West Coast it's shorter via the Pacific; but either way it's a long haul, involving one or more intermediate stops, and you'll arrive fresher and less jet-lagged if you can manage to fit in a few days' lay-over somewhere en route.

Most North American travellers arrive at **Mumbai** (Bombay), one of India's busiest – and, in general, cheapest – air gateway. You can also get flights from North America to Chennai, the main port of entry for the south, to Goa on the west coast and to Thiruvananthapuram in the far south.

There are no nonstop flights to India from North America, but Air India has direct flights from New York and Chicago to Mumbai, all via London, and Air Canada has a direct flight from Vancouver to Delhi via London. Many more airlines offer services to India from North America with a change of planes either in Asia or Europe. Your choice of airline is likely to depend on whether you fly from the east or the west (with the exception of the above-mentioned Vancouver–Delhi direct flight), with a variety of Asian airlines making the trip from the West Coast, and several European and Middle Eastern carriers doing the trip from the Midwest and the East Coast (for more details see box on p.8).

Air fares from North America to India are highest from the beginning of June to late August. They drop during the "shoulder" seasons (Sept to early Dec and the last half of May), but you'll get the best deals during low season (mid-Dec to mid-May, excluding Christmas). Direct flights are no more expensive than those where you'll have to change planes, but flying on weekends ordinarily adds about $100 to the round-trip fare; price ranges quoted in the sections below assume midweek travel.

If India is only one stop on a longer journey, you might want to consider buying a **round-the-world ticket**. Some travel agents can sell you an "off-the-shelf" RTW ticket, touching down in about half a dozen cities; tailor-made RTW tickets usually work out more expensive. Figure on paying at least $1300 for a regular RTW ticket including India and Europe. A more extensive RTW ticket will cost up to $3000.

FROM EASTERN AND CENTRAL US

Flying east, you'll stop over somewhere in Europe (most often London), the Gulf or both. Figure on at least eighteen hours' total travel time from the East Coast.

Air India and PIA discount their tickets heavily through a few specialist, understaffed New York consolidators. Marked-down tickets on European carriers – notably British Airways, Air France and Lufthansa – are frequently sold by other discount agents. Other airlines flying between the eastern US and India include KLM, Aeroflot, Gulf Air, Kuwait Airways and Egypt Air. Or you can simply hop on any of the dozens of airlines that fly to London and pick up a flight to India from there.

Prices are most competitive out of New York, where the cheapest low-season fares to Mumbai hover around $1300 ($1400 high season). From **Washington** or **Miami**, figure on $1550/$1750; from **Chicago**, $1200/$1550; and from and from **Dallas/Ft. Worth**, $1700/$2300. Fares to Chennai or Goa run about $100 to $150 higher.

FROM THE WEST COAST

From the West Coast, it takes about as long to fly east or west – a minimum of 22 hours' total travel time – and if you're booking through a consolidator there may not be much difference in price

MAJOR AIRLINES IN NORTH AMERICA

Aeroflot ☎1-800/995-5555, in Canada ☎514/288-2125, *www.aeroflot.com* Flights from several US cities and Montreal to Moscow with onward connections to Delhi and Calcutta.

Air Canada ☎1-800/776-3000, *www.aircanada.ca* Shoulder and high season flights from all major Canadian cities to London, with onward connections to Delhi. The rest of the year they book via Zurich with Swiss Air.

Air France ☎1-800/237-2747, *www.airfrance.fr* Flights to Paris from several US cities, Montreal and Toronto with onward connections to Mumbai.

Air India ☎1-800/223-7776 or 212/751-6200, *www.airindia.com* Direct flights to Mumbai (via London) from New York and Chicago, with onward connections to Chennai, Bangalore, Hyderabad and Thiruvananthapuram. One direct flight weekly from New York to Bangalore via London and Mumbai.

British Airways ☎1-800/247-9297 in US, ☎1-800/668-1059 in Canada, *www.british-airways.com* Flights from major US cities, Montreal and Toronto to London with onward connections to Mumbai and Chennai.

Cathay Pacific ☎1-800/233-2742, *www.cathay-usa.com* Flights from New York, LA, San Francisco, Toronto and Vancouver to Hong Kong with onward connections to Mumbai.

Egypt Air ☎1-800/334-6787 or ☎212/315-0900 Weekly flights from New York and LA to Cairo with onward connections to Mumbai.

Gulf Air ☎1-800/553-2824, *www.gulfairco.com* Flights from New York and Houston to various Gulf capitals with onward connections to Mumbai, Chennai and Thiruvananthapuram.

KLM ☎1-800/447-4747 in US, ☎1-800/361-5073 in Canada; *www.klm.com* Flights from major US and Canadian cities to Amsterdam with daily connections to Mumbai.

Kuwait Airways ☎1-800/458-9248 or 212/308-5707 Flights from New York to London, London to Kuwait and onward connections to Delhi and Mumbai.

Lufthansa ☎1-800/645-3880 in US, ☎1-800/563-5954 in Canada; *www.lufthansa.com* Flights from twelve US cities and Toronto, Vancouver and Calgary to Frankfurt with onward connections to Mumbai and Chennai.

Malaysia Airlines ☎1-800/552-9264, *www.malaysia-airlines.com* Flights from LA and Vancouver to Kuala Lumpur with onward connections to Chennai.

Northwest Airlines ☎1-800/225-2525 domestic, ☎1-800/447-474 7 international, *www.nwa.com* Flights to Amsterdam from several US and Canadian cities, with daily onward connections to Mumbai, in co-operation with KLM.

PIA ☎1-800/221-2552, *www.piac.com* Flights from New York to Karachi/Lahore with onward connections to Mumbai.

Singapore Airlines ☎1-800/742-3333, *www.singaporeair.com* Flights from LA, San Francisco, New York or Vancouver to Singapore with onward connections to Mumbai and Chennai.

DISCOUNT AGENTS, CONSOLIDATORS AND TRAVEL CLUBS

Air Brokers International ☎1-800/883-3273, *www.airbrokers.com* Round-the-world ticket specialist with good rates for itineraries that include India.

Council Travel ☎1-888-COUNCIL, *www.counciltravel.com* Student/budget travel agency.

Discount Airfares Worldwide On-Line *www.etn.nl/discount.htm* A hub of consolidator and discount agent Web links, maintained by the non-profit European Travel Network.

Educational Travel Centre ☎1-800/747-5551 or ☎608/256-5551, *www.edtrav.com* Student/youth and consolidator fares.

Fly Time ☎212/760 3737 Consolidator specializing in tickets to India.

Hari World Travel ☎212/997 3300, *www.hariworld.com* Biggest Indian consolidator; agent for Indrail passes.

HighTime Travel ☎212/684 7700 Consolidator specializing in tickets to India.

STA Travel ☎1-800/777-0112, *www.sta-travel.com* Worldwide discount travel firm specializing in student/youth fares; also student IDs, travel insurance and car rental.

Travel CUTS ☎1-800/667-2887 Canada only, or ☎416/979-2406, *www.travelcuts.com* Organization specializing in student fares, IDs and other travel services.

Travelocity *www.travelocity.com* Online consolidator whose website has a special India section, where you'll find tour operators, accommodation options and cheap airfares.

Vijay ☎1-800/892-0027, *www.pltravel.com* Consolidator offering bargain airfares to India.

SPECIALIST TOUR OPERATORS IN NORTH AMERICA

Adventure Center ☎1-800/227-8747 Trekking and cultural tours.

Cox & Kings ☎1-800/999-1758, *www.zenonet.com/cox-kings/* Deluxe and special-interest sightseeing.

Geographic Expeditions ☎1-800/777-8183, *www.geoex.com* Remote mountain treks and unusual tours including sea kayaking in the Andamans.

Journeyworld International ☎1-800/635-3900 Fifteen- and twenty-day regional tours across the country, some including Sri Lanka and Nepal.

Mercury Travels Limited ☎1-800/223-1474 A variety of regional and custom tours to each region of India.

either. Thai Airways, Cathay Pacific, Malaysia Airlines and Singapore Airlines are the main carriers flying over the Pacific to India, via their respective hubs. Air India doesn't do the trans-Pacific route, but can book passengers on Northwest to any of several Asian capitals and then fly them the rest of the way.

From **Los Angeles** or **San Francisco**, you're looking at a minimum of $1600 to fly to Mumbai in low season ($1700 in high season). Flights to Chennai or Calcutta cost about $50 more.

FROM CANADA

At the time of writing, the only **direct flight** from Canada to India was Vancouver–Delhi on Air Canada. All other routings involve a plane change and more layover time. Air Canada flies during shoulder and high season from all major Canadian cities to London, where passengers can join the Vancouver–Delhi flight; the rest of the year they fly through Zurich. Other airlines offering services to India, via their capitals, include British Airways, Air France, Lufthansa, KLM and Aeroflot. This list doesn't convey the full range of possibilities, however. A discount agent will probably break the journey into two, using one of dozens of carriers for the transatlantic (or trans-Pacific) leg.

Typical discounted low and high season fares to Mumbai: from **Montreal** or **Toronto**, CDN$2200/$2400; from **Vancouver**, CDN$2500/$2700. Add $100 for Chennai, or Goa.

PACKAGES AND ORGANIZED TOURS

Wrapping South India up into a tidy **package** makes it less daunting and more comprehensible to many first-time tourists. A tour company can also shield you from the subcontinent's many little frustrations, enabling you to cover more ground than if you were going it alone. However, tour prices are wildly out of line with the cost of living in India, and whether you take one will depend on which is tighter, your budget or your schedule. Excluding airfare, a two-week tour is likely to cost at least $2000, and a three-week trip can cost $3500 or more. Your local travel agent should be able to book any tour for you at no additional cost.

GETTING THERE FROM AUSTRALIA AND NEW ZEALAND

Some of the best-value air fares from Australia to India are on the jointly operated Ansett/Air India flights from the east coast, Perth and Darwin. Flying (via Hong Kong) to Mumbai or Delhi, with the option of flying into one city and out of the other, costs from around A$1250 in low/shoulder season (Feb 1–Nov 21), and from around A$1650 during high season (Nov 22–Jan 31). Qantas also offers a competitive fare from the east coast to Mumbai of around A$1400 low season. There are daily departures connecting with these flights from most Australian cities, with less frequent departures from Cairns and Darwin (2–3 times a week).

Of possible alternatives, Singapore Airlines flies to Mumbai and Chennai for A$1429/A$1699 from eastern Australia, A$1299 (low season) from Perth or Darwin and Cathay Pacific at a cost of A$1400 (low season) flies to Mumbai via Hong Kong from the east coast, or Perth.

AIRLINES AND SPECIALIST AGENTS

AIRLINES

Air India Level 18, 44 Market St, Sydney (☎02/9299 2026); 214-218 Queen St, Auckland (☎09/303 301)

Air New Zealand 5 Elizabeth St, Sydney (☎13 2476); 139 Queen St, Auckland (☎09/357 3000)

British Airways Level 19, 259 George St, Sydney (☎02/8904 8800); 154 Queen St, Auckland (☎09/356 8690)

Cathay Pacific Level 12, 8 Spring St, Sydney (☎13 1747); 11/205 Queen St, Auckland (☎09/379 0861)

Malaysia Airlines 16 Spring St, Sydney (☎13 2627); 12–26 Swanson St, Auckland (☎09/373 2741)

Qantas 70 Hunter St, Sydney (☎13 1211); 154 Queen St, Auckland (☎09/357 8900, toll-free 0800/808 767)

Singapore Airlines 17–19 Bridge St, Sydney (☎13 1011); Lower Ground Floor, West Plaza Building, cnr Customs and Albert streets, Auckland (☎09/379 3209)

SPECIALIST AGENTS

Flight Centres 82 Elizabeth St, Sydney (☎02/9235 3522); 19 Bourke St, Melbourne (☎03/9650 2899), plus branches nationwide (☎13 1600 for nearest branch); 205–225 Queen St, Auckland (☎09/309 6171); nearest branch (☎0800/FLIGHTS) Branches throughout Australia and New Zealand.

STA Travel 855 George St, Sydney (☎02/9212 1255); 256 Flinders St, Melbourne (☎03/9654 7266), for nearest branch (☎13 1776); 10 High St, Auckland (☎09/309 0458); 132 Cuba St, Wellington (☎04/385 0561); 90 Cashel St, Christchurch (☎03/379 9098). Branches throughout Australia and New Zealand, specialists in youth travel.

Abercrombie and Kent 90 Bridport St, Albert Park, Victoria (☎03/9699 9766). Specialist in individual mid- to upmarket holidays, away from the main tourist trails.

Adventure World 73 Walker St, Sydney (☎02/9956 7766, toll-free ☎1800/221 931), plus branches in Melbourne, Adelaide, Brisbane and Perth; 101 Great South Rd, Remuera, Auckland (☎09/524 5118) Tailor-made air and accommodation packages, rail passes and regional tours. NZ agents for Peregrine.

India/Nepal Adventure Travel Level 13, 92 Pitt St, Sydney (☎02/9223 6000); Level 7, 333 Adelaide St, Brisbane (☎07/3221 4788); branches in Melbourne and Perth. Adventure holiday specialists.

Peregrine Adventures 258 Lonsdale St, Melbourne (☎03/9663 8611); offices in Brisbane, Sydney, Adelaide and Perth. Wide range of tailored group and individual tours; trekking specialists.

San Michele Travel Level 5, 83 York St, Sydney (☎02/9299 1111, toll-free 1800/222 244), plus branches in Melbourne and Perth. Budget to upmarket packages, rail tours and land-based designer tours for groups or individual travellers.

Flying from **New Zealand**, the cheapest fares to India are: Singapore Airlines daily from Auckland and Christchurch via Singapore to Mumbai, or Chennai (NZ$1900/NZ$2200); Air New Zealand/Air India from Auckland to Mumbai via Singapore, Hong Kong or Bangkok (NZ$2000/$2300). Add on approximately NZ$150 for flights from Wellington.

Round-the-world fares from Australia and New Zealand using the above airlines can include India; for example, Air New Zealand, Qantas or Malaysia Airlines can route you through Mumbai as part of a RTW deal from around A$2200/NZ$2600.

VISAS AND RED TAPE

Gone are the days when Commonwealth nationals could stroll visa-less into India and stay for as long as they pleased: nowadays everybody, except Nepalis and Bhutanis, needs a visa.

If you're going to India on business or to study, you'll need to apply for a special student or business visa, otherwise a standard tourist visa will suffice. These are valid for six months from the date of issue (not of departure from your home country or entry into India), and cost £19/$50/CAN$47/A$45/NZ$55. As you're asked to specify whether you need a single-entry or a multiple-entry visa, and the same rates apply to both, it makes sense to ask for the latter, just in case you make a side-trip to Nepal or another neighbouring country.

Much the best place to get a visa is in your country of residence, from the embassies and high commissions listed on p.12. In Britain and North America, you'll need two passport photographs and an application form, obtainable in advance by post, or on the day. In Australia and New Zealand, one passport-sized photo and your flight/travel itinerary are required, together with the visa application form. As a rule, visas are issued in a matter of hours. Embassies in India's neighbouring countries, however, often drag their feet, demand letters of recommendation from your embassy (expensive if you are, for example, British), or make you wait and pay for them to send your application to Delhi. Tourist visas are available by post in most countries, though in the US, for example, this takes a month as opposed to two days if you do it in person – check your nearest embassy, high commission or consulate to be sure. Make sure that your visa is signed by someone at the embassy or you may be refused entry into the country.

It's also possible in many countries to pay a visa agency to obtain them on your behalf, in the UK this costs from around £24 (plus the price of the visa). In Britain, try The Visa Service, 2 Northdown St, Kings Cross, London N1 (☎0171/833 2709), or Visa Express, 31 Corsham St, London N1 (☎0171/251 4822). In the US, try Express Visa Service, 2150 Wisconsin Ave, Suite 20, Washington (☎202/337 2442).

It is no longer possible to extend a visa in India, though exceptions may be made in special circumstances. Most people whose standard six-month tourist visas are about to expire head for Colombo, capital of neighbouring Sri Lanka. However, in recent years this has been something of a hit-and-miss business, with some tourists having their requests turned down for no apparent reason. Try to find out from other travellers what the visa situation is, and always allow enough time on your current permit to re-enter India and catch a flight out of the country in case your request is refused.

If you do stay more than 180 days, before you leave the country you are supposed to get a tax clearance certificate, available at the foreigners' section of the income tax department in every major city. They are free, but you should take bank receipts to show you have changed your money legally. In practice, tax clearance certificates are rarely demanded, but you never know.

For details of other kinds of visas – foreigners of Indian origin, business travellers and even students of yoga can get five-year visas – contact your nearest Indian embassy.

Duty-free allowances for travellers arriving in India are covered on p.69.

SPECIAL PERMITS

In addition to a visa, **special permits** are required for travel to the Andaman Islands and Lakshadweep. Arriving by plane, you'll be issued them at the airport, but tourists travelling to the Andamans by ship have to obtain permits before leaving the port of origin (Chennai, Calcutta or Vishakapatnam). Full details of how to do this appear in the relevant chapter of the Guide.

INDIAN EMBASSIES AND CONSULATES

Australia High Commission: 3–5 Moonah Place, Yarralumla, Canberra, ACT 2600 (☎02/6273 3999, fax 6273 3328). Consulates: Level 27, 25 Bligh St, Sydney, NSW 2000 (☎02/9223 9500, fax 9223 9246); 13 Munro St, Coburg, Melbourne, Vic 3058 (☎03/9384 0141, fax 9384 1609). Honorary consulates: Perth (☎08/9221 1485, fax 9221 1206) and Brisbane (☎07/3260 2825, fax 3260 2826).

Bangladesh House 120, Rd 2, Dhanmondi Residential Area, Dhaka (☎02/503606, fax 863662); 1253–1256 Nizam Rd, Mehdi Bagh, Chittagong (☎031/211007, fax 225178).

Burma (Myanmar) Oriental Assurance Building, 545-547 Merchant St (PO Box 751), Rangoon (☎01/82550).

Canada High Commission: 10 Springfield Rd, Ottawa, ON K1M 1C9 (☎613/744 3751, fax 744 0913). Consulates: 2 Bloor St W, #500, Toronto, ON M4W 3E2, (☎416/960 0751); 325 Howe St, 2nd floor, Vancouver, BC V6C 1Z7 (☎604/662 8811).

Japan 2-11, Kudan Minami 2-Chome, Chiyoda-ku, Tokyo 102 (☎03/3262 2391, fax 3234 4866).

Malaysia 2 Jalan Taman Dlita (off Jalan Duta), PO Box 10059, 50704 Kuala Lumpur (☎03/253 3504, fax 253 3507).

Nepal Lainchaur (off Lazimpath), PO Box 92, Kathmandu (☎01/410940, fax 413132). Mon–Fri 9.30–11am. Allow a week – plus extra fee – to fax Delhi; British nationals and some Europeans need letters of recommendation.

New Zealand Indian High Commission: 180 Molesworth St (PO Box 4005), Wellington (☎04/473 6390, fax 499 0665).

Pakistan G-5, Diplomatic enclave, Islamabad, (☎051/814371, fax 820742); India House, 3 Fatima Jinnah Rd (PO Box 8542), Karachi (☎021/522275, fax 568 0929).

Singapore India House, 31 Grange Rd (PO Box 9123), Singapore 0923 (☎737 6777, fax 732 6909).

Sri Lanka 36–38 Galle Rd, Colombo 3 (☎01/421605, fax 446403); 31 Rajapihilla Mawatha, PO Box 47, Kandy (☎08/24563).

Thailand 46 Soi 23 (Prasarn Mitr), Sukhumvit Rd, Bangkok 10110 (☎02/258 0300, fax 258 4627); 113 Bumruangrat Rd, Chiang Mai 50000 (☎053/243066, fax 247879). Visas take five working days to issue.

UK High Commission: India House, Aldwych, London WC2B 4NA (☎0171/836 8484, fax 836 4331). Consulates: 20 Augusta St, Birmingham B18 6GL (☎0121/212 2782, fax 212 2782); St Andrew House 141 West Nite St, Glasgow G1 2RN (☎0141/331 0777, fax 331 0666). All open Mon–Fri 8.30am–noon.

USA Embassy of India (Consular Services): 2536 Massachusetts Ave NW, Washington DC 20008 (☎202/939 9839, fax 939 7027). Consulates: 3 East 64th St, New York, NY 10021 (☎212/774-0600, fax 988 6423); 540 Arguello Blvd, San Francisco, CA 94118 (☎415/668 0657, fax 668 2073); 150 N Michigan Ave, Suite 1100, Chicago, IL 60601 (☎312/595-0405); 201 St Charles Ave, New Orleans, LA 70170 (☎504/582 8106); 2051 Young St, Honolulu, HI 96826 (☎808/947 2618).

TRAVEL INSURANCE

In the light of the potential health risks involved in a trip to India – see p.14 – travel insurance is essential. In addition to covering medical expenses and emergency flights, it also insures your money and belongings against loss or theft.

Flights paid for with a major credit or charge card offer some automatic cover, but usually only while travelling to and from your destination. Some package tours may also include insurance, but package operators more commonly offer an insurance deal as an extra: it might be worth checking against alternative policies, though differences in price and cover are likely to be slight.

Always **check the fine print** of a policy. A 24-hour medical emergency contact number is a must, and one of the rare policies that pays your medical bills directly is better than one that reimburses you on your return home. The per-article limit for loss or theft should cover your most valuable possession (a camera for example) but, conversely, don't pay for cover you don't need – such as too much baggage or a huge sum for personal liability. Make sure, too, that you are covered for all the things you intend to do. Activities such as trekking or rafting are usually specifically excluded, but can be added on for a supplement. Another variable to check when you are shopping around is the level of the excess – the amount you'll be liable for if you ever need to make a claim. With some of the cheaper policies, this can be considerable.

Frequent travellers may benefit from **annual** insurance policies, but these almost invariably put an upper limit on the duration of any single trip, likely to be ninety days at most.

Among **UK insurers**, Columbus (☎0171/375 0011) is about the cheapest, offering one-month's standard cover for around £38, or £99 for three months. Their main competitors are Worldwide Travel Insurance Services Ltd, whose policies are sold direct from their head branch (☎01892/833338, fax 837744). Also worth phoning for a quote are: Endsleigh, who sell policies through most major youth/student travel agents, or through their office (☎0171/436 4451); and worth a call are Club Direct (☎01243/817 711).

Travellers from the **US** should carefully check their current insurance policies before taking out a new one. You may discover that you are already covered for medical and other losses while abroad. Holders of ISIC cards are entitled to be reimbursed for $3000-worth of accident coverage, and sixty days of in-patient benefits of up to $100 a day for the period the card is valid. If you do want a specific travel insurance policy, there are numerous kinds to choose from: short-term combination policies covering everything from baggage loss to broken legs are the best bet. $150 for up to thirty days, plus $5 per day – per extra day – will buy you coverage of prepaid airfare and accommodation expenses of up to US$2,500, plus US$10,000 primary medical coverage. Companies you might try, include: Travel Guard (☎1-800/826-1300, *www.noelgroup.com*); Access America International (☎1-800/284-8300); and Worldwide Assistance (☎1-800/821-2828).

In **Australia** and **New Zealand**, travel insurance is put together by airlines and travel agent groups, which include: UTAG, at 122 Walker St, North Sydney (☎02/9956 8399, toll-free ☎1800/809 462), Cover-More, at 32 Walker St, Sydney (☎02/9202 8000, toll-free ☎1800/251 881) and Ready Plan, at 141–147 Walker St, Victoria (☎1300/555 017) or 63 Albert St, Auckland (☎09/379 3208). Most adventure sports are covered, but check your policy first. A typical policy will cost AUS$150/NZ$170 for one month.

If you need **to claim**, you *must* have a police report in the case of theft or loss, and supporting evidence of medical treatment in the form of bills, although with some policies, doctors and hospitals will be able to bill your insurers direct. Keep photocopies of everything you send to the insurer and don't allow months to elapse before informing them. Write immediately and tell them what's happened; you can usually claim later.

HEALTH

A lot of visitors get ill in South India just as in the rest of the country, and some of them get very ill. However, if you are careful, you should be able to get through the region with nothing worse than a mild dose of "Delhi belly". The important thing is to keep your resistance high and to be very aware of health risks such as poor hygiene, untreated water, mosquito bites and undressed open cuts.

What you **eat** and **drink** is crucial: a poor diet lowers your resistance. Ensure you eat a balance of protein, energy, vitamins and minerals. Meat and fish are obvious sources of protein for non-vegetarians in the West, but not necessarily in India; eggs, pulses (lentils, peas and beans), rice and curd are all protein sources, as are nuts. Overcooked vegetables lose a lot of their vitamin content; eating plenty of peeled fresh fruit – provided this is fruit you have peeled yourself – helps keep up your vitamin and mineral intake. With all that sweating, too, make sure you get enough salt – put a bit extra on your food – and drink enough water. This is especially important in the consistently hot and humid south. It's also worth taking daily multivitamin and mineral tablets with you. Above all, make sure you eat *enough* – an unfamiliar diet may reduce the amount you eat – and **get enough sleep** and rest: it's easy to get run down if you're on the move a lot, especially in a hot climate.

PRECAUTIONS

The lack of sanitation in India can be exaggerated. It's not worth getting too worked up about, though, as you'll never enjoy anything. A few **common-sense precautions**, however, are in order, bearing in mind that things such as bacteria multiply far more quickly in a tropical climate, and your foreign body will have little immunity to Indian germs.

For details on **water**, see the box on p.15. When it comes to **food**, it's quite likely that tourist restaurants and Western dishes will bring you grief. Be particularly wary of prepared dishes that have to be reheated – ask yourself how long they've been on display in the heat and the flies. Anything that is boiled or fried (and thus sterilized) in your presence is usually all right, though meat can sometimes be dodgy, especially in towns or cities where the electricity supply (and thus refrigerators) frequently fails. Any food that has been left out for any length of time is definitely suspect. Raw unpeeled fruit and vegetables should always be viewed with suspicion, and you should avoid salads unless you know they have been soaked in an iodine or potassium permanganate solution. Wiping down a plate before eating is sensible, and avoid straws as they are usually dusty or second-hand. As a rule of thumb, stick to cafés and restaurants that are doing a brisk trade, and where the food is thus freshly cooked, and you should be fine.

Be vigilant about **personal hygiene**. Wash your hands often, especially before eating. Keep all cuts clean – treat them with iodine or antiseptic – and cover them up to prevent infection. Be fussier about sharing things like drinks and cigarettes, and never share a razor or toothbrush. It is also not advisable to go around barefoot – and best to wear flip-flop sandals, including in the shower.

Among items you might wish to take with you – though all are available in India itself, at a fraction of what you might pay at home – are hypodermic needles and sterilized skin wipes (more for the security of knowing you have them with you, than any fear that an Indian hospital would fail to observe basic sanitary precautions), antiseptic cream, plasters, lints and sealed bandages, a course of Flagyl antibiotics, a box of Immodium (Lomotil) for emergency diarrhoea treatment, rehydration sachets, insect repellent and cream such as Anthisan for soothing bites, paracetamol or aspirin (useful for combating the effects of altitude) and a mild oral anaesthetic such as Bonjela for soothing ulcers or mild toothache.

Advice on avoiding **mosquitoes** is offered under the section on Malaria on p.16. If you do get bites or itches try not to scratch them: it's hard, but infection and tropical ulcers can result if you do. Tiger balm and even dried soap may relieve the itching.

Finally, especially if you are going on a long trip, have a **dental check-up** before you leave home – you don't want to go down with unexpected tooth trouble in India. If you do, and it feels serious, head for Delhi, Mumbai or Calcutta, and ask a foreign consulate to recommend a dentist.

WHAT ABOUT THE WATER?

One of the chief concerns of many prospective visitors to India is whether the water is safe to drink. To put it simply, no, though your unfamiliarity with Indian micro-organisms is generally more of a problem rather than any great virulence in the water itself.

It is generally not a good idea to drink **tap water**, although in big cities it is usually chlorinated. However, it is almost impossible to avoid untreated tap water completely: it is used to make ice, which may appear in drinks without being asked for, lassis are made with it, utensils are washed with it, and so on. **Bottled water** is widely available. Always check that the seal is intact, as refilling bottles is not uncommon.

If you plan to go somewhere with no access to bottled drinks (which really only applies to travellers venturing well off the beaten track) find an appropriate method of **treating water**, whether your source is tap water or natural groundwater such as a river or stream. **Boiling** it for a minimum of five minutes (longer at higher altitudes) is sufficient to kill micro-organisms, but is not always practical and does not remove unpleasant tastes. **Chemical sterilization** is cheap and convenient, but dirty water remains dirty, and still contains organic matter or other contamination. You can sterilize water by using chlorine or iodine tablets, but these leave a nasty after-taste (which can be masked with lemon or lime juice) and are not effective in preventing such diseases as amoebic dysentery and giardia. Tincture of iodine is better, although it still doesn't do much for the taste; add five drops to one litre of water and leave it to stand for thirty minutes. If the water is cloudy, filter it before adding the iodine or add ten drops per litre. Pregnant women, babies and people with thyroid problems should avoid using iodine sterilizing tablets or iodine-based purifiers, or use an additional iodine-removal filter. The various kinds of **filter** only remove visible impurities and the larger pathogenic organisms (most bacteria and cysts). However fine the filter, it will not remove viruses, dissolved chemicals, pesticides, herbicides etc.

Purification, a two-stage process involving both filtration and sterilization, gives the most complete treatment. Portable water purifiers range from pocket-size units weighing 60g, up to 800g. Some of the best water purifiers on the market are made in Britain by Pre-Mac. For suppliers contact:

Pre-Mac (Kent) Ltd Unit 5 Morewood Close, Sevenoaks, Kent TN13 2HU England (☎01732/460333, fax 460222).

All Water Systems Ltd Unit 2018 Citywest Business Campus, Faggart, Co. Dublin, Ireland (☎01/466 0133).

Travel Medicine 351 Pleasant St, Suite 312, Northampton, MA 01060, US (☎1-800/872 8633).

VACCINATIONS

No **inoculations** are legally required for entry into India, but meningitis, typhoid and hepatitis A jabs are recommended, and it's worth ensuring that you are up to date with tetanus, polio and other boosters. All vaccinations can be obtained in Mumbai, Chennai and other major cities if necessary; just make sure the needle is new.

Hepatitis A is not the worst disease you can catch in India, but the frequency with which it strikes travellers makes a strong case for immunization. Transmitted through contaminated food and water, or through saliva, it can lay a victim low for several months with exhaustion, fever and diarrhoea – and may cause liver damage. The Havrix vaccine has been shown to be extremely effective; though expensive, it lasts for up to ten years. The protection given by gamma-globulin, the traditional serum of hepatitis antibodies, wears off quickly and the injection should therefore be given as late as possible before departure: the longer your planned stay, the larger the dose.

Symptoms by which you can recognize hepatitis include a yellowing of the whites of the eyes, nausea, general flu-like malaise, orange urine (though dehydration could also cause that) and light-coloured stools. If you think you have it, avoid alcohol, try to avoid passing it on and get lots of rest. More serious is **hepatitis B**, passed on like AIDS through blood or sexual contact (though it is more virulent than AIDS). There is a vaccine, but it is only recommended for those planning to work in a medical environment. Otherwise, your chances of getting hepatitis B are low – assuming you take the precautions you should be taking to avoid AIDS.

Typhoid, also spread through contaminated food or water, is endemic in India, but rare outside the monsoon. It produces a persistent high fever with malaise, headaches and abdominal pains, followed by diarrhoea. Vaccination can be by injection (two shots are required, or one for a booster), giving three years' cover, or orally – tablets, which are more expensive but easier on the arm.

Cholera, spread the same way as hepatitis A and typhoid, causes sudden attacks of watery diarrhoea with cramps and debilitation. However, its periodic epidemics are not too common in South India. If you do get it, take copious amounts of water with rehydration salts and seek medical treatment. There is currently no effective vaccination against cholera.

Most medical authorities now recommend vaccination against **meningitis** too. Spread by airborne bacteria (through coughs and sneezes for example), it attacks the lining of the brain and can be fatal. Symptoms include fever, a severe headache, stiffness in the neck and a rash on the stomach and back. If you think you may have meningitis, seek immediate medical attention.

You should have a **tetanus** booster every ten years whether you travel or not. Tetanus (or lockjaw) is picked up through contaminated open wounds and causes severe muscular spasms; if you cut yourself on something dirty and are not covered, get a booster as soon as you can.

Assuming that you were vaccinated against **polio** in childhood, only one (oral) booster is needed during your adult life. Immunizations against mumps, measles, TB and rubella are a good idea for anyone who wasn't vaccinated as a child and hasn't had the diseases.

Although **rabies** is a problem in India, the best advice is to give dogs and monkeys a wide berth, and not to play with animals at all, no matter how cute they might look. A bite, a scratch or even a lick from an infected animal could spread the disease; wash any such wound immediately but gently with soap or detergent, and apply alcohol or iodine if possible. Find out what you can about the animal and swap addresses with the owner (if there is one) just in case. If the animal might be infected, or, if the wound begins to tingle and fester, act immediately to get treatment – rabies is invariably fatal once symptoms appear. There is a vaccine, but it is expensive, is only effective for a maximum of three months and only serves to shorten the course of treatment you need anyway.

Diseases you won't need vaccinations for include: smallpox (now virtually eradicated in India), cholera (because the vaccine offers very little protection) and yellow fever (only necessary if you're visiting Africa).

MALARIA

Protection against **malaria** is absolutely essential. The disease, caused by a parasite carried in the saliva of female Anopheles mosquitoes, is endemic everywhere in South India and is nowadays regarded as the big killer in the subcontinent. It has a variable incubation period of a few days to several weeks, so you can become ill long after being bitten. Programmes to eradicate the disease by spraying mosquito-infested areas and distributing free preventative tablets have proved disastrous; within a short space of time, the Anopheles mosquitoes develop immunities to the insecticides, while the malaria parasite itself constantly mutates into drug-resistant strains, rendering the old cures ineffective.

It is vital for travellers to take **preventative tablets** according to a strict routine, and to cover the period before and after your trip. The drug used is chloroquine (trade names include Nivaquin, Avloclor and Resochin), and you usually take two tablets weekly, but India has chloroquine-resistant strains, and you'll need to supplement it with daily proguanil (Paludrine) or weekly Maloprim. A new weekly drug, mefloquine (Lariam), is supposed to replace all these, but is not currently recommended for journeys of more than two months because of its side-effects (see below). Australian authorities are now prescribing the antibiotic Doxycycline instead.

As the malaria parasite can incubate in your system without showing symptoms for more than a month, it is essential that you continue to take preventative tablets for at least four weeks after you return home: the most common way of catching malaria is when travellers forget to do this.

If you do go down with malaria, you'll know soon enough. The shivering, burning fever and headaches are like severe flu and come in waves, usually beginning in the early evening. Anyone who develops such symptoms should get to a doctor for a blood test as soon as possible. Malaria is not infectious, but some strains are dangerous and can occasionally be fatal when not treated promptly, in particular, the choloquine-resistant **cerebral malaria**. This virulent and lethal strain of the disease, which affects the brain and often proves fatal if left untreated, is treatable, but has to be diagnosed early. Erratic body temperature, lack of energy and aches are the first key signs, and if you get diagnosed at such an early stage, you have a much better chance of being treated without complications and the onset of more unpleasant symptoms.

Side-effects of antimalaria drugs may include itching, rashes, hair loss, sight problems and even (in the case of Lariam) depression, and it is probably not advisable to use them for prolonged periods. However, on a three-month trip, it is just common sense. Chloroquine and quinine are safe during pregnancy, but Maloprim, Fansidar, mefloquine and Doxycycline should be avoided at that time. Note that the doses we quote apply to adults: children will want reduced dosages.

The most important thing, however, is to **avoid mosquito bites**. Sleep under a net if possible – one which can hang from a single point is best (you can usually find a way to tie a string across your room to hang it from), burn mosquito coils (easily available, but easy to break in transit) and use repellent. An Indian brand of mosquito repellent, Odomos, is widely available and very effective, though most travellers bring their own from home, usually one containing the noxious but effective compound DEET. DEET can cause rashes and a strength of more than thirty percent is not advised for those with sensitive skin. Mosquito "buzzers", which plug into the electricity supply, are pretty useless but the new wrist and ankle bands are as effective as spray and a good alternative for sensitive skin. Although they are active from dusk till dawn, female Anopheles mosquitoes prefer to bite in the evening, so be especially careful at that time. Wear long sleeves, skirts and trousers, avoid dark colours, which attract mosquitoes, and put repellent on exposed skin.

Another illness spread by mosquito bites is **dengue fever**, whose symptoms are similar to those of malaria, plus aching bones. There is no vaccine available and the only treatment is complete rest, with drugs to assuage the fever. **Japanese encephalitis** (yet another mosquito-borne viral infection causing fever, muscle pains and headaches) has been on the increase in recent years in wet, rural rice-growing areas. However, there have been no reports of travellers catching the disease, and you shouldn't need the vaccine (which is expensive and has several potentially nasty side-effects) unless you plan to spend much time around paddy fields during and immediately after the monsoons.

INTESTINAL TROUBLES

Diarrhoea is the most common bane of travellers. When mild and not accompanied by other major symptoms, it may just be your stomach reacting to unfamiliar food. Accompanied by cramps and vomiting, it could well be food poisoning. In either case, it will probably pass of its own accord in 24–48 hours without treatment. In the meantime, it is essential to replace the fluids and salts you're losing, so take lots of water with oral rehydration salts (commonly referred to as ORS, or called Electrolyte in India). If you can't get ORS, use half a teaspoon of salt and eight of sugar in a litre of water, and if you are too ill to drink, seek medical help immediately. While you are suffering, it's a good idea to avoid greasy food, heavy spices, caffeine and most fruit and dairy products. Some say bananas and pawpaws are good, as is rice soup and coconut water, while curd or a soup made from Marmite or Vegemite (if you happen to have some with you) are forms of protein that can be easily absorbed by your body when you have the runs. Drugs like Lomotil or Immodium simply plug you up –undermining the body's efforts to rid itself of infection – though they can be useful if you have to travel. If symptoms persist for more than a few days, a course of antibiotics may be necessary; this should be seen as a last resort, and following medical advice.

Sordid though it may seem, it's a good idea to look at what comes out when you go to the toilet (and it makes an endless topic of polite meal-time conversation with your fellow travellers). If your diarrhoea contains blood or mucus, and other symptoms include rotten-egg belches and farts, the cause may be dysentery or giardia. With a fever, it could well be **bacillic dysentery**, and it may clear up without treatment. If you're sure you need it, a course of antibiotics such as tetracycline should sort you out, but they destroy "gut flora" in your intestines (which help protect your stomach, although, curd can replenish them to some extent). If you start a course, be sure to finish it, even after the symptoms have gone. Similar symptoms without fever indicate **amoebic dysentery**, which is much more serious and can damage your gut if untreated. The usual cure is a course of Metronidazole (Flagyl) or Fasigyn, both antibiotics, which may themselves make you feel ill and must not be taken with alcohol. Symptoms of **giardia** are similar – including frothy stools, nausea and constant fatigue – for which the treatment again is Metronidazole. If you suspect that you have any of these, seek medical help, and only start on the Metronidazole (750mg three times daily for a week for adults) if there is blood in your diarrhoea and it is impossible to see a doctor.

Finally, bear in mind that oral drugs, such as malaria pills and the Pill, are likely to be largely ineffective if taken while suffering from diarrhoea.

BITES AND CREEPY-CRAWLIES

Worms may enter your body through skin (especially the soles of your feet) or food. An itchy anus is a common symptom, and you may even see them in your stools. They are easy to treat: if you suspect you have them, get some worming tablets such as Mebendazole (Vermox) from any pharmacy.

Biting insects and similar animals other than mosquitoes may also aggravate you. The obvious ones are **bed bugs** – look for signs of squashed ones around cheap hotel beds. An infested mattress can be left in the hot sun all day to get rid of them, but they often live in the frame or even in walls or floors. Head and body **lice** can also be a nuisance, but medicated soap and shampoo (preferably brought with you from home) usually see them off. Avoid scratching bites, which can lead to infection. Bites from ticks and lice can spread **typhus**, characterized by fever, muscle aches, headaches, and later, red eyes and a measles-like rash. If you think you have it, seek treatment (tetracycline is usually prescribed – for adults, a single 1g dose followed by 300mg four times daily for five days).

Snakes are unlikely to bite unless accidentally disturbed, and most are harmless in any case. To see one at all, you will need to search stealthily – if you walk heavily, they usually oblige by disappearing. If you do get bitten, remember what the snake looked like (kill it if you can), try not to move the affected part and seek medical help: antivenoms are available in most hospitals.

A few **spiders** have poisonous bites too. Remove **leeches**, which may attach themselves to you in jungle areas, with salt or a lit cigarette rather than just pulling them off.

HEAT TROUBLE

The sun and the heat can cause a few unexpected problems, especially in the tropical south. Many people get a bout of **prickly heat** rash before they've acclimatized. It's an infection of the sweat ducts caused by excessive perspiration that doesn't dry off. A cool shower, zinc oxide powder (sold in India) and loose cotton clothes should help. **Dehydration** is another possible problem, so make sure you're drinking enough liquid, and drink rehydration salts frequently, especially when hot and/or tired. The main danger sign is irregular urination (only once a day for instance), but dark urine could probably mean you should drink more, although it could indicate hepatitis (see above).

The **sun** can burn, or even cause sunstroke, and a high-factor sunblock is vital on exposed skin, especially when you first arrive, and on areas newly exposed by haircuts or changes of clothes. A light hat is also a very good idea, especially if you're doing a lot of walking around.

Finally, be aware that overheating can cause **heatstroke**, which is potentially fatal. Signs are: a very high body temperature without a feeling of fever, accompanied by headaches and disorientation. Lowering body temperature (a tepid shower for example) and resting in an air-conditioned room is the first step in treatment.

Some of the illnesses and parasites you can pick up in India may not show themselves immediately. If you become ill within a year of returning home, tell whoever treats you where you have been and when you went there.

HIV AND AIDS

The rapidly increasing presence of **AIDS** (acquired immune deficiency syndrome) has only recently been acknowledged by the Indian government as a national problem, and as yet only foreign agencies have embarked on awareness and prevention campaigns. As elsewhere in the world, high-risk groups include prostitutes and intravenous drug users. It is extremely unwise to contemplate casual sex without a condom – carry some with you (preferably brought from home as Indian ones may be less reliable, and also, be aware that heat affects the durability of condoms), and insist on using them.

Should you need an injection or a blood transfusion in India, make sure that new, sterile equipment is used; any blood you receive should be from voluntary rather than commercial donor banks. If you have a shave from a barber, make sure he uses a clean blade, and don't submit to processes such as ear-piercing, acupuncture or tattooing unless you can be sure that the equipment is sterile.

GETTING MEDICAL HELP

Pharmacies can usually advise on minor medical problems, and most doctors in India speak English. Also, many hotels have a doctor on call. Basic medicaments are made to Indian Pharmacopoeia (IP) standards, and most medicines are available without prescription – although always check the sell-by date. Hospitals vary in standard. Private clinics and mission hospitals are often better than state-run ones, but may not have the same facilities. Hospitals in the big cities are generally pretty good; university or medical-school hospitals are best of all. Private hospitals require patients (even emergency cases) to buy necessities such as medicines, plaster casts and vaccines and to pay for X-rays, before procedures can be carried out. However, government hospitals provide all surgical and aftercare services free of charge, and in most other state medical institutions, charges are usually so low that for minor treatment the expense may well be lower than the initial "excess" on your insurance. You will need a companion to stay, or you'll have to come to an arrangement with one of the hospital cleaners, to help you out in hospital – relatives are expected to wash, feed and generally take care of the patient. Addresses of foreign consulates (who will advise in an emergency), and of clinics and hospitals can be found in the Listings sections for major towns in this book.

AYURVEDIC MEDICINE

Ayurved, a five-thousand-year-old holistic medical system, is widely practised in India and especially popular in the South, where Kerala is a particular stronghold. Ayurvedic doctors and clinics in large towns deal with foreigners as well as their usual patients, and some pharmacies specialize in ayurvedic preparations, including toiletries such as soaps, shampoos and toothpaste.

The "knowledge of life", as *ayurveda* means in Sanskrit, assumes the fundamental sameness of self and nature. Thus, man as microcosm reflects the universe as macrocosm. As such it is a sister science to yoga and stems from the same period of Vedic philosophy. Consequently, it accords great importance to the harmony of mind, body and spirit and acknowledges the psychosomatic causes behind many diseases. Unlike the allopathic medicines of the West, which depend on finding out what's ailing you and then killing it, *ayurveda* looks at the whole patient: disease is regarded as a symptom of imbalance, so it's the imbalance that's treated, not the disease.

Ayurvedic theory holds that the body is controlled by three *doshas* (forces), themselves made up of the basic elements of space, fire, water, earth and air, which reflect the forces within the self. The three *doshas* are: *pitta*, the force of the sun, which is hot and rules the digestive processes and metabolism; *kapha*, likened to the moon, the creator of tides and rhythms, which has a cooling effect, and governs the body's organs and bone structure; and *vata*, wind, which relates to movement, circulation and the nervous system. People are classified according to which *dosha* or combination of them is predominant. The healthy body is one that has the three forces in the correct balance for its type. To diagnose an imbalance, the ayurvedic doctor not only goes into the physical complaint but also into family background, daily habits and emotional traits.

Imbalances are typically treated with herbal remedies designed to alter whichever of the three forces is out of whack. This commonly involves the application of oils or ingestion of specially prepared medicines. Made according to traditional formulae, using indigenous plants, ayurvedic medicines are cheaper than branded or imported ones. Traditional, strictly vegetarian diets are also advised for long-term benefits. In addition, the doctor may prescribe various forms of yogic cleansing to rid the body of waste substances. To the uninitiated, these techniques will sound rather off-putting – for instance, swallowing a long strip of cloth, a short section at a time, and then pulling it back up again to remove mucus from the stomach.

Many places advertising ayurvedic treatments in the more touristic spots are just glorified massage parlours using a few herbal oils and traditional techniques; however, even these can provide welcome relaxation. Those who seek out more bona fide clinics for lengthier purification regimes, or for the treatment of individual ailments, are often full of praise for the efficacy of these ancient methods.

INFORMATION AND MAPS

The Indian government maintains a number of tourist offices abroad, where you can pick up a range of pamphlets. Their main purpose is to advertise rather than inform, but they can be extremely helpful and knowledgeable.

Other sources of information include travel agents (who are in business for themselves, so their advice may not always be totally unbiased), and the Indian Railways representatives listed in the box on p.29.

Inside India, both national and local governments run **tourist information offices**, providing general travel advice and handing out an array of printed material, from city maps to glossy leaflets covering specific destinations. The Indian government's tourist department – whose main offices are opposite Churchgate train station, Mumbai – has branches in most regional capitals. These, however, operate independently of the information counters and bureaux run by the **state tourism development corporations**, usually referred to by their initials (eg KTDC in Kerala), who offer a wide range of travel facilities, including **guided tours**, **car rental** and their own **hotels** (which we identify with the relevant acronyms throughout this book).

Just to confuse things more, the Indian government's tourist office has a go-ahead corporate wing too. **ITDC** (Indian Tourism Development Corporation), is responsible for the Ashok chain of hotels and operates tour and travel services, frequently competing with its state counterparts.

SOUTH INDIA ON THE INTERNET

General

www.123india.com
India-specific search engine providing links to a wide choice of India-related Web sites.

http://travel.indiamart.com
Comprehensive site providing tourist information on India's forts, monuments, museums and temples.

www.indev.org
India Development Information Network Web site for information on Indian development issues: discussions, news regarding NGOs and useful links.

Government of India, Ministry of Tourism

www.tourisminindia.com
A very useful site providing a vast range of information, includin`g rail and air travel timetables, details and dates of festivals. (Also, check out *www.tourismindia.com* a site which links up with all the regional Indian Tourist Boards.)

www.tourindia.com
The Web site – originating from the US – of the Government of India Tourist Office, which is easier to navigate than the main site.

News and media

www.mahesh.com/india/media
Excellent resource for links to the Web sites of

INDIAN GOVERNMENT TOURIST OFFICES ABROAD

Australia Level 2, Piccadilly, 210 Pitt St, Sydney NSW (☎02/9264 4855, fax 4860).

Canada 60 Bloor St West, #1003, Toronto, Ontario M4W 3B8 (☎416/ 962-3787).

Netherlands Rokin 9–15, 1012 KK, Amsterdam (☎020/620 8991, fax 638 3059).

Singapore 20 Karamat Lane, 01–01A United House, Singapore 0922 (☎065/235 3800, fax 235 8677).

Thailand Singapore Airlines Bldg, 3rd floor, 62/5 Thaniya Rd, Bangkok (☎02/235 2585).

UK 7 Cork St, London W1X 1PB (☎0171/437 3677, fax 494 1048).

US 3550 Wiltshire Bd, Suite #204, Los Angeles, CA 90010 (☎213/380-8855, fax 380-6111); Suite 1808, 1270 Ave of Americas, NY 10020 (☎212/751-6840, fax 582-3274).

both national and regional Indian newspapers and magazines.

www.timesofindia.com
www.hinduonline.com
The Web sites of *The Times of India* and *The Hindu* provide the most up-to-date and detailed national news coverage.

South India
www.mumbaimart.com
www.mumbai-central.com
www.bangaloreonline.com
www.chennainow.com
www.hyderabadnetizens.com
www.mangalore.com
www.pondicherry.com
Besides our own extensive site on India (*www.roughguides.com*), these are some useful Web sites on South Indian cities, some with search engines, listings and news.

www.andhraworld.com
www.goacom.com
www.karnataka.com
www.kerala.com
Useful state-wide Web sites with search engines and some good links.

www.thekkady.com
www.alappuzha.com
Some of the best of a host of town and regional Web sites now available on Kerala.

Travel advice
www.fco.gov
The British Foreign Office Web site is useful for checking potential or actual dangerous areas.

http://travel.state.gov/travel–warnings.html
The US State Department's travel advice for potential hot spots.

MAPS

Getting good **maps** of India, in India, can be difficult; the government forbids the sale of detailed maps of border areas, which include the entire coastline. Geocentre produces an excellent map of South India at a scale of 1:2,000,000, showing good road detail.

Another excellent map of South India is the Nelles' India 4 (South) 1:1,500,000, which shows colour contours, road distances, inset city plans and even the tiniest places. Ttk, a Chennai-based company, publishes basic state maps, which are widely available in India, and in some specialized travel and map shops in the UK such as Stanfords (see box on p.22). Regional Automobile Associations based in Delhi, Calcutta, Mumbai and Chennai produce books of road maps which are useful for those planning overland routes across India. For basic state-by-state and city road maps off the Internet try the extensive Web site: *http://mapsofindia.com/maps/*.

If you need larger-scale **city maps** than the ones we provide in this book – which are keyed to show recommended hotels and restaurants – you can sometimes get them from tourist offices. Both Ttk and the official Indian mapping organization, the Survey of India, Janpath Barracks A, New Delhi 110 001 (☎011/332 2288), have town plans at scales of 1:10,000 and 1:50,000. Some of the city and regional maps they have for sale are grossly out of date.

BOOK AND MAP OUTLETS

IN THE UK AND IRELAND

Blackwell's Map and Travel Shop 53 Broad St, Oxford OX1 3BQ (☎01865/792792, *bookshop.blackwell.co.uk*).

Heffers Map Shop 3rd Floor, Heffers Stationery Department, 19 Sidney St, Cambridge CB2 3HL (☎01223/568467, *www.heffers.co.uk*). Also offers mail-order service.

John Smith and Sons 57–61 St Vincent St, Glasgow G2 5TB (☎0141/221 7472, *www.johnsmith.co.uk*).

The Map Shop 30 Belvoir St, Leicester LE1 6QH (☎0116/247 1400).

National Map Centre 22–24 Caxton St, London SW1H 0QU (☎0171/222 2466, *www.mapsworld.com*).

Newcastle Map Centre 55 Grey St, Newcastle upon Tyne NE1 6EF (☎0191/261 5622).

Stanfords 12–14 Long Acre, London WC2E 9LP (☎0171/836 1321, email *sales@stanfords.co.uk*). Also offers mail-order service.

IN AUSTRALIA AND NEW ZEALAND:

Mapland 372 Little Bourke St, Melbourne, VIC 3000 (☎03/9670 4383).

The Map Shop 16a Peel St, Adelaide, SA 5000 (☎08/8231 2033).

Perth Map Centre 884 Hay St, Perth, WA 6000 (☎08/9322 5733).

Speciality Maps 58 Albert St, Auckland (☎09/307 2217).

Travel Bookshop Shop 3, 175 Liverpool St, Sydney, NSW 2000 (☎02/9261 8200).

Worldwide Maps and Guides 187 George St, Brisbane, QLD 4000 (☎07/3221 4330).

IN NORTH AMERICA AND CANADA:

Adventurous Traveler Bookstore PO Box 1468, Williston, VT 05495 (☎1-800/282-3963).

Book Passage 51 Tamal Vista Blvd, Corte Madera, CA 94925 (☎415/927-0960).

The Complete Traveler Bookstore 199 Madison Ave, New York NY 10016 (☎212/685-9007); 3207 Fillmore St, San Francisco CA 94123 (☎415/923 1511).

Curious Traveller Travel Bookstore 101 Yorkville Ave, Toronto ON M5R 1C1 (☎1-800/268-4395).

Elliot Bay Book Company 101 South Main St, Seattle WA 98104 (☎206/624 6600).

Map Link 30 S La Petera Lane, Unit #5, Santa Barbara, CA 93117 (☎805/692-6777).

The Map Store, Inc. 1636 I St Washington, DC 20006 (☎202/628-2608).

Open Air Books and Maps 25 Toronto St, Toronto M5C 2R1 (☎416/363 07190).

Phileas Fogg's Books & Maps #87 Stanford Shopping Center, Palo Alto, CA 94304 (☎1-800/533-FOGG).

Rand McNally 444 N Michigan Ave, Chicago IL 60611 (☎312/321 1751); 150 East 52nd St, New York NY 10022 (☎212/758 7488); 595 Market St, San Francisco CA 94105 (☎415/777 3131); with additional branches across the US. For other locations and maps by mail order (☎1-800/220-2665).

Ulysses Travel Bookshop 4176 St-Denis, Montreal (☎514/843 9447).

World Wide Books and Maps 552 Seymour St, Vancouver BC V6B 3J5 (☎604/687 3320).

COSTS, MONEY AND BANKS

India is, unquestionably, one of the least expensive countries for travellers in the world – and generally the South is even cheaper than the North so a little foreign currency goes a long way. That means you can be confident of getting consistently good value for money, whether you're setting out to keep your budget to a minimum or to enjoy the opportunities that spending a bit more will make possible.

While we attempt to suggest the kind of sums you can expect to pay for varying degrees of comfort, it is vital not to make a rigid assumption at the outset of a long trip that whatever money you bring to India will last for a certain number of weeks or months. On any one day it may be possible to spend very little, but cumulatively you won't be doing yourself any favours if you don't make sure you keep yourself well rested and properly fed.

What you spend depends on you: where you go, where you stay, how you get around, what you eat and what you buy. On a budget of as little as £5/US$8 per day, you'll manage if you stick to the cheapest of everything and don't move about too much; double that, and you can permit yourself a few splurge meals, the occasional mid-range hotel and some souvenirs. If you're happy spending £15–20/US$20–30 per day, however, you can really pamper yourself; to spend much more than that, you'd have to be doing a lot of travelling, consistently staying in the best hotel in town and eating in the top restaurant.

Accommodation ranges from £1.50/US$2per night upwards (see p.34), while a mid-range **meal** in an ordinary restaurant is unlikely to cost even that much. Filling eat-all-you-can vegetarian "meals" are available throughout the southern states at no more than 30p/50¢ but not many people want to live on them alone. Transport in town costs pence (even by taxi or the most over-charging rickshaw), while a twelve-hour train journey might cost £2/$3 in second class, £8/$12 in first.

Where you are makes a difference: Mumbai is notoriously pricey, especially for accommodation, while tourist enclaves like the Goa beaches will not be cheap for things like food, and there will be more souvenirs to tempt you. Out in the sticks, on the other hand, and particularly away from your fellow tourists, you will find things incredibly cheap, though your choices will obviously be more limited.

Some independent travellers tend to indulge in wild and highly competitive penny-pinching, which Indian people find rather pathetic – they know how much an air ticket to Delhi or Mumbai costs, and they have a fair idea of what you can earn at home. Bargain where appropriate, but don't begrudge a few rupees to someone who's worked hard for them: consider what their services would cost at home, and how much more valuable the money is to them than it is to you. Even if you get a bad deal on every rickshaw journey you make, it will only add at most one percent to a £1000/$1500 trip. Remember too, that every pound or dollar you spend in India goes that much further, and luxuries you can't afford at home become possible here: sometimes it's worth spending more simply because you get more for it. At the same time, don't pay well over the odds for something if you know what the going rate is. Thoughtless extravagance can, particularly in remote areas that see a disproportionate number of tourists, contribute to inflation, putting even basic goods and services beyond the reach of local people.

CURRENCY

India's unit of currency is the **rupee**, usually abbreviated "Rs" and divided into a hundred paise. Almost all money is paper, with notes of 1, 2, 5, 10, 20, 50, 100 and 500 rupees. Coins start at 5 paise (for temple offerings), then range up to 10, 20, 25 and 50 paise, and 1, 2 and 5 rupees.

Banknotes, especially lower denominations, can get into a terrible state, but don't accept banknotes torn down the centre; no one else will be prepared to take them, so you will be left saddled with the things. You can change them at the Reserve Bank of India and large branches of other big banks, or slip them into the middle of a wad when paying for something (which is probably how they'll have been passed to you). Don't pass them on to beggars; they can't use them either, so it amounts to an insult. However, notes full of holes (from the obligatory bank staples), tatty edges or covered in plastic pass without comment.

Large denominations can also be a problem, as change is often in short supply, particularly in small towns. Many Indian people cannot afford to keep much lying around, and you shouldn't necessarily expect shopkeepers or rickshaw-*wallahs* to have it (and they may – as may you – try to hold onto it if they do). Paying for your groceries with a Rs100 note may well entail waiting for the grocer's errand boy to go off on a quest around town trying to change it. Keeping a wad of Rs1 notes handy isn't a bad idea (you can get bundles of a hundred stapled together in banks).

At the time of writing, the **exchange rate** was approximately Rs69 to £1, or Rs43 to US$1.

TRAVELLERS' CHEQUES AND CREDIT CARDS

Carry a mixture of cash and travellers' cheques to cover all eventualities, with a few small denominations for the end of your trip and for the odd foreign-currency purchase. US dollars are the easiest **currency** to convert, with pounds sterling coming a close second. Major hard currencies can be changed easily in tourist areas and big cities, less so elsewhere. If you enter the country with over US$10,000 or the equivalent, you are supposed to fill in a currency declaration form.

Travellers' cheques aren't as liquid as cash, but obviously more secure (and you get a slightly better exchange rate for them at banks). Not all banks, however, accept them, and those that do can be quirky about exactly which ones they *will* change. Well-known brands such as Thomas Cook and American Express are your best bet, but in some places even American Express is only accepted in US dollars and not as pounds sterling.

A **credit card** is a handy backup, as an increasing number of hotels, restaurants, large shops and tourist emporia as well as airlines now take plastic, with American Express, Access/Mastercard, Visa and Diners Club being the most commonly accepted brands. If you have a selection of cards, take them all; you'll get much the same exchange rate as you would in a bank, and bills can take a surprisingly long time to be charged to your account at home. The Bank of Baroda issues rupees against a Visa card at all its branches. Even train tickets can now be paid for by credit card.

It is illegal to carry rupees into or out of India, and you won't get them at a particularly good rate in the West anyhow (though you might in Thailand, Malaysia or Singapore).

TRAVELLERS' CHEQUES AND CREDIT CARDS

American Express

Lost and stolen cards ☎011/687 5050 (open 24hr).

Bangalore Janardhan Tower, 2 Residency Rd (☎080/2271485).

Chennai G-17, Spencer Plaza, 768–769 Anna Salai (☎044/852 3573).

Mumbai Regal Cinema Building, Chatrapati Shivaji Maharaj Rd, Colaba (☎022/204 8291).

Thomas Cook

Bangalore 70 Mahatma Gandhi Rd (☎080/558 8038).

Chennai Ceebros Centre, 45 Montieth Rd, Egmore (☎044/855 3263).

Mumbai Dr D Naoroji Rd, Fort (☎022/204 8556).

Both American Express and Thomas Cook have offices in other major cities throughout India; see the relevant accounts in the guide and collect a full list when you purchase your travellers' cheques.

BANKS

Changing money in regular banks can be a time-consuming business, involving lots of form-filling and queuing at different counters, so change substantial amounts at any one time. Banks in main cities are likely to be most efficient, though not all change foreign currency, and some won't take travellers' cheques or currencies other than dollars or sterling. You'll have no such problems with private companies such as Thomas Cook and American Express who have offices in most state capitals. In small towns, the State Bank of India is your best bet. Note that if you arrive at a minor airport you may not be able to change anything, except cash US dollars or sterling.

Outside **banking hours** (Mon–Fri 10am–2pm, Sat 10am–noon), large hotels may change money, probably at a lower rate. Banks at Mumbai and Chennai airports stay open **24 hours** but none of these is conveniently located. Otherwise, there's always the black market.

Hold on to **exchange receipts** ("encashment certificates"); they will be required if you want to change back any excess rupees when you leave the country, and to buy air tickets and reserve train-berths with rupees. The State Bank of India now charges for tax clearance forms (see p.11 to find out if you'll need one.)

Wiring money to India is a lot easier than it used to be. Indian banks with branches abroad, such as the State Bank of India and the Bank of Baroda, can wire money by telex from those branches to large ones in India within two working days. Western Union (information on ☎1-800/325 6000 in the US or ☎0800/833833 in the UK) can transfer cash or banker's drafts paid into their overseas branches to any one of 43 offices in India within fifteen minutes, for a typical fee of around 7.5 percent of the total amount. Similar transfer services are offered by American Express, Thomas Cook and foreign banks with branches in India such as ANZ Grindlays.

THE BLACK MARKET

A **black market** still exists today, but only in the major tourist areas of the biggest cities, with little if any premium over the bank rate, though it is a lot faster. Small denominations are not popular, with the best rates given for notes of £50, US$100 or DM1000; you will, of course, have to haggle.

Always do this kind of business with shopkeepers rather than shady "hello my friend" types on the street, and proceed with caution. Never hand over your pile until you *yourself* have counted and checked the rupees and have them in your hand; make sure they really are the denominations they should be. Unusually high rates suggest a con, as does any attempt to rush you, or sudden claims that the police are coming. Remember what you are doing is illegal; you can be arrested and you may be set up.

BAKSHEESH

As a presumed-rich sahib or memsahib, you will, like wealthy Indians, be expected to be liberal with the **baksheesh**, which takes three main forms.

The most common is **tipping**: a small reward for a small service, which can encompass anyone from a waiter or porter to someone who lifts your bags onto the roof of a bus or keeps an eye on your vehicle for you. Large amounts are not expected – five rupees should satisfy all the aforementioned. Taxi drivers and staff at cheaper hotels and restaurants do not necessarily expect tips, but always appreciate them, of course, and they can keep people sweet for the next time you call. Some may take liberties in demanding *baksheesh*, but it's often better just to acquiesce rather than spoil your mood and cause offence over trifling sums.

More expensive than plain tipping is paying people to **bend the rules**, many of which seem to have been invented for precisely that purpose. Examples might include letting you into a historical site after hours, finding you a seat or a sleeper on a train that is "full" or speeding up some bureaucratic process. This should not be confused with bribery, a more serious business with its own risks and etiquette, which is best not entered into.

The last kind of *baksheesh* is **alms-giving**. In a country without a welfare system, this is an important social custom. People with disabilities and mutilations are the traditional recipients, and it seems right to join local people in giving out small change to them. Kids demanding money, pens or the like are a different case, pressing their demands only on tourists. In return for a service it is fair enough, but to yield to any request encourages them to go and pester others.

GETTING AROUND

Inter-city transport in South India may not be the fastest or the most comfortable in the world, but it's cheap, goes more or less everywhere and generally gives you the option of train or bus, sometimes plane, and occasionally even boat. Transport around town comes in even more permutations, ranging from cycle rickshaws just about everywhere to double-decker buses in Mumbai.

Whether you're on road or rail, public transport or your own vehicle, India offers the chance to try out some classics: narrow-gauge railways, steam locomotives, the Ambassador car and the Enfield Bullet motorbike, they're all here. Some people come to India for these alone.

BY TRAIN

Travelling by train is one of the great experiences of South India. There may be railway systems that are faster, more punctual and more comfortable (though perhaps none cheaper), but nowhere will you find one that is more, well, Indian!

Indian railways are a frenetic, crowded, yet in some ways rather quaint world of "up" trains and "down" trains, carrying untold masses of people in barrack-like carriages, echoing to the ubiquitous cries of the *chai-wallahs* as they dispense tea in disposable clay cups, and food hawkers whose stalls spring into action on every railway platform as each train arrives and they jostle for position with sellers of *bidis*, newspapers and magazines. From tiny country stations, where the daily train is the big event, to massive labyrinthine city terminals where families make their homes on the platforms, the new wave of computer technology now sweeps through the dusty offices of railway functionaries. It's a system which looks like chaos, but it works, and well. Trains are often late of course, sometimes by hours rather than minutes, but they do run, and with amazing efficiency too: when the train you've been waiting for rolls into the station, the reservation you made halfway across the country several weeks ago will be on a list pasted to the side of your carriage, and when it's time to eat, the packed meal you ordered down the line will be ready at the next station, put on the train and delivered to your seat.

Once rolling, you can settle down to enjoy an excellent view of the countryside as it slips past, fall into conversation with your fellow passengers, enjoy a nice cup of *chai* or relax with a book or newspaper. It's worth bearing in mind too, with journeys frequently lasting twelve hours or more, that an overnight train can save you a day's travelling and a night's hotel bill, assuming you sleep well on trains. While sleeper carriages can be more crowded during the day, between 9pm and 6am anyone with a bunk reservation is entitled to exclusive use of their bunk. When travelling overnight, however, always padlock your bag to your bunk.

> At the end of each chapter in this book, you'll find a Travel Details section summarizing major transport connections in the relevant state. In addition, boxes at the end of each major city detail Moving On from that city.

ROUTES AND CLASSES

The rail network covers almost the whole of South India; only a few places (such as most of Goa and some parts of the Ghats) are inaccessible by train. **Inter-city** trains, called "**express**" or "**mail**", vary a lot in the time taken to cover the same route. Slow by Western standards, they're still much faster than local "**passenger**" trains, which you need only use to get right off the beaten track. There is also an increasing number of special "**super-fast**" a/c trains, usually named *Rajdhani* or *Shatabdi Express*, which cover routes between major cities in as little as half the normal time.

Note that express and mail trains cost a fair amount more than ordinary passenger trains, so if travelling unreserved you must buy the right ticket to avoid being fined.

Most lines are either metre-gauge or broad-gauge (1.676m, or 4ft 6in), the latter being faster; many metre-gauge lines are now being converted to broad-gauge. The only narrow-gauge line (often referred to as "the toy train"), in the South, runs to Ootacamund, and you will only find **steam locomotives** in routinely scheduled service on the steep sections of this narrow-gauge mountain railway.

Indian Railways distinguishes between no fewer than seven **classes** of travel, though you'll seldom have more than the following four to choose from on mainline services: second-class unreserved, second-class sleeper, first and a/c first (or a/c two- or three-tier sleeper class). In general, most travellers (not just those on low budgets) choose to travel second class, and prefer not to be in a/c compartments; an open window keeps you cool enough, and brings you into contact with the world outside, while air-conditioning by definition involves being sealed away behind glass, which is often virtually opaque. Doing without a sleeper on an overnight journey is, however, a false economy. Bed rolls (sheet, blanket and pillow) are available in first class and a/c second for that extra bit of comfort – book these with your ticket, or before you board the train.

Second-class unreserved is painfully crowded and noisy with no chance of a berth overnight, but incredibly cheap, for example, just Rs77 (that's just over £1 or under $2) for a thousand-kilometre journey. However, the crush and hard wooden seats (if you are lucky or nifty enough to get one) make it viable only for short hops or for the extremely hardy. Far more civilized, and only around thirty percent more expensive, is second-class sleeper, which must be booked in advance even for daytime journeys. If you have an unreserved ticket and travel in a sleeper carriage, even if it is not full, you will be charged a Rs60 fine as well as the difference in fare. Sleeper class can be pretty crowded during the day but never lacks activity, be it peanut-, *chai-* or coffee-sellers, travelling musicians, beggars or sweepers passing through each carriage. Overnight trips in second-class sleeper compartments are reasonably comfy (provided the berths are foam and not wooden), and there's the option of more privacy for women in ladies' compartments on most long-haul journeys. First class, in comfortable compartments of two to four berths, is used mainly by English-speaking business travellers. It costs about three and a half times as much as second-class sleeper and insulates you to a certain extent from the chaotic hustle and bustle – which you may or may not consider to be an advantage.

Air-conditioned travel falls into four categories but only one or two will be available on any particular service. The best value is a/c chair car, with comfortable reclining seats at only double the price of second-class sleeper. The famous "super-fast" *Rajdhani* and *Shatabdi* expresses mostly consist of such compartments, and you will also find the odd carriage tacked onto some normal expresses. Air-conditioned three-tier sleepers cost slightly less than normal first class, but are not all that common, while a/c two-tier sleepers are more abundant and cost half as much again as first class. Top of the tree and costing around two and a half times as much as first class is a/c first class, which offers little more than extra space on top of the obvious cool air.

TIMETABLES AND TICKETS

Indian Railways publish an annual **timetable** of all mail and express trains – in effect, all the trains you are likely to use. Called *Trains at a Glance*, it is available from information counters and news-stands at all main stations, and from Indian Railways agents abroad. *Thomas Cook's International Timetable Vol II* (the blue one) has a limited selection of timetables, while the elusive monthly *Indian Bradshaw* covers every scheduled train in the country. In theory, this is available at major termini, but it is often difficult to get hold of; complete regional timetables are widely available, however. Southern Railways' timetable is ample for the region and contains a summary of routes in the rest of the country.

All rail **fares** are calculated according to the exact distance travelled; *Trains at a Glance* prints a chart of fares by kilometres, and also gives the distance in kilometres of stations along each route in the timetables, making it possible to calculate what the basic fare will be for any given journey. Endless pouring over the columns reveals little more than that fares are very cheap indeed.

Each individual train has its own name and number, which is prominently displayed in station booking halls. When buying a ticket, it makes sense to pay the tiny, extra fee to reserve a seat or sleeper (the fee is already included in the price of a first-class sleeper). To do so, you fill in a form specifying the train you intend to catch, its number, your date of travel and the stations you are travelling to and from, plus, amusingly to most travellers, your age and sex.

Most stations (listed in *Trains at a Glance*) have computerized booking counters, and you will be told immediately whether or not seats are available. These **reservation offices** are often in a separate building and generally open Mon–Sat 8am–8pm and Sun 8am–2pm. In larger cities, the major stations have special **tourist sections**, to cut the queues for foreigners and Indian citizens resident abroad buying tickets, with helpful English-speaking staff; however, if you don't pay in pounds sterling or US dollars (travellers' cheques or cash), you must produce an encashment certificate to back up your rupees. Elsewhere, buying a ticket can often involve a long wait, though women get round this at ticket counters which have "ladies' queues". Some stations also operate a numbered system of queuing, allowing you to repair to the *chai* stall or check the timetable until your number is called. Alternatively, many travel agents will secure tickets for a reasonable Rs25–50 fee. Failure to buy a ticket at the point of departure will result in paying a stiff penalty when the ticket inspector finds you.

It's important to plan your train journeys in advance, as demand often makes it impossible to buy a long-distance ticket on the same day that you want to travel. Travellers following tight itineraries tend to buy their departure tickets from particular towns the moment they arrive, to avoid having to trek out to the station again. At most large stations, it's possible to reserve tickets for journeys starting elsewhere in the country. You can even book tickets for specific journeys (if you buy an Indrail pass) before you leave home, with Indian Railways representatives abroad (see box on p.29). They accept bookings of up to six months in advance, with a minimum of one month for first class, and three months for second.

If you have to **cancel your ticket**, the fare is refunded up to a day before departure, minus a fee for the reservation (Rs10 in second class, Rs20 in sleeper, Rs30 a/c chair car or first, and, Rs50 in a/c first). Cancelling between a day and four hours before scheduled departure, gets you 75 percent back; you can still claim a fifty percent refund if you present your ticket up to twelve

INDRAIL PASSES

Indrail passes – sold to foreigners and Indians resident abroad – cover all fares and reservation fees for periods ranging from half a day to ninety days. Even if you travel a lot, this works out considerably more expensive than buying your tickets individually (especially in second class), but it will save you queuing for tickets, and allow you to make and cancel reservations with impunity (and without charge). It will also generally smooth your way in, for example, finding a seat or berth on a "full" train: pass-holders, for example, get priority for tourist quota places. Indrail passes are available, for pounds sterling or US dollars, at main station tourist counters in India, and outside the country at Indian Railways agents (see box on p.29). If you're travelling from Britain, Mr Dandapani of SD Enterprises Ltd (see box on p.29) is an excellent contact, providing information on all aspects of travel on Indian railways.

RATES IN US$

	a/c First Class		First Class or a/c Sleeper or a/c Chair Car		Second Class	
	Adult	Child	Adult	Child	Adult	Child
1 day*	86	43	39	20	17	9
4 days*	220	110	110	55	50	25
7 days	300	150	150	75	80	40
15 days	370	185	185	95	90	45
21 days	440	220	220	110	100	50
30 days	550	275	275	140	125	65
60 days	800	400	400	200	185	95
90 days	1060	530	530	265	235	120

*For sale outside India only; half-day & two-day passes are also available. Note that these prices are liable to rise a further ten percent.

INDIAN RAILWAYS SALES AGENTS ABROAD

Australia: Adventure World, 73 Walker St (PO Box 480), North Sydney, NSW 2059 (☎02/9956 7766).

Bangladesh: Omaitrans International, 70/1 Inner Circular Rd, Kakrail, Dhaka (☎02/834401).

Canada: Hari World Travel Inc, 1 Financial Place, Adelaide St East, Toronto M5C 2V8 (☎416/366 2000).

Malaysia: City East West Travels, Sdn Bhd No 135-A, Jalan Bunus, 50100 Kuala Lumpur (☎03/293 0569).

Thailand: SS Travels Service, 10/12–13, SS Building, Convent Rd, Bangkok 10500 (☎02/236 7188).

UK: SD Enterprises Ltd, 103 Wembley Park Drive, Wembley, Middx HA9 8HG (☎0181/903 3411).

USA: Hari World Travels Inc, 25 W 45th St # 1003 New York, NY 10036 (☎212/957 3000); with additional locations in Atlanta (☎404/233 5005), and Chicago (☎773/381 5555).

hours after the train actually leaves on a journey of over 500km, six hours on 200–500km trips or three hours on a short journey.

If there are **no places available** on the train you want, you have a number of choices. First, some seats and berths are set aside as a "tourist quota" – ask at the tourist counter if you can get in on this, or try the stationmaster. This quota is usually only available at major or originating stations. Failing that, other special quotas, such as one for VIPs, may remain unused – however, if you get a booking on the VIP quota and a pukka VIP turns up, you lose the reservation. Alternatively, a "reservation against cancellation" (RAC) ticket will give you priority if sleepers do become available – the ticket clerk should be able to tell you your chances – or you could get a plain, wait-listed ticket, get on the train and go and see the ticket inspector as soon as possible. You may be able to persuade them to find you a place if one is free: something usually is, but you'll be stuck in unreserved if it isn't. In practice, if your number on the waiting list is not far into double figures, you have a good chance of getting a place. Alternatively, and especially if you get on where the train starts its journey, *baksheesh* may persuade a porter to "reserve" you an unreserved seat, or, better still, a luggage rack where you can stretch out for the night. You *could* even fight your way on and grab one yourself, although don't rate your chances. As for attempting to **travel unreserved**, for journeys of any length, it's too uncomfortable to be worth seriously considering.

Ladies' compartments exist on all overnight trains for women travelling on their own or with other women; they are usually small and can be full of noisy kids, but can give untold relief to women travellers who otherwise have to endure incessant staring in the open section of the carriage. On the other hand, particularly if you like (or are with) children, they can be a good place to meet Indian women. Some stations also have ladies-only waiting rooms.

CLOAKROOMS

Most stations in India have "cloakrooms" (sometimes called "parcel offices"), for passengers to leave their baggage. These can be extremely handy if you want to go sightseeing in a town and move on the same day. In theory, you need a train ticket or Indrail pass to deposit luggage, but they don't always ask; they may however refuse to take your bag if you can't lock it. Losing your reclaim ticket causes problems; the clerk will be assumed to have stolen the bag if he can't produce it, so there'll be untold running around to obtain clearance before you can get your bag without it. Make sure, when checking baggage in, that the cloakroom will be open when you need to pick it up. The standard charge is currently Rs5 per 24 hours.

BY AIR

Though obviously more expensive than going by train or bus, **flying** can save a lot of time: Mumbai–Chennai, for example, can take around thirty hours' hard travelling by train, yet a mere 1hr 45min by plane. Delays and cancellations can whittle away the time advantage, especially over small distances, but if you're short of time and plan to cover a lot of ground, you should definitely consider flying for longer journeys.

India has just one national internal air carrier, **Indian Airlines** (IA), which serves 147 routes country-wide and also flies to Southeast

Asia. In addition, Air India runs shuttles between the four main cities (from the international, not the domestic, terminals), which provides useful links to Mumbai and Chennai for those entering India via Delhi or Calcutta. Jet Airways is the only private operator with an extensive and constantly expanding network throughout the country and standards compare favourably with IA. Sahara also has some schedules for southern cities. Prices are similar whichever company you use. Short flights can be cheap, often less than £40/$50, but longer ones are hardly less than equivalent distances anywhere else. IA has a number of special deals that are worth knowing about: in addition to 25 percent discount for under-30s and students, and 50 percent for over-65s, they offer two multi-flight discounts (see box). Jet Airways also has similar deals.

One problem with flying is that you may have to spend a massive amount of time queuing at the airline office to get a reservation; it's often quicker to book through a hotel or travel agent, which is the norm for booking on private carriers. If you haven't got a confirmed seat, be sure to get to the airport early and keep checking your position in the queue; even if you *have* got a confirmed seat, be sure to always reconfirm 72 hours before your flight.

Airlines have offices or representatives in all the places they fly to; all are listed in this book in the relevant city sections. IA tickets must be paid for in hard currency or with a credit card. Children under twelve pay half fare, and under-twos (one per adult) pay ten percent. There are no cancellation charges if you pay in foreign currency, but tickets are not replaceable if lost. **Timetables** for all internal flights (with fares) are published in *Divan* and *Excel* magazines, and shown on teletext in the UK, while all operators stock their own timetables.

INDIAN AIRLINES MULTI-FLIGHT DEALS

Discover India Fare: Unlimited travel on all internal flights; $500 for fifteen days or $750 for 21 days (no single route twice). **India Wonderfare**: Seven days' travel in one given region; $300.

JET AIRWAYS MULTI-FLIGHT DEAL

Visit India Fare: Unlimited travel on their routes: fifteen days $550; 21 days $800.

BY BUS

Although trains are the definitive form of transport in South India, and generally more comfortable than **buses**, there are places where trains don't go, where they are awkward and inconvenient, or where buses are simply faster (as in most places without broad-gauge track). Alternatively, you might just fancy a change or the train you want might be booked up. In that case, the bus is for you; and you'll be pleased to know that they go almost everywhere, more frequently than trains (though mostly in daylight hours), and there are state-government-operated services everywhere, and plenty of private firms besides.

Buses vary somewhat in price and standards. Government-run ramshackle affairs, packed to the gunwales with people, livestock and luggage, cover both short and very long distances. In more widely travelled areas there usually tend to be additional private buses offering more leg-room and generally travelling faster – not necessarily a plus point when you consider the dilapidated state of the vehicles.

Some clue as to comfort can be gained from the description given to the bus. "**Ordinary**" buses usually have minimally padded fixed upright seats arranged with a double and triple on either side of the aisle. "**Deluxe**", or "**luxury**", and even "**super-deluxe**", are fairly interchangeable terms and when applied to government buses may hardly differ from "ordinary". Usually they refer to private services, though, and should then guarantee a softer, sometimes reclining, individual seat. You can check this out when booking, and it's also worth asking if your bus has a video or music system, as their deafening noise ruins any chances of sleep. The South generally has fewer smart private buses, and those available are aimed primarily at foreigners. However, smaller private bus companies may be only semi-legal and have little backup in case of breakdown. You should also bear in mind that even luxury coaches can have broken seats, recliners that don't recline and windows that don't close, so be prepared, and always try to avoid the back seats – they accentuate bumpy roads, launching you into the air several times a minute.

Luggage travels in the hatch on private buses, but you can usually squeeze it into an unobtrusive corner inside state-run vehicles, although you may sometimes be requested to have it travel on the roof (you may be able to travel up there yourself if the bus is too crowded, though it's dangerous and illegal); check that it's well secured (ideally, lock it there) and not liable to get squashed. *Baksheesh* is in order for whoever puts it up there for you.

Buying a bus ticket is usually less of an ordeal than buying a train ticket, although at large city bus stations there may be twenty or so counters, each assigned to a different route. When you buy your ticket you'll be given the registration number of the bus and, sometimes, a seat number. As at train stations, there is usually a separate, quicker, ladies' queue, although the sign to indicate it may not be in English. You can always get on ordinary state buses without a ticket, and at bus stands outside major cities you can usually only pay on board, so you have to be sharp to secure a seat. Prior booking is usually available and preferable for express and private services and it is a good idea to check with the agent exactly where the bus will depart from. You can usually pay on board private buses too, though that reduces your chances of a seat.

BY BOAT

Apart from flat-bottomed river ferries, which are common along the Konkan coast (particularly in Goa), the boat services you're most likely to use in South India are those plying the backwaters of **Kerala**, where the majority of settlements are still most easily reached by water. Foreign visitors generally stick to the route connecting the area's two main towns, Alappuzha and Kollam, along which the local tourist office operates popular sightseeing boats, but it can be fun to catch run-of-the-mill village ferries to smaller, less developed areas.

The other region of South India still heavily reliant on ferries is the **Andaman Islands**, around a thousand kilometres east of Chennai in the Bay of Bengal. A new road runs the length of this remote archipelago, crossing larger estuaries by means of small river ferries, but to reach any of the offshore islands you'll have to wait around in the capital, Port Blair, for one of the sporadic government ferry services. If you can't afford the air fare (or can't get a ticket on the over-subscribed flight), boats – from Chennai or Vishakapatnam (and Calcutta) – are the only other way to reach the Andamans. The crossing is long, frequently uncomfortable and lasts three or four days (see p.525).

A decade or so ago, you could catch a rusty old steamer from Mumbai to **Goa**, but the Indian Navy requisitioned the boat for the invasion of Sri Lanka in 1989, and since then the service has been suspended. A private company, Frank Damania Shipping, introduced a fast hydrofoil link direct to Panjim from Mumbai in 1995, but in the winter of 1998 this too was suspended. It is thought that the new Konkan Railway (which covers the same route in less time for a fraction of the cost) has all but forced the hydrofoil link out of business.

For more detailed information on the routes outlined above, see the relevant chapter of the guide. At the time of writing, these were the only ferry services in operation in South India. Sri Lanka can for the moment only be reached by air, while the scheduled ferry crossing to the Lakshadweep Islands from Kochi (Kerala) is closed to foreign-passport holders.

BY CAR OR MOTORBIKE

It is much more usual for tourists in South India to be driven than it is for them to drive; car rental firms operate on the basis of supplying **chauffeur-driven vehicles**, and taxis are available at cheap daily rates. Arranged through tourist offices, local car rental firms, or branches of Hertz, Budget or Europcar, a chauffeur-driven car will run to about £20/US$30 per day. On longer trips, the driver sleeps in the car. The big international chains are the best bet for self-drive car rental; in India they charge around thirty percent less than chauffeur-driven, with a Rs1000 deposit against damage, though if you pay in your home country it can cost a whole lot more. In one or two places, motorbikes or mopeds may be rented out for local use, but for biking around the country, it is a much better idea to buy (see below).

Driving in India is not for beginners. If you do drive yourself, expect the unexpected, and expect other drivers to take whatever liberties they can get away with. Traffic circulates on the left, but don't expect road regulations to be obeyed. Traffic in the cities is heavy and undisciplined; vehicles cut in and out without warning, and pedestrians, cyclists and cows wander nonchalantly down the middle of the road as if you don't exist. In the country the roads are narrow, in terrible repair and hogged by overloaded Tata trucks that move aside for nobody, while something slow-moving like a bullock cart or a herd of goats can easily take up the whole road. To overtake, sound your horn – the driver in front will signal if it is safe to do so; if not, he will wave his hand, palm downwards, up and down. A huge number of potholes don't make for a smooth ride either. Furthermore, during the monsoon, roads can become flooded and dangerous; rivers burst their banks and bridges get washed away. Ask local people before you set off, and proceed with caution, sticking to main highways if possible.

You should have an **international driving licence** to drive in India, but this is often overlooked if you have your licence from home (but beware of police in Goa, who are quick to hand out fines). Insurance is compulsory, but not expensive. Car seat-belts and motorcycle crash-helmets are not compulsory but very strongly recommended; helmets are best brought from home. Accident rates are high, and you should be on your guard at all times. It is very dangerous to drive at night – not everyone uses lights, and bullock carts don't have any. If you have an **accident**, it might be an idea to leave the scene quickly and go straight to the police to report it; mobs can assemble fast, especially if pedestrians or cows are involved.

Fuel is reasonably cheap, but the state of the roads will take its toll, and mechanics are not always very reliable, so a knowledge of **vehicle maintenance** is a help, as is a check-over every so often to see what all those bone-shaking journeys are doing to your conveyance. Luckily, if you get a flat tyre, puncture-*wallahs* can be found almost everywhere.

To import a car or motorbike into India, you'll have to show a *carnet de passage*, a document intended to ensure that you don't sell the vehicle illegally. These are available from foreign motoring organizations such as the AA. It's also worth bringing a few basic spares, as spare parts for foreign makes can be hard to find in India, although low-quality imitations are widely available. All in all, the route is arduous, and bringing a vehicle to India something of a commitment.

The classic Indian automobile is the Hindustan Ambassador (basically a Morris Oxford), nowadays largely superseded by more modern vehicles such as the Japanese-style Maruti. Renting a car, you'll probably have a choice of these two or others. If you're interested in buying one, the Ambassador is not famed for its mod cons or low mpg, but has a certain style and historical interest, and later models make little sense as prices are higher and quality lower than in the West.

Buying a motorbike is a much more reasonable proposition, and again, if it's an old British classic you're after, the Enfield Bullet (350 model), sold cheapest in Pondicherry on the coast of Tamil Nadu, leads the field. If low price and practicality are your priorities, however, a smaller model, perhaps even a moped or a scooter, might better fit the bill. Many Japanese bikes are now made in India, as are Vespas and Lambrettas, and motorbikes of various sorts can easily be bought new or second-hand. Garages and repair shops are a good place to start; Bales Rd in Chennai is particularly renowned. Obviously, you will have to haggle for the price, but you can expect to pay half to two-thirds the original price for a bike in reasonable condition. Given the right bargaining skills, you can sell it again later for a similar price – perhaps to another foreign traveller, by advertising it in hotels and restaurants. A certain amount of bureaucracy is involved in transferring vehicle ownership, but a garage should be able to put you on to a broker ("auto consultant") who, for a modest commission (around Rs300), will help you find a seller or a buyer, and do the necessary paperwork. A motorbike can be taken in the luggage car of a train for the same price as a second-class passenger fare.

Some knowledge of mechanics is necessary to ensure that you are not being sold a pup so if you are not too savvy yourself, make sure you take someone with you to give the engine, forks, brakes and suspension the once-over. Bear in mind that experienced overlanders often claim that making sure the seat is comfy is the crucial element to an enjoyable trip.

BY BICYCLE

Ever since Dervla Murphy's *Full Tilt*, a steady but increasing trickle of travellers has either done the overland trip **by bicycle**, or else bought a bike in India and ridden it around the country. In many ways it is the ideal form of transport, offering total independence without loss of contact with local people. You can camp out, though there are cheap lodgings in almost every village – take the bike into your room with you – and, if you get tired of pedalling, you can put it on top of a bus as luggage, or transport it by train (it goes in the luggage van: get a form and pay a small fee at the station luggage office).

Bringing a bike from abroad requires no *carnet* or special paperwork, but spare parts and accessories may be of different sizes and standards in India, and you may have to improvise. Bring basic spares and tools and a pump. Panniers are the obvious thing for carrying your gear, but fiendishly inconvenient when not attached to your bike, and you might consider sacrificing ideal load-bearing and streamlining technology for a backpack you can lash down on the rear carrier.

Buying a bike in India presents no great difficulty; most towns have cycle shops and even cycle markets. The advantages of a local bike are that spare parts are easy to get, locally produced tools and parts will fit and your vehicle will not draw a crowd every time you park it. Disadvantages are that Indian bikes tend to be heavier and less state-of-the-art than ones from abroad – bikes with gears, let alone mountain bikes, are unheard of. Selling should be quite easy: you won't get a tremendously good deal at a cycle market, but you may well be able to sell privately, or even to a rental shop.

Bicycles can be **rented** in most towns, usually for local use only: this is a good way to find out if your legs and bum can survive the Indian bike before buying one. Rs10–25 per day is the going rate, occasionally more in tourist centres, and you may have to leave a deposit, or even your passport as security.

IBT, 4887 Columbia Drive S, Seattle WA 98108-1919 (☎206/628-9314) publishes information and offers advice on bicycle travel around the world. In India, the Cycle Federation of India, C-5A/262, DDA Flats, Janak Puri, New Delhi 110058 (☎553006) is the main cycle-sports organization.

CITY TRANSPORT

Transport around town takes various forms, with **buses** the most obvious. These are usually single-decker, though double-deckers (some articulated) exist in Mumbai and elsewhere. City buses can get unbelievably crowded, so beware of pickpockets, razor-armed pocket-slitters and "Eve-teasers" (see p.65); the same applies to **suburban trains** in Mumbai (Chennai is about the only other place where you might want to use trains for local city transport).

You can also take **taxis**, usually rather battered Ambassadors (painted black and yellow in Mumbai). With any luck, the driver will agree to use the meter; in theory you're within your rights to call the police if he doesn't, but the usual compromise is to agree a fare for the journey before you get in. Naturally, it helps to have an idea in advance what the fare should be, though any figures quoted in this or any other book should be treated as being the broadest of guidelines only. From places such as main stations, you may be able to find other passengers to share a taxi to the town centre; many stations, and certainly most airports, operate pre-paid taxi schemes with set fares that you pay before departure; more expensive pre-paid limousines are also available.

The **auto-rickshaw**, that most Indian of vehicles, is the front half of a motor-scooter with a couple of seats mounted on the back. Cheaper than taxis, better at nipping in and out of traffic, and usually metered (again, in most places they probably won't use them and you should agree a fare before setting off), auto-rickshaws are a little unstable and their drivers often rather reckless, but that's all part of the fun. In major tourist centres rickshaws can, however, hassle you endlessly on the street, often shoving themselves right in your path to prevent you ignoring them, and once they've got you on board, they may take you to several shops before reaching your destination. Moreover, agreeing a price before the journey will not necessarily stop your rickshaw-*wallah* reopening discussion when the trip is under way, or at its end. In general it is better to hail a rickshaw than to take one that's been following you, and to avoid those that hang around outside posh hotels.

One or two cities also have larger versions of auto-rickshaws known as **tempos**, with six or eight seats behind, which usually ply fixed routes at flat fares. Here and there, you'll also come across horse-drawn carriages, or **tongas**. Tugged by underfed and often lame horses, these are the least popular with tourists.

Slower and cheaper still is the **cycle rickshaw** – basically a glorified tricycle. Foreign visitors often feel squeamish about travelling this way, and with good reason; except in the major tourist cities, cycle rickshaw-*wallahs* are invariably emaciated pavement dwellers who earn only a pittance for their pains. In the end, though, to deny them your custom on those grounds is spurious logic; they will earn even less if you don't use them. Also, you will invariably pay a rupee or two more than a local would.

If you want to see a variety of places around town, consider hiring a taxi, rickshaw or auto-rickshaw for the day. Find a driver who speaks English reasonably well, and agree a price beforehand. You will probably find it a lot cheaper than you imagine: the driver will invariably act as a guide and source of local knowledge, and tipping is usually in order.

ACCOMMODATION

There are far more Indians travelling around South India at any one time – whether for holidays, on pilgrimages or for business – than there are foreign tourists, and a vast infrastructure of hotels and guesthouses caters for their needs. On the whole, accommodation, like so many other things in South India, provides extremely good value for money, though in the major cities, especially, prices are soaring for luxury establishments that provide Western-style comforts and service.

Throughout this book we recommend places to stay in cities, towns and villages that range from lavish lakeside palaces to the most basic dormitory accommodation. Travellers on all budgets are looking to get the best return for what they're prepared to spend, and we set out to highlight bargains in every category.

INEXPENSIVE HOTELS

While accommodation prices in India are generally on the up, there's still an abundance of **cheap hotels**, catering for backpacking tourists and less well-off Indians. Most charge Rs100–200 for a double room, and some outside the big cities have rates below Rs100 (£1.50/$2.50). The cheapest option is usually in a dormitory of a hostel or hotel, where you'll be charged anything from Rs30 to Rs100. With prices as low as Rs20 per person, ashrams and *dharamshalas* are even better value.

Budget accommodation varies from filthy fleapits to homely guesthouses and, naturally, tends to be cheaper the further you get off the beaten track; it's at its most expensive in Mumbai, where prices are at least double those for equivalent accommodation in most other cities.

Cold showers or "bucket baths" are the order of the day – not really a problem in most of South India for most of the year. It's always wise, though, to check out the state of the bathrooms and toilets before taking a room. Bed bugs and mosquitoes are other things to check for – splotches of blood around the bed and on the walls where people have squashed them are telltale signs.

If a taxi driver or rickshaw-*wallah* tells you that the place you ask for is full, closed or has moved, it's more than likely that it's because he wants to take you to a hotel that pays him commission – added, in some cases, to your bill. Hotel touts,

ACCOMMODATION PRICE SYMBOLS

All **accommodation prices** in this book are coded using the symbols below. The prices given are for a double room, except in the case of categories ① and ② where the price can refer to dorm accommodation per bed. Most mid-range and all expensive and luxury hotels charge a luxury tax of around ten to fifteen percent, and a local tax of around five percent. All taxes are included in the prices we quote.

India doesn't have a "tourist season" as such, and most accommodation keeps the same prices throughout the year. Certain resorts, however, and some spots on established tourist trails do experience some variation and will be more expensive, or less negotiable, when demand is at its peak. For the hill stations, this will be in the summer (April–July); for Goa and other beach resorts in the South, it'll be the winter (Dec–Jan), especially around Christmas and New Year. We indicate such fluctuations where appropriate.

① up to Rs100	④ Rs300–400	⑦ Rs900–1500
② Rs100–200	⑤ Rs400–600	⑧ Rs1500–2500
③ Rs200–300	⑥ Rs600–900	⑨ Rs2500 and upwards

more prevalent in the North than in the South, operate in some major tourist spots, working for commission from the hotels they take you to. This can become annoying, but sometimes paying the little extra can be well worth it, especially if you arrive alone in a new place at night. One way to avoid the hassle is to stay put – some of the airports have retiring rooms and so do most of the larger train stations.

MID-RANGE HOTELS

Even if you value your **creature comforts**, you don't need to pay through the nose for them. A large clean room, freshly made bed, your own spotless (often sit-down) toilet and hot and cold running water can still cost under Rs300 (£4/$7). Extras that bump up the price include local taxes, TV, mosquito nets, a balcony and, above all, **air-conditioning**. Abbreviated in this book and in India itself as **a/c**, air-conditioning is not necessarily the advantage you might expect – in some hotels you can find yourself paying double for a system that is so dust-choked, wheezy and noisy as to preclude any possibility of sleep – but providing it entitles a hotel to consider itself mid-range. Some also offer a halfway-house option known as "**air-cooled**" found in drier climes as coolers do not work in areas of extreme humidity such as along the coasts of South India and the Bay of Bengal. Additionally, many medium-priced hotels have attached restaurants, and even room service.

New hotels tend to be lined inside, on floors and walls, with marble (or some imitation), which can make them feel totally characterless. They are, however, much cleaner than older hotels, where dirt and grime clings to cracks and crevices, and damp quickly devours paint. Some mid-range hotels feel compelled to furnish their rooms with wall-to-wall carpeting which often smells due to the humidity and damp caused by heavy rains.

Most state governments run their own "**tourist bungalows**" – similar to mid-range hotels – either directly, or through their Tourist Development Corporation. These usually offer pricier a/c rooms as well as cheaper dorms, and are usually good value, though the standard varies a lot from state to state and even within states. Some, such as Karnataka's, for example, tend to be rather run-down, whereas Tamil Nadu's – all called *Hotel Tamil Nadu* – are very well kept, and Kerala's range even includes four-star luxury.

If you're on a medium budget, it's not a bad idea to consider staying at the state-run hotel in any town; we've consistently indicated such places throughout this guide by including the state acronym in the name – eg KTDC (Kerala Tourist Development Corporation) *Surya*. Bookings for state-run hotels can be made in advance by telephone, through state tourist offices or with most of the state Tourist Development Corporation offices or hotels.

UPMARKET HOTELS

Most luxury hotels in India fall into one of two categories: old-fashioned institutions brimming with class, and modern jet-set chain hotels, on the whole confined to large cities and tourist resorts. Most luxury hotels belong to a chain, although there are now several independent hotels, especially around Goa and Kerala, that offer superb facilities. The faded grandeur of the **Raj** lingers on in the venerable edifices of British imperial hangouts, more prevalent in the north than in South India where you are more likely to come across it in the timeless atmosphere of clubs, most of which are in hill stations.

Modern deluxe establishments – slicker, brighter, faster and far more businesslike – tend to belong to chains, which can be Indian as often as they are international. The *Taj* in Mumbai for example, the country's grandest hostelry, has a number of offshoots, including hotels in Chennai, Kochi, Bangalore, Hyderabad and several "Garden Retreats", including Kumarakom and Varkala. Other chains include Oberoi, Hilton International, Meridien, Hyatt and Sheraton, the Welcomgroup and the India Tourist Development Corporation's Ashok chain. You'll find such hotels in most state capitals and some resorts favoured by rich Indian and foreign tourists. It's becoming more common for these to quote tariffs in US dollars, starting at $90, and sometimes bringing the price for a double room up to an astonishing $450. In palaces and heritage hotels, however, you'll still get excellent value for money, with rates only just beginning to approach those of their counterparts back home.

Heritage hotels, combine traditional-style, and in some cases, antique architecture with modern amenities, to offer an interesting and much more attractive alternative than the large deluxe hotels. They are located along the popular western coastal strip, especially in Kerala. Although some – especially those along the sea –

tend to shun air-conditioning and come with "open to the sky" showers, standards are generally very high. In fact, most feature Ayurvedic massage treatment. A handful of old mansions in Kochi have been converted very successfully into hotels, and the Kochi-based Casino Group runs several heritage hotels in Kerala and one in Lakshadweep. You can expect to pay around $100 for a double room low season (roughly Jan–Jun & Nov), and up to $250 for the most luxurious rooms in high season (July, Aug & Dec).

Bookings for many of the larger hotel chains can be made in offices around the world. The Taj, Oberoi and Sheraton chains are among those with outlets in the UK and the US. Otherwise, bookings can be made by mail or fax to:

Casino Group, Casino Hotel, Willingdon Island, Kochi 682003 (☎0484/668 221, fax 668001).

ITDC Ashok Group, Ashok Reservation Service, ITDC, Jivan Vihar, 3 Sansad Marg, Delhi 110001 (☎011/336 0923, fax 334 3167).

Oberoi Group, Oberoi Towers, Nariman Point, Mumbai 400021 (☎022/202 5757, fax 204 3282); UK reservations (☎0800 962096, fax 0181/789 5369).

Taj Group, Taj Mahal Mumbai, Apollo Bunder, Mumbai 400001 (☎022/202 2626, fax 287 2719); UK reservations (☎0800 282699, fax 0171/834 8629).

Welcomgroup (Sheraton), Welcomnet, 25 Community Centre, Vasant Lok, Vasant Vihar, New Delhi 100057 (☎011/614 3199, fax 614 6147); UK reservations (☎0800 962096, fax 00353 21/279211).

YOUTH HOSTELS

Official and non-official **youth hostels**, some run by state governments, are spread haphazardly across the country. Often run-down and often full (though on occasion completely empty), they'll give HI cardholders a discount, but rarely exclude non-holders, nor do they usually impose daytime closing or other silly rules. Prices match the cheapest hotels. Where there is a youth hostel, it usually has a dormitory and may well be the best budget accommodation available – which goes especially for the Salvation Army ones.

YMCAs and **YWCAs**, confined to big cities, are plusher and pricier, and comparable to a mid-range hotel. They are usually good value, but often full, and sometimes only take members of one sex.

OTHER PLACES

Many train stations have "**retiring rooms**" for passengers to sleep in, but you have to put up with station noises. These rooms can be particularly handy if you're catching an early morning train, but tend to get booked up well in advance. They vary in price, but generally charge roughly the same as a budget hotel, and have large, clean, if somewhat institutional rooms; dormitories, where you can bank on being woken at the crack of dawn by a morning chorus of throat-clearing, are often available. Occasionally you may come across a main station with an a/c room, in which case you will have found a real bargain.

YOUTH HOSTEL ASSOCIATIONS

Australia

Australian YHA, 422 Kent St, Sydney (☎02/9261 1111).

Canada

HI Canadian Hostelling Association, #400, 205 Catherine St, Ottawa, Ontario K2P 1C3 (☎613/237 7884 or ☎1-800/663 5777).

England and Wales

Youth Hostel Association (YHA), Trevellyan House, 8 St Stephen's Hill, St Alban's, Herts AL1 2DY (☎017278/45047). London shop and information office, 14 Southampton St, London WC2 (☎0171/836 1036).

Ireland

An Oige, 61 Mountjoy St, Dublin 7 (☎01/830 4555).

New Zealand

YHA of New Zealand, 173 Gloucester St, Christchurch 1 (☎03/379 9970).

Northern Ireland

YHA of Northern Ireland, 22 Djonegall Rd, Belfast BT12 5JN (☎01232/324 733).

Scotland

Scottish YHA, Glebe Crescent, Stirling, FK8 2JA (☎01786/891 400).

USA

American Youth Hostels (HI-AYH), 733 15th St NW, PO Box 37613, Washington DC 20005 (☎202/783 6161, *www.hiah.org*).

In one or two places, you can **rent rooms in people's homes**. Munjeeta Travel in Woking (see box on p.6) organize "Home-stay Tours" across India – an excellent way to get to know an Indian family and see how they live.

Camping is possible too, although in most of the country it's hard to see why you'd want to be cooped up in a tent overnight, when you could be sleeping on a cool *charpoi* (a sort of basic bed) on a roof terrace for a handful of rupees – let alone why you'd choose to carry a tent around India in the first place, except possibly on treks. It's not usual simply to pitch a tent in the countryside, though many hotels allow camping in their grounds. The YMCA runs a few sites, as do state governments (Maharashtra in particular), and the Scouts and Guides.

Finally, some temples offer accommodation for pilgrims and visitors, and may put up tourists. A donation is often expected, and certainly appreciated. Pilgrimage sites, especially those far from other accommodation, also have **dharamshalas** where visitors can stay – very cheap and very simple, almost always with basic, communal washing facilities. Some of the Jain as well as Hindu sites in South India are very well organized, with booking offices in town that offer quite reasonable budget accommodation for very little.

PRACTICALITIES

Check-out time at most hotels is noon. Always confirm this when you arrive: some expect you out by 9am, while others operate a 24-hour system, under which you are simply obliged to leave by the same time as you arrived. Some places let you use their facilities after the official check-out time, sometimes for a small charge, others won't even let you leave your baggage after then unless you pay for another night.

Unfortunately, not all hotels offer **single rooms**, so it can often work out more expensive travelling alone; in hotels that don't, you may be able to negotiate a slight discount. However, it's not unusual to find rooms with three or four beds – great value for families and small groups.

In cheap hotels and hostels, you needn't expect any **additions to your basic bill**, but as you go up the scale, you'll find taxes and service charges creeping in, sometimes adding as much as a third on top of the original tariff. Service is generally ten percent, but taxes are a matter for state governments and as such, vary from state to state.

Like most other things in India, the price of a room may well be open to **negotiation**. If you think the price is too high, or if all the hotels in town are empty, try haggling. You may get nowhere – but nothing ventured, nothing gained.

EATING AND DRINKING

Indian food has a richly deserved reputation throughout the world for being aromatic and delicious. The broad spectrum of cultures in South India is reflected in the cuisine of the various regions, and a culinary tour will prove that food in the South is some of the finest there is in the subcontinent. South India can be particularly special if you're a vegetarian. Indians are used to people having special dietary requirements: yours will be respected, and no one will think you strange for having them. Indeed, some of the very best food in India – and especially the South – has to offer is vegetarian, and even the most confirmed meat-eaters will find themselves tucking into delicious lentils and veg curries with relish.

For the first-time visitor, South India, with its bewildering range of regional cuisine (see below), can challenge all pre conceptions of Indian food. What Westerners call a **curry** covers a variety of dishes, each made with a different *masala* or mix of spices. The word curry probably originates from the *karhi* leaf, a type of laurel, found in much of Indian cooking especially in the South. Curry powder does not exist in India, the nearest equivalent being the northern *garam masala* ("hot mix"), a combination of dried, ground black pepper and other spices, added to a dish at the last stage of cooking to spice it up. Commonly used **spices**, most grown along the lush spice belt of the Western Ghats particularly in Kerala, include pepper, cardamom, cloves, cinnamon, chilli, turmeric, garlic, ginger, coriander – both leaf and seed – cumin and saffron. Some are used whole, so beware of chewing on them.

It's the Indian penchant for **chilli** that alarms many Western visitors. The majority of foreigners develop a tolerance for it, but if you don't, stick to mild dishes and eat rice and plenty of *dahi* (curd) to counter the effects. Fresh lime squeezed onto hot curries, also tends to reduce the fire. Curd rice, a typical southern dish, is calming and good for an upset stomach, as is tender coconut water (*yellaniru* in Kanada). Beer is one of the best things for washing chilli out of your mouth; the essential oils that cause the burning sensation dissolve in alcohol, but not in water. A softer option – a *lassi* (sweet or salty curd drink) – to accompany your meal can also help cool things down.

Most religious Hindus, and a large majority of people in the far South, do not consume the flesh of animals, while some orthodox Brahmins will not eat food cooked by anyone outside their household (or onions or garlic, as they inflame the baser instincts). Jains are even stricter and will go as far as shunning tomatoes, which remind them of blood. Veganism as such is not common, however, so if you're vegan keep your eyes open for dairy products which are prevalent in all forms of cooking, from sweets to *ghee* (the unclarified butter often used in more elaborate cuisine).

Many eating places state whether they are vegetarian or non-vegetarian – "**veg**" and "**non-veg**" – and we have adopted these terms throughout our eating reviews. Sometimes, especially in the South, you will come across restaurants advertising both "veg" and "non-veg", indicating they have two separate kitchens and, often, two distinct parts to the restaurant so as not to contaminate and offend their vegetarian clientele. You'll also see "**pure veg**" advertised, which means that no eggs or alcohol are served. As a rule, meat-eaters should exercise caution in India: even when meat is available, especially in the larger towns, its quality is not assured and you won't get much in a dish anyway – especially in railway canteens where it's mainly there for flavouring. Note, what is called "mutton" is in fact goat. Hindus, of course, do not eat beef, and Muslims shun pork, so you'll only find those in a few Christian enclaves such as the beach areas of Goa, and amongst the Kodavas of the Kodagu

(Coorg) hill country of Karnataka who love pork. In Kerala, due to a liberal mix of religions and cultures, attitudes to food can be more relaxed, and both beef and pork appear on the same menu. Fish, especially along the coast, is popular and is consumed by most, except strict vegetarians.

Set "**meals**" – rather more plain food usually served on a banana leaf instead of a plate – are served all over South India. After the meal, the banana leaf is either assigned to compost or as fodder for cows. In some circles, tradition is so entrenched, that the banana leaf is preferred even in an urban environment. "Meals" restaurants are usually found clustered around major bus stations and busy bazaars; they serve endless quantities of rice and vegetables and are normally excellent value. Not all "meals" restaurants are vegetarian. Some serve chicken and fish, and a good way of approaching a "meal" is to order a vegetarian meal, with fish or chicken on the side. Most "meals" restaurants often come with a plain canteen and a more upmarket section, some with air-conditioning. You may even encounter "meals" restaurants that come with vegetarian and non-vegetarian sections. Occasionally found along main highways, though more prevalent in north India, *dhabas*, are a Punjabi tradition and cater mainly to truck drivers serving basic but delicious wholesome food including *dal* (a lentil soup pronounced "da'al") and *roti* (an oven-baked unleavened bread).

In the South – perhaps even more so than elsewhere – **eating with your fingers** is *de rigueur* (you want to feel the food as well as taste it), and cutlery may not always be available. Wherever you eat, however, remember to use only your right hand (see p.53), and wash your hands before you start. Use the tips of your fingers to avoid getting food on the palm of your hand.

Restaurants, as such, vary in price and quality, and offer a wide variety of dishes. If you're in a group, order a variety of dishes and sample each one. Deluxe restaurants, such as those in five-star hotels, are expensive by Indian standards, but they offer the chance to sample top-quality classic Indian cuisine: rich, subtle and mouthwatering, at a fraction of the price you'd pay at home – assuming you could find Indian food that good. Try one out at least once but avoid the wine, which is invariably overpriced.

An alternative type of eating-place – catering specifically for foreign travellers with unadventurous tastebuds, or simply a hankering for home – is the **tourist restaurant**; found in beach resorts, hill stations and travellers' meccas. Here you can get Western food galore: pancakes and fritters, omelettes and toast, chips, fried prawns, cereal, and fruit salad. They tend to be pricey, can miss the mark by a long way and are not, of course, authentically Indian.

Finally, should you be lucky enough to be invited into someone's home, you will get to taste the most authentic Indian food of all. Most Indian women are expert cooks, trained from childhood by mothers, grandmothers and aunties, and aided by daughters and nieces. They can quite easily spend a whole day cooking – grinding and mixing the spices themselves – and using only the freshest ingredients.

For advice on water in India, see p.15.

SOUTH INDIAN FOOD

Occasionally, a sweeping generalization is made, that the cuisine of North India is rich and spicy, while that of the South is plain. Considering the incredible **regional variety**, ranging from the rich northern-style Mughlai cooking, developed within the opulent courts of Muslim Hyderabad, to more simple vegetarian dishes in Tamil Nadu, this generalization is quite simply not true. The street food of Mumbai is renowned; Goan cuisine reflects strong Portuguese influences; and Karnataka draws heavily from the plain cooking of its southern neighbours as well as from the rich, aromatic cooking of Hyderabad. Kerala's cuisine is remarkably varied. Tamil Nadu, the most vegetarian and perhaps the most austere, however, offers pockets of variety in regions such as Chettinad – with its memorable version of fried chicken – and the small, diminishing Franco-Indian population of Pondicherry – whose unique cuisine, now rare outside the family home, threatens to disappear altogether.

Most quintessential of all South Indian food are *iddlis* (steamed rice cakes), *vadas* (deep-fried lentil cakes) and *dosas* (rice pancakes), which come either with filling (*masala*) or plain (*sada*) – dished up with *sambar* (lentil soup) and coconut chutney. They are served as breakfast, snacks and frequently as part of "meals" dishes, throughout South India.

Those with a penchant for North Indian food and **tandoori** (clay oven) preparations will find dishes such as chicken *tikka* (boneless cubes of *tandoori* chicken, marinated with yoghurt, spices and herbs) feature on the menus of more upmarket restaurants and five-star hotels.

GOAN CUISINE

The hot and sour curry **vindaloo**, found on menus in Indian restaurants worldwide, is possibly the most famous of all Goan dishes. *Vindaloo* originates from the Portuguese *vinho d'alho*, literally "garlic wine", and consists of meat or fish seasoned with vinegar, but is traditionally made with pork. Goan food is particularly distinctive in that it uses palm vinegar, a Portuguese introduction, in many of its preparations. In fact, the **Portuguese influence** spread far beyond the borders of their once colonial enclave, when they introduced vegetables and spices from the New World. These included green and red peppers – chillies – which eventually replaced black pepper as the source of heat in Indian cooking.

Pork specialities from Goa, include: *chouriço* (red sausages), *leitao* (suckling pig) and *balchao* (pork in a rich brown sauce). Essentially a *vindaloo*, *sarpotel* (pork with liver and heart, vinegar, chillies, spices and tamarind) combines the best of both Portuguese and Indian influences, as does *assado* (a spicy, pan-cooked beef preparation, usually served with salad and potatoes). Although meats like pork and beef feature heavily in Goan cuisine, being a coastal region, its seafood is exceptional. Much like the food of Kerala, Goan cooking relies heavily on coconuts especially ground coconut, an ingredient that appears in assorted dishes, from fish curries to cakes. Best prepared with *pomfret*, a flat fish found in coastal waters throughout India, the classic Goan fish curry is cooked with spices mixed with coconut and tamarind, and is usually served with plain, boiled rice. Another fish curry, *caldeen*, marinades the fish in vinegar before cooking it in a spicy sauce made with coconut and chillies. Goa's wonderfully fresh seafood includes shellfish such as clams, lobster and prawn cooked in a variety of ways. Specialities are pies, hot curries and soups such as *sopa de camarão,* a prawn soup cooked with puréed potatoes, egg yolk and milk, and *apa de camarão*, a spicy prawn pie with a rice and semolina crust. Goa is also celebrated for its cakes and desserts such as *bebinca*, a custard made with *gram* (chickpea) flour, eggs and coconut juice.

HYDERABADI HAUTE CUISINE

Some connoisseurs may argue, and not without a certain justification, that haute cuisine originating from Hyderabad, Andhra Pradesh, represents the **pinnacle** of all **Indian Muslim cooking**. Although the grandeur of a once luxurious court has faded, traditions still linger on and if you find yourself in the city, a culinary tour will leave indelible impressions. Many Hyderabadi dishes will already be familiar to visitors. Preparations such as *korma* (an aromatic but mild and creamy curry), *pilaf* (aromatic fried rice also known as *pilau*) and *biryani* (aromatic baked rice) feature prominently in India and are recognized worldwide.

During the height of the Nizam's rule (nineteenth/early twentieth century) Hyderabad attracted Muslims from all over India and abroad, who left their influence on food preparation in the region. Spice mixtures present in some preparations are derived from Persian recipes, and, with the city's proximity to the spice belts of the Malabar Coast, are combined with indigenous ingredients to give a unique, rich and aromatic cuisine. With the help of tamarind and local spices, Persian dried lamb with beans is recreated as the delicious *dalcha*, and the fiery *til ki chutney*, inspired by the Middle Eastern *tahini*, is made of sesame seeds. Common ingredients used in Hyderabadi cuisine include: cassia buds, *karhi* leafs, chillies, cinnamon, cardamom, tamarind, peanuts, coconut milk and curds (*dahi*). Mixing these spices is a high art, best illustrated by *potli ka masala*, an unusual mixture consisting of *khas* (vetivert) and dried rose petals, ground and sprinkled onto prepared food, and sometimes present on meat dishes such as *nahari* (a slow cooked stew of lamb with tongue and trotters). Other meat dishes include *lukmi*, which is a type of deep fried ravioli, and *chippe ka gosht*, where lamb, marinated in yoghurt and coconut, is cooked slowly in an earthenware pot to give it its distinctive earthy flavour. As with Muslim cooking everywhere, Hyderabadi cuisine is heavily meat-orientated with a large variety of kebabs and meat preparations. However, there are delicious vegetarian dishes such as *bagheri baingan*, also known as *Hyderabadi baingan* (small aubergines cooked with peanut paste), as well as several rice preparations including *khichari* (rice cooked with lentils and *ghee*), which is traditionally served at breakfast.

FOOD FROM KARNATAKA

Sandwiched between the meat-loving Muslim enclaves of Hyderabad and the central Deccan and the lush, rice-eating coastal regions to the south, Karnataka enjoys the **best of both worlds** in terms of food. In restaurants in Bangalore, you can eat the most sumptuous chicken *biryanis* inspired by Andhra Pradesh cuisine and served on banana leafs, while your neighbour on the next table tucks into a vegetarian "meal" complete with unlimited quantities of vegetables, *sambar* (lentil soup), rice and *rasam* (pepper water). By far the most famous of all of Karnataka's cooking comes from the town of Udupi, to the north of Mangalore, where the Udupi Brahmins have gained a legendary reputation as excellent restaurateurs and hotel-keepers and for their vegetarian cuisine developed, in part, as offerings made to their famous Krishna temple at Udipi. They have become synonymous with quality, and, throughout the South, restaurants and hotels boast they are "Udupi-run". Udupi food is presented as a classic "meal" on a banana leaf but complemented with excellent rice preparations and a variety of delicious vegetable curries, liberally sprinkled with *ghee* (clarified butter) and accompanied by pickle. Udupi "meals" restaurants are well worth seeking out, not just because of their legendary food, but also for their excellent value. Their restaurants are also good for the ubiquitous *iddlis*, *vadas* and *dosas*, and, it is said, the *masala dosa*, wrapped around a filling of potatoes and vegetables, was invented by an Udupi Brahmin. While Bangalore offers the most choice, a visit to Mysore is an opportunity to sample a good selection of Karnatakan cuisine, offering a handful of good Andhra and Udupi restaurants. The city's best-known dish is its Mysore *pak*, a sweet made from a rich, crumbly mixture of maize flour and *ghee*. Regional variety within Karnataka includes the meat-dominated specialties of the Kodavas (see p.220) and the North Indian-style food of the central Deccan in the north of the state, where spicy curries are accompanied by *joleata roti*, a *chapatti* (unleavened flat bread) made from a locally grown maize.

KERALAN COOKING

Colourful communities living in close proximity to each other have given Kerala a legacy of a rich and varied cuisine, complemented by the great spice belts along the Western Ghats and the rich source of **fish** to be had along the Malabar Coast and the Kuttanad backwaters. Kerala has always been a key centre for the **spice trade**, and as such, attracted traders throughout history from all over the world. These different cultures, including Arabs, Phoenicians, Egyptians, Greeks, Romans and Chinese, were all instrumental in the development of Keralan cuisine. Syrian Christians and an ancient Iraqi Jewish community, along with indigenous Keralan Christians, Hindus and Muslims have, more recently, helped create a tolerant and liberal atmosphere that is reflected in the food – Kerala is, in fact, the only state in India where the slaughter of beef is tolerated. A veritable hothouse enclosed by a lush mountain range and the highest tea estates in the world, Kerala offers a huge variety of vegetables, from beans to bitter gourds, and fruit, including mangoes, bananas and jackfruit, which lie at the heart of the diverse cuisine of this region. One dish that is universally Keralan is *appam* – rice pancakes mixed with coconut, and cooked in a wok, known as *cheena chatti* (Chinese pot), to give it a soft centre and crisp edges which can make it look like a large fried egg. Variously known as *kallappam* or *wellayappam*, *appam* is traditionally served with an "*eshtew*" (a stew) of chicken and potatoes in a creamy white sauce, flavoured with spices such as pepper and cloves and complemented with coconut milk. While the *eshtew* may or may not have been inspired by European imports, the Malabar pudding – made of sago and topped with liquid jaggery and coconut milk instead of sugar and cream – has far more obvious European roots. The most famous of all Keralan dishes, however, is its wonderful fish curry or *molee*, cooked in a delicious cream of tomatoes, ground coconut and coconut milk. The coastal waters proffer a huge variety of seafood including marlin and shark. The day's catch is proudly displayed on the stands of the many seaside tourist restaurants of Kovalam and Varkala. Some of the best fish comes from the backwaters, where the black *karimeen*, a flat sole-like fish that hugs the muddy bottoms, is justifiably prized. Also known as fish tamarind, *kodampoli* (*Garcinia indica*) provides the distinctive flavour in the fiery fish curry *meen vevichathu*, which is cooked in an earthenware pot.

Muslim fishermen of the Mopla community favour shellfish, as well as beef, while the

Christian fishing communities around Kovalam specialize in catching pomfret, mackerel, squid, prawns and other seafood, which they then sell on the beach to the highest bidder.

Rice features heavily in various forms in the Keralan diet. The *pilaf* (aka *pulau*) is especially popular among Muslims, and is served with seafood, especially prawns along the coast; occasionally tapioca appears as an alternative staple to accompany coastal fish curries.

SNACKS AND STREET FOOD

Feeling peckish should never be a problem, with all sorts of **snack meals** and **finger food** to choose from. Served in restaurants and cafés throughout the South, *vadas*, *iddlis* and *dosas*, are the most popular snacks, and are available during the day but not in the evening. *Appams*, offered along the seafront at Kochi, are served by vendors from portable stands, and are a favoured regional snack.

Street finger food includes *bhel puris* (a Mumbai speciality of small vegetables – stuffed *puris* with tamarind sauce), *pani puris* (the same *puris* dunked in peppery and spicy water – only for the seasoned), *bhajis* (deep-fried cakes of vegetables in chickpea flour), *samosas* (meat or vegetables in a pastry triangle, fried) and *pakoras* (vegetables or potato dipped in chickpea flour batter and deep-fried). Kebabs are common in the north and around Hyderabad, most frequently *shish kebab* (minced lamb grilled on a skewer) but also *shami kebab* (small minced lamb cutlets). With all street snacks, though, remember that food left lying around attracts germs – make sure it's freshly cooked. Be especially careful with snacks involving water such as *pani puris* and cooking oil that is often recycled. Generally, it's a good idea to acclimatize to Indian conditions before you start eating street snacks.

You won't find anything called "Bombay mix" in India, but there's no shortage of dry spicy snack mixes, often referred to as *channa chur*. Jackfruit chips are sometimes sold as a savoury snack, though they are rather bland, and cashew nuts are a real bargain. Peanuts, also known as "monkey nuts", usually come roasted and unshelled. Look out for *gram* vendors who sell dry roasted chickpeas – known as *gram*.

NON-INDIAN FOOD

Chinese food has become widespread in towns all over the country, where it is generally cooked by Indian chefs and not what you'd call authentic. However, India does have a small Chinese population, and in Mumbai, Bangalore and Chennai, you can expect to come across very good Chinese cuisine. Chinese communities tend to adapt their cooking to their environment and, in India, Chinese food comes with a hint of spice.

Outside of upmarket hotels, **Western food** is often dire, and expensive compared to Indian food, although the international chains serve the same standard fare as elsewhere in the world at much cheaper prices. Branches of Pizza Hut, Domino's, KFC and McDonalds can be found in Mumbai, Chennai and Bangalore in ever-increasing numbers. Wimpy's, home-grown chains such as Kwality's and independently owned fast-food cafés can be found in most cities and large towns. Tourist centres, however, such as Goa and Kovalam offer a reasonable choice of Western food, from patisseries serving

PAAN

You may be relieved to know that the red stuff people spit out all over the streets – predominantly in the North and major cities in the South – isn't blood, but juice produced by chewing **paan** – a digestive, commonly taken after meals, and also a mild stimulant.

A *paan* consists of chopped or shredded nut (always referred to as *betel* nut, though in fact it comes from the areca palm), wrapped in a leaf (which *does* come from the betel tree). It is prepared with ingredients such as *katha* (a red paste), *chuna* (slaked white lime), *mitha masala* (a mix of sweet spices, which can be ingested) and *zarda* (chewing tobacco, not to be swallowed on any account, especially if made with *chuna*). The triangular package thus formed is wedged inside your cheek and chewed slowly, and in the case of *chuna* and *zarda paans*, spitting out the juice as you go. *Paan* is an acquired taste; novices should start off, and preferably stick with, the sweet and perfectly harmless *mitha* variety, which is perfectly all right to ingest.

Paan and *paan masala* (a mix of betel nut, fennel seeds, sweets and flavourings) are sold by *paan-wallahs*, often from tiny stalls squeezed between shops. *Paan-wallahs* develop big reputations and some of the more extravagant concoctions come with silver and, in some rare cases, even gold foil.

cakes and croissants to restaurants offering lasagna on candle-lit terraces. Small cheese factories are beginning to emerge, providing an alternative to the dreary processed cheese produced by Amul. Cities such as Bangalore and Mumbai also offer a choice of **Tex-Mex**, **Thai**, **Japanese**, **Italian** and **French** cuisine, but these are usually only available in the restaurants of luxury hotels.

BREAKFAST

Unreconstructed Westerners seem to get especially homesick around breakfast time; but getting your fry-ups and hash browns is likely to be a problem. Each region has its own **traditional** way of greeting the day and in the South *iddli*, *vada*, *dosa* and *uppma* (semolina and nuts) is the most common equivalent, while members of the *India Coffee House* chain can be depended upon for some decent coffee and toast.

In those towns which have established a reputation as hangouts for "travellers", budget hotels and restaurants serve up the usual hippy fare – banana pancakes, muesli, etc – as well as omelettes, toast, porridge (not always oatmeal), cornflakes and even bacon and eggs.

SWEETS

Most Indians have rather a sweet tooth and Indian **sweets**, usually made of milk, can be very sweet indeed. Although the emphasis on milk products is stronger in the North than in the South, sweets, including regional specialties, are popular throughout the country, with sweet shops thriving in all cities and large towns.

Of the more solid type, *barfi*, a kind of fudge made from boiled-down and condensed milk, varies from moist and delicious to dry and powdery. It comes in various flavours, from plain, creamy white to livid green *pista* (pistachio), and is often sold covered with silver leaf (which you eat). Smoother-textured, round *penda* and thin diamonds of *kaju katri*, plus moist *sandesh* and the harder *paira*, are among many other sweets made from boiled-down milk. Numerous types of gelatinous *halwa*, are especially popular in Hyderabad, all of which are totally different in taste and texture to the Middle Eastern variety. Of the regional varieties, Mysore *pak*, made from a rich crumbly mixture of maize flour and *ghee*, is one South Indian sweet that is exported to the rest of India.

Getting softer and stickier, those circular orange tubes, dripping syrup in sweet-shop windows, called *jalebis*, and made of deep-fried treacle, are as sickly as they look. *Gulab jamuns* (deep-fried cream cheese sponge balls soaked in syrup) are just as unhealthy. Common in both the North and the South, *ladu* consists of balls made from semolina flour with raisins and sugar and sometimes made of other grains and flour.

Chocolate is improving rapidly in India, and Cadbury's and Amul bars are now available. None of the indigenous brands of imitation Swiss and Belgian chocolates appearing on the cosmopolitan markets are worth eating.

Among the large **ice-cream** vendors, Kwality (now owned and branded as Walls), Vadilal's, Gaylord and Dollops stand out. Uniformed men push carts of ice-cream around and the bigger companies have many, usually quite obvious, imitators. Some have no scruples – stay away from water ices unless you have a seasoned constitution. Now common throughout southern towns and cities, ice-cream parlours selling elaborate concoctions including sundaes have really taken off. When travelling, especially around coastal Karnataka and parts of Kerala, look out for a local variation known as *gad-bad* (literally "mix-up") where layers of ice-cream come interspersed with chopped nuts and dried and glacéd fruit. Be sure to try *kulfi*, a pistachio- and cardamom-flavoured frozen sweet which is India's answer to ice-cream but is more popular in the north than in South India. *Bhang kulfi*, not available everywhere but popular during the festival of Holi, is laced with cannabis, so has an interesting kick to it, but should be approached with caution.

FRUIT

What fruit is available varies with region and season, but there's always a fine choice. Ideally, you should **peel all fruit** including apples, or soak it in a strong iodine or potassium permanganate solution for thirty minutes. Roadside vendors sell fruit which they often cut up and serve sprinkled with salt and even *masala*. Don't buy anything that looks as if it's been hanging around for a while.

Mangoes are usually on offer, but not all are sweet enough to eat fresh – some are used for pickles or curries. Indians are picky about their mangoes, which they feel and smell before buying; if you don't know the art of choosing the fruit, you could be sold the leftovers. Among the varieties appearing at different times in the season –

A GLOSSARY OF DISHES AND COOKING TERMS

Due to the very distinct languages of South India, an effective glossary of food terms is almost impossible, but the following list represents a highlight of food and the terms you are likely to come across as a visitor.

apa de camarão	spicy prawn pie with a rice and semolina crust (Goa)
appam	wok-cooked rice pancake speckled with holes, soft in the middle; a speciality of the Malabar coast of Kerala (Kerala)
assado	a spicy pan-cooked beef preparation (Goa)
bagheri baingan	small aubergine cooked with peanut paste and spices (Hyderabad)
bebinca	custard made with *gram* (chickpea) flour, eggs and coconut juice (Goa)
biryani	rice baked with saffron or turmeric, whole spices and meat (sometimes vegetables), and often hard-boiled egg (North India and Hyderabad)
Bombay duck	dried bummelo fish (Mumbai)
caldeen	fish marinated in vinegar and cooked in a spicy sauce of coconut and chillies (Goa)
chapati	unleavened bread made of wholewheat flour and baked on a round griddle-dish called a *tawa* (universal)
chop	minced meat or vegetable surrounded by breaded mashed potato (universal)
cutlet	cutlet – often minced meat or vegetable fried in the form of a flat cake (universal)
dahi rice	a pleasant and light preparation – sometimes lightly spiced – of boiled rice with yoghurt (*dahi*)
dal	lentils, pronounced "da'al" and found in one form or another throughout India; in the South often replaced by *sambar* (universal)
dhansak	meat and lentil curry, a Parsi speciality; medium-hot (Mumbai)
dosa	rice pancake – should be crispy; when served with a filling it is called a *masala dosa* and when plain, a *sada dosa* (Andhra Pradesh, Karnataka, Tamil Nadu, universal)
eshtew	a stew, usually made with chicken, cooked with potatoes in a creamy white sauce of coconut milk (Kerala)
ghee	clarified butter sometimes used for festive cooking, and often sprinkled onto food before eating (universal)
iddli	steamed rice cake, usually served with *sambar*; *malligi* (jasmine) *iddlis* around Mysore are exceptionally fluffy and so named because of their lightness – the scent of jasmine is said to waft on the breeze (Andhra Pradesh, Karnataka, Kerala, Tamil Nadu, universal)

from spring to summer – look out for Alphonso, which is grown in the vicinity of Mumbai, and, Langra, which is grown all over South India. Oranges and tangerines are generally easy to come by, as are sweet melons and thirst-quenching watermelons, although the South is famous for its numerous kinds of bananas on sale all year round. Some bananas, such as the *nendrakai* variety of Kerala, come raw and are meant for cooking. Try the delicious red bananas of Kovalam, or the *nanjangod* variety grown in the vicinity of Mysore, which are considered by many Mysore city-dwellers as the best and most extravagant at around Rs4 per fruit! Certainly, while travelling on the buses through the Western Ghats, bananas provide a good fallback, especially for upset stomachs, complemented by tender-coconut water. After you drink the coconut juice, the vendor will split the coconut with a machete and fashion you a spoon from the outer layer so that you can scoop the delicate unhardened flesh of the coconut.

Tropical fruits such as coconuts, papayas (pawpaws) and pineapples are common, while things such as lychees and pomegranates are very seasonal. Among less familiar fruit, the *chiku*, which looks like a kiwi and tastes a bit like a pear, is

jaggery	unrefined sugar made from palm sap (universal)
jeera rice	rice cooked with cumin seeds (*jeera*) (universal)
karhi leaf	a type of laurel from which the leaf and the seeds are widely used as a spice throughout South India (universal)
keema	minced meat (Hyderabad)
khichari	rice cooked with lentils in various ways, from plain, to aromatic and spicy (Hyderabad, universal)
kofta	balls of minced vegetables or meat in a curried sauce (Hyderabad)
korma	meat braised in yoghurt sauce, mild (Hyderabad)
kulcha	fried flat bread to accompany curries (Hyderabad)
molee	curry with coconut, usually fish, originally Malay (hence the name), now a speciality of Kerala; hot (Kerala)
mulligatawny	curried vegetable soup, a classic Anglo-Indian dish rumoured to have come from "Mulligan Aunty" but probably South Indian; medium-strength (universal)
naan	white, leavened bread kneaded with yoghurt and baked in a *tandoor* (universal)
papad or *poppadum*	crisp, thin chickpea flour cracker (universal)
paratha	wholewheat bread made with butter, rolled thin and griddle-fried; a little bit like a chewy pancake, sometimes stuffed with meat or vegetables (universal)
pomfret	a flatfish popular in Bombay and Calcutta (universal)
pulau	also known as *pilaf* or *pullao*, rice, gently spiced and pre-fried (universal)
puri	crispy, puffed-up, deep-fried wholewheat bread (universal)
rasam	spicy, pepper water often drunk to accompany "meals" in the South
roti	loosely used term; often just another name for *chapati*, though it should be thicker, chewier and baked in a *tandoor* (universal)
sambar	soupy lentil and vegetable curry with asafoetida and tamarind; used as an accompaniment to *dosas*, *iddlis* and *vadas* (universal)
sarpotel	pork dish with liver and heart, cooked in plenty of vinegar and spices (Goa)
uppma	popular breakfast cereal made from semolina, spices and nuts, and served with *sambar* (Kerala, Tamil Nadu)
uttapam	thick rice pancake often cooked with onions (Karnataka, Tamil Nadu, Kerala, universal)
vada	also known as *vadai*, a doughnut-shaped deep-fried lentil cake, which usually has a hole in its centre
vindaloo	Goan meat – seasoned with vinegar – (sometimes fish) curry, originally pork; very hot (but not as hot as the kamikaze UK version) (Goan, universal)

worth a mention, as is the watermelon-sized jackfruit (*chakkai* in Malayalam), a favourite with Keralans, whose spiny green exterior encloses sweet, slightly rubbery yellow segments, each containing a seed.

DRINKS

With some of the world's prime coffee-growing areas, **coffee** is certainly more common than tea in South India. South Indian coffee is traditionally prepared with sugar, topped with large quantities of milk to produce a distinctive taste. A whole ritual is attached to the drinking of milky Keralan coffee, poured in flamboyant sweeping motions between tall glasses to cool it down. One of the best places to get a decent cup of South Indian coffee is in the India Coffee House co-operative chain, found in every southern town, and occasionally in the North, where the coffee is not nearly as good. In the North, most coffee is instant, even though advertised as "espresso" while in the South expect the real thing. Good vacuum-packed filter coffee from Coorg (Kodagu) in Karnataka is now available but is yet to have an impact in cafés and restaurants.

The rest of India sometimes seems to run on **tea** (**chai**) – grown in Darjeeling, Assam and in the Nilgiri Hills in South India – and sold by *chai-wallahs* on just about every street corner. Ginger and/or cardamoms are often added. If you're quick off the mark, you can get them to hold the sugar. English tea it isn't, but most travellers get used to it: "Just don't think of *chai* as tea," advise some. Sometimes, especially in tourist spots and upmarket hotels, you might get a pot of European-style "tray" tea, generally consisting of a tea bag in lukewarm water – you'd do better to stick to the pukka Indian variety, unless you are in a traditional tea-growing area. In some of the highest estates in the world, on the borders of Kerala and Tamil Nadu, the tea gardens of the Nilgiris produce fine, strong tea with a long tradition and a justifiable reputation.

With **bottled water** so widely available, you may have no need of **soft drinks**. These have long been surprisingly controversial in India. Coca Cola and Pepsi returned to India in the early Nineties after being banned from the country for seventeen years. That policy was originally instigated, in part, to prevent the expatriation of profits by foreign companies; since their return, militant Hindu groups such as the RSS have threatened to make them the focus of a new boycott campaign against multinational consumer goods. The absence of Coca Cola and Pepsi spawned a host of Indian colas such as Campa Cola (innocuous), Thums Up (not unpalatable), Gold Spot (fizzy orange) and Limca (rumoured to have dubious connections to Italian companies and to contain additives banned there). All contain a lot of sugar but little else: adverts for Indian soft drinks have been known to boast "Absolutely no natural ingredients!" None will quench your thirst for long.

More recommendable are straight water (treated, boiled or bottled; see also p.15), and cartons of Frooti Jumpin, Réal and similar brands of fruit juice drinks, which come in mango, guava, apple and lemon varieties. If the carton looks at all mangled, it is best not to touch it as it may have been recycled. At larger stations, there will be a stall on the platform selling Himachali apple juice. Better still, tender-coconut water from **green coconuts**, common around coastal areas especially in the South, are cheaper than any of these, and sold on the street by vendors who will hack off the top of the coconut for you with a machete and give you a straw to suck up the coconut water (you then scoop out the flesh and eat it).

India's greatest cold drink, **lassi** – originally from the north but now available throughout India – is made with beaten curd and drunk either salted, sweetened with sugar or mixed with fruit. It varies widely from smooth and delicious to insipid and watery, and is sold at virtually every café, restaurant and canteen in the country. Freshly made milk shakes are also common at establishments with blenders. They'll also sell you what they call a fruit juice, which is usually fruit, water and sugar (or salt) liquidized and strained; also, street vendors selling fresh fruit juice in less than hygienic conditions are apt to add salt and garam masala! In central and northern cities, especially in Hyderabad, *sharbat*, flavoured drinks made with sugar, fruit and, often, rose essence, are inspired by Middle Eastern roots and remain popular especially among Muslim communities.

With all such drinks, however appetizing they may seem, exercise great **caution** in deciding where to drink them; find out where the water is likely to come from.

ALCOHOL

Prohibition, once widespread in India, is now only fully enforced in a few states, including Tamil Nadu which retains partial prohibition in the form of "dry" days, high taxes, restrictive licences and health warnings on labels ("Liquor – ruins country, family and life," runs Tamil Nadu's). Kerala's licensing laws have also resulted in restrictive licences and prohibitive fees to all except the government agencies, such as the Kerala Tourist Development Corporation, who have a virtual monopoly on the beer parlours throughout the state.

Except for the new pub scene in cosmopolitan cities such as Bangalore, most Indians drink to get drunk as quickly as possible and this trend has had a terrible toll on family life, especially among the working classes and peasantry. Because of this, politicians searching for votes have from time to time played the prohibition card. In states like Tamil Nadu, which persist with draconian drinking policies, the illicit trade in liquor flourishes, and every now and then papers report cases of mass contamination from illicit stills that have led tragically to an extraordinary number of deaths.

Alcoholic enclaves in prohibition states can become major drinking centres: Pondicherry and

Karaikal in Tamil Nadu are the main ones. Goa and Mahé (Kerala) join them as places where the booze flows especially freely and cheaply. Interestingly, all were outside the British Raj. **Liquor permits** – free, and available from Indian embassies, high commissions and tourist offices abroad, and from tourist offices in Mumbai and Chennai, and even at airports on arrival – allow those travellers who bother to apply for one, to evade certain restrictions in prohibition states.

Beer is widely available, if rather expensive by local standards. Price varies from state to state, but you can usually expect to pay around Rs50–70 for a 650ml bottle. Kingfisher and Black Label are the leading brands, but there are plenty of others. All lagers, which tend to contain chemical additives including glycerine, are usually pretty palatable if you can get them cold. In certain places, notably unlicensed restaurants in Tamil Nadu, beer comes in the form of "special tea" – a teapot of beer, which you pour into and drink from a teacup to disguise what it really is. A cheaper, and often delicious, alternative to beer in Kerala and one or two other places is *toddy* (palm wine).

Spirits usually take the form of "Indian Made Foreign Liquor" (IMFL), although the recently legitimized foreign liquor industry is expanding rapidly. Some Scotch, such as Seagram's Hundred Pipers, is now being bottled in India and sold at a premium; Smirnoff vodka is also available and other known brands are soon to follow. Some of the brands of Indian whisky are not too bad and are affordable in comparison; gin and brandy can be pretty rough, while Indian rum is sweet and distinctive. In Goa, *feni* is a spirit distilled from coconut or cashew fruit. Steer well clear of illegally distilled arak, however, which often contains methanol (wood alcohol) and other poisons. A look through the press, especially at festival times, will soon reveal numerous cases of blindness and death as a result of drinking bad hooch (or "spurious liquor" as it's called). Licensed country liquor, sold in several states under such names as *bangla*, is an acquired taste.

MAIL, TELECOMMUNICATIONS AND MEDIA

There is no need to be out of touch with the rest of the world while you're in India. The mail service is pretty reliable if a little slow; international phone calls are surprisingly easy; and email services are nowadays widely available. In addition, there are a number of decent English-language newspapers, and more people and places than you might imagine have access to satellite TV in English.

MAIL SERVICES

Mail can take anything from three days to four weeks to get to or from India, depending largely on where exactly you are; ten days is about the norm. Stamps are not expensive, and aerogrammes and postcards cost the same to anywhere in the world. Ideally, you should have mail franked in front of you. Most post offices are open Mon–Fri 10am–5pm and Sat 10am–noon, but big city GPOs where the Poste Restante is usually located, keep longer hours (Mon–Fri 9.30am–6pm, Sat 9.30am–1pm). You can also buy stamps at big hotels.

Poste restante (general delivery) services throughout the country are pretty reliable, though exactly how long individual offices hang onto letters is more or less at their own discretion; for periods of longer than a month, it makes sense to mark mail with your expected date of arrival. Letters are filed alphabetically; in larger offices, you sort through them yourself. To avoid misfiling, your name should be printed clearly, with the surname in large capitals and underlined, but it is still a good idea to check under your first name too, just in case. Have letters addressed to you c/o Poste Restante, GPO (if it's the main post office you want), and the name of the town and state. Sometimes too, as in Chennai, local tourist offices might be more convenient than the GPO. Don't forget to take ID with you to claim your mail. American Express offices also keep mail for holders of their charge card or travellers' cheques.

Having parcels sent out to you in India is not such a good idea – chances are they'll go astray. If you do have a parcel sent, have it registered.

Sending a parcel out of India can be quite a performance. First you have to get it cleared by customs at the post office (they often don't bother, but check), then you take it to a tailor and agree a price to have it wrapped in cheap cotton cloth (which you may have to go and buy yourself), stitched up and sealed with wax. In big city GPOs, people offering this service will be at hand. Next, take it to the post office, fill in and attach the relevant customs forms (it's best to tick the box marked "gift" and give its value as less than Rs1000 or "no commercial value", to avoid bureaucratic entanglements), buy your stamps, see them franked, and dispatch it. Parcels should not be more than a metre long, nor weigh more than 20kg. Surface mail is incredibly cheap, and takes an average of six months to arrive – however, it may take half, or four times that. It's a good way to dump excess baggage and souvenirs, but don't send anything fragile this way.

As in Britain, North America and Australasia, books and magazines can be sent more cheaply, unsealed or wrapped around the middle, as **printed papers** ("book post"). Alternatively, there are numerous courier services, although it is safest to stick to known international companies such as DHL. Packages sent by air are expensive. Couriers are not as reliable as they should be, and there have been complaints of packages going astray. Remember that all packages from India are likely to be suspect at home, and searched or X-rayed: don't send anything dodgy.

PHONES

Privately run **phone services** with international direct dialling facilities are widespread. Advertising themselves with the acronyms STD/ISD (standard trunk dialling/international subscriber dialling), they are extremely quick and easy to use; some stay open 24 hours per day. Both national and international calls are dialled direct. To call abroad, dial the international access code (00), the code for the country you want – 44 for the UK, for example – the appropriate area code (leaving out any initial zeros), and the number you want; then you speak, pay your bill, which is calculated in seconds, and leave. Prices vary between private places and are slightly cheaper at official telecommunications offices; many have fax machines too. Calling from hotels is usually more expensive. "Call back" (or "back call", as it is often known) is possible at most phone booths and hotels, although check before you call and be aware that this facility rarely comes without a charge of between Rs3 and 10 per minute at booth, usually free at hotels.

Direct dialling rates are very expensive during the day – Monday to Saturday 8am to 7pm – but this falls to half rate on Sundays, national holidays, and daily from 7am to 8am and 7pm to 8.30pm, when the charge is reduced further.

Home country direct services are now available from any phone to the UK, the US, Canada, Ireland, Australia, New Zealand and a growing number of other countries. These allow you to make a collect or telephone credit card call to that country via an operator there. If you can't find a phone with home country direct buttons, you can use any phone toll-free, by dialling 000, your country code and 17 (except Canada which is 000-127).

To **call India** from abroad, dial the international access code 00, followed by 91 for India, the local code minus the initial zero, then the number you want.

International Codes

	From India:	To India:
UK	☎00 44	☎00 91
Irish Republic	☎00 353	☎00 91
US and Canada	☎001	☎011 91
Australia	☎00 61	☎0011 91
New Zealand	☎00 64	☎00 91

INTERNET AND EMAIL

In all the large cities there are **Internet** and **email** facilities accessible to the general public, usually at cybercafés, though many hotels and STD booths offer this service as well. The charges for Internet use range from Rs40 to Rs150 per hour for reading mail and browsing, extra for printing and sending emails (especially if you do not have access to a registered account); most centres offer membership deals which can cut costs. The shops that advertise email alongside unrelated business concerns are cheaper, but you have to send and receive mail through their own private account, which means your messages are open to public scrutiny.

If you're planning to be away from home for a while, you may want to set up an **free email** account before leaving. This takes five or ten minutes, costs nothing and allows you to receive electronic mail wherever you are in the world. All you have to pay is the cybercafé's charges after you've finished using their machine. Microsoft own the phenomenally popular Hotmail service (*www.hotmail.com*), but due the volume of traffic through this server, smaller Web-based email providers such as Yahoo (*www.yahoo.com*) tend to be quicker and less prone to interruptions. To sign up, access the Internet and key in one of site addresses listed above in italics. For more advice on using the Internet, see *Rough Guide to the Internet*.

THE MEDIA

India has a large number of **English-language daily newspapers**, both national and regional. The most prominent of the nationals are *The Hindu*, *The Statesman*, *The Times of India*, *The Independent*, the *Economic Times*, and the *Indian Express* (usually the most critical of the government). All are pretty dry and sober, and concentrate on Indian news; *The Independent* and the *Calcutta Telegraph* tend to have better coverage of world news than the rest. *Asian Age*, published simultaneously in India, London and New York, is a conservative tabloid that sports a motley collection of the world's more colourful stories. All the major Indian newspapers have **Web sites**, with *The Times of India* and *The Hindu* providing the most up-to-date and detailed news services; see p.21 for addresses.

India's press is the freest in Asia, and attacks on the government are often quite outspoken. However, as in the West, most papers can be seen as part of the political establishment and are unlikely to print anything that might upset the "national consensus".

In recent years, a number of *Time*/*Newsweek*-style **news magazines** have hit the market with a strong emphasis on politics. The best of these are *India Today*, published independently, and *Frontline*, published by *The Hindu*. Others include *Outlook*, which presents the most readable broadly themed analysis, *Sunday* and *The Week*. As they give more of an overview of stories and issues than the daily papers, you will probably get a better idea from them of what is going on in Indian politics, and most tend to have a higher proportion of international news too. *Business India* is more financially orientated, and *The India Magazine* more cultural. Film fanzines and gossip mags are very popular (*Screen* and *Filmfare* are the best, though you'd have to be reasonably *au fait* with Indian movies to follow a lot of it), but magazines and periodicals in English cover all sorts of popular and minority interests, so it's worth having a look through what's available. One publication of special interest is *Amar Chitra Katha*'s series of Hindu legends, Indian history and folk tales in comic form for children.

Foreign publications such as the *International Herald Tribune*, *Time*, *Newsweek*, *The Economist* and the international edition of the British *Guardian* are all available in the main cities and in the most upmarket hotels, but they are rather costly. For a read through the British press, try the British Council in Mumbai and Chennai, the USIS being the American equivalent. Expat-orientated bookstalls stock slightly out-of-date and expensive copies of magazines like *Vogue* and *NME* for homesick Westerners.

BBC World Service radio can be picked up on short wave, although reception quality is highly variable. The wavelength also changes at different times of day. In the morning, try 5965Khz (49m/5.95–6.20Mhz) or 9605Khz (31m/9.40–9.90Mhz); in the afternoon, 9740Khz (31m/9.40–9.90Mhz) or 11750 (25m/11.70Mhz). A full list of the World Service's many frequencies appears on the BBC website (*www.bbc.uk/worldservice/*).

The government-run **TV** company, Doordarshan, which broadcasts a sober diet of edifying programmes, has tried to compete with the onslaught of mass access to **satellite TV**. The main broadcaster in English is Rupert Murdoch's **Star TV** network, which incorporates the BBC World Service, and Zee TV, which presents a progressive blend of Hindi-orientated chat, film, news and music programmes. Others include CNN, some sports channels, the Discovery Channel, the immensely popular Channel V hosted by scantily-clad Mumbai models and DJs, and a couple of American soap and chat stations.

SPORTS

India is not perhaps a place that most people associate with sports, but cricket, hockey and football (soccer, that is) all have their place.

Cricket is by far the most popular of these, and a fine example of how something quintessentially British (well, English) has become something quintessentially Indian. Travellers to India will find it hard to get away from cricket – it is everywhere and enjoys extensive coverage on television. Cricketing heroes such as the maestro batsman Sachin Tendulkar are held in the highest esteem and live under the constant scrutiny of the media and public. Expectations are high and disappointments acute; India versus Pakistan matches are especially emotive. In 1999, the right-wing Hindu group Shiv Sena threatened to disrupt Pakistan's tour of India and even dug up the pitch in Delhi but to no avail. Despite the occasional riot, the tour was a resounding success and one of the most exciting and eagerly fought cricketing contests ever held between the two sides. Test matches are rare but inter-state cricket is easy to catch – the most prestigious competition is the Ranji Trophy. Besides spectator cricket, you'll see games being played on open spaces all around the country. Occasionally, you may even come across a match blocking a road, and will have to be patient as the players grudgingly let your vehicle continue.

Horseracing can be a good day out, especially if you enjoy a flutter. There are several racecourses around the country, mostly in larger cities such as Mumbai, Hyderabad, Mysore and Bangalore; look in local newspapers, such as *Bangalore Today*, and any local listings magazine to find out when race meetings are being held. Other (mainly) spectator sports include **polo**, originally from upper Kashmir, but taken up by the British to become one of the symbols of the Raj. Princes of Rajasthan were considered in the Thirties, Forties and Fifties to be the best polo players in the world but since the Sixties, when the Privy Purses were cut, they have been unable to maintain their stables, and the tradition of polo has declined. Today, it is mainly the army which plays polo.

After years in the doldrums, Indian **hockey**, which used regularly to furnish India with Olympic medals, is making a strong comeback. The haul of medals dried up in the Sixties when international hockey introduced astro-turf which was, and still is, a rare surface in India. However, hockey is still very popular, especially in schools and colleges and, interestingly, amongst the tribal girls of Orissa who supply the Indian national team with a regular influx of players. Indian **athletics** are improving all the time and, today, India boasts world-class women sprinters who bagged several medals at the 1998 Asian Games.

Volleyball is very popular throughout India. Standards aren't particularly high, and joining a game should be quite easy. **Football** (soccer) is similarly liked, with a keenly contested national championship. The best teams are based in Calcutta and include three legendary clubs – Mohan Bagan, East Bengal and Mohamadan Sporting – who all command fanatical support. Unlike most of the league, these teams employ professional players and even include some minor internationals, mostly from Africa.

Amongst the contact sports unique to India **kushti**, a form of Indian wrestling, has a small but dedicated following and is a favourite of devotees of the monkey god, Hanuman. However, the most dramatic and ferocious of all is the popular Keralan martial art of **kalarippayat** (see p.285) which utilizes both hand-to-hand combat and the use of weapons.

CRIME AND PERSONAL SAFETY

In spite of the crushing poverty and the yawning gulf between rich and poor, India is on the whole a very safe country in which to travel. As a tourist, however, you are an obvious target for the tiny number of thieves (who may include some of your fellow travellers), and stand to face serious problems if you do lose your passport, money and ticket home. Common sense, therefore, suggests a few precautions.

If you can tolerate the encumbrance, carry valuables in a money belt or in a pouch around your neck at all times. In the latter case, the cord should be hidden under your clothing and not be easy to cut through (a metal guitar string is good). Beware of crowded locations, such as packed buses or trains, in which it is easy for pickpockets to operate – slashing pockets or bags with razor blades is not unheard of in certain locations – and don't leave valuables unattended on the beach when you go for a swim. Backpacks in dormitory accommodation are also obvious targets.

Budget travellers would do well to carry a padlock, as these are usually used to secure the doors of cheap hotel rooms and it's reassuring to know you have the only key; strong combination locks are ideal. You can also lock your bag to seats or racks in trains, for which a length of chain also comes in useful. Don't put valuables in your luggage for bus or plane journeys: keep them with you at all times. If your baggage is on the roof of a bus, make sure it is well secured. On trains and buses, the prime time for theft is just before you leave, so keep a particular eye on your gear then, beware of deliberate diversions and don't put your belongings next to open windows. Remember that routes popular with tourists tend to be popular with thieves too.

However, don't get paranoid. Crime levels in India are a long way below those of Western countries, and violent crime against tourists is extremely rare. Virtually none of the people who approach you on the street intend any harm: most want to sell you something (though this is not always made apparent immediately), some want to practise their English, others (if you're a woman) to chat you up, while more than a few just want your address in their book or a snap taken with you. Anyone offering wonderful-sounding money-making schemes, however, is almost certain to be a con artist.

Be wary of **credit card fraud**; a credit card can be used to make duplicate forms to which your account is then billed for fictitious transactions, so don't let shops or restaurants take your card away to process – insist they do it in front of you. Even **monkeys** rate a mention here: it is not unknown for them to steal things from hotel rooms with open windows or even to snatch bags from unsuspecting shoulders. It's not a bad idea to keep US$100 or so separately from the rest of your money, along with your travellers' cheque receipts, insurance policy number and phone number for claims and a photocopy of the pages in your passport containing personal data and your Indian visa. This will cover you in case you do lose all your valuables.

If the worst happens and you get robbed, the first thing to do is report the theft as soon as possible to the local **police**. They are very unlikely to recover your belongings, but you need a report from them in order to claim on your travel insurance. Dress smartly and expect an uphill battle; city cops in particular tend to be jaded from too many insurance and travellers' cheque scams.

Losing your passport is a real hassle, but does not necessarily mean the end of your trip. First, report the loss immediately to the police, who will issue you with the all-important "complaint form" you need to travel around and check into hotels, as well as claim back any expenses incurred in replacing your passport from your insurer. A complaint form, however, will not allow you to change money or travellers' cheques. If you've run out of cash, your best bet is to ask your hotel manager to help you out (staff will have seen your passport when you checked in, and the number will be in the register). The next thing to do is telephone your nearest embassy or consulate in India (see p.113). Normally, passports have to be applied for and collected in person, but if you are stranded, it is usually possible to arrange to receive the necessary forms in the post. However, you still have to go to the embassy or consulate to pick it up. "Emergency passports" are the cheapest form of replacement, but are normally only valid for the few days of your return flight. If you're not sure when you're leaving India, you'll have to obtain a more costly "full passport"; these can only be issued by embassies and larger consulates in Mumbai, and not those in Chennai or Panjim.

DRUGS

Future is black if sugar is brown – Indian anti-drugs poster.

India is a centre for the production of **cannabis** and to a lesser extent **opium**, and derivatives of these drugs are widely available. *Charas* (hashish) is produced all along the Himalaya, where the harvest is around September, and Kerala is famous for its *ganja* (marijuana).

Charas and *ganja* are normally smoked in a *chillum*, originally the bowl of a hookah pipe, used by the poor, who would cup their hands around it to make a smoke-cooling chamber. Nowadays, *chillum*-making has become something of an art form, with centres at Pondicherry and Hampi.

The use of cannabis is frowned upon by respectable Indians – if you see anyone in a movie smoking a *chillum*, you can be sure it's the baddie. *Sadhus*, on the other hand, are allowed to smoke *ganja* legally as part of their religious devotion to Shiva, who is said to have originally discovered its narcotic properties.

Bhang (a preparation made from marijuana leaves, which, it is claimed, sometimes contains added hallucinogenic ingredients such as datura) is legal: it is used to make sweets and drinks such as the notoriously potent *bhang lassis* which have waylaid many an unwary traveller. Use of other illegal drugs such as LSD, ecstasy and cocaine is largely confined to tourists in party locations such as Goa. All of these drugs except *bhang* are strictly controlled under Indian **law**, with a minimum sentence of ten years for possession. Anyone arrested with less than three grams of cannabis, which they are able to *prove* is for their own use, is liable to a six-month maximum, but cases can take years to come to trial (two is normal and eight not unheard of). Police raids and searches are particularly common in the beach areas of Goa, and around Idukki and Kumily in Kerala. "Paying a fine now" *may* be possible with one or two officers upon arrest – though it will probably mean *all the money* you have – but once you are booked in at the station, your chances are slim. A minority of the population languishing in Indian jails are foreigners on drugs charges.

CULTURAL HINTS AND ETIQUETTE

Cultural differences extend to all sorts of little things. While allowances will usually be made for foreigners, visitors unacquainted with Indian customs may need a little preparation to avoid causing offence or making fools of themselves. The list of do's and dont's here is hardly exhaustive: when in doubt, watch what the Indian people around you are doing.

EATING AND THE RIGHT HAND RULE

The biggest minefield of potential faux pas has to do with **eating**. This is usually done with the fingers, and requires practice to get absolutely right. Rule one is: **eat with your right hand only**. In India, as right across Asia, the left hand is for wiping your bottom, cleaning your feet and other unsavoury functions (you also put on and take off your shoes with your left hand), while the right hand is for eating, shaking hands, and so on.

Quite how rigid individuals are about this tends to vary, with *brahmins* (who at the top of the hierarchical ladder are one of only two "right-handed castes") and southerners likely to be the strictest. While you can hold a cup or utensil in your left hand, and you can usually get away with using it to help tear your *chapati*, you should not eat, pass food or wipe your mouth with your left hand. Best is to keep it out of sight below the table.

This rule extends beyond food. In general, do not pass anything to anyone with your left hand or point at anyone with it either, and Indians definitely won't be impressed if you put it in your mouth. In general, you should accept things given to you with your right hand – though using both hands is a sign of respect.

The other rule to beware of when eating or drinking is that your lips should not touch other people's food – *jhuta* or sullied food is strictly taboo. Don't, for example, take a bite out of a *chapati* and pass it on. When drinking out of a cup or bottle to be shared with others, don't let it touch your lips, but rather pour it directly into your mouth. This custom also protects you from things like hepatitis. It is customary to wash your hands before and after eating.

TEMPLES AND RELIGION

Religion is taken very seriously in South India; it's important always to show due respect to religious buildings, shrines, images and people at prayer. When entering a temple or mosque, remove your shoes and leave them at the door (socks are OK and protect your feet from burning-hot, stony ground). Some temples – Jain ones in particular – do not allow you to enter wearing or carrying leather articles and forbid entry to menstruating women. Dress conservatively (see below), and try not to be obtrusive; cover your head with a cap or cloth when entering a *dargah* (Sufi shrine) or Sikh *gurudwara*. At a mosque, you'll not normally be allowed in at prayer time and women are sometimes not let in at all. In a Hindu temple, you are not usually allowed into the inner sanctum. At a Buddhist *stupa* or monument, you should always walk round clockwise (with the *stupa* on your right). Hindus are very superstitious about taking **photographs** of images of deities and inside temples; if in doubt, resist. Do not take photos of funerals or cremations.

DRESS

Indian people are very conservative about **dress**. Women are expected to dress modestly, with legs and shoulders covered. Trousers are acceptable, but shorts and short skirts are offensive to many. Men should not walk around bare-chested and should avoid wearing shorts (a sign of low caste). These rules go double in temples and mosques.

Never mind sky-clad Jains or *naga sadhus*, **nudity** is not acceptable in India. The mild-mannered people of Goa may not say anything about nude bathing (though it is in theory prohibited), but you can be sure they don't like it.

In general, Indians find it hard to understand why rich Western sahibs should wander round in ragged clothes or imitate the lowest ranks of Indian society, who would love to have something more decent to wear. Staying well groomed and dressing "respectably" vastly improves the impression you make on local people, and reduces sexual harassment too.

OTHER POSSIBLE GAFFES

Kissing and **embracing** are regarded in India as part of sex: do not do them in public. It is not even a good idea for couples to hold hands, though

Indian men can sometimes be seen holding hands as a sign of "brotherliness". Be aware of your feet. When entering a private home, you should normally remove your shoes (follow your host's example); when sitting, avoid pointing the soles of your feet at anyone. Accidental contact with someone's foot is always followed by an apology.

Indian English can be very formal and even ceremonious. Indian people may well call you "sir" or "madam", even "good lady" or "kind sir". At the same time, you should be aware that your English may seem rude to them. In particular, **swearing** is taken rather seriously in India, and casual use of the F-word is likely to shock.

MEETING PEOPLE

Westerners have an ambiguous status in Indian eyes. In one way, you represent the rich sahib, whose culture dominates the world, so the old colonial mentality has not completely disappeared: in that sense, some Indians may see you as "better" than them. On the other hand, as a non-Hindu, you are an outcast, your presence in theory polluting to an orthodox or high-caste Hindu, while to members of all religions, your morals and your standards of spiritual and physical cleanliness are suspect: in that sense Indians may see themselves as "better" than you. Even if you are of Indian origin, you may be considered to suffer from Western corruption, and people may test you out on that score.

As a traveller, you will constantly come across people who want to strike up a conversation. English not being their first language, they may not be familiar with the conventional ways of doing this, and thus their opening line may seem abrupt if at the same time very formal. "Excuse me gentleman, what is your mother country?" is a typical one. It is also the first in a series of questions that Indian men seem sometimes to have learnt from a single book in order to ask Western tourists. Some of the questions may baffle at first – "What is your qualification?" "Are you in service?" – some may be queries about the ways of the West or the purpose of your trip, but mostly they will be about your family and your job.

You may find it baffling or even intrusive that complete strangers should want to know that sort of thing, but these subjects are considered polite conversation between strangers in India and help people place one another in terms of social position. Your family, job, even income, are not considered "personal" subjects in India, and it is completely normal to ask people about them. Asking the same questions back will not be taken amiss – far from it. Being curious does not have the "nosy" stigma in India that it has in the West.

Things that Indian people are likely to find strange about you are: lack of religion (you could adopt one), travelling alone, leaving your family to come to India, being an unmarried couple (letting people think you are married can make life easier) and travelling second class or staying in cheap hotels when, as a tourist, you are relatively rich. You will probably end up having to explain the same things many times to many different people; on the other hand, you can ask questions too, so you could take it as an opportunity to ask things you want to know about India. English-speaking Indians, and members of the large and growing middle class in particular, are usually extremely well informed and well educated and often far more *au fait* with world affairs than Westerners, so you may even be drawn into conversations that are way out of your depth.

SHOPPING

So many beautiful and exotic souvenirs are on sale in South India, at such low prices, that it's sometimes hard to know what to buy first. On top of that, all sorts of things (such as made-to-measure clothes) that would be vastly expensive at home are much more reasonably priced. Even if you lose weight during your trip, your baggage might well put on quite a bit – unless of course you post some of it home.

WHERE TO SHOP

Quite a few items sold in tourist areas are made elsewhere and, needless to say, it's more fun (and cheaper) to pick them up at source. Best buys are noted in the relevant sections of the guide, along with a few specialties that can't be found outside their regions. South India is awash with street and beach **hawkers**, often very young kids. Although they can be annoying and should be dealt with firmly if you are not interested, do not write them off completely as they sometimes have decent souvenirs at lower than shop prices and are open to hard bargaining.

Virtually all the state governments in India run handicraft "**emporia**". There is also an exceptionally well-stocked Central Cottage Industries Emporium in Mumbai. Goods in these places are generally of a high quality, even if their fixed prices are a little expensive, and they are worth a visit to get an idea of what crafts are available and how much they should cost.

Other famous places to shop in South India include the weekly flea market in **Anjuna**, Goa, where goods from all over the country are sold alongside the latest fluoro rave gear and techno tapes, and **Kovalam**, in southern Kerala, where vendors import handicrafts from northern states such as Rajasthan and Gujarat. For sheer variety, however, **Mumbai** is hard to beat. With its tourist-orientated streetside boutiques, swish CD and fashion shops, antique markets and huge *khadi* store, the Maharashtran capital is the perfect place to stock up on souvenirs before you leave.

BARGAINING

Whatever you buy (except food and cigarettes), you will almost always be expected to **haggle** over the price. Bargaining is very much a matter of personal style, but should always be light-hearted, never acrimonious. There are no hard and fast rules – it's really a question of how much something is worth to you. It's a good plan, however, to have an idea of how much you want, or ought, to pay. "Green" tourists are easily spotted, so try and look as if you know what you are up to, even on your first day, or leave it till later.

Don't worry too much about initial prices. Some guidebooks suggest paying a third of the opening price, but it's a flexible guideline depending on the shop, the goods and the shopkeeper's impression of you. You may not be able to get the seller much below the first quote; on the other hand, you may end up paying as little as a tenth of it. If you bid too low, you may be hustled out of the shop for offering an "insulting" price, but this is all part of the game, and you'll no doubt be welcomed as an old friend if you return next day.

Don't start haggling for something if you know you don't want it, and never let any figure pass your lips that you are not prepared to pay. It's like bidding at an auction. Having mentioned a price, you are obliged to pay it. If the seller asks you how much you would pay for something, and you don't want it, say so.

METALWARE AND JEWELLERY

South Indian artisans have been casting **bronze statues** of Hindu deities for over two thousand years – notably in the Kaveri (Cauvery) Delta, where the Chola dynasty took the form to heights never since surpassed. Traditionally, bronzes were commissioned by wealthy temples, but today the casters are kept busy by demand from rich NRIs (Non-Resident Indians) and tourists who can afford to pay the huge sums for these striking metal icons. The images are produced by the "lost-wax" process, used since medieval times, in which a model is first carved out of beeswax, then surrounded in clay, and finally fired. The wax melts to leave a terracotta mould. Top quality images will have finely detailed fingers and eyes, and the metal should not have pits or spots. Still the best place to watch bronze casters in action is the village of **Swamimalai**, near Kumbakonam in Tamil Nadu (see p.431), where showrooms display awesome dancing Shivas and other Chola-style bronzes. Some Chola bronzes are priceless, such as those in the temples of Tamil Nadu, but affordable miniatures are available direct from the artisans. For more on Chola bronzes, see p.588.

Brass and copperware can be exquisitely worked, with trays, plates, ashtrays, cups and bowls among the products available. **Bidri** work (see box on page p.271), named after Bidar (Karnataka), where it originated, is a method of inlaying a gunmetal alloy with fine designs in brass or silver, then blackening the gunmetal with sal ammoniac, to leave the inlay work shining. *Bidri* jewellery boxes, dishes and hookah pipes, among other things, are widely sold, particularly in Karnataka and Andhra Pradesh. **Stainless steel** is less decorative and more workaday: *thali* sets, tiffin and spice tins are among the possible buys, available throughout the region.

Among precious metals, silver is generally a better buy than **gold**. The latter is usually 22 carat and very yellow, but relatively expensive due to taxes (smuggling from the Gulf to evade taxes is rife), added to this is its investment value – women traditionally keep their wealth in this form, and a bride's jewellery is an important part of her dowry. **Silver** varies in quality, but is usually reasonably priced, with silver jewellery generally heavier and rather more folksy than gold. Gold and silver are usually sold by weight, the workmanship costing very little. While silversmiths are ubiquitous in South India, goldsmiths are thinner on the ground, with the largest single concentration around the Kaplishvara temple in the Mylapore district of Chennai (see p.377). This is also a prime place to sight the gaudy but distinctively Tamil **dance jewellery** worn by Bharatiya Natyam performers. Made from gold-coated silver, studded with artificial rubies, the most striking items are the headpiece, or *thalasaman*, the *adigay*, a long chain worn around the neck with a large floral or peacock-shaped pendant known as a *padakkam*, and the heavy ornamental belt, or *odyanan*.

Gemstones can be something of a minefield; scams abound, and you would be most unwise to even consider buying gems for resale or as an investment without a basic knowledge of the trade. That said, some precious and semi-precious stones can be a good buy in India, particularly those which are indigenous, such as garnets, black stars and moonstones.

WOODWORK AND STONE CARVING

Ornate carvings of gods and goddesses are a specialty of Mysore, where members of the *gudigar* caste work with fragrant **sandalwood**, their preferred medium for a thousand years or more. At one time, deities could *only* be figured from this rare wood, but dwindling forests have forced the price up, and these days fake sandalwood – cheaper soft wood that's been rubbed with essential oil – is almost as common as the real thing. In Kerala, deep red **rosewood**, inlaid with lighter coloured woods to create geometric patterns, is used for carving elephants and heavy furniture, samples of which are to be found at most state-run emporia. For more authentic Kathakali masks and old wooden jewellery **boxes**, however, the bric-a-brac and antiques market in the former Jewish quarter of Kochi (Fort Cochin) is the best place to look. Embossed with brass, these traditionally contained a woman's dowry goods. Metal trunks have largely superseded them, but Keralan cabinet-makers still turn out reproductions for the tourist market.

The fishing village of **Mamallapuram** (see p.397), just south of Chennai, is renowned as India's **stone-carving** capital. Countless workshops line its sandy lanes, and the sound of chisels chipping granite is a constant refrain from dawn until well into the night. Pieces range from larger-than-life-size icons for temples to pocket-size gods sold to the hundreds of tourists who pour through every day. Whatever their size, though, the figures are always precisely carved according to measurements meticulously set out in ancient canonical texts, which explains why little innovation has taken place over the centuries. The only recent developments in Mamallapuram's stone carving has been in the design of *chillums*, and small pendants, bought wholesale for the summer festival hippy market back in Europe.

TEXTILES AND CLOTHING

Textiles are so much a part of Indian culture that Gandhi wanted a spinning wheel put on the flag. The kind of cloth he had in mind was the plain white homespun material worn by Nehru, whose hat, jacket and *dhoti* remain a mark of support for the Congress Party to this day. Homespun, hand-loom-woven, hand-printed cloth is called **khadi**, and is sold in government shops called Khadi Gramodyog all over India. Methods of dying and printing this and other cloth vary from the tie-dying (*bhandani*) of Rajasthan to block printing and screen printing of calico (from Calicut – now Kozhikode, Kerala) cotton and silk.

Saris are normally made of cotton for everyday use, although **silk** is used for special occasions (worn more frequently throughout the South). Western women are notoriously inept at wearing this most elegant of garments – it takes years of practice to carry one off properly – but silk is usually a good buy in India, provided you make sure it is the real thing (the old test was to see whether it was possible to pull the whole garment straight through a wedding ring; however, some synthetics apparently go through too, so burn a thread and sniff it to be sure). The best silk in India comes from **Kanchipuram** (see p.406), in northern Tamil Nadu, whose hallmarks are contrasting borders (known as Ganga-Jamuna borders after India's two most sacred rivers) and ornate designs featuring *gopurams* (temple gate towers). Kanchi's weavers are also famous for **brocade** – top-quality silk hand-woven with expensive gold or silver thread.

In Andhra Pradesh, cloth is more likely to be patterned using the **ikat** technique, where yarn is resist- or tie-dyed before being woven. The geometric images of flowers, animals and birds that result have attractive blurred, or "flame", edges that conjure up Southeast Asia, to where *ikat* was exported in the medieval era.

Less expensive cloth to look out for, especially while you're in Goa, includes that touted by the **Lamanis** – the seminomadic low-caste minority from northern Karnataka who traditionally lived by transporting salt across the Deccan Plateau. These days, the women and girls make most of the family money through the sale of textiles carefully tailored for the tourist trade. Their rainbow cloth, woven with geometric designs and inlaid with cowrie shells or fragments of mirror and mica, is fashioned into shoulder bags, caps and money belts. If you haggle hard and can put up with all the shouting and tugging that inevitably accompanies each purchase, you can usually pick up it up at bargain prices.

From Tamil Nadu, an authentic souvenir to take home is the kind of **Madras-check lunghis** worn by most of the men (at least in the countryside); Keralans tend to prefer jazzier varieties, with dayglo colours rendered on slinky polyester. For women, **salwar kamise**, the elegant pyjama suits worn by Muslims, unmarried girls and middle-class students, make ideal travel outfits, although in the sticky heat of the far south you may find them too heavy. Long loose shirts – preferably made of khadi, and known as *kurta* or *panjabi* – are more practical. Tourist shops sell versions in various fabrics and colours. Block-printed bedsheets, as well as being useful, make good wall-hangings. You will find every region has its own fabrics, its own methods of colouring them and making them up – the choice is endless.

CARPETS AND RUGS

South India is generally less renowned for its carpets than the north, but the former Muslim kingdoms of the Deccan, notably around Eluru and Warangal in Andhra Pradesh, have retained weaving traditions dating from the seventeenth century, when Moghul artisans drifted south in the wake of their conquering armies. They brought with them techniques and designs from medieval Persia, and these still feature prominently in today's flat-weave durries. The colours tend to be pale pastels, with floral motifs overlaid on cameo backgrounds. In accordance with an old Persian tradition, each design is named after a patron of the weaving industry. The carpets themselves are hard to come by – they are only produced in small numbers by a few families – but you can usually track some down in the Muslim bazaars of Hyderabad, the Andhran capital.

For everyday domestic use, **rag rugs**, made from recycled clothing, are good buys. Available just about everywhere, they cost little enough in Europe and North America, but in India are fantastically cheap; many visitors buy large ones and post them home by sea mail.

PAINTINGS AND ANTIQUES

The former Chola capital of Thanjavur (Tanjore), in the Kaveri (Cauvery) Delta area of Tamil Nadu, is famous throughout the South for its school of religious painting, which emerged in the nineteenth century under patronage from the local maharaja. "Painting" is actually something of a misnomer, as the images are partly raised in low plaster relief, and inlaid with precious stones, glass pieces, pearls, mica and ivory. The Tanjore school's preferred subject is Balakrishna (Krishna as a crawling baby stealing butter balls), and depictions of Vishnu's other incarnations. You'll come across these all over the region, but only in **Thanjavur** itself (see p.476) are you likely to see the artists in action. Prices range from around

Rs2000 to Rs200,000 depending on the size, the quality of the painting and the value of the inlays and gold leaf.

The villages of Machilipatnam and Kalahasti, southeast of Vijayawada in Andhra Pradesh, are the source of a rare kind of devotional painting known as **Kalamkari**. Stylized images of deities and mythological scenes are outlined in black on lengths of thick cotton and coloured with beautiful natural dyes. Ochre, russet, blue-green, soot black and red are the predominant colours of the ornate hangings, which were traditionally produced for temples.

At the opposite end of the market, **leaf skeleton paintings** from southern Kerala are widely available in handicraft and souvenir shops, though they too vary somewhat in quality.

When it comes to **antiques**, if they really are genuine – and, frankly, that is unlikely – you'll need a licence to export them, which is virtually impossible to get. The age and status of antiques can be verified by the **Archaeological Survey of India**, Sion Fort, Sion, Mumbai 400022 (☎022/407 1102); Fort St George, Chennai 600009 (☎044/560396); 5th floor, F Wing, Kendriya Sadan, 17th Main Rd, Keramangala, Bangalore 560034 (☎080/5537348). These offices also issue export clearance certificates.

TOYS AND PUPPETS

Wooden **toys** crop up in various craft villages around Andhra Pradesh, among them Kondapalli, near Vijayawada, and Ettikopakka in the Vishakaptnam district, where brightly coloured figures, thought to have originally been made for temple rituals, are produced on lathes. Sticks of lac dye are used to decorate them; the heat generated by friction as the crayons are pressed against the revolving wood causes the pigment to melt. When this dries it forms a hard, bright shell. A similar technique has been refined in the village of Chennapatna, between Mysore and Bangalore in Karnataka, where artisans fashion toy replicas of buses, trains, planes and everyday household objects for children to play with.

Shadow puppets, *tolu bommalaatam* in Tamil, are another traditional South Indian means to amuse and instruct kids. Made of translucent leather, dyed and decorated with geometric perforations, they are manipulated with bamboo sticks by teams of puppeteers seated behind a back-lit cloth screen – a technique that was exported by medieval Tamil traders and which has subsequently taken root in parts of Indonesia, including Bali. Music and percussion accompanies the performances of mythological epics such as the *Ramayana* and *Mahabharata*. Squeezed out by cinema, puppetry is sadly a dying art in South India these days, but you can still see performances at the Dakshina Chitra folk museum near Chennai (see p.614), while souvenir-sized shadow puppets are sold at most government emporia in Tamil Nadu.

ODDS AND SODS

Of course, not everything typically Indian is old or traditional. **CDs** and **audio cassettes** of Hindustani classical, Carnatic, *Bhangra*, *filmi* and Western music are available in most major towns and cities for a fraction of what you'd pay back home. By far the best-stocked stores are in Mumbai, Bangalore and Chennai.

Books are also excellent buys in India, whether by Indian writers (see Contexts p.600) or writers from the rest of the English-speaking world. Once again, they are usually much cheaper than at home, if not so well printed or bound. Hardback volumes of Indian sacred literature are particularly good value.

Bamboo flutes are incredibly cheap, while other **musical instruments** such as *tabla*, *sitar* and *sarod* are sold in music shops in the larger cities. The quality is crucial; there's no point going home with a *sitar* that is virtually untunable, even if it does look nice. Students of music purchase their instruments from master craftsmen or established shops. A good place to start looking is Chennai, where you can pick up quality Carnatic percussion instruments such as *mridangam*, the double-headed drum that gives South Indian music its distinctive rhythms, *vinas*, the southern cousin of the sitar, and *nadasvaram*, a kind of over-sized oboe used in temple rituals. For more on Carnatic music, see Contexts p.603.

Other possible souvenirs include kitchen implements like tiffin boxes, wind-up clockwork tin toys, film posters, tea (especially Orange Pekoe from the plantations of the Nilgiri mountains), essential oils (such as eucalyptus, citronella or sandalwood) from Coonor in Tamil Nadu (see p.478), spices and peacock feather fans (though these are considered unlucky).

Things not to bring home include ivory and anything made from a rare or protected species, including snakeskin and turtle products. As for drugs – don't even think about it.

FESTIVALS AND HOLIDAYS

Virtually every temple in every town or village across the country has its own festival. While mostly religious in nature, merrymaking rather than solemnity are generally the order of the day, and onlookers are usually welcome. Indeed, if you are lucky enough to coincide with a local festival, it may well prove to be the highlight of your trip. Music and dance, originally nurtured within the temple environment, are often key features of temple festivals and in winter, multi-day music festivals known as "conferences", spring up in most major southern cities where you can hear the cream of Carnatic classical music. The biggest and most splendid of festivals, such as Madurai's three annual festivals and Mysore's celebrated Dussehra festival around September or October, are major attractions. In Karnataka, the focus of a temple festival is usually a *rath* (chariot) in which the deities are borne aloft in procession through the streets. However, further south and especially in Kerala, instead of a *rath*, the deity is carried on a pageant of elephants. A few festivals feature elephant races while others, especially along the coast of Kerala, host spectacular boat races and regattas. These are only a few of the festivals which occur, and as we cannot list every festival in every village across South India here, look to the body of the guide for listings of local festivals.

Below is a list of the main national and regional celebrations. It requires a little explanation. Hindu, Sikh, Buddhist and Jain festivals follow the Indian **lunar calendar** and their dates therefore vary from year to year against the plain old Gregorian calendar. Determining them more than a year in advance is a highly complicated business best left to astrologers. Each lunar cycle is divided into two *paksa* (halves): "bright" (waxing) and "dark" (waning), each consisting of fifteen *tithis* ("days" – but a *tithi* might begin at any time of the solar day). The *paksa* start respectively with the new moon (*ama* or *bahula* – the first day of the month) and the full moon (*purnima*). Lunar festivals, then, are observed on a given day in the "light" or "dark" side of the month. The lunar calendar adds a leap month every two or three years to keep it in line with the seasons. Muslim festivals follow the **Islamic calendar**, whose year is shorter and which thus loses about eleven days per annum against the Gregorian. Christianity – following the Gregorian calendar – is especially strong in Goa and Kerala where the feasts of saints are celebrated and carols are sung in churches packed to the brim during Christmas.

You may, while in India, have the privilege of being invited to a **wedding**. These are jubilant affairs with great feasting, always scheduled on auspicious days. Although there are numerous regional variations, at a Hindu wedding celebration the bride wears red for the ceremony and marks the parting of her hair with red *sindhur* and her forehead with a *bindu*. She is adorned with gold or bone bangles, which she wears for the rest of her married life. Although the practice is officially illegal, large dowries change hands. These are usually paid by the bride's family to the groom, and can be contentious; poor families feel obliged to save for years to get their daughters married.

Funeral processions are much more sombre affairs, and should be left in peace. In Hindu funerals, the body is normally carried to the cremation site within hours of death by white-shrouded relatives (white is the colour of mourning). The eldest son, whose responsibility it is to light the pyre, is expected to shave his head and wear white following the death of a parent.

PRINCIPAL SOUTH INDIAN FESTIVALS

India has only four national public holidays as such: January 26 (Republic Day); August 15 (Independence Day); October 2 (Gandhi's birthday); and December 25 (Christmas Day). Each state, however, has its own calendar of public holidays, and you can expect most businesses to close on the major holidays of their own religion, marked with an asterisk below.

The Hindu calendar months are given in brackets below as most of the festivals listed are Hindu.

Key: **B**=Buddhist; **C**=Christian; **H**=Hindu; **J**=Jain; **M**=Muslim; **N**=non-religious; **P**=Parsi; **S**=Sikh.

Jan–Feb (Magha)

H Pongal (1 Magha): Tamil harvest festival celebrated with decorated cows, processions and *rangolis* (chalk designs on the doorsteps of houses). *Pongal* is a sweet porridge made from newly harvested rice and eaten by all, including the cows. The festival is also known as Makar Sankranti and is celebrated in Karnataka, Andhra Pradesh and the east of India.

H Vasant Panchami (5 Magha): One-day spring festival in honour of Saraswati, the goddess of learning, celebrated with kite-flying, yellow saris and the blessing of schoolchildren's books and pens by the goddess.

C Feast of Mar Thoma: A colourful procession of decorated carts leads to this ancient site where St Thomas first landed.

N Republic Day (Jan 26)*: A military parade in Delhi typifies this state celebration of India's republic-hood, followed on Jan 29 by the "Beating the Retreat" ceremony outside the Presidential Palace in Delhi.

N Goa Carnival: Goa's own Mardi Gras features float processions and *feni*-induced mayhem in the state capital, Panjim.

N International Kite Festival at Aurangabad (Maharashtra).

H Floating Festival (16 Magha) at Madurai (Tamil Nadu).

N Elephanta Music and Dance Festival (Mumbai).

H Elephant Festival at Thiruvananthapuram's Shiva temple which boasts a spectacular elephant procession.

Feb–March (Phalguna)

B Losar (1 Phalguna): Tibetan New Year celebrations among Tibetan communities throughout India including Karnataka.

H Shivratri (10 Phalguna): Anniversary of Shiva's *tandav* (creation) dance, and his wedding anniversary. Popular family festival but also a *sadhu* festival of pilgrimage and fasting, especially at important Shiva temples.

H Holi (15 Phalguna)*: Water festival held during Dol Purnima (full moon) to celebrate the beginning of spring, most popular in North India where you can expect to be bombarded with water, paint, coloured powder and other mixtures.

C Carnival (Mardi Gras): The last day before Lent, forty days before Easter, is celebrated in Goa, as in the rest of the Catholic world.

H Puram, Guruvayur: Although the temple here is off-limits to non-Hindus, the elephant procession with over forty elephants and the elephant race are well worth the visit.

March–April (Chaitra)

H Ramanavami (9 Chaitra)*: Birthday of Rama, the hero of the *Ramayana*, celebrated with readings of the epic and discourses on Rama's life and teachings.

C Easter (movable feast)*: Celebration of the resurrection of Christ. Good Friday is a particularly celebrated day.

P Pateti: Parsi new year, also known as No Ruz, celebrating the creation of fire. Feasting, services and present-giving.

P Khorvad Sal (a week after Pateti): Birthday of Zarathustra (aka Zoroaster).

H Chittirai, Madurai (Tamil Nadu): Elephant-led procession.

H Arat Festival, Thiruvananthapuram: Held again during Oct/Nov, this festival celebrates the deities of the rajas of Travancore who are led to the sea in a procession of elephants.

April–May (Vaisakha)

HS Baisakhi (1 Vaisakha): To the Hindus, it's the solar new year, celebrated with music and dancing; to the Sikhs, it's the anniversary of the foundation of the *Khalsa* (Sikh brotherhood).

J Mahavir Jayanti (13 Vaisakha)*: Birthday of Mahavira, the founder of Jainism. The main Jain festival of the year.

H Puram Festival, Thrissur (Kerala): frenzied drumming and elephant parades.

B Buddha Jayanti (16 Vaisakha)*: Buddha's birthday. He achieved enlightenment and *nirvana* on the same date.

July–Aug (Shravana)

H Naag Panchami (3 Shravana): Snake festival in honour of the *naga* snake deities. Mainly celebrated in Rajasthan and Maharashtra.

H Raksha Bandhan/Narial Purnima (16 Shravana): Festival to honour the sea god Varuna. Brothers and sisters exchange gifts, the sister tying a thread known as a *rakhi* to her brother's wrist. Brahmins, after a day's fasting, change the sacred thread they wear.

N Independence Day (15 Aug)*: India's biggest secular celebration, on the anniversary of its Independence from Britain.

Aug–Sept (Bhadraparda)

H Ganesh Chaturthi (4 Bhadraparda): Festival dedicated to Ganesh, especially celebrated in Maharashtra. In Mumbai, huge processions carry images of the god to immerse in the sea.

H Onam: Keralan harvest festival, celebrated with snake-boat races. The Nehru Trophy snake-boat race at Alappuzha (held on the second Saturday of August), is the most spectacular, with long boats each crewed by 150 rowers.

H Janmashtami (23 Bhadraparda)*: Krishna's birthday, an occasion for feasting and celebration, especially in the Vaishnava heartlands of northwest UP and in Mumbai.

H Avani Mula festival, Madurai (Tamil Nadu): Celebration of the coronation of Shiva.

Sept–Oct (Ashvina)

H Dussehra (1–10 Ashvina)*: Ten-day festival (usually two days' public holiday) most popular in the North and associated with vanquishing demons, in particular Rama's victory over Ravana in the *Ramayana*, and Durga's over the buffalo-headed Mahishasura. Dussehra celebrations include performances of the *Ram Lila* (life of Rama). Best seen in the South in Mysore (Karnataka).

N Mahatma Gandhi's Birthday (2 Oct)*: Rather solemn commemoration of Independent India's founding father.

Oct–Nov (Kartika)

H Diwali (Deepavali) (15 Kartika)*: Festival of lights, especially popular in the North, to celebrate Rama and Sita's homecoming in the *Ramayana*. Festivities include the lighting of oil lamps and firecrackers and the giving and receiving of sweets.

J Jain New Year (15 Kartika): Coincides with Diwali, so Jains celebrate alongside Hindus.

S Nanak Jayanti (16 Kartika)*: Guru Nanak's birthday marked by prayer readings and processions, especially in the Punjab.

Nov–Dec (Margashirsha, or Agrahayana)

N Hampi Festival (Karnataka): Government-sponsored music and dance festival.

Dec–Jan (Pausa)

CN Christmas (Dec 25)*: The Christian festival the whole world celebrates, popular in Christian areas of Goa and Kerala, and in big cities.

N Carnatak Music Festivals, Chennai: For around a month every year, the city hosts around thirteen large music programmes called conferences, each lasting several days.

N Kerala Kalamandalam Festival, Cheruthuruthy: The annual festival of music and dance is a showcase for this leading arts institution, featuring the best of Kerala and attracting musicians and dancers from all over the country.

Movable

H Kumbh Mela: Major three-yearly festival held at one of four holy cities: Nasik, Ujjain, Haridwar or Prayag. The Maha Kumbh Mela or "Great" Kumbh Mela, the largest religious fair in India, is held every twelve years in Allahabad; the next festival is due to take place in 2001.

M Ramadan (first day: Dec 9, 2000; Nov 28, 2001): The start of a month during which Muslims may not eat, drink or smoke from sunrise to sunset, and should abstain from sex. Towards the end of the month it takes its toll, so be gentle with Muslims you meet at this time.

M Id ul-Fitr (Jan 8, 2000; Dec 28, 2001)*: Feast to celebrate the end of Ramadan, after 28 days.

M Id ul-Zuha: Pilgrimage festival to commemorate Abraham's preparedness to sacrifice his son Ismail. Celebrated with slaughtering and consumption of sheep.

M Muharram: Festival to commemorate the martyrdom of the (Shi'ite) Imam, the Prophet's grandson and popular saint, Hussain.

YOGA, MEDITATION AND ASHRAMS

Of all India's exports, the ancient techniques of yoga and meditation, refined over more than two thousand years of tradition and still widely practised as part of everyday religious life in the subcontinent, have arguably been the most influential. The source of many Western stereotypes about the "mystic east", they have also ensured a steady supply of spiritual questers over the centuries — particularly since Allen Ginsberg's drug-fuelled visions in Varanasi and the Beatles' much-publicized sojourn with Maharishi Yogi in Rishikesh.

The West's long-standing obsession with Indian gurus and godmen doubtless says more about the shortcomings of occidental culture than the essence of the subcontinent, but the modern India remains – despite the rampant materialism that has taken hold in the late twentieth century – a land of countless living saints, wandering *sadhus* and yogis with mysterious powers. This is particularly true of the South, which even more than the famous religious sites of the Ganges plains, has always attracted foreigners seeking spiritual nourishment. While you may not be tempted to don saffron and disappear into the forest for a decade, a short spell in an ashram learning yoga and meditation can, if nothing else, be an ideal antidote to the chaos and pollution of the southern cities.

COURSES AND ASHRAMS

Ashrams range in size from several thousand people to just a handful, and their rules, regulations and restrictions vary enormously. While some offer on-site accommodation, charge Western prices and have set programmes, others will require you to stay in the nearest town or village, operate on a donations basis and only offer guidance and teaching as and when requested. The following well-known establishments routinely welcome foreign visitors:

Astanga Yoga Nilayam, 876 1st Cross, Lakshmipuram, Mysore, Karnataka 570004. Run by Pattabhi Jois, courses last at least a month and need to be booked in advance. The great yoga master Sri Tirumalai Krisnamacharya taught here until his death in 1989.

Auroville, near Pondicherry, Tamil Nadu (see p.424). Along with Osho's *ashram* in Pune, this Utopian planned settlement, which sprawls over a vast site near the Coromandel coast, is the best known New Age centre in India. After a protracted and acrimonious split with the Shri Aurobindo Ashram (see below), the community continues to develop experimental, ecologically sensitive ways of living. Its centre is a huge spherical meditation room known as the Matri Mandir. Volunteers and visitors are welcome; guesthouse accommodation is available.

Mata Amritananda Mayi Math, between Kollam and Alappuzha, Kerala (see p.311). Dubbed the "Hugging Guru" because she ritually embraces all who come to see her, Amritananda Mayi is a self-proclaimed reincarnation of Lord Krishna, and the focal point of a rapidly growing cult with a huge following in the US. Her ashram, in the depths of the Keralan backwaters, has a large contingent of Westerners, and a sizeable transient population who come here by boat en route between Kollam and Alappuzha for the daily *darshan* (literally "viewing") sessions, when the guru goes into hugging mode.

Prasanthi Nilayam, Puttaparthi, Andhra Pradesh (☎08555/87583); see p.519. The ashram of Sai Baba, one of India's most revered and popular gurus, with a worldwide following of millions. Puttaparthi is four–five hours by bus from Bangalore. Visitors sometimes comment on the strict security staffing and rigid rules and regulations. Cheap accommodation is available at the ashram in dormitories or "flats" for four people. There is no need to book in advance though phone to check availability; see p.578 for more details. Sai Baba also has a smaller ashram in Bangalore and one in Kodaikanal.

Saccidananda Ashram, Thanneepalli, Kullithalai near Tiruchirapelli, Tamil Nadu (☎04323/3060); see p.451. Also known as Shanivanam (meaning "Peace Forest" in Sanskrit), this unusual ashram is situated on the banks of the sacred Cauvery River in the heart of Tamil Nadu. It was founded by Father Bede Griffiths, a visionary Benedictine monk, to develop a sympathetic fusion of Christianity and

Yoga is taught virtually everywhere in the South, and in addition, there are several internationally known yoga centres where you can train to become a teacher. **Meditation** is similarly practised all over the region and specific courses are available in temples, meditation centres and monasteries. South India also has innumerable **ashrams** — communities where people work, live and study together, drawn by a common (usually spiritual) goal. The most established of these is the Shri Aurobindo Ashram in Pondicherry, but there are dozens of others dotted around the southern states, from the headquarters of India's most famous living holy man, Sai Baba, in Andhra Pradesh, to the home of the celebrated "Hugging Guru", Amritananda Mayi, in the backwaters of Kerala.

Details of yoga and meditation courses and ashrams are provided throughout the guide section of the book. Most centres offer courses that you can enroll on at short notice; however, many of the more popular ones included in the box below, need to be booked well in advance.

YOGA

The word "yoga" literally means "to unite" and the aim of the discipline is to help the practitioner unite his or her individual consciousness with the Divine. This is achieved by raising awareness of one's self through spiritual, mental and physical discipline. *Hatha* yoga is based on physical postures called **asanas**, and although the most popular form in the West, it is traditionally just the first

Hinduism. Visitors can join in the services and rituals or just relax here. Accommodation is in simple huts dotted around the grounds and meals are communal. Very busy during the major Christian festivals.

Sankaramandam Math, Kanchipuram, Tamil Nadu (see p.406). The sacred city of Kanchipuram is the seat of a line of holy men, or Archaryas, dating back more than two thousand years. Their monastery, or *math*, houses the *samadhi* of the highly revered Sri Chandrasekharendra Sarasvati Swami, the sixty-eighth Archarya, who died in January 1994 at the age of a hundred and one. His successor gives *darshan* to the public during the morning. All are welcome.

Shri Aurobindo Ashram, Pondicherry, Tamil Nadu (see p.422). The anti-imperial revolutionary, Aurobindo Ghose, fled the British and his native Bengal in 1910 to settle in the French colony of Pondicherry, where he ditched politics to propagate his tortuous amalgamation of Hinduism and occultism. In this, he was aided by his half-Egyptian, half-Turkish chief organizer, Mirra Alfassa, known to her devotees as "The Mother". Their massive marble sarcophagi form the focal point of the ashram today, patronized by a predominantly Bengali following. Accommodation available in Western-style guest houses; see also Auroville, above.

Shri Ramana Maharishi Ashram, Tiruvannamalai, Tamil Nadu (see p.413). Ramana Rishi, one of twentieth-century India's most famous saints, spent the best part of two decades meditating in a cave on the lower slopes of Arunachala, a sacred "red" mountain overlooking a vast Chola temple complex. Later, he founded an ashram nearby, where his *samadhi* now attracts devotees from all over the world. In addition, around half a dozen other ashrams have sprung up in the town, offering a range of courses.

Sivananda Yoga Vedanta Dhanwanthari Ashram, PO Neyyar Dam, Thiruvanthapuram Dist, Kerala, 695 576 (☎0471/290493, email *YogaIndia@sivananda.org*); see p.297. This yoga-based ashram, deep in the Keralan hills, was set up by a swami known as "The Flying Guru" (because he used to throw flowers and peace leaflets into war zones from a small airplane). In addition to excellent introductory courses in yoga and meditation for beginners, it offers more advanced training for teachers. The regime is also very strict.

Vipassana. The Vipassana movement has three regional centres in South India: Dhamma Khetta, Nagarjun Sagar Rd, Kusum Nagar Vanasthali Puram, Hyderabad 500 070 Andhra Pradesh (☎040/402 0290, fax 241-005, email *bprabhat@hd1.vsnl.net.in*); Dhamma Setu, c/o Sri Roopchand Agarwal, Gotewalla R.G. Brothers, 148 Mint St, Chennai 600 079, Tamil Nadu (☎044/587399); Bangalore Vipassana Centre, Dhamma Sumana, c/o Mrs. Jaya Sangoi, 13/1 Vijaya II Main, 5th Block; Kumara Park (W), Bangalore, Karnataka 560 020 (☎080/336 0896, fax 221-5776, email *maitri@cyberspaceindia.com*).

step leading on to more subtle stages of meditation which commence when the energies of the body have been awakened and sensitized by stretching and relaxing. Other forms of yoga include *raja* yoga which includes moral discipline and *bhakti* yoga, the yoga of devotion which entails a commitment to one's guru or teacher. Traditional centres for yoga in the South include Mysore, in Karnataka (see p.195) and Tiruvanammalai in Tamil Nadu (see p.413), but numerous institutions throughout the region have good teachers and advanced practitioners. In many of the travellers' haunts, such as Goa and Kovalam, posters in cafés advertise local teachers.

MEDITATION

Meditation is often practised after a session of yoga, when the energy of the body has been awakened, and is an essential part of both Hindu and Buddhist practices. It is considered the most powerful tool for understanding the true nature of mind and self, an essential step on the path to enlightenment. **Vipassana** meditation is a technique originally taught by the Buddha, whereby practitioners learn to become more aware of physical sensations and mental processes. Courses last for a minimum of ten days and are austere, involving 4am kick-offs, around ten hours of meditation a day, no solid food after noon, segregation of the sexes and no talking for the duration (except with the leaders of the course). Courses are free for all first-time students to allow everyone an opportunity to learn and benefit from the technique. Vipassana is taught in more than 25 centres throughout India including ones in Bangalore, Chennai and Hyderabad.

WOMEN TRAVELLERS

India is not a country that provides huge obstacles to women travellers, petty annoyances being more the order of the day. In the days of the Raj, upper-class eccentrics started a tradition of lone women travellers, taken up enthusiastically by the flower children of the hippy era. Nineties women still do it, and most come through the challenge perfectly unscathed. However, few women get through their trip without any hassle, and it's good to prepare yourself to be a little thick-skinned.

South Indian streets are almost without exception male-dominated – something that may take a bit of getting used to, particularly when you find yourself subjected to incessant staring, whistling and name-calling. This can usually be stopped by ignoring the gaze and quickly moving on, or by firmly telling the offender to stop looking at you. Most of your fellow travellers on trains and buses will be men who may start up most unwelcome conversations about sex, divorce and the freedom of relationships in the West. These cannot often be avoided, but demonstrating too much enthusiasm to discuss such topics can lure men into thinking that you are easy about sex, and the situation could become threatening. At its worst in larger cities, all this can become very tiring. You can get round it to a certain extent by joining women in public places, and you'll notice an immense difference if you join up with a male travelling companion. In this case, however, expect Indian men to approach him (assumed, of course, to be your husband – an assumption it is sometimes advantageous to go along with - you could even consider wearing a wedding ring) and talk to him about you quite happily as if you were not there. Beware, however, if you are (or look) Indian with a non-Indian male companion: this may well cause you grief and harassment, as you will be seen to have brought shame on your family by adopting the loose morals of the West.

In addition to staring and suggestive comments and looks, sexual harassment, or "Eve teasing" as it is bizarrely known, is likely to be a nuisance, but not generally a threat. North Indian men are particularly renowned for their disregard of women's rights, and it is on the plains of Uttar Pradesh and Bihar that you are most likely to experience physical hassle. Expect to get groped in crowds, and to have men "accidentally" squeeze past you at any opportunity. It tends to be worse in cities than in small towns and villages, but anywhere being followed can be a real problem.

In time you'll learn to gauge a situation – sometimes wandering around on your own may attract so much unwanted attention that you may prefer to stay in one place until you've recharged your batteries or your male fan club has moved on. It's always best to dress modestly whenever in public – a *salwar kamise* is perfect or baggy clothing – and refrain from smoking and drinking in public, which only reinforces suspicions that Western women are "loose" and "easy".

Returning an unwanted touch with a punch or slap is perfectly in order (Indian women often become aggressive when offended), and does serve to vent a little frustration. It should also attract attention and urge someone to help you, or at least deal with the offending man – a man transgressing social norms is always out of line, and any passer-by will want to let him know it. If you feel someone getting too close in a crowd or on a bus, brandishing your left shoe in his face can be very effective.

To go and watch a Bollywood movie at the cinema is a fun and essential part of your trip to India, but unfortunately such an occasion is rarely without hassle. The crowd is predominantly male and mostly young at that. A combination of male testosterone and the excitement of gaudy and tacky love scenes leaves you the target of hormone over-charge. If you do go and see a film, go with a group of people and/or sit in the balcony area – it's a bit more expensive but the crowd is much more sedate up there.

Violent sexual assaults on tourists are extremely rare, but unfortunately the number of reported cases of rape is rising. Though no assault can be predicted, you can take precautions: at night avoid quiet, dimly lit streets and alleys, if you find a trustworthy rickshaw/taxi driver in the day keep him for the night journey, and try to get someone to accompany you to your hotel whenever possible. While Indian women are still quite timid about reporting rape – it is considered as much a disgrace to the victim as to the perpetrator – Western victims should always report it to the police, and before leaving the area try to let other tourists, or locals, know, in the hope that pressure from the community may uncover the offender and see him brought to justice. At present there's nowhere for tourists who've suffered sexual violence to go for sanctuary (though you could try the Feminist Resource Centre (FRC) in Mumbai); most victims seek support from other travellers, or go home.

WOMEN'S ORGANIZATIONS IN SOUTH INDIA

Feminist Resource Centre (FRC) 13 Carol Mansion, 35 Sitladevi Temple Rd, Mahim, Mumbai 400016. A centre for feminist-perspective research on a wide range of issues (health, sexuality, violence against women, discrimination at work).

Forum against the Oppression of Women 29 Bhatia Bhawan, Babrekan Rd, Gokale Rd (North), Dadar, Mumbai 400028 (☎022/422 2436). Support centre which also organizes workshops.

Streelekha (International Feminist Bookshop and Information Centre), 15/55, 1st floor, Cambridge, Jeevan Kendra Layout, Bangalore 560 008, Karnataka. Stocks books, journals, posters; provides space for women to meet.

Women's Centre 104B Sunrise Apartments, Nehru Rd, Valoka, Santa Cruz East, Mumbai 400055 (☎022/614 0403). A drop-in centre for women to meet, hold workshops and gain access to literature on women's issues.

The practicalities of travel take on a new dimension for lone women travellers. Often you can turn your gender to your advantage. For example, on buses the driver and conductor will often take you under their wing, watch out for you and buy you *chai* at each stop, and there will be countless other instances of kindness wherever you travel. You'll also be more welcome in some private houses than a group of Western males, and may find yourself learning the finer points of Indian cooking round the family's clay stove. Women frequently get preference at bus and train stations where they can join a separate "ladies' queue", and use ladies' waiting rooms. On overnight trains you can aim for the enclosed ladies' compartments, which are peaceful havens – unless filled with noisy children – or share a berth section with a family so as to draw you into the security of the group, making you less exposed to lusty gazing. In hotels watch out for "peep-holes" in your door (and in the common bathrooms), be sure to cover your window when changing and when sleeping, and avoid the sleazy permit-room hotels of the southern cities.

Lastly, bring your own supply of tampons, not widely available outside Indian cities.

GAY TRAVELLERS

Homosexuality is not generally open or accepted in India, and "carnal intercourse against the order of nature" (anal intercourse) is a ten-year offence under article 377 of the penal code. Laws against "obscene behaviour" are used to arrest gay men for cruising or liaising anywhere that could be considered a public place. The same law could in theory be used against lesbians, but that is unlikely as lesbian liaisons are much more clandestine.

The homosexual scene in India was brought into the spotlight in 1998 with the nationwide screening of the highly controversial film *Fire* by Deepa Mehta, about two sisters-in-law living together under the same roof who become lesbian lovers. Flying in the face of the traditional emphasis on heterosexual family life, the film created a storm. Right-wing extremists attacked cinemas that showed it, and in the wake of the attacks, many gays and lesbians came out for the first time to hold candlelit protest vigils in Delhi, Mumbai, Calcutta, Chennai and Bangalore.

For lesbians, **making contacts** will be rather difficult; even the Indian Women's Movement does not readily promote lesbianism as an issue that needs confronting. The only public faces of a hidden scene are the organizations listed below and a few of the nationwide women's organizations (see p.65).

Meeting places for gay men are marginally easier to find, with established gay bars cropping up in the more Westernized cities such as Mumbai and Bangalore. Contact the organizations listed given below, and they will tell you about gay events and parties.

CONTACTS IN SOUTH INDIA

(Write in advance for information – most addresses are PO boxes):

Bombay Dost 105A Veena-Beena Shopping Centre, Bandra Station Rd, Bandra (West), Mumbai 400050. Publish a newsletter and have contacts nationwide.

Khush Club, PO Box 573551, Mumbai 400058. Organizes gay social events regularly in Mumbai.

Sneha Sangama PO Box 3250, Bangalore 560032, Karnataka. Gay men's support group.

Stree Sangam PO Box 16613, Matunga, Mumbai 400019. A support group for lesbian and bisexual women.

Gay Info Centre c/o Owais, PO Box 1662, Secunderabad HPO 500003, Andhra Pradesh. Provides literature, contacts and resources on homosexuality in India.

Good As You 201 Samaraksha, 2nd Floor Royal Corner, 1+2 Lalbang Rd, Bangalore, Karnataka. Gay support group.

Saathi PO Box 571, Putlibowli PO, Hyderabad, Andhra Pradesh. Gay support group.

Men India Movement PO Box 885, Kochi 682005, Kerala. Gay men's support group.

DISABLED TRAVELLERS

Disability is common in India; many conditions that would be treatable in the West, such as cataracts, are permanent disabilities here because people can't afford the treatment. Disabled people are unlikely to get jobs (though there is a famous blind barber in Delhi), and the choice is usually between staying at home being looked after by your family and going out on the street to beg for alms.

For the disabled traveller, this has its advantages: disability and disfigurement, for example, do not get the same embarrassed reaction from Indian people that they do from able-bodied Westerners. On the other hand, you'll be lucky to see a state-of-the-art wheelchair or a disabled loo (major airports usually have both, though the loo may not be in a usable state), and the streets are full of all sorts of obstacles that would be hard for a blind or wheelchair-bound tourist to negotiate independently. Kerbs are often high, pavements uneven and littered, and ramps non-existent. There are potholes all over the place and open sewers. Some of the more expensive hotels have ramps for the movement of luggage and equipment, but if that makes them accessible to wheelchairs, it is by accident rather than design.

If you walk with difficulty, you will find street obstacles and steep stairs hard going. Another factor that can be a problem is the constant barrage of people proffering things at you (hard to wave aside if you are for instance on sticks or crutches), and all that queuing, not to mention heat, will take it out of you if you have a condition that makes you tire quickly. A light, folding camp-stool is one thing that could be invaluable if you have limited walking or standing power.

DISABLED ORGANIZATIONS

BRITAIN AND IRELAND

RADAR, 12 City Forum, 250 City Rd, London EC1V 8AS (☎0171/250 3222).

Can Be Done, 7-11 Kensington High St, London W8 5NP (☎0181/907 2400). Specialist tour operators for the disabled.

Carefree Holidays, 64 Florence Rd, Northampton NN1 4NA (☎01604/634301). Specialist tour operators for the disabled.

Holiday Care Service, 2nd Floor, Imperial Buildings, Victoria Rd, Horley, Surrey RH6 7PZ (☎01293/774535). Provides information and lists of tour operators and should be able to help you get in touch with someone.

National Rehabilitation Board, 25 Clyde Rd, Ballsbridge, Dublin 4 (☎01/668 4181).

Tripscope (☎0181/994 9294) is a free telephone information service giving advice and assisting with journeys.

AUSTRALIA AND NEW ZEALAND

ACROD, PO Box 60, Curtin, ACT 2605 (☎02/6682 4333).

Barrier Free Travel, 36 Wheatley St, North Bellingen, NSW 2454 (☎02/6655 1733).

Disabled Persons Assembly, 173 Victoria St, Wellington (☎04/801 9100).

US AND CANADA

Jewish Rehabilitation Hospital, 3205 Place Alton Goldbloom, Chomedy Laval, Quebec, H7V 1RT (☎450/688-9550 ext 226). Their medical library provides guidebooks and travel information on India and various other countries for travellers with disabilities.

Society for the Advancement of Travel for the Handicapped (SATH), 347 Fifth Ave, Suite 610, New York NY10016 (☎212/447 7284, *www.sit-travel.com*).

Travel Information Service, Moss Rehab Hospital, 1200 West Tabor Rd, Philadelphia PA 19141 (☎215/456 9600).

Twin Peaks Press, Box 129, Vancouver, WA 98666 (360/694-2462 or 1-800/637-2256). Publisher of *Directory of Travel Agencies for the Disabled, Travel for the Disabled, Directory of Accessible Van Rentals,* and *Wheelchair Vagabond*, which is loaded with personal tips.

INDIA

India Rehabilitation Co-ordination – India, A–2 Rasadhara Co-operation Housing Society, 385 SVP Rd, Mumbai 400004.

Then again, Indian people are likely to be very helpful if, for example, you need their help getting on and off buses or up stairs. Taxis and rickshaws are easily affordable and very adaptable; if you rent one for a day, the driver is certain to help you on and off, and perhaps even around the sites you visit. If you employ a guide, they may also be prepared to help you with steps and obstacles.

If complete independence is out of the question, going with an able-bodied companion might be on the cards. Contact one of the specialist organizations listed below for further advice on planning your trip. Otherwise, some package tour operators try to cater for travellers with disabilities – Bales and Somak among them – but you should always contact any operator and discuss your exact needs with them before making a booking. You should also make sure you are covered by any insurance policy you take out.

TRAVELLING WITH KIDS

Travelling with kids can be both challenging and rewarding. Indians are very tolerant of children so you can take them almost anywhere without restriction, and they always help break the ice with strangers.

The main problem with children, especially small children, is their extra vulnerability. Even more than their parents, they need protecting from the sun, unsafe drinking water, heat and unfamiliar food. All that chilli in particular may be a problem, even with older kids, if they're not used to it. Remember too, that diarrhoea, perhaps just a nuisance to you, could be dangerous for a child: rehydration salts (see p.17) are vital if your child goes down with it. Make sure too, if possible, that your child is aware of the dangers of rabies; keep children away from animals, and consider a rabies jab.

For babies, nappies (diapers) and places to change them can be a problem. For a short visit, you could bring disposable ones with you; for longer journeys, consider going over to washables. A changing mat is another necessity. And if your baby is on powdered milk, it might be an idea to bring some of that; you can certainly get it in India, but it may not taste the same. Dried baby food too could be worth taking – mix it with hot (boiled) water that any café or *chai-wallah* should be able to supply you with.

For touring, hiking or walking, child-carrier backpacks are ideal; they start at around £35 and can weigh less than 2kg. If the child is small enough, a fold-up buggy is also well worth packing – especially if they will sleep in it (while you have a meal or a drink...). If you want to cut down on long journeys by flying, remember that children under two travel for ten percent of the adult fare, and under-twelves for half price.

DIRECTORY

Airport Departure Tax There is a standard departure tax of either Rs500 – for most international flights – or Rs210, for domestic flights and flights to Pakistan, Bangladesh, Nepal, Sri Lanka, Myanmar (Burma), the Maldives and Afghanistan. Recently the tax has started to be included in the ticket price of all flights, wherever purchased, but there is no harm in double-checking that it has been covered when you reconfirm your flight. This tax also applies to international sea departures.

Cigarettes Indian cigarettes, such as Wills, Gold Flake, Four Square and Charms, are okay once you get used to them, and hardly break the bank (Rs5–Rs18 per pack), but if you find them too rough, stock up on imported brands such as Marlboro and Benson and Hedges, or some rolling tobacco, available in the bigger towns and cities. One of the great smells of India is the *bidi*, the cheapest smoke, made of a single low-grade tobacco leaf. If you smoke roll-ups, stock up on good papers as Indian Capstan cigarette papers are thick and don't stick very well and Rizlas, where available, are pretty costly.

Duty Free Allowance Anyone over seventeen can bring in one US quart (0.95 litre – but nobody's going to quibble about the other 5ml) of spirits, or a bottle of wine and 250ml spirits; plus 200 cigarettes, or 50 cigars, or 250g tobacco. You may be required to register anything valuable on a Tourist Baggage Re-export Form to make sure you can take it home with you, and to fill in a currency declaration form if carrying more than US$10,000 or the equivalent. There is a market for duty-free spirits in big cities: small retailers are the best people to approach.

Electricity Generally 220V 50Hz AC, though direct current supplies also exist, so check before plugging in. Most sockets are triple round-pin (accepting European-size double round-pin plugs). British, Irish and Australasian plugs will need an adaptor, preferably universal; American and Canadian appliances will need a transformer too, unless multi-voltage. Power cuts and voltage variations are very common; voltage stabilizers should be used to run sensitive appliances such as laptops.

Initials and acronyms Widely used in Indian English. Thus, the former Prime Minister, Vishwana Pratap Singh, was always "VP", and many middle-class Indian men bear similar monikers. Similarly, Andhra Pradesh (not Arunchal Pradesh) is AP and MG Rd anywhere you go means Mahatma Gandhi Rd. State and national organizations such as ITDC, RTDC and so on are always known by their acronyms.

Laundry In India, no one goes to the laundry: if they don't do their own, they send it out to a *dhobi-wallah*. Wherever you are staying, there will either be an in-house *dhobi-wallah*, or one very close by to call on. The *dhobi-wallah* will take your dirty washing to a *dhobi ghat*, a public clothes-washing area (the bank of a river for example), where it is shown some old-fashioned discipline: separated, soaped and given a damn good thrashing to beat the dirt out of it. Then it's hung out to dry in the sun and, once dried, taken to the ironing sheds where every garment is endowed with razor-sharp creases and then matched to its rightful owner by hidden cryptic markings. Your clothes will come back from the *dhobi-wallah* absolutely spotless, though this kind of violent treatment does take it out of them: buttons get lost and eventually the cloth starts to fray. For more on *dhobi-wallahs*, see our box on p.95 in the Mumbai chapter. If you'd rather not entrust your Saville Row made-to-measure to their tender mercies, there are dry-cleaners in large towns.

Numbers A hundred thousand is a *lakh* (written 1,00,000); ten million is a *crore* (1,00,00,000). Millions, billions and the like are not in common use.

Opening Hours Standard shop opening hours in India are Mon–Sat 9.30am–6pm. Most big stores, at any rate, keep those hours, while smaller shops vary from town to town, religion to religion and one to another, but usually keep longer hours. Government tourist offices are open in principle Mon–Fri 9.30am–5pm, Sat 9.30am–1pm, though these may vary slightly; state tourist offices are likely to be open Mon–Fri 10am–5pm.

Photography Beware of pointing your camera at anything that might be considered "strategic", including airports, anything military and even bridges, train stations and main roads. Remember too that some people prefer not to be photographed, so it is wise to ask before you take a snapshot of them. More likely, you'll get people, especially kids volunteering to pose. Camera film, sold at average Western prices, is widely available in India (but check the date on the box, and note that false boxes containing outdated film are often sold – Konica have started painting holograms on their boxes to prevent this). It's fairly easy to get films developed, though they don't always come out as well as they might at home. If you're after slide film, slow film or fast film, buy it in the big cities, and don't expect to find specialist brands such as Velvia. Also, remember to guard your equipment from dust.

Time India is all in one time zone: GMT+5hr 30min, all year round. This makes it 5hr 30min ahead of London, 10hr 30min ahead of New York, 13hr 30min ahead of LA, 4hr 30min behind Sydney and 6hr 30min behind NZ; however, summer time in those places will vary the difference by an hour.

Toilets A visit to the loo is not one of India's more pleasant experiences: toilets are often filthy and stink. They are also major potential breeding grounds for disease. In addition, there is the squatting position to get used to, as the traditional Asian toilet has a hole in the ground, with two small platforms either side for feet instead of a seat. Paper, if used, often goes in a bucket next to the loo rather than down it. Indians use a jug of water and their left hand instead of paper, a method you may also come to prefer, but if you do use paper, keep some handy – it isn't usually supplied, and it might be an idea to stock up before going too far off the beaten track as it is not available everywhere.

THINGS TO TAKE

Most things are easy to find in India and cheaper than at home, but here is a list of useful items worth bringing with you:

A padlock and chain (to lock rooms in budget hotels, and attach your bag to train fittings)

A universal electric plug adaptor and a universal sink plug (few sinks or bathtubs have them)

A mosquito net

A sheet sleeping bag (made by sewing up a sheet – so you don't have to worry about the state of the ones in your hotel room)

A pillowcase

A small flashlight

Earplugs (for street noise in hotel rooms and music on buses)

High-factor sunblock

A pocket alarm clock

An inflatable neck-rest, to help you sleep on long journeys

A multi-purpose penknife

A needle and some thread (but dental floss is better than cotton for holding baggage together)

Plastic, or nylon, bags (to sort your baggage, make it easier to pack and unpack, and keep out damp and dust)

A small umbrella (local ones tend not to retract)

Tampons

Condoms

A first-aid kit

Multivitamin and mineral tablets

PART TWO

THE GUIDE

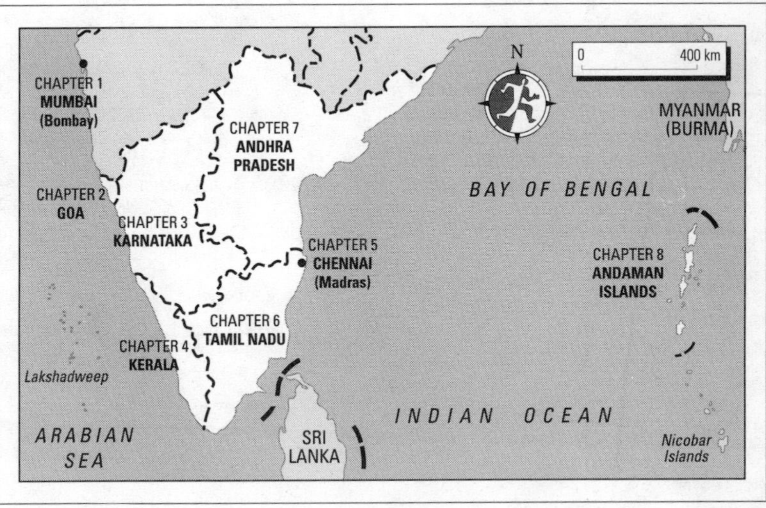

CHAPTER ONE

MUMBAI

Young, brash and oozing with the cocksure self-confidence of a maverick money-maker, **MUMBAI** (formerly Bombay) revels in its reputation as India's most dynamic and westernized city. Behind the hype, however, intractable problems threaten the Maharashtran capital, foremost among them a chronic shortage of **space**. Crammed onto a narrow spit of land that curls from the swamp-ridden coast into the Arabian Sea, Mumbai has, in less than five hundred years since its "discovery" by the Portuguese, metamorphosed from an aboriginal fishing settlement into a sprawling megalopolis of thirteen million people. Whether you are being swept along broad boulevards by endless streams of commuters, or jostled by coolies and hand-cart pullers in the teeming bazaars, Mumbai always feels as if it is about to burst at the seams.

The roots of the population problem lie, paradoxically, in the city's enduring ability to create **wealth**. Mumbai alone generates 35 percent of India's GNP, its port handles half the country's foreign trade, and its movie industry is the biggest in the world. Symbols of prosperity are everywhere: from the phalanx of office buildings clustered on Nariman Point, Maharashtra's Manhattan, to the yuppie couples nipping around town in their shiny new Maruti hatchbacks. The flip side to the success story, of course, is the city's much-chronicled **poverty.** Each day, hundreds of economic refugees pour into Mumbai from the Maharashtran hinterland. Some find jobs and secure accommodation; many more (around a third of the total population) end up living on the already overcrowded streets, or amid the appalling squalor of Asia's largest slums, reduced to rag-picking and begging from cars at traffic lights.

However, while it would definitely be misleading to downplay its difficulties, Mumbai is far from the ordeal some travellers make it out to be. Once you've overcome the major hurdle of finding somewhere to stay, you may even begin to enjoy its frenzied pace and crowded, cosmopolitan feel.

Conventional **sights** are thin on the ground. After a visit to the most famous colonial monument, the **Gateway of India**, and a look at the antiquities in the **Prince of Wales Museum**, the most rewarding way to spend time is simply to wander the city's atmospheric streets. **Downtown**, beneath the rows of exuberant **Victorian Gothic** buildings, the pavements are full of noisy vendors and office-*wallahs* hurrying through clouds of wood-smoke from the *gram*-sellers' braziers. In the eye of the storm, encircled by the roaring traffic of beaten-up red double-decker buses, lie other vestiges of the Raj, the **maidans**. Depending on the time of day, these central parks are peppered with cricketers in white flannels, or the bare behinds of squatting pavement-dwellers relieving themselves on the parched brown grass. North of the city centre, the broad thoroughfares splinter into a maze of chaotic streets. The **central bazaar** districts afford glimpses

MUMBAI/BOMBAY

In 1996, the name of city was changed from Bombay to Mumbai, as part of a wider policy instigated by the conservatives to replace names of all places, roads and features in the city that echoed of the Raj. Mumbai is the Marathi name of the local deity, the mouthless "Maha-amba-aiee" (Mumba for short), who is believed to have started her life as an obscure aboriginal earth goddess; see also p.96.

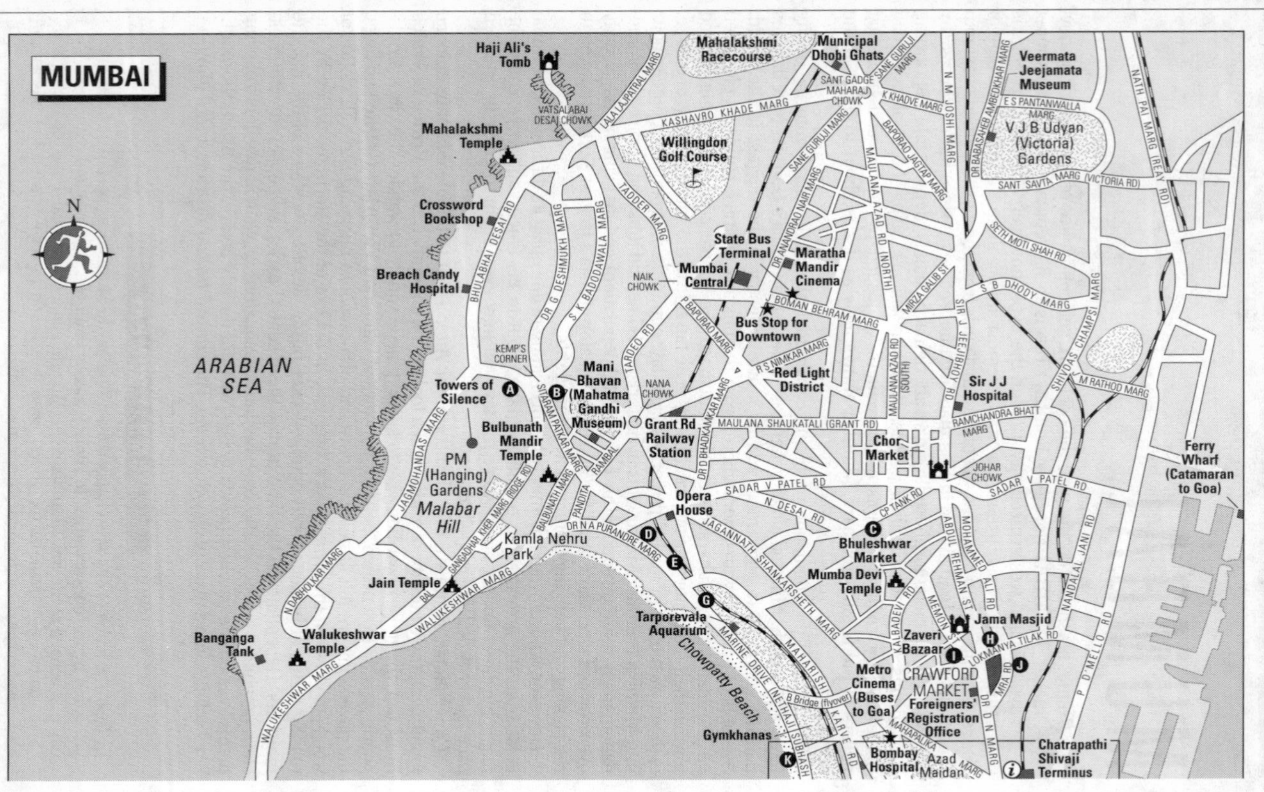
MUMBAI
N
ARABIAN SEA
Haji Ali's Tomb
Mahalakshmi Temple
Crossword Bookshop
Breach Candy Hospital
Towers of Silence
Bulbunath Mandir Temple
PM (Hanging) Gardens
Malabar Hill
Kamla Nehru Park
Jain Temple
Walukeshwar Temple
Banganga Tank
Mahalakshmi Racecourse
Willingdon Golf Course
Municipal Dhobi Ghats
Mani Bhavan (Mahatma Gandhi Museum)
Grant Rd Railway Station
Mumbai Central
State Bus Terminal
Bus Stop for Downtown
Maratha Mandir Cinema
Red Light District
Opera House
Tarporevala Aquarium
Chowpatty Beach
Gymkhanas
Chor Market
Bhuleshwar Market
Mumba Devi Temple
Sir J J Hospital
Zaveri Bazaar
Jama Masjid
CRAWFORD MARKET
Metro Cinema (Buses to Goa)
Foreigners' Registration Office
Bombay Hospital
Azad Maidan
Chatrapathi Shivaji Terminus
Veermata Jeejamata Museum
V J B Udyan (Victoria) Gardens
Ferry Wharf (Catamaran to Goa)
NATH PAI MARG (REAY RD)
N M JOSHI MARG
MAULANA AZAD RD (NORTH)
MAULANA AZAD RD (SOUTH)
SIR J JEEJIBHOY RD
MAULANA SHAUKATALI (GRANT RD)
JAGANNATH SHANKARSHETH MARG
MAHARISHI KARVE RD
MARINE DRIVE (NETHAJI SUBHASH
B Bridge (flyover)
TARDEO RD
TADDER MARG
KASHAVRO KHADE MARG
BHULABHAI DESAI RD
L JAGMOHANDAS MARG
WALUKESHWAR MARG
N DABHOLKAR MARG
SITARAM PATKAR MARG
DR G DESHMUKH MARG
S K BADODAWALA MARG
LALA LAJPATRAI MARG
DR N A PURANDRE MARG
GANGADHAR KHER MARG (RIDGE RD)
BALBUNATH MARG
PANDITA
RAMBAL
SADAR V PATEL RD
N DESAI RD
CP TANK RD
MOHAMMED ALI RD
ABDUL REHMAN ST
MEMON
KALBADEVI RD
LOKMANYA TILAK RD
MRA RD
DR D N MARG
MAHAPALIKA MARG
P D MELLO RD
NANDALAL JANI RD
SHIVDAS CHAMPSI MARG
M RATHOD MARG
S B DHODY MARG
SETH MOTI SHAH RD
SANT SAVTA MARG (VICTORIA RD)
E S PANTANWALLA MARG
DR BABASAHEB AMBEDKHAR MARG
BAPORAO JAGTAP MARG
K KHADVE MARG
SANE GURUJI MARG
DR ANANDRAO NAIR MARG
J BOMAN BEHRAM MARG
P BAPURAO MARG
R S NIMKAR MARG
DR D BHADKAMKAR MARG
MIRZA GALIB ST
RAMCHANDRA BHATT MARG
SANT GADGE MAHARAJ CHOWK
VATSALABAI DESAI CHOWK
KEMP'S CORNER
NANA CHOWK
NAIK CHOWK
JOHAR CHOWK

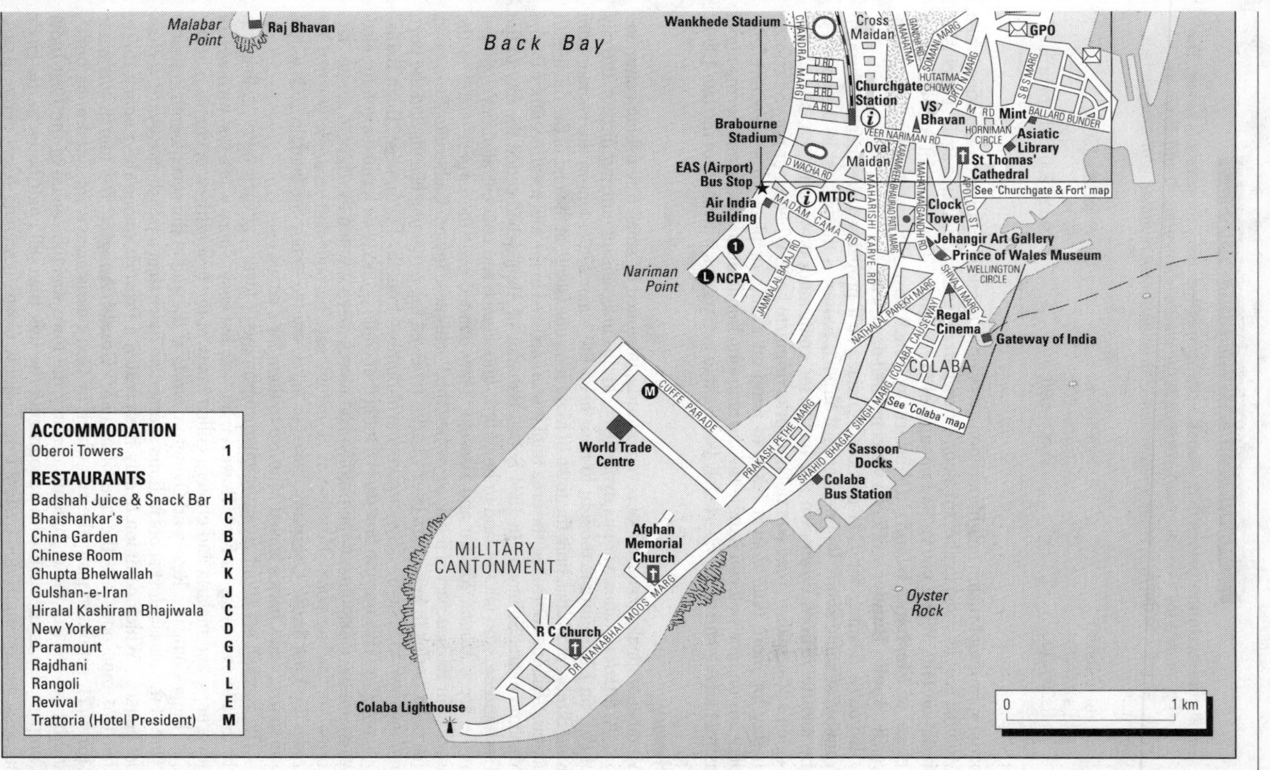
Malabar Point
Raj Bhavan
Back Bay
Wankhede Stadium
Cross Maidan
Churchgate Station
VS Bhavan
Mint
GPO
Asiatic Library
St Thomas' Cathedral
See 'Churchgate & Fort' map
Brabourne Stadium
Oval Maidan
EAS (Airport) Bus Stop
Air India Building
MTDC
Clock Tower
Jehangir Art Gallery
Prince of Wales Museum
WELLINGTON CIRCLE
Nariman Point
NCPA
Regal Cinema
Gateway of India
COLABA
See 'Colaba' map
CUFFE PARADE
World Trade Centre
Sassoon Docks
Colaba Bus Station
Afghan Memorial Church
MILITARY CANTONMENT
Oyster Rock
R C Church
Colaba Lighthouse
CHANDRA MARG
HUTATMA CHOWK
P M RD
BALLARD BUNDER
S B S MARG
HORNIMAN CIRCLE
VEER NARIMAN RD
D WACHA RD
MADAM CAMA RD
MAHARISHI KARVE RD
KARAMVEER BHAURAO PATIL MARG
MAHATMA GANDHI RD
APOLLO ST
SHIVAJI MARG
NATHALAL PAREKH MARG
JAMNALAL BAJAJ RD
SHAHID BHAGAT SINGH MARG (COLABA CAUSEWAY)
PRAKASH PETHE MARG
DR NANABHAI MOOS MARG
ACCOMMODATION
Oberoi Towers 1
RESTAURANTS
Badshah Juice & Snack Bar H
Bhaishankar's C
China Garden B
Chinese Room A
Ghupta Bhelwallah K
Gulshan-e-Iran J
Hiralal Kashiram Bhajiwala C
New Yorker D
Paramount G
Rajdhani I
Rangoli L
Revival E
Trattoria (Hotel President) M
0
1 km

ACCOMMODATION PRICE CODES

All **accommodation prices** in this book have been coded using the symbols below. The prices given are for a double room, except in the case of categories ① and ② where the price can refer to dorm accommodation per bed. All taxes are included. For more details, see p.34.

① up to Rs100	④ Rs300–400	⑦ Rs900–1500
② Rs100–200	⑤ Rs400–600	⑧ Rs1500–2500
③ Rs200–300	⑥ Rs600–900	⑨ Rs2500 and upwards

of the sprawling Muslim neighbourhoods, as well as exotic **shopping** possibilities, while Mumbai is at its most exuberant along **Chowpatty Beach**, which laps against exclusive **Malabar Hill**. When you've had enough of the mayhem, the beautiful rock-cut Shiva temple on **Elephanta Island** – a short trip by launch across the harbour from the promenade, **Apollo Bunder** – offers a welcome half-day escape.

If you're heading for Goa or South India, you'll probably have to pass through Mumbai at some stage. Its international airport, **Sahar**, is the busiest in the country; the **airline offices** downtown are handy for confirming onward flights, and all the region's principal air, road and rail networks originate here. Whether or not you choose to stay for more time than it takes to jump on a train or plane to somewhere else depends on how well you handle the burning sun, humid atmosphere and perma-fog of petrol fumes – and on how seriously you want to get to grips with India of the late 1990s.

History

Mumbai originally consisted of seven **islands**, inhabited by small Koli fishing communities. At different times, various dynasties held this insignificant outlying district; the city of Puri on **Elephanta** is thought to have been the major settlement in the region, until King Bimba, or Bhima, built the town of Mahim on one island, at the end of the thirteenth century. Hindus controlled the area until it was captured in the fourteenth century by the Muslim Gujarat Sultanate. In 1534 Sultan Bahadur of Ahmedabad ceded the city to the **Portuguese**, who felt the land to be of little importance and concentrated development in the areas around Mahim and Bassein. They handed over the largest island to the English in 1661, as part of the dowry when the Portuguese Infanta Catherine of Braganza married Charles II; four years later Charles received the remaining islands and the port, and the town took on the anglicized name of Bombay from the Portuguese "Buan Bahia" or Good Bay. This was the first part of India that could properly be termed a colony; elsewhere on the subcontinent the English had merely been granted the right to set up "factories", or trading posts. Because of its natural safe harbour and strategic position for trade, the **East India Company**, based at Surat, wanted to buy the land; in 1668 a deal was struck, and Charles leased Mumbai to them for a pittance.

The English set about an ambitious programme of fortifying their outpost, living in the area known today as Fort. However, life was not easy. There was a fast turnover of governors, and malaria and cholera culled many of the first settlers. A chaplain of the East India Company, Reverend Ovington, wrote at the end of the seventeenth century: "One of the pleasantest spots in India seemed no more than a parish graveyard, a charnel house… Which common fatality has created a Proverb among the English there, that two monsoons are the age of a man." **Gerald Aungier**, the fourth governor (1672–77), set out to plan "the city which by God's assistance is intended to be built", and by the start of the eighteenth century the town was the capital of the East India Company. He is credited with encouraging the mix that still contributes to the city's success, welcoming Hindu traders from Gujurat, Goans (escaping Jesuit persecution), Muslim weavers and, most visibly, the business-minded Zoroastrian **Parsis**.

THE DONS AND THE BOMBS

For many years, despite intense competition for jobs and living space among its diverse ethnic and social groups, Mumbai boasted of being one of India's most stable cities. While Delhi and Calcutta reeled under communal riots and terrorist attacks in the early 1980s, the great Maharashtran melting-pot remained outwardly calm. However, as early as 1982, Mumbai's infrastructure was starting to buckle under the tensions of overpopulation. A bitter and protracted **textile strike**, or *bandh*, had impoverished tens of thousands of industrial workers. Unemployment and crime were spiralling, and the influx of immigrants into the city showed no signs of abating. Among the few beneficiaries of mounting discontent was the extreme right-wing Maharashtran party, the **Shiv Sena**. Founded in 1966 by Bal "the Saheb" Thackery, a self-confessed admirer of Hitler, the Sena's uncompromising stand on immigration and employment (jobs for "Sons of the Soil" first), found favour with the disenchanted mass of lower-middle-class Hindus in the poorer suburbs. The party's venom, at first focused on the city's sizeable South Indian community, soon shifted to its fifteen percent Muslim minority. Communal antagonism flared briefly in 1984, when ninety people died in riots, and again in 1985 when the Shiv Sena routed the Congress Party in municipal elections, thereby sweeping into the mainstream.

The rise of the right coincided with an intensification of **organized crime**. Previously, the city's gangsters had confined their activities to small-scale racketeering in poor neighbourhoods. After the post-1970s real estate boom, however, many petty "landsharks" became powerful godfather figures, or "**dons**", with multi-*crore* drug- and gold-smuggling businesses. Moreover, the corrupt politicians who had employed the gangs' muscle-power to rig elections, were now highly placed political puppets with debts to pay – a phenomenon dubbed "**criminalization**". The dividing line between the underworld and politics grew increasingly blurred as the decade progressed: in 1992, no fewer than forty candidates in the municipal elections had criminal records. Meanwhile, Shiv Sena had consolidated its support by striking up an alliance with the up-and-coming and equally extreme-right Hindu party, the BJP.

Even to those who had been charting the communal situation, the events that followed the destruction by Hindu extremists of the **Babri Masjid** mosque in Ayodhya, UP, came as a shock. Between December 1992 and late January 1993 two waves of **rioting** in Mumbai, affected not only the Muslim ghettos and poor industrial suburbs, but, for the first time, much of downtown too. Around 150,000 citizens fled into the countryside, while 100,000 more moved into refugee camps. According to (conservative) official statistics, 784 people died and around 5000 were injured – seventy percent of them Muslim. Although a great deal of blame for the madness must accrue to right-wing Hindu political groups such as Shiv Sena, some commentators believe other factions stood to gain from the situation, notably slum landlords whose tenants are protected under rent freezes imposed by the Bombay Rent Act. The thousands of slum-dwellers who fled Mumbai and their burning homes following the riots conveniently cleared the way, it is suggested, for property development.

Just as Mumbai was regaining its composure, disaster struck again. Around mid-afternoon on March 12, 1993, ten massive **bomb blasts** ripped through the heart of the city, killing 317 people and gutting the Stock Exchange, the Air India building, the passport office and three swanky hotels near the airports. No one claimed responsibility, but the involvement of "foreign hands" (such as, Pakistan) was suspected. Investigators claimed the bombs had been smuggled into India and planted by Muslim mobsters. The name of India's most wanted criminal, the *don* Dawood Ibrahim, was bandied about in the press at the time, yet it took until 1998 to arrest him and a number of his associates.

The city recovered from the explosions with astonishing speed. Most banks and offices reopened the next day, and slowly the paranoia, or "fear psychosis", subsided. The hoardings erected beside the motorways ("Bombay Bounces Back!", "It's My Bombay", "Bombay, I Love You") attempted to restore the pride and ebullience with which India's most confident city had formerly gone about its business, and to an extent peaceful security has now been achieved for the average Bombayite. However, the city is still the playground for infamous mafia gangs – each with their own personalities and legends – with the newspapers revelling in the shocking and bloodthirsty details of the latest cat-and-mouse encounters between rival gangs or the police. The unfolding sagas run like an Al Pacino and Robert de Niro blockbuster, and all who stay a while in Mumbai get hooked on the latest shoot-out.

Much of the British settlement in the old Fort area was destroyed by a devastating fire in 1803, and the European population remained comparatively low well into the 1800s. The arrival of the **Great Indian Peninsular Railway** in the 1850s improved communications, encouraging yet more immigration from elsewhere in India. In 1852 the first of many land-reclamation projects (still on-going) fused the seven islands; just a year later the rail link between Bombay and the cotton-growing areas of the Deccan plateau opened. This crucial railway, coupled with the cotton crisis in America following the Civil War, gave impetus to the great Bombay cotton boom and established the city as a major industrial and commercial centre. With the opening of the Suez Canal in 1859 and the construction of enormous docks, Bombay's access to European markets improved further. **Sir Bartle Frere**, governor from 1862 to 1867, oversaw the construction of the city's distinctive colonial-Gothic buildings; the most extravagant of all, Victoria Terminus train station, now Chatrapathi Shivaji Terminus or CST, is a fitting testimony to this extraordinary age of expansion.

Not all Mumbai's grandest architecture is owed to the Raj; wealthy Jains and Parsis have also left their mark throughout the downtown area. As the most prosperous city in the nation, Bombay was at the forefront of the Independence struggle; Mahatma Gandhi used a house here, now a museum, to co-ordinate the struggle through three decades. Fittingly, the first British colony took pleasure in waving the final goodbye to the Raj, when the last contingent of British troops passed through the Gateway of India in February 1948.

Despite its recent communal tensions and growing crime-related violence, Mumbai approaches the twenty-first century as the financial and commercial centre of India, with a cost of living almost equal to that in the US, and, in Malabar Hill in particular, some of the most expensive property in the world.

Arrival

Unless you arrive in Mumbai by train at Chatrapathi Shivaji Terminus (formerly Victoria Terminus), be prepared for a long slog into the centre. The international and domestic airports are north of the city, way off the map, and ninety minutes or more by road from the main hotel areas, while from Mumbai Central railway or bus stations, you face a laborious trip across town. **Finding a place to stay** can be even more of a hassle; phone around before you set off into the traffic.

By air

For many visitors, **Sahar**, Mumbai's busy **international airport**, provides their first experience of India. The complex is divided into two "modules", one for Air India flights and the other for foreign airlines. Once through customs and the lengthy immigration formalities, you'll find a 24-hour State Bank of India exchange facility, rather unhelpful government (ITDC) and state (MTDC) tourist information counters, car rental kiosks, cafés and a pre-paid taxi stand in the chaotic arrivals concourse. If you're on one of the few flights to land in the afternoon or early evening – by which time most hotels tend to be full – it's worth paying on the spot for a room at the **accommodation booking desk** in the arrivals hall. All of the domestic airlines also have offices outside the main entrance, and there's a handy 24-hour **left luggage** "cloakroom" in the car park nearby (Rs5–15 per day, depending on the size of your bag; maximum duration 90 days).

Many of the more upmarket hotels, particularly those near the airport, send out **courtesy coaches** to pick up their guests. **Taxis** are comfortable and not too extravagant. To avoid haggling over the fare or being done by the private taxi companies outside the airport, pay in advance at the taxi desk in the arrivals hall. The price on the receipt, which you hand to the driver on arrival at your destination, is slightly more than the normal meter rate, (around Rs250 to Colaba, or Rs150 to Juhu), but at least you can be sure you'll be taken by the most direct route. Taxi-*wallahs* invariably try to persuade you to stay at a different hotel from the one you ask for. Don't agree; their commission will be added onto the price of your room.

Internal flights land at Mumbai's more user-friendly **domestic airport, Santa Cruz**, which is divided into separate, modern terminals: the cream-coloured one (Module 1A) for Indian Airlines, and the blue-and-white (Module 1B) for private carriers. If you're transferring directly from here to an international flight at Sahar, 3km northeast, take the free "fly-bus" that shuttles every fifteen minutes between the two. The Indian government and MTDC both have 24-hour information counters in the arrivals hall, and there's a foreign exchange counter and accommodation desk tucked away near the first floor exit. Use the yellow and black metered taxis that queue outside the exit. The touts that claim to be running a pre-paid taxi system overcharge hugely – a journey to Colaba should cost around Rs250, no more.

Don't be tempted to use the **auto-rickshaws** that buzz around outside the airports; they're not allowed downtown and will leave you at the mercy of unscrupulous taxi drivers on the edge of Mahim Creek, the southernmost limit of their permitted area.

By train

Trains to Mumbai from most central, southern and eastern regions arrive at **Chatrapathi Shivaji Terminus** (CST), the main train station at the end of the Central Railway line. From here it's a ten- or fifteen-minute ride to Colaba; either pick up a taxi at the busy rank outside the south exit, opposite the new reservation hall, or make your way to the main road and catch one of the innumerable buses.

Mumbai Central, the terminus for Western Railway trains from northern India, is farther out from the centre; take a taxi from the main forecourt, or cross the hectic road junction next to the station and catch a BEST bus from the top of Dr DN Marg

CHATRAPATHI SHIVAJI TERMINUS (VICTORIA TERMINUS)

Inspired by St Pancras station in London, F.W. Stevens designed **Victoria Terminus**, the most barmy of Mumbai's buildings, as a paean to "progress". Built in 1887 as the largest British edifice in India, its extraordinary amalgam of domes, spires, Corinthian columns and minarets was succinctly defined by the journalist James Cameron as "Victorian-Gothic-Saracenic-Italianate-Oriental-St-Pancras-Baroque". In keeping with the current re-indianization of the city's roads and buildings, this icon of British imperial architecture has been renamed **Chatrapathi Shivaji Terminus**, in honour of a Maratha warlord who dedicated his life to fighting the Muslim Moghuls and professing Hindu cultural identity.

Few of the two million or so passengers who fill almost a thousand trains every day notice the mass of decorative detail. A "British" lion and Indian tiger stand guard at the entrance, and the exterior is festooned with sculptures executed at the Bombay Art School by the Indian students of John Lockwood Kipling, Rudyard's father. Among them are grotesque mythical beasts, monkeys, plants and medallions of important personages. To minimize the sun's impact, stained glass was employed, some designed with locomotives and elephant images. Above it all, "Progress"stands atop the massive central dome.

An endless frenzy of activity goes on inside: scuttling passengers, hundreds of porters in red with impossibly oversized headloads, TTEs (Travelling Ticket Examiners) wearing black jackets and white trousers clasping clipboards detailing reservations, spitting checkers busy handing out fines to those caught in the act, *chai-wallahs* with trays of tea, trundling magazine stands, crowds of bored soldiers smoking *bidis* and the inexorable progress across the station of sweepers bent double. Amid it all, whole families spread out on the floor, eating, sleeping or just waiting and waiting.

(Lamington Rd); #66 and #71 run to CST, #70 to Colaba Causeway. Equally cheap, take a suburban train from Mumbai Central's local platform, across the footbridge. Four stops on is Churchgate station, the end of the line, a short taxi ride from Colaba (Rs15).

Some trains from South India arrive at more obscure stations. If you find yourself at **Dadar**, way up in the industrial suburbs, and can't afford a taxi, cross the Tilak Marg road bridge onto the Western Railway and catch a suburban train into town, or take BEST bus #70 to Colaba. **Kurla** station, where a few Bangalore trains pull in, is even farther out, just south of Santa Cruz airport. The only alternative to a cab from here is to catch bus #91 to Mumbai Central Station and change there to #70 for Colaba or a suburban train for Churchgate. Trying anything so complicated during a rush hour, however – especially if you're carrying heavy luggage – is more trouble than it's worth.

By bus

Nearly all inter-state **buses** arrive at **Mumbai Central** bus stand, a stone's throw from the train station of the same name. Again, you have a choice between municipal black and yellow taxis, the BEST buses (#66, #70 & #71), which run straight into town from the stop on Dr DN Marg (Lamington Rd), two minutes' walk west from the bus station, or a suburban train from Mumbai Central's local platform over the footbridge.

Most Maharashtran state buses terminate at the **ASIAD** bus stand, a glorified parking lot beside the main street in **Dadar**. Taxis are on hand for the thirty- to sixty-minute trip down to Colaba, or you can make your way over Tilak Marg road bridge to Dadar train station and pick up a local train to Churchgate.

Buses from Goa drop off at various points between central and downtown Mumbai. Most of the private companies currently work from the roadside in front of the Metro Cinema, at the north end of MG Rd, while Kadamba (the Goan state transport corporation) buses stop nearby on the opposite (east) side of Azad Maidan, where they have a small ticket kiosk. Both places are an inexpensive taxi ride from the main hotel district.

ONWARD TRANSPORT

For onward transport from Mumbai, including routes to Goa, see p.114 onwards.

Information and communications

The best source of **information** in Mumbai is the excellent **Government of India tourist office** (Mon–Fri 8.30am–6pm, Sat 8.30am–2pm; ☎022/203 3144) at 123 M Karve Rd, opposite Churchgate station's east exit. The staff here are exceptionally helpful and hand out a wide range of leaflets, maps and brochures both on Mumbai and the rest of the country. The office has recently established the first 24-hour tourist enquiry telephone line, which can be reached on ☎1913. There are also 24-hour tourist **information counters** at Sahar International (☎022/832 5331) and Santa Cruz (☎022/614 9200) airports.

Maharashtra State Tourism Development Corporation's (**MTDC**) main office, on Madam Cama Rd (☎022/202 6731), opposite the LIC Building in Nariman Point, sells tickets for city sightseeing tours and long-distance "luxury" buses (see p.118), and can reserve rooms in MTDC hotels. They too have information counters at Sahar International and Santa Cruz airports, as well as at CST train station and near the Gateway of India.

Local publications

If you need detailed information about **what's on** in Mumbai, ask at the Government of India tourist office for a fortnightly listings pamphlet, or check out the "Entertainments" page in the *Indian Express*, whose city edition, and that of *The Times of India*, is available from street vendors around Colaba and the downtown area. For a picture of what Mumbai has to offer the socialite, *The Bombay Experience* is a glossy booklet available at all bookstalls that gives a detailed insight into the haunts and activities of the rich and famous.

For a detailed **map** of Mumbai, look for Karmarkar Enterprise's *Most Exhaustive A–Z* street plan (Rs60). It's fiendishly hard to find in bookstores (Crossword on Bhulabai Desai Rd usually have one or two in stock), but the pavement guidebook- and magazine-*wallahs* along VN Rd, between Churchgate and Flora Fountain, may have copies. Otherwise, the Discover India Series has produced a good, up-to-date map and listings book called the *Road Guide to Mumbai*, that is widely available. For full listings of bus services, local train times and useful telephone numbers, you'll find the *Pocket Mumbai Guide* (Rs5) on sale at every stall, which is utterly essential if you want to spend any time in the city.

Banks

The logical place to change money when you arrive in Mumbai is at the State Bank of India's 24-hour counter in Sahar airport. Rates here are standard but you'll have to pay for an encashment certificate – essential if you intend to buy tourist quota railway tickets or an Indrail pass at the special counters in Churchgate or CST stations.

All the major **banks** downtown change foreign currency (Mon–Fri 10.30am–2.30pm, Sat 10.30am–12.30pm); some also handle **credit cards**, increasingly by way of 24-hour ATM cash machines. The Andhra Bank (☎022/204 4535), 18 Homi Modi St, near Hutama Chowk, takes Visa, and the Bank of America (☎022/285 2882), in the Express Towers building, Nariman Point, deals with Mastercard. The fast and efficient American Express office (daily 9.30am–7.30pm; ☎022/204 8278), on Shivaji Marg, around the corner from the Regal cinema in Colaba, offers all the regular services (including poste restante) to travellers' cheque and card holders and is open to anyone wishing to change cash; they also have an office at 364 Dr DN Marg, near Hutama Chowk. Hong Kong Bank (☎022/274921), offers 24-hour instant global ATM transactions on Visa, Delta and Mastercard. Thomas Cook's big Dr DN Marg branch (Mon–Fri 9.30am–5.30pm, Sat 9.30am–4.30pm; ☎022/204 8556), between the Khadi shop and Hutama Chowk, can also arrange money transfers from overseas, and is a good place to change money and cash travellers' cheques.

Mail and telecommunications

The **GPO** (Mon–Sat 9am–8pm, Sun 9am–4pm) is around the corner from CST station, off Nagar Chowk. Its **poste restante** counter (Mon–Sat 9am–6pm, Sun 9am–3pm) is among the most reliable in India, although they trash the letters after four weeks. The much less efficient parcel office (10am–4.30pm) is behind the main building on the first floor. Packing-*wallahs* hang around on the pavement outside.

STD booths abound in Mumbai. For rock-bottom **phone** and **fax** rates however, head for Videsh Sanchar Bhavan (open 24hr), the swanky new government telecom building on MG Marg, where you can make **reversed charge calls** to destinations such as the UK, US and Australia. Receiving incoming calls costs a nominal Rs5. Numbers in the city change constantly, so if you can't get through after several attempts, try directory enquiries on ☎197.

You can send **emails** and access the **Internet** at an increasing number of "cafés" and STD booths across Mumbai (see *Listings*, p.113).

City transport

Only a masochist would travel on Mumbai's hopelessly overtaxed public **transport** for fun. For much of the day, traffic on the main roads crawls along at little more than walking speed, or grinds to a halt in endless jams at road junctions. On the plus side, it might take forever to ride across town on a dusty red double-decker **bus**, but it will never set you back more than a few rupees. Local **trains** get there faster, but are a real endurance test even outside rush hours. **Rickshaws** do not run downtown.

Buses

BEST (Bombay Electric Supply and Transport) operates a **bus** network of labyrinthine complexity, extending to the farthest-flung corners of the city. Unfortunately, neither route booklets, maps nor "Point-to-Point" guides (which you can consult at the tourist office or at news-stands) make things any clearer. Finding out which bus you need is difficult enough. Recognizing it in the street can be even more problematic, as the numbers are written in Maharathi (although in English on the sides). Aim, wherever possible, for the "Limited" services, which stop less frequently, and avoid rush hours at all costs. Tickets should be bought from the conductor on the bus.

USEFUL BUS ROUTES

#1/3/6(Ltd)/11(Ltd)/103/124 Colaba bus station to Mahatma Phule (Crawford) Market, via CST (Nagar Chowk).

#43 Colaba bus station to GPO.

#70 Colaba to Dadar Station (W), via Mumbai Central.

#103/106/107 Colaba to Kamala Nehru Park, via Chowpatty Beach.

#124 Colaba to Vatsalabai Desai Chowk, via Mumbai Central.

#132 Colaba to Breach Candy, via Vatsalabai Desai Chowk.

#81 Churchgate to Santa Cruz, via Vatsalabai Desai Chowk (for Haji Ali's tomb and Mahalakshmi temple).

#66 CST to Mumbai Central.

#91 (Ltd) Mumbai Central to Kurla station.

Trains

Mumbai would be paralysed without its local **trains**, which carry millions of commuters each day between downtown and the sprawling suburbs in the north. One line begins at CST, running up the east side of the city as far as Thane. The other leaves Churchgate, hugging the curve of Back Bay as far as Chowpatty Beach, where it veers north towards Mumbai Central, Dadar, Santa Cruz and Vasai, beyond the city limits. Services depart every few minutes from 5am until midnight, stopping at dozens of small stations. Carriages remain packed solid virtually the whole time, with passengers dangling precariously out of open doors to escape the crush, so start to make your way to the exit at least three stops before your destination. The apocalyptic peak hours are worst of all. Women are marginally better off in the "ladies' carriages"; look for the crowd of saris and *salwar kamises* grouped at the end of the platform.

Taxis

With rickshaws banished to the suburbs, Mumbai's ubiquitous black and yellow **taxis** are the quickest and most convenient way to nip around the city centre. In theory, all should have meters and a current rate card (to convert the amount shown on the meter to the correct fare); in practice, particularly at night or early in the morning, many drivers refuse to use them. If this happens, either flag down another or haggle out a fare. As a rule of thumb, expect to be charged Rs5 per kilometre after the minimum fare of around Rs10, together with a small sum for heavy luggage (officially Rs1 per article). The latest addition to Mumbai's hectic roads is the cool cab, a blue taxi that boasts air-conditioning and charges higher rates for the privilege.

Boats

Ferry-boats regularly chug out of Mumbai harbour, connecting the city with the far shore and some of the larger islands in between. The most popular with visitors is the **Elephanta Island** launch (see p.97) which departs hourly (9am–noon; Rs50 for just the boat ride, Rs70 for the boat ride plus an English-speaking MTDC guide at the caves) from the Gateway of India. Boats to **Rewas**, the jetty across the bay which is the transport hub for Chaul, Murud-Janjira and the rarely used coastal route south, leave from Ferry Wharf, 4.5km north of Colaba up P D'Mello (Frere) Rd.

Car rental

Cars with drivers can be rented per day (around Rs600 for a non-a/c Ambassador, upwards of Rs1000 for more luxurious a/c cars), or per kilometre, from ITDC's counter at the Government of India tourist office, or through good travel agents (see p.114). Ramniranjan Kedia Tours and Travels (☎022/437 1112) is recommended if you want to book a vehicle on arrival at Sahar international airport.

Self-drive is also now available in Mumbai, though the service seems to be intended more for middle-class Indians out to impress their friends – "They'll never know it's rented!" – than tourists. You will be a lot safer if you leave the driving to someone more at home with the city's racetrack rules of the road. If you are willing to risk it, Autoriders International Ltd (in association with Hertz), at 139 Auto World, Tardeo Rd (☎022/4921838, fax 492 1172), is recommended.

Guided Tours

Of MTDC's sightseeing tours around Mumbai, the **city** tour (Tues–Sun 2–6pm; Rs75) is the most popular, managing to cram Colaba, Marine Drive, Jehangir Art Gallery, the Hanging Gardens, Kamla Nehru Park and Mani Bhavan into half a day; the "Suburban" tour (Tues–Sun 9.15am–6.15pm; Rs130) takes in Kanheri caves, Krishnagiri Upavan National Park, a lion safari and Juhu in a full day. Every Monday, the **city-suburban** tour combines the highlights of both, but wastes a lot of time in stationary traffic. **Tickets** should be booked in advance from the MTDC counter next to the Gateway of India (the main departure point). MTDC have also just begun an hour-long **evening** tour of the illuminated sights on an open-deck bus, departing on Saturday and Sunday at 7.30pm from the *Oberoi* hotel, Nariman Point.

MTDC also run four-day **outstation tours** to the caves at Ellora, Ajanta and Aurangabad, and to Nasik and Mahabaleshwar. Either book all-in tickets, which include the cost of accommodation (Rs1000), or else pay the one-way fare of Rs150.

The City

Between the airports to the north and the southern tip of Mumbai there lies a thirty-kilometre-long, seething mass of streets, suburbs and relentless traffic. Even during the relatively cool winter months, exploring it can be hard work, requiring plenty of pit stops at cold drink stalls along the way. The best place to start is down at the far south end of the peninsula in **Colaba**, home to most of the hotels, restaurants and best-known sights, including the **Gateway of India**. Fifteen minutes' walk north takes you past the **Prince of Wales Museum** to the **Fort** area, home of all the banks and big stores, plus the cream of Mumbai's ostentatious Raj-era buildings. The extravagant **Chatrapathi Shivaji Terminus** overlooks its northern limits, close to the impressive onion-dome of the **GPO**. The hub of the suburban train network, **Churchgate station**, stands 4km west, across the big *maidans* that scythe through the centre of town. Churchgate, and the **tourist office**, is a stone's throw from the sweeping curve of Back Bay. With **Nariman Point**'s skyscrapers at one end, lively **Chowpatty Beach** and the affluent apartment buildings of **Malabar Hill** at the other, the Bay is Mumbai at its snazziest. But the area immediately north and east is ramshackle and densely populated. The **central bazaars** extend from **Crawford Market**, beyond CST station, right up to **J Boman (JB) Behram Marg**, opposite the other mainline train station, **Mumbai Central**.

Colaba

At the end of the seventeenth century, **Colaba** was little more than the last in a straggling line of rocky islands extending to the lighthouse that stood on Mumbai's southernmost point. Today, the original outlines of the promontory (whose name derives from the **Koli** who first lived here) have been submerged under a mass of dilapidated colonial tenements, hotels, bars, restaurants and handicraft shops. If you never venture beyond the district, you'll get a very distorted picture of Mumbai. In spite of being the main tourist enclave and a trendy hangout for the city's rich young things, Colaba has retained the distinctly sleazy feel of the bustling port it used to be, with dodgy money-changers, dealers and pimps hissing at passers-by from doorways.

The Gateway of India

Mumbai's most famous landmark, the **Gateway of India**, was built in 1924 by George Wittet, responsible for many of the city's grandest constructions. Commemorating the visit of King George V and Queen Mary in 1911, India's own honey-coloured Arc de Triomphe was originally envisaged as a ceremonial disembarkation point for passengers alighting from the P&O steamers. Ironically, today it is more often remembered as the place the British chose to stage their final departure from the country: on February 28, 1948, the last detachment of troops remaining on Indian soil set sail from here. Nowadays, the only boats bobbing about at the bottom of its stone staircase are the launches that ferry tourists across the harbour to Elephanta Island (see p.97).

The recently spruced-up square surrounding the Gateway is a popular place for a stroll during the evenings. At one end, an equestrian statue of **Shivaji**, the Maratha military adventurer who dogged the last years of the Moghul emperor Aurangzeb in the second half of the seventeenth century, looks sternly on. Shivaji has been appropriated as a nationalist symbol (the prototypical "Son of the Soil") by the extreme right-wing Shiv Sena, which explains the garland of marigolds often draped around the statue's neck as a sign of respect.

Behind the Gateway

Directly behind the Gateway, the older hotel in the **Taj Mahal Intercontinental Hotel** complex stands as a monument to native hubris in the face of colonial oppression. Its patron, the Parsi industrialist J.N. Tata, is said to have built the old *Taj* as an act of revenge after he was refused entry to what was then the best hotel in town, the "whites only" *Watson's*. The ban proved their undoing. *Watson's* disappeared long ago, but the

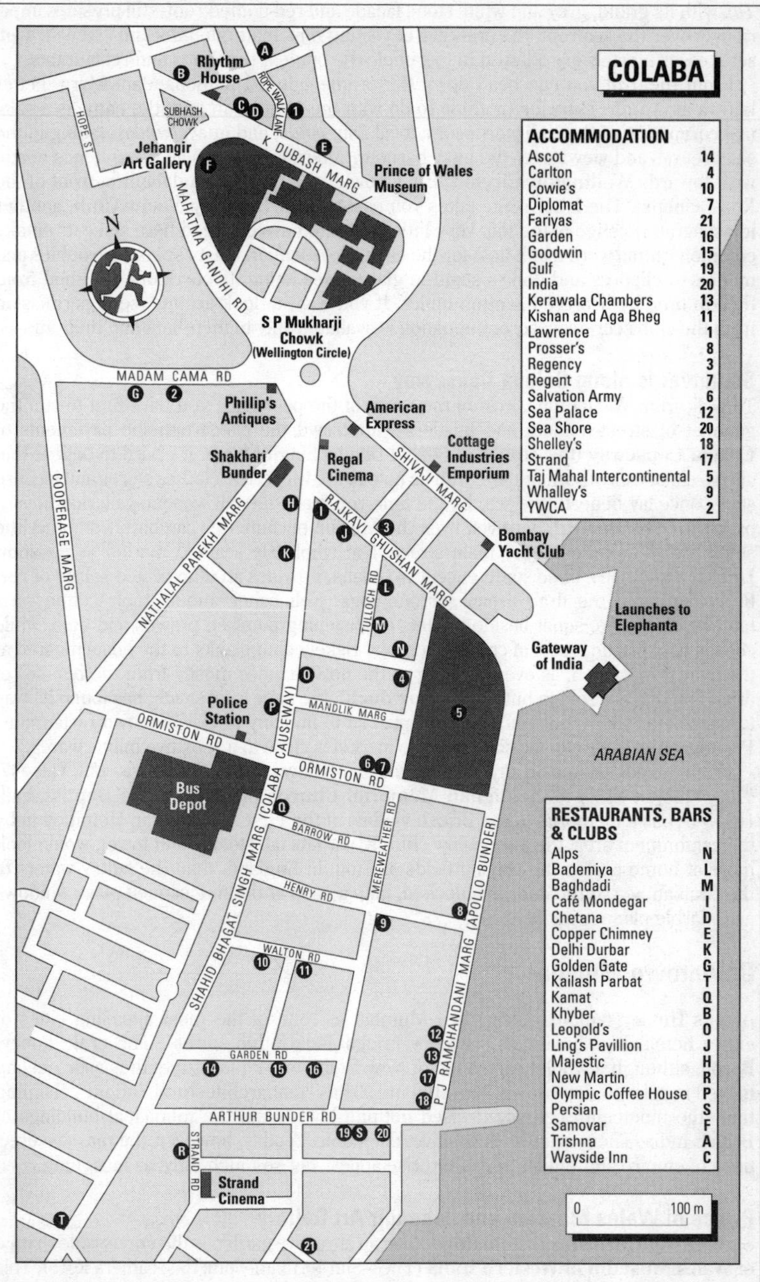
COLABA
ACCOMMODATION
Ascot 14
Carlton 4
Cowie's 10
Diplomat 7
Fariyas 21
Garden 16
Goodwin 15
Gulf 19
India 20
Kerawala Chambers 13
Kishan and Aga Bheg 11
Lawrence 1
Prosser's 8
Regency 3
Regent 7
Salvation Army 6
Sea Palace 12
Sea Shore 20
Shelley's 18
Strand 17
Taj Mahal Intercontinental 5
Whalley's 9
YWCA 2
RESTAURANTS, BARS & CLUBS
Alps N
Bademiya L
Baghdadi M
Café Mondegar I
Chetana D
Copper Chimney E
Delhi Durbar K
Golden Gate G
Kailash Parbat T
Kamat Q
Khyber B
Leopold's O
Ling's Pavillion J
Majestic H
New Martin R
Olympic Coffee House P
Persian S
Samovar F
Trishna A
Wayside Inn C
Rhythm House
Subhash Chowk
Hope St
Rope Walk Lane
K Dubash Marg
Jehangir Art Gallery
Prince of Wales Museum
Mahatma Gandhi Rd
S P Mukharji Chowk (Wellington Circle)
Madam Cama Rd
Phillip's Antiques
American Express
Cottage Industries Emporium
Shakhari Bunder
Regal Cinema
Shivaji Marg
Cooperage Marg
Nathalal Parekh Marg
Rajkavi Ghushan Marg
Bombay Yacht Club
Tulloch Rd
Launches to Elephanta
Gateway of India
Police Station
Mandlik Marg
Ormiston Rd
Colaba Causeway
Arabian Sea
Bus Depot
Barrow Rd
Merewether Rd
Henry Rd
Shahid Bhagat Singh Marg
P J Ramchandani Marg (Apollo Bunder)
Walton Rd
Garden Rd
Arthur Bunder Rd
Strand Rd
Strand Cinema
0 100 m

Taj, with its grand, grey and white stone facade and red-domed roof, still presides imperiously over the seafront, the preserve of visiting diplomats, sheikhs and Mumbai's jet-set. Lesser mortals are allowed in to sample the opulent tea-shops and restaurants.

From the *Taj*, you can head down the promenade, PJ Ramchandani Marg, better known as **Apollo Bunder** (nothing to do with the Greek sun god, the name is a colonial corruption of the Koli words for a local fish, *palav*, and quay, *bunda*), taking in the sea breezes and views over the busy harbour. Alternatively, Shivaji Marg heads north-west towards **Wellington Circle** (SPM Chowk), the hectic roundabout in front of the Regal cinema. The latter route takes you past the old **Bombay Yacht Club**, another idiosyncratic vestige of the Raj. Very little seems to have changed here since its smoky common rooms were a bolt hole for the city's *burra-sahibs*. Dusty sporting trophies and models of clippers and dhows stand in glass cases lining its corridors, polished from time to time by bearers in cotton tunics. If you want to look around, seek permission from the club secretary; accommodation is available only to members and their guests.

Southwards along Colaba Causeway

To walk from Wellington Circle to the south of the peninsula, you have first to run the gauntlet of street-vendors and hustlers who crowd the claustrophobic pavements of **Colaba Causeway** (this stretch of Shahid Bhagat Singh Marg). It's hard to believe that such a chaotic city thoroughfare, with its hole-in-the-wall cafés, clothes stores and incense stalls, once lay beneath the sea. By the time you reach the tall wooden-galleried houses of **Arthur Bunder Rd**, however, even the Muslim perfumeries can barely smother the smell of fish wafting up the main street. The wholesale seafood market at **Sassoon Docks**, a kilometre or so south of central Colaba, provides an unexpected splash of rustic colour amid the drab urban surroundings. Koli fisherwomen, their cotton saris hitched *dhoti*-style, squat beside baskets of glistening pomfret, prawns and tuna, while coolies haul plastic crates of crushed ice over rickety gangplanks to the boats moored at the quay. The stench, as overpowering as the noise, comes mostly from the bundles of dried fish that are sold in bulk. "**Bombay duck**", the salty local snack, has found its way to many a far shore, but you'll be hard pushed to find any in Colaba's own restaurants. **Photography** is strictly forbidden, as the market is close to a sensitive military area.

From the docks, hop on any bus heading south down Colaba Causeway (#3, #11, #47, #103, #123, or #125) to the **Afghan Memorial Church of St John the Baptist**, built (1847–54) as a memorial to the British victims of the First Afghan War. Hemmed in by the cantonment area, the pale yellow church, with its tall steeple and tower, would look more at home beside the playing fields of Eton, in England, than the sultry waters of the Arabian Sea. If the door is unlocked, take a peep at the fine stained-glass windows and marble plaques inside.

Downtown Mumbai

Aldous Huxley famously described Mumbai as "one of the most appalling cities of either hemisphere", with its "lavatory bricks and Gothic spires". The critic Robert Byron, although a wholehearted fan of New Delhi, was equally unenthusiastic, feeling moved to refer to **downtown Mumbai** in 1931 as "that architectural Sodom", claiming that "the nineteenth century devised nothing lower than the municipal buildings of British India. Their ugliness is positive, daemonic." Today, however, the massive erections of empire and Indian free enterprise appear not so much ugly, as intriguing.

Prince of Wales Museum and Jehangir Art Gallery

Set back from Mahatma Gandhi (MG) Rd in an attractive garden is the unmissable **Prince of Wales Museum of Western India** (Tues–Sun 10.15am–6pm; Rs3; camera Rs15). This

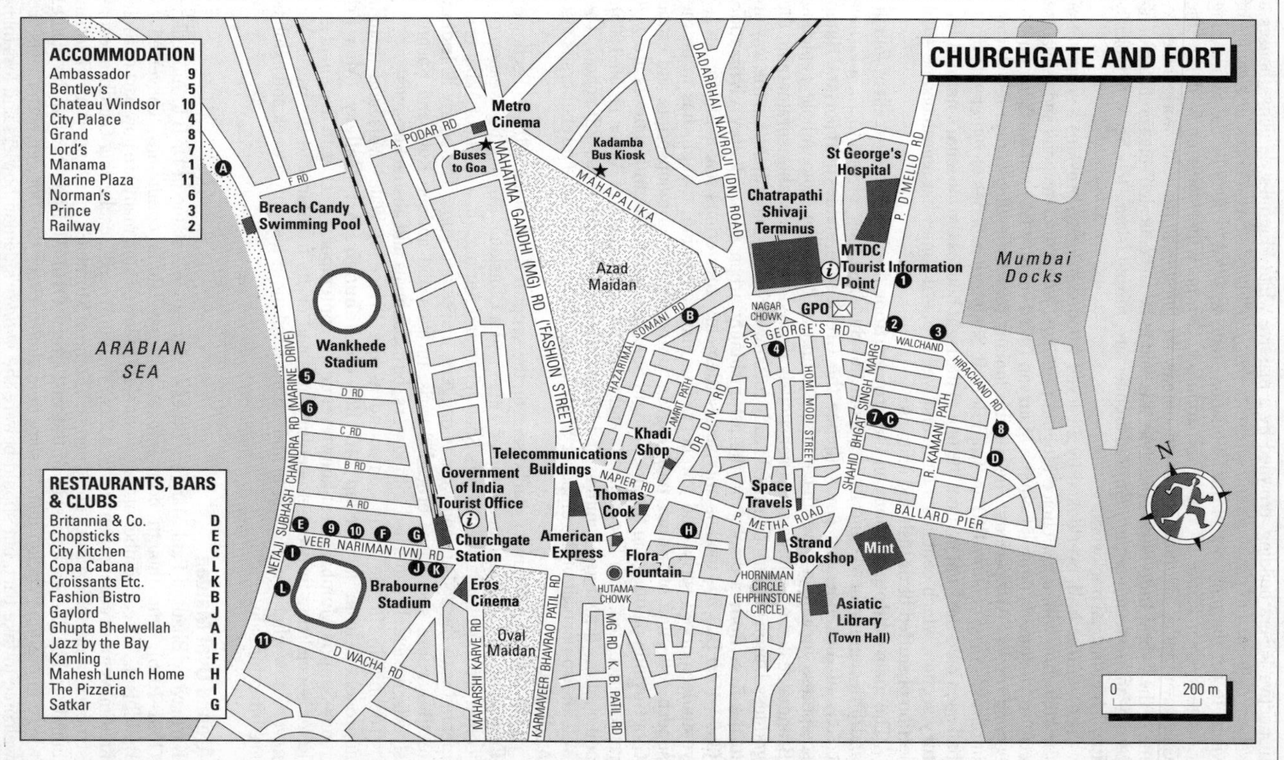
CHURCHGATE AND FORT
ACCOMMODATION
Ambassador 9
Bentley's 5
Chateau Windsor 10
City Palace 4
Grand 8
Lord's 7
Manama 1
Marine Plaza 11
Norman's 6
Prince 3
Railway 2
RESTAURANTS, BARS & CLUBS
Britannia & Co. D
Chopsticks E
City Kitchen C
Copa Cabana L
Croissants Etc. K
Fashion Bistro B
Gaylord J
Ghupta Bhelwellah A
Jazz by the Bay I
Kamling F
Mahesh Lunch Home H
The Pizzeria I
Satkar G
ARABIAN SEA
Mumbai Docks
N
0
200 m
P. D'MELLO RD
St George's Hospital
MTDC Tourist Information Point
GPO
Chatrapathi Shivaji Terminus
NAGAR CHOWK
ST GEORGE'S RD
WALCHAND HIRACHAND RD
R. KAMANI PATH
SHAHID BHGAT SINGH MARG
HOMI MODI STREET
BALLARD PIER
P. METHA ROAD
Space Travels
Strand Bookshop
Mint
HORNIMAN CIRCLE (EPHINSTONE CIRCLE)
Asiatic Library (Town Hall)
DADARBHAI NAVROJI (DN) ROAD
DR D.N. RD
AMRIT PATH
HAZARIMAL SOMANI RD
Khadi Shop
NAPIER RD
Thomas Cook
Telecommunications Buildings
American Express
Flora Fountain
HUTAMA CHOWK
MG RD
K. B. PATIL RD
KARMAVEER BHAVRAO PATIL RD
Azad Maidan
MAHAPALIKA
Kadamba Bus Kiosk
MAHATMA GANDHI (MG) RD ('FASHION STREET')
Metro Cinema
A. PODAR RD
Buses to Goa
Government of India Tourist Office
Churchgate Station
Eros Cinema
Oval Maidan
MAHARSHI KARVE RD
VEER NARIMAN (VN) RD
Brabourne Stadium
D WACHA RD
Wankhede Stadium
D RD
C RD
B RD
A RD
F RD
Breach Candy Swimming Pool
NETAJI SUBHASH CHANDRA RD (MARINE DRIVE)

distinctive Raj-era building, crowned by a massive white Moghul-style dome, houses a superb collection of paintings and sculpture that you'll need several hours, or a couple of visits, to get the most out of. Its foundation stone was laid in 1905 by the future King George V, then Prince of Wales; the architect, George Wittet, went on to design the Gateway of India. The museum is undoubtedly the finest example of his work; the epitome of the hybrid **Indo-Saracenic** style, it is said to be an "educated" interpretation of fifteenth- and sixteenth-century Gujarati architecture, mixing Islamic touches with typically English municipal brickwork.

The **central hall**, overlooked by a carved wooden balcony, provides a snapshot of the collection with a few choice Moghul paintings, jade work, weapons and miniature clay and terracotta figures from the Mauryan (third century BC) and Kushana (first to second century AD) periods. The horrible-looking *yakshis* (godlings or sprites) devouring lizards (first century BC) are from Bengal. Sculpture galleries on either side of the hall open onto the front garden; the one to the right houses the museum's **natural history** section, which contains a large and well-kept – if somewhat unfashionable – collection of stuffed birds, fish and animals.

The main **sculpture room** on the **ground floor** displays some excellent fourth- and fifth-century heads and figures from the Buddhist state of Gandhara, a former colony of Alexander the Great (hence the Greek-style statues). Important Hindu sculptures include a seventh-century Chalukyan bas-relief from Aihole depicting Brahma seated on a lotus and a sensuously carved torso of Mahisasuramaraini, the goddess Durga with tripod raised ready to skewer the demon buffalo. On the way up to the **first floor** a display on the astonishingly urban **Indus Valley civilization** (3500–1500 BC) has models of typical settlements, mysterious seal moulds in an as-yet-undeciphered script and jewellery. The main attraction, though, has to be the superb collection of **Indian painting**, including illustrated manuscripts and erotic Gita Govinda paintings in the pre-Mohgul Sultanate style. **Moghul schools** are well represented, too, with fine portraits and folios from the reign of Akbar (1556–1605), and sublime drawings of animals and birds from the Jehangir (1605–28) school. The well-known portrait of the emperor Shah Jehan (1628–58) and his forefathers is also on display.

Jade, porcelain and ivory can be seen on the **second floor**, along with a collection of **European art** that includes a minor Titian and a Constable. Among the weapon collection are the swords of emperors Shah Jehan and Aurangzeb, a shield of Akbar ornamented with the zodiac, and various daggers, maces and guns. The poorly lit **Indian textiles room** showcases brocaded saris, turbans and antique Kulu and Kashmiri shawls, intricately patterned with flowers, birds, animals and abstract designs.

Technically in the same compound as the Prince of Wales Museum, though approached from farther up MG Rd, the **Jehangir Art Gallery** (Mon–Fri 10am–5pm) is Mumbai's best-known venue for contemporary art, with five small galleries specializing in twentieth-century arts and crafts from around the world. You never know what you're going to find – most exhibitions last only a week and exhibits are often for sale.

Around Oval Maidan

Karmaveer Bhaurao Patil Marg's southern edge holds a statue of Dr B.R. Ambedkar (1891–1956), who though born into an outcast Hindu community, converted to Buddhism. A great number of "untouchables" followed suit; many are now part of a militant movement calling themselves *dalits*, "the oppressed", eschewing Gandhi's reconstructed name of *Harijans*, "god's people". Some of Mumbai's most important Victorian buildings line the eastern side of the vast green **Oval Maidan**, behind the statue, where impromptu cricket matches are held almost every day (foreign enthusiasts are welcome to take part, but should beware the *maidan*'s demon bowlers and less-than-

DABA-WALLAHS

Mumbai's size and inconvenient shape create all kind of hassles for its working population – not least having to stew for over four hours each day in slow municipal transport. One thing the daily tidal wave of commuters does not have to worry about, however, is finding an inexpensive and wholesome home-cooked lunch. In a city with a *wallah* for everything, it will find them. The members of the **Mumbai Tiffin Box Suppliers Association**, known colloquially, and with no little affection, as "**daba-wallahs**", see to that.

Every day, around four thousand *daba-wallahs* deliver freshly cooked food from 125,000 suburban kitchens to offices in the downtown area. Each lunch is prepared early in the morning by a devoted wife or mother while her husband or son is enduring the crush on the train. She arranges the rice, *dhal*, *subzi*, curd and *parathas* into cylindrical aluminium trays, stacks them on top of one another and clips them together with a neat little handle. This **tiffin box**, not unlike a slim paint tin, is the lynchpin of the whole operation. When the runner calls to collect it in the morning, he uses a special colour code on the lid to tell him where the lunch has to go. At the end of his round, he carries all the boxes to the nearest train station and hands them over to other *daba-wallahs* for the trip into town. Between leaving the wife and reaching its final destination, the tiffin box will pass through at least half a dozen different pairs of hands, carried on heads, shoulder-poles, bicycle handlebars and in the brightly decorated handcarts that plough, with such insouciance, through the midday traffic. Tins are rarely, if ever, lost, and always find their way home again (before the husband returns from work) to be washed up for the next day's lunch.

To catch *daba-wallahs* in action, head for **CST** or **Churchgate** stations around late morning time, when the tiffin boxes arrive in the city centre. The event is accompanied by a chorus of "*lafka! lafka!*" – "hurry! hurry!" – as the *daba-wallahs*, recognizable in their white Nehru caps and baggy khaki shorts, rush to make their lunch-hour deadlines. Most collect about one rupee for each tin they handle, netting around Rs1000 per month in total. *Daba* lunches still work out a good deal cheaper than meals taken in the city restaurants, saving precious paise for the middle-income workers who use the system, and providing a livelihood for the legions of poorer immigrants from the Pune area who operate it.

even pitches). Partially obscured by police huts, the dull yellow **Old Secretariat** now serves as the City Civil and Sessions Court. Indian civil servant G.W. Forrest described it in 1903 as "a massive pile whose main features have been brought from Venice, but all the beauty has vanished in transhipment." Inside, you can only imagine the originally highly polished interior, which no longer shines, but buzzes with activity. Lawyers in black gowns, striped trousers and white tabs bustle up and down the staircases, whose corners are emblazoned with expectorated *paan* juice, and offices with perforated swing-doors give glimpses of text-book images of Indian bureaucracy – peons at desks piled high with dusty be-ribboned document bundles.

Across AS D'Mello Rd from the Old Secretariat, two major buildings belonging to **Mumbai University** (established 1857) were designed in England by Sir Gilbert Scott, who had already given the world the Gothic extravaganza of London's St Pancras train station. Access through the main gates is monitored by caretakers who only allow you in if you say you're using the library. Funded by the Parsi philanthropist Cowasjee "Readymoney" Jehangir, the **Convocation Hall** greatly resembles a church. Above its entrance, a huge circular stained-glass window features a wheel with spokes of Greek pilasters that separate signs of the zodiac. The library (open daily 10am–10pm) is beneath the 79.2-metre-high **Rajabhai clock tower** which is said to be modelled on Giotto's campanile in Florence. Until 1931, it chimed tunes such as *Rule Britannia* and *Home Sweet Home*. It's worth applying for a visitor's ticket to the library (Rs5 a day,

Rs10 for three days) just to see the interior. The magnificent vaulted wooden ceiling of the reading room, high Gothic windows and stained glass still evoke a reverential approach to learning.

Hutama Chowk (Flora Fountain)

A busy five-point intersection in the heart of the Fort area, the roundabout formerly know as **Flora Fountain**, has been renamed **Hutama Chowk** (Martyrs' Square) to commemorate the freedom fighters who died to establish the state of Maharashtra in the Indian Union. The *chowk* centres on a statue of the Roman goddess **Flora**, erected in 1869 to commemorate Sir Bartle Frere. It's hard to see quite why they bothered: the Raj architecture expert, Philip Davies, was not being unkind when he said "The fountain was designed by a committee, and it shows."

Facing Hutama Chowk is a **statue of Dadabhai Naoroji** (1812–1917) the first Indian member of the British parliament (1892–95). You may want to tarry here a while to consult Machindra Govind Pawar, who for years has sat next to the statue every day except Sundays, from 8am to 8pm. Signs explain his business, offering cures for "rheumatism, hair falling, piles, fistula and sex weakness". Sri Pawar, who hails from Pune, says he is a practitioner of ayurvedic medicine, and operates on a basis that sounds like commercial suicide: he accepts no payment until his patients are cured.

Horniman Circle and the Town Hall

Horniman Circle, formerly Elphinstone Circle, is named after a pro-Independence newspaper editor. It was conceived in 1860 as the centrepiece of a newly planned Bombay by the Municipal Commissioner, Charles Forjett, on the site of Bombay "Green". Forjett, a Eurasian, had something of a peculiar reputation; he was fond of disguising himself in "native" dress and prowling about certain districts of the city to listen out for seditious talk. In 1857, at the time of the First War of Independence (as it is now known by Indians; the British call it the Indian Mutiny), Forjett fired two suspected revolutionaries from a cannon on the Esplanade (roughly the site of the modern *maidans*).

It is often said that the design of Horniman Circle was based on Tunbridge Wells or Leamington Spa in England, with elegant Neoclassical buildings centring on a garden with a fountain. East of here, the impressive Doric **Town Hall** on SBS Marg houses the vast collection of the **Asiatic Library** (see p.113).

St Thomas's Cathedral

The small, simple **St Thomas's Cathedral** (daily 6.30am–6pm), on Tamarind St, is believed to be the oldest English building in Mumbai, blending Classical and Gothic styles. Governor Aungier self-righteously envisaged it with "the main design of inviting the natives to repair thereunto, and observe the gravity and purity of our own devotions". After his death, the project was abandoned; the walls stood five metres high for years until enthusiasm was rekindled by Richard Cobbe, a chaplain to the East India Company in the second decade of the eighteenth century. He believed the church's unfinished walls represented "a mark of derision for the natives for whose conversion they were partly raised [and] a reproach and a scandal to the English in Bombay". It was finally opened on Christmas Day 1718, complete with the essential "cannon-ball-proof roof". In those days, the seating was divided into useful sections for those who should know their place, including one for "Inferior Women".

St Thomas's whitewashed and polished brass-and-wood interior looks much the same as when the staff of the East India Company worshipped here in the eighteenth century. Lining the walls are memorial tablets to English parishioners, many of whom died young, either from disease or in battle.

Marine Drive and Chowpatty Beach

Netaji Subhash Chandra Marg, better known as **Marine Drive**, is Mumbai's seaside prom, an eight-lane highway with a wide pavement built in the 1920s on reclaimed land. Sweeping in an arc from the skyscrapers at Nariman Point in the south, Marine Drive ends at the foot of Malabar Hill and the old Chowpatty Beach. The whole stretch is a favourite place for a stroll; the promenade next to the sea has uninterrupted views virtually the whole way along, while the apartment buildings on the land side – most of which are ugly, unpainted concrete and called something-or-other Mahal – are some of the most desirable and expensive addresses in the city.

It's a great place for people-watching. Early in the morning yuppies in shorts speed-walk or jog before breakfast while street kids, mothers and babies and limbless beggars take up position at the traffic lights at major junctions to petition drivers and passengers for a rupee. Those one rung farther up the social ladder have something to sell: twisted fun balloons or a newspaper. Some kids perfunctorily wipe a rag over car bodywork and do their best to wrest a few coins from momentarily captive people, ninety percent of whom stare resolutely ahead.

Evening sees servants walking their bosses' pekinese or poodles, and children playing under the supervision of their *ayahs* (nannies). Sometime after 6pm the place magically transforms; the British called it the "Queen's Necklace". The massive red sun disappears into the sea, street lights snap on, five-star hotels glow and neon lights blink. Innumerable couples materialize to take romantic strolls down to the beach, stopping on the way to buy from a peanut vendor or to pay off a *hijra* or eunuch, threatening to lift up his sari and reveal all.

Just beyond the huge flyover, B Bridge, are a series of cricket pitches known as **gymkhanas**, where there's a good chance of catching a match any day of the week. A number are exclusive to particular religious communities. The first doubles as a swanky outdoor wedding venue for Parsi marriages; others include the Catholic, Islamic and Hindu pitches, the last of which has a classic colonial-style pavilion.

At the northern end of the gymkhanas, the **Tarporevala Aquarium** (Tues–Sat 10am–7pm, Sun & hols 10am–8pm) is less notable for its sea snakes, vibrant green and yellow trigger fish and turtles, than its two aquatic miracles: the "Koran fish", inscribed with a line from the Koran, and the "Christ Crab", which has a holy cross on his back. No photography is allowed.

Chowpatty Beach

Chowpatty Beach is a Mumbai institution, which really comes to life at night and on Saturday. People do not come here to swim (the sea is foul) but to wander, sit on the beach, let the kids ride a pony or a rusty Ferris wheel, have a massage, get ears cleaned or hair cut, listen to musicians, buy drugs, have a go on a rifle range, consult an astrologer, watch dreadlocked ascetics perform public austerities, get conned and most importantly picnic on *bhel puri* and cups of *kulfi.* Gupta Bhelwalla's *bhel puri* stall has been satisfying the discerning Mumbai palate with a secret concoction of the sunset snack for over a century – watch a legend turn pastry, *masala* and yoghurt into an art form. There are also plenty of good ice-cream bars and restaurants on Marine Drive, opposite the beach (see above), where you'll find Wagh's Fine Art Studio, whose curious collection of plaster figures in the window includes a much-larger-than-life Gandhi plus Alsatian dog.

Amazingly enough, Chowpatty Beach is still home to a small Koli fishing village that carries on as if the vast city of Mumbai didn't exist. Once a year in September the **Ganesh Chathurthi** festival (see p.61) draws gigantic crowds to participate in the immersion of idols, both huge and small, of the elephant-headed god Ganesh.

Just west of Chowpatty Beach is the **Breach Candy swimming pool**, where membership is strictly restricted to the upper echelons of society. However, tourists are allowed to join for the day (Rs200), and use both the British-style indoor pool and the India-shaped outdoor pool. The complex overlooks the beach, has relaxing sun loungers and a good restaurant.

Mani Bhavan Mahatma Gandhi Museum

Mani Bhavan, 19 Laburnum Rd (daily 9.30am–6pm), was Gandhi's Bombay base between 1917 and 1934. Set in a leafy upper-middle-class road, the house is now a permanent memorial to the Mahatma with an extensive research library. Within the lovingly maintained polished wood interior, the walls are covered with photos of historic events and artefacts from the man's extraordinary life – the most disarming of which is a friendly letter to Hitler suggesting world peace. Gandhi's predictably simple sitting-cum-bedroom is preserved behind glass. Laburnum Rd is a few streets along from the Bharatiya Vidya Bhavan music venue on KM Munshi Marg (see p.107) – if coming by taxi ask for the nearby Gamdevi police station.

Malabar Hill

Malabar Hill, the long, steep-sided promontory enfolding Chowpatty Beach at the north end of Back Bay, is Mumbai's ritziest neighbourhood. Since the eighteenth century, its lush forests, fresh sea breezes and panoramic views have made the hill an attractive location for the grand mansions and bungalows of the city's merchants and governors. These days however, high-rise, high-rent apartment buildings have squeezed out all but a handful of the old colonial buildings to make way for Mumbai's "new money" set – the in-crowd of politicians, millionaires, film stars and gangsters who flit across the glossy pages and gossip columns of India's popular magazines. Somehow, though, a few remnants of the city's past have managed to weather the changes.

Before heading up the hill from the busy roundabout at the far end of Chowpatty Beach, make a short diversion through the narrow backlanes to **Balbunath Mandir**, one of Mumbai's most important Hindu temples. You'll have no trouble finding the entrance: just look for the melee of stray cattle and flower-sellers that forms here around *puja* times. The building itself, a clumsy modern agglomeration of towers, turquoise arches and staircases, makes a much less interesting spectacle than the stream of *pujaris* (priests) and pilgrims on the greasy stone steps leading to it.

The municipal parks and the Jain temple

From the Balbunath temple, the most pleasant and direct route up to Malabar Hill's main thoroughfare, **Ridge Rd**, now re-named **Bal Gangadhar** (or **BG**) **Kher Marg**, is via the tangle of crumbling concrete paths through the woods below it. The trail emerges near a pair of dull but popular public parks. The larger, known as the "**Hanging Gardens**" (recently renamed "Pherozeshah Mehta Gardens") is full of loving couples smooching ostentatiously around its gravel paths and manicured flowerbeds. By contrast, the smaller **Kamala Nehru Children's Park** (across the road) is unlikely to appeal to anyone over the age of seven. The views of Back Bay are, in any case, better admired from the congenial terrace bars of the *Naaz Café* nearby.

A kilometre or so straight down the ridge from the parks stands Malabar Hill's **Jain temple**. Mumbai's Jains originally came from Gujarat in the late seventeenth century to escape persecution by the Hindu Marathas. Since then, their legendarily sharp business sense has helped make these ultra-strict vegetarians one of the city's most prosperous minorities. According to an ancient dictum, Jains should, every day after bathing, walk barefoot to their local temple in a length of stitchless cloth to pray, a gesture of humility

THE TOWERS OF SILENCE

High on the top of Malabar Hill, screened from prying eyes by an imposing wall and a dense curtain of vegetation, stand the seven Parsi **Towers of Silence**, or *dokhmas*. If you know only one thing about the Parsis, it is probably that they dispose of their dead by leaving the corpses on top of tall cylindrical enclosures for their bones to be picked clean by vultures. This ancient mortuary ritual, thought to predate the 2500-year-old faith, was advocated by the prophet Zoroaster as a means of avoiding pollution of the four sacred elements (air, water, earth, and the holiest of all, fire). Recently, Parsis have been debating whether to switch to electric cremation as a sound, and more sanitary, alternative – supposedly because scraps of human flesh discarded by the over-fed vultures have been appearing on balconies, roof-tops and gardens near the Towers. Whatever they decide, no one will thank you for trying to peep at the *dokhmas* themselves, which are off-limits to all living people other than the pall-bearers who put the corpses in place. Not to be put off, *Time-Life* once published a colour photograph of a funeral taken from the buildings overlooking the site. Enraged Parsis retorted by asking how the photographer would feel if he saw pictures of *his* mother's body being pecked to bits by birds?

and renunciation that contrasts with the lavish decoration of the temples themselves. This temple, though on the small side, is no exception. Mirrors and colourful paintings cover the walls surrounding the approach to the central chamber, where the polished marble image of **Adinath**, the first of the twenty-four Jain teacher-prophets, or *tirthankaras*, is enshrined. In front of the image, devotees make rice patterns as offerings. The temple also runs a stall selling freshly baked pure-veg biscuits, sweets and cakes. It's to the left of the main entrance, near the racks where shoes and leather articles have to be deposited.

Walukeshwar Mandir and Banganga tank

Beyond the Jain temple, Malabar Hill tapers off to a narrow spit that shelves steeply down to Back Bay on one side, and the rocky sea shore on the other. **Walukeshwar Mandir**, among the few of Mumbai's ancient Hindu sites not buried under layers of conurbation, can be reached via a lane left off the main road. According to the *Ramayana*, Rama paused here during his journey south to rescue Sita from the clutches of the evil Ravana, and fashioned a *lingam* out of sand to worship Shiva. Over time, the Walukeshwar, or "Sand-Lord" shrine, became one of the western Indian coast's most important religious centres, venerated even by the marauding Malabar pirates who menaced the islands. Today's temple, erected in 1715 after the original had been destroyed by the Portuguese, is unremarkable and best bypassed in favour of the more impressive **Banganga tank**, below it. Hemmed in by a towering wall of apartment buildings, the spring that feeds the tank is believed to have been created by an arrow fired from Rama's own fabled bow. Today, it's a minor pilgrimage site, busy only on "white" (full-) or "black" (no-) moon days of the month. At other times, Banganga's stone *ghats*, numerous subsidiary shrines and scum-covered greenish waters see little more than a trickle of bathers, drawn mostly from the slum encampments which have sprung up on the broken land lining the shore. A path picks its way past these shacks, and the washing lines of the *dhobis* who live in them, to the **cremation ghats** nearby.

North of Malabar Hill

Two of Mumbai's most popular religious sites, one Hindu, the other Muslim, can be reached by following Bhulabhai Desai Rd north from Malabar Hill as far as Prabhu Chowk, through the exclusive suburb of **Breach Candy** (bus #132 from Colaba).

Alternatively, make for Mumbai Central and head due northwest to **Vatsalabai Desai Chowk** (also bus #132 from Colaba).

Mahalakshmi Mandir is joined to Bhulabhai Desai Rd by an alley lined with stalls selling *puja* offerings and devotional pictures. Mumbai's favourite *devi*, **Lakshmi**, goddess of beauty and prosperity – the city's most sought-after attributes – is here propitiated with coconuts, sweets, lengths of shimmering silk and giant lotus blooms. At weekends, queues for *darshan* extend right the way across the courtyard and down the main steps beyond. Gifts pile so high that the temple *pujaris* run a money-spinning sideline reselling them. Their little shop, to the left of the entrance, is a good place to buy cut-price saris and brocades infused with lucky Lakshmi-energy. While you're here, find out what your future holds by joining the huddle of devotees pressing rupees onto the rear wall of the shrine room. If your coin sticks, you'll be rich.

A temple has stood on this rocky outcrop for well over a thousand years. Not until the eighteenth century however, when the hitherto swampy western edge of the city was drained, was the present building erected. Legend has it that the goddess herself told a contractor working on the project that unless her icon – which she said would soon reappear from the sea where it had been cast by Muslim invaders – was reinstated in a temple on the site, the breach-wall would not hold back the waves. Sure enough, the next day a Lakshmi deity was fished out of the silt by workmen, to be installed on this small headland, where it has remained to the present day.

Another site shrouded in myth is the mausoleum of the Muslim saint, **Haji Ali**, occupying a small islet in the bay just north of the Mahalakshmi temple. Islamic lore says that the Afghan mystic lived and meditated on this spot, or more picturesquely, that Haji Ali's coffin was washed ashore on these rocks after it had, on strict instructions from the saint, been cast into the sea off the coast of what is now Pakistan. The tomb is connected to the mainland by a narrow concrete **causeway**, only passable at low tide. When not immersed in water, its entire length is lined with beggars who change one-rupee pieces into ten-*paise* coins for pilgrims. The prime sites, closer to the snack bars that flank the main entrance, near the small mosque, and the gateway to the **tomb** itself, are allocated in a strict pecking order. If you want to make a donation, spare a thought for the unfortunates in the middle. After all the commotion, the tomb itself comes as something of a disappointment. Its white Moghul domes and minarets look a lot less exotic close up than when viewed from the shore, silhouetted against the sun as it drops into the Arabian Sea.

A couple of kilometres farther up the coast, the densely packed districts of central Mumbai are broken by a huge, empty expanse of dusty brown grass. The optimistically named **Mahalakshmi racecourse**, founded in 1879, is the home of the Mumbai Turf Club and a bastion of the city's Anglophile elite. Regular meetings take place here on weekends between November and March. If you fancy a hack yourself, the Amateur Riding Club also rents out horses during the week (except Wednesdays).

The central bazaars

Lining the anarchic jumble of streets north of Lokmanya Tilak (formerly Carnac) Rd, Mumbai's teeming **central bazaars** are India at its most intense. You could wander around here for months without seeing the same shopfront twice. In practice, most visitors find a couple of hours mingling with the crowds in the heat and din quite enough. Nevertheless, the market districts form a fascinating counterpoint to the wide and Westernized streets of downtown, even if you're not buying.

In keeping with traditional divisions of guild, caste and religion, most streets specialize in one or two types of merchandise – a pain if you want to see a smattering of all the goods on offer in a relatively short time. If you lose your bearings, the best way out

THE MUNICIPAL DHOBI GHATS

On the face of it, the idea of going out of your way to ogle Mumbai's dirty washing sounds like a very perverse pastime. If you're passing, however, the **municipal dhobi ghats**, near Mahalakshmi suburban train station, are well worth hopping off the train to see. This huge open-air laundry is the centre of one of those miraculous Indian institutions which, like the *daba-wallah*'s operation (see p.89), is usually regarded by Westerners with disbelief. Each morning, washing from all over Mumbai is brought here to be thrown into soapy piles and thumped by the resident *dhobi-wallahs* in the countless concrete tanks, barrels and shanty shacks inside the compound. The next day, after being aired, pressed, folded in newspaper and bound with cotton thread, the bundles are returned to whence they came. The secret behind this smooth operation is a symbol marked on each item of clothing; all *dhobi-wallahs* have their own code – invisible to the untrained eye but understood by all in the washing business – that ensures the safe passage of laundry. The bird's-eye view over the V-shaped rows of *dhobi ghats* from Mahalakshmi Rd bridge is one of Mumbai's most bizarre photo opportunities.

is to ask someone to wave you in the direction of **Abdul Rehman St**, the busy road through the heart of the district, from where you can hail a taxi.

Crawford Market

Crawford (aka Mahatma Phule) **Market**, ten minutes' walk north of CST station, is an old British-style covered market dealing in just about every kind of fresh food and domestic animal imaginable. Thanks to its pompous Norman Gothic tower and prominent position at the corner of Lokmanya Tilak Rd and Dr DN Marg, the Crawford Market is also a useful landmark and a good place to begin a foray into the bazaars.

Before venturing inside, check out the **friezes** wrapped around its exterior – a Victorian vision of sturdy-limbed peasants toiling in the fields designed by Rudyard Kipling's father, Lockwood, as principal of the Bombay School of Art in 1865. The **main hall** is still divided into different sections: pyramids of polished fruit and vegetables down one aisle; sacks of nuts or oil-tins full of herbs and spices down another. Sitting cross-legged on a raised platform in front of each stall, is its eagle-eyed owner, wearing starched *khadi* pyjamas and a Nehru cap, with a fresh red *tilak* smeared on his forehead.

Around the back of the market, in the atmospheric **wholesale wing**, the pace of life is more hectic. Here, noisy crowds of coolies mill about with large reed-baskets held high in the air (if they are looking for work) or on their heads (if they've found some).

One place animal-lovers should definitely steer clear of is Crawford Market's **pet** and **poultry** section, on the east side of the building. You never quite know what creatures will turn up here, cringing in rank-smelling, undersized cages. The **tobacco** market, by contrast, is altogether more fragrant. Look out for the Muslim *hookah* merchants selling picturesque smoking paraphernalia.

Heading north of Crawford Market to Bhuleshwar Market

The streets immediately **north of Crawford Market** and west of **Mohamed Ali Rd**, the main drag through Mumbai's Muslim ghettos, form one vast bazaar area. Ranged along both sides of narrow **Mangaldas Lane**, the cloth bazaar, are small shops draped with lengths of bright silk and cotton. Low doorways on the left open onto a colourful **covered market** area, packed with tiny stalls where you'll be badgered to sit and take tea while the merchants tempt you with dozens of different saris and scarves.

Eastwards along Mangaldas Lane from Lokmanya Tilak Rd, the pale green-washed domes, arches and minarets of the **Jami Masjid**, or "Friday Mosque" (*c.*1800), mark the start of the Muslim neighbourhoods. Memon St, cutting north from the mosque, is the site of the **Zaveri Bazaar**, the jewellery market.

By the time the gleaming golden spire that crowns the **Mumba-Devi temple**'s cream and turquoise tower appears at the end of the street, you're deep in a maze of twisting lanes hemmed in by tall, wooden-balconied buildings. The temple is one of the most important centres of Devi-worship in India. Reached via a tiny courtyard where *pujaris* regale devotees with religious songs, its shrine houses a particularly revered, and unusual, deity, Mumba Devi. Her present resting place was built early in the nineteenth century, when she was relocated from her former home to make way for the CST station. Mumba Devi's other claim to fame is that her name is the original root of the word "Bombay", as well as the newer, and more politically correct, Maharashtran version, "Mumbai".

Continuing farther north, you reach **Bhuleshwar market**, which draws thousands of Bombayites for vegetables in the early morning or clothes bargains later in the day. The small turning to the left at the next junction north of Buleshwar is Phool Galli or "Flower Lane", a short, narrow street devoted to supplying elaborate flower arrangements to temples and wedding functions. The skilled artists use jasmine, spider lilies, roses, hibiscus, ladies lace, a rare flower known as "snake champa" and blue, purple, orange and yellow marigolds, along with banana, *tulsi* and *gol pada* (round foot) leaves. When admiring the blooms remember that to smell or touch them will render them useless for a temple and will lead to them being discarded. It is for the god to smell them first.

Further north: Chor Bazaar, Mutton Rd and the red-light district

Jump in a taxi at the Mumba-Devi temple for the two-kilometre trip north to the other concentration of markets around **Johar Chowk**, just north of SP Patel Rd. The most famous of these, **Chor** (literally "thieves") **Bazaar** (where vendors peevishly insist the name is a corruption of the Urdu *shor*, meaning "noisy"), is the city's largest **antiques**-cum-flea-market. Friday, the Muslim holy day, is the best day to be here. From 9am onwards, the neighbourhood is cluttered with hawkers and handcarts piled high with bric-a-brac and assorted junk being eagerly rummaged by men in skullcaps. At other times, the antique shops down on **Mutton Rd** are the main attraction. Once, you could hope to unearth real gems in these dark, fusty stores, but your chances of finding a genuine bargain nowadays are minimal. Most of the stuff is pricey Victoriana – old gramophones, chamber pots, chipped china – salvaged from the homes of Parsi families on the decline. The place is also awash with **fakes**, mainly small bronze votive statues, which make good souvenirs if you can knock the price down.

Press on north through Chor Bazaar and you'll eventually come out onto **Grant Rd** (Maulana Shaukatali Rd). Further north and west, in the warren of lanes below JB Behram Marg, lies the city's infamous **red-light district**. **Kamathipura**'s rows of luridly lit, barred shopfronts, from where an estimated 25,000 prostitutes ply their trade, are one of Mumbai's more degrading and unpleasant spectacles. Many of these so-called "**cage girls**" are young teenagers from poor tribal areas and from across the border in Nepal, who have been sold by desperate parents into **bonded slavery** until they can earn the money to pay off family debts. The area is definitely no place to wander around on foot.

Elephanta

An hour's boat ride from Colaba, the tranquil, forested island of **ELEPHANTA** is one of the most atmospheric places in Mumbai. Populated only by a small fishing community, it makes a wonderful contrast to the seething claustrophobia of the city, even when crowded with day-trippers at weekends. Originally known as **Gharapuri** ("city of Ghara priests"), the island was renamed in the sixteenth century by the Portuguese in honour of the carved elephant they found at the port (see p.98). Its chief attraction is its unique **cave temple**, whose massive **Trimurti** (three-faced) **Shiva sculpture** is as fine an example of Hindu architecture as you'll find anywhere.

"**Deluxe**" and "**ordinary**" **boats**, run by the MTDC, set off from the Gateway of India (Oct–May hourly 9am–noon; Rs70 including guide); book through MTDC on Madam Cama Rd or at their kiosk near the Gateway of India. Three "deluxe" boats leave with an MDTC English-speaking guide on board (8.45am, 11am & 2pm); if you take any of the others you can ask for your guide at the MTDC ticket office on arrival. **Ordinary boats** (hourly 9am–noon; Rs50) do not include guides, and are usually packed. The journey takes about an hour on either boat.

Cool drinks and souvenir stalls line the way up the hill, and at the top, the MTDC *Chalukya* restaurant offers food and beer, and a terrace with good views out to sea but you cannot stay overnight on the island.

The Cave

Elephanta's impressive excavated **cave** (eighth century), covering an area of approximately 5000 square metres, is reached by climbing more than one hundred steps to the top of the hill. Inside, the massive columns, carved from solid rock, give the deceptive impression of being structural. To the right, as you enter, note the panel of **Nataraj**, Shiva as the cosmic dancer (see p.564). Though spoiled by the Portuguese who, it is said, used it for target practice, the panel remains magnificent; Shiva's face is rapt, and in one of his left hands he removes the veil of ignorance. Opposite is a badly damaged panel of Lakulisha, Shiva with a club (*lakula*).

Each of the four entrances to the simple square main **shrine** – unusually, it has one entrance on each side – is flanked by a pair of huge, fanged *dvarpala* guardians (only those to the back have survived undamaged), while inside a large *lingam* is surrounded by coins and smouldering joss left by devotees. Facing the northern wall of the shrine another panel shows Shiva impaling the demon **Andhaka**, who wandered around as though blind, symbolizing his spiritual blindness. Shiva killed him as he attempted to steal a divine tree from heaven. The panel behind the shrine on the back wall portrays the marriage of **Shiva and Parvati**. Moving east, the next panel shows Ganghadaran, Shiva receiving the descending river Ganga, his lover, to live in his hair, while Parvati, his wife, looks on. A powerful six-metre-high bust of **Trimurti**, the three-faced Shiva, who embodies the powers of creator, preserver and destroyer, stands nearby, and to the west a sculpture shows Shiva as **Ardhanarishvara**, half male and half female. Near the second entrance on the east, another panel shows Shiva and Parvati on **Mt Kailasha** with Ravana about to lift the mountain. His curved spine shows the strain.

Uptown and the outskirts

Greater Mumbai has crept inexorably northwards to engulf villages and swampland in a pall of chimneys, motorways and slums. These grim industrial areas hold few attractions, but possibilities for full- or half-day excursions include the quirky **Victoria and Albert Museum** and **botanical gardens** in Byculla, and the **beach** at Juhu. All lie within reach of a suburban train station, although you will, in most cases, have to take a rickshaw or taxi for the last few kilometres. Beyond them to the north lie the Buddhist caves chiselled out of the hillside at **Kanheri**, and the crumbling Portuguese fort at **Bassein**.

Byculla and the Veermata Jeejamata (Victoria and Albert) Museum

As the bedrock of Mumbai's once-gigantic weaving industry, **Byculla**, immediately north of the central bazaar, epitomizes the grim legacy of nineteenth-century industrialization: idle chimney stacks, overcrowded pavements strewn with ragged, sleeping bodies. The cotton-mills and sweat-shops are still here, churning out cheap clothes for the massive domestic market, but few can claim the turnovers they enjoyed a hundred years ago. Today, eclipsed by their old Gujarati rivals in Surat and Ahmedabad, all but the larger nationalized mills teeter on the brink of bankruptcy.

Visitors are welcome to look around the few of Byculla's cotton-mills still in business, but a more common reason to come up here is to see the **Victoria and Albert Museum** (daily except Wed 10am–5pm; free) on Dr Babasaheb Ambedkar Marg, which has now been renamed Veermata Jeejamata museum. Inspired by its namesake in London, this grand Victorian Gothic building was built in 1871 to house artefacts relating to Mumbai's history and development. Engravings, photographs and old maps are displayed in a small gallery on the first floor, along with sundry *objets d'art*. Downstairs in the main hall, the exhibits are more eclectic. Among the Victorian china and modest assortment of South Indian bronzes, are cases filled with papier-mâché parakeets, pick-axe heads and plastic models of vegetables. More instructive is the scale model of a Parsi Tower of Silence (see box on p.93), with a gruesome description of the mortuary rituals performed on the real ones on Malabar Hill.

The museum's oldest and most famous exhibit, however, is the **stone elephant** in the small garden to the rear of the building. Now somewhat forlorn and neglected in the shadows, this was the very beast that inspired the Portuguese to name the island in the harbour "Elephanta" (see p.96). The crumbling figure was brought here for safe-keeping in 1863 from its original, and more fittingly prominent site alongside the landing stage that leads up to the cave temple.

A wrought-iron gateway beyond the elephant opens onto one of Mumbai's most popular venues for an old-fashioned family day out. The peaceful and green **botanical gardens** (daily except Wed 8am–6pm) hold a huge collection of South Asian flora, plus Mumbai's only **zoo**, where, after a trip around the predictably small and smelly cages, kids can enjoy an elephant or camel ride.

Both museum and botanical gardens can be reached either by BEST **bus** #3 or #11(Ltd) from Colaba, or #19 from Flora Fountain and Crawford Market; or by suburban train to Byculla station, on the opposite (western) side of the motorway.

Juhu Beach

With its palm trees, glamorous seaside apartment buildings and designer clothes stores, **Juhu**, 30km north of downtown, is Mumbai's answer to Sunset Boulevard. Unless you're staying in one of the many five-star hotels lining its five-kilometre strip of white sand, however, this affluent suburb holds little appeal. Sunbathing and swimming are out of the question, thanks to an oily slick of raw sewage that seeps into the Arabian Sea from the slum *bastis* (temples) surrounding Mahim Creek to the south. A more salubrious way to enjoy Juhu is to walk along the strand after office hours, when young families turn out in droves to enjoy the sunsets and sea breezes, attracting a bevy of *bhel puri-wallahs*, side shows, mangy camels and carts, and lads hawking cheap Taiwanese toys. The rows of brightly painted stalls along the beach whip up delicious varieties of *falooda*, a fruit, ice cream and sugar-macaroon milkshake unique to Mumbai.

Further north up Juhu Rd, the headquarters of the International Society for Krishna Consciousness (ISKCON) deals with matters more spiritual. Its richly appointed **Krishna temple** (daily 4am–1pm & 4–9pm) draws local Hindus in their Sunday-best shirtings and saris, and well-heeled Westerners wearing kaftans, *kurtas* and *dhotis*. Rich visitors get to stay in what must surely rank as the world's most glamorous *dharamshala* – a modern, multistorey hotel complex with its own veg restaurant, conference hall and theatre.

Kanheri Caves

The chief reason to make the day's excursion to the suburb of Borivli, 42km out at the northern limits of Mumbai's sprawl, is to visit the Buddhist **caves** of **Kanheri** (daily 9am–5.30pm), ranged over the hills in virtually unspoilt forest. It's an interminable journey by road, so catch one of the many **trains** (50min) on the suburban line from Churchgate (marked "BO" on the departure boards; "limited stop" trains are 15min faster). When you arrive, take the Borivli East exit, and pick up an **auto-rickshaw** (about Rs10) to the entrance of the Sanjay Gandhi National Park (Rs5), formerly the Borivli National Park. Bring water and food as the stalls here only sell warm soft drinks.

Kanheri may not be as spectacular as other cave sites, but some of its sculpture is superb – though to enjoy the blissful peace and quiet that attracted its original occupants you should avoid the weekend and the crowds of day-trippers. Most of the caves, which date from the second to the ninth centuries AD, were used simply by monks as *viharas* for accommodation and meditation during the four months of the monsoon, when an itinerant life was impractical – the season when the forest is at its most beautiful. They are connected by steep winding paths and steps; engage one of the friendly local guides at the entrance to find your way about, but don't expect any sort of lecture as their English is limited.

In **Cave 1**, an incomplete *chaitya* hall (a hall with a *stupa* at one end, an aisle and row of columns at either side), you can see where the rock was left cut, but unfinished. Two *stupas* stand in **Cave 2**, one was vandalized by a certain N. Christian, whose carefully incised Times Roman graffiti bears the date 1810. A panel shows seated Buddhas, portrayed as teachers. Behind, and to the side, is the *bodhisattva* of compassion, Padmapani, while to the right the *viharas* feature rock-cut beds.

Huge Buddhas, with serenely joyful expressions and unfeasibly large shoulders, stand on either side of the porch of the spectacular **Cave 3**. Between them, you'll see the panels of "donor couples", thought to have been foreigners that patronized the community. Inside, leading to a *stupa* at the back, octagonal columns in two rows, some decorated with animal motifs, line the magnificent Hinayana *chaitya* hall.

The sixth-century **Cave 11** is a large assembly hall, where two long "tables" of rock were used for the study of manuscripts. Seated at the back, in the centre, is a figure of the Buddha as teacher, an image repeated in the entrance, to the left, with a wonderful flight of accompanying celestials. Just before the entrance to a small cell in **Cave 34**, flanked by two standing Buddhas, an unfinished ceiling painting shows the Buddha touching the earth. There must be at least a hundred more Buddha images on panels in **Cave 67**, a large hall; on the left side, and outside in the entrance, these figures are supported by *nagas* (snakes representing *kundalini*, yogic power).

Bassein Fort

Trundling over the rickety iron bridge that joins the northern fringes of Mumbai to the Maharashtran mainland, you could easily fail to notice the ruined fort at **Bassein** (or Vasai), 61km north of the city centre. Yet these mouldy stone walls, obscured by a carpet of palms and lush tropical foliage at the mouth of the milky-blue River Ulhas, once encompassed India's most powerful and prosperous colonial settlement. It was ceded to the Portuguese by Sultan Bahadur of Gujarat in 1534, in return for help in the Gujarati struggle against the Moghuls, and quickly became the hub of the region's maritime trade, "The Court of the North", from which the Portuguese territories at Goa, Daman and Diu were administered. In 1739, however, the **Marathas** laid siege to the city for three months, eventually wiping out the garrison, and a final deathblow was dealt in 1780 by the cannons of the **British**. Bassein's crumbling remnants were left to be carried off for raw building material or reclaimed by the coastal jungle, and only a handful of weed-infested buildings still stand today.

If you don't mind travelling in a crowded suburban **train** (around 1hr 15min from Churchgate), Bassein makes an atmospheric day-trip from the city. Only a few express trains stop at the nearest mainline station, Vasai Rd, from where the onward trip (11km) involves jumping in and out of **shared auto-rickshaws**. These stop halfway at a busy market crossroads, where you catch another ride for the last stretch from a stand one hundred metres up a road left from the crossroads. Ask for the "*kila*", the Marathi word for "fort". Stock up on food and drink at Vasai Rd; there's nowhere very sanitary to eat in Bassein.

The **fort** is entered through a large gateway in its slanting stone battlements. Once inside, the road runs past a modern monument to the Maratha leader, Shivaji, before heading towards the woods and the old Portuguese town. The ruins are a melancholy sight: *peepal* and tall palm trees poke through the chancels of churches and convents, while water buffalo plod listlessly past piles of rubble, and monkeys leap and crash through the canopy overhead.

By contrast, the small **fishing village**, under the archway from the rickshaw stand, is thriving. The spiritual legacy of the Portuguese has endured here longer than their architectural one, as shown by the painted Madonna shrines tucked into wall-niches and crucifixes gleaming on the singlets of the fishermen lounging in the local bar. On the **beach**, a short way down the narrow sandy footpath through the main cluster of huts, large wooden frames are hung with pungent-smelling strips of dried pomfret, while nearby, fishing boats bob around in the silt-laden estuary water.

Accommodation

Even though Mumbai offers all kinds of **accommodation**, finding a room at the right price when you arrive can be a real problem. Budget travellers, in particular, can expect a hard time; standards at the bottom of the range are grim and room rates exorbitant. A windowless cell, with wood-partition walls and no running water costs Rs300 and above, while a comfortable room in the centre of town, with an attached toilet and shower, and a window, will set you back the best part of Rs1000. The best of the relatively inexpensive places tend to fill up by noon, which can often mean a long trudge in the heat with only an overpriced flea-pit at the end of it, so you really should phone ahead as soon as (or preferably well before) you arrive. Prices in upmarket places are farther inflated by the state-imposed "**luxury tax**" (between four and thirty percent depending on how expensive the room is), and "**service charges**" levied by the hotel itself; such charges are included in the price symbols indicated.

Colaba, down in the far, southern end of the city, has dozens of possibilities in each price range and is where the majority of foreign visitors head first. A short way across the city centre, **Marine Drive**'s accommodation is generally a little more expensive, but more salubrious, with Back Bay and the promenade right on the doorstep. If you're arriving by train and plan to make a quick getaway, a room closer to **CST** station is worth considering. Alternatively, **Juhu**, way to the north near the airports, boasts a string of flashy four- and five-stars, with a handful of less expensive places behind the beach. For those who just want to crawl off the plane and straight into bed, there are plenty of options in the suburbs around **Sahar** and **Santa Cruz** airports, a short taxi ride from the main terminal buildings.

Finally, if you would like to **stay with an Indian family**, ask at the Indian Government tourist office in Churchgate, or at their information counters in Sahar and Santa Cruz (see p.80) about the popular "paying guest" scheme. Bed and breakfast-style accommodation in family homes, vetted by the tourist office, is available throughout the city at rates ranging from Rs200–1000.

Colaba

A short ride from the city's main commercial districts, train stations and tourist office, **Colaba** makes a handy base. It also offers more in the way of food and entertainment than neighbouring districts, especially along its busy main thoroughfare, **"Colaba Causeway"** – Shahid Bhagat Singh (SBS) Marg. The streets immediately south and west of the Gateway of India are chock-full of accommodation, ranging from grungy guesthouses to India's most famous five-star hotel, the *Taj Mahal Intercontinental*. Avoid at all costs the nameless lodges lurking on the top storeys of wooden-fronted houses along **Arthur Bunder Rd** – the haunts of not-so-oil-rich Gulf Arabs and touts who depend on commission from these rock-bottom hostels to finance their heroin habits. If, like many, you find all this sleaze a turn-off, Colaba's quieter, leafier back-streets harbour plenty of respectable mid-range hotels.

For a map of Colaba, see p.85.

INEXPENSIVE

Carlton, 12 Mereweather Rd (☎022/202 0259). Popular budget hotel in an advanced state of decrepitude, with a verandah. Pricier rooms have attached baths and TV. ④–⑤.

India, 4th Floor, 1/39 Kamal Mansion, Arthur Bunder Rd (☎022/283 3769). Ceilingless, partitioned rooms with shared baths (only those on the sea-facing side have windows). A bit seedy for single women. ⑤.

Kishan and Aga Bheg, Ground Floor, Shirin Manzil, Walton Rd (☎022/283 3886). Lurid pink walls and little wooden blue beds, clean, cool with a thankfully quiet and relaxed atmosphere. ④–⑤.

Lawrence, 3rd Floor, 33 Rope Walk Lane, off K Dubash Marg, opposite Jehangir Art Gallery (☎022/284 3618). Mumbai's best-value cheap hotel if you don't mind the great hike up the stairs. Six immaculate double rooms (one single) with fans, and not so clean shared shower-toilet. Breakfast included in the price. Best to book in advance. ④–⑤.

Prosser's, 2–4 Henry Rd (☎022/283 4937). Noisy, with mostly wood-partitioned rooms that are clean and air-cooled. ④–⑤.

Salvation Army, Red Shield House, 30 Mereweather Rd, directly behind the *Taj* (☎022/284 1824). Rock-bottom bunk beds in cramped, stuffy dorms (lockers available), good-value doubles (some a/c) and a sociable travellers' scene. Cheap canteen food. Priority given to women; stay limited to one week or less. ①–⑤.

Sea Shore, 4th Floor, 1/49 Kamal Mansion, Arthur Bunder Rd (☎022/287 4237). Among the best budget deals in Colaba. The sea-facing rooms with windows are much better than the airless cells on the other side. Friendly management and free, safe baggage store. Try the *India* or *Sea Lord* downstairs if it's full. Common baths only. ④–⑤.

Whalley's, Jaiji Mansion, 41 Mereweather Rd (☎022/287 4237). Well-established, popular hotel in rambling colonial building, with 26 rooms (some very small), shared or attached shower-toilets, pleasant verandah and some a/c. Reasonable value with breakfast included. ⑤–⑥.

MODERATE

Ascot, 38 Garden Rd (☎022/284 6006, fax 204 6449). One of Mumbai's oldest hotels. Comfortable, spacious rooms, with cable TV and room service. ⑦–⑧.

Cowie's, 15 Walton Rd (☎022/284 0232). Promising facade and friendly staff, but rooms are windowless and non-a/c. ⑦–⑧.

Gulf, 4/36 Kamal Mansion, Arthur Bunder Rd (☎022/285 6072). Seedy neighbourhood, but respectable and grandly decorated, with clean, modern rooms. ⑥–⑦.

Kerawala Chambers, 3rd and 4th Floors, 25 PJ Ramchandani Marg (☎022/282 1089). Decent hotel tucked away above *Strand*; with sea-facing rooms. ⑥–⑦.

Regency, 18 Lansdowne House, Mahakari Bhusan Marg, behind the Regal cinema (☎022/202 0292, fax 287 3375). Well-appointed rooms, some rather cramped, and cheaper attic garrets with character. ⑥.

Strand, 25 PJ Ramchandani Marg (☎022/288 2222). Simple, spacious and reasonably comfortable rooms, although the sea-facing ones are way overpriced. Common or attached bathrooms. ⑥–⑧.

YWCA, 18 Madam Cama Rd (☎022/202 0445). Relaxing, secure and quiet hostel with spotless dorms, doubles or family rooms. Rate includes membership, breakfast and filling buffet dinner. One month's advance booking (by money order) advisable. ⑤–⑦.

EXPENSIVE

Diplomat, 24–26 PK Boman Behram Marg (☎022/202 1661). Hemmed in by the *Taj* across the road and in need of a face-lift, but the rooms are pleasant. ⑧.

Fariyas, 35 Arthur Rd (☎022/204 2911, fax 283 4492). Next on the scale down from the *Taj*. Relaxing roof garden, luxurious decor with themed suites, pool, health club, business centre, central a/c and all the trimmings. *Geoffrey's* pub is very popular with trendy Bombayites. Rates in dollars only. ⑨.

Garden, 42 Garden Rd (☎022/824 1476, fax 204 4296). Rather bland option, with no single occupancy rates for its comfortable a/c rooms. Has a reasonable restaurant and bar. ⑧–⑨.

Goodwin, Jasmine Building, Garden Rd (☎022/287 2050, fax 287 1592). Top-class three-star with restaurant, bar and 24hr room service. ⑧.

Regent, 8 Best Rd (☎022/287 1854, fax 202 0363). Luxurious, international-standard hotel on smaller scale, with all mod cons but smallish rooms and a dark, expensive restaurant. ⑧.

Sea Palace, 26 PJ Ramchandani Marg (☎022/285 4404, fax 284 1828). A touch shabby from the outside, but rooms are well furnished and have bath tubs. Sea views at a premium. ⑦–⑧.

Shelley's, 30 PJ Ramchandani Marg (☎022/284 0229). Charmingly old-fashioned hotel in the colonial mould. Period furniture, pukka dining hall and (more expensive) sea views. ⑦–⑧.

Taj Mahal Intercontinental, PJ Ramchandani Marg (☎022/202 3366, fax 287 2711). The stately home among India's top hotels, and the haunt of Mumbai's *beau monde*. Opulent suites in an old wing or a modern skyscraper; shopping arcades, outdoor pool, swish bars and restaurants. ⑨.

Marine Drive and Nariman Point

At the western edge of the downtown area, Netaji Subhash Chandra Marg, or **Marine Drive**, sweeps from the skyscrapers of Nariman Point in the south to Chowpatty Beach in the north. Along the way, four- and five-star hotels take advantage of the panoramic views over Back Bay and the easy access to the city's commercial heart, and a couple of inexpensive guest houses are worth trying here if Colaba's cheap lodges don't appeal. Compared with Colaba, Marine Drive and the arterial **VN Rd** that connects it with Churchgate are more open and relaxed. Families and office cronies plod along the promenade in the evening, approached more often by *gram-* and balloon-*wallahs* than junkies and money-changers. The hotels below are marked on the maps on p.85 and p.87.

Ambassador, VN Rd (☎022/204 1131, fax 204 0004). Luxurious four-star with excellent views from upper front-side rooms and a revolving rooftop restaurant. Dollars only. ⑨.

Bentley's, 3rd Floor, Krishna Mahal, Marine Drive (☎022/203 1244). Run-down hotel on the corner of D Rd. No lift, no a/c, no attached bathrooms and no frills (except windows), but clean rooms, some of which have sea-facing balconies – at a price. Breakfast included. ⑤–⑥.

Chateau Windsor, 5th Floor, 86 VN Rd (☎022/204 3376, fax 202 6459). Spotless single, double or group rooms (some are on the small side), shared or attached bathrooms, optional a/c and self-catering for vegetarians. Very popular, reservations recommended. ⑧–⑨.

Marine Plaza, 29 Marine Drive (☎022/285 1212, fax 282 8585). Glitzy pad on the seafront, with every luxury mod con, glass-bottomed swimming pool, health club, restaurants and a very trendy nightclub. ⑨.

Norman's, 127 Marine Drive (☎022/281 4234). Small, moderately priced ground-floor guesthouse, with neat, clean rooms, some attached shower-toilets and a/c. ⑦.

Oberoi Towers, Nariman Point (☎022/202 4343). The *Taj*'s main competitor – India's most expensive hotel – is glitteringly opulent, with a pool and a Polynesian restaurant. ⑨.

Around Chatrapathi Shivaji Terminus (CST)

Arriving in Mumbai at **CST** after a long train journey, you may not feel like embarking on a room-hunt around Colaba. Unfortunately, the area around the station and the nearby GPO, though fairly central, has little to recommend it. The majority of places worth trying are mid-range hotels grouped around the crossroads of P D'Mello (Frere) Rd, St George's Rd and Shahid Bhagat Singh (SBS) Marg, immediately southeast of the post office (five minutes on foot from the station). CST itself also has **retiring rooms** (②–④), although these are booked up by noon. The hotels below are marked on the map on p.87.

City Palace, 121 City Terrace (☎022/261 5515, fax 267 6897). Large and popular hotel, bang opposite the station. "Ordinary" rooms are tiny and windowless, but have a/c, are perfectly clean and proudly sport "electronic push button telephone instruments". ⑤–⑦.

Grand, 17 Sprott Rd, Ballard Estate (☎022/269 8211, fax 262 6581). Solid and very comfortable with faintly 1930s feel left by the British. Central a/c, restaurant and foreign exchange. ⑧.

Lord's, 301 Adi Mazban Path (Mangalore St) (☎022/261 8310). Above *City Kitchen* restaurant. Drab, but reasonably clean and cheap for the area. Mostly shared bathrooms. ④–⑤.

Manama, opposite George Hospital, 221/5 P D'Mello Rd (☎022/261 3412, fax 261 3860). Very friendly, clean, popular budget option with run-of-the-mill rooms. Book ahead. ④–⑥.

Prince, 34 Walchand Hirachand Rd, near Red Gate (☎022/261 2809). The best all-round economy deal in this area: modest, neat and respectable. Avoid the airless partition rooms upstairs. ⑤–⑥.

Railway, 249 P D'Mello Rd (☎022/261 6705, fax 265 8049). Spacious, clean and friendly, and the pick of the mid-range bunch around CST, though correspondingly pricey. ⑦–⑧.

Juhu Beach

Since the early 1970s, a crop of exclusive **resort-hotels** has been creeping steadily down the road that runs behind **Juhu Beach**, twenty minutes' drive from Santa Cruz airport. Most offer the predictable hermetically sealed five-star package, with bars, restaurants and a pool to lounge beside. It's hard to believe that anyone would come to India expressly for this sort of thing, but if money's no object and you want to keep well away from all the hustle, bustle and poverty, you'll be spoiled for choice.

Vile Parle (pronounced *Veelay Parlay*) is the nearest suburban train station to Juhu. All the hotels below lay on courtesy coaches from the airports.

Centaur Juhu Beach, Juhu Tara Rd (☎022/611 3040, fax 611 6343). Gigantic five-star with palatial foyer, sea views, pool, jogging track and various specialty restaurants. ⑨.

Guestline, 462 AB Nair Rd (☎022/625 2254, fax 620 2821). Very plush, efficient and pricey. Rooftop restaurant and pool among the mod cons. ⑨.

Holiday Inn, Balraj Sahani Marg (☎022/620 4444, fax 4452). This recently re-vamped five-star boasts two pools, terrace garden, shops, bars and formula furnishings. Dollars only. ⑨.

Sea Princess, Juhu Beach (☎022/611 7600, fax 611 3973). Five-star with pool, smack on the beach. ⑨.

Sun-n-Sand, 39 Juhu Beach (☎022/620 1811, fax 620 2170). Longest established of the big five-stars, with all amenities, including a pool. ⑨.

Around the airports

Hotels near Sahar and Santa Cruz **airports** cater predominantly for transit passengers and flight crews, at premium rates. If you're picking up your own tab, and arrive in Mumbai at an inconvenient hour when most of the hotels in the city proper are closed or full, you may want to arrange less expensive accommodation in the nearby suburbs of **Santa Cruz**, **Vile Parle** or **Andheri**. Bookings can be made through the accommodation desk in the arrivals concourse at Sahar, or by phone. Nearly all the "moderate to expensive" hotels below have courtesy buses to and from the terminal building.

Airlines International, Plot #111, Fourth Rd, Prabhat Colony, Santa Cruz East (☎022/618 2222). Businessperson-orientated hotel near domestic airport with smart, if dark rooms. ⑧.

Airport Palace, Vakola Bridge, Bull's Royce Colony Rd (☎022/614 0057). Small, airless rooms, but all with fresh bed linen and lockable doors. ⑤.

Air View, 12th Nehru Rd, Santa Cruz (East) (☎022/612 0060). Quiet hotel near rail and bus stations. Clean rooms with either fan or a/c. ⑤–⑥.

Ashwin, near Marol fire station, Andheri Kurla Rd, Andheri East (☎022/836 7267, fax 836 7258). One of several medium-sized, international-standard hotels right outside Sahar. Rooms are deluxe and there is a good multicuisine restaurant. ⑧.

Centaur, Western Express Highway, Santa Cruz (☎022/611 6660, fax 611 3535). Circular building directly outside the domestic airport, a five-star hotel with three restaurants, two bars and one pool. ⑨.

Kamat's Plaza, 70-C Nehru Rd, Vile Parle (☎022/612 3390, fax 612 5974). Plush four-star with pool. ⑧–⑨.

Kumaria Presidency, Andheri Kurla (☎022/835 2601, fax 837 3850). Facing the international airport. One of a string of three-stars bookable through the accommodation desk in the airport arrivals hall. ⑧.

Leela Kempinski, Sahar (☎022/836 3636, fax 836 0606). Ultra-luxurious, has an art gallery, four restaurants, a nightclub and amazing sports facilities. Dollars only. ⑨.

Samrat, Seventh Rd, Khar, Santa Cruz East, near Khar train station (☎022/649 6806, fax 649 3501). Another comfortable transit hotel in a quiet suburban backstreet. No courtesy bus. ⑥–⑦.

Shangri-La, Nanda Parker Rd, Vile Parle (East) (☎022/612 8983). Cheerful budget hotel near the domestic airport with lots of clean and basic a/c and non-a/c rooms. Good Chinese restaurant tacked alongside. ④–⑥.

Eating and drinking

In keeping with its cosmopolitan credentials, Mumbai (and Colaba above all) is crammed with interesting **places to eat and drink**, whether you fancy splashing out on a buffet lunch-with-a-view from a flashy five-star revolving restaurant, or simply tucking into piping-hot *roti kebab* by gaslight in the street.

Restaurants, bars and cafés are listed below by district. The most expensive restaurants, particularly in the top hotels, will levy "service charges" that can add thirty percent to the price of your meal. Phone numbers have been given where we recommend you reserve a table for dinner.

Colaba

Colaba (see map on p.85) has even more places to eat than it does hotels. In the space of just one kilometre, you can sample an amazing array of **regional cuisines**: pure veg "Hindu hotels" serving delicious Gujarati and South Indian food stand cheek by jowl with Muslim cafés whose menus will delight die-hard carnivores. Nearby, within a stone's throw of the *Taj* and its expensive gourmet restaurants, are Mumbai's oldest and best-loved Chinese joints. Other than during the monsoons (when choppy seas keep the fishing fleet in the polluted waters of the harbour), these offer fresh, safe **seafood** dishes of tiger prawns, crab or delicate white pomfret. Still in Colaba, tradi-

STREET FOOD

Mumbai is renowned for distinctive street foods – and especially **bhel puri**, a quintessentially Mumbai *masala* mixture of puffed-rice, deep-fried vermicelli, potato, crunchy puri pieces, chilli paste, tamarind water, chopped onions and coriander. More hygienic, but no less ubiquitous, is **pao bhaji**, a round slab of flat-bread stuffed with meat or vegetables simmered in a vat of hot oil, and **kanji vada**, savoury doughnuts soaked in fermented mustard and chilli sauce. Even if all that doesn't appeal, a pit stop at one of the city's hundreds of **juice bars** probably will. There's no better way to beat the sticky heat than with a glass of cool milk shaken with fresh pineapple, mango, banana, *chikoo* (small brown fruit that tastes like a pear) or custard apple. Just make sure they hold on the ice – made, of course, with untreated water.

tional Iranian restaurants serve minced lamb and mutton specialities, while revamped café-bars dish up draught beer and reasonable Western food for tourists and local yuppies. Non-vegetarians will enjoy succulent meats, smothered in the split lentil stew known as *dhansak*, in Parsi restaurants, while Goan and Mangalorean "lunch-homes" crop up everywhere too – good for a pork *vindaloo* or a fiery fish curry.

The majority of Colaba's best cafés, bars and restaurants – among them the popular travellers' haunts, *Leopold's* and the *Café Mondegar* – are located up at the north end of the Causeway. Those mentioned below are divided into price categories, which are based on the cost of a main dish: inexpensive (below Rs50), moderate (Rs50–200), and expensive (above Rs200).

INEXPENSIVE

Bademiya, behind the *Taj* on Tulloch Rd (open daily 7.30pm until late). Legendary Colaba *kebab-wallah*; delicious flame-grilled chicken, mutton and fish steaks, in hot *tandoori rotis*, from benches on the sidewalk.

Kailash Parbat, 1 Pasta Lane, near the Strand cinema. Uninspiring on the outside, but the *alu parathas* for breakfast, pure veg nibbles, hot snacks and sweets are worth the walk. Try their famous *makai-ka* (corn) *rotis*.

Kamat, Colaba Causeway. Friendly little eatery serving the cheapest and best South Indian breakfasts in the area.

Majestic, near Regal cinema, Colaba Causeway. Large, traditional South Indian joint patronized by off-duty taxi-*wallahs*, junior office staff and backpackers. Among the best value in this price range.

New Martin, near the Strand cinema, Strand Rd. Unpromising formica booths, but famed for delicious Goan dishes such as prawn *pulao*, sausages, pork *vindaloo* and spicy fish curry. Also does takeaways.

Olympic Coffee House, 1 Colaba Causeway. *Fin-de-siècle* Iranian café with marble table-tops, wooden wall panels and a mezzanine floor for "ladies". Decor more alluring than the menu of greasy meat dishes, but nonetheless, a good place for a coffee break.

Persian, Arthur Bunder Rd, off Colaba Causeway. Cheap but delicious Persian food, especially the *biryani* and the *prawn pulao*. There's also a roadside snack counter with freshly baked *tandoori* items-to-go.

MODERATE

Alps, Nawroji Fardunji Rd. Trendy, ersatz American restaurant serving lamb-burgers, fries, sizzling steaks and copious "mixed-grills".

Baghdadi, Tulloch Rd. Male-dominated place famous for its meat: mostly mutton and chicken steeped in spicy garlic sauce. Chauffeurs pick up takeaways here for their bosses in the *Taj*.

Café Mondegar, 5a Colaba Causeway, next to the Regal cinema. Small, Western-style café-bar serving snacks (including tasty pizza) and light meals. Loud CD juke box and murals by a famous Goan cartoonist are the main attractions, though it's worth a mention that the small tables can make life difficult for women on their own.

Delhi Durbar, Colaba Causeway (☎022/202 0235). Popular branch of the reputed Grant Rd restaurant specializing in classic Mughlai food with some vegetarian and Chinese alternatives. *Biryanis* still cooked in a traditional way – slowly over a charcoal fire. Very reasonable prices.

Leopold's, Colaba Causeway. Colaba's most famous café-bar is determinedly Western, with a clientele and prices to match. Three hundred items on the menu from scambled eggs to "drunken chicken", washed down with cold beer. There's also a bar upstairs.

EXPENSIVE

Golden Gate, Madam Cama Rd, next to the YWCA (☎022/202 6306). Classy a/c restaurant, best known for its buffet salad lunches. Also North Indian dishes, plus seafood and Chinese.

Ling's Pavillion, 19/21 Lansdowne Rd, behind the Regal cinema (☎022/285 0023). Swanky Chinese restaurant: soft lighting, marble floors and gourmet Cantonese cuisine.

Tanjore, *Taj Hotel* (☎022/202 3366). Opulent interior, rich Mughlai cuisine and classical Indian music and dance in the evening. Expense account prices.

Downtown

In the following list *Britannia & Co*, *City Kitchen* and *Mahesh Lunch Home* feature on the Churchgate and Fort map (see p.87); the others appear on the Colaba map (see p.85).

Britannia & Co, Sprott Rd, Ballard Estate. Definitive Iranian/Parsi food and decor. Try their special "*berry pulao*" or Bombay duck dishes. A real find, and cheap too.

Chetana, 34 K Dubash Marg (☎022/284 4968). Painstakingly prepared Rajasthani/Gujarati food, including set *thalis* at lunchtime and numerous à la carte dishes – absolutely the last word in fine veg cuisine. Expensive, but not extravagant. Reserve for dinner.

City Kitchen, 301 SBS Marg. Highly rated hole-in-the-wall Goan restaurant. Serves all the usual dishes – mostly fish and meat simmered in coconut milk and fiery spices. Inexpensive.

Copper Chimney, 18 K Dubash Marg (☎022/204 1661). Renowned *tandoori* house, recently renovated with wonderful ceramic murals; stylish renditions of standard North Indian dishes. Superb but expensive. Reservations essential.

Khyber, opposite Jehangir Art Gallery, Kala Ghoda (☎022/267 3227). Ultra-fashionable, with opulent Arabian Nights interior and uncompromisingly rich Mughlai/Punjabi cuisine. The chicken *makhanwallah* is legendary. Reservations essential.

Mahesh Lunch Home, 8-B Cawasji Patel St, Fort. Inexpensive Keralan restaurant serving authentic veg "meals" and delicious non-veg options – chicken fried in ginger or fish *masala* on groaning platefuls of rice.

Samovar, Jehangir Art Gallery, MG Rd. Very pleasant, peaceful semi-open-air café, with varying menu: *roti kebabs*, prawn curry, fresh salads and *dhansak*, chilled guava juice – and beer.

Trishna, 7 Ropewalk Lane, Kala Ghonda (☎022/267 2176). Visiting dignitaries and local celebs from the president of Greece and Imran Khan to Bollywood stars have eaten here (as shown in the photographic evidence). Wonderful fish preparations in every sauce going, and prices to match the clientele. Very small, so book in advance.

Wayside Inn, opposite Jehangir Art Gallery, K Dubash Marg. Upmarket Parsi café, with red-chequered table cloths and solid English cooking. Nice place for a coffee after visiting the museum.

Churchgate and Nariman Point

The restaurants listed below are marked on either the Churchgate and Fort map (see p.87) or the Mumbai map (see p.74).

Chopsticks, 90a VN Rd (☎022/204 9284). Wide choice of pricey meat, seafood and veg in fiery Szechuan and milder Cantonese style offered here. Try the excellent *dim sum* or "ant climbing up the tree".

Croissants Etc, Industrial Insurance Building, opposite Churchgate station. Filled croissants, pricey pastries and other Western food, including delicious cakes, in an a/c setting.

Gaylord, VN Rd (☎022/282 1259). Parisian-style terrace café in the heart of Mumbai. *Tandoori*, sizzlers and some Western food. Wholewheat bread, baguettes and delicious sticky buns are sold in the patisserie.

Kamling, VN Rd (☎022/204 2618). Favourite for the title of oldest, best and most authentic Chinese in town. Southeast Asian flight crews and well-heeled locals tuck into delicious Cantonese dishes – try the mouthwatering "chimney soup" or the (expensive) seafood specialities.

The Outrigger, *Oberoi Hotel*, Nariman Point (☎022/202 4343). Offering Polynesian specialities (Chinese with more fruit thrown in), tribal masks and a full-size canoe. Expensive.

The Pizzeria, 143 Marine Drive. Delicious freshly baked pizzas, either served on a newly renovated terrace overlooking Back Bay or to take away. Plenty of choice and moderate prices.

Rangoli, Nariman Point (☎022/202 3366). Excellent-value buffet lunches are its forte, but the à la carte menu (including fish and strict Jain veg dishes) is gourmet standard and reasonably priced.

Satkar, opposite Churchgate station's western exit. Busy pure veg terrace restaurant: great for South Indian "fast food" and crowd-watching.

The Top, *Ambassador Hotel*, VN Rd (☎022/291131). Revolving restaurant in glam four-star hotel with panoramic views. Excellent lunch buffets are just the thing for a splurge. Reserve for dinner.

Trattoria, *Hotel President*, 90 Cuffe Parade (☎022/215 0808). Surprisingly authentic Italian cuisine. Pizza and pasta with fresh herbs, real Parmesan, bitter chocolate ice cream and a big buffet lunch on Sundays (noon–3pm).

Crawford Market and the central bazaars

Badshah Juice and Snack Bar, opposite Crawford Market, Lokmanya Tilak Rd. Mumbai's most famous *falooda* joint also serves delicious *kulfi*, ice-creams and dozens of freshly squeezed fruit juices. The ideal place to round off a trip to the market.

Bhaishankar's, CP Tank Circle, near Bhuleshwar Market. One of Mumbai's oldest and most respected sweet shops. Try their Bengali *barfi*, cashew *kalingar* or *masala* milk (made with pistachio, almonds, saffron and nutmeg).

Gulshan-e-Iran, Palton Rd (☎022/265183). Popular Muslim breakfast venue on the main road that does inexpensive *biryanis*, kebabs, chutneys and fresh bread. Open all day.

Hiralal Kashiram Bhajiwala, Kumbhar Tukda, Bhuleshwar Market. Cheap restaurant serving great *farsan* savouries, including *ponk vadas* (millet and garlic balls), *batata vadas* (made with sweet potatoes) and *kand bhajis* (deep-fried purple yam), all with a tasty, fiery chutney.

Rajdhani, Mangaldas Lane (in the silk bazaar opposite Crawford market). Outstanding, eat-till-you-burst Gujarati *thalis* dished up by barefoot waiters to discerning aficionados. A little more expensive than usual, but well worth it.

Chowpatty Beach and Kemp's Corner

Chowpatty Beach is a popular venue for a picnic, crowded with vendors selling *kulfi* in clay cups and *bhel puri*, *kanji vada* and *pao bhaji*. Kemp's Corner, crouched under the hectic G Deshmukh flyover, fifteen minutes' walk north, boasts a clutch of very good places to eat – handy for visitors to Malabar Hill. The restaurants listed below feature on the Mumbai map (see p.74).

China Garden, Om Chambers, 123 August Kranti Marg (☎022/363 0841). Malabar Hill's glitterati don their finest for this place, which has expensive, authentic Chinese, Korean, Thai and Japanese food.

Chinese Room, Kwality House, Kemp's Corner (☎022/380 6771). A much less expensive alternative to *China Garden*, specializing in quality Sezchuan, Hunan and Cantonese cooking, with great seafood.

Ghupta Bhelwallah, first stall in front row, Chowpatty Beach. *The* most legendary stall in India; colourful variations of hot/cold, sweet/sour *bhel puri* are whipped up in front of you with flair. Utterly delicious (see p.91).

New Yorker, Fulchand Niwas, 25 Chowpatty Seaface. Western food – baked potatoes, pizzas, burgers and some Tex-Mex options – dished up in a bustling a/c café. Moderate.

Paramount, Marine Drive, near the Aquarium. Small Iranian café, which while it has a certain charm, with marble-top tables, wood-panelled and mirrored walls, applies strict rules: signs request that you "Do not spit", "Do not comb your hair", "Do not stretch legs on other pieces of furniture" and, most advisedly, "Do not sit unnecessarily a long time".

Revival, above *London Pub*, Chowpatty Seaface, near the footbridge. Fairly pricey 1930s retro-decor restaurant serving imaginative and tasty Western and Indian dishes.

Nightlife and entertainment

Mumbai never sleeps. No matter what time of night you venture out, there are bound to be others going about some business or other. The city has always led the nightlife scene in India and there are bars and clubs to suit every taste; jazz dens compete with salsa, *tabla*-dance fusions mixes and funk. Mumbai's alternative but decidely yuppy crowd meet at the *Ghetto Bar* before heading down to the gay, glitzy or groovy clubs around Colaba and Juhu.

Of course, Mumbai is also a cultural centre attracting the finest **Indian classical music** and **dance** artists from all over the country. Venues such as Bharatiya Vidya

Bhavan, KM Munshi Marg – the headquarters of the international cultural (Hindu) organization – Cowasjee Jehangir (CJ) Hall, Birla Matushri, Tejpal Auditorium, Shanmukhananda Hall and the National Centre for the Performing Arts (NCPA) auditorium frequently present concerts and recitals. NCPA also offers modern Gujarati, Hindi, Marathi and English-language **plays** as well as Western **chamber music**, while a smattering of platinum-selling Western rock artists appear at Mumbai stadium.

Bars and cabarets

Mumbai has an unusually easy-going attitude to **alcohol**; popping into a bar for a beer is very much accepted (for men at least) even at lunchtime. Chowpatty Beach and Colaba Causeway, with *Leopold's* and the *Café Mondegar*, form the focus of the travellers' social scene, but if you want to sample the heart and throb of the city's nightlife, venture up to Bandra and Juhu.

There is also a seamier side to the city's nightlife, concentrated around (illegal) late-night cabarets in the Grant Rd area. In these dens of iniquity, women dance before men-only crowds in clothes that might in the West be considered Victorian in their propriety but would be unheard of anywhere else in India.

Café Mondegar, 5a Colaba Causeway. Draught beer by the glass or pitcher, imported beer and deliciously fruity cocktails in a small café-bar. The atmosphere is very relaxed, the music tends towards rock classics and the clientele is a mix of Westerners and students.

BOLLYWOOD: THE CAPITAL OF THE HINDI FILM

For anyone brought up on TV, it's hard to imagine the power that films continue to wield in India. Every village has a cinema within walking distance, and with a potential audience in the hundreds of millions, film companies seem to have virtually cast-iron guarantees of vast profits. The Indian film industry is the **largest in the world**, producing around 750 full-length features each year. Regional cinema, catering for different language groups (in particular, the Tamil cinema of Chennai), though popular locally, has little national impact. Only Hindi film – which accounts for one-fifth of films made in India – has crossed regional boundaries to great effect, most particularly in the north. The home of the Hindi blockbuster, the "all-India film", is Mumbai, formerly Bombay, famously known as "**Bollywood**".

To overcome differences of language and religion, the Bollywood movie follows **rigid conventions and genres**; as in myth, its characters have predetermined actions and destinies. Knowing a plot need not detract from the drama, and indeed, it is not uncommon for Indian audiences to watch films numerous times. Unlike the Hollywood formula, which tends to classify each film under one genre, the Hindi film follows what is known as a "*masala* format", including during its luxurious three hours a little bit of everything – especially romance, violence and comedy. Frequently the stories feature dispossessed male heroes fighting evil against all odds with a love interest thrown in. The sexual element is repressed, with numerous wet sari scenes and dance routines featuring the tensest pelvic thrusts. Other typical themes include male bonding and betrayal, family melodrama, separation and reunion and religious piety. Dream sequences are almost obligatory, too, along with a festival or celebration scene – typically Holi, when people shower each other with colour – a comic character passing through and a depraved, alcoholic and mostly Western "cabaret", filled with strutting villains and lewd dancing. One way in which Bollywood has moved closer to Hollywood in recent years, however, has been the development, alarming to traditionalists, of films in which the "hero" is no longer necessarily a moral exemplar; violence can be fun, and good does not always triumph.

The Mumbai film industry is however now entering a new phase. Bollywood has gone arty as foreign-educated film-school graduates struggle to make an impact. Recent English-language films, such as *Bombay Boys* and *Hyderabad Blues*, raise contemporary

The Ghetto, 30 Bhulabhai Desai Rd, near Breach Candy, Mahalaxmi. The alternative Mumbai scene where young arty theatre-types gather to play their music with attitude and write profound thoughts on the walls. Cheap beer by the pitcher.

The Inside Story, *Café Mondegar*, Colaba Causeway, next to the Regal cinema. The *Mondegar's* exclusive inner sanctum is a pricey English pub with a dark atmosphere and mostly male clientele plus bouncers.

Jazz by the Bay, next to *The Pizzeria*, 143 Marine Drive. The official Channel V pad is a convenient place to crawl to after pizza. There are often jazz festivals with both Indian and foreign artists performing, as well as a DJ spinning the latest chart hits at weekends.

Leopold Pub, 1st Floor, *Leopold's*, Colaba Causeway. Swanky, self-consciously Western-style bar-nightclub, with bouncers, serving expensive beers to Mumbai's smart set. No single men admitted.

London Pub, 39D Chowpatty Seaface. Designer frosted-glass bar with prog-rock murals, quality sound system and uncomfortable bar stools.

The Tavern, *Fariyas Hotel*, Colaba. Another "English-style" pub, complete with wooden beams, loud music, and the local equivalent of lager louts.

Nightclubs

The nightclub scene in Mumbai has come a long way from the *filmi* dance and chart-busting discos of a few years ago, as the moneyed jet-set now expect the latest house, trance, fusion and funk hitting the decks in the US and the UK. The five-star hotels tend to operate "couple-only" policies, and entry is restricted to hotel guests

issues that traditional Indian society tries to hide – homosexuality, pre-marital relationships, hard drugs, liberated women and the mafia dons, for example. Critically acclaimed films like *Fire* and *The Last Train to Pakistan* are emerging from the same studios that continue to spew the garish and glorious Bollywood classics, and for the first time are being received with the same level of popular interest.

Film song is the most popular form of music in India; an average of six songs play an essential part in the narrative of each film. A song can transcend its filmic context, remaining popular years after the film it was composed for has been forgotten. Equally, a good song released before the film acts as a trailer to help fill the theatres. The songs are created through the artistic collaboration of a film director, lyricist, music composer, arranger, studio instrumentalists, the "playback" singers (the most famous, Lata Mangeshkar, is in the *Guinness Book of Records* for the number of songs she has recorded) and finally the actor who mimes the song on screen.

The exploits of Mumbai's **film stars** – on and off screen – and their lavish lifestyles in the city's clubs and millionaires' ghetto of Malabar Hill are the subject of endless titillating gossip. Fanzines such as *Stardust*, *Star and Style*, *Film World* and *Cine Blitz* are snaffled up by millions, while the industry looks to the more sober *Screen*. Following the careers of the stars requires dedication; each may work on up to ten movies at once.

At one time specially arranged tours made it easy to get into a film studio to see a movie being made, but those days are gone. If you're very keen, try contacting Mehboob Studios, Hill Rd, Bandra West (☎022/642 8045); Natraj Studios, Western Express Highway, Andheri East (☎022/834 2371); or Film City, Goregaon East, Mumbai 65 (☎022/840 1533). Otherwise you may well come across violent action scenes being filmed on Sunday afternoons, in the broad backstreets around Ferry Wharf for example.

Visitors to Mumbai should have ample opportunity to sample the delights of a movie. To make an educated choice, buy *Bombay* magazine, which contains extensive listings and reviews. Otherwise, look for the biggest, brightest hoarding, and join the queue. Seats in a comfortable a/c cinema cost around Rs20, or less if you sit in the stalls (not advisable for women). Of the two hundred or so **cinemas**, only eight regularly screen **English-language** films. The most central and convenient are the Regal in Colaba, the Eros opposite Churchgate station and the Sterling, the New Excelsior and the New Empire, which are all a short walk west of CST station.

and members. Other discos and clubs charge per couple on the door, and many operate "ladies' nights" when women get in free.

The 1900s, *Taj Mahal*. Pounding disco, free to guests but otherwise for members only. If you can get in, you will see the cream of Mumbai society at their air-kissing best.

Copa Cabana, Marine Drive. Dark, smoky atmosphere, Latino music and lots of Tequilla. Free shots for the ladies.

Fashion Bistro, 16 Marzban Rd, next to Sterling cinema. The latest arrival on the nightclub scene and definitely *the* place to be seen. Mannequins display designer creations in one room, with a bar and dance floor in another. Deafeningly loud music and steep prices.

Go Bananas, *Kamat's Plaza* hotel near Santa Cruz airport. Plays hit records and, on certain nights, allows singles onto its small dance floor.

Razzberry Rhinoceros, *Juhu Hotel*, Juhu Beach. A good size dance floor. Entrance is for couples only, and they serve fairly pricey Chinese, Western and Indian food. The club closes at 12am on week nights, and at 1am at weekends.

Sheetal Again, Juhu. Small pub with an enthusiastic crowd, tiny dance floor, loud sound system and DJs playing international dance hits. The barmen dress in denim dungarees and confederate caps. Although singles are allowed in, the comfortable seating is reserved for the paired-up. Woe betide any man who tries to dance on his own; the DJ will call for him to leave.

Three Flights Up, Apollo Bunder, Colaba. Claims to have the longest bar in Asia, and is certainly the biggest club in Mumbai. There is a no-smoking policy on the dance floor and fantastic a/c, which, along with the innovative food on offer, makes the place definitely worth trying.

THE FESTIVALS OF MUMBAI

Mumbai has its own versions of all the major Hindu and Muslim festivals, plus a host of smaller neighbourhood celebrations imported by its immigrant communities. Exact dates vary from year to year; check in advance at the Indian Government tourist office.

Makar Sankranti (Jan). A celebration of prosperity, when sweets, flowers and fruit are exchanged by all, and kites are flown in the parks as a sign of happiness.

Elephanta Music and Dance Festival (Feb). MTDC-organized cultural event including floodlit performances by classical artists with the Shiva cave temple as backdrop.

Gudi Padva (March/April). The Maharashtran New Year.

Gokhulashtami (July/Aug). Riotous commemoration of Krishna's birthday; terracotta pots filled with curd, milk sweets and cash are strung from tenement balconies and grabbed by human pyramids of young boys.

Nowroz (July/Aug). The Parsi New Year is celebrated with special ceremonies in the fire temples and feasting at home.

Ganesh Chathurthi (Aug/Sept). Huge effigies of Ganesh, the elephant-headed god of prosperity and wisdom, are immersed in the sea at Chowpatty Beach in a ritual originally promoted by freedom-fighters to circumvent British anti-assembly legislation. Recently it has seemed in danger of being hijacked by Hindu extremists such as the Shiv Sena, tinging it more with chauvinism than celebration.

Nariel Purnima (Sept). Koli fishermen launch brightly decorated boats to mark the end of the monsoon.

Dussehra (Oct). Rama's victory over the evil king of Lanka, Ravana, is marked in Mumbai by re-enactments of scenes from the *Ramayana* on Chowpatty.

Shopping

Mumbai is a great place to shop, whether for last-minute souvenirs or essentials for the long journeys ahead. Locally produced **textiles** and export-surplus clothing are among the best buys, as are **handicrafts** from far-flung corners of the country. With the exception of the swish arcades in the five-star hotels, **prices** compare surprisingly well with other Indian cities. In the larger shops, rates are fixed and **credit cards** are often accepted; elsewhere, particularly dealing with street-vendors, it pays to haggle. Uptown, the **central bazaars** – see p.94 – are better for spectating than serious shopping, although the **antiques** and Friday flea-market in the Chor, or "thieves" bazaar, can sometimes yield the odd bargain. The **Zaveri** (goldsmiths') **bazaar** opposite Crawford Market is the place to head for new gold and silver jewellery. **Opening hours** in the city centre are Monday to Saturday, 10am to 7pm. The Muslim bazaars, quiet on Friday, are otherwise open until around 9pm.

Antiques

The Chor Bazaar area, and Mutton Rd in particular, is the centre of Mumbai's antique trade; for a full account, see p.96. Another good, if much more expensive, place to sift through the fakes for a real gem or two is Phillip's famous antique shop, on the corner of Madam Cama Rd, opposite the Regal cinema in Colaba. This fascinating old-fashioned store has changed little since it opened in 1860. Innumerable glass lamps and chandeliers hang from the ceiling, while antique display cases are stuffed with miniature brass, bronze and wood Hindu sculpture, silver jewellery, old prints and aquatints. Most of the stuff on sale dates from the twilight of the Raj – a result of the Indian government's ban on the export by foreigners of items more than a century old.

In the Jehangir Art Gallery basement, a branch of the antiques chain Natesan's Antiqarts offers a tempting selection of antique (and reproduction) sculpture, furniture, paintings and bronzes.

Clothes and textiles

Mumbai produces the bulk of India's clothes, mostly the lightweight, light-coloured "shirtings and suitings" favoured by droves of uniformly attired office-*wallahs*. For cheaper Western clothing, you can't beat the long row of stalls on the pavement of MG Rd, opposite the Mumbai Gymkhana. "**Fashion Street**" specializes in reject and export-surplus goods ditched by big manufacturers, selling off T-shirts, jeans, leggings, summer dresses, and trendy sweatshirts. Better-quality cotton clothes (often stylish designer-label rip-offs) are available in shops along Colaba Causeway, such as Cotton World, down Mandlik Marg.

If you're looking for more traditional Indian clothes, head for the Khadi Village Industries Emporium at 286 Dr DN Marg, near the Thomas Cook office. As Whiteaway & Laidlaw, this rambling Victorian department store used to kit all the newly arrived *burra-sahibs* out with pith helmets, khaki shorts and quinine tablets. These days, its old wooden counters and shirt and sock drawers stock dozens of different hand-spun cottons and silks, sold by the metre or made up as vests, *kurtas* or block-printed *salwar kamises*. Other items include the ubiquitous white Nehru caps, *dhotis*, Madras-check *lunghis* and fine brocaded silk saris. Actually buying the stuff requires a number of separate manoeuvres: you select an item, get a chit, go to the cash desk, have the additions checked, pay for the goods, get a receipt, and go to the collection point, where your goods will be beautifully wrapped in paper bags just bursting to fall apart.

Another good place to pick up quality Indian clothes is the cloth bazaar on Mangaldas Lane, opposite Crawford Market, where touts lead you through a maze of stalls to backstreet shops crammed with inexpensive silk scarves, embroidered Kashmiri shawls and Gujarati tie-dyed wall-hangings.

Handicrafts

Regionally produced **handicrafts** are marketed in assorted state-run emporia at the World Trade Centre, down on Cuffe Parade, and along PM Rd, Fort. The quality is consistently high – as are the prices, if you miss out on the periodic holiday discounts. The same goes for the Central Cottage Industries Emporium, 34 Shivaji Marg, near the

Gateway of India in Colaba, whose size and central location make it the single best all-round place to hunt for souvenirs. Downstairs you'll find inlaid furniture, wood- and metalwork, miniature paintings and jewellery, while upstairs specializes in toys, clothing and textiles: Gujarati appliqué bedspreads, hand-painted pillowcases and Rajasthani mirrorwork, plus silk ties and Noel Coward dressing-gowns. **Mereweather Rd**, directly behind the *Taj*, is awash with Kashmiri handicraft stores stocking overpriced papier-mâché pots and bowls, silver jewellery, woollen shawls and rugs. Avoid them if you find it hard to shrug off aggressive sales pitches.

Perfume is essentially a Muslim preserve in Mumbai. Down at the south end of Colaba Causeway, around Arthur Bunder Rd, shops with mirrored walls and shelves are stacked with cut-glass carafes full of syrupy, fragrant essential oils. **Incense** is hawked in sticks, cones and slabs of sticky *dhoop* on the sidewalk nearby (check that the boxes haven't already been opened and their contents sold off piecemeal). For bulk buying, the hand-rolled, cottage-made bundles of incense sold in the Khadi Village Industries Emporium on Dr DN Marg (see p.111) are a better deal; it also has a handicraft department where, in addition to furniture, paintings and ornaments, you can pick up glass bangles, block-printed and calico bedspreads and wooden votive statues produced in Maharashtran craft villages.

Books

Mumbai's excellent English-language **bookshops** and bookstalls are well stocked with everything to do with India, and a good selection of general classics, pulp fiction and travel writing. Indian editions of popular titles cost a fraction of what they do abroad and include lots of interesting works by lesser-known local authors. If you don't mind picking through dozens of trigonometry textbooks, back issues of *National Geographic* and salacious 1960s paperbacks, the street-stalls between Flora Fountain and Churchgate station can also be good places to hunt for secondhand books.

Chetana, 34 Dubash Rd (Rampart Row). Exclusively religion and philosophy.

Crossword, Mahalakshmi Chambers, 22 Bhulabhai Desai Rd, Breach Candy (☎022/492 2548). Mumbai's largest and most reputed retailer, a bus ride (#132) from the downtown area.

Nalanda, Ground Floor, *Taj*. An exhaustive range of coffee-table tomes and paperback literature.

Pustak Bharati, Bharatiya Vidhya Bhavan, KM Munshi Marg. Excellent small bookshop specializing in Hindu philosophy and literature, plus details of Bhavan's cultural programmes.

Shankar Book-Stand, outside the *Café Mondegar*, Colaba Causeway. Piles of easy-reads, guidebooks, classic fiction and most of the old favourites on India.

Strand, next door to the Canara Bank, off PM Rd, Fort. The best bookshop in the city centre, with the full gamut of Penguins and Indian literature.

Music

The most famous of Mumbai's many good **music shops** are near the Moti cinema along SV Patel Rd, in the central bazaar district. Haribhai Vishwanath, Ram Singh and RS Mayeka are all government-approved retailers of traditional Indian instruments, including *sitars, sarods, tablas* and flutes.

For **cassettes and CDs** try Rhythm House, Subhash Chowk, next to the Jehangir Art Gallery. This is a veritable Aladdin's cave of classical, devotional and popular music from all over India, with a reasonable selection of Western rock, pop and jazz.

Listings

Ambulance ☎022/266 2913 or ☎022/610836 for general emergencies or ☎105 for heart cases.

Airport enquiries Sahar International Airport (☎022/836 6700). Santa Cruz Domestic Airport: Terminal 1A for Indian Airlines (☎022/611 3300); 1B for all other airlines (☎022/610 5923).

Consulates and High Commissions Although the many consulates and High Commissions in Mumbai can be useful for replacing lost travel documents or obtaining visas, most of India's neighbouring states, including Bangladesh, Bhutan, Burma, Nepal and Pakistan, only have embassies in New Delhi and/or Calcutta (office hours 9am–5pm). Australia, 16th Floor, Maker Tower "E", Cuffe Parade (☎022/218 1071); Canada, 41/42 Maker Chambers VI, Nariman Point (☎022/287 6028); Denmark, L & T House, Narottam Moraji Marg, Ballard Estate (☎022/261 8181); Germany, 10th Floor, Hoechst House, Nariman Point (☎022/283 2422); Netherlands, 16 Queen's Rd (☎022/201 6750); Norway, Navroji Mansion, 31 Nathelal Parekh Marg (☎022/284 2042); Philippines, 116 Free Press House, Nariman Point (☎022/202 0375); Singapore, 9th Floor, 941 Sakhar Bhavan, 230 Nariman Point (☎022/204 3209); Sri Lanka, Sri Lanka House, 34 Homi Modi St, Fort (☎022/204 5861); Sweden, 85 Sayani Rd, Subash Gupta Bhavan, Prabhadevi (☎022/436 0493); Switzerland, 7th Floor, Manekh Mahal, 90 VN Rd (☎022/204 3003); Thailand, 2nd Floor, Krishna Bagh, 43 Bhulabhai Desai Rd (☎022/363 1404); UK, 2nd Floor, Maker Chamber IV, Nariman Point (☎022/283 0517); US, Lincoln House, 78 Bhulabhai Desai Rd (☎022/363 3611).

Email All cybercentres charge Rs100–200 for an hour on the net, but will charge by the quarter hour if you just want to send an email. Three friendly and professional places are: the *Net Express Cyber Café*, Express Tower, Nariman Point (8am–7pm; ☎022/202 2627); DBS Corporate Travel, Raheja Chambers, 213 Nariman Point (☎022/287 2641); and the *Cyber Café*, which is behind *Berry's Restaurant*, 82 Veer Nariman (VN) Rd, Churchgate.

Hindi lessons Kalina University, in north Mumbai, and a number of private academies run short courses. Ask at the tourist office in Churchgate (☎022/203 3144) for more details.

Hospitals The best hospital in the centre is the private Mumbai Hospital (☎022/286 3343), New Marine Lines, just north of the Indian Government tourist office on M Karve Rd. Breach Candy Hospital (☎022/822 3651) on Bhulabhai Desai Rd, near the swimming pool, is also recommended by foreign embassies.

Left luggage If your hotel won't let you store bags with them, try the cloakrooms at Sahar and Santa Cruz airports (see p.78), or the one in CST station. Anything left here, even rucksacks, must be securely fastened with a padlock and can be left for a maximum of twelve weeks.

Libraries Asiatic Society, SBS Marg, Horniman Circle, Ballard Estate (Mon–Sat 10am–5.30pm); British Council (for British newspapers), "A" Wing, Mittal Towers, Nariman Point; Alliance Française, Theosophy Hall, 40 New Marine Lines; Max Mueller Bhavan, Prince of Wales Annexe, off MG Rd. The KR Cama Oriental Institute, 136 Mumbai Samachar Marg (Mon–Fri 10am–5pm, Sat 10am–1pm), specializing in Zoroastrian and Iranian studies has a public collection of 22,000 volumes in European and Asian languages. Mumbai Natural History Society, Hornbill House (Mon–Fri 10am–5pm, Sat 10am–1pm, closed 1st & 3rd Sat of the month), has an international reputation for the study of wildlife in India. Visitors may become temporary members which allows them access to the library, natural history collection, occasional talks and the opportunity to join organized walks and field trips.

Pharmacies Real Chemist, 50/51 Kaka Arcade (☎022/201 2497) and Royal Chemists, M Karve Rd (☎022/202 14970), both close to Mumbai Hospital, are open 24hr. Kemps in the *Taj* hotel also opens late.

Photographic studios and equipment The Javeri Colour Lab, opposite the Regal cinema in Colaba, stocks colour-print and slide film, as do most of the big hotels. A small boutique behind the florists in the Shakhari Bunder covered market does instant Polaroid passport photographs.

Police The main police station in Colaba (☎022/262 1855) is on the west side of Colaba Causeway, near the crossroads with Ormiston Rd.

State tourist offices in Mumbai include: Goa, Mumbai Central Railway Station (☎022/308 6288); Gujarat, Dhanraj Mahal, PJ Ramchandani Marg (Mon–Sat 10am–5pm; ☎022/202 4925); Himachal Pradesh, World Trade Centre, Cuffe Parade (Mon–Sat 10am–5pm; ☎022/218 1123); Jammu and Kashmir, World Trade Centre (Mon–Fri 10am–3pm; ☎022/218 6249); Madhya Pradesh, World Trade Centre (Mon–Sat 10am–5pm; ☎022/218 7603); Rajasthan, 230 Dr DN Marg (☎022/204 4162); Tamil Nadu, c/o Peerless Hotels and Travels Ltd, Ground Floor, Churchgate Chambers, New Marine Lines (Mon–Sat 9am–6pm; ☎022/266 6400); and Uttar Pradesh, World Trade Centre (Mon–Sat 10.30am–5.30pm, closed 2nd Sat of each month; ☎022/218 5458).

Swimming pools The snooty sports club at Breach Candy, north of Malabar Hill, is a popular place to beat the heat. A day's membership costs around Rs200.

Travel agents The following travel agents are recommended for booking domestic and international flights, and long-distance private buses where specified; most also sell tickets for Frank Demania Shipping's popular catamaran service to Goa (see box on p.117). Ambassador Travels, 14 Embassy Centre, Nariman Point (☎022/283 1046); Cox and Kings India Ltd, 270/272, Dr DN Rd (☎022/204 3065); M/S Magnum International Tours & Travels, Frainy Villa, Henry Rd, Colaba (☎022/287 1037); Peerless Hotels & Travels Ltd, Ground Floor, Churchgate Chambers, 5 New Marine Lines (☎022/265 1500); Sita Travels Pvt Ltd, 8 Atlanta Building, Nariman Point (☎022/284 0666); Thomas Cook, Thomas Cook Building, Dr DN Rd (☎022/204 8556).

Visa extensions & permits Contact Foreigners' Registration Office, Office of the Police Commissioner, opposite Crawford Market (Mon–Fri 10am–5pm; ☎022/262 0446). Standard three-month extensions cost around Rs650, and take 24 hours to process.

Onwards from Mumbai

Most visitors feel like getting out of Mumbai as soon as they can. Fortunately, Mumbai is equipped with "super-fast" services to arrange or confirm onward travel. All the major international and domestic airlines have offices in the city, the rail networks operate special tourist counters in the main reservation halls and dozens of travel agents and road transport companies are eager to help you on your way by bus.

Travel within India

Mumbai is the nexus of several major internal flight routes, train networks and highways, and is the main transport hub for traffic heading towards South India. The most-travelled trails lead north up the Gujarati coast to **Rajasthan** and **Delhi**; northwest into the **Deccan** via Aurangabad and the caves at Ellora and Ajanta; and south, through Pune and the hills of Western Ghats towards **Goa** and the Malabar Coast. Public transport is cheap and frequent, but book in advance and be prepared for delays.

By plane

Indian Airlines and other domestic carriers fly out of Santa Cruz to destinations all over India. Computerization has made booking less of a lottery than it used to be, but availability on popular routes (eg Mumbai–Goa–Mumbai) should never be taken for granted. Check with the airlines as soon as you arrive; **tickets** can be bought directly from their offices (see box on p.115), or through any reputable travel agent, although you will have to pay the mandatory Rs300 **airport tax** when you get to Santa Cruz.

In theory, it is also possible to book domestic air tickets abroad when you buy your original long-haul flight. However, as individual airlines tend to have separate agreements with domestic Indian carriers, you may not be offered the same choice (or rates) as you will through agents in Mumbai. Note, too, that Indian Airlines is the only company offering 25-percent discounts (on all flights) to customers under the age of thirty.

By train

Two main networks converge on Mumbai: the Western Railway runs to north and west India; the Central Railway connects Mumbai to central, eastern and southern regions.

Nearly all services to Gujarat, Rajasthan, Delhi and the far north leave from **Mumbai Central** station, in the mid-town area. Second-class tickets can be booked here through the normal channels, but the quickest place for foreign nationals to make reservations is at the efficient tourist counter (counter no. 28) on the first floor of the Western Railway's booking hall, next door to the Indian Government tourist office in Churchgate (Mon–Fri 9.30am–4.30pm, Sat 9.30am–2.30pm; ☎022/2038016, ext. 4577 for foreigners). This

AIRLINE OFFICES IN MUMBAI

International Airlines

Aeroflot, Ground Floor, 241/242 Nirmal Building, Nariman Point (☎022/287 1942).

Air France, 1st Floor, Maker Chambers VI, Nariman Point (☎022/202 5021).

Air India, Air India Building, Nariman Point (☎022/202 4142).

Air Lanka, Ground Floor, Mittal Tower, C Wing, Nariman Point (☎022/282 3288).

Alitalia, Industrial Insurance Building,VN Rd, Churchgate (☎022/204 5018).

British Airways, 202-B Vulcan Insurance Building,VN Rd, Churchgate (☎022/282 0888).

Canadian Airlines International, Podar House, 10 Marine Drive (☎022/204 4552).

Cathay Pacific, Ground Floor, *Taj Hotel*, Colaba (☎022/202 9112).

Continental Airlines (US), Ground Floor, 6 Maker Arcade, Cuffe Parade (☎022/2181440).

Delta, *Taj Hotel*, Colaba (☎022/283 7314).

Emirates, 228 Mittal Chambers, Nariman Point (☎022/287 1649).

Gulf Air, Maker Chamber VI, Nariman Point (☎022/202 1777).

KLM, Khaitan Bhavan, 198 J Tata Rd, Churchgate (☎022/283 3338).

Kuwait Airways, Chateau Windsor, 86 Veer Nariman Rd, Churchgate (☎022/204 5351).

Lufthansa, 4th Floor, Express Towers, Nariman Point (☎022/287 5264).

Pakistan International Airlines, 7 Stadium House, VN Rd, Churchgate (☎022/202 1373).

Qantas Airways, 42 Sakhar Bhavan, Nariman Point (☎022/202 0343).

Royal Nepal Airlines, Sherbanoo, 111 M Karve Rd (☎022/283 6198).

Saudia, Ground Floor, Express Towers, Nariman Point (☎022/202 0199).

Scandinavian Airlines, Ground Floor, Podar House, 10 Marine Drive, Churchgate (☎022/204 4552).

South African Airways, Podar House, 10 Marine Drive (☎022/202 2661).

Swissair, Maker Chamber VI, 220 Nariman Point (☎022/287 2210).

Syrian Arab Airlines, 7 Stadium House, VN Rd, Churchgate (☎022/282 6043).

Thai Airways, Ground Floor, Podar House, 10 Marine Drive (☎022/202 2661).

Domestic Airlines

Damania, Terminal B, Santa Cruz (☎022/610 2545).

Goa Way Aviation Pvt. Ltd, Runwal Chamber, Rd 1, Chembur (☎555/8064).

Indian Airlines, Air India Building, Nariman Point (Mon–Sat 8.30am–7.30pm, Sun 10am–1pm & 1.45–5.30pm; ☎022/202 3031); counter at the airport (☎022/611 2850).

Jet Airways, Amarchand Mansion, Madam Cama Rd (☎022/287 5086).

Sahara Airlines, Unit 7, Ground Floor, Tulsiani Chambers, Nariman Point (☎022/283 5671); counter at the airport (☎022/611 9402).

counter also has access to special "**tourist quotas**", which are released the day before departure if the train leaves during the day, or the morning of the departure if the train leaves after 5pm. If the quota is "closed" or already used up, and you can't access the "**VIP quota**" (always worth a try), you will have to join the regular queue.

Mumbai's other "Tourist Ticketing Facility" is in the snazzy new air-conditioned Central Railway booking office to the rear of CST (Mon–Sat 9am–1pm & 1.30–4pm; counter no. 22, or no. 21 on Sun), the departure point for most trains heading east and south. Indrail passes can also be bought here, and there's an MTDC tourist information kiosk in the main concourse if you need help filling in your reservation slips.

RECOMMENDED TRAINS FROM MUMBAI

The services listed below are the **most direct** and/or the **fastest**. This list is by no means exhaustive and there are numerous slower trains that are often more convenient for smaller destinations; see p.118.

Destination	Name	No.	From	Frequency	Departs	Total time
Agra	*Punjab Mail*	#2137	CST	Daily	7.10pm	21hr 30min
Aurangabad	*Devagiri Express*	#1003	CST	Daily	9.20pm	7hr 25min
Bangalore	*Shatabdi Express*	#2027	CST	Daily	6.40am	24hr 40min
Bhopal	*Pushpak Express*	#2133	CST	Daily	8.10am	14hr
Calcutta	*Gitanjali Express*	#2859	CST	Daily	6am	33hr 10min
	Mumbai–Howrah Express	#8001	CST	Daily	8.15pm	36hr
Chennai	*Mumbai–Chennai Express*	#6011	CST	Daily	2pm	26hr 45min
Cochin*	*Kanniya kumari Express*	#1081	CST	Daily	3.35pm	38hr 10min
Delhi	*Rajdhani Express*	#2953	MC	Daily**	5.40pm	17hr
	Paschim Express	#2925	MC	Daily	11.35am	23hr 20min
	Punjab Mail	#2137	CST	Daily	7.10pm	25hr 40min
Gorakhpur	*Kushi Nagar Express*	#1015	Kurla	Daily	10.45pm	33hr 35min
Hyderabad	*Hussainsagar Express*	#7001	CST	Daily	9.55pm	15hr 15min
Jaipur	*Bandra–Jaipur Express*	#9707	Bandra	Daily	11.25pm	22hr 20min
Jodhpur	*Bandra–Bikaneer Express*	#4708	Bandra	Tues, Thurs, Sat, Sun	3.10pm	19hr 20min
Pune	*Shatabdi Express*	#2027	CST	Daily	6.40pm	3hr 15min
Trivandrum	*Kanniya kumari Express*	#1081	CST	Daily	3.35pm	44hr 45min
Udaipur	*Saurashtra Express****	#9215	MC	Daily	7.45am	24hr 40min
Varanasi	*Mahanagiri Express*	#1093	CST	Daily	11.55pm	28hr

*details also applicable for Ernakulam Junction
**except Wednesday
***change at Ahmedabad to the *Delhi Sarai Rohila Express* #9944

Just to complicate matters, some Central Railway trains to South India, including the fast *Dadar–Madras Chennai Express* #6063 to Chennai, do not depart from CST at all, but from Dadar station, way north of Mumbai Central. Seats and berths for these trains are reserved at CST. Finally, if you're booking tickets to Calcutta, make sure your train doesn't leave from Kurla station, which is even more inconvenient, up near the airports. Getting to either of these stations on public transport can be a major struggle.

By bus

The main departure point for long-distance **buses** leaving Mumbai is the frenetic **State Transport Terminal** on JB Behram Marg, opposite Mumbai Central train station. State bus companies with counters here (daily 8am–8pm), include Maharashtra, Karnataka, Madhya Pradesh, Goa and Gujarat. Few of their services compare favourably with train travel on the same routes. Reliable timetable information can be difficult to obtain, reservations are not available on standard buses, and most long-haul journeys are gruelling overnighters. Among the exceptions are the **deluxe buses** run

GETTING TO GOA

By plane

At present, six domestic airline companies operate daily services to Goa (see p.119). If you can afford it, this is the most painless way to go, but competition for seats is fierce (particularly around Christmas–New Year) and you may well have to wait several days. The journey takes an hour and costs around Rs1700.

By train

The new Konkan Railway line is now up and running with daily express trains sprinting from Mumbai to Goa. The best of the services are the *Kurla Superfast Express* #2619 (11hr) and the *Kurla–Ernakulam* #6635 (10hr), both of which run between Kurla and Madgaon. The more practical but heavily booked overnight *CSTM–Madgaon Express* #0111 takes 12 hours. There are other fast services to Goa from Panvel, a large station two hours out of town on the suburban train: the *Trivandrum Rajdhani Express* #2432 (7hr 30min) and the *Rajkot–Trivandrum Express* #6333 (9hr; overnight) are your best options.

By bus

The Mumbai–Goa **bus** journey ranks among the very worst in India. Don't believe travel agents who assure you it takes thirteen hours. Clapped-out coaches and appalling road surfaces along the sinuous coastal route make fourteen to eighteen hours a more realistic estimate.

Bus tickets start at around Rs240 for a push-back seat on a beaten-up Kadamba (Goan government) or MSRTC coach. Tickets for these services are in great demand in season, so book in advance at Mumbai Central or Kadamba's kiosks on the north side of Azad Maidan, near St Xavier's College (just up from CST station). More and more **private** overnight buses also run to Goa, costing from around Rs270 for a noisy front-engined Tata bus to Rs450 for a place on a top-of-the-range imported a/c coach with pneumatic suspension, video and onboard toilet. Tickets should be booked at least a day in advance through a reputable travel agent (see p.114), though it's sometimes worth turning up at the car park opposite the Metro cinema, Azad Maidan, where most buses leave from, on the off-chance of a last-minute cancellation. Make sure, in any case, that you are given both your seat and the bus registration numbers, and that you confirm the exact time and place of departure with the travel agent, as these frequently vary between companies.

By catamaran

Ever since the old steamer service ended, the powerful Goan bus lobby has managed to block any comeback by the Mumbai–Goa passenger ferry. However, it's still possible to reach Goa by sea on the recently inaugurated **catamaran** service, operated by Frank Damania Shipping. This is a fairly quick and comfortable way to do the trip, but feels more like air travel than an ocean cruise. Sailing just fifteen kilometres off shore, the Scandinavian-built catamaran, its reclining seats sealed inside a/c cabins, takes seven hours to reach Panjim, leaving Mumbai's **Baucha Chakka Ferry Wharf** dock every morning at 7am. Seats in economy class (lower deck) cost around US $45; a ticket in business class (upper deck with headphones and a choice of meals) will set you back US $60. Tourists are encouraged to pay in foreign currency, but note that the separate tariff works out more expensive than the rupee rate of Rs1400 for economy or Rs1600 for business class.

Tickets for the catamaran, which **does not operate during the monsoon** (roughly June–Sept), include the cost of two excellent meals, snacks and drinks, and are sold through most reputable travel agents in Mumbai (see p.114). Alternatively, book through Frank Damania's shipping office on Ferry Wharf (☎022/373 5562 or 373 5562 for timetable information). Be sure to arrive at the dock, 3km north of CST along P D'Mello Rd at least 45 minutes before departure; buses run there from Colaba and Fort, but the trip is a lot less hassle by taxi.

by MSRTC to Pune, Nasik and Kolhapur; the small extra cost buys you more leg-room, fewer stops and the option of advance booking. The only problem is, most leave from the **ASIAD** bus stand in Dadar, half an hour or so by road north of Mumbai Central.

Other possibilities for road travel include the "super-fast" **luxury coaches** touted around Colaba. Most are run by private companies, guaranteeing breakneck speeds and noisy Hindi film videos. MTDC and ITDC also operate similarly priced, video-less services to the same destinations, which you can book direct from their main offices downtown or through the more conveniently situated Government of India tourist office, 123 M Karve Rd, Churchgate. Two night buses leave Nariman Point every evening for the twelve-hour trip to **Aurangabad**, and there are morning departures to **Nasik** and **Mahabaleshwar**, which take six and seven hours respectively.

Leaving India

In spite of its prominence on trans-Asian flight routes, Mumbai is no longer the bargain basement for **international air tickets** it used to be. Discounted fares are very hard to come by – a legacy of Rajiv Gandhi's economic reforms of the 1980s. If you do need to book a ticket, stick to one of the tried and tested agents listed on p.114.

All the major airlines operating out of Mumbai have offices downtown where you can buy scheduled tickets or confirm your flight. The majority are grouped around VN Rd, opposite the *Ambassador Hotel*, or else on Nariman Point, a short taxi ride west of Colaba.

travel details

Note that no individual route appears more than once in this chart; for any specific journey, check against where you want to get to as well as where you're coming from. More information on onwards travel from Mumbai appears on p.114, and for detailed information on getting to Goa from Mumbai see box on p.117.

Trains

Mumbai to: Agra (4 daily; 23hr 30min–27hr); Ahmedabad (4 daily; 8–12hr); Aurangabad (2 daily; 14hr); Bangalore (3 daily; 8–11hr); Bhopal (4 daily; 14–20hr); Calcutta (7 daily; 28–36hr); Calicut (6 daily; 18–20hr); Chennai (4 daily; 21–31hr); Cochin (1 daily; 13hr); Coimbatore (1 daily; 10hr); Delhi (11 daily; 17–33hr); Hyderabad (2 daily; 16–18hr); Indore (2 daily; 12–15hr); Jaipur (1 daily; 19hr); Jodhpur (1 daily; 22hr; change at Ahmedabad); Kolhapur (3 daily; 10–12hr); Madurai (4 weekly; 35hr); Mangalore (1 daily; 16hr); Nagpur (3 daily; 14–15hr); Nasik (20 daily; 4hr); Pune (25 daily; 3hr 15min–5hr); Trivandrum (5 daily; 24–43hr); Udaipur (1 daily; 25hr; change at Ahmedabad); Ujjain (2 daily; 15hr); Varanasi (2 daily; 29–35hr). Unless stated, all of the above are direct services.

Buses

Only state bus services are listed here; for details of private buses, see above.

Mumbai Central to: Bangalore (3 daily; 24hr); Bijapur (3 daily; 12hr); Goa (2 daily; 14–18hr); Indore (2 daily; 16hr); Ujjain (1 daily; 17hr).

Mumbai ASIAD Dadar to: Kolhapur (4 daily; 10hr); Nasik (6 daily; 4hr); Pune (hourly; 4hr 30min).

Flights

Mumbai (Santa Cruz airport) to: Ahmedabad (3 daily; 1hr); Aurangabad (1 daily; 40min); Bangalore (5 daily; 1hr 30min); Bhopal (1 daily; 2hr); Calcutta (3 daily; 2hr 25min–4hr); Calicut (2 daily; 2hr); Chennai (4 daily; 1hr 45min); Cochin (1 daily; 1hr 50min); Coimbatore (1 daily; 1hr 50min); Delhi (7 daily; 1hr 45min–2hr); Goa (2 weekly; 1hr 55min); Hyderabad (3 daily; 1hr 15min); Indore (1 daily; 1hr 5min); Jaipur (2 daily 2hr 25 min–3hr 25min); Jodhpur (1 daily; 1hr 20min–2hr 20min); Madurai (4 weekly; 1hr 50min); Mangalore (1 daily; 1hr 15min); Nagpur (2 daily; 1hr 15min); Pune (3–4 daily; 30–75min); Trivandrum (2 daily; 1hr 55min); Udaipur (1 daily; 2hr 15min); Varanasi (2 weekly; 3hr 5min).

CHAPTER TWO

GOA

Famous for its white sand beaches and mesmeric sunsets, the state of **GOA** has been renowned as one of India's most irresistible destinations ever since the Portuguese navigator Vasco da Gama sailed down the Malabar coast in 1498, in search of "Christians and spices". He found neither, but the fort he founded at Cochin resulted, twelve years later, in the erstwhile Muslim port and its hinterland becoming a **Portuguese colony**, which it remained until 1961. These days, the region's easy-going ambience, good food and salubrious winter climate have made it one of the most popular spots in South Asia to unwind and enjoy the simple, undemanding pleasures of life on the beach.

The very word "Goa" may be synonymous in some circles with hedonistic hippy holidays, but in reality, each of the countless beaches of this hundred-kilometre-long state seems to attract its own different kind of tourists, from Bombayites on weekend breaks to fortnighting European holidaymakers, as well as long-stay shoestring travellers. Moreover, the fabled palm-fringed coastline, lapped by the warm waters of the Arabian Sea, is only part of the picture. Separated from the rest of India by the jungle-covered hills of the Western Ghats, Goa's heartland and most densely populated area is the alluvial strip **inland** from the beaches – a lush patchwork of paddy fields, coconut plantations, whitewashed churches and gently meandering rivers.

Goa's 450 years under Portuguese domination produced a unique, syncretic blend of East and West that is at once exotic and strangely familiar: Christmas and Carnival are celebrated as enthusiastically by the thirty percent Christian minority as Diwali and Durga *puja* are by the mainly Konkani-speaking Hindus. The state's separate identity is discernible in other ways too, most visibly in its Latin-influenced architecture, but also in a fish- and meat-rich cuisine that would be anathema to most Indians. Another marked difference is the prevalence of **alcohol**. Beer is cheap, and six thousand or more bars around the state are licensed to serve it, along with the more traditional tipples of *feni*, the local hooch, and *toddy*, a derivative of palm sap.

Thanks to a fecund tropical climate and the well-watered soil of its seaward side, Goan (as against "Goanese", which has undesirable colonial connotations) farmers grow a wide array of **crops**, ranging from rice, the main staple, to cashew, areca (the source of betel nuts) and fruit for export. On the coast itself, coconut cultivation and **fishing** (both in-shore, with small boats, canoes and hand-nets, and off-shore, with modern trawlers) are still the main sources of income. The recent discovery of **iron** in the hills to the east has also generated considerable revenue, and the economy is further fuelled by the

ACCOMMODATION PRICE CODES

All **accommodation prices** in this book have been coded using the symbols below. The prices given are for a double room, except in the case of categories ① and ② where the price can refer to dorm accommodation per bed. All taxes are included. For more details, see p.34.

① up to Rs100	④ Rs300–400	⑦ Rs900–1500
② Rs100–200	⑤ Rs400–600	⑧ Rs1500–2500
③ Rs200–300	⑥ Rs600–900	⑨ Rs2500 and upwards

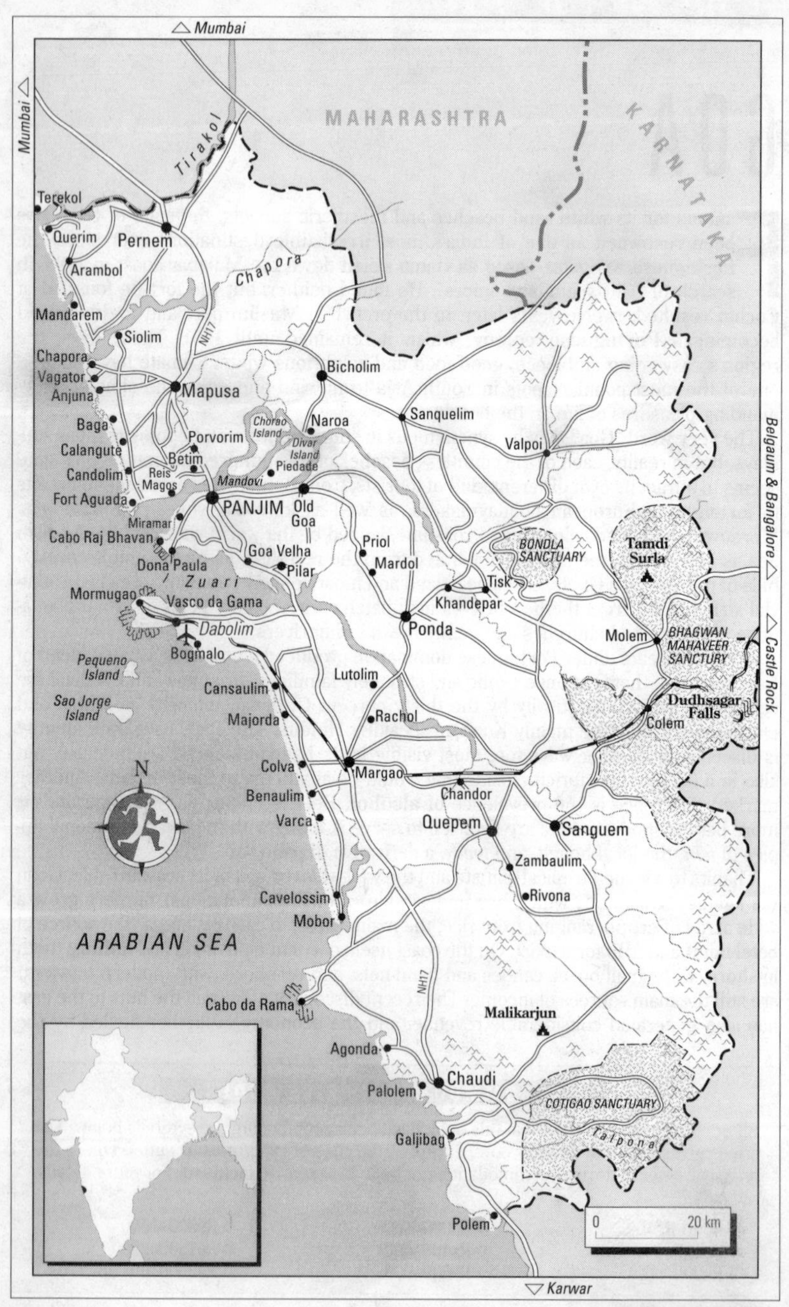
Mumbai
Mumbai
MAHARASHTRA
KARNATAKA
Tirakol
Terekol
Querim
Pernem
Arambol
Chapora
Mandarem
Siolim
NH17
Chapora
Vagator
Anjuna
Mapusa
Bicholim
Baga
Calangute
Candolim
Fort Aguada
Porvorim
Betim
Reis Magos
Chorao Island
Divar Island
Naroa
Piedade
Mandovi
Sanquelim
Valpoi
Belgaum & Bangalore
PANJIM
Old Goa
Miramar
Cabo Raj Bhavan
Dona Paula
Zuari
Goa Velha
Pilar
Priol
Mardol
BONDLA SANCTUARY
Tamdi Surla
Tisk
Khandepar
Mormugao
Vasco da Gama
Dabolim
Bogmalo
Ponda
Molem
BHAGWAN MAHAVEER SANCTURY
Castle Rock
Pequeno Island
Sao Jorge Island
Cansaulim
Majorda
Lutolim
Rachol
Dudhsagar Falls
Colem
N
Colva
Margao
Benaulim
Chandor
Varca
Quepem
Sanguem
Zambaulim
Rivona
Cavelossim
Mobor
ARABIAN SEA
NH17
Cabo da Rama
Malikarjun
Agonda
Palolem
Chaudi
COTIGAO SANCTUARY
Galjibag
Talpona
Polem
0
20 km
Karwar

PARTIES

Hedonism has been a feature of the expatriate Westerners' social scene in Goa since the mid-sixteenth century, when mariners and merchants returned to Lisbon with tales of unbridled drunkenness and debauchery among the colonists. Following the Inquisition, a semblance of morality was restored, but the traditional Catholic life of Goa's coastal villages sustained a rude shock in the 1960s with the first influx of "hippies" to Calangute and Baga beaches. Much to the amazement of the locals, the preferred pastime of these would-be *sadhus* was to cavort naked on the sands together on full-moon nights, amid a haze of *chillum* smoke and loud rock music blaring from makeshift PAs. The villagers took little notice of these bizarre gatherings at first, but with each season the scene became better established, and by the late 1970s the **Christmas and New Year** parties, in particular, had become huge events, attracting thousands of foreign travellers from all over Asia.

It was around that time that DJs such as **Goa Gill** made a name for themselves, playing the kind of dismal Pink Floyd and Grateful Dead discs you still occasionally hear in the sadder cafés of south Calangute. By the mid-1980s, however, acid rock had given way to the driving rhythms and electronically generated sounds of acid house and techno, and the party scene received a dramatic face-lift. Mirroring the shift from LSD to Ecstasy as the preferred dance drug, tight lycra and fluoro fractal prints supplanted floppy cotton, and the drifty dope-and-dub-reggae scene succumbed to rave culture, with ever greater numbers of young clubbers pouring in for the season on cheap charter flights.

Goa's now legendary party scene has even spawned its own distinctive brand of psychedelic dance music, known as "**Goa Trance**". Artists such Juno Reactor and Hallucinogen added the fine touches that coined the new sound, but when household-name DJs Danny Rampling and Paul Oakenfold started playing Goa Trance in clubs and on national radio stations back in the UK, they generated a huge following among listeners who would otherwise never have even heard of the Indian state.

In spite of the growing interest in Goa Trance, the plug was effectively pulled on the state's party scene by the police in 1994–95. For years, drug busts and bribes provided the notoriously corrupt local cops with a lucrative source of *baksheesh*. But after a spate of sensational newspaper articles in the regional press, the police began to demand impossibly large bribes to allow the parties to go ahead – sums that the organizers could not hope to recoup. Although the big New Year and Christmas events continued unabated, smaller parties started to peter out, much to the annoyance of local people, many of whom had become financially dependent on the raves and the punters they pulled into the villages. This is particularly true of the "*chai* ladies", local women who sell cakes, snacks and hot tea through the small hours, sitting on palm-leaf mats in the glow of gas lamps.

The winter of 1996–97 saw something of a revival in the party scene, as police and government officals acquiesced to local complaints, while in 1998-99, a hard-core Italian sound system, complete with giant PA, lights and lasers, drove overland and set up for the Christmas festivities. Even so, Goa is still a far cry from Ibiza and the island of Ko Pha Ngan in southern Thailand, and if you're expecting full-on raves every night, you'll be disappointed. Parties are only certain to take place at Christmas and New Year, when the hilltop above Vagator and an expanse of paddy behind Anjuna host big events. At other times, keep your ear to the ground for the tell-tale roar of massed Enfields, as hard-core Israeli ravers ride off to secret locations in the countryside.

stream of remittance cheques sent home by expatriate Goans working in Mumbai and the Gulf states. The consequent higher standard of living has, inevitably, stimulated a massive influx of **immigrants** from elsewhere in India, who comprise around a third of the total population.

Goa's other big money-spinner, of course, is **tourism**. Lured here in the 1960s by the locals' apparently permissive stance on drink, drugs and nudity – not to mention abundant cheap food and accommodation – the first foreigners to take advantage of the new state's pristine beaches were the "**hippies**". As the region's fame spread, however, the marginal minority was gradually squeezed out, leaving the more accessible stretches of coastline near Panjim free for development as **mainstream resorts**. Today, budget travellers taking time out from trips around the subcontinent and package tourists over for a dose of winter sun flock here in roughly equal numbers. The "alternative" contingent, meanwhile, has fled up the coast, ditching Pink Floyd along the way in favour of hard-edged, chest-thumping techno music. The legendary **full-moon parties** have also survived, despite numerous police crackdowns, and continue to attract thousands of revellers, especially around the Christmas–New Year period.

Which **beach** you opt for when you arrive largely depends on what sort of holiday you have in mind. Heavily developed resorts such as **Calangute** and **Baga**, in the North, and **Colva** (and to a lesser extent **Benaulim**), in the South, offer more "walk-in" accommodation, shopping and tourist facilities than elsewhere. Even if you don't fancy crowded bars and purpose-built hotels, it can be worth heading for these centres at first, as finding places to stay in less commercialized corners is often difficult. **Anjuna**, **Vagator** and **Chapora**, where accommodation is generally more basic and harder to come by, are the beaches to aim for if you've come to Goa to party. To get a taste of what most of the state must have been like twenty or thirty years ago, however, you'll have to travel farther afield – to **Arambol**, a sleepy fishing-village-cum-hippy-hangout in the far north; or to **Agonda** and **Palolem**, near the Karnatakan border, where, as yet, tourism has made very little impact.

Foremost among worthwhile attractions **away from the coast** are the ruins of the Portuguese capital at **Old Goa**, 10km from Panjim – a sprawl of Catholic cathedrals, convents and churches that draws crowds of Christian pilgrims from all over India. Another popular day-excursion is to Anjuna's Wednesday **flea market**, a sociable place to shop for souvenirs and the latest rave gear. Farther inland, the thickly wooded countryside around **Ponda** harbours numerous temples, where you can check out Goa's peculiar brand of Hindu architecture. The *taluka* (district) of Salcete and its main market town, **Margao**, are also littered with Portuguese mansions, churches and seminaries, whose gabled baroque facades nose tantalizingly above the tropical treeline. Finally, wildlife enthusiasts may be tempted into the interior to visit the nature reserve at **Cotigao** in the far south.

The best **time to come** to Goa is during the dry, relatively cool winter months between late September and early March. At other times, either the sun is too hot for comfort, or the monsoon rains make life miserable for everyone except the fisherfolk and hoteliers, who get to sit around all day snoozing and playing backgammon. During peak season, from mid-December to the end of January, the weather is perfect, with the temperature gauge rarely nudging above a manageable 32°C. Finding a room or a house to rent at that time, however – particularly over the Christmas and New Year fortnight when the tariffs double, or triple – can be a real hassle.

Some history

The sheer inaccessibility of Goa by land has always kept it out of the mainstream of Indian history; on the other hand, its control of the seas, and above all of the lucrative spice trade, made it a much-coveted prize for rival colonial powers. Until a century before the arrival of the Portuguese adventurer **Vasco da Gama**, who landed near Kozhikode in Kerala in 1498, Goa had belonged for over a thousand years to the kingdom of Kadamba. In the interim it had been successfully conquered by the Karnatakan Vijayanagars, the Muslim Bahmanis and Yusuf 'Adil Shah of Bijapur, but the capture of the fort at Panjim by **Afonso de Albuquerque** in 1510 signalled the start of a Portuguese occupation that was to last for 450 years.

POLICE, TROUBLE AND NUDISM

While the vast majority of visitors to Goa never encounter any **trouble**, tourism-related crime is definitely more prevalent than in other parts of the country. **Theft** is the most common problem – usually of articles left unattended on the beach. Don't assume your valuables are safe in a padlocked house or hotel room, either. Break-ins, particularly on party nights, are on the increase. The most secure solution is to rent a deposit box in a bank, which costs around Rs50, or to opt for one of the few guesthouses with lockers.

The other eventuality to avoid, at all costs, is getting on the wrong side of the law. **Drugs** are the most common cause of serious trouble. Many travellers imagine that, because of Goa's free-and-easy reputation, drug use is legal; it isn't. Possession of even a small amount of cannabis is a criminal offence, punishable by large fines or prison sentences of up to ten years. Arrests, however, rarely result in court appearances. The Goan police like to ensure that offenders are given the opportunity of leaving the country first, having relieved them of nearly all their spare cash and valuables. That said, Fort Aguada prison had, at the last count, half a dozen foreigners serving long sentences for drugs offences.

Though violent crime is rare, women should think twice before wandering down deserted beaches and dark tracks on their own. **Sexual harassment** usually takes the form of a bit of unsubtle ogling, but there have also been several incidents of **rape** in recent years, the most publicized of them in **Anjuna** where, in 1996, a British woman was violently attacked by two men (one of whom was her taxi driver). In March of the same year, two Swedish motorcyclists were also gang-raped after seven men armed with sticks and knives stopped them on their way home from a beach party. Wherever you're staying, therefore, take the same common-sense precautions as you would at home: keep to the main roads when travelling on foot or by bicycle, avoid dirt tracks and unfrequented beaches (particularly on party nights) unless you're in a group, and when you're in your house after dark, ensure that all windows and doors are locked.

Finally, remember that **nudism** is prohibited. In case tourists miss the "NO NUDISM" signs posted at the entrances to most beaches, police regularly patrol the busier resorts to ensure that decorum is maintained. If you are tempted to drop your togs, check that there are no families within eyeshot. No one is likely to object openly, but when you consider that wet Y-fronts and saris are about as risqué as beachwear gets for most Indians, you'll understand why men in G-strings and topless women cause such a stir.

As Goa expanded, its splendid capital (now Old Goa) came to hold a larger population than either Paris or London. Though Ismail 'Adil Shah laid siege for ten months in 1570, and the Marathas under Shivaji and later chiefs came nail-bitingly close to seizing the region, the greatest threat was from other European maritime nations. While the Dutch made several unsuccessful attacks, the British at first preferred the avenue of diplomacy. Their **East India Company** signed the **Convention of Goa** in 1642, granting them the right to trade with the colony and to use its harbours.

Meanwhile, conversions to **Christianity**, started by the Franciscans, gathered pace when St Francis Xavier founded the **Jesuit** mission in 1542. With the advent of the **Inquisition** soon afterwards, laws were introduced censoring literature and banning any faith other than Catholicism – even the long-established Syrian Christian community were branded heretics. Hindu temples were destroyed, and converted Hindus adopted Portuguese names, such as da Silva, Correa and de Sousa, which remain common in the region. The transnational influence of the Jesuits eventually alarmed the Portuguese government; the Jesuits were expelled in 1749, which made it possible for Indian Goans to take up the priesthood. However, standards of education suffered, and Goa entered a period of decline. The Portuguese were not prepared to help, but neither would they allow native Goans equal rights. An abortive attempt to establish a Goan republic was quelled with the execution of fifteen Goan conspirators.

A spin-off of the British conflict with Tipu Sultan of Mysore (an ally of the French), at the end of the eighteenth century, was the **British occupation** of Goa, a little-known period of the region's history, which lasted sixteen years from 1797. The occupation was solely military; the Goan authorities never gave up their administration. Despite a certain liberalization, such as the restoration of Hindus' right to worship, the nineteenth century saw widespread civil unrest. During British occupation many Goans moved to Bombay, and elsewhere in British India, to find work.

The success of the post-Independence Goan struggle for freedom from Portugal owed as much to the efforts of the Indian government, who cut off diplomatic ties with Portugal, as to the work of freedom fighters such as **Menezes Braganza** and **Dr Cunha**. After a "liberation march" in 1955 resulted in a number of deaths, the state was blockaded. Trade with Bombay ceased, and the railway was cut off, so Goa set out to forge international links, particularly with Pakistan and Sri Lanka. That led to the building of Dabolim airport and a determination to improve local agricultural output. In 1961, Prime Minister Jawaharlal Nehru finally ran out of patience with his opposite number in Lisbon, the right-wing dictator Salazar, and sent in the armed forces. Mounted in defiance of a United Nations resolution, "**Operation Vijay**" met with only token resistance, and the Indian army overran Goa in two days. Thereafter, Goa (along with Portugal's other two enclaves, Daman and Diu) became part of India as a self-governing **Union Territory**, with minimum interference from Delhi.

Since Independence, Goa has continued to prosper, bolstered by receipts from iron-ore exports and a booming tourist industry, but it is struggling to hold its own against a tidal wave of **immigration** from other Indian states. Its inhabitants voted overwhelmingly to resist a merger with neighbouring Maharashtra in the 1980s, and successfully lobbied for Konkani to be granted official-language status in 1987, when Goa was finally declared a fully-fledged state of the Indian Union.

Getting around Goa

Before Independence, the many rivers that drain across Goa made **getting around** a problem. Nowadays, however, thanks to a network of road bridges (and the recent two-wheeler revolution), life is a lot easier.

For tourists, white Maruti van **taxis** serve as the main means of travelling between resorts. You'll find them lined up outside most charter hotels, where a board invariably displays "fixed rates" to destinations in and around the region. These fares only apply to peak season, however, and at other times you should be able to negotiate a hefty reduction.

By ferry

If auto-rickshaws are the quintessentially Indian mode of transport, flat-bottomed **ferries** are their Goan equivalent. Crammed with cars, buses, commuters on scooters, fisherwomen and clumps of bewildered tourists, these rusting blue-painted hulks provide an essential service, crossing the coastal backwaters where bridges have not yet been built. They're also incredibly cheap, and run from the crack of dawn until late in the evening.

The most frequented river crossings in Goa are Panjim to Betim, across the Mandovi (every 15min); Old Goa to Divar Island (every 15min); Siolim to Chopdem, across the

Chapora River for Arambol and Pernem (every 15min); Querim to Terekol, over the Terekol River (every 30min); and Cavelossim, in the far south of Salcete *taluka*, to Assolna (every 20–30min).

By train

Following years of controversy, the **Konkan Railway** was completed in 1997, running down the coast from Mumbai to link with the southern rail network at Mangalore. This now serves as Goa's principal long-distance transport artery, but is rarely convenient for shorter journeys within the state. The relative infrequency of services and distance of the line from most of the resorts means you're invariably better off catching the bus.

By bus

The Goan transport corporation, **Kadamba**, runs long-distance services throughout the state from their main stands at Panjim, Mapusa and Margao. Private buses, serving everywhere else including the coastal resorts, are cheap, frequent and more relaxed than many in India, although you should still brace yourself for a crush on market days and when travelling to major towns and tourist centres. Details on how to get around by bus are listed in the relevant accounts, and on p.178.

By motorcycle taxi

Goa's unique pillion-passenger **motorcycle taxis**, known locally as **"pilots"**, are ideal for nipping between beaches or into town from the resorts. Bona fide operators ride black bikes (usually *Rajdoots*) with yellow mudguards and white number plates. Fares, which should be settled in advance, are comparable with auto-rickshaw rates: roughly Rs5 per km.

By rented motorcycle

Renting a motorcycle in Goa gives a lot of freedom but can be perilous. Every season, an average of one person a day dies on the roads; many of them are tourists on two-wheelers. Make sure, therefore, that the lights and brakes are in good shape, and be especially vigilant at night: many Goan roads are appalingly pot-holed and unlit, and stray cows and bullock carts can appear from nowhere.

Officially, you need an **international driver's licence** to rent, and ride, anything more powerful than a 25cc moped. Owners and rental companies rarely enforce this, but some local **police** use the rule to extract exorbitant *baksheesh* from tourists. If you don't have a licence with you, the only way around the problem is to avoid big towns such as Panjim, Margao and Mapusa (or Anjuna on market day), and only to carry small sums of money when driving. If you are arrested for not having the right papers, it's no big deal, though police officers may try to convince you otherwise; keep cool, and be prepared to negotiate. Some unlicensed operators attempt to rent out machines to unwary visitors; always make sure you get some evidence of rental and insurance.

Rates vary according to the season, the vehicle and how long you rent it for; most owners also insist on a deposit and/or passport as security. The range is pretty standard, with the cheapest choice, a 50cc **moped**, costing Rs50–100 per day. These are fine for buzzing to the beach and back, but to travel farther try the stalwart **Enfield Bullet 350cc**, popular mainly for its pose value (upwards of Rs250 per day); the smaller but more reliable **Honda Kinetic 100cc**, which has automatic gears and is a good first-time choice (Rs100–120 per day); or the best all-rounder, the **Yamaha RD 100cc**: light, fast enough, reliable, economical and with manual gears (Rs150–200 per day). The notoriously unreliable Indian makes, **Rajdoot** and **Bajaj**, are best avoided.

Guided tours

On paper, GTDC's guided **tours** from Panjim, Margao, Calangute and Colva seem like a good way of getting around Goa's highlights in a short time. However, they're far too rushed for most foreign tourists, appealing essentially to Indian families wishing to combine a peek at the resorts with a whistlestop *puja* tour of the temples around Ponda. Most also include a string of places inland you wouldn't otherwise consider visiting. Leaflets giving full itineraries are available at any GTDC office, where you can also buy tickets: half-day tours cost Rs80, full-day excursions Rs150.

Crossing the Goa–Karnataka border

If you're heading south from Goa towards Jog Falls (see p.234) or the Hindu pilgrimage town of Gokarn (see p.235), you'll have to cross the state border at a road barrier a short way before the river bridge, near the town of Karwar. For travellers on buses, or in cars, this is a straightforward procedure; you probably won't even have to fill in the requisite form. Anyone who is crossing into Karnataka on a rented motorcycle, however, can expect some **hassle from the police**. The standard scam is to take your passport, scrutinize it with a very stern face and then inform you that you can't continue south because of some directive from Panjim. Of course, this is all a ploy to extract *baksheesh*; like it or not, you'll probably have to shell out at least Rs100 to continue. Curiously enough, the cops are honest when it comes to recognizing you on the return trip, and will politely wave you through the barrier after signing the ledger in their office.

Panjim and central Goa

Take any middle-sized Portuguese town, add a sprinkling of banana trees and auto-rickshaws, drench annually with torrential tropical rain, and leave to simmer in fierce humid sunshine for at least one hundred and fifty years, and you'll end up with something like **PANJIM** (also known by its more politically correct Maharathi name, **Panaji** – "land that does not flood"). The Goan capital has a completely different feel from any other Indian city. Stacked around the sides of a lush terraced hillside at the mouth of the Mandovi River, its skyline of red-tiled roofs, whitewashed churches and mildewing concrete apartment buildings has more in common with Lisbon than Lucknow. This lingering European influence is most evident in the small squares and cobbled lanes of the town's old Latin quarter, **Fontainhas**. Here, Portuguese is still very much the lingua franca, the shopfronts sport names like *José Pinto* and *de Souza*, and the women wear knee-length dresses that would turn heads anywhere else in the country.

For centuries, Panjim was little more than a minor landing stage and customs house, protected by a hilltop fort, and surrounded by stagnant swampland. It only became capital in 1843, after the port at Old Goa had silted up and its rulers and impoverished inhabitants had fled the plague. Although the last Portuguese viceroy managed to drain many of the nearby marshes and erect imposing public buildings on the new site, the town never emulated the grandeur of its predecessor upriver – a result, in part, of the Portuguese nobles' predilection for erecting their mansions in the countryside rather than the city. Panjim expanded rapidly in the 1960s and 1970s, without reaching the unmanageable proportions of other Indian state capitals. After Mumbai, or even Bangalore, its uncongested streets seem easy-going and pleasantly parochial. Sights are thin on the ground, but the palm-lined squares and atmospheric Latin quarter, with its picturesque Neoclassical houses and Catholic churches, make a pleasant backdrop for aimless wandering.

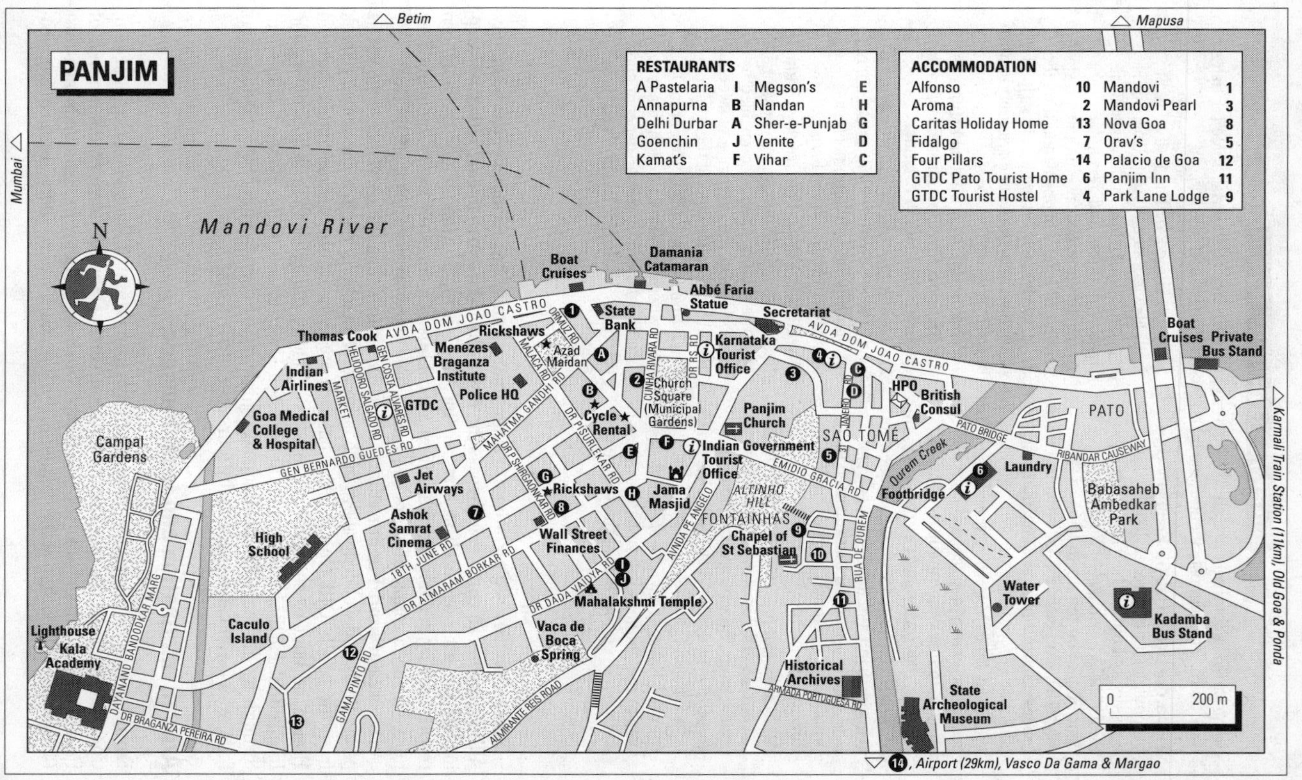
PANJIM
RESTAURANTS
A Pastelaria I
Annapurna B
Delhi Durbar A
Goenchin J
Kamat's F
Megson's E
Nandan H
Sher-e-Punjab G
Venite D
Vihar C
ACCOMMODATION
Alfonso 10
Aroma 2
Caritas Holiday Home 13
Fidalgo 7
Four Pillars 14
GTDC Pato Tourist Home 6
GTDC Tourist Hostel 4
Mandovi 1
Mandovi Pearl 3
Nova Goa 8
Orav's 5
Palacio de Goa 12
Panjim Inn 11
Park Lane Lodge 9
Betim
Mapusa
Mumbai
Karmali Train Station (11km), Old Goa & Ponda
Airport (29km), Vasco Da Gama & Margao
Mandovi River
N
Boat Cruises
Damania Catamaran
Abbé Faria Statue
Secretariat
State Bank
Rickshaws
Thomas Cook
AVDA DOM JOAO CASTRO
ORMUZ RD
Azad Maidan
MALACA RD
Menezes Braganza Institute
Police HQ
Indian Airlines
MARKET
HELIODORO SALGADO RD
GEN COSTA ALVARES RD
GTDC
Goa Medical College & Hospital
Campal Gardens
GEN BERNARDO GUEDES RD
MAHATMA GANDHI RD
DR PISURLEKAR RD
Cycle Rental
CUNHA RIVARA RD
Church Square (Municipal Gardens)
DR RS RD
Karnataka Tourist Office
Panjim Church
Indian Government Tourist Office
Jet Airways
DR P SHIRGAONKAR RD
Rickshaws
Jama Masjid
Ashok Samrat Cinema
18TH JUNE RD
Wall Street Finances
High School
DR ATMARAM BORKAR RD
DR DADA VAIDYA RD
Mahalakshmi Temple
AVDA PE ANGELO
ALTINHO HILL
FONTAINHAS
Chapel of St Sebastian
EMIDIO GRACIA RD
SAO TOMÉ
31 JANEIRO RD
RUA DE OUREM
HPO
British Consul
PATO BRIDGE
Ourem Creek
Footbridge
Laundry
PATO
RIBANDAR CAUSEWAY
Babasaheb Ambedkar Park
Boat Cruises
Private Bus Stand
Water Tower
Kadamba Bus Stand
Lighthouse
Kala Academy
DAYANAND BANDODKAR MARG
Caculo Island
GAMA PINTO RD
Vaca de Boca Spring
ALMIRANTE REIS ROAD
DR BRAGANZA PEREIRA RD
Historical Archives
ARMADA PORTUGUESA RD
State Archeological Museum
0 200 m

THE FESTIVALS OF GOA

Some of Goa's **festivals** are on fixed dates each year; ask at a tourist office for dates of the others. The biggest celebrations take place at Panjim and Margao.

Festa dos Reis (Jan 6). Epiphany celebrations include a procession of young boys decked out as the Three Kings to the Franciscan chapel of Reis Magos, near Panjim on the north bank of the Mandovi, 3km east of Fort Aguada. Other processions are held at Cansaulim and Chandor.

Carnival (Feb/March). Three days of *feni*-induced mayhem, centring on Panjim, to mark the run-up to Lent.

Shigmo (Feb/March). The Goan version of Holi is celebrated with big parades and crowds; drum and dance groups compete, and huge floats, that threaten to bring down telegraph wires, trundle through the streets.

All Saints (March). On the fifth Monday in Lent, 26 effigies of saints, martyrs, popes, kings, queens and cardinals are paraded around the village of Velha Goa, near Panjim. A fair also takes place.

Igitun Chalne (May). *Dhoti*-clad devotees of the goddess Lairya enter trances and walk over hot coals at the village of Sirigao, Bichloim.

Sanjuan (June 24). The festival of St John is celebrated all over Goa, but is especially important in the coastal villages of Arambol and Terekol. Youngsters torch straw dummies (representing St John's baptism, and thus the death of sin), while revellers in striped pants dive into wells after drinking bottles of *feni*.

Janmashtami (Aug). Ritual bathing in the Mandovi River, off Diwadi Island, to celebrate the birth of Krishna.

Dussehra (Sept/Oct). Nine days of festivities in which more effigies are burned on bonfires, and children perform episodes from the life of Rama.

Diwali (Oct/Nov). The five-day Hindu "festival of lights" features processions all over the region, often accompanied by fireworks, and the exchange of sweets by neighbours, regardless of their faith.

Christmas (Dec 24/25). Celebrated everywhere in Goa. Late-night mass is usually followed by music, dancing and fireworks, while tourist ravers party in Anjuna.

Some travellers see no more of Panjim than its noisy bus terminal – which is a pity. Although you can completely bypass the town when you arrive in Goa, either by jumping off the train or coach at Margao (for the South), or Mapusa (for the northern resorts), or by heading straight off on a local bus, it's definitely worth spending time here – if only a couple of hours en route to the ruined former capital at Old Goa.

The area **around Panjim** attracts far fewer visitors than the coastal resorts, yet its paddy fields and wooded valleys harbour several attactions worth a day or two's break from the beach. **Old Goa** is just a bus ride away, as are the unique temples around **Ponda**, an hour or so southeast, to where Hindus smuggled their deities during the Inquisition. Farther inland still, the forested lower slopes of the Western Ghats, cut through by the main Panjim–Bangalore highway, shelter the impressive **Dudhsagar falls**, which you can reach only by four-wheel-drive jeep.

Arrival, information and local transport

European charter planes and domestic flights from Mumbai, Bangalore, Cochin, Delhi, Chennai and Thiruvananthapuram arrive at Goa's **Dabolim airport**, 29km south of Panjim on the outskirts of Vasco da Gama, Goa's second city. Pre-paid taxis into town (45min; Rs450), booked at the counter in the forecourt, can be shared by up to four people. In theory, Kadamba buses (Rs25) should meet domestic flights, dropping passengers at the main bus stand and outside the Indian Airlines office on Dr D Bandodkar Rd, in the northwest of town; in practice, however, they rarely show up.

GTDC's **information** counter, inside the concourse at the main Kadamba bus stand (Mon–Fri 8am–6pm, Sat & Sun 9am–1pm & 2–5pm; ☎0832/232169) is useful for checking train and bus timings, but little else. The more efficient **India Government tourist office** is across town on Church Square (Mon–Fri 9.30am–5.45pm, Sat 9.30am–1pm; ☎0832/43412).

Long-distance and local **buses** pull into Panjim at the town's busy **Kadamba bus terminal**, 1km east of the centre in the district of Pato. Ten minutes' walk from here across Ourem Creek to Fontainhas, brings you to several budget hotels. If you plan to stay in the more modern west end of town, flag down a **motorcycle taxi** or jump into an auto-rickshaw at the rank outside the station concourse. The only city buses likely to be of use to visitors run to Dona Paula from the main bus stand via several stops along the esplanade (including the Secretariat) and Miramar beachfront. The most convenient way of getting around Panjim is by **auto-rickshaw**; flag one down at the roadside or head for one of the ranks around the city. If you feel up to taking on Panjim's anarchic traffic, **bicycles** can be rented (Mon–Sat only; Rs3 per hour) from a stall up the lane opposite the GPO.

A popular alternative to watching the sunset from a beach bar – at least for most Indian tourists – is an evening **river cruise** along the Mandovi from Panjim. GTDC runs two return trips every day from Santa Monica jetty: the first at 6pm, and the second at 7.15pm. Snacks and drinks are available, and the price (Rs60) includes a display of Konkani and Portuguese dance accompanied by folk singers in traditional Goan costume, and sometimes a live Hindi cover band. Two-hour "Full Moon" cruises also leave daily at 8.30pm, regardless of the lunar phase. Operating in direct competition to GTDC are Emerald Waters cruises from the quay outside the *Hotel Mandovi* (daily 5.45pm, 7pm, 8.15pm & 9.30pm; Rs70); they also offer longer sightseeing trips during the day.

Bookings for the GTDC cruises can be made through their agents, Goa Sea Travels, opposite the *Tourist Hostel*. Emerald Waters' ticket counter is opposite the *Hotel Mandovi*.

The Town

Until a decade ago, most visitors' first glimpse of **Panjim** was from the decks of the old Bombay steamer as it chugged into dock at the now-defunct ferry ramp. These days, however, despite the recent inauguration of the Konkan Railway and Damania's catamaran service from Mumbai, the town is most usually approached by road – from the north via the huge ferroconcrete bridge that spans the Mandovi estuary, or from the south on the recently revamped NH7, which links the capital with the airport and railhead at Vasco da Gama. Either way, you'll have to pass through the suburb of **Pato**, home of the main Kadamba bus terminal, before crossing Ourem Creek to arrive in Panjim proper. West of **Fontainhas**, the picturesque Portuguese quarter, the commercial centre's grid of long straight streets fans out west from Panjim's principal landmark, **Church Square**. Farther north, the main thoroughfare, **Avenida Dom Joao Castro**, sweeps past the GPO and **Secretariat** building, before bending west along the waterfront.

Church Square

The leafy rectangular park opposite the India Government tourist office, known as **Church Square** or the **Municipal Garden**, forms the heart of Panjim. Presiding over its east side is the town's most distinctive and photogenic landmark, the toothpaste-white Baroque facade of the **Church of Our Lady of the Immaculate Conception**. Flanked by rows of slender palm trees, at the head of a criss-crossing laterite walkway, the church was built in 1541 for the benefit of sailors arriving here from Lisbon. The weary mariners would stagger up from the quay to give thanks for their safe passage before proceeding to the capital at Old Goa – the original home of the enormous bell that hangs from the church's central gable.

The Secretariat

The road that runs north from the church brings you out at the riverside near Panjim's oldest surviving building. With its sloping tiled roofs, carved-stone coats of arms and wooden verandahs, the stalwart **Secretariat** looks typically colonial. Yet it was originally the summer palace of Goa's sixteenth-century Muslim ruler, the Adil Shah. Later, the Portuguese converted it into a temporary rest house for the territory's governors (who used to overnight here en route to and from Europe) and then a residence for the viceroy. Today, it accommodates the Goan State Legislature, which explains the presence of so many shiny chauffeur-driven Ambassador cars outside and the armed guards at the door.

A hundred metres east, a peculiar statue of a man holding his hands over the body of an entranced, reclining woman shows **Abbé Farin** (1755–1819), a Goan priest who emigrated to France to become one of the world's first professional hypnotists.

Fontainhas and Sao Tomé

Panjim's oldest and most interesting district, **Fontainhas**, lies immediately west of Pato, overlooking the banks of the oily green Ourem Creek. From the footbridge between the bus stand and town centre, a dozen or so blocks of Neoclassical houses rise in a tangle of terracotta rooftops up the sides of **Altinho Hill**. At siesta time, Vespas stand idle on deserted street corners, while women in Western clothes exchange pleasantries with their neighbours from open windows and leafy verandahs. Many buildings have retained their traditional coat of ochre, pale yellow, green or blue – a legacy of the Portuguese insistence that every Goan building (except churches, which had to be white) should be colour-washed after the monsoons.

At the southern end of the neighbourhood, the pristine whitewashed **Chapel of St Sebastian** is one of many Goan churches to remain faithful to the old colonial decree. It stands at the end of a small square where Fontainhas' Portuguese-speaking locals hold a lively annual street *festa* to celebrate their patron saint's day in mid-November. The eerily lifelike crucifix inside the chapel, brought here in 1812, formerly hung in the Palace of the Inquisition in Old Goa. Unusually, Christ's eyes are open – allegedly to inspire fear in those being interrogated by the Inquisitors.

Sao Tomé ward is the other old quarter, lying north of Fontainhas on the far side of Emilio Gracia Rd. This is the area to head for if you fancy a bar crawl: the narrow streets are dotted with dozens of hole-in-the-wall taverns, serving cheap, stiff measures of rocket-fuel *feni* under strip lights and the watchful gaze of colourful Madonnas. You'll feel less conspicuous, however, in the neighbourhood's best known hostelry, the *Hotel Venite* (see p.133).

The State Archeological Museum

The most notewothy feature of Panjim's **State Archeological Museum** (Mon–Fri 9.30am–1.15pm & 2–5.30pm) is its imposing size, which stands in glaringly inverse proportion to the scale of the collection inside. In their bid to erect a structure befitting a state captial, Goa's status-obsessed bureaucrats ignored the fact that there was precious little to put in it. The only rarities to be found amid the lame array of temple sculp-

GOAN FOOD AND DRINK

Goa has few of the dietary restrictions or taboos that apply in other regions of India, both Hindu and Muslim. Here the idea of vegetarianism is probably more equated with poverty than purity, and drinking alcohol is not the shameful activity it is elsewhere. The Goan palate relishes meat, especially pork, and all kinds of fresh seafood.

Not unnaturally, after 450 years of colonization, Goan cooking has absorbed a strong **Portuguese influence**. Palm vinegar (unknown elsewhere in India), copious amounts of coconut, garlic, tangy tamarind and fierce local chillies all play their part. Goa is the home of the famous *vindaloo* (from the Portuguese *vinho d'alho*, literally "garlic wine"), originally an extra-hot and sour pork curry, but now made with a variety of meat and fish. Other **pork** specialties include *chouriço* (red sausages), *sarpotel* (a hot curry made from pickled pig's liver and heart), *leitao*, (suckling pig), and *balchao* (pork in a rich brown sauce). Delicious alternatives include vinegar **chicken**, spicy chicken or **mutton** *xacutti*, made with a sauce of lemon juice, peanuts, coconut, chillies and spices. The choice of **seafood**, often cooked in fragrant *masalas*, is excellent – clams, mussels, crab, lobster, giant prawns – while **fish**, depending on the type, is either cooked in wet curries, grilled or baked in tandoor clay ovens. Try *apa de camarão*, a spicy prawn pie with a rice and semolina crust. *Sannam*, like the South Indian *iddli*, is a steamed cake of fermented rice flour, but here fermented with palm *toddy*. Sweet tooths will adore *bebinca*, a rich, delicious solid egg custard with coconut.

As for **drinks**, locally produced wine, spirits and beer are **cheaper** than anywhere in the country, thanks to lower rates of tax. The most famous and widespread beer. is, of course, Kingfisher, which tastes less of glycerine perservative than it does elsewhere in India. Goan port, a sweeter, inferior version of its Portuguese namesake, is ubiquitous, served chilled in large wine glasses with a slice of lemon. Local whiskies, brandies, rums, gins and vodkas come in a variety of brand names for less than Rs20 a shot, but at half the price, local speciality **feni**, made from distilled cashew or from the sap of coconut palms, offers strong competition. Cashew *feni* is usually drunk after the first distillation, but you can also find it double-distilled, flavoured with ginger, cumin or sarsparilla to produce a smooth liqueur.

ture, hero stones and dowdy colonial-era artefacts are a couple of beautiful Jain bronzes rescued by Customs and Excise officials from smugglers and, on the ground floor, photos of the pre-historic rock carvings at Usgalimal.

Accommodation

The town centre has plenty of **accommodation**, and finding a place to stay is only a problem during Dusshera (Sept/Oct), the festival of St Francis in early December and during peak season (mid-Dec to mid-Jan), when tariffs double. At other times, hotels try to fill rooms by offering substantial discounts. The best inexpensive options are in Fontainhas, down by Ourem Creek and in the backstreets behind the esplanade. Standards are generally good, and even the cheapest rooms should have a window, a fan, running water and clean sheets. Most other hotels are bland places in the more modern, west end of town.

Note that **checkout times** here vary wildly. Find out what yours is as soon as you arrive, or your hard-earned lie-in could end up costing you an extra day's rent.

The price codes quoted below refer to peak season.

Inexpensive

Alfonso, St Sebastian Chapel Square, Fontainhas (☎0832/222359). Recently refurbished colonial-era building in a picturesque backstreet. Spotlessly clean, cool en-suite rooms, friendly owners and a rooftop terrace with views. Single occupancy rates available. ⑤.

Four Pillars, Rua de Ourem (☎0832/225240 or 229463). A bit of a trek away from the centre, and an uninspiring location, but the rooms are very good value. ④.

GTDC Pato Tourist Home, around the corner from the bus stand, overlooking Ourem Creek, Pato (☎0832/225715 or 227972). Run-of-the-mill dorm beds and inexpensive doubles – fine for a night if you can't face a room hunt. ①–④.

Mandovi Pearl, PO Box #329, behind GTDC *Tourist Hostel* (☎0832/223928). Eccentric lodge for salesmen and budget travellers, close to the riverfront, run by a garrulous landlord. The rooms are roughish but good value. ③–⑤.

Orav's, 31 Janeiro Rd (☎0832/46128). Bland modern building in Sao Tomé, with good-sized, comfortable rooms and small balconies. ④.

Park Lane Lodge, near the chapel of St Sebastian (☎0832/220238). Spotless, characterful but cramped guesthouse in an old colonial-style family home. Pot plants, stuffed parrots, safe-deposit facilities and a relaxed, friendly atmosphere. Good off-season discounts, too. ④.

Moderate to expensive

Aroma, Cunha Rivara Rd (☎0832/43519, fax 224330). Very central and long-established hotel with a popular *tandoori* restaurant. Some rooms look onto Church Square. ⑤.

Caritas Holiday Home, south of the Caculo Island intersection, St Inez (☎0832/220496). Well-maintained place west of the town centre with clean rooms but little character. ④.

Fidalgo, 18 June Rd (☎0832/22629, fax 2250612). Large, upscale hotel with all mod cons, including central a/c, exchange facilities, a health club, a shopping arcade and a travel agency. ⑦–⑧.

GTDC Tourist Hostel, Avda Dom Joao Castro (☎0832/227103 or 223396). Spacious rooms in popular government-run hotel overlooking a busy thoroughfare and the river. Shops, a hair salon and tourist information in the lobby. Some a/c. ⑤–⑥.

Mandovi, Dr D Bandodkar Rd (☎0832/226270, fax 225451). Grand waterside hotel with river views from the front rooms, central a/c, shops, an in-house travel agent and a pool. The best deal in this category. ⑦–⑨.

Nova Goa, Dr Atmaram Borkar Rd (☎0832/46231, fax 224958). Panjim's newest top hotel, in the heart of the shopping area. The usual comforts, plus bathtubs and a pool. ⑨.

Palacio de Goa, Gama Pinto Rd (☎0832/44289). Kitsch, five-storey Neoclassical facade and pleasant but plain rooms with balconies, and a pure veg restaurant. ⑥.

Panjim Inn, E-212, 31 Janeiro Rd, Fontainhas (☎0832/226523, fax 228136). Grand old colonial-era town house, managed as an upmarket but homely hotel, with period furniture, sepia family photos, individual balconies and a verandah where meals and drinks are served to guests. An equally beautiful recently renovated Hindu house across the road, offers more of the same with the added bonus of a leafy courtyard. Easily the best place in its class. ⑤–⑥.

Eating and drinking

Panjim is packed with good **places to eat**. Most are connected to a hotel (the *Hotel Venite* restaurant is the most popular with foreigners), but there are also plenty of smaller family-run establishments in the backstreets of Sao Tomé, where a plate of fish curry and rice and a cold Kingfisher will set you back less than Rs50; vegetarians will do better at the numerous South Indian-style caféterias. Two of these, the *Satkar* and the *Vihar*, open at around 7am for blow-out **breakfasts** – great if you have just staggered into town after a night on the bus. Beer, *feni* and other spirits are available in all but the purest "pure veg" places, especially in the hole-in-the-wall taverns around Sao Tomé.

A Pasteleria, Dr Dada Vaidya Rd. Panjim's best bakery does dozens of Western-style cakes, biscuits and sticky buns, including brownies and fruit loaves. Takeaway only.

Annapurna, Ormuz Rd. Traditional inexpensive South Indian *thalis* and snacks dished up by cotton-clad waiters in a large, clean, cool dining hall.

Delhi Durbar, behind the *Hotel Mandovi*. A provincial branch of the famous Mumbai restaurant, and the best place in Panjim to sample traditional Mughlai cuisine: mainly meat steeped in rich, spicy sauces. Patronized by an expense account crowd, but you can eat well here for under Rs200.

Goenchin, off Dr Dada Vaidhya Rd. Glacial a/c and dim lighting, but unquestionably the best and most authentic Chinese food to be found in Goa. Count on Rs200-250 per head.

Kamat's, near the India Government tourist office, Municipal Gardens, 31 Janeiro Rd. Busy Indian fast-food caféteria with formica booths and barefoot waiters. Their filling South Indian *thalis* (Rs35) consist of six dishes (including some delicious coconut-flavoured local specialties), or you can order the usual range of *iddlis*, *dosas* and *vada*.

Megson's, next to *Moti Mahal*, 18 June Rd. The state's top deli, with a great selection of traditional Goan foods: spicy sausages, prepared meats, tangy cheese from the Nilgiris, olive oil and the best *bebinca* you can buy (ask for *Linda* brand).

Nandan, ground floor of *Rajdhani Hotel*, Dr Atmaram Borkar Rd. The classiest *thali* joint in town, with comfortable upholstered furniture and a/c. They offer a choice of Gujarati, Punjabi, South Indian or Chinese meals – all pure vegetarian.

Sher-e-Punjab, 18 June Rd, near the *Satkar*. North Indian food served up in crowded city-centre restaurant. Their specialty – butter chicken – is delicious, and there's a reasonable veg menu. The same outfit also has a more upmarket branch in the *Hotel Aroma* on Cunha Rivara Rd.

Venite, 31 Janeiro Rd. Deservedly popular hotel restaurant, serving great, fresh seafood, including affordable lobster and crab, along with Western dishes, desserts, *feni* and cold beers. Wooden floors, balcony seats, candles and an eclectic cassette collection add to the ambience. Good breakfasts, too. Closed Sun.

Vihar, 31 Janeiro Rd, around the corner from *Venite*. Arguably the best South Indian snack café in Panjim, and more conveniently situated than *Kamat's*. Try their tasty *rawa masala dosas*.

Listings

Airline offices in Panjim include: Air India, *Hotel Fidalgo*, 18 June Rd (☎0832/224081); British Airways, 2 Excelsior Chambers, MG Rd (☎0832/& fax 228681); Indian Airlines, Dempo Building, Dr D Bandodkar Rd (☎0832/223831); Jet Airways, Rizvi Chambers, office #102, Caetano Albuquerque Rd (☎0832/221476); KLM (also PIA), 18 June Rd, near Titan showroom (☎0832/226678); Sahara, *Hotel Fidalgo* Room 132, 18 June Rd (☎0832/230634).

Banks and exchange The most efficient place to change money in Panjim is Thomas Cook, near the Indian Airlines office, at 8 Alcon Chambers, Devanad Bandodkar Rd (☎0832/221312, fax 221313). For Visa withdrawals, you have to go to the Bank of Baroda on Azad Maidan, or the Andhra Bank, opposite the Ashok Samrat cinema. The Corporation Bank on Church Square, around the corner from the GTDC tourist office, also has a foreign exchange section that's much faster than the State Bank of India opposite the *Hotel Mandovi*. American Express are at Menezes Air Travel, Rua de Ourem, near Pato Bridge (☎ & fax 0832/225081).

Books The bookshops in the *Hotel Fidalgo* and the *Hotel Mandovi* stock a range of English-language fiction in paperback, and special-interest titles and coffee-table tomes on Goa.

Consulate The British High Commission of Mumbai has a consular assistant who can be useful in emergencies. Agnelo Godinho's office/home is at 189 Avda Dom Joao Castro, around the corner from the GPO (☎0832/432829).

Hospital Panjim's largest hospital, the Goa Medical College (aka GMC), in the west of town at the far end of Avda Dom Joao Castro, is grim and overstretched; if you're able to travel, head for the more modern and better-equipped Salgaonkar Hospital, 12km south on the Vasco road.

Music and dance Regular recitals of classical Indian music and dance are held at Panjim's school for the performing arts, the Kala Academy in Campal, at the far west end of town on Devanand Bandodkar Rd. For details of forthcoming events, consult the boards in front of the auditorium or the listings page of local newspapers.

Pharmacies Panjim's best pharmacy is Hindu Pharma (☎0832/43176), next to the *Hotel Aroma* on Church Square, which stocks ayurvedic, homeopathic and allopathic medicines.

Police The Police Headquarters is on Malacca Rd, central Panjim.

Post Panjim's reliable poste restante counter (Mon–Sat 9.30am–1pm & 2–5.30pm) is in the GPO, 200m west of Pato Bridge. To get your stamps franked, walk around the back of the building and ask at the office behind the second door on the right. For parcel stitching, ask at Deepak Stores on the corner of the next block north.

Travel agents Reliable Panjim travel agents include: AERO Mundial, *Hotel Mandovi*, Dr D Bandodkar Rd (☎0832/223773); Menezes Air Travel, Rua de Ourem (☎ & fax 0832/222214); TPH Travel, Padmavati Towers, 18 June Rd (☎0832/235365); and Rauraje Deshprabhu, Cunha Rivara Rd (☎0832/221840). For details of catamaran tickets, see box on p.176.

Old Goa (Velha Goa)

At one time a byword for splendour, with a population of several hundred thousand, Goa's erstwhile capital, **OLD GOA (Velha Goa)**, was virtually abandoned following malaria and cholera epidemics that plagued the city from the seventeenth century onwards. Today you need considerable imagination to picture the once-great capital as it used to be. The maze of twisting streets, piazzas and ochre-washed villas has gone, and all that remains are a score of extraordinarily grandiose churches and convents. Granted World Heritage Status by UNESCO, Old Goa today attracts bus-loads of foreign tourists from the coast and Christian pilgrims from around India, in roughly equal numbers. While the former come to admire the gigantic facades and gilt altars of the beautifully preserved churches, the main attraction for the latter is the tomb of **St Francis Xavier**, the renowned sixteenth-century missionary, whose remains are enshrined in the **Basilica of Bom Jesus**.

If you are staying on the coast and contemplating a day-trip inland, this is the most obvious and accessible option. Just thirty minutes by road from the state capital, Old Goa is served by buses every fifteen minutes from Panjim's Kadamba bus stand; alternatively, hop into an auto-rickshaw, or rent a taxi. GTDC also slot the site's highlights into several of their guided coach **tours**; further details and tickets are available at any GTDC hotel or tourist office.

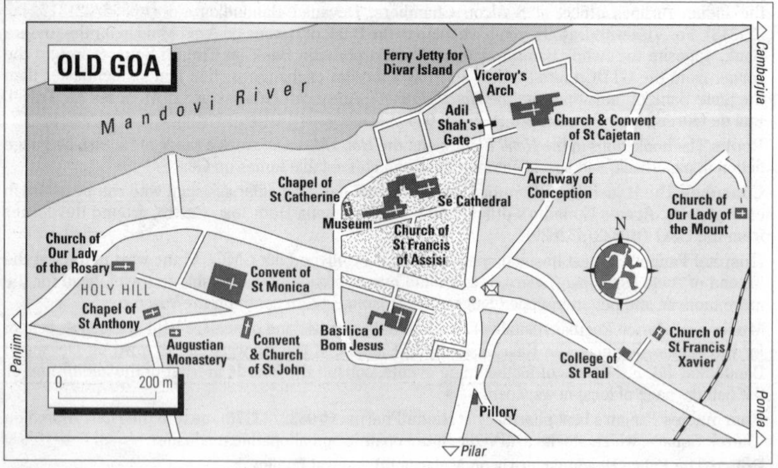

Arch of the Viceroys and the Church of St Cajetan

On arriving at the river landing stage to the north, seventeenth-century visitors passed through the **Arch of the Viceroys** (1597), constructed to commemorate Vasco da Gama's arrival in India and built from the same porous red laterite as virtually all Old Goa's buildings. Above it, a bible-toting figure rests his foot on the cringing figure of a "native", while its granite facade, facing the river, holds a statue of da Gama himself. It is hard to imagine today that these overgrown fields and simple streets with a few cool drinks stands were once the focus of a lively market, with silk and gem merchants, horse dealers and carpet weavers. The one surviving monument, known as **'Adil Shah's Gate**, predates the Portuguese and possibly even the Muslim period. Hindu in style, it consists simply of a lintel supported by two columns in black basalt, to which are attached the remains of perforated screens. You can find it by turning left at the crossroads immediately above the Arch of the Viceroys.

A short way up the lane from the Gate, the distinctive domed **Church of St Cajetan** (1651) was modelled on St Peter's in Rome by monks from the Theatine order, who believed in Divine Providence; they never sought charity, but simply expected it. While it does boast a Corinthian exterior, you can also spot certain non-European elements in the decoration, such as the cashew-nut designs in the carving of the pulpit. Hidden beneath the church is a crypt where the embalmed bodies of Portuguese governors were once kept in lead coffins before they were shipped back to Lisbon. Forgotten for over thirty years, the last batch (of three) was only removed in 1992 on the eve of the state visit to Goa of Portuguese President Mario Soares.

The Sé (St Catherine's Cathedral)

The Portuguese viceroy Redondo (1561–64) commissioned the **Sé**, or **St Catherine's Cathedral**, southwest of St Cajetan's, to be "a grandiose church worthy of the wealth, power and fame of the Portuguese who dominated the seas from the Atlantic to the Pacific". Today it stands larger than any church in Portugal, although it was beset by problems, not least a lack of funds and Portugal's temporary loss of independence to Spain. It took eighty years to build and was not consecrated until 1640.

On the Tuscan-style exterior, the one surviving tower houses the **Golden Bell**, cast in Cuncolim (south Goa) in the seventeenth century. During the Inquisition, its tolling announced the start of the gruesome *auto da fés* that were held in the square outside, when suspected heretics were subjected to public torture and burned at the stake. Reconstruction of parts of the roof, which once had overhanging eaves, has damaged some paintings inside. The scale and detail of the Corinthian-style interior is overwhelming; huge pillars divide the central nave from the side aisles, and no fewer than fifteen altars are arranged around the walls, dedicated among others to Our Ladies of Hope, Anguish and Three Needs. An altar to St Anne treasures the relics of the **Blessed Martyrs of Cuncolim**, whose failed mission to convert the Moghul emperor Akbar culminated in their murder by Muslims, while a chapel behind a highly detailed screen holds the **Miraculous Cross**, which stood in a Goan village until a vision of Christ appeared on it. Said to heal the sick, it is kept in a box; a small opening on the side allows devotees to touch it. The staggeringly ornate, gilded main **altar** comprises nine carved frames and a splendid crucifix. Panels depict episodes from the legend of St Catherine of Alexandria (believed to have been martyred in the fourth century), including an interchange of ideas with the pagan Roman emperor Maxentius, who wished to marry her, and her subsequent flogging and martyrdom.

The Church of St Francis of Assisi and Archeological Museum

Southwest of the cathedral is the ruined **Palace of the Inquisition**, in operation up until 1774, while to the west stands the **Convent of St Francis of Assisi**, built by Franciscan monks in 1517 and restored in the mid-eighteenth century. Today, the core of its **Archeological Museum** (daily except Fri 10am–5pm) is a gallery of portraits of Portuguese viceroys, painted by local artists under Italian supervision. Other exhibits include coins, domestic Christian wooden sculpture and, downstairs in the cloister, pre-Portuguese Hindu sculpture. Next door, the **Church of St Francis** (1521), features fine decorative frescoes and paintings on wood showing the life of St Francis of Assisi.

Basilica of Bom Jesus

Close to the convent of St Francis, the 1605 church of **Bom Jesus**, "Good" or "Menino Jesus" (Mon–Sat 9am–6.30pm, Sun 10am–6.30pm), is known principally for the **tomb of St Francis Xavier**. In 1946, it became the first church in India to be elevated to the status of Minor Basilica. On the west, the three-storey Renaissance facade encompasses Corinthian, Doric, Ionic and Composite styles.

The interior is entered beneath the choir, supported by columns. On the northern wall, in the centre of the nave, is a cenotaph in gilded bronze to **Dom Jeronimo Mascaranhas**, Captain of Cochin and benefactor of the church. The main altar, extravagantly decorated in gold, depicts the infant Jesus under the protection of St Ignatius Loyola; to each side are subsidiary altars to Our Lady of Hope and St Michael. In the southern transept, lavishly decorated with twisted gilded columns and floriate carvings, stands the **Chapel and Tomb of St Francis Xavier**. Constructed of marble and jasper in 1696, it was the gift of the Medici Grand Duke of Tuscany, Cosimo III. An ornate domed reliquary in silver contains his remains and the middle tier has panels detailing the saint's life; on his feast day, December 3, the saint's finger is displayed to devotees.

Holy Hill

A number of other important religious buildings, some in ruins, stand opposite Bom Jesus on **Holy Hill**. The **Convent of St Monica**, constructed in 1627, destroyed by fire in 1636 and rebuilt the following year, was the only Goan convent at the time and the largest in Asia. It housed around a hundred nuns, the Daughters of St Monica, and also offered accommodation to women whose husbands were called away to other parts of the empire. The **church** adjoins the convent on the south. As they had to remain away from the public gaze, the nuns attended mass in the choir loft and looked down upon the congregation.

Inside, a **Miraculous Cross** rises above the figure of St Monica at the altar. In 1636, it was reported that the figure of Christ had opened his eyes, motioned as if to speak and blood had flowed from the wounds made by his crown of thorns. The last Daughter of St Monica died in 1885, and since 1964 the convent has been occupied by the Mater Dei Institute for nuns.

Nearby, the **Convent of St John of God**, built in 1685 by the Order of Hospitallers of St John of God to tend to the sick, was rebuilt in 1953. At the top of the hill, the **Chapel of Our Lady of the Rosary**, built in 1526 in the Manueline style (after the Portuguese king Manuel I, 1495–1521), features Ionic plasterwork with a double-storey portico, cylindrical turrets and a tower that commands fine views across the river.

Ponda and around

Characterless, chaotic **PONDA**, 28km southeast of Panjim and 17km northeast of Margao, is Ponda *taluka*'s administrative headquarters and main market town, but

ST FRANCIS XAVIER

Francis Xavier, the "Apostle of the Indies", was born in 1506 in the old kingdom of Navarre, now part of Spain. After taking a master's degree in philosophy and theology at the University of Paris, where he studied for the priesthood until 1535, he was ordained two years later in Venice. He was then recruited by (St) **Ignatius Loyola** (1491–1556) along with five other priests into the new "Society of Jesus", which later became known as the **Jesuits**.

When the Portuguese king, Dom Joao III (1521–57), received reports of corruption and dissolute behaviour among the Portuguese in Goa, he asked Ignatius Loyola to despatch a priest who could influence the moral climate for the better. In 1541 Xavier was sent to work in the diocese of Goa, constituted seven years before and comprising all regions east of the Cape of Good Hope. Arriving after a year-long journey, he embarked on a busy programme throughout southern India. Despite frequent obstruction from Portuguese officials, he founded numerous churches, and is credited with converting 30,000 people and performing such miracles as raising the dead and curing the sick with a touch of his beads. Subsequently he took his mission farther afield to Sri Lanka, Malacca (Malaysia), China and Japan, where he was less successful.

When Xavier left Goa for the last time, it was with the ambition of evangelizing in China; however, he contracted dysentery aboard ship and died on the island of San Chuan (Sancian), off the Chinese coast, where he was buried. On hearing of his death, a group of Christians from Malacca exhumed his body – which, although the grave had been filled with lime, they found to be in a perfect state of preservation. Reburied in Malacca, it was later removed and taken to Old Goa, where it has remained ever since, enshrined in the Basilica of Bom Jesus.

However, St Francis Xavier's incorruptible corpse has never rested entirely in peace. Chunks of it have been removed over the years by relic hunters and curious clerics: in 1614, the right arm was dispatched to the pope in Rome (where it allegedly wrote its name on paper), a hand was sent to Japan and parts of the intestines to Southeast Asia. One Portuguese woman, Dona Isabel de Caron, even bit off the little toe of the cadaver in 1534; apparently, so much blood spurted into her mouth, it left a trail to her house and she was discovered.

Every ten years, the saint's body is carried in a three-hour ceremony from the Basilica of Bom Jesus to the Sé Cathedral, where visitors file past, touch and photograph it. During the 1995 "**Exposition**", which was rumoured to be the last one, an estimated two million pilgrims flocked for *darshan* or ritual viewing of the corpse, these days a shrivelled and somewhat unsavoury spectacle.

not somewhere you're likely to want to stay. Straddling the busy Panjim–Bangalore highway (NH4), the town's ugly concrete centre is permanently choked with traffic and guaranteed to make you wonder why you ever left the coast. Of the few visitors who stop here, most do so en route to the nearby **Hindu temples** or **wildlife reserves** farther east, or to take a look at Goa's best-preserved sixteenth-century Muslim monument, the **Safa Masjid**, 2km west on the Panjim road. Built in 1560 by the Bijapuri ruler Ibrahim 'Adil Shah, this small mosque, with its whitewashed walls and pointed terracotta tile roof, is renowned less for its architecture than for being one of only two Islamic shrines in Goa to survive the excesses of the Portuguese Inquisition.

Practicalities

Ponda is served by regular **buses** from Panjim (via Old Goa) and Margao, and lies on the main route east to Karnataka. The Kadamba bus stand is on the main square, next to the auto-rickshaw rank.

There are plenty of **places to stay** if you get stuck here. Best of the budget lodges is the *Padmavi* (no phone; ①) at the top of the square. For more comfort, try the *President* (☎08343/312287; ③–⑤), a short rickshaw ride up the Belgaum road, which has large, clean en-suite rooms (some with a/c). More upmarket is the three-star *Atash* (☎08343/313224; ⑥), 4km northwest on the NH4 at Farmagudi, whose comfortable a/c rooms have satellite TV, and there's also a restaurant and parking facilities. However, the best mid-range deal within striking distance of Ponda has to be GTDC's *Tourist Cottages* (☎08343/312922 or 312037; ②–④), also at Farmagudi (look for the signpost on the roundabout below the Shivaji memorial), stacked up the side of a steep hill overlooking the highway, with spacious and clean en-suite chalets, and a small terrace restaurant serving a standard menu of spicy mixed cuisine.

Temples around Ponda

Scattered among the lush valleys and forests **around Ponda** are a dozen or so **Hindu temples** founded during the seventeenth and eighteenth centuries, when this hilly region was a Christian-free haven for Hindus fleeing persecution by the Portuguese. Although the temples themselves are fairly modern by Indian standards, their deities are ancient and held in high esteem by both local people and thousands of pilgrims from Maharashtra and Karnataka.

The temples are concentrated in two main clusters: the first to the north of Ponda, on the busy NH4, and the second deep in the countryside, around 5km west of the town. Most people only manage the **Shri Manguesh** and **Shri Mahalsa**, between the villages of **Mardol** and **Priol**. Among the most interesting temples in the state, they lie just a stone's throw from the main highway and are passed by regular **buses** between Panjim and Margao via Ponda. The others are farther off the beaten track, although they are not hard to find on motorbikes: locals will wave you in the right direction if you get lost.

MARDOL AND PRIOL

Although the **Sri Manguesh** temple originally stood in a secret location in Cortalim, and was moved to its present site between **MARDOL** and **PRIOL** during the sixteenth century, the structure visitors see today dates from the 1700s. A gateway at the roadside leads to a paved path and courtyard that gives onto a water tank, overlooked by the white temple building, raised on a plinth. Also in the courtyard is a seven-storey *deepmal*, a tower for oil lamps. Inside, the floor is paved with marble, and bands of decorative tiles emblazon the white walls. Flanked by large *dvarpala* guardians, embossed silver doorways with floriate designs lead to the sanctum, which houses a *shivalingam*.

Two kilometres south, the **Mahalsa Marayani** temple was also transferred from its original site, in this case Salcete *taluka* farther south, in the seventeenth century. Here, the *deepmal* is exceptionally tall, with twenty-one tiers rising from a figure of Kurma, the tortoise incarnation of Vishnu. Original features include a marble-floored wooden *mandapa* (assembly hall) with carved pillars, ceiling panels of parakeets and, in the eaves, sculptures of the incarnations of Vishnu.

Dudhsagar waterfalls

Measuring a mighty 600m from head to foot, the famous **waterfalls** at **DUDHSAGAR**, on the Goa–Karnataka border, are some of the highest in India and a spectacular enough sight to entice a steady stream of visitors from the coast into the rugged Western Ghats. After pouring across the Deccan plateau, the headwaters of the Mandovi River form a foaming torrent that fans into three streams, then cascades down a near-vertical cliff-face into a deep green pool. The Konkani name for the falls, which literally translated means "sea of milk", derives from clouds of foam kicked up at the bottom when the water levels are at their highest. Overlooking a steep, crescent-shaped head of a valley carpeted with pristine tropical forest, Dudhsagar is set amid breathtaking **scenery** that is most easily accessed by jeep; the old Vasco–Castle Rock railway actually passes over the falls on an old stone viaduct, but has been closed for the past three years while track conversion work is carried out.

Practicalities

The best time to visit Dudhsagar is immediately after the monsoons, from October until mid-December, although the falls flow well into April. Until the new broad-gauge railway line is finished, the only way to get there is by four-wheel-drive **Jeep** from the railway junction village of **Colem** (reached by taxi from the north coast resorts for around Rs1000; or by train from Vasco). The cost of the onward thirty- to forty-minute Jeep trip from Colem to the falls, which takes you across rough forest tracks and two or three river fords, is around Rs250–350 per person; the drive ends with an enjoyable fifteen-minute hike, for which you'll need a sturdy pair of shoes. Finding a Jeep-*wallah* is easy; just turn up in Colem and look for the "Controller of Jeeps" near the station. However, if you're travelling alone or in a couple, you may have to wait around until the vehicle fills up, or else fork out Rs2000 or so to cover the cost of hiring the whole Jeep yourself. Note that it can be difficult to arrange transport of any kind from Colem crossroads, where regular taxis are in short supply.

North Goa

Beyond the mouth of the Mandovi estuary, the Goan coast sweeps **north** in a near-continuous string of beaches, broken only by the odd salt-water creek, rocky headland and three tidal rivers – two of which, the Chapora and Arondem, have to be crossed by ferry. The most developed resorts, **Calangute** and **Baga**, occupy the middle and northern part of the seven-kilometre strip of pearl-white sand that stretches from the Aguada peninsula in the south to a sheer laterite promontory in the north. Formerly, the infamous colonies of Goa hippies gathered in these two villages during their annual winter migration; now both heave during high season with British charter tourists, bus-loads of trippers from out-of-state and itinerant vendors hawking fruit and trinkets on the beach. The "scene", meanwhile, has shifted northwards, to the beaches around **Anjuna**, **Vagator** and **Chapora**, where most Christmas–New Year parties take place.

Most of the tourist traffic **arriving in north Goa** from Bombay is syphoned off towards the coast through **Mapusa**, the area's main market town. For short hops between towns and resorts, **motorcycle taxis** are the quickest and most convenient way to get around, but **buses** also run to all the villages along the coast, via the **ferry crossings** at Siolim, 7km north of Anjuna, and Querim (for Terekol).

Mapusa

The ramshackle market town of **MAPUSA** (pronounced *Mapsa*) is the district headquarters of Bardez *taluka*. If you arrive by road from Mumbai and plan to stay in one

HAWKERS

Hawkers are a feature of **beach life** in all but the most remote of Goa's resorts these days, and you'll be pestered by a steady stream of them in the course of any day. The large majority are kids from Karnataka, flogging cheap cotton clothes, coconuts and cold drinks, but you'll also come across Kashmiris selling papier-mâché boxes, Rajasthani girls with sacks of dodgy silver jewellery, Tamil stone carvers, buskers, painted bulls led around by their turbaned, oboe-blowing owners and, most distinctive of all, **Lamani tribal women** from the Gadag-Hubli-Hampi area, with their coin necklaces, cowrie-shell anklets and rainbow-coloured mirrorwork.

Initially, this parade can be a novel distraction. The hawkers are usually polite and pleasant to chat with; and it is, after all, convenient to have a slice of melon or fresh pineapple cut for you just when you fancy one. Eventually, though, the constant attention will start to wear your patience, and you'll find yourself experimenting with different ways to shake off the hawkers, who, given half the chance, will congregate in tight huddles around you. An "I've-been-here-a-while-already" tan helps, as does feigning sleep or burying yourself in a book. Failing that, a stern shake of the head or wave of the hand should send the vendor on his or her way. Occasionally, however, one comes along who won't take no for an answer, in which case, you'll either have to buy something (which will inevitably attract every other hawker on the beach) or else start shouting – neither of which is likely to bring you much peace and quiet the following day.

The best ploy if you're going to spend much time on the same beach is to hook up with one or two hawkers and always do "beesness" with them; that way, the others will more often than not leave you alone.

of the north Goan resorts, you can jump off the bus here and pick up a local service straight to the coast, rather than continue on to Panjim, 13km south.

A dusty collection of dilapidated modern buildings scattered around the west-facing slope of a low hill, Mapusa is of little more than passing interest in itself, although on Fridays it hosts a lively **market** (hence the town's name, which derives from the Konkani words for "measure", *map*, and "fill up", *sa*). Calangute and Anjuna may be better stocked with souvenirs, but this bazaar is more authentic. Visitors who have flown straight to Goa, and have yet to experience the rest of India, wander in on Friday mornings to enjoy the pungent aromas of fish, incense, spices and exotic fruit stacked in colourful heaps on the sidewalks. Local specialties include strings of spicy Goan sausages (*chouriço*), bottles of fermented palm sap (*toddy*) and large green plantains. You'll also encounter sundry freak shows, from run-of-the-mill snake charmers and kids dressed up as *sadhus* to wide-eyed flagellants, blood oozing out of slashes on their backs.

Practicalities

Other than to shop, you may want to visit Mapusa to arrange **onward transport**. All buses between Goa and Maharashtra pass through here, so you don't need to travel to Panjim to book a ticket to Mumbai, Pune, Bangalore or Mangalore. Reservations for private buses can be made at the numerous agents' stalls at the bottom of the square, next to where the buses pull in; the **Kadamba terminal** – the departure point for both long-distance state buses, and local services to Calangute, Baga, Anjuna, Vagator, Chapora and Arambol – is five minutes' walk down the main road, on the southwest edge of town. You can also get to the coast from Mapusa on one of the **motorcycle taxis** that wait at the bottom of the square. Rides to Calangute and Anjuna take twenty minutes and cost Rs30–40. **Taxis** charge considerably more, but you can split the fare with up to five people.

As soon as you step off the bus, you'll be pestered by touts trying to get you to rent a **motorbike**. They'll tell you that rates here are lower than on the coast – they're not. Another reason to wait a while is that Mapusa is effectively a "no-go zone" for rented motorbikes, especially on Friday, when the police set up road-blocks on the outskirts of town to collar tourists without international licences (see p.125).

ACCOMMODATION AND EATING

Nearly all long-distance buses pull into Mapusa in the morning, leaving plenty of time to find **accommodation** in the coastal resorts nearby. If you have to spend the night here, though, there are plenty of places within easy walking distance of the Kadamba bus stand. The best budget deal is GTDC's *Tourist Hotel* (☎0832/262794; ③–⑤), on the roundabout below the square, which has spacious and clean rooms, a Goa **tourist information** counter and a small Damania Shipping office. The *Vilena*, across town near the Muncipality Building on Mapsa Rd (☎0832/263115: ③–⑤), also offers good-value economy rooms (with or without attached bathrooms), in addition to more comfortable a/c ones, and has a dimly lit bar and small rooftop restaurant. On the north side of the main square, the *Hotel Satyaheera* (☎0832/262849; ⑤–⑥), is the town's top hotel, with mostly a/c rooms.

Mapusa's most relaxing **restaurant** is the *Ruchira*, on the top floor of the *Hotel Satyaheera*, which serves a standard Indian menu with Goan and Chinese alternatives and cold beer. The *Hotel Vrindavan*, on the east side of the main square, dishes up Mapusa's best inexpensive South Indian snacks, along with an impressive range of ice-creams and shakes. Cheaper but less salubrious Goan *thali* joints can be found in the streets east of the main square. Excellent fresh fruit and juice bars are dotted around the market.

Candolim and Fort Aguada

Four or five years ago, **CANDOLIM**, at the far southern end of Calangute beach, was a surprisingly sedate resort, appealing to an odd mixture of middle-class Bombayites, and burgundy-clad *sannyasins* taking a break from the Rajneesh ashram at Pune. Times, however, have changed. Now, large-scale package holiday complexes jostle for space behind the dunes, and the increasingly crowded beach has sprouted ranks of sun-beds. Worse still is the constant swoosh of speedboats, jet skis and huge inflatable banana-rafts through the surf: tourist Goa at its most gruesome. On the plus side, Candolim has plenty of pleasant places to stay, many of them tucked away down quiet sandy lanes and better value than comparable guesthouses in nearby Calangute, making this a good first stop if you've just arrived in Goa and are planning to head farther north after finding your feet.

Immediately south of Candolim, a long peninsula extends into the sea, bringing the seven-kilometre white sandy beach to an abrupt end. **FORT AGUADA**, which crowns the rocky flattened top of the headland, is the best-preserved Portuguese bastion in Goa. Built in 1612 to protect the northern shores of the Mandovi estuary from Dutch and Maharatha raiders, it is home to several natural springs, the first source of drinking water available to ships arriving in Goa after the long sea voyage from Lisbon. On the north side of the fort, a rampart of red-brown laterite juts into the bay to form a jetty between two small sandy coves. This picturesque spot, known as **Sinquerim Beach**, was among the first places in Goa to be singled out for upmarket tourism. Taj Group's *Fort Aguada* resorts, among the most expensive hotels in India, lords over the beach from the lower slopes of the steep-sided peninsula.

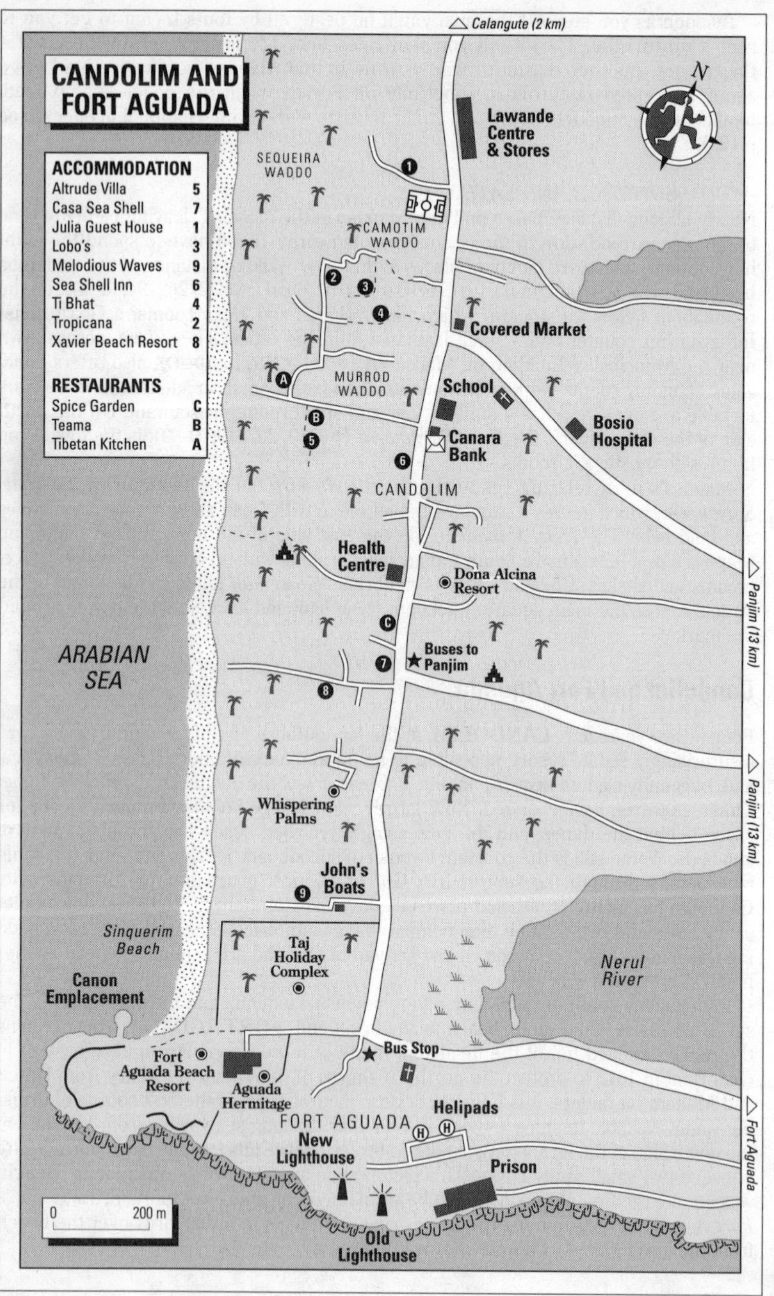
CANDOLIM AND FORT AGUADA
ACCOMMODATION
Altrude Villa 5
Casa Sea Shell 7
Julia Guest House 1
Lobo's 3
Melodious Waves 9
Sea Shell Inn 6
Ti Bhat 4
Tropicana 2
Xavier Beach Resort 8
RESTAURANTS
Spice Garden C
Teama B
Tibetan Kitchen A
Calangute (2 km)
N
SEQUEIRA WADDO
Lawande Centre & Stores
CAMOTIM WADDO
Covered Market
MURROD WADDO
School
Bosio Hospital
Canara Bank
CANDOLIM
Health Centre
Dona Alcina Resort
Panjim (13 km)
ARABIAN SEA
Buses to Panjim
Panjim (13 km)
Whispering Palms
John's Boats
Singuerim Beach
Taj Holiday Complex
Nerul River
Canon Emplacement
Fort Aguada Beach Resort
Aguada Hermitage
Bus Stop
Fort Aguada
Helipads
FORT AGUADA
New Lighthouse
Prison
0
200 m
Old Lighthouse

The ruins of the **fort** can be reached by road; head through the *Taj* village, and turn right when you see the sign. Nowadays, much of the site serves as a prison, and is therefore closed to visitors. It's worth a visit, though, if only for the superb views from the top of the hill where a four-storey Portuguese **lighthouse**, erected in 1864 and the oldest of its kind in Asia, looks down over the vast expanse of sea, sand and palm trees of Calangute beach on one side, and across the mouth of the Mandovi to Cabo Raj Bhavan and the tip of the Mormugao peninsula, on the other.

Practicalities

Buses to and from Panjim stop every twenty minutes or so at the stand opposite the *Casa Sea Shell*, in the middle of Candolim. A few also continue south to the the *Fort Aguada Beach Resort* terminus, from where services depart every thirty minutes for the capital via Nerul village. **Taxis** wait outside the major resort hotels and can be flagged down on the main road.

ACCOMMODATION

Candolim is charter-holiday land, so **accommodation** tends to be expensive for most of the season. That said, if bookings are down you can find some great bargains here. The best place to start looking is at the end of the lane that leads to the sea opposite the Canara Bank, at the north side of the village.

Altrude Villa, Murrod Vaddo (☎0832/277703). Airy rooms with attached tiled bathrooms and verandahs. The larger ones on the first floor have sea views. ④.

Casa Sea Shell, Fort Aguada Rd, near *Bom Successo* restaurant (☎0832/277879). A new building with its own pool, picturesquely situated beside a small chapel. The rooms are large, with spacious tiled bathrooms, and the staff and management welcoming and courteous. The best choice in this class. ⑥.

Fort Aguada Beach Resort, including *Aguada Hermitage* and *Taj Holiday Village*, Sinquerim Beach (☎0832/277501, fax 277733). Five-star opulence in hermetically sealed, manicured vacation campus. Pools, but no private beach. Recently lost a legal battle for infringing environmental laws. ⑨.

Julia, Escrivao Vaddo (☎0832/277219). At the north end of the village. Comfortable en-suite rooms, tiled floors, balconies, a relaxing, sociable garden, and easy access to the beach. ④.

Lobo's, Camotim Vaddo (no phone). In a peaceful corner of the village, this is a notch up from *Manuel's*, opposite (☎0832/277729), with larger rooms and a long verandah on the ground floor. ④.

Melodious Waves, Dando Vaddo (☎0832/277711, fax 217421). A dozen recently built rooms with balconies in a quiet location, well back from the main road and two minutes' walk through the dunes to a relatively peaceful stretch of beach. Tariffs reflect its proximity to the *Taj*, though still good value. ⑥.

Sea Shell Inn, Fort Aguada Rd, opposite the Canara Bank (☎0832/276131). Homely, comfortable hotel on the roadside with large, immaculately clean rooms, safety lockers, laundry facility and a popular terrace restaurant. The tariff includes use of a nearby pool. Well worth shelling out a little extra for. ⑤.

Ti Bhat, Murrod Vaddo (no phone). Simple but clean attached rooms with fans in one of Candolim's few remaining small, family-run guesthouses. Their rates are low for the area, and they do single occupancy. ③.

Tropicana Beach Resort, 835/b Camotim Vaddo (☎0832/277732). Modern but tastefully designed chalets made of local stone with traditional oyster-shell windows, grouped around a leafy lawn. Very pleasant. ⑥.

Xavier Beach Resort, Vaddy, off Fort Aguada Rd (☎ & fax 0832/276911). Peaceful, with luxurious rooms, large verandahs and sea views. They also have a popular rooftop cocktail bar, and a terrace restaurant on the ground floor. ⑥.

EATING AND DRINKING

Candolim's numerous beach **cafés** are a cut above your average seafood shacks, with pot plants, state-of-the-art sound systems and prices to match. Basically, the farther from the *Taj* complex you venture, the more realistic the prices become. The main road is also dotted with restaurants serving the usual selection of fresh fish dishes, with a handful of continental options thrown in.

Casa Sea Shell, in the hotel of the same name. This is the place to head for topnotch *tandoori* and North Indian dishes, although they also offer a good choice of Chinese and European food. Excellent service and moderate prices.

Spice Garden, opposite Canara Bank. The food here's not up to much, but the live music is well worth dropping in for. A local guitarist does singalong numbers (and beautiful Konkani wedding songs if cajoled), interspersed with Tom Jones covers from the owner, complete with dramatic gestures and heavy vibrato; a must.

Sea Shell, at the *Sea Shell Inn*, Fort Aguada Rd. A congenial terrace restaurant that cooks seafood and sizzling meat meals to order – also good for vegetarians and anyone fed up with spicy Indian food. Try one of their delicious cocktails.

Teama, Murrod Vaddo, opposite *Holiday Beach Resort*. One of the best places in the area to sample authentic Goan food. Try their prawn curry and rice house specialty, or milder fish *caldin* (a spicy stew). Most main meals cost around Rs80, and they have a good breakfast menu. Occasional live music from folk string trio during the season.

Tibetan Kitchen, Murrod Vaddo. A swish offshoot of the established Calangute restaurant, serving filling and tasty (but non-spicy) Tibetan and Chinese specialties, and a good range of Western dishes, in comfortable surroundings behind the dunes. Most main dishes cost under Rs75.

Xavier's, Vaddy, off Fort Aguada Rd. The à la carte menu in this popular hotel restaurant (run by an ex-British Airways caterer) features mostly seafood, but they do regular barbecues, lots of Mughlai-style Indian dishes, *baltis* (ask for a "*karai*") and even slap-up roast beef Sunday lunches (most main courses around Rs100). In addition, the rooftop terrace houses a lively cocktail bar with jazzy lights and a sound system. Happy hour 6–7pm.

Calangute

A mere 45-minute bus ride up the coast from the capital, **CALANGUTE** is Goa's busiest and most commercialized resort, and the flagship of the state government's bid for a bigger slice of India's package-tourist pie. In the 1970s and early 1980s, this once peaceful fishing village epitomized Goa's reputation as a haven for hedonistic hippies. Indian visitors flocked by the bus-load from Mumbai and Bangalore to giggle at the tribes of dreadlocked Westerners lying naked on the vast white sandy beach, stoned out of their brains on local *feni* and cheap *charas*. Calangute's flower-power period, however, has long passed. Hoteliers today joke about the days when they used to rent out makeshift shacks on the beach to backpackers. Now many of them manage tailor-made tourist settlements, complete with air-conditioned rooms, swimming pools and lush lawns, for groups of suitcase-carrying fortnighters.

The charter boom, combined with a huge increase in the number of Indian visitors, has placed an impossible burden on Calangute's rudimentary infrastructure. Each year, as another crop of construction sites blossoms into resort complexes, what little charm the village has retained gets steadily more submerged under ferroconcrete and heaps of garbage. The pollution problems are compounded by an absence of adequate provision for waste disposal and sewage treatment, and ever-increasing water consumption levels. One worrying sign that Calangute has already started to stew in its own juices has been a dramatic rise in **malaria** cases: virex and the more serious falciparum strain are now both endemic here, and rife during the early part of the season.

The town and beach

The road from the **town** to the beach is lined with Kashmiri-run handicraft boutiques and Tibetan stalls selling Himalayan curios and jewellery. The quality of the goods –

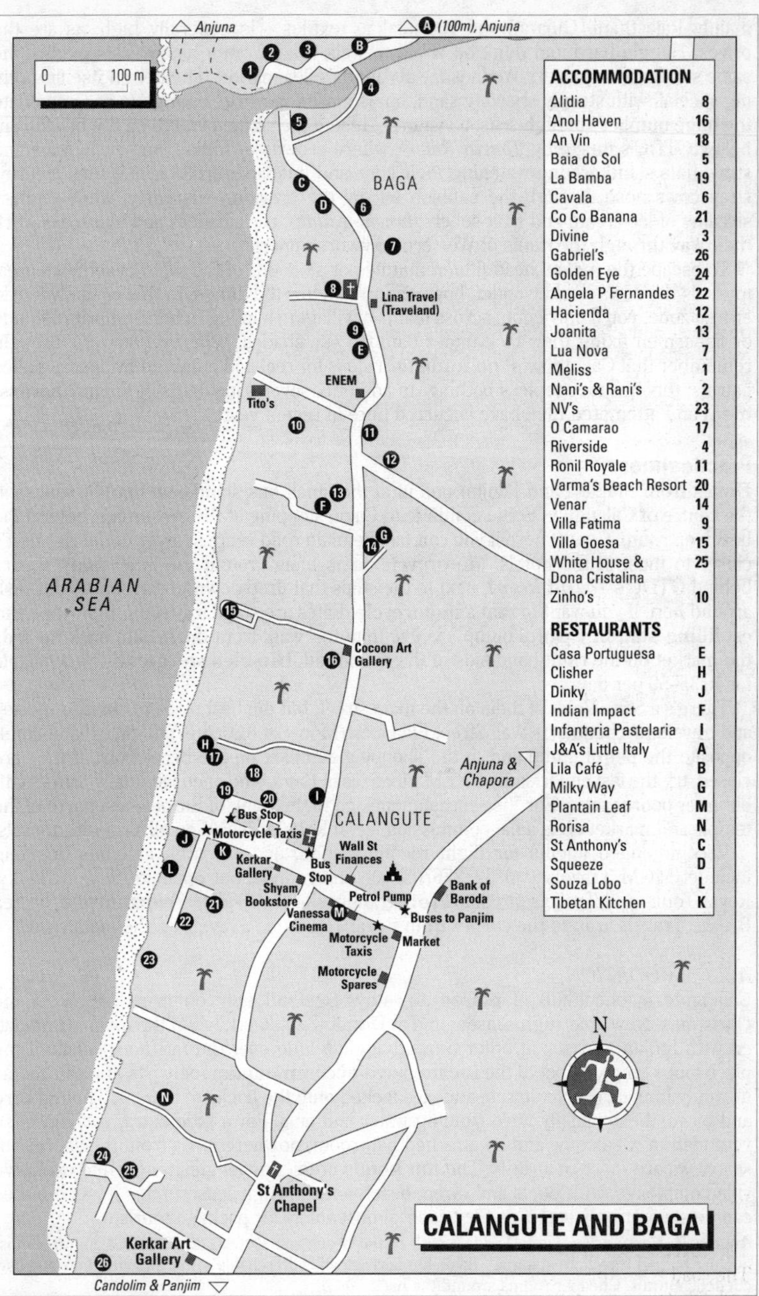
Anjuna
A (100m), Anjuna
0 100 m
ACCOMMODATION
Alidia 8
Anol Haven 16
An Vin 18
Baia do Sol 5
La Bamba 19
Cavala 6
Co Co Banana 21
Divine 3
Gabriel's 26
Golden Eye 24
Angela P Fernandes 22
Hacienda 12
Joanita 13
Lua Nova 7
Meliss 1
Nani's & Rani's 2
NV's 23
O Camarao 17
Riverside 4
Ronil Royale 11
Varma's Beach Resort 20
Venar 14
Villa Fatima 9
Villa Goesa 15
White House & Dona Cristalina 25
Zinho's 10
RESTAURANTS
Casa Portuguesa E
Clisher H
Dinky J
Indian Impact F
Infanteria Pastelaria I
J&A's Little Italy A
Lila Café B
Milky Way G
Plantain Leaf M
Rorisa N
St Anthony's C
Squeeze D
Souza Lobo L
Tibetan Kitchen K
BAGA
Lina Travel (Traveland)
ENEM
Tito's
ARABIAN SEA
Cocoon Art Gallery
Anjuna & Chapora
CALANGUTE
Bus Stop
Motorcycle Taxis
Wall St Finances
Kerkar Gallery
Bus Stop
Shyam Bookstore
Petrol Pump
Bank of Baroda
Vanessa Cinema
Buses to Panjim
Motorcycle Taxis
Market
Motorcycle Spares
N
St Anthony's Chapel
CALANGUTE AND BAGA
Kerkar Art Gallery
Candolim & Panjim

mainly Rajasthani, Gujarati and Karnatakan textiles – is generally high, as are the prices. Haggle hard and don't be afraid to walk away from a heavy sales pitch – the same stuff crops up every Wednesday at Anjuna's flea market. The **beach** itself is nothing special, with steeply shelving sand, but is more than large enough to accommodate the huge numbers of high-season visitors. Most of the action centres on the beachfront below GTDC's unsightly *Tourist Resort*, where crowds of Indian women in *saris* and straw hats stand around watching their sons and husbands frolic in the surf. Nearby, stray cows nose through the rubbish left by the previous bus party, while endless streams of ice-cream and fruit sellers, *lunghi-wallahs*, ear cleaners and masseurs work their way through the ranks of Western sun-worshippers.

To escape the melee, head fifteen minutes or so south of the main beachfront area, towards the rows of old wooden boats moored below the dunes. In this virtually hawker-free zone, you'll only come across teams of villagers hauling in hand-nets at high tide or fishermen fixing their tack under bamboo sun-shades. Wherever you go, though, remember that Calangute's "**no nudism**" rule is for real and enforced by special police patrols; this includes topless bathing. In addition, several incidents of **sexual harassment** and attempted rape have occurred here in recent years.

Practicalities

Buses from Mapusa and Panjim pull in at the small bus stand-cum-market square in the centre of Calangute. Some continue to Baga, stopping at the crossroads behind the beach en route. Get off here if you can (as the main road veers sharply to the right); it's closer to most of the hotels. **Motorcycle taxis** hang around the little sandy square behind GTDC's *Tourist Resort*, next to the steps that drop down to the beachfront. Ask around here if you want to rent a **motorcycle**. Rates are standard (see p.125); the nearest **filling station** ("petrol pump") is five minutes' walk from the beach, back towards the market on the right-hand side of the main road. **Bicycles** are also widely available for Rs35–50 per day.

There's a State Bank of India on the main street, but the best place to **change money** and travellers' cheques is Wall Street Finances (Mon–Sat 8.30am–7pm, Sun 10am–2pm), opposite the petrol pump and in the shopping complex on the beachfront. If they are closed, try the fast and friendly ENEM Finances in Baga, who open late (daily 8am–9pm), but offer poorer rates. For Visa encashments, go to the Bank of Baroda, just north of the temple and market area; a flat commission fee of Rs100 is levied on all Visa withdrawals.

Recommended agents for flight reconfirmation, and air, train and bus ticketing include: MGM Travels (☎0832/276703), on the roundabout opposite Shyam Books; Royal Tours and Travels (☎0832/276109), opposite the GTDC *Tourist Resort*; or Sea Breeze Travels around the corner from Royal Tours and Travels on the main road.

ACCOMMODATION

Calangute is chock-full of **places to stay**. Demand only outstrips supply in the Christmas–New Year high season, and at Diwali (Sept/Oct), when the town is inundated with Indian tourists; at other times, haggle a little over the tariff, especially if the place looks empty. Most of the **inexpensive accommodation** consists of small rooms in family homes, or in concrete annexes tacked onto the backs of houses. Though bare and basic, these usually have running water and fans. For a little extra, you can get a verandah or a balcony, and an attached bathroom; nowhere is far from the shore, but sea views are more of a rarity. The **top hotels** are nearly all gleaming white exclusive villa complexes, with pools and direct beach access. High-season rates in such places can be staggeringly steep, as they cater almost solely for package tourists.

Angela P. Fernandes, Umta Vaddo, south of the beachfront (☎0832/277269). Calangute's most popular budget travellers' hangout. Basic but fairly clean, with reliable water supplies, fans and psychedelic murals. Cheaper rooms around the back. ②–③.

Anol Haven, 6/85A Cobra Vaddo (☎0832/276532). Seven newish, airy rooms with balconies and en-suite bathrooms, just off the main drag in a quiet district. An improbably named place, but among the best deals in this category. ⑥.

An Vin, 5/193 Umta Vaddo, behind the bus park (☎0832/276519). Eight neat, clean rooms (some with attached bathrooms) in a hospitable family guesthouse, and good home cooking on request from a garrulous landlady. ④.

La Bamba, next to GTDC *Tourist Resort* (☎0832/276108). Small, cosy and well-maintained guesthouse close to the beach with some sea-facing rooms. Breakfast available on request. ⑥.

CoCo Banana, 1/195 Umta Vaddo, down the lane past *Meena Lobo's* restaurant (☎0832/276478). Very comfortable, spacious chalets, all with bathrooms, Swiss mosquito nets, extra-long mattresses and balconies, grouped around a central garden. ⑧.

Gabriel's, just south of the *Golden Eye* near the ice factory, Gaura Vaddo (☎0832/279486). A congenial, quiet, family-run guesthouse, with an excellent in-house restaurant, midway between Calangute and Candolim. Close to the beach with a shady garden and pleasant views from the back across the *todi* dunes. ③.

Golden Eye, A-1/189 Gaura Vaddo (☎0832//fax 276187). Large rooms, balconies, sea views and a terrace restaurant, all smack on the beach. One of the first purpose-built hotels in Calangute. ⑥.

NV's, south Calangute (☎0832/279749). Homely, traditional Goan guesthouse right on the beach, run by a fishing family and holding its own despite proximity to a large package resort. A good budget option. ③–⑤.

O Camarao, 5/201 Umta Vaddo, just north of GTDC *Tourist Resort* (☎0832/276229). Spruce, blue and white bungalow with immaculate rooms, verandahs and a restaurant. Very good value, but a little too close to the scruffy, busy beachfront area. ⑤.

Varma's Beach Resort, two minutes' east of GTDC *Tourist Resort* (☎0832/276077, fax 276022). Attractive a/c rooms, with immaculate mosquito nets and balconies overlooking a leafy garden. Secluded but close to the centre of the village. ⑧.

Villa Goesa, Cobravaddo (☎0832/277535, fax 276182). A stone's throw from the beach and very swish, set around a lush garden with young palms and lawns. Occasional live music and a cocktail bar. All rooms have balconies. ⑧.

White House, 185/B, near *Goan Heritage* resort, Gaura Vaddo (☎0832/277938, fax 276308). Immaculate, large rooms in a modern block close to the beach, with balconies, bathrooms and some views. They also have a lovely old traditional house next door, which would suit a family or group. If full, try the equally comfortable *Dona Cristalina* (☎0832/279012; ⑤) along the lane. ⑤–⑥.

EATING AND DRINKING

Calangute's **bars** and **restaurants** are mainly grouped around the entrance to the beach and along the Baga Rd. As with most Goan resorts, the accent is firmly on **seafood**, though many places tack on a few token vegetarian dishes. Western breakfasts (pancakes, porridge, muesli, eggs, etc) also feature prominently.

Clisher, north of GTDC *Tourist Resort*, behind the beach. Among the best of the inexpensive beachside bar-restaurants, with the usual fresh seafood, good breakfasts, cold beer and sea views.

Dinky, beside the steps to the beach. Standard seafood and beer bar, with a pleasant verandah for crowd watching. Popular with budget travellers.

Gabriel's, just south of *Golden Eye* near the ice factory, Gaura Vaddo. Authentic Goan cooking (pork *sarpotel*, chicken *xacuti*, stuffed squid and prawn *masala*), and very popular Italian dishes (with homemade pasta) served on a cosy roof terrace well away from the main road; and they do pukka espresso coffee. Bring mosquito repellent.

Infantaria Pastelaria, near St John's Chapel, Baga Rd. Small roadside terrace that gets packed out for breakfast – piping hot croissants or freshly baked apple pie.

NV's, in the guesthouse of the same name, south Calangute. A ten-minute trek down the beach, but well worth it for no-nonsense platefuls of grilled fish, calamari and crab, all fresh from the family boat.

Plantain Leaf, near Vanessa Cinema, market area. Arguably the best South Indian restaurant outside Panjim, serving the usual range of delicious *dosas* and other spicy snacks in a clean, cool, marble-lined canteen, with relentless background *filmi* music.

Rorisa, up the lane west of St Anthony's chapel. Quiet café serving tasty Goan and Western food, including great Mumbai *allu* and green fish curry; their banana pancakes are a must for breakfast.

Souza Lobo, on the beachfront. One of Goa's oldest restaurants and deservedly famous for its superb seafood; try their blow-out fish sizzlers or mouthwatering tiger prawns. Get there early, and avoid weekends; moderate prices.

Tibetan Kitchen, off the beach road. Filling, inexpensive Tibetan food, including tasty cheese-fried *momo* and home-made cakes. Also offers Western and Chinese options, full breakfasts, New Age music and chess sets.

NIGHTLIFE

Thanks to repeated crackdowns by the Goan police on beach parties and loud music, Calangute's **nightlife** is surprisingly tame. All but a handful of the **bars** wind up by 10pm, leaving punters to prolong the short evenings back at their hotels. One notable exception is *Tito's*, at the Baga end of the beach, which stays open until 11pm off-season and into the small hours in late December and January (see Baga "Nightlife" p.149). Unfortunately, the only other places that consistently stay open through the night are a couple of dull hippy hangouts in the woods to the south of the beach road: *Pete's Bar*, a perennial favourite next door to *Angela P. Fernandes*, is generally the most lively, offering cheap drinks, backgammon sets and relentless reggae. Farther afield, *Bob's Inn*, between Calangute and Candolim, is another popular bar, famed less for its tasty Western food and extrovert owner than the group of ageing "heads" that holds court around a large table in the front bar.

Finally, don't miss the chance to sample some real Indian culture while you are in Calangute. The Kerkar Art Gallery, in Gaura Vaddo, at the south end of town (☎0832/276017), hosts evenings of **classical music and dance** every Tuesday and Saturday from 6.30 to 8pm, held in the back garden on a sumptuously decorated stage, complete with incense and evocative candlelight. The recitals, performed by students and teachers from Panjim's Kala Academy, are kept comfortably short for the benefit of Western visitors, and are preceded by a short introductory talk. Tickets, available in advance or at the door, cost Rs250.

Baga

BAGA, 10km west of Mapusa, is basically an extension of Calangute; not even the locals agree where one ends and the other begins. Lying in the lee of a rocky, wooded headland, the only difference between this far northern end of the beach and its more congested centre is that the scenery here is marginally more varied and picturesque. A small river flows into the sea at the top of the village, below a broad spur of soft white sand, from where a dirt track strikes across an expanse of paddy fields towards Anjuna. The old red-tiled fishers' houses behind the dunes have long been swamped by gaudily lit bars, *tandoori* terrace restaurants and handicraft shops, but you don't feel quite so hemmed in as at Calangute. That said, Baga can get horrendously congested, especially at the height of the season in December and early January, when the sealed road running through it to the sandy bus park at the top of the village is clogged all evening with streams of Maruti-van taxis and sunburnt tourists from the huge new resorts on the outskirts.

Accommodation

Accommodation is harder to arrange on spec in Baga than in Calangute, as most of the hotels have been carved up by the charter companies; even rooms in smaller guesthouses tend to be booked up well before the season gets under way. If you're keen to stay, you may have to hole up farther down the beach for a night while you hunt around for a vacancy. The rough-and-ready places dotted around the fishing village usually have space; look for signs on the main square. Cheap houses and rooms for rent are also available on the quieter north side of the river, although these are like gold dust in peak season.

INEXPENSIVE

Divine, near *Nani's and Rani's* (☎0832/279546). Quiet, new and friendly family guesthouse north of the river, run by fervent Christians (the sign board features a burning cross and bleeding heart). Rooms are on the small side, but clean; some have attached shower-toilets. ④.

Joanita, Baga Rd (☎0832/277166). Clean, airy rooms with attached baths and some double beds, ranged around a quiet garden. A good choice if you want to be in the village centre, but off the road. ④.

Meliss, 620 Anjuna Rd (no phone). Eight rooms in a clean, quiet block on the north side of the river, all with attached shower-toilets. Good off-season discounts, too. ④.

Nani's and Rani's, north of the river (☎0832/276313 or 277014). A handful of red-tiled, white-washed cottages in a secluded back garden, perenially popular with long-staying guests. Fans, shared toilets, well-water and an outdoor shower. ③.

Venar, 1963 Cobra Vaddo (☎0832/276867). Large, immaculate rooms (some with attached baths) in an old Portuguese-style house. Discount for singles. One of the best budget deals in town. ③.

Villa Fatima, Baga Rd (☎0832/277418). Thirty-two rooms with attached baths in a large, three-storey backpackers' hotel centred on a sociable garden terrace. Their rates are very reasonable, varying with room size. All attached bathrooms. ④–⑥.

Zinho's, 7/3 Saunta Vaddo (☎0832/277`383). Tucked away off the main road, close to *Tito's* nightclub. Half a dozen good-value, modest-size, clean rooms near the beach. ④.

MODERATE TO EXPENSIVE

Alidia (Alirio & Lidia), Baga Rd, Saunta Vaddo (☎0832/276835). Attractive modern chalet rooms with good-sized verandahs looking onto the dunes. Double or twin beds. Quiet and friendly. ⑤–⑥.

Baia do Sol, on the square (☎0832/276085). Modern, immaculate and surrounded by a well-kept garden. No single occupancy in high season. Some a/c. ⑧.

Cavala, Baga Rd (☎0832/277587). Modern building in tastefully traditional mould; simple rooms, attached bathrooms and separate balconies. ⑦.

Hacienda, Baga Rd (☎0832/277348). Nothing special but with big, airy rooms, balconies and a well-tended garden. ⑤.

Lua Nova, north of Baga Rd, near the *Cavala Hotel* (☎0832/276288, fax 277173). Peaceful and cosy; pool, sunbeds on the lawn and individual balconies, though somewhat boxed in by its multistorey neighbour. ⑦.

Riverside, on the river bank (☎0832/276062). Newish, tasteful hotel with large comfy rooms, a good restaurant and river views. Moving into the package bracket, but the best value at this price. ⑦.

Ronil Royale, Baga Rd (☎0832/276101, fax 276068). Baga's most upmarket hotel has ersatz Portuguese apartments overlooking two small pools, and a swish restaurant. ⑨.

Eating, drinking and nightlife

Baga arguably has the best range of **restaurants** in Goa, from standard beach shacks to swish pizzerias and terrace cafés serving real espresso coffee. Because of the stiff competition, prices are generally reasonable and the quality of cooking high. Even if they wouldn't be seen dead here during the day, many old Goa hands come to Baga to eat in the evenings. For a splurge, splash out on a candle-lit dinner at *J&A*'s riverside trattoria, or a traditional Goan meal at the eccentric *Casa Portuguesa*.

Thanks to the droves of predominantly British package tourists who stay here, Baga's nightlife is the liveliest in the area. Most of the revellers end up at *Tito's* which has the only dance floor and hefty sound system outside a big hotel for miles. Women are allowed in for free; "unaccompanied" men have to pay whatever the management think they can get away with (between Rs100 and Rs250, depending on the crowd). Be warned, however, that in recent years this has become something of a pickup joint, plagued by groups of so-called "rowdies" from Delhi and Mumbai, and the same loutish, lager-fuelled antics you'd expect of a Costa del Sol nightclub.

Casa Portuguesa, Baga Rd. Traditional Portuguese and Goan food served by candlelight inside this romantic colonial villa or al fresco on a leafy lawn. The gregarious owner serenades diners with Amelia Rodrigues *fados* most evenings. Overpriced, but worth it for the atmosphere.

Indian Impact, on the road towards *CSM* resort. Quality *tandoori* fish and meat dishes prepared and served on a dimly lit terrace; moderate prices.

J&A's (formerly *Little Italy*), north side of the river. Mouthwatering, authentic Italian food (down to the imported parmesan and olive oil) served in the riverside garden of an old fisherman's cottage. Cooked in a wood-fired oven, their pizzas are delicious (try the amazing "smoked beef" house specialty), and dishes of the day often include fresh lasagne. Count on Rs250 per head for the works; extra for wine (at Rs55 per glass).

Lila Café, north side of the river. Tastefully decorated bakery-cum-snack bar, run by a German couple. Their healthy homemade breads and cakes are great, and there's an adventurous lunch menu featuring spinach *à la creme*, rounded off with real espresso coffee.

Milky Way, midway between Calangute and Baga. Baga's best breakfast venue, serving mountainous bowls of fresh fruit and homemade curd, as well as pancakes, muesli and omelettes. In the evening, a resident French chef turns out imaginative Western dishes in an atmospheric illuminated garden.

Nani's and Rani's, in the hotel of the same name, on the north side of the river. Friendly family-run restaurant serving unremarkable but inexpensive food on a sociable verandah overlooking the river. Popular with budget travellers.

Squeeze, north end of the village. One of the best places around for inexpensive, healthy Italian food: fresh pasta, tasty sauces, filling portions and a full range of coffees. Their cool, fruit milk shakes are delicious, too.

St Anthony's, off the square. The place to watch the sunset accompanied by an icy beer and Indian classical music on a better-than-average sound system.

Valerio's, next door to *Hotel Baia do Sol*. Sophisticated bar-restaurant with good sea and river views from a pleasant first-floor terrace. Live reggae music on Wednesdays after the flea market.

Anjuna

With its fluorescent-painted palm trees and infamous full-moon parties, **ANJUNA**, 8km west of Mapusa, is Goa at its most "alternative". Designer leather and lycra may have superseded cotton kaftans, but most people's reasons for coming are the same as they were in the 1970s: drugs, dancing and lying on the beach slurping tropical fruit. Depending on your point of view, you'll find the headlong hedonism a total turn-off or heaven-on-sea. Either way, the scene looks here to stay, despite government attempts to stamp it out, so you might as well get a taste of it while you're in the area, if only from the wings, with a day-trip to the famous **flea market**.

One of the main sources of Anjuna's enduring popularity as a hippy hangout is its superb **beach**. Fringed by groves of swaying coconut palms, the curve of soft white sand conforms more closely to the archetypal vision of paradise than any other beach on the Goan north coast. Bathing is generally safer than at most of the nearby resorts, too, especially at the more peaceful southern end, where a rocky headland keeps the sea calm and the undertow to a minimum. North of the market ground, the beach broadens, running in an uninterrupted kilometre-long stretch of steeply shelving sand to a low red cliff. The village bus park lies on top of this high ground, near a crop of small cafés, bars and Kashmiri handicraft stalls. Every lunchtime, tour parties from Panjim pull in here for a beer, before heading home again, leaving the ragged army of sun-weary Westerners to enjoy the sunset.

The season in Anjuna starts in early November, when most of the long-staying regulars show up, and peters out in late March, when they drift off again. During the Christmas and New Year rush, the village is inundated with a mixed crowd of round-the-world backpackers, refugees from the British club scene and revellers from all over India, lured by the promise of the big beach parties. A large contingent of these are young Israelis fresh out of the army and full of devil-may-care attitude to drugs and other people's sleep. Outside peak season, however, Anjuna has a surprisingly simple, unhurried atmosphere – due, in no small part, to the shortage of places to stay. Most

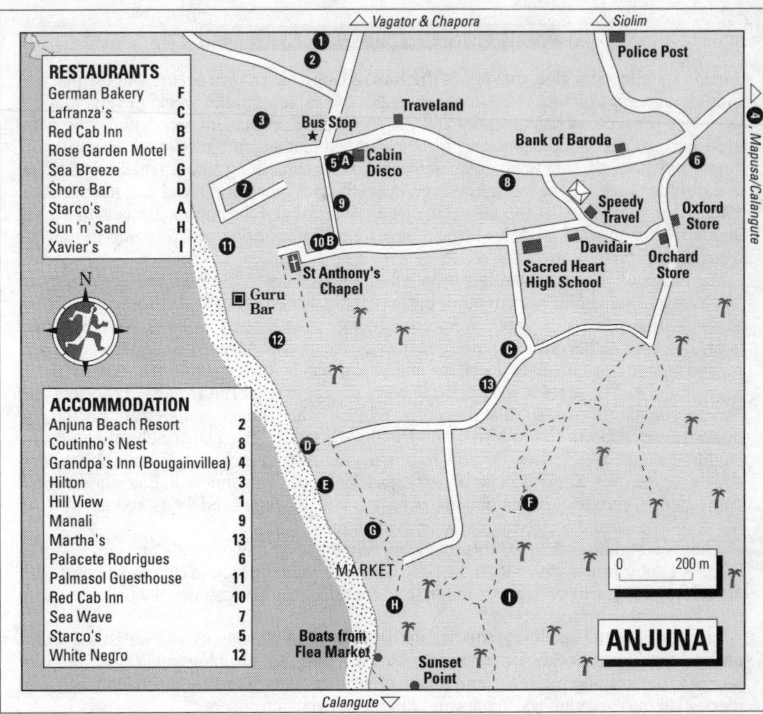

visitors who come here on market day or for the raves travel in from other resorts. That said, a couple of large package-tour hotels have appeared over the past couple of years (the swishest of them on the headland overlooking the village), and this is bound to alter radically the mix of visitors here.

Whenever you come, keep a close eye on your valuables. **Theft**, particularly from the beach, is a big problem. Party nights are the worst; if you stay out late, keep your money and papers on you, or lock them somewhere secure (see below). Thieves have even been known to break into local houses by lifting tiles off the roof.

Practicalities

Buses from Mapusa and Panjim drop passengers at various points along the tarmac road across the top of the village, which turns right towards Chapora at the main Starco's crossroads. If you're looking for a room, get off here as it's close to most of the guesthouses. The crossroads has a couple of small **stores**, a **motorcycle-taxi** rank, and functions as a *de facto* village square and **bus stand**.

The *Manali Guesthouse* and Oxford Stores **change money** (at poor rates). The Bank of Baroda on the Mapusa road will make encashments against Visa cards, but doesn't do foreign exchange, nor is it a good place to leave valuables, as thieves have previously climbed through an open window and stolen a number of "safe custody" envelopes. The **post office,** on the Mapusa road, 1km inland, has an efficient poste restante counter.

THE ANJUNA FLEA MARKET

Anjuna's Wednesday **flea market** is the hub of Goa's alternative scene, and *the* place to indulge in a spot of souvenir shopping. A decade or so ago, the weekly event was the exclusive preserve of backpackers and the area's semi-permanent population, who gathered here to smoke *chillums*, and to buy and sell clothes and jewellery they probably would not have the nerve to wear anywhere else: something like a small pop festival without the stage. These days, however, everything is more organized and mainstream. Pitches are rented out by the metre, drugs are banned and the approach roads to the village are choked solid all day with a/c buses and Ambassador cars ferrying in tourists from resorts farther down the coast.

The range of goods on sale has broadened, too, thanks to the high profile of migrant hawkers and stall-holders from other parts of India. Each region or culture tends to stick to its own corner. At one end, Westerners congregate around racks of New Age rave gear, Balinese batiks and designer beachwear. Nearby, hawk-eyed Kashmiris sit cross-legged beside trays of silver jewellery and papier-mâché boxes, while Tibetans, wearing jeans and T-shirts, preside over orderly rows of prayer wheels, turquoise bracelets and sundry Himalayan curios. Most distinctive of all are the Lamani women from Karnataka, decked from head to toe in traditional tribal garb and selling elaborately woven multi-coloured cloth, which they fashion into everything from jackets to money belts, and which makes even the Westerners' party gear look positively funereal. Elsewhere, you'll come across dazzling Rajasthani mirrorwork and block-printed bedspreads, Keralan woodcarvings and a scattering of Gujarati appliqué.

What you end up paying for this exotic merchandise largely depends on your ability to **haggle**. Lately, prices have inflated as tourists not used to dealing in rupees will part with almost anything. Be persistent, though, and cautious, and you can usually pick things up for a reasonable rate.

Even if you're not spending, the flea market is a great place to sit and watch the world go by. Mingling with the sun-tanned masses are bands of strolling musicians, itinerant beggars, performing monkeys and snake charmers, as well as the inevitable hippy jugglers, clad in regulation waistcoats and billowing pyjama trousers.

ACCOMMODATION

Most of Anjuna's very limited **accommodation** consists of small unfurnished houses, although finding one is a problem at the best of times – in peak season it's virtually impossible. By then, all but a handful have been let to long-staying regulars who book by post several months in advance. If you arrive hoping to sort something out on the spot, you'll probably have to make do with a room in a guesthouse at first, although most owners are reluctant to rent out rooms for only one or two days at a time. Basically, unless you mean to stay for at least a couple of months, you're better off looking for a room in Calangute, Baga or nearby Vagator or Chapora.

Anjuna Beach Resort, De Mello Vaddo (☎ & fax 0832/ 274499). Fifteen spacious, comfortable rooms with balconies, fridges and attached bathrooms, in a new concrete building at the north edge of the village. Those on the upper floor are best. Good value. ⑤.

WATER SHORTAGES

Because of the extra inhabitants it attracts over the winter, Anjuna has become particularly prone to **water shortages**. These tend not to affect many visitors, as the drought only begins to bite towards the end of March when the majority have already left. For the villagers, however, the problem causes genuine hardship. Use well-water very sparingly and avoid water toilets if possible – traditional "dry" (ie "pig") ones are far more ecologically friendly.

Coutinho's Nest, Soronto Vaddo (☎0832/274386). Small, very respectable family guesthouse on the main road, in the centre of Anjuna. Their immaculately clean rooms are among the village's best budget deals. Shared shower-toilets only. ②.

Grandpa's Inn (Bougainvillea), Gaunwadi, at the east side of the village on the main Mapusa road (☎0832/274370 or 2743271, fax 252624). Colonial-era building stylishly converted for well-heeled party lovers, with ten tasteful rooms, a terrace-restaurant, a wet-bar, a billiards room and a pool. ⑧.

Hill View, De Mello Vaddo (☎0832/273235). One of the newer and more pleasant budget places, quiet location, and good value. ③.

Hilton, on the main road near the bus park (☎0832/274432). Rooms in a characterless outbuilding, 500m behind the beach, all with attached shower-toilets. ④.

Manali, south of *Starco's* (☎0832/274421). Anjuna's best all-round budget guesthouse has simple rooms with fans opening onto a yard, shared bathrooms and a sociable terrace restaurant. Facilities include a safe deposit, money-changing and Internet access. Very good value, so book in advance. ②.

Martha's, 907 Montero Vaddo (☎0832/273365). Five well-kept rooms, and one pleasant house to rent, run by a welcoming family. Basic amenities include kitchen space and running water. ③–⑤.

Palacete Rodrigues, near Oxford Stores (☎0832/273358). Old Portuguese-style residence converted into an upmarket guesthouse. Carved, wooden furniture, and a relaxed, traditional Goan feel. Single occupancy available. ⑥–⑦.

Palmasol Guesthouse, Praia de St Anthony, behind the middle of the beach (☎0832/273258). Huge, comfortable rooms in an immaculately kept old house with a relaxing garden, very near the beach. The larger ones have running water, verandahs, cooking space; cheaper alternatives are in the back yard. ④–⑤.

Red Cab Inn, De Mello Vaddo (☎0832/273312, fax 274427). Run-of-the-mill rooms ranged around a courtyard and busy restaurant. Check out their overpriced "Executive Chalet" – a lurid confection of red-painted concrete with blue lights and Day-Glo mobiles. ⑤.

Sea Wave, De Mello Vaddo (☎0832/274455). Smart, spacious, high-ceilinged rooms in a new block. Tiled bathrooms and balconies. Not the best location, but good value at this price. ⑥.

Starco's, on the crossroads (no phone). Dark, cramped rooms around a yard, but with a good restaurant and an owner with the longest fingernails in India. ③.

White Negro, 719 Praia de St Anthony, south of the village (☎0832/273326). A row of spotless back-to-back chalets catching sea breezes, all with attached bathrooms and 24hr running water. Also a lively restaurant and friendly management. Very good value. ⑤–⑥.

EATING AND DRINKING

Both the beachfront and village at Anjuna are awash with good **places to eat and drink**. Most are simple semi-open-air, thatched palm-leaf affairs, specializing in fish and Western food. All serve cold beer, invariably with thumping techno music in the background. On the beach, you'll also be approached every ten minutes by women selling fresh **fruit**, including watermelons, pineapples and locally grown coconuts.

German Bakery, east of the market ground (look for the sign on the main road). Pricey but mouth-watering main meals and wholefood snacks, with real cream cheese, peanut butter, hummus, honey slices, sophisticated sounds and relaxing wicker chairs.

Lafranza's, south end of the village on the road to the market ground. The budget travellers' choice: big portions of tasty fresh fish and fries, with plenty of veg options.

Martha's Breakfast Home, near *Lafranza's*, off the road to the market. Secluded breakfast garden serving fresh Indian coffee, crepes and American waffles, in addition to a regular menu.

Red Cab Inn, south of *Starco's*. The multicuisine menu here's particularly strong on Goan specialties, and in season they do a range of popular pasta and wholefood dishes, as well as imported German beer. Most main meals under Rs120.

Rose Garden Motel, on the beach south of the *Shore Bar*. Not to be confused with the *Rose Garden Restaurant* in the village. The exhaustive menu here features superb, reasonably priced seafood sizzlers and tasty Indian-vegetarian dishes.

Sea Breeze, market ground. Does a roaring trade in cold beer and snacks on Wednesdays. At other times the huge *tandoori* fish is tasty and good value, especially for groups; order in advance.

Shore Bar, in the middle of the beach. Draws a dope-smoking crowd for sunset after the flea market and most Saturdays, with the best sound system in Anjuna. Light and main meals served as well as drinks.

Starco's, on the crossroads. Somewhat sophisticated bar-restaurant serving tasty *tandoori* seafood and Western dishes, inside or on the roadside terrace.

Sun 'n' Sand, market ground. Renowned for its whopping fresh-fruit salads served with crumbled coconut and curd. Great for inexpensive, healthy breakfasts.

Xavier's, east of market ground. Difficult to find, but worth it for its classy seafood and Chinese menu. Deservedly among Anjuna's most popular restaurants; *the* place for a splurge.

NIGHTLIFE

Thanks to the killjoy attitude of the local police, Anjuna no longer deserves the reputation it gained through the 1980s as a legendary rave venue, but big **parties** do still take place here from time to time, especially around the Christmas–New Year full-moon period. Smaller events may also happen whenever the organizers can muster the increasingly large pay-offs demanded by local police. At other times, **nightlife** centres on the *Shore Bar*, in the middle of the beach, which has a pounding sound system. The biggest crowds show up on Wednesdays after the market to watch the sunset from the steps in front of the bar, accompanied by the latest ambient trance mixes from London. The music gains pace as the evening wears on, winding up around 11pm, when there's an exodus over to the *Guru Bar*, farther up the beach, or to the *Primrose Café* in Vagator, both of which stay open until after midnight. When it eventually gets its act together, the *Alcove*, overlooking Ozran Vagator beach, will be another worthwhile night spot, although its owners are still seeking "permission" from the local police to install a serious sound system. More mainstream musical entertainment is on offer at *Temptations*, in the *Red Cab Inn* just below *Starco's* crossroads, where Indian classical recitals and guitar-based cover bands feature with fire dancers on Mondays, starting at 7pm.

Vagator

Barely a couple of kilometres of clifftops and parched grassland separate Anjuna from the southern fringes of its nearest neighbour, **VAGATOR**. A desultory collection of ramshackle farmhouses and picturesque old Portuguese bungalows scattered around a network of leafy lanes, the village is entered at the east via a branch off the Mapusa road, which passes a few small guesthouses and restaurants before running down to the sea. Dominated by the red ramparts of Chapora fort, Vagator's broad white sandy beach – **Big Vagator beach** – is undeniably beautiful, spoiled only by the daily deluge of whisky-swilling, snap-happy tour parties that spill across it at lunchtimes.

Far better, then, to head to the next cove south. Backed by a steep wall of crumbling palm-fringed laterite, **Ozran** (or "Little") **Vagator beach** is more secluded and much less accessible than either of its neighbours. To get there, walk ten minutes from Big Vagator, or drive to the end of the lane off the main Chapora–Anjuna road, from where a footpath drops sharply down to a wide stretch of level white sand (look for the mopeds and bikes parked at the top of the cliff). At this southern end of the beach (dubbed "Tel Aviv Beach"), a row of makeshift **cafés** provides shade and sustenance (and relentless trancy techno music) for a predominantly Israeli crowd. In spite of the Goan nudism laws, topless bathing is the norm; not that the locals, nor the odd groups of inebriated men that file past around mid-afternoon, seem in the least bit perturbed.

Like Anjuna, Vagator is a relaxed, comparatively undeveloped resort that appeals, in the main, to budget travellers with time on their hands. Accommodation is limited, however, and visitors frequently find themselves travelling to and from Baga every day until a vacancy turns up in one of the guesthouses.

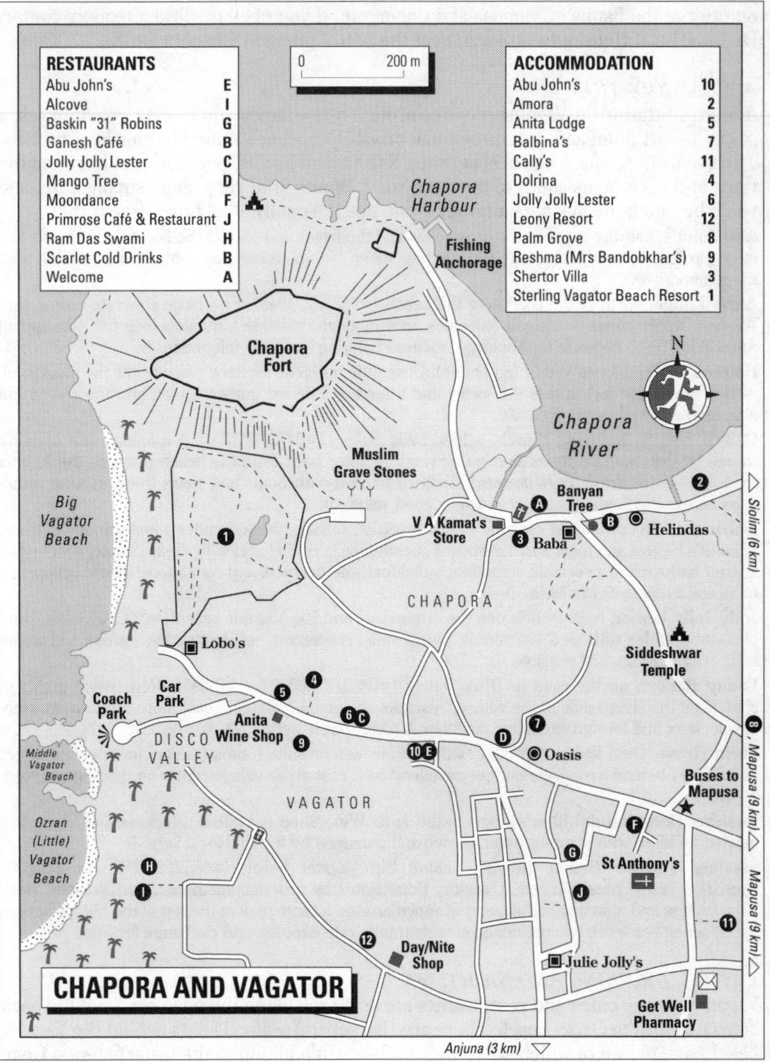

Practicalities

Buses from Panjim and Mapusa, 9km east, pull in every fifteen minutes or so at the crossroads on the far northeastern edge of Vagator, near where the main road peels away towards Chapora. From here, it's a one-kilometre walk over the hill and down the other side to the beach, where you'll find most of the village's accommodation, restaurants and cafés. The *Primrose Café*, on the south side of the village, has a **foreign exchange** licence (for cash and travellers' cheques) but their rates are well above those on offer at the banks in Mapusa and Calangute. If you need medical attention, contact Dr Jawarhalal Henriques at Zorin, near the petrol pump in Chapora (☎0832/274308).

ACCOMMODATION

Accommodation in Vagator revolves around a few family-run budget guesthouses, a pricey resort hotel and dozens of small private properties rented out for long periods. The usual charge for a house is between Rs2000 and Rs4500 per month; ask around the cafés and back lanes south of the main road. **Water** is in very short supply here, and you'll be doing the villagers a favour if you use it frugally at all times (see p.152).

Abu John's, halfway between the crossroads and the beach (no phone). Self-contained chalets in a quiet garden; all with bathrooms and running water. No off-season discounts. A comfortable mid-range option. ⑤.

Anita Lodge, north of the road near the beach (☎0832/274348). Five basic concrete rooms with Western water toilets and small balconies, in a modern roadside bungalow. See the manager of Anita Wine Shop opposite for bookings, money-changing and STD telephone. ②.

Balbina's, Menndonca Vaddo (no phone). Cosy little budget-travellers' place below the main road, with views of the fort across the valley and a terrace café for guests. Quiet, and the rooms (all attached) are well maintained. ③.

Cally's, near St Anthony's church, behind *Bella Bakery* (☎0832/273704). A spanking new building owned by the same family as *Dolrina's*, twenty minutes back from the beach (turn off the Anjuna road just before *Scarlett's Restaurant*), with clean tiled bathrooms and views from relaxing verandahs across the fields. Secluded and very good value. ③.

Dolrina, north of the road near the beach (☎0832/273382). Nestled under a lush canopy of trees, Vagator's largest and most popular budget guesthouse is run by a friendly Goan couple; attached or shared bathrooms, a sociable verandah, individual safe deposits and roof space. Single occupancy rates and breakfasts available. ③–④.

Jolly Jolly Lester, halfway between the crossroads and Big Vagator beach (☎0832/273620). Nine pleasant doubles with tiled bathrooms, plus a small restaurant, set in attractive garden and woodland. Single occupancy possible. ④.

Leony Resort, on the road to Disco Valley (☎0832/273634, fax 273595). New, swish group of chalets on the sleepy side of the village. Spacious octagonal "cottages" cost more. Restaurant, laundry, lockers and foreign exchange facilities. A comfortable option. ⑦–⑨.

Palm Grove, Deul Vaddo (☎0832/2274388). Fourteen en-suite rooms (the pricier ones are larger and newer) behind a roadside budget-travellers' café, east of the village centre on the Mapusa road. ④–⑤.

Reshma (Mrs Bandobkhar's), next to the Anita Wine Shop (no phone). Inexpensive rooms in a newish building with running water, owned and managed by friendly local lady. ④.

Sterling Vagator Beach Resort, behind Big Vagator beach (☎0832/273276, fax 273314). Upmarket resort hotel pitched at wealthy Bombayites by new management. A/c "cottages" (with TVs, fridges and attached bathrooms) grouped around a large pool at the top of the hill, or behind the beach at sea level; two multicuisine restaurants, safe deposits and exchange facilities. ⑨.

EATING, DRINKING AND NIGHTLIFE

Vagator's many **cafés** and **restaurants** are scattered along the main road and the back lanes that lead to Ozran beach. There are also several seafood joints behind Big Vagator beach, one or two of which serve Indian dishes in addition to the usual fish-rich Goan specialties. **Nightlife** focuses on the *Primrose Café*, out towards Anjuna, which boasts a beefier-than-average sound system and a late bar.

Abu John's, between the crossroads and the beach. Moderately priced, relaxing terrace restaurant specializing in seafood and meat barbecues.

Alcove, next to *Ram Das Swami's*, above Ozran beach. This unsightly new clifftop complex enjoys the best location for miles, with spellbinding sea views through the palms. The food is also a cut above the competition, and the service slick. Try their fish dish of the day, washed down with a cocktail.

Baskin "31" Robins, near the *Primrose Café*. Thirty-one flavours of melt-in-the-mouth imported American ice-cream. The nut crunch is to die for.

Jolly Jolly Lester, halfway between the village crossroads and Big Vagator beach. Not to be confused with *Julie Jolly's*, near the *Primrose*. This one's smaller, offering a better selection of inexpensive seasonal seafood, salads and tasty Western-style veg dishes.

Mango Tree, near the crossroads and bus stop. Moderately-priced sizzlers, seafood and deliciously spicy stir-fries prepared in front of you. Not the cheapest place around, but the food is consistently good.

Moondance, near St Anthony's church. A large shack restaurant set back off the main road, and offering Vagator's most eclectic menu: Mexican, Italian and Chinese main meals starting at around Rs80 per head.

Primrose Café and Restaurant, on the southern edge of the village. Goa's posiest café-bar livens up around 8pm and serves tasty German wholefood snacks, light meals and cakes, as well as drinks.

Ram Das Swami, above Ozran beach. Boasting a crystal clear, trance sound system, this clifftop café enjoys a prime location, with fine sea views from its terrace through the palm canopy, where Nepali waiters serve up cold beer and the usual range of budget-travellers' grub to a generally spaced-out clientele. The sort of place you'll either love or hate.

Chapora

Crouched in the shadow of a Portuguese fort on the opposite, northern side of the headland from Vagator, **CHAPORA**, 10km from Mapusa, is a lot busier than most north-coast villages. Dependent on fishing and boat-building, it has, to a great extent, retained a life of its own independent of tourism. The workaday indifference to the annual invasion of Westerners is most evident on the main street, lined with as many regular stores as travellers' cafés and restaurants. It's unlikely that Chapora will ever develop into a major resort, either. Tucked away under a dense canopy of trees on the muddy southern shore of a river estuary, it lacks both the space and the white sand that have pulled crowds to Calangute and Colva.

If you have your own transport, however, Chapora is a good base from which to explore the region: Vagator is on the doorstep, Anjuna is a short ride to the south, and the ferry crossing at Siolim – gateway to the remote north of the state – is barely fifteen minutes away by road. The village is also well connected by bus to Mapusa, and there are plenty of sociable bars and cafés to hang out in. The only drawback is that accommodation tends, again, to be thin on the ground. Apart from the guesthouses along the main road, most of the places to stay are long-stay houses in the woods.

Chapora's chief landmark is its venerable old **fort**, most easily reached from the Vagator side of the hill. At low tide, you can also walk around the bottom of the headland, via the anchorage, and the secluded coves beyond it, to Big Vagator, then head up the hill from there. The red laterite bastion, crowning the rocky bluff, was built by the Portuguese in 1617 on the site of an earlier Muslim structure (whence the village's name – from *Shahpura*, "town of the Shah"). Deserted in the nineteenth century, it lies in ruins today, although the **views** up and down the coast from the weed-infested ramparts are still superb.

Practicalities

Direct **buses** arrive at Chapora three times daily from Panjim, and every fifteen minutes from Mapusa, with departures until 7pm. **Motorcycle taxis** hang around the old banyan tree at the far end of the main street, near where the buses pull in. Air, train, bus and catamaran **tickets** may be booked or reconfirmed at Soniya Tours and Travels, next to the bus stand.

If you want to check into a cheap guesthouse while you sort out more permanent **accommodation**, try the popular *Shertor Villa* (①–②), off the west side of the main street. Nearly all its rooms, ranged around a sheltered back yard, come with fans and running water. If this place is full, try the *Helinda* (①–③), at the opposite end of the village, which has both rock-bottom options and more comfortable rooms with attached shower-toilets, and a good restaurant. As a last resort, the dilapidated *Amora* (①), between the *Helinda* and the chapel down the lane, has grotty rooms in an extension to the local fishing-tackle shop.

Finding somewhere to **eat** in Chapora is easy: just take your pick from the crop of inexpensive little cafés and restaurants on the main street. The popular *Welcome*, halfway down, offers a reasonable selection of cheap and filling seafood, Western and veg dishes, plus relentless reggae and techno music, and backgammon sets. The *Preyanka*, nearby, is in much the same mould, but has a few more Indian and Chinese options. If you're suffering from chilli-burn afterwards, *Scarlet Cold Drinks* and the *Sai Ganesh Café*, both a short way east of the main street, knock up deliciously cool fresh-fruit milkshakes.

Pernem and the far north

Sandwiched between the Chapora and Arondem rivers, the predominantly Hindu *taluka* of **Pernem** – in the *Novas Conquistas* area – is Goa's northernmost district and one of its least explored regions. Apart from the fishing village of **Arambol**, which attracts a trickle of backpackers seeking a rustic alternative to the resorts south of the Chapora River, the beautiful Pernem coastline of long sandy beaches, lagoons and coconut plantations has few settlements equipped to cope with visitors. However, the picturesque, if bumpy, journey north from Arambol to **Terekol Fort**, on the Maharashtran border, provides ample incentive to spend a day away from the beach.

Heading to Pernem from Anjuna, Vagator or Chapora, you have to travel a few kilometres inland to pick up the main Calangute road, as it runs north over a low ridge of laterite hills, to the river crossing at **Siolim**. Boatmen sometimes paddle tourists over the estuary from Chapora too, although their dugouts are unstable when laden with passengers and they can't carry motorbikes. Pending the completion of the road bridge, the two **car ferries** that chug back and forth across the river from the ramp at Siolim remain the only dependable link, and one of the high points of the journey north.

Once across the river, head straight on until you reach a fork in the road, where a sign to "Harmal/Terekol" marks the quick route to Arambol.

Arambol (Harmal)

Of the fishing settlements dotted along the north coast, only **ARAMBOL** (also known as **Harmal**), 32km northwest of Mapusa, is remotely geared to tourism – albeit in a very low-key, low-impact fashion. If you're happy with basic amenities, the village offers two very fine **beaches** and a healthy dose of peace and quiet. Parties are occasionally held here, drawing revellers across the river from Anjuna and Vagator, but these are rare intrusions into an otherwise tranquil, out-of-the-way enclave.

Modern Arambol is scattered around an area of high ground west of the main coast road, where most of the buses pull in. From here, a bumpy lane runs downhill, past a large school and the village church, to the more traditional end of the village, clustered under a canopy of widely spaced palm trees. The main **beach** lies 200m farther along the lane. Strewn with dozens of old wooden fishing boats and a line of tourist café-bars, the gently curving bay is good for bathing, but much less picturesque than its neighbour around the corner.

The smaller and less frequented of Arambol's two beaches can only be reached on foot by following the stony track over the headland to the north. Beyond an idyllic, rocky-bottomed cove, the trail emerges to a broad strip of soft, white sand hemmed in on both sides by steep cliffs. Behind it, a small freshwater lake extends along the bottom of the valley into a thick jungle. Hang around the banks of this murky green pond for long enough, and you'll probably see a fluorescent-yellow human figure or two appear from the bushes at its far end. Fed by boiling hot springs, the lake is lined with sulphurous mud, which, when smeared over the body, dries to form a surreal, butter-coloured shell. The resident hippies swear it's good for you and spend much of the day tiptoeing naked around the shallows like refugees from some obscure tribal initiation ceremony – much to the amusement of Arambol's Indian visitors. Nearby, in the woods immediately behind the lake, other members of the eccentric fringe have taken to living in the branches of an old tree; the scene resembles a cross between *Lord of the Flies* and *Apocalypse Now*.

PRACTICALITIES

Buses to and from Panjim (via Mapusa) pull into Arambol every half-hour until noon, and every ninety minutes thereafter, at the small bus stand on the main road. A faster private **minibus** service from Panjim arrives daily opposite the *chai* stalls at the beach end of the village. **Boats** leave here every Wednesday morning for the ninety-minute trip to the Anjuna flea market. Tickets should be booked in advance from the *Welcome Restaurant* by the beach (Tues–Sun 8–9am & 8–9pm; Rs150), which also rents out **motorcycles**. The **post office**, next to the church, has a poste restante box; to **change money**, however, you'll have to head for Vagator, as Arambol's State Bank of India has no foreign exchange facility.

Apart from a couple of purpose-built chalets on the edge of the village, most of Arambol's **accommodation** consists of simple houses in the woods behind the beach. Some of the more expensive places have fully equipped kitchens and showers, but the vast majority are standard-issue bare huts, with "pig" toilets and a well in the back garden. Long-stay visitors either bring their own bedding and cooking stuff, or kit themselves out at Mapusa market. The best place to stay if you only have a couple of days, however, is the *Ganesh Bar* (②–③), in the cove between the two main beaches. Scattered over the hillside directly above the café, it consists of a handful of small, new chalets with clean outhouses and superb sea views from their verandahs. The bar is also the best place in Arambol to enjoy the sunset over a chilled beer.

Finding **food** is, as ever, less problematic than finding a bed. The *Welcome Restaurant*, next to the main entrance to the beach, is a popular and sociable café serving a good range of locally caught seafood, with *toddy* to order. The palm-leaf bar-restaurants on the beach itself are slightly pricier, but still good value. Best of the bunch, on the south side of the main beach, is *Jah Kingdom*. Run by a couple of Senegalese Rastas, it serves copious salads, seafood and fruit cocktails with an African accent, and is a popular place to congregate at sunset. For simple, filling Indian food, though, you can't beat the no-nonsense *chai* stalls at the bottom of the village. *Sheila's* and *Siddi's* cheap and tasty *thalis* both come with *puris*, and they have a good travellers' breakfast menu of pancakes, eggs and curd. *Dominic's*, also at the bottom of the village (near where the road makes a sharp ninety-degree bend), is renowned for its fruit juices and milkshakes, while *Sai Deep*, a little farther up the road, does generous fruit salads with yoghurt. Over towards "Paradise" beach, *Lakes Paradise* is the best pit stop, serving good espresso coffee and sublime apple pie made by a local Dutch expatriate.

Terekol

North of Arambol, the sinuous coast road climbs to the top of a rocky, undulating plateau, then winds down through a swathe of thick woodland to join the River Arondem, which it then follows for 4km through a landscape of vivid paddy fields, coconut plantations and temple towers protruding from scruffy red-brick villages. The tiny enclave of **TEREKOL**, the northernmost tip of Goa, is reached via a clapped-out car ferry (every 30min; 5min) from the hamlet of Querim, 42km from Panjim.

After the long and scenic drive, the old **fort** that dominates the estuary from the north is a bit of an anticlimax. Hyped as one of the state's most atmospheric historic monuments, it turns out to be little more than a down-at-heel country house recently converted into a low-key luxury hotel. If your visit coincides with the arrival of a guided tour, you may get a chance to look around the gloomy interior of the **Chapel of St Anthony**, in the fort's claustrophobic cobbled square; at other times it's kept locked.

PRACTICALITIES

The few visitors that venture up to Terekol tend to do so by motorbike, heading back at the end of the day to the relative comfort of Calangute or Baga. If you run out of fuel, the nearest service station is at Arambol. One of GTDC's daily **tours** from Panjim (see p.125) comes up here, as does one daily Kadamba **bus** from the capital; alternatively, the 7am bus from Siolim, on the Chapora River, pulls in at the Querim ferry an hour later.

Accommodation is limited to the posh *Tirakhol Fort Heritage* (☎0834/782240, fax 782326; ⑦–⑧), whose rooms are pleasant and comfortable, but way overpriced at Rs800 for the no-frills (windowless) options, and around Rs1800 (plus taxes) for a luxury suite with sea views. The **restaurant** downstairs, kept busy in the daytime by bus parties, offers seafood, Indian and Chinese dishes, as well as beer.

South Goa

At present, tourism is a good deal less developed in **south Goa** than in the north. However, beyond the unattractive port city of **Vasco da Gama**, and its nearby airport, the southern reaches of the state offer some of the region's finest **beaches**, with attractive Portuguese-style villages nestled in a hilly interior.

Many visitors base themselves initially at **Colva**, 6km west of Goa's second city, **Margao**. The most developed resort in the area, Colva stands slap in the middle of a spectacular 25-kilometre stretch of pure white sand, backed by a broad band of coconut plantations. Although increasingly carved up by the British charter industry, accommodation here is plentiful, with hotels and guesthouses to suit most pockets. Longer-staying budget travellers, however, tend to steer clear of Colva in favour of neighbouring **Benaulim**, 2km farther south, which remains a low-key resort despite recent encroachments by the package-tour trade.

To escape the tourist scene altogether, rent a motorcycle or jump on a long-distance bus bound for Goa's **far south**. Less than a couple of hours by road from Margao, **Canacona** district sees few visitors, yet its rocky coast shelters a string of beautiful beaches, set against a backdrop of forest-cloaked hills. **Palolem**, 2km west of the district's main settlement, **Chaudi**, is the only one really geared up for visitors.

Vasco da Gama

VASCO DA GAMA (commonly referred to as "Vasco"), 29km by road southwest of Panjim, sits on the narrow western tip of the Mormugao peninsula, overlooking the mouth of the Zuari River. Acquired by the Portuguese in 1543, this strategically important site was formerly among the busiest ports on India's west coast. It remains a key shipping centre, with container vessels and iron-ore barges clogging the choppy river mouth, but holds nothing of interest for visitors, particularly since the completion of the Konkan Railway, when Goa's main railhead shifted from here to Margao. The only conceivable reason you might want to come to Vasco is to catch a bus to **Dabolim airport**, or **Bogmalo beach**, 8km southeast.

DABOLIM AIRPORT

Dabolim, Goa's airport, lies on top of a rocky plateau, 4km southeast of Vasco da Gama. A large new civilian terminal was recently constructed at this naval airfield to accommodate Goa's rapidly increasing air traffic, but long delays are still common – so if you're catching a flight from here, aim to check in well in advance.

Facilities in the terminal buildings include State Bank of India **foreign exchange desks** (open for flights), post office counters and counters for domestic airlines. There's also a handy pre-paid **taxi counter** outside the main exit. Fixed fares to virtually everywhere in the state are displayed behind the desk; pay here and give the slip to the driver when you arrive.

Kadamba **buses** for Panjim are supposed to meet domestic Indian Airlines flights, but don't bank on one being here when you arrive. If your budget won't stretch to a taxi ride, catch a regular bus from the intersection immediately outside the airport to Vasco, from where there are services to Margao and Panjim, Goa's principal transport hubs.

Practicalities

Vasco is laid out in a grid, bordered by Mormugao Bay to the north, and by the railway line on its southern side. Apart from the cluster of oil storage tanks, the town's most prominent landmark is the **train station** at the south end of the main Dr Rajendra Prasad Ave. **Arriving** by **bus** from Panjim or Margao, you'll be dropped off in the inconveniently situated inter-state Kadamba terminus, 3km east of the town centre. Local **minibuses** ferry passengers from here to the more central market bus stand, at the top of the square, where buses from Dabolim airport also pull in. **Auto-rickshaws**, and Ambassador and motorcycle **taxis**, hang around on the corner of Swatantra Path and Dr Rajendra Prasad Ave, near the station and the small **cycle rental** stall. If you need to **change money**, head for the State Bank of India (Mon–Fri 10am–2pm, Sat 10am–noon) at the north end of FL Gomes Rd. GTDC's **tourist information** counter is in the lobby of their *Tourist Hostel* (daily 9.30am–5pm).

Thanks to its business city status, Vasco boasts a better-than-average batch of **hotels**. Most are plush mid-range places, although there are several no-frills lodges near the railway station. Best of the budget bunch is the neat and clean *Annapurna*, on Dattatreya Deshpande Rd (☎0834/513655; ③). If it's full, try either the GTDC *Tourist Hostel*, off Swatantra Path near the station (☎0834/510009 or 513119; ③–⑤), or the well-maintained *Urvashi*, east of the main square on FL Gomes Rd (☎0834/511625; ②). Moving upscale, the *Citadel*, Pe Jose Vaz Rd (☎0834/512097, fax 513036; ⑤), currently offers the best value for money among Vasco's many modern mid-range places. At the other end of town, opposite Hindustan Petroleum, the *Maharaja* (☎0834/513075, fax 512559; ④–⑤) has similar tariffs and spotless rooms, but dismal views over the refinery. Finally, for fully air-conditioned comfort, complete with plush bars, restaurants and a gym, check in to Vasco's top hotel, *La Paz*, on Swatantra Path (☎ & fax 0834/512121; ⑦–⑧).

All of the hotels listed above have **restaurants**, but for traditional Indian snacks and *thalis*, the *Annapurna*'s ground-floor vegetarian cafeteria is hard to beat. At the other end of the centre, next door to *La Paz*, the excellent *Welcome Restaurant*, a more modern snack bar, serves a huge selection of *dosas*, as well as the usual range of *bhajis* and a full Punjabi menu; most main dishes cost between Rs30 and Rs50.

Bogmalo

Immediately south of the airport, the Mormugao peninsula's sun-parched central plateau tumbles to a flat-bottomed valley lined with coconut trees and red-brick huts.

The sandy **beach** at the end of the cove would be even more picturesque if not for the monstrous multistorey edifice perched above it. Until *Oberoi* erected a huge five-star hotel here, **BOGMALO** was just another small fishing village, hemmed in by a pair of palm-fringed headlands at the northern end of Colva Bay. The village is still here, complete with a tiny whitewashed chapel and gangs of hogs nosing through the rubbish, but its environs have been transformed. Pricey café-bars blaring Western music have crept up the beach, while the clearing below the hotel is prowled by assiduous Kashmiri handicraft vendors.

Even so, compared with Calangute or Colva, Bogmalo is still a small-scale resort. As long as you haven't come to Goa to get away from it all or party all night, then you'll find it congenial enough. The beach is clean and not too crowded, the water reasonably safe for swimming, and there are plenty of places to eat, drink and shop. If, on the other hand, you're looking for somewhere not yet on the package-tourist map, you'll be better off farther south, at the far end of Colva beach or beyond.

Practicalities

Bogmalo can be reached by **bus** or **taxi** from Vasco da Gama, 8km northwest. It's also near enough to the airport for a last-minute dip before catching a plane. As this is primarily a package-tour destination, walk-in **accommodation** is very limited and best booked ahead. Costing around $160 per night for full board, the most luxurious option here is the *Sarovar Park Plaza* (☎0834/513291, fax 513311; ⑨), overlooking the beach, which offers formula five-star luxury, with a pool, central a/c and a sun terrace. A stone's throw up the beach, *Sarita Guesthouse* (☎0834/555965; ⑤) is altogether more humble, and much better value for money, with well-furnished, comfortable rooms and a terrace bar-restaurant. You're more likely to find a vacancy here than at nearby *Joet's* (☎0834/514997; ⑤), Bogmalo's other mid-range guesthouse, which is invariably block-booked by charter companies.

There's no shortage of places **to eat and drink** in the village. Those dotted along the beach depend on a steady trickle of refugees from the *Park Plaza*, and have whacked up their prices accordingly. The *Full Moon Kneipe*, outside the main hotel entrance, takes the lion's share of the overspill, though the menu, mainly seafood and chicken, is predictably expensive, and the portions are not overly generous. The *Sea Cuisine* opposite offers identical dishes and prices, but tends to be less crowded at lunchtimes. Farther up the beach, all the café-bars are in much the same mould; only the music changes.

DIVING AT BOGMALO

A small **dive school** recently opened up in Bogmalo and is one of the few places in India where you can do PADI-approved Open Water Diving Courses. Operating out of *Joet's Guesthouse*, at the far end of the beach, the British-run outfit also offers half-day "Try-Dives" for novices, guided dives to shipwreck sites and coral beds off the coast and tuition for more advanced qualifications. Prices range from Rs1300 for a one-tank guided dive, to Rs12,500 for the three-day PADI Open Water course. For more information, contact Goa Diving, House no. 145P, Chapel Bhat, Chicalim, near Bogmalo (☎0834/555117 or 555036).

Margao (Madgaon) and around

MARGAO, the capital of prosperous Salcete *taluka*, is regarded as Goa's second city, even though it's marginally smaller than Vasco da Gama, 30km northwest. Surrounded by fertile farmland, the town has always been an important agricultural market, and was once a major religious centre, with dozens of wealthy temples and *dharamshalas* – however, most of these were destroyed when the Portuguese absorbed the area into their Novas Conquistas (New Conquests) during the seventeenth century. Today, Catholic churches still outnumber Hindu shrines, but Margao has retained a distinctly cosmopolitan feel, largely due to a huge influx of migrant labour from neighbouring Karnataka and Maharashtra. The resultant overcrowding has become a real problem in the town centre, whose 1950s municipal buildings and modern concrete structures stew under a haze of traffic pollution.

If you're arriving in Goa on the Konkan Railway from Mumbai or South India, you'll almost certainly have to pause in Margao to pick up onwards transport by road. The other reason to come here is to shop at the town's excellent **market**. Stretching from the south edge of the main square to within a stone's throw of the old train station, the bazaar centres on a labyrinthine covered area that's a rich source of authentic souvenirs and a good place to browse. While you're here, take a short rickshaw ride north to the stately **Church of the Holy Spirit**, in the heart of a dishevelled but picturesque colonial enclave. Presiding over the dusty Largo de Igreja square, the church, built by the Portuguese in 1675, is one of the finest examples of late Baroque architecture in Goa, boasting a pristine white facade and an interior dripping with gilt, crystal and stucco.

The picturesque farming villages strewn across the verdant countryside **around Margao** host a scattering of evocative colonial monuments and a handful of Hindu temples that can be visited on day-trips from the coast.

Practicalities

Margao's new **train station**, the only stop in Goa for most long-distance express services on the Konkan Railway, lies 3km south of the centre. The reservation office (Mon–Sat 8am–4.30pm, Sun 8am–2pm) is divided between the ground and first floor; bookings for the superfast Rajdhani Express to Delhi are made at the hatch to the left of the main entrance. Tickets for trains to Mumbai are in short supply – so

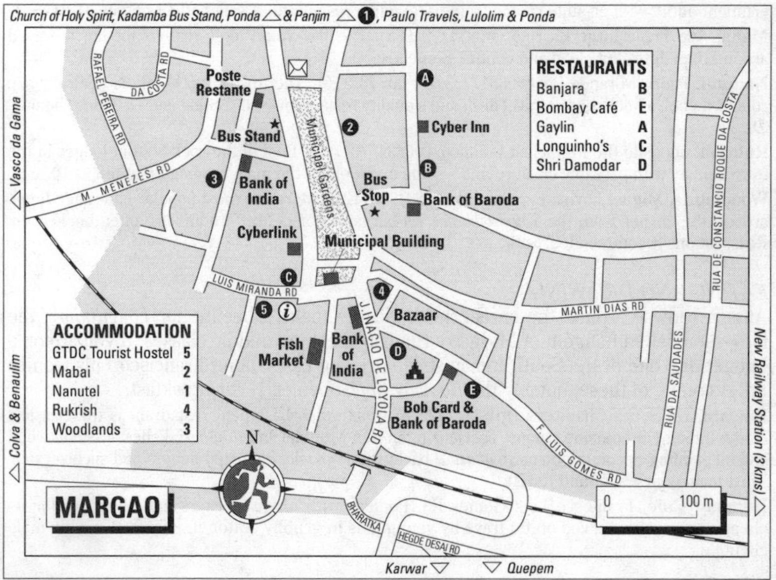

make your reservation as far in advance as possible, get here early in the day to avoid agonizingly long queues, and bring a book. **Several** of the principal trains that stop in Margao do so at unsociable times of the night, but there's a 24-hour information counter (☎0832/712790) and around-the-clock pre-paid auto-rickshaw stand outside the exit.

Local private buses to Colva and Benaulim leave from in front of the *Kamat Hotel*, on the east side of Margao's main square. Arriving on long-distance government services you can get off either here or (at a more leisurely pace) at the main **Kadamba bus stand**, 3km farther north, on the outskirts of town. The latter is the departure point for inter-state services to Mangalore, via Chaudi and Gokarn, and for services to Panjim and north Goa. Paulo Travel's deluxe coach to and from Hampi works from a lot next to the *Nanutel Hotel*, one kilometre or so south of the Kadamba bus stand on Padre Miranda Rd.

GTDC's **information office** (Mon–Fri 9.30am–5.30pm; ☎0834/222513), which sells tourist maps and keeps useful lists of train and bus times, is inside the lobby of the *Tourist Hostel*, on the southwest corner of the main square. **Exchange** facilities are available at the State Bank of India (Mon–Fri 10am–2pm, Sat 10am–noon), off the west side of the square; the Bobcard office in the market sub-branch of the Bank of Baroda, on Luis Gomes Rd, does Visa encashments. The **GPO** is at the top of the municipal gardens, although its **poste restante** is in a different building, 200m west on the Rua Diogo da Costa. Margao's least expensive **internet café** is *CyberLink*, in the Rangavi Building, opposite the Municipal Building in the centre of town; they charge Rs4/minute, or Rs200/hour.

ACCOMMODATION

With Colva and Benaulim a mere twenty-minute bus ride away, it's hard to think of a reason why anyone should choose to **stay** in Margao. If you do get stuck here, however, one of the following hotels should have a vacancy.

GTDC Tourist Hostel, behind the Municipal Building (☎0834/721966). Standard good-value government outfit, with en-suite rooms (some a/c) and a restaurant. A safe budget option. ④–⑤.

Mabai, 108 Praca Jorge Barreto (☎0834/721658). The *Woodlands*' only real competitor is frayed around the edges, but clean and central. Some a/c. ④.

Nanutel, Padre Miranda Rd (☎0834/733176, fax 733175). The town's top hotel: 55 centrally a/c rooms, a pool, a bookshop, a travel desk and a quality restaurant (see "Eating and Drinking" below). ⑦–⑧.

Rukrish, opposite the Municipal Building (☎0834/721709). Best of the rock-bottom lodges in the town centre, with passably clean rooms – some overlooking the main road and market. ①–②.

Woodlands, Miguel Loyola Furtado Rd (☎0834/721121). Margao's most popular mid-range hotel, around the corner from the *Tourist Hostel*. Its bargain "non-deluxe" rooms are often booked up. Reservations recommended. Some a/c. ③–④.

EATING AND DRINKING

After a browse around the bazaar, most visitors make a beeline for *Longuinho's*, the long-established hangout of Margao's English-speaking middle classes. If you are on a budget, try one of the South Indian-style pure veg cafés along Francisco Luis Gomes Rd. A couple of these, notably the *Bombay Café*, open early for breakfast.

Banjara, De Souza Chambers (☎0834/722088). This swish basement restaurant is the classiest North Indian joint outside Panjim, specializing in rich Mughlai and *tandoori* dishes. Tasteful wood and oil-painting decor, unobtrusive *ghazaal* background music, imported liquors and slick service. Most main courses around Rs100.

Bombay Café, Francisco Luis Gomes Rd. Popular with office workers and shoppers for its cheap veg snacks, served on tin trays by young lads in grubby cotton uniforms. A mostly male clientele.

Gaylin, behind Grace Church. Smart, air-conditioned Chinese restaurant serving a good selection of Cantonese and Schezuan dishes (most of them steeped in hot, red Goan chilli paste). Count on around Rs150-200 for three courses; extra for drinks.

Longuinho's, opposite the *Tourist Hostel*, Rua Luis Miranda. Relaxing, old-fashioned café serving a reasonable selection of moderately priced meat, fish, and vegetarian main meals, freshly baked savoury snacks (including moreish veg and prawn patties), cakes and drinks.

Shri Damodar, opposite Gandhi Market, Francisco Luis Gomes Rd. One of several inexpensive café and ice-cream parlours ranged around the temple square. This one is the cleanest, and has an air-cooled "family" (read "women's") room upstairs.

Lutolim

Peppered around the leafy lanes of **LUTOLIM**, 10km northeast of Margao, are several of Goa's most beautiful **colonial mansions**, dating from the heyday of the Portuguese empire when this was the country seat of the territory's top brass. Lying just off the main road, the village is served by eight daily **buses** from Margao, which drop passengers off on the square in front of a lopsided-looking church. The cream of Lutolim's houses lie within walking distance of here, nestled in the woods, or along the road leading south. However, you shouldn't turn up at any of them unannounced; **visits have to be arranged in advance** through the Margao tourist office.

Pick of the crop in Lutolim is **Miranda House**, a stone's throw from the square. Fronted by a plain classical facade, the mansion was built in the 1700s, though renovated later following raids by a clan of rebel Rajput bandits. Today, it is occupied by a famous Goan cartoonist, and his family, direct descendants of the wealthy areca planters who originally owned the surrounding estate. **Roque Caetan Miranda House**, two minutes' walk south of the square, and **Salvador Costa House**, tucked away on the western edge of the village, are other mansions worth hunting out; the latter is occupied by an elderly lady who only welcomes visitors by appointment.

Lutolim's other attraction is the quirky model village-cum-heritage centre, a short way east of the square, called **Ancestral Goa** (daily 9am–6pm; Rs20). Set up to show visitors a cross-section of local village life a hundred years ago, it's a well-meaning but ultimately dull exhibition of miniature houses and dressed dummies.

Chandor

Thirteen kilometres east of Margao across the fertile rice fields of Salcete lies sleepy **CHANDOR** village, a scattering of tumbledown villas and farmhouses ranged along shady tree-lined lanes. The main reason to venture out here is the splendid **Perreira-Braganza/Menezes-Braganza house** (daily except holidays; donation), regarded as the grandest of Goa's colonial mansions. Dominating the dusty village square, the house, built in the 1500s by the wealthy Braganza family for their two sons, has a huge double-storeyed facade, with 28 windows flanking its entrance. Braganza de Perreira, the great-grandfather of the present owner, was the last knight of the king of Portugal; more recently, Menezes Braganza (1879–1938), a famous journalist and freedom fighter, was one of the few Goan aristocrats actively to oppose Portuguese rule. Forced to flee Chandor in 1950, the family returned in 1962 to find their house, amazingly, untouched. The airy tiled interiors of both wings contain a veritable feast of **antiques**. Furniture enthusiasts and lovers of rare Chinese porcelain, in particular, will find plenty to drool over, while anyone interested in religious relics should request a glimpse of St Francis Xavier's diamond-encrusted toenail, recently retrieved from a local bank vault and enshrined in the east wing's tiny chapel.

Visitors generally travel to Chandor by taxi, but you can also get there by bus from Margao (8 daily; 45min), or by train via Chandragoa station, 1km northwest. While many people turn up without an appointment, it is still a good idea to call ahead through the tourist office.

Colva

A hot-season retreat for Margao's moneyed middle classes since long before Independence, **COLVA** is the oldest and largest – but least appealing – of south Goa's resorts. Its leafy outlying *vaddos*, or wards, are pleasant enough, dotted with colonial-style villas and ramshackle fishing huts, but the beachfront is dismal: a lacklustre collection of concrete hotels, souvenir stalls and fly-blown snack bars strewn around a bleak central roundabout. Each afternoon, bus-loads of visitors from out of state mill around here after a paddle on the crowded foreshore, pestered by postcard-*wallahs* and the little urchins whose families camp on the outskirts. The atmosphere is not improved by heaps of rubbish dumped in a rank-smelling ditch that runs behind the beach, nor by the stench of drying fish wafting from the nearby village. If, however, you steer clear of this central market area, and stick to the cleaner, greener outskirts, Colva can be a pleasant and convenient place to stay for a while. Swimming is relatively safe, while the sand, at least away from the beachfront, is spotless and scattered with beautiful shells.

Practicalities

Buses leave Margao (from outside the *Kamat Hotel* on Praça Jorge Barreto) every thirty minutes for Colva, dropping passengers at the main beachfront, and at various points along the main road. The thirty- to forty-minute trip costs virtually nothing, but can be a real endurance test towards the end of the day when the conductors pack on punters like sardines. Far better to jump in an **auto-rickshaw** for Rs50, or squeeze into a shared **taxi**. Heading in the opposite direction, from Colva to Margao, these pick up passengers at the entrance to the beach, along the main road leading to the village and

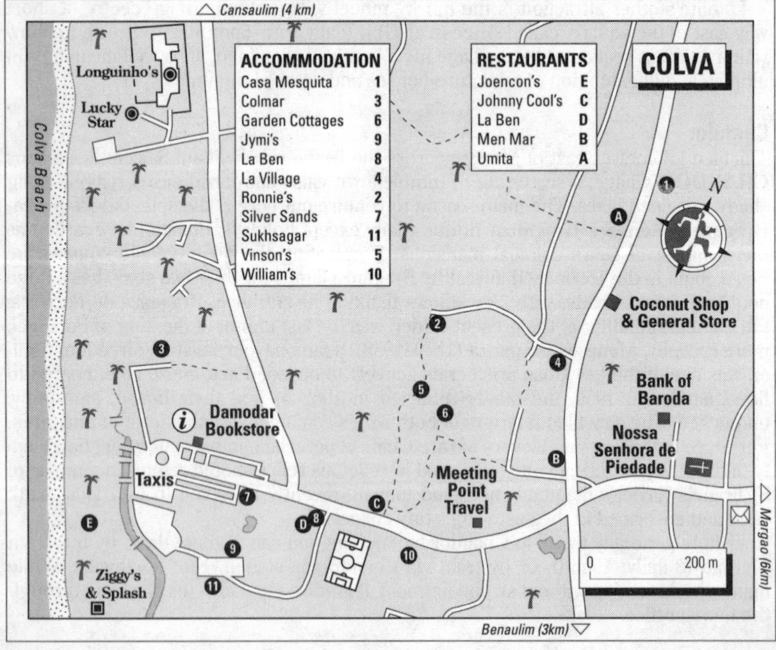

from the crossroads 200m west of the church. Regular mini-van and Ambassador taxis line up on the north side of the beachfront, next to the public toilets and outside several of the upmarket resort hotels, including the *Silver Sands* and *Penthouse*.

To rent a **motorcycle**, ask around the taxi rank or in front of *Vincy's Hotel*, where 100cc Yamahas are on offer at the usual rates (see p.125). Their owners will advise you to avoid Margao if you haven't got a valid international driver's licence, as the approach road passes the police post. **Fuel** is sold by the Bisleri bottle from a little house behind the Menino Jesus College, just east of *William's Resort*. This is the only fuel stop in Colva, but the stuff they sell may well be adulterated with kerosene.

Meeting Point Travel (☎0834/723338, fax 732004), between *William's Resort* and the crossroads, exchanges **travellers' cheques** and **cash** at a little under bank rates, and Sanatan Travel Agency, 200m east of the church does encashments on Visa and Mastercard. Both also book and reconfirm domestic and international flights, and arrange deluxe bus, catamaran and train tickets to other parts of India.

The **post office**, opposite the church in the village, has a small but reliable **poste restante** box. Damodar Book Store, on the beachfront, stocks a good selection of reasonably priced secondhand paperbacks in English. They also do part-exchange, and have the best range of postcards in Colva.

ACCOMMODATION

Mirroring the village's rapid rise as a package tour resort, Colva's plentiful **accommodation** ranges from bare cockroach-infested cells to swish campuses of chalets and swimming pools, with a fair selection of good-value guesthouses in between. Most of the mid- and top-of-the-range places are strung out along the main beach road or just behind it. Budget rooms lie amid the more peaceful palm groves and paddy fields north of here: the quarter known as Ward 4, which is accessible via the path that winds north from *Johnny Cool's* restaurant, or from the other side via a lane leading west off the main Colva–Vasco road.

Casa Mesquita, 194 Vasco Rd, Ward 3 (no phone). Large rooms, with rickety four-poster beds, no fans or attached shower-toilets, in fading old colonial-style house. Relaxing mosaic-floored verandahs, Western water toilet and some cheap dorm beds available on request. Good value. ①–②.

Colmar, on the beachfront (☎0834/220485). Colva's oldest purpose-built hotel overlooks the beach, comprising comfortable chalets, and some cheaper non-attached rooms, grouped around a central lawn. No advance bookings, but good off-season discounts. Some a/c. ⑤–⑥.

Garden Cottages, Ward 4 (no phone). Immaculately maintained, attractive budget guesthouse in Colva's most tranquil quarter. Spacious twin-bedded en suite rooms with fans, and a garden. Very popular and excellent value. ②.

Jymi's, opposite *Sukhsagar* (☎0834/712502). Large, established budget-travellers' hotel, with passable en-suite rooms. A good place until you find somewhere nicer, as it usually has vacancies. ③.

La Ben's, on the beach road (☎0834/222009). Neat, clean, and good value, though better known for its rooftop restaurant. ⑤–⑥

La Village, 333 Vasco Rd, Ward 4 (no phone). Relaxed and friendly roadside guesthouse geared to budget backpackers, with clean rooms (some attached), good wooden beds, mosquito nets and a safe-deposit facility. Ultra basic, but the cheapest place in Colva. ①.

Ronnie's, Ward 4 (no phone). Standard cell-block rooms, all with attached shower-toilets, and idyllic views west over the paddy fields from verandahs. ①.

Silver Sands, on the beach road (☎0834/721645). Average rooms (some a/c) ranged around a pool, with restaurant and health club. Facilities include car rental, foreign exchange and a courtesy bus to the airport. Popular with package companies, but much shabbier than the others at this price. ⑥.

Sukhsagar, opposite the *Penthouse* (☎0834/220224, fax 731666). Nothing special from the outside, but its en-suite rooms are clean, light and airy, and the best deal in this price range. ⑤–⑥.

Vinson's, Ward 4 (no phone). Newest of this ward's good-value cheap options; quiet and secluded. ①–②.

William's, on the beach road (☎0834/221077, fax 222852). Flashy package-tour complex, 400m from the beach, with good facilities, some a/c, and a pool. Accepts walk-in customers. ⑦–⑧.

EATING, DRINKING AND NIGHTLIFE

When the season's in full swing, Colva's beachfront sprouts a row of large seafood **restaurants** on stilts, some of them very ritzy indeed, with tablecloths, candles and smooth music. The prices in these places are top-whack, but the portions are correspondingly vast and standards generally high. Budget travellers are equally well catered for, with a sprinkling of **shack-cafés** at the less frequented ends of the beach, and along the Vasco Rd.

Although never an established rave venue, Colva's **nightlife** is livelier than anywhere else in south Goa, thanks to its ever-growing contingent of young package tourists. The two most happening nightspots are down in the dunes south of the beachfront area: *Splash* boasts a big MTV satellite screen and music to match, and a late bar and disco that liven up around 10pm. A sandy plod just south of here, posier *Ziggy's* boasts Goa's only air-conditioned dance floor, a thumping Indian-ragga and techno sound system and a sociable terrace littered with wicker easy chairs. If you'd prefer to get plastered somewhere cheaper and less pretentious, try *Johnny Cool's*, midway between the beach and Colva crossroads. *Men Mar*, on the Vasco Rd, also serves beers, snacks and *lassis* until around 10.30pm.

Joencon's, second restaurant south from the beachfront. The classiest of Colva's beach restaurants. Agonizingly slow service and pricey, but the food is superb: try their flamboyant fish sizzlers, mouthwatering *tandoori* sharkfish or Chinese and Indian vegetarian specialties.

Johnny Cool's, opposite *William's Resort*, on the beach road. Inexpensive roadside café-bar with views across the fields behind. Serves different beers and spirits and tasty pizzas.

La Ben's, on the beach road. Pleasant rooftop restaurant located in the hotel of the same name, with a predictable moderately priced menu and sea views. A good sunset spot.

Men Mar, Vasco Rd. Their *lassis*, prepared with fresh fruit and homemade curd, are delicious. Open for breakfast.

Umita, Vasco Rd. Down-to-earth Goan and Indian veg cooking served up by a friendly Hindu family. Try their blow-out "special" *thalis* or whopping fresh-fruit-and-curd breakfasts. Opens early.

COBRA WARNING

You'll rarely see a villager in Colva or Benaulim crossing a **rice field at night**. This is because paddy is prime territory for snakes, especially cobras. If you do intend to cut across the fields after dark, take along a strong flashlight, make plenty of noise and hit the ground ahead of you with a stick to warn any lurking serpents of your approach.

Benaulim

According to Hindu mythology, Goa was created when the sage Shri Parasurama, Vishnu's sixth incarnation, fired an arrow into the sea from the top of the Western Ghats and ordered the waters to recede. The spot where the shaft fell to earth, known in Sanskrit as *Banali* ("place where the arrow landed") and later corrupted by the Portuguese to **BENAULIM**, lies in the centre of Colva Beach, 7km west of Margao. Only a decade ago, this fishing and rice-farming village, scattered around the coconut groves and paddy fields between the main Colva–Mobor road and the dunes, had barely made it onto the backpackers' map. Now, the shady lane leading through it is studded with guesthouses and souvenir stalls, while the paddy fields on the outskirts are gradually disappearing under a rash of gigantic luxury resorts and time-share apartment buildings. If these eventually attract the huge number of

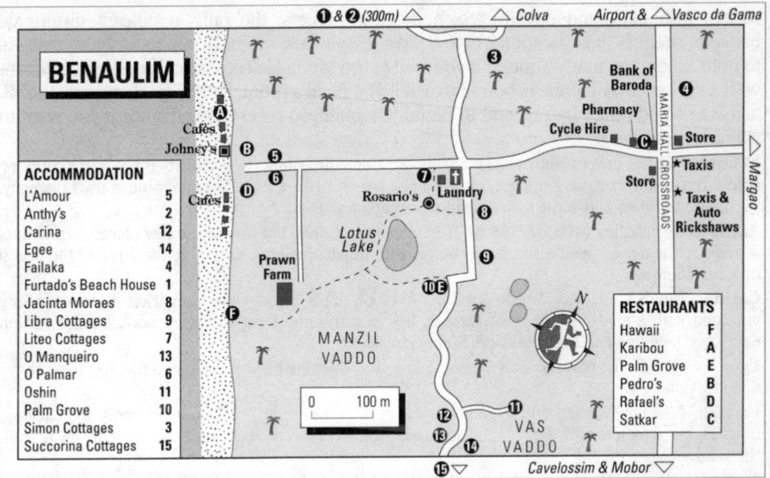

package tourists they are intended to, Benaulim's days as a sleepy village will soon be over. For the time being, however, this remains a peaceful and welcoming place to unwind.

Either side of the sand-blown beachfront, the gently shelving sands shimmer away almost to the horizon, littered with photogenic wooden fishing boats that provide welcome shade if the walk from the palm trees to the sea gets too much. Hawkers, itinerant masseurs and fruit-*wallahs* appear from time to time, but you can easily escape them by heading south towards neighbouring **Varca**, where tourism has thus far made little impact. Moreover, the sea is safe for swimming, being generally jellyfish-free, while the village itself boasts a few serviceable bars and restaurants, several telephone booths and a couple of stores.

Practicalities

Buses from Margao, Colva, Varca, Cavelossim and Mobor roll through Benaulim every half-hour, dropping passengers at the Maria Hall crossroads. Ranged around this busy junction are two well-stocked **general stores**, a couple of **café-bars**, a **bank**, **pharmacy**, **laundry** and the taxi and auto-rickshaw rank, from where you can pick up **transport** to the beach 2km west.

Signs offering **bicycles** and **motorbikes** for rent are dotted along the lane leading to the sea: rates are standard, descending in proportion to the length of time you keep the vehicle. The nearest place to **change money** is the Sanatan Travel Agency in Colva (see p.167), or one of the banks in Margao (see p.164). Benaulim's Bank of Baroda (Mon–Fri 9am–1pm, Sat 9am–noon) only handles Visa card encashments; the *L'Amour Beach Resort* has a foreign exchange counter for guests. Finally, international and domestic flights can be booked or reconfirmed at Meeting Point Travel, in the centre of the village, which also does deluxe bus, train and catamaran ticketing for cities elsewhere in India.

ACCOMMODATION

Benaulim's **accommodation** consists largely of small budget guesthouses, scattered around the lanes 1km or so back from the beach. Most are featureless annexes of spartan rooms with fans, and usually attached shower-toilets; the only significant difference between them is their location. As few have telephones, the best way to find a vacancy is to hunt around on foot, although if you wait at the Maria Hall crossroads or the beachfront with a rucksack, someone is bound to ask if you need a room. During peak season, the village's few mid-range hotels tend to be fully booked, so reserve in advance if you want to stay in one of these.

L'Amour, on the beachfront (☎0834/737961-2). Benaulim's longest-established hotel is a comfortable thirty-room/cottage complex, close to the beach, with a terrace restaurant, a travel agency, exchange facilities and some a/c. No single occupancy. ⑤–⑥.

Anthy's, Sernabatim (☎0834/733824). Technically in Colva, but one of the few places hereabouts actually in the dunes. Well-maintained rooms, with tiny bathrooms, breezy verandahs and the beach on your doorstep. ③.

Carina, Tamdi-Mati, Vas Vaddo (☎0834/734166). This good-value upmarket hotel, recently enlarged with a spacious roadside annexe, lies in a tranquil location with a pool, bar-restaurant, exchange facilities and room service. Some a/c. ⑤–⑦.

Egee, Vas Vaddo (no phone). Half a dozen nicer-than-average budget rooms on the first floor above a family house. ②.

Failaka, Adsulim Nagar (☎0834/734416). Large new roadside hotel built primarily for package tourists, but which usually has some vacancies. Ask for a room on the quieter east side, away from the road. ⑤.

Furtado's Beach House, Sernabatim (no phone). Not to be confused with *Furtado's* in the village proper. This one is slap on the beach, with en-suite rooms and road access. Very popular, mainly with refugees from Colva. The best fallback if nearby *Anthy's* is full. ③.

Jacinta Moraes, 1608/A Vas Vaddo (☎0834/722706). Half a dozen largish, clean rooms with fans, attached shower-toilets and sound plumbing. Some Western toilets. Very good value. ②.

Libra Cottages, Vas Vaddo (☎0834/731740). In much the same mould as *Jacinta Moraes*, only marginally cheaper, and with a couple of larger, self-contained family rooms around the back. ②.

Liteo Cottages, opposite a tailor's shop, on the beach road (☎0834/721173). Very large, clean rooms (all en suite and with balconies) in the centre of the village. Hardly the most inspiring location, but good value if tariffs are maintained. ③.

O Manqueiro, Vas Vaddo (☎0834/734164). Very basic budget accommodation in the secluded south of the village, run by a family with a predilection for plastic fruit. Mostly shared shower-toilets. The rooms on the top floor are the best. ②.

O Palmar, opposite *L'Amour* (no phone). A row of slightly shabby sea-facing chalets, virtually on the beach, with their own verandahs. Those at the rear are the most appealing, as they're not plagued by wind-blown rubbish from the beachfront. ④.

Oshin, Mazil Vaddo (☎0834/722707). Large, triple-storey complex set well back from the road, with balconies looking over the tree from top-floor rooms. Spacious and clean, with en-suite bathrooms. A notch above most places in this area, and good value. ④.

Palm Grove, Tamdi-Mati, 149 Vas Vaddo (☎0834/722533). Secluded hotel surrounded by beautiful gardens, with a luxurious new annexe around the back; some a/c, pleasant terrace restaurant and friendly management. A bike ride back from the beachfront, but by far the most pleasant place in its class. ④–⑦.

Simon Cottages, Sernabatim Ambeaxir (☎0834/734283). Currently the best budget deal in Benaulim: large rooms, all with shower-toilets and sit-outs, opening on to a sandy courtyard in a secluded spot. You can book through Silver Stores at Maria Hall crossroads during shop hours. ②–③.

Succorina Cottages, House no. 1711/A, Vas Vaddo, Vaddi (☎0834/712072). Immaculate rooms in a new house, 1km south of the crossroads in the fishing village. You'll need some form of transport to stay here, but it's a perfect place to get away from the tourist scene. ②.

EATING AND DRINKING

Benaulim's proximity to Margao market, along with the presence of its Christian fishing community, means its restaurants serve the most succulent, competitively priced seafood in Goa. The most popular places to **eat** are the shack cafés in the beachfront area, where *Johncy's* catches most of the passing custom. However, you'll find better food at lower prices in the smaller terrace restaurants farther along the beach and scattered around the village. Arguably the best of bunch is the *Palm Grove*'s congenial garden restaurant, and there is a string of lookalike café-bars which dot the lane leading to it. For fresh seafood, though, the *Hawaii* shack is hard to beat.

Hawaii, south of the village behind the beach. Among the best shack restaurants for miles, run by a warm local family. Their seafood, grilled or flash-fried in tasty Worcester sauce, is straight off the boats, the portions huge and the prices fair, and they serve stiff pegs of the village's finest *feni*. To find it, head south down the beach, or walk down the lane leading south off the beach road to the government prawn farm, and head across the dunes from there.

Karibou, the last shack in the row running north from *Johncy's* at the beachfront. Easily the best seafood in this area, served by a friendly American-Israeli/Goan couple. Try one of their fish steaks steeped in rich, garlic butter sauce. A good venue for a sundowner, too. They've had trouble getting a licence in recent years, so the shack may not be at the location marked on the map.

Pedro's, on the beachfront. Long waits, but the food – mostly fish steaks served with homemade sauces – is freshly cooked, tasty and inexpensive.

Rafael's, on the beachfront. Rough-and-ready beach café serving all the usual dishes, plus fried rice, salads and deliciously stodgy oven-hot coconut pudding.

Palm Grove, Tamdi-Mati, Vas Vaddo. Mostly Goan seafood, with some Indian and Continental options, dished up al fresco in a cosy garden café-restaurant. Worth the trip out here.

Varca

If you're staying in Benaulim, you're bound at some point to visit **VARCA**. The row of beached wooden fishing boats 2 kilometres south of Benaulim belong to its community of Christian fisher-folk, whose palm-thatched long houses line the foot of the grassy dunes. Of the tourists that pedal past, few stay longer than a few hours crashed in the shade of an outrigger. However, it is possible to find **rooms to rent** in family houses by asking around the village. Facilities are ultra-basic, with well-water and "pig" toilets, but if you're looking for somewhere authentically Goan, yet not too far off-track, Varca is worth considering. A bicycle and cooking equipment are essential for long spells.

The only blots on the otherwise unspoiled landscape around Varca are the *Resorte de Goa* (☎0834/245066; ⑨), a three-star resort, whose rooms and chalets cluster around a pool and sun terrace, with two bars and a restaurant, along with the large and swish *Ramada Renaissance* (☎0834/745208; ⑧–⑨), which boasts a palatial reception, nine-hole golf course, Polynesian restaurant, poolside disco and casino.

Cavelossim and Mobor

Sleepy **CAVELOSSIM**, straddling the coast road 11km south of Colva, is the last major settlement in southwest Salcete – its only claim to fame. A short way beyond the village's picturesque church square, a narrow lane veers left (east) across an open expanse of paddy fields to the Cavelossim–Assolna **ferry crossing** (last departures: 8.30pm from Cavelossim, 8.45pm from Assolna), near the mouth of the Sal River. If you're heading south to Canacona, turn left off the ferry – *not* right as indicated on local maps – and carry on as far as Assolna bazaar, clustered around a junction on the main road. A right turn at this crossroads puts you on track for Canacona.

Carry straight on at the junction just past the square in Cavelossim and you'll eventually arrive at **MOBOR**, where Colva beach fades into a rounded sandy spur at the mouth of the Assolna River. This would be an exquisite spot if it weren't the site of south Goa's largest, and most obtrusive, package-tourist enclave. Crammed together on to a narrow spit of dunes between the surf and estuary, the controversial *Leela Beach*, *Holiday Inn* and *Dona Sylvia* resort hotels combine to create a holiday-camp ambience that has as little to do with Goa as their architecture. Moreover, most have at some time been served writs by the region's green lobby for infringing environmental laws. The best place to stay here is the friendly family-run place *Gaffino's* (☎0834/746385 or 746430; ⑤–⑥); the smallest of Mobor's hotels, with sixteen immaculate rooms (with river views) and a small restaurant, it's great value considering the cost of other accommodation in the area. If *Gaffino's* is full and you don't have hundreds of dollars to waste on the hugely inflated tariffs they charge walk-in customers elsewhere, it's best to look for accommodation farther south.

The far south: Canacona

Ceded to the Portuguese by the Rajah of Sund in the Treaty of 1791, Goa's **far south – Canacona district** – was among the last parts of the territory to be absorbed into the the Novas Conquistas, and has retained a distinctly Hindu feel. The area also boasts some of the state's most outstanding scenery. Set against a backdrop of the jungle-covered Sahyadri Hills (an extension of the Western Ghat range), a string of pearl-white coves and sweeping beaches scoop its indented coastline, enfolded by laterite headlands and colossal piles of black boulders.

So far, tourism has made little impression on this beautiful landscape. With the exception of the village of **Palolem**, whose near-perfect beach attracts a steady flow of day-trippers and longer-staying travellers during high season, the coastal settlements remain rooted in a traditional fishing and *todi*-tapping economy. However, the red gash of the **Konkan Railway** threatens to bring its days as a tranquil rural backwater to an end. For the last year or two, it has been possible to reach Canacona by direct "superfast" express trains from Mumbai, Panjim and Mangalore: the developers' bulldozers and concrete mixers are sure to follow.

The region's main transport artery is the NH17, which crawls across the Sahyadri and Karmali Ghats towards Karnataka via the district headquarters, **Chaudi**. Bus services between here and Margao are frequent; off the highway, however, bullock carts and bicycles far outnumber motor vehicles. The only way to do the area justice, therefore, is by motorcycle, although you'll have to rent one farther north (Benaulim's your best bet for this) and drive it down here as few are available on the spot.

Palolem

PALOLEM, 2km west of Chaudi, pops up more often in glossy holiday brochures than any other beach in Goa; not because the village is a major package-tour destination, but because its crescent-shaped bay, lined with a swaying curtain of coconut palms, is irresistibly photogenic. Hemmed in by a pair of wooded headlands, a perfect curve of white sand arcs north from a pile of huge boulders to the spur of **Sahyadri Ghat**, which here tapers into the sea.

Until recently, foreign tourists were few and far between in Palolem. Over the past five or six years, however, increasing numbers of budget travellers have begun to find their way here, and the village is now far from the undiscovered idyll it used to be, with a string of cafés, Karnatakan hawkers and a tent camp crowding the beachfront. Souvenir stalls have also sprung up, catering mainly for the mini-van and boat parties of charter tourists on day-trips from resorts farther north. In spite of these encroachments, Palolem remains a resolutely traditional village, where the easy pace of life is dictated more by the three daily rounds of *todi*-tapping than the exigencies of tourism.

ARRIVAL, INFORMATION AND LOCAL TRANSPORT

Buses run between Margao and Karwar (in Karnataka) via Chaudi (every 30min; 2hr), where you can pick up an **auto-rickshaw** (Rs30) or **taxi** (Rs50) to Palolem. Alternatively, get off at the Char Rostay (Four-Way) crossroads, 1.5km before Chaudi, and walk the remaining kilometre or so to the village. A couple of buses each day also go all the way to Palolem from Margao; these stop at the end of the lane leading from

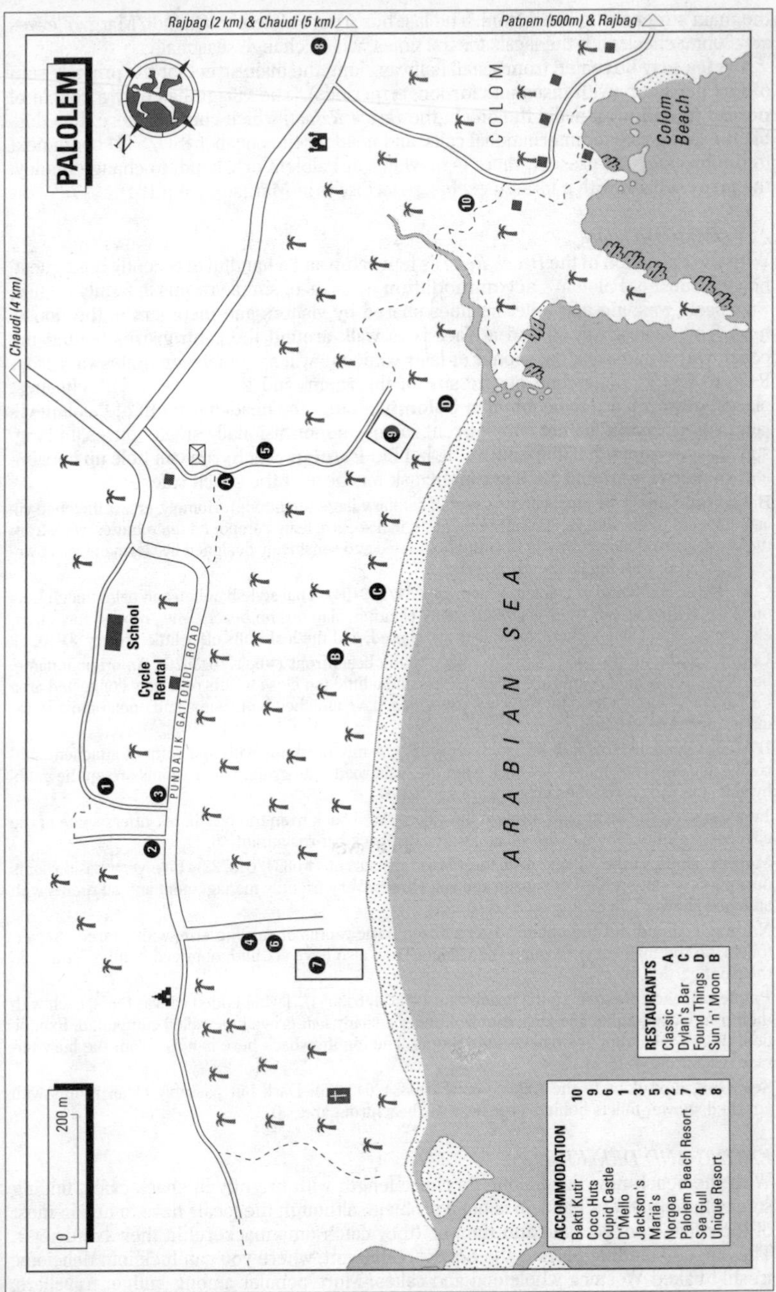
PALOLEM
Rajbag (2 km) & Chaudi (5 km)
Patnem (500m) & Rajbag
Chaudi (4 km)
COLOM
Colom Beach
ARABIAN SEA
School
Cycle Rental
PUNDALIK GAITONDE ROAD
0
200 m
ACCOMMODATION
Bakti Kutir 10
Coco Huts 9
Cupid Castle 6
D'Mello 1
Jackson's 3
Maria's 5
Norgoa 2
Palolem Beach Resort 7
Sea Gull 4
Unique Resort 8
RESTAURANTS
Classic A
Dylan's Bar C
Found Things D
Sun 'n' Moon B

the main street to the beachfront. The last bus from Palolem to Chaudi/Margao leaves at 4.30pm; check with the locals for the times, which change seasonally.

Cycles may be rented from a stall halfway along the main street for the princely sum of Rs3 per hour (with discounts for longer periods). The village has only a couple of **public telephones**: avoid the one in the *Beach Resort*, which charges more than double the going rate for international calls, and head for the cheaper ISD/STD booth next to the bus stop. At present, there is nowhere in Palolem or Chaudi to change money; the nearest bank with a foreign exchange facility is in Margao (see p.164).

ACCOMMODATION

With the exception of the *Beach Resort*'s tent camp and a handful of recently built guesthouses, most of Palolem's **accommodation** consists of simple rooms in family homes, with basic washing and toilet facilities shared by visitors and members of the household. The easiest way to find a place is to walk around the palm groves behind the beach with a rucksack on; sooner or later someone will approach you. Rates vary from Rs75 to Rs150, depending on the size of the room, and time of year. The cheapest places, however, are to be found in **Colomb**, around the headland south of Palolem village, where Hindu fishing families rent rooms, and occasionally small houses, to long-staying foreigners. Farther south still, behind **Patnem** beach, you can hole up in palm-leaf shelters for around Rs40 per night; ask for these at the shack cafés.

Bakti Kutir, on the headland above Colomb fishing village (no phone). Homely, ersatz thatched village huts equipped with eco-friendly amenities, in a secure, leafy compound ten minutes' walk from the south end of Palolem beach. Beautifully situated and sensitively designed by German-Goan owners to blend in with the landscape. ④–⑥.

Coco Huts, south end of Palolem beach. (☎0834/643104). Thai-style bamboo and palm-thatch huts on stilts, lashed to *todi* trees around a sandy clearing, slap on the beach. The "rooms" have fans, electric light and safe lockers, but toilets are shared, and the leaf walls offer little privacy. ④–⑤.

Cupid Castle, on the road from the village to the beachfront (☎0834/643326). An original name, but these newly built rooms are characterless and a little too close to this relatively congested area for comfort. Nonetheless, they're clean, spacious, have attached bathrooms and open onto a relaxing garden. ④.

D'Mello, Pundalik Gaitondi Rd (☎0834/643057). A mix of rooms with and without attached bathrooms in a concrete annexe set back from the main road. The ground-floor rooms are on the grubby side, but the newer ones upstairs are fine. ②–④.

Jackson's, on the main road through the village. Well back from the beach, but offers some of the cheapest en-suite rooms in the village, with a laid-back bar-restaurant. ②.

Maria's, south of the village, near the *Classic* restaurant (☎0834/643732). Five very basic rooms opening on to an orchard of banana and spice trees. Very friendly management and all rooms with attached shower-toilets. A good deal. ②.

Norgoa, Gaitondi Rd (no phone). Half a dozen basic rooms of varying size, with shared shower-toilets, on the main road through the village. They also have six budget-priced bamboo "huts" in the front garden. ①–③.

Palolem Beach Resort, on the beachfront (☎0834/643054). Twin-bedded canvas tents, each with their own locker, lights and fans, grouped under a shady *todi* grove in a walled compound. In addition, there's a handful of small en-suite rooms. The big drawback here is noise from the busy terrace restaurant. ③–④.

Sea Gull, next door to the *Cupid Castle* (☎0834/643326). Dark but passably clean rooms with attached shower-toilets behind a bar near the beachfront area. ④.

EATING AND DRINKING

With the beach now lined along its entire length with brightly lit shack cafés, finding somewhere to **eat** in Palolem is not a problem, although the locals have to buy in most of their fish from Margao and Karwar (they catch only mackerel in their hand-nets). The one outstanding place is the *Classic* restaurant, where you can tuck into delicious, freshly baked Western wholefood and cakes. More popular among budget travellers, though, is *Sun 'n' Moon*, behind the middle of the beach; when it closes, the die-hard drinkers head through the palm trees to nearby *Dylan's Bar*, which stays open until the last customer has staggered home. For optimum sunset views of the bay, head for the obscurely named *Found Things* bar and restaurant, at the far southern end of Palolem beach, which faces west. Travellers on tight budgets should also note the row of tiny **bhaji stalls** outside the *Beach Resort*, where you can order tasty and filling breakfasts of *pao bhaji*, fluffy bread rolls, omelettes and *chai* for next to nothing.

Bakti Kutir, between Palolem beach and Colomb fishing village. Laid-back terrace café-cum-restaurant with wooden tables and a German-bakery style menu. Cooked dishes here are pricey, but delicious, and most of the ingredients are local and organically produced.

Beach Resort, Palolem beachfront. The one place to definitely avoid: indifferent, overpriced food and grating background music.

Classic (aka "German Bakery"), south of the centre. Tucked away in a quiet corner of Palolem village, this is the most sophisticated café in the area, with tablecloths, smooth fusion sounds and attentive staff. The food – freshly baked cakes, Indian main meals and mouthwatering desserts (including tiramisú to die for) – is equally appealing, though expensive.

Maria's, south side of the village, near the *Classic* restaurant. Authentic Goan food, such as chicken *vindaloo*, fried calamari (*ambot tik*) and spicy vegetable side dishes, prepared entirely with local produce and served al fresco on a terrace. Maria's garrulous husband, Joseph, serves a mean *feni*, too, flavoured with cummin, ginger or lemongrass.

Sun 'n' Moon, Gaitondi Rd. This restaurant's terrace gets packed out in the evenings, thanks to the consistently good, inexpensive food, served by friendly staff. Mountainous seafood sizzlers are the house specialty, but they also do tasty *tandoori* meat, fish and vegetarian dishes.

Chaudi

CHAUDI (aka Chauri, or Canacona), 33km south of Margao, is Canacona district's charmless headquarters. Packed around a noisy junction on the main Panjim–Mangalore highway, it is primarily a transport hub, of interest to visitors only because of its proximity to Palolem, 2km west. Buses to and from Panjim, Margao and Karwar in Karnataka *taluka* trundle in and out of a scruffy square on the main street, from where taxis and auto-rickshaws ferry passengers to the villages scattered across the surrounding fields. The area's only **pharmacy** stands just off the crossroads, handy if you're staying in Palolem.

Agonda

AGONDA, 10km north of Chaudi, can only be reached along the sinuous coast road connecting Cabo de Rama with NH14 at Chaudi. No signposts mark the turning and few of the tourists that whizz past en route to Palolem pull off here, but the beach, fringed along its entire length by *toddi* trees, is superb. Its remote location is not the only reason why this three-kilometre spread of white sand has been bypassed by the bulldozers. Villagers here are opposed to any kind of tourist development. In 1982, when a group of absentee landlords sold off a chunk of the beach to a Delhi-based hotel chain, the locals refused to vacate the plot, insisting the proposed five-star hotel and golf course would ruin their traditional livelihoods. Faced with threats of violent resistance and protracted legal battles, the developers eventually backed down, and the unfinished concrete hulk they left behind is today the only unsightly structure for miles.

This acrimonious episode may in part explain the relative scarcity in Agonda of facilities for visitors. At present, there are only two **places to stay**, both situated at the far (south) end of the beach. The better of the pair is the *Dunhill Bar & Restaurant* (☎0834/647328; ②), which has a handful of basic rooms with breezy verandahs. It's a clean and peaceful place, and the family who run it serve spicy Goan-fried mackerel, rice and curry to order on their small terrace. If they're full, *Caférns* (☎0834/647235; ②) down the road is a good fallback.

MOVING ON FROM GOA

To Mumbai

If you're heading north to **Mumbai**, the quickest and easiest way is to **fly**. Between three and four planes leave Goa's Dabolim airport daily. One-way fares range from $75 (or $58 if you're under thirty) with Indian Airlines and Sahara, to $90 ($67 for under 30s) with swisher Jet Airways. In addition, Air India operate an Airbus service to Mumbai on Mondays and Thursdays. Few people seem to know about this flight, so you can nearly always get a seat on it.

Since the inauguration of the Konkan Railway in 1997, journey times to Mumbai from Goa by **train** have been slashed from 24 to twelve hours. Three services run daily, the most convenient of them being the *Madgaon–Mumbai Express* #0112 which departs from Margao at 6.25pm, arriving at CST (still commonly known as "Victoria Terminus", or "VT") at 6.35am the following day. The other two trains, the *Mangalore–Kurla Express* #2620 and the overnight *Netravati Express* #6636, both arrive at Kurla station.

If your budget won't stretch to a flight and the trains are all booked up, Frank Damania Shipping's **catamaran** is the next best option. Leaving from the ferry quay opposite the *Hotel Mandovi* in Panjim at 10am (Mon, Wed, Fri, Sat & Sun only), the Scandanavian-built vessel takes seven and a half hours to reach Mumbai (so make sure you have a room reserved in advance). Once again, tickets (around Rs1250 in economy class) are in great demand and should be booked as far in advance as possible. The seats are comfortable enough, and meals are served en route, but the journey can be less than comfortable; even passengers with proven sea legs find the sealed-in, glacially cold a/c cabins a trial. It's also a boring voyage as the catamaran has to sail fifteen kilometres from the coast to avoid trawlers, so there's nothing of particular interest to see out of the window.

The cheapest, though the most uncomfortable and nightmarish way to get to Mumbai is by night **bus** (14–18hr), covering 500km of rough road at often terrifying speeds. Fares vary according to levels of comfort, and luxury buses arrive two or three hours sooner. For more on the different ways to travel between Mumbai and Goa, see p.117.

To Hampi and northern Karnataka

Getting to **Hampi** from Goa will be more straightforward with the completion of work on the line running east from Vasco; in the meantime, the only way to travel across the Ghats into Karnataka (unless you can afford a taxi) is by **bus**. Two direct services each day leave Panjim for **Hospet** (9am & 10.30am). However, seats can be in short supply during peak season, and many travellers end up on the following day's service to **Hubli** (6.30am), from where you can pick up hourly buses on to Hospet. Note that the buses KSRTC use for this route are even more decrepit than normal, and breakdowns are par for the course. The only private alternative is Paulo Travel's direct night bus to Hampi, which leaves from a lot next to the *Nunutel Hotel* on Padre Miranda Rd, Margao, at 6pm and arrives at dawn the following day; tickets cost Rs350, and are available through most reputable travel agents. The luxury coach has reclining seats, bunk beds and

Cotigao Wildlife Sanctuary

The **Cotigao Wildlife Sanctuary**, 10km southeast of Chaudi, was established in 1969 to protect a remote and vulnerable area of forest lining the Goa–Karnataka border. Encompassing 86 square kilometres of mixed deciduous woodland, the reserve is certain to inspire tree lovers, but less likely to yield many wildlife sightings: its tigers and leopards were hunted out long ago, while the gazelles, sloth bears, porcupines, panthers and hyenas that allegedly lurk in the woods rarely appear. You do, however, stand a good chance of spotting at least two species of monkey, a couple of wild boar and the odd *gaur* (the primeval-looking Indian bison). Best visited between October and March, Cotigao is a peaceful and scenic park that makes a pleasant day-trip from pneumatic suspension, but there have been complaints from women readers about sexual harassment from other passengers during the journey.

To Mangalore and southern Karnataka

The journey south down the Konkan coast towards **Mangalore** in Karnataka is a lot less gruelling, with better road surfaces and plenty of worthwhile places to pull over for a day or two. One direct **bus** per day leaves Panjim for **Gokarna** (see p.235); alternatively, catch one of the more frequent Kadamba services to **Mangalore** (10–11hr) and jump off at Ankola, from where private mini-vans run the last leg to the coast. This route is also covered by three to four daily services on the Konkan Railway. The fastest train is the twice weekly *Trivandrum Rajdhani Express* #2432, which takes just over four hours to reach Mangalore en route to Kerala. For Gokarn and Udupi, catch the *KR0001 "Down"* from Margao at 2.10pm. As most of the southbound trains along this stretch run during the day, tickets are plentiful, although you should still book at least a day in advance.

To Delhi

The Konkan Railway has also improved **train** services to **Delhi**, which can now be reached on the superfast *Rajdhani Express* #2431 in a little under 26 hours (Sat & Sun only). A slower daily service, the *Mangala Lakshadweep Express* #2616, takes nearly 38 hours to cover the same distance. Alternatively, you can **fly** to the capital with Indian Airlines or Sahara in two and a half hours for around Rs6400.

Reservations, tickets and information

Wherever possible, try and book plane tickets directly through the **airline** as private agents charge the dollar fare at poor rates of exchange; addresses of airline offices in Panjim are listed on p.133. **Catamaran** tickets can be booked direct at Damania's office in Panjim on Avda Dom Joao Castro, opposite the State Bank of India (☎0832/228711–4). Otherwise, try MGM International, Mamai Camotim Building (near the Secretariat), or Tradewings Ltd, Mascarenhas Buildings (near Jolly Shoes), Dr Akmaram Borkar Rd (☎0832/22243), who both specialize in catamaran and air tickets. In Mapusa, there's a Damania Shipping Office at the GTDC's *Tourist Hotel*.

Seats on all **Konkan Railway** services can be booked at the KR reservation office on the first floor of Panjim's Kadamba bus stand (Mon–Fri 9–11.30am & 1.30–5pm, Sun 9am–2pm), or at KR's main reservation hall in Margao station (Mon–Sat 8am–4.30pm, Sun 8am–2pm; ☎0832/712780). Make your bookings as far in advance as possible, and try to get to the offices soon after opening time – the queues can be horrendous. Seats on the Konkan Railway from Goa to Mumbai are in notoriously short supply as the lion's share of the quotas goes to longer-distance (ie more lucrative) travellers from Kerala, with the result that peak periods tend be reserved up to two months in advance.

Book Kadamba **bus tickets** at their offices in Panjim and Mapusa bus stands (daily 9–11am & 2–5pm); private companies sell theirs through the many travel agents immediately outside the bus stand in Panjim, and at the bottom of the square in Mapusa. **Information** on all departures and fares is available from Goa Tourism's counter inside Panjim's bus stand.

Palolem, 12km northwest. Any of the buses running south on NH14 to Karwar via Chaudi will drop you within 2km of the gates. However, to explore the inner reaches of the sanctuary, you really need your own transport. The wardens at the reserve's small **Interpretative Centre** will show you how to get to a 25-metre-high treetop watchtower, overlooking a **waterhole** that attracts a handful of animals around dawn and dusk. Written permission for an overnight **stay**, either in the watchtower or the Forest Department's small *Rest House* (①), must be obtained from the Deputy Conservator of Forests, 3rd Floor, Junta House, Panjim (☎0832/45926), as far in advance of your visit as possible. If you get stuck, however, the wardens can arrange a tent, blankets and basic food.

travel details

Note that no individual route appears more than once in this chart; for any specific journey, check against where you want to get to as well as where you're coming from. More information on onwards travel from Goa appears on p.176, and for detailed information on getting to Goa from Mumbai see p.117.

Trains

Margao to: Canacona/Chaudi for Palolem (3 daily; 50min); Delhi (1–2 daily; 25hr 45min–35hr 10min); Ernakulam for Kochi (5 daily; 12hr–15hr 40min); Gokarna (1 daily; 2hr 10min); Hampi via Hospet (1 nightly; 10hr); Kanakadi, Mangalore (5 daily; 4–6hr); Mumbai (3 daily; 12hr); Thiruvanantapuram (2 daily; 16hr 15min); Udupi (4 daily; 3hr 40min).

Buses

Margao to: Agonda (4 daily; 2hr); Benaulim (every 15min; 20min); Canacona/Chaudi for Palolem (every 30min: 1hr 40min); Cavelossim (8 daily; 45min); Colva (every 15min; 20–30min); Gokarna (1 daily; 4hr 30min); Mangalore (5 daily; 10–11hr); Mapusa (10 daily; 2hr); Mumbai (2 daily; 16–18hr); Panjim (every 30min; 1hr 30min); Udupi (5 daily; 9–10hr).

Panjim to: Arambol (12 daily; 1hr 45min); Badami (1 daily; 10hr); Baga (every 30min; 45min); Bangalore (3 daily; 13hr); Bijapur (3 daily; 16hr); Calangute (every 30min; 40min); Canacona/Chaudi (hourly; 2hr 15min); Candolim (every 30min; 30min); Chapora (4 daily; 1hr); Kolhapur (2 daily; 9hr); Hampi via Hospet (2 daily; 9–10hr); Mahabaleshawar (1 daily; 12hr); Mangalore (5 daily; 11–12hr); Mapusa (every 15min; 25min); Mumbai (24 daily; 14–18hr); Mysore (2 daily; 16–17hr); Old Goa (every 30min; 30min); Pune (5 daily; 13hr).

Mapusa to: Anjuna (hourly; 30min); Arambol (12 daily; 1hr 45min); Baga (hourly; 30min); Calangute (hourly; 45min); Chapora (every 30min; 30–40min); Mumbai (24 daily; 14–17hr); Vagator (every 30min; 25–35min).

Flights

Dabolim airport (Vasco da Gama) to: Bangalore (3 weekly; 1hr); Chennai (3 weekly; 2hr 20min); Delhi (2 daily; 2hr 35min); Kochi (daily; 1hr); Mumbai (3–4 daily; 50min); Pune (3 weekly; 45min).

CHAPTER THREE

KARNATAKA

Created in 1956 from the princely state of Mysore, **KARNATAKA** – the name is a derivation of the name of the local language, Kannada, spoken by virtually all of its 46 million inhabitants – marks a transition zone between northern India and the Dravidian deep south. Along its border with Maharashtra and Andhra Pradesh, a string of medieval walled towns, studded with domed mausoleums and minarets, recall the era when this part of the Deccan was a Muslim stronghold, while the coastal and hill districts that dovetail with Kerala are quintessential Hindu South India, profuse with tropical vegetation and soaring temple *gopuras*. Between the two are scattered some of the peninsula's most extraordinary historic sites, notably the ruined Vijayanagar city at Hampi, whose lost temples and derelict palaces stand amid an arid, boulder-strewn landscape of surreal beauty.

Karnataka is one of the wettest regions in India, its **climate** dominated by the seasonal monsoon, which sweeps in from the southwest in June, dumping an average of 4m of rain on the coast before it peters out in late September. Running in an unbroken line along the state's palm-fringed coast, the **Western Ghats**, draped in dense deciduous forests, impede the path of the rain clouds east. As a result, the landscape of the interior – comprising the southern apex of the triangular Deccan trap, known here as the **Mysore Plateau** – is considerably drier, with dark volcanic soils in the north, and poor quartzite-granite country to the south. Two of India's most sacred rivers, the Tungabhadra and Krishna, flow across this sun-baked terrain, draining east to the Bay of Bengal.

Broadly speaking, Karnataka's principal attractions are concentrated at opposite ends of the state, with a handful of lesser-visited places dotted along the coast between Goa and Kerala. Road and rail routes dictate that most itineraries take in the brash state capital, **Bangalore**, a go-ahead, modern city that epitomizes the aspirations of the country's new middle classes, with glittering malls, fast-food outlets and a nightlife unrivalled outside Mumbai. The state's other major city, **Mysore**, appeals more for its old-fashioned ambience, nineteenth-century palaces and vibrant produce and incense markets. It also lies within easy reach of several important historical monuments. At the nearby fortified island of **Srirangapatnam** – site of the bloody battle of 1799 that finally put Mysore state into British hands, with the defeat of the Muslim military genius **Tipu Sultan** – parts of the fort, a mausoleum and Tipu's summer palace survive.

A cluster of other unmissable sights lies further northeast, dotted around the dull railroad town of **Hassan**. Around nine centuries ago, the Hoysala kings sited their grand dynastic capitals here, at the now middle-of-nowhere villages of **Belur** and **Halebid**, where several superbly crafted temples survive intact. More impressive still, and one of India's most extraordinary sacred sites, is the eighteen-metre Jain colossus at **Sravanabelgola**, which stares serenely over idyllic Deccani countryside.

West of Mysore, the Ghats rise in a wall of thick jungle cut by deep ravines and isolated valleys. You can either traverse the range by rail, via Hassan, or explore some of its scenic backwaters by road. Among these, the rarely visited coffee- and spice-growing region of **Kodagu (Coorg)** has to be the most entrancing, with its unique culture and lush vistas of misty wooded hills and valleys. Most Coorgi agricultural produce is shipped out of **Mangalore**, the nearest large town, of little interest except

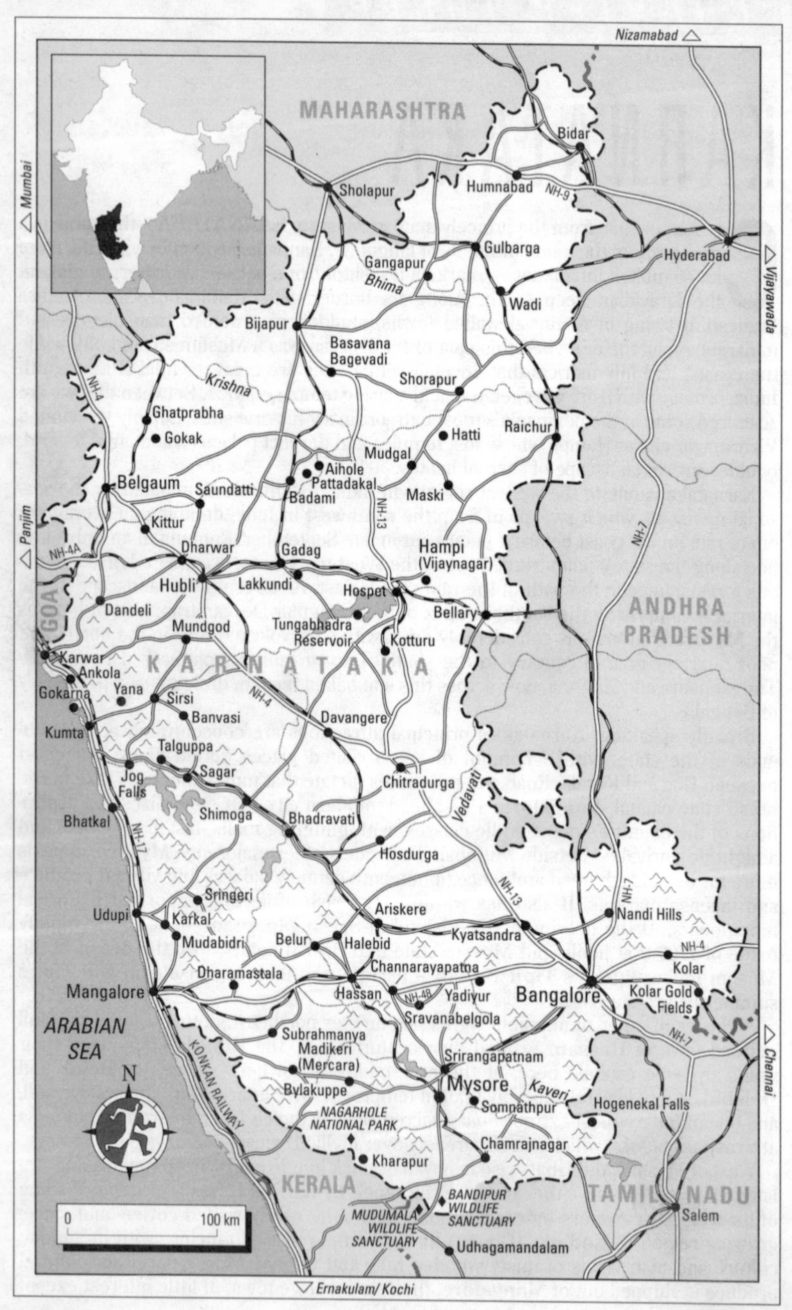

MAHARASHTRA
ANDHRA PRADESH
KARNATAKA
KERALA
TAMIL NADU
GOA
ARABIAN SEA
Nizamabad
Mumbai
Panjim
Vijayawada
Chennai
Ernakulam/ Kochi
Bidar
Humnabad
NH-9
Sholapur
Gulbarga
Hyderabad
Gangapur
Bhima
Wadi
Bijapur
Basavana Bagevadi
Shorapur
Krishna
NH-4
Ghatprabha
Gokak
Hatti
Raichur
Mudgal
Aihole
Pattadakal
Badami
Belgaum
Saundatti
Maski
NH-13
NH-7
Kittur
Dharwar
Gadag
Hampi (Vijaynagar)
NH-4A
Hubli
Lakkundi
Hospet
Dandeli
Tungabhadra Reservoir
Bellary
Mundgod
Kotturu
Karwar
Ankola
Gokarna
Yana
Sirsi
Banvasi
Kumta
Davangere
Talguppa
Sagar
Jog Falls
Chitradurga
Vedavati
Shimoga
Bhatkal
NH-17
Bhadravati
Hosdurga
Sringeri
Udupi
Karkal
Ariskere
Nandi Hills
Mudabidri
Belur
Halebid
Kyatsandra
NH-4
Kolar
Dharamastala
Channarayapatna
Mangalore
Hassan
NH-48
Yadiyur
Bangalore
Kolar Gold Fields
Sravanabelgola
NH-7
Subrahmanya
Madikeri (Mercara)
Srirangapatnam
Mysore
KONKAN RAILWAY
Bylakuppe
Kaveri
Somnathpur
Hogenekal Falls
NAGARHOLE NATIONAL PARK
Kharapur
Chamrajnagar
BANDIPUR WILDLIFE SANCTUARY
MUDUMALA WILDLIFE SANCTUARY
Salem
Udhagamandalam
N
0
100 km

as a transport hub whose importance can only increase when the new Konkan Railway starts operating to its full potential (see p.229). Situated mid-way between Goa and Kerala, it's also a convenient – if uninspiring – place to pause on the journey along Karnataka's beautiful **Karavali coast**. Interrupted by countless mangrove-lined estuaries, the state's 320-kilometre-long red laterite coast has always been difficult to navigate by land, and traffic along the recently revamped highway remains relatively light. Although there are plenty of superb beaches, facilities are, with rare exceptions, nonexistent, and locals often react with astonishment at the sight of a foreigner. Again, that may well change with the arrival of the Konkan Railway – with as-yet-unguessable consequences for the fishing hamlets, long-forgotten fortresses and pristine hill and cliff scenery along the way. For now, few Western tourists visit the famous Krishna temple at **Udupi**, an important Vaishnavite pilgrimage centre, and fewer still venture into the mountains to see India's highest waterfall at **Jog Falls**, set amid some of the region's most spectacular scenery. However, atmospheric **Gokarn**, farther north up the coast, is an increasingly popular beach hideaway for budget travellers. Harbouring one of India's most famous *shivalinga*, this seventeenth-century Hindu pilgrimage town enjoys a stunning location, with a high headland dividing it from a string of exquisite beaches.

Winding inland from the mountainous Goan border, NH4A and the rail line comprise sparsely populated **northern Karnataka**'s main transport artery, linking a succession of grim industrial centres. This region's undisputed highlight is the ghost city of Vijayanagar, better known as **Hampi**, scattered around boulder hills on the south banks of the Tungabhadra River. The ruins of this once splendid capital occupy a magical site, while the village squatting the ancient bazaar is a great spot to hole up for a spell. The jumping-off place for Hampi is **Hospet**, from where buses leave for the bumpy journey north across the rolling Deccani plains to **Badami**, **Aihole** and **Pattadakal**. Now lost in countryside, these tiny villages were once capitals of the **Chalukya** dynasty (sixth–eighth centuries). The whole area is littered with ancient rock-cut caves and finely carved stone temples.

Farther north still, in one of Karnataka's remotest and poorest districts, craggy hilltop citadels and crumbling wayside tombs herald the formerly troubled buffer zone between the Muslim-dominated northern Deccan and the Dravidian Hindu south. The bustling, walled market town of **Bijapur**, capital of the Bahmanis, the Muslim dynasty that oversaw the eventual downfall of Vijayanagar, harbours South India's finest collection of Islamic architecture, including the world's second largest free-standing dome, the Golgumbaz. The first Bahmani capital, **Gulbarga**, site of a famous Muslim shrine and theological college, has retained little of its former splendour, but the more isolated **Bidar**, to which the Bahmanis moved from Gulbarga in the sixteenth century, definitely deserves a detour en route to or from Hyderabad, four hours east by bus. Perched on a rocky escarpment, its crumbling red ramparts harbour Persian-style mosaic-fronted mosques, mausoleums and a sprawling fort complex evocative of Samarkhand and the great silk route.

ACCOMMODATION PRICE CODES

All **accommodation prices** in this book have been coded using the symbols below. The prices given are for a double room, except in the case of categories ① and ② where the price can refer to dorm accommodation per bed. All taxes are included. For more details, see p.34.

① up to Rs100	④ Rs300–400	⑦ Rs900–1500
② Rs100–200	⑤ Rs400–600	⑧ Rs1500–2500
③ Rs200–300	⑥ Rs600–900	⑨ Rs2500 and upwards

A little history

Like much of southern India, Karnataka has been ruled by successive Buddhist, Hindu and Muslim dynasties. The influence of Jainism has also been marked; India's very first emperor, **Chandragupta Maurya**, is believed to have converted to Jainism in the fourth century BC, renounced his throne, and fasted to death at Sravanabelgola, now one of the most visited Jain pilgrimage centres in the country.

During the first millennium AD, this whole region was dominated by power struggles between the various kingdoms, such as Vakatakas and the Guptas, who controlled the western Deccan and at times extended their authority as far as the Coromandel coast, in Tamil Nadu. From the sixth to the eighth centuries, briefly interrupted by thirteen years of Pallava rule, the **Chalukya** kingdom included Maharashtra, the Konkan coast on the west, and the whole of Karnataka. The **Cholas** were powerful in the east of the region from about 870 until the thirteenth century, when the Deccan kingdoms were overwhelmed by General Malik Kafur, a convert to Islam.

By the medieval era, Muslim incursions from the north had forced the hitherto warring and fractured Hindu states of the south into close alliance, with the mighty **Vijayanagars** emerging as overlords. Founded by the brothers Harihara and Bukka, their lavish capital, Vijayanagar, ruled an empire stretching from the Bay of Bengal to the Arabian Sea, and south to Cape Comorin. The Muslims' superior military strength, however, triumphed in 1565 at the Battle of Talikota, when the **Bahmanis** laid siege to Vijayanagar, reducing it to rubble and plundering its opulent palaces and temples.

Thereafter, a succession of Muslim sultans held sway over the north, while in the south of the state the independent **Wadiyar Rajas** of Mysore, whose territory was comparatively small, successfully fought off the Marathas. In 1761, the brilliant Muslim campaigner Haider Ali, with French support, seized the throne. Haider Ali and his son, Tipu Sultan, turned Mysore into a major force in the south, before Tipu was killed by the British at the **battle of Srirangapatnam** in 1799.

Following Tipu's defeat, the British restored the Wadiyar family to the throne, which they kept until riots in 1830 led the British to appoint a commission to rule in their place. Fifty years later, the throne was once more returned to the Wadiyars, who remained governors until Karnataka was created by the merging of the states of Mysore and the Madras Presidencies in 1956.

Bangalore and around

Once across the Western Ghats the cloying air of Kerala and the Konkan coast gradually gives way to the crisp skies and dry heat of the dusty **Mysore Plateau**. The setting for E.M. Forster's acclaimed Raj novel, *A Passage to India*, this southern tip of the Deccan – a vast, open expanse of gently undulating plains dotted with wheat fields and dramatic granite boulders – formed the heartland of the region's once powerful princely state. Today it remains the political hub of the region, largely due to the economic importance of **BANGALORE**, Karnataka's capital, which, with a population racing towards eight million is one of the fastest-growing cities in Asia. A major scientific research centre at the cutting edge of India's technological revolution, Bangalore has a trendy high-speed self-image quite unlike anywhere else in South India.

In the 1800s, Bangalore's gentle climate, broad streets, and green public parks made it the "Garden City". Until well after Independence, senior citizens, film stars and VIPs flocked to buy or build dream homes amid this urban idyll, which offered such unique amenities as theatres, cinemas and a lack of restrictions on alcohol. However, during the last decade or so, Bangalore has undergone a massive transformation. The wide avenues, now dominated by tower blocks, are teeming with traffic,

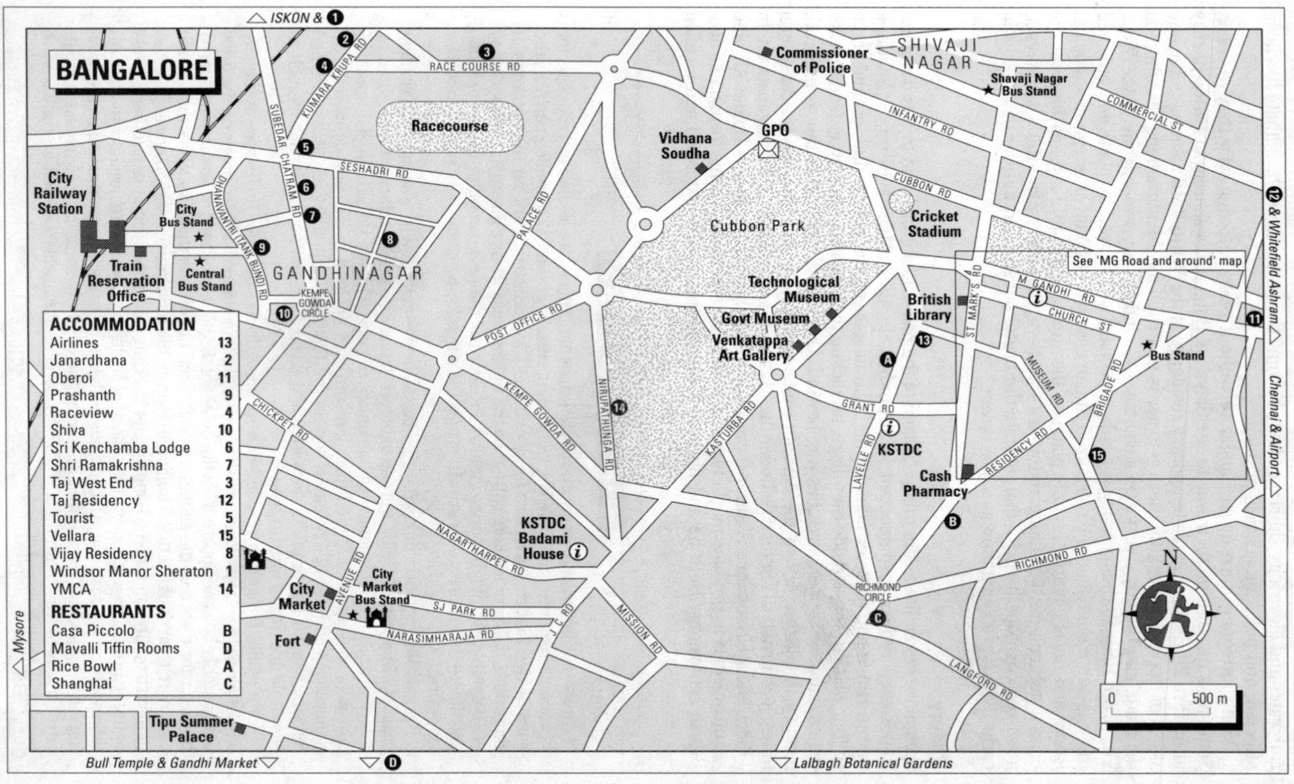
BANGALORE
ACCOMMODATION
Airlines 13
Janardhana 2
Oberoi 11
Prashanth 9
Raceview 4
Shiva 10
Sri Kenchamba Lodge 6
Shri Ramakrishna 7
Taj West End 3
Taj Residency 12
Tourist 5
Vellara 15
Vijay Residency 8
Windsor Manor Sheraton 1
YMCA 14
RESTAURANTS
Casa Piccolo B
Mavalli Tiffin Rooms D
Rice Bowl A
Shanghai C
ISKON & 1
12 & Whitefield Ashram
Chennai & Airport
Mysore
Bull Temple & Gandhi Market
D
Lalbagh Botanical Gardens
See 'MG Road and around' map
SHIVAJI NAGAR
Shavaji Nagar Bus Stand
Commissioner of Police
GANDHINAGAR
City Railway Station
Train Reservation Office
City Bus Stand
Central Bus Stand
Racecourse
Vidhana Soudha
GPO
Cubbon Park
Cricket Stadium
Technological Museum
Govt Museum
Venkatappa Art Gallery
British Library
KSTDC
Cash Pharmacy
KSTDC Badami House
City Market Bus Stand
City Market
Fort
Tipu Summer Palace
Bus Stand
KEMPE GOWDA CIRCLE
RICHMOND CIRCLE
RACE COURSE RD
KUMARA KRUPA RD
SUBEDAR CHATRAM RD
SESHADRI RD
DHANAVANTRI (TANK BUND) RD
PALACE RD
POST OFFICE RD
KEMPE GOWDA RD
NIRUPATHUNGA RD
KASTURBA RD
INFANTRY RD
CUBBON RD
COMMERCIAL ST
M GANDHI RD
CHURCH ST
ST MARK'S RD
MUSEUM RD
BRIGADE RD
RESIDENCY RD
RICHMOND RD
LANGFORD RD
LAVELLE RD
GRANT RD
MISSION RD
J C RD
NAGARTHARPET RD
SJ PARK RD
NARASIMHARAJA RD
AVENUE RD
CHICKPET RD
N
0 500 m

and water and electricity shortages have become the norm. Even the climate has been affected, and pollution is a real problem.

Many foreigners turn up in Bangalore without really knowing why they've come. Some pass through on their way to see Satya Sai Baba at his ashram in **Puttarparthy** in Andhra Pradesh, or at his temporary residence at the **Whitefield** ashram on the outskirts of the city. What little there is to see is no match for the attractions elsewhere in the state, and the city's very real advantages for Indians are two-a-penny in the West. That said, Bangalore is a transport hub, especially well served by plane and bus, and there is some novelty in a Westernized Indian city that not only offers good shopping, eating and hotels, but is the only place on the subcontinent to boast anything resembling a pub culture. For dusty and weary travellers, Bangalore can offer a few days in a relaxed cosmopolitan city that, despite the brutal but isolated murder of a tourist in early 1998, has a reputation as a safe haven.

History

Bangalore began life as the minor "village of the half-baked *gram*" and to this day *gram* (chickpeas) remain an important local product. In 1537, Magadi **Kempe Gowda**, a devout Hindu and feudatory chief of the Vijayanagar empire, built a mud fort and erected four watchtowers outside the village, predicting that it would, one day, extend that far; the city now, of course, stretches way beyond. During the first half of the seventeenth century, Bangalore fell to the Muslim Sultanate of Bijapur; changing hands several times, it returned to Hindu rule under the Mysore Wadiyar Rajas of Srirangapatnam. In 1758, Chikka Krishnaraja Wadiyar II was deposed by the military genius Haider Ali, who set up arsenals to produce muskets, rockets and other weapons for his formidable anti-British campaigns. Both he and his son, **Tipu Sultan**, greatly extended and fortified

THE SILICON RUSH

It comes as a surprise to many visitors to learn that India is the second-largest exporter of computer software after the US. Generating sales of around $720 million per year, the apex of this hi-tech boom was the Electronic City Industrial Park on the outskirts of Bangalore, dubbed "**Silicon Valley**" by the Indian press. Today, due to the meteoric rise of Hyderabad, in neighbouring Andhra Pradesh, as the new computer capital of India, and due to Bangalore's own growth pangs, the city is losing some of its attraction to new investors.

Bangalore's meteoric industrial rise began in the early 1980s. Fleeing the crippling costs of Mumbai and Delhi, a group of hi-tech Indian companies relocated here, lured by the comparatively cool climate and an untapped pool of highly skilled, English-speaking labour (a consequence of the Indian government's decision to concentrate its telecommunications and defence research here in the 1960s). Within a decade, Bangalore had become a major player in the software market, and a magnet for multinationals such as Motorola and Texas Instruments.

For a while, Bangalore revelled in a spending frenzy that saw the centre of the city sprout gleaming skyscrapers, swish stores and shopping malls. Soon, however, the price of prosperity became apparent. At the height of the boom, millions of immigrants poured in, eager for a slice of the action; it is estimated that in less than five years the population more than doubled to 7.5 million. However, too little municipal money was invested in infrastructure, and today, Bangalore is buckling under the weight of numbers; levels of traffic **pollution** are approaching those of Delhi and **power cuts** are now routine. All this is having a disastrous effect on business and industry: the multinationals are moving out as quickly as they moved in, forcing the city's big-spending ex-pats and computer whiz kids to leave with them. Old Bangaloreans, meanwhile, are left to wonder what became of their beloved "Garden City".

Bangalore, but Tipu was overthrown by the British in 1799. The British set up a cantonment, which made the city an important military station, and passed the administration over to the Maharaja of Mysore in 1881. After Independence, the erstwhile Maharaja became Governor of Mysore state. Bangalore was designated capital of Mysore in 1956, and retained that status when Karnataka state was created in 1973.

Arrival, information and getting around

Recently expanded and revamped to accommodate increased traffic and planned international flights, **Bangalore airport**, 13km north of the city centre, serves cities in South India and beyond; for details of departures, see p.273. The **KSTDC desk** in the arrivals hall (daily 7.30am–1.30pm & 2–7.30pm; ☎080/526 8012) stocks leaflets on Karnataka and can book hotel rooms. Branches of the State Bank of Mysore (daily 8am–7pm) and Vijaya Bank (daily 8.30am–12.30pm) **change money**, and there's an STD telephone booth. You can get **into the city** by taxi (Rs150; book at the pre-paid desk), by one of the auto-rickshaws (Rs40) that gather outside or by bus – the Pushpak bus service (Rs10) meets most flights and travels to the Central bus stand, there are also regular KSRTC buses (Rs15).

Bangalore City train station is west of the centre, near Kempe Gowda Circle, and across the road from the main bus stands (for the north of the city, get off at Bangalore Cantonment train station). As you come into the entrance hall from the platforms, the far left-hand corner holds an **ITDC booth** (daily 7am–5.30pm; ☎080/220 4277), where you can rent cars and book tours; they will book you a hotel for a fee of ten percent of the day's room rate. The **KSTDC tourist information office** (daily 10am–8pm; ☎080/287 0068), to the right, also books tours and can provide useful advice. You'll find a rank of metered taxis outside or, alternatively, auto-rickshaws charge around Rs25 to travel to MG Rd – drivers are generally honest and their meters usually work.

Innumerable **long-distance buses** arrive at the big, busy **Central (KSRTC) bus stand**, opposite the train station. A bridge divides it from **City bus stand**, used by local services and by long-distance private operators.

Information

For information on Bangalore, Karnataka and neighbouring states, go to the excellent **Government of India tourist office** (Mon–Fri 9.30am–6pm, Sat 9am–1pm; ☎080/558 5417), in the KSFC Building, 48 Church St (parallel to MG Rd between Brigade and St Mark's roads). You can pick up a city map here for Rs5 and the staff will help you put together tour itineraries.

Apart from the desks at the City train station and airport (see above), **Karnataka State Tourist Development Corporation** has two city offices: one at Badami House, NR Square (☎080/227 5883), where you can book the tours outlined below, and another on the second floor of 10/4 Mitra Chambers, Kasturba Rd, Queen's Circle (☎080/221 2901).Their useful *Downtown Bangalore* map (Rs30) features the latest bars and restaurants. For up-to-the-minute information about **what's on**, check the trendy and ubiquitous free listings paper *Bangalore This Fortnight*, and their monthly magazine, *Bangalore*, features articles, reviews and, occasionally, environmental issues. The *Bangalore Trail Blazer*, another monthly, is a good source of information, with a directory, listings and review section.

If you want to visit any of Karnataka's **national parks**, try the Wildlife Office, Forest Department, Aranya Bhavan, Malleswaram (☎080/334 1993) or better still approach Jungle Lodges & Resorts, Floor 2, Shrungar Shopping Centre, just off MG Rd (☎080/559 7021, fax 558 6163, *jungle@giasbg01.vsnl.net.in*). A quasi-governmental body, Jungle Lodges & Resorts promotes "Eco-Tourism" through several upmarket forest lodges (see box on p.186). You should book all these through their Bangalore office.

Getting around

The easiest way of getting around Bangalore is by metered **auto-rickshaw**, with fares starting at Rs7 for the first kilometre and Rs3.60 per km thereafter. Most meters do work, although you will occasionally be asked for a flat fare, especially during rush hours. The night rate starts at 9pm and is charged at one and a half times of the meter reading. Bangalore's extensive **bus** system, run by the Bangalore Metropolitan Transport Corporation, radiates from the **Kempe Gowda bus stand** (aka City bus stand) (☎080/222 2542) near City train station. Along with regular buses, they also operate a deluxe express service, "Pushpak", on a number of set routes and a handful of night buses. Buses are numbered and depart from marked platforms. Other important city bus stands include the KR Market bus stand (☎080/670 2177) to the south of the train station and Shivajinagar bus stand (☎080/286 5332) to the north of Cubbon Park.

You can find self-drive **car rental** at Europcar, Sheriff House, 85 Richmond Rd (☎080/221 9502) and at Hertz, 167 Richmond Rd, near Trinity Circle (☎080/559 9408). Most visitors, however, opt for **chauffeur-driven cars** and **taxis** booked through several agencies including the Cab Service, Sabari Complex, 24 Residency Rd (☎080/558 7341), Dial-a-Car, *Hotel Airlines*, Madras Bank Rd (☎080/221 7628), and Brindavan Travels, 62/3 Mission Rd (☎080/223 3692). Typical rates are around Rs100 per hour, Rs300 for four hours (includes 40km) and Rs500 for eight hours (includes 80km); the extra mileage charge is around Rs5 per kilometre.

A word of warning: most taxi companies start calculating their time and distance fare from when the car leaves their depot until it returns there, you are best advised to find out first how far the you are from the depot before ordering the cab. If you need a taxi for a one-way journey be prepared to pay for the return fare as well.

For **long-distance car rental** and **tailor-made itineraries**, try Gullivers Tours & Travels, South Black 201/202 Manipal Centre, 47 Dickenson Rd (☎080/558 8001), Clipper Holidays, 406 Regency Enclave, 4 Magrath Rd (☎080/559 9032), any KSTDC office or the ITDC booth at the train station.

GUIDED TOURS

KSTDC operates a string of guided **tours** from Bangalore. Though rushed, these can be handy if you're short of time. The twice-daily **City tour** (7.30am–2pm or 1.30–7.30pm; Rs85), calls at the museum, Vidhana Soudha, Ulsoor Lake, Lalbagh Gardens, Bull temple and Tipu Sultan's palace, and winds up with a long stop at the government handicrafts emporium. **Outstation tours** include a long day-trip to Srirangapatnam and Mysore (daily 7.15am–11pm; Rs200) and a weekend tour to Hampi (Fri 8pm–Sun 10pm; Rs675). Their day-trip to Belur, Halebid and Sravanabelgola is not recommended unless you're happy to spend more than eight hours on the bus. Other tours on offer include a three-day trip to Jog Falls.

Jungle Lodges & Resorts, Shrungar Shopping Centre, MG Rd (☎080/558 6163, fax 558 6163), under the banner of "Eco Tourism", offers package holidays to several **wildlife destinations** throughout the state. These include well-situated, luxury camps at the Biligiri Rangaswamy Wildlife Sanctuary (see box on p.204), the Dandeli Wildlife Sanctuary (see p.242), the Cauvery Fishing Camp at Bheemeshwari, and the Kabini River Lodge near Nagarhole National Park (see p.208). In addition they run the Devbagh Beach Resort at Karwar (see p.242). Their charges are all-inclusive and also cover excursions into the forests and local sightseeing, but transport to and from the sanctuaries is extra. However, while their charges to Indians in rupees are good value, foreigners have to pay much higher rates in US dollars; typical prices are Rs1000 per night for Indians and $60 per night for foreigners.

The City

The **centre** of modern Bangalore lies about 5km east of Kempe Gowda Circle, and the principal train and bus stations, at the area around **MG Rd**. On MG Road you'll find most of the mid-range accommodation, restaurants, shops, tourist information and banks. Leafy **Cubbon Park**, with its less than exciting museums, lies on its western edge, while the oldest, most "Indian" part of the city extends south from the City train station, a warren of winding streets at their most dynamic in the hubbub of the **City** and **Gandhi markets**. Bangalore's tourist attractions are well spread out; monuments such as **Tipu's Summer Palace** and the **Bull temple** are some way south of the centre. Most, if not all, can be seen on a half-day tour (see box opposite).

Cubbon Park and museums

A welcome green space in the heart of the city, shaded by massive clumps of bamboo, the entrance to **Cubbon Park**, at the western end of MG Rd, is presided over by a statue of Queen Victoria. On Kasturba Rd, which runs along its southern edge, the poorly labelled and badly maintained **Government Museum** (daily except Wed 10am–5pm; free) features Vijayanagar, Hoysala and Chalukya sculpture, musical instruments, Thanjavur paintings and Deccani and Rajasthani miniatures. Next door, the missable **Venkatappa Art Gallery** (also free), exhibits twentieth-century landscapes and abstract wood sculpture, and occasional contemporary art shows. A little farther along the same road, the **Technological and Industrial Museum** (daily except Mon 10am–5pm; Rs10), is a showpiece of Indian technology with interactive displays popular with visiting schoolchildren.

Vidhana Soudha

Built in 1956, Bangalore's vast State Secretariat, Vidhana Soudha, northwest of Cubbon Park, is the largest civic structure of its kind in the country. K. Hanumanthaiah, chief minister at the time, wanted a "people's palace" that, following the transfer of power from the royal Wadiyar dynasty to a legislature, would "reflect the power and dignity of the people". In theory its design is entirely Indian, combining local models from Bangalore, Mysore and Somnathpur with features from Rajasthan and the rest of India. Its overall effect, however, is not unlike bombastic colonial architecture built in the so-called Indo-Saracenic style – a style incorporating onion-domes and mixed-oriental features on a large public building.

Lalbagh Botanical Gardens

Inspired by the splendid gardens of the Moghuls and the French botanical gardens at Pondicherry in Tamil Nadu, Sultan Haider Ali set to work in 1760 laying out the **Lalbagh Botanical Gardens** (daily 8am–8pm), south of the centre. Originally covering forty acres, just beyond his fort – where one of Kempe Gowda's original watchtowers can still be seen – the gardens were expanded under Ali's son Tipu, who introduced numerous exotic species of plants. Today, the gardens house an extensive horticultural seedling centre. The British brought in gardeners from Kew in 1856 and – naturally – built a military bandstand and a glasshouse, which hosts wonderful flower shows and is based on London's Crystal Palace. Now spreading over 240 acres, the gardens are pleasant to visit during the day, but tend to attract unsavoury characters after 6pm.

Tipu's Summer Palace

A two-storey structure built in 1791, mostly of wood, **Tipu's Summer Palace** (9am–5pm), southwest of the City Market and 3km from MG Rd, is similar to the Daria

Daulat Palace at Srirangapatnam (see p.204), but in a far worse state, with most of its painted decoration destroyed. Next door, the **Venkataramanaswamy temple**, dating from the early eighteenth century, was built by the Wadiyar Rajas. The *gopura* entrance way was erected in 1978.

ISKCON temple

A hybrid of ultramodern glass and vernacular South Indian temple architecture, the gleaming new temple of the ISKCON (International Society of Krishna Consciousness), the **Sri Radha Krishna Mandir**, Hare Krishna Hill, Chord Rd (daily 7am–1pm & 4pm–8.30pm), 8km from the centre, is a fantastic and lavish showpiece crowned by a gold-plated dome. Barriers, designed with huge crowds in mind, guide visitors on a one-way journey through the huge, well-organized complex to the inner sanctum displaying images of the god Krishna and his consort Radha. Collection points throughout and inescapable merchandizing on the way out are evidence of the organization's highly successful commercialization. Regular **buses** to the temple depart from both the City and Shivajinagar bus stands.

Bull temple

About 6km south of the City bus stand (buses #34 and #37), in the Basavanagudi area, Kempe Gowda's sixteenth-century **Bull temple** (open to non-Hindus; daily 7.30am–1.30pm & 2.30–8.30pm) houses a massive monolithic Nandi bull, its grey granite made black by the application of charcoal and oil. The temple is approached along a path lined with mendicants and snake charmers; inside, for a few rupees, the priest will offer you a string of fragrant jasmine flowers. For more information on Kempe Gowda, the city's founder, see p.184.

Accommodation

Arrive in Bangalore towards the end of the day, and you'll be lucky to find a room at all, let alone one at the right price, so book at least a couple of days ahead or at least phone around as soon as you arrive. **Budget accommodation** is concentrated around the City train station (which itself has good-value, but often full, retiring rooms; ①–④) and

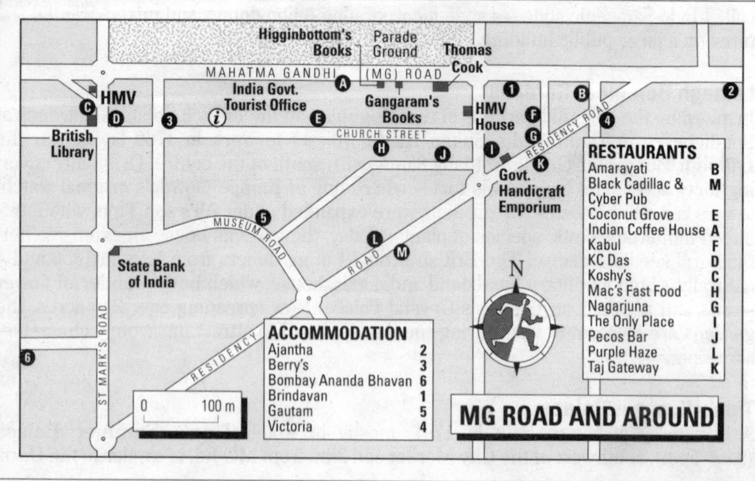

Central bus stand. Standards in this area can be very low; better options are dotted around Subedar Chatram Rd and Dhanavantri Rd, five minutes' walk west, and the Racecourse, a short rickshaw trip east. **Mid-range hotels** are more scattered and of the many near MG Rd, the *Victoria* is definitely the most characterful.

Around the City train station and Central bus stand

Prashanth, 21 E Tank Rd (☎080/287 4041). Among the better lodges opposite the Central bus stand. All rooms with windows and shower-toilets. The *Mayura* nearby is the best fallback. ⑤.

Shiva, 14 Dhanavantri (formerly "Tank Bund") Rd (☎080/228 1778). The poshest option in the vicinity of the bus stand. Balconies cost extra. ⑥–⑦.

Shri Ramakrishna, Subedar Chatram Rd (☎080/226 3041). Modern mega-lodge with 250 simple (en-suite) rooms in a colossal concrete block with a good South Indian restaurant. ④.

Sri Kenchamba Lodge, Subedar Chatram Rd (☎080/225 4131). Clean rooms in a large concrete complex, ranged around a courtyard (the top floor has great views). The best budget deal in the area. Near the Kapali cinema. ③.

Vijay Residency, 18 3rd Cross, Main Rd (☎080/220 3024). A chain hotel and the most plush and comfortable – if a bit ostentatious. Within striking reach of the train station, with foreign exchange and restaurant. ⑦–⑧.

Around the Racecourse and Cubbon Park

Janardhana, Kumara Krupa Rd (☎080/225 4444). Neat, clean and spacious rooms with balconies and baths. Well away from the chaos, and good value at this price (despite hefty service charges). ④–⑤.

Raceview, 25 Race Course Rd (☎080/220 3401). Run-of-the-mill mid-range hotel whose upper front rooms overlook the racecourse. Safe deposit, foreign exchange and some a/c. ⑤.

Taj West End, Race Course Rd (☎080/225 5055, fax 220 0010). Dating back to 1887 with fabulous gardens and long colonnaded walkways. The most characterful rooms are in the old wing, where deep verandahs overlook acres of grounds. ⑨.

Tourist, Ananda Rao Circle (☎080/226 2381). One of Bangalore's best all-round budget lodges, with 120 small rooms, long verandahs and friendly family management. No reservations. ②.

Windsor Manor Sheraton, 25 Sankey Rd (☎080/226 9898, fax 226 4941). Ersatz palace run by Welcomgroup as a luxurious five-star, mainly for businesspeople. Facilities include voice mail, modems, gym, jacuzzi and pool. ⑨.

YMCA, Nirupathunga Rd, Cubbon Park, midway between the bus stand and MG Rd (☎080/221 1848). Large, clean rooms and cheaper dorm beds for men. Rock-bottom rates, but often full. ②–④.

Around MG Road

These hotels are featured on the Bangalore (see p.183) and also MG Rd and around (see p.188) maps.

Airlines, 4 Madras Bank Rd (☎080/227 3783). Respectable budget hotel in its own grounds, with lively terrace restaurant. Among the best options at this end of town, so it's usually full. Some a/c. ③–⑤.

Ajantha, 22-A MG Rd (☎080/558 4328). Good value, with larger than average en-suite rooms. Close to the shops, and often booked up days in advance. ④.

Berry's, 46 Church St (☎080/558 7211). Not a particularly good deal (the rooms are a bit musty), but the views are great, and there are nearly always vacancies. ⑥.

Bombay Ananda Bhavan, 68 Vittal Mallya (☎080/221 4581). Family-run, Raj-era mansion in a lovely garden, with large characterful rooms (bath tubs, shutters and stucco ceilings). Recommended. ⑥–⑦.

Brindavan, 40 MG Rd (☎080/558 4000). Old-style economy hotel with some a/c rooms and an excellent South Indian "meals" restaurant. A little dowdy, but still excellent value for money. ③–⑥.

Gautam, 17 Museum Rd (☎080/558 8764). Large, faceless concrete building south of MG Rd. The biggest of the "economy" hotels in this area, so more likely than most to have vacancies. Overpriced. ⑤.

Oberoi, 37–9 MG Rd (☎080/558 5858, fax 558 5960). Ultra-luxurious five-star, with a group of swish restaurants, a beautiful landscaped garden and a pool. ⑨.

Taj Residency, 41–3 MG Rd (☎080/558 4444, fax 558 4748). Not quite in the same league as the *Oberoi*, but a fully fledged five-star, with all the trimmings. ⑨.

Vellara, 283 Brigade Rd, opposite Brigade Towers (☎080/556 9116). Good-value rooms from no-frills "standard", to light and airy "deluxe" on the top floor (with sweeping city views). ④–⑥.

Victoria, 47–8 Residency Rd (☎080/558 4077, fax 558 4945). Set in its own leafy compound in the centre of town, with heaps of old-world style and a popular garden restaurant. Single rooms are good value, the doubles adequate, while "deluxe" buys you a verandah. Book well ahead. ⑦.

Eating

With unmissable sights thin on the ground, but tempting cafés and restaurants on every corner, you could easily spend most of your time in Bangalore **eating**. Nowhere else in South India will you find such gastronomic variety. Around **MG Rd**, pizzerias (including *Pizza Hut*), ritzy ice-cream parlours and gourmet French restaurants stand cheek by jowl with regional cuisine from Andhra Pradesh and Kerala, Mumbai *chaat* cafes and snack bars where, in true Bangalorean style, humble *thalis* from as little as Rs20 masquerade as "executive mini-lunches".

Amaravati, Residency Rd Cross, MG Rd. Excellent Andhra cooking with "meals" served on banana leafs and specialities including *biryanis* and fried fish. Hectic at lunchtime but well worth any wait.

Casa Piccolo, Devata Plaza, 131 Residency Rd. A dozen different tasty pizzas, *wienerschnitzel*, steaks, fried chicken and ice-cream. Tables outside and flower baskets give the place a European ambience. Patronized by the well-heeled, sunglasses-wearing studenty set and travellers.

Coconut Grove, Church St (☎080/558 8596). Mouthwatering and moderately priced gourmet Keralan coastal cuisine: vegetarian, fish and meat preparations served in traditional copper *thalis* on a leafy terrace; try their tender coconut juice cocktail, *thala chickory bom*. Recommended.

Indian Coffee House, MG Rd. The usual cheap South Indian snacks, egg dishes and good filter coffee, served by waiters in turbans and cummerbunds. Best for breakfast.

Kabul, 43–4 Gopal Krishna Complex, Residency Rd. One of two northwest frontier restaurants in Bangalore, serving Afghan *biryanis*, kebabs and Muslim-style mutton in rich almond and cream sauces. Moderately priced.

KC Das, 38 Church St (corner of St Mark's Rd). Part of the legendary chain of Bengali sweet shops serving traditional steam-cooked sweets, many soaked in syrup and rose-water. Try their definitive *rasgullas*. Eat in or take away.

Koshy's, St Mark's Rd, next to British Library. Spacious old-style café with cane blinds, pewter tea pots and cotton-clad waiters. Bangalore's most congenial meeting place. Serves snacks and alcohol.

Mac's Fast Food, Church St. Cramped, not at all bad burger joint that also does stroganoffs, passable pizzas and fish and chips.

Mavalli Tiffin Rooms, Lalbagh Rd. Indian fast-food restaurant, serving superb-value set menus (4–8.30pm), and good snacks (including the best *masala dosas* in Bangalore) during the day. Also pure fruit juices and *lassis* sweetened with honey.

Nagarjuna, Residency Rd. Traditional and popular Andhra "meals" restaurant serving food on a banana leaf with *rasam*, vegetables, chutney and unlimited rice at very reasonable prices.

The Only Place, Mota Royal Arcade, Brigade Rd. Highly rated Western food, including a near-legendary lasagne, pizzas and great apple pie, at reasonable prices.

Rice Bowl, 40–2 Lavelle Rd. Plush air-conditioned Chinese restaurant and one of the best in town; try their *chop suey* and, for dessert, the "leechies" with ice-cream.

Shanghai, G3–4 Shiva Shankar Plaza, 19 Lalbagh Rd, Richmond Circle. Among the city's top Chinese restaurants. Excellent beancurd veg soup and Hunan peppered fish, deep-fried with ginger, garlic and spring onions in a black pepper sauce.

Shiva Refreshments, *Brindavan Hotel*, MG Rd. Deservedly popular traditional South Indian "meals" restaurant, packed out for unlimited *thalis* served on plantain leaves.

Taj Gateway, 66 Residency Rd (☎080/558 4545). The *Peacock* serves a fairly undistinguished selection of Mughlai and other North Indian dishes, while the *Karavalli* specializes in west coast dishes from Goa to Kerala, including seafood and veg. Very attractive room in traditional southern style with wooden ceiling – plus tables outside under an old tamarind tree. Reservations essential. Expensive.

Victoria, 47–8 Residency Rd. The hotel is equally popular as a garden restaurant and bar; they run a "breakfast club" featuring English breakfast with bacon, sausages and eggs, Keralan *iddlis*, Goan sausages and, the chef's special, chicken liver and bacon on toast.

Nightlife

The big boom may be over, but Bangalore's bright young things still have money to spend, and **nightlife** in the city is thriving. A night on the town generally kicks off with a bar crawl along **Brigade Rd**, **Residency Rd** or **Church St**, where there are scores of swish "**pubs**", complete with MTV, lasers and thumping sound systems. If you persevere, you can get away from the noise, and find a spot to have a quiet drink. Drinking alcohol does not have the seedy connotations here as it does elsewhere in India; you'll even see young Indian women enjoying a beer with their mates. There is, however, a ban on alcohol sales between 2.30 and 5.30pm, imposed in 1993 by ex-Chief Minister Veerappa Moily because of the number of schoolkids skipping school to booze. Pubs close at 11pm but, once in, you generally get served till later. For quiet, elegant drinking head for the bars of five-star **hotels** such as the *Jockey Club* at the *Taj Residency* or its competition, the *Polo Club* at the *Oberoi*, and for a taste of colonial grandeur, the *Colonnade* at the *Taj West End*.

Check the listings magazines to catch Bangalore's small but steady stream of **live music** and **theatre**, some of which is homegrown; there are also a handful of **discos**, which usually follow a couples-only policy.

Bangalore is also a major centre for **cinema**, with a booming industry and dozens of theatres showing the latest releases from India and abroad. Check the listings page of the *Deccan Herald*, the *Evening Herald*, the free listings monthly, *Trail Blazer*, and *Bangalore Fortnightly*, to find out what's on. Western movies are often dubbed into Hindi, although their titles may be written in English; check the small print in the newspaper. Cinema fans should head for **Kempe Gowda Circle**, which is crammed with posters, hoardings and larger-than-life-size cardboard cutouts of the latest stars, strewn with spangly garlands. To arrange a visit to a local movie studio phone Chamundeshwari Studio (☎080/226 8642) or Shree Kanteera Studio (☎080/337 1008).

Pubs & clubs

Black Cadillac, 50 Residency Rd. Long-term favourite theme pub with some tables outside that also attract families.

The Club, Mysore Rd (☎080/337 1008). The talk of the town, 14km from the centre, and popular with a wealthy young crowd. Features regular discos and the occasional live gig with a few big names passing through. You'll need to take a taxi.

Cyber Pub, above Black Cadillac, Residency Rd. If you can cope with extremely loud music in a high-tech bar while surfing the World Wide Web, head up here for a unique experience.

Down Town, opposite Pub World, Residency Rd. Large pub that also serves food and wine, and has a couple of pool tables at the back.

Guzzlers Inn, 48 Rest House Rd, off Brigade Rd. Popular and established pub offering MTV, Star Sport and draught beer.

High Spirits, Brigade Rd, below *Kwality Restaurant*. Loads of mirrors and glass, quasi-tribal terracotta designs and TV sets, but ludicrously loud sounds. Mostly men.

JJ's, MSIL Building, Airport Rd Cross (☎080/526 1929). A café which offers a varied evening programme including discos, folk dance and live jazz nights on Sunday nights led by the musician-owner.

Nasa, 1/4 Church St. Karaoke and space-age decor, with the usual combination of big-screen MTV and in-your-face music, however, now declining in popularity.

Oasis, Church St. Low light and unobtrusive sound system: the chill-out option.

Pecos, Rest House Rd, off Brigade Rd. Small and relaxed pub on two floors with 60s and 70s music, popular with a mixed arty set.

A Pinch of Jazz, The Central Park, 47 Dickenson Rd (☎080/558 4242). Upmarket jazz café serving Cajun cuisine and live soft-jazz covers.

Pub World, opposite Galaxy Cinema, Residency Rd. A well-presented newish place popular with trendy young professionals offering the usual high-volume music.

Purple Haze, opposite Black Cadillac, Residency Rd. Currently the trendiest of the downtown pubs with a smart but jumping upstairs bar sporting Jimi Hendrix theme graphics.

Shopping

Bangalore has many fine shops, particularly if you're after **silk**. A wide range of silk is available at Karnataka Silk Industries Corporation and Vijayalakshmi Silk Kendra, both on Gupte Market, Kempe Gowda Rd, and at Deepam Silk Emporium on MG Rd. **Handicrafts** such as soapstone sculpture, brass, carved sandalwood and rosewood are also good value; emporia include: Central Cottage Industries Emporium, 144 MG Rd; the expensive Cottage Industries Exposition Ltd, 3 Cunningham Rd; Gulshan Crafts, 12 Safina Plaza, Infantry Rd, and the Karnataka's own state emporium, Cauveri, at the MG Rd and Brigade Rd crossing. For **silver**, try looking on and around Commercial St (north of MG Rd) and at KR Market, on Residency Rd as well as at Jewel Paragon between MG Rd and Kasturba Rd. The long-established Natesan's Antiqarts, 64 MG Rd, sells antiques and beautifully made reproduction sculpture, furniture and paintings, at international art house prices. If you want to take a look at expensive Indian *haute couture* try Ffolio at Embassy Chamber, Vittal Mallya Rd, which features several well-known Indian designers.

Bangalore is also a great place for **bookshops**. The first floor of Gangarams, 72 MG Rd, offers a wide selection on India (coffee-table art books and academic) plus the latest paperback fiction, and a great selection of Indian greetings cards. Another good option is Higginbotham's, 68 MG Rd; while you can browse in air-conditioned comfort at LB Publishers, 91 MG Rd. Around the corner from the ITDC office, Premier, 46/1 Church St, crams a huge number of books into a tiny space. The shop belonging to established publishers Motilal Banarsidas at 16 St Mark's Rd, close to the junction with MG Rd, offers a superb selection of heavyweight Indology and philosophy titles. The best **music** shops in the city centre, selling Indian and Western tapes, are HMV, on Brigade Rd or St Mark's Rd, where you can pick up an excellent four-cassette pack introducing South Indian or Carnatic music, and Rhythms, at 14 St Mark's Rd, beneath the *Nahar Heritage* hotel.

Listings

Airlines: Domestic: Indian Airlines, Cauvery Bhavan, Kempegowda Rd (☎080/221 1914); Jet Airways, 1-4 M Block, Unity Building, JC Rd (☎080/229 0465); NEPC, 138A Brigade Gardens, Church St (☎080/526 2842); Sahara Indian Airlines, 101 Nirvana, Richmond Rd, Richmond Circle (☎080/224 6435). **International:** Air Canada, Sunrise Chambers, 22 Ulsoor Rd (☎080/558 5394); Air France, Sunrise Chambers, 22 Ulsoor Rd (☎080/558 9397); Air India, Unity Building, JC Rd (☎080/227 7747); British Airways, St Mark's Rd (☎080/227 1205); Gulf Air, Sunrise Chambers, 22 Ulsoor Rd (☎080/558 4702); KLM, *Taj West End*, Race Course Rd (☎080/226 8703); Lufthansa, 44/2 Dickenson Rd (☎080/558 8791); Malaysian Airlines, Richmond Circle (☎080/221 3030); Pakistan International Airlines, ABC International, 108 Commerce House, 9/1 Cunningham Rd (☎080/226 0667); Qantas, Westminster, Cunningham Rd (☎080/226 4719); Royal Brunei, Stic Travels, Imperial Court, Cunningham Rd (☎080/226 7613); Singapore Airlines, 51 Richmond Rd (☎080/221 2822); Swiss Air, 51 Richmond Rd (☎080/221 1983); Thai Airlines, Stic Travels, Imperial Court, Cunningham Rd (☎080/226 7613); United Airlines, Richmond Towers, 12 Richmond Rd (☎080/224 4620).

Banks and exchange The best place to change money is Thomas Cook, 55 MG Rd, on the corner of Brigade Rd; the slower State Bank of India, is farther down at 87 MG Rd (Mon–Fri 10.30am–2.30pm & Sat 10.30am–12.30pm). ANZ Grindlays at Raheja Towers on MG Rd (same hours) changes money and advances cash on credit cards or, alternatively, try the fast and efficient Wall Street Finances, 3 House of Lords, 13/14 St Mark's Rd (Mon–Sat 9.30am–6pm; ☎080/227 1812). Also for Visa and Mastercard advances – but not travellers' cheques – go to Bank of Baroda, 70 MG Rd (same hours).

Car rental You can find self-drive car rental at Europcar, Sheriff House, 85 Richmond Rd (☎080/221 9502) and at Hertz, 167 Richmond Rd, near Trinity Circle (☎080/559 9408) with charges from Rs850 per day. For long-distance car rental and tailor-made itineraries, try Gullivers Tours & Travels, South Black 201/202 Manipal Centre, 47 Dickenson Road (☎080/558 8001), Clipper Holidays, 406 Regency Enclave, 4 Magrath Rd (☎080/559 9032), any KSTDC office and the ITDC booth at the train station.

Email There is no shortage of email/internet bureaux – most charge around Rs60 per hour and offer half-hour and, some, even shorter slots. The Cyber Café, 13-15 Brigade Rd (☎080/550 0949), is the most obvious and the most popular; you will need to get a ticket at the door to book your slot on the machines and there is coffee, but they don't encourage more than one person per computer. Other alternatives include Cyber Inn, Residency Rd Brigade Rd Cross (☎080/559 9962), Cyber Craft, Brigade Rd (☎080/559 6441) and Cyber's Den, First Floor, S112A Manipal Centre, Dickenson Rd (☎080/558 8792).

Libraries The British Council (English-language) library, 39 St Mark's Rd (☎080/221 3485) (Tues–Sat 10.30am–6.30pm), has newspapers and magazines that visitors are welcome to peruse in a/c comfort, as does the Alliance Française, (French), 16 GMT Rd (☎080/225 8762), and Max Mueller Bhavan (German), 3 Lavelle Rd (☎080/227 5435).

Pharmacies Open all night: Al-Siddique Pharma Centre, opposite Jamia Masjid near City Market; Janata Bazaar, in the Victoria Hospital, near City Market; Sindhi Charitable Hospital, 3rd Main S R Nagar. During the day, head for Santoshi Pharma, 46 Mission Rd.

Photographic equipment Adlabs, Mission Rd, Subbaiah Circle, stocks transparency film. GG Welling, 113 MG Rd, and GK Vale, 89 MG Rd, sell transparency and Polaroid film.

Police ☎100.

Post office on the corner of Raj Bhavan Rd and Cubbon St, at the northern tip of Cubbon Park, about ten minutes' walk from MG Rd (Mon–Sat 10am–7pm, Sun 10.30am–1.30pm).

Swimming pools Five-star hotel pools open to non-residents include: the *Taj Residency* (Rs400 includes sauna, jacuzzi and health club) and *Taj West End* (Rs400).

Travel agents For flight booking and reconfirmation and other travel necessities, try Gullivers Tours & Travels, South Black 201/202 Manipal Centre, 47 Dickenson Road (☎080/558 8001); Merry Go Round Tours, 41 Museum Rd, opposite *Berry's Hotel* (☎/fax 080/558 6946); Marco Polo Tours, Janardhan Towers, 2 Residency Rd (☎080/227 4484, fax 223 6671; or Sita Travels, 1 St Mark's Rd (☎080/558 8892).

Visa extensions Commissioner of Police, Infantry Rd (Mon–Sat 10am–5.30pm; ☎080/225 6242).

Around Bangalore

Bangalore is surrounded by some very pleasant countryside, which includes good walking country in the Nandi Hills to the north, and the Bannerghatta National Park to the south. Many visitors to Bangalore, however, are on their way to or from Mysore. The **Janapada Loka Folk Arts Museum**, between the two, gives a fascinating insight into Karnataka culture, while anyone wishing to see or study classical dance in a rural environment should check out the **Nrityagram Dance Village**.

Janapada Loka Folk Arts Museum

The **Janapada Loka Folk Arts Museum** (daily 9am–6pm; free), 53km southwest of Bangalore on the Mysore road, includes an amazing array of Karnatakan agricultural, hunting and fishing implements, weapons, ingenious household gadgets, masks, dolls

MOVING ON FROM BANGALORE

Bangalore is South India's principal transport hub. Fast and efficient computerized booking facilities make **moving on** relatively hassle-free, although availability of seats should never be taken for granted; book as far in advance as possible. For an overview of travel services to and from Bangalore, see Travel Details on p.273.

Bangalore's recently upgraded **airport** is the busiest in South India, with international and domestic departures and plans for more. The most frequent flights are to **Mumbai**, operated by Air India, Jet Airways, Indian Airlines and Sahara Indian, and there are also six or seven daily flights to **Delhi**. Both Jet and Indian Airlines operate daily flights to **Calcutta** and several flights a day to **Chennai**.

Most of the wide range of long-haul **buses** from the Central stand can be booked in advance at the computerized counters near bay #13 (7.30am–7.30pm). Aside from KSRTC, state bus corporations represented include Andhra Pradesh, Kerala, Maharashtra, Tamil Nadu and the Kadamba Transport Corporation, a Government of Goa undertaking. Timings and ticket availability for the forthcoming week are posted on a large board left of the main entrance. For general enquiries, call ☎080/287 3377. Several private bus companies run luxury coaches to destinations such as Mysore, Bijapur, Ooty, Chennai, Kochi/Ernakulam, Trichur, Kollam and Thiruvananthapuram. Agencies opposite the bus stand sell tickets for private coach companies such as Sharma (c/o MM Travels), National and Shama, and several advertise overnight deluxe buses to Goa (Rs225) as well as a/c (Rs375) and sleeper coaches (Rs420). The most reliable of the private bus companies is Vijayananda Travels at Sri Saraswathi Lodge, 3rd Main 2nd Cross, Gandhinagar (☎080/228 7222), with several other branches in Bangalore, who operate their distinctive yellow and black luxury coaches to destinations such as Mangalore and Hospet for those going to Hampi.

While Southern Railways converts to broad gauge, some **rail** routes in Karnataka continue to suffer disruption especially along the route from Hassan to Mangalore. Check the situation when you arrive. Bangalore City station's reservations office (Mon–Sat 8am–2pm & 2.15–8pm, Sun 8am–2pm; phone enquiries 7am–2pm & 2.15–9pm; ☎132) is in a separate building, east of the main station (to the left as you approach). Counter #14 is for foreigners. If you have an Indrail Pass, go to the Chief Reservations Supervisor's Office on the first floor (turn left at the top of the stairs), where "reservations are guaranteed". If your reservation is "waitlisted", or you are required to confirm the booking,

and shadow puppets, carved wooden *bhuta* (spirit-worship) sculptures and larger-than-life temple procession figures, manuscripts, musical instruments and *Yakshagana* theatre costumes. In addition, an incredible 1600 hours of **audio and video recordings** of musicians, dancers and rituals from the state are available for viewing on request.

To get to the museum, take one of the many slow Mysore buses (not the nonstop ones) from Bangalore. After the town of Ramanagar, alight at the 53km stone by the side of the road. A small **restaurant** serves simple food, and dorm **accommodation** (①) is available, though you can just jump back onto a bus to Mysore. For more details contact the Karnataka Janapada Trust, 7 Subramanyaswami Temple Rd, 5th Cross, 4th Block, Kumara Park West, Bangalore.

Nrityagram Dance Village

NRITYAGRAM DANCE VILLAGE is a delightful, purpose-built model village, 30km west of Bangalore. It was designed by the award-winning Goan architect Gerard de Cunha, and founded by the late Protima Gauri – who died in an avalanche during a pilgrimage to Kailash in Tibet in 1998. Protima Gauri, who had left Nrityagram sometime before her death, had enjoyed a colourful career in media and film, and eventually came to be well respected as an exponent of Odissi dance. The school continues without her you may have to go on the day of departure to the Commercial Officer's office, in the Divisional Office – yet another building, this time to the west, accessible from the main road. There are two 24 hr telephone information lines; one handles timetable enquiries (☎131), the other reels off a recorded list of arrivals and departures (☎133).

RECOMMENDED TRAINS FROM BANGALORE

The following trains are recommended as the fastest and/or most convenient from Bangalore:

Destination	Name	Number	Departs	Total time
Mumbai	*Udyan Express*	#6530	daily 8.30pm	24hr
Delhi	*Rajdhani Express**	#2429	daily 6.35pm	33hr 15min
	Karnataka Express	#2627	daily 6.25pm	41hr 45min
Chennai	*Shatabdi Express**	#2008	daily except Tues 4.20pm	4hr 45min
	Lalbagh Express	#2608	daily 6.30am	5hr 15min
Hospet (for Hampi)	*Hampi Express*	#6592	daily 10pm	10hr
Hyderabad	*Rajdhani Express**	#2429	daily 6.35pm	12hr
(Secunderabad)	*Kanyakumari Express*	#6526	daily 9pm	16hr 25min
Kochi (Ernakulam)	*Shatabdi Express**	#2007	daily except Tues 10.45am	2hr 5min
Mysore	*Chennai Mysore Express*	#6222	daily 6.35am	3hr 20min
	Tippu Express	#6206	daily 2.25pm	2hr 25min
	Chamundi Express	#6216	daily 6.15pm	3hr
Thiruvananthapuram	*Kannyakumari Express*	#6526	daily 9pm	15hr 10min

*= a/c only

and attracts pupils from all over the world. It hosts regular performances, as well as lectures on Indian mythology and art, and also offers courses in different forms of Indian dance. **Guided tours** of the complex cost Rs250. **Accommodation** for longer stays (⑦) promises "oxygen, home-grown vegetables and fruits, no TV, telephones, newspapers or noise". Contact their Bangalore office for further details (☎080/558 5440 or 226188).

Mysore

A centre of sandalwood-carving, silk and incense production, 159km southwest of Bangalore, **MYSORE**, the erstwhile capital of the Wadiyar Rajas, is one of South India's most-visited places. Considering the clichés that have been heaped upon the town, however, first impressions can be disappointing. Like anywhere else, you are not so much greeted by the scent of jasmine blossom or gentle wafts of sandalwood when you stumble off the bus or train, as by the usual cacophony of careering auto-rickshaws and noisy buses, bullock carts and tongas. Nevertheless, Mysore is a charming, old-fashioned and undaunting town, dominated by the spectacular **Maharaja's Palace**, around which the

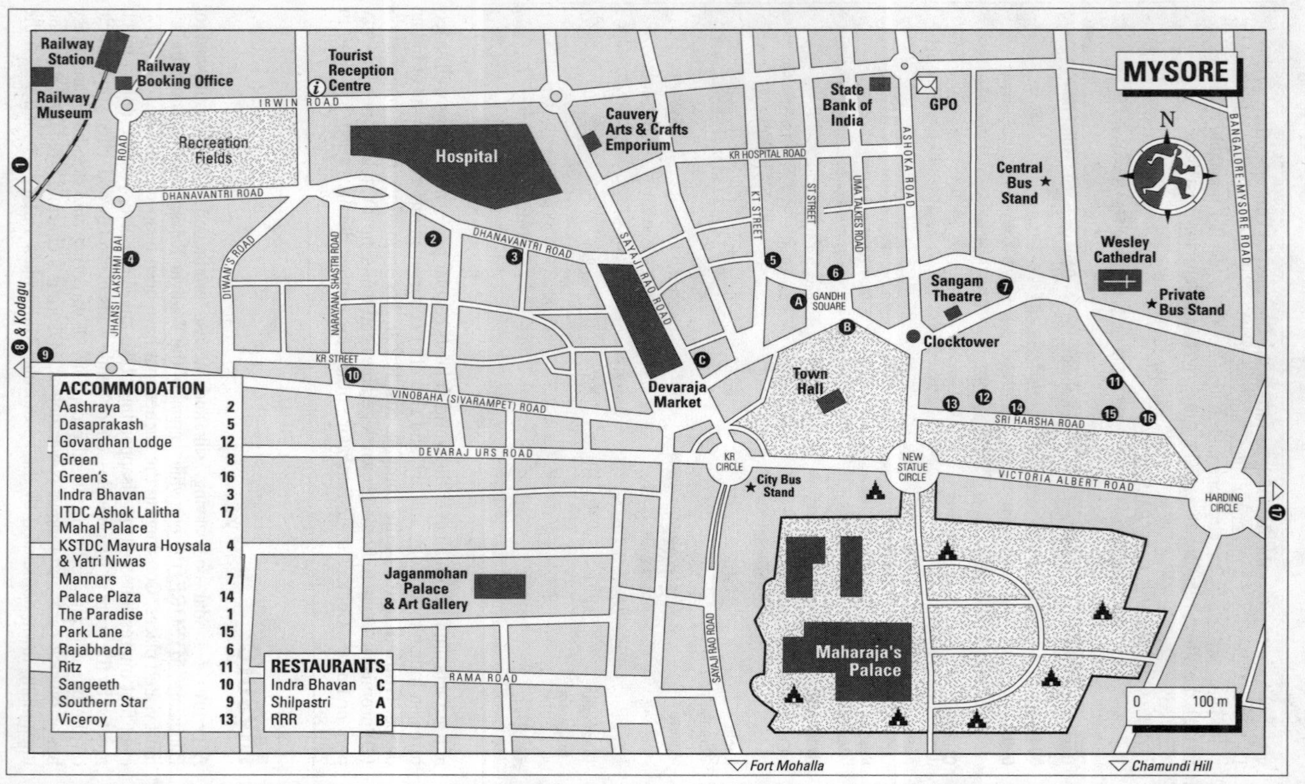
MYSORE
N
Railway Station
Railway Booking Office
Railway Museum
Tourist Reception Centre
IRWIN ROAD
Recreation Fields
Hospital
DHANAVANTRI ROAD
Cauvery Arts & Crafts Emporium
KR HOSPITAL ROAD
State Bank of India
GPO
ASHOKA ROAD
KT STREET
ST STREET
UMA TALKIES ROAD
Central Bus Stand
BANGALORE-MYSORE ROAD
Wesley Cathedral
Private Bus Stand
Sangam Theatre
GANDHI SQUARE
Clocktower
JHANSI LAKSHMI BAI ROAD
DIWAN'S ROAD
NARAYANA SHASTRI ROAD
SAYAJI RAO ROAD
& Kodagu
KR STREET
VINOBAHA (SIVARAMPET) ROAD
Devaraja Market
Town Hall
SRI HARSHA ROAD
DEVARAJ URS ROAD
KR CIRCLE
NEW STATUE CIRCLE
VICTORIA ALBERT ROAD
HARDING CIRCLE
City Bus Stand
Jaganmohan Palace & Art Gallery
Maharaja's Palace
RAMA ROAD
0
100 m
Fort Mohalla
Chamundi Hill
ACCOMMODATION
Aashraya 2
Dasaprakash 5
Govardhan Lodge 12
Green 8
Green's 16
Indra Bhavan 3
ITDC Ashok Lalitha 17
Mahal Palace
KSTDC Mayura Hoysala 4
& Yatri Niwas
Mannars 7
Palace Plaza 14
The Paradise 1
Park Lane 15
Rajabhadra 6
Ritz 11
Sangeeth 10
Southern Star 9
Viceroy 13
RESTAURANTS
Indra Bhavan C
Shilpastri A
RRR B

boulevards of the city radiate. Nearby, the city centre with the colourful and frenetic **Devaraja Market** is an inviting stroll. On the outskirts of Mysore, **Srirangapatnam** still harbours architectural gems from the days of the great Indian hero, Tipu Sultan, and the magnificent Hoysala temple of **Somnathpur** lies little more than an hour's drive away.

In the tenth century Mysore was known as "Mahishur" – "the town where the demon buffalo was slain" (by the goddess Durga). Presiding over a district of many villages, the city was ruled from about 1400 until Independence by the Hindu **Wadiyars**, and its fortunes were inextricably linked with those of Srirangapatnam, which became the Wadiyar headquarters from 1616 (see p.204). Their rule was only broken from 1761, when the Muslim Haider Ali and his son Tipu Sultan took over. Two years later, the new rulers demolished the labyrinthine old city to replace it with the elegant grid of sweeping, leafy streets and public gardens that survive today. However, following Tipu Sultan's defeat in 1799 by the British colonel Arthur Wellesley (later the Duke of Wellington), Wadiyar power was restored. As the capital of Mysore state, the city thereafter dominated a major part of southern India. In 1956, when Bangalore became capital of newly formed Karnataka, its maharaja was appointed governor.

Arrival and information

Mysore's nearest airport is at Bangalore. Four or five daily trains to the state capital serve the **train station**, 1500m northwest of the centre, with connections to and from Chennai. Mysore has three **bus** stands: Central, Private and City. Major long-distance KSRTC services pull in to the **Central bus stand**, near the heart of the city, where there's a friendly KSTDC booking counter for their tours, which is also good for information regarding bus times. The **Private bus stand**, which is basically just a dusty patch of road, lies a little way south, opposite the *Ritz Hotel*, and is used by buses to and from Somnathpur. Local buses, including services for Chamundi Hill and Srirangapatnam, stop at the **City bus stand**, next to the northwestern corner of the Maharaja's Palace.

Ten minutes' walk east of the train station, on a corner of Irwin Rd in the Old Exhibition Building, the helpful **tourist reception centre** (daily 10am–5.30pm) will make an effort to answer queries, though there's not much you can take away with you. The **KSTDC office** (daily 7.30am–8.30pm), at the hotel *Mayura Hoysala*, 2 Jhansi Laxmi Bai Rd, is of little use except to book one of their **tours**. The whistle-stop city tour (7.30am–8.30pm; Rs100) makes for a long day, covering Jaganmohan Palace Art Gallery, Maharaja's Palace, St Philomena's Cathedral, the Zoo, Chamundi Hill, Somnathpur, Srirangapatnam and Brindavan Gardens. It only leaves with a minimum of ten passengers, so you may not know for sure whether it will run when you buy your ticket. Their long-distance tour to Belur, Halebid and Sravanabelgola (7.30am–9.00pm; Rs180) is not recommended as it is too long for a single day and you spend far too much time on the bus; it's a similar story with their Ooty tour (7.30am–9.00pm; Rs180). However, their **car rental** rates at Rs3.50 per km (for a minimum of 250km per day) are quite reasonable if you want to put together your own itinerary. The Tourist Corporation of India at Gandhi Square (☎0821/443023) can also act as KSTDC agents and arranges tours and car rental.

The main **post office** (poste restante) is on the corner of Ashoka and Irwin roads (Mon–Sat 10am–7pm, Sun 10.30am–1.30pm). If you need to **change money**, there's a State Bank of Mysore on the corner of Sayaji Rao and Sardar Patel Rd, and the Indian Overseas Bank, Gandhi Square, opposite *Dasaprakash Hotel*. Seagull Travels, Ramanashri Hotel Complex, near Woodland Cinema, Harding Circle, are also licensed moneychangers. Unlike many of South India's cities, Mysore is slow in making cyber progress and besides the small Pepsi Cyber Club (☎0821/538455), tucked down a lane in Fort Mohallato to the south of the centre, there are few **email** bureaus around.

The City

In addition to its official tourist attractions, Mysore is a great city simply to stroll around. The characterful, if dilapidated, pre-Independence buildings lining market areas such as **Ashoka Rd** and **Sayaji Rao Rd** lend an air of faded grandeur to the busy centre, teeming with vibrant street life. The best place to get a sense of what's on offer is the Government Cauvery Arts and Crafts Emporium, Sayaji Rao Rd (closed Thurs), which stocks a wide range of local crafts that can be shipped overseas. Elsewhere, souvenir stores spill over with the famous **sandalwood**. The city's famous **Devaraja Market**, on Sayaji Rao Rd, is one of South India's most atmospheric produce markets: a giant complex of covered stalls bursting with bananas (the delicious *nanjangod* variety), luscious mangoes, blocks of sticky jaggery and conical heaps of lurid *kunkum* powder.

As an important centre of silk production, Mysore has several silk factories, the most prestigious of which is the Karnataka Silk Industries Corporation's **Silk Weaving Factory** (Mon–Sat 10am–4pm) on HD Kote Rd, 4km from the centre. Visitors are welcome and the showroom offers silk – mostly saris – at fixed but competitive prices. You will need a chit from the office to enter the complex; there are no conducted tours and don't expect a cottage industry. The large factory founded in the 1920s by the Maharaja of Mysore, runs in shifts signalled by wailing sirens, and consists of huge workshops filled with automated machines. You can see the silk being loomed, some batches with pure gold thread, before it goes into the dyeing process. The machine tenders are happy to explain the operation to you but with the machines working flat out, you will be lucky if you can hear a word over the deafening din. They also have a showroom at KSTDC hotel *Yatri Niwas*.

Maharaja's Palace

Mysore centre is dominated by the walled **Maharaja's Palace** (daily 10.30am–5.30pm; Rs10), a fairytale spectacle, topped with a shining brass-plated dome surmounting a single tower; it's especially magnificent on Sunday nights and during festivals, when it is illuminated by no fewer than five thousand light bulbs. Designed in the hybrid Indo-Saracenic style by Henry Irwin, the British consultant architect of Madras state, it was completed in 1912 for the twenty-fourth Wadiyar Raja, on the site of the old wooden palace that had been destroyed by fire in 1897. Twelve temples surround the palace, some of them of much earlier origin. Although there are six gates in the perimeter wall, entrance is on the south side only. Shoes and cameras must be left at the cloakroom inside.

An extraordinary amalgam of styles from India and around the world crowds the lavish **interior**. Entry is through the Gombe Thotti or **Dolls' Pavilion**, once a showcase for the figures featured in the city's lively Dussehra celebrations and now a gallery of European and Indian sculpture and ceremonial objects. Halfway along the pavilion, the brass **Elephant Gate** forms the main entrance to the centre of the palace, through which the Maharaja would drive to his car park. Decorated with floriate designs, it bears the Mysore royal symbol of a double-headed eagle, now the state emblem. To the north, past the gate, are dolls dating from the turn of the century, a wooden *mandapa* glinting with mirrorwork, and at the end, a ceremonial wooden elephant *howdah* (frame to carry passengers). Elaborately decorated with 84kg of 24-carat gold, it appears to be inlaid with red and green gems – in fact the twinkling lights are battery-powered signals to let the *mahout* know when the Maharaja wished to stop or go.

Walls leading into the octagonal **Kalyana Mandapa**, the royal wedding hall, are lined with a meticulously detailed frieze of oil paintings illustrating the great Mysore Dussehra festival of 1930, executed over fifteen years by four Indian artists. The hall itself is magnificent, a cavernous space featuring cast-iron pillars from Glasgow, Bohemian chandeliers and multicoloured Belgian stained glass arranged in peacock designs in the domed ceiling. A mosaic of English floor-tiles repeats the peacock motif. Beyond here lie small rooms cluttered with grandiose furniture, including a pair of silver chairs and others of Belgian cut-crystal made for the Maharaja and Lord Mountbatten, the last Viceroy of India. One of the rooms has a fine ceiling of Burma teak carved by local craftsmen.

Climbing a staircase with Italian marble balustrades, past an unnervingly realistic life-size plaster-of-Paris figure of Krishnaraja Wadiyar IV, lounging comfortably with his bejewelled feet on a stool, you come into the **Public Durbar Hall**, an orientalist fantasy often compared to a setting from *A Thousand and One Nights*. A vision of brightly painted and gilded colonnades, open on one side, the massive hall affords views out across the parade ground and gardens to Chamundi Hill. The Maharaja gave audience from here, seated on a throne made from 280kg of solid Karnatakan gold. These days, the hall is only used during the Dussehra festival, when it hosts classical concerts. Paintings by the celebrated artists Shilpi Siddalingaswamy and Raja Rama Varma, from the Travancore (Kerala) royal family, adorn the walls. The whole is crowned by white marble, inlaid with delicate floral scrolls of jasper, amber and lapis lazuli in the Moghul style. Somewhat out of sync with the opulence, a series of ceiling panels of Vishnu, painted on fire-proof asbestos, date from the 1930s. The smaller **Private Durbar Hall** features especially beautiful stained glass and gold-leaf painting. Before leaving you pass two embossed silver doors – all that remains of the old palace.

Nearby, behind the main palace building but within the same compound, a line of tacky souvenir shops leads to a small **museum** run by the royal family which shows paintings from the Thanjavur and Mysore schools, some inlaid with precious stones and gold leaf. After a lengthy judicial tussle, in 1998 the courts decided in favour of formally placing the main palace in the hands of the Karnataka state government but the royal family, who still hold a claim, are set to appeal.

MYSORE DUSSEHRA FESTIVAL

Following the tradition set by the Vijayanagar kings, the ten-day festival of **Dussehra** (Sept/Oct), to commemorate the goddess Durga's slaying of the demon buffalo, Mahishasura (see p.61), is celebrated in grand style at Mysore. Scores of cultural events occur, including concerts of south Indian classical (Carnatic) music and dance performances, in the great Durbar Hall of the **Maharaja's Palace**. On Vijayadasmi, the tenth and last day of the festival, a magnificent procession of mounted guardsmen on horseback and caprisoned elephants – one carrying the palace deity, Chaamundeshwari, on a gold *howdah* – marches 5km from the palace to Banni Mantap. There's also a floating festival in the temple tank at the foot of **Chamundi Hill** and a procession of chariots around the temple at the top. A torchlight parade takes place in the evening, followed by a massive firework display and much jubilation on the streets. Check out the excellent Web site at *www.dasara.com*.

Jaganmohan Palace: Jayachamarajendra Art Gallery

Built in 1861, the **Jaganmohan Palace** (daily 8am–5pm; Rs5; no cameras), 300m west of the Maharaja's Palace, was used as a royal residence until turned into a picture gallery and museum in 1915 by the Maharaja Krishnaraja Wadiyar IV. Most of the "contemporary" art on show seems to date from the 1930s, when a revival of Indian painting was spearheaded by E.B. Havell and the Tagore brothers Abandrinath and Ganganendranath in Bengal.

On the ground floor, a series of faded black-and-white photos of ceremonial occasions shares space with elaborate imported clocks. Nineteenth- and twentieth-century paintings dominate the first floor; among them is the work of the pioneering oil painter Raja Ravi Varma who, although not everyone's cup of tea, has been credited with introducing modern techniques to Indian art. Inspired by European masters, Varma gained a reputation in portraiture and also depicted epic Indian themes from the classics, such as the demon king Ravana absconding with Rama's wife Sita. Games on the upper floor include circular *ganjeeb* playing cards illustrated with portraits of royalty or deities and board games delicately inlaid with ivory. There's also a cluster of musical instruments, among them a brass *jaltarang* set and glass xylophone, and harmonicas and clarinet played by Krishnaraja Wadiyar IV himself. Another gallery, centring on a large wooden Ganesh seated on a tortoise, is lined with paintings, including Krishnaraja Wadiyar sporting with the "inmates" of his *zenana* (women's quarter of the palace) during Holi.

Chamundi Hill

Chamundi Hill, 3km southeast of the city, is topped with a temple to the chosen deity of the Mysore Rajas: the goddess Chamundi, or Durga, who slew the demon buffalo Mahishasura. It's a pleasant, easy bus trip (#101 from the City bus stand) to the top; the walk down, past a huge Nandi – Shiva's bull – takes about thirty minutes. Pilgrims, of course, make the trip in reverse order. The walk isn't very demanding, but by the end of it, after more than a thousand steps, your legs are likely to be a bit wobbly. Take plenty of drinking water, especially if walking in the middle of the day.

Don't be surprised if, at the top of the hill, which is dominated by the temple's forty-metre *gopura*, you're struck by a feeling of *déja vu*: at the **Godly Museum** there, one of the highly educational displays states, "5000 years ago at this time you had visited this place in the same way you are visiting now. Because world drama repeats itself identically every 5000 years." Another exhibit goes to the heart of our "problematic world: filthy films, lack of true education, blind faith, irreligiousness, bad habits and selfishness". Suitably edified, proceed along a path from the bus stand, past trinket and tea stalls, to the temple square. Immediately to the right, at the end of this path, are four bollards painted with a red stripe; return here after visiting the temples, when you want to take the path back down the hill.

Non-Hindus can visit the twelfth-century **temple** (daily 8am–noon & 5–8pm; leave shoes opposite the entrance), staffed by friendly priests who will plaster your forehead in vermilion paste. The Chamundi figure inside is solid gold; outside, in the courtyard, stands a fearsome, if gaily coloured, statue of the demon Mahishasura. On leaving, if you continue by the path instead of retracing your steps, you can return to the square via two other temples and various buildings storing ceremonial paraphernalia and animal figures used during Dussehra. You'll also come across loads of scampering monkeys and the odd dreadlocked *sadhu*, who will willingly pose for your holiday snaps – for a consideration. The magnificent five-metre **Nandi**, carved from a single piece of black granite in 1659, is an object of worship himself, adorned with bells and garlands and tended by his own priest. Minor shrines, dedicated to Chamundi and the monkey god Hanuman among others, line the side of the path, and at the bottom, a little shrine to Ganesh lies near a *chai*-shop. From here it's usually possible to pick up an auto-rickshaw or bus, back into the city, but at weekends the latter are often full. If you walk on towards the city, passing a temple on the left, with a big water tank (the site of the floating festival during Dussehra), you come after ten minutes to the main road between the *Lalitha Mahal Palace* and the city; there's a bus stop, and often auto-rickshaws, at the junction.

Accommodation

Mysore has plenty of **hotels** to suit all budgets. Finding a room is only a problem during Dussehra (see box on p.199),when popular places are booked up weeks in advance.

Cheap lodges are concentrated on and around **Dhanavantri Rd**, a little way south of the tourist reception centre on Irwin Rd, and close to **Gandhi Square** further east. Most, however, are pokey and not particularly clean. Mid-range to expensive hotels are more spread out, but a good place to start is **Jhansi Lakshmi Bai Rd**, which runs south from the train station. If you're looking for a palace, then head straight for ITDC's opulent *Ashok Lalitha Mahal*.

Inexpensive

Govardhan Lodge, opposite the Opera cinema, Sri Harsha Rd (☎0821/434118). Basic budget rooms close to Gandhi Square. Frayed around the edges, but clean enough. ②–③.

Green's, Sri Harsha Rd, next to *Park Lane* (☎0821/422415). Not to be confused with the palace hotel (see below). This place has small but clean rooms that come with high ceilings and attached baths. Simple food is available in the dining room which also serves as a popular local bar. ①.

Indra Bhavan, Dhanavantri Rd (☎0821/423933). Dilapidated and characterful old lodge popular with Tibetans, with en-suite singles and doubles. Their "ordinary" rooms are a little grubby, but the good-value "deluxe" have clean tiled floors and open on to a wide common verandah. ②–③.

KSTDC Yatri Niwas, 2 Jhansi Llaxmi Bai Rd (☎0821/423492). The government-run *Mayura Hoysala*'s economy wing: simple rooms around a central garden, with beer garden and terrace restaurant next door, and a cheap dorm for Rs70. ③.

Mannars, Chandragupta Rd (☎0821/448060). Budget hotel near the bus stand and Gandhi Square. No frills, except the TV and sofas in reception. Deservedly popular with backpackers. ②–③.

Park Lane, Sri Harsha Rd (☎0821/434340). Six pleasant rooms over a popular beer-garden/restaurant. One of the best deals at this price, but with some drawbacks: clouds of mozzies, noise from the bar until 11.30pm and dodgy plumbing. Avoid room 8 (it's next to the generator). ②.

Rajabhadra, Gandhi Square (☎0821/423023). Best value of several look-a-like lodges on the square. The front rooms are great if you don't mind being in the thick of things. Some singles. ②.

Ritz, Bangalore–Nilgiri Rd (☎0821/422668). Wonderful colonial-era hotel, a stone's throw from the Private bus stand. At the top of this category, but worth the extra. Only four rooms, so book ahead. ④.

Sangeeth, 1966 Narayana Shastry Rd, near the Udipi Krishna temple (☎0821/424693). Mysore's best all-round budget deal: bland and a bit boxed in, but central, friendly and very good value. ②.

Moderate to expensive

Aashraya, Rajmal Talkies Rd, Dhanavantri Rd Cross (☎0821/427088). Run-of-the-mill hotel on the edge of the market area. Attached rooms are small, but comfortable and reasonable value. ③–⑤.

Dasaprakash, Gandhi Square (☎0821/442444). Modern multistorey hotel; busy, clean and efficient, though lacking character. Some a/c rooms, cheap singles and a veg restaurant. ③–⑤.

Green, Chittaranjan Palace, 2270 Vinoba Rd, Jayalakshmipuram (☎0821/512536, fax 516139). On the western outskirts, a former royal palace refurbished as an elegant, eco-conscious two-star, in large gardens, awarded the prize for best garden in Mysore in 1998. Spacious rooms, lounges, verandahs, a croquet lawn and well-stocked library. All profits to charities and environmental projects. Their auto-rickshaw will pick you up with prior arrangement and they can also be contacted through the Charities Advisory Trust in London (☎0171/794 9835). ⑥–⑧.

ITDC Ashok Lalitha Mahal Palace, T Narasipur Rd (☎0821/571265, fax 571770). On a slope overlooking the city in the distance, and visible for miles around, this white, Neoclassical palace was built in 1931 to accommodate the Maharaja's foreign guests. Now it's a Raj-style fantasy, popular with tour groups and film crews. Tariffs are astronomical by Indian standards, ranging from $160 to $740 per night for the "Viceroy Suite". The tea lounge, restaurant and pool are open to non-residents. ⑨.

KSTDC Mayura Hoysala, 2 Jhansi Laxmi Bai Rd (☎0821/425349). Reasonably priced rooms and suites in a colonial-era mansion. Terrace restaurant and beer garden. Good value but the food is uninspiring and there is no room service. ④–⑦.

Palace Plaza, Sri Harsha Rd (☎0821/430034). A modern multistoried block close to all amenities where the cheaper rooms are pokey but reasonable value and there are a few a/c deluxes with extraordinary round beds and mirrored ceilings no doubt meant for the honeymoon crowd. The restaurant is good. ④–⑥.

The Paradise, 104 Vivekananda Rd, Yadavgiri (☎0821/410366). Dasaprakash's upmarket hotel; new and modern with luxurious rooms and all facilities including an excellent South Indian vegetarian restaurant. ⑥–⑧.

Southern Star, Vinobha Rd (☎0821/438141, fax 421689). Modern and comfortable monolithic hotel with all facilities including two restaurants, a bar and a swimming pool. ⑨.

Viceroy, Sri Harsha Rd (☎0821/428001, fax 433391). Snazzy new business-oriented hotel, with most mod cons and views over the park to the palace from front rooms. Mostly a/c. ⑥–⑦.

Eating

Mysore has scores of **places to eat**, from numerous South Indian "meals" joints dotted around the market to the opulent *Lalita Mahal*, where you can work up an appetite for a gourmet meal with a few lengths of the pool. To sample the celebrated Mysore

MOVING ON FROM MYSORE

For an overview of travel services to and from Mysore, see Travel Details on p.273.

If you're contemplating a long haul, the best way to travel is by **train**, usually with a change at **Bangalore**. Four express services leave Mysore each day for the Karnatakan capital, taking between 2hr and 3hr 30min to cover the 139km. The fastest of these, the a/c *Shatabdi Express* #2008 (daily except Tues) continues on to Chennai (6hr 55min); the others terminate in Bangalore, where you can pick up long-distance connections to a wide range of Indian cities (see p.194). **Reservations** can be made at Mysore's computerized booking hall inside the station (Mon–Sat 8am–2pm & 2.15–8pm, Sun 8am–2pm). There's no tourist counter; take a good book. Due to sporadic work upgrading the line, trains to **Hassan** are subject to disruption but when the service is operating there are four passenger trains a day (2hr 25min–4hr), the best of which leaves at 10.10am and arrives at Hassan at 12.35pm.

Reservations are not required for Bangalore (except on the *Shatabdi Express*), so you shouldn't ever have to do the trip by **bus**, which takes longer and is a lot more terrifying. If you do have to take a bus, there are numerous services to Bangalore including several private coaches run by the likes of Sardar Travels or Sharma from near the Central bus stand. Most destinations within a day's ride of Mysore can only be reached by road. Long-distance services operate out of the Central bus stand, where you can book computerized tickets up to three days in advance. English timetables are posted on the wall inside the entrance hall, and there's a helpful enquiries counter in the corner of the compound. Regular buses leave here for **Hassan**, jumping-off place for the Hoysala temples at **Belur** and **Halebid**, and for Channarayapatna/**Saravanabelgola** (hourly; 2–3hr). Heading south to **Ooty** (5hr), there's a choice of a dozen or so buses, all of which stop at **Bandipur National Park**. Direct services to **Hospet**, the nearest town to **Hampi** (the overnight bus leaves at 7pm and takes 10hr), and several cities in Kerala, including **Kannur**, **Kozhikode** and **Kochi** also operate from Mysore. Even though the coastal Konkan Railway line has been completed, the service is not yet running smoothly and so the only way to travel direct to **Goa** is on the 4pm overnight bus that arrives at **Panjim** at 9am. Most travellers, however, break this long trip into stages, heading first to **Mangalore** (12–15 daily; 7hr), and working their way north from there, usually via **Gokarn** – which you can also reach by direct bus (1 daily; 14hr) – or **Jog Falls**. Mangalore-bound buses and coaches tend to pass through **Madikeri**, capital of Kodagu (Coorg), which is also served by hourly buses most of which travel through the Tibetan enclave of **Bylakuppe**. For details of services to **Somnathpur** and **Srirangapatnam**, see the relevant accounts below.

Mysore doesn't have an airport (the nearest one is at Bangalore), but you can confirm and book Indian Airlines flights at their office in the *KSTDC Mayura Hoysala* (Mon–Sat 10am–1.30pm & 2.15–5pm; ☎0821/421846).

pak, a sweet, rich, crumbly mixture made of *ghee* and maize flour, queue at *Guru Sweet Mart*, a small stall at KR Circle, Savaji Rao Rd, which is considered the best sweet shop in the city. Another specialty from this part of the world is *malligi iddli* a delicate light fluffy *iddli* usually served in the mornings and at lunch at several of the downtown "meals" restaurants.

Akshaya, *Hotel Dasaprakash*, Gandhi Square. Very good South Indian veg "meals" joint, serving various *thalis* (try the "special"), ice-creams and cold drinks. Low on atmosphere, but the food is delicious and cheap.

Gopika, *Govardhan Lodge*, Sri Harsha Rd. Inexpensive "meals" restaurant on the ground floor of a busy hotel; opens early for Indian breakfasts of *iddlis*, *wada*, *pakora* and big glasses of hot-milk coffee.

Indra Bhavan, Savaji Rao Rd. Comfortable and popular veg restaurant that serves both South and North Indian cuisine. Their other branch on Dhanavanti Rd (see Accommodation) is equally if not more popular and also has an a/c section.

KSTDC Bamboo Grove, *Mayura Hoysala*, 2 Jhansi Laxmi Bai Rd. Terrace-garden restaurant and bar, with split-cane blinds and the usual multicuisine menu but uninspiring food; more popular as a bar in the evenings.

ITDC Ashok Lalitha Mahal. Sample the charms of this palatial five-star with an expensive hot drink in the turn-of-the-century tea lounge, or an à la carte lunch in the grand dining hall, accompanied by live sitar music. The old-style bar also boasts a full-size billiards table.

Park Lane, Sri Harsha Rd. Congenial courtyard restaurant-cum-beer-garden (see under Accommodation), with moderately priced veg and non-veg food (meat sizzlers are a specialty), pot plants and loud *filmi* music. Popular with travellers, but they actively discourage Indians and foreigners from sitting together.

Ritz, Bangalore–Nilgiri Rd. Central and secluded hotel restaurant, and a nice escape from the city streets for a drink or veg and non-veg meals. The best tables are in courtyard at the back. Opens at 8.30am for "omelette-bread-butter-jam" breakfasts.

RRR, Gandhi Square. A plain "meals" restaurant in front with a small but plush a/c room at the back which gets packed at lunchtimes and at weekends. Well worth the wait for its excellent set menus on banana leaves, chicken *biryani* and fried fish.

Shilpastri, Gandhi Square. Quality North Indian-style food, with particularly tasty *tandoori* (great chicken *tikka*). Plenty of good veg options, too, including lots of *dals* and curd rice. Serves alcohol.

Around Mysore

Mysore is a jumping-off point for some of Karnataka's most popular destinations. At **Srirangapatnam**, the fort, palace and mausoleum date from the era of Tipu Sultan, the "Tiger of Mysore", a perennial thorn in the side of the British. The superb **Hoysala temples** of **Somnathpur**, and farther out, **Belur** and **Halebid**, are architectural masterpieces. Also near Hassan, the Jain site of **Sravanabelgola** attracts bus-loads of pilgrims and tourists to see the monolithic, naked statue of **Gomateshvara**. Mysore's own Jain shrine of **Gomatagiri** is not nearly as dramatic but makes a pleasant day-trip from the city centre.

If you're heading south towards Ooty, **Bandipur National Park**'s forests and hill scenery offer another escape from the city, although your chances of spotting any rare animals are actually quite slim. The same is true of **Nagarhole National Park**, three hours southwest of Mysore in the Coorg region.

Srirangapatnam

The tiny island of **Srirangapatnam**, in the Kaveri (Cauvery) River, 14km north of Mysore, measures only 5km by 1km. Long a site of Hindu pilgrimage, it is named for its tenth-century Sriranganathaswamy Vishnu temple, which in 1133 served as a

WILDLIFE SANCTUARIES AROUND MYSORE

Mysore lies within striking distance of three major wildlife sanctuaries – **Bandipur**, **Nagarhole** and across the border in Tamil Nadu, **Madumalai** – all part of the vast **Nilgiri Biosphere Reserve**. In recent years, however, all three have been affected by the presence of the bandit **Veerapan** (see p.490), and large parts of these forest tracts are often closed to visitors. If you are thinking of going there, check with the tourist office to see which areas are open. You will require a good deal of forward planning if you want to get the most out of the sanctuaries. A few upmarket private "resorts" on the edge of the parks and one or two tourist complexes, allow visitors to experience some of the delights in an area famous for its **elephants**. For others, Forest Department accommodation at Bandipur (see p.207) and Nagarhole (see p.208) must be booked as far in advance as possible through the Chief Warden, *Aranya Bhavan*, Ashokpuram (☎0821/520901), 6km south of the centre, on bus #61 from the City stand. To arrange accommodation at Madumalai, you'll have to phone ahead (see p.487). Note that the Forest Department's *Rest Houses* can only be booked in Ooty.

One of several lesser wildlife sanctuaries within striking distance of Mysore, the **Biligiri Rangaswamy Wildlife Sanctuary**, 90km to the east, lies in an unspoiled corner of the state inhabited by the Soliga tribe. Covering an area of 525 square kilometres, the deciduous forests spread over the picturesque Biligiri Rangaswamy Hills harbour a myriad forms of wildlife, including elephant, panther, tiger, wild dog, sloth bear and several species of deer. Despite the thick cover, the sanctuary is a **bird-watcher's dream** with over 270 species including the majestic crested hawk eagle. Accessible by bus via Nanjangod and Chamarajnagar, the sanctuary is being promoted by Jungle Lodges & Resorts, Bangalore (☎080/558 6163), a government-sponsored organization which aims to promote wildlife in the state through comfortable, upmarket camps and resorts. For an all-inclusive stay including elephant ride and forest walks, their luxurious camp at the sanctuary charges Indians Rs1000 per person per night but foreigners an extraordinary US$60.

refuge for the philosopher Ramanuja, a staunch Vaishnavite, from the Shaivite Cholas in Tamil Nadu. The Vijayanagars built a fort here in 1454, and in 1616 it became the capital of the Mysore Wadiyar Rajas. However, Srirangapatnam is more famously associated with **Haider Ali**, who deposed the Wadiyars in 1761, and even more so with his son, **Tipu Sultan**. During Tipu's seventeen-year reign – which ended with his death in 1799, when the future Duke of Wellington took the fort at the bloody battle of "Seringapatnam" – he posed a greater threat than any other Indian ruler to British plans to dominate India.

Tipu Sultan and his father were responsible for transforming the small state of Mysore into a major Muslim power. Born in 1750, of a Hindu mother, Tipu Sultan inherited Haider Ali's considerable military skills. However, unlike his illiterate father, he was an educated, cultured man who introduced radical agricultural reforms. His burning life-long desire to rid India of the hated British invaders naturally brought him an ally in the French. He obsessively embraced his popular name of the **"Tiger of Mysore"**, surrounding himself with symbols and images of tigers; much of his memorabilia is decorated with the animal or its stripes, and, like the Romans, he is said to have kept tigers for the punishment of criminals.

Tipu Sultan's Srirangapatnam was largely destroyed by the British, but parts of the fort area in the northwest survive, including gates, ramparts, arsenals, the grim dungeons (where chained British prisoners were allegedly forced to stand neck-deep in water) and the domed and minareted Jami Masjid mosque.

The former summer palace, the **Daria Daulat Bagh** (Sat–Thurs 10am–5pm; Rs2), literally meaning "wealth of the sea", is situated 1km east of the fort and was used to entertain Tipu Sultan's guests. At first sight, this low, wooden colonnaded building set in an attractive formal garden fails to impress because most of it is obscured by sunscreens. However, the superbly preserved interior, displaying ornamental arches, tiger-striped columns and floral decoration on every inch of the teak walls and ceiling, is remarkable. A much-repainted mural on the west wall relishes every detail of Haider Ali's victory over the British at Pollilore in 1780. Upstairs, a small collection of Tipu Sultan memorabilia, European paintings, Persian manuscripts on handmade paper and a model of Srirangapatnam are on show.

An avenue of cypress trees leads from an intricately carved gateway to the **Gumbaz mausoleum**, 3km east of the palace. Built by Tipu Sultan in 1784 to commemorate Haider Ali, and to serve as his own resting place later, the lower half of the grey granite edifice is crowned by a dome of white-washed brick and plaster. Ivory-inlaid rosewood doors lead to the tombs of Haider Ali and Tipu Sultan, each covered by a pall (tiger stripes for Tipu), and an Urdu tablet records Tipu Sultan's martyrdom. Today, the mausoleum is at the centre of a bitter contest between the family of Tipu Sultan and the government-appointed caretakers. Visitors may have the good fortune to meet, at one corner of the cloisters, the erudite direct descendant of the Sultan himself, who has set up camp there to further his campaign.

At the heart of the fortress, the great temple of **Sriranganathaswamy** still stands proud and virtually untouched by the turbulent history that has flowed around it, and remains, for many devotees, the prime draw. Developed by succeeding dynasties, the temple consists of three distinctive sanctuaries and is entered via an impressive five-storeyed gateway and a hall that was built by Haider Ali. The innermost sanctum, the oldest part of the temple, contains an image of the reclining Vishnu.

THE RANGANATHITTU SANCTUARY

Some 2km southwest of Srirangapatnam, the **Ranganathittu Bird Sanctuary** (daily 9am–6pm; Rs100) is a must for ornithologists, especially during October/November, when the lake, fed by the Kaveri River, attracts huge flocks of migrating birds. At other times it's a tranquil spot to escape the city, where you can enjoy boat rides through the backwaters to look for crocodiles, otters and dozens of species of resident waders, wildfowl and forest birds. The easiest way to get there is by **rickshaw** from Srirangapatnam.

Practicalities

Frequent **buses** from Mysore City bus stand and all the Mysore–Bangalore **trains** pull in near the temple and fort. Srirangapatnam is a small island, but places of interest are quite spread out; tongas, auto-rickshaws and bicycles are available on the main road near the bus stand. The KSTDC **hotel**-cum-restaurant, *Mayura River View* (☎0821/52114; ④), occupies a pleasant spot beside the Cauvery River, 3km from the bus stand and there are a couple of alternatives nearby.

Gomatagiri

Few of Mysore's residents have ever been out to the hill of **Gomatagiri**, 18km to the northwest of the city near the small town of Bettadoor, where on a rocky granite outcrop, a monolithic ten-metre-high statue of **Gomateshvara** stands gazing serene over the surrounding countryside. Also known as Bahubali, the son of the first Jain *tirthankara*, Gomateshvara is shown here, as he is in sites all over southern Karnataka, naked and in a state of deep meditation with his arms limp by his sides. An idyllic spot among eucalyptus groves, Gomatagiri sees no tourists and the only other building here besides the temple on top of the hill, is the Jain guesthouse where the welcoming caretaker-cum-priest lives; he will gladly open the temple for you. Small shrines litter the base of the outcrop and house the footprints of the 24 Jain *tirthankaras*. Steps hewn out of rock lead up to the temple and the eleventh-century statue with distant views out towards the Brindavan Gardens and the Krishnaraja Sagar dam on the Kaveri River. The only time the peace of the place is at all disturbed is during the **Mastakabhisheka ceremony** around September every year, when the statue is anointed with a nectar of milk.

Practicalities

If you are tempted to stay here, the **accommodation** is limited to the very basic rooms of the guesthouse (①) none of which have beds, so bring a mat. With ample notice, the caretaker priest will provide simple vegetarian food. Bus 264 from Mysore's City bus stand, runs past Gomatagiri five times a day with the first bus at 6.30am and the last at 6.30pm. The journey takes one hour and the bus continues to a village a short distance past Gomatagiri; after a short break the bus returns the way it came to Mysore.

Bandipur National Park

Situated among the broken foothills of the Western Ghat mountains, **Bandipur National Park**, (6am–6pm; Rs150 foreigners, Rs10 Indians; Rs10 extra for camera, Rs100 for video) 80km south of Mysore, covers 880 square kilometres of dry deciduous forest, south of the Kabini River. The reserve was created in the 1930s from the local Maharaja's hunting lands, and expanded in 1941 to adjoin the Nagarhole National Park to the north, and Madumalai and Wynad Sanctuaries to the south in Tamil Nadu. These now collectively comprise the huge **Nilgiri Biosphere Reserve**, one of India's most extensive areas of protected forest.

Access to Bandipur National Park is **severely restricted** at present, due to activities of the bandit, Veerapan – an alleged kidnapper and smuggler – although parts, such as Gopalswamy Betta, remain open to visitors with their own vehicles. Visitors should check, however, with forest authorities before travelling around the park. In any case, Bandipur, in spite of its good accommodation and well-maintained metalled jeep tracks, is a disappointment as a tourist destination. Glimpses of anything rarer than a langur or spotted deer are infrequent outside the core area, which is off-limits to casual visitors, and the noisy diesel bus laid on by the Forest Department to transport tourists around the accessible areas of the park scares off what little fauna remain. If you're hoping to spot a tiger, forget it.

On the plus side, Bandipur is one of the few reserves in India where you stand a good chance of sighting wild **elephants**, particularly in the wet season (June–Sept), when water and forage are plentiful and the animals evenly scattered. Later in the monsoon, huge herds congregate on the banks of the Kabini River, in the far north of the park, where you can see the remnants of an old stockade used by one particularly zealous nineteenth-century British hunter as an elephant trap. Bandipur also boasts some fine scenery: at **Gopalswamy Betta**, 9km from the park headquarters, a high ridge looks north over the Mysore Plateau and its adjoining hills, while to the south, the "**Rolling Rocks**" afford sweeping views of the craggy, 260-metre-deep "**Mysore Ditch**".

Practicalities

The **best time to visit** is during the rainy season (June–Sept); unlike neighbouring parks, Bandipur's roads do not get washed out by the annual deluge, and elephants are more numerous at this time. By November/December, however, most of the larger animals have migrated across the state border into Madumalai, where water is more plentiful in the dry season. If possible, **avoid weekends**, as the park attracts bus-loads of noisy day-trippers.

Getting to Bandipur by bus is easy; all the regular KSRTC services to Ooty from Mysore's Central bus stand (12 daily; 2hr 30min) pass through the reserve (the last one back to Mysore leaves at 5pm), stopping outside the Forest Department's reception centre (daily 9am–4.30pm). If you miss the last bus from Mysore you can change at Gundulapet 18km and take a taxi to the main reception centre (Rs180).

KSTDC's *Mayura Prakruthi* at Melkamanahally (☎08229/7301; ①–⑤), 4km before Bandipur, has pleasant cottages with large, comfortable rooms and a restaurant. If the park is officially open, you can confirm accommodation bookings at their Forest Department's reception centre. The rooms on offer are basic, but good value, ranging from the "VIP" *Gajendra Cottages*, which have en-suite bathrooms and verandahs, to beds in large, institutional dorms. The *chowkidars* will knock up simple meals by arrangement. Upmarket options include *Tusker Trails*, at Mangala Village, 3km from Bandipur (booked through their office at Hospital Cottage, Bangalore Palace, Bangalore; ☎080/353 0748, fax 334 2862; ⑨), which is a **resort** run by members of the royal family of Mysore and offers cottages, a swimming pool, a tennis court and organizes trips into the forest. *Bush Betta*, off the main Mysore highway (booked through Gainnet, Raheja Plaza, Richmond Rd, Bangalore; ☎080/551 2631; ⑨), has comfortable cottages and organizes guided tours. It is essential to book accommodation in advance through the **Forest Department** office in Bangalore (Aranya Bhavan, 18th Cross, Malleswaram; ☎080/334 1993), or at Mysore (Project Tiger, Aranya Bhavan, Ashokpuram; ☎0821/520901).

Unless you have your own vehicle, the only **transport around the park** – although at the time of writing, even this had been suspended due to the Veerapan situation – is the hopeless Forest Department bus, which makes two tours daily (7.30am & 4.30pm; 1hr; Rs15). If you decide to take the half-hour **elephant ride** around the reception compound you may see a deer or two, but nothing more. Visitors travelling to Gopalswamy Betta should note that car rental is not available at Bandipur, but at Gundulapet, from where they will try and charge a lot more than the official Rs500. You must exit the park before nightfall.

Nagarhole National Park

Bandipur's northern neighbour, **Nagarhole** (Snake River) **National Park**, extends 640 square kilometres north from the Kabini River, which was dammed in 1974 to form a picturesque artificial lake. During the dry season (Feb–June), this perennial water source attracts large numbers of animals, making it a potentially prime spot for sighting wildlife. The forest here is of the moist-deciduous type – thick jungle with a thirty-metre-high canopy – and more impressive than Bandipur's drier scrub.

However, disaster struck Nagarhole in 1992, when friction between local pastoralist "tribals" and the park wardens over grazing rights and poaching erupted into a spate of arson attacks. Thousands of acres of forest were burned to the ground. The trees have grown back in places, but it will be decades before animal numbers completely recover. An added threat to the fragile jungle tracts of the region is a notorious gang of female wood-smugglers from Kerala, which has developed a fearsome and almost mythical, Amazon-like reputation. Meanwhile, Nagarhole is only worth visiting at the height of the dry season, when its muddy river banks and grassy swamps, or *hadlus*, offer better chances of sighting *gaur* (Indian bison), elephant, *dhole* (wild dog), deer, boar and even the odd tiger or leopard, than any of the neighbouring sanctuaries.

Practicalities

Nagarhole is open year-round, but avoid the monsoons, when floods wash out most of its dirt tracks and a proliferation of leeches makes hiking impossible. To get there from Mysore, catch one of the two daily **buses** from the Central stand to **Hunsur** (3hr), which is 10km from the park's north gate, where you can pick up transport to the Forest Department's two *Rest Houses* (①–②). The **rest houses** have to be booked well in advance through the Forest Department offices in Mysore or Bangalore (see p.207). Turn up on spec, and you'll be told accommodation is "not available". It is also important to arrive at the park gates well before dusk, as the road through the reserve to the lodges closes at 6pm, and is prone to "elephant blocks".

The Nagarhole **visitor centre** is open 24 hours and charges foreigners Rs150 for entrance for the park, plus Rs10 for a camera. They do not organize elephant rides, but schedule four bus tours – two in the morning starting at 6am, and two in the afternoon – for a minimum of two people.

Other **accommodation** around Nagarhole includes the highly acclaimed and luxurious, *Kabini River Lodge* (book through Jungle Lodges & Resorts in Bangalore; ☎080/559 7021; ⑨), approached via the village of Karapura, 3km from the park's south entrance. Set in its own leafy compound on the lakeside, this former maharaja's hunting lodge offers expensive all-inclusive deals that include transport around the park with expert guides. It's impossible to reach by public transport, so you'll need to rent a taxi – in rural South India, this signifies a car with no meter – to get there and you will also have to book well in advance. Another upmarket option but not quite in the same league, the *Jungle Inn* at Veerana Hosahalli (☎08222/52781; ⑨; booked through their Bangalore office on ☎080/224 3172), is close to the park entrance and arranges wildlife safaris, with a very hefty surcharge for foreign visitors. Some tour groups prefer the luxury of *Orange County* (see p.224), near the town of Siddapura in Kodagu 75km to the north, despite the long drive.

Somnathpur

Built in 1268 AD, the exquisite **Keshava Vishnu temple**, in the sleepy hamlet of **SOMNATHPUR**, was the last important temple to be constructed by the Hoysalas; it is also the most complete and, in many respects, the finest example of this singular style (see p.586). Somnathpur itself, just ninety minutes from Mysore by road, is little more than a few neat tracks and some attractive simple houses with pillared verandahs.

Like other Hoysala temples, the Keshava is built on a star-shaped plan, but, as a triple shrine, it represents a mature development from the earlier constructions. ASI staff can show you around and also grant you permission to clamber on the enclosure walls, to get a marvellous bird's-eye view of the modestly proportioned structure. It's best to do this as early as possible, as the stone gets very hot to walk on in bare feet.

The temple is in the style of a *trikutachala* or "three-peaked hill", with a tower on each shrine – a configuration also seen in certain Chalukya temples, and three temples on Hemakuta hill at Vijayanagar (Hampi; see p.253). Each shrine, sharing a common hallway, is dedicated to a different form of Vishnu. In order of "seniority" they are Keshava in the central shrine, Venugopala to the proper right and Jagannath to the left. The Keshava shrine features a very unusual *chandrasila* or "moonstone" step at its entrance, and, diverging from the usual semi-circular Hoysala style, has two pointed projections.

The Keshava's high plinth (*jagati*) provides an upper ambulatory, which on its outer edge reproduces the almost crenellated shape of the structure and allows visitors to approach the upper registers of the profusely decorated walls. Among the many superb images here are an unusually high proportion of Shaivite figures for a Vishnu temple.

As at Halebid, a lively frieze details countless episodes from the *Ramayana*, *Bhagavata Purana* and *Mahabharata*. Intended to accompany circumambulation, the panels are "read" (there is no text) in a clockwise direction. Unusually, the temple is autographed; all its sculpture was the work of one man, named Malitamba.

Outside the temple stands a *dvajastambha* column, which may originally have been surmounted by a figure of Vishnu's bird-vehicle Garuda. The wide ground-level ambulatory that circles the whole building is edged with numerous, now empty, shrines.

Practicalities

Very few Mysore **buses**, if any, go direct to Somnathpur. Buses from the Private stand, at Mysore, run to T Narasipur (1hr), served by regular buses to Somnathpur (20min). Everyone will know where you want to go, and someone will show you which scrum to join. Alternatively, join one of KSTDC's guided tours (see p.197).

Aside from the odd coconut- or watermelon-seller, the only **food** and **drink** on offer in Somnathpur is at the government-owned but privately run *Tourist Canteen and Rest House* (no phone; ②), which serves basic snacks until 5pm and meals by arrangement later in the day. Their two basic rooms, with attached bathrooms, cannot be booked in advance; you'll have to go back to the cheap "meals" hotels at T Narasipur if necessary.

Hassan

The unprepossessing town of **HASSAN**, 118km northwest of Mysore, is visited in disproportionately large numbers because of its proximity to the Hoysala temples at **Belur** and **Halebid**, both northwest of the town, and the Jain pilgrimage site of **Sravanabelgola**, southeast. Some travellers end up staying a couple of nights, killing time in neon-lit *thali* joints and dowdy hotel rooms, but with a little forward planning you shouldn't have to linger here for longer than it takes to get on a bus somewhere else. Set deep in the serene Karnatakan countryside, Belur, Halebid and Sravanabelgola are much more congenial places to stay.

Practicalities

Hassan's **KSRTC bus stand** is in the centre of town, at the northern end of Bus Stand Rd which runs south past the post office to **Narsimharaja Circle**. Here you'll find the State Bank of Mysore, where you can change money, but not Thomas Cook travellers' cheques, and also most of the town's accommodation. Local auto-rickshaws operate without meters and charge a minimum of Rs8. Winding its way east–west via the Narsimharaja Circle, is the Bangalore–Mangalore Rd (BM Rd) along which you will find the **tourist office** (1km) at Wartah Bhavan (Mon–Sat 10am–5.30pm) good for information on bus and railway timings and the usual cluster of booklets, but not much else. The **train station**, served by four slow passenger trains a day to Mysore, is a further 2km down the road. Note that at the time of going to press, the line from here across the Ghats to Mangalore on the coast, had been temporarily suspended due to engineering work involved with upgrading the line. See the Moving on from Hassan box (p.211) for details of how to get to Sravanabelgola, Belur and Halebid.

ACCOMMODATION

Considering the number of tourists who pass through, Hassan is oddly lacking in good accommodation. Most of the budget options are of a pitiful standard: the few exceptions are within walking distance of the bus stand, around **Narsimharaja Circle**. Wherever you stay, call ahead, as most hotels tend to be full by early evening.

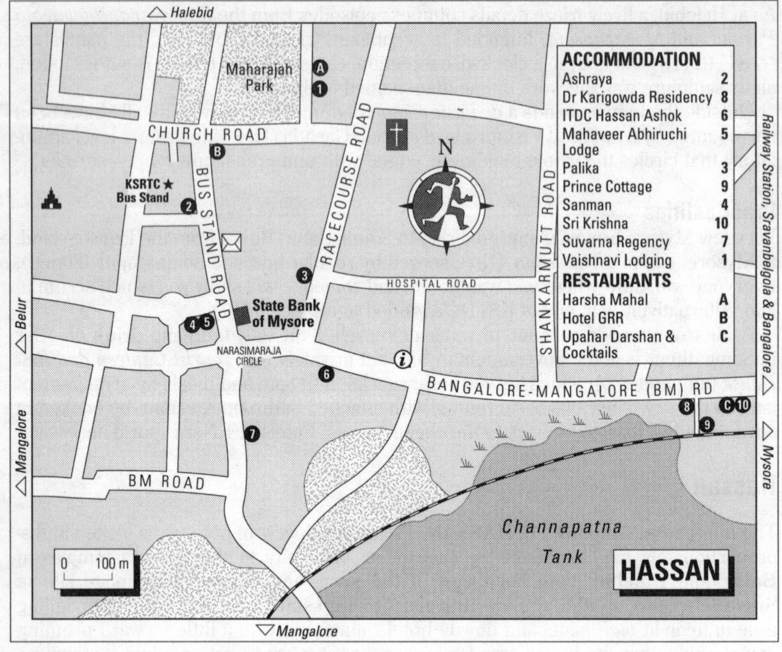

Ashraya, near the bus stand (☎08172/68024). Run-of-the-mill rooms, some literally overlooking the bus stand. Clean enough, but noisy. ①.

DR Karigowda Residency, BM Rd, 1km from train station (☎08172/64506). Immaculate mid-range place: friendly, comfortable and amazing value. Single occupancy possible; no a/c. ③.

ITDC Hassan Ashok, BM Rd, near Narsimharaja Circle (☎08172/68731, fax 68324). On the left as you approach from the train station. Overpriced hotel for tour groups and VIPs. Uninspiring but comfortable veg and non-veg restaurant, craft shops and bar. ⑧–⑨.

Mahaveer Abhiruchi Lodge, BM Rd, near Narsimharaja Circle (☎08172/68885). Cleanish rooms (some with TVs and mosquito nets) and good but dilapidated veg restaurant, the *Abhiruchi*. ②–③.

Palika, Race Course Rd (☎08172/67145). Large somewhat characterless building with sizeable rooms; the cheaper ones are good value. ④.

Prince Cottage, BM Rd, behind Bhanu Theatre (☎08172/65385). Small, neat guesthouse tucked away off the main road. Good value and handy for the train station. ②.

Sanman, Municipal Office Rd (☎08172/68024). Above a busy restaurant, decent rooms with squeaky-clean white-tiled floors, frames for mozzie nets, attached bath and small balconies looking on to main bazaar. ②.

Sri Krishna, BM Rd (☎08172/63240). A large new hotel with some a/c rooms. The spacious non-a/c rooms are a great deal and the restaurant downstairs produces excellent South Indian cooking. ⑤–⑥.

Suvarna Regency, PB 97, BM Rd (☎08172/64006, fax 63822). The swankiest hotel in town, with lots of lights, shiny marble lobby, comfortable rooms and a rooftop BBQ. Good value and a better choice than the *Ashok*. Some a/c. ⑤.

Vaishnavi Lodging, Harsha Mahal Rd (☎08172/63885). Hassan's best budget lodge, with big clean rooms and veg restaurant. Reservations essential. Turn left out of the bus stand, right onto Church Rd and it's on the corner of the first left turn. ②.

MOVING ON FROM HASSAN

Hassan is well connected to most points in southwest Karnataka with frequent **buses** to Mysore from the KSRTC bus stand. Hassan lies midway on the main bus route between Mangalore (180km) and Bangalore (187km) serviced by several ordinary and occasional luxury buses, and more comfortable private buses of which Vijayananda Travels, *Suvarna Regency*, PB 97, BM Rd (☎08172/65807) which runs the VRL service, is by far the best.

Apart from taking a tour, the only way to see Sravanabelgola (53km), Belur (37km) and Halebid (30km) in one day is **by car**, which some visitors share; most of the hotels can fix this up (around Rs1000 per day or Rs3.50 per km for a minimum of 250km). Travelling **by bus**, you'll need at least two days. Belur and Halebid can be comfortably covered in one day; it's best to take the first (8am) of fifteen daily buses to Halebid (1hr) and move on to Belur (30min; 16km), from where services back to Hassan during the evening are more frequent (6.30am–6.15pm; 1hr 10min). **Sravanabelgola**, however, is in the opposite direction, and not served by direct buses; you have to head to **Channarayapatna** aka "CR Patna" (from 6.30am; 1hr) on the main Bangalore highway and pick up one of the regular buses (30min) or any number of minibuses from there. If you want to get to Sravanabelgola in time to visit the site and move on the same day (to Mysore or Bangalore), aim to catch one of the private luxury buses to Bangalore that leave from the road just below the *Vaishnavi Lodge* before dawn (5.30–6am); they all stop briefly in Channarayapatna. Bear in mind, too, that there are places to stay in both Belur and Halebid; arrive in Hassan early enough, and you can travel on to the temple towns before nightfall, although you should phone ahead to check rooms are available.

EATING

Most of the **hotels** listed above have commendable restaurants, or you can take your pick from the string of cheap snack bars and *thali* joints outside the bus stand.

Cocktails, BM Rd near Krishna. A new multistorey development with a terraced restaurant and bar offering a run-of-the-mill but varied menu.

Golden Gate, *Suvarna Regency*, PB 97, BM Rd. Plush restaurant and bar with a garden extension, and the best Hassan has to offer; the varied menu is not cheap.

Harsha Mahal, below *Harsha Mahal Lodge*, Harsha Mahal Rd. No-nonsense veg canteen that serves freshly cooked *iddli* and *dosa* breakfasts from 7.30am.

Hotel GRR, opposite the bus stand. Traditional, tasty and filling "mini-meals" served on plantain leaves, with a wide choice of non-veg dishes and some ice-creams.

Upahar Darshan, BM Rd. A cheap South Indian restaurant serving good "meals" and fresh *dosas* and *iddlis*.

Halebid

Now little more than a scruffy hamlet of brick houses and *chai* stalls, **HALEBID**, 32km northwest of Hassan, was once the capital of the powerful Hoysala dynasty, who held sway over south Karnataka from the eleventh until the early fourteenth centuries. Once known as **Dora Samudra**, the city's name was changed to *Hale-bidu*, or "Dead City", in 1311 when Delhi Sultanate forces under the command of Ala-ud-Din-Khalji swept through and reduced it to rubble. Despite the sacking, several large Hoysala temples survive, two of which, the Hoysaleshvara and Kedareshvara, are covered in exquisite carvings. A small **archeological museum** (daily except Fri 10am–5pm) next to the Hoysaleshvara temple houses a collection of Hoysala art and other finds from the area.

The Hoysaleshvara temple

The **Hoysaleshvara** temple was started in 1141, and after some forty years of work was left unfinished, which possibly accounts for the absence of the type of towers that feature at Somnathpur. It is no longer known which deities were originally worshipped, though the double shrine is thought to have been devoted at one time to Shiva and his consort. In any event, both shrines contain *shivalingam* and are adjoined by two linked, partly enclosed *mandapa* hallways in which stand Nandi bulls.

Like other Hoysala temples, it is raised on a high plinth (*jagati*) which follows the star-shaped plan and provides an upper ambulatory; the *mandapas* are approached by flights of steps flanked by small, free-standing, towered shrines. Inside, the lower portions of the black polished stone pillars were lathe-turned, though the upper levels appear to have been hand-carved to reproduce the effect of turning.

Hoysaleshvara also features many Vaishnavite images. The **sculptures**, which have a fluid quality lacking in the earlier work at Belur, include Brahma aboard his goose-vehicle Hamsa, Krishna holding up Mt Govardhana, Krishna playing the flute and Vishnu (Trivikrama) bestriding the world in three steps. One of the most remarkable images is of the demon king **Ravana** shaking Shiva's mountain abode, Mt Kailasa: the mount is populated by numerous animals and figures, and Shiva is seated atop with Parvati. Secular themes, among them dancers and musicians, occupy the same register as the gods, and you'll come across the odd erotic tableau featuring voluptuous, heavily bejewelled maidens. A narrative frieze, on the sixth register from the bottom, follows the length of the Nandi *mandapas* and illustrates scenes from the *Bhagavata* and Vishnu *Puranas*, *Mahabharata* and *Ramayana*.

The Jain *bastis* and the Kedareshvara temple

About 600m south of the Hoysaleshvara, a group of Jain *bastis* (temples) stands virtually unadorned; the only sculptural decoration consists of ceiling friezes inside the *mandapas* and elephants at the entrance steps, where there's an impressive donatory plaque. The thirteenth-century temple of **Adi Parshwanatha**, marked by a large entrance *mandapa*, is dedicated to the twenty-third *tirthankara*, while the newer **Vijayanatha** built in the sixteenth-century, easily recognized by its predominant *manasasthamba* pillar in front, is dedicated to the *tirthankara* Shantinatha. The *chowkidar* at the Parshwanatha temple will demonstrate various tricks made possible by the carved pillars' highly polished surfaces; some are so finely turned they sound metallic when struck.

To the east, there's a smaller Shiva temple, **Kedareshvara** (1217–21), also built on a stellate plan. Unfortunately, due to instability, it's not possible to go inside. Many fine images decorate the exterior, including an unusual stone Krishna dancing on the serpent demon Kaliya – more commonly seen in bronze and painting.

Practicalities

Frequent **buses** run between Halebid (the last at 6.15pm) and Hassan, and to Belur (the last at 8.45pm). The private minibuses that work from the crossroads outside the Hoysaleshvara temple take a lot longer and only leave when crammed to bursting.

The monuments lie within easy walking distance of each other, but if you fancy exploring the surrounding countryside, rent a **bicycle** from the stalls by the bus stand (Rs3 per hour). The road running south past the temples leads through some beautiful scenery, with possible side-hikes to hilltop shrines while the road to Belur (16km) makes for another pleasant bicycle ride.

Accommodation in the village is limited to KSTDC *Mayura Shantala* (☎08177/73224; ②–③), which is opposite the main temple and set in a small garden by the road it offers two comfortable doubles with verandahs, plus a four-bedded room, all of which should be booked in advance. Plans are afoot to construct a larger complex farther south; ask at any KSTDC tourist office. After 6pm, when the *chai* stalls at the crossroads are closed, the only place to **eat** is at the KSTDC *Mayura Shantala* where the food, including *thalis*, is uninspiring but the garden's pleasant.

Belur

BELUR, 37km northwest of Hassan, on the banks of the Yagachi, was the Hoysala capital – prior to Halebid – during the eleventh and twelfth centuries. Still in use, the **Chennakeshava temple** (7.30am–8.30pm; open to non-Hindus), is a fine and early example of the singular Hoysala style (see Contexts p.586). The temple was built by King Vishnuvardhana in 1117 to celebrate his conversion from Jainism, victory over Chola forces at Talakad and independence from the Chalukyas. Today, its grey-stone *gopura* (gateway tower) soars above a small, bustling market town – a popular pilgrimage site from October to December, when bus-loads of Ayappan devotees stream through en route to Sabarimala (see p.323). The **car festival** held around March or April takes place over twelve days and has a pastoral feel, attracting farmers from the surrounding countryside, who conduct a bullock-cart procession through the streets to the temple. If you have time to linger, Belur, with marginally better facilities than those found at Halebid, is a far better place to base yourself in order to explore the Hoysala region.

Built on a star-shaped plan, Chennakeshava stands in a huge walled courtyard, surrounded by smaller shrines and columned *mandapa* hallways. Lacking any form of superstructure, and terminating at the first floor, it has the appearance of having a flat roof. If it ever had a tower, it would have disappeared by the Vijayanagar (sixteenth-century) period; above the cornice, a plain parapet, presumably added at the same time as the east entrance *gopura*, shows a typically Vijayanagar Islamic influence. Both the sanctuary and *mandapa* are raised on the usual plinth (*jagati*). Double flights of steps, flanked by minor towered shrines, afford entry to the *mandapa* on three sides; this hallway was originally open, but in the 1200s, pierced stone screens, carved with geometric designs and scenes from the *Puranas*, were inserted between the lathe-turned pillars. The main shrine opens four times a day for worship (8.30–10pm, 11am–1pm, 2.30–5pm & 6.30–8.30pm) and it's worth considering using one of the guides who offer their services at the gates (Rs30) to explain the intricacies of the carvings.

The quantity of **sculptural decoration**, if less mature than in later Hoysala temples, is staggering. Carvings on the plinth and lower walls, in successive and continuous bands, start at the bottom with depictions of elephants, followed by garlands and arches with lion heads. As you progress, the carvings illustrate stylized vegetation with dancing figures; birds and animals; pearl garlands; projecting niches containing male and female figures and seated *yakshas*, or spirits; miniature pillars alternating with female figures dressing or dancing; miniature temple towers interspersed with dancers, and above them lion heads. Above the screens, a series of 42 figures, added later, shows celestial nymphs hunting, playing music, dancing and beautifying themselves.

Columns inside, each unique, feature extraordinarily detailed carving, with more than a hundred deities on the central **Narasimha pillar**. The inner sanctum contains a black image of Chennakeshava, a form of Krishna who holds a conch (*shankha*, in the upper right hand), discus (*chakra*, upper left), lotus (*padma*, lower right) and mace (*gada*, lower left). He is flanked by consorts Shri Devi and Bhudevi. Within the same enclosure, the **Kappe Channigaraya temple** has some finely carved niche images and a depiction of Narasimha (Vishnu as man-lion) killing the demon Hiranyakashipu. Farther west, fine sculptures in the smaller **Viranarayana** shrine include a scene from the *Mahabharata* of Bhima killing the demon Bhaga.

Practicalities

Buses from Hassan and Halebid pull into the small bus stand in the middle of town, ten-minutes' walk along the main street from the temple, whereas some through buses don't bother to pull into the bus stand but stop on the highway next to it. There are auto-rickshaws available, but a good way to explore the area, including Halebid, is to rent a **bicycle** (Rs3 per hour) from one of the stalls by the bus stand. The **tourist office** (Mon–Sat 10am–5pm) is located within the KSTDC *Mayuri Velapuri* compound near the temple. They have all the local bus times, and sometimes the tourist officer is available as a guide – his knowledge of the temples is quite remarkable.

The KSTDC *Mayuri Velapuri* (☎08177/22209; ②–③) is the best **place to stay**, with immaculately clean and airy rooms in its new building, or dingy ones in the older wing. The two dorms are rarely occupied (Rs35 per bed), other than between March and May, when the hotel tends to be block-booked by pilgrims. Down the road, the *Annapurna* (☎08177/22039; ②), has adequate, if dull, rooms above an uninspiring restaurant and the *Swagath Tourist Home* (no phone; ①), farther up the road towards the temple, is basic, boxed in and does not have hot water, but is fine as a fallback. For a bit more comfort try the *Hotel Parimala* (no phone; ②), a few metres behind the public baths near the temple. It's a good budget option where the rooms come with small attached baths and there's a canteen downstairs serving South Indian veg meals. Of the hotels around the bus stand, the *Vishnu Prasad* (☎08177/22263; ②) above a restaurant and sweet shop, is the best bet with spacious rooms but tiny attached bathrooms where hot water is only available in the mornings.

The most salubrious **place to eat** is at KSTDC *Mayuri Velapuri*'s newly built restaurant, but the menu is limited. There are several other options, many located beneath hotels strung along the main road, in addition to the veg *dhabas* by the temple, and the *Indian Coffee House* on the main road by the temple gates. If you have a weakness for Indian sweets, head for *Poonam's* below the *Vishnu Prasad*.

Sravanabelgola

The sacred Jain site of **SRAVANABELGOLA**, 49km southwest of Hassan and 93km north of Mysore, consists of two hills and a large tank. On one of the hills, Indragiri (also known as Vindhyagiri), stands an extraordinary eighteen-metre-high monolithic statue of a naked male figure, **Gomateshvara**. Said to be the largest free-standing sculpture in India, this tenth-century colossus, visible for miles around, as well as the nearby *bastis* (Jain temples), make Sravanabelgola a key pilgrimage centre, though surprisingly few Western travellers find their way out here. Spend a night or two in the village, however, and you can climb Indragiri Hill before dawn to enjoy the serene spectacle of the sun rising over the sugar-cane fields and outcrops of lumpy granite that litter the surrounding plains – an unforgettable sight.

Sravanabelgola is linked in tradition with the Mauryan emperor Chandragupta, who is said to have starved himself to death on the second hill in around 300 BC, in accordance with a Jain practice. The hill was renamed Chandragiri, marking the arrival of Jainism in southern India. At the same time, a controversy regarding the doctrines of Mahavira, the last of the 24 Jain **tirthankaras** (literally "crossing-makers", who assist the aspirant to cross the "ocean of rebirth"), split Jainism into two separate branches. *Svetambara*, "white-clad" Jains, are more common in North India, while *digambara*, "sky-clad", are usually associated with the south. Truly ascetic *digambara* devotees go naked, though few do so away from sacred sites.

All the *tirthankaras* are represented as naked figures, differentiated only by their individual attributes: animals, inanimate objects (such as a conch shell), or symbols (such as the *swastika*). Each of the 24 is also attached to a particular *yaksha* (male) or *yakshi* (female) spirit; such spirits are also evident in Mahayana Buddhism, suggesting a strand of belief with extremely ancient origins. *Tirthankaras* are represented either sitting cross-legged in meditation – resembling images of the Buddha, save for their nakedness – or *kayotsarga*, "body upright", where the figure stands impassive; here Gomateshvara stands in the latter, more usual posture.

The monuments at Sravanabelgola probably date from no earlier than the tenth century, when a General Chamundaraya is said to have visited Chandragiri in search of a Mauryan statue of Gomateshvara. Failing to find it, he decided to have one made. From the top of Chandragiri he fired an arrow across to Indragiri Hill; where the arrow landed he had a new Gomateshvara sculpted from a single rock.

Indragiri Hill

Gomateshvara is approached from the tank between the two hills by 620 steps, cut into the granite of **Indragiri Hill**, which pass numerous rock inscriptions on the way up to a walled enclosure. Shoes must be deposited at the stall to the left of the steps, and you can leave bags at the site office nearby. Anyone unable to climb the steps can be carried up by a chair known as a *dholi*. Take plenty of water, especially on a hot day, as there is none available on the hill. Entered through a small wagon-vaulted *gopura*, the **temple** is of the type known as *betta*, which, instead of the usual *garbhagriha* sanctuary, consists of an open courtyard enclosing the massive sculpture. Figures and shrines of all the *yaksha* and *yakshi* spirits stand inside the crenellated wall, but the towering figure of Gomateshvara dominates. With his elongated arms and exaggeratedly

GOMATESHVARA AND MAHAMASTAKABHISHEKA

Gomateshvara, or Bahubali, who was the son of the legendary King Rishabdev of Ayodhya (better known as Adinath, the first *tirthankara*), had a row with his elder brother, Bharat, over their inheritance. After a fierce fight, he lifted his brother above his head, and was about to throw him to the ground when he was gripped by remorse. Gently setting Bharat down, Gomateshvara resolved to reject the world of greed, jealousy and violence by meditating until he achieved *moksha*, release from attachment and rebirth. This he succeeded in doing, even before his father.

As a *kevalin*, Gomateshvara had achieved *kevalajnana*, or "sole knowledge", acquired through solitude, austerity and meditation. While engaged in this non-activity, he stood "body upright" in a forest. So motionless was he that ants built their nest at his feet, snakes coiled happily around his ankles, and creepers began to grow up his legs.

Every twelve years, at an auspicious astrological conjunction of certain planets, the Gomateshvara statue is ritually anointed in the Mahamastakabhisheka ceremony – the next one is scheduled for some time between September and December of 2005 (the precise date has yet to be announced). The process lasts for several days, culminating on the final morning when 1008 *kalashas* (pots) of "liberation water", each with a coconut and mango leaves tied together by coloured thread, are arranged before the statue in a sacred diagram (*mandala*), on ground strewn with fresh paddy. A few priests climb scaffolding, erected around Gomateshvara, to bathe him in milk and *ghee*. After this first bath, prayers are offered. Then, to the accompaniment of temple musicians and the chanting of sacred texts, a thousand priests climb the scaffold to bathe the image in auspicious unguents including the water of holy rivers, sandal paste, cane juice, saffron and milk, along with flowers and jewels. The ten-hour 1993 ceremony reached a climax when a helicopter dropped 20kg of gold leaf and 200 litres of milk on the colossus, along with showers of marigolds, gem stones and multi-hued powders. The residue formed a cascade of rainbow colours down the statue's head and body, admired by *lakhs* of devotees, Jain *sadhus* and *sadhvis* (female *sadhus*) and the massed cameras of the world. A satellite township, Yatrinagar, provides accommodation for 35,000 during the festival, and eighteen surrounding villages shelter pilgrims in temporary *dharamshalas*.

wide shoulders, his proportions are decidedly non-naturalistic. The sensuously smooth surface of the white granite "trap" rock is finely carved: particularly the hands, hair and serene face. As in legend, ant-hills and snakes sit at his feet and creepers appear to grow on his limbs.

Bhandari Basti and monastery (*math*)

The road east from the foot of the steps at Chandragiri leads to two interesting Jain buildings in town. To the right, the **Bhandari Basti** (1159), housing a shrine with images of the 24 *tirthankaras,* was built by Hullamaya, treasurer of the Hoysala Raja Narasimha. A high wall encloses the temple, forming a plain ambulatory which contains a well. Two *mandapa* hallways, where naked *digambara* Jains may sometimes be seen discoursing with devotees clad in white, lead to the shrine at the back. Pillars in the outer *mandapa* feature carvings of female musicians, while mythical beasts adorn the entrance to the inner, *navaranga*, hallway.

At the end of the street, the *math* (monastery) was the residence of Sravanabelgola's senior *acharya*, or guru. Thirty male and female monks, who also "go wandering in every direction", are attached to the *math*; normally a member of staff will be happy to show visitors around. Among the rare palm-leaf manuscripts in the library, some more than a millennium old, are works on mathematics and geography, and the *Mahapurana*, hagiographies of the *tirthankaras*. Next door, a covered walled courtyard contains a number of shrines; the entrance is elaborately decorated with embossed brass designs of *yali* mythical beasts, elephants, a two-headed eagle and an image of Parshvanath, the twenty-third *tirthankara*, here shown as Padmavati. Inside, the courtyard is edged by a high platform on three sides, on which a chair is placed for the *acharya*. A collection of tenth-century bronze *tirthankara* images is housed here, and vibrant murals detail the various lives of Parshvanath. The hills where the *tirthankaras* stood to gain *moksha* are represented in a model, somewhat resembling a jelly mould, with tacked-on footprints.

Chandragiri Hill

Leaving your shoes with the keeper at the bottom, take the rock-cut steps to the top of the smaller **Chandragiri Hill**. Miraculously, the sound of radios and rickshaws down below soon disappears. Fine views stretch south to Indragiri and, from the north on the far side, across to a river, paddy and sugar-cane fields, palms and the village of **Jinanathapura**, where there's another ornate Hoysala temple, the Shantishvara *basti*.

Rather than a single large shrine, as at Indragiri, Chandragiri holds a group of *bastis* in late Chalukya Dravida style, within a walled enclosure. Caretakers, who don't speak fluent English, will take you around and open up the closed shrines. Save for pilasters and elaborate parapets, all the temples have plain exteriors. Named after its patron, the tenth-century **Chamundaraya** is the largest of the group, dedicated to Parshvanath. Inside the **Chandragupta** (twelfth century), superb carved panels in a small shrine tell the story of Chandragupta and his teacher Bhadrabahu. Traces of painted geometric designs survive and the pillars feature detailed carving. Elsewhere in the enclosure stands a 24-metre-high *manastambha*, or "pillar of fame", decorated with images of spirits, *yakshis* and a *yaksha*. No fewer than 576 inscriptions dating from the sixth to the nineteenth centuries are dotted around the site, on pillars and the rock itself.

Practicalities

Sravanabelgola, along with Belur and Halebid, features on **tours** from Bangalore and Mysore (see p.186 and p.197). However, if you want to look around at a civilized pace, it's best to come independently (see p.211). The **tourist office** (Mon–Sat 10am–5.30pm), at the bottom of the steps, has little to offer and the management committee office next door only serves to collect donations and hand out tickets for the *dholis*.

If you want **accommodation**, there are plenty of **dharamshalas**, managed by the temple authorities, offering simple, scrupulously clean rooms, many with their own bathrooms and sit-outs, ranged around gardens and courtyards, and most costing less than Rs125 per night. The 24-hour accommodation office (☎08176/57258) is located inside the *SP Guest House*, next to the bus stand (look for the clock tower); they will allocate you a room here. The *Yatri Niwas* (③), which is close by and also booked through the accommodation office, is about as expensive as it gets, but even so, is only marginally better than the best of the guesthouses. *Hotel Raghu*, opposite the main tank, houses the best of the many small local **restaurants**.

Crisscrossed by winding, back roads, the idyllic (and mostly flat) countryside around Sravanabelgola is perfect cycling terrain. **Bicycles** are available for hire (Rs3 per hour) at Saleem Cycle Mart, on Masjid Rd, opposite the northeast corner of the tank or stalls on the main road. If you're returning to Hassan, you'll have to head to **Channarayapatna** aka "CR Patna" by bus or in one of the shared vans that regularly ply the route and depart only when bursting; change at CR Patna for a bus to Hassan.

Kodagu (Coorg)

The hill region of **Kodagu**, formerly known as **Coorg**, lies 100km west of Mysore in the Western Ghats, its eastern fringes merging with the Mysore Plateau. Comprising rugged mountain terrain interspersed with cardamom jungle, coffee plantations and swathes of lush rice paddy, it's one of South India's most beautiful areas. Little has changed since Dervla Murphy spent a few months here with her daughter in the 1970s (the subject of her classic travelogue, *On A Shoestring To Coorg*), and was entranced by the landscape and people, whose customs, language and appearance set them apart from their neighbours.

Today tourism is still virtually nonexistent, and the few travellers that pass through rarely venture beyond **Madikeri** (Mercara), Kodagu's homely capital. However, if you plan to cross the Ghats between Mysore and the coast, the route through Kodagu is definitely worth considering. Most of the area around Kodagu is swathed in lush coffee plantations. Some coffee-plantation owners open their doors to visitors; to find out more contact the Codagu Planters Association, Mysore Road, Madikeri (☎08272/29873). A good time to visit is during the festival season in early December or during the **Blossom Showers** around March and April when the coffee plants bloom with white flowers, although for some the strong scent can be overpowering.

Kodagu is relatively undeveloped, and "sights" are few, but the countryside is idyllic and the climate refreshingly cool, even in summer. With the help of local operators, there is now a growing trickle of visitors who come to Kodagu to **trek** through the unspoilt forest tracts and ridges that fringe the district (see box on p.219). On the eastern borders of Kodagu on the Mysore Plateau, large **Tibetan settlements** around Kushalnagar have transformed a once barren countryside into fertile farmland dotted with busy monasteries some of which house thousands of monks.

Some history

Oblique references to Kodagu crop up in ancient Tamil and Sanskrit scriptures, but the first concrete evidence of the kingdom dates from the eighth century, when it prospered from the salt trade passing between the coast and the cities on the Deccan Plateau. Under the Hindu **Haleri Rajas**, the state repulsed invasions by its more powerful neighbours, including Haider Ali and his son Tipu Sultan, the infamous Tiger of

Mysore. A combination of hilly terrain, absence of roads (a deliberate policy on the part of defence-conscious Kodagu kings) and the tenacity of its highly trained army, ensured that Kodagu was the only Indian kingdom never to be conquered.

Peace and prosperity prevailed through the 1700s, when the state was ruled by a line of eccentric rajas, among them the paranoid Dodda Vira (1780–1809), who reputedly murdered most of his relatives, friends, ministers and palace guards. The monarchy was more accountable during the reign of his successor, Chickavirarajah Rajendra, known as **Vira Raja**, but eventually lapsed into decadence and corruption. Emulating his father's brutal example, Vira Raja imprisoned or assassinated his rivals and indulged his passion for women and spending. The king's ministers eventually appealed to the British Resident in Mysore for help to depose the despot. Plagued by threats from Vira Raja, the colonial administration was eager for an

WALKS AROUND KODAGU

With long high ridges and large forest cover, Kodagu has great **trekking** potential which, due to the lack of infrastructure, remains largely untapped. Much of the forest cover seen from vantage points such as Madikeri, belongs to coffee plantations which need the canopy to protect coffee from the intense heat. There are few trails through the plantations, and, to the south, the Nagarhole National Park does not even allow access on foot. However, trails, some of which are ancient byways, do exist and are best explored with the help of the small handful of **agencies**, some working out of Madikeri, who run treks in the area. If you want to try and arrange your own itinerary approach the Conservator of Forests, Deputy Commissioner's Office, at the fort (☎08272/25708), for permission to enter the forests and to stay at their forest bungalows, and for a mandatory guide. Because of the lack of reliable maps and infrastructure, you are better off arranging your trek through one of the local operators in Madikeri such as Ganesh Aiyanna at the *Hotel Cauvery Capitol* (☎08272/25492), who is very informative and helpful, or Coorg Travels at *Vinayaka Lodge* (☎08272/25817). Even if you intend to do it yourself, it is well worth talking to Ganesh Aiyanna and to the part-time, voluntary association, the Kodagu Wildlife Society, c/o the Kodagu Planters Association on Mysore Rd (☎08272/29873), as they can provide useful information on the area. Although not local, the experienced Clipper Holidays, with offices in Bangalore (☎080/559 9032) and Cochin (☎0484/364443), have been organizing forest treks in Kodagu for years, while Madhushudan Shukla at Woody Adventures in Bangalore (☎080/225 9159) specializes in a variety of outdoor sports, including trekking in Kodagu. The best **season** to trek here is between October and March; April and May are not as hot as some other parts of Karnataka, but avoid the monsoons between June and September, when the trails can get muddy and the leaches rampant.

The finest of Kodagu's treks lie to the south of the region along the Kerala border where an ancient path snakes through forests and across mountain ridges linking **Nagarhole to Talakaveri** in the southwest. The trek, which takes around a week, starts at the entrance to Nagarhole National Park and continues, with interesting diversions, to Talakaveri. The trail passes by the Shri Ramneshwarna Temple with a diversion through forest to the Irpu Falls, before continuing to Nalaknod Palace, an old hunting lodge now used as a camp and for bee-keeping. The trail continues to the hill temple of Nishani Motte before arriving at Brahmagiri Hill and Talakaveri (see p.225). Between Kakkabe, the small town near the Nalaknod Palace, there are two alternative routes to Talakaveri – one takes a more gentle, lower route while the other tackles challenging high ground over Kodagu's highest peak, **Tadiandamol** (1745m), and the peak of **Iggutappa** (1590m), where there are a couple of old temples. You are best advised to take a guide to help avoid elephants and for route-finding through sometimes difficult terrain.

Kakkabe is a good base for climbing both Tadiandamol and Iggutappa, with excellent accommodation and food at the *Palace Estate* (☎08272/38346; ③), where Mr A.P. Pooramma will assist in planning treks and negotiating guides who charge around Rs125 per day. One direct bus leaves Madikeri at 7am to Kakkabe 50km to the south. Other possible treks in Kodagu include a climb to the hill of Devasi Betta close to Irpu Falls, through the **Brahmagiri Wildlife Sanctuary**, for which you will need permission. Elsewhere, connecting trails from Talakaveri can be taken to the top of Kodagu's second highest peak, **Pushpagiri** (1712m), to the north of the region. Pushapagiri can also be climbed via the village of Heggademane to the north of Madikeri and is accessible by bus.

excuse to intervene; they got it in 1834, when the unruly raja killed his cousin's infant son. Accusing him of maladministration, the British massed troops on the border and forced a short siege, at the end of which Vira Raja (and what remained of his family) fled into exile.

THE KODAVAS

Theories abound as to the origins of **the Kodavas**, or **Coorgis**, who today comprise less than one sixth of the hill region's population. Fair-skinned and with their own language and customs, they are thought to have migrated to southern India from Kurdistan, Kashmir and Rajasthan, though no one knows exactly why or when. One popular belief holds that this staunchly martial people, who since independence have produced some of India's leading military brains, are descended from Roman mercenaries who fled here following the collapse of the Pandyan dynasty in the eighth century; some even claim connections with Alexander the Great's invading army. Another theory is that the Kodavas were originally from Arabia having been pushed out by the early Muslims and made to flee into exile. Whatever their origins, the Kodavas have managed to retain a distinct identity apart from the freed plantation slaves, Moplah Muslim traders and other immigrants who have settled here. More akin to Tamil than Kannada, their language is Dravidian, yet their religious practices, based on ancestor veneration and worship of nature spirits, differ markedly from those of mainstream Hinduism. Land tenure in Kodagu is also quite distinctive, with taxation based on type of land and, unlike in some other traditional societies, women have a right to inheritance and ownership; they are also allowed to remarry. Kodava martial traditions are grounded in the family where, according to custom, one son was raised to work the land while another joined the army and even today, they are allowed to carry weapons without licence.

Spiritual and social life for traditional Kodavas revolves around the **Ain Mane**, or ancestral homestead. Built on raised platforms to overlook the family land, these large, detached houses, with their beautiful carved wood doors and beaten-earth floors, generally have four wings and courtyards to accommodate various branches of the extended family, as well as shrine rooms, or **Karona Kalas**, dedicated to the clan's most important forebears. Key religious rituals and rites of passage are always conducted in the *Ain Mane*, rather than the local temple. However, you could easily travel through Kodagu without ever seeing one, as they are invariably away from roads, shrouded in thick forest.

You're more likely to come across traditional Kodava **costume**, which is donned for all auspicious occasions, such as marriages, funerals, harvest celebrations and clan get-togethers. The men wear dapper knee-length coats called *kupyas*, bound at the waist with a scarlet and gold cummerbund, and daggers (*peechekathis*) with ivory handles. Most distinctive of all, though, is the unique flat-bottomed turban; sadly, the art of tying these is dying, and most men wear ready-made versions (which you can buy in Madikeri bazaar). Kodava women's garb of long, richly coloured silk saris, pleated at the back and with a *pallav* draped over their shoulders, is even more stunning, enlivened by heaps of heavy gold and silver jewellery, and precious stones. Women also wear headscarves, in the fields as well as for important events, tying the corners behind the head, Kashmiri style.

The Kodava diet is heavily carnivorous, their favourite meat being pork which is an important dish at festive occasions where it is often served as a dryish dish known as *pandi curry*, but sometimes substituted by *nooputtakoli curry* made with chicken, and usually accompanied with a rice preparation, *tumbuttu pandi*. Their traditional breakfast, consisting of a type of chapati known as *aki oti* served with honey and *pajji*, a chutney, is far lighter.

Like all traditional Indian cultures, this one is on the decline, not least because young Kodavas, predominantly from well-off land-owning families, tend to be highly educated and move away from home to find work, weakening the kinship ties that have for centuries played such a central role in the life of the region. However, in recent years there has been a rekindling of Kodava pride with calls for a state separate from Karnataka.

Thereafter, Kodagu became a princely state with nominal independence, which it retained until the creation of Karnataka in 1956. During the Raj, **coffee** was introduced and, despite plummeting prices on the international market, this continues to be the linchpin of the local economy, along with pepper and cardamom. Although Kodagu is Karnataka's wealthiest region, providing the highest revenue, it does not reap the rewards, and this, coupled with the distinct identity and fiercely independent nature of the Kodavas, has resulted in the Kodagu freedom movement, known as **Kodagu Rajya Mukti Morcha**, seeking its own statehood. Methods used by the KRMM include cultural programmes and occasional strikes, known as *bandhs*, designed to close down all commercial activity in protest; they rarely use violence but a new order is emerging within the movement which has left some of the older members disgruntled.

Madikeri (Mercara) and around

Nestling beside a curved stretch of craggy hills, **MADIKERI (Mercara)**, capital of Kodagu, is 117m up in the Western Ghats, roughly midway between Mysore and the coastal city of Mangalore. Few foreigners travel up here, but it's a pleasant enough town, with red-tiled buildings and undulating roads that converge on a bustling bazaar.

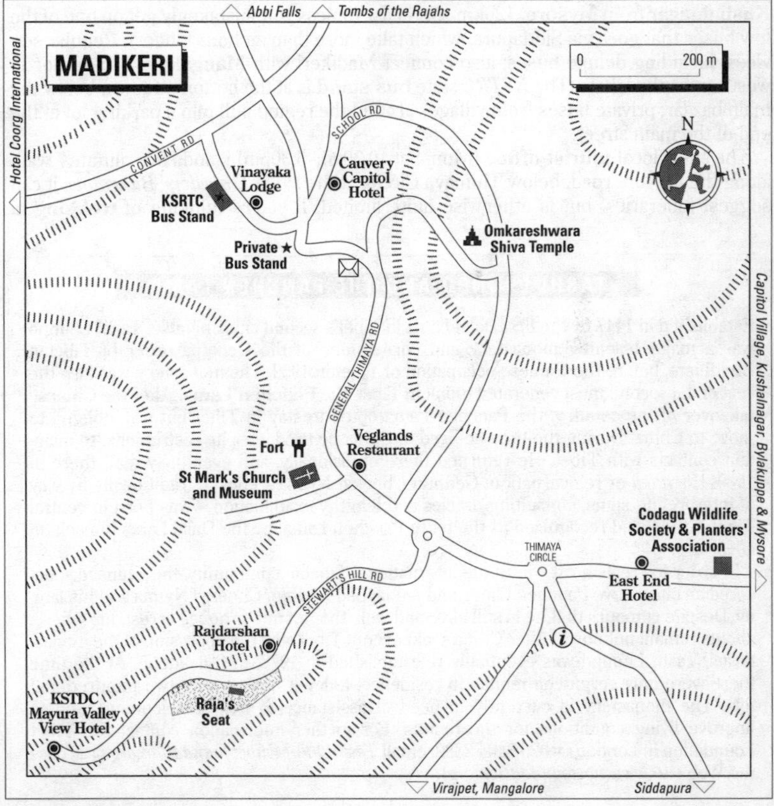

The **Omkareshwara Shiva** temple, built in 1820, features an unusual combination of red-tiled roofs, Keralan Hindu architecture, Gothic elements and Islamic-influenced domes. The fort and palace, worked over by Tipu Sultan in 1781 and rebuilt in the nineteenth century, now serve as offices and a prison. Also worth checking out are the huge square **tombs of the Rajas** which, with their Islamic-style gilded domes and minarets, dominate the town's skyline. **St Mark's church** holds a small **museum** of British memorabilia, Jain, Hindu and village deity figures and weapons (daily except Mon 9.30am–1.30pm & 2.30am–5.30pm). At the western edge of town, **Rajas' Seat**, next to *KSTDC Hotel Mayura Valley View*, is a belvedere, said to be the Kodagu kings' favoured place to watch the sunset.

Madikeri is the centre of the lucrative coffee trade, and although auto-rickshaws will take you there and back for around Rs150, a walk to **Abbi Falls** (8km) is a good introduction to coffee-growing country. The pleasant road, devoid of buses, winds through the hill country past plantations and makes for a good day's outing. At the littered car park at the end of the road, a gate leads through a private coffee plantation sprinkled with cardamom sprays and pepper vines, to the bottom of the large stepped falls that are most impressive during the monsoons.

Practicalities

You can only reach Madikeri by road, but it's a scenic three-hour **bus** ride via **Kushalnagar** from **Mysore**, 120km southeast (unless you mistakenly get on one of the few buses that goes via Siddapura, which take more than an hour longer). Regular services, including deluxe buses, also connect Madikeri with **Mangalore**, 135km northwest across the Ghats. The *KSTRC* state **bus stand** is at the bottom of town, below the main bazaar; private buses from villages around the region pull into a parking lot at the end of the main street.

The small local **tourist office** (Mon–Sat 10.30am–5.30pm) stands five minutes' walk along the Mysore road, below Thimaya Circle, at the *PWD Travellers' Bungalow*; it can suggest itineraries, but is otherwise quite limited. If you're thinking of **trekking** in

TASHI LHUNPO AND THE PANCHEN LAMA

Established in 1447 by the first Dalai Lama in Tibet's second city, Shigatse, Tashi Lhunpo was a major teaching monastery and cornerstone of the Gelugpa order of Tibetan Buddhism, before the Chinese occupation of Tibet in 1959. The monastery was also the seat of the second most venerated monk in Tibet, the **Panchen Lama**. After the Chinese takeover of the country, the Panchen Lama opted to stay in Tibet but was obliged to move to China. During the time he lived in China he tried, despite restrictions, to maintain contacts with Tibet. He returned there occasionally, and eventually died there in 1989. His *tulku* or reincarnation, Gedhun Choekyi Nyima – chosen traditionally by way of interpreting signs, consulting oracles and lengthy examination – was born in central Tibet in 1989 and recognized as the tenth Panchen Lama, by the Dalai Lama himself, in 1995.

In order to create a rift within the international Tibetan community, the Chinese sponsored an alternative Panchen Lama, and kidnapped Gedhun Choekyi Nyima and his family. Despite rumours that he is still alive and well, though under house arrest, his whereabouts remain unknown. After China's takeover of Tibet, and the oppresion of the monasteries, Tashi Lhunpo was eventually re-established in 1972, in Bylakuppe. At the time there were only seventeen monks in residence; today it houses over two hundred and fifty. The monastery is currently in need of assistance to help development, and to improve living conditions for the monks. For further information contact the Tibet Foundation in London (☎020 7404 2889, email *TashiLhunp@tibet-foundation.org* or access the Web site *www.tibet-foundation.org*).

Kodagu contact Ganesh Aiyanna at the *Hotel Cauvery Capitol* (☎08272/25492) who is very helpful and organizes itineraries and trips for around Rs500 per day. Coorg Travels at *Vinayaka Lodge* (☎08272/25817), is also flexible and friendly and will help put together a tour. For information on Kodagu's **forests** and forest bungalows contact the Conservator of Forests, Deputy Commissioner's Office, at the fort (☎08272/25708).

ACCOMMODATION AND EATING

Accommodation in Madikeri can be hard to come by, particularly in the budget range, most of which is concentrated around the bazaar and bus stand. The better-class and some of the budget hotels generally have **restaurants**. The moderately expensive restaurant at *Rajdarshan* is one of the best; surprisingly, they do not serve coffee although they do have a good bar. There are a couple of "meals" joints on the main road and in the centre of town, *Veglands* is a good and highly popular vegetarian restaurant.

Capitol Village (☎08272/25492). Six kilometres from the centre and booked through the *Hotel Cauvery Capitol* in Madikeri, this is the best place to stay in the area, but you'll need your own transport. The "village" consists of a cottage complex surrounded by a splendid variety of horticulture on the edge of a coffee plantation. It's quiet and secluded and excellent value, except when booked for weddings. ⑤–⑥.

Cauvery Capitol, School Rd (☎08272/25492). Below the Private bus stand, this large and friendly place is almost hidden behind their *Capitol* restaurant. ③.

Coorg International, Convent Rd (☎08272/28071). Ten minutes by rickshaw from the centre, this is one of the few upmarket options. It's a large but slightly characterless hotel with comfortable Western-style rooms, a multicuisine restaurant, exchange facilities and shops. ⑦–⑧.

East End, General Thimaya (aka Mysore) Rd (☎08272/29996). A large, plain, tiled-roof colonial bungalow turned into a hotel with a hint of character, but better known for its popular bar and restaurant. ③.

KSTDC Hotel Mayura Valley View (☎08272/28387). Well away from the main road, past Raja's Seat, and with excellent views. The rooms are huge and the restaurant serves beer. Hail a rickshaw to get there, as it's a stiff 20 min uphill walk from the bus stand. ④–⑤.

Rajdarshan (☎08272/29142). A modern and salubrious place with a restaurant and bar, just down the hill on the left from the *Hotel Mayura Valley View*. ⑤–⑥.

Vinayaka Lodge (☎08272/29830). To the left outside the KSRTC bus stand, this is adequate for a night, and they offer single rates. ②–③.

Tibetan settlements and coffee plantations

Madikeri provides an excellent base from which to explore the delights of Kodagu including the **Tibetan settlements** that straddle the district border to the east. Co-operatives line the Madikeri–Mysore highway and maroon-clad monks ride tractors to work the fields around the town of **Kushalnagar**, 22km from Madikeri, and the Tibetan villages, known as "camps", scattered around **Bylakuppe**, 6km across the district border. Although the term "camp" suggests a sense of transition, the Tibetans who first settled here as refugees in the 1960s represent one of the largest settlements outside their homeland and have adapted remarkably well to a starkly different environment.

Today, several key monasteries punctuate the landscape and chief amongst these is the great *gompa* of **Sera Je**, 5km to the south of the main highway, a huge complex which acts as a university for around two thousand monks. At the centre of Sera is a large main hall built on three floors, designed to accommodate a vast congregation of monks who gather here for instruction and ceremony. Despite the colossal image of the Buddha Shakyamuni at the head of the hall, there is nothing attractive about the monastery, which has a functional air to it; however, the village has a buzz and the monks are welcoming. Sera Je's new and welcoming *Guest House* (②), which serves to raise funds, has pleasant clean rooms and a café, and is one of the few places to stay and eat around **BYLAKUPPE**. The only transport to and from the main highway is by shared **auto-rickshaws** that regularly ply the route; the turn-off to Sera Je is midway between Bylakuppe and Kushalnagar. Another important monastery in the vicinity of Bylakuppe is Tashi Lhunpo, which is one kilometre off the main road past the police station. Tashi Lhunpo is much smaller than Sera Je, and is renowned as the seat of the Panchen Lama – Tibet's second most revered spiritual leader after the Dalai Lama (see box on p.222). If you're arriving by bus from Mysore, ask to be let down at Bylakuppe, recognizable by the Tibetan farm co-operatives. If you're coming from the west, however, you'll reach Kushalnagar first, where there are more auto-rickshaws available at the bus stand. If you want an auto-rickshaw all to yourself, it'll cost Rs50 to Sera.

There's more **accommodation** at **KUSHALNAGAR**, but nothing wonderful. The most comfortable of the hotels is the *Kannika International* (☎08276/74728; ④–⑤) set back from the main road near the bus stand, with its own garden, a restaurant and bar with tables on the porch, and airy rooms with televisions. Cheaper options on the main road around the bus stand include the *Radhakrishna Lodge* (②) with adequate budget rooms and the basic *Ganesh* (②). For a bit more quiet follow the lane along the side of the bus stand past the communications tower to the *Mahalaxmi Lodge* (②). If you've come specifically to visit the monasteries of Bylakuppe, a good place to start is at the *Tibet Restaurant*, popular with young monks, above a small shopping complex at St Philomena's Complex, IB Rd, past the *Kannika International*. Namgyal, the proprietor, is welcoming and a fount of local information, and serves great *thukpas*, *momos*, *shabhaleys*, *mothuk* and fried rice. Although in close proximity to Madikeri and feasible on long day-trips, Kushalnagar is also well connected **by bus** to Mangalore (via Madikeri), Bangalore, Mysore and Hassan as well as to several destinations in Tamil Nadu. Bus times are posted in English and deluxe and express buses stop here as well.

The sleepy coffee town of **SIDDAPURA** on the banks of the Kaveri (Cauvery) River, lies 32km to the south of Madikeri in the heart of coffee country and provides the delights of staying on a plantation, but at a price. Across the river, the **Dubare Reserve Forest** makes for good short exploratory treks with the chance of seeing wildlife and the occasional elephant, but contact the Conservator of Forests, Deputy Commissioner's Office, The Fort, Madikeri (☎08272/25708) for more information and take a guide. Alternatively, the resort of *Orange County* at Karadigodu, 3km from Siddapura (☎08274/58481; ⑨), arranges forest walks for guests. Approached by a small road that winds through lush plantations where tall trees provide essential cover for the coffee plants, *Orange County* lies at the edge of a wealthy estate and is

LAMA OSEL

A Spanish boy born in Granada in 1985, was discovered, through traditional methods and oracles, as the incarnation of Lama, by Lama Yeshe's former disciple Lama Zopa. The boy was recognised as the reincarnation (*tulku*) of Yeshe Rinpoche by the Dalai Lama and given the name **Lama Osel** after Osel Ling, a small Tibetan monastery high in the Alpujarras in Andalucia. Today, Lama Osel, studies Buddhism under Lama Zopa at Sera Je – the tables have turned and the reincarnation of the master is now studying under the former student. Although he is being brought up as a high lama, he also has to receive a Western education. Lama Osel is unique in that he is the first Westerner to be recognized as a high reincarnate lama. However, he will probably not be the last. According to Tibetan belief, Maitreya, the Buddha of the future, will be born in the West, and so is often portrayed as having blue eyes and, unlike traditional Tibetan custom, sitting on an upright chair.

CATHERINE KARNOW / CORBIS

Daba wallahs, Mumbai (M)

RAVI SHAKAR / IMAGES OF INDIA

Film hoardings, Mumbai (M)

MAHENDRA PATIL / IMAGES OF INDIA, DPA

Dhobi ghat, Mumbai (M)

ALAN LEWIS / TRAVEL INK

Hauling in nets, Palolem, Goa

AMAR GROVER

Carved pillars, Hampi (Kar)

ALAN BEDDING / TRAVEL INK

Karnatakan boy busking with a cow.

JEROEN SNIJDERS / IMAGES OF INDIA

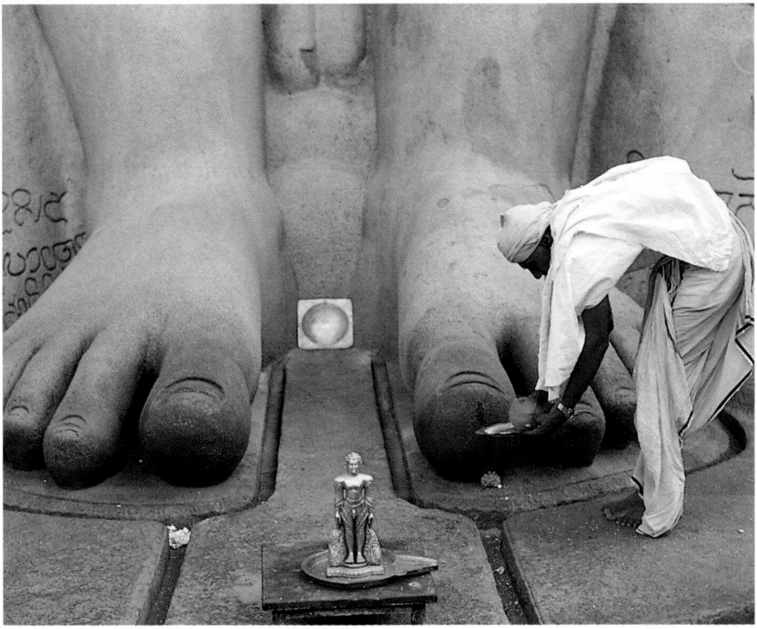

Worshipper at Sravanabelgola (Kar)

SIMON REDDY / TRAVEL INK

Temple gopura, Mysore (Kar)

STEPHEN COYNE / TRAVEL INK

Nandi bull, pilgrimage site, Mysore (Kar)

FREDRIK ARVIDSSON / AXIOM

Canoeing in the backwaters of Kerala

JEROEN SNIJDERS / IMAGES OF INDIA

Chinese fishing nets, Kochi (Ker)

the most luxurious place to stay in the whole of Kodagu. Booked through their Bangalore office (☎080/240550), *Orange County* offers mock-Tudor cottages set within a manicured estate where activities include treks and horse-riding and there's a pleasant pool (for residents only) and a good restaurant serving some Kodava dishes as part of a varied menu. Popular with affluent Indians, some of whom come on a time-share basis, and tour groups, *Orange Country* can provide a base from which to visit Nagarhole National Park 75km to the south (see p.207), and should be booked in advance.

Bhagamandala and Talakaveri

A good bus excursion from Madikeri takes you to the quiet village of **BHAGAMANDALA** (35km west), and from there to the sacred site of **TALAKAVERI**, which is said to be the source of the holy Kaveri (Cauvery) River. The hill scenery is superb, and you can opt to walk part of the way on blissfully quiet country roads.

Wear something warm, and take the 6.30am bus from Madikeri's private stand to Bhagamandala. You should arrive around 8am, with just enough time to grab a good breakfast of *parathas* and local honey at the *Laxmi Vilas* tea shop, next to the bus stop from which the bus to Talakaveri leaves at 8.30am. At Bhagamandala, the holy spot where the Kaveri merges with two streams, Kanike and Sujyothi, the **Bhagandeshwara temple** is a fine example of Keralan-style architecture, with tiled roofs and courtyards.

At Talakaveri the bus stops on the slopes of Brahmagiri Hill by the entrance to the sacred tank and **temple**. During **Kaveri Shankrama** in October, thousands of pilgrims come here to witness a spring – thought to be the goddess Kaveri, known as Lopamudra, the local patron deity – suddenly spurting into a small well. To bathe in the tank at this time is considered especially sin-absolving. The belief is that, if one year, the spring dries up all the rivers of southern India will dry up too. Whenever you come, you're likely to find wild-haired *sadhus* and bathing pilgrims, and the surrounding walls swathed in drying *dhotis* and saris. Two small shrines stand at the head of the tank, one containing an image of Ganesh and the other a metal *lingam* with a *naga* snake canopy. Steep granite steps to the right lead up to the peak of **Brahmagiri Hill**, which affords superb 360° views over Kodagu.

Mangalore

Many visitors only come to **MANGALORE** on their way somewhere else. As well as being fairly close to Madikeri and the Kodagu (Coorg) hill region, it's also a stopping-off point between Goa and Kerala, and is the nearest coastal town to the Hoysala and Jain monuments near Hassan, 172km east.

Mangalore was one of the most famous ports of South India. It was already famous overseas in the sixth century, as a major source of pepper, and the fourteenth-century Muslim writer Ibn Battuta noted its trade in pepper and ginger and the presence of merchants from Persia and the Yemen. In the mid-1400s, the Persian ambassador Abdu'r-Razzaq saw Mangalore as the "frontier town" of the Vijayanagar empire (see p.250) – which was why the Portuguese captured it in 1529. In Haider Ali's time, during the eighteenth century, the city became a shipbuilding centre. Nowadays, the modern port, 10km north of the city proper, is principally known for the processing and export of coffee and cocoa (much of which comes from Kodagu), and cashew nuts from Kerala and Karnataka, as well as granite. It is also a centre for the production of *bidi* cigarettes. Mangalore's heady ethnic mix lived more or less in harmony until 1998, when communal riots saw sections of the large Christian community in the city attacked by right-wing Hindu fundamentalists.

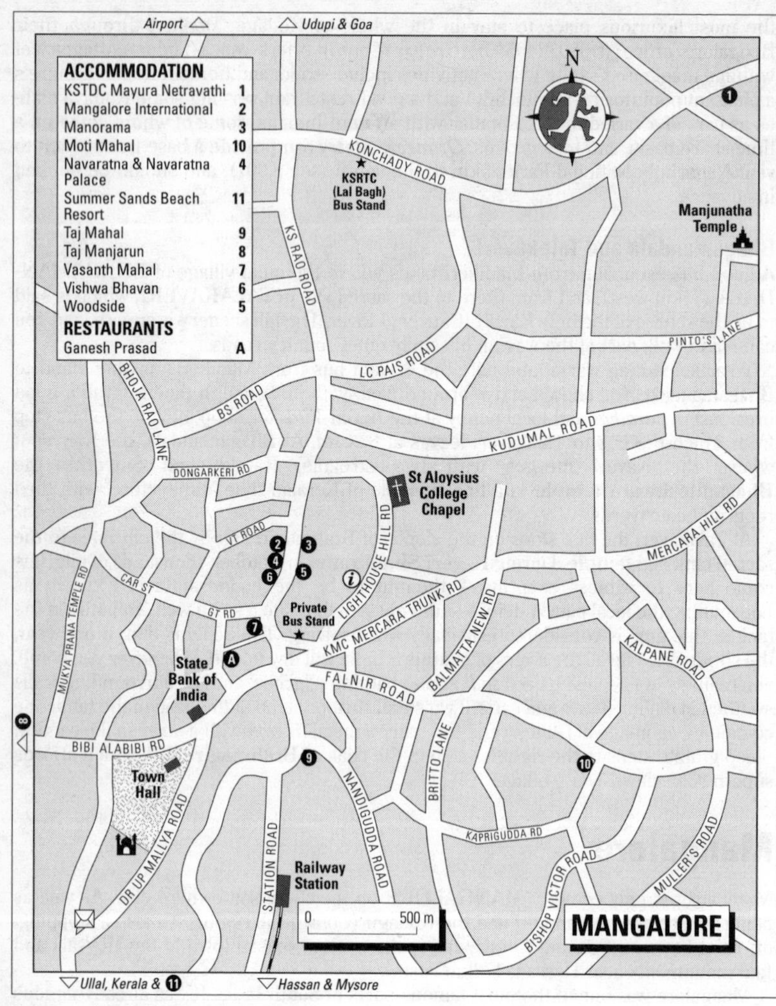

Arrival and information

Mangalore's busy KSRTC **bus stand** (known locally as the "Lal Bagh" bus stand) is 2km north of the town centre, Hampankatta, at the bottom of Kadri Hill. **Bajpe airport**, 22km north of the city (bus #47A, Indian Airlines city bus or taxis for Rs200), is served by both Indian Airlines and Jet Airways from Mumbai and Bangalore. The **train station**, on the south side of the city centre, sees daily services from cities all over India, including Delhi, Agra, Hyderabad, Bangalore, Chennai and Thiruvananthapuram.

Hampankatta, close to the facilities of Light House Hill Rd, acts as the traffic hub of the city from where you can catch **city buses** to most destinations or **auto-rickshaws** (but note their drivers prefer not to use their meters). The **tourist office** (Mon–Sat 10am–1.30pm & 2–5.30pm; ☎0824/442926) on the ground floor of the *Hotel Indraprashta* on Light House Hill Rd is helpful for general information and some bus times, but carries no information on trains, for which you will need to go to the train station.

You can **change money** at Trade Wings, Light House Hill Rd (Mon–Sat 9.30am–5.30pm; ☎0824/426817) who encash travellers' cheques, and at TT Travels (Mon–Sat 9.30am–5.30pm; ☎0824/426817), inside the *Poonja International* shopping mall on KS Rao Rd. The State Bank of India (Mon–Fri 10.30am–2.30pm & Sat 10.30am–12.30pm), near the Town Hall on Hamilton Circle is somewhat slower.

Mangalore's **GPO** (Mon–Sat 10am–7pm, Sun 10.30am–1.30pm) is a short walk from the centre, at Shetty Circle. For **email** try the friendly and popular Kohinoor Computer Zone, Plaza Towers, Light House Hill Rd (Mon–Sat 8am–2am; ☎0824/429340) down the road from the tourist office, or the tiny Indepth Cyber Solutions, Shop 9, Kerala Samajam Complex, KS Rao Rd (Mon–Sat 9.30am–6.30pm; ☎0824/428347).

The city and beaches

Mangalore's strong Christian influence can be traced back to the arrival farther south of St Thomas (see p.316). Some 1400 years later, in 1526, the Portuguese founded one of the earliest churches on the coast close to the old port; the present **Most Holy Rosary church**, however, with a dome based on St Peter's in Rome, dates only from 1910. Fine restored fresco, tempera and oil murals, the work of an Italian artist, Antonio Moscheni, adorn the Romanesque-style **St Aloysius College chapel**, built in 1885, on Lighthouse Hill Rd, near the centre.

At the foot of Kadri Hill, 3km north, Mangalore's tenth-century **Manjunatha temple** is an important centre of the Shaivite and Tantric **Natha-Pantha cult**. Thought to be an outgrowth of Vajrayana Buddhism, the cult is a divergent species of Hinduism, similar to certain cults in Nepal. Enshrined in the sanctuary, a number of superb **bronzes** include a 1.5-metre-high seated Lokeshvara (Matsyendranatha), made in 958 AD and considered the finest southern bronze outside Tamil Nadu. To see it you'll have to visit at *darshan* times (6.30–9am & 6.30–9pm). Manjunatha's square and towered sanctuary, containing an unusual *lingam*, is surrounded by two tiled and gabled colonnades with louvred windows, showing strong affinity with the temple complexes further south in Kerala. Nine water tanks adjoin the temple. Opposite the east entrance, steps lead via a laterite path to a curious group of minor shrines. Beyond this complex stands the **Shri Yogishwar Math**, a hermitage of Tantric *sadhus* set round two courtyards, one of which contains shrines to Kala Bhairava (a form of Dakshinamurti, the southern aspect of Shiva and deity of death), Durga and god of fire, Agni. Nearby, cut into the side of the hill, a tiny unadorned cave is credited with being one of the "night halts" for the Pandava brothers from the *Mahabharata*.

If you're looking to escape the city for a few hours, head out to the village of **ULLAL**, 10km south, whose long sandy **beach**, backed by wispy fir trees, stretches for miles in both directions. It's a deservedly popular place for a stroll, particularly in the evening when families and courting couples come out to watch the sunset, but a strong undertow makes swimming difficult, and at times unsafe. You're better off using the pool at the excellent *Summer Sands Beach Resort* (see p.230), immediately behind the beach (Rs60 for non-residents). A further 2km past the *Summer Sands*, a banyan-lined road leads to the Shiva temple of **Someshwar**, built in Keralan style, overlooking a rocky promontory, and another popular beach which is subject to gangs of gawking youths. Towards the centre of Ullal and around 700m from the main bus stand, is the *dargah* (burial shrine) of **Seyyid Mohammad Shareeful Madani**, a sixteenth-century saint who is said to have come from Medina in Arabia and floated across the sea on a handkerchief. The extraordinary nineteenth-century building with garish onion-domes

KAMBLA

If you're anywhere between Mangalore and Bhatkal from October to April and come across a crowd gathering around a water-logged paddy field, pull over and spend a day at the races – Karnatakan style. Few Westerners ever experience it, but the unique and spectacular rural sport of **kambla**, or **bull racing**, played in the southernmost district of coastal Karnataka (known as Dakshina Kannada), is well worth seeking out.

Two contestants, usually local rice-farmers, take part in each race, riding on a wooden plough-board attached to a pair of prize bullocks. The object is to reach the opposite end of the field first, but points are also awarded for style, and riders gain extra marks – and roars of approval from the crowd – if the muddy spray kicked up from the plough-board splashes the special white banners, or *thoranam*, strung across the course at a height of 6 to 8m.

Generally, race days are organized by wealthy landowners on fields specially set aside for the purpose. Villagers flock in from all over the region, as much for the fair, or *shendi*, as the races themselves: men huddle in groups to watch cock fights (*korikatta*), women haggle with bangle sellers, and the kids roam around sucking sticky *kathambdi goolay*, the local bon-bons. It is considered highly prestigious to be able to throw such a party, especially if your bulls win any events or, better still, come away as champions. Known as *yeru* in Kannada, racing bulls are thoroughbreds who rarely, if ever, are put to work. Pampered by their doting owners, they are massaged, oiled and blessed by priests before big events, during which large sums of money are often won and lost.

houses the saint's tomb, which is one of the most important sufi shrines in southern India. Visitors are advised to follow custom and cover their heads and limbs and wash their feet before entering. Local **buses** (#44A) run to Ullal from the junction at the south end of KS Rao Rd. As you cross the Netravathi River en route, look out for the brick chimney-stacks clustered on the banks at the mouth of the estuary. Using quality clay shipped downriver from the hills, these factories manufacture the famous terracotta red **Mangalorean roof tiles**, which you see all over southern India.

Accommodation and eating

Mangalore's **accommodation** standards seem to be forever improving; it even has a modern five-star hotel. The main area for hotels, **KS Rao Rd**, runs south from the bus stand and has an ample choice to suit most pockets. You can also stay out of town by the beach in **Ullal**.

The best **places to eat** are in the bigger hotels. If you're on a tight budget, try one of the inexpensive café-restaurants opposite the bus stand, or the excellent canteen inside the bus stand itself, which serves great *dosas* and other South Indian snacks. Also recommended for delicious, freshly cooked and inexpensive "meals" is the *Ganesh Prasad*, down the lane alongside of the *Poonja International*. For something a little more sophisticated, head for the a/c *Xanadu*, connected to the *Woodside Hotel*, also on KS Rao Rd, which offers classy non-veg cuisine and alcohol. It's too dingy for lunch, but fine for dinner, when its kitsch fish tanks and resident duck colony are illuminated. One of the best of the hotel restaurants, however, is the *Moghul Darbar* at the *Mangalore International*, also on KS Rao Rd, which has both a plush a/c and a comfortable and non-a/c section. Although they do not serve alcohol, they offer an excellent mixed menu – if you order a vegetarian *thali* and add fish to it, you have a feast.

KSTDC Mayura Netravathi, 1km north of the bus stand, Kadir Hill (☎0824/211192). Rambling old government hotel, the best of the budget bunch, with large, good-value en-suite rooms (most with twin beds and mozzie nets), although some are a little on the grubby side. None of the rickshaw *wallahs* knows where it is, so ask for the "Circuit House", next door. ②.

Mangalore International, KS Rao Rd (☎0824/444860). Friendly, new hotel with slightly expensive economy rooms but better-value, comfortable a/c doubles and two very good restaurants; strictly no alcohol. ⑤–⑥.

Manorama, KS Rao Rd (☎0824/440306). A 65-room concrete building with spartan, large and very clean rooms (some a/c). Good value; the best fallback if the *Mayura Netravathi* is full. ③–⑤.

Moti Mahal, Falnir Rd (☎0824/441411). Large hotel (some a/c) with 24hr room service and coffee shop, bar, pool, shops, exchange and travel desk. *Mangala* non-veg and *Madhuvan* veg restaurants serve Indian, Chinese and Western food. ⑥–⑦.

MOVING ON FROM MANGALORE

Mangalore is a major crossroads for tourist traffic heading along the Konkan coast between Goa and Kerala, and between Mysore and the coast. The city is also well connected **by air** to **Mumbai**, **Bangalore** and **Chennai**. Jet Airways flies to Mumbai (Mon–Sat) and to Bangalore (daily), while Indian Airlines flies to Mumbai (daily), Bangalore (Mon–Sat) and Chennai (Mon–Sat). The Indian Airlines office is at Airlines House, Hat Hill, Lalbagh (☎0824/454669), and the Jet Airways office at DS Ram Bhavan Complex, Kodiabail (☎0824/441181).

With the inauguration of the single-track coastal **Konkan Railway**, services are opening up to Goa and Mumbai but these have been subject to severe teething problems, and, at the time of going to press, the promise of regular express passenger trains up the coast has not yet materialized. One passenger train departs Mangalore at 7.10am travelling north along the coast and takes 6hr 20min to travel to **Goa** via Udupi and **Gokarn**. The *Mangalore–Madgaon Express* #0022 departs at 2.45pm is only marginally faster (6hr), but does not stop at Gokarn. The service south is more established and if you're travelling to Kerala, the **train** is far quicker and more relaxing than the bus. Two services leave Mangalore station every day for **Thiruvananthapuram**, via **Kozhikode**, **Ernakulam/Cochin**, **Kottayam** and **Kollam**. Leaving at the red-eyed time of 3.50am, the *Parsuram Express* #6350 is the fastest of the two but the *Malabar Express* #6330 which leaves at 5pm is convenient as an overnight train to Thiruvananthapuram, arriving there at 9.25am. A better choice of train connections for the coastal run south can be had from **Kasargode**, an easy bus ride across the Kerala border. For those travelling to **Chennai**, the overnight *Mangalore–Chennai Mail* #6602 departs at 12.15pm and follows the Kerala coast till Shoranur where it turns east to **Palakaad** before journeying on to **Coimbatore** and arriving at Chennai at 6.40am. The *West Coast Express* #6628 follows the same route and departs Mangalore at 7.25pm.

The traditional way to travel on to **Goa** is by **bus**, at least until the Konkan Railway has a more established service. Six buses leave the KSRTC Lal Bagh stand daily, taking around 10hr 30min to reach Panjim. You can jump off at Chaudi (for Palolem) en route, and some buses also go via Margao (for Colva beach), but it's best to check, as most travel direct to the Goan capital. Tickets should be booked in advance (preferably the day before) at KSRTC's well-organized computer booking hall (daily 7am–8pm), or from the Kadamba office on the main concourse. The Goa buses are also good for **Gokarn**; hop off at **Kumta** on the main highway, and catch an onward service from there. The only direct bus to Gokarn leaves Mangalore at 1.30pm. There are plenty of buses to **Udupi** and several south along the coast to **Kasargode** and **Kannur** in Kerala.

For **Mysore**, **Bangalore**, **Hassan** and **Madikeri**, take the bus as the train service inland to Hassan is slow and, at the time of going to press, has been disrupted due to work on the line. The best private bus service to Bangalore is on the distinctive yellow luxury coaches of VRL; two buses leave at night (10pm; 8hr; Rs170) and tickets are available through Vijayananda Travels, PVS Centenary Building, Kodiyalbail, Kudmulranga Rao Rd (☎0824/493536). Agents along Pale Rd including Kohinoor Travels (☎0824/426400) and Ideal Travels (☎0824/424899) who also run luxury buses to Bangalore and a bus to **Ernakulam** (9pm; 9hr; Rs200). Bangalore-bound luxury buses travel through Madikeri and there are several KSRTC buses to Mysore.

Navaratna, KS Rao Rd (☎0824/440520). Clean, dependable, good-value hotel, slap in the centre. Some deluxe rooms with TV, 24hr room service and laundry. ④–⑦.

Navaratna Palace, KS Rao Rd (☎0824/441104). Close to the *Navaratna*, but more upmarket, with two good a/c restaurants: *Heera Panna* and *Palimar* (pure veg). ④–⑦.

Summer Sands Beach Resort, Chota Mangalore, Ullal, 10km south of the city (☎0824/467690, fax 467693). Spacious rooms and cottages (some a/c) near the beach, originally built as a campus for ex-pats, with pool, and bar-restaurant serving local specialties, Indian and Chinese food. Foreign exchange for guests. Recommended. Take bus #44A from town. ⑥–⑧.

Taj Mahal, Hampankatta (☎0824/421751). Large economy hotel overlooking a busy crossing; the restaurant, including a plain canteen and an a/c section, is known for its wholesome *thalis*. ③–④.

Taj Manjarun, Old Port Rd, 2km from train station (☎0824/420420, fax 420585). Modern business hotel; some rooms with sea view and all a/c. Travel desk, exchange, pool, bar and 24hr coffee shop. The pricey restaurant, *Galley*, serves Indian and Western food; *Embers* is a poolside BBQ. ⑦–⑧.

Vasanth Mahal, KS Rao Rd (☎0824/22311). Large but run-down budget lodge, with bathrooms and few frills. The best that can be said about it is that it's handy for the train station. ②.

Vishwa Bhavan, KS Rao Rd (☎0824/440822). Cheap, plain rooms, some with attached baths, around a courtyard close to all amenities. ①–②.

Woodside, KS Rao Rd (☎0824/440296). Old-fashioned hotel offering a range of rooms (their economy doubles are the best deal), but "no accommodation for servants". Some a/c. ③–⑥.

Around Mangalore: Jain bastis and temple towns

The Jain shrines of southwest Karnataka, some of which date back to the ninth century, continue to form part of a pilgrimage circuit attracting Jains from all over India. Many of them feature a statue of Gomateshvara – also known as Bahubali – a key Jain figure, who was the son of the first *tirthankara*. Although the most famous of all the Jain *bastis* (temples) is at Sravanabelgola on the outskirts of Hassan (see p.214), the greatest concentration of these shrines lies within striking distance, to the east and northeast, of Mangalore and can be taken in on long day-trips.

Of the important Hindu pilgrimage centres near Mangalore, the great *matha* (a centre of pilgrimage and learning), at Sringeri to the east, continues to play a pivotal role in Hindu theology.

Mudabidri

The most extensive of these *bastis* can be found in the small, quiet town of **MUDABIDRI**, 35km to the north. According to legend, a Jain ascetic settled here in the eighth century when he saw significance in the sight of a tiger playing with a cow. Most of the eighteen *bastis* and several *mathas* (monasteries) at Mudabidri were built between the fifteenth and sixteenth centuries. The most impressive of these, close to the town centre, is the **Chandranatha Basti**, completed in 1430 AD and known as Tribhuvana Tilaka Chudamani Basti, or more commonly as the "thousand-pillar hall". Approached by an imposing entrance gate and fronted by a tall, multistoried stone lamp, the main temple consists of two large interconnected columned halls. The surrounding verandah has stone columns supporting a sloping stone roof that is, in turn, crowned by a roof coated with copper tiles supported by carved wooden angle brackets.

Karkala

A short 18km bus ride to the north of Mudabidri and 52km from Mangalore, the small town of **KARKALA** is famous for the thirteen-metre high statue of **Gomateshvara**, standing placid and naked atop a rocky granite outcrop on the outskirts, a kilometre away from the town centre. Steps hewn out of rock lead up to the dramatic freestanding image, which was built in 1432 by Veerapandyadeva, a local ruler, and inspired by the monolith at Sravanabelagola (see p.214). At the bottom of the hill lies the **Chaturmukha Basti**, built in 1586 and so called because of its identical four (*chatur*) faces (*mukha*) or directions. The main object of the symmetry is the columned hall where four doors punctuate the porch, each with a view of three deities within the inner sanctum. By circumambulating the sanctuary, the devotee is thus able to take in twelve *tirthankaras* in all.

Dharamastala

A popular Hindu pilgrimage town set against a pleasant backdrop of paddy fields, wooded hills and plantations, **DHARAMASTALA**, 75km east of Mangalore, has another monolithic image, made out of stone from Karkalaa, of **Gomateshvara**, albeit one that was completed quite recently (1973) by the artist Ranjal Gopal Shenoy. Although impressive, the statue, which borrows heavily from its predecessors and took five years to make, lacks the refinement of those seen at Karkalaa and Sravanabelgola. The fourteen-metre-high statue stands on a slight hill, above the frenetically busy **Manjunatha temple** (daily 6.30am–1pm & 7–8pm), where Hindus and Jains co-exist in the same place of worship. An important Shaivite shrine, managed by Vaishnava priests, it was founded in 1780 by the influential Hegdes, a family of Jains who still run the temple and were responsible for the statue of Gomateshvara. According to custom, pilgrims to Dharamastala bathe in the **Netravati River**, 3km away. Across from the temple gates, two temple chariots stand at the entrance to the **Manjusha Museum** (daily 6.30am–1pm & 7–8pm), which boasts a diverse collection ranging from religious objects including bells and bronzes to household goods such as sewing machines and spectacles.

Sringeri

On the banks of the Tunga River, the scenic village of **SRINGERI**, on the edge of coffee plantations 100km northeast of Mangalore, is notable for its ancient *matha*, established in the ninth century by the great Hindu reformer and theologian, Shankara (see box below). Shankara is supposed to have spent twelve years of his life in Sringeri. The village itself has been at the centre of religious and social events throughout history, formerly exerting a strong influence over the Vijayanagar empire based at Hampi. During the festival of Navaratri, held each September/October, which commemorates the goddess Sharada's triumph over evil, the village swells with the influx of pilgrims, and the quiet tranquillity of the place turns into frenetic activity.

The modern **Sharada temple** at Sringeri, devoted to a form of the goddess Saraswati, receives a steady stream of pilgrims. Steps lead down to the Tunga River,

SHANKARA

Shankara, whom some historians see as a quasi-Buddhist, used existing models, mainly Buddhist and Jain, to establish the Hindu system of *sannyas* (monkhood). He reinterpreted the Upanishads, originally composed just prior to the Buddhist era around 7BC, and wrote commentaries that provide much of the foundation of the philosophy of Advaitya Vedanta, which aims to realize the non-dual self or consciousness otherwise known as Brahman. Politically, Shankara was to help establish the religious institutions of Hinduism and provide a religious geography that stretched between the extremities of India. To the north he established Joshimath, to the west Dwarka and to the east Puri. Governed by a long line of successors known as Shankaracharyas, these *mathas* became influential centres of learning and wielded, as they still do today, a strong political, religious and spiritual influence.

where devotees congregate to feed the sacred fish. More interesting, architecturally at least, a short distance to the south of the Sharada temple, on a picturesque location above the river, is the **Vidyashankara temple**, which dates back to the sixteenth century. Built on a high plinth decorated with friezes of animals, figures and gods, the temple enshrines a *lingam* that is considered to be the *samadhi* (memorial) to Shankara. The twelve pillars of the *mandapa* support a set of heavy ceiling-slabs and feature lavish details including riders on mythical beasts, depicting each of the twelve signs of the zodiac. The walls of the temple are richly adorned with carvings depicting the gods, while the niches hold various aspects of Shiva and the incarnations of Vishnu, including Krishna playing the flute.

Practicalities

Regular buses from the KSRTC bus stand in Mangalore ply the route to Dharamastala, Mudabidri and Karkalaa, which can also be approached directly from Udupi 35km to the southeast. Several buses continue on to Sringeri, but if you miss these you can change at Karkalaa. The road between Karkalaa and Sringeri is particularly beautiful, as it passes through a lush forest-belt on its way up the Western Ghats. Mudabidri and Karkalaa can be taken in as long day-trips from the coast. At both places **accommodation** is limited to the form of basic government-run *Tourist Cottages* (②), which you can book in the tourist office in Mangalore. Both Dharamastala and Sringeri have **room reservation offices** located near the temple entrances, which will assign you temple-run rooms (①). These are usually excellent value and can range from very basic rooms with shared bathrooms to comfortable doubles with attached baths. Private accommodation (②–③), is available near the bus stands, where the choice of restaurants is limited to basic "meals".

North of Mangalore: coastal Karnataka

Until the Konkan Railway is fully operational, transport along the **Karnatakan (Karavali) coast** is confined to the busy NH14, southern India's smoothest highway. The ten-hour bus journey between Goa and Mangalore ranks among the most scenic anywhere in the country. Crossing countless palm- and mangrove-fringed estuaries, the recently upgraded road, dubbed by the local tourist board as "The Sapphire Route", scales several spurs of the Western Ghats, which here creep to within a stone's throw of the sea, with spellbinding views over long, empty beaches and deep blue bays. Highlights are the pilgrim town of **Udupi**, site of a famous Krishna temple, and **Gokarn**, a bustling village that provides access to exquisite unexploited beaches. A couple of bumpy back roads wind inland through the mountains to **Jog Falls**, India's biggest waterfall, most often approached from the east. Infrequent buses crawl from the coast through rugged jungle scenery to this spectacular spot, but you'll enjoy the trip more by motorbike; it is possible to rent one in Goa and ride down the coast from there, stopping off at secluded beaches, falls and viewpoints en route.

Udupi

UDUPI (also spelt Udipi), on the west coast, 58km north of Mangalore, is one of South India's holiest Vaishnavite centres. The Hindu saint **Madhva** (1238–1317) was born here, and the **Krishna temple** and *mathas* (monasteries) he founded are visited by *lakhs* of pilgrims each year. The largest numbers congregate during the late winter, when the town hosts a series of spectacular **car festivals** and gigantic, bulbous-domed chariots are hauled through the streets around the temple. Even if your visit doesn't coincide with a festival, Udupi is a good place to break the journey along the Karavali coast. Thronging with *pujaris* and pilgrims, its small sacred enclave is wonderfully atmospheric, and you can take a boat from the nearby fishing village at **Malpé beach** to **St Mary's Island**, the deserted outcrop of hexagonal basalt where Vasco da Gama erected a crucifix prior to his first landfall in India.

Incidentally, Udupi also lays proud claim to being the birthplace of the nationally popular **masala dosa**; these crispy stuffed pancakes, made from fermented rice flour, were first prepared and made famous by the Udupi *brahmin* hotels. Certainly, the food in Udupi is excellent.

The Krishna temple and mathas

Udupi's **Krishna temple** lies five minutes' walk east of the main street, surrounded by the eight **mathas** founded by Madhva in the thirteenth century. Legend has it that the idol enshrined within was discovered by the saint himself, after he prevented a shipwreck. The grateful captain of the vessel concerned offered Madhva his precious cargo as a reward, but the holy man asked instead for a block of ballast, which he broke open to expose a perfectly formed image of Krishna. Believed to contain the essence (*sannidhya*) of the god, this deity draws a steady stream of pilgrims and is the focus of almost constant ritual activity. It is cared for by *acharyas*, or pontiffs, from one or other of the *mathas*. The only people allowed to touch the idol, they perform *pujas* (5.30am–8.45pm) that are open to non-Hindus; men are only allowed in the main shrine bare chested. As the *acharya* approaches the shrine, the crowd divides to let him through, while *brahmin* boys fan the deity with cloths, accompanied by a cacophony of clanging bells and clouds of incense smoke.

A stone tank adjacent to the temple, known as the **Madhva Sarovara**, is the focus of a huge festival every two years (usually Jan 17/18), when a new head priest is appointed. Preparations for the **Paryaya Mahotsava** begin thirteen months in advance, and culminate with the grand entry of the new *acharya* into the town, at the head of a huge procession. Outside in the street, a window in the wall affords a view of the deity; according to legend, this is the spot where a Harijan, or "untouchable", devotee, denied entry due to his caste, was worshipping Krishna from outside when the deity turned to face him. A statue of the devotee stands opposite. Nearby, there's a magnificent gold-painted temple chariot (*rath*), wood-carved in the distinctive Karnatakan style, its onion-shaped tower decked with thousands of scraps of paper, cloth and tinsel.

At the **Regional Resources Centre for the Performing Arts**, in the MGM College, staff can tell you about local festivals and events that are well off the tourist trail; the collection includes film, video and audio archives. The pamphlet *Udupi: an Introduction*, on sale in the stalls around the sacred enclave, is another rich source of background detail on the temple and its complex rituals.

Malpé, Thottam and St Mary's Island

Udupi's weekend picnic spot, **Malpé beach**, 5km north of the centre, is disappointing, marred by a forgotten concrete structure that was planned to be a government-run hotel. After wandering around the smelly fish market at the harbour you could haggle to arrange a boat (Rs800) to take you out to **St Mary's Island**, an extraordinary rock face of hexagonal basalt. Vasco da Gama is said to have placed a cross here in the 1400s, prior to his historic landing at Kozhikode in Kerala. From a distance, the sandy beach at **Thottam**, 1km north of Malpé and visible from the island, is tempting; in reality it's an open sewer.

Practicalities

Udupi's three **bus stands** are a short walk from the main street in the centre of town: the City stand handles private services to nearby villages, including Malpé, while the adjacent Service stand is for long-distance private buses, including numerous services to Mangalore. The KSRTC stand is for long-distance government buses to and from Mangalore, Bangalore, Gokarn, Jog Falls and Goa, and other towns along the coastal highway. Udupi's **train station** is at Indrali on Manipal Road 3km from the centre, but at the time of going to press, no local trains were stopping here.

Udupi has a good choice of **places to stay**. The *Hotel Sharada International* (☎08252/22910; ③–⑤), 1km out of town on the highway, has a range of rooms from singles to carpeted a/c, as well as veg and non-veg restaurants and a bar. *Kediyoor*, near the bus stand (☎08252/22381; ④–⑥) is much the same, but with three restaurants – the a/c *Janata* serves excellent *thalis* – while the *Shri Ramakrishna Hotel* (☎08252/23189; ③–⑤) with a/c and ordinary rooms, also has a good, but slow, non-veg restaurant and bar. The new *Hotel Swadesh Heritage*, Maruthi Vethika (☎08252/29605; ④–⑦), close to the Service and City bus stands, is Udupi's most luxurious hotel with complimentary breakfasts, reasonable a/c rooms and two restaurants and a bar. Their vegetarian *thalis* are excellent. If you're looking for somewhere cheaper, try the *Vyavahar Lodge*, on Kankads Rd (☎08252/22568; ②), between the bus stand and temple. This excellent, if bland, hotel has simple, clean rooms, some of them en suite and looking over the temple precinct. The small restaurant serves good "meals".

Jog Falls

Hidden in a remote, thickly forested corner of the Western Ghats, **Jog Falls**, 240km northeast of Mangalore, are the highest **waterfalls** in India. These days, they are rarely as spectacular as they were before the construction of a large dam upriver, which impedes the flow of the Sharavati River over the sheer red-brown sandstone cliffs. However, the surrounding scenery is spectacular at any time, with dense scrub and jungle carpeting sparsely populated, mountainous terrain. The views of the falls from the scruffy collection of *chai* stalls on the opposite side of the gorge is also impressive, unless, that is, you come here during the monsoons, when mist and rain clouds envelop the cascades. Another reason not to come here during the wet season is that the extra water, and abundance of leeches at this time, make the excellent **hike** to the valley floor dangerous. So if you can, head up here between November and January, and bring stout footwear. The trail starts just below the bus park and winds steeply down to the water. Confident hikers also venture farther downriver, clambering over boulders to other pools and hidden viewpoints, but you should keep a close eye on the water level and take along a local **guide** to point out the safest path.

Practicalities

Getting to and from Jog Falls by public transport is not easy. There are two **buses** to Udupi (7.30am & 8.15pm; 6hr), two to Karwar (5am & noon; 8hr), one to Gokarn (5am), two unreliable buses to Sirsi (7.30am & 1.30pm) for those visiting to Banvasi, and several to Shimoga where you can change onto buses for Hospet and Hampi. Better connections can be had at nearby Sagar (30km southeast) with buses to Shimoga, Udupi, Mysore, Hassan and Bangalore. Of the two direct buses to Bangalore from Jog Falls, the "semi-deluxe" departs at 7.30pm (9hr) and the ordinary at 8.30am. The **tourist office** at the *Tunga Tourist Home* (Mon–Sat 10am–5.30pm) is good for bus times and advice in case you need to rent a **car** or a jeep, both available at Jog Falls. With a car or motorbike, you can approach the falls from the coast along one of several scenic routes through the Ghats. The easiest and best maintained of these heads inland from Bhatkal to Jog Falls, but for a truly unforgettable experience, risk the tortuous, bumpy back route from **Kumta**, which takes you through some breathtaking landscape. There are very few villages, and no fuel stops, along the way, so stock up beforehand, and make sure your vehicle is in good shape.

Accommodation is limited. If you can get in, the *PWD Inspection Bungalow* (①), on the north side of the gorge, has great views from its spacious, comfortable rooms, but is invariably full and has to be booked in advance from Shimoga. Across the falls on the main side of the settlement, the large concrete complex of the KSTDC *Mayura Gerusoppa* (☎08186/4732; ②–④), located past the non-functioning public swimming pool, has vast rooms with fading plaster and bathrooms with rickety plumbing, but the staff are friendly and there's an adequate restaurant. Their annexe, the KSTDC *Tunga Tourist Home* at the bus stand is more basic (②) and doesn't have the garden or view. The *Youth Hostel* (①), ten minutes' walk down the Shimoga road, has basic facilities, but is having a new wing added, which should enhance its poor reputation. Most travellers make do with a raffia mat on the floor of one of the houses behind the *chai* stalls, known here as "*petty*" shops, ranged around the square; the government has been threatening to clear them as they are considered to be illegal.

The KSTDC canteen next to the *Tunga Tourist Home* at the bus stand serves reasonable South Indian vegetarian **food** including *iddlis* and *dosas*. The KSTDC *Mayura Gerusoppa* has a more comfortable restaurant with a varied menu but still manages to remain uninspiring, while the *chai* stalls around the square serve basic *thalis* and (eggy) snacks.

Gokarn

Set behind a broad white-sand beach, with the forest-covered foothills of the Western Ghats forming a blue-green backdrop, **GOKARN** (also spelled Gokarna), seven hours by bus north of Mangalore, is among India's most scenically situated sacred sites. Yet this compact little coastal town – a Shaivite centre for more than two millennia – remained largely "undiscovered" by Western tourists until a little under a decade ago, when it began to attract dreadlocked and didgeridoo-toting travellers fleeing the commercialization of Goa. Now, it's firmly on the tourist map, although the Hindu pilgrims pouring through still far outnumber the foreigners that flock here in winter.

Even if you're not tempted to while away weeks on isolated beaches, Gokarn is well worth a short detour from the coastal highway. Like Udupi, it is an old-established pilgrimage place, with a markedly traditional feel: shaven-headed *brahmins* sit cross-legged on their verandahs murmuring Sanskrit verses, while Hindu pilgrims file through a bazaar crammed with religious paraphernalia to the sea for a holy dip.

Arrival and information

The new KSRTC **bus stand**, 300m from the main road and within easy walking distance of Gokarn's limited accommodation, means that buses no longer have to negotiate the narrow streets of the bazaar. Gokarn's **train station**, served by the occasional passenger train, is at Madanageri from where buses and tempos are available to take you the 9km into town.

If you're on a short visit and want to take a close look at the temples, **hiring a guide** (Rs50 for a half-day) can be a good idea; look out for the wiry, grey-haired Mr VG Pai. The nearest State Bank of India is in Karwar, but you can **change money** at the versatile *Prema Restaurant* opposite the main gates of the Mahabaleshwar temple in Gokarn, or try the *Om Hotel* near the new bus stand. **Bicycles** are available for rent from a stall next to the *Pai Restaurant*, for Rs3 per hour or Rs30 for a full day. However, due to the roughness of the tracks you will find it near impossible to cycle to beaches other than the town beach, or along the long route to Om beach.

The Town

Gokarn **town**, a hotchpotch of wood-fronted houses and red terracotta roofs, is clustered around a long L-shaped bazaar, its broad main road – known as **Car Street** – running

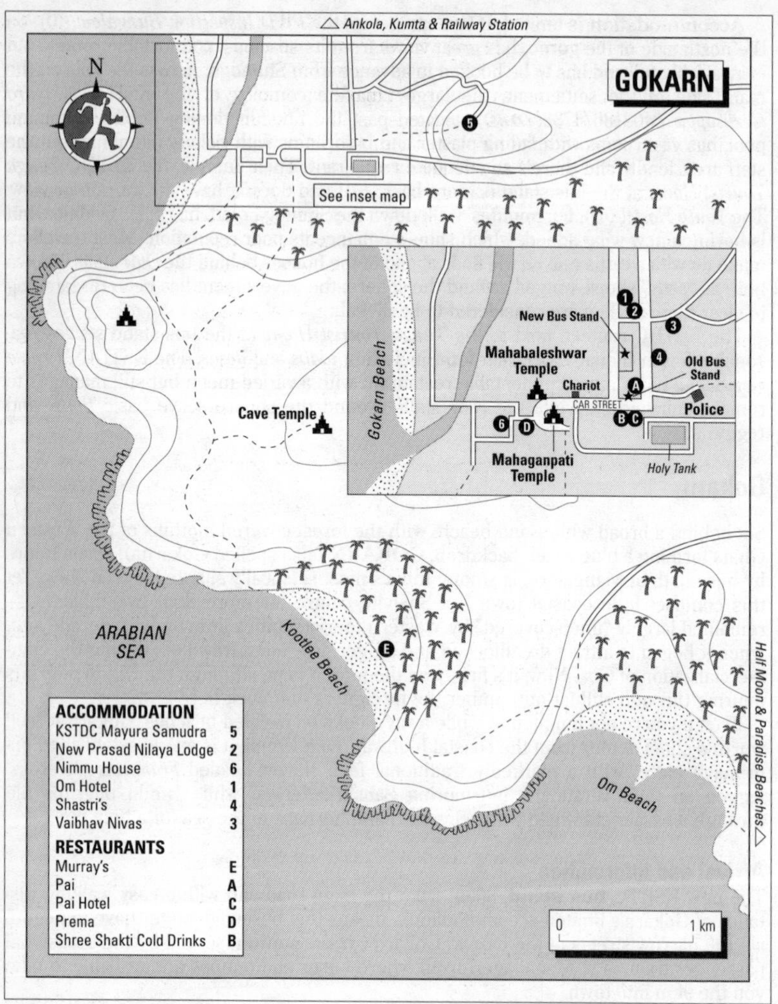

west to the town beach, a sacred site in its own right. Hindu mythology identifies it as the place where Rudra (another name for Shiva) was reborn through the ear of a cow from the underworld after a period of penance. Gokarn is also the home of one of India's most powerful *shivalingam* – the **pranalingam**, which came to rest here after being carried off by Ravana, the evil king of Lanka, from Shiva's home on Mt Kailash in the Himalaya. Sent by the gods to reclaim the sacred object, Ganesh, with the help of Vishnu, tricked Ravana into letting him look after the *lingam* while he prayed, knowing that if it touched the ground it would take root and never be moved. When Ravana returned from his meditation, he tried to pick the *lingam* up, but couldn't, because the gods had filled it with "the weight of three worlds".

The *pranalingam* resides in Gokarn to this day, enshrined in the medieval **Shri Mahabaleshwar temple**, at the far west end of the bazaar. It is regarded as so auspicious that a mere glimpse of it will absolve a hundred sins, even murder of a *brahmin*. Local Hindu lore also asserts that you can maximize the *lingam*'s purifying power by shaving your head, fasting and taking a holy dip in the sea before *darshan*, or ritual viewing of the deity. For this reason, pilgrims traditionally begin their tour of Gokarn with a walk to the beach. They are aided and instructed by their personal *pujari* – one of the bare-chested priests you see around town, wearing sacred caste threads and with single tufts of hair sprouting from their shaven heads – whose job it is to guide the pilgrims. Next, they visit the **Shri Mahaganpati temple**, a stone's throw east of Shri Mahabaleshwar, to propitiate the elephant-headed god Ganesh; non-Hindus are welcome to visit both shrines. En route, check out the splendid **rath**, or chariot, that stands at the end of the bazaar next to the Mahaganpati temple. During important festivals, notably Shiva's "birthday", **Shivratri** (Feb), deities are installed inside this colossal carved-wood cart and hauled by hand along the main street, accompanied by drum bands and watched by huge crowds.

The beaches

Notwithstanding Gokarn's numerous temples, shrines and tanks, most Western tourists come here for the beautiful **beaches** situated south of the more crowded town beach, beyond the lumpy laterite headland that overlooks the town. The hike to them takes in some superb coastal scenery, but be sure to carry plenty of water and wear a hat.

To pick up the trail, head along the narrow alley opposite the south entrance to the Mahaganpati temple, and follow the path uphill through the woods. After twenty minutes, you drop down from a sun-baked rocky plateau to **Kootlee beach** – a wonderful kilometre-long sweep of pure white sand sheltered by a pair of steep-sided promontories. Despite appearances, locals consider the water here to be dangerous. The palm-leaf *chai* stalls and seasonal cafés that spring up here during the winter, offer some respite from the heat of the midday sun and some of the villagers offer very basic accommodation in huts.

It takes around twenty minutes to hike from Kootlee to the next beach, scaling the headland to the south and following the steep gravel path as it zig-zags down the other side to the sea. The views along the way are stunning, especially when you first glimpse exquisite **Om beach**, so-named because its distinctive twin crescent-shaped bays resemble the auspicious Om symbol. For the past decade or so, this has been the all but exclusive preserve of a hard-core hippy fringe, many of whom spend months here wallowing in a *charas*-induced torpor. However, the arrival of a dirt road from Gokarn (7km), and the recent acquisition of the land by developers, may well squeeze the scene out. If the concrete mixers ever do descend, it's unlikely they'll ever reach Gokarn's two most remote beaches, which lie another forty- to sixty-minute walk over the hill. Tantalizingly inaccessible and virtually devoid of fresh water, **Half-Moon** and **Paradise** beaches, reached via difficult dirt paths across a sheer hillside, are, despite the presence of the occasional shack, only for intrepid sun lovers happy to pack in their own supplies. If you're looking for near-total isolation, this is your best bet.

Accommodation

Gokarn has a small, but not bad, choice of **guesthouses**. After staying in the village for a couple of days, however, many visitors strike out for the **beaches**, where apart from a few picturesque brick-and-mortar huts on the north side of Kootlee beach (invariably booked out to long-staying tourists from late Sept through March), accommodation consists of primitive palm-leaf shacks with beaten-earth floors, scattered in the trees. One exception is *Murray's Tea Shop* (aka the "Spanish tea shop" after his wife) set behind a line of neatly planted palms midway down the beach. Fresh water has been a perennial problem but bottled water is widely available. Om beach has also got its share of shacks while Half-Moon beach has one seasonal *chai* shop as does Paradise where long-term regulars usually occupy the thatched shelters. Some people end up sleeping rough on the beaches, but the nights can be chilly and robberies are common. Leave your luggage and valuables behind in Gokarn (most guesthouses will store your stuff for a fee), and if you plan to spend any time on the beaches, consider investing in a cheap mattress from the bazaar – you can always sell it on when you leave.

As a last resort, you can nearly always find a bed in one of the pilgrims' hostels, or **dharamshalas**, dotted around town. With dorms, bare, cell-size rooms and basic washing facilities, these are intended mainly for Hindus, but Western tourists are welcome if there are vacancies: try the *Prasad Nilaya*, just down the lane from *Om Hotel*.

KSTDC Mayura Samudra, high on a bald hill above Gokarn (look for the sign on the left as you arrive) (☎08386/56236). Large rooms with crumbling plaster and bathrooms with rickety plumbing, each with sit-out and garden overlooking the coast and out to sea. The staff are friendly and helpful and serve meals to order. Good option if you have your own transport or are willing to tackle the short but steep hike up from the bazaar past the police barracks. ②.

New Prasad Nilaya Lodge, near the new bus stand (☎08386/56675). A recently opened hotel with clean, bright spacious rooms with attached baths and food to order. Very reasonable. ②.

Nimmu House, a minute's walk from the temples, Gokarn beach (☎08386/56730). Gokarn's best budget guesthouse and handy for the town beach, with clean rooms (shared showers). The new building has very reasonable doubles and there is a reliable left-luggage facility. ①.

Om Hotel, near the new bus stand (☎08386/56445). A conventional economy hotel pitched at middle-class Indian pilgrims, with plain, good-sized en-suite rooms, some a/c, and a dingy bar that serves cold beer – a rarity in Gokarn. They will change money. ②–④.

Shastri's, 100m from the new bus stand (☎08386/56220). The best of the uniformly drab and run-down guesthouses lining the main street, this is a quiet place offering some rooms with attached bath and rock-bottom single occupancy rates. ①–②.

Vaibhav Nivas, off the main road, five minutes from the bazaar (☎08386/56714). Friendly, cheap and justifiably popular place despite the tiny rooms, most with shared baths. The new extension includes some rooms with attached baths. You can eat here, too, and leave luggage if you're heading off to the beaches (Rs5 per locker including a shower on return). ①–②.

Eating

Gokarn town offers a good choice of **places to eat**, with a crop of busy "meals" joints along Car St and the main road. Most popular, with locals and tourists, is the brightly lit *Pai Restaurant*, which dishes up fresh and tasty veg *thalis*, *masala dosas*, crisp *wadas*, teas and coffees until late. The other commendable "meals" canteen, around the corner on Car St, is also called the *Pai Hotel*; it's much smaller, but their snacks are excellent and the milk coffee delicious. *Shree Shakti Cold Drinks*, also on Car St, serves mouth-watering fresh cheese, hygienically made to an American recipe and served with rolls, garlic and tomato; the friendly owner also makes his own peanut butter, and serves filling toasties and *lassis*. Round this off with an ice-cream, either here or at any number of places along the road. Every café does its own version of *gad-bads*, several layers of different ice-creams mixed with chopped nuts and chewy dried fruit. One of the best places for a *gad-bad* is the tiny *Prema Restaurant* opposite the Mahabaleshwar temple's main gates, which has a traveller-friendly menu. Even if you are not staying on the beach, the trek out to *Murray's Tea Shop* on Kootlee beach is well worth the effort for fresh food and delicious *lassis*.

MOVING ON FROM GOKARN

Gokarn is well connected by direct daily **bus** to Goa (5hr), and several towns in Karnataka, including Bangalore (13hr), Hospet/Hampi (10hr) and Mysore (14hr), via Mangalore (7hr) and Udupi (6hr). Although there are only three direct buses north along the coast to Karwar (2hr), close to the border with Goa, you can change at Ankola on the main highway for more services. For more buses to Hospet and Hampi, change at Kumta; **tempos** regularly ply the route between Gokarn and Kumta (32km) as well as Ankola. The KSRTC counter on Car St, soon to be transferred to the new bus stand, is helpful for current bus timings.

You'll get the best **train** connections to Goa, Mangalore, Udupi and Kerala by going first to either Kumta or Ankola.

Sirsi and around

The large, bustling administrative centre of **SIRSI**, 110km east of Gokarn, sees few visitors, but with interesting temples in the vicinity and several great budget hotels, the town can be a rewarding and convenient pause on long journeys to and from the coast. An essential transport hub on a vital crossroad, Sirsi offers good onward connections to the Tibetan settlements of Mundgod and Hubli in the north, Jog Falls to the south, and distant Hospet to the east (for those travelling on to Hampi). Although the town's main point of interest, the striking **Marikamba temple**, lies in the heart of town, a short walk away from the bustling centre leads to pleasant tree-lined avenues. The chief reason for stopping here, however, is to use the town as a base to visit the fascinating temple complex at the quiet town of **BANVASI**.

The Town

The popular **Marikamba temple**, 500m from the bus stand in Sirsi, sees a steady stream of devotees who come to propitiate Durga, the ferocious multi-armed goddess who, as usual, is depicted slaying a demon and astride a tiger. Although the most frenetic period of activity is in the evenings, the temple is best seen during the day so as to appreciate the remarkable murals, which are some of the finest surviving examples of **Kavi art**. A rare form of wall-art once prevalent throughout the coastal Konkan region of west Karnataka but now practically extinct, Kavi art utilizes an unusual technique where the top layer of plaster, dyed with a blood-red pigment, is etched away to create detail revealed by the lower white layer of plaster. An imposing nineteenth-century facade, finished in red, leads into a grand courtyard with the temple at its centre. The cloisters within the courtyard are lavishly decorated with Kavi art details of gods and goddesses. Parts of the inner sanctum, which houses an image of Durga, date back to the sixteenth century, but numerous additions hide any traces of the original structure. Marikamba's *rath* (chariot) festival is held here only once every other year in February, and is one of the grandest in Karnataka; the next *rath* festival here will be held in 2001. During the festival the deity is led, on the *rath*, through the town in a procession.

Banvasi

The ancient town of **BANVASI**, 22km to the southeast of Sirsi, dates back to the third century BC when it was a centre of Buddhist learning. However, little remains of that period and the brick *stupas* that once graced the banks of the Varada River have all but disappeared. From the fourth century onwards, under the Kadambas, a dynasty that ruled the region for around two hundred years, Banvasi became the capital of Kannada, the forerunner of modern Karnataka, and is still held in high esteem as the home of the Kannada script created during that period.

The **Madhukeshvara temple**, at the far end of Banvasi's Car St, 1500m from the bus stand, is still in use today. It exudes a timeless atmosphere and dates back to the Kadamba period, although most of the major additions are attributed to the late Chalukya period of the twelfth century. The inner sanctum of the main temple – dedicated to Shiva as the lord (*ishvara*) of the bees (*madhuka*), who is represented here with a honey-coloured *lingam* – is said to date back to the fourth century and the adjoining stone, pillared hall to the sixth century. To the right of the inner sanctum stands a marble image of Datatreya, a three-headed combination representing the Hindu trinity of Brahma the creator, Vishnu the preserver and Shiva the destroyer. A most imposing Nandi, Shiva's bull and vehicle, as always, sits outside in ever-faithful attendance facing the *lingam*. The entrance hall (*mukhamandapa*) has numerous pillars, all unique in style except for the four highly polished granite, reflective pillars that surround the stone dance circle, now, alas, no longer in use. Leading to the middle chamber, a stone throne with lavishly carved pillars, built in 1628, is still used for placing idols during special occasions such as Vasant Utsava, the summer festival held around April every year. Immediately to the right of the main temple, the temple dedicated to Parvati was built in the late twelfth century. The extensive courtyard has an interesting collection of stone images, including gods known as the Ashtadigpalakas (the guardians of the eight directions), each with his own animal vehicle. The Ashtadigpalakas, who predate modern Hinduism and represent the sacrificial Vedic period, include: Indra (east) on his elephant; Agni (southeast) on his ram; Yama, the god of death (south), on his buffalo; Niraruti (southwest), whose vehicle is a man; Varuna (west) on a crocodile; Yayu (northwest) on a deer; Kubera (north) on a horse and Ishana, one of the prototypes of Shiva (northeast), on his bull. Each of the gods is shown with his consort and the overall display is impressive. At one side of the courtyard, stands a small temple dedicated to Shiva's son, the elephant god Ganapati (aka Ganesh). A small museum by the main gates has a collection of sculpture from around Banvasi, including a striking image of the Jain Gomateshvara dated to the fifteenth century and Buddhist plaques from the second century. Outside the main temple stands the majestic temple *rath* (chariot) built in 1608 and used to transport the gods during Vasant Utsava.

Practicalities

Several **buses** travel between Sirsi and Banvasi but none after 6pm. Buses from Sirsi's KSRTC bus stand connect the town to numerous destinations including Gokarn via Kumta, Hospet, Jog Falls, Karwar, Mundgod and Hubli. Private companies operate deluxe buses from near the bus stand to destinations such as Hubli and Bangalore.

The best mode of transport around town is by **auto-rickshaw**; **taxis** are available near the bus stand, and if you book through a hotel, you may find them cheaper. Although there is no accommodation in Banvasi, hotels in Sirsi are good value. Ignore the dives around the bus stand and head two kilometres out to College Rd, where you will find a handful of good options, including the *Madhuvana* (☎08384/27496; ②–④), a large, clean and well-run hotel with excellent-value suites and a very good vegetarian restaurant. The *Samrat* next door (☎08384/26278; ①–④), has a good range of rooms available, even though it is beginning to show its age. By far the best of Sirsi's hotels, the *Panchavati* on Yellapur Rd (☎08384/26755; ②–⑥), is four kilometres from the centre but well worth the ride. This well-presented hotel is set in large, pleasant grounds on the edge of town and offers good facilities, including a restaurant and some a/c rooms.

Karwar

On the coastal route south from Goa, the busy but uninspiring town of **KARWAR**, 105km from Panjim, provides good connections for those travelling to Gokarn (56km farther south) or inland towards Hampi via Hubli. Those travelling to the interior may want to avail themselves of the only foreign exchange facilities for miles. The natural harbour at Karwar is about to be developed by the navy, who are in the process of building one of the biggest bases in the world. When completed, the base will stretch for around 20km south and engulf the pristine, unspoiled beaches that have lain undiscovered by tourists for years – mainly because they are relatively hard to reach. One of the only beaches accessible to the public is **Devbagh beach**, 5km to the north across the mouth of the Kali River, a pleasant stretch of sand, some of it taken by the up-market *Devbagh Beach Resort*. The only way to get to Devbagh beach, if you are not a guest at the resort, is to take a bus or auto-rickshaw across the bridge and walk along the Kali River towards the sea. The beach shelters a brackish backwater, home to several species of birds, and makes a pleasant change from the grime of the town. There is nowhere to eat at the beach except at the expensive restaurant at the resort, which only opens during the winter.

Practicalities

The KSRTC **bus stand** close to the centre of town, is well connected to Goa with several buses a day to Margoa and Panjim. Four buses a day travel to Dandeli and several to Hubli and Sirsi. There are a few direct buses to Gokarn, and if you miss the direct bus you can change at Ankola on the coastal highway – NH17 – which extends all the way from Goa to Kerala. Long-distance buses travel south along the highway to Mangalore, Mysore and Bangalore as well as Mumbai and Pune, to the north.

Lying on the new **Konkan Railway**, Karwar's **train station** lies 10km to the southeast at Shirwad, and is connected to the town centre by buses, shared tempos and auto-rickshaws (Rs40). Several express trains travel to Goa, Mangalore, Kerala and Thiruvananthapuram. The **rail booking office** is next door to the **tourist office** at Mini Vidhan Sandha, DC Compound (Mon–Sat 10am–5.30pm). The tourist office is pretty low-key, although Mr Hegde is very obliging and a fountain of knowledge on the local area; he is also helpful with bus times. You can **change money** at either the Indian

IMPORTANT TRAINS FROM KARWAR

The services listed below are the **most direct** and/or the **fastest**. This list is by no means exhaustive and there are numerous slower trains, that are often more convenient for smaller destinations – see p.273.

Destination	Train	Number	Frequency	Departs	Total Time
Ernakulam	*Mangala–Lakshadweep Express*	#2618	Daily	10.18pm	12hr 12min
Madgaon (Margao)	*Netravati Express*	#6636	Daily	7.27pm	1hr 8min
Mangalore	*Madgaon–Mangalore Express*	#0021	Daily	9.08am	7hr 23min
Thiruvananthapuram	*Rajkot–Trivandrum Express*	#6333	Sat	9.08am	19hr 52min

Bank (Mon–Fri 10am–2pm, Sat 10am–noon) or the State Bank of India; both are in the town centre.

The most luxurious **accommodation**, and the reason why many come to Karwar, is the *Devbagh Beach Resort* (☎08382/26596; ⑥–⑧) booked through the Jungle Lodges & Resorts office in Bangalore (☎080/559 7021). A motorboat takes you out there from the town-side jetty next to the bridge. Set within a secluded five-acre development under the canopy of the dense casuarina forest, the resort offers eight cottages and a beautiful beach, which at an all-inclusive full-board price of Rs700 per head for Indians is excellent value, although the US$40 per head for foreigners is over-the-top. However, they do organize tours, and the resort could be used as a base from which to discover the Dandeli Wildlife Sanctuary and Gokarn's beaches and temples. The *Krishna Guest House* (☎08382/21613; ②), on Binaga Beach, 5km to the south of town, in marked contrast is a relaxed family-run guesthouse, with limited accommodation and food to order. As the beach is part of the navy's scheme for development, access to it is under threat. Accommodation in the town centre includes *Navarathna* (☎08382/26927; ②–④), on Main Rd, with plain rooms, and *Shri Ram Lodge* on Cutinho Rd (☎08382/21178; ②), which is set in a quiet location and offers basic rooms with attached baths. The *Bhadra*, next to the Kali River bridge(☎08382/25212; ③–⑧), 4km from the centre, is a huge rambling complex with large rooms and two new buildings with Western bathrooms. By far the best deal in the centre of Karwar is the *Dwarka* on Kaiga Rd (☎08382/20344; ②), on the way to the train station, which offers clean rooms, some with balconies, a quiet location and a good vegetarian restaurant; it's excellent value and well worth the short auto-rickshaw ride. Most of the best **eating** options in Karwar are along Main Rd. The *Savita* and *Udipi*, owned by the same management, serve excellent vegetarian South Indian food, while the *Amrut*, which also has a bar, serves meat and local fish – try the bangade or pomfret. The *Rajasthani* specializes in good North Indian vegetarian food.

Dandeli Wildlife Sanctuary

Lying between Hubli 75km to the east and Panjim 145km to the west, the scruffy town of **DANDELI** on the banks of the Kali River in Uttar Kanada (Northern Karnataka), provides access to the **Dandeli Wildlife Sanctuary** (Dec–April, closed June–Sept), an extensive, unspoiled forest on the edge of the Deccan Plateau. Despite its close proximity to Goa and its situation at a major crossroads on the route to Hampi via Hubli, the sanctuary sees few visitors except for occasional jeeploads from nearby Maharashtra, and it remains a low-key and undeveloped wildlife destination. This, however, is part of its charm.

The forest checkpost, at the gate, is around 18km from the town of Dandeli and you will need to arrange your own vehicle, either privately or through the Forest Department in Dandeli, before getting here. Spread across 834 square kilometres, the large mixed-deciduous forest, famed for its teak, spills over the lip of the Deccan Plateau where it gives way to the hills, ravines and deep river valleys of the Western Ghats. At the heart of the forest, 22 kilometres from the forest gateway, the huge 100-metre-high **Cyntheri Rock** rises out of the **Kanari River**. The river provides an excellent vantage point for observing the animals. **Sunset Point**, 6km from the gate, and the remote **Sykes Point** provide sweeping views of the jungle-covered ridges of the Western Ghats. The sanctuary is famous for its black panthers, but sightings are rare, especially with the deep cover; you stand a better chance of seeing sambar deer, spotted deer, flying squirrels, wild boar and Indian bison – distinguished by the distinctive white bands across parts of their body. Dandeli also shelters elephants, sloth bears and a small handful of tigers, while the rivers, including the **Kali River**, which sweeps past the town of Dandeli, is home to mugger crocodiles.

The main Hubli–Karwar highway, moving on from Dandeli, is one of the most beautiful in Karnataka as it descends through the evergreen **Anasi National Forest**, which forms part of the same forest-belt as that of the Dandeli Wildlife Sanctuary. Travelling through the area you may notice the striking features of the **Siddis**, a **tribe** of Africans who live in the region and maintain their own customs and language. The Siddis were brought over in the nineteenth century as bodyguards by a local raja.

Practicalities

Dandeli's KSRTC bus stand, in the centre of town, is well connected, with frequent buses to Hubli and to Karwar on the coast; in addition the two KSRTC buses a day travelling between Goa and Hubli stop here. Cheap, simple **accommodation** is available around the bus stand, but for a little more comfort try the popular but often full, *Government Guest House* (☎08284/31299; ③), which has attractive clean rooms. The Forest Department have their own camp, *Nature Camp* (①), located at the forest gates next to the Interpretation Centre. Permanent tented accommodation is offered here at a rate of Rs100 for a four- to five-person tent; however, the camp does seem to be geared towards accommodating groups of schoolchildren. If you want to stay at any of the Forest Department's rest houses in the sanctuary, you will need to arrange it through the Deputy Conservator of Forests at the department's office, on the main Karwar road, near the Kali River. Across the Kali River from Dandeli, lies the *Kali Wilderness Camp and Visitors Centre* (☎08284/30266; ⑦), with ten spacious rooms in the main concrete building and nine luxurious tents with attached baths along the river – bring plenty of mosquito repellent.

Jungle Lodges & Resorts (☎080/559 7021) offer a package that includes accommodation, jeep safari and a coracle ride along the Kali River. The food at the *Kali Wilderness Camp*, served in an open thatched restaurant, is excellent. Their jeep safaris, however, are the best informed, with a better chance of viewing wildlife; rates vary according to time and distance. Jeeps, which cost from Rs150 per hour to hire, can be arranged through the Deputy Conservator of Forests' office. Two new ventures should be opening soon. At the time of writing, the *Dandeli Resort*, run by Indian Adventures, was being built near Ganeshgudi Dam on the Kali River and a different *Nature Camp*, this time at Panasoli 9km from Dandeli, was about to begin operations; both plan to cater for upmarket tours.

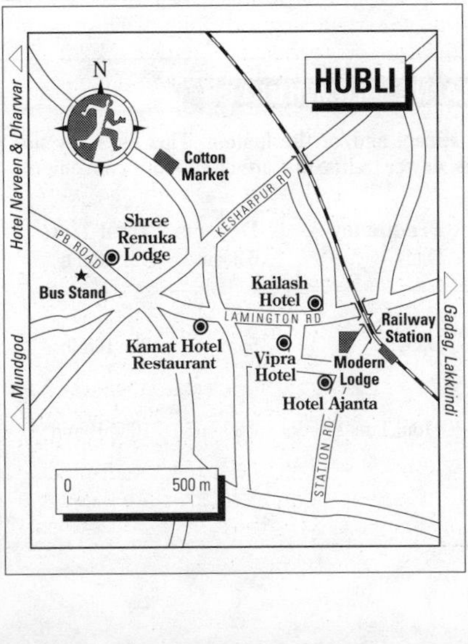

Hubli and around

Karnataka's second most industrialized city, **HUBLI**, 418km northwest of Bangalore, has little to offer tourists except for its transport connections for those travelling between Mumbai, Goa, the coast of Uttar Kanada (Northern Karnataka), Hampi and other points in the interior. However, the city is pleasant enough to use as a base from which to explore some interesting sites in the area.

These sites include the large Tibetan monastery of **Drepung** on the outskirts of the town of Mundgod

48km to the south of Hubli. Improbably located in the rolling countryside of central Karnataka, where summer temperatures can soar well above 40°C – a stark contrast to the cold climate of Tibet – the busy and rarely visited complex at Drepung is home to several hundred monks. Representing the ancient scholastic monastery that once flourished outside Lhasa, along with Sera Je at Bylakuppe (see p.223), Drepung is one of the most important Tibetan monasteries in India today and plays a vital role in continuing religious traditions. The environs of Drepung, as around Bylakuppe, have been settled by Tibetan refugees since the 1960s, who have industriously farmed the once barren land. Although few travellers come this way, visitors are welcome.

Immediately to the west of Hubli, the leafy university town of **DHARWAR**, is far less polluted than the city, and, although it attracts little tourist interest, is best known for its Hindustani classical music connections, as it is home to several famous musicians and vocalists. In musical terms, this region marks the watershed between the Carnatic classical music system of South India, and the Hindustani system of North India (see Contexts p.60). The main concert season is in winter, and performances are held at various venues around Dharwar and Hubli; check local papers for listings.

Travelling east towards Hospet and Hampi, the cotton town of **GADAG**, 53km from Hubli, is an important stop on the train line as well as the highway. During the cotton season, between February and June, the town is a hive of activity, but at other times the town returns to its quiet ways. Few travellers stop here but for those with the time and inclination, Gadag and its environs make an interesting diversion from the main route to and from Hampi, with a handful of rarely visited Chalukya temples dating back to the eleventh century. The best of the Gadag monuments are the **Trikuteshwara** and **Saraswati** temples, which share a compound in the southern part of the town. The inner sanctum of the Trikuteshwara temple houses a triple *lingam*; the adjoining Saraswati temple shares the same hall and boasts a porch with impressive carvings. You may find parts of the complex locked, in which case you will need to look for the priest, who will unlock it for you.

Gadag's other temples are in a terrible state of repair and travelling to the village of **LAKKUNDI**, a further 11km east along the Hospet highway, is more rewarding. Less threatened with urban growth, Lakkundi's Chalukya temples, from the same period as those in Gadag, include a **Jain Basti**, dominating the north of the village, with an impressive tower and sanctuary walls. A short distance away the **Kashi Vishwanatha**

IMPORTANT TRAINS FROM HUBLI

The services listed below are the **most direct** and/or the **fastest**. This list is by no means exhaustive and there are numerous slower trains, that are often more convenient for smaller destinations – see p.273.

Destination	Train	Number	Frequency	Departs	Total Time
Bangalore	*Hubli–Bangalore Inter City Express*	#2726	Daily	6.20am	7hr 30min
Hospet	*Bangalore–Hubli Parbhani Hampi Express*	#6591	Daily	5pm	3hr 10min
Mumbai	*Bangalore CST–Mumbai Express*	#1018	Mon, Tue, Fri, Sat	2.50pm	16hr 10min**

* Stops in Pune.

** Stops at Pune (in the middle of the night).

temple, dedicated to Shiva as lord of Kashi (Varanasi), consists of two temples facing each other sharing the same plinth. Unfortunately, the connecting porch has collapsed, but the animal and flower friezes along the plinth are impressive and so are the carvings along the doorways and pillars. Close to the bus stand, a square stepped bathing tank with a columned bridge half-way through was designed to provide privacy for women bathers.

Practicalities

Hubli's **train station**, close to the town centre and within walking distance of several of the hotels, is well connected to Bangalore, Mumbai, Pune and Hospet (see box opposite). For the time being, rail services to and from Goa are suspended while conversion work is carried out on the line – work should be finished by late 2000. Hubli's frenetic KSRTC **bus stand**, 1500m northwest of the station, has good bus connections with regular services linking the city with Goa, coastal Karnataka, Badami, Hospet, Mumbai and Bangalore. There are more buses than trains for Hospet, numerous buses to Dharwar and several to Dandeli and Karwar. Many buses connect Lakkundi to Gadag as well as to Hospet. Most long-distance services are overnight and private operators can be found across the main road from the bus stand. Janata Travel (☎0836/354968) operate buses for Mumbai and Pune. Perhaps the most reputable of the private outfits, Vijayananda Travels (☎0836/350630), distinguishable by their yellow and black signs, operate luxury buses to Mumbai, Pune, Gulbharga, Bijapur, Sirsi and Bangalore. To Drepung, there are several buses from the KSRTC bus stand to Mundgod or you should head for the *Modern Lodge* opposite the train station, where the Tibetan community congregates, and two or three shared jeeps depart every morning. Hubli's **airport**, a 6km auto-rickshaw ride from the centre, is serviced by the new airline Gujarat Airways, booked though Fly Wing Trade and Travel, Shri Krishna Bhavan, Lamington Rd (☎0836/362251), which flies nineteen-seater aircraft to Mumbai. The best method of getting around the city is by **auto-rickshaw**; these have meters, but at the train station and bus stands they are controlled by *dalals* (middlemen) who fix high prices.

Accommodation around the train station includes the *Hotel Ajanta* in Jayachamaraj Nagar (☎0836/362216; ②), which has small, plain rooms and rickety plumbing, and, opposite the bus stand the large and well-organized *Shree Renuka Lodge* (☎0836/251384; ②–④), which offers a range of reasonable budget rooms. Between the train station and the bus stand, Lamington Rd has a few more options, including the pleasant *Kailash* (☎0836/352235; ⑤), an efficient business hotel, which has comfortable clean rooms but a rather plain restaurant. The *Vipra*, opposite, is a bit cheaper with a range of simple rooms (☎0836/362336; ②–④). For a lot more comfort the *Naveen* at Unkal (☎0836/372283; ⑦–⑨), 6km out from the centre, despite its lavish use of concrete, is quite attractive, with cottages, a pleasant lakeside setting and a swimming pool; transport can be provided from the train station or bus stand by prior arrangement.

Most hotels have their own **restaurants**, for example, the *Shree Renuka*, which has two sections, one serving South Indian vegetarian food and the other serving Chinese and North Indian cuisine. The best of the independent restaurants is the vegetarian *Kamat Hotel*, at the traffic island at the head of Lamington Rd towards the bus stand. The downstairs restaurant serves excellent South Indian food, while the plush restaurant upstairs, *Kosher*, serves vegetarian North Indian and Chinese dishes.

Hospet

Charmless **HOSPET**, ten hours by bus east of Goa, is of little interest except as a transport hub: in particular, it is the jumping-off place for the extraordinary ruined city of Hampi (Vijayanagar), 13km northeast. If you arrive late, or want somewhere fairly comfortable to sleep, it makes sense to stay here and catch a bus or taxi out to the ruins the following morning. Otherwise, hole up in Hampi, where the setting more than compensates for the basic facilities.

Practicalities

Hospet's **train station**, 1500m north of the centre, is served by the overnight *Hampi Express* #6592 from Bangalore and services from Hyderabad, via Guntakal Junction. The line north continues to Hubli for connections to the coast and Goa. For connections to Badami and Bijapur, travel to Gadag and change onto the slow single track running north. Auto-rickshaws are thin on the ground, and often the only way to get into town is by cycle rickshaw (Rs10).

The **long-distance bus stand** is nearer the centre, 250m down MG (Station) Rd, which runs south from the train station. The most frequent services are from Bangalore and Hubli, and there are daily arrivals from Mysore, Badami, Bijapur, Hassan, Gokarn (via Kumta), Mangalore and Goa. For a summary of services see Travel Details on p.273. **Bookings** for long-distance routes can be made at the ticket office on the bus stand concourse (daily 8am–noon & 3–6pm), where there's also a **left luggage** facility.

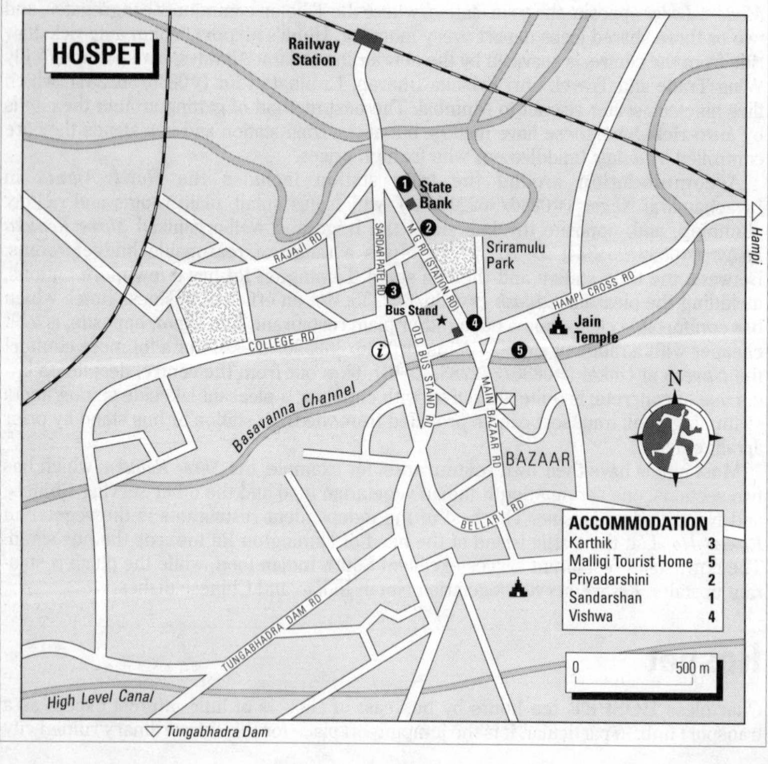

The **tourist office** at the Rotary Circle (Mon–Sat: June–March 10am–5.30pm & April & May 8am–1pm; ☎08394/28537) offers limited information and sells tickets for the KSTDC conducted tours (see below). You can **change currency** at the State Bank of India (Mon–Fri 10.30am–2.30pm & Sat 10.30am–12.30pm). The State Bank of Mysore (same hours) on MG Rd next to the tourist office, changes travellers' cheques and cash; or try the reception desk at the *Hotel Malligi*. *Neha Travels* (☎08394/25838) at the Elimanchate Complex situated next to the *Hotel Priyadarshini* on MG Rd also changes any currency, travellers' cheques and advances money on credit cards. They also have branches in Hampi and book airline and train tickets and cars and run private **luxury buses to Goa**. Their sleeper coach departs at 7pm, costs Rs350 and takes fourteen hours. Luxury buses are also available for Bangalore (10hr; Rs190) departing between 10pm and 11pm at night. You can also buy tickets for these buses at Malleshwara Travels (☎08394/25696) opposite the bus stand.

Accommodation and eating

Accommodation in Hospet, concentrated around MG Rd, ranges from budget to mid-price. By far the most popular place to stay is the incredibly versatile *Malligi Tourist Home*, with something to suit most budgets, but the *Priyadarshini* is also good value and nearer the bus and train stations.

There's little to do in Hospet, so you'll probably pass a fair amount of time **eating and drinking**. Many of the hotels have good dining rooms, but in the evening, the upscale though affordable *Waves*, a terrace restaurant opposite and owned by the *Malligi*, is the most congenial place to hang out, serving *tandoori* and chilled beer from 7pm to 11pm (bring lots of mosquito repellent). *Shanbhog*, an excellent little Udupi restaurant next to the bus station, is a perfect pit stop before heading to Hampi, and opens early for breakfast.

Karthik, Pampa Villa, off MG Rd (☎08394/24938). A new, characterless structure featuring unremarkable rooms but with a surprise around the back in the form of an extraordinary nineteenth-century stone villa housing four huge suites. ④–⑧.

Malligi Tourist Home, 6/143 Jambunatha Rd, 2min walk east of MG Rd (look for the signs) and the bus stand (☎08394/28101, fax 27038). Friendly, well-managed hotel with cheaper, clean, comfortable rooms (some a/c) in the old block and two new wings across the immaculate lawn, with luxurious a/c rooms. There is also a great new swimming pool in their *Waves* complex beneath the restaurant/bar. They sell the otherwise hard-to-find journal *Homage to Hampi*, and offer foreign exchange. The al fresco *Madhu Paradise* restaurant/bar in the old building serves great veg food and they have an efficient travel service. ②–⑧.

Priyadarshini, MG Rd, over the road from the bus stand, towards the train station (☎08394/28838). Rooms from rock-bottom singles to doubles with TV and a/c (some balconies). Large, and bland, but spotless and very good value. They have two good restaurants: the veg *Chalukya* and, in the garden, non-veg *Manasa*, which has a bar. Their travel service handles bus and train tickets. ②–⑥.

Sandarshan, MG Rd, between the train station and bus stand (☎08394/29175). Budget rooms, some with bathrooms and hot water only in the mornings. ②.

Vishwa, MG Rd, right opposite the bus stand (☎08394/27171). No-frills lodge, with mostly en-suite rooms. The *Shanthi* canteen serves breakfast, South Indian snacks, and unlimited veg "meals". ②.

Getting to Hampi

KSTDC's daily guided **tour** only stops at three of the sites in Hampi and spends an inordinate amount of time at the far less interesting Tungabhadra Dam. Even so, it can be worth it if you're short of time. It leaves from the tourist office at Rotary Circle (Taluk Office Circle), east of the bus station (9.30am–5.30pm; Rs60 including lunch).

Frequent **buses to Hampi** run from the bus stand between 6.30am and 7.30pm; the journey takes thirty minutes. If you arrive late, either stay in Hospet, or take a taxi or one of the rickshaws that gather outside the train station. It is also possible to catch a bus to **Kamalpura**, at the south side of the site, and explore the ruins from there, catching a bus back to Hospet from Hampi Bazaar at the end of the day. **Bicycles** are available for rent at several stalls along the main street, but the trip to, around and back from the site is a long one in the heat. Auto-rickshaws, best arranged through hotels such as the *Malligi* or the *Priyadarshini*, will also take you to Hampi and back and charge up to Rs150. For the adventurous, Bullet **motorbikes** are available on rent (or sale) from Bhurat Motors (☎08394/24704) near Rama Talkies. Finally, some hotels in Hospet can also organize for you to hook up with **trained guides** in Hampi; ask at the *Malligi* or *Priyadarshini*.

Hampi (Vijayanagar)

> *The city of Bidjanagar [Vijayanagar] is such that the pupil of the eye has never seen a place like it, and the ear of intelligence has never been informed that there existed anything to equal it in the world.. .. The bazaars are extremely long and broad.. .. Roses are sold everywhere. These people could not live without roses, and they look upon them as quite as necessary as food.. .. Each class of men belonging to each profession has shops contiguous the one to the other; the jewellers sell publicly in the bazaars pearls, rubies, emeralds and diamonds. In this agreeable locality, as well as in the king's palace, one sees numerous running streams and canals formed of chiselled stone, polished and smooth.. .. This empire contains so great a population that it would be impossible to give an idea of it without entering into extensive details.*
>
> Abdu'r-Razzaq, the Persian ambassador who visited Vijayanagar in 1443

The ruined city of **Vijayanagar**, (the City of Victory) – also known as **HAMPI**, the name of a local village – spills from the south bank of the Tungabhadra River, littered among a surreal landscape of golden-brown granite boulders and leafy banana fields. According to Hindu mythology, the settlement began its days as Kishkinda, the monkey kingdom of the *Ramayana*, ruled by the monkey kings Vali and Sugriva and their ambassador, Hanuman; the weird rocks – some balanced in perilous arches, others heaped in colossal, hill-sized piles – are said to have been flung down by their armies in a show of strength.

Between the fourteenth and sixteenth centuries, this was the most powerful Hindu capital in the Deccan. Travellers such as the Portuguese chronicler Domingo Paez, who stayed for two years after 1520, were astonished by its size and wealth, telling tales of markets full of silk and precious gems, beautiful, bejewelled courtesans, ornate palaces and joyous festivities. However, in the second half of the sixteenth century, the dazzling city was devastated by a six-month Muslim siege. Only stone, brick and stucco structures survived the ensuing sack – monolithic deities, crumbling houses and abandoned temples dominated by towering *gopuras* – as well as the sophisticated irrigation system that channelled water to huge tanks and temples.

Thanks to the Muslim onslaught, most of Hampi's monuments are in disappointingly poor shape, seemingly a lot older than their four or five hundred years. Yet the serene riverine setting and air of magic that lingers over the site, sacred for centuries before a city was founded here, make it one of India's most extraordinary locations. Even so, mainstream tourism has thus far made little impact: along with streams of Hindu pilgrims and tatty-haired *sadhus* who hole up in the more isolated rock crevices and shrines, most visitors are budget travellers straight from Goa. Many find it difficult to leave, and spend weeks chilling out in cafés, wandering to whitewashed hilltop temples and gazing at the spectacular sunsets.

The **best time to come** to Hampi, weather-wise, is from October to March, when daytime temperatures are low enough to allow long forays on foot through the ruins.

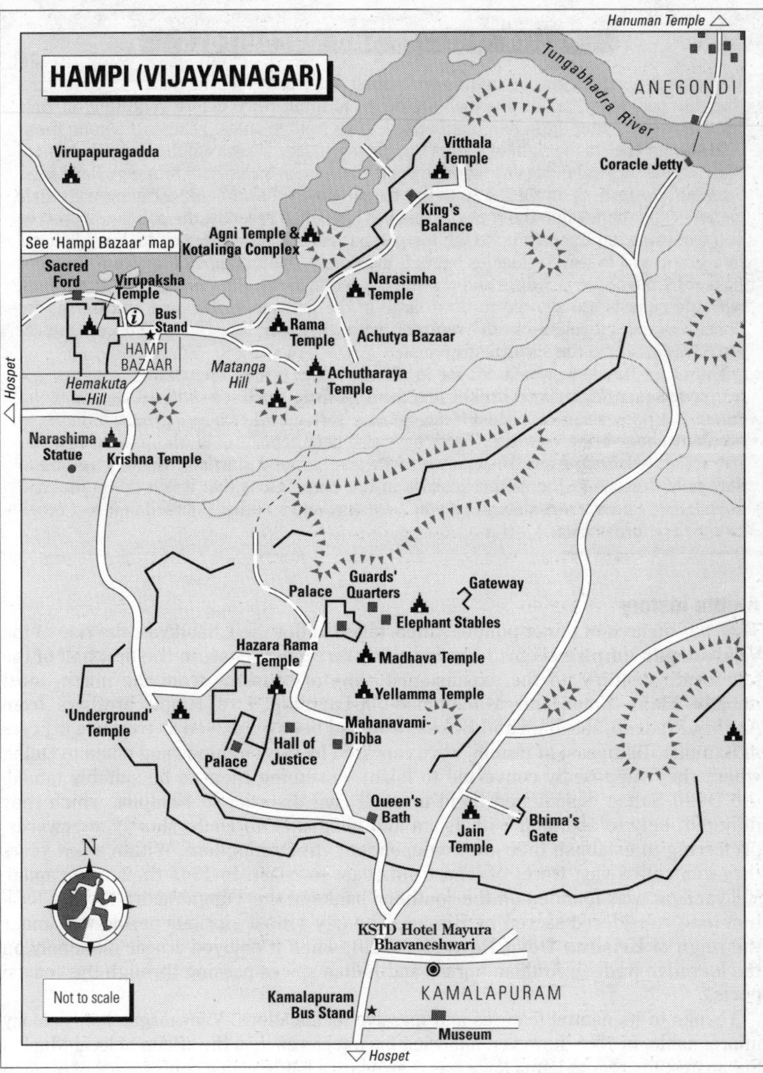

From Christmas through early January, however, the site is swamped by an exodus of travellers from Goa that has been increasing dramatically over the past few years; there have even been Anjuna-style full-moon parties, complete with techno sound systems and bus-loads of ravers, mostly from Israel. The influx also attracts its share of dodgy characters, and crime has become a problem in the village at this time; so if you want to enjoy Hampi at its best, come outside peak season.

POLICE, THIEVES AND MOSQUITOES

Hampi is generally a safe site to wander around, but a spate of armed attacks on tourists over the past few years means that you ought to think twice before venturing on your own, especially after dark, to a number of known trouble spots. Foremost among these is **Matanga Hill**, to the right of Hampi Bazaar as you face away from the Virupaksha temple, dubbed by local guides as "sunrise point" because it looks east. Muggers have been jumping Westerners on their way to the temple before dawn here, escaping with their cameras and money into the rocks. If this has happened recently, the police will prevent you from walking the path up to the temple, but even at other times it's advisable to go in a group and to leave valuables behind. Incredibly, photographs of known rogues are posted by the police at lodges and one must wonder, as the thieves are familiar to them, why the culprits are allowed to be at large in the first place. As some precaution, the police request **foreigners to register** with them at the Hampi Police Outpost (☎08394/41240) at the Virupaksha temple.

The other hassle to watch out for in Hampi is the **police** themselves, who are not averse to squeezing the odd backhander from tourists. You'll see *chillums* smoked in the cafés, but possession of hashish (*charas*) is a serious offence in Karnataka, liable to result in a huge bribe, or worse. There have also been reports of local cops arresting and extracting *baksheesh* from Western men who walk around shirtless. Another reason to stay fully dressed in Hampi, particularly in the evenings, is that it is a prime **malaria** zone. Sleep under a mosquito net if you have one, and smother yourself in insect repellent well before sunset.

A little history

This was an area of minor political importance under the Chalukyas; the rise of the **Vijayanagar empire** seems to have been a direct response, in the first half of the fourteenth century, to the expansionist aims of Muslims from the north, most notably Malik Kafur and Muhammad-bin-Tughluq. Two Hindu brothers from Andhra Pradesh, Harihara and Bukka, who had been employed as treasury officers in Kampila, 19km east of Hampi, were captured by the Tughluqs and taken to Delhi, where they supposedly converted to Islam. Assuming them to be suitably tamed, the Delhi Sultan despatched them to quell civil disorder in Kampila, which they duly did, only to abandon both Islam and allegiance to Delhi shortly afterwards, preferring to establish their own independent Hindu kingdom. Within a few years they controlled vast tracts of land from coast to coast. In 1343 their new capital, Vijayanagar, was founded on the southern banks of the Tungabhadra River, a location long considered sacred by Hindus. The city's most glorious period was under the reign of **Krishna Deva Raya** (1509–29), when it enjoyed a near monopoly on the lucrative trade in Arabian horses and Indian spices passing through the coastal ports.

Thanks to its natural features and massive fortifications, Vijayanagar was virtually impregnable. In 1565, however, following his interference in the affairs of local Muslim Sultanates, the regent Rama Raya was drawn into a battle with a confederacy of Muslim forces, 100km away to the north, which left the city open to attack. At first, fortune appeared to be on the side of the Hindu forces, but there were as many as 10,000 Muslims in their number, and loyalties may well have been divided. When two Vijayanagar Muslim generals suddenly deserted, the army fell into disarray. Defeat came swiftly; although members of his family fled with untold hoards of gold and jewels, Rama Raya was captured and suffered a grisly death at the hands of the Sultan of Ahmadnagar. Vijayanagar then fell victim to a series of destructive raids, and its days of splendour were brought to an abrupt end.

The site

Although spread over 26 square kilometres, the ruins of Vijayanagar are mostly concentrated in two distinct groups: the first lies in and around **Hampi Bazaar** and the nearby riverside area, encompassing the city's most sacred enclave of temples and *ghats*; the second centres on the "**royal enclosure**" – 3km south of the river, just northwest of **Kamalapuram** village – which holds the remains of palaces, pavilions, elephant stables, guard houses and temples. Between the two stretches a long boulder-choked hill and swathe of banana plantations, fed by ancient irrigation canals.

Frequent buses run from Hospet to Hampi Bazaar and Kamalapuram, and you can start your tour from either; most visitors prefer to set out on foot or bicycle from the former. After a look around the soaring **Virupaksha temple**, work your way east along the main street and river bank to the beautiful **Vitthala temple**, and then back via the **Achyutaraya** complex at the foot of Matanga Hill. From here, a dirt path leads south to the royal enclosure, but it's easier to return to the bazaar and pick up the tarred road, calling in at **Hemakuta Hill**, a group of pre-Vijayanagar temples, en route.

On KSTDC's whistle-stop **guided tour** (see p.247) it's possible to see most of the highlights in a day. If you can, however, set aside at least two or three days to explore the site and its environs, crossing the river by **coracle** to **Anegondi** village, with a couple of side-hikes to hilltop viewing points: the west side of Hemakuta Hill, overlooking Hampi Bazaar, is best for sunsets, while **Matanga Hill**, though plagued by thieves in recent years, offers what has to be one of the world's most exotic sunrise vistas.

Hampi Bazaar, the Virupaksha temple and riverside path

Lining Hampi's long, straight main street, **Hampi Bazaar**, which runs east from the eastern entrance of the Virupaksha temple, you can still make out the remains of Vijayanagar's ruined, columned bazaar, partly inhabited by today's lively market. Landless labourers live in many of the crumbling 500-year-old buildings.

Dedicated to a local form of Shiva known as Virupaksha or Pampapati, the functioning **Virupaksha temple** (daily 8am–12.30pm & 3–6.30pm; Rs2) dominates the village, drawing a steady flow of pilgrims from all over southern India. Also known as **Sri Virupaksha Swami**, the temple is free for all who come for *arati* (worship; daily 6.30–8am & 6.30–8pm) when the temple has the most atmosphere. The complex consists of two courts, each entered through a towered *gopura*. The larger gateway, on the east, is approximately 56m high, each storey with pilastered walls and sculptures flanking an open window. It is topped by a single wagon-vault and *kalasha*, pot-shaped finial. In the southwest corner a water channel runs along a large columned *mandapa*.

FESTIVALS AT VIJAYANAGAR

Vijayanagar's main **festivals** include, at the Virupaksha temple, a **Car Festival** with street processions each February, and in December the marriage ceremony of the deities, which is accompanied by drummers and dances. The **Hampi Festival**, organized by the tourist department, takes place in early November usually between the 3rd and the 5th and involves classical music and dance from both Carnatic and Hindustani (North Indian) traditions performed on temple stages and at Anegondi. The festival, which is beginning to attract several well-known musicians and dancers, has been growing in size and prestige and hotels in the area can get booked well in advance. Unfortunately, the traditional music festival, **Purandaradas Aradhana** (Jan/Feb), which is usually held at the Vitthala temple, to celebrate the birth anniversary of the poet-composer Purandaradasa, had been temporarily suspended.

A colonnade surrounds the inner court, usually filled with pilgrims dozing and singing religious songs; in the middle the principal temple is approached through a *mandapa* hallway whose carved columns feature rearing animals. Rare Vijayanagar-era paintings on the *mandapa* ceiling include aspects of Shiva, a procession with the sage Vidyaranya, the ten incarnations of Vishnu and scenes from the *Mahabharata*; the style of the figures is reminiscent of local shadow puppets. Faced by a brass image of Nandi, a *shivalingam* is housed in the small sanctuary, its entrance decorated with painted *makaras*, semi-aquatic mythical animals whose bodies end with foliage instead of a tail. Blue water spouts from their mouths, while above them flicker yellow flames. Just outside the main temple's wall, immediately to the north, is a small earlier temple, thought to have been the "ancestor" of the Virupaksha.

The sacred **ford** in the river is reached from the Virupaksha's north *gopura*; you can also get there by following the lane around the temple past *Shanti Lodge*. A *mandapa* overlooks the steps that originally led to the river, now some distance away. Although threatened by a new footbridge, **coracles** ply from this part of the bank, just as they did five centuries ago, ferrying villagers to the fields and tourists to the popular *Uma-Shankar Café* on the other side. The path through the village also winds to an impressive ruined bridge, and on to the hilltop Hanuman shrine – a recommended round walk described opposite.

To reach the Vitthala temple, walk east from the Virupaksha, the length of Hampi Bazaar. At the end, a path on the left, staffed at regular intervals by conch-blowing *sadhus* and an assortment of other ragged mendicants, follows the river past a café and numerous shrines, including a Rama temple – home to hordes of fearless monkeys. Beyond at least four Vishnu shrines, the paved and colonnaded **Achutya Bazaar** leads due south to the **Tiruvengalanatha temple**, whose beautiful stone carvings – among them some of Hampi's famed erotica – are being restored by the ASI. Back on the main path again, make a short detour across the rocks leading to the river to see the little-visited waterside **Agni temple**; next to it, the Kotalinga complex consists of 108 (an auspicious number) tiny *linga*, carved on a flat rock. As you approach the Vitthala temple, to the south is an archway known as the **King's Balance**, where the rajas were weighed against gold, silver and jewels to be distributed to the city's priests.

Vitthala temple

Although the area of the **Vitthala temple** (daily 6am–6pm; Rs6, the ticket is also valid for the Lotus Mahal) does not show the same evidence of early cult worship as Virupaksha, the ruined bridge to the west probably dates from before Vijayanagar times. The bathing *ghat* may be from the Chalukya or Ganga period, but as the temple has fallen into disuse it seems that the river crossing (*tirtha*) here has not had the same sacred significance as the Virupaksha site. Now designated a World Heritage Monument by UNESCO, the Vitthala temple was built for Vishnu, who according to legend was too embarrassed by its ostentation to live there. The tower of the principal Vishnu shrine is made of brick – unusual for South India – capped with a hemispherical roof; in front is an enclosed *mandapa* with carved columns, the ceiling of which has partly collapsed. Two doorways lead to a dark passageway surrounding the sanctuary.

The open *mandapa* features slender monolithic granite **musical pillars** which were constructed so as to sound the notes of the scale when struck. Today, due to vandalism and erosion from being repeatedly beaten, heavy security makes sure that no one is allowed to play them. Guides, however, will happily demonstrate the musical resonance of other pillars on an adjacent structure. Outer columns sport characteristic Vijayanagar rearing horses, while friezes of lions, elephants and horses on the moulded basement display sculptural trickery – you can transform one beast into another simply by masking one portion of the image.

In front of the temple, to the east, a stone representation of a wooden processional **rath**, or chariot, houses an image of Garuda, Vishnu's bird-vehicle. Now cemented, at one time the chariot's wheels revolved. The three *gopura* entrances, made of granite at the base with brick and stucco multistorey towers, are now badly damaged.

Anegondi and beyond

With more time, and a sense of adventure, you can head across the Tungabhadra to **ANEGONDI**, a fortress town predating Vijayanagar and the city's fourteenth-century headquarters. The most pleasant way to go is to take a **putti**, a circular rush-basket coracle, from the ford 1500m east of the Vitthala temple; the *puttis* which are today reinforced with plastic sheets, also carry bicycles.

Forgotten temples and fortifications litter Anegondi village and its quiet surroundings. The ruined **Huchchappa-matha temple**, near the river gateway, is worth a look for its black stone lathe-turned pillars and fine panels of dancers. **Aramani**, a ruined palace in the centre, stands opposite the home of the descendants of the royal family; also in the centre, the **Ranganatha temple** is still active.

A huge wooden temple chariot stands in the village square. To complete the five-kilometre loop back to Hampi from here (best attempted by bicycle), head left (west) along the road, winding through sugar-cane fields towards the sacred **Pampla Sarovar**, signposted down a dirt lane to the left. The small temple above this square bathing tank, tended by a *swami* who will proudly show you photos of his pilgrimage to Mt Kailash, is dedicated to the goddess Lakshmi and holds a cave containing a footprint of Vishnu. If you are staying around Anegondi, this quiet and atmospheric spot is best visited early in the evening during *arati* (worship).

Another worthwhile detour from the road is the hike up to the tiny whitewashed **Hanuman temple**, perched on a rocky hilltop north of the river, from where you gain superb views over Hampi especially at sunrise or sunset. The steep climb up to it takes around half an hour. Keep following the road west for another 3km and you'll eventually arrive at an impressive old **stone bridge** dating from Vijayanagar times. The track from the opposite bank crosses a large island in the Tungabhadra, emerging after twenty minutes at the sacred ford and coracle jetty below the Virupaksha temple. This rewarding round walk can, of course, be completed in reverse, beginning at the sacred ford. With a bike, it takes around three hours, including the side-trips outlined above; allow most of the day if you attempt it on foot, and take plenty of water.

Hemakuta Hill and around

Directly above Hampi Bazaar, **Hemakuta Hill** is dotted with pre-Vijayanagar temples that probably date from between the ninth and eleventh centuries (late Chalukya or Ganga). Three are of the *trikutachala* (three-peaked hills) type, with three shrines facing into a common centre. Aside from the architecture, the main reason to clamber up here is to admire the **views** of the ruins and surrounding countryside. Looking across miles of boulder-covered terrain and banana plantations, the sheer western edge of the hill is Hampi's number one sunset spot, attracting a crowd of blissed-out tourists most evenings, along with a couple of entrepreneurial *chai-wallahs*.

A couple of interesting monuments lie on the road leading south towards the main, southern group of ruins. The first of these, a walled **Krishna temple complex** to the west of the road, dates from 1513. Although dilapidated in parts, it features some fine carving and shrines. On the opposite side of the road, a fifty-metre-wide processional path leading east through what's now a ploughed field, with stray remnants of colonnades straggling on each side, is all that remains of an old market place.

Hampi's most-photographed monument stands just south of the Krishna temple in its own enclosure. Depicting Vishnu in his incarnation (*avatar*) as the Man-Lion, the monolithic **Narashima** statue, with its bulging eyes and crossed legs strapped into meditation pose, is one of Vijayanagar's greatest treasures.

The southern and royal monuments

The most impressive remains of Viyayanagar, the city's **royal monuments**, lie some 3km south of Hampi Bazaar, spread over a large expanse of open ground. Before tackling the ruins proper, it's a good idea to get your bearings with a visit to the small **Archeological Museum** (daily except Fri 10am–5pm; free) at Kamalapuram, which can be reached by bus from Hospet or Hampi. Turn right out of the Kamala puram bus stand, take the first turning on the right and the museum is on the left – two minutes' walk. Among the sculpture, weapons, palm-leaf manuscripts and painting from Vijayanagar and Anegondi, the highlight is a superb scale-model of the city, giving an excellent bird's-eye view of the entire site.

To walk into the city from the museum, go back to the main road and take the nearby turning marked "Hampi 4km". After 200m or so you reach the partly ruined massive **inner city wall**, made from granite slabs, which runs 32km around the city, in places as high as 10m. The outer wall was almost twice as long. At one time, there were said to have been seven city walls; coupled with areas of impenetrable forest and the river to the north, they made the city virtually impregnable.

Just beyond the wall, the **citadel area** was once enclosed by another wall and gates of which only traces remain. To the east, the small *ganigitti* (oil-woman's) fourteenth-century **Jain temple** features a simple stepped pyramidal tower of undecorated horizontal slabs. Beyond it is **Bhima's Gate**, once one of the principal entrances to the city, named after the Titan-like Pandava prince and hero of the *Mahabharata*. Like many of the gates, it is "bent", a form of defence that meant anyone trying to get in had to make two 90° turns. Bas-reliefs depict episodes such as Bhima avenging the attempted rape of his wife, Draupadi, by killing the general Kichaka. Draupadi vowed she would not dress her hair until Kichaka was dead; one panel shows her tying up her locks, the vow fulfilled.

Back on the path, to the west, the plain facade of the fifteen-metre-square **Queen's Bath** belies its glorious interior, open to the sky and surrounded by corridors with 24 different domes. Eight projecting balconies overlook where once was water; traces of Islamic-influenced stucco decoration survive. Women from the royal household would bathe here and umbrellas were placed in shafts in the tank floor to protect them from the sun. The water supply channel can be seen outside.

Continuing northwest brings you to **Mahanavami-Dibba**, or "House of Victory", built to commemorate a successful campaign in Orissa. A twelve-metre pyramidal structure with a square base, it is said to have been where the king gave and received honours and gifts. From here he watched the magnificent parades, music and dance performances, martial art displays, elephant fights and animal sacrifices that made celebration of the ten-day Dussehra festival famed throughout the land (the tradition of spectacular Dussehra festivals is continued at Mysore; see p.199). Carved reliefs of dancers, elephant fights, animals and figures decorate the sides of the platform. Two huge monolithic doors on the ground nearby may have once been part of a building atop the platform, of which no signs remain. To the west, another platform – the largest at Vijayanagar – is thought to be the basement of the **King's Audience Hall**. Stone bases of a hundred pillars remain, in an arrangement that has caused speculation as to how the building could have been used; there are no passageways or open areas.

The two-storey **Lotus Mahal** (daily 6am–6pm; Rs6, the ticket is also valid for the Vitthala temple), a little farther north and part of the **zenana enclosure** (women's quarters), was designed for the pleasure of Krishna Deva Raya's queen: a place where she could relax, particularly in summer. Displaying a strong Indo-Islamic influence, the pavilion is open on the ground floor, whereas the upper level (no longer accessible by stairs) contains windows and balcony seats. A moat surrounding the building is thought to have provided water-cooled air via tubes.

Beyond the Lotus Mahal, the **elephant stables**, a series of high-ceilinged, domed chambers, entered through arches, are the most substantial surviving secular buildings at Vijayanagar – a reflection of the high status accorded to elephants, both ceremonial and in battle. An upper level, with a pillared hall, is capped with a tower at the centre; it may have been used by the musicians who accompanied the royal elephant processions. Tender coconuts are usually for sale under the shade of a nearby tree. East of here, recent archeological excavations have revealed what are thought to have been the foundations of a series of Vijayanagar administration offices, which until 1990 had remained buried under earth deposited by the wind.

Walking west of the Lotus Mahal, you pass two temples before reaching the road to Hemakuta Hill. The rectangular enclosure wall of the small **Hazara Rama** (One Thousand Ramas) temple, thought to have been the private palace temple, features a series of medallion figures and bands of detailed friezes showing scenes from the *Ramayana*. The inner of two *mandapas* contains four finely carved, polished, black columns. Many of the ruins here are said to have been part of the Hazara Rama Bazaar, which ran northeast from the temple. Much of the so-called **Underground Temple**, or Prasanna Virupaksha, lies below ground level and spends part of the year filled with rainwater. Turning north (right) onto the road that runs west of the Underground Temple will take you back to Hampi Bazaar, via Hemakuta Hill.

Practicalities

Buses from Hospet terminate halfway along the main street in Hampi Bazaar, a little east of the Virupaksha temple. On the opposite side of the street, the **tourist office** (Mon–Sat 10am–5.30pm; ☎08394/41339) can put you in touch with a **guide** – ask for Shankar – but not much else. Shankar runs a convenience store just behind the office. Most visitors coming from Hospet organize a guide from there (see p.248).

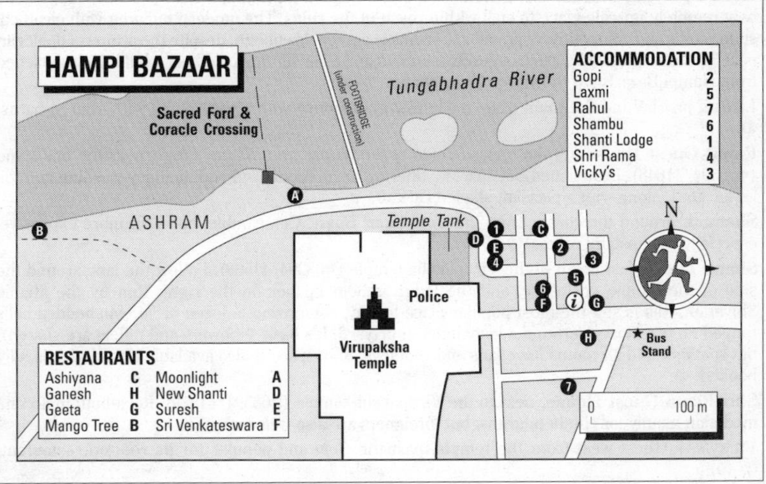

Rented **bicycles**, available from stalls near the lodges cost Rs5 per hour or Rs25 per day and Rs30 for a 24-hour period. Bikes are really of use if you're planning to explore Anegondi across the river, accessible by **coracle** for Rs2, or if you want to explore Hampi by road. You can also rent bicycles at Kamalapuram for Rs35 per day or a motorcycle from Ravi Garage, also in Kamalapuram, for Rs250 per day not including fuel. You can **change money** (including travellers' cheques) at Neha Travels who have three outlets in Hampi with the main office at D131/11 Main St (☎08394/41580), near the Virupaksha temple. They also advance cash on credit cards and book airline and **train tickets** as well as run **luxury buses** to Bangalore and luxury sleeper coaches to Goa. You can also book these through their Hospet office.

Run by Shri Swamy Sadashiva Yogi, the Shivananda Yoga Ashram overlooking the river past the site of the new footbridge and coracle crossing, offers courses in **yoga and meditation** as well as homeopathic treatment, magnetotherapy and **Ayurvedic treatment** specializing in snakebites.

Accommodation

If you're happy to make do with basic amenities, Hampi is a far more enjoyable place to stay than Hospet, with around fifty congenial **guesthouses** and plenty of cafés to hang out in after a long day in the heat. As you wander through the lanes, you may find yourself solicited by local residents offering rooms in their own homes. Staying in the village also means you can be up and out early enough to catch the sunrise over the ruins – a mesmerizing spectacle. Some travellers shun Hampi Bazaar for more basic amenities at one of several new lodges at **Virupapuradadda** across the river or at the more comfortable *Kiskinda Resorts* at Hanomana Halli, 2km from Anegondi, which has been the scene of several raves. During the high season that lasts for six weeks starting around Christmas, expect to pay almost double for a room. The relaxed atmosphere of Hampi is under threat, however, as the government, including the tourist authorities and the ASI, wants to strip the entire site of all guesthouses and cafés in a bid to extend their dream of a gigantic museum open only to daytime visitors.

Gopi Guest House, a short walk down the lanes behind *Shanti*. There's a pleasant rooftop café here, and some of the rooms have attached baths. ①–②.

KSTDC Mayura Bhavaneshwari, Kamalapuram, 2.5km from Hampi Bazaar (☎08394/41574). The only remotely upscale place to stay within reach of the ruins. The modern building with clean en-suite rooms and competitively priced a/c rooms is agreeable enough, despite the aroma of dank carpets. There's a pleasant garden, a good restaurant and a bar serving cold beers, but it feels detached from Hampi Bazaar and the village lacks charm. ③–⑤.

Laxmi, just behind the main drag, a friendly guesthouse with clean rooms with shared baths. ①.

Rahul Guest House, on the opposite side of the bazaar from *Shanti Lodge*, near the bus stand (☎08394/41648). Established but spartan, offering small rooms and rudimentary washing and toilet facilities, along with a pleasant shaded café. ①.

Shambu, around the corner from the *Gopi Guest House*. Comparable, but a bit more expensive, especially the upstairs rooms. ②–③.

Shanti Lodge, just north of the Virupaksha temple (☎08394/41568). Follow the lane around the side of the temple enclosure, and the lodge is 30m further on the right. Run by the affable Shivaram, this is still the most popular place to stay, comprising a dozen or so twin-bedded cells ranged on two storeys around a leafy inner courtyard. It's basic (showers and toilets are shared), but spotless, and all rooms have fans and windows. Roof space is also available if the lodge is fully booked. ①.

Shri Rama Guest House, next to the Virupaksha temple (☎08394/41219). Rock-bottom accommodation mainly for Hindu pilgrims, but foreigners are also welcome. ①.

Vicky's, furthest west from the temple, past the *Gopi* and popular for its rooftop restaurant. ②–③.

Eating

During the season, Hampi spawns a rash of travellers' cafés and temporary tiffin joints, as well as a number of laidback shack bars tucked away in more secluded corners. Among the many **restaurants** in the bazaar, *Welcome* near the bus stand and *Sri Vendateswara* on the main street, are firm favourites with Western tourists, serving a predictable selection of pancakes, porridge, omelettes and veg food. Other popular restaurants include the *Geeta* and *Ganesh*, also on the main street, and the *New Shanti Restaurant*, opposite *Shanti Lodge* (but not the same ownership), is another typical travellers' joint, renowned for its fresh pasta and soft cheese. Steer clear of the latter if there have been lots of power cuts. The friendly *Suresh* behind the *Shri Rama Tourist Home*, serves delicious *shak-shuka* on banana leaves and is a good place for breakfast.

You can also get filling *thalis* and a range of freshly cooked snacks in the *Rahul Guest House*; other lodges with restaurants include *Vicky's* and *Gopi*. The *Moonlight*, a thatched café overlooking the river and the coracle jetty, offers the usual travellers' menu, but has a pleasant location a short walk past the Shanti. However, the prize for Hampi's best all-round café has to go to the *Mango Tree*, hidden away in the banana plantations beyond the coracle jetty and the Shivananda Yoga Ashram. The food is fairly run-of-the-mill, but the relaxing riverside location is hard to beat.

You can get authentic Western-style bread and **cakes** through *Shanti Lodge*; place your order by early evening, and the cakes and pies are delivered the following day.

Monuments of the Chalukyas

Now quiet villages, **BADAMI**, **AIHOLE** and **PATTADAKAL**, in northwest Karnataka, were once the capital cities of the **Chalukyas**, who ruled much of the Deccan between the fourth and eighth centuries. The astonishing profusion of **temples** in the area beggars belief, and it is hard to imagine the kind of society that can have made use of them all. Most visitors use Badami, which can offer a few basic lodges, as a base; Aihole boasts a single rest house, and no rooms are available at Pattadakal. The **best time to visit** is between October and early March; in April and May, most of this part of northwest Karnataka becomes much too hot and all government offices only work between 8am and 1pm.

Badami and Aihole's cave temples, stylistically related to those at Ellora, are some of the most important of their type. Among the many structural temples are some of the earliest in India, and uniquely, it is possible to see both northern (*nagari*) and southern (Dravida) architectural styles side by side. Clearly much experimentation went on, as several other temples (commonly referred to, in art historical terms, as "undifferentiated") fit into neither system. None is now thought to date from before the late sixth century, but at one time scholars got very excited when they believed the famous Lad Khan temple at Aihole, for example, to be even older.

Although some evidence of **Buddhist** activity around Badami and Aihole exists, the earliest cave and structural temples are assigned to the period of the Chalukya rise to power in the mid-sixth century, and are mostly **Hindu**, with a few Jain examples. The first important Chalukyan king was Pulakeshin I (535–66), but it was Pulakeshin II (610–42) who captured the Pallava capital of Kanchipuram in Tamil Nadu and extended the empire to include Maharashtra to the north, the Konkan coast on the west and the whole of Karnataka. Although the Pallavas subsequently, and briefly, took most of his territory, including Badami, the capital, at the end of his reign, Pulakeshin's son, Vikramaditya I (655–81) later recovered it, and the Chalukyas continued to reign until the mid-eighth century. Some suggest that the incursion of the Pallavas accounts for the southern elements seen in the structural temples.

Badami and around

Surrounded by a yawning expanse of flat, farmed land, **BADAMI**, capital of the Chalukyas from 543 AD to 757 AD, extends east into a gorge between two red sandstone hills, topped by two ancient fort complexes. The south is riddled with cave temples, and on the north stand early structural temples. Beyond Badami, to the east, is an artificial lake, **Agastya**, said to date from the fifth century. The small selection of places to stay and restaurants makes Badami an ideal base from which to explore the Chalukyan remains at Mahakuta, Aihole and Pattadakal as well as the temple village of Banashankari on the outskirts of town.

Southern Fort cave temples

Badami's earliest monuments, in the Southern Fort area, are a group of sixth-century **caves** (daily, sunrise to sunset; Rs2) cut into the hill's red sandstone, each connected by steps leading up the hillside. About 15m up the face of the rock, **Cave 1**, a Shiva temple, is probably the earliest. Entrance is through a triple opening into a long porch raised on a plinth decorated with images of Shiva's dwarf attendants, the *ganas*. Outside, to the left of the porch, a *dvarpala* door guardian stands beneath a Nandi bull. On the right is a striking 1.5m-high image of a sixteen-armed dancing Shiva. He carries a stick-zither-type *vina*, which may or may not be a *yal*, a now-extinct musical instrument, on which the earliest Indian classical music theory is thought to have been developed. In the antechamber, a panel on the left shows Harihara (Shiva and

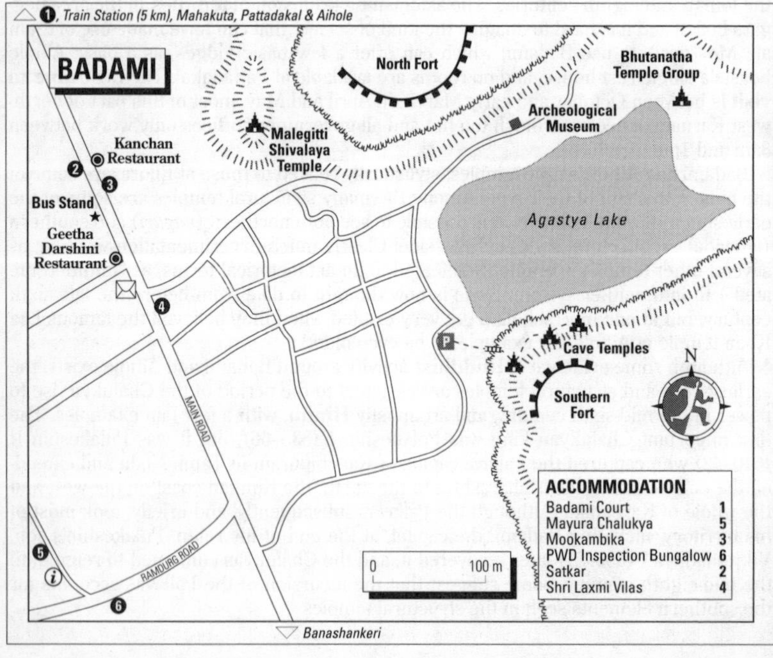

Vishnu combined), accompanied by consorts Lakshmi and Parvati and the gods' vehicles Nandi and Garuda. On the right Ardhanarishvara (Shiva combined with Parvati; half-male, half-female) is accompanied by Nandi and the skeleton Bringi. Ceiling panels include a coiled Naga snake deity, flying couples and Shiva and Parvati. Inside, a columned hall, divided into aisles, leads to a small, square sanctuary at the back, containing a *lingam*.

A little higher, the similar **Cave 2**, a Vishnu shrine, is approached across a courtyard with two *dvarpala* door guardians at the end. The porch contains a panel to the left of Varaha, the boar incarnation of Vishnu, and, to the right, of Trivikrama, Vishnu as a dwarf *brahmin* who inflates in size to cross the earth in three steps. On the ceiling nearby, Vishnu is shown riding his bird Garuda. A central square of the ceiling features a lotus encircled by sixteen fish; other decoration includes swastika designs and flying couples. Traces of painting show how colourful the caves originally were.

Steps and slopes lead on upwards, past a natural cave containing a smashed image of the Buddhist Bodhisattva, Padmapani (He who Holds the Lotus), and steps on the right in a cleft in the rock lead up to the fort. **Cave 3** (578 AD) stands beneath a thirty-metre-high perpendicular bluff. The largest of the group, with a facade measuring 21m from north to south, it is also considered the finest, for the quality of its sculptural decoration. Eleven steps lead up to the plinth decorated with dwarf *ganas*. Treatment of the pillars is extremely elaborate, featuring male and female figures, lotus motifs and medallions portraying amorous couples.

To the east of the others, a Jain temple, **Cave 4**, overlooks Agastya Lake and the town. It's a much simpler shrine, dating from the sixth century. Figures, both seated and standing, of the 24 *tirthankaras*, mostly without their identifying emblems, line the walls. Here, the rock is striped.

After seeing the caves you can climb up to the fort and walk east where, hidden in the rocks, a carved panel shows Vishnu reclining on the serpent Adisesha, attended by a profusion of gods and sages. Continuing, you can skirt the gorge and descend on the east to the Bhutanatha temples at the lakeside. Before you get to them, there's another rock carving of a reclining Vishnu and his ten incarnations.

North Fort

North of Agastya Lake a number of structural temples can be reached by steps. The small **Archeological Museum** (daily except Fri 10am–5pm) nearby contains sculpture from the region. Although now dilapidated, the **Upper Shivalaya temple** is one of the earliest Chalukyan buildings. Scenes from the life of Krishna decorate the base and various images of him can be seen between pilasters on the walls. Only the sanctuary and tower of the **Lower Shivalaya** survive. Perched on a rock, the **Malegitti Shivalaya** (late seventh century) is the finest southern-style early Chalukyan temple. Its shrine is adjoined by a pillared hallway with small windows hewn out of stone and a single image on each side: Vishnu on the north and Shiva on the south.

Banashankari

A pleasant, short excursion, 5km to the northwest of Badami, leads to the temple village of **Banashankari**, believed to date back to the sixth century – although much of it was built during the Maratha period of the eighteenth century. Banashankari is worth a visit more for the gentle atmosphere that prevails, than for its architectural interest. Dedicated to Shiva's consort Parvati, the shrine, with large bathing tank, is the most important living temple of the region. It attracts a steady stream of devotees throughout the year, especially during the *rath* (chariot) festival (held according to the lunar calendar, either during January or February), when the deity is led through the streets in a procession. At this time the quiet atmosphere of the village gives way to the fun and excitement of a large and hectic country fair, complete with circus acts, stalls selling everything from toys to food and a colourful cattle fair down the road towards Badami.

Practicalities

Badami **bus stand** – in the centre of the village on Main (Station) Rd – sees daily services to Gadag (2hr), Hospet (5hr), Hubli (3hr), Bijapur (4hr) and Kolhapur, and frequent buses to Aihole and Pattadakal. The **train station** is 5km north, along a road lined with *neem* trees; *tongas* (Rs30 or Rs5 per head shared) as well as buses and auto-rickshaws are usually available for the journey into town. A slow metre-gauge line connects Badami to Bijapur to the north and to Gadag in the south, from where you can change for trains or buses to Hospet and Hampi.

The new and friendly **tourist office** (Mon–Sat: June–March 10am–5.30pm & April–May 8am–1pm; ☎08357/65414) on Ramdurg Rd next to KSTDC *Hotel Mayura Chalukya*, can put you in touch with a **guide**. If you need to **change money**, *Hotel Mookambika* opposite the bus stand will change US dollars and sterling, but no travellers' cheques; the other place to try is the *Hotel Badami Court*.

Ambika Tours & Travels at *Hotel Mookambika* runs **tours** taking in Badami, Mahakuta, Aihole and Pattadakal and charge Rs150 per head for a minimum of three people. One of the best ways of exploring the closer sites of Mahakuta as well as the temple village of Banashankari, is to rent a **bicycle**, available at Rs3 per hour from stalls in front of the bus stand, but Aihole and Pattadakal will prove a challenging day.

ACCOMMODATION AND EATING

Of Badami's handful of **places to stay and eat**, by far the most comfortable is the *Hotel Badami Court* (☎08357/65230; ⑧), 2km west of town towards the train station. Ranged around a garden on two storeys, its 27 en-suite rooms are plain, but spacious; they serve meals and beer which, paid in dollars, is expensive. Their swimming pool should be finally ready and, despite being owned by a Bangalore travel agent who uses the hotel for his tour groups, they nearly always have vacancies. Far cheaper, the KSTDC *Hotel Mayura Chalukya* (☎08357/65046; ③), at the south side of town on Ramdurg Rd, has ten basic rooms with decrepit plumbing and peeling plaster, but, despite fearless scavenging monkeys, the gardens are pleasant and there's a restaurant. Next door, rooms are going to be available in the tourist complex, which, with attached baths and more up-to-date plumbing, should present a welcome alternative. Opposite the bus stand, the *Hotel Mookambika* (☎08357/65067; ③–⑥), is the best option in the centre of town, offering a wide range from simple doubles on the ground floor to comfortable new a/c rooms upstairs, accompanied by a restaurant where the food is good. Their *Kanchan* bar and restaurant next door is a bit more down to earth and a lot more popular with the locals. Other options are the grungy budget lodges near the bus stand such as the *Satkar* (☎08357/65417; ②) and the *Shri Laxmi Vilas* (☎08357/65077; ②); the latter has a reasonable restaurant. You may be able to talk the *chowkidar* of the spartan but clean *PWD Inspection Bungalow* (①) on Ramdurg Rd, into letting you have one of his four double rooms for a night, but these should in theory be booked ahead through the Assistant Engineer, Badami.

For food, and especially breakfast, try the *Geetha Darshini*, 50m from the bus stand; it's a South Indian fast-food restaurant without seating, but there are counters to stand at. The *iddlis*, *vadas* and *dosas* are out of this world.

Mahakuta

Another crop of seventh-century Chalukyan temples lies 15km out of Badami on the route to Pattadakal at **Mahakuta**. Four buses a day and the occasional shared tempo run to the site, but the two- to three-hour **walk** there, via an ancient, paved pilgrim trail, is well worth while, although it can get very hot; take plenty of water and an umbrella to keep off the sun. The path starts a short way beyond the museum, just before you reach the first temple complex and tank. Peeling left up the hill, it winds past a series of crumbling shrines, gateways and old watercourses and peters out into the flat plateau. The turning down to Mahakuta is easy to miss: look for a stone marker-post that reads "RP", which leads you to a steep, roughly paved stairway. At the bottom, the main temple complex is ranged around a crystal-clear spring-fed tank, popular with bathers (it is open to all) and an enjoyable dip at the end of a hot walk. On a rise above the tank next to a shady courtyard dominated by a huge banyan tree, stands the white-washed **Mahakutesvara temple** with its silver-crowned lingam. Around the base of the temple are wrapped some fine stone friezes – those on the southwest corner, depicting Shiva and Parvati with Ravana, the demon king of Lanka, are particularly accomplished. More carvings adorn the entrance and ceilings of the **Mallikarjuna temple** on the opposite side of the tank, while in the clearing outside the nearby **Sangameshwar temple** stands a gigantic stone-wheeled chariot used during the annual festival in May.

A living Shiva temple, attracting local devotees, pilgrims and a sprinkling of *sadhus*, Mahakuta may be in the minor league of Chalukyan architecture, but has, with its brooding banyan trees, a timeless atmosphere. There are a couple of teashops but no official guesthouse; if you want to stay, you may be able to negotiate one of the very basic rooms outside the temple gates.

Aihole

No fewer than 125 temples, dating from the Chalukyan and the later Rashtrakuta periods (sixth–twelfth centuries), are found in the tiny village of **AIHOLE** (Aivalli), near the banks of the Malaprabha River. Lying in clusters within the village, in surrounding fields and on rocky outcrops, many of the temples are remarkably well preserved, despite being used as dwellings and cattle-sheds. Reflecting both its geographical position and spirit of architectural experimentation, Aihole boasts northern (*nagari*) and southern (Dravida) temples, as well as variants that failed to survive subsequent stylistic developments.

Two of the temples are **rock-cut caves** dating from the sixth century. The Hindu **Ravanaphadigudi**, northeast of the centre, a Shiva shrine with a triple entrance, contains fine sculptures of Mahishasuramardini, a ten-armed Nateshan (the precursor of Shiva Nataraja) dancing with Parvati, Ganesh and the Sapta Matrikas (Seven Mothers). A central lotus design, surrounded by mythical beasts, figures and foliate decoration, adorns the ceiling. Near the entrance is Gangadhara (Shiva with the Ganga River in his hair) accompanied by Parvati and the skeleton Bringi. A two-storey cave, plain save for decoration at the entrances and a panel image of Buddha in its upper verandah, can be found partway up the hill to the southeast, overlooking the village. At the top of that hill, the Jain **Meguti** temple, which may never have been completed, bears an inscription on an outer wall dating it to 634 AD. The porch, *mandapa* hallway and upper storey above the sanctuary, which contains a seated Jain image, are later additions. You can climb up to the first floor for fine views of Aihole and surrounding country.

The late seventh to early eighth century **Durga temple** (daily 6am–6pm; Rs2, Fri free), one of the most unusual, elaborate and large in Aihole, stands close to others on open ground in the Archeological Survey compound, near the centre of the village. It derives its name not from the goddess Durga but from the Kannada *durgadagudi*, meaning "temple near the fort". Its apsidal-ended sanctuary shows influence from earlier Buddhist *chaitya* halls; another example of this curved feature, rare in Hindu monuments, can be seen in one of the *rathas* at Mamallapuram in Tamil Nadu (see p.585). Here the "northern"-style tower is probably a later addition, and is incongruously square-backed. The temple is raised on a plinth featuring bands of carved decoration. A series of pillars – many featuring amorous couples – forms an open ambulatory that continues from the porch around the whole building. Other sculptural highlights include the decoration on the entrance to the *mandapa* hallway and niche images on the outer walls of the now-empty semicircular sanctum. Remains of a small and early *gopura* gateway stand to the south. Nearby, a small **Archeological Museum** (daily except Fri 10am–5pm) displays early Chalukyan sculpture and sells the booklet *Glorious Aihole*, which includes a site map and accounts of the monuments.

Farther south, beyond several other temples, the **Ladh Khan** (the name of a Muslim who made it his home) is perhaps the best known of all at Aihole. Now thought to have been constructed at some point between the end of the sixth century and the eighth, it was dated at one time to the mid-fifth century and was seen as one of the country's temple prototypes. The basic plan is square, with a large adjoining rectangular pillared porch. Inside, twelve pillars support a raised clerestory and enclose a further four pillars; at the centre stands a Nandi bull. A small sanctuary containing a *shivalingam* is next to the back wall. Both *lingam* and Nandi may have been later additions, with the original inner sanctum located at the centre.

Practicalities

Regular **buses** run to Aihole from Badami (2hr) via Pattadakal (30min), leaving Badami at 5.30am, 7.30 am and 9pm; returning buses leave Aihole at 8am, 9am and 4pm. The only place to **stay and eat** (apart from a few *chai*-shops) in Aihole is the small, clean and spartan KSTDC *Tourist Rest House* (☎08351/68041; ①) about five minutes' walk up the main road north out of the village, next to the ASI offices. They have a "VIP" room, two doubles with bath plus two doubles and four singles without. Simple, tasty food is available by arrangement – and by candlelight during frequent power cuts. The *Kiran Bar* on the same road, but in the village, serves beer and spirits and has a restaurant.

Pattadakal

The village of **PATTADAKAL**, on a bend in the Malaprabha River 22km from Badami, served as the site of Chalukyan coronations between the seventh and eighth centuries; in fact it may only have been used for such ceremonials. Like Badami and Aihole, Pattadakal boasts fine Chalukyan architecture, with particularly large mature examples; as at Aihole, both northern and southern styles can be seen. Pattadkal's main group of monuments (daily 6am–6pm; Rs5, Fri free) stands in a well-maintained compound, next to the village, and has recently attained the status of a World Heritage Site.

Earliest among the temples, the **Sangameshvara**, also known as **Shri Vijayeshvara** (a reference to its builder, Vijayaditya Satyashraya; 696–733), shows typical southern features, such as the parapet lined with barrel-vaulted miniature roof forms and walls divided into niches flanked by pilasters. To the south, both the **Mallikarjuna** and the enormous **Virupaksha**, side by side, are in the southern style, built by two sisters who were successively the queens of Vikramaditya II (733–46). The temples were inspired by the Pallava Kailashanatha temple at Kanchipuram in Tamil Nadu, complete with enclosure wall with shrines and small *gopura* entrance way. Along with the Kanchi temple, the Virupaksha was probably one of the largest and most elaborate in India at the time. Interior pillars are carved with scenes from the *Ramayana* and *Mahabharata*, while in the Mallikarjuna the stories are from the life of Krishna. Both temples have open Nandi *mandapa* hallways and sanctuaries housing black polished stone *lingam*.

The largest northern-style temple, the **Papanatha**, farther south, was probably built after the Virupaksha in the eighth century. It features two long pillared *mandapa* hallways adjoining a small sanctuary with a narrow internal ambulatory. Outside walls feature reliefs (some of which, unusually, bear the sculptors' autographs) from the *Ramayana*, including, on the south wall, Hanuman's monkey army.

About 1km south of the village, a fine **Rashtrakuta** (ninth–tenth century) **Jain temple** is fronted by a porch and two *mandapa* hallways with twin carved elephants at the entrance. Inexplicably, the sanctuary contains a *lingam*. In the first *mandapa*, on the right, a stone staircase leads up to the roof, where there's a second, empty sanctuary. The porch is lined with bench seats interspersed with eight pillars; the doorway is elaborately decorated with mythical beasts.

Pattadakal is connected by regular state **buses** and hourly private buses to Badami (45min) and Aihole (22km; 45min). Aside from a few tea-shops and cold drinks and coconut stalls, there are no facilities. Between January 27 and 29, Pattadakal hosts an annual **dance festival** featuring dancers from all over the country.

Bijapur and the north

Boasting some of the Deccan's finest Muslim monuments, **BIJAPUR** is often billed as "The Agra of the South". The comparison is partly justified: for more than three hundred years, this was the capital of a succession of powerful rulers, whose domed mausoleums, mosques, colossal civic buildings and fortifications recall a lost golden age of unrivalled prosperity and artistic refinement. Yet there the similarities between the two cities end. A provincial market town of just 210,000 inhabitants, modern Bijapur is a world away from the urban frenzy of Agra. With the exception of the mighty **Golgumbaz**, which attracts bus-loads of day-trippers, its historic sites see only a slow trickle of tourists, while the ramshackle town centre is surprisingly laidback, dotted with peaceful green spaces and colonnaded mosque courtyards. The best **time to come** here is between November and early March; in summer Bijapur gets unbearably hot and in April and May offices shut at 1pm. Between February 6 and 7 Bijapur hosts an annual **music festival** which attracts several well-known musicians from both the Carnatic (South Indian) and the Hindustani (North Indian) classical music traditions.

Some history

Bijapur began life in the tenth century as **Vijayapura**, the Chalukyas' "City of Victory". Taken by the Vijayanagars, it passed into Muslim hands for the first time in the thirteenth century with the arrival of the Sultans of Delhi. The Bahmanis administered the area for a time, but it was only after the local rulers, the **Adil Shahis**, won independence from Bidar by expelling the Bahmani garrison and declaring this their capital that Bijapur's rise to prominence began.

Burying their differences for a brief period in the late sixteenth century, the five Muslim dynasties that issued from the breakdown of Bahmani rule – based at Galconda, Ahmednagar, Bidar and Gulbarga – formed a military alliance to defeat the Vijayanagars. The spoils of this campaign, which saw the total destruction of Vijayanagar (Hampi), funded a two-hundred-year building boom in Bijapur during which the city acquired its most impressive monuments. However, old emnities between rival Muslim sultanates on the Deccan soon resurfaced, and the Adil Shahis' royal coffers were gradually squandered on fruitless and protracted wars. By the time the British arrived on the scene in the eighteenth century, the Adil Shahis were a spent force, locked into a decline from which they and their capital never recovered.

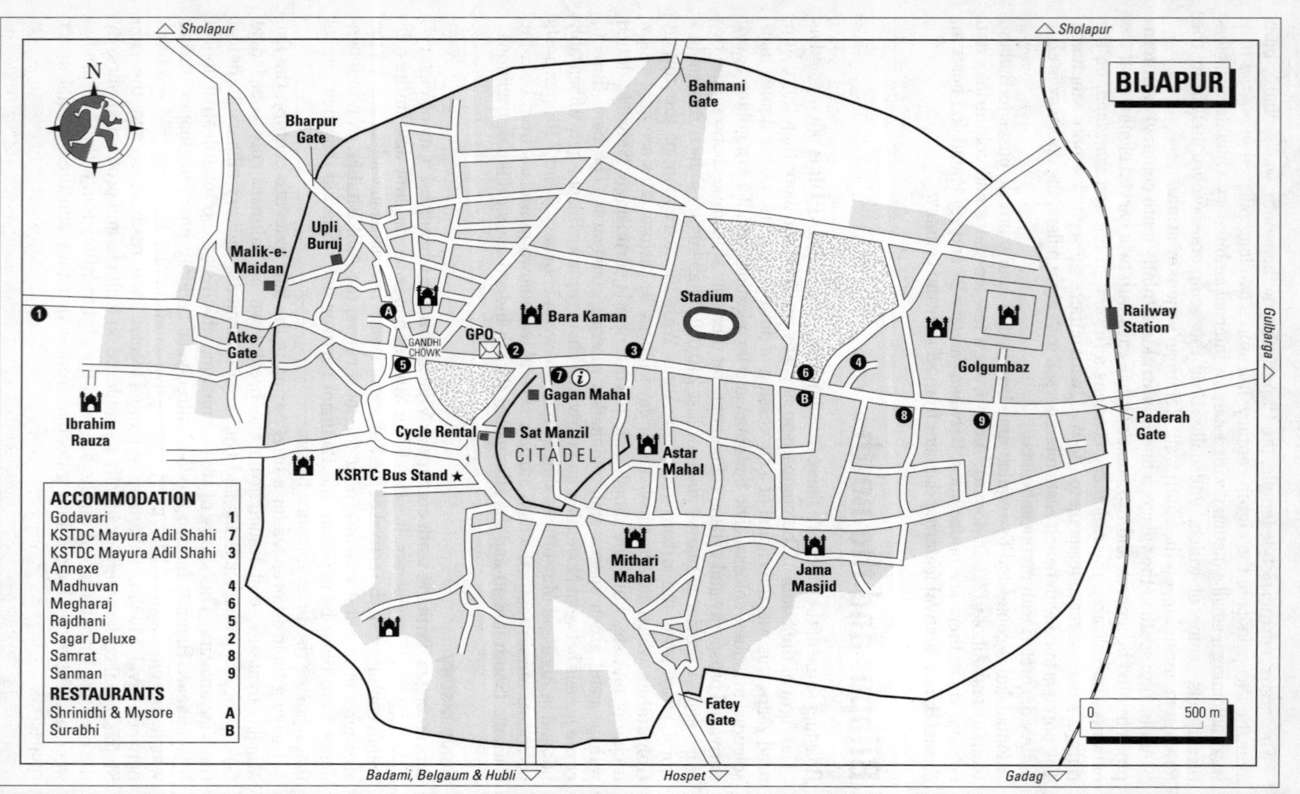
BIJAPUR
Sholapur
Sholapur
N
Bahmani Gate
Bharpur Gate
Upli Buruj
Malik-e-Maidan
Atke Gate
Ibrahim Rauza
Bara Kaman
GPO
GANDHI CHOWK
Stadium
Railway Station
Gulbarga
Golgumbaz
Paderah Gate
Gagan Mahal
Cycle Rental
Sat Manzil
CITADEL
Astar Mahal
KSRTC Bus Stand
Mithari Mahal
Jama Masjid
Fatey Gate
0
500 m
Badami, Belgaum & Hubli
Hospet
Gadag
ACCOMMODATION
Godavari 1
KSTDC Mayura Adil Shahi 7
KSTDC Mayura Adil Shahi Annexe 3
Madhuvan 4
Megharaj 6
Rajdhani 5
Sagar Deluxe 2
Samrat 8
Sanman 9
RESTAURANTS
Shrinidhi & Mysore A
Surabhi B

The town and monuments

Unlike most medieval Muslim strongholds, Bijapur lacked natural rock defences and had to be strengthened by the Adil Shahis with huge **fortified walls**. Extending some 10km around the town, these ramparts, studded with cannon emplacements (*burjes*) and watchtowers, are breached in five points by *darwazas*, or strong gateways, and several smaller postern gates (*didis*). In the middle of the town, a further hoop of crenellated battlements encircled Bijapur's **citadel**, site of the sultans' apartments and durbar hall, of which only fragments remain. The Adil Shahis' **tombs** are scattered around the outskirts, while most of the important **mosques** lie southeast of the citadel.

It's possible to see Bijapur's highlights in a day, although most people stay for three or four nights, taking in the monuments at a more leisurely pace. Our account covers the sights from east to west, beginning with the Golgumbaz – which you should aim to visit at around 6am, before the bus parties descend – and ending with the exquisite Ibrahim Rauza, an atmospheric spot to enjoy the sunset.

The Golgumbaz

The vast **Golgumbaz** mausoleum (daily 6am–6pm; Rs2, Fri free), Bijapur's most famous building, soars above the town's east walls, visible for miles in every direction. Built towards the end of the Adil Shahis' reign, the Golgumbaz is a fitting monument to a dynasty on its last legs – pompous, decadent and ill-proportioned, but conceived on an irresistibly awesome scale.

The cubic tomb, enclosing a 170-square-metre hall, is crowned with a single hemispherical **dome**, the largest in the world after St Peter's in Rome (which is only 5m wider). Spiral staircases wind up the four seven-storey octagonal towers that buttress the building to the famous **Whispering Gallery**, a three-metre-wide passage encircling the interior base of the dome from where, looking carefully down, you can get a real feel of the sheer size of the building. Get here just after opening time and you can experiment with the extraordinary acoustics; by 7am, though, the cacophony generated by bus-loads of whooping and clapping tourists means you can't hear yourself think, let alone make out whispering 38m away. A good antidote to the din is the superb **views** from the mausoleum's ramparts, which overlook the town and its monuments to the dark-soiled Deccan countryside beyond, scattered with minor tombs and ruins.

Set on a plinth in the centre of the hall below are the gravestones of the ruler who built the Golgumbaz, **Muhammed Adil Shahi**, along with those of his wife, daughter, grandson and favourite courtesan, Rambha. At one corner of the grounds stands the simple gleaming white shrine to a sufi saint of the Adil Shahi period, **Hashim Pir** which, around February, attracts *qawwals* (singers of devotional *qawwali* music) to the annual *urs* which lasts for three days.

The Jama Masjid

A little under 1km southwest of the Golgumbaz, the **Jama Masjid** (Friday Mosque) presides over the quarter that formed the centre of the city during Bijapur's nineteenth-century nadir under the Nizam of Hyderabad. It was commissioned by Ali Adil Shahi, the ruler credited with constructing the city walls and complex water-supply system, as a monument to his victory over the Vijayanagars at the Battle of Talikota in 1565, and is widely regarded as one of the finest mosques in India. As it is a living mosque, you should cover your head and limbs when entering.

Approached via a square *hauz* (ablutions tank), the main **prayer-hall** is surmounted by an elegantly proportioned central dome, with thirty-three smaller shallow domes ranged around it. Simplicity and restraint are the essence of the colonnaded hall below, divided by gently curving arches and rows of thick plaster-covered pillars. Aside from the odd geometric design and trace of yellow, blue and green tile-work, the only ornamentation is found in the mihrab, or west- (Mecca-)facing prayer niche, which is smothered in gold leaf and elaborate calligraphy. The marble floor of the hall features a grid of 2500 rectangles, known as *musallahs* (after the *musallah* prayer mats brought to mosques by worshippers). These were added by the Moghul emperor Aurangzeb, allegedly as recompense for making off with the velvet carpets, long golden chain and other valuables that originally filled the prayer-hall.

The Mithari and Astar Mahals

Continuing west from the Jama Masjid, the first monument of note is a small, ornately carved gatehouse on the south side of the road. Although of modest size, the delicate three-storey structure, known as the **Mithari Mahal**, is one of Bijapur's most beautiful buildings, with ornate projecting windows and minarets crowning its corners. Once again, Ali Adil Shahi erected it, along with the mosque behind, using gifts presented to him during a state visit to Vijayanagar. The Hindu rajas' generosity, however, did not pay off. Only a couple of years later, the Adil Shahi and his four Muslim allies sacked their city, plundering its wealth and murdering most of its inhabitants.

The lane running north from opposite the Mithari Mahal brings you to the dilapidated **Asar Mahal**, a large open-fronted hall propped up by four green-painted pillars and fronted by a large stagnant step-well. Built in 1646 by Muhammed Adil Shahi as a Hall of Justice, it was later chosen to house hairs from the Prophet's beard, thereby earning the title **Asar-i-Sharif** (Place of Illustrious Relics). In theory, women are not permitted inside to view the upper storey, where fifteen niches are decorated with mediocre, Persian-style pot-and-foliage murals, but for a little *baksheesh*, one of the girls who hang around the site will unlock the doors for you.

The citadel

Bijapur's **citadel** stands in the middle of town, hemmed in on all but its north side by battlements. Most of the buildings inside have collapsed, or have been converted into government offices, but enough remains to give a sense of how imposing this royal enclave must once have been.

The best-preserved monuments lie along, or near, the citadel's main north–south artery, Anand Mahal Rd, reached by skirting the southeast wall from the Asar Mahal, or from the north side via the road running past KSTDC's *Mayura Adil Shahi Hotel*. The latter route brings you first to the **Gagan Mahal**. Originally Ali Adil Shahi's "Heavenly Palace", this now-ruined hulk later served as a durbar hall for the Sultans, who would sit in state on the platform at the open-fronted north side, watched by crowds gathered in the grounds opposite. West off Anand Mahal Rd, the five-storeyed **Sat Manzil** was the pleasure palace of the courtesan Rambha, entombed with Muhammed Adil Shahi and his family in the Golgumbaz. In front stands an ornately carved water pavilion, the **Jal Mandir**, now left high and dry in an empty tank.

Malik-i-Maidan and Upli Buruj

Guarding the principal western entrance to the city is one of several bastions (*burje*) that punctuate Bijapur's battlements. This one, the Burj-i-Sherza (Lion Gate) sports a colossal cannon, known as the **Malik-i-Maidan**, literally "Lord of the Plains". It was brought here as war booty in the sixteenth century, and needed four hundred bullocks, ten elephants and an entire battalion to haul it up the steps to the emplacement. Inscriptions record that the cannon, whose muzzle features a relief of a monster swallowing an elephant, was cast in Ahmednagar in 1551.

A couple more discarded cannons lie atop the watchtower visible a short walk northwest. Steps wind around the outside of the oval-shaped **Upli Burj** (Upper Bastion), to a gun emplacement that affords unimpeded views over the city and plains.

The Ibrahim Rauza

Set in its own walled compound less than 1km west of the ramparts, the **Ibrahim Rauza** represents the high watermark of Bijapuri architecture (daily 6am–6pm; Rs2, Fri free). Whereas the Golgumbaz impresses primarily by its scale, the appeal of this tomb complex lies in its grace and simplicity. Beyond the reach of most bus parties, it's also a haven of peace, with cool colonnaded verandahs and flocks of viridescent parakeets careering between the mildewed domes, minarets and gleaming golden finials.

Opinions differ over whether the tomb was commissioned by Ibrahim Adil Shah (1580–1626), or his favourite wife, Taj Sultana, but the former was the first to be interred here, in a gloomy chamber whose only light enters via a series of exquisite pierced-stone (*jali*) windows. Made up of elaborate Koranic inscriptions, these are the finest examples of their kind in India. More amazing stonework decorates the exterior of the mausoleum and the equally beautiful **mosque** opposite, the cornice of whose facade features a stone chain carved from a single block. The two buildings, bristling with minarets and domed cupolas, face each other from opposite sides of a rectangular raised plinth, divided by a small reservoir and fountains. Viewed from on top of the walls that encloses the complex, you can see why its architect, Malik Sandal, added a self-congratulatory inscription in his native Persian over the tomb's south doorway, describing his masterpiece as "… A beauty of which Paradise stood amazed".

Practicalities

State and inter-state **buses** from as far afield as Mumbai and Aurangabad (see Travel Details on p.273) pull into the KSRTC bus stand on the southwest edge of the town centre; ask at the enquiries desk for exact timings, as the timetables are all in Kannada. Most of the Bangalore buses travel through Hospet, including two overnight superdeluxe coaches. Other connections include Hyderabad, several to Gulbarga and to Bidar and to Badami to the south. Most visitors head off to their hotel in a horse-drawn *tonga*, and there are plenty of (unmetered) auto-rickshaws. Just a stone's throw away from the Golgumbaz, outside the old city walls, the **train station**, 3km northeast of the bus stand, is a more inspiring point of arrival. However, services have been severely disrupted over the past few years by track conversion work, and only five passenger trains per day pass through in either direction. You can change at Gadag for Hospet and for onward express services to Bangalore; and north to Sholapur, for Mumbai and most points north. The only reliable source of information on train departures is the station itself, although most hotels keep a timetable in reception.

Besides the usual literature, the **tourist office** (Mon–Sat 10am–5.30pm; ☎08352/50359) behind the *Hotel Adil Shahi Annexe* on Station Rd can help with arranging itineraries and guides. If you need to **change money** (or travellers' cheques), head for the Canara Bank, a short walk north up the road from the vegetable market; service is painfully slow and you will need to take photocopies of the relevant pages of your passport.

Bijapur is flat, compact, relatively uncongested and generally easy to negotiate by **bicycle**; rickety Heros are available for rent from several stalls outside the bus stand for around Rs2 per hour, or staff at the KSTDC *Mayura Adil Shahi* can sort you out a bike. **Auto-rickshaws** don't have meters and charge a minimum of Rs10, with most of Bijapur covered within Rs30; they are a much more expensive way of getting around the monuments, and charge around Rs200 for a four-hour tour. **Taxis**, available from near the bus stand, charge Rs4 per kilometre.

Moving on from Bijapur is getting easier with the efficient private services such as VRL, recognizable by their distinctive yellow and black luxury coaches, travelling to Bangalore (3 buses from 7pm); a single bus to Udupi and Mangalore departs at 3pm. VRL can be booked through Vijayanand Travel, Terrace Floor, Shastri Market, Gandhi Circle (☎08352/20943). KSRTC also runs deluxe buses to Bangalore, Hubli, Mumbai and Hyderabad (via Sholapur). Trains to Gadag depart at 4.10am, 12.10pm, 6.15pm and 0.25am, while services to Sholapur leave at 7.30am, 9.40am, 3.20pm and 9.05pm.

Accommodation and eating

Accommodation standards are pretty low in Bijapur, although finding a room is rarely a problem. Most budget tourists head for the KSTDC *Mayura Adil Shahi*, which, despite its shabbiness, has a certain charm; it's also cheap and central. **Eating** is largely confined to the hotels, with the *Mayura Adil Shahi*'s dingy beer-bar-restaurant cleaning up most of the foreign tourist trade. At Gandhi Chowk, the *Shrinidhi Hotel* and the *Mysore Hotel* both serve good south Indian vegetarian food, while the *Surabhi* on Station Rd serves meat. The *Hotel Megharaj*, also on Station Rd, has a good cheap vegetarian "meals" restaurant, and the *Sagar Deluxe*, at Busreshwar Chowk, has a vegetarian and a non-vegetarian restaurant as well as a bar.

Godavari, Athani Rd (☎08352/53105). Monolithic modern but fading hotel and something of a landmark, but with pretensions beyond its class and expensive for what it is. ③–⑥.

KSTDC Mayura Adil Shahi, Anand Mahal Rd (☎08352/20934). Stone-floored rooms ranged around a leafy courtyard-garden could be a lot nicer; all have very grubby attached bathrooms, fans, holed mozzie nets, clean sheets and towels. Hot and cold drinks from the restaurant are served on the verandahs by helpful staff. The service at the restaurant itself is incredibly slow, and the food – a standard mix of veg and non-veg Indian, with some Chinese and Continental dishes – is very ordinary, but they do serve chilled beer. ②–④.

KSTDC Mayura Adil Shahi Annexe, Station Rd (☎08352/20401). Almost as dowdy as the main wing, but with larger, cleaner rooms and individual sit-outs. No restaurant. ⑤.

Madhuvan, Station Rd (☎08352/25571). The cleanest and best-appointed place in town, with a variety of rooms, from ordinary doubles to more comfortable a/c "deluxe" options but expensive for what it is. The restaurant, however, serves good-value *thalis* at lunchtime. ⑤–⑦.

Megharaj, Station Rd (☎08352/21458). Run by the affable ex-wrestler Sundara who unfortunately doesn't speak a word of English, the hotel has good-value doubles upstairs and there are even some a/c rooms. The vegetarian restaurant in the basement is cheap and good. ②–④.

Rajdhani, opposite Laxmi Talkies, near Old Head Post Office, Station Rd (☎08352/23468). Most bearable of the rock-bottom lodges in the centre, with clean rooms and a 24hr checkout. Sandwiched between two cinemas. ②.

Sagar Deluxe, next to Bara Kaman, Busreshwar Chowk (☎08352/59234). New centrally located hotel with unremarkable doubles and some a/c rooms, plus two restaurants and a bar. ③–⑤.

Samrat, Station Rd (☎08352/21620). Newish lodge at the east end of town. Institutional and not all that neat, but a fallback if the *Mayura Adil Shahi* is full. However, you can do better, and the restaurant is best avoided. ②–③.

Sanman, opposite the Golgumbaz, Station Rd (☎08352/21866). Best value among the budget places, and well placed for the train station. Good-sized rooms with mozzie nets and clean attached shower-toilets. The Udupi canteen is a stop for the bus parties, so their South Indian snacks are all freshly cooked; try the popular *puri korma* or delicious *sadar masala dosas*. ②.

Gulbarga

GULBARGA, 165km northeast of Bijapur, was the founding capital of the Bahmani dynasty and the region's principal city before the court moved to Bidar in 1424. Later captured by the Adil Shahis and Moghuls, it has remained a staunchly Muslim town, and bulbous onion-domes and mosque minarets still soar prominently above its ramshackle concrete-box skyline. The town is also famous as the birthplace of the *chisti*, or saint, Hazrat Bandah Nawaz Gesu Daraz (1320–1422), whose tomb, situated next to one of India's foremost Islamic theological colleges, is a major shrine.

In spite of Gulbarga's religious and historical significance, its **monuments** pale in comparison with those at Bijapur, and even Bidar. Unless you're particularly interested in medieval Muslim architecture, few are worth breaking a journey to see. The one exception is the tomb complex on the northeast edge of town, known as the **Dargah**. Approached via a broad bazaar, this marble-lined enclosure, plastered in mildew-streaked limewash, centres on the tomb of Hazrat Gesu Daraz, affectionately known to his devotees as "**Bandah Nawaz**", or "the long-haired one who brings comfort to others". The saint was spiritual mentor to the Bahmani rulers, and it was they who erected his beautiful double-storeyed mausoleum, now visited by hundreds of thousands of Muslim pilgrims each year. Women are not allowed inside, and must peek at the tomb – surrounded by a mother-of-pearl-inlaid wooden screen and draped with green silk – through the pierced-stone windows. Men, however, can enter to leave offerings and admire the elaborate mirror-mosaic ceiling. The same gender bar applies to the neighbouring tomb, whose interior has retained its exquisite Persian paintings. The Dargah's other important building, open to both sexes, is the **madrasa**, or theological college, founded by Bandah Nawaz and enlarged during the two centuries after his death. The syllabus here is dominated by the Koran, but the saint's own works on sufi mysticism and ethics are also still studied.

After mingling with the crowds at the Dargah, escape across town to Gulbarga's deserted **fort**. Encircled by sixteen-metre-thick crenellated walls, fifteen watchtowers and an evil-smelling stagnant moat, the great citadel now lies in ruins. Its only surviving building is the beautiful fourteenth-century **Jama Masjid**, whose elegant domes and arched gateways preside over a scrubby wasteland. Thought to have been modelled by a Moorish architect on the great Spanish mosque of Cordoba, it is unique in India for having an entirely domed prayer-hall.

Practicalities

Daily KSRTC **buses** from Bijapur, Bidar and Hospet pull in to the state bus stand on the southwest edge of town. Private mini-buses work from the roadside opposite, their conductors shouting for passengers across the main concourse. Don't be tempted to take one of these to Bidar; they only run as far as the fly-blown highway junction of Humnabad, 40km short, where you'll be stranded for hours. Gulbarga's main-line **train station**, with services to and from Mumbai, Pune, Hyderabad, Bangalore and Chennai, lies 1km east of the bus stand. **Station Road**, the town's main artery, runs due north of here past three hotels and a large artificial lake to the busy **Chowk** crossroads, at the heart of the bazaar.

Gulbarga's main sights are well spread out, so you'll need to get around by **auto-rickshaw**; fix fares in advance. For medical help, head for the town **hospital**, east of the centre next door to the *Hotel Santoosh*, which has a well-stocked pharmacy. There is nowhere in Gulbarga to change money.

ACCOMMODATION AND EATING

Gulbarga is well provided with good-value **accommodation**, and even travellers on tight budgets should be able to afford a clean room with a fan and small balcony. The one place to avoid is the grim and neglected KSTDC *Mayura Bahmani*, set in the public gardens, more of a drinking den than a hotel, and plagued by mosquitoes, although a new annexe under construction looks promising.

All the hotels listed below have **restaurants**, mostly pure veg places with a no alcohol rule. *Kamat*, the chain restaurant, has several branches in Gulbarga including a pleasant one at Station Chowk, specializing in vegetarian "meals" as well as *iddlis* and *dosas*; try *joleata roti*, a local bread cooked either hard and crisp or soft like a chapatti.

Adithya, 2-244 Main Rd, opposite Public Gardens (☎08472/24040). Unbeatable value economy doubles, or posher a/c options, in a new building. Their impeccably clean pure veg Udupi restaurant, *Pooja*, on the ground floor does great *thalis* and snacks. ③–⑥.

Pariwar, Station Rd, near the train station (☎08472/21522, fax 22039). One of the town's top hotels, and excellent value with singles for Rs125. Book ahead if you want an economy room, as these fill up by noon. The *Kamakshi Restaurant* (6am–10pm) serves quality vegetarian South Indian food, but no beer. Some a/c. ③–⑥.

Raj Rajeshwari, Vasant Nagar, Mill Rd (☎08472/25881). Just 5min from the bus stand, and good value. Well-maintained modern building with large en-suite rooms with balconies, plus a reasonable veg restaurant (strictly no alcohol). ②–③.

Santosh, Bilgundi Gardens, University Rd (☎08472/22661). Upscale, efficient chain hotel peacefully located on the eastern outskirts, with big, comfortable rooms (some a/c), sit-outs, veg and non-veg restaurants and a bar. Recommended. ③–⑤.

Southern Star, near the fort, (☎08472/24093). New and comfortable with two restaurants and a bar and some a/c rooms; the rooms at the back look onto the ramparts of the fort but across the stagnant and putrid moat. ③–⑤.

Bidar

In 1424, following the break-up of the Bahmani dynasty into five rival factions, Ahmad Shah I shifted his court from Gulbarga to a less constricted site at **BIDAR**, spurred, it is said, by grief at the death of his beloved spiritual mentor, Bandah Nawas Gesu Daraz (see p.268). Revamping the town with a new fort, splendid palaces, mosques and ornamental gardens, the Bahmanis ruled from here until 1487, when the Barid Shahis took control. They were succeeded by the Adil Shahis from Bijapur, and later the Moghuls under Aurangzeb, who annexed the region in 1656, before the Nizam of Hyderabad finally acquired the territory in the early eighteenth century.

Lost in the far northwest of Karnataka, Bidar, 284km northwest of Bijapur, is nowadays a provincial backwater, better known for its fighter-pilot training base than the monuments gently decaying in, and within sight of, its medieval walls. Yet the town, half of whose 140,000 population are still Muslim, has a gritty charm, with narrow red-dirt streets ending at arched gates, with vistas across the plains. Littered with tile-fronted tombs, rambling fortifications and old mosques, it merits a visit if you're travelling between Hyderabad (150km east) and Bijapur, although expect little in the way of Western comforts, and more than the usual amount of curious approaches from locals. Lone women travellers, especially, may find the attention more hassle than it's worth.

Bidar's sights are too spread out to be comfortably explored on foot. However, autorickshaws tend to be thin on the ground away from the main streets, and are reluctant to wait while you look around the monuments, so it's a good idea to rent a **bicycle** for the day from Rouf's only 50m east of the bus stand next to the excellent *Karnatak Juice Centre*.

The old town

The heart of Bidar is its medieval **old town**, encircled by crenellated ramparts and eight imposing gateways (*darwazas*). This predominantly Muslim quarter holds many Bahmani-era mosques, *havelis* and *khanqahs* – "monasteries" set up by the local rulers for Muslim cleric-mystics and their disciples – but its real highlight are the impressive ruins of **Mahmud Gawan's Madrasa**, or theological college, whose single minaret soars high above the city centre. Gawan, a scholar and Persian exile, was the *wazir*, or prime minister, of the Bahmani state under Muhammed Bahmani III (1463–82). A talented linguist, mathematician and inspired military strategist, he oversaw the dynasty's expansion into Karnataka and Goa, bequeathing this college as a thank-you gift to his adoptive kingdom in 1472. The distinctively Persian-style building, originally surmounted by large bulbous domes, once housed a world-famous library. However, this burnt down after being struck by lightning in 1696, while several of the walls and domes were blown away when gunpowder stored here by Aurangzeb's occupying army caught fire and exploded. Today, the *madrasa* is little more than a shell, although its elegant arched facade has retained large

BIDRI

Bidar is celebrated as the home of a unique damascene metalwork technique known as **Bidri**, developed by the Persian silversmiths that came to the area with the Bahmani court in the fifteenth century. These highly skilled artisans engraved and inlaid their traditional Iranian designs onto a metal alloy composed of lead, copper, zinc and tin, which they blackened and polished. The resulting effect – swirling silver floral motifs framed by geometric patterns and set against black backgrounds – has since become the hallmark of Muslim metalwork in India.

Bidri objets d'art are displayed in museums and galleries all over the country. But if you want to see pukka *bidri-wallahs* at work, take a walk down Bidar's **Siddiq Talim Rd**, which cuts across the south side of the old town, where skull-capped artisans tap and burnish vases, goblets, plates, spice boxes, betel-nut tins and ornamental *hookah* pipes, as well as less traditional objects – coasters, ashtrays and bangles – that crop up (at vastly inflated prices) in silver emporiums as far away as Delhi and Calcutta.

patches of the vibrant Persian glazed tile-work that once covered most of the exterior surfaces. This includes a beautiful band of Koranic calligraphy, and striking multi-coloured zigzags wrapped around the base of the one remaining *minar*, or minaret.

The fort

Presiding over the dark-soiled plains from atop a sheer-faced red laterite escarpment, Bidar's **fort**, at the far north end of the street running past the *madrasa*, was founded by the Hindu Chalukyas and strengthened by the Bahmanis in the early fifteenth century. Despite repeated sieges, it remains largely intact, encircled by 10km of ramparts that drop away in the north and west to three-hundred-metre cliffs. The main southern entrance is protected by equally imposing man-made defences: gigantic fortified gates and a triple moat formerly crossed by a series of drawbridges. Once inside, the first building of note (on the left after the third and final gateway) is the exquisite **Rangin Mahal**. Mahmud Shah built this modest "Coloured Palace" after an unsuccessful uprising of Abyssinian slaves in 1487 forced him to relocate to a safer site inside the citadel. The palace's relatively modest proportions reflect the Bahmanis' declining fortunes, but its interior comprises some of the finest surviving Islamic art in the Deccan, with superb wood-carving above the door arches and Persian-style mother-of-pearl inlay on polished black granite surfaces. If the doors to the palace are locked, ask for the keys at the nearby *ASI* **museum** (daily 8am–1pm & 2–5pm; free), which houses a missable collection of Hindu temple sculpture, weapons and Stone Age artefacts.

Opposite the museum, an expanse of gravel is all that remains of the royal gardens. This is overlooked by the austere **Solah Khamb** mosque (1327), Bidar's oldest Muslim monument, whose most outstanding feature is the intricate pierced-stone *jali* calligraphy around its central dome. From here, continue west through the ruins of the former royal enclosure – a rambling complex of half-collapsed palaces, baths, *zenanas* (women's quarters) and assembly halls – to the fort's west walls. You can complete the round of **the ramparts** in ninety minutes, taking time out to enjoy the views over the red cliffs and across the plains.

Ashtur: the Bahmani tombs

As you look from the fort's east walls, a cluster of eight bulbous white domes floats alluringly above the trees in the distance. Dating from the fifteenth century, the mausoleums at **Ashtur**, 3km east of Bidar (leave the old town via Dulhan Darwaza gate), are the final resting places of the Bahmani Sultans and their families, including the son of the ruler who first decamped from Gulbarga, Alauddin Shah I. His remains by far the most impressive **tomb**, with patches of coloured glazed tiles on its arched facade and a large dome whose interior surfaces writhe with sumptuous Persian paintings. Reflecting sunlight on to the ceiling with a small pocket mirror, the *chowkidar* picks out the highlights, among them a diamond, barely visible among the bat droppings.

The tomb of Allaudin's father, the ninth and most illustrious Bahmani Sultan, Ahmad Shah I, stands beside that of his son, decorated with Persian inscriptions. Beyond this are two more minor mausoleums, followed by the partially collapsed tomb of Humayun the Cruel (1458–61), cracked open by a bolt of lightning. Continuing along the line, you can chart the gradual decline of the Bahmanis as the mausoleums diminish in size, ending with a sad handful erected in the early sixteenth century, when the Sultans were no more than puppet rulers of the Barid Shahis.

Crowning a low hillock halfway between Ashtur and Bidar, on the north side of the road, the **Chaukhandi of Hazrat Khalil Ullah** is a beautiful octagonal-shaped tomb built by Allaudin Shah for his chief spiritual adviser. Most of the tiles have dropped off the facade, but the surviving stonework and calligraphy above the arched doorway, along with the views from the tomb's plinth, deserve a quick detour from the road.

The Badri Shahi tombs

The **tombs of the Badri Shahi** rulers, who succeeded the Bahmanis at the start of the sixteenth century, stand on the western edge of town, on the Udgir road, 200m beyond and visible from the bus stand. Although not as impressive as those of their predecessors, the mausoleums, mounted on raised plinths, occupy an attractive site. Randomly spaced rather than set in a chronological row, they are surrounded by lawns maintained by the *ASI*. The most interesting is the tomb of **Ali Barid** (1542–79), whose Mecca-facing wall was left open to the elements. A short distance southwest lies a mass grave platform for his 67 concubines, who were sent as tribute gifts by vassals of the Deccani overlord from all across the kingdom.

Practicalities

Bidar lies on a branch line of the main Mumbai–Secunderabad–Chennai rail route, and can only be reached by slow passenger **train**. The few visitors that come here invariably arrive **by bus**, at the KSRTC bus stand on the far western edge of town, which has hourly direct services from Hyderabad (3hr 30min) and Gulbarga (3hr 30min), and several a day between Bijapur (8hr) and Bangalore (12hr).

Auto-rickshaws are on hand for the short hop east along the main road to the town's only decent **hotels**. By far the best hotel in Bidar, is the *Ashoka* (☎08482/26249; ②–③), 1500m from the bus stand past Dr Ambedkar Chowk, which is comfortable and has good-value deluxe rooms, some with a/c. The same management is also due to open the *Hotel Mayura* opposite the bus stand. The KSTDC *Mayura Barid Shahi* (☎08482/26571; ②) on Udgir Rd, less than 1km from the bus stand, has been undergoing extensive renovation and should now be much improved.

Finding somewhere good to **eat** is not a problem in Bidar, thanks to the open-air garden restaurant next to the *Mayura Barid Shahi*. The food here – mostly North Indian with a handful of Chinese options – is commendable and the service attentive (try the veg *malai kofta*, or chicken *tikka*); they also do chilled beer and ice-cream. Equally good, the restaurant at the *Ashoka* offers a good selection of North Indian veg and meat dishes and serves cold beer. Also recommended, and much cheaper, is the popular *Udupi Krishna* restaurant, five minutes east of the *Mayuri Badri Shahi*, overlooking the *chowk*, which serves up unlimited pure veg *thalis* for lunch; they have a "family room" for women, too, and open early (around 7.30am) for piping hot South Indian breakfasts.

travel details

When this book went to press, the changeover from metre- to broad-gauge track was disrupting some **train services** in Karnataka especially those to Hassan; check the current situation with Indian Railways. Note that no individual route appears more than once in these listings; check against where you want to get to as well as where you're coming from.

Trains

Bangalore to: Ahmedabad (6 weekly; 37hr); Calcutta (1 weekly; 26hr 15min); Chennai (4–5 daily; 5–7hr); Coimbatore (3 daily; 18–20hr); Delhi (2 daily; 33hr 15min–41hr 45min); Gulburga (2 daily; 12hr); Hospet (1 daily; 10hr); Hubli (3 daily; 7hr 30min–11hr 45min); Hyderabad (1 daily; 16hr 15min); Kochi (Ernakulam) (2 daily; 13hr 10min–16hr 20min); Mangalore (3 weekly; 18–24hr); Mumbai (4 daily; 22hr 30min–24hr); Mysore (3–4 daily; 2hr 30min–3hr); Pune (2 weekly; 20hr); Thiruvananthapuram (1 daily; 18hr).

Bijapur to: Badami (5 daily; 4hr 20min); Gadag (5 daily; 6hr); Sholapur (5 daily; 3hr 30min).

Hassan to: Mangalore (1 daily, but subject to disruptions in service; 8hr); Mysore (3 daily; 4hr).

Hubli to: Hospet (1 daily; 3hr 10min); Mumbai (4 weekly; 16hr 10min); Pune (5 weekly; 12hr 35min–13hr).

Karwar to: Ernakulam (2–3 daily; 14hr 10min–16hr); Goa (6 daily; 1hr 10min–2hr); Mangalore (3 daily; 4hr 20min–6hr); Thiruvananthapuram (1 weekly; 20hr).

Mangalore to: Chennai (2 daily; 15–16hr); Kochi (Ernakulam) (3 daily; 7hr 45min); Goa (2 daily; 6–7hr); Gokarn (1 daily; 4hr); Kollam (3 daily; 15hr 50min); Kozhikode (3 daily; 5hr); Thiruvananthapuram (3 daily; 16hr).

Mysore to: Bangalore (4 daily; 2hr–3hr 30min); Hassan (4 daily; 2hr 25min–4hr).

Buses

Bangalore to: Bidar (2 daily; 12hr); Chennai (9 daily; 9hr); Coimbatore (2 daily; 9hr); Goa (5 daily; 14hr); Gulburga (2 daily; 15hr); Hassan (every 30min; 4hr); Hospet (3 daily; 8hr); Hubli (6 daily; 9hr); Hyderabad (10 daily; 16hr); Jog Falls (1 nightly; 8hr); Karwar (3 daily; 12hr); Kodaikanal (1 nightly; 12hr); Kochi (Ernakulam) (6 daily; 12hr); Kozhikode (Calicut) (6 daily; 10hr); Madikeri (16 daily; 6hr); Madurai (2 daily; 8hr); Mangalore (10 daily; 8hr); Mumbai (3 daily; 24hr); Mysore (every 15min; 3hr); Pondicherry (2 daily; 9hr); Udhagamandalam (7 daily; 8hr).

Bijapur to: Aurangabad (2 daily; 14hr); Badami (5 daily; 4hr); Bidar (2 daily; 8hr); Gulbarga (4 daily; 3hr 30min); Hospet (4 daily; 5hr); Hubli (hourly; 6hr); Hyderabad (1 daily; 1hr 30min); Mumbai (3 daily; 12hr); Pune (1 daily; 8hr); Sholapur (9 daily; 3hr).

Hassan to: Channarayapatna (hourly; 1hr); Halebid (15 daily; 1hr); Hospet (1 daily; 10hr); Mangalore (hourly; 4hr); Mysore (15 daily; 7–8hr).

Hospet to: Badami (4 daily; 5hr); Bidar (1 nightly; 10hr); Gokarn (1 daily; 10hr); Hampi (every 30min; 20min); Hyderabad (2 daily; 12hr); Mangalore (2 daily; 10hr); Mysore (3 daily; 7–8hr); Panjim (1 daily; 10hr); Vasco da Gama (1 daily; 10hr).

Hubli to: Goa (8 daily; 5hr); Hospet (hourly; 4hr); Mumbai (6 daily; 12–15hr); Sirsi (hourly; 3hr).

Mangalore to: Bijapur (1 daily; 16hr); Chaudi (6 daily; 8hr); Gokarn (1 daily; 7hr); Kannur (6 daily; 4hr); Karwar (9 daily; 8hr); Kasargode (hourly; 1hr); Kochi (Ernakulam) (1 daily; 9hr); Madikeri (hourly; 4hr); Mysore (hourly; 7hr); Panjim (6 daily; 10hr 30min); Udupi (every 10 min; 45min).

Mysore to: Channarayapatna (hourly; 2hr); Jog Falls (via Shimoga) (hourly; 7hr); Kannur (5 daily; 7hr); Kochi (5 daily; 12hr); Kozhikode (hourly; 8hr); Madikeri (hourly; 2hr 30min); Somnathpur (every 30min; 20min); Srirangapatnam (every 30 min; 20min); Udhagamandalam (12 daily; 5hr).

Flights

Bangalore to: Ahmedabad (6 weekly; 2hr 5min); Calcutta (1–2 daily; 2hr 20min); Chennai (3–5 daily; 40min–1hr); Coimbatore (8 weekly; 40min); Delhi (6–7 daily; 2hr 20min); Goa (3 weekly; 1hr); Hyderabad (2 daily; 50min); Kochi (Ernakulam) (1 daily; 50min); Kozhikode (Calicut) (2 weekly; 45min); Mangalore (3 weekly; 40min); Mumbai (9–10 daily; 1hr 20min); Pune (6 weekly; 1hr 25min); Thiruvananthapuram (4 weekly; 50min).

Hubli to: Mumbai (3 weekly; 45 min).

Mangalore to: Chennai (6 weekly; 1hr); Mumbai (1–2 daily; 1hr 15min).

CHAPTER FOUR

KERALA

Isolated at the southwestern tip of India, sandwiched between the Arabian Sea and the forested Western Ghat mountains, the state of **KERALA**, around 550km long and 120km wide at its broadest point, is blessed with unique geographical and cultural features. Its overpowering tropical greenness, with 41 rivers and countless waterways fed by two annual monsoons, intoxicates every new visitor. Equally, Kerala's arcane rituals and spectacular festivals stimulate even the most jaded traveller, continuing centuries of tradition that have never strayed far from the realms of magic.

Travellers weary of daunting metropolises find welcome respite here. Kerala's cities are small-scale, relaxed and generally a good deal less expensive than elsewhere. The most popular is undoubtedly the great port of **Kochi** (Cochin), where Kerala's extensive history of peaceable foreign contact is evident in the atmospheric old quarters of Mattancherry and Fort Cochin – hubs of a still-thriving tea and spice trade. The capital, **Thiruvananthapuram** (Trivandrum), almost as far south as you can go, and a gateway to the nearby palm-fringed beaches of **Kovalam**, provides varied opportunities to sample Kerala's rich cultural and artistic life.

More so than anywhere else in India, the greatest joy of exploring Kerala is actually in the travelling itself, above all, by **boat,** in the spell-binding **Kuttanad** region near historic **Kollam** (Quilon) and **Alappuzha** (Alleppey) – on the southern tip of the huge **Vembanad Lake** that stretches northwards to **Kochi**. Vessels including ferries, cruisers, wooden longboats and even houseboats ply the **backwaters** in voyages which offer the chance of a close-up view of village life in India's most densely populated state. It's always easy to escape the heat of the lowlands, however, by taking off to the **hills**. Roads through a landscape dotted with churches and temples pass spice, tea, coffee and rubber plantations, as well as natural forest, en route to wildlife reserves such as **Peppara** or **Periyar**, roamed by herds of mud-caked elephants. To the north, the beautiful, forested hill district of **Wayanad** – with a large tribal population – lies within easy reach of the coast and harbours rewarding wildlife sanctuaries off the beaten track. Roads leading to the hills can be slow and in poor repair, however, and although a bus journey doesn't have the charm of a Kuttanad boat ride, you will remember it all the same, as Kerala's private bus drivers are notoriously competitive and pass each other in the most improbable of places.

Kerala is short on the historic monuments prevalent elsewhere in India, mainly because wood is the building material of choice. Moreover, the ancient temples which remain are still in use, and are more often than not closed to non-Hindus. Nonetheless, distinctive buildings throughout the state eschew grandiosity in favour of elegant understatement. Following an unwritten law, few buildings, whether houses or temples, are higher than the surrounding trees; from high ground in urban areas this creates the illusion you're surrounded by forest. Typical features of both domestic and temple architecture include long, sloping tiled and gabled roofs that minimize the excesses of both rain and sunshine, and pillared verandahs. The definitive example of such architecture, is the **Padmanabhapuram palace,** just south of the border in neighbouring Tamil Nadu, easily reached from Thiruvananthapuram.

Phenomenal amounts of money are lavished upon many, varied and often all-night **entertainments** associated with Kerala's temples. Fireworks fill the sky, while processions of gold-bedecked elephants are accompanied by some of the loudest (and

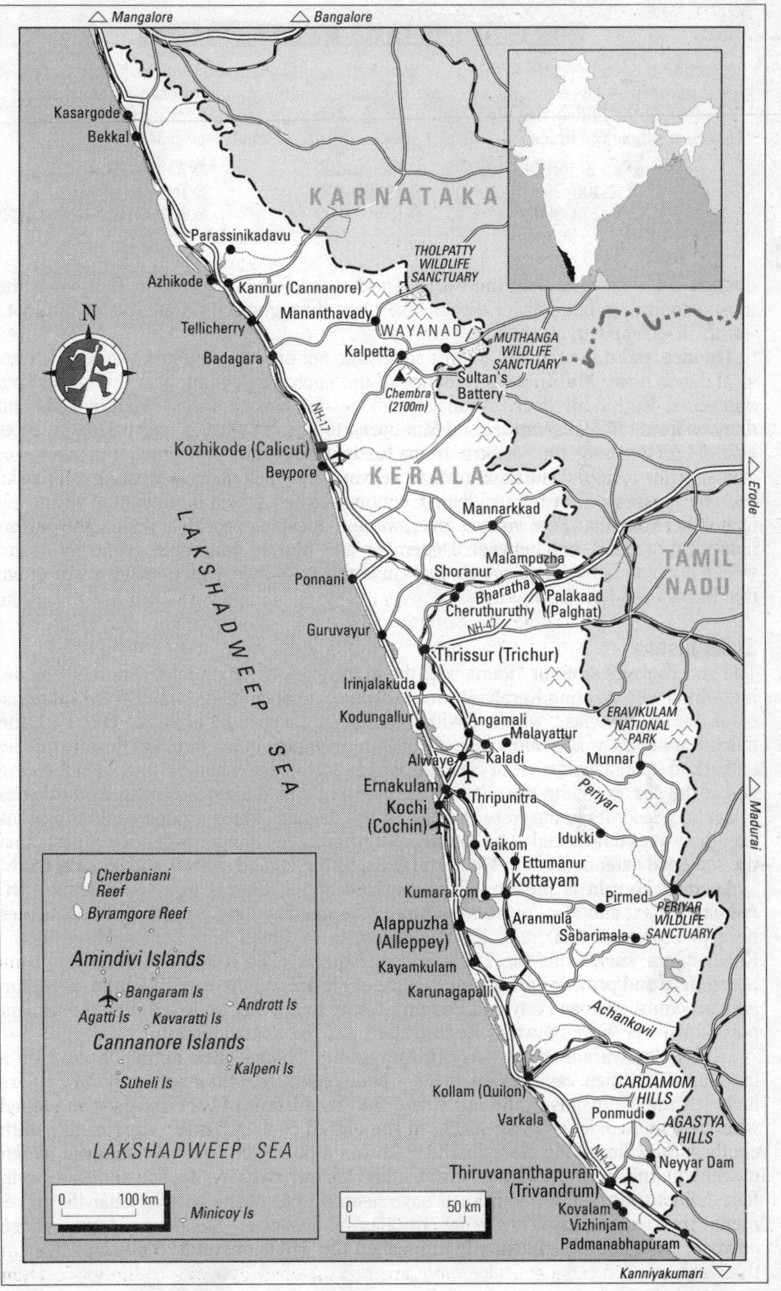
Mangalore
Bangalore
Kasargode
Bekkal
KARNATAKA
Parassinikadavu
THOLPATTY WILDLIFE SANCTUARY
Azhikode
Kannur (Cannanore)
Tellicherry
Mananthavady
WAYANAD
MUTHANGA WILDLIFE SANCTUARY
Badagara
Kalpetta
Sultan's Battery
Chembra (2100m)
NH-17
Kozhikode (Calicut)
Beypore
KERALA
Erode
LAKSHADWEEP SEA
Mannarkkad
Malampuzha
TAMIL NADU
Ponnani
Shoranur
Bharatha
Palakaad (Palghat)
Cheruthuruthy
NH-47
Guruvayur
Thrissur (Trichur)
Irinjalakuda
ERAVIKULAM NATIONAL PARK
Kodungallur
Angamali
Malayattur
Alwaye
Kaladi
Munnar
Periyar
Ernakulam
Thripunitra
Madurai
Kochi (Cochin)
Idukki
Vaikom
Ettumanur
Kottayam
Kumarakom
Pirmed
PERIYAR WILDLIFE SANCTUARY
Alappuzha (Alleppey)
Aranmula
Sabarimala
Kayamkulam
Karunagapalli
Achankovil
Cherbaniani Reef
Byramgore Reef
Amindivi Islands
Bangaram Is
Andrott Is
Agatti Is
Kavaratti Is
Cannanore Islands
Kalpeni Is
Suheli Is
LAKSHADWEEP SEA
0 100 km
Minicoy Is
0 50 km
CARDAMOM HILLS
Kollam (Quilon)
Ponmudi
Varkala
AGASTYA HILLS
NH-47
Neyyar Dam
Thiruvananthapuram (Trivandrum)
Kovalam
Vizhinjam
Padmanabhapuram
Kanniyakumari

ACCOMMODATION PRICE CODES

All accommodation prices in this book have been coded using the symbols below. In principle the prices given are for the least expensive double rooms in each establishment; however, some hotels, usually in category ①, offer rates per bed rather than per room. Taxes are included unless specifically stated. For more details, see p.34.

① up to Rs100	④ Rs300–400	⑦ Rs900–1500
② Rs100–200	⑤ Rs400–600	⑧ Rs1500–2500
③ Rs200–300	⑥ Rs600–900	⑨ Rs2500 and upwards

deftest) drum orchestras in the world. The famous **Puram** festival in Thrissur is the most astonishing, but smaller events take place throughout the state – often outdoors – with all welcome to attend.

Theatre and **dance** styles abound in Kerala; not only the region's own female classical dance form, **Mohiniattam** (dance of the enchantress), but also the martial-art-influenced **Kathakali** dance drama, which has for four centuries brought gods and demons from the *Mahabharata* and *Ramayana* to Keralan villages (see p.610). Its 2000-year-old predecessor, the Sanskrit drama **Kutiyattam**, is still performed by a handful of artists, while localized rituals known as **Teyyam**, in which dancers wearing tall masks become "possessed" by temple deities, continue to be a potent ingredient of village life in northern Kerala. Few visitors ever witness these extraordinary all-night performances first hand, but between December and March, you could profitably spend weeks hopping between village festivals in northern Kerala, experiencing a way of life that has altered little in centuries.

Some history

The god **Parasurama**, or "Rama with the battle axe", the sixth incarnation of Vishnu, is credited with creating Kerala. Born a *brahmin*, he set out to re-establish the supremacy of the priestly class, whose position had been usurped by arrogant *kshatryas*, the martial aristocracy. *Brahmins* were forbidden to engage in warfare, but despite this he embarked upon a campaign of carnage, which only ended when Varuna, the all-seeing god of the sea, gave him the chance to create a new land from the ocean, for *brahmins* to live in peace. Its limits were defined by the distance Parashurama could throw his axe; the waves duly receded up to the point where it fell. Fossil evidence suggests that the sea once extended to the Western Ghats, so the legend reflects a geological truth.

Ancient Kerala is mentioned as the land of the Cheras in a third-century BC Ashokan edict, and also in the *Ramayana* (the monkey king Sugriva sent emissaries here in search of Sita), and the *Mahabharata* (a Chera king sent soldiers to the Kurukshetra war), while the Tamil *Silappadikaram* (The Jewelled Anklet) was composed here and provides a valuable picture of life around the time of Christ. Early foreign accounts, such as Pliny and Ptolemy, testify to thriving trade between the ancient port of Muziris (now known as Kodungallur) and the Roman empire.

Little is known about the early history of the Cheras; their dominion covered a large area, but their capital Vanji has not been identified. Other contemporary rulers included the Nannanas in the north and the Ay chieftains in the south, who battled with the Pandyas from Tamil Nadu, in the eighth century. At the start of the ninth century, the Chera king Kulashekhara Alvar – a poet-saint of the Vaishnavite *bhakti* movement known as the *alvars* – established his own dynasty. His son and successor, Rajashekharavarman, is thought to have been a saint of the parallel Shaivite movement, the *nayannars*. The great Keralan philosopher Shankaracharya, whose *advaitya* (non-dualist) philosophy influenced the whole of Hindu India, also lived at this time.

Eventually, the prosperity acquired by the Cheras through trade with China and the Arab world proved too much of a temptation for the neighbouring **Chola** empire; at the end of the tenth century, they embarked upon a hundred years of sporadic warfare with the Cheras. Around 1100, the Cheras lost their capital at Mahodayapuram in the north, and shifted south to establish a new capital at Kollam (Quilon).

When the **Portuguese** ambassador/general Vasco da Gama and his fleet first arrived in India in 1498, people were as much astounded by their recklessness in sailing so close to Calicut during monsoon, as by their physical and sartorial strangeness. Crowds filled the streets of Calicut to see them, and a Moroccan found a way to communicate with them. Eager to meet the king – whom they believed to be a Christian –

THE FESTIVALS OF KERALA

Catching one of the numerous festivals – **Utsavam** – held throughout the year, will make a visit to Kerala all the more rewarding. Perhaps one of the greatest spectacles of the festivals are the **elephant processions**, which feature particularly strongly in temple festivals known as **Puram** – the celebration of local deities, usually a goddess. One of the highlights of the elephant parades is the Kudamattom ritual, when the colourful parasols atop the elephants are changed in synchronized motion. The *Puram* festivals originate from the tradition of taking the local deity in a procession, accompanied by drums and fanfare, to receive offerings at the end of the harvest period. The most remarkable of all the *Puram* festivals are held in the town of **Thrissur** (April/May), when deities from the surrounding countryside are brought together in celebration. *Puram* festivals are not exclusive to Thrissur, they are held in several towns and villages throughout central Kerala including Cherai on the northern outskirts of Kochi/Ernakulam, and in and around Palakaad. The annual eight-day elephant procession at Ernakulam's Shiva temple (Jan/Feb) is not to be missed, and neither is the **Arat** festival held in Thiruvananthapuram when the deity is led to sea escorted by elephants (March/April & Oct/Nov). At Guruvayur (Feb/March), an **elephant race** is held, and, although the temple itself is off-limits to non-Hindus, the public part of the festival showcases over forty elephants. **Onam**, the annual harvest festival found throughout Kerala (Aug/Sept), also features elephant processions and water carnivals – one of the best of these is at **Aranmula**, near the town of Kottayam, which holds a **snakeboat race** consisting of long boats each with two lines of rowers. The most famous and spectacular of all the snakeboat races, the **Nehru Trophy Boat Race**, is held at Alappuzha (Aug), and unlike the light-hearted festival spirit of Aranmula, is taken very seriously.

Many Keralan festivals feature **classical music** and **dance**, and provide an excellent opportunity to catch a **Kathakali** performance, in a genuine setting (see p.610 for further detail on Kathakali dance). On the outskirts of Ernakulam, the **Shri Purnatrayisa temple** in the small town of Thripunitra, runs an all-night Kathakali performance during its annual festival (Oct/Nov). The royal family of Travancore are great patrons of the arts and hold a yearly **Carnatic music** festival, at the Puttan Malika palace in Thiruvananthapuram. Probably the best place to experience one of the numerous performing art forms of Kerala and other regions of South India, however, is at Cheruthuruthy near Thrissur, where an annual performing arts festival is held every year towards the end of December. **Christmas**, when the climate is pleasant, is also a good time to travel in Kerala and gives you the opportunity to attend a Christian church service. Fort Cochin has several churches, including the historic church of St Francis, which hosts an extremely popular carol service where the attendance is large and the crowds spill onto the street. Another notable Christian festival is held yearly in early January at Mar Thoma Pontifical Shrine near Kodungallur; devotees process to the ancient site, with colourfully decorated carts laden with gifts. Unfortunately, the festivals of Kerala are too numerous to list here, but local tourist offices usually provide current information, and the Kerala Government's tourist department publishes a useful little booklet, *Fairs and Festivals of Kerala*, every year.

the Portuguese were escorted in torrential rain to his palace. However, Vasco da Gama soon established that the gifts he had brought from the king of Portugal had not made the good impression he had hoped for. The *zamorin* (raja) wanted silver and gold, not a few silk clothes and a sack of sugar.

Vasco da Gama, after such diplomatic initiatives as the kidnapping, mutilation and murder of assorted locals, came to an agreement of sorts with the *zamorin*, after which he pressed on to demand exclusive rights to the spice trade. He was determined to squeeze out the Keralan Muslim (Mappila) traders who for centuries had been a respected section of the community – acting as middlemen between local producers and traders in the Middle East. Exploiting an existing enmity between the royal families of Cochin and Calicut, Vasco da Gama turned to Cochin, which became the site of India's first Portuguese fortress in 1503. The city's strategic position enabled the Portuguese to break the Middle Eastern monopoly of trade with western India. Unlike previous visitors, they introduced new agricultural products such as cashew and tobacco, and for the first time turned coconut into a cash crop, having recognized the value of its by-products: coir rope and matting.

The rivalry between Cochin and Calicut also allowed other colonial powers to move in; both the Dutch, who forcibly expelled the Portuguese from their forts, and the British, in the shape of the East India Company, firmly established themselves early in the seventeenth century. During the 1700s, first Raja Marthanda Varma, then Tipu Sultan of Mysore, carved out independent territories, but the defeat of Tipu Sultan by the British in 1792 left the British in control right up until Independence.

Kerala today can claim some of the most startling **radical** credentials in India. In 1957 it was the first state in the world to elect a communist government democratically, and, despite having one of the lowest per capita incomes in the country, it currently has the most equitable land distribution, due to uncompromising reforms made during the 1960s and 1970s. In 1996, the Left Democratic Front, led by the Communist Party of India (Marxist), retook the state from the Congress-led United Democratic Front, which had been in power for five years. Poverty is not absent, but it appears far less acute than in other parts of India. Kerala is also justly proud of its reputation for health care and education, with a literacy rate that stands, officially at least, at one hundred percent. Industrial development is negligible, however, with potential investors from outside tending to fight shy of dealing with a politicized workforce. Many Keralans find themselves obliged to leave home to seek work, especially in the Gulf. The resultant influx of petro-dollars seems only to have the negative effect of increasing inflation.

Thiruvananthapuram (Trivandrum)

Kerala's capital, the coastal city of **THIRUVANANTHAPURAM** (still widely and more commonly known as **TRIVANDRUM**), is set on seven low hills, 87km from the southern tip of India. Despite its administrative importance – demonstrated by wide roads, multi-storey office blocks and gleaming white colonial buildings – it's a decidedly easy-going city, with an attractive mixture of narrow backstreets, traditional red-tiled gabled houses and acres of palm trees and parks breaking up the bustle of its modern concrete centre.

Although it has few monuments as such, as a window on Keralan culture Thiruvananthapuram is an ideal first stop in the state. The oldest, most interesting, part of town is the **Fort** area, which encompasses the **Shri Padmanabhaswamy temple** and **Puttan Malika palace** to the south. Important showcases for painting, crafts and sculpture, the **Shri Chitra Art Gallery** and **Napier Museum**, stand together in a park to the north. In addition, schools specializing in the martial art Kalarippayat, and the dance/theatre forms of Kathakali and Kutiyattam, showcase the Keralan obsession with physical training and ability.

THIRUVANANTHAPURAM (TRIVANDRUM)
ACCOMMODATION
Greenland Lodging 13
Hazeen 9
Highland 12
Horizon 7
Jas 10
KTDC Chaithram 14
KTDC Mascot 1
Lucia Continental 15
Manacaud 11
Navratna 5
Pankaj 4
Prasanth 8
Residency Tower 6
South Park 2
YWCA 3
RESTAURANTS
Anand Bhavan C
Arya Niwas D
Indian Coffee House A
Indian Coffee House II F
Kalavara B
Prime Restaurant E
Kollam & NH17
General Hospital
Airport (6 km)
Kovalam
Indian Airlines
Sri Chitra Art Gallery
Vellayambalam Palace
Air India
Zoo
MUSEUM RD
Museum of Science & Technology
Napier Museum, Open Air Theatre & Natural History Museum
MAIN CENTRAL RD
Library
Stadium
VAZHUTHACUD
Forest Museum
Connemara Market
SPENCER JCTN
BAKERY JCTN
VAZHUTHACUD ROAD
Air Lanka
DC Books
Secretariat
STATUE RD
MAHATMA GANDHI (MG) RD
Foreigners Registration Office
Telegraph Office
YMCA RD
VANCHIYUR
Aries Travel
PRESS RD
Chachu Nehru Children's Museum
THYCAUD
TAIKKAD HOSPITAL RD
MANJALIKULAM RD
Swastik Tours
GPO
Ayurveda College
COLLEGE JCTN
SS COIL RD
ARISTO ROAD
CHETTIKULANGARA RD
Tourist Reception Centre
KSRTC Bus Stand
New Theatre
CENTRAL STATION RD
Railway Station
THAMPANOOR
THAKARAPARAMBU RD
POWER HOUSE RD
PADMAVILASAM RD
FORT
Tank
City & Local Bus Stand
CHENTITTA
N
Sri Padmanabhaswamy Temple
CHALI BAZAR RD
CHALAI
Wall Street Finances
Buses to Kovalam
Puttan Malika Palace
0
250 m

Many travellers, however, choose to pass straight through Thiruvananthapuram, lured by the promise of **Kovalam**'s palm-fringed beaches. A mere twenty-minute bus ride south, this popular resort is close enough to use as a base to see the city, although the recent upsurge in package tourism means it's far from the low-key, inexpensive travellers' hangout it used to be.

Arrival

The airport (connected to most major Indian cities, as well as to Sri Lanka, the Maldives and the Middle East), with information and foreign exchange facilities, is 6km southwest of town and serviced by an airport bus and bus #14 to and from the **City bus stand**. Auto-rickshaws will run you into the centre for around Rs40, and there is also a handy pre-paid taxi service.

If you are heading straight out to Kovalam, you may find that a pre-paid taxi is almost as cheap as an auto-rickshaw. **Auto-rickshaws**, who don't always like using their meters – which start at Rs6 – run to Kovalam for around Rs60–80, and normal **taxis** charge around Rs150. **Local buses** (to Kovalam for example) go from the City bus stand, East Fort.

In the city the long-distance *KSRTC* **Thampanoor bus stand** (☎0471/323886) and **train station** (☎0471/329246 & 132) face each other across Station Rd in the southeast – a short walk east of Overbridge Junction, where the long north–south **MG Road** bisects the city.

Information, tours and communications

There are a couple of **tourist offices** at the **airport**, which are open during flight times. The Government of India has a counter (☎0471/501498), which offers general information regarding Kerala and the adjacent states, while the Government of Kerala has two counters – one at the domestic terminal (☎0471/501085), and the other at the international terminal (☎0471/502298), offering Kerala-specific information, including details of backwater cruises. The Government of Kerala also has an information office in the main block at the Thampanoor **bus stand** (Mon–Sat 10am–5pm; ☎0471/327224), which in addition to providing information and maps, also sells tickets for backwater cruises between Kollam and Alappuzha. They have another counter at the **train station** (☎0471/334470).

The best organized of all the South Indian tourist corporations, the **Kerala Tourist Development Corporation** (KTDC) runs several key hotels and organizes guided tours throughout the region. For further information, try one of their offices listed below, or contact them through their head office at Mascot Square (☎0471/308976, fax 314406; *www.ktdc.com*). They have an office in the KTDC *Chaithram Hotel*, Station Rd

THE CITY OF THE SNAKE ANANTHA

Thiruvananthapuram was the capital of the kingdom of Travancore from 1750 until 1956, when the state of Kerala was created. Its name (formally readopted to replace "Trivandrum"), derives from *thiru-anantha-puram*, or "the holy city of Anantha", the coiled snake on which the god Vishnu reclines in the midst of the cosmic ocean.

Vishnu is given a special name for this non-activity – *Padma-nabha* (lotus-navel) – and is invariably depicted lying on the sacred snake with a lotus growing umbilically from his navel. The god Brahma sits inside the lotus, which represents the beginning of a new world age. Padmanabha is the principal deity of the royal family of Travancore and of Thiruvananthapuram's **Shri Padmanabhaswamy temple**.

(daily 6am–10pm; ☎0471/330031), which primarily handles bookings for hotels and sells tickets for their **guided tours**, but is also good for general information. The KTDC's main visitor centre (☎0471/321132), opposite the Napier Museum at Park View, is not so conveniently located. Most of the KTDC tours, including the city tour (daily 8am–7pm; Rs95), are far too rushed, but if you're pushed for time try the **Cape Comorin** tour (daily 7.30am–9pm; Rs230), which takes in Padmanabhapuram palace (except Mon), Kovalam, Suchindram temple and Kanniyakumari.

Several smaller independent companies are starting **backwater cruises** within striking distance of Thiruvananthapuram, for those without the time to explore the much more rewarding Kuttanad region; try Island Queen at Pazhikkara, Pachalloor (☎0471/481559).

The **GPO**, with poste restante (daily 8am–6pm), is in the Vanchiyur district, a short distance west of MG Rd. The **Telegraph Office**, opposite the Secretariat on MG Rd, is open around the clock. Several banks and agencies **change money**, including the State Bank of India, near the Secretariat on MG Rd (Mon–Fri 10am–2pm, Sat 10am–noon), the very efficient Wall Street Finances, behind the *Lucia Continental Hotel* in East Fort (Mon–Sat 10am–6pm; ☎0471/450659) and the Central Reserve Bank in the lobby of the KTDC *Chaithram Hotel*. At the Great Indian Tour Company, Mullassery Tavern, Vanross Junction, east off MG Rd (☎0471/331422 or 331516, fax 330579), American Express will make encashments on credit cards and travellers' cheques. Thomas Cook has a counter at the airport and an office at Tourindia, MG Rd (☎ & fax 0471/331507).

The City

The historical and spiritual heart of Thiruvananthapuram is in the **Fort area**, at the southern end of **MG Road**, which encloses the **Shri Padmanabhaswamy Vishnu temple**. Following MG Rd north leads you through the main shopping district, which is busy all day, and especially choked when one of the frequent, but generally orderly, political demonstrations converges on the grand colonial **Secretariat** building halfway along. The whole centre can be explored easily on foot, though you might be glad of a rickshaw ride back from the museums and parks, which are close to the top end of the road.

Fort area

The solid but unremarkable fort gateway leads from near the Kovalam bus stand at East Fort to the **Shri Padmanabhaswamy temple**, which is still controlled by the Travancore royal family. Unusually for Kerala it is built in the Dravidian style of Tamil Nadu, with a tall *gopura* gateway, surrounded by high fortress-like walls. It is closed to non-Hindus, and little can be seen from outside, apart from that is, the seven-storey *gopura*.

Most of the temple buildings date from the eighteenth century, and were additions made by Raja Marthanda Varma to a much older shrine. According to legend, the temple was founded after Vishnu – disguised as a beautiful child – merged into a huge tree in the forest, which immediately crashed to the ground. There it transformed into an image of the reclining Vishnu, a full 13km long. Divakara, a sage who witnessed this, was frustrated by his limited human vision, and prayed to Vishnu to assume a form that he could view in its entirety. Vishnu complied, and the temple appeared. The area in front of the temple, where devotees bathe in a huge tank, is thronged with stalls selling religious souvenirs such as shell necklaces, *puja* offerings, jasmine and marigolds, as well as the ubiquitous plaster-cast models of Kathakali masks. As you approach the temple, the red-brick CVN Kalari Sangam, a **Kalarippayat martial arts** gymnasium, is on the left. Here you can watch the students practising Kalarippayat fighting exercises (Mon–Sat 6.30–8am). Visitors may join courses held in the gym, although prior experience of martial arts and/or dance is a prerequisite; three-month courses are also available for Rs500, although the fee does not cover accommodation – see the head teacher for details. You can also come here for a traditional **Ayurvedic massage**, and to consult the gym's expert Ayurvedic doctors (Mon–Sat 10am–1pm & 5–7.30pm, Sun 10am–1pm).

A path along the north side of the tank leads past the north, west and southern entrances to the temple, all guarded by bare-chested doormen armed with sticks – apparently to keep dogs away. It's an atmospheric walk, particularly in the early morning and at dusk, when devotees make their way to and from prayer (a closed iron gate bars the northern side, but everybody climbs through the gap). These little streets, in the old days of Kerala's extraordinary caste system, would have been a "no go" area – possibly on pain of death – to some members of the community.

Behind the temple on West Fort, set back from the road across open ground, the Margi School of **Kathakali** dance drama and **Kutiyattam** theatre (see p.612) is housed in Fort High School. With prior notice you can watch classes, and this is the place to ask about authentic Kathakali performances.

Puttan Malika palace

The **Puttan Malika palace** (daily 8.30am–12.30pm & 2–5.30pm; no cameras; Rs5), immediately southeast of the temple, became the seat of the Travancore rajas after they left Padmanabhapuram at the end of the nineteenth century. To generate funds for much-needed restoration, the Travancore royal family have opened the palace to the public for the first time in more than two hundred years. Although much of it remains off-limits, you can wander around some of the most impressive wings, which have been converted into a **museum**. Cool chambers, lined with delicately carved wooden screens and with highly polished plaster floors, house a crop of dusty Travancore heirlooms. Among the predictable array of portraits, royal regalia and weapons are some genuine treasures, such as a solid crystal throne given by the Dutch and some fine murals. The real highlight, however, is the typically understated, elegant Keralan architecture. Beneath sloping red-tiled roofs, hundreds of wooden pillars, carved into the forms of rampant horses, prop up the eaves, with airy verandahs projecting onto the surrounding lawns.

The royal family have always been keen patrons of the arts, and the tradition is upheld with an open-air **Carnatic music festival**, held in the grounds during the festival of Navaratri (Oct/Nov). Performers sit on the palace's raised porch, flanked by the main facade, with the spectators seated on the lawn. For details, ask at the KTDC tourist office.

MG Road: markets and shopping

An assortment of **craft shops** along **MG Road**, north of Station Rd, sell sandalwood, brass and Keralan bell-metal oil lamps (see box on p.351). The Gandhian **Khadi Gramodyog**, between Pazhavangadi and Overbridge junctions, stocks handloom cloth (dig around for the best stuff), plus radios and cassette machines manufactured by the Women's Federation. **Natesan's Antique Arts**, further up, is part of a chain that specializes in paintings, temple wood-carvings and so forth. Prices are high, but they usually have some beautiful pieces, among them some superb reproduction Thanjavur paintings and traditional inlaid chests for Kathakali costumes.

At first glance most of the **bookstores** in the area seem largely intended for exam entrants but some, such as the a/c **Continental Books** on MG Rd, stock a good choice of titles in English – mostly relating to India – and a fair selection of fiction too. Smaller, but with a wide array of English-language fiction and assorted subjects, such as philosophy, history and music, **DC Books**, on Statue Rd, on the first floor of a building above Statue Junction, is well worth a browse. Other bookshops along MG Rd include the chain store **Higginbothams** and **Paico Books**.

Almost at the top of MG Rd, on the right-hand side, the excellent little **Connemara Market** is the place to pick up odds and ends, such as dried and fresh fish, fruit, vegetables, coconut scrapers, crude wooden toys, coir, woven winnowing baskets and Christmas decorations. The workshops of several **tailors** are within the market.

Public Gardens, Zoo and museums

A minute's walk east from the north end of MG Rd, opposite the KTDC's visitor centre, you come to the entrance of Thiruvananthapuram's **Public Gardens**. As well as serving as a welcome refuge from the noise of the city – its lawns are usually filled with courting couples, students and picnicking families – the city's best museums are here in the park. The **Zoo** is in a nice enough location, but the depressing state of the animals, and the propensity of some visitors to get their kicks by taunting them, make it eminently missable (daily except Mon 9am–4.45pm; tickets sold at the Shri Chitra Art Gallery, Rs5).

The extraordinary **Government (Napier) Museum** of arts and crafts (Tues & Thurs–Sun 9am–5pm, Wed 1–5pm), completed in 1880, was an early experiment in what became known as the "Indo-Saracenic" style. The building features tiled double-storey gabled roofs, garish red, black and salmon-patterned brickwork, tall slender towers and, above the main entrance, a series of pilasters forming Islamic arches. The spectacular interior boasts stained-glass windows, a wooden ceiling and loud turquoise, pink, red and yellow stripes on the walls. The architect, Robert Fellowes Chisolm (1840–1915), set out to incorporate Keralan elements into colonial architecture; the museum was named after his employer, Lord Napier, the governor of the Madras Presidency. Highlights include fifteenth-century Keralan wood-carvings from Kulathupuzha and Thiruvattar, gold necklaces and belts, minutely detailed ivory work, a carved temple chariot (*rath*), wooden models of Guruvayur temple and an oval temple theatre (*kuttambalam*), plus twelfth-century Chola and fourteenth-century Vijayanagar bronzes.

The attractive **Shri Chitra Art Gallery** (same opening times), with its curved verandah and tiled roof, houses some splendid paintings from the Rajput, Moghul and Tanjore schools, as well as China, Tibet and Japan. The oil paintings by Raja Ravi Varma (1848–1906), who is widely credited with having introduced the medium of oil painting to India, have been criticized for their sentimentality and Western influence, but his treatment of Hindu mythological themes is both dramatic and beautiful. Also on display are the paintings of the Russian artist-philosopher and mystic, Nicholas Roerich, who arrived in India at the turn of the century. His paintings draw heavily on the deep, strong colours of his Russian background, amalgamating them with the mythical landscape of the Himalayas, where he died in 1947.

In the ethnographic collection at the **Natural History Museum** (same hours), there's a model of a Nayar *taravad* (manor house). Traditional houses that follow this *nalekettu* (four-sided) design, built around an open courtyard, are scattered throughout Kerala. Grander ones can have as many as four such courtyards – all hidden from prying eyes.

Away from the centre

The **Chachu Nehru Children's Museum** (Mon–Fri 10am–5pm), in Thycaud in the east of the city, serves as a rather dusty testament to the enthusiasm of some anonymous donor, presumably back in the 1960s. One room contains ritual masks, probably from Bengal, Rajasthan and Orissa, but the rest of the place is taken up with stamps, health-education displays and over two thousand dolls featuring figures in Indian costume, American presidents, Disney characters and British Beefeaters.

Also on the eastern side of town, visitors can, by arrangement, watch classes in the martial art of **Kalarippayat** (see box on p.285), at the PS Balachandran Nair Kalari martial arts gymnasium, Kalariyil, TC 15/854, Cotton Hill, Vazhuthakad (daily 6–8am &

FESTIVALS OF THIRUVANANTHAPURAM

The **Arat** festival, centred around the Shri Padmanabhaswamy temple, takes place bi-annually – in Meenam (March/April) and Thulam (Oct/Nov). Each time, ten days of festivities inside the temple (open to Hindus only) culminate in a procession through the streets of the city, taking the deity, Padmanabhaswamy, to the sea for ritual immersion. Five caparisoned elephants, armed guards and a *nagasvaram* (double-reed wind instrument) and *tavil* drum group are led by the Maharaja of Travancore, in his symbolic role as *kshatrya*, the servant of the god. Instead of the richly apparelled figure that might be anticipated, the Maharaja, no longer officially recognized, wears a simple white *dhoti*, with his chest bare save for the sacred thread. Rather than riding, he walks the whole way, bearing a sword. To the accompaniment of a twenty-one-gun salute and music, the procession sets off from the east gate of the temple at around 5pm, moving at a brisk pace to reach Shankhumukham Beach at sunset, about an hour later. The route is lined with devotees, many of whom honour both the god and the Maharaja. After the seashore ceremonies, the cavalcade returns to the temple at about 9pm, to be greeted by another gun salute. An extremely loud firework display rounds off the day.

For ten days in March, Muslims celebrate **Chandanakkutam** at the Beemapalli mosque, 5km southwest of the city on the coastal road towards the airport. The Hindu-influenced festival commemorates the anniversary of the death of Beema Beevi, a woman revered for her piety. On the first, most important, day, pilgrims converge on the mosque carrying earthenware pots decorated with flowers and containing money offerings. Activities such as the sword form of *daharamuttu* take place inside the mosque, while outside there is dance and music. In the early hours of the morning, a flag is brought out from Beema Beevi's tomb and taken on a procession, accompanied by a *panchavadyam* drum and horn orchestra and caparisoned elephants, practices normally associated with Hindu festivals. Once more, the rest of the night is lit up with fireworks.

6–7.30pm). Built in 1992, along traditional lines, in stone, the *kalari* fighting pit is overlooked from a height of 4m from a viewing gallery. Students, some as young as eight, train both in unarmed combat and in the use of weapons. Traditionally, the art of battle with long razorblade-like *urumi* is only taught to the teacher's successor. The school arranges short courses in Kalarippayat, and can also provide guides for forest trekking.

Accommodation

Thiruvananthapuram's mid-range and expensive **hotels** are generally cheaper than those in most state capitals, but they are not concentrated around any one district. Budget hotels, however, are grouped primarily in the streets around **Central Station Rd**; good areas to start looking include **Manjalikulam Rd**, five minutes' walk west from the train station, or the lanes off **Aristo Junction**. Note that the best of the budget places tend to be full by late afternoon. If you prefer to base yourself at the beach, head for Kovalam (see p.289).

Inexpensive

Greenland Lodging, Aristo Rd, Thampanoor (☎0471/328114). Large, efficient budget lodge, and the best there is within a stone's throw of both the bus stand and the train station; it has a 24hr checkout policy, but even so, get there early. ①.

Hazeen, off Aristo Rd (☎0471/325181). Among the best of the budget lodges, which is within easy reach of the station. There are the usual green-walled rooms, the bed linen is fresh and the tiled bathrooms immaculate. ②.

Manacaud, Manjalikulam Rd (☎0471/330360). Nothing special this one, but the best maintained of several cheap hotels on this lane. It has attached bathrooms, but the windows are small and there are no balconies. ②.

Prasanth Tourist Home, Aristo Rd, opposite *Horizon Hotel* (☎0471/327181). One of a crop of rock-bottom guesthouses built around a courtyard near the station. Reputable and family-run. *Satil* and *Salvha*, next door, are of a similar standard. ②.

YWCA, MG Rd, Spencer Junction (☎0471/477308). Offering spotless en-suite doubles in modern block. Friendly, efficient and central, this place is by far the city's best economy deal, so book ahead by phone. Men are welcome too, and single rates are available. ③.

Moderate to expensive

Highland, Manjalikulam Rd (☎0471/333200). A dependable mid-range option, which is clean, well run and a short walk from the stations. As it is part of a multistorey block, it's also the easiest place in the area to find. ③–⑥.

Horizon, Aristo Rd, 10min by taxi north from the train station (☎0471/326888). Plush and efficient business hotel, which offers good-value non-a/c rooms and a/c suites, two restaurants and a bar. There is 24hr checkout. ④–⑦.

Jas, Thycaud, Aristo Junction (☎0471/324881, fax 324443). This is a reasonable two-star place, situated in a quiet central location near the stations. The rooms are plain but pleasant, and all have TVs, Western toilets and easy chairs. ⑥–⑧.

KTDC Chaithram, Station Rd (☎0471/330977). A large, modern hotel, which is opposite the train station and adjacent to Thampanoor bus stand. It has spacious rooms (some a/c), an a/c-veg restaurant, bank, travel agent, car rental, beauty parlour, bookshop and bar. It's a good-value option, for its price range. ⑥–⑦.

KTDC Mascot, Museum Rd, near Indian Airlines (☎0471/318990). Housed in a period building with long corridors, it has huge rooms and a swimming pool but the service is rather low-key. ⑦–⑨.

Lucia Continental, East Fort (☎0471/463443, fax 463347). An upscale complex tucked away in a warren of streets near the temple, with 104 rooms plus "fantasy suites". Facilities include a restaurant, coffee shop, disco, swimming pool and a travel agent. ⑧–⑨.

KALARIPPAYAT

Started in the thirteenth-century, **Kalarippayat**, the ferocious martial art of Kerala, which uses both hand-to-hand combat and weapons, is now widely believed to have been developed by the bodyguards of medieval warlords and chieftains. There are many other theories surrounding the origins, however, including one that the martial art was introduced by the warrior sage **Parasuram**, who reclaimed the land of Kerala from the ocean by throwing his *mazhu* (battle axe) into the ocean. Others believe that **Lord Shiva** himself was the founder of Kalarippayat, and that Parasuram and **Agasthya**, another illustrious sage linked to the form, were Shiva's disciples. Yet another theory amongst the practitioners of Kalarippayat is that **Bodhi Dharma**, the Buddhist monk from South India, took the form to China and the Far East, when he made his epic journey to spread the faith.

In the eighteenth century Kalarippayat was banned by the British, but it made a strong comeback after their departure. Kalarippayat has two distinct schools – the southern system and the northern system. The southern system places particular emphasis on footwork and the use of hands in combat, involving a complicated range of moves, blows and locks. The northern system is more complex and uses four basic stages of training for battle. The first stage, **Meythari**, is a series of twelve levels of body exercise. The second stage, **Kothari**, uses wooden replica weapons. The third stage, **Ankathari**, involves training with real medieval weapons such as the *udaval* (sword), *paricha* (shield), *kadaras* (dagger), *kuntham* (spear), *gadha* (mace) and *urumi* (a long flexible sword). The final stage, **Verum Kaythari**, involves barehanded combat against an armed enemy and is for advanced practitioners only. Kalarippayat demonstrations are never dull, and injuries, although rare, do happen. Traditionally practised by the martial Nair caste, Kalarippayat is popular today with Hindus, Muslims and Christians alike.

Navaratna, southeast of Secretariat, YMCA Rd (☎0471/331784). Run-of-the-mill place, which has pleasant enough rooms and is located in the centre of town. The restaurant is reasonably priced, if dull, and serves everything from beef and pork to duck. ④–⑥.

Pankaj, opposite Secretariat, MG Rd (☎0471/464645). Stylish, well-maintained, modern hotel. Some rooms have beautiful views over trees, as does the fifth-floor restaurant. Some a/c. ⑧.

Residency Tower, Press Rd (☎0471/331661). A centrally located, mid-range business hotel with reasonable rooms and good facilities including a restaurant and a bar. ⑤–⑦.

South Park, MG Rd (☎0471/333333, fax 331861). Comfortable, business-orientated four-star with a/c rooms, restaurant and 24-hr coffee shop. Central reservation through any Welcomgroup hotel. ⑨.

Eating

Thiruvananthapuram is crying out for a **restaurant** specializing in delicious Keralan home-cooking. In the meantime, the upscale hotels, notably *South Park*, have the best **restaurants**, with Indian and Western cuisine at moderate prices. Some, such as the *Pankaj*, have rooftop restaurants with views over the city. Alternatively, try some of the roadside vans around Thattukada, which serve local cuisine including *dosas*, *parathas*, *chapattis* and Keralan beef curries – popular with Hindus as well.

Anand Bhawan, opposite Secretariat, MG Rd. Cheap, simple restaurant near the *Pankaj Hotel*, which serves up regional veg "meals".

Arya Niwas, Aristo Rd, Aristo Junction, Thampanoor. Spotless veg restaurant where you can get "meals" for less than Rs30 and an assortment of dishes such as *biryani*.

Indian Coffee House, Spencer Junction, MG Rd. Small, colonial-style building, set back from the road; a sociable place to meet local students. Serves good-value snack meals and coffee.

Indian Coffee House (II), Station Rd. This place is unbeatable for breakfast or a quick snack. Turbaned waiters serve *dosas*, *wadas*, omelettes and hot drinks in a bizarre spiral building designed by an eccentric British architect. Makes for a fascinating pit stop.

Kalavara, Press Rd. Situated on the same stretch as several bookshops, *Kalavara* is an upstairs restaurant, above a fast-food counter, which features a mixed menu and local cuisine, including pork and beef dishes. You can expect to pay around Rs70.

KTDC Chaithram, Station Rd. Two restaurants: one pure veg and the other Mughlai-style. The former, a tastefully decorated air-cooled place, is the best of the two, offering good-value Keralan specialties and a standard range of rice-based North Indian dishes. Recommended.

Prime Restaurant, Prime Square, near the train station. A comfortable restaurant with a mixed menu, generous helpings and attractive prices.

Sandha, *Pankaj Hotel*, opposite Secretariat, MG Rd. A fifth-floor restaurant with a mixed menu and good-value lunch buffet; there is also a ground-floor restaurant open for breakfast.

Listings

Ayurvedic health centres Ayurvedic treatment in one form or another is to be found throughout Kerala but for more information contact the Ayurvedic Medical College Hospital, MG Rd; for *Kayachikistsa* or traditional Ayurvedic massage and foot therapy contact Agastheswara, Ayurvedic Health Centre, Jiji Nivas, Killi, Kattakkada (☎0471/291270).

Car rental Inter-Car, Ayswarya Buildings, Press Rd (☎0471/330964); Nataraj Travels, Thampanoor (☎0471/323034); Travel India, Convent Rd (☎0471/78208); The Great Indian Tour Company, Mullassery Towers, Vanross Junction (☎0471/331516); and Travel India, opposite the Secretariat, MG Rd (☎0471/461212).

Dance and drama For Kathakali and Kutiyattam check with the Margi School (see p.282), or the tourist office on Station Rd (see pp.280–1), which organizes free dance performances at the open-air Nishagandhi Auditorium (Sept–March Sat 6.45pm).

Email Internet charges are high around Thiruvananthapuram at Rs2 per minute or Rs120 per hour. Bureaus include: the *Cyber Café*, tucked into a corner of the *Gokulum Restaurant* at KTDC *Hotel Chaitram*, as well as Tandem Communications and Panackal Enterprises, both at Statue Junction, MG Rd.

Hospitals General Hospital, near Holy Angels Convent, Vanchiyur; Ramakrishna Mission Hospital, Sastamangalam (☎0471/322125).

Pharmacies Statue Medicals, amongst others, at Statue Junction, MG Rd.

Travel agents Aries Travels (specialists for tours to the Maldives), Ayswarya Building, Press Rd (☎0471/330964); Swastik Tours and Travel, Puthenchantai, MG Rd (☎0471/331713, fax 331270); The Great Indian Tour Company, Mullassery Towers, Vanross Junction (☎0471/331516); Airtravel Enterprises (good for air tickets), New Corporation Building, MG Rd, Palayam (☎0471/327627); Tourindia (pioneering cruise and tour operators), MG Rd (☎ & fax 0471/331507); and Travel India, opposite the Secretariat, MG Rd (☎0471/461212).

Visa extension The City Police Commissioner's office (Mon–Sat 10am–5pm; ☎0471/60555), on Residency Rd, near the Women's College, Thycaud. The process takes three days to one week.

MOVING ON FROM THIRUVANATHAPURAM

Thiruvananthapuram is the main transport hub for traffic both along the coast and cross-country. Towns within a couple of hours of the capital – such as Varkala and Kollam – are most quickly and conveniently reached by **bus**, although for longer hauls you're better off travelling by **train** as both the private and state (KSRTC) buses tend to hurtle along the recently upgraded coastal highway at terrifying speeds; they're also more crowded.

For an overview of travel services to and from Thiruvananthapuram, see Kerala Travel Details, on p.365.

By air

Thiruvananthapuram's airport, 6km south of the centre, sees daily Jet Airways flights to **Chennai**, while Indian Airlines flies the same route four days a week, and twice a day to **Delhi** via **Mumbai** as well as three days a week to **Bangalore**. Air India flies to Mumbai six days a week to connect with international flights to European and other destinations. Both Gulf Air and Air India fly to Abu Dhabi, Bahrain, Doha, Dubai and Muscat in the **Gulf**, while Air India also flies to **Dhahran** and **Kuwait** as well as to Riyadh in **Saudi Arabia**. Indian Airlines flies four times a week to Malé in the **Maldives**, and Air Maldives flies the same route daily with additional flights on Fridays and Sundays. Both Indian Airlines (3 weekly) and AirLanka (6 weekly) fly to Colombo in **Sri Lanka**.

Airline offices

Indian Airlines has offices at Air Centre, Mascot Junction (☎0471/438288), and at the airport (☎0471/451537), while Jet Airways is at Akshaya Towers, first floor, Sasthamangalam Junction (☎0471/321018). Air India is on Museum Rd, Velayambalam Circle (☎0471/310310 & 328767), and the airport (☎0471/501426), while Air Lanka is based at Spencer Building, Palayam, MG Rd (☎0471/471810) and has an office at the airport (☎0471/501147). Air Maldives is on Spencer Rd (☎0471/461315) with an office at the airport too (☎0471/501344). Gulf Air, which operates regular flights to various Gulf states, is across town in Vellayambalam (☎0471/322156 & 327579). Other Middle Eastern airlines include Saudi Arabian Airlines at Baker Junction (☎0471/321321) and Oman Airways at Sasthamangalam (☎0471/328137). British Airways is at Vellayambalam (☎0471/326604) and KLM at Spencer Junction (☎0471/463531).

By bus

From the long-distance KSRTC Thampanoor **bus stand** (☎0471/323886), frequent services run north through Kerala to Kollam and Ernakulam/Kochi via Alappuzha (3hr 15min). Three buses a day go up to Kumily for the Periyar Wildlife Reserve, and one an hour to Kanniyakumari. Most buses running south are operated by the Tamil Nadu state road transport corporation, Thiruvallar; these include regular services to Madurai and Chennai. **Tickets** for all the services listed above may be booked in advance at the reservations hatch on the main bus stand concourse; note that Thiruvallar has its own counter.

continued overleaf

MOVING ON FROM THIRUVANATHAPURAM (contd)

By train

Kerala's capital is well connected **by train** to other towns and cities in the country; although getting seats at short notice on long-haul journeys can be a problem. **Reservations** should be made as far in advance as possible from the computerized booking office at the station (Mon–Sat 8am–2pm & 2.15–8pm, Sun 8am–2pm). Sleepers are sold throughout Kerala on a first-come, first-served basis, not on local stations' quotas.

The following trains are recommended as the **fastest** and/or **most convenient** from Thiruvananthapuram.

Recommended trains from Thiruvananthapuram

Destination	Name	Number	Frequency	Departs	Total time
Bangalore	*Kanniyakumari–Bangalore Express*	#6525	daily	9.10am	19hr 25min
Calcutta	*Trivandrum–Howrah Express**	#6323	Wed & Sat	12.45pm	48hr
	*Trivandrum–Guwahati Express**	#5627	Sun	12.45pm	47hr
Chennai	*Trivandrum–Chennai Mail**	#6320	daily	1.30pm	17hr 45min
	*Trivandrum–Guwahati Express**	#5627	Sun	12.45pm	18hr 55min
Delhi	*Rajdhani Express***	#2431	Fri	7.30pm	44hr 30min
	Kerala Express	#2625	daily	11am	52hr 30min
Ernakulam/Kochi	*Kerala Express*	#2625	daily	11am	4hr 30min
Kanniyakumari	*Kanniyakumari Express*	#1081	daily	12.30pm	2hr 15min
Kollam	*Kanniyakumari Express***	#1082	daily	7.30am	1hr 30min
Kozhikode	*Trivandrum–Cannanore Express*	#6347	nightly	9pm	9hr 50min
Mangalore	*Trivandrum-Mangalore-Parasuram Express****	#6349	daily	6am	15hr 30min
	*Malabar Express****	#6329	daily	5.40pm	17hr 25min
Mumbai	*Trivandrum–Mumbai Express*	#6332	Sat	4.20am	40hr
	*Kanniyakumari Express**	#1082	daily	7.30am	45hr 35min

* via Kollam, Kottayam, Ernakulam, Palakaad and Chennai
** a/c only
*** via Varkala, Kollam, Kottayam, Ernakulam, Thrissur, Kozhikode, Kannur, Kasargode

Yoga The Sivananda Yoga Ashram at 37/1929 Airport Rd, Palkulangara, West Fort (☎0471/450942), holds daily classes at various levels, which you can arrange on spec. Better still, head for Neyyar Dam, 28km east of town, where their world-famous Dhanwanthari ashram offers excellent two-week introductory courses amid idyllic mountain surroundings (see box on p.297 for more).

Around Thiruvananthapuram

Although for virtually its entire 550-kilometre length the **Keralan coast** is lined with sandy beaches, rocky promontories and coconut palms, **Kovalam** is one of the only places where swimming in the sea is not considered eccentric by locals – but watch out for the strong undertow – and which offers accommodation to suit all budgets. When it gets too hot at sea level, **Ponmudi** and the **Peppara Wildlife Sanctuary**, both a bus ride away – through forest and spice and tea plantations – in the Cardamom hills, make a refreshing break. The picturesque **Agastya Hills** could be a pleasant day-trip, or a longer excursion if you want to explore the unspoilt forest tracts. Another easy excursion from Thiruvananthapuram is to its predecessor as capital of Travancore, **Padmanabhapuram**, site of a magnificent palace.

Kovalam and around

The coastal village of **KOVALAM** may lie just ten kilometres south from Thiruvananthapuram, but as Kerala's most developed **beach resort** it's becoming ever more distanced from the rest of the state. Each year greater numbers of Western visitors – budget travellers and jet-setters alike – arrive in search of sun, sea and palm-fringed beaches. For many travellers it has become, with Goa and Mamallapuram, the third essential stop on a triangular tour of tropical South Indian "paradises" – or indeed another leg of the trail along the coasts of South Asia.

Europeans have been visiting Kovalam since the 1930s, but not until hippies started to colonize the place some thirty years later were any hotels built. As the resort's popularity began to grow, more and more paddy fields were filled and the first luxury holiday complexes sprang up. These soon caught the eye of European charter companies scouting for "undiscovered" beach hideaways to supplement their Goa brochures, and by the mid 1990s plane-loads of fortnighting package tourists were flown here direct from the UK. This influx has had a dramatic impact on Kovalam. Prices have rocketed, rubbish lies in unsightly piles at the roadsides, and in high season the beach – recently enlarged to make way for even more cafés, souvenir stalls and fish restaurants – is packed nose-to-tail. Add to this a backdrop of rapidly deteriorating concrete hotels, and you can see why Kovalam's detractors call it "the Costa del Kerala".

Arrival, information and getting around

Heading along the recently upgraded approach road from the capital (now littered with stone-breakers and publicity hoardings), the frequent #9 **bus** from Thiruvananthapuram (East Fort; 20min) loops through Kovalam, and stops at the gates of the *Ashok* complex, at the northern end of the middle bay. Anyone carrying heavy bags who wants to stay by the sea (and not at the *Ashok*), should alight earlier, either at the road to the lighthouse, or the road leading down to the *Sea Rock* hotel. It's also possible to take an **auto-rickshaw** or **taxi** all the way from Thiruvananthapuram; auto-rickshaws cost between Rs60 and Rs80 but will try to get away with a lot more, while taxis charge around Rs150.

Opposite the bus stand, Western Travels (daily 8am–8pm; ☎0471/481334) is a reliable agent for flight confirmations and ticketing, and can arrange **car rental**. Great Indian is another all-round agency, which also arranges **motorbike rental** (an Enfield Bullet costs around Rs550 per day, and a scooter Rs350). **Surfboards** can be rented on Lighthouse Beach for Rs50 per hour, and for around Rs300 you can also take a ride on a traditional **kettumaran** (*kettu*, tied *maran* logs), which gave the catamaran its name. Popular with the fishermen of Kovalam, the rudimentary boat consists of five logs tied together and feels fairly fragile in a choppy sea.

There are now several places to **change money** in Kovalam; private exchange rates tend to vary, however, and so it is best to do some research first. Of the **banks**, the Central Bank of India (Mon–Fri 10.30am–2pm, Sat 10.30am–noon) is at the *Ashok* and there is a branch of the Andhra Bank at the KTDC *Samudra* complex near the main gates (same hours). You can also change money at Great Indian Travel Services, Lighthouse Beach (☎0471/481110); at *Wilson's Beach Resort* any time (the most competitive rates); and at the *Moonlight Tourist Home*, amongst others. Several agencies offer **internet** services with charges of around Rs200 per hour or Rs4 per minute, rates which are even higher than at Thiruvananthapuram; these include Great Indian (mail-*zigi@keralaonline.com*), Alphanet and Yes Internet on Lighthouse Beach and Aquarius Internet at the *Hotel Aquarius* on Lighthouse Beach Rd. Kovalam doesn't have a major **bookshop** but opposite the *Lonely Planet* restaurant is Jungle Books, run

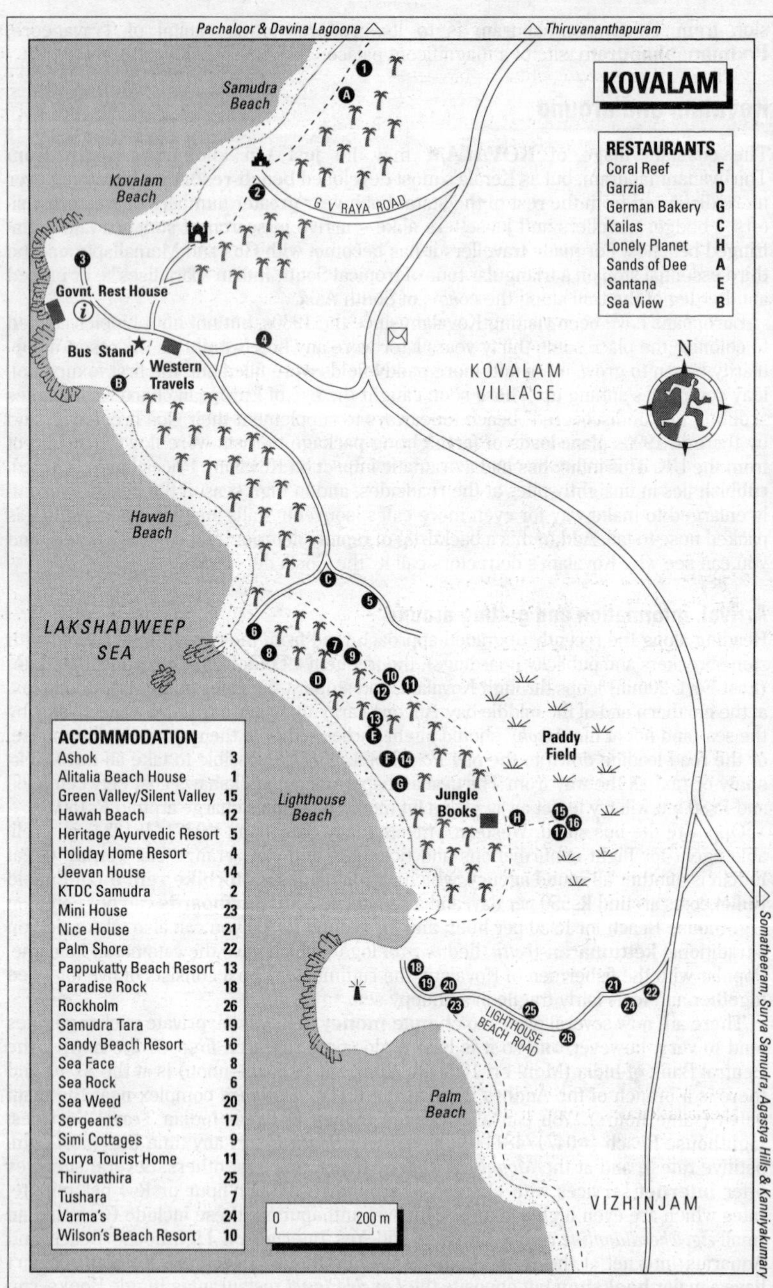
KOVALAM
Pachaloor & Davina Lagoona
Thiruvananthapuram
Samudra Beach
Kovalam Beach
G V RAYA ROAD
Govnt. Rest House
Bus Stand
Western Travels
KOVALAM VILLAGE
Hawah Beach
LAKSHADWEEP SEA
Lighthouse Beach
Paddy Field
Jungle Books
LIGHTHOUSE BEACH ROAD
Palm Beach
VIZHINJAM
Somatheeram, Surya Samudra, Agastya Hills & Kanniyakumary
0 200 m
N
RESTAURANTS
Coral Reef F
Garzia D
German Bakery G
Kailas C
Lonely Planet H
Sands of Dee A
Santana E
Sea View B
ACCOMMODATION
Ashok 3
Alitalia Beach House 1
Green Valley/Silent Valley 15
Hawah Beach 12
Heritage Ayurvedic Resort 5
Holiday Home Resort 4
Jeevan House 14
KTDC Samudra 2
Mini House 23
Nice House 21
Palm Shore 22
Pappukatty Beach Resort 13
Paradise Rock 18
Rockholm 26
Samudra Tara 19
Sandy Beach Resort 16
Sea Face 8
Sea Rock 6
Sea Weed 20
Sergeant's 17
Simi Cottages 9
Surya Tourist Home 11
Thiruvathira 25
Tushara 7
Varma's 24
Wilson's Beach Resort 10

by an Englishwoman, which has a small but interesting selection, for rent or for sale, and a noticeboard where you can find out what's on. You can't get away from **Ayurvedic massage**, which is advertised everywhere in Kovalam, but some places are more salubrious than others; the best places for Ayurvedic treatment are in the specialist clinics, some of which are attached to upmarket hotels such as the KTDC *Samudra* and *Somatheeram* at Chowera.

Kovalam's beaches

Kovalam consists of a succession of small crescent beaches; the southernmost, known for obvious reasons as **Lighthouse Beach**, is where most visitors spend their time. Roughly five minutes' amble through the sand from end to end, it's bordered with cheek-to-cheek low-rise guesthouses and restaurants. The red-and-white **lighthouse** (daily 2–4pm; max stay 15min), on the promontory at the southern end of the beach, gives superb views across to Vizhinjam mosque (see p.295). On Lighthouse Beach you can hire surfboards and also take a ride out on a wooden outrigger (see p.289).

Hawah, the middle beach, overlooked from a rocky headland by the five-star *Ashok* resort, functions each morning as a base for local fishermen, who drag a massive net through the shallows to scoop up thrashing multi-hued minnows, coiling endless piles

KERALAN AYURVEDIC TREATMENT

The ancient system of **Ayurvedic herbal medicine**, dating back to the sixth century BC, has been making a healthy resurgence over the last few decades (see p.19), and nowhere more so than in Kerala. Institutes such as the Ayurvedic Medical College, on MG Rd in Thiruvananthapuram, have been making tremendous steps with their research, which has resulted in Keralan Ayurveda being well regarded.

The most common form of Ayurveda in Kerala is massage, which uses oils and herbs in a course of treatment, either for rejuvenation or as remedies. Ayurveda, which aims to eliminate toxic imbalances, believes in the well-being of the individual as a whole and not just the affected part. The best time for treatment is during the monsoon from June till November, when the atmosphere remains cool and free of dust. Rejuvenation therapy, or *Rasayan Chikitsa*, advocates face and head massage using medicated oils and creams, body massage using hands and feet, and medicated baths. *Kayakalpa Chikitsa*, whose primary objective is to control the ageing process, concentrates on diet. *Sweda Karma*, used in the treatment of certain rheumatic illnesses, uses medicated steam baths to improve tone and reduce fat. Other therapeutic treatments include: *Dhara*, for mental disorders, and *Pizhichil*, for the treatment of rheumatic diseases and nervous disorders, which involve courses of between seven and twenty-one days. Among numerous remedies available in Keralan Ayurveda, *Snehapanam* prescribes medicated ghee and is aimed at curing osteoarthritis and leukemia.

Ayurvedic massage has become intensely popular recently, and when travelling around Kerala you will find it offered everywhere, from small establishments – some with questionable training – to more elaborate sessions offered by several of the upmarket hotels; you can even pick up an Ayurvedic holiday package. Costs for Ayurvedic massage start from around Rs300 per session in smaller places, to far more expensive treatments in specialist clinics, although the specialist clinics should offer a more reliable diagnosis. Although not exclusive to these hotels, the best Ayurvedic treatment to be found in the Kovalam area is at the *Somatheeram* resort at Chowara (☎0471/481601); *KTDC Samudra*, Kovalam (☎0471/480089, fax 480242); and the *Keraleeyam* at Alappuzha (☎0477/241468), which is owned by the well-established family firm of SD Pharmacy. In Thiruvananthapuram, Agastheswara, a clinic at Jiji Nivas, Killi, Kattakkada (☎0471/291270), uses a course of treatment called *Kayachikistsa* that relies heavily on *Chavittihirumal* (foot therapy), which has the masseur walking over your body.

of coir rope as they work. North of the *Ashok*, in full view of its distinctive sloping terraces, the final, northernmost beach, **Samudra**, is the least affected of all by the changing times, dotted only with a few rudimentary wooden fishing vessels.

WARNING: SWIMMING SAFETY

Due to unpredictable **rip currents** and an often **strong undertow**, especially during the monsoons, swimming from Kovalam's beaches is not always safe. The recent introduction of lifeguards (noticeable by their blue shirts), has reduced the annual death toll, but at least a couple of tourists drown here each year, and many more get into difficulties. Follow the warnings of the safety flags at all times, and keep a close eye on children.

Accommodation

Kovalam is crammed with **accommodation**, ranging from sandy-floored cells to five-star hilltop chalets. Only decent rock-bottom rooms are hard to find, as all but a handful of the many budget travellers' guesthouses that formerly crowded the beachfront have been recently upgraded. Touts hang around the bus stand, but if you follow one remember that their "commission" tends to be tacked onto the room tariff. The most varied range of hotels is concentrated around the lively Lighthouse Beach area, the quieter Samudra Beach has a couple of upmarket hotels and few simple ones to offer, and the best of the resorts, such as *Davina Lagoona, Treasure Island, Somatheeram* and *Surya Samudra,* are a little further away and require transport.

Prices are extortionate compared with the rest of Kerala, soaring in peak season (Dec to mid-Jan), when you'll be lucky to find a basic room for less than Rs250. At other times, haggling should bring the rate down, especially if you stay for over a week.

INEXPENSIVE

Green Valley/Silent Valley, Lighthouse Beach (☎0471/480636). Set amid the paddy fields, this pair of jointly owned hotels still offers the best budget accommodation in Kovalam, with pleasant en-suite rooms ranged around leafy and secluded courtyards. There's a restaurant on site. ⑤.

Alitalia Beach House, Samudra Beach (☎0471/480042). Simple rooms in one of the few budget places on Samudra Beach, where the advantage is being away from the razzmatazz of the main strip further south. ③–⑤.

Hawah Beach, behind *Hawah Beach Restaurant*, Lighthouse Beach (☎0471/480431). Cheap and cheerful rooms with small verandahs but no views. Situated behind a good seafood restaurant. ③.

Heritage Ayurvedic Resort, behind Hawah Beach (☎0471/481990). One of several similar little cottages tucked away behind the beach; three good, cheap rooms but disregard the name. ③.

Jeevan House, behind *Coral Reef Café*, Lighthouse Beach (☎0471/480662). This place offers large plain rooms, each equipped with a fridge; the more expensive rooms have views of the sea. ④–⑤.

Nice House, Lighthouse Beach Rd, opposite *Varma's* (☎0471/480684). Clean hotel with a pleasant rooftop café, where the cheaper rooms at the back are good value and share a verandah, but don't expect any views. ④–⑤.

Sandy Beach Resort, Lighthouse Beach (☎0471/480012). Pleasant garden and sizeable rooms – a good fallback if *Green Valley* is full. ④–⑤.

Sergeant's, Lighthouse Beach (no phone). This is a dilapidated guesthouse run by a garrulous retired army sergeant. Rooms are basic, but the atmosphere is sociable, and the rates rock-bottom. ②–③.

Simi Cottages, Lighthouse Beach (☎0471/480925). A pleasant little place with four plain rooms within a stone's throw of the beach. ④.

Surya Tourist Home, Lighthouse Beach (☎0471/481012). One of a clutch of no-frills places tucked behind the main beach, with small-ish rooms, low tariffs and long-term discounts. Plenty of fallbacks nearby. ②–③.

Thiruvathira, Lighthouse Beach Rd (☎0471/480787). A good-value option, which has attached rooms with verandahs and sea views, though slightly boxed in; the rooms at the back are cheaper. Martial arts and massage courses are available. ②–⑤.

Wilson's Beach Resort, Lighthouse Beach (☎0471/480051). At the top of its range, but worth the extra for spacious en-suite rooms, balconies, garden, friendly staff and proximity to the beach. The massage parlour is also recommended (for men or women), and they do foreign exchange. ⑤–⑦.

MODERATE TO EXPENSIVE

Ashok, on the headland by Samudra Beach (☎0471/480101, fax 481522). Four complexes of chalets and "cottages" in Charles Correa's award-winning hilltop block. Bars, restaurants, pools, yoga centre and tennis courts should make this Kovalam's swankiest option, but it seems to be plagued by indifferent management. ⑨.

Holiday Home Resort, Beach Rd (☎0471/480497). Disregard the main block which has a range of rooms including some with a/c, as behind it lie eight new, attractive and comfortable cottages with verandahs and shared cooking facilities. The hotel boasts the only dormitory in Kovalam. ③–⑧.

KTDC Samudra, Samudra Beach (☎0471/480089, fax 480242). Posh government-run three-star, set away from other hotels, and the best there is in Kovalam. Tastefully manicured grounds, lovely swimming pool and good access to beach. Restaurant, bar and a good ayurvedic massage centre with friendly but slow service. ⑨.

Mini House, Lighthouse Beach Rd (☎0471/330417). There are two large rooms with balconies, set in a great location right over the rocks and breaking sea – which can be loud. A third room without the view is much cheaper. ④–⑥.

Palm Shore, Lighthouse Beach Rd (☎0471/481481, fax 480495). New management putting some life back into an ailing hotel, which is full of potential and in a good location – surrounded by palms and with fine views from individual terraces. It is a bit overpriced though. ⑨.

Pappukutty Beach Resort, behind *Santana Restaurant*, Lighthouse Beach (☎0471/480235). A large complex, which is popular with package groups. The main block has sizeable airy rooms, but the two cottages are cheaper, one of which is particularly good value and is usually booked out. ③–⑦.

Paradise Rock, Lighthouse Beach Rd (☎0471/480658) Variously priced, large en-suite rooms which overlook the main beach. It's a clean and welcoming place, though no single occupancy is available. ④–⑥.

Rockholm, Lighthouse Beach Rd (☎0471/480636). One of the best options along this stretch with a range of well-appointed rooms, some of which have great views. ⑦.

Samudra Tara, Lighthouse Beach Rd (☎0471/481608). Set in a three-storey concrete block just back from the beach, it has comfortable rooms and individual balconies. A peaceful, and popular choice with older visitors. ④–⑥.

Sea Face, Lighthouse Beach (☎0471/481835). A rather ugly, modern block with three-star pretensions and comfortable, if nondescript, rooms. Its saving grace is that it is the only hotel along this strip with a swimming pool. ⑦–⑧.

Sea Rock, Hawah Beach (☎0471/480422). One of Kovalam's oldest, established hotels. Slap on the seafront, with views of Hawah Beach from the more expensive front rooms (those at the back cost half the tariff). There are good off-season discounts. ⑦.

Sea Weed, Lighthouse Beach Rd (☎0471/480391). Neat, clean and breezy hotel with rooftop restaurant and leafy central courtyard. Some rooms have a/c, and again, rooms with views cost extra. ⑤–⑧.

Tushara, behind Lighthouse Beach (☎0471/481693). A moderately comfortable hotel where the sizeable rooms come with balconies, but face onto a courtyard with no views. ⑥.

Varma's, Lighthouse Beach Rd (☎0471/480478). This is the most attractive of the upper-range places, offering superb views from sea-facing terraces. The rooms are tastefully furnished with carved wood and tiled interiors. ⑦–⑧.

Eating, drinking and nightlife

Lighthouse Beach is lined with identikit cafés and restaurants like *Garzia*, *Hawah* and *Coral Reef*. Most specialize in **seafood**: you pick from the fresh fish, lobster, tiger prawns, crab and mussels on display, which are then weighed, grilled over a charcoal fire, and served with salad and chips. Meals are pricey by Indian standards – typically around Rs150 per head for fish, and double that for lobster or prawns – and the service is often painfully slow, but the ambience of the beachfront terraces is convivial. Beer, spirits and local *feni* (distilled palm wine) are served, to a background of soft reggae or Pink Floyd. For upmarket service and more comfort try the restaurants at one of the more expensive hotels, such as the excellent terrace restaurant at the *Rockholm* and the popular rooftop restaurant at the *Hotel Sea Weed*; for even more upmarket options, try the *Ashok* or the *Surya Samudra* (see p.295). For **breakfast** you can chose from any number of typical trans-Asia-budget-traveller cafés with the usual brown bread menus, or you can search out a traditional breakfast of *iddli* and *sambar* at one of the cheap local cafés along the main road and near the bus stand.

Nightlife in Kovalam is pretty laid-back, and revolves around the beach where Westerners lounge about drinking and playing backgammon until the wee hours. A couple of restaurants also offer **video nights**, screening pirate copies of the latest American hits. You may be offered *charas*, but bear in mind cannabis is illegal in Kerala, as everywhere else in India, and that the local police regularly arrest foreigners for possession.

German Bakery, Lighthouse Beach. Breezy rooftop terrace at the south end of the beach, serving tasty (mostly healthy), Western food and lots of tempting cakes (try the waffles with chocolate sauce). Breakfasts include a "full English" and "French" (croissants with espresso and a cigarette).

Kailas, above Hawah Beach. Owned by the same people as the *Lonely Planet* restaurant, with the same congenial atmosphere but unlike its sister concern, it serves meat.

Lonely Planet, behind Lighthouse Beach, near *Green Valley/Silent Valley*. Congenial, generally inexpensive, veg restaurant tucked away in the paddy fields. The place to come if you're pining for Indian food, and one of the few places you can get *iddlis* for breakfast.

Sands of Dee, Samudra Beach. Run-of-the-mill place, but situated on the less developed Samudra Beach, it is the best of the few seafood restaurants and organizes a beach party and a bonfire on Sunday evenings. They have rooms as well.

Santana, Lighthouse Beach. The best of the seafood joints on this beach, with a great BBQ, *tandoori* fish and chicken, and Kovalam's best sound system. Stays open later than most.

Sea View, Hawah Beach. Congenial atmosphere; good place for a snack lunch, or, notably for the day's catch – from lobster to huge king prawns – which is on the menu in the evenings.

Pozhikkara beach and Pachalloor village

Heading north along Samudra for around 3km, you'll pass through fishing hamlets before eventually arriving at a point where the sea merges with the backwaters to form a salt-water lagoon. Although only thirty minutes' walk from the *Ashok*, the sliver of white sand dividing the two, known as **Pozhikkara beach**, is a world away from the headlong holiday culture of Kovalam. Here, the sands are used primarily for landing fish and fixing nets, while the thick palm canopy shelters a mixed community of Hindu fishermen and Christian coir-makers. The tranquil village of **PACHALLOOR**, behind the lagoon, is a good alternative base to Thiruvananthapuram or Kovalam. Two guesthouses, including the original and idyllic – and now upmarket – *Lagoona Davina* (☎0471/480049 or 462935; ⑨), featured in *Tatler* magazine and owned by an English woman Davina Taylor Phillips, where the six en-suite rooms open onto the water. Price includes full board. The guesthouse organizes its own **backwater trips** at a cost of Rs300 per head for two hours. Accompanied by a knowledgeable guide, you're punted around the neighbouring villages, with stops to see coir being made and to identify an amazing wealth of tropical fruit trees, spices and birds. The **food** served at *Lagoona Davina* is exceptional, authentic Keralan village dishes that you're unlikely to encounter elsewhere, and, power-cuts permitting, chilled beer. You can also sample

Ayurvedic massage or take yoga lessons. If you book in advance, you will be met at the airport. If you are making your own way there, however, take an auto-rickshaw six kilometres along the highway towards Kovalam, and bear right along the "by-pass" where the road forks (just after the Thiruvallam bridge). After another kilometre or so, a sign on the right-hand-side of the road points through the trees to the guesthouse. The other guesthouse at Pachalloor, the *Beach Lake* (⑧), lies across the water from *Lagoona Davina* on the beach side, and has five rooms but no restaurant and little atmosphere.

South of Kovalam: Vizhinjam (Vilinjam)

The unassuming village of **VIZHINJAM** (pronounced Virinyam), on the opposite (south) side of the headland from Lighthouse Beach, was once the capital of the Ay kings, the earliest dynasty in south Kerala. During the ninth century the Pandyans intermittently took control, and it was also the scene of major Chola–Chera battles in the eleventh century. A number of small, simple shrines survive from those times, and can be made the focus of a pleasant afternoon's stroll along quiet paths. They're best approached from the village centre, beyond a fishing community, rather than via the coast road. However, if you do walk along the coast road from Kovalam to the north side of Vizhinjam, you can't fail to be struck by the contrast: from the conspicuous consumption of a tourist resort to a poor fishing village, where a huge modern pink **mosque** on the promontory overlooks a bay of tightly packed thatched huts.

For centuries, the Muslim fishermen here were kept at arm's length by the Hindu orthodox, perpetually forced into debt by the combination of low prices for their produce and exorbitant interest charged by moneylenders on loans for boats and nets (as much as ten percent per day). Co-operatives have recently started to arrange interest-free loans and sell fish on behalf of individuals, but the mutual antipathy between the two communities persists. A flare-up occurred as recently as the early 1990s, when a series of violent riots resulted in the deaths of numerous local people. Today, Hindus and Muslims are divided by a three-hundred-metre stretch of no-man's-land, patrolled by police, which only tourists can cross without risking a severe beating. Needless to say, you're not likely to be popular if you use Vizhinjam as a photo opportunity.

On the far side of the fishing bay, in the village centre, fifty metres down a road opposite the police station, a small unfinished eighth-century rock shrine features a carved figure of Shiva with a weapon. The **Tali Shiva** temple, reached by a narrow path from behind the government primary school, may mark the original centre of Vizhinjam. This simple shrine is accompanied by a group of *naga* snake statues, a reminder of Kerala's continuing cult of snake worship that survives from pre-Brahminical times.

The grove known as **Kovil Kadu** (temple forest) lies near the sea, ten minutes' walk from the main road in the village, along Hidyatnagara Rd. Here a small enclosure contains a square Shiva shrine and a rectangular shrine dedicated to the goddess **Bhagavati**. Thought to date from the ninth century, these are probably the earliest structural temples in Kerala, although the Bhagavati shrine has been renovated.

Accommodation south of Kovalam

Two of the most luxurious of Kovalam's resorts lie around 8km to the south, by road. The German-run *Surya Samudra* at **Pulinkudi** (☎0471/480413 or 481124; ⑨) consisting of antique Keralan wood cottages, beautifully presented but without air-conditioning, and with baths open to the sky, has spawned several imitators. The exquisite development, spread discretley along a rocky hillside, looks down onto two small beaches and has an extraordinary swimming pool cut into the rock that is open to non-residents – for a price (Rs400). You can get **Ayurvedic massage** treatment here, but you'd be better off trying the nearby *Somatheeram* at Chowera (☎0471/480049 or 462935; ⑨; *www.richsoft.com/soma*), which specializes in Ayurvedic treatment. This place has cottages spilling down the fifteen-acre landscaped hillside. Their Ayurvedic hospital and yoga centre offer an extensive range of treatments, either on the basis of two-week courses (for around US$600) or single sessions (from US$24). Accommodation ranges from simple, round cottages to elaborate stone bungalows. If full, try their sister concern around the corner, *Manatheeram* (☎0471/481610; ⑨), which is marginally cheaper but shares the same Ayurvedic facilities. Next to *Surya Samudra*, the *Bethsaida Hermitage* (☎0471/481554; ⑧) prides itself, justifiably, as an eco-friendly beach resort built in 1996 without sacrificing a single tree. Set in a superb location, within a twenty-acre spread, the resort is made up of pleasant but small cottages built in traditional style, its own beach and a great restaurant which serves both South and North Indian dishes. *Bethsaida Hermitage* also offers Ayurvedic treatment and yoga. The resort belongs to a Christian charitable trust and profits go to several projects including an orphanage. For a bit of quiet, head south to **Poovar** at the mouth of the River Neyyar, 20km south of Kovalam (taxis charge Rs200). Here, the *Treasure Island* (☎0471/210019; ⑨), pre-booked through *Wilson Beach Resort* at Kovalam (☎0471/480051), occupies a secluded spot on a palm-studded island with pleasant but not grand cottages set in a coconut plantation; there is a swimming pool and opportunities to explore this stretch of the coast.

Agastya Hills

Within easy distance of Kovalam, 25km to the northeast and feasible on a day-trip, the jagged, forested **AGASTYA HILLS** form an unspoilt backdrop to a large artificial lake created by the **Neyyar Dam**. This area would be idyllic, except for the ornamental gardens at its base which are decorated by outsize, garishly painted plaster images of gods and heroes. Thankfully, very few people come here, except on weekends when it is invaded by day-trippers from Thiruvananthapuram. Signs warn you not to take photographs of the dam itself. The Neyyar Dam's greatest asset is the opportunity to walk away from it. Stretching north for 32km to Meenmutty near Ponmudi, the **Neyyar Lake** is, for the most part, surrounded by thick jungle, which makes it difficult to glimpse **wildlife**. Many travellers who come this way, do so to visit the **Sivananda Yoga Vedanta Dhanwanthari Ashram**, one of the country's leading **yoga** ashrams situated overlooking the lake (see box opposite and p.288).

Across the lake the forest beckons. The only way to enter the Agastya Hills reserve, however, is through the Forest Department, who will, on request, organize a **boat** and an obligatory **guide**. The guide service is free but you should have prior permission to **trek** in the park from the Forest Department offices at Vazhuthacud in Thiruvananthapuram. On occasions, the local range officer does give permission, especially if you arrange it through the manager at the tourist bungalow, *KTDC Agastya House* (see below). Longer treks into the forest can be arranged through the department or through the *Agastya Garden Hill Resort* (see below) but, so far, there has been little demand.

The Forest Department's **crocodile** breeding pens located behind the Wildlife Information Office (Tue–Sun 10am–5pm), near the *KTDC Agastya House*, are thankfully going to be closed – a mercy for the wretched animals who exist in pitiful, dilapidated conditions. You are strongly advised not to swim in the waters of the lake as it is **infested** by the creatures. A tiny, two-acre safari park on a corner of the lake, approached by boats from near the Forest Department, is home to seven lions, whose roars during feeding time at sunset echo through the hills; their presence here is entirely inexplicable.

SIVANANDA YOGA VEDANTA DHANWANTARI

Located amid the serene hills and tropical forests, around the Neyyar Dam, the **Sivananda Yoga Vedanta Dhanwanthari** is one of India's leading **yoga** ashrams. It was founded by Swami Shivananda – dubbed the "Flying Guru" because he used to pilot light aircraft over war-stricken areas of the world scattering flowers and leaflets calling for peace – as a centre for meditation, yoga and traditional Keralan martial arts and medicine. Sivananda was a renowned exponent of Advaitya Vedanta, the philosophy of non-duality, as espoused by the Upanishads and promoted later by Shankara in the eleventh century.

Aside from training teachers in advanced *raja* and *hatha* yoga, the ashram offers excellent **introductory courses** for beginners. These comprise four hours of intensive tuition per day (starting at 5.30am), with background lectures that provide helpful theory. During the course, you have to stay at the ashram and comply with a regime that some Western students find disconcertingly strict (smoking, alcohol, drugs, sex and even "rock music" are prohibited, the diet is pure veg, and you have to get up at the crack of dawn). However, if you are keen to acquire the basic techniques and knowledge of yoga, this is a good place to start. For more details, contact either the ashram itself (☎0471/290493) or its branch in Thiruvananthapuram, 37/1929 Airport Rd, West Fort (☎0471/450942). You can also consult its publication, *Sivananda Yoga Life*, published by the Sivananda Yoga Vedanta centre, 51 Felsham Rd, London SW15 1AZ (☎0181/780 0160; *Siva@dial.pipex.com*).

Practicalities

Buses from the KSRTC Thampanoor bus stand in Thiruvananthapuram depart every half hour for the Neyyar Dam. If you are coming from Kovalam, take a bus to Balaramapuram or Neyyattinkara on NH47, then change for Aruvikara and the Neyyar Dam. The only decent **accommodation** at Neyyar Dam, is the *KTDC Agastya House* (☎0471/272160; ③), which has huge rooms and verandahs (with views), and a restaurant. During the weekend, avoid the rooms upstairs as the popular beer bar below gets noisy. For a bit more comfort, head for **Kalipara**, the large, black, rocky hill with a small temple on top. The recently opened *Agastya Garden Hill Resort* (☎0471/273151; ⑦–⑧) has comfortable, mock-rustic cottages with incredible views, albeit expensive for what it is. On the downside, it is situated next to a rocky cliff-face and gets very hot in summer. The resort has introduced treks in the Agastya Hills reserve forest, and boat tours, but with a dearth of competition, these are vastly overpriced.

Ponmudi and Peppara Wildlife Sanctuary

In the tea-growing region of the **Cardamom** (or Ponmudi) **Hills**, about 60km north-east of Thiruvananthapuram and 77km from Kovalam, at an altitude of 1066m, the hill station of **PONMUDI** – not a town, or even a village, but merely some accommodation of a pretty minimal standard – commands breathtaking views out across the range as far as the sea.

The main reason anyone comes up here is that it serves as the only practical base for visits to the fifty-three square kilometres of forest set aside as the **Peppara Wildlife Sanctuary**, which protects elephants, *sambar*, lion-tailed macaques, leopard and other assorted wildlife. Although Peppara is theoretically open all year, the main season is from January until May; check before you go with the District Forest Officer, Thiruvananthapuram Forest Division, Thiruvananthapuram (☎0471/320674).

The beautiful drive up, via the small towns of Nedumangad and Vithura, runs along very narrow roads past areca nut, clove, rubber and cashew plantations, with first the

Kavakulam and then the Kallar River close at hand. The bridge at **Kallar Junction** marks the start of the real climb. Twenty-two hairpin bends (numbered at the roadside) lead slowly up, starting in the foothills, heading up past great lumps of black rock and thick clumps of bamboo (*iramula*), then through the Kallar teak forest. Finally you emerge into tea plantations; the temperature is noticeably cooler and, once out of the forest, the views across the hills and the plains below become truly spectacular – on a clear day you can see the sea. There really is very little to do up here, but the high ridges and tea estates make good rambling country.

Practicalities

Four daily **buses** run from Thiruvananthapuram to Ponmudi, via Vithura; the first is at 5.30am and the last at 3.30pm. They return between 12.30pm and 6.30pm. In 1992, the Kallar River broke its banks in freak December rains, killing a number of people, and the havoc caused may still be evident in the state of the roads. Check that the road is safe before attempting the journey in your own vehicle.

The KTDC *Ponmudi Guest House* (☎0472/890230; closed June & July; ①) has twenty-four **rooms**, a dorm and seven cottages. Meals have to be ordered in advance, so it's worth bringing some provisions; if you forget to, walk a short way down the road to a tea-shop on the bend. The main building, which originally belonged to the raja of Travancore, has lost any charm it may once have possessed, and the huge plate-glass windows of its canteen-like restaurant rattle disconcertingly in the wind. Views from the terrace do make up for all that, and, thanks to the beer parlour, weekends get lively.

Padmanabhapuram

Although now officially in Tamil Nadu, **PADMANABHAPURAM**, 63km southeast of Thiruvananthapuram, was the capital of Travancore between 1550 and 1750, and therefore has a far more intimate connection with the history of Kerala and is administered by the Government of Kerala. For anyone with even a minor interest in Keralan architecture, the small palace here is an irresistible attraction. However, **avoid weekends**, when the complex gets overrun with bus parties. Occasionally parts of the palace are closed to visitors for restoration.

Set in neat, gravelled grounds in a quiet location away from the main road, the predominantly wooden **Padmanabhapuram Palace** (daily except Mon 9am–4.30pm; Rs6; cameras Rs10) epitomizes Keralan architecture. It is reached by crossing the main road from the bus station, turning left, and then following a road on the right for a pleasant ten- to fifteen-minute walk through the paddy fields. The substantial walls of the palace compound delimit a small village.

Against a backdrop of steep-sided hills, the exterior of the palace displays a perfect combination of clean lines and gentle angles, with the sloping tiled roofs of its various interconnecting buildings broken by triangular projecting gables which enclose delicately carved screens. The palace is excellently maintained by the Archaeological Survey of India. All visitors have to be shown around by the informative **guides**, who do not charge a fee but expect a tip. At busy times they will rush you through the palace, especially if there are only a few of you, so as to catch up with the next group.

In the **entrance hall** (a verandah), a brass oil lamp hangs from an ornate teak, rosewood and mahogany ceiling and is carved with ninety different lotus flowers. Beautifully ornamented, the revolving lamp inexplicably keeps the position in which it is left, seeming to defy gravity. The raja rested from the summer heat on the cool, polished-granite bed in the corner. On the wall is a collection of *onamvillu* (ceremonial bows) decorated with images of Padmanabha – the god Vishnu reclining (see box opposite) – which local chieftains would present to him during the Onam festival.

Directly above the entrance hall, on the first floor, is the **mantrasala** (council chamber), gently illuminated by the light filtering through panes of coloured mica. Herbs soaking in water were put into the boxed bench seats along the front wall, as a natural air-cooling system. The highly polished black floor was made from a now-lost technique using burnt coconut, sticky sugar-cane extract, egg whites, lime and sand.

The oldest part of the complex is the **Ekandamandapam**, or "the lonely place". Built in 1550, it was used for rituals for the goddess Durga which typically employed elaborate floor paintings known as *kalam ezhuttu* (see p.590). A loose ring attached to a column is a tour de force of the carpenter: both ring and column are carved from a single piece of jackwood. Nearby is a *nalekettu*, a four-sided courtyard found in many Keralan houses, open to the sky and surrounded by a pillared walkway. A trapdoor once served as the entrance to a secret passageway leading to another palace, since destroyed.

The Pandya-style stone-columned **dance hall** stands directly in front of a shrine to the goddess of learning, Saraswati. The women of the royal household had to watch performances through screens on the side, and the staff, through holes in the wall from the gallery above. Typical of old country houses, steep, wooden ladder-like steps, ending in trapdoors, connect the floors. Belgian mirrors and Tanjore miniatures of Krishna adorn the chamber forming part of the **women's quarters**, where a swing hangs on plaited iron ropes. A four-poster bed, made from sixteen kinds of medicinal wood, dominates the **raja's bedroom**. Its elaborate carvings depict a mass of vegetation, human figures, birds and, as the central motif, the snake symbol of medicine, associated with the Greek physician deity Asclepius.

The **murals** for which the palace is famous – alive with detail, colour, graceful form and religious fervour – adorn the walls of the **meditation room** directly above the bedroom, which was used by the raja and the heirs apparent. Unfortunately, this is now closed – allegedly because the stairs are shaky, but in fact to preserve the murals, which have been severely damaged by generations of hands trailing along the walls.

Further points of interest in the palace include a **dining hall** intended for the free feeding of up to two thousand *brahmins*, and a 38-kilo stone which, it is said, every new recruit to the raja's army had to raise above his head 101 times.

Practicalities

Frequent buses run to Padmanabhapuram from Thiruvananthapuram's Thampanoor station; hop on any service heading south towards Nagercoil or Kanniyakumari and get down at Thakkaly (sometimes written Thuckalai). If you're determined to see Padmanabhapuram, Kanniyakumari and Suchindram in one day, leave the city early to arrive when the palace opens at 9am. Seats are harder to come by on the way back, but with luck not all the passengers will be going right the way to Thiruvananthapuram. Note that two express buses leave Thakkaly for the capital during the afternoon, at

TRAVANCORE AND THE SERVANTS OF VISHNU

In front of a depiction of the god in the meditation, or prayer room, at Padmanabhapuram Palace lies a sword. In 1750, **Raja Marthanda Varma** symbolically presented this weapon to Padmanabha – the god Vishnu – who reclines on the sacred serpent Anantha in the midst of the cosmic ocean, thereby dedicating the kingdom of Travancore to Vishnu. From that day, the raja took the title of Padmanabhadasa ("servant of Padmanabha"), and ruled as a servant of the god.

Thus Travancore belonged to Vishnu, and the raja was merely its custodian – a spiritual, and presumably legal, loophole which is said to have proved invaluable in restricting the power of the British in Travancore. Travancore, therefore, remained under direct control of the raja, with the British presence restricted to that of a resident only.

2.30pm and 3.30pm. Another way to see Padmanabhapuram is on KTDC's Kanniyakumari tour which starts at Thiruvananthapuram (Tues–Sun 7.30am–9pm; Rs230) but you can pick it up at Kovalam where it stops en route.

The area around the bus station, being on the NH47, is noisy and dirty. It's better to get **refreshment** from the *chaiya*-cum-food and "cool drinks" shops inside the outer walls of the palace. Just outside the inner gate you can usually find tender **coconuts**.

Varkala

Long known to Keralans as a place of pilgrimage, **VARKALA**, 54km northwest of Thiruvananthapuram and 20km southeast of Kollam, is drawing more and more foreign visitors, who see the beautiful beach and cliffs, just beyond the village, as a quiet, unspoiled alternative to Kovalam. Centred on a handful of budget guesthouses and palm-thatch cafés, the tourist scene has so far been relatively low-key, despite the arrival of the *Taj Group*'s luxury resort and the occasional package tour group. Varkala is developing, albeit slowly, so enjoy it while you can; this tranquil spot could well go the same way as Kovalam. The best time to get here is between October and early March; during the monsoons the beach is virtually unusable.

Arrival and information

Varkala's train station, two kilometres east of the village, is served by some express and mail **trains** from Thiruvananthapuram, Kollam and most other Keralan towns on the main coastal line. Regular **buses** run from Thiruvananthapuram's Thampanoor stand, and from Kollam. Some go all the way to the beach, but most stop in the village centre, a five-minute auto-rickshaw ride away. Some buses take a painfully slow route, so, if you can't get a direct bus, take any "superfast" or "limited stop" bus along the main highway NH47, and change at Kallamballam from where you can hop onto a local bus to Varkala, or take an auto-rickshaw (Rs70) or a taxi (Rs100).

For general **tourist information** head for the privately run *Tourist Helping Centre*, where Beach Rd meets the beach, who can arrange motorbike rental and advise you on train times. Their main raison d'être, however, is to recruit punters for their **elephant trips** through the forest thirty kilometres away. The full day-trip costs a little over Rs800 per person, which includes all food and travel, and is well worthwhile. They also arrange backwater trips for Rs600 per person, and longer wildlife and plantation excursions. The government's tourist office at the *Tourist Bungalow* (Mon–Sat 10am–5pm), is new and untested. There are now several places to **change money** in Varkala, including the friendly and versatile Bureau de Change (daily 9am–10pm), on the corner of Temple Junction (aka Holy Cross), the main temple square at the centre of town. They also run an **Internet** service for Rs150 per hour, with a minimum charge of Rs40, or Rs25 per **email** message. There is another Internet bureau, which is opposite the *Akshay Beach Resort* on Beach Rd. Cliff Tours & Travels (☎0472/604659), up on the clifftop, arranges tours and airline tickets. The *JA Tourist Home* near the Janardhana Swamy temple rents out a range of bicycles and motorcycles.

The village

Known in Malayalam as Papa Nashini (sin destroyer), Varkala's beautiful white-sand **beach** known as **Papanasam Beach** has long been associated with ancestor worship. Devotees come to the beach after praying at the **Janardhana Swamy temple** (said to be over two thousand years old), to bring the ashes of departed relatives for their "final rest". Non-Hindus are not permitted to enter the sanctum sanctorum but are welcome in the grounds. A small government hospital at its north end, opened by Indira Gandhi in 1983, was set up to benefit from being built on the same site as three **natural**

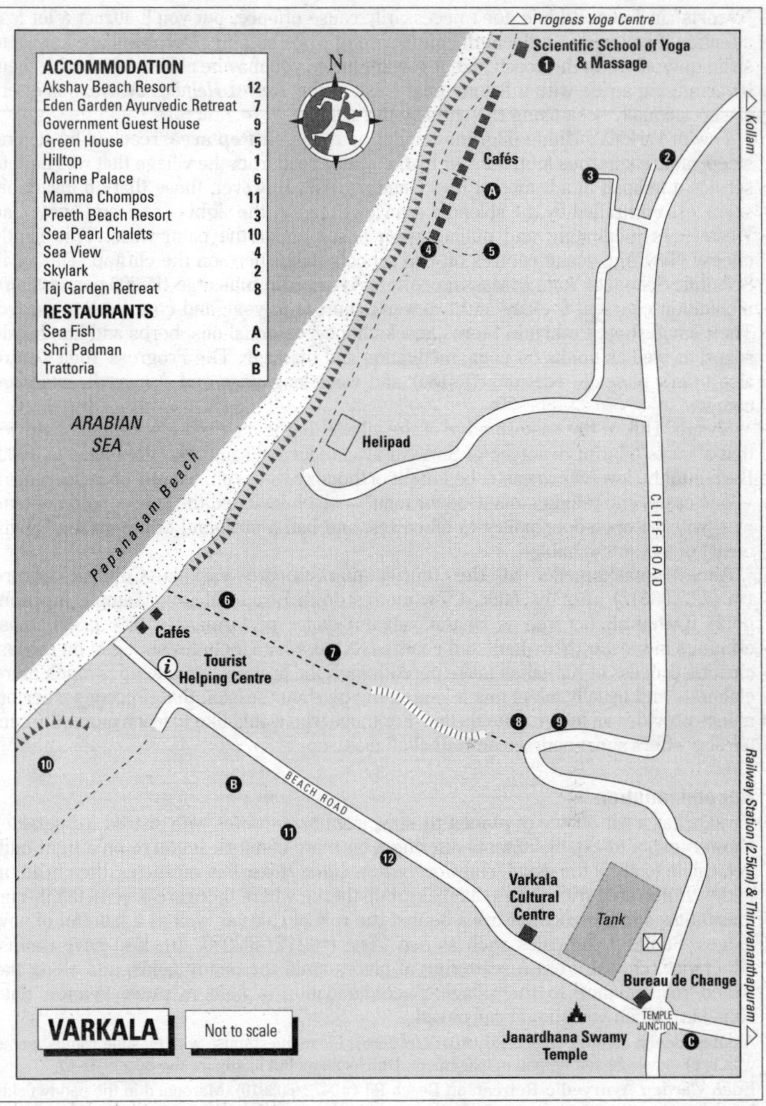

springs, and to take advantage of the sea air, which is said to boost the health of asthma sufferers.

Backed by sheer red laterite cliffs and drenched by rolling waves off the Arabian Sea, Papa Nashini is imposingly scenic and still a relatively peaceful place to soak up the sun, with few hawkers and only the odd group of ogling men. Its religious significance means attitudes to (female) public nudity are markedly less liberal than other coastal "resorts" in India. Bikinis don't necessarily cause offence, but you'll attract a lot less attention if you wear a full-length cotton sarong while bathing. **Dolphins** are known to swim quite close to the coast, and, if you are lucky, you may be able to swim with them by arranging a ride with a fishing boat – ask at the *Tourist Helping Centre*. Sea otters are occasionally seen along the cliffs by the sea.

Few of Varkala's Hindu pilgrims wander up to the **clifftop area**, reached by several steep and treacherous footpaths, or by the sealed road from the village that was built to service a helipad in advance of Mrs Gandhi's visit. However, those that do invariably seem less enthralled by the splendid sea views than by the sight of *sari-* and *kurta*-clad Westerners meditating and pulling **yoga** poses under the palm trees. This faintly cheesy New Age scene centres on two schools based here on the clifftop. The small Scientific School of Yoga & Massage, offers **Ayurvedic massage** (Rs200 per session), meditation courses, five-day and two-week courses in yoga and courses in massage. Their small shop, Prakruthi Stores, stocks honey, essential oils, herbs and handmade soaps, as well as books on yoga, meditation and massage. The Progress Yoga Centre also offers massage sessions (Rs180) and week-long yoga and Ayurvedic massage courses.

Sivagiri Hill, at the eastern edge of the village, harbours a more traditional **ashram** that attracts pilgrim devotees of Shri Narayana Guru, a saint who died here in 1922. Born into the low *ezhava* caste, he fought orthodoxy with a philosophy of social reform – "one caste, one religion, one God for man" – which included the consecration of temples, with an open-door policy to all castes, and had a profound effect on the "upliftment" of the untouchables.

Aimed unashamedly at the tourist market, the Varkala Cultural Centre (☎0472/603612) near the tank, a few metres down Beach Rd from Temple Junction, holds **Kathakali** (as well as Bharatanatyam) dance performances (see p.336) most evenings in season (Nov–Jan), and charges Rs100, which includes sitting in on the fascinating process of Kathakali make-up. Although the process of make-up is much more elaborate and usually takes much longer, the two-hour session that precedes a performance provides an insight into the art. For those who would like to learn more, the centre also offers short courses on Kathakali make-up.

Accommodation

Varkala has a fair choice of **places to stay**, from basic rooms with shared (or outside) shower-toilets to establishments offering a bit more comfort. If you're on a tight budget, call in to see if the wonderful *Government Guest House* has vacancies, then head up to the clifftop area (rickshaws can make it up there), where there are several family-run guesthouses in the coconut trees behind the row of cafés as well as a handful of new lodges. Some of the cafés such as *Sea View* (☎0472/602050; ①), also have rooms. Otherwise, choose from a scattering of places amid the paddy fields, and along the sealed road leading to the village. Accommodation is tight in **peak season** (late Nov–Jan), when you should call ahead.

Akshay Beach Resort, Beach Rd (☎0472/602668). Clean guesthouse with en-suite rooms (some with a/c), massage and helpful management. Dull location, but handy for the beach. ⑤–⑥.

Eden Garden Ayurvedic Retreat, off Beach Rd (☎0472/603910). Marooned in the paddy fields behind the beach, with cosy en-suite rooms ranged around a fishpond (watch out for mosquitoes). Offers Ayurvedic treatment including massage and food. ④–⑤.

Government Guest House/Tourist Bungalow, near the steps up the cliff, off Cliff Rd (☎0472/602227). Former maharajah's holiday palace, converted into a characterful guesthouse, with eight enormous rooms and meals available on request. Superb value but a bit run-down. For more comfort try the new *Tourist Bungalow*, which is next door and part of the same complex – the large plain rooms are excellent value. ①.

Green House, clifftop area (☎0472/604659). Secluded place, situated behind a small temple, in an unhurried and friendly hamlet. There are plenty of similarly priced fallbacks nearby (try *White House* or *Red House*). ②–③.

Hilltop, northernmost end of the clifftop area (☎0472/601237). A great spot, with pleasant, breezy rooms, attached shower-toilets and relaxing terrace restaurant. There are cheaper rooms at the back, while the upstairs rooms – quite a bit more expensive – have views. Good value. ③–⑥.

Mamma Chompos, Beach Rd (☎0472/603995). Rock-bottom rooms in a converted farm compound with shared toilets. There's the recent addition of a restaurant, and also a new block up on the hill, where the rooms are plain, but adequate and reasonably good value. ①–③.

Marine Palace, behind Papanasam Beach (☎0472/603204). En-suite rooms in a modern, pale green building near the sea. Pricier front rooms have sea views and balconies; the thatched annexe is cheaper and the restaurant is very pleasant. ③–⑥.

Preeth Beach Resort, clifftop area, off Cliff Rd (☎0472/600942). Large, well-maintained complex shaded by a palm grove, with a range of rooms including some a/c and a restaurant. ⑥–⑦.

Sea Pearl Chalets, Papanasam Beach (☎0472/605875). The closest to the sea with a nice location on the cliff overlooking the beach. The attractive, small, round, single-room cottages are expensive though, especially in season. ⑥.

Skylark, clifftop area, off Cliff Rd (☎0472/602107). Quiet guesthouse away from the sea with plain but comfortable rooms, and within easy walking distance of the clifftop restaurants.

Taj Garden Retreat, near the *Government Guest House*, off Cliff Rd (☎0472/603000, fax 602996; toll-free UK 0800/282699, USA/Canada 1 0800 458 8825). Total luxury with comfortable rooms, a good restaurant and bar and a pleasant swimming pool, but all a bit ostentatious for a laid-back place like Varkala. ⑨.

Eating

Seafood lovers will do well in Varkala's increasingly sophisticated clifftop café-restaurants, some of which have upper storeys raised on stilts for better sea views. Prices are quite high and the service slow, but the superb location more than compensates especially in the evenings when the sea twinkles with the lights of countless fishing boats. Most of the restaurants offer identical menus with fresh fish, including shark and marlin, on display. The further you go along the clifftop the cheaper the restaurants get. Due to Kerala's antiquated licensing laws which involve huge amounts of tax, **beer** is discreetly available but at a price (Rs75–90), as none of the cafés are supposed to sell it and periodically get raided, resulting in official or unofficial fines. One alternative is to retire to the comforts of the *Taj Garden Retreat's* bar and superb restaurant but you will have to pay through the nose.

Sea Fish, clifftop area. The largest of the clifftop cafés, serving moderately priced tandoori meat and fish on a sandy terrace with relaxing wicker chairs and optimum views.

Shri Padman, next to the Janardhana Swamy temple. The large rear terrace of this unpromising, grubby-looking "meals" joint is the main travellers' hangout in Varkala. The veg food is cheap and delicious, try the coconut-rich *navrattan*, deep-fried cheese, garlic *chapatis* or filling *biryani*. The location is very atmospheric, especially at breakfast time, when villagers come to the tank to bathe.

Trattoria, off Beach Rd. Hut restaurant above the beach with good views of the sea and, like its sister concern *Mamma Chompos*, features a strong Italian menu.

Kollam (Quilon)

One of the oldest ports on the Malabar Coast, **KOLLAM** (pronounced *Koillam*, and previously known as Quilon), 74km northwest of Thiruvananthapuram and 85km southeast of Alappuzha, was formerly at the centre of the international spice trade. The sixteenth-century Portuguese writer Duarte Barbossa described it as a "very great city with a right good haven", which was visited by "Moors, Heathen and Christians in great numbers", and stated that "a great store" of pepper was to be found there. In fact, the port flourished from the very earliest times, trading amicably with the Phoenicians, Arabs, Persians, Greeks, Romans and Chinese.

Nowadays, Kollam is chiefly of interest as one of the entry or exit points to the backwaters of Kerala (see box on p.310), and most travellers simply stay overnight en route to or from Alappuzha. The **town** itself, sandwiched between the sea and the Ashtamudi (eight inlets) lake, is less exciting than its history might suggest. It's a typically sprawling Keralan market community, with a few characterful old tiled wooden houses and winding backstreets, kept busy with the commercial interests of coir, cashew nuts (a good local buy), pottery, aluminium and fishery industries. The missable ruins of **Tangasseri** fort (three kilometres from the centre) are the last vestiges of colonial occupation.

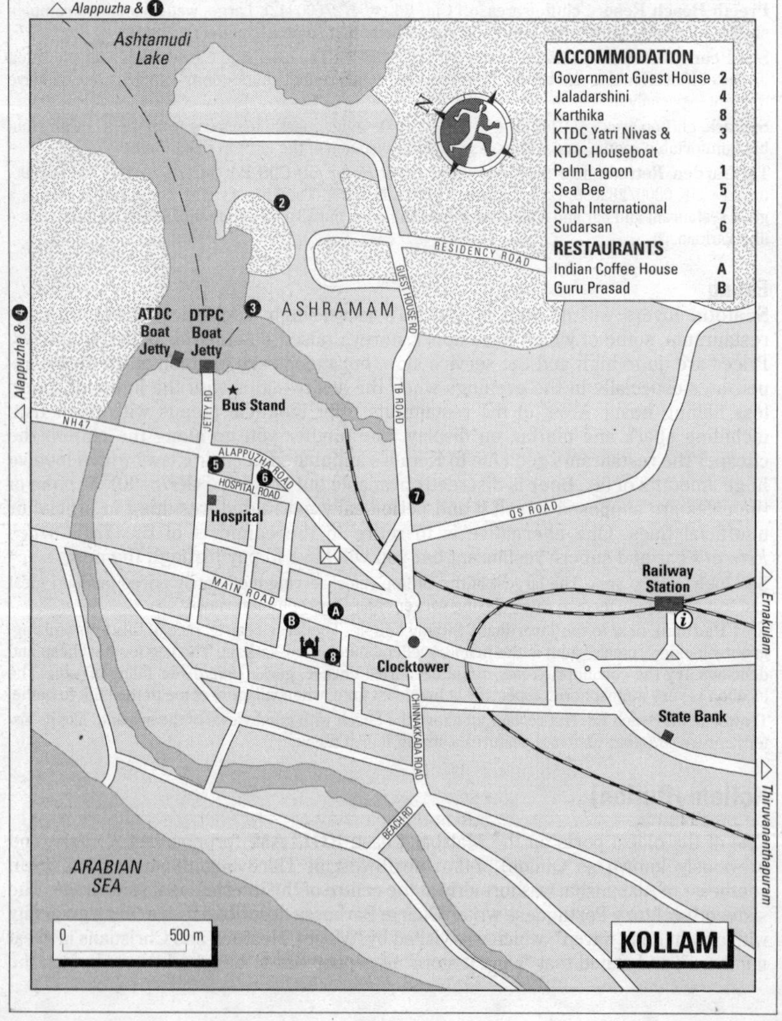

Arrival and information

An important stop on the main coastal route, Kollam is served by numerous daily trains connecting north to Ernakulam and south to Thiruvananthapuram and beyond. The **train station** is on the east side of town, a two-kilometre auto-rickshaw ride (Rs10) from the jetty. On platform 4, the tiny District Tourism Promotion Council (DTPC) **Tourist Information Counter** (Mon–Sat 9am–12.30pm & 1.30–5pm), provides an excellent service. They will book hotels for you; you have to pay one night in advance, but the only extra charge is for the phone calls. There is also a DTPC tourist office (Mon–Sat 9am–5.30pm; ☎0474/742558), at the **DTPC boat jetty** (for boat details, see box on p.310). The jetty and **bus stand** are close together on the edge of Ashtamudi Lake. Bookable express buses are available south to Thiruvananthapuram, and north to Kochi (see "Travel Details" on p.366).

Note, however, that the rival Alappuzha Tourism Development Council (ATDC) ferry leaves from the **ATDC boat jetty**, 100m to the west, which is booked at the pier or through their Alappuzha office (☎0477/243462). The DTPC centre at their boat jetty will **change money** at bank rates during bank hours. The DTPC organizes **guided tours** (daily 9am–1pm; Rs250), by boat and by foot, through the complex of waterways and footpaths of nearby Monroe Island on Ashtamudi Lake, providing a fascinating glimpse of Keralan village life.

Accommodation and eating

The most congenial **places to stay** are outside the town, across Ashtamudi Lake from the DTPC main boat jetty (easy to get to by auto-rickshaw, but more difficult to return from). You could stay on a **houseboat** such as the one moored at the *Yatri Nivas*. Apart from the hotel restaurants, other places to **eat** include the *Indian Coffee House* on Main Rd, and *Guru Prasad*, a little further along the same road, which serves great South Indian veg "meals". The best of the hotel restaurants can be found in the *Sudarsan*, which has a good-value "meals" restaurant along with its more upmarket a/c restaurant.

Government Guest House, north of the centre, off Guest House Rd, by Ashtamudi Lake (☎0474/743620). Characterful, Euro-Keralan building, once the British Residency, with curved tiled roof and verandahs, in a vast compound. Ye olde British furniture in cavernous spaces, but just five rooms (unbelievable value at Rs150). Boats are available for rent on the lake, simple meals are served by arrangement, and you can reserve your backwater tickets here. Book in advance; some travellers come to Kollam purely to stay here. ①.

Jaladarshini, Thevally, 2km west of town (☎0474/743414). Beautiful lakeside location but the new management uses it more for weddings and daytime visitors who come for the low-key recreational facilities. This is unfortunate, as the rooms are now neglected and abysmally maintained, although the a/c room on the corner overlooking the lake is still attractive. ③–⑥.

Karthika, next to the temple, Chinnakadan (☎0474/76241). Large and popular budget hotel with plain rooms, some a/c, ranged around a courtyard; handy for the train station. ③–⑤.

KTDC Houseboat, *KTDC Yatri Nivas* (☎0474/745538). The KTDC houseboats are distinctive in that they have a traditional Keralan-style wood cottage as a cabin rather than the usual rattan cabins of the other tourist boats. Each boat comes with two cabins – one on either side. You can rent these boats for short cruises, or to go along the backwaters to Alappuzha. ⑦.

KTDC Yatri Nivas, across from the DTPC boat jetty (☎0474/745538). Modern, clean rooms (two are a/c) in a great location overlooking the lake; the best fallback if the *Government Guest House* is full. Good restaurant with South Indian snacks but plagued in the evenings by louts from the beer parlour. ②–⑤.

Palm Lagoon, Vellimon West (☎0474/523974). A beautiful location on Ashtamudi Lake but a good 15km from town. Pleasant thatched cottages, with breakfast or full board plus good Ayurvedic treatment and the opportunity to explore the backwaters. Book directly or through DTPC for directions and a discount. ⑧.

Railway Retiring Rooms, first floor, train station. Spacious, clean and very cheap. ①.

Sea Bee, Jetty Rd (☎0474/744371). Big, recently renovated hotel, near the bus station and jetty. Some a/c rooms, restaurant, bar and foreign exchange. ③–⑤.

Shah International, TB Rd (☎0474/742362). A large, modern-looking hotel with three-star pretensions, but a flash exterior hides some quite dull rooms. ④–⑤.

Sudarsan, Alappuzha Rd (☎0474/744322). Central and popular, with varying standards of rooms, some with a/c and TV. Busy, dark a/c restaurant with a white plaster model of the "Last Supper" at one end and a TV at the other. Extensive Indian and Chinese menu, though not all is necessarily available, and a bar. ③–⑥.

Around Kollam: Kayamkulam and Karunagapalli

KAYAMKULAM, served by (non-express) buses between Kollam and Alappuzha, was once the centre of its own small kingdom, which after a battle in 1746 came under the control of Travancore's king Marthanda Varma. In the eighteenth century the area was famous for its spices, particularly pepper and cinnamon. The Abbé Reynal claimed that the Dutch exported some two million pounds of pepper each year, one-fifth of it from Kayamkulam. At this time, the kingdom was known also for the skill of its army of fifteen thousand Nayars (Kerala's martial caste).

Set in a tranquil garden, the dilapidated eighteenth-century **Krishnapuram palace** (Tues–Sat 10am–4.30pm) is imbued with Keralan grace, and constructed largely of wood, with gabled roofs and rooms opening out onto internal courtyards. It's now a museum, but unlike the palace at Padmanabhapuram (see p.298), with which it shares some similarities, the whole place is in great need of restoration. So few visitors ever find their way here that the motivation for upkeep must be minimal.

The collection inside is dusty, poorly labelled and neglected. A display case contains *puja* ceremony utensils and oil lamps, some of which are arranged in an arc known as a *prabhu*, placed behind a temple deity to provide a halo of light. Fine miniature *panchaloha* ("five-metal" bronze alloy, with gold as one ingredient) figures include the water god Varuna, several Vishnus and a minuscule worshipping devotee. Small stone columns carved with serpent deities were recovered from local houses.

The prize exhibit is a huge **mural** of the classical Keralan school, in muted ochre-reds and blue-greens, measuring over fourteen square metres, which depicts **Gajendra Moksha** – the salvation of Gajendra, king of the elephants. In the tenth-century Sanskrit *Bhagavata Purana*, the story is told of a Pandyan king, Indrayumna, a devotee of Vishnu cursed by the sage Agastya to be born again as an elephant. One day, while sporting with his wives at the edge of a lake, his leg was seized by a crocodile whose grip was so tight that Gajendra was held captive for years. Finally, in desperation the elephant called upon his chosen deity Vishnu, who immediately appeared, riding his celestial bird/man vehicle, Garuda, and destroyed the crocodile.

The centre of the painting is dominated by a dynamic portrayal of Garuda about to land, with huge spread wings and a facial expression denoting *raudra* (fury), in stark contrast to the compassionate features of the multi-armed Vishnu. Smaller figures of Gajendra, in mid-trumpet, and his assailant are shown to the right. As with all paintings in the Kerala style, every inch is packed with detail. Bearded sages, animals, mythical beasts and forest plants surround the main figures. The outer edges are decorated with floriate borders which, at the bottom, form a separate triptych-like panel showing Balakrishna, the child Krishna, attended by adoring females.

At a quiet spot just outside the small town of **KARUNAGAPALLI**, 23km north of Kollam towards Alappuzha, it is still possible to watch the construction and repair of traditional **kettu vallam**, or "tied boats". These long cargo boats, a familiar sight on the backwaters, are built entirely without nails. Each jackwood plank is **sewn** to the next with coir rope, and then the whole is coated with a caustic black resin made from boiled cashew kernels. With careful maintenance they last for generations.

Karunagapalli is best visited as a day-trip from Kollam; regular **buses** pass through on the way to Alappuzha. One daytime **train**, #6525, leaves Kollam at 11.55am, arriving at Karunagapalli at 12.30, but you have to get a bus back. On reaching the bus stand or

KETTU VALLUM CRUISES

Groups of up to ten can charter a *vallam* moored at **Karunagapalli** for a day's **cruise** on the backwaters (see box on p.310). The boat has comfortable cane chairs and a raised central platform where passengers can laze on cushions, and a toilet on board. Cool drinks can be made available. Sections of the curved roof of wood and plaited palms open out to provide shade and allow uninterrupted views. Whether powered by local gondoliers or by sail, the trip is as quiet and restful (at least for the passengers), as you could possibly want. Though not cheap (around Rs3000 for the day), the luxury is well worth it. For longer trips a second *vallam* has been converted into a houseboat with two bedrooms and a kitchen. A cook will also be provided. To book, call Tourindia, MG Rd, Thiruvananthapuram (☎0471/331507).

KTDC also rent out houseboats for cruises on Vembanad Lake, moored at their *Kumarakom Tourist Village*, near the Kumarakom Bird Sanctuary (see p.315), Alappuzha (☎0481/92258). Rates start at around Rs3000 per boat per day, which includes the services of crew and cook. These *kettu vallam* can also be rented for shorter cruises (Rs600 per hour).

train station, take an auto-rickshaw to the boatyard of the *vallam asharis*, the boat carpenters. The boatbuilders are friendly and willing to let visitors watch them work. In the shade of palm trees at the edge of the water, some weave palm leaves, others twist coir strands into rope, and craftsmen repair the boats. Soaking in the shallows nearby are palm leaves, used for thatch, and coconut husks for coir rope. If you wanted to buy a *vallam*, it would set you back around two *lakh* (Rs200,000).

Alappuzha

Under its former appellation of Alleppey, **ALAPPUZHA**, roughly midway between Kollam 85km south and Kochi 64km north, is another romantic and historic name from Kerala's past. It was one of the best-known ports along the Malabar Coast, and tourist literature is fond of referring to it as the "Venice of the East", but while it may be full of interconnecting **canals**, there the resemblance ends. Alappuzha is a bustling, messy town of ramshackle wood and corrugated-iron-roof houses, chiefly significant in the coir industry, which accounts for much of the traffic on its oily, green-brown waterways. Emanating from the slicks of raw sewage, diesel spills and aquatic weed that coagulate on their surfaces, the stomach-churning stench these give off each time a ferry chugs through is something many travellers wince about for weeks afterwards.

Despite its insalubrious canals and frequent power cuts, Alappuzha is prominent on the tourist trail as one of the major centres for **backwater boat trips**, served by ferries to and from Kollam and Kottayam in particular. Most visitors stay just one night, catching a boat or bus out early the next morning. However, a short distance away from the centre, the congestion of Alappuzha eases and palm-fringed roads lead to the pleasant **lakeside** where Keralan life appears much more attractive. No special sights demand attention here, but the bazaar along the main street, **Mullakal Rd**, is worth a browse, with a better-than-average crop of lurid Keralan *lunghis*.

Alappuzha really comes alive on the second Saturday of August, in the depths of the rainy season, when it serves as the venue for one of Kerala's major spectacles – the **Nehru Trophy snakeboat race**. This event, first held in 1952, is based on the traditional Keralan enthusiasm for racing magnificently decorated longboats, with raised rears designed to resemble the hood of a cobra. More than enthusiastically powered by a maximum of one hundred and fifty singing and shouting oarsmen, scores of boats take part, and Alappuzha is packed with thousands of spectators. Similar races can be

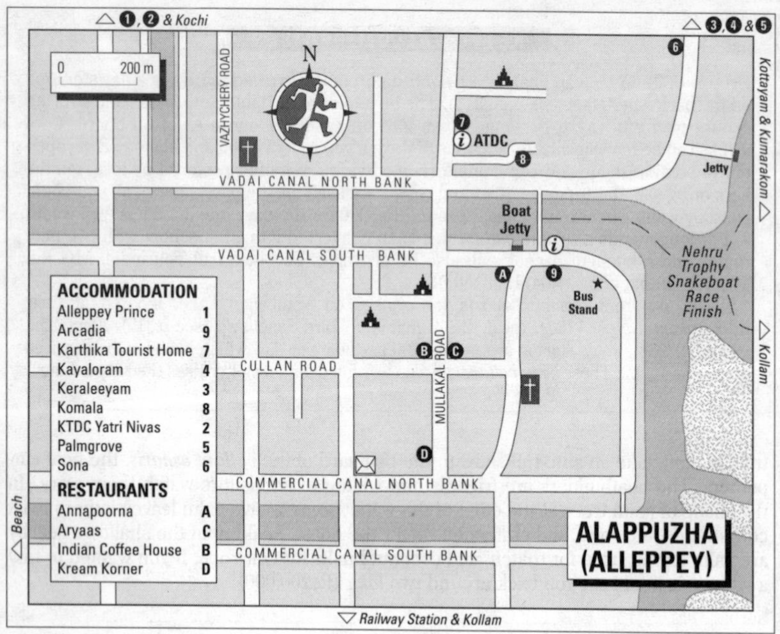

seen at Aranmula (p.316), and at Champakualm, 16km by ferry from Alappuzha. The ATDC information office (see below) will be able to tell you the dates of these other events, which change every year.

Arrival and information

The KSRTC **bus stand**, on the east of the town, has reasonably good local and long-distance connections. The **boat jetty** is just one minute's walk west from the bus stand. The **train station**, 3km southwest of the jetty, sees few major services. For recommended bus, boat and train services out of Alappuzha, see p.312 "Moving on from Alappuzha".

Among Alappuzha's two rival **tourist departments**, the ATDC tourist information office (daily 8am–8pm; ☎0477/2433462) is a short walk across the canal from the jetty, on Komala Rd. The DTPC office (daily 7.30am–9pm; ☎0477/251796), at the DTPC boat jetty, is handier and handles **hotel bookings** for all KTDC and private hotels throughout Kerala, and other parts of South India, for the charge of the telephone call and on receipt of a day's tariff. Both the ATDC and the DTPC are co-operative societies, and are friendly and helpful, both sell tickets for their **ferries**, **backwater cruises** and **charter boats** (maximum 20 people); the latter are good for group excursions into less-visited backwaters. The Government of Kerala also has a tourist office at the DTPC jetty (Mon–Sat 10am–5pm; ☎0477/260722), which is good for travel information and has a useful stack of literature. Another ferry and charter organization worth mentioning is Kerala Backwaters, at Choondapally Buildings, near the Nehru Trophy finishing point (☎0477/241693). **Money-changing** facilities are available at the Bank of India on

Mullakal Rd, the State Bank of India on Beach Rd, or the Canara Bank, next to the Zion Food Shop, near the jetty, which accepts travellers' cheques but not cash.

Accommodation

If you need to stay near the town centre, Alappuzha's choice of **lodgings** is uninspiring but there are some great places to stay if you are willing to travel. For traditional atmosphere, try *Sona* or *Keraleeyam,* which specialize in Ayurvedic treatment. The *Alleppey Prince*, which has a pool, is an old favourite and within striking distance of town, while the luxurious *Kayaloram* on the southern edge of the lake ranks amongst Kerala's finest settings.

Alleppey Prince, AS Rd (aka Ernakulam Rd or NH47), 2km north of the jetty (☎0477/243752). The poshest option close to the town centre, all rooms are a/c. Private backwater trips, and classical music or Kathakali dance performances are staged by the pool. Book ahead. ⑦.

Arcadia, by the KSRTC bus stand (☎0477/241354). Revamped hotel (previously the *Kuttanad*) with plain but acceptable rooms (some are a/c), situated close to the jetty. The restaurant serves excellent fish. ③–⑥.

Karthika Tourist Home, Kathiyani Rd, off Komala Rd, across the canal, opposite the jetty (☎0477/245524). Run-down and plain rooms, some with bath and wicker chairs. Room 31 has large bay windows. ②.

Kayaloram, Punnamada Kayal (☎0477/242040). Set in the incredible location of a palm grove, with views onto the lake; these twelve wood cottages are built in Keralan Theravad style with open to-the-sky baths, and are ranged around a pool. Book through their city office at Punchiri Buildings, Jetty Rd (☎0477/260573), and you will be taken there by boat from the Nehru Trophy jetty. ⑨.

Keraleeyam, Nehru Trophy Rd, Thathampally (☎0477/241468). A traditional Keralan house with oodles of character offering genuine Ayurvedic treatment. Located right on Punnamada Kayal, the Nehru Trophy channel. You get here by boat from the jetty. Four-day Ayurvedic rejuvenation and all-inclusive holidays also available. Recommended. ⑦.

Komala, Zilla Court Ward, north of the jetty canal, five minutes by rickshaw from the bus stand (☎0477/243631). This is a large hotel, which is easily the best in its class, and has the town's nicest restaurant. A good range of rooms are available including some a/c. ②–⑥.

KTDC Yatri Nivas, AS Rd, near the *Alleppey Prince* (☎0477/244460). Brand new complex with good-value, sizeable rooms. There's a restaurant and beer parlour next door at their *Aaram Motel*. ②.

Palmgrove, Punnamada (☎0477/245004 & 243474). On Punnamada Kayal, 2.5km from the jetty. Set in a quiet two-and-a-half acre plot, it has quaint bamboo huts and attached open-to-the-sky baths, which are dotted around a manicured palm grove. This place isn't in the same league as some other "resorts" along the backwaters, but then it is a lot more affordable. You can get here by bus or by boat. ⑥.

Sona, Lakeside, Thathampally (☎0477/245211). A beautiful old Keralan home, which once belonged to Swiss lady, this place has a beautiful garden and offers four rooms with mosquito nets. There's plenty of family atmosphere here. Recommended. ⑤.

Eating

One of the most popular places to eat in Alappuzha is the *Komala Hotel*'s *Arun* restaurant, but there are plenty of other adequate, and cheaper, places including the restaurant and snack bar at the DTPC jetty. For a splurge, slip on some clean clothes and catch a rickshaw out to the *Alleppey Prince,* whose a/c *Vembanad* restaurant offers the town's classiest menu, and beer by the pool. The KTDC *Aaram Motel*, however, around the corner, is a lot cheaper and also serves beer.

Annapoorna, opposite the DTPC jetty. A good cheap vegetarian "meals" restaurant.

KUTTANAD: THE BACKWATERS OF KERALA

One of the most memorable experiences available to travellers in India – even those on the lowest of budgets – is the opportunity to take a boat journey on the **backwaters of Kerala**. The area known as **Kuttanad** stretches for 75km from Kollam in the south to Kochi in the north, sandwiched between the sea and the hills. This bewildering labyrinth of shimmering waterways, composed of lakes, canals, rivers and rivulets, is lined with dense tropical greenery and preserves rural Keralan lifestyles that are completely hidden from the road.

Views constantly change from narrow canals and dense vegetation to open vistas and dazzling green paddy fields. Homes, farms, churches, mosques and temples can be glimpsed among the trees, and every so often you might catch the blue flash of a kingfisher or the green of a parakeet. Pallas fishing eagles cruise above the water looking for prey, and cormorants perch on logs to dry their wings. If you're lucky enough to be in a boat without a motor, at times the peace will be broken only by the squawking of crows and the occasional film song from a distant radio. Day-to-day life is lived on and beside the water. Some families live on tiny pockets of land, with just enough room for a simple house, yard and boat. They bathe and wash their clothes – sometimes their buffaloes too, muddy from ploughing the fields – at the water's edge. Traditional Keralan longboats, *kettu vallam*, glide along, powered both by gondolier-like boatmen with poles and by sail. Often they look on the point of sinking, with water lapping perilously close to the edge, and laden with heavyweight cargo. Fishermen work from rowing boats or operate massive Chinese nets on the shore.

Coconut trees at improbable angles form shady canopies, and occasionally you pass under simple curved bridges. Here and there basic drawbridges can be raised on ropes, but major bridges are few and far between; most people rely on boatmen to ferry them across the water to connect with roads and bus services, resulting in a constant crisscrossing of the waters from dawn until dusk (a way of life beautifully represented in the visually stunning film *Piravi*, by Keralan director Shaji). Poles sticking out of the water indicate dangerous shallows.

Threats to the fragile ecosystem

The **African moss** that often carpets the surface of the narrower waterways, incidentally, may look attractive, but is a menace to small craft traffic and starves underwater life of light. It is also a symptom of the many serious **ecological problems** currently affecting the region, whose population density ranges from between two and four times that of other coastal areas in southwest India. This has put growing pressure on land, and hence a greater reliance on fertilizers, which eventually work their way into the water causing the buildup of moss. Illegal land reclamation, however, poses the single greatest threat to this fragile ecosystem. In a little over a century, the total area of water in Kuttanad has been reduced by two-thirds, while mangrove swamps and fish stocks have been decimated by pollution and the spread of towns and villages around the edges of the backwater region.

Routes and practicalities

There are numerous backwater routes to choose from, on vessels ranging from local ferries, through chauffeur-driven speedboats run by the KTDC, to customized *kettu vallam* (see box on p.307) cruises offered by numerous agencies as well as upmarket hotels such as the *Malabar* in Kochi (see p.339). Much the most popular excursion is the full-day journey between **Kollam** and **Alappuzha**; you can cover part or all of the route in a day, returning to your original point of departure by bus during the evening, or, more comfortably, staying the night at either end. All sorts of private hustlers offer their ser-

Arun, *Komala Hotel*, Zilla Court Ward. Tasty Chinese noodles and Indian veg (including delicious *dal makhini*, *malai kofta* and *subzis*), but avoid the continental food. If it's busy, settle in for a wait.

vices, but the basic choice lies between boats run by the Alappuzha Tourism Development Co-op (ATDC) and the District Tourism Promotion Council (DTPC), which run one boat daily on alternate days from Monday through Saturday (there is **no service on Sundays**); additionally, from December to May, they lay on two boats per day. The double-decker boats depart at 10.30am, and tickets, which can be bought in advance at the jetties, or from ATDC/DTPC counters in Alappuzha and Kollam, cost Rs150. Both companies make around five stops during the 8hr 30min journey, including one for lunch, and another at the renowned **Mata Amritanandamayi Mission** at Amritapuri. Foreigners are welcome to stay at the ashram, which is the home of the renowned female guru, Shri Amritanandamayi Devi, known as the "Hugging Guru" because she gives each of her visitors and devotees a big, power-imparting hug during the daily *darshan* sessions (see p.62).

Although it is by far the most popular backwater trip, many tourists find the Alappuzha–Kollam route overlong and at times uncomfortable, with crowded decks and intense sun. There's also something faintly embarrassing about being cooped up with a crowd of fellow tourists madly photographing any signs of life on the water or canal banks, while gangs of kids scamper alongside the boat screaming "one pen…! one pen…!" You can sidestep the tourist scene completely, however, by catching **local ferries**. These are a lot slower, and the crush can be worse, but you're far less conspicuous than on the ATDC/DTPC boats and you are exposed to a more intimate experience of life on the water. The trip from Alappuzha to Kottayam (7.30am, 10am, 11.30am, 2.30pm & 5.30pm; Rs6) is particularly recommended; take the 2.30pm departure for the best light, and arrive early so you can get a place on the bow, which affords uninterrupted views. The scenery on this route is more varied than between Alappuzha and Kollam, beginning with open lagoons and winding up on narrow canals through densely populated coconut groves and islands, and the ticket costs one tenth of the price of the ATDC/DPTC tour.

Whichever boat you opt for, take a sun hat and plenty of water, and **check the departure times** in advance, as these can vary from year to year.

From Alappuzha, the ATDC tour departs on Mon, Wed and Fri at 10.30am. From November to March, they lay on two boats per day. You can book tickets at their office on Komala Rd, Alappuzha (☎0477/2433462). There are eleven daily departures by local ferry to Kottayam (Rs6; 2hr 30min; first at 5am, last 9pm). Noisy speedboats can be chartered from ATDC and from the DTPC (☎0477/251796) from Rs400 per hour.

From Kollam, the ATDC boat departs at 10.30am on Tuesday, Thursday and Saturday only. Shorter ferry trips are available to Kapapuzha and Guhanandapuram (2hr), if you don't have time for a full-day excursion.

From Kottayam, there are eleven daily ferries to Alappuzha (Rs5; 2hr 30min; first at 7.30am, last 8.30pm).

Houseboats

Although expensive by Keralan standards, the best way of seeing the backwaters – and getting a taste of Keralan life on the Kuttanad – is by hiring a customized rattan-covered *kettu vallam* **houseboat**. They cost upwards of Rs3000 for a day cruise, usually sleep four, and come equipped with cook and crew. The journey from Kollam to Alappuzha can take around eight hours and a further eight from Alappuzha to Kochi. Several agencies now hire boats, but the original pioneer, and one of the best operators in Kerala is Tourindia, with offices in Thiruvananthapuram (☎0471/331507) and Kochi (☎0484/668053). Other upmarket operators include the *Casino Hotel*, Willingdon Island, Kochi (☎0484/668221, fax 668001). The KTDC, ATDC and DTPC can also arrange houseboats, and the Tourist Desk at the main jetty at Kochi (☎0484/371761) has a small operation and is slightly cheaper (see p.330).

Aryaas, Mullakal Rd. The town's best Udupi restaurant, serving South Indian breakfasts, and excellent *rawa masala dosas* after 6pm. Recommended if you're on a tight budget.

Indian Coffee House, Mullakal Rd. Part of the all-India chain of co-operatives, which has a predictable menu of *dosas* and *iddlis,* but with the addition of meat dishes.

Kream Korner, Mullakal Rd. Recently revamped non-veg-restaurant-cum-ice-cream parlour. Mostly serves chicken and mutton, but also has a selection of snacks, milkshakes and ice-creams.

Thoppi, *Karthika Tourist Home.* Very modest, clean and friendly place with an ambitious, inexpensive Indian and Chinese menu. They open early for standard omelette with bread and butter and jam breakfasts.

MOVING ON FROM ALAPPUZHA

As Alappuzha is not on the main railway network, but rather on a branch line, the choice of trains servicing the town is limited, but bus connections are adequate especially to Kochi/Ernakulam where there is a greater choice of trains to northern destinations and Tamil Nadu. There are, however, adequate train connections to Thiruvananthapuram and Kollam in the south, and to Kochi/Ernakulam, Thrissur, Palakaad and other points in the north. Although buses travel to Kollam, the best way of getting there is by boat. Regular ferry services connect to Kottayam from where you can get buses to Periyar, or several destinations along the coastal highway.

By bus

The shambolic KSRTC bus stand, on the east of town, is served by half-hourly buses to **Kollam** (3hr) and **Thiruvananthapuram** (3hr 15min), and to **Kochi/Ernakulam** (2hr); less frequent buses run to **Kottayam** (4hr), **Thrissur** (8hr) and **Palakaad** (11hr).

By boat

Tourist boats travel regularly to **Kollam** with the ATDC and DTPC boats operating with a similar schedule on alternate days (Mon–Sat) departing at 10.30am and arriving at Kollam at 6.30pm. Regular **ferries** travel to **Kottayam**, the first starting at 5am and the last at 5.30pm.

By train

As the backwaters prevent trains from continuing south beyond Alappuzha, only a few major daily services and a handful of passenger trains depart from the train station, 3km southwest of the jetty. For points further north along the coast including **Mangalore**, take an early train and change at Ernakulam, as the Alleppey Cannanore Express #6307, which continues to **Kozhikode** and **Kannur**, arrives at those destinations far too late at night. Most trains south to Thiruvananthapuram leave at inconvenient hours except for the Ernakulam Trivandrum Express #6341.

The following trains are recommended as the **fastest** and/or **most convenient** from Alappuzha.

Recommended trains from Alappuzha

Destination	Name	Number	Frequency	Departs	Total time
Kochi/Ernakulam	**Bokaro/Tata Express*	#8690	daily	6am	1hr 3min
	**Alleppey–Chennai Express*	#6042	daily	3pm	1hr
	**Trivandrum–Mumbai CST Express*	#6332	Fri	7.20am	1hr 15min
Chennai	**Alleppey–Chennai Express*	#6042	daily	3pm	15hr 30min
Thiruvananthapuram	*Ernakulam–Trivandrum Express*	#6341	daily	7.25am	3hr 20min

* these trains continue to **Thrissur** and **Palakaad**

Kottayam and around

The busy commercial centre of **KOTTAYAM**, 76km southeast of Kochi and 37km northeast of Alappuzha, is strategically located between the backwaters to the west and the spice, tea and rubber plantations, forests and mountains of the Western Ghats to the east. Most visitors come here on the way to somewhere else – foreigners take short backwater trips to Alappuzha or set off to the **Periyar Wildlife Sanctuary**, while Ayappa devotees pass through en route to the forest temple at Sabarimala (see box on p.320).

Kottayam's long history of **Syrian Christian** settlement is reflected by the presence of two thirteenth-century churches on a hill, five kilometres northwest of the centre, which you can get to by rickshaw. Two eighth-century Nestorian stone crosses with Pahlavi and Syriac inscriptions, on either side of the elaborately decorated altar of the **Valliapalli** (big) church, are probably the earliest solid evidence of Christianity in India. The visitors' book in the church contains entries from as far back as the 1890s, including one by the Ethiopian emperor, Haile Selassie, and a British viceroy. The interior of the nearby **Cheriapalli** (small) church is covered with lively, naive paintings,

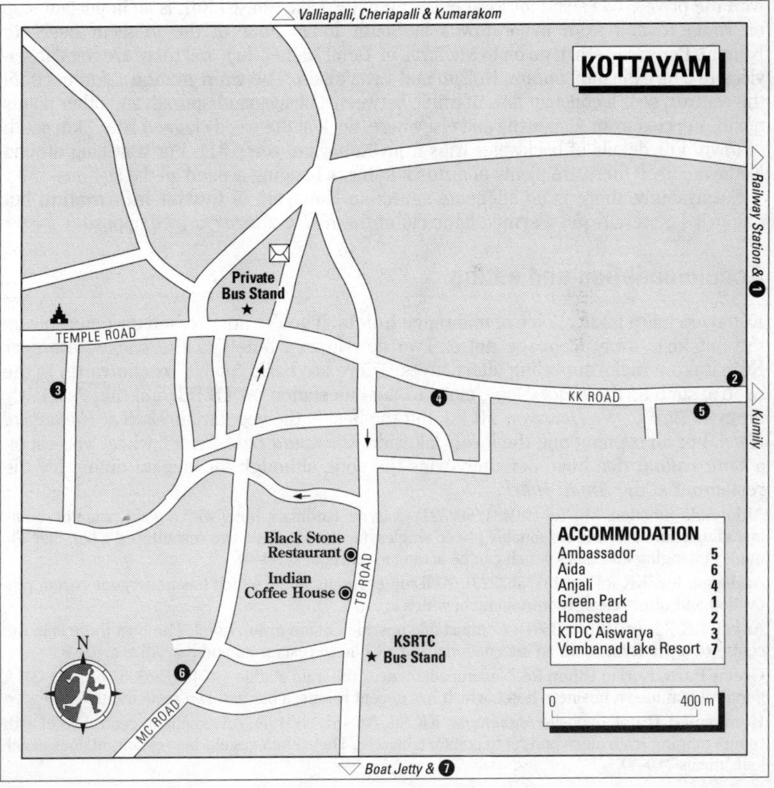

GOD OF SMALL THINGS

Arunadhati Roy's remarkable novel, **God of Small Things**, published in 1997, is set in a riverside village on the outskirts of Kottayam. It earned her the Booker Prize as well as the ire of certain sections of the local populace who reacted strongly to her description of small-town Kerala. The intricate, haunting and intensely personal tale gives a chilling glimpse of social tensions in Keralan life, and has an astutely observed interplay of character and environment. Roy was brought up in the same village as Ayemenem, the protagonist, and some of her family still live there. An architect by training, Arunadhati Roy became an important spokesperson for the anti-nuclear campaign that followed the "blast" – India's nuclear tests – in 1998, and she has also taken up the cause of the 33 million or so people who have been displaced by India's hydroelectric dam projects.

thought to have been executed by a Portuguese artist. If the doors are locked, ask for the key at the church office (9am–1pm & 2–5pm).

Arrival and information

Kottayam's *KSRTC* **bus stand**, 500m south of the centre on TB Rd (not to be confused with the private bus stand for local buses on KK Rd aka Shastri Rd), is an important stop en route to and from major towns in South India. Four of the frequent buses to Kumily/Periyar (3–4hr), go on to Madurai, in Tamil Nadu (7hr), and there are regular services to Thiruvananthapuram, Kollam and Ernakulam. The **train station** (2km north of the centre), sees a constant flow of traffic between Thiruvananthapuram and other points north. **Ferries** from Alappuzha and elsewhere, dock at the weed-clogged jetty, 3km south of town. For details of backwater trips from Kottayam, see p.311. For travelling around Kottayam itself there are plenty of **auto-rickshaws** hanging around all the stations.

Surprisingly, there is no adequate source in Kottayam of **tourist information** but enquiries generally get a sympathetic ear at the *KTDC Aiswarya* (see opposite).

Accommodation and eating

Kottayam has a good choice of mid-range **hotels**. If you're not pressed for time, stay on the outskirts away from the noise. Two new luxury hotels in the backwaters near Kumarakom make appealing alternatives. There are basic "meals" **restaurants** in the centre, such as the *Black Stone*, close to the bus station on TB Rd, and there's a fairly dingy *Indian Coffee House* on TB Rd, but the best is the vegetarian *Thali* at *Homestead Hotel*. For an evening out, the lovely lakeside *Vembanad Lake Resort*, where you eat on a *kettu vallam* rice boat, definitely wins the vote, although for elegant dining try the restaurant at the *Anjali Hotel*.

Aida, Aida Junction, MC Rd (☎0481/568391). A large, landmark hotel with a good range of rooms including some a/c, and reasonably priced singles; facilities include two restaurants, a bar, Star TV, money-changing and tours which can be arranged on request. ④–⑤.

Ambassador, KK Rd (☎0481/563293). Well-run economy hotel, which has undergone recent renovation and offers clean rooms, some of which are a/c. ②.

Anjali, KK Rd, (☎0481/563661). Comfortable upscale Casino group hotel. The best there is in the centre of town. It has both an international and a Chinese restaurant and bar. All a/c. ⑦–⑧.

Green Park, Kurian Uthup Rd, Nagampadam, near the train station (☎0481/563331 or 563243). A good-value modern business hotel, which has decent rooms, a bar and two restaurants. ⑤–⑥.

Homestead Hotel, opposite *Manorama*, KK Rd, (☎0481/560467). An excellent, central hotel with rooms ranging from clean budget to comfortable a/c. Their *Thali* vegetarian restaurant does excellent "meals". ③–⑥.

KTDC Aiswarya, just off Temple Rd (☎0481/581255 or 581254). Simply furnished modern tower block, which lacks character, but the staff are friendly and the rooms (a/c and non-a/c) are spacious. There are superb views from the upper storeys. Facilities include a restaurant, beer parlour and 24hr room service. ④–⑥.

Vembanad Lake Resort, Kodimatha, 5min walk from the boat jetty, and 2km from the centre of town (☎0481/564298). Western-style motel, with large, simply furnished modern chalets (four are a/c), set in pleasant gardens beside an inlet of Lake Vembanad. The restaurant has good Indian, Western and Chinese dishes, including seafood. Eat outside in a lakeside garden or on a moored *kettu vallam* longboat – gorgeous at night. ⑥–⑦.

Around Kottayam

Some of Kerala's most attractive scenery lies within easy access of Kottayam. Probably the ideal destination for a day-trip – it also has some wonderful accommodation – is the **Kumarakom** bird sanctuary, in the backwaters to the west. **Aranmula**, to the south, is one of the last villages still making *kannady* metal mirrors, and has a Krishna temple that organizes a ritual "non-competitive" boat race. The Mahadeva temple at **Ettumanur**, a short way north of Kottayam, is known to devotees as the home of a dangerous and wrathful Shiva and to art lovers as a sublime example of temple architecture, adorned with wood-carvings and murals.

Kumarakom

KUMARAKOM, 16km west of Kottayam, is technically an island on Vembanad Lake. Although right in the thick of a tangle of lush tropical waterways, it can be reached quite easily by bus from Kottayam (every 10min). The peak time to visit the **Bird Sanctuary**, which is no longer negotiable by boat as the channels are choked by African moss, is between November and March when it serves as a winter home for many migratory birds, some of which come from as far away as Siberia. Species include the darter or snakebird, little cormorant, night heron, golden-backed woodpecker, crow pheasant, white-breasted water hen and tree pie. Enthusiasts should seek permission to enter the sanctuary at dawn, the best time for bird viewing. Although quite small, a guide is useful and you can arrange one through the *KTDC Tourist Village* or through one of the hotels.

Next to the sanctuary, set in lovely waterside gardens, a refurbished colonial bungalow that once belonged to a family of Christian missionaries and rubber planters, forms the nucleus of a luxury **hotel**. The *Taj Garden Retreat* (☎0481/524377; ⑨) has two dozen "cottages", and a *kettu vallam* longboat, grouped around a landscaped garden. It also has direct water access to the lake. However, it's not nearly as impressive as the Casino group's *Coconut Lagoon Hotel* (☎0481/524491, fax 524495; ⑨), 1km northwest and reached by launch (you can telephone for the boat from a kiosk at the canal side). Superbly crafted from fragments of ruined Keralan palaces, with beautiful wood-carvings and brass work, the building alone merits a visit. It was designed in traditional Keralan style, and its air of low-key elegance is set off perfectly by its location on the edge of Vembanad Lake. Even if you can't afford to stay here, consider eating Keralan specialties at the **restaurant**. *KTDC's Tourist Village*, right on the lake (☎0481/524258; ⑧), has been completely rebuilt and now consists of comfortable a/c cottages built on stilts. You can stay on one of their *kettu vallams* moored at the jetty for Rs1500 per day for a double with bathroom, or for Rs5000 if you fancy a day's cruise across the lake (see box on p.307). Besides the hotels, the only other place to eat is KTDC's uninspiring café at the *Tourist Complex*, near where the bus from Kottayam pulls in, close to the gates of the *Taj Garden Retreat*.

Aranmula

The village of **ARANMULA** is another appealing day-trip – so long as you start early – from Kottayam, 30km south of the town and 10km beyond Chengannur. Its ancient temple is dedicated to Parthasarathy, which was the name under which Krishna acted as Arjuna's charioteer during the bloody Kurekshetra war recorded in the *Mahabharata* (see p.562), and the guise in which he expounded the *Bhagavad Gita*. Each year, towards the end of the Onam festival (Aug/Sept), a **Snakeboat Regatta** is celebrated as part of the temple rituals, and crowds line the banks of the Pampa River to cheer on the thrusting longboats (similar to those seen at Alappuzha; see p.307).

Aranmula is also known for manufacturing extraordinary *kannady* **metal mirrors**, produced, using the "lost wax" technique, with an alloy of copper, silver, brass, lead and bronze (see p.588). Once a perquisite of royal households, these ornamental mirrors are now exceedingly rare; only two master craftsmen, Subramanian and Arjun Asary, and their families, still make them. The most modest models cost in the region of Rs300, while custom-made mirrors can cost as much as Rs50,000.

The **Vijana Kala Vedi Cultural Centre** in Aranmula, offers ways of "experiencing traditional India through the study of art and village life". Introductory courses are offered in Kathakali, Mohiniattam and Bharatanatyam dance, wood-carving, mural painting, cooking, Kalarippayat, Ayurvedic medicine and several Indian languages. Courses cost upwards of US$200 per week and are booked by writing to: The Director, *Vijana Kala Vedi Cultural Centre*, Tarayil Mukku Junction, Aranmula, Kerala 689533.

CHRISTIANITY IN KERALA

The history of Kerala's **Christians** – who today represent 21 percent of the population – is said to date back to the first century AD, which is some three centuries before Christianity received official recognition in Europe. These days, the five main branches, among a bewildering assortment of churches, are the **Nestorians** (confined mainly to Thrissur), **Roman Catholics** (found throughout Kerala), **Syrian Orthodox Church** (previously known as the Jacobite Syrians), **Marthoma Syrians** (a splinter group of the Syrian Orthodox) and the Anglican **Church of South India**.

A legend, widely believed in Kerala but the object of academic scepticism, states that **St Thomas** the Apostle – "Doubting Thomas" – landed on the Malabar Coast in 52AD, where he converted several *brahmins* and others, and founded seven churches. Muziris, his first port of call, has been identified as **Kodungallur** (see p.351); the traditional accounts of Jews who arrived there in 68AD state that they encountered a Christian community. Their number was augmented in the fourth century by an influx of Syrians belonging to seven tribes from Baghdad, Nineveh and Jerusalem, which were under the leadership of the merchant Knayi Thoma (Thomas of Cana).

Christians gradually came to the forefront as traders, and eventually gained special privileges from the local rulers. The early communities followed a liturgy in the **Syriac language** (a dialect of Aramaic). Latin was introduced by missionaries who visited Kollam in the Middle Ages, and once the Portuguese turned up, in 1498, a large community of **Latin Christians** developed, particularly on the coast, and came under the jurisdiction of the pope. In the middle of the seventeenth century, with the ascendancy of the Dutch, part of the Church broke away from Rome, and local bishops were appointed through the offices of the Jacobite patriarch in Antioch.

During the nineteenth century, the Anglican Church amalgamated with certain "free" Churches, to form the Church of South India. At the same time, elements in the Syrian Church advocated the replacement of Syriac with the local language of Malayalam. The resultant schism led to the creation of the new Marthoma Syrian Church.

Christmas is an important festival in Kerala; during the weeks leading up to December 25, innumerable star-shaped lamps are put up outside shops and houses, illuminating the night and identifying followers of the faith.

Ettumanur

The magnificent Mahadeva temple at **ETTUMANUR**, 12km north of Kottayam on the road to Ernakulam, features a circular shrine, fine wood-carving and one of the earliest (sixteenth-century) and most celebrated of Keralan **murals**. The deity is Shiva in one of his most terrible aspects, described as *vaddikasula vada*, "one who takes his dues with interest" and is "difficult to please". His predominant mood is *raudra* (fury). Although the shrine is open to Hindus only, foreigners are allowed to see the painting, which may be photographed only after obtaining a camera ticket from the hatch to the left of the main, *gopura* entranceway. The four-metre mural depicts Nataraja – Shiva – executing a cosmic *tandava* dance, trampling evil underfoot in the form of a demon. Swathed in cobras, he stands on one leg in a wheel of gold, with his matted locks fanning out amid a mass of flowers and snakes. Outside the wheel, a crowd of celestials are in attitudes of devotion. Musical accompaniment is courtesy of Krishna on flute, three-headed Brahma on cymbals, and, playing the copper *mizhavu*, the holiest and most ancient of Keralan drums, Shiva's special rhythm expert Nandikesvara.

Ettumanur's ten-day **annual festival** (Feb/March) reflects the wealth of the temple, with elaborate celebrations including music. On the most important days, the eighth and tenth, priests bring out figures of elephants, fashioned from 460kg of gold, presented in the eighteenth century by Marthanda Varma, Raja of Travancore.

Periyar Wildlife Sanctuary

One of the largest and most visited wildlife reserves in India, the **Periyar Wildlife Sanctuary** occupies 777 square kilometres of the Cardamom Hills region of the Western Ghats. The majority of its many visitors come in the hope of seeing **tigers** and **leopards** – and are disappointed, as the few that remain very wisely keep their distance, and there's only a slight chance of a glimpse even at the height of the dry season (April/May). However, there are plenty of other animals and Periyar is a good place to see **elephants**; if you are lucky, you may come across a herd swimming across a channel. Other animals include wild pig, *sambar*, Malabar flying squirrel, *gaur*, stripe-necked mongoose, numerous species of birds and wild boar, which are plentiful and easily visible on the shores of the lake. Located close to the Kerala–Tamil Nadu border, the park makes a convenient place to break the long journey across the Ghats between Madurai and the coast. It's also a good base for day-trips into the Cardamom Hills, with a couple of tea factories, spice plantations, view points and forest waterfalls, and even the trailhead for the Sabarimala pilgrimage (see box on p.320), within striking distance.

Periyar lies at cool altitudes of 900m to 1800m with temperatures between 15°C and 30°C, and is located just over 100km east of Kottayam. The sanctuary centres on a vast artificial **lake**, created by the British in 1895 to supply water to the drier parts of neighbouring Tamil Nadu, around Madurai. The royal family of Travancore, anxious to preserve favourite hunting grounds from the encroachment of tea plantations, declared it to be a forest reserve, and built the Edapalayam Lake Palace to accommodate their guests in 1899. It expanded as a wildlife reserve in 1933, and once again when it became part of **Project Tiger** in 1979 (see Contexts, p.595).

Seventy percent of the protected area, which is divided into core, buffer and tourist zones, is covered with evergreen and semi-evergreen forest. The **tourist zone** – logically enough, the part accessible to casual visitors – surrounds the lake, and consists mostly of semi-evergreen and deciduous woodland interspersed with grassland, both on hilltops and in the valleys. Although excursions on the lake are the standard way to experience the park, you can get much more out of a visit by **walking** with a local guide in a small group, or, especially, staying in basic accommodation away from the crowd.

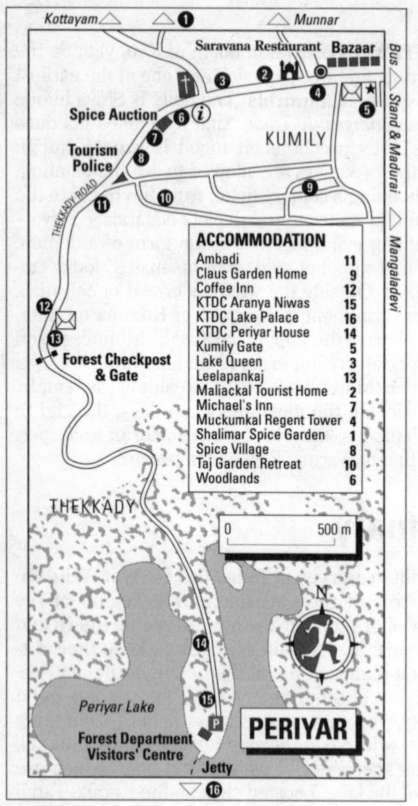

However, avoid the period immediately after the monsoons, when **leeches** make hiking virtually impossible. The **best time to visit** is from December until April, when the dry weather draws animals from the forest to drink at the lakeside.

Getting to Periyar

Travellers heading for the sanctuary have first to make their way to the tea and spice market village of **Kumily**, 4km short of the park entrance at **Thekkady**, on the northwest of the reserve. Kumily is served by state and private **buses** from Kottayam (every 30 min; 4hr), Ernakulam (10 daily; 6hr), and Madurai in Tamil Nadu (frequent service; 5hr 30min). Most of these buses terminate at the scruffy bus stand east of Kumily bazaar, from where a minibus shuttles visitors to the park, although some continue through to the KTDC *Aranya Nivas* at Thekaddy, inside the sanctuary. **Auto-rickshaws** will also run you from the bus stand to the Aranya Nivas for Rs25 plus Rs5 (to take the auto into the park), but if you are arriving late remember the gates close at 6pm after which you will have to show proof of your accommodation before they will let you in. If you are staying at the KTDC *Lake Palace*, the last boat is officially at 4pm, but they will arrange a boat for you as long as it is not dark. The **entrance fee** to the park is Rs10 for Indians, but is only good for one day, whereas the Rs50 fee for foreigners is valid for three – so hang on to your ticket.

The pothole-filled road that winds through the undulating hills up to Kumily, from Ernakulam and Kottayam, makes for a very long, slow drive, but it gives wonderful views across the Ghats. The route is dotted with grand churches among the trees, and numerous jazzy roadside shrines to St Francis, St George or the Virgin Mary – a charming Keralan blend of ancient and modern. Once you've climbed through the rubber-tree forests into Idukki District, the mountains get truly spectacular, and the wide-floored valleys are carpeted with lush tea plantations.

KTDC runs hectic and uncomfortable **weekend tours** to Periyar from Kochi, calling at Kadamattom and the Idukki Dam en route (see p.280; Sat 7.30am–Sun 8pm), and an even more rushed tour from Thiruvananthapuram. Unless you love being cooped up for days in video buses, give them a miss. Numerous tour operators in Thiruvananthapuram, Kovalam and Kochi also offer tailor-made packages.

THE BIRDS OF PERIYAR

Although animals are not often visible due to the dense forest cover, **birds** are plentiful in Periyar and there are over 260 species known to be in the sanctuary. The most notable amongst these are the darters, which are also known as snakebirds due to the snake-like appearance of their neck while swimming. They belong to the cormorant family, and can be seen perching on top of dead tree trunks protruding from the water, sometimes allowing boats to get quite close. Other common aquatic birds include the cormorant, grey heron, squat and tailless little grebe – also known as dabchick. Of the several types of kingfisher, the lesser pied kingfisher has distinctive white flashes around its neck, and the blue-eared and storkbilled kingfishers are both a more common blue. The osprey or fish hawk is a common sight, cruising above the water. Occasionally, you may be fortunate enough to see a grey-headed fishing eagle, recognizable by its white body, which contrasts with its deep brown back and wings. Other common birds of prey in Periyar include the *brahminy* kite, which is a handsome gold-coloured bird with a regal, white neck and crest. Amongst many of Periyar's other birds, are: the Nilgiri wood pigeon, blue-winged parakeet, white-bellied tree pie, laughing thrushes and flycatchers, the white-necked stork and the white cattle egret. You will be very lucky, however, if you catch site of the great Indian hornbill, a majestic multi-coloured bird with a large yellow beak.

Information

Based in Kumily, Idduki's DTPC has a low-key **tourist office** (Mon–Sat 10am–5pm; ☎04863/22620) on the first floor of the Panchayat Building, Thekkady Junction, Kumily. Besides information on the district itself, it organizes conducted tours. Their tour to Munnar costs Rs200, and they also run tours to spice plantations, which are charged according to time. Their rates are quite competitive compared to some of the prices quoted around Kumily; a one-hour tour inclusive of guide costs Rs150, two hours Rs250 and three hours Rs350. The other source of information is the Tourism Police, staffed by friendly, English-speaking graduates, with an office at the bus stand and the main office at Ambady Junction. Although their prime purpose is law and order, they are give general information as well as assistance in booking hotels. While scouring the information offices you may have the good fortune to come across the sociologist Guruvayurappan, who is connected to the Forestry Department and has been working on the fascinating **India Eco Development Project**. The project lays emphasis on the role of forest-dwellers to help protect their own environment through awareness programmes.

Both the State Bank of Travancore (☎04863/22041), near the bus stand, and the Central Bank of India, KK Rd (☎04863/22053), **change money**. For general information on Thekkady look up the local website *www.thekkady.com*. For **Internet** facilities try Rissas Communications/Media at Thekkady Junction, Kumily (☎04863/22103), where the charges are Rs65 for 30min, Rs125 for 1hr, and for sending and receiving email, Rs20 and Rs10 respectively. Although hilly, Kumily and Thekkady make good cycling territory, and **bicycle rental** is available from stalls in the market for around Rs30 per day. DC Books in Thekkady has a good selection of **books** on religion, culture and art.

Boat trips and walking in the park

Tickets for the **boat trips** (7am & 4pm; 2hr; Rs50 for open upper deck; Rs25 enclosed lower deck; plus Rs10 entrance fee) on the lake are sold through the Forest

THE AYAPPA CULT

During December and January, Kerala is jam-packed with crowds of men in black or blue *dhotis*, milling about train stations and filling up trains on their way to the Shri Ayappa forest temple (also known as Hariharaputra or Shasta) at **Sabarimala**, in the Western Ghat mountains, around 200km from both Thiruvananthapuram and Kochi. The **Ayappa devotees** can seem disconcertingly ebullient, chanting "*Swamiyee Sharanam Ayappan*" (give us protection, god Ayappa) in a call and response style reminiscent of Western sports fans.

Although he is primarily a Keralan deity, Ayappa's appeal has spread phenomenally in the last thirty years across South India, to the extent that this is said to be the **second largest pilgrimage in the world**, with as many as a million devotees each year. A curious story relates to the birth of Ayappa. One day, when the two male gods, Shiva and Vishnu, were together in a pine forest, Shiva asked to see Vishnu's famed female form Mohini, the divine enchantress. Vishnu refused, having a fair idea of what this could lead to. However, Shiva was undeterred, and used all his powers of persuasion to induce Vishnu to transform. As a result of the inevitable passionate embrace, Vishnu became pregnant, and the baby Ayappa emerged from his thigh.

Pilgrims, however, are required to remain celibate; they must abstain from intoxicants, keeping to a strict vegetarian diet for a period of 41 days prior to setting out on the four-day walk through the forest from the village of **Erumeli** (61km, as the crow flies, north-west), to the shrine at Sabarimala. Rather less devoted devotees take the bus to the village of Pampa, and join the five-kilometre queue. When they arrive at the modern temple complex – a surreal spread of concrete sheds and walkways in the middle of the jungle – pilgrims who have performed the necessary penances may ascend the famous eighteen **gold steps** to the inner shrine. There they worship the deity, throwing donations down a chute that opens onto a subterranean conveyor belt, where the money is counted and bagged for the bank. In recent years, the mass appeal of the Ayappa cult has brought in big bucks for the temple, which now numbers among India's richest, despite being open for only a few months each year. Funds also pour in from the shrine's innumerable spin-off businesses, such as the sale of coconut oil and milk (left by every pilgrim) to a soap manufacturer.

The pilgrimage reaches a climax during the festival of **Makara Sankranti** when massive crowds of over 1.5 million, congregate at Sabarimala. On 14 January 1999, 51 devotees were buried alive when part of a hill crumbled under the crush of a stampede. The devotees had gathered at dusk to catch a glimpse of the final sunset of *Makara Jyoti* (celestial light) on the distant hill of Ponnambalamedu.

Although males of any age and even of any religion can take part in the pilgrimage, females between the ages of nine and fifty are barred. This rule, still vigorously enforced by the draconian temple oligarchy, was contested in 1995 by a bizarre court case. Following complaints to local government that facilities and hygiene at Sabarimala were sub-standard, the Local Collector, a 42-year-old woman, insisted she be allowed to inspect the site. The temple authorities duly refused, citing the centuries-old ban on women of menstrual age, but the High Court, which earlier upheld the gender bar, was obliged to overrule the priests' decision. The Collector's triumphant arrival at Sabarimala soon after made headline news, but she was still not allowed to enter the shrine proper.

For advice on how to visit Sabarimala, via a back route beginning at Kumily near the Periyar Sanctuary, see p.323.

Department at their hatch just above the main visitor centre. Although it is unusual to see many animals from the boats – engine noise and the presence of a hundred other people make sure of that – you might spot a family group of elephants, wild boar and *sambar* deer by the water's edge. The upper deck is best for game viewing, although the seats are invariably block-booked by the upscale hotels. Turn up half-an-hour early, however, and you may be allocated any no-show places, either at the ticket hatch, or by slipping the boatman some *baksheesh.* To maximize your chances, take the earliest boat at 7am (wear something warm). At this hour, the mist rises over the lake and hills as you chug past dead trees, now bird perches, that were never cleared when the valley was flooded. You could also consider renting your own boat (from Rs400 for 6 passengers, again at the jetty). Note that after heavy rain, chances of good sightings are very slim as the animals only come to the lake when water sources inside the forest have dried up.

Group trekking is possible (7.30am–noon; Rs50 per head), but it's more enjoyable by far to hire a **private guide** to take you walking in the forest (under Rs100 for 3hr for two or three people; longer trips are negotiable). They'll approach you in Kumily or near the park gates at Thekkady. Guides point out anything of interest, reassuring you that the fresh elephant dung on the path is nothing to worry about. The Forest Department also offers overnight trips and more elaborate weeklong programmes. **Elephant rides** into the park cost Rs50 per head for an hour. For more information contact the Wildlife Preservation Officer (☎04863/22620) at Thekkady.

Accommodation and eating inside the sanctuary

The star attraction of Periyar has to be the prospect of staying in the Forest Department **watchtowers**, reached by boat from Thekkady and the best way to get a hands-on experience of the jungle. For the *Lake Palace*, *Periyar House* and the *Aranya Nivas* you should book in advance at the KTDC offices in Thiruvananthapuram or Ernakulam – essential if you plan to come on a weekend or a public holiday or during **peak season** (Dec–March), when rooms are often in short supply.

Forest Department Rest House, Edappalayam. Very basic accommodation in the woods on the far side of the lake (you have to catch the 4pm boat and then hike, so a guide is recommended). Bring your own food and bedding. Reserve in advance at the Forest Department's visitor centre in Thekkady, above the boat jetty; you'll be lucky to get in on a weekend or in December. ③.

Forest Department Watchtowers, Edappalayam and Manakkavala. Even more primitive than the Rest House, but the best way of sighting game: the towers overlook waterholes in the buffer zone. Book through the visitor centre, and take along food, candles, matches, a torch, a sleeping bag and warm clothes. Again, you have to catch the 4pm boat and trek from the jetty, so a guide is useful. Don't consider this if it's been raining, as leeches plague the trail. ①.

KTDC Aranya Nivas, just above the boat jetty, Thekkady (☎04863/22023, fax 22282). Plusher than *Periyar House*, a colonial manor with some huge rooms, a pleasant garden, a great swimming pool, a multi-cuisine restaurant with indifferent food and a cosy bar. The off-season (Jun & Jul) discounts are especially tempting. Upper deck tickets on the boat trips are included in the tariff. ⑧–⑨.

KTDC Lake Palace, across the lake (booked through *Aranya Nivas*). The sanctuary's most luxurious hotel with six suites, in a converted maharajah's game lodge surrounded by forest, with wonderful views. Charming old-fashioned rooms, great dining and a lovely lawn. This has to be one of the few places in India where you stand a chance of spotting tiger and wild elephant while sipping tea on your own verandah. Rates start at Rs4658 for a double in low season to over Rs8000 in peak season around Christmas and January. ⑨.

KTDC Periyar House, midway between the park gates and the boat jetty, Thekkady (☎04863/22026, fax 22526). This comfortable mid-range hotel is close to the lake, with a restaurant, bar, and balcony overlooking the monkey-filled woods leading down to the waterside. Not as nice a location as its neighbour *Aranya Nivas*, but then a lot cheaper. Ask for a lake-facing room. ⑤–⑧.

Accommodation outside the sanctuary: Kumily

With beds inside the sanctuary in such short supply, most visitors end up staying in or near **Kumily**, 2km north of the park gates. With several new "resorts" and hotels appearing periodically, Kumily is a growing town where tourism seems to be slowly replacing the spice trade as the main source of income. However, the spice industry is alive and well, and several agencies offer tours to plantations. In addition, shops such as Spices Centre on the Thekkady Rd offer spices as fresh as they can be. Clustered along the main trans-ghat highway, the village centre is a long, gritty bazaar full of raucous traffic and lined with hardware and spice shops. In the middle of the melee stands the area's main **cardamom auction**, where you can watch tribal women sifting and sorting the fragrant green pods in heart-shaped baskets; it's easy to find – just follow your nose.

Kumily has **accommodation** to suit all pockets. Thankfully, most of the accommodation lies well outside the bazaar area, dotted along Thekkady Rd leading to the park. Nearly every establishment has its own café-restaurant, ranging from the *Spice Village*'s smart à la carte terrace to the more traveller-oriented *Coffee Inn*. If you're on a really tight budget, however, the best place to eat in Kumily is the *Hotel Saravana*, one of several no-frills "meals" joints on the main bazaar. Their *thalis*, served on plantain leaves, are tasty, cheap and always freshly cooked, and they serve up deliciously crisp *dosas* too.

Ambadi, Thekkady Rd (☎04863/22193). Pleasant hotel which has seen better times, but whose non-a/c "cottages", are good value. It's furnished with attractive coir mats and wood-carvings. The restaurant here is satisfactory. ⑤–⑦.

Claus Garden Home, five minutes' walk south of the main bus stand (no phone) behind the *Taj Garden Retreat*. Difficult to find, but worth the effort. This place is German-owned, and consists of simple, pleasant rooms, with sociable verandahs, in a cosy house decorated with mandala murals. It is surrounded by pepper plantations. ②.

Coffee Inn, Thekkady Rd, near the post office (no phone). Good budget accommodation: a handful of simple rooms (one en suite), ranged around a covered terrace and garden. Their "Wild Huts" annexe has six rooms (and two rafia tree houses), with shared shower and toilet, and a spacious enclosed garden with a pond. The (pricey) café serves delicious homemade Western food including fresh bread. ①–③.

Kumily Gate, Main Rd, behind the bus stand (☎04863/22279). Greenish, modern block with clean, large rooms, a restaurant and a popular and noisy bar. Expensive for what it is, but good for late arrivals. ⑥.

Lake Queen, opposite the Thekkady turn-off, Kumily Bazaar (☎04863/22084). Dilapidated, multi-storey hotel, with good views from the top floors, but a far cry from the forest. ②–③.

Leelapankaj, Thekkady Rd, near the post office (☎04863/22392). Quaint, but tiny and disappointing, thatched cottages next to the forest gate and checkpost. ⑤.

Maliackal Tourist Home, Kumily Bazaar (☎04863/22589). Good clean rooms, with TVs and some with balconies. Handy place for the bus stand. ③–⑤.

Michael's Inn, Thekkady Rd, next to the spice auction (☎04863/22355). A brash, new hotel with a garden and decent rooms. Unfortunately, it makes no attempt to blend in with its surroundings, and the more expensive rooms are overpriced. ⑥–⑨.

Muckumkal Regent Tower, Main Rd, near the bus stand (☎04863/22570). A monolithic hotel handy for late or early buses, with a range of rooms including some a/c, and a decent restaurant. They also run the *Tourist Home* next door, which is smaller and marginally cheaper, though a bit noisier. ②–⑥.

Shalimar Spice Garden, Murikaddy (☎ & fax 04863/22132). Secluded spot on the edge of a cardamom and pepper estate, 5km from Kumily (Rs50 by jeep). Beautiful and tasteful campus, run by an Italian. It has attractive cottages, a small pool, and features some traditional Keralan wood structures. Recommended. ⑨.

Spice Village, Thekkady Rd (☎04863/22315, fax 22317). Stylish and friendly (and terrifically eco-conscious), accommodation run by the Casino group. Thatched huts and traditional Keralan wood cottages, spread out over a well-planted spice garden with a good restaurant and an attractive pool. If you are into Keralan cooking and would like to know more, join the master chef's evening classes. ⑨.

Taj Garden Retreat, Ambalambika Rd (☎04863/22273). Luxurious, mock-rustic cottages, and a main building built to emulate a jungle lodge, which has great views, a pleasant pool and elegant dining. Tours can be arranged. ⑨.

Woodlands, Thekkady Rd (☎04863/22077). One of the cheapest places to stay in Kumily, and very rudimentary, although clean enough for a short stay, and the management are friendly. ①–②.

Around Periyar and Kumily: the Cardamom Hills

Nestled amid soaring, mist-covered mountains and dense jungles, Periyar and Kumily are convenient springboards from which to explore Kerala's beautiful **Cardamom Hills**. Guides will approach you at Thekkady with offers of trips by jeep-taxi; if you can get a group together, these work out to be pretty good value. Among the more popular destinations is the **Mangaladevi temple**, 14km east of Kumily. The rough road to this tumbledown ancient ruin deep in the forest is sometimes closed due to flood damage, but when open the round trip takes about five hours. With a guide, you can also reach remote waterfalls and mountain view points, offering panoramic vistas of the Tamil Nadu plains. Rates vary according to the season, but expect to pay around Rs500 for the jeep-taxi, and an additional Rs150 for the guide.

Of places that can be visited under your own steam, the fascinating **High Range Tea Factory** (☎04868/77038 or 77043), at Puttady (pronounced "Poo-*tee*-dee"), 19km north, is a rewarding diversion on the road to Munnar. Regular buses leave from Kumily bus stand; get down at Puttady crossroads, and pick up a rickshaw from there to the factory. Driven by whirring canvas belts, old-fashioned English-made machines chop, sift, and ferment the leaves, which are then dried by wood-fired furnaces and packed into sacks for delivery to the tea auction rooms in Kochi. The affable owner, Mr P.M. James, or one of his clerks, will show you around; you don't have to arrange the visit, but it's a good idea to phone ahead to check they are open.

The other possible day-trip from Kumily, though one that should not be undertaken lightly (or, because of Hindu lore, by pre-menopausal women), is to the Sri Ayappan forest shrine at **Sabarimala** (see box on p.320). This remote and sacred site can be reached in a long day-trip, but you should leave with a pack of provisions, as much water as you can carry and plenty of warm clothes in case you get stranded. Jeep-taxis wait outside Kumily bus stand to transport pilgrims to the less frequented of Sabarimala's two main access points – a windswept mountaintop 13km above the temple (2hr; Rs50 per person if the jeep is carrying ten passengers). Peeling off the main Kumily–Kottayam road at **Vandiperiyar**, the route takes you through tea estates to the start of an appallingly rutted forest track. After a long and spectacular climb, this emerges at a grass-covered plateau where the jeeps stop. You proceed on foot, following a well-worn path through superb, old-growth jungle – complete with hanging creepers and monkeys crashing through the high canopy – to the temple complex at the foot of the valley. Allow at least two hours for the descent, and an hour or two more, for the climb back up to the road head, for which you'll need plenty of drinking water. The alternative route from Kumily to Sabarimala takes a jeep ride on a forest road to **Uppupara** (42km), with a final walk of 6km through undulating country. Given the very real risks involved with missing the last jeep back to Kumily (the mountaintop is prime elephant and tiger country), it's advisable to get a group together and rent a 4WD for the day (Rs560 or Rs4 per km, plus waiting time).

Munnar and around

MUNNAR, 130km east of Kochi and 60km by bus north of the Periyar Wildlife Sanctuary, is the centre of Kerala's principal tea-growing region. Although billed in tourist bumpf as a "hill station", these days it is becoming less of a Raj-style resort than a scruffy, workaday settlement of corrugated-iron-roofed cottages and factories, surrounded by mile upon mile of rolling green **tea plantations**. The town still has

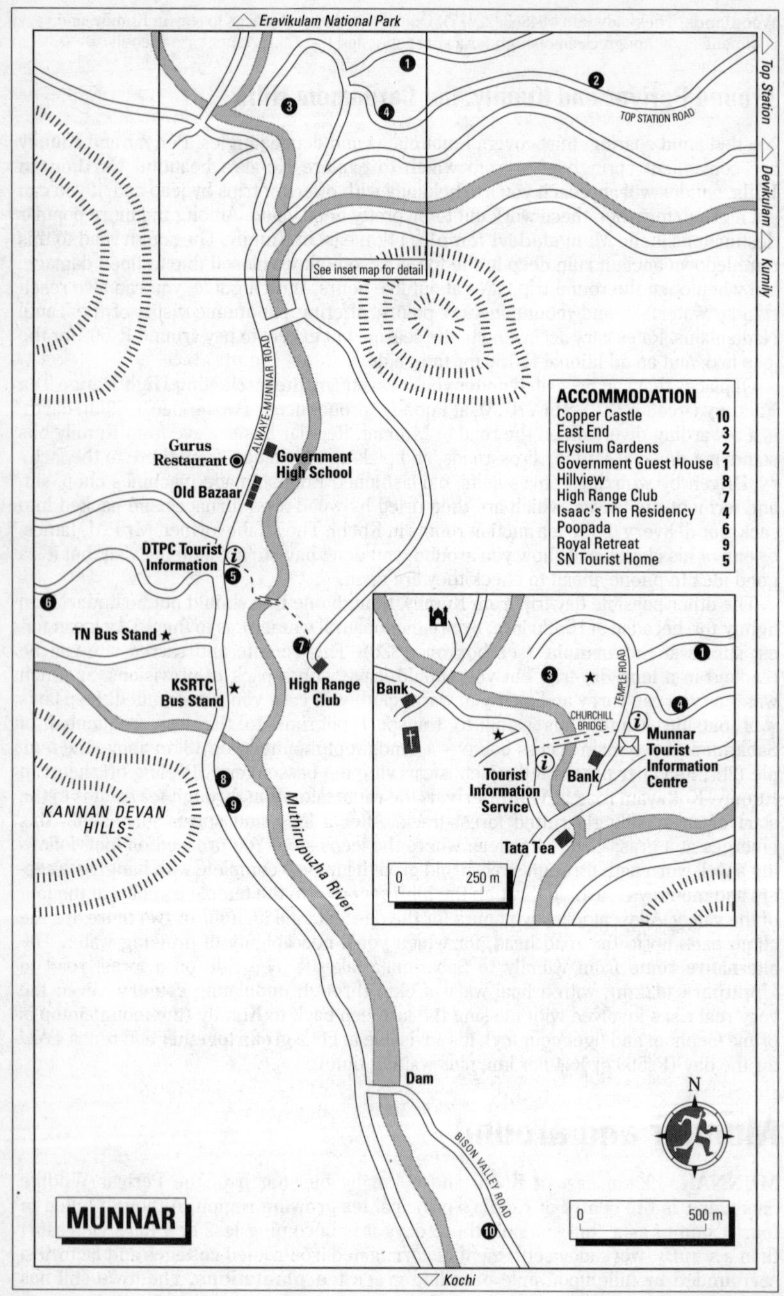

Eravikulam National Park
Top Station
Devikulam
Kumily
TOP STATION ROAD
See inset map for detail
ALWAYE-MUNNAR ROAD
ACCOMMODATION
Copper Castle 10
East End 3
Elysium Gardens 2
Government Guest House 1
Hillview 8
High Range Club 7
Isaac's The Residency 4
Poopada 6
Royal Retreat 9
SN Tourist Home 5
Gurus Restaurant
Government High School
Old Bazaar
DTPC Tourist Information
TN Bus Stand
KSRTC Bus Stand
High Range Club
Bank
TEMPLE ROAD
CHURCHILL BRIDGE
Munnar Tourist Information Centre
Tourist Information Service
Bank
Tata Tea
0 250 m
KANNAN DEVAN HILLS
Muthirupuzha River
Dam
N
BISON VALLEY ROAD
MUNNAR
0 500 m
Kochi

something of a colonial look about it, however, with verandahed British bungalows clinging to the valley's sides, and the famous **High Range Club** on the southeast edge of town, with its manicured lawns and golfcourse. Beyond the club sprawl some of the valley's 37 thousand-acre plantations, most of which are owned by the industrial giant, Tata. It's regional headquarters in the centre of town is the place to arrange visits to **tea factories** in the area.

In spite of more recent developments, it's easy to see why the pioneering Scottish planters that first developed this hidden valley in the 1900s felt so at home here. At an altitude of around 1600m, the town enjoys a refreshing climate, with crisp winter mornings and relentlessly heavy rain during the monsoons. Hemmed in by soaring mountains – including peninsular India's highest peak, **Anamudi** (2695m) – it also boasts a spectacular setting. When the river mist clears, the surrounding summits form a wild backdrop to the carefully manicured plantations carpeting the valley floor and sides.

Munnar's greenery and cool air have attracted increasing numbers of well-heeled honeymooners from Mumbai and Bangalore. Foreign visitors, however, remain few and far between. Those that do make it up here tend to come for the spell-binding bus ride from Periyar, which takes you across the high ridges and lush tropical forests of the Cardamon Hills, or, for the equally spectacular climb across the Ghats from Madurai. Once in the town, there's little to do other than enjoy the views and fresh air, although several interesting excursions, and hiking opportunities, to the scenic hamlet of **Top Station** and to **Eravikulam National Park** lie within reach of day-trips.

Arrival and information

Munnar can be reached by **bus** from Kochi, Kottayam, Kumily and Madurai (see "Travel Details", p.366). The service to Madurai is either direct, or involves changing at Tehni. State-run and private services pull into the stand in the bazaar at the northern end of town, near the Tourist Information Service. For hotels south of the centre, you should ask to be dropped off at Old Munnar, at the friendly but ineffectual **DTPC Tourist Information** (Mon–Sat 10am–5pm; ☎0486/530679). If you need information on transport, accommodation or day-trips, seek out the helpful Joseph Iype, who runs the more efficient Tourist Information Service (☎0486/530349) in the main bazaar. Immortalized in Dervla Murphy's *On a Shoestring to Coorg*, this self-appointed tourist officer has become something of a legend. In addition to handing out useful **maps** and newspaper articles, he'll arrange **auto-rickshaws** and **taxis** for excursions, and will bombard you with background information on the area. Unfortunately, the accommodation he has on offer is expensive and disappointing.

A short walk across Churchill Bridge, over the filthy Muthirupuzha River, the Munnar Tourist Information Centre (☎0486/530249) is a government-sponsored private body which offers information services, although its primary function appears to be the promotion of its own half-day **guided tours** (daily 9am–2pm; Rs125), which run throughout high season. One of the tours covers Top Station and some waterfalls nearby, and includes the hire of a pedalo on the lakes, but is targeted at Indian tourists. The best of their other tours takes in the Eravikulam National Park and the adjacent Chinnar Wildlife Sanctuary but like the others, it is far too fleeting (daily 2.30pm–8pm; Rs125).

You can **change money** at the State Bank of Travancore on Temple Rd, or the State Bank of India. **Cycle rental** is catching on and the DTPC Tourist Information rents out bicycles for Rs10 per hour; ask around, however, and you will find one cheaper.

Accommodation and eating

Thanks to its status as an up-and-coming hill resort, Munnar has plenty of **accommodation**, although budget options are limited. Visitors generally **eat** in their hotels. The

Royal Retreat's plush, à la carte restaurant has an eclectic menu and attentive service, and comes particularly recommended. *Gurus*, in the old bazaar, opposite the government High School, is a characterful old-style coffee shop serving South Indian snacks. For tasty, filling and cheap meals, however, you can't beat the *Poopada*, whose small, no-frills restaurant is open to non-residents. *Saravana*, in the main market serves good vegetarian "meals", and the *East End's* plush, mid-priced restaurant is the best in the town centre, with a very varied menu.

Copper Castle, Bison Valley Rd, Kannan Devan hills (☎0486/530633, fax 30438). Large, well-run and comfortable hotel on the side of a hill high above the valley, with an excellent restaurant. ⑦.

East End, Temple Rd, (☎0486/530451, fax 30227). Immaculate, upmarket hotel close to the centre of town, which has cottages set in a big garden, and a plush mid-price multi-cuisine restaurant with a good varied menu. ⑥–⑦.

Elysium Gardens, Top Station Rd (☎0486/530510). A quiet, pleasant spot with cottages and good rooms, which during low season, are offered at an amazing eighty percent discount. There is room service but no restaurant. ⑤–⑧.

Government Guest House, Mattupatty Rd, near the main bazaar (☎0486/530385). Completely revamped and characterful old British bungalow, offering comfortable rooms and meals by arrangement. ⑥.

Hillview, Kannan Devan hills (☎0486/530567, fax 30241). Large, well-run Western-style hotel with forty rooms, at the southern end of town. All rooms are en suite and some have good views. ⑤–⑦.

High Range Club, Kannan Devan hills (☎0486/530253). A celebrated club, and the place to stay to enjoy tea or gin in an old-world ambience – hung with hunting trophies. You can play billiards, golf, tennis or squash and the tariff is full board; spoil yourself. ⑧–⑨.

Issac's The Residency, Top Station Rd (☎0486/530501). A large concrete hotel with adequate rooms and a commanding view over the town. Unfortunately, it makes no attempt to blend in with its surroundings. ⑥–⑦.

Poopada, Kannan Devan hills, on the Manukulam Rd (☎0486/530223). Good-sized, en-suite rooms, and about the best cheap eating in town, along with fine valley views and secluded location. Booking recommended on weekends. ⑤.

Royal Retreat, Kannan Devan hills (☎0486/530240). Spacious rooms and cottages, set in a pleasant complex at the south end of town. Some of the rooms have brick fireplaces and are furnished with cane furniture. The best upscale option, although its north side has been boxed in by the *Hillview* next door. ⑥–⑦.

Shree Narayana ("SN") Tourist Home, Kannan Devan hills, near the tourist office (☎0486/530212). Far and away Munnar's best economy lodge, with shared or en-suite bathrooms. If it's full there are much cheaper (and grottier) places further north in the bazaar as fallbacks. ④–⑤.

Eravikulam National Park

Encompassing a hundred square kilometres of moist evergreen forest and grassy hilltops in the Western Ghats, **Eravikulam National Park** (foreigners Rs50 & Indians Rs10; taxis Rs10 & auto-rickshaws Rs5 vehicle fee), 13km northeast of Munnar (auto-rickshaws charge Rs150 return), is the last stronghold of one of the world's rarest mountain goats, the **Nilgiri tahr**, whose innate friendliness made it pathetically easy prey during the hunting frenzy of the colonial era (during a break in his campaign against Tipu Sultan in the late 1790s, the future Duke of Wellington reported that his soldiers were able to shoot the unsuspecting goats as they wandered through his camp), and by Independence it was virtually extinct. Today, however, numbers are healthy, and the animals are as relaxed as ever, largely thanks to the efforts of the American biologist, Clifford Rice, who studied them here in the early 1980s. Unable to get close enough to observe the creatures properly, Rice followed the advice of locals and attracted them using salt. Soon, whole herds were congregating around his camp. The tahrs' salt addiction also explains why so many hang around the park gates at **Vaguvarai**, where visitors – despite advice from rangers – slip them salty snacks.

The park gates mark the start of an excellent **hike** up the most accessible of the Anamudi massif's three peaks, for which you'll need sturdy footwear, plenty of water, a fair amount of stamina and a head for heights. Officially, due to erosion and environmental damage caused by trekkers, at the time of going to press the hike had been temporarily closed; so if you do wish to do it, check first at Munnar to see whether it has reopened. When open, follow the road as it winds through the sanctuary, cutting across the switchbacks until you reach the pass forming the Kerala–Tamil Nadu border (autorickshaws and jeep-taxis will drive you this far, although you can enter the park by paying the extra vehicle fee). Leave the road here and head up the ridge to your right; the path, which becomes very steep, peters out well before you reach the summit, and many hikers find the gradient too hair-raising to continue. But the panoramic views from the top are well worth the effort, and you may be rewarded with a glimpse of tahr grazing the high slopes.

Another popular excursion is the 34-kilometre uphill climb by bus through the subcontinent's highest tea estates to **TOP STATION**, a tiny hamlet on the Kerala–Tamil Nadu border, which has superb views across the plains. It's renowned for the very rare **Neelakurunji plant** (*Strobilatanthes*), which grows in profusion on the mountainsides but only flowers once every twelve years, attracting crowds who come to admire the cascades of violet blossom spilling down the slopes. Top Station can be reached by **bus** from Munnar (8 daily; 1hr), and jeep-taxis will do the round trip for Rs600.

TREK TO KODAIKANAL

A superb **trek**, one which is probably best done with a guide, takes around three days and follows the forested hill country to the town of **Kodaikanal**, 85km to the southeast in Tamil Nadu. Joseph Iype of the Tourist Information Service will be happy to assist with organization, and several agencies such as Clipper Holidays in Kochi (☎0484/364443) as well as Trio Travels, also in Kochi (☎0484/369571), will also organize the trek on request.

Kochi (Cochin) and Ernakulam

The venerable city of **KOCHI** (long known as Cochin), Kerala's prime tourist destination, spreads across islands and promontories in a stunning location between the Arabian Sea and the backwaters. Its main sections – modern **Ernakulam**, in the east, and the old districts of **Mattancherry** and **Fort Cochin** on a peninsula in the west – are linked by a complex system of ferries, and distinctly less romantic bridges. Although most visitors end up staying in Ernakulam, Fort Cochin and Mattancherry are the focus of interest, where the city's extraordinary history of foreign influence and settlement is reflected in an assortment of architectural styles. During a wander through their narrow lanes, you'll stumble upon spice markets, Chinese fishing nets, a synagogue, a Portuguese palace, India's first European church, Dutch homes and a village green that could have been transported from England's Home Counties. The city is also one of the few places in Kerala where, at any time of year, you can be assured of seeing **Kathakali dance**, either in one of several special tourist theatres or at a more authentic performance by a temple-based company (see box on p.336).

Kochi sprang into being in 1341, when a flood created a natural safe port that swiftly replaced Muziris (Kodungallur, 50km north), as the chief harbour on the Malabar Coast. The royal family transferred here from Muziris in 1405, after which the city grew rapidly, attracting Christian, Arab and Jewish settlers from the Middle East. Its name probably derives from *kocchazhi*, meaning the new, or small, harbour.

The history of European involvement in Kochi from the early 1500s onwards is dominated by the aggression of, successively, the Portuguese, Dutch and British, competing to control the port and its lucrative spice trade. From 1800, the state of Cochin was part of the British Madras Presidency; from 1812 until Independence in 1947, its administration was made the responsibility of a series of *diwans*, or financial ministers. In the 1920s, the British expanded the port to make it suitable for modern ocean-going ships; extensive dredging created Willingdon Island, between Ernakulam and Fort Cochin.

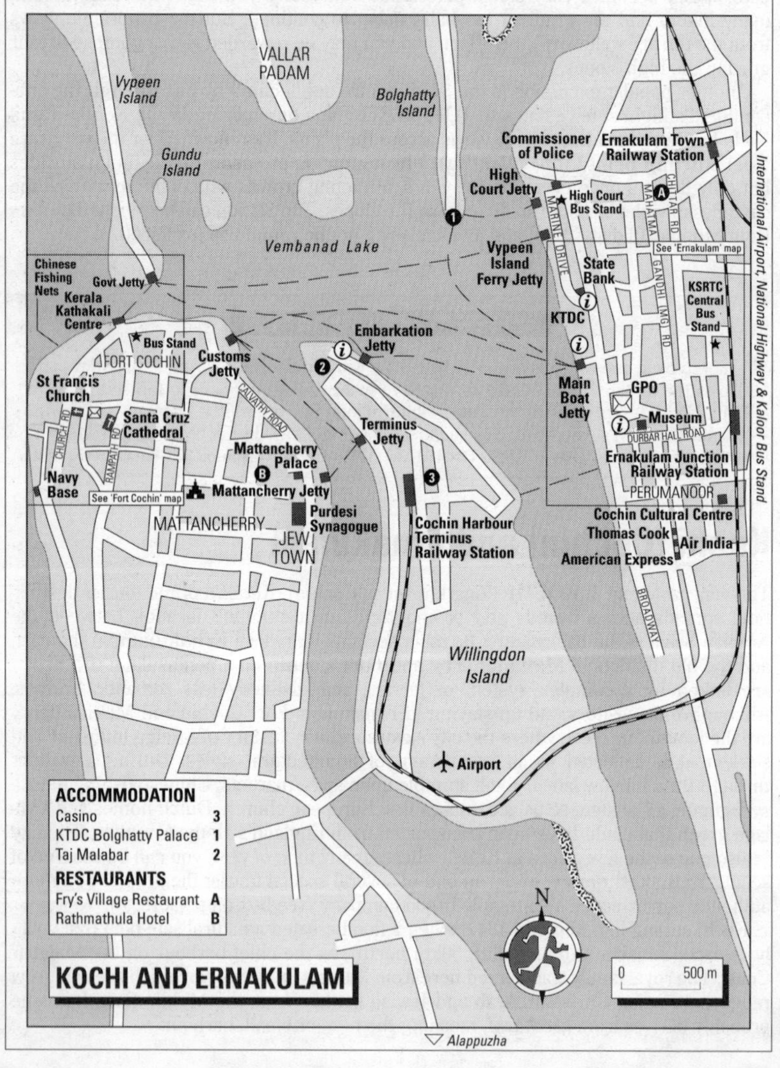

Arrival and local transport

Kochi's brand new **international airport** at Nedumbassery, near Alwaye (aka Alua), 26km to the north of Ernakulam, was inaugurated in May 1999. Only partly funded by the government, the airport project, initiated by local businesses, promises to be one of South India's finest airports designed to take the bulk of international flights, especially from the Gulf. The busy old airport, shared with the navy, is at the southern end of Willingdon Island, connected to Ernakulam (5km) by buses, taxis and auto-rickshaws, but will cease to carry civilian traffic once the new airport is in full operation. Kochi is served by several flights daily from **Mumbai**, one each from **Kozhikode** and **Chennai**, flights most days from **Delhi**, and twice weekly from **Goa** as well as the **Lakshadweep Islands** and **Bangalore**. There are three **train stations**: Ernakulam Junction, closest to the centre, is the most important; Ernakulam Town lies 4km to the north; and the Cochin Harbour Terminus, on Willingdon Island, is useful only for people using the airport or staying in one of the luxury hotels on the island. No trains run to Fort Cochin or Mattancherry.

The KSRTC **Central bus stand** (☎0484/372033), is the principal station for long-distance buses. There are two bus stands for private buses, which are not officially permitted to use the state highways; these buses have been responsible for several horrendous accidents; they stop more frequently and compete with each other over-taking dangerously; they also tend to be more crowded than KSRTC buses. The **Kaloor bus stand** (rural destinations to the south and east) is across the bridge from Ernakulam Town train station on the Alwaye Rd, and the **High Court bus stand** (buses to Kumily, Periyar Wildlife Reserve, Thrissur, Guruvayur and Kodungallur) is opposite the High Court boat jetty.

Although **auto-rickshaws** are plentiful and reliable in Ernakulam, and to a slightly lesser extent across the water in Mattancherry and Fort Cochin, everyone uses Kochi's **ferry system**. **Bicycles** for exploring Mattancherry and the rest of Fort Cochin can be rented from a small shop on Bazaar Rd between the *Hotel Seagull* and Fort Cochin or from *Adams Old Inn* (at a rate of Rs5 per hour).

Tours and backwater trips

KTDCs half-day **Kochi boat cruise** (daily 9am–12.30pm & 2–5.30pm; Rs50) is a good way to orientate yourself, though as it doesn't stop long in Mattancherry or Fort Cochin. Departing from the High Court Jetty on Shanmugham Rd, Ernakulam, it calls at the Synagogue, Mattancherry Dutch Palace, St Francis Church, the Chinese fishing nets and Bolghatty Island. Book at the KTDC Tourist reception centre on Shanmugham Rd (☎0484/353234).

KTDC and a couple of private companies also operate popular **backwater trips** (see p.311) out of Kochi. Taking in a handful of coir-making villages north of the city, these are a leisurely and enjoyable way to experience rural Kerala from small hand-punted canoes. KTDC's cost Rs300, including the car or bus trip to the departure point, 30km north, and a knowledgeable guide. Better value is a similar trip run by the Tourist Desk at the Main Boat Jetty (daily depart 9am, return 1.30pm or depart 2pm, return 6.30pm; Rs275; ☎0484/371761). Reserve at least a day in advance for either tour. They also offer *kettu vallam* **houseboat** cruises for Rs2500 – for the boat – for a 24-hour trip, which, in comparison, is a great deal. Among other tour operators, Titus of Trio Travels, XL/180 Hospital Rd, Ernakulam (☎0484/353234) organizes all-inclusive, backwater cruises from Cherai Beach, 35km to the north, taking in sights along the way plus hospitality at a traditional Keralan home; it's interesting but expensive at Rs950 per head.

KOCHI BY FERRY

Half the fun of visiting Kochi is getting about on the cheap **local ferries**. When it's not downright impossible, catching a bus, rickshaw or taxi the long way round to most parts of the city takes much longer and is far less interesting.

The map of Kochi and Ernakulam on p.328 shows the four main jetties. Theoretically, the routes below should work in reverse. However, play safe, and don't rely on getting the last boat. Timings are available from the ticket hatches by the jetties, and from the helpful Tourist Desk at the Main Boat Jetty in Ernakulam.

Ernakulam to Mattancherry
From Ernakulam (Main Jetty), via **Fort Cochin** (Customs Jetty), for Chinese fishing nets, St Francis Church, Dutch Cemetery; Willingdon Island (Terminus Jetty); and **Mattancherry Jetty** for Jewish Synagogue and Dutch Palace. Journey time 20min. First boat 7am, last 9.30pm.

Ernakulam to Vypeen
From Ernakulam (Main Jetty). This frequent service has two routes: one via Willingdon Island (Embarkation Jetty; 25min), and a fast one to Vypeen (Government Jetty; 15min). First boat 7am, every 30min until 9.30pm.

Fort Cochin to Vypeen
Privately operated service, intended mainly for locals. Journey time 10min. First boat 6.30am, every 30min until 9pm.

Willingdon Island to Fort Cochin
From the Embarkation Jetty (Willingdon Island) to Customs Jetty (Fort Cochin). Journey time 10min. First boat 6.30am, every 30min until 6.15pm.

Ernakulam to Bolghatty Island
Journey time 10min. From High Court Jetty, first boat at 6.30am, last 9pm; there are also speed boat taxis (Rs20).

Ernakulam to Varapuzha
Local ferry service that provides a chance to see the **backwaters** (see box on p.310) if you can't travel further south than Kochi. First boat 7.40am, last 6.45pm; 2hr each way. There's little to see at Varapuzha, apart from paddy fields and coconuts, so it makes sense to take the 2.30pm boat and stay on it, returning to Ernakulam just after dusk at 6.30pm.

Information, communications and banks

The helpful Government of India **Tourist Office** (Mon–Fri 9am–5.30pm, Sat 9am–noon; ☎0484/668352), between the *Malabar Hotel* and Embarkation Jetty on Willingdon Island, offers information on Kerala and beyond, and can provide guides; they also have a desk at the airport. KTDC's **Tourist Reception Centre**, on Shanmugham Rd, Ernakulam (daily 8am–7pm; ☎0484/353234), will book hotels in their chain (including the popular *Bolghatty Palace Hotel*) and runs sightseeing and backwater tours (see above). Further KTDC counters can be found at the airport and at the Old Collectorate, Park Ave, Ernakulam. The tiny independent **Tourist Desk** (daily 8am–7pm; ☎0484/371761), located at the entrance to the Main Boat Jetty in Ernakulam, is extremely helpful and friendly, and is the best place to check ferry and bus timings. It is run by P.J. Varghese, and is the only place to get free city maps. Varghese is a mine of information on ritual theatre and temple festival dates around the state. He publishes a useful South India information guide and offers daily boat tours and houseboats at very competitive rates. Other useful **publications** include the Jaico Timetable (Rs7), which is not exhaustive but lists details of bus, train, ferry and flight times, and the Cochin *Shopper's Digest* published every two months. The city's **tourist police** have a counter at the train station and are on hand at to answer queries and assist if you get into difficulties.

The **Head Post Office** is on Hospital Rd, not far from the Main Jetty (Mon–Fri 8.30am–8pm, Sat 9.30am–2.30pm & 4–8pm, Sun 10am–4pm); the city's **poste restante** is at the **GPO**, behind St Francis Church in Fort Cochin.

Banks along MG Rd in Ernakulam include: ANZ Grindlays (☎0484/361301); the State Bank of India (☎0484/366376), which also has a branch opposite the KTDC Tourist Reception Centre; the efficient Andhra Bank, which makes encashments on Visa cards; and the State Bank of Travancore (☎0484/352309). The State Bank of Travancore is virtually the only place in the state where you can trade in torn bank notes; it also has an evening counter (4–6pm). To exchange travellers' cheques, however, the best place is Thomas Cook (Mon–Sat 9.30am–6pm; ☎0484/373829), near the Air India Building at Palal Towers, MG Rd; Surana Financial Corporation (☎0484/353724), next door, is also good and so is the Jyotiss Exchange Bureau, Shop 10, KTDC Shopping Complex, Shanmugham Rd.

Mattancherry

With high-rise development restricted to Ernakulam, across the water, the old-fashioned character of **Mattancherry** and **Fort Cochin** remains intact. Within an area small enough to cover on foot, bicycle or auto-rickshaw, glimpses of Kochi's variegated history greet you at virtually every turn. As you approach by ferry (get off at Mattancherry Jetty), the shoreline is crowded with tiled buildings painted in pastel colours – a view that can't have changed for centuries.

Despite the large number of tourists visiting daily, trade is still the most important activity here. Many of the streets are busy with barrows, loaded with sacks of produce, trundling between *godowns* (warehouses), and there are little shops everywhere with dealers doing business in tea, jute, rubber, chillies, turmeric, cashew, ginger, cardamom and pepper.

Jew Town

The road heading left from Mattancherry Jetty leads into the district known as **Jew Town**, where *NX Jacob's* tailor shop and the offices of *JE Cohen*, advocate and tax consultant, serve as reminders of a once-thriving community. Nowadays many of the shops sell antiques, Hindu and Christian wood-carvings, oil lamps, wooden jewellery boxes and other bric-a-brac.

Turning right at the India Pepper & Spice Trade Building, usually resounding with the racket of dealers shouting the latest spice prices, and then right again, brings you into Synagogue Lane. The **Pardesi (White Jew) Synagogue** (daily except Sat 10am–noon & 3–5pm) was founded in 1568, and rebuilt in 1664. Its interior is an attractive, if incongruous, hotchpotch; note the floor, paved with hand-painted eighteenth-century blue and white tiles from Canton, each unique, depicting a love affair between a mandarin's daughter and a commoner. The nineteenth-century glass oil-burning chandeliers suspended from the ceiling were imported from Belgium. Above the entrance, a gallery supported by slender gilt columns was reserved for female members of the congregation. Opposite the entrance, an elaborately carved Ark houses four scrolls of the *Torah* (the first five books of the Old Testament), encased in silver and gold, on which are placed gold crowns presented by the maharajas of Travancore and Cochin, testifying to good relations with the Jewish community. The synagogue's oldest artefact is a fourth-century copperplate inscription from the Raja of Cochin.

An attendant is usually available to show visitors around and answer questions, and his introductory talk features as part of the KTDC guided tour (see p.329). Outside, in a small square, several antique shops are well worth a browse but don't expect a bargain.

THE JEWS OF KOCHI

According to tradition, the first Jews to arrive on the Malabar Coast were fleeing from the occupation of Jerusalem by Nebuchadnezzar, in 587 BC. Trading in spices, they remained respected members of Keralan society until the Portuguese embarked upon a characteristic "Christian" policy of persecution of non-believers, early in the sixteenth century.

At that time, when Jews were being burned at the stake in Goa, and forced to leave their settlements elsewhere on the coast, the Raja of Cochin gave them a parcel of land adjoining the royal palace in Mattancherry. A new Jewish community was created in the area now known as Jew Town, and a synagogue was built.

There were formerly three distinct groups of Jews in Kochi: **Black** (Myuchasim), **Brown** (Meshuchrarim) and **White** (Pardesi, "foreign") Jews. The Black Jews were employed as labourers in the spice business, and their community – of some thousands – resulted from the earliest Jewish settlers marrying and converting Indians; the Brown Jews are thought to have been slave converts. Both groups were considered inferior by the White Jews. In the early 1950s, however, most of Kochi's Jews disappeared, when they were given free passage to Israel. The remaining White Jews are on the verge of extinction. At the time of writing, only seven families survive, a total of twenty-two people with just enough males over the age of thirteen to perform the rituals in the synagogue – and no rabbi.

Draavidia, on Jew St, is a small but active art **gallery**, which has an emphasis on contemporary art. Draavidia also puts on daily live Indian **classical music**, the programme is called Sadhana (6–7pm), and admission is on a membership basis of Rs100.

Mattancherry Palace

Mattancherry Palace (daily except Fri 10am–5pm; free, but donations are welcome), stands on the left side of the road a short walk from the Mattancherry Jetty in the opposite direction to Jew Town. The gateway on the road is, in fact, its back entrance; although the most sensible side to approach from the ferry, it inexplicably remains locked with a loose chain. Visitors slim enough can, and do, enter through the gap, saving the walk around the block. In the walled grounds stands a circular, tiled Krishna temple (closed to non-Hindus).

Although known locally as the **Dutch Palace**, the two-storey palace was built by the Portuguese as a gift to the Cochin Raja, Vira Keralavarma (1537–61), and the Dutch were responsible for subsequent additions. While its appearance is not particularly striking – squat with whitewashed walls and tiled roof – the interior is captivating.

The **murals** that adorn some of its rooms are among the finest examples of Kerala's much underrated school of painting (see Contexts, p.589): friezes illustrating stories from the *Ramayana*, on the first floor, date from the sixteenth century. Packed with detail and gloriously rich colour, the style is never strictly naturalistic; the treatment of facial features is pared down to the simplest of lines for the mouth, and characteristically aquiline noses. Downstairs, the women's bedchamber holds several less complex paintings, possibly dating from the 1700s. One shows Shiva dallying with Vishnu in his female form, the enchantress Mohini; a second portrays Krishna holding aloft Mount Govardhana; another features a reclining Krishna surrounded by *gopis*, or cowgirls. His languid pose belies the activity of his six hands and two feet, intimately caressing adoring admirers.

While the paintings are undoubtedly the highlight of the palace, the collection also includes interesting Dutch maps of old Cochin, coronation robes belonging to past maharajas, royal palanquins, weapons and furniture. Without permission from the Archaeological Survey of India, photography is strictly prohibited.

Fort Cochin

Moving northwest from Mattancherry Palace along Bazaar Rd, you pass wholesale emporia where owners, sitting behind scales surrounded by sacks of spices, may well be prepared to talk about their wares. After about half an hour's leisurely walk, cross the canal to find yourself in **Fort Cochin**. The architecture of the quiet streets in this enclave is very definitely European, with fine houses built by wealthy British traders and Dutch cottages with split farmhouse doors. At the water's edge there's a bus stand, boat jetty and food and drinks stalls. This area and nearby Princess St (which has a few budget hotels) attract backpackers and the consequent local hustlers.

Fort Cochin is home to a unique community of Eurasians, commonly known as "**Anglo-Indians**", who have developed a distinct and lively culture. With the development of tourism and the arrival of guesthouses, the changes to Fort Cochin are threatening the fragile infrastructure of this community and altering the face of the area. Fort Cochin was being preserved as a **"Heritage Zone"** with the help of a grant by US Aid which was unfortunately cut as a result of India's nuclear tests in 1998. The map and leaflet *Walking Through Fort Cochin* is excellent but difficult to get hold of since US Aid

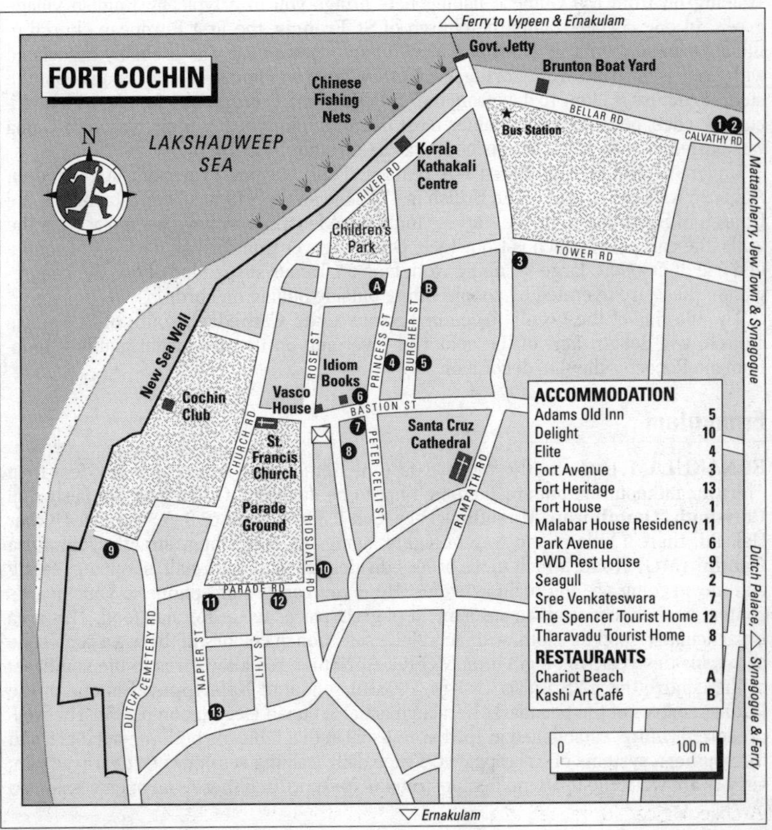

terminated their programme, but try the Tourist Desk at the ferry jetty in Ernakulam. The Gulbenkian Foundation, however, has put forward plans for an exciting new museum in Fort Cochin to showcase Portuguese heritage.

The Kashi Art Café on Burgher St is an interesting and lively contemporary art **gallery**. The Kerala Kathakali Centre at the Cochin Aquatic Club holds Kathakali performances everyday (see box on p.336).

Chinese fishing nets

The huge, elegant **Chinese fishing nets** that line the northern shore of Fort Cochin – adding grace to an already characterful waterside view, and probably the single most familiar photographic image of Kerala – are said to have been introduced to the region by traders from the court of Kublai Khan. Known in Malayalam as *cheena vala*, they can also be seen throughout the backwaters further south. The nets, which are suspended from arced poles and operated by levers and weights, require at least four men to control them. You can buy fresh fish from the tiny market here and have it grilled on the spot at one of the ramshackle stalls.

St Francis Church

Walking on from the Chinese fishing nets brings you to a typically English village green. In one corner stands the church of **St Francis**, the first European church in India. Originally built in wood and named Santo Antonio, it was probably associated with Franciscan friars from Portugal. Exactly when it was founded is not known, but the stone structure is likely to date from the early sixteenth century. The facade, with multi-curved sides, became the model for most Christian churches in India. Vasco da Gama was buried here in 1524, but his body was later removed to Portugal.

Under the Dutch, the church was renovated and became Protestant in 1663, then Anglican with the advent of the British in 1795 and since 1949 has been attached to the Church of South India. Inside, various tombstone inscriptions have been placed in the walls, the earliest of which is from 1562. One hangover from British days is the continued use of *punkahs*, large swinging cloth fans on frames suspended above the congregation; these are operated by people sitting outside pulling on cords.

The interior of the twentieth-century **Santa Cruz Cathedral**, south of St Francis church, will delight fans of the colourful – verging on the downright gaudy – Indo-Romano-Rococo school of decoration.

Ernakulam

ERNAKULAM presents the modern face of Kerala, with more of a city feel than Thiruvananthapuram, but small enough not to be daunting. Other than the fairly dull **Parishath Thamburan Museum** (Tues–Sun 9.30am–noon & 3–5.30pm) in Durbar Hall Rd, there's little in the way of sights; along the busy, long, straight **Mahatma Gandhi (MG) Road**, which more or less divides Ernakulam in half, shopping, eating and movie-going are the main activities. Here you can fax and phone to your heart's content, and choose from an assortment of great places to eat Keralan food. This area is particularly good for cloth, with an infinite selection of colours. If there's a jazzy style in *lunghis* this year, you'll get it on MG Rd. At Netoor, ten kilometres to the southeast of the centre, the ENS Kalari (☎0484/700810) school of **Kalarippayat** is one of the leading centres of the peculiarly Keralan martial art form (see box on p.285). The well-organized centre, established in 1954, is unusual in that it blends both the northern and the southern systems of Kalarippayat. Twice daily training sessions start early at 4am; visitors are welcome to attend demonstrations (6–7pm), and there's an open session on

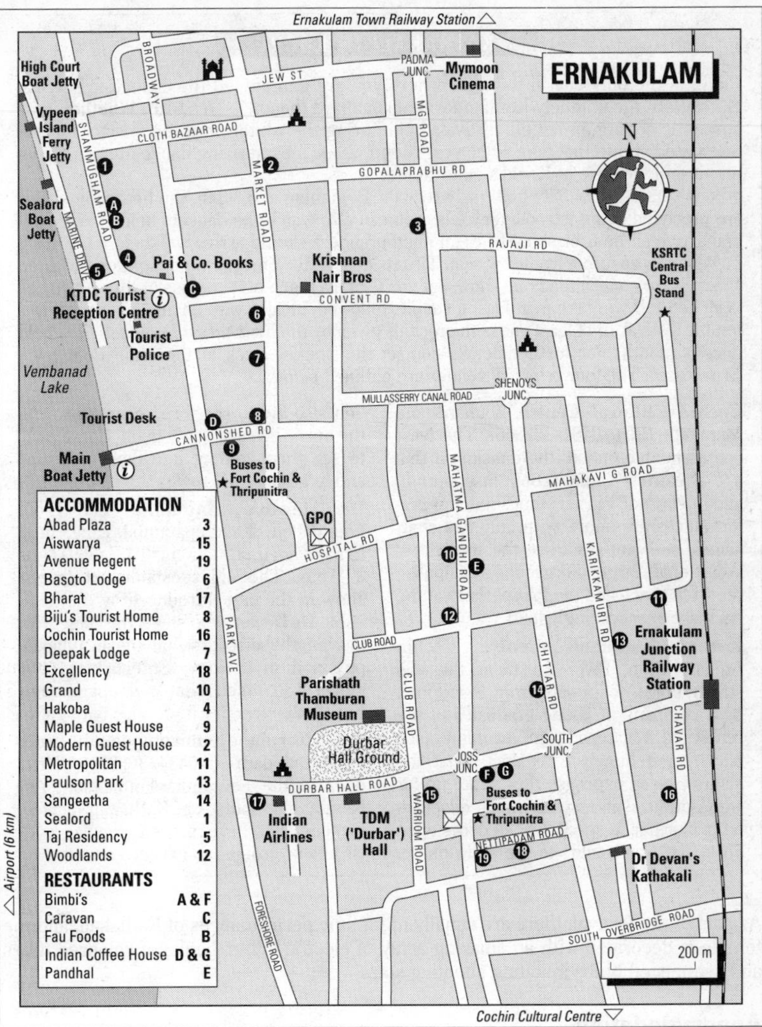

Sundays (3–7pm). The centre also offers **Uzhichil massage** – a treatment derived from Ayurvedic medicine, designed as a cure to Kalari-related injuries – which concentrates on the lymph glands to improve tone and circulation. To get to the school take a bus from the KSRTC or the Kaloor bus stands to the Netoor INTUC bus stand, and walk down the road for half a kilometre; the school is opposite the Mahadevar Temple.

An eight-day annual **festival** at the Shiva temple in Ernakulam (Jan/Feb) features elephant processions and *panchavadyam* (drum and trumpet groups) out in the street.

KATHAKALI IN KOCHI

Kochi is the only city in the state where you are guaranteed the chance to see live **Kathakali**, the uniquely Keralan form of ritualized theatre (see p.610). Whether in its authentic setting, in temple festivals held during the winter or at the shorter tourist-orientated shows that take place year round, these mesmerizing dance dramas are an unmissable feature of Kochi's cultural life.

Four venues in the city hold daily recitals. Beginning at 6.30pm, the hour-long shows are preceded by an introductory talk. You can also watch the dancers being made up if you arrive an hour or so early. Keen photographers should arrive well before the start, however, to ensure a front-row seat. Tickets cost Rs100 and can be bought on the door. Most visitors only attend one show, but you'll gain a much better sense of what Kathakali is all about if you take in at least a couple, followed, ideally, with an all-night recital at a temple festival, or at least one of the recitals given by the *Ernakulam Kathakali Club* held once a month. For further details contact the Tourist Desk at the Main Boat Jetty, Ernakulam. The four principal venues are outlined below.

Cochin Cultural Centre, Souhardham, Manikath Rd (☎0484/367866). The least commendable option: the dancing at this a/c theatre ("sound-proof, insect-proof, and dust-proof") is accomplished, but performances are short, with only two characters, and you can't see the musicians. Worst of all, large tour groups monopolize the front seats, and the PA speakers at the back are excruciatingly loud.

Kerala Kathakali Centre, Cochin Aquatic Club, River Rd (near the bus stand), Fort Cochin waterfront. Performed by a company of young graduates of the renowned Kalamandalam Academy (see p.354), and hugely enjoyable. What the actors lack in expertise they make up for with enthusiasm, and the small, dilapidated performance space, whose doors open on to the water, adds to the atmosphere. You also get to see three characters, and the music is particularly good. Come early to see them getting into their costumes and to grab a front-row seat.

Dr Devan's Kathakali, See India Foundation, Kalathiparambil Lane, near Ernakulam train station (☎0484/369471 or 371759). The oldest-established tourist show in the city, introduced by the inimitable Dr Devan, who steals the stage with his lengthy discourse on Indian philosophy and mythology. Entertaining, but maybe too much chat and not enough Kathakali.

Art Kerala, Kannanthodathu Lane, Valanjambalam (☎0484/366231). Next door to the See India Foundation, Art Kerala also puts on Kathakali performances that have proved popular with large tour groups; so expect a crowd.

As part of the festival, there are usually night-time performances of Kathakali, and the temple is decorated with an amazing array of electric lights: banks of coloured tubes and sequenced bulbs imitating shooting stars.

Accommodation

The romantic atmosphere of **Fort Cochin** is slowly being exploited, with a small but growing number of budget guesthouses and some upmarket hotel developments which promise to displace sections of the original community and to drastically alter the face of this quaint town. Most visitors still end up staying in **Ernakulam**, which, although it lacks the old-world ambience, is far more convenient. **Bolghatty Island**, site of the city's most congenial and best-value mid-price hotel, is a comfortable, but isolated, alternative. If you would like to stay on a **house boat**, contact the Tourist Desk (☎0484/371761; ⑨) at the Main Boat Jetty in Ernakulam, who charge Rs3500 for two; other options include the more expensive but well-organized house boats and cruises run by the *Casino Hotel*.

Ernakulam

Ernakulam has plenty of accommodation, although its guesthouses and hotels tend to fill up by late afternoon, so book in advance.

INEXPENSIVE

Basoto Lodge, Market Rd (☎0484/352140). Clean, dependable backpackers' lodge with twelve cheap rooms and no restaurant. Two rooms have small balconies and attached shower-toilets. Advance booking is recommended. ②.

Biju's Tourist Home, corner of Cannonshed and Market roads (☎0484/381881). Pick of the budget bunch, close to the main boat jetty, which has thirty basic but clean and spacious rooms, some with a/c. TVs may be rented, and they have an inexpensive same-day laundry service. ③–⑤.

Cochin Tourist Home, Chavar Rd (☎0484/364577). Cleanest of the cheap hotels lined up outside Ernakulam Junction, but often full. Single occupancy is available, and there's a resident astro-palmist. If it's full, try *KK International* (☎0484/366010; ③–⑤) or *NM Hotel* (☎0484/353641; ③–⑥) nearby, both of which have a few a/c rooms. ②.

Deepak Lodge, Market Rd (☎0484/353882). One of a handful of budget lodges on this road, offering cheap basic rooms. ②.

Hakoba, Shanmugham Rd (☎0484/369839). Dowdy, but adequate for a night, with a good "meals" joint on the ground floor. The front rooms overlooking the street and harbour are the best deals. ③–⑤.

Maple Guest House, XL/271 Cannonshed Rd (☎0484/355156). After Biju's, the best deal in the district. The rooms are spartan, but clean, cheap and central and there are some a/c. ③–⑤.

Modern Guest House, XL/6067, Market Rd (☎0484/352130). Simple rooms, above (noisy) Keralan veg restaurant, all en suite and with fans. Popular budget option; book ahead. If full try their annexe, the Modern Rest House (☎0484/361407), with sixteen plain but pleasant rooms which are slightly more expensive. ②.

MODERATE TO EXPENSIVE

Abad Plaza, MG Rd (☎0484/381122). Comfortable and pleasant business-style high-rise, the facilities include a restaurant and bar, swimming pool and well-equipped health club. ⑧.

Aiswarya, Durbar Hall Rd (☎0484/364454). All-round hotel where the cheaper rooms are excellent value and there is a good and versatile restaurant downstairs serving "meals" and fish *molee* (fish in coconut sauce). The a/c rooms on the top floors have balconies. ④–⑥.

Avenue Regent, MG Rd, Jos Junction (☎0484/372660, fax 370129). Very comfortable, centrally a/c four-star, close to the train station and main shopping area. There's a restaurant, 24hr coffee shop, and most mod cons. ⑧.

Bharat, Gandhi Square, Durbar Hall Rd (☎0484/353501, fax 370502). Large, well-run hotel near the harbour and city centre. The rooms are clean and comfortable, and there's a 24-hr coffee shop and three restaurants. ⑥–⑦.

Excellency, Nettipadam Rd, Jos Junction (☎0484/374001, fax 374009). Smart, modern mid-range place, which has mostly a/c rooms. Credit cards are accepted. ⑦.

Grand, MG Rd (☎0484/382061). Two-part hotel near Woodlands Junction, which has undergone recent extensive refurbishment; the cheaper rooms are on the bottom floors, which have a faintly 1950s feel. There's a restaurant on site. ⑦–⑧.

Metropolitan, near Ernakulam Junction (☎0484/369931). Smart middle-market business hotel with good facilities including restaurant, coffee-shop and bar. ⑦

Paulson Park, Karikkamuri Rd (☎0484/382179). Close to Ernakulam Junction. Good value, with large, well-appointed rooms, some with a/c, and a ground-floor restaurant featuring a surreal fake rock garden. ⑤–⑥.

Sangeetha, 36/1675 Chittar Rd, South Junction (☎0484/368736). Comfortable rooms, if small for the price; the non-a/c ones can be stuffy. Left luggage and foreign exchange. ⑤–⑥.

Sealord, Shanmugham Rd (☎0484/382472, fax 370135). Modern, comfortable high-rise near Sealord Boat Jetty. Standard rooms are excellent value; the best are on the top floor. Rooftop restaurant, bar and foreign exchange. ⑥–⑧.

Taj Residency, Marine Drive (☎0484/371471, fax 371481). Erankulam's top hotel enjoys a prime location overlooking the harbour. All the luxuries provided here, minus a pool. ⑨.

Woodlands, Woodlands Junction, MG Rd (☎0484/382051). Central, stylish Indian-style middle-class hotel with a fine veg restaurant. The rooms are a/c and non-a/c and have sofas, easy chairs and spotless marble bathrooms. Recommended. ⑤–⑦.

Fort Cochin

Fort Cochin has a congenial atmosphere not equalled anywhere else in the city, but the fragile infrastructure is being threatened by overdevelopment and an explosion of hotels, most in the budget range, but some like the Casino Group's *Brunton Boatyard*, under construction, in the luxury bracket.

Adams Old Inn, Burgher St (☎0484/229495). Great little guesthouse full of character, situated in an expertly restored period building. It has small ordinary rooms, one of which has a/c. ③–④.

Delight, opposite the Parade Ground (☎0484/228658). Beautiful home, with distinctive blue lattice-work, which overlooks the ground. One of the best all-round budget options in Fort Cochin, and run by a friendly family. Six spacious, airy rooms are ranged around a leafy courtyard, and breakfast is available. Book ahead. ③–⑥.

Elite, Princess St (☎0484/225733). Small, cheap rooms in a friendly guesthouse, above a popular restaurant. ②.

Fort Avenue, Tower Rd (☎0484/221219). A family house, with small but pleasant rooms upstairs, and a quiet but convenient location. ③.

Fort Heritage, 1/283 Napier St (☎0484/225333). A seventeenth-century beautifully restored Dutch mansion, with comfortable airy rooms, a restaurant and loads of character. However, the walls are hung with tacky and inescapable imitations of Rubens, and the management is a little surly. ⑧.

Fort House, 2/6A Calvathy Rd (☎0484/226103). Next to *Seagull* and a lot better. Five rooms, in an interesting if eccentric compound littered with pots and statues; there's also a good café and a brilliant jetty but none of the rooms looks onto the water. ⑥.

Malabar House Residency, 1/268 Parade Rd (☎0484/221199). Beautifully renovated, historic mansion with a highly successful mix of old-world charm, and bright and brash European designer chic. Recommended. ⑨.

Park Avenue, Princess St (☎0484/222671). This building has been badly restored and is now an eyesore; previously beautiful features have been drowned out by the need for modern comfort. Rooms are small and uninspiring, some have a/c ⑥.

PWD Rest House, Dutch Cemetery Rd. A dilapidated place with three gigantic rooms full of colonial furniture. Although it's intended for government employees, others can stay when it's not busy. ①.

Seagull, Calvathy Rd (☎0484/228128). Assorted rooms, a couple with a/c, but none makes the most of the location next to the water's edge (stand on a chair to see out of the window). It also suffers from noise from its own popular bar and restaurant. ③–⑤.

Spencer Tourist Home, 1/298 Parade Rd (☎0484/225049). A place with loads of character set in an old, rambling Portuguese house. It has five large rooms to offer, but no food, and it's not as well maintained as the *Delight* close by. ⑤.

Sree Venkateswara, 1/653B Peter Celli St (☎0484/369839). Small, but clean, guesthouse along this popular strip. ③.

Tharavadu Tourist Home, Quinose St, on the road behind the post office (☎0484/226897). Eight simple, clean rooms (two without bath), in an old house, where breakfast and cool drinks are available and there's a cheap laundry service. They do not always, however, honour advance bookings. ②–③.

Willingdon and Bolghatty islands

Casino, Willingdon Island, 2km from airport, close to Cochin Harbour Terminus train station (☎0484/668221, fax 668001). Fairly modern, efficient and comfortable option, with good service; facilities include swimming pool, travel agent, foreign exchange and a choice of excellent restaurants. ⑨.

KTDC Bolghatty Palace, Bolghatty Island (☎0484/355003 or 354879). Extensively renovated palace in a beautiful location, a short hop by ferry from the High Court Jetty, Ernakulam. Huge rooms in four massive suites with massive ceilings in main building, built by the Dutch in 1744 and later home of the British Resident. The annexe has also been completely renovated. Their "honeymoon" cottages, which suffer from poor plumbing, stand on stilts right on the water's edge and ferries go by in almost spitting distance. Check by phone, or at the KTDC office on Shanmugham Rd, to make sure they have vacancies, and arrive armed with mosquito repellent. During the day, the adjacent canteen and grounds are invaded by day-trippers. ⑦–⑨.

Taj Malabar, Willingdon Island, by the Embarkation Jetty (☎0484/666811, fax 668297). A 20min ferry ride from Ernakulam, it is one of India's best hotels, owned by the Taj group. Superb location with waterside gardens and views of old Mattancherry. There are two restaurants, a swimming pool and excellent service. ⑨.

Eating

Unusually for Keralan cities, Kochi offers a wide choice for **eating out**, from the delicious fresh-cooked fish by the Chinese fishing nets at Fort Cochin, to the sophistication of the *Malabar Hotel*. Between the two extremes, various popular, modest places in Ernakulam serve real Keralan food.

Ernakulam

Bimbi's, Shanmughan Rd and Jos Junction. Brisk new Indian-style fast-food joints. Hugely popular for inexpensive Udupi, North Indian and Chinese snacks and meals, and the tangiest *wada-sambars* in town. They also do a great selection of shakes and ice-creams.

The Brasserie, *Taj Residency*, Marine Drive. Luxury coffee shop serving snacks and a particularly good range of Western cakes (Dundee, plum, palmettes and fudge). Expensive.

Caravan, Broadway, near the KTDC tourist reception centre. An a/c ice-cream parlour that's a good place to chill out over a banana split or milkshake. Closes at midnight so you can nip in for a late dessert.

Fau Foods, Shanmughan Rd. Busy, clean and popular roadside restaurant serving veg and non-veg meals, including blow-out *thalis* and good-value "dish of the day". For dessert, try their Mumbai-style *faloodas*, vermicelli steeped in syrup.

Fry's Village Restaurant, adjacent to Mymoor Cinema, Chittar Rd. Moderately priced, ultra-spicy Keralan and "ethnic" specialities you rarely find served in such style, including Calicut Muslim delicacy *patthri*, wafer-thin rice pancakes, *idliappam* dumplings, and *puthoo*, steamed rice cakes.

Indian Coffee House, on the corner of Cannonshed Rd and Park Ave, and on Durbar Hall Rd. The usual excellent coffee (ask for "pot coffee" if you don't want it with sugar), and simple snacks such as *dosa* and scrambled egg.

Lotus Cascades, *Woodlands Hotel*, Woodlands Junction, MG Rd. Classy veg Indian food, with plenty of *tandoori* options, at bargain prices. Great service, too. Recommended.

Pandhal, MG Rd. Very smart upmarket restaurant, run by the same catering family which owns the Casino Group of hotels. Excellent Keralan fish dishes, as well as good North Indian cuisine and a sprinkling of continental food.

Sealord, in the hotel *Sealord*, Shanmugham Rd. Pricey rooftop restaurant serving good Chinese, Indian and sizzlers – but the portions are not too generous, and the view is not what it was since the shopping centre opposite was built. Great for a beer, though.

Utsav, *Taj Residency*, Marine Drive. Top Indian restaurant with great views over the harbour, and an à la carte menu at expense-account prices. Their lunch-time buffets are better value.

Fort Cochin and Mattancherry

Chariot Beach, Princess St. Huge seafood and Chinese menu, at reasonable prices, and you can eat al fresco on their small terrace.

Elite, Princess St. Popular and lively travellers' haunt where locals come to check out the scene; however, as a place to eat, the café has had mixed reviews.

Kashi Art Café, Burgher St. Great café and exhibition space, in a restored old building with a cosmopolitan atmosphere, run by an American woman. A good place to check the notice boards. It serves healthy food, an excellent breakfast and the best coffee in town, but the menu has little local flavour.

Rahmathula Hotel (aka **Kaika's**), New Rd, near Mattancherry Palace. Kaika, the chef, is renowned for his mutton and chicken *biryanis* cooked in traditional Keralan style and served at breakfast and at lunch; you will need to ask directions as it is tucked away and difficult to find.

Seagull, Calvathy Rd. Average restaurant, in a good location overlooking the water. Their seafood in Chinese sauces is particularly tasty, but be prepared for a long wait. Serves beer and spirits.

Willingdon Island

Fort Cochin, *Casino Hotel* (☎0484/6688421). Exceptional seafood restaurant, considered to be one of the best in India. Pleasant garden ambience and the opportunity to choose from the catch of the day. Although expensive, it is well worth the treat. In season, book in advance. Their indoor restaurant is good for lunchtime buffets.

Taj Malabar, *Taj Malabar Hotel* (☎0484/666811). Two restaurants to choose from here: the *Jade Pavilion* for Chinese, and *Rice Boats* serving Western, North Indian and Keralan cuisines, in a beautiful waterside location. The food is excellent and prices reflect this; the lunchtime buffet is less expensive.

Listings

Audio cassettes Sargam, XL/6816 GSS Complex, Convent Rd, opposite Public Library (☎0484/374216), stocks the best range of music tapes in the state, mostly Indian (Hindi films and lots of Keralan devotional music), with a couple of shelves of Western rock and pop. Sound of Melody, DH Rd, near the Ernakulam Junction station, also has a good selection of traditional South Indian and contemporary Western music. Sea Breeze, 248, GCDA Complex, Marine Drive (☎0484/362561), is a smart upmarket shop with a strong emphasis on Western music.

Ayurvedic treatment Although widely advertised, the following two come highly recommended – Kerala Ayurveda Pharmacy, Warriom Rd, off MG Rd (Rs350–400 for 1hr 30min sessions) with trained doctors, and PNVM Shanthigiri, Thrikkakara (☎0484/558879), on the northern outskirts (Rs250 per session).

Bookstores Bhavi Books, Convent Rd (☎0484/354003); Higginbothams, TD Rd (☎0484/368834); and Pai & Co, MG Rd (☎0484/355835), Broadway (☎0484/361020), New Rd (☎0484/225607). One of the best for travel, religion and art, Idiom, opposite the Synagogue, Jew Town, Mattancherry and also on Bastion St near Princess St, Fort Cochin, which also deals in second-hand books.

Cinemas Sridhar Theatre, Shanmughan Rd, near the Hotel Sealord, screens English-language movies daily; check the listings pages of the *Indian Express* or *Hindu* (Kerala edition) to find out what's on. For the latest Malayalam and Hindi releases, head for the comfortable a/c Mymoon Cinema at the north end of Chitoor Rd, or the Saritha Savitha Sangeetha, at the top of Market Rd.

Handicrafts CI Company, Broadway (☎0484/352405). Kairali (☎0484/354507), Khadi Bhavan (☎0484/355279), Khataisons Curio Palace (☎0484/367472), Surabhi Kerala State Handicrafts (☎0484/353063), Coirboard Showroom, are all on MG Rd.

Hospitals General, Hospital Rd (☎0484/361251); Lissie, Lissie Junction (☎0484/352006); Lourdes, Pachalam (☎0484/351507).

Internet Raiyaan Communications, Raiyaan Complex, Padma Junction, MG Rd (☎0484/351387; *raiyaan@giasmd01.vsnl.net.in*), Rs60 per hour and Rs10 for incoming and Rs20 for outgoing email. *Rendezvous Cyber Café*, Burger St, opposite St Mary's School, Fort Cochin (☎0484/220342; *gks@giasmd01.vsnl.net.in*).

Musical instruments Manual Industries, Bannerji Rd, Kacheripady Junction (☎0484/352513), is the best for Indian classical instruments. For traditional Keralan drums, ask at Thripunitra bazaar (see p.341).

Photography City Camera, Lovedale Building, Padma Junction, MG Rd (☎0484/380109), repair cameras and come recommended; Krishnan Nair Bros, Convent Rd (☎0484/352098), stocks the best range of camera film, including black-and-white, Kodachrome and Fujichrome and professional colour transparency; Royal Studio, Shanmugham Rd (☎0484/351614), is also worth a try. Several others around MG Rd.

Tour & Travel Agents Clipper Holidays, 40/6531 Convent Rd (☎0484/364443), are experienced agents good for wildlife and adventure tours in Kerala and Karnataka. Trio Travels, XL/180 Hospital Rd (☎0484/369571), is a friendly tour operator who organizes local sightseeing and backwater tours as well as trips into the interior. Other all-round travel agents specializing in tours and air-ticketing include Travel Corporation of India, MG Rd (☎0484/351646), Princy World Travels, Marine Drive (☎0484/352751), Trade Wings, MG Rd (☎0484/367938), and Pioneer Travels, Bristow Rd (☎0484/666148).

Visa extensions Apply in person to City Police Commissioner, Marine Drive (Shanmugham Rd), near the Vypeen Island ferry (☎0484/360700); take two passport photos. Extensions normally take between five and ten working days to process.

Around Kochi and Ernakulam

Within easy distance of Kochi and Ernakulam are the small suburban town of **Thripunitra**, which harbours a former royal seat, and the three-kilometre stretch of sand called **Cherai Beach**, which offers a taste of both beach- and backwater-life. Visitors to Kochi and Ernakulam who really want to get away from it all, however, and have time and a lot of money to spare, could do no better than to head for **Lakshadweep**, the "one hundred thousand islands", which lie between 200 and 400km offshore, in the deep blue of the Arabian Sea.

Thripunitra

THRIPUNITRA, 12km southeast of Ernakulam, is worth a visit for its dilapidated colonial-style **Hill Palace** (Tues–Sun 9am–12.30pm & 2–4pm), now an eclectic museum a short auto-rickshaw ride from the busy bus stand. The royal family of Cochin – "Honour is our family treasure" – at one time maintained around forty palaces. This one was confiscated by the state government after Independence, and has slipped into dusty decline over the past decade.

One of the museum's finest exhibits is an early seventeenth-century wooden *mandapa* removed from a temple in Pathanamthitta, featuring excellent carvings of the coronation of the monkey king Sugriva and other themes from the *Ramayana*. Of interest too are silver filigree jewel boxes, gold and silver ornaments, and ritual objects associated with grand ceremonies. The **epigraphy** gallery contains an eighth-century Jewish *Torah*, and Keralan stone and copperplate inscriptions. Sculpture, ornaments and weapons in the **bronze** gallery include a *kingini katti* knife, whose decorative bells belie the fact that it was used for beheading, and a body-shaped cage in which condemned prisoners would be hanged for birds to peck them to death. Providing the place isn't crowded with noisy school groups here to see the nearby deer park, the **garden** behind the palace is a peaceful spot to picnic beneath the cashew trees.

Performances of theatre, classical music and dance, including consecutive all-night Kathakali performances, are held over a period of several days during the annual **festival** (Oct/Nov) at the **Shri Purnatrayisa** temple, on the way to the palace. Inside the temple compound, both in the morning and at night, massed drum orchestras perform *chenda melam* in procession with fifteen caparisoned elephants (decked out in golden regalia). At night, the outside walls of the sanctuary are covered with thousands of tiny oil lamps. Although the temple is normally closed to non-Hindus, admittance to appropriately dressed visitors is usually allowed at this time.

Cherai Beach

The closest decent beach to Kochi is **Cherai Beach**, 35km to the north. However, despite the fact it's three kilometres long, don't expect it to be deserted, especially at weekends. The beach shelters a backwater and supports an active fishing community, some of whom use Chinese fishing nets (see p.334). The **Sri Goureeswara Temple**, closed to non-Hindus, is dedicated to the deity Sri Subramanya Swami and holds its

MOVING ON FROM KOCHI/ERNAKULAM

For an overview of travel services to and from Kochi/Ernakulam, see Travel Details on pp.365–6.

By Air

Kochi airport, 5km south of the city centre on Willingdon Island, is in the process of being shifted to the new international airport at Nedumbassery, near Alwaye (aka Alua) 26km to the north of Ernakulam which has been designed to attract international flights especially from the Gulf. In the meantime, Jet Airways has two flights a day and Indian Airlines, one daily to **Mumbai**; Alliance NEPC and Indian Airlines both have one flight a day to **Bangalore** and Indian Airlines one to **Goa** which continues to **Delhi**; while Indian Airlines flies to **Chennai** four times a week, Jet Airways flies there everyday. If you want to fly to the **Lakshadweep Islands** contact *Casino Hotel*, Willingdon Island (☎0484/666821) who operate a private aircraft on demand. For details of airlines see below, and for travel agents, see Listings on p.340.

Domestic and International Airline Offices

Domestic: Indian Airlines, Durbar Hall Rd (daily 9.45am–1pm & 1.45–4.45pm; ☎0484/370242 & 141); Jet Airways, Bab Chambers, Atlantis, MG Rd (☎0484/369423); and Alliance NEPC in the Chandrika Building, also on MG Rd (☎0484/367720).

International: Air India, 35/1301 MG Rd, Ravipuram (☎0484/351295); British Airways, c/o Nijhwan Travels, MG Rd (☎0484/364867); Air France, Alard Building, Wariam Rd (☎0484/361702); Egypt Air, c/o ABC International, Old Thevara Rd (☎0484/353457); Gulf Air, Jet Air, Bab Chambers, Atlantice Junction, MG Rd (☎0484/369142); Kuwait Airways, c/o National Travels, Pulinat Building, MG Rd (☎0484/360123); PIA, c/o ABC International, Old Thevara Rd (☎0484/353457); Saudia, c/o Arafat Travels, MG Rd (☎0484/352689); Singapore Airlines & Swissair, Aviation Travels, 35/2433 MG Rd, Ravipuram (☎0484/367911 or 360380). Spencer & Co, Arya Vaidya Sala Buildings, 35/718 MG Rd (☎0484/373997) are the local agents for Air Maldives, Cathay Pacific, KLM and Northwest Airlines.

By Bus

Buses leave Ernakulam's KSRTC Central bus stand for virtually every town in Kerala, and some beyond; most, but not all, are bookable in advance. Travelling south, dozens of buses per day run to **Thiruvananthapuram**; most go via **Alappuzha** and **Kollam**, but a few go via **Kottayam**. It is also possible to travel all the way to Kanniyakumari (9hr). However, for destinations further afield in Karnataka and Tamil Nadu, you're much better off on the train, although KSRTC's "super express" and private "luxury" buses travel to these destinations. If travelling to **Mysore** get there early to book a seat on the 8pm bus which takes ten hours. One of several private luxury bus companies travelling between Kochi/Ernakulam and **Mangalore** as well as to **Bangalore**, is Sharma Transports, based at the Grand Hotel near Jos Junction, MG Rd (☎0484/350712); NTC Travels at Jos Junction (☎0484/370046) runs luxury buses to **Madurai**; Indira Travels,

annual nine-day festival (*utsavam*) between January and February each year. The *utsavam* is a great time to see traditional dance, including Kathakali performances, but the highlight of the festival is on the seventh day, when eighteen caparisoned elephants take to the streets in a spectacular procession.

To get to Cherai Beach, take a ferry to Vypeen Island and then a bus for 18km to the Devaswamnada Junction near Cherai, from where an auto-rickshaw will cost around Rs15 for the three-kilometre journey to the beach. You can stay here at the north end of the beach, at *Sea Men's Cottage* (☎0484/489795; ③–④), a quiet place offering a cou-

Jos Junction (☎0484/360693) travels to Mangalore; and SMP Travels, Jos Junction (☎0484/353080) travels to **Chennai**.

By Train

Kochi lies on Kerala's main broad-gauge line, and sees frequent trains down the coast to Thiruvananthapuram, via Kottayam, Kollam and Varkala. Heading north, there are plenty of services to Thrissur, and thence northeast across Tamil Nadu to Chennai, but only a couple run north to Mangalore, where a poorly served branch line veers inland to Hassan and Mysore in Karnataka.

Although most long-distance express and mail trains depart from **Ernakulam Junction**, a short way southeast of the city centre, a couple of key services leave from **Ernakulam Town**, 2km north. To confuse matters further, some also start at Cochin Harbour station, on Willingdon Island, so be sure to check the departure point when you book your ticket. The main reservation office, good for trains leaving all three stations, is at Ernakulam Junction (☎390920 & 131 for general enquiries); take a good book with you as there is no special fast-track counter for tourists.

The trains listed below are recommended as the fastest and/or most convenient services from Kochi. If you're heading to **Alappuzha** for the backwater trip to Kollam, take the bus, as the only train that can get you there in time invariably arrives late. With the opening of the Konkan Railway, there is now a handful of trains that travel along the coast to Goa and beyond.

Recommended trains from Kochi/Ernakulam

Destination	Name	Number	Station	Frequency	Departs	Total time
Bangalore	*Kanniyakumari–Bangalore Express*	#6525	ET	daily	2.40pm	14hr
Mumbai	*Kanniyakumari Express*	#1081	EJ	daily	12.45pm	40hr
Delhi	*Rajdhani Express**	#2431	EJ	Fri & Sat	11.40pm	40hr 30min
	Kerala Express	#2625	EJ	daily	11am	48hr 45min
Goa	*Rajdhani Express**	#2431	EJ	daily	11.40pm	12hr 35min
	Mangala Lakshadweep Express	#2617	EJ	daily	12.15pm	16hr 18min
Chennai	*Trivandrum–Chennai Mail*	#6320	ET	daily	6.20pm	13hr
Mangalore	*Malabar Express*	#6329	ET	daily	10.53pm	10hr 30min
	Parasuram Express	#6349	ET	daily	10.50am	10hr
Thiruvan-anthapuram	*Parasuram Express*	#6350	EJ	daily	1.55pm	4hr 55min
Varkala	*Parasuram Express*	#6350	EJ	daily	1.55pm	3hr 43min

EJ = Ernakulam Junction
ET = Ernakulam Town
* = a/c only, Fri & Sat

ple of double rooms and a café, which serves up seafood on demand. Trio Travels in Ernakulam (☎0484/353234) organizes trips to the area including boat trips on the backwaters.

Lakshadweep

LAKSHADWEEP, the smallest Union Territory in India, consists of lagoons, reefs, sand banks and 27 tiny coconut-palm-covered **coral islands**. Only ten are inhabited, with a total population of just over 50,000, the majority of whom are Malayalam-speaking Sunni Muslims, said to be descended from seventh-century Keralan Hindus who converted to Islam. The main sources of income are fishing, coconuts and related products. Fruit, vegetables and pulses are cultivated in small quantities but staples such as rice and many other commodities have always had to be imported. The Portuguese, who discovered the value of coir rope, a by-product of the coconut, controlled Lakshadweep during the sixteenth century; when they imposed an import tax on rice, locals retaliated by poisoning some of the forty-strong Portuguese garrison. Terrible reprisals followed. As Muslims, the islanders enjoyed friendly relations with Tipu Sultan of Mysore, something which naturally aroused the ire of the British, who moved in at the end of the eighteenth century and remained until Independence, when Lakshadweep became a Union Territory.

Practicalities

At present, accommodation is available for non-residents of India on one island only. The teardrop-shaped uninhabited 128-acre islet of **Bangaram** welcomes a limited number of tourists, and expects them to pay handsomely for the privilege. Bangaram is the archetypal tropical paradise and a scuba diver's dream, edged with pristine white sands and sitting in a calm lagoon where the average water temperature stays around 26°C. Beyond the lagoon lie coral reefs and the technicolour world of the deep, home to sea turtles, dolphins, eagle rays, lionfish, parrotfish, octopus and predators like barracudas and sharks. Islanders come to Bangaram and its uninhabited neighbours, devoid of animal and bird life, to fish and to harvest coconuts.

It's theoretically possible to visit Bangaram all year round; during the hottest time (April–May), the temperature can reach 33°C; the monsoon (May–Sept) attracts approximately half the rainfall seen in Kerala, in the form of passing showers, not a deluge, although seas are rough. The island remains staggeringly peaceful, and compared to other resorts, at least attempts to minimize the ecological impact of tourism. The *Bangaram Island Resort* (⑨) accommodates thirty couples in simple thatched cottage rooms, each with a verandah. Cane tables and chairs sit outside the restaurant on the beach, and a few hammocks are strung up between the palms. There's no air-conditioning, TV, radio, telephone, newspapers or shops, let alone discos. The tariff, if expensive for India, compares favourably with other exotic holiday destinations; during the peak season (21 Dec–20 Jan) it rises to US$275 full board for a double room; in low season (April–Sept except Aug) it may be as much as twenty-five percent less. Facilities include scuba diving (from US$40 per dive; lessons are available with qualified instructor); glass-bottomed boat trips to neighbouring uninhabited islands; and deep-sea fishing trips (Oct to mid-May; US$50–75). Kayaks, catamarans and a sail boat are available free. Day-trips are possible to the inhabited island of **Kadmat**, the only other island where foreigners are allowed but one, along with Kavarattu and Minicoy, which is being developed as a tourist destination for Indian visitors.

At present, the only way for foreigners to reach Bangaram is on the staggeringly expensive twice daily flights (Mon–Sat 7.30 & 12.30pm; 1hr 30min), on small aircraft run by Taneja Aviation out of **Kochi**, and booked through the *Casino Hotel* on Willingdon Island (see below). Foreigners pay US$350 and Indians Rs10,000 for the privilege of a round trip but the aircraft times and departures are flexible and depend on demand. Flights arrive in Lakshadweep at the island of Agatti, 8km southwest, from where the connecting boat journey to Bangaram takes two hours, picking its way through the shallows to avoid the corals. During the monsoon (May–Sept), helicopters are used so as to protect the fragile coral reefs that lie just under the surface. All arrangements, including accommodation and the necessary entry permit, are handled by the *Casino Hotel*, Willingdon Island, Kochi (☎0484/668221, fax 668001). Some foreign tour operators, however, offer all-in packages combining Lakshadweep with another destination, usually Goa.

The Society for Promotion of Recreational Tourism and Sports (SPORTS) on IG Rd, Willingdon Island (☎0484/668245 & 668387, fax 668155) organizes five-day packaged **cruises** for domestic tourists on either one of the two ships, the *Tipu Sultan* or the *Bharat Seema*, that ply between Kochi and Lakshadweep, but the service is far from reliable. As the body in charge of tourism in Lakshadweep, SPORTS, who are in the process of gradually opening up tourism, will be able to provide up-to-date information on tourism on the islands. At the time of going to press, no foreign tourists had yet taken any of their boats, but in theory you should be able to sail, armed with a permit, to Kadmat, but check with SPORTS.

Thrissur

The welcoming town of **THRISSUR** (Trichur), roughly midway between Kochi, 74km south, and Palakaad, 79km northeast, is an obvious base for exploring the cultural riches of central Kerala. Situated near the Palghat (Palakaad) Gap – an opening in the natural border made by the Western Ghat mountains – it presided over the main trade route into the region from Tamil Nadu and Karnataka, and was for years the capital of Cochin State, controlled at various times by both the *zamorin* of Kozhikode and Tipu Sultan of Mysore. Today, Thrissur prides itself as the cultural capital of Kerala and is home to several influential art institutions. The town centres on Kerala's largest temple complex, **Vaddukanatha**, surrounded by a *maidan* (green) that sees all kinds of public gatherings, not least Kerala's most extravagant, noisy and sumptuous festival, **Puram**.

Arrival and information

The principal point of **orientation** in Thrissur is the Round, a road subdivided into North, South, East and West, which encircles the Vaddukanatha temple and *maidan* at the centre. Once you've established which side of the Round you're on, you can save yourself long walks along the busy pavement by striking out across the green.

Thrissur's **train station**, 1km southwest of Round South, is on the mainline to Chennai and other points in Tamil Nadu, and also has good connections to Kochi and Thiruvananthapuram. There are three main bus stands in Thrissur; the **KSRTC long-distance bus stand**, near the train station; **Priya Darshini** (also known as "North", "Shoranur" and "Wadakkancheri") bus stand, close to Round North, which serves Palakaad and Shoranur, and the **Shakthan Thampuran** stand, on TB Rd, 1km from Round South, which serves local destinations south of Thrissur such as Irinjalakuda, Kodungallur and Guruvayur.

The DTPC **tourist office** on Palace Rd, opposite the Town Hall (Mon–Sat 10am–5pm), is where you can pick up maps of Thrissur, but little else. It's run on a voluntary basis and its primary purpose is to promote the elephant festival. KTDC have a small information counter at their hotel *Yatri Niwas*, Stadium Rd (Mon–Sat 10am–5pm; ☎0487/332333). If you need to **change money**, the main branch of the State Bank of Travancore, next to the Paramekkavu temple (Mon–Fri 10am–2pm, Sat 10am–noon), accepts American Express travellers' cheques, but not Thomas Cook or Mastercard. Opposite the same temple near the Sapna Theatre, the State Bank of India (same hours) changes dollars and sterling, as well as travellers' cheques. The Canara Bank on Round South also changes money. The GPO is on the southern edge of town, near the *Casino Hotel* off TB Road. **Internet** facilities are available at the *Trichur Internet Café* on the first floor of the Shah Complex near the north bus stand (☎0487/421033) at a cost of Rs100 per hour or Rs55 for 30min. Space Net at the United Shopping Complex, Shankar Agar Rd, Poothole (☎0487/385813), is friendlier and a lot cheaper at Rs70 per hour and Rs35 for 30min.

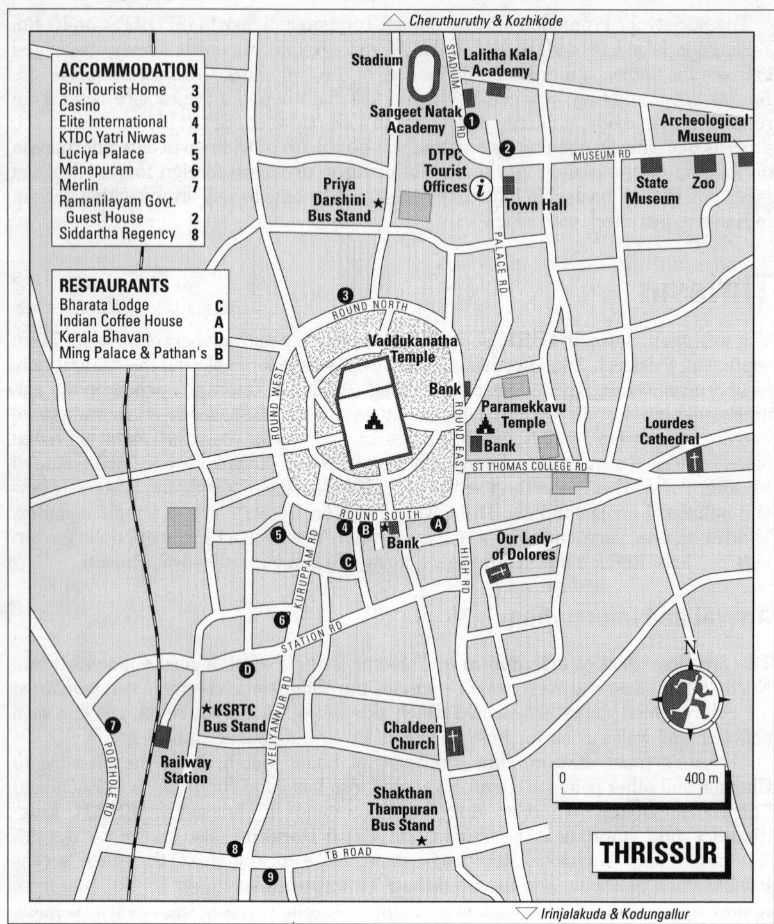

The Town

The focus of Thrissur is the **Vaddukanatha temple** (closed to non-Hindus) a walled complex of fifteen shrines, dating from the twelfth century and earlier, the principal of which is dedicated to Shiva. Inside the walls, the grassy compound is surprisingly quiet and spacious, with a striking apsidal shrine dedicated to Ayappa (see box on p.320). Sadly, many of the temple's treasures, such as wood-carving and murals, are not as well maintained as they might be. Once an essential ingredient of the temple's cultural life, but now under-used and neglected, the long, sloping-roofed **Kuttambalam theatre** (closed to non-Hindus) with carved panels and lathe-turned wooden pillars, is the venue for the ancient Sanskrit performance forms Chakyar Kuttu and Kutiyattam.

The **State Museum** and **Zoo** (both daily except Mon 10am–5pm) stand together on Museum Rd, ten minutes' walk from the temple. Although small, the museum has

PURAM

Thrissur is best known to outsiders as the venue for Kerala's biggest festival, **Puram**, which takes place on one day in April/May. Introduced by the Kochi (Cochin) Raja, Shaktan Tampuran (1789–1803), Puram is today the most extreme example of the kind of celebration seen on a smaller scale all over Kerala, whose main ingredients invariably include **caparisoned elephants**, **drum music** and **fireworks**.

On this day, at the hottest time of year, the centre of Thrissur fills to capacity with a sea of people gravitating towards Round South, where a long wide path leads to the southern entrance of the **Vaddukanatha temple** complex. Two processions, representing the Tiruvambadi and Paramekkavu temples in Thrissur, compete to create the more impressive sights and sounds. They eventually meet, like armies on a battlefield, facing each other at either end of the path. Both sides present fifteen tuskers sumptuously decorated with gold ornaments, each ridden by three *brahmins* clutching objects symbolizing royalty: silver-handled whisks of yak hair, circular peacock feather fans and orange, green, red, purple, turquoise, black, gold or patterned silk umbrellas fringed with silver pendants. At the centre of each group, the principal elephant carries an image of the temple's deity. Swaying gently, the elephants stand still much of the time, ears flapping, seemingly oblivious to the mayhem engendered by the crowds, bomb-like firework bangs and the huge orchestra that plays in front of them.

Known as **chenda melam**, this quintessentially Keralan music, featuring as many as a hundred loud, hard-skinned, cylindrical *chenda* drums, crashing cymbals and wind instruments, mesmerizes the crowd while its structure marks the progress of the procession. Each kind of *chenda melam* is named after the rhythmic cycle (*tala* or, in Malayalam, *talam*) in which it is set. Drummers stand in ranks, the most numerous at the back often playing single beats. At the front, a line of master drummers, the stars of Keralan music, try to outdo each other with their speed, stamina, improvisational skills and showmanship. Facing the drummers, musicians play long double-reed, oboe-like *kuzhals* (similar to the North Indian *shehnai*) and C-shaped *kompu* bell-metal trumpets. The fundamental structure is provided by the *elatalam* – medium-sized, heavy, brass hand cymbals that resolutely and precisely keep the tempo, essential to the cumulative effect of the music. Over an extended period, the *melam* passes through four phases of tempo, each a double of the last, from a majestic dead slow through to a frenetic pace.

The arrival of the fastest tempo is borne on a wave of aural and visual stimulation. Those astride the elephants stand at this point, to manipulate their feather fans and hair whisks in co-ordinated sequence, while behind, unfurled umbrellas are twirled in flashes of dazzling colour and glinting silver in the sun. Meanwhile, the cymbals crash furiously, often raised above the head, requiring extraordinary stamina (and causing nasty weals on the hands). The master drummers play their loudest and fastest, frequently intensified by surges of energy emanating from single players, one after another. A chorus of trumpets, in ragged unison, makes an ancient noise.

All this is greeted by firework explosions and roars from the crowd. Many people punch the air, some fairly randomly much like heavy metal fans in the West, while others are clearly *talam branthans*, rhythm "madmen", who follow every nuance of the structure. When the fastest speed is played out, the slowest tempo returns and the procession edges forward, the *mahouts* leading the elephants by the tusk. Stopping again, the whole cycle is repeated. At night, the Vaddukanatha temple entrances are a blaze of coloured lights and a spectacular firework display takes place in the early hours of the morning.

If you venture to Thrissur for Puram, be prepared for packed buses and trains. Needless to say, accommodation should be booked well in advance. An umbrella or hat is recommended. Women travellers should be aware that the densest parts of the crowd are almost entirely male; Keralan women usually look on from a distance.

Similar but much smaller events take place, generally from September onwards, with most during the summer (April & May). Enquire at a tourist office or your hotel, or ask someone to check a local edition of the newspaper, *Mathrabhumi*, for local performances of *chenda melam*, and other drum orchestras such as *panchavadyam* and *tyambaka*.

excellent local bronzes, jewellery, fine wood-carvings of fanged temple guardians and a profusion of bell-metal oil lamps. The zoo, however, houses a miserable set of tenants, and although it can be grimly fascinating to observe the variety of snakes that slither locally (king cobra, krait, viper), you may also be expected to watch an attendant prod cobras with a stick so they spit at the glass that separates you from them. Next door to the *Yatri Niwas*, the **Kerala Sangeet Natak Academy** (☎0487/332548) has a large auditorium where occasional music and dance concerts are held, as well as Keralan theatre, which has an enthusiastic following and tends to be heavily political. Around the corner is the **Kerala Lalitha Kala Academy**, whose gallery often holds exhibitions of contemporary Indian art.

One of the most important churches for Thrissur's large Christian population is the Syrian Catholic **Lourdes Cathedral**, along St Thomas College Rd. Three daily masses serve a regular congregation of nine hundred. Like many of Kerala's Indo-Gothic churches, the exterior of dome and spires is more impressive than the interior, with its unadorned metal rafters and corrugated-iron ceiling. Steps lead down from the altar to the crypt, a rather dilapidated copy of the grotto in Lourdes. The **Church of Our Lady of Dolores**, a short way to the south of the Round, is another important Catholic church and boasts Neo-Gothic spires and the largest interior of any church in South India. Slightly further south, the **Chaldean Church** (services Mon–Sat 7am–9am & Sun 7.30am–9.30am), dedicated to Mary, is the most ancient of all Keralan Christian centres as it is the focal point of the unique Nestorian Syrian community which also runs a school here. Not much of the original structure remains, as the church was extensively renovated in the nineteenth century. However, the gabled facade is in evi-

CHRISTIANITY IN THRISSUR

Ever since the arrival of the Apostle St Thomas at the ancient Roman port of Muziris (now known as Azhikode near Kodungallur, see p.352), Thrissur and its environs have been an important centre of Christianity. Today, along with numerous roadside shrines known as *kurisupalli*, or "chapels of the cross", large and popular churches in and around the city bear testimony to the continuing strength of the Christian communities of the region. Early Keralan Christians, known as **Nazranis**, or "followers of the Nazarene" (Jesus), found little opposition from the largely Hindu population, and were able to amalgamate some age-old indigenous Hindu religious practices into their newfound religion. Later in the fourth century, according to local belief, a wealthy merchant named Kanai Thoma led a group of **Syrian Christians** fleeing persecution from the ruling Persians here to Muziris. Assisted by the development of commerce, the Syrian Christians were to play a vital role in the spread of Christianity in Kerala. The Syrians introduced architectural conventions from the Middle East, and so incorporated the nave and chancel with a gabled façade, resulting in a distinctive style of Keralan Christian church. They also absorbed some architectural styles from the Nazranis by retaining the *dhwajastamba* (flag mast), the *kottupura* (gate house) and the *kurisuthara* (altar with a mounted cross).

The **Nestorians** (after Nestorius, the patriarch of Constantinople), were part of the Chaldean Syrian Christian community. They were the dominant Christian group in Kerala after the sixth century and once had centres in various parts of India. Despite the assertive spread of **Portuguese Catholicism** centuries later, a small and unique pocket of Nestorians survives to the present day in Thrissur.

In the eighteenth century, Raja Rama Varma (aka the Maharajah Sakthan Thampuran), renowned as the "architect of Thrissur", developed the city, laying out roads and establishing markets with which Christian merchants were invited to trade. Although a Hindu himself, the Raja helped further ensure the welfare of the Christian communities by establishing Christian enclaves to the east and to the south of the city centre.

dence, albeit in Baroque style. The friendly and welcoming office will open the door to the church for you. Inside, the plain chamber is hung with chandeliers and the extraordinary pulpit is ornately carved in teak.

Shopping

Thrissur is a great place to pick up distinctive Keralan **crafts**. The main shopping area is on the Round; on Round West, the Kerala State Handicraft Emporium specializes in wood, while a few doors along, a small branch of Khadi Gramodyog sells a limited range of handloom cloth. A far better selection of handloom can be found in Co-optex at the top of Palace Rd. At Chemmanur's, Round South, near the *Elite International Hotel*, you'll find the usual carved-wooden-elephant-type souvenirs, and, on the ground floor, a high kitsch Aladdin's Cave of nodding dogs, Jesus clocks, Mecca table ornaments and parabolic nail-and-string art. Sportsland, further west on Round South, aside from sports equipment, also sells crudely painted wooden toys, such as buses and cars. Alter Media at Utility Building, Nehru Bazaar, Nayarangadi, is a small but interesting bookshop, devoted to women's studies.

Kuruppam Rd, which leads south towards the train station from the western end of Round South, is one of the best places in Kerala to buy **bell-metal** products, particularly oil lamps made in the village of Nadavaramba, near Irinjalakuda (see box on p.351). Nadavaramba Krishna & Sons and Bell-metal Craft both specialize in brass, bronze and bell-metal. Lamps cost Rs80–25,000, and "superfine" bell-metal is sold by weight, at over Rs250 per kilo. Continuing south on Kuruppam Rd to the next junction with Railway Station Rd, you'll find a number of small shops selling cheap Christian, Muslim and Hindu pictures etched on metal, and places that supply festival accessories, including umbrellas similar to those used for Puram (see p.347).

Accommodation

Thrissur has a fair number of mid-price hotels, but there's a dearth of decent budget places. The one bargain in this bracket is the palatial *Government Rest House*, which offers star-hotel comfort at economy lodge rates but the constant stream of government officials gets priority. Almost all of Thrissur's hotels follow a 24-hour checkout policy.

Bini Tourist Home, Round North (☎0487/335703). Overpriced ordinary and some a/c rooms with a restaurant and bar, a fallback if the *Rest House* and *Yatri Niwas* are full, but not recommended for women. ④–⑤.

Casino, TB Rd, near the train station (☎0487/424699, fax 442037). Once Thrissur's poshest hotel but has since seen better days. Facilities include a multi-cuisine restaurant, bar and foreign exchange for residents (they'll accept travellers' cheques as partial payment if you eat here). ⑤–⑦.

Elite International, Chembottil Lane, off Round South (☎0487/421033). Pronounced *Ee-light*. Thrissur's first "modern" hotel, with 82 rooms. Friendly staff, good restaurant and very central; some balconied rooms overlook the green. Gets booked up months ahead, however, for Puram, when the rooms cost ten times more than normal. ③–⑥.

KTDC Yatri Niwas, Stadium Rd (☎0487/332333). Clean and reasonable place with a beer parlour and a simple restaurant good for a "meal". The best budget option after the *Government Rest House*. ②–⑤.

Luciya Palace, Marar Rd (☎0487/424731). Recently revamped Neoclassical/traditional Keralan fantasy; a highly rated mid-range choice. Some a/c rooms, but the standard non-a/c rooms, with coir mats and cane furniture, are the best deals. Single occupancy possible. ⑤–⑦.

Manapuram, Kuruppam Rd (☎0487/440933). A modern and efficient two-star business hotel with a lively location in the heart of the market. A good range of rooms with some a/c and a few singles, and two restaurants; credit cards accepted. ⑤–⑦.

Merlin, opposite the train station, Poothole Rd (☎0487/385520). New hotel within site of the station, which has a large garden and some reasonable rooms, some of which are a/c, and a restaurant and coffee shop. Pity about the proximity of the open drain, though. ④–⑤.

Ramanilayam Government Guest House, on the corner of Palace Rd and Museum Rd (☎0487/332016). Very good-value, huge, clean, comfortable suites with balconies. It's officially for

VIPs, and they're not obliged to give you a room, but smart dress will help. It's hugely popular, and often full; if you're alone, the rate doubles after three nights. Breakfast is served, but other meals are by advance order only. ①–③.

Siddartha Regency, Veliyannur Rd, Kokkalai, near the train station (☎0487/424773). Modernish, centrally a/c, comfortable hotel. Restaurant, bar and garden. ⑥.

Eating and drinking

Thrissur's big **hotels** offer Indian, Western and Chinese food, and Keralan lunches, while several quality, inexpensive "meals" places are clustered near **the Round**. Late at night, on the corner of Rounds South and East, opposite the Medical College Hospital, you'll find a string of *chai* and omelette stalls, frequented by auto-rickshaw *wallahs*, hospital visitors, itinerant mendicants, Ayappa devotees and student revellers.

Bharata Lodge, Chembottil Lane, next door to *Elite International Hotel*. Inexpensive, good-quality South Indian breakfasts, snacks and "meals" at lunchtime.

Indian Coffee House, Round South. The better of the two in town. Very busy, serving snacks and the usual excellent coffee. The branch on Station Rd is very run-down.

Kerala Bhavan, Station Rd. Recommended for breakfast and low-priced regional "meals". A 10min walk south of Round South (most rickshaw *wallahs* know where it is).

Luciya Palace, Marar Rd (☎0487/424731). Indian and Chinese dishes. The main appeal is that they serve food at night in a pleasant garden illuminated by fairy lights.

Ming Palace, Pathan Building, Round South. Inexpensive "Chindian", serving chop suey, noodles and lots of chicken and veg dishes, under dim light and with cheesy muzak.

Pathan's, Round South. Deservedly popular veg restaurant, with a cosy a/c family (female) annexe and a large canteen-like dining hall. Generous portions and plenty of choice, *koftas*, *kormas* and lots of *tandoori* options, as well as Keralan *thalis* and wonderful Kashmiri *naan*.

Around Thrissur

The chief appeal of exploring the area around Thrissur is for the chances it provides to get to grips with Kerala's cultural heritage. Countless festivals, at their peak before the monsoon hits in May, enable visitors to catch some of the best drummers in the world, **Kathakali** dance drama (see p.610) and **Kutiyattam**, the world's oldest surviving theatre form (see p.612).

Irinjalakuda

The village of **IRINJALAKUDA**, 20km south of Thrissur, has a unique temple, five minutes' walk west from the bus stand, dedicated to **Bharata**, the brother of Rama. Visitors are usually permitted to see inside (men must wear a *dhoti*), but as elsewhere, the inner parts of the temple are closed to non-Hindus. It boasts a superbly elegant tiled *kuttambalam* **theatre** within its outer courtyard, built to afford an unimpeded view for the maximum number of spectators (drawn from the highest castes only), and known for excellent acoustics. A profusion of painted wood-carvings of mythological animals and stories from the epics decorates the interior. On the low stage, which is enclosed by painted wooden columns and friezes of female dancers, stand two large copper *mizhavu* drums, for use in the Sanskrit drama Kutiyattam (see p.612), permanently installed in wooden frames into which a drummer climbs to play. Traditionally, *mizhavus* were considered sacred objects; Nandikeshvara, Shiva's rhythm expert and accompanist, was said to reside in them. The drama for which they provided music was a holy ritual, and in the old days the instrument was never allowed to leave the temple and only played by members of a special caste, the Nambyars. Since then, outsiders have learned the art of *mizhavu* playing; some are based near the temple, but the orthodox authorities do not allow them to play inside.

Natana Kairali is an important cultural centre dedicated to the performance, protection and documentation of Kerala's lesser-known, but fascinating and vibrant theatre arts, including Kutiyattam, Nangiar Koothu (female mono-acting) and shadow and puppet theatres. Left of the Bharata temple as you leave, it is based in the home of one of Kerala's most illustrious acting families, Ammanur Chakyar Madhom; cite that name when you ask for directions. *Natana Kairali*'s director, Shri G Venu, is a mine of information about Keralan arts, and can advise on forthcoming performances.

Irinjalakuda is best reached by **bus** from the Shakthan Thampuran stand at Thrissur rather than by train, as the train station is an inconvenient 8km east of town.

Kodungallur

Virtually an island, surrounded by backwaters and the sea, the small country town of **KODUNGALLUR** (Cranganore), 35km south of Thrissur, is rich in Keralan history. The dearth of information regarding the modern town contrasts with tales of its illustrious past, and travellers may find that Kodungallur's "sights", with one exception, require some imagination. The town is best visited in a day-trip by **bus** from Thrissur's Shakthan Thampuran stand (1hr 30min), or en route between Thrissur and Kochi.

Standing on a large piece of open ground at the centre of Kodungallur, the ancient and typically Keralan **Kurumba Bhagavati temple** is the site of an extraordinary annual event that some residents would prefer didn't happen at all. The **Bharani** festival, held during the Malayalam month of Meenom (March/April), attracts droves of devotees, both male and female, mainly from "low caste" communities previously excluded from the temple. Their devotions consist in part of drinking copious amounts of alcohol and taking to the streets to sing Bharani *pattu*, sexually explicit songs about, and addressed to, the goddess Bhagavati, which are considered obscene and highly offensive by many other Keralans. On Kavuthindal, the first day, the pilgrims run en masse around the perimeters of the temple three times at breakneck speed, beating its walls with sticks. Until the mid-1950s, chickens were sacrificed in front of the temple; today, a simple red cloth symbolizes the bloody ritual. An important section of the devotees are the crimson-clad village oracles, wielding scythe-like swords with which they sometimes beat themselves on the head in ecstatic fervour, often drawing blood. Despite widespread disapproval, the festival draws plenty of spectators.

Cheraman Juma Masjid, 1500m south of Kodungallur centre on NH17, is thought to be the earliest mosque in India, founded in the seventh century. The present building, which dates from the sixteenth century, was until recently predominantly made of wood, of a style usually associated with Keralan Hindu temples. Unfortunately, due to weather damage, it has recently had to be partly rebuilt, and the facade, at least, is now

NADAVARAMBA BELL-METAL OIL LAMPS

Keralan nights are made more enchanting by the use of **oil lamps**; the most common type, seen all over, is a slim floor-standing metal column surmounted by a spike that rises from a circular receptacle for coconut oil, and using cloth or banana plant fibre wicks. Every classical theatre performance keeps a large lamp burning centre-stage, all night. The special atmosphere of temples is also enhanced by innumerable lamps, some hanging from chains; others, *deepa stambham*, are multi-tiered and stand metres-high.

The village of **Nadavaramba**, near Irinjalakuda, is an important centre for the manufacture of oil lamps and large cooking vessels, known as *uruli* and *varppu*. Alloys made from brass, copper and tin are frequently used, but the best are from bell-metal, said to be eighty percent copper, and give a sonorous chime when struck. Shops in Thrissur that specialize in Nadavaramba ware arrange visits to see the craftsmen at work.

rather mundane, with concrete minarets. The wooden interior remains intact, however, with a large Keralan oil lamp in the centre. Introduced five centuries ago for group study of the Koran, the lamp has taken on great significance to other communities, and Muslims, Christians and Hindus alike bring oil for the lamp on the auspicious occasion of major family events. In an anteroom, a small mausoleum is said to be the burial place of Habib Bin Malik, an envoy sent from Mecca by the convert king Cheraman Perumal. Women are not allowed into the mosque at any time ("they pray at home"), but interested male visitors should contact the assistant *mukhari* (*imam*, or priest), K.M. Saidumohamed, who lives directly opposite and will show you around.

Less than 500m south from the Cheraman Juma Masjid, past a bend in the main highway (NH17), a short but wide avenue leads past tall multi-staged lamps to the **Mahadeva Temple** dedicated to the god Shiva at Thirvanchikulam. A fine example of Keralan temple architecture, the temple allows access to the outer courtyard via a majestic gateway with a sloping roof and carvings of elephants, protective deities, gods and goddesses. Inside the enclosure, past a large multi-tiered metal lamp, a porch adorned with carvings dedicated to the heroes of the great Hindu epic, the *Ramayana*, marks the furthest non-Hindus are allowed. Within the restricted enclosure, an impressive, columned hall shelters Shiva's ever faithful bull Nandi, and the inner sanctum houses a plain stone *lingam*. Despite the restriction, low retaining walls allow a good view of the extensive complex, which is well worth the short detour. Be careful of the heavy traffic, however, when walking along the narrow highway between the mosque and the temple.

The **Mar Thoma Pontifical Shrine**, fronted by a crescent of Neoclassical colonnades at Azhikode (pronounced "Arikode") Jetty (6km), marks the place where the Apostle Thomas is said to have arrived in India, soon after the death of Christ. Despite the ugly waterside promenade and the tacky visitor centre, it is a moving spot, on the edge of backwaters, but not worth a detour unless you're desperate to see the shard of the saint's wrist bone enshrined within the church.

If you want **to stay** at Kodungallur, the *Hotel Indraprastham* close to the town centre (☎0488/602678; ②–④) has ordinary and competitively priced a/c rooms as well as an ordinary "meals" restaurant and an a/c "family" restaurant and they also have a bar.

ANCIENT KODUNGALLUR

Kodungallur has been identified as the site of the ancient cities of **Vanji**, one-time capital of the Chera kingdom, and **Muziris**, described in the first century AD by the Roman traveller, Pliny, as *primum emporium Indiae*, the most important port in India. Other accounts describe the harbour as crowded with great ships, warehouses, palaces, temples and *Yavanas* (a generic term for foreigners) who brought gold and left with spices, sandalwood, teak, gems and silks. The Romans are said to have built a temple in Kodungallur; nothing remains, but their presence has been shown through finds of coins, the majority of which date from the reigns of Augustus to Nero (27 BC–68 AD). Its life as a great port was curtailed in 1341 by floods that silted up the harbour, leading to the development of Kochi (Cochin).

Kodungallur is also reputed to be the site where the Apostle Thomas ("**Doubting Thomas**") landed in 52 AD, bringing Christianity to the subcontinent. Jews fleeing the fall of Jerusalem arrived in 69 AD, and, although the advent of Islam in India is usually associated with invading land armies arriving from the northwest in the twelfth century, Kerala claims an earlier date. The region had long enjoyed peaceable relations with the Arab world, thanks to its sea trade. **Cheraman Perumal**, the legendary Keralan king who converted to Islam, abdicated and emigrated to Mecca, is said to have founded the Cheraman Juma Masjid in Kodungallur in the seventh century, making it the earliest mosque in India. The supposed site of his palace, Cheraman Parambu, is today nothing more than a few broken columns on open ground.

Guruvayur

Kerala's most important Krishna shrine, the high-walled temple of **GURUVAYUR**, 29km northwest of Thrissur, attracts a constant flow of pilgrims, second only in volume to Ayappa's at Sabarimala (see box on p.320). Its deity, **Guruvayurappan**, has inspired numerous paeans from Keralan poets, most notably Narayana Bhattatiri, who wrote the *Narayaniyam* during the sixteenth century, when the temple, whose origins are legendary, seems to have first risen to prominence.

One of the richest temples in Kerala, **Guruvayur temple** (3am–1pm & 4–10pm) is from very early morning to late at night awash with pilgrims in their best white clothes, often trimmed with gold. Some visitors find the intense activity of the market around the temple perimeter too commercial, full of glitter and trinkets such as two-rupee plastic Guruvayurappan signet rings, but nevertheless there is a palpable air of excitement, particularly when events inside spill out into the streets. A temple committee stall outside the main gates auctions off the gifts, including bell-metal lamps, received at the shrine but, according to superstition, if you buy any of these items they must be returned to the temple as gifts. **Closed to non-Hindus**, the temple has turned away many famous people in its time, including, ironically, the most vocal of Guruvayurappan's devotees, the Keralan film-song artist Jesudas. Though born into a Christian family (his name literally means "servant of Jesus"), Jesudas has earned millions of fans by his sincere rendition of Hindu devotional songs. Many temples, including this one, play his records, but he is not allowed past the door unless he formally converts and produces a certificate to prove it. One of his songs describes how he has, in any event, already had *darshan* of Guruvayurappan "in his mind".

Of the temple's 24 **annual festivals**, the most important are Ekadashi and Ulsavam. During the eighteen days of Ekadashi, in the month of Vrischikam (Nov/Dec), marked by processions of caparisoned elephants outside the temple, the exterior of the building may be decorated with the tiny flames of innumerable oil lamps. On certain days (check dates with a KTDC office) programmes staged in front of the temple attract the cream of South Indian classical music artists.

During Ulsavam, in the month of Kumbham (Feb/March), tantric rituals are conducted inside, an **elephant race** is run outside on the first day, and elephant processions take place during the ensuing six days. On the ninth day, the Palivetta, or "hunt" occurs; the deity, mounted on an elephant, circumambulates the temple accompanied by men dressed as animals, who represent human weaknesses such as greed and anger, and are vanquished by the god. The next night sees the image of the god taken out for ritual

THE FOUNDING OF GURUVAYUR TEMPLE

The founding of the Guruvayur temple is associated with the end of Krishna's life. After witnessing the massacre of family and compatriots, Krishna returned to his capital, Dvarka, in Gujarat, to end his earthly existence. However, knowing that Dvarka would disappear into the sea on his death, he was concerned that the form of Vishnu there, which he himself worshipped, should be spared its fate.

Krishna invited Brihaspati, also known as Guru, the preceptor of the gods, and a pupil, Vayu, the god of wind, to help him select a new home for Vishnu. By the time they arrived at Dvarka, the sea (Varuna) had already claimed the city, but the wind managed to rescue Vishnu. Krishna, Guru and Vayu travelled south, where they met Parashurama, who had just created Kerala by throwing his axe into the sea (see p.276). On reaching a beautiful lake of lotuses, Rudratirtha, they were greeted by Shiva and Parvati who consecrated the image of Vishnu; Guru and Vayu then installed it, the temple was named after them, and so the deity received the title Guruvayurappan ("Lord of Guruvayur").

immersion in the temple tank; devotees greet the procession with oil lamps and throw rice. It is considered highly auspicious to bathe in the tank at the same time as the god.

The Punnathur Kotta Elephant Sanctuary

When they are not involved in races and other arcane temple rituals, Guruvayur's tuskers hang out at the **Punnathur Kotta Elephant Sanctuary** (daily 9am–6pm; free; camera Rs25), 4km north of town. Forty animals, aged from three to ninety-three, live here, munching for most of the day on specially imported piles of fodder. Most were either gifted by wealthy patrons or else rescued from slavery and starvation in other parts of India. Though hobbled for much of day, they appear content enough, cared for by their two personal *mahoots*, who wash and scrub them each evening in the sanctuary pond – a great photo opportunity. One exception is the giant bull elephant that rocks maniacally back and forth in the corner of the compound, making menacing noises at passers-by; he killed two people a few years back, and it's a credit to the animal-loving temple authorities that they haven't put him down. Just don't get too close to any of the elephants unless their handlers say it's safe to do so.

Practicalities

Buses from Thrissur (40min) arrive at the main **bus stand** at the top end of E Nada St, five minutes east of the temple. **Accommodation** is concentrated along this street; it's often packed to the gills with pilgrims, but the two KTDC hotels are usually good bets. *Mangalya* (②–⑤) has a/c and non-a/c rooms, but can be noisy as it is so near the temple entrance; *Nandanam* (☎0487/556266; ③–⑤) is a better option, with a pleasant garden in a quiet spot near the bus stand. Rooms are spacious, if a little dowdy, and there's a restaurant and laundry on site. As you'd expect, the town is crammed with pure veg "meals" **restaurants**, and an *Indian Coffee House* on the southern side of E Nada St serves South Indian snacks.

Cheruthuruthy

The village of **CHERUTHURUTHY** is an easy day-trip 32km north of Thrissur through gently undulating green country. It consists of a few lanes and one main street, which runs south from the bank of Kerala's longest river, the **Bharatapuzha** (pronounced *Bharatapura*). Considered holy by Hindus, the great river has declined in recent years, leaving a vast expanse of sand. Although of little consolation to locals, who have to deal with the problems of a depleted water supply, it has produced a landscape of incomparable beauty.

Cheruthuruthy is famous as the home of **Kerala Kalamandalam**, the state's flagship training school for Kathakali and other indigenous Keralan performing arts, which was founded in 1927 by the revered Keralan poet Vallathol (1878–1957). At first patronized by the Raja of Cochin, the school has been funded by both state and national governments and has been instrumental in the large-scale revival of interest in Kathakali, and other unique Keralan art forms. Despite conservative opposition, it followed an open-door recruitment policy, based on artistic merit, which produced "scheduled caste", Muslim and Christian graduates along with the usual Hindu castes, something that was previously unimaginable. During the 1960s Kalamandalam's dynamic leadership forged international links with cultural organizations. Foreign students were accepted and every attempt was made to modernize, extending into the way in which the traditional arts were presented. Kalamandalam artists perform in the great theatres of the world, many sharing their extraordinary skills with outsiders; luminaries of modern theatre, such as Grotowski and Peter Brook, are indebted to them. Nonetheless, many of these trained artists are still excluded from entering, let alone performing in, temples, a popular venue for Hindu art forms, especially music.

Non-Hindus can see Kathakali, Kutiyattam and Mohiniattam performed in the school's superb theatre, which replicates the wooden, sloping-roofed traditional theatres, known as *kuttambalams*, found in Keralan temples. If you've got more than a passing interest in how this extraordinary technique is taught, don't miss the chance to sit in on the rigorous training sessions, which have to be seen to be believed (Mon–Fri 4.30–6.30am & 3–5pm; closed March 31, June 1, public hols, April & May). A handful of foreigners each year also come to the Kalamandalam academy to attend full-time **courses** in Kathakali and other traditional dance and theatre forms. Those interested should first apply in writing, and if accepted could attend short courses for a minimum of one month, or condensed courses of between three and six months. Full-time courses usually last between four and six years, and foreign students, with the necessary student visas, are allowed to attend for a maximum of four years. Applicants need to be interviewed and will be chosen on merit; previous experience of a related discipline is normally required. The enrolment fee is Rs100 and, for foreigners, the monthly fee is Rs850 plus room rent – if needed – in their new international hostel, which has cooking facilities and costs Rs1000 per month. Applications may be made from abroad (write to the Secretary, Kerala Kalamandalam, Vallathol Nagar, Cheruthuruthy, Thrissur Dist, Kerala 679 531), but it's a good idea to visit before committing yourself. The students' lot here is not an easy one – to say the least. For information contact the school office (☎ & fax 0492/622418).

A good time to visit is during their weeklong festival starting on Christmas Day. Held at the *kuttambalam* and at their original riverside campus amongst the trees, the festival presents all the art forms of Kerala and is free, although the limited accommodation can be a problem. A short walk past the old campus leads to a small but exquisite **Shiva temple** in classic Keralan style, where the early evening worship, when the exterior is lit with candles, is particularly rewarding.

Practicalities

Cheruthuruthy's **accommodation** is limited, with some students staying as guests in private accommodation. The village has a couple of simple guesthouses and there is the basic but atmospheric *Government Rest House* (☎0492/622498; ①) in the village a short distance along the Shoranur road from Kalamandalam, where eight simple doubles, some with Western-style toilets, share a verandah. The bustling and unattractive town of Shoranur has more options but none that could capture the charm of Cheruthuruthy and its environs. **Food** may be available by arrangement, and there are simple "meals" shops in the village; of these, the *Mahatma*, serving vegetarian food is much the best but if you want meat try the *Shalimar* close by.

Buses heading to Shoranur from Thrissur's Wadakkancheri stand stop outside Kalamandalam, just before Cheruthuruthy. The nearest **train station** is Shoranur Junction, 3km south. It's on the main line and served by express trains to and from Mangalore, Chennai and all major stations south of here on the coastal route through Kerala.

Palakaad

PALAKAAD (Palghat), surrounded by paddy fields, lies on NH47 between Thrissur (79km) and Coimbatore, Tamil Nadu (54km) and on the railway line from Karnataka and Tamil Nadu. Historically, thanks to the natural twenty-kilometre-wide Palakaad Gap in the Western Ghats, this area has been one of the chief entry points into Kerala. The environs are beautiful, but the town itself, which has the distinction of being the only Keralan town where the traffic lights actually work, doesn't warrant a stop, unless to break a journey. Arriving from Tamil Nadu, Palakaad, with its dry, Deccan-like landscape, unlike most of the state, gives a misleading first impression of Kerala. The well-preserved **fort**, built in 1766 by Haider Ali of Mysore, is the nearest thing to a "sight";

it gets plenty of visitors at weekends, despite having little to offer. However, many travellers in search of **Kathakali** and **Teyyam** performances find themselves directed here. Particularly during April and May, hundreds of one-off events take place in the area. The local Government Carnatic Music College has an excellent reputation, and a small open-air amphitheatre next to the fort often hosts first-class music and dance performances. Ask at the tourist office (see below) for details. A short journey north, the landscaped gardens and amusement park at **Malampuzha** (10km), watered by the large adjacent dam, is a great attraction during the weekends when crowds come to ride the cable car (known as the "ropeway"), or look at the fantasy rock garden created by the artist Nek Chand of Chandigarh fame.

Practicalities

Palakaad is well connected to the rest of Kerala, and most of the main express trains travelling through to Chennai, Bangalore and points further north stop at Palakaad's **train station** (☎0491/535231), 6km to the northeast. The KSRTC **bus stand** is slap in the centre of town, around which most **accommodation** is in budget Indian-style lodges. *Hotel Kairali* (☎0491/534611; ②–④), near the KSRTC bus stand, is pokey but one of the better budget options in the centre and there are some a/c rooms as well. For a bit more comfort try the *Ammbadi*, on TB Rd, opposite the town bus stand and 500m from the KSRTC bus stand (☎0491/531244; ③–⑤) where the restaurant serves Indian and Chinese food and the rooms, some with a/c, are adequate. Far more upmarket, the modern *Hotel Indraprastha*, English Church Rd (☎0491/534641; ⑥–⑦), boasts large rooms, some with a/c, a gloomy but blissfully cool a/c restaurant serving a mixed menu of Indian, Western and Chinese cuisine, a bar and a pleasant lawn. *Fort Palace*, W Fort Rd (☎0491/534621; ⑤–⑥), is also reasonable, with some a/c rooms, a bar and a restaurant for good Indian food. Another alternative is to head out to KTDC's *Garden House* at Mallampuzha (☎0491/815217; ⑥–⑦) which has a range that includes large, ordinary doubles as well as some comfortable a/c rooms.

Around the corner from the *Indraprastha*, the DTPC's **tourist office** is at Fort Maidan (Mon–Sat 10am–5.30pm; (☎0491/538996); it offers colourful leaflets but not much else though you can coax the staff for travel information. Both the *Indraprastha* and the *Fort Palace* **change money** for residents and, in theory, so does the State Bank of India, next door to the *Indraprastha*.

Kozhikode (Calicut)

The busy coastal city of **KOZHIKODE** (Calicut), 225km north of Kochi, occupies an extremely important place in Keralan legend and history. It is also significant in the story of European interference in the subcontinent, as Vasco da Gama first set foot in India at Kozhikode in 1498. However, as a tourist destination, it's a dud, with precious few remnants of its historic past. The few foreigners that pause here invariably do so only to break the long journey between Mysore and Kochi.

Kozhikode's roots are shrouded in myth. According to Keralan tradition, the powerful king Cheraman Perumal is said to have converted from Hinduism to Islam and left for Mecca "to save his soul", never to return. Before he set sail he divided Kerala between his relatives, all of whom were to submit to his nephew, who was given the kingdom of Kozhikode and the title *zamorin*, equivalent to emperor. The city prospered and, perhaps because of the story of the convert king, became the preferred port of Muslim traders from the Middle East in search of spices, particularly pepper. During the Raj, it was an important centre for the export of printed Indian cotton, whence the term "calico", an English corruption of the name Calicut – itself an anglicized version of the city's original Malayalam name, now reinstated. Today, due to strong ties with the

Gulf, where numerous sons of the city work, Kozhikode is flourishing with the injection of new wealth.

Arrival and information

The **train station** (☎0495/701234), served by a handful of coastal expresses and several passenger trains, is close to the centre. Trains north on the Konkan Railway include the fast *Rajdhani Express* #2431 (Fri & Sat 3am), which stops at Madgaon on the way to Delhi, but the most convenient in terms of departure time is the *Netravati Express* #6636 (daily 9.45am); neither stops at Mangalore but at nearby Kankanadi. Trains south include the *Mangala Lakshadweep Express* #2618 (daily 7.35am) to Ernakulam and the overnight *Malabar Express* #6330 (daily 10.40pm) to Thiruvananthapuram. Of the three **bus stands**, the most important is the KSRTC stand, Mavoor Rd (aka Indira Gandhi Rd), from where buses run to destinations as far afield as Bangalore, Mysore, Ooty, Madurai, Coimbatore and Mangalore. From the New Mafussil private stand, 500m away, on the other side of Mavoor Rd, you can get local buses and services to northern Kerala. The Palayam stand is for city and the infrequent long-haul buses and destinations further south, such as Palakaad, Thrissur and Guruvayur. Private deluxe buses to Thiruvananthapuram or Kochi leave from in front of the KSRTC bus stand.

Kozhikode's **airport** (nearly always referred to as Calicut in timetables) lies at Karippur, 29km south of the city. Taxis cost Rs300, or take an **auto-rickshaw**, which in the city charge from Rs6 (and their meters work), to the Kozhikode–Palakaad highway and catch a bus. Indian Airlines flies two **flights** a day to **Mumbai**, one via **Coimbatore**, and flies to **Chennai** three days a week; Jet Airways also flies two flights a week to Mumbai. Indian Airlines flies two flights a week (Mon & Fri) to **Goa** and has several international flights to Sharjah, Kuwait and Bahrain in the **Gulf**. Air India also flies to the Gulf (Abu Dhabi, Dubai and Muscat). For airline tickets, try Century Travels, Bank

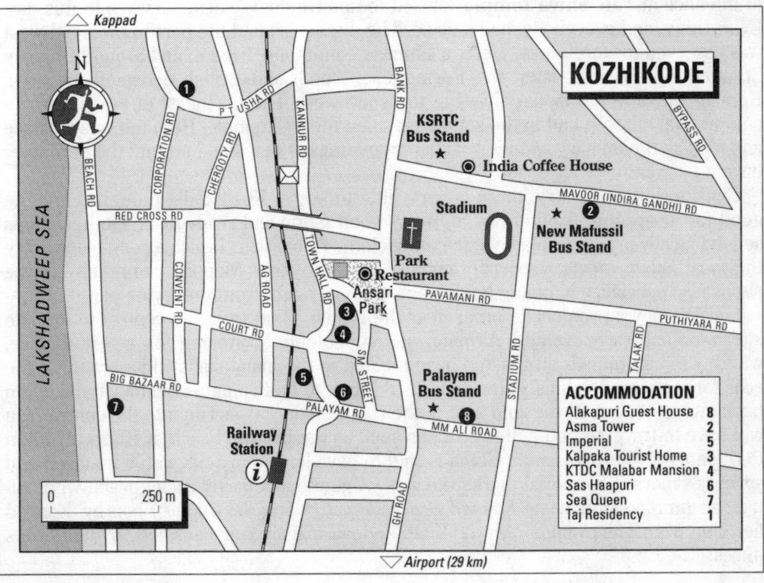

Rd (☎0495/766522); or directly at Indian Airlines, Eroth Centre, 5/2521 Bank Rd (☎0495/753966); or Jet Airways, 29 Mavoor Rd (☎0495/356518); or Air India also at Eroth Centre (☎0495/673001).

The friendly Government of Kerala **tourist information** booth (Mon–Sat 10am–pm), at the train station, is useful for travel connections and sites around Kozhikode. KTDC Information Centre (☎0495/722392) in their *Malabar Mansion Hotel*, at the corner of SM St, can supply limited information and "sketch maps" of the centre and sell their own products including tours and bookings in their many hotels across the state. There is a **left luggage** facility at the train station but, as is always the case, they only accept locked luggage. With so much Gulf money floating around, you shouldn't have any difficulty **changing money** in Kozhikode. A good place to change any currency or travellers' cheques is at PL Worldways, Semma Towers, Third Floor, Mavoor Rd Junction (☎0495/722564), or try Wall Street Financers, also on Mavoor Rd. Banks that change money include the Standard Chartered Bank on Town Hall Rd, and the State Bank of India at Manachira Park. **Internet** facilities are available at the Telegraph Office, Central Bank Building, Mavoor Rd (☎0495/723919), which charges Rs125 per hour and a minimum of fifteen minutes. Telephone numbers in the area have been changed several times over the last few years, and will no doubt continue to do so, sometimes with the same number of digits.

For **backwater cruises** in the Kozhikode region try the small, friendly and efficient Malabar House Boats at either of their three city offices including 1/335 Purakkatri, Thalakalthur (☎0495/766124), and another c/o Prime Land Holdings, 5/2486 Bank Rd (☎0495/765066). Their *kettu vallam* cruises start at Purakkatri, 12km north of the city, but they will arrange transport to the boat with prior notice.

The City

Few traces remain of the model city laid out in the fourteenth century, which followed a Hindu grid formula based on a sacred diagram containing the image of the cosmic man, Purusha. The axis and energy centre of the diagram was dictated by the position of the ancient **Tali Shiva temple** (closed to non-Hindus), which survives to this day. Everything, and everybody, had a place. The district around the port in the northwest was reserved for foreigners. Here, a Chinese community lived in and around Chinese St (now Silk St) and, later, the Portuguese, Dutch and British occupied the area. Keralan Muslims (Mappilas) lived in the southwest. The northeast of the city was a commercial quarter, and in the southeast stood the Tali temple. Here too was a palace and fort; all the military *kalaris* (martial art gymnasia) that stood around the perimeter have now gone.

Considering its history, there is very little to see in Kozhikode, though it is quite good for **shopping**. Around SM St, many good fabric and ready-made clothes shops sell the locally produced plain white cotton cloth. This district is also a good place to try the local *halva* sweets, especially popular with the large Mappila community. Some shops also specialize in piping-hot banana chips, straight from the frying pan.

Locals enjoy a promenade on or near the **beach** (3km from the centre) in the late afternoon and early evening. Although not suitable for swimming, it's a restful place, where you can munch on roasted peanuts sold in the many stalls while scanning the seas for jumping dolphins. After dark it's difficult to find an auto-rickshaw to take you back into town, but on the land side of the road regular buses run into the centre. You will have to travel to find better beaches such as the historic beach of **Kappad**, 16km to the north, where Vasco de Gama is said to have landed in 1498 with a hundred and seventy sailors; a memorial marks the spot. A gentle and partly rocky beach with cottage accommodation at the *Kappad Beach Resort* (☎0496/683760; ⑦) nearby, Kappad lies 4km from Thiruvangoor on the Kozhikode–Badagara route serviced by numerous buses.

The **Pazhassirajah and Krishnamenon Museums and Art Gallery** (Thurs–Tues 10am–12.30pm & 2.30–5pm, Wed 2.30–5pm) stand together 5km from the centre on East Hill. The Pazhassirajah collection includes copies of murals, coins, bronzes and models of the umbrella-shaped, stone megalithic remains peculiar to Kerala, while the museum houses a collection of memorabilia associated with the left-wing Keralan politician VK Krishnamenon, and a gallery of works by Indian artists.

Accommodation and eating

Kozhikode's reasonably priced city-centre **hotels**, most of which operate a 24-hour check-out, can fill up by evening, especially during conventions. The beach area is a quiet alternative. Your best bet for a proper **meal** is to eat at your hotel, though you can get snacks in town at the dependable *Indian Coffee House* on Mavoor (Indira Gandhi) Rd. The open-air *Park Restaurant*, by Mananchira tank, makes an appealing oasis in the evenings in the city centre. *Mezban* at the *Asma Tower* on Mavoor Rd is comfortable with a tasteful a/c section where you can get continental and local breakfasts and the strong menu includes excellent local Malabari cuisine – try the fish.

Alakapuri Guest House, MM Ali Rd (☎0495/723451). Built around a courtyard, some rooms have huge bathtubs, polished wood and easy chairs; the cheaper, non-a/c options are rather spartan. The first-floor café serves great South Indian food all day; in the evening go to the restaurant on the ground floor. Singles rooms are available. ②–⑥.

Asma Tower, Mavoor (Indira Gandhi) Rd (☎0495/723560). Close to the bus stands and the best along this stretch. An efficient new hotel with well-appointed rooms and an excellent restaurant. Very good value. ④–⑥.

Imperial, Town Hall Rd (☎0495/753966). Large hotel around a courtyard with plain and cheap rooms and a very good vegetarian restaurant. ①.

Kalpaka Tourist Home, Town Hall Rd (☎0495/720222). Five storeys ranged around a weirdly shaped courtyard-cum-sari store, make for a space-station-like interior, which is now ageing. The views from the east side are best. Some a/c, and 24-hour checkout. ③–⑥.

KTDC Malabar Mansion, SM St (☎0495/722391). Modern high-rise hotel, which has huge a/c suites, reasonable non-a/c rooms, beer parlour and restaurant. Good value, but usually block-booked weeks in advance. ③–⑤.

Sas Haapuri, off Palayam Rd (☎0495/723281). Small, functional, well-maintained rooms; the best budget option near the station. It's tucked away down a side-street off the main road (MM Ali/Jail Rd) that runs east into town from the train station. ②–⑤.

Sea Queen, Beach Rd (☎0495/366604). Quiet, comfortable, but slightly ageing middle-class hotel close to the beach, whose prime location is marred only by the nasty smells from across the road. A/c and non-a/c rooms are available, plus popular ground-floor restaurant and bar. ⑤–⑦.

Taj Residency, PT Usha Rd (☎0495/766448) Kozikhode's most luxurious address, which offers all the mod cons associated with this luxury group. ⑨.

Wayanad

One of the most beautiful regions of Kerala is the hill district of **WAYANAD**, situated 70km east of Kozhikode, which is clad with large tracts of forest along the western flanks of the Nilgiris. Wayanad is home to several exotic tribes and is rarely visited due to its comparative isolation and lack of express bus connections. The scenery is rich and varied, ranging from plantations of tea, spice, coffee and cocoa to the dry scruffy jungles of the **Muthanga Wildlife Sanctuary** and the rain forests of the **Tholpatty Wildlife Sanctuary**. For those with time on their hands Wayanad makes an alternative and rewarding route between coastal Kerala and Mysore in neighbouring Karnataka, or Ooty in Tamil Nadu. Travelling from Kozhikode, a beautiful but tortuous road climbs a series of hairpin bends up the Western Ghats, through unspoiled forests, where macaques forage along the roadside, impervious to the groaning, diesel-belching trucks and buses going past. As the road arrives at the lip of the great plateau, there are sweeping views back towards the coast of lush, green cover, and a glimpse of the sea is visible in the hazy distance. On the highway to Mysore and Ooty, **Kalpetta**, the district capital makes a good base from which to discover most of Wayanad, but **Mananthavady**, 35km from Kalpetta, is more convenient for exploring the northern jungles.

Kalpetta and Around

Surrounded by plantations and rolling hills, **KALPETTA**, 72km east of Kozhikode, is a quiet market town with little to commend it except its pleasant location and access to the **Muthanga Wildlife Sanctuary**. Along with the settlement of **Vythiri** 5km to the west, Kalpetta provides ample amenities and excellent walking country, including the ranges around the spectacular **Chembra Peak** (2100m), the highest mountain in Wayanad.

Although not as evocative as Periyar, the Muthanga Wildlife Sanctuary, 40km southeast of Kalpetta, also forms part of the **Nilgiri Biosphere Reserve** along with national parks such as Bandipur and Nagarhole in Karnataka, and Madumalai, across the border in Tamil Nadu. Like neighbouring Bandipur National Park, Muthanga with its dry deciduous forests, is noted for its elephants and also shelters, deer, wild boar, bear and the ever-elusive tiger. The highway from Kalpetta to Mysore and Ooty via the scruffy town of **Sultan's Battery** passes through part of the sanctuary, and provides an opportunity if you are lucky, to see elephants crossing the road on long-used migratory trails. However, if you want to explore the inner reaches and visit the old elephant stockades, which are now rarely used thanks to the controls on elephant catching, the main Muthanga sanctuary gates lie 16km east of Sultan's Battery for which you will require your own transport – Rs5 & Rs100 entry per vehicle – jeeps are available for hire from Sultan's Battery.

Accessible from Meppady and 12km south of Kalpetta, **Chembra Peak** (2100m) has soaring ridges and expansive meadows on one side, thick forests on the other. It makes an interesting and stiff climb but take plenty of water. The peak towers over Vythiri, dominating the countryside, and provides stunning views over Wayanad, as well as over the Western Ghats down to the sea. To get to Meppady, turn off the main Kozhikode highway at Chundale and follow the Ooty road for a further 8km; you can take a bus from Kalpetta. **Pookot Lake** 7km to the west of Kalpetta, cupped in a mountain hollow and surrounded by forest, is a pretty and popular spot and makes a good walk, but is spoiled by the tourist centre (daily 7am–6pm; Rs3; Rs5 for camera), which includes a café and even pedalos for hire on the lake.

Practicalities

The **bus** stand at Kalpetta in the centre of town, has connections to Kozhikode (72km; 2hrs), Ooty (115km; 3hr), Mysore (42km; 4hr), and Mananthavady (35km; 1hr); none of these are deluxe. **Auto-rickshaws** and **jeeps** are available for local transport. The DTPC **tourist office** (Mon–Sat 10am–5pm; ☎0493/602134) is in Kalpetta North, 1km from the bus stand; although they are not accustomed to foreign visitors, with a little encouragement, they will supply information on buses and the area in general. They also organize **guided tours** by minibus whenever there is enough demand. Their day tour (Rs100) takes in the **Edakkal caves**, 12km south of Sultan's Battery, with prehistoric carvings dating back to around 1000BC, and some nearby waterfalls, but doesn't spend nearly enough time at Muthanga. They also organize longer two-day tours which include Muthanga and Mananthavady wildlife sanctuaries, which are a little less frenetic and offer more time at the sanctuaries. The tourist office is able to assist with hiring a forest guide at Rs250 a day, and negotiating a jeep with driver (Rs4.25 per km) for those going independently to the wildlife sanctuaries.

Kalpetta has ample **accommodation**, most within easy striking distance of the bus stand, including the *Arun Tourist Home* on Main Rd (☎0493/602039; ①–②) which has cheap basic rooms. For a bit more comfort, try the large, rambling modern *Haritagiri*, close by on Emily Rd (☎0493/602673; ②–⑥). Although the hotel has seen better days it offers a wide range of rooms from budget (including singles) to deluxe a/c suites; there is a garden, bar and a restaurant and they arrange tours on demand. By far the best hotel in town, however, is the *Green Gates* above the tourist office, TB Rd, Kalpetta North (☎0493/602001; ⑥–⑦). The hotel offers well-appointed standard and a/c rooms and has a pleasant restaurant. Cheaper **eating** can be found at the *India Coffee House*, with its dependable "meals" menu and good coffee, opposite the tourist office.

For a lot more luxury head out to **Vythiri** where, tucked away on tea, coffee and spice plantations, lie two excellent resorts. The first and most accessible is the *Vythiri Resort* (☎0493/602039; ⑦). To reach the *Vythiri*, turn off the main road, which runs south to Kozhikode, by the well-stocked spice shop onto an estate road and continue for 3km; jeeps from Kalpetta out to the resort charge Rs100. Managed by, and booked through, Prime Holdings in Kozhikode (☎0493/655366), the resort is set in a beautiful seven-acre plot, which has three boulder-strewn mountain streams flowing through it – one waterfall has created a wonderful plunge pool. Tasteful "cottages" are scattered throughout the lush development, and exquisite Keralan cuisine is provided in the restaurant. The resort will arrange forest and sightseeing tours, including a visit to the Harrison Malayalam Tea Factory. The nature resort *Green Magic* (⑧–⑨), a further 4km up the same track, only accessible by four-wheel drive with the final 1.5km on foot, is even more exotic. The resort consists of luxurious tree houses nestled under a canopy of lush rain forest. The tree houses are accessed by a unique pulley system made with cane which relies on a counter-weight of water to lift you into the tree house twenty-six metres off the ground. Energy sources include solar power and *gobar* (cow-dung) gas, and meals are prepared from organically grown vegetables and served, according to Keralan tradition, on banana leaves. Several forest trails lead out from the resort offering plenty of opportunities for guided walks; tours of the sanctuaries can also be arranged. Accommodation and transport bookings to the resort should be made through the pioneering agency Tourindia, MG Rd, Thiruvananthapuram (☎0471/330437; *www.richsoft.com/tourindia*).

Mananthavady and Around

Although there's not much to see in the small, sleepy town of **MANANTHAVADY**, 35km to the north of Kalpetta, it is ideally placed for visiting the wildlife reserves, islands and temples of northern Wayanad which surround it. The **Nagarhole National Park**, 40km northeast in Karnataka (see p.207), and the **Tholpatty Wildlife Sanctuary,** 25km north, are within striking distance, as are the beautiful jungles along the **Kabini River** 14km east, where the **Kuruva Islands** shelter a unique ecology abundant with rare plants, orchids and wildlife. Although it doesn't appear on many tourist maps, the smaller and little-known **Tholpatty Wildlife Sanctuary** (Rs5 & Rs100 entry per vehicle), is far more picturesque and rewarding than the Muthanga Wildlife Sanctuary, and there's a much greater chance of sighting wildlife. Tholpatty, adjacent to Nagarhole National Park in Karnataka, forms part of the **Nilgiri Biosphere Reserve** and shelters elephants as well as a large variety of deer including *sambar*, cheetal and barking deer. Unlike the dry deciduous Muthanga reserve, Tholpatty is a lush rain forest, best visited outside the monsoons, during the winter (Dec–Feb). Although it lies on the main road to Kodagu, in order to discover the inner sanctuary, you will need to arrange your own vehicle before arriving (see p.362).

One of Wayanad's most celebrated temples, the **Thirunelli temple** lies in a remote part of the district 32km north, off the Kodagu road. The temple is dedicated to the god

Vishnu and is often referred to as the "Kashi of the South", which equates it in veneration with the holy city of Varanasi. The temple is an unusual mix of Keralan-style tiled roofs and northern-style pillared halls. Like Kashi, Thirunelli temple is considered to be a *tirtha*, or crossing, between the mundane world and the divine, and, following tradition, devout pilgrims bathe in the nearby **Papanasini River**, which is said to absolve them of their worldly sins. Buses to Thirunelli are available from Mananthavady. More interesting still – especially during the annual festival (14–28 Mar) when it comes alive with tribal colour – is the **Valliyurkavu Bhagavathi temple**, 8km east. It's an unassuming Keralan-style temple in a pastoral setting, dedicated to the goddess Durga. For the last hundred years, however, the temple has played host to a tribal labour mart, and although bonded labour is now extinct, the festival continues as a celebration and attracts tribal people from all over Wayanad.

Practicalities

Buses from Kalpetta, Kozhikode and Kannur pull into the **bus stand** in the centre of town. There are also bus connections, although these are by ordinary express rather than deluxe buses, to Kodagu and Mysore in Karnataka. There is no official tourist office, and whatever information you need can be had from the town's limited **accommodation** mostly centred around the bus stand. The best option in Mananthavady is *Haksons* at KT Junction (☎0493/540118; ②–④), a short distance down the Kozhikode road, which has a restaurant and is excellent value with clean doubles and deluxe rooms. Jeep rental, essential for Tholpatty, is available around the bus stand or ask at *Haksons*.

THE TRIBES OF WAYANAD

There are sixteen tribes in Wayanad, which make up over seventeen percent of the region's population, and travelling through the area you won't fail to notice the variety of its people. Surrounded by a sea of change, many have found their traditional way of life under threat; as a result some tribes are adapting to modern life and others are resisting change.

One of the largest of the Wayanad tribes is the **Paniya** who, until early this century, were sold as **bonded labour** to plantation owners. Traditional Paniya women are distinctive, as they wear large round earrings made of palmyra leaves studded with bright red *kunnikkuru* seeds. Like the Paniyas, the **Adiyas** were another tribe who worked as bonded labour. "Adiyar" literally means "slave" and some of their songs celebrate their serfdom. However, Adiya legends also trace their roots back to the legend of the hero Maveli who lived at time when there was no caste or divisions of tribes. The legend relates the coming of outsiders in the form of three celestial beings who, with the help of the ferocious mother goddess Mali, helped subjugate the people and create the tribes of Wayanad.

The **Kattunaykan** live in the forests of Wayanad and adjacent districts, and are more shy and primitive. Resisting change, the Kattunaykan continue to live, by and large, as hunter-gatherers and honey-collectors. In contrast, the **Mullukurman** were once hunter-gatherers but now thrive as subsistence farmers and live in small hamlets, called *kudis*, consisting of ten to twelve houses. The Mullukurman practice a form of ritualistic religion centred on the *daivapura*, a sacred meeting place found in every *kudi*. Some Mullukurman have abandoned their roots and now work in modern-day India, in areas such as local and state government. Although a small section of **Kurichiyans** has followed a similar direction, for the most part they continue to live within matrilineal joint families and to work the land. The Kurichiyans have baffled modern medicine with their longevity, as many live to be a hundred, a fact which has been put down to healthy living, hard work and the pleasant climate of Wayanad.

North of Kozhikode

The beautiful coast of Kerala **north of Kozhikode** is a seemingly endless stretch of coconut palms, wooded hills and virtually deserted beaches. However, the towns hold little of interest for visitors, most of whom bypass the area completely. The main reason to stop here today is to look for **Teyyam**, the extraordinary masked trance dances that take place in villages throughout the region during winter.

Kannur (Cannanore)

KANNUR (Cannanore), 92km north of Kozhikode, was for many centuries the capital of the Kolathiri rajas, who prospered from the thriving maritime spice trade through its port. In the early 1500s, after Vasco da Gama passed through, the Portuguese took it and erected an imposing bastion, **St Angelo's fort**, overlooking the harbour, but this is today occupied by the Indian army and closed to visitors. If you come to Kannur at all, it will probably be on the trail of **Teyyam**, spectacular spirit-possession rituals that are an important feature of village life in the area from late December until March (see p.612). Locating them is not always easy, but if you ask at the local tourist office, they should be able to point you in the right direction, and it's well worth heading out to the daily ritual at **Parassinikadavu** (see p.364). The popular town beach can get quite crowded and so for a bit more quiet head down to the small **Baby Beach** (4km) which, lying in the army's cantonment area of large bungalows set in leafy gardens, is protected by restricted access (9am–5pm).

Practicalities

Straddling the main coastal transport artery between Mangalore and Kochi/ Thiruvananthapuram, Kannur is well connected by **bus** and **train** to most major towns and cities in Kerala. In addition buses also travel to Mysore, turning inland at Thalassery (aka Tellychery) and climbing the beautiful wooded ghats to Virajpet in Kodagu. Metered **auto-rickshaws** are easily available and their rates start at Rs6. Modest, good-value **accommodation** is available at KTDC's *Yatri Niwas* (☎0497/700717; ③–⑤), near the Police Club, across the tracks from the train station, or a five-minute rickshaw ride from the bus stand; it has large, clean en-suite rooms and a simple restaurant and beer parlour. It has suffered from a history of strikes in the recent past, so you should phone or book in advance, preferably through a KTDC outlet. *Plaza Tourist Home* (☎0497/360031; ②), close to the train station gates, on Fort Road is a good budget option with reasonable rooms and the India Coffee House **restaurant** downstairs. *Madan* (②), a few metres up the road is a friendly budget lodge set in a courtyard with plain but adequate rooms. *Swadeshi Woodlands Lodge* a few minutes away on Aarat Rd (☎0497/501434; ②), is a quiet old hotel with character, set in a large yard with basic rooms but a reasonable restaurant. More upscale is the business-orientated *Kamala International* (☎0497/766910; ⑥–⑦), in the town centre on SM Rd, which has been undergoing a complete overhaul and where most rooms are a/c, with colour TVs and room service; they also have a rooftop garden restaurant. By far the best option is the brilliantly located *Mascot Beach Resort* (☎0497/708445; ⑥–⑧), 300m before Baby Beach, right on top of a rocky shoreline with large well-appointed rooms with splendid windows to catch the sea breeze and views to the lighthouse across the cove. A swimming pool is in progress and there is great food in their restaurant but no bar. But for peace and quiet, head 8km south to *Costa Malabari*, booked through the Tourist Desk at Ernakulam (☎0497/766910; ⑤–⑥), where a cottage among the palms provides access to an unspoilt beach and three attractive coves. They will pick you up from the station with prior arrangement.

The *Mascot* offers **foreign exchange** for guests and they also have email. For full **Internet** services try Internet at Wheat House Building, opposite the Civil Station (☎0497/472181).

Parassinikadavu

The only place you can be guaranteed a glimpse of Teyyam is the village of **PARASSINIKADAVU**, 20km north of Kannur beside the Valapatanam River, where the head priest, or *madayan*, of the **Parassini Madammpura** temple performs every day during winter before assembled devotees. Elaborately dressed and accompanied by a traditional drum group, he becomes possessed by the temple's presiding deity – Lord Muthappan, Shiva in the form of a *kiratha*, or hunter – and enacts a series of complex offerings. The two-hour ceremony culminates when the priest/deity dances forward to bless individual members of the congregation. Even by Keralan standards, this is an extraordinary spectacle, and well worth taking time out of a journey along the coast for.

Regular local buses leave Kannur **for Parassinikadavu** from around 7am, dropping passengers at the top of the village, ten minutes on foot from the temple. However, if you want to get there in time for the dawn Teyyam, you'll have to splash out on one of the Ambassador taxis that line up outside Kannur bus stand. The cabbies sleep in their cars, so you can arrange the trip on the spot by waking one up; you can also arrange a taxi through one of the more upmarket hotels but you will have leave around 4.30am. Alternatively, head out to Parassinikadavu for the early afternoon ritual, which starts around 2pm, allowing you plenty of time to get there and back by bus, with half an hour or so to browse the temple bazaar (whose stalls do a great line in kitsch Lord Muthappan souvenirs). Note that the second performance of the day does not always take place; if you should miss the ritual and are still determined to see it at dawn the following day, but can't afford a taxi from Kannur, look for accommodation in one of the village's small *dharamshalas* grouped around the temple at the riverside. Plenty of small *dhabas* serve *dosas* and other spicy vegetarian snacks in the temple bazaar.

Kasargode and Bekal

The old-fashioned little town of **KASARGODE**, 153km north of Kozhikode, near the Karnataka border, with a predominantly Muslim population, is principally a fishing community – though some say smuggling is not unknown. It currently gets few foreign visitors, but the number is increasing, as it is the nearest town of any size to the beaches and fort at **BEKAL** (16km south), gradually being developed for tourism. At present, this is as unexploited an area as you could hope to find, with nary a beachside shack café, let alone a five-star hotel. However, don't come expecting an undiscovered Kovalam. The local fishermen are completely unused to the sight of semi-naked Westerners, while some stretches of sand serve as communal toilets. The undertow can also be dangerously strong in some places.

A popular weekend day-trip destination, Bekal's **fort** (daily 9am–5.30pm; Rs2, Fri free) stands on a promontory between two long, classically beautiful palm-fringed **beaches**. Although this is one of the largest forts in Kerala and has been under the control of various powers including Vijayanagar, Tipu Sultan and the British, it's nothing to get excited about. The bastion's commanding position, with views across the bays to north and south, is impressive enough, but only four watchtowers and the outer walls survive. An adjacent Hindu temple, next to the gates, with garish stucco images of the gods, draws a steady stream of visitors, while others clamber along the battlements or climb down to the beach through hidden passages. A short walk south of the main gates leads to Bekal Resort's visitor centre where the café and shops only open at the weekends.

Practicalities

The nearest major town to Kasargode is Mangalore, 50km north in Karnataka, a ninety minute bus ride away. Long-distance **buses** usually call at both its bus stands: a new private one on the main highway (NH17) on the outskirts and the KSRTC city bus stand at the centre of town. Among regular buses along the smaller coastal road, those south to Kanhangad, also on NH17, stop at Bekal. Kasargode **train station** is 3km from town. Bekal Resorts (☎0499/736937), a government-funded project to promote the area with careful consideration of environmental and social issues, runs a **tourist information office** at their visitor centre next to Bekal Fort, which is only manned sporadically and at weekends. When open, they are happy to give you advice about the area and to give you information on transport and accommodation.

The most atmospheric **place to stay** at **Bekal** is limited to the *Travellers Bungalow*, which has two basic rooms in a superb location at the furthest point of the promontory inside the fort. It's a great place to spend a night, except at weekends, when bus-loads of ghetto-blaster-toting day-trippers hang out on the verandah. If you want to stay here, you have to book through the Kasargode District Collector, Civil Station, Kasargode; ☎0499/430400. *Eeyam Lodge* (☎0499/736343; ②–④) at Palakannu, 2km from the fort in the direction of Kasargode, is friendly and not too far from the sea at Kappil Beach, with very reasonable rooms including some value-for-money a/c, a restaurant and the ability to **change money**. So does the *Fortland Tourist Home* (☎0499/736600; ①–④) at Udma, 6km from the fort, which has very cheap doubles and a dorm plus four a/c rooms, but it is 2km from the sea.

Near the bus stand in **Kasargode**, the *Enjay Tourist Home* (☎0499/421164; ②) has some a/c rooms, a South Indian restaurant and car rental, while *Aliya Lodge* (☎0499/430744; ①–②), near the town centre on MG Rd, has very cheap doubles, which get booked early, and a restaurant. *Ceeyal Tourist Home* on MG Rd (☎0499/430177; ①), conveniently placed next to the city bus stand, is a popular budget hotel with cheap, plain rooms which are often full. At the top (east) end of MG Rd, near the new bus stand, the easily recognizable monolith of the *City Tower* (☎0499/430400; ③–⑤) is Kasargode's fanciest hotel with reasonably priced doubles, some a/c rooms and a travel desk, but their "meals" restaurant is disappointingly dull.

travel details

Note that most individual routes appear only once; check against where you want to get to as well as where you're coming from. For details of ferry services on the backwaters – primarily between Alappuzha and Kollam – see p.311.

Trains

Kochi/Ernakulam to: Alappuzha (2 daily; 1hr 20min); Bangalore (1 daily; 13hr); Chennai (3–4 daily; 13–14hr); Coimbatore (5–6 daily; 4hr 45min–5hr); Delhi (2 daily; 40hr 30min–49hr); Kanniyakumari (4 daily; 7hr); Kollam (8–9 daily; 3–4hr); Kottayam (8–9 daily; 1hr 5min); Kozhikode (5 daily; 4–5hr); Mumbai (1–2 daily; 40–58hr); Palakaad (5–6 daily; 3hr 20min); Thrissur (9–10 daily; 1hr 30min–2hr).

Kozhikode to: Kannur (7 daily; 2hr 30min–3hr 30min); Mangalore (7 daily; 6–7hr 30min); Thrissur (6 daily; 1hr 50min–2hr 20min).

Thiruvananthapuram to: Alappuzha (3 daily; 2hr 50min–3hr 30min); Bangalore (1–2 daily; 18hr 30min); Chennai (1–2 daily; 17hr 45min–18hr 20min); Calcutta (3 weekly; 47–48hr); Delhi (2–3 daily; 44hr 30min–56hr 40min); Kanniyakumari (3 daily; 2hr 15min); Kochi (8 daily; 4hr–4hr 30min); Kollam (hourly; 1hr 30min–1hr 50min); Kozhikode (3 daily; 9hr 30min–10hr 30min); Mumbai (1–2 daily; 40hr–45hr 30min); Thrissur (5–6 daily; 5hr 30min–6hr 45min); Varkala (8 daily; 55min).

Thrissur to: Chennai (3–4 daily; 11hr 30min).

Buses

Kochi/Ernakulam to: Alappuzha (15 daily; 2hr); Kanniyakumari (6 daily; 9hr); Kollam (15 daily; 3hr); Kottayam (15 daily; 1hr 30min–2hr); Kozhikode (7 daily; 5hr); Periyar (10 daily; 6hr); Thrissur (10 daily; 2hr).

Kozhikode to: Kalpetta (6 daily; 3hr); Kannur (15–20 daily; 2–3hr); Mananthavady (4 daily; 4hr); Mysore (2 daily; 10hr); Ooty (4 daily; 6hr); Thrissur (10 daily; 4hr).

Munnar to: Kochi (5 daily; 4hr 30min); Kottayam (5 daily; 5hr); Kumily (4 daily; 4hr 30min); Madurai (6 daily; 5hr).

Periyar to: Kottayam (every 30min; 3–4hr); Kozhikode (hourly; 8hr); Madurai (10 daily; 5hr 30min); Munnar (4 daily; 4hr 30min).

Thiruvananthapuram to: Alappuzha (15 daily; 3hr 15min); Chennai (4 daily; 17hr); Kanniyakumari (12 daily; 2hr); Kochi (20 daily; 5–6hr); Kollam (15 daily; 1hr 30min); Kottayam (20 daily; 4hr); Madurai (10 daily; 7hr); Periyar (3 daily; 8hr); Ponmudi (4 daily; 2hr 30min); Varkala (hourly; 1hr 30min).

Thrissur to: Chennai (1 daily; 14hr); Guruvayur (10 daily; 40min); Mysore (2 daily; 10hr); Palakaad (6 daily; 2hr).

Flights

Kochi/Ernakulam to: Bangalore (1–2 daily; 50min); Chennai (1–2 daily; 40min–1hr 35min); Delhi (1 daily; 4hr); Goa (1 daily; 1hr 15min); Kozhikode (1 daily; 30min); Lakshadweep (2 daily except Sun; 1hr 30min); Mumbai (3 daily; 1hr 30min).

Kozhikode to: Chennai (3 weekly; 1hr 15min); Coimbatore (1 daily; 45min); Goa (2 weekly; 1hr 20min); the Gulf (1–2 daily; 4–7hr); Mumbai (2–3 daily; 1hr 40min–3hr).

Thiruvananthapuram to: Bangalore (3 weekly; 1hr 5min); Chennai (1–2 daily; 40min); Colombo (Sri Lanka) (1–2 daily; 50min); Delhi (1–2 daily; 4hr 30min); the Gulf (1–2 daily; 4hr); Malé (Maldives) (1–2 daily; 40min); Mumbai (2–3 daily; 1hr 55min).

CHAPTER FIVE

CHENNAI (MADRAS)

In the northeastern corner of Tamil Nadu, on the Bay of Bengal, **CHENNAI** (still commonly referred to by its former British name, **Madras**) is India's fourth largest city, with a population nudging six million. Hot, congested and noisy, it is the major transportation hub of the South – the international airport makes a marginally less stressful entry point to the subcontinent than Mumbai or Delhi – but most travellers stay just long enough to book a ticket for somewhere else. The attractions of the city itself are sparse, though it does boast fine specimens of Raj architecture, pilgrimage sites connected with the apostle "Doubting Thomas", superb Chola bronzes at its chief (Government) museum and plentiful music and dance performances.

The capital of Tamil Nadu, Chennai is, like Mumbai and Calcutta, a comparatively modern creation. It was founded by the **British East India Company** in 1639, on a narrow five-kilometre strip of land between the Cooum and Adyar rivers, a few kilometres north of the ancient Tamil port of **Mylapore** and the Portuguese settlement of San Thome, which was established in 1522. The site had no natural harbour; it was selected by Francis Day, the East India Company agent, in part because he enjoyed good relations with the Nayak governor Dharmala Ayyappa, who could intercede with the Vijayanagar Raja of Chandragiri, to whom the territory belonged. In addition, the land was protected by water on the east, south and west; cotton could be bought here twenty percent cheaper than elsewhere; and, apparently, Day had acquired a mistress in San Thome. A fortified trading post, completed on St George's Day (April 23) 1640, was named **Fort St George**. By 1700, the British had acquired neighbouring territory including Triplicane and Egmore, while over the course of the next century, as capital of the **Madras Presidency**, which covered most of South India, the city mushroomed to include many surrounding villages. The British were repeatedly challenged by the French who, in 1746, destroyed much of the city. **Robert Clive** ("Clive of India"), then a clerk, was taken prisoner, an experience said to have inspired him to become a campaigner. Clive was among the first to re-enter Madras when it was retaken three years later, and continued to use it as his base. Following this, fortifications were strengthened and the British survived a year-long French siege in 1759, completing the work in 1783. By this time, however, Calcutta was in the ascendancy and Madras lost its national importance.

The city's renaissance began after Independence, when it became the centre of a thriving Tamil **movie industry**, and a hotbed of **Dravidian nationalism**. The rise of Annadurai's DMK — which ousted Nehru's Congress government in 1967 and has

ACCOMMODATION PRICE CODES

All **accommodation prices** in this book have been coded using the symbols below. The prices given are for a double room, except in the case of categories ① and ② where the price can refer to dorm accommodation per bed. All taxes are included. For more details, see p.34.

① up to Rs100	④ Rs300–400	⑦ Rs900–1500
② Rs100–200	⑤ Rs400–600	⑧ Rs1500–2500
③ Rs200–300	⑥ Rs600–900	⑨ Rs2500 and upwards

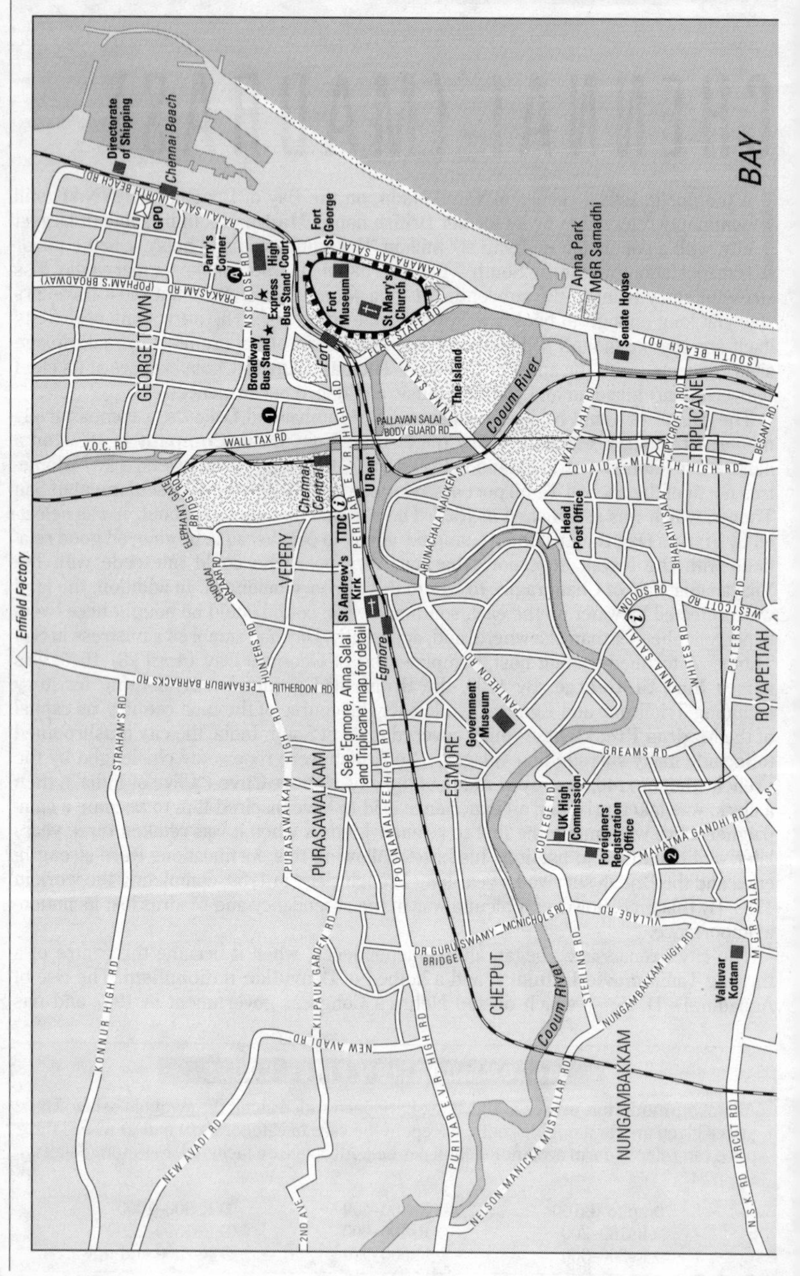
BAY
Directorate of Shipping
Chennai Beach
GPO
Parry's Corner
High Court
Fort St George
Fort Museum
St Mary's Church
Express Bus Stand
Broadway Bus Stand
Fort
GEORGE TOWN
Anna Park
MGR Samadhi
Senate House
The Island
Coom River
TRIPLICANE
Chennai Central
TTDC
U Rent
VEPERY
St Andrew's Kirk
Egmore
Head Post Office
See 'Egmore, Anna Salai and Triplicane' map for detail
Government Museum
EGMORE
PURASAWALKAM
UK High Commission
Foreigners' Registration Office
ROYAPETTAH
CHETPUT
NUNGAMBAKKAM
Valluvar Kottam
Enfield Factory
RAJAJI SALAI (NORTH BEACH RD)
PRAKASAM RD (POPHAM'S BROADWAY)
NSC BOSE RD
KAMARAJAR SALAI
FLAG STAFF RD
(SOUTH BEACH RD)
ANNA SALAI
WALL TAX RD
V.O.C. RD
PALLAVAN SALAI
BODY GUARD RD
WALLAJAH RD
QUAID-E-MILLETH HIGH RD
PYCROFTS RD
BESANT RD
BHARATHI SALAI
ELEPHANT GATE BRIDGE RD
CHOOLAI BAZAAR RD
PERIYAR E.V.R. HIGH RD
ARUNACHALA NAICKEN ST
WOODS RD
WESTCOTT RD
WHITES RD
PETERS RD
HUNTERS RD
PERAMBUR BARRACKS RD
RITHERDON RD
PANTHEON RD
GREAMS RD
STRAHAM'S RD
PURASAWALKAM HIGH RD
(POONAMALLEE HIGH RD)
COLLEGE RD
MAHATMA GANDHI RD
VILLAGE RD
MCNICHOLS RD
DR GURUSWAMY BRIDGE
STERLING RD
NUNGAMBAKKAM HIGH RD
M.G.R. SALAI
KILPAUK GARDEN RD
NEW AVADI RD
KONNUR HIGH RD
PURIYAR E.V.R. HIGH RD
NELSON MANICKA MUSTALLAR RD
2ND AVE
N.S.K. RD (ARCOT RD)

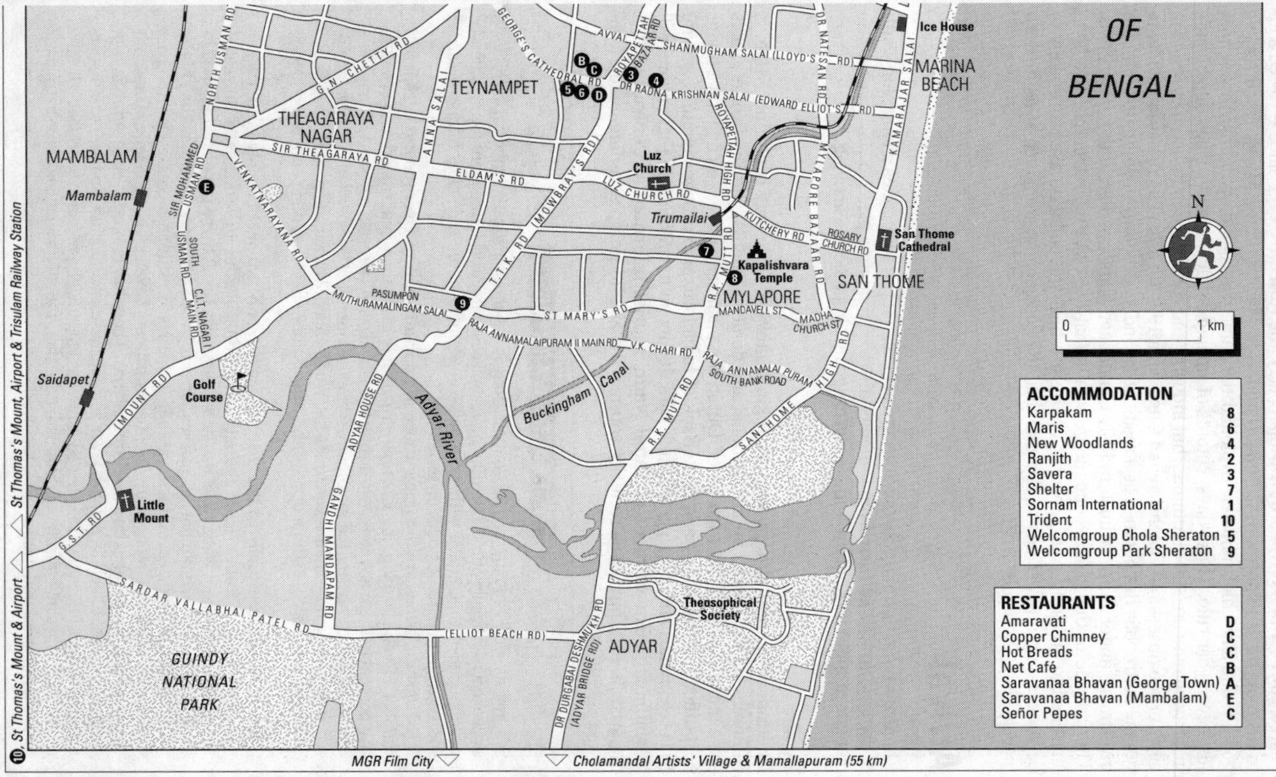
OF
BENGAL
N
0
1 km
ACCOMMODATION
Karpakam 8
Maris 6
New Woodlands 4
Ranjith 2
Savera 3
Shelter 7
Sornam International 1
Trident 10
Welcomgroup Chola Sheraton 5
Welcomgroup Park Sheraton 9
RESTAURANTS
Amaravati D
Copper Chimney C
Hot Breads C
Net Café B
Saravanaa Bhavan (George Town) A
Saravanaa Bhavan (Mambalam) E
Señor Pepes C
Ice House
MARINA BEACH
KAMARAJAR SALAI
San Thome Cathedral
SAN THOME
SANTHOME HIGH RD
ROSARY CHURCH RD
MYLAPORE BAZAAR RD
DR NATESAN RD
KUTCHERY RD
Kapalishvara Temple
MYLAPORE
MADHA CHURCH ST
MANDAVELL ST
RAJA ANNAMALAI PURAM SOUTH BANK ROAD
R.K. MUTT RD
Tirumailai
ROYAPETTAH HIGH RD
SHANMUGHAM SALAI (LLOYD'S RD)
DR RADNA KRISHNAN SALAI (EDWARD ELLIOT'S RD)
ROYAPETTAH BAZAAR RD
AVVAI
Luz Church
LUZ CHURCH RD
GEORGE'S CATHEDRAL RD
MOWBRAY'S RD
TEYNAMPET
ELDAM'S RD
T.T.K. RD
ST MARY'S RD
V.K. CHARI RD
RAJA ANNAMALAIPURAM II MAIN RD
Buckingham Canal
Theosophical Society
ADYAR
DR DURGABAI DESHMUKH RD (ADYAR BRIDGE RD)
ELLIOT BEACH RD
Adyar River
ANNA SALAI
PASUMPON MUTHURAMALINGAM SALAI
ADYAR HOUSE RD
GANDHI MANDAPAM RD
G.N. CHETTY RD
THEAGARAYA NAGAR
SIR THEAGARAYA RD
VENKATNARAYANA RD
NORTH USMAN RD
SIR MOHAMMED USMAN RD
SOUTH USMAN RD
C.I.T. NAGAR I MAIN RD
Golf Course
(MOUNT RD)
Little Mount
SARDAR VALLABHAI PATEL RD
GUINDY NATIONAL PARK
MAMBALAM
Mambalam
Saidapet
G.S.T. RD
MGR Film City
Cholamandal Artists' Village & Mamallapuram (55 km)
St Thomas's Mount, Airport & Trisulam Railway Station
St Thomas's Mount & Airport
10, St Thomas's Mount & Airport

shared power with its rival pro-Dravidian party, the AIADMK, ever since — owed a lot to his movement's control of the major studios in Madras. Later, **MGR**, Tamil Nadu's godlike film-star chief minister, exploited the same propaganda potential throughout his eleven-year rule. These days, cutouts of smiling politicians and strings of pennants in party colours are still ubiquitous, but industry and commerce have taken over as the city's prime obsessions. Rechristened Chennai in 1997 (to assert its pre-colonial identity), the metropolis has boomed as a result of the Indian economy opening up to foreign investment under Prime Ministers Rajiv Gandhi and Narasima Rao in the early 1990s. The flip side of this rapid economic growth is that the city's infrastructure has been stretched to breaking point; poverty, oppressive heat and pollution are more likely to be your lasting impressions of Chennai than the conspicuous affluence of its modern marble shopping malls.

Arrival

Chennai's main bus and train stations are central, but the airport lies a long slog south of the city, around an hour from the hotel districts. Finding a place to stay can be difficult late at night so hunt around for a vacancy by phone before arriving.

By air

Chennai Meenambakkam airport 16km southwest of the city centre on NH45, is comprehensively served by international and domestic flights, and the two terminals are a minute's walk from each other. Out in the main concourse, you'll find a 24-hour post office, Thomas Cook and State Bank of India foreign exchange counters, several STD telephones and a couple of snack bars. It's by no means certain that anyone will be staffing the **Government of Tamil Nadu Tourist Information Centre** booth at the arrivals exit, but if you're lucky you may be able to fix up accommodation from

HEALTH WARNING

It's just as well Chennai boasts some of India's most sophisticated medical facilities, because it is officially one of the unhealthiest places in the world. Exponential, unplanned economic growth, coupled with inadequate investment in the municipal infrastructure, has resulted in chronic pollution problems.

Exhaust emissions are the prime cause of **poor air quality**. Over the last decade the number of vehicles clogging Chennai's roads has more than quadrupled, and seventy-five percent of them are dirty, two-stroke two-wheelers. As a result, carbon monoxide levels are double the permitted maximum, while the amount of "suspended particulate matter" in the air is more than seven times the World Health Organization prescribed limits. So, if you suffer from asthma or any other respiratory disorders, don't aim to spend long here.

Water quality is equally bad: in a recent survey, only two out of twenty groundwater samples collected from around the city were drinkable due to leakages of untreated sewage from the main waterways into reservoirs. As a result there is a disturbing rise in the incidence of mosquito-borne diseases. Chennai alone accounts for around half of the total number of reported **malaria** cases in Tamil Nadu, with an increase over the past three years of sixty percent in the number of patients developing the deadly falciparum strain (which can develop into cerebral malaria). There has also been an upsurge in less common diseases such as dengue fever and Japanese encephalitis. So take extra malaria precautions while you're in Chennai – always sleep under a net and cover yourself with repellent – especially during, and immediately after, the monsoons, and take extra care over what you eat and drink.

NAME CHANGES

The city's former name, "Madras", is not the only one to have been weeded out over the last few years by **pro-Dravidian politicians**. Several major roads in the city have also been renamed as part of an on-going attempt to "Dravidify" the Tamil capital (most of the new names immortalize former nationalist politicians). However, far from all of Chennai's inhabitants are in favour of the recent changes, while some (notably a large contingent of auto-rickshaw *wallahs*) seem completely oblivious to them. The confusing result of this is that both old and new names remain in use. We have used the new ones throughout the chapter. Thus Mount Rd, the main shopping road through the centre of town, is now Anna Salai; to the east, Triplicane High Rd, near *Broadlands Hotel*, has become Quaide Milleth Salai; Poonamallee High Rd, running east–west across the north of the city is Periyar EVR High Rd; North Beach Rd, along the eastern edge of George Town is now known as Rajaji Salai; South Beach Rd, the southern stretch of the coastal road, is Kamaraj Salai; running west, Edward Elliot's Rd has been renamed Dr Radha Krishnan Salai; Mowbray's Rd is also known as TTK Rd, and Nungabamkkam High Rd is now Uttamar Gandhi Salai.

Although, for the sake of political correctness, we've adopted the new names, it's safe to say that the old ones are still more commonly understood, and that using them will not cause offence – unless, of course, you happen to be talking to a pro-Dravidian activist.

here, or at the "Free Fone" desk nearby. Also worth knowing about if you plan to leave Chennai by train is Southern Railways' handy computerized **ticket reservation** counter (daily 10am–5pm), immediately outside the domestic terminal exit.

To **get away from the airport**, there are pre-paid minibus and taxi counters at the international arrivals exit. **Taxis** cost around Rs220–250 for the thirty-five-minute ride to the main hotels or train stations; rickshaws charge around Rs100, but you'll have to lug your gear out to the main road as they're not allowed to park inside the airport forecourt. A taxi to **Mamallapuram** is in the region of Rs850. Shuttle **buses** run to Egmore and Central train stations and the Thiruvalluvar (Express) bus stand and cost Rs75, but they call at several of the large hotels en route, and are certainly not "Express". The cheapest way to get downtown is to walk to the main road and take any bus marked Broadway from the near side. Ask to be let off at the central LIC (Life Insurance Company) stop, on Chennai's main thoroughfare in the downtown area, close to hotels, restaurants and tourist information.

Trains run every 15 or 20 minutes (4.30am–11pm) from **Trisulam** station, 500m from the airport on the far (east) side of the road, to Park, Egmore and North Beach stations, taking roughly 45 minutes.

By train

Arriving in Chennai by train, you come in at one of two **long-distance train stations**, 1.5km apart on Periyar EVR High Rd, towards the north of the city. **Egmore station**, in the heart of the busy commercial Egmore district, is the arrival point for most trains from Tamil Nadu and Kerala; on the whole, others pull in at **Central station**, further east, on the edge of George Town, which has a 24-hour left luggage office and STD phone booths outside the exit. Information kiosks at both stations are poorly staffed and badly equipped, but both have plentiful taxis and auto-rickshaws; Central has a pre-paid auto-rickshaw booth in the forecourt.

By bus

Buses from elsewhere in Tamil Nadu arrive at two bus stands, **Thiruvalluvar** (also known as **Express**) and **Broadway**, opposite each other in George Town, near the

High Court complex off NSC Bose Rd. Both stations are unbearably crowded and confusing but Broadway, which also sees services from Karnataka, Kerala and Andhra Pradesh, is the worst: little more than a dirty, chaotic, pot-holed yard, and a nightmare to negotiate with luggage. It can also be a real problem to pick up a rickshaw. For details of buses to **Mamallapuram** from Broadway, see p.391.

Information and communications

At the highly efficient and very helpful **Government of India Regional Tourist Office** (GIRTO) at 154 Anna Salai (Mon–Fri 9.15am–5.45pm, Sat 9am–1pm; ☎044/852 4785 or 852 4295), you can pick up leaflets, arrange accommodation and organize tours by rented car. They also supply approved **guides** by the day (Rs350–750) or half-day (Rs250–500).

A ten-minute walk across town, the **Tamil Nadu Tourism Development Corporation** (TTDC), 4 Periyar EVR High Rd (Mon–Fri 10am–5pm; ☎044/560294) organizes guided tours of the city. Advance bookings for **ITDC** hotels can be made, and tours of the city arranged, at the ITDC office at 29 Victor Crescent, C-in-C Rd (Mon–Sat 6am–8pm, Sun 6am–2pm; ☎044/827 8884). Tourist offices for other states, including Himachal Pradesh, Kerala, Rajasthan and Uttar Pradesh, are at 28 C-in-C Rd; *Hallo! Chennai* (see opposite) has full details of these and other state offices, as does the GIRTO on Anna Salai.

Banks and exchange

Tourists have few difficulties **changing money** in Chennai: there are plenty of banks, and the major hotels offer exchange facilities to residents. A conveniently central option is American Express, G-17, Spencer Plaza, 769 Anna Salai (daily 9.30am–5.30pm, Sat 9.30am–2.30pm). Thomas Cook (Mon–Sat 9am–6pm) have offices at: the Ceebros Centre, 45 Monteith Rd, Egmore; and at the G-4 Eldorado Building, 112 Nungambakkam High Rd; and also at the airport (open to meet flights). For encashments on Visa cards, go to Bobcards, next door to the Bank of Baroda on Monteith Rd, near the *Ambassador Pallava Hotel.*

Post and telephone

Chennai's **Head Post Office** is on Anna Salai (daily 8am–8pm). If you're using it for poste restante, make sure your correspondents mark the envelope "Head Post Office, Anna Salai", or your letters could well end up across town at the General Post Office, north of Parry's Corner on Rajaji Salai (same hours). The post office on Quaide Milleth Salai, in Triplicane (Mon–Sat 7am–3pm) is convenient if you're staying at *Broadlands* or the *Comfort Hotel.*

Telegram and **telephone** services are most efficient at the Head Post Office on Anna Salai. Trying to make a local or international call from Rajaji Salai Post Office requires tiresome form-filling, queuing and deposits – if you're in the area head for a phone booth advertising STD/PCO/ISD on a yellow sign, where you'll rarely have to wait.

Internet access

Chennai has no shortage of places offering **Internet access**, albeit at wildly varying rates. The snazziest option, with its own ISDN line, is the *Net Café*, at 101/1 Kanakasri Nagar, down an alleyway off Cathedral Rd (daily 7am–midnight) – look for the neon @ sign. Staff are helpful, you rarely wait long for a machine but rates are high (Rs100/hr) and they're reluctant to let you compose offline. *SRIS Netsurfing Café* on the first floor of Spencer Plaza is a cheaper, though smaller, alternative, and if you're staying at

Broadlands or one of the other hotels in Triplicane, *Internet Point*, 61 CNK Rd, is conveniently located opposite the *Maharaja Restaurant*.

Publications

The long-established *Hallo! Chennai* (monthly; Rs5) is an accurate directory to all the city's services, with full-moon dates (useful for estimating temple festivals), a guide to Tamil Nadu for tourists, exhaustive flight and train details and an outline of Chennai bus timetables. It doesn't have a "What's On" section: for forthcoming music and dance performances, consult the events column on page three of the *Hindu*, or ask at the tourist office.

City transport

The offices, sights, train stations and bus stands of Chennai are spread over such a wide area that it's impossible to get around without using some form of **public transport**. Most visitors jump in auto-rickshaws, but outside rush hours you can travel around comfortably by **bus** or suburban **train**.

Incidentally, the city's drastic dry-season water shortage explains the **water carriers** trundling along its congested streets. Watch out for unofficial ones as you cross the road; tractors pull tankers so heavy that they either topple over or fail to stop when brakes are applied, causing fatal accidents.

Buses

To ride the bus in most Indian cities you need to be incredibly resilient and a master of the art of hanging onto open doorways with two fingers. Buses in Chennai, on the other hand, are regular, reliable, inexpensive, well-labelled and only cramped during rush-hours. On Anna Salai, they have special stops; on smaller streets, flag them down, or wait with the obvious crowd. Buses in Egmore gather opposite the train station. The numbers of services to specific places of interest in the city are listed in the relevant account.

Trains

If you want to travel south from central Chennai to Guindy (Deer Park), St Thomas Mount or the airport, the easiest way to go is by **train**. Services run every 15 minutes (on average) between 4.30am and 11pm, prices are minimal, and you can guarantee a seat at any time except rush hour (9am & 5pm). First-class carriages substitute padded seats for wooden slatted benches and are a little cleaner. Buy a ticket before boarding.

City trains follow the route: North Beach (opposite the general post office), Fort, Park (for Central), Egmore, Nungambakkam, Kodambakkam, Mambalam (for T Nagar and silk shops), Saidapet (for Little Mount Church), Guindy, St Thomas Mount and Trisulam (for the airport).

Taxis and rickshaws

Chennai's yellow-top Ambassador **taxis** gather outside Egmore and Central train stations, and at the airport. All have meters, but they often prefer to set a fixed price before leaving, and invariably charge a return fare, whatever the destination. At around Rs150 for Central to Triplicane, they're practically pricing themselves out of business.

Flocks of auto- and cycle-rickshaws wait patiently outside tourist hotels, and not so patiently outside train stations. **Auto-rickshaw** drivers in Chennai are notorious for their demand for high fares from locals and tourists alike. All rickshaws have meters; a few drivers use them if asked, but in many cases you'll save a lot of frustrating bargaining by offering a small sub above the meter-reading (a driver may offer you a rate of "meter plus 5", meaning Rs5 above the final reading). If you need to get to the airport or station early in the morning, book a rickshaw, and negotiate the price, the night before (the driver may well sleep in his vehicle outside your hotel).

Only take **cycle-rickshaws** on the smaller roads; riding amid Chennai traffic on a fragile tricycle seat can be extremely hair-raising.

Bicycle rental

Bicycles may be rented by the hour from dozens of stalls around the city, but you'll have to keep your wits about you riding through the centre. The traffic on Anna Salai, in particular, can feel like a scene from *Rollerball*, so avoid this main drag, or stick to its less dangerous service lanes.

Car and motorcycle rental

Car rental, with driver, can be arranged through the Government Tourist Office, ITDC (see p.372), or many of the upmarket hotels. It's a great, relatively stress-free way to get about if you can afford it. Ambassadors cost Rs650–800 per day (or Rs1100–1200 for a/c).

Anyone brave enough to rent a **moped** or **motorcycle** for short rides around the city, or tours of Tamil Nadu, should head for U-Rent Services, at the *Picnic Hotel*, 1132 Periyar EVR High Rd (Mon–Sat 6am–10pm; ☎044/567398). You'll need an international driving licence. Prices range from Rs150 to Rs350 per day, and you have to pay a flat Rs250 annual membership fee regardless of how long you rent a bike for.

Bus tours

One good way to get around the sights of Chennai is on a TTDC **bus tour**; bookings are taken in the relevant offices. Albeit rushed, they're good value, and the guides can be very helpful.

The **TTDC half-day tour** (daily; 8am–1pm or 1–6.30pm; Rs75) starts at their office on Periyar EVR High Rd. It takes in Fort St George, the Government Museum, the Snake Park, Kapalishvara temple, Elliot's Beach and lastly Marina Beach (on Friday, the Government Museum is closed, so the tour goes to the Birla Planetarium instead.)

The City

Chennai divides into three main areas. The northern district, separated from the rest by the Cooum River, is the site of the first British outpost in India, **Fort St George**, and the commercial centre, **George Town**, that grew up during British occupation. At the southern end of Rajaji Salai, is **Parry's Corner**, George Town's principal landmark – look for the tall grey building labelled "Parry's". It's a major stop for city buses.

Central Chennai, sandwiched between the Cooum and Adyar rivers, and crossed diagonally by the city's main thoroughfare, **Anna Salai**, is dominated by modern commercial and residential areas, and gives way in the east to a long straight **Marina** where fishermen mend nets and set small boats out to sea, and tourists hitch up saris and trousers for a quick paddle. South of here, near the coast, **Mylapore**, inhabited in the 1500s by the Portuguese, boasts **Kapalishvara Temple** and **San Thome Cathedral**, both tourist attractions and places of pilgrimage. Further out, south of the Adyar, the Portuguese church on **St Thomas Mount** overlooks **Guindy National Park**, the only city national park in India.

Fort St George

Quite unlike any other fort in India, **Fort St George** stands amid state offices facing the sea in the east of the city, just south of George Town on Kamaraj Salai. It looks more like a complex of well-maintained colonial mansions than a fort; indeed many of its buildings are used today as offices, roamed during the week by businessmen passing between the Secretariat and State Legislature.

The fort was the first structure of Madras city, and the first territorial possession of the British in India. Construction began in 1640, but most of the original buildings had to be replaced later that century, after being damaged during French sieges. The most imposing structure is the eighteenth-century colonnaded **Fort House**, coated in deep-slate-grey and white paint. Next door, in the more modestly proportioned **Exchange Building** – site of Madras's first bank – is the excellent fort **museum** (daily except Fri; 10am–5pm; R2). The collection within faithfully records the central events of the British occupation of Madras with portraits, regimental flags, weapons, coins minted by the East India Company, medals, stamps and thick woollen uniforms that make you wonder how the Raj survived as long as it did. Some of the most evocative momentos are letters written by figures such as Robert Clive, reporting on life in the colony. The squat cast-iron cage on the ground floor was brought to Madras from China, where for more than a year in the nineteenth century it was used as a particularly sadistic form of imprisonment for a British captain. The upper floor, once the public exchange hall where merchants met to gossip and trade, is now an **art gallery**, where portraits of prim officials and their wives sit side by side with fine sketches of the British embarking at Madras in aristocratic finery, attended by Indians in loin cloths. Also on display are etchings by the famous artist **Thomas Daniells**, whose work largely defined British perceptions of India at the end of the eighteenth century.

South of the museum, past the State Legislature, stands the oldest surviving Anglican church in Asia, **St Mary's Church** (daily 9am–5pm), built in 1678, and partly renovated after a battle with the French in 1759. The church, built with thick walls and a strong vaulted roof to withstand the city's many sieges, served as a store and shelter in times of war. It's distinctly English in style, crammed with plaques and statues in memory of British soldiers, politicians and their wives. The grandest plaque, made of pure silver, was presented by Elihu Yale, former Governor of Fort St George (1687–96) and founder of Yale University in the USA. A collection of photographs of visiting dignitaries, including Queen Elizabeth II, is on display in the entrance porch. Nearby, **Robert Clive's house** is in a rather sorry state, and is currently used by the Archaeological Survey of India as offices.

George Town

North of Fort St George, the former British trading centre of **George Town** (bus #18 from Anna Salai) remains a focus for banks, offices and shipping companies. This confusing – if well-ordered – grid of streets harbours a fascinating medley of architecture: eighteenth- and nineteenth-century churches, Hindu and Jain temples and a scattering of mosques, interspersed with grand mansions. However, despite its potential charm, this is Chennai's most chaotic and crowded area, a dirty and uninviting warren clogged by particularly persistent hawkers and thick traffic. Probably the best way to appreciate the area is from its edges. In the east, on Rajaji Salai, the **General Post Office** (daily 8am–8pm) occupies a robust earth-red Indo-Saracenic building, constructed in 1884. George Town's southern extent is marked by the bulbous white domes and sandstone towers of the **High Court** and the even more opulent towers of the **Law College**, both showing strong Islamic influence.

It can be fun to take a quick rummage around George Town's **bazaars**, lines of rickety stalls selling clothes, bags, umbrellas, watches, shoes and perfume, concentrated along Rajaji Salai and NSC Bose Rd.

Government Museum

It's well worth setting aside at least half a day to explore the Chennai **Government Museum** (daily except Fri; 9.30am–5pm; Rs3; camera Rs20), hop on bus #11H from Anna Salai for Pantheon Rd, south of Egmore train station. It has remarkable archeological finds from South India and the Deccan, stone sculptures from major temples and an unsurpassed collection of Chola bronzes.

A deep red circular structure, fronted by Italian-style pillars and built in 1851, the **main building** stands opposite the entrance and ticket office. The first gallery is devoted to archeology and geology, with tools, pots, jewellery and weapons from the Stone and Iron Ages, and maps of principal excavations. Later exhibits include a substantial assortment of dismantled panels, railings and statues from the second century AD *stupa* complex at **Amaravati**, Andhra Pradesh (see p.514). Depicting episodes from the Buddha's life and scenes from the *Jataka* stories from ancient Hinayana Buddhist texts, these sensuously carved marble reliefs are widely regarded as the finest achievements of early Indian art, outshining even the Sanchi *toranas*. Sadly, they are poorly lit and inadequately labelled; some have even been defaced with graffiti, while others are blackened and worn from constant rubbing. To the left of the Amaravati gallery, high, arcaded halls full of stuffed animals and the like lead to the **ethnology gallery**, where models, clothes and weapons, along with photographs of expressionless faces in orderly lines, illustrate local tribal societies, some long since wiped out. A fascinating display of wind and string instruments, drums and percussion includes the large predecessor of today's *sitar* and several very old *tabla*. Nearby, a group of wooden doors and window frames from Chettinad, a region near Madurai, are exquisitely carved with floral and geometric designs much like those found in Gujarati *havelis*.

The museum's real treasure, however, is the modern, well-lit gallery, left of the main building, which contains the world's most complete and impressive selection of **Chola bronzes** (see p.508). Large statues of Shiva, Vishnu and Parvati stand in the centre, flanked by glass cases containing smaller figurines, including several sculptures of Shiva as **Nataraja**, the Lord of the Dance, encircled by a ring of fire and standing with his arms and legs poised and head provocatively cocked. One of the finest models is **Ardhanarishvara**, the androgynous form of Shiva (united with Shakti in transcendence of duality), the left side of the body is female and the right male, and the intimacy of detail is astounding. A rounded breast, a delicate hand and tender bejewelled foot are counterpoints to the harsher sinewy limbs and torso, and the male side of the head is crowned with a mass of matted hair and serpents.

A **children's museum** demonstrates the principles of electricity and irrigation with marginally diverting, semi-functional models, while the magnificent Indo-Saracenic **art gallery** houses old British portraits of figures such as Clive and Hastings, Rajput and Moghul miniatures and a small display of ivory carvings.

St Andrew's Kirk

Just northeast of Egmore station, off Periyar EVR High Rd, **St Andrew's Kirk**, consecrated in 1821, is a fine example of Georgian architecture. Modelled on London's St Martin-in-the-Fields, it is one of just three churches in India which has a circular seating plan, laid out beneath a huge dome painted blue with gold stars and supported by a sweep of Corinthian columns. A staircase leads onto the flat roof, surrounding the dome, from where you can climb further up into the steeple past the massive bell to a tiny balcony affording excellent views of the city.

Valluvar Kottam

In the south of the Nungambakkam district, just off Village Rd, the **Valluvar Kottam** is an intriguing construction, built in classical style in 1976 as a memorial to the first-century Tamil poet Thiruvalluvar. Most impressive is the 34-metre-high stone chariot, carved from just three blocks of granite, into a likeness of the great temple car of Thiruvarur. Adjoining this veritable juggernaut is a vast public auditorium, one of the largest in Asia, with a capacity of four thousand. A stroll along the auditorium roof past shallow rectangular ponds brings you to a large statue of the poet saint, within a shrine carved into the upper reaches of the chariot. Among the many reliefs around the monument, look out for the cat in human pose, reminiscent of the figure at Arjuna's Penance in Mamallapuram.

Marina Beach

One of the longest city beaches in the world, the **Marina** (Kamarajar Salai) stretches 5km from the harbour at the southeastern corner of George Town, to San Thome Cathedral. The impulse to transform Chennai's "rather dismal beach" into a Marina, styled "from old Sicilian recollections" to function as a "lung" for the city, was conceived by Mountstuart Elphinstone Grant-Duff (Governor 1881–86) who had otherwise won himself the reputation for being "feeble, sickly" and a "failure". Over the years, numerous buildings, some of which undoubtedly would not have figured in memories of Sicily, have sprung up, among them surreal modern memorials to Tamil Nadu's chief political heroes and freedom fighters.

The **beach** itself is a sociable stretch, peopled by idle paddlers, picnickers and pony-riders; on Sunday afternoons crowds gather for a market. Swimming and sunbathing are neither recommended nor approved – if you're desperate, however, you could try one of the shabby swimming pools. There's also a rather neglected aquarium, and two parks at the northern end, the **Anna Park** and **MGR Samadhi**, where Tamil tourists flock in droves to pay their respects at the shrine of the state's most illustrious movie actor and chief minister, **MGR** (see box on p.382). At the northern end, one of the oldest of the city's university buildings is the **Senate House** (1879), an uncharacteristically Byzantine-influenced design by Robert Fellowes Chisholm (1840–1915). He was one of the British leaders in developing the Indo-Saracenic hybrid style, incorporating Hindu, Jain and Muslim elements along with solid Victorian, British brickwork.

Continuing south, past the Indo-Saracenic **Presidency College** (1865–71), a number of stolid Victorian university buildings include the **Lady Willingdon Teacher Training College**. Next door, the college's hostel, a huge lump of a building with a semicircular frontage painted white and yellow, was during the nineteenth century the Madras depot of the Tudor Ice Company (see box on p.378).

Mylapore

Long before Madras came into existence, **Mylapore**, south of the Marina (buses #4, 5 or 21 from the LIC building on Anna Salai), was an major settlement; the Greek geographer Ptolemy mentioned it in the second century AD as a thriving port. During the Pallava period (fifth to ninth centuries) it was second only to Mamallapuram (see p.397).

An important stop – with Little Mount and St Thomas Mount – on the St Thomas pilgrimage trail, **San Thome Cathedral** (daily 6am–8pm) marks the eastern boundary of Mylapore, lying close to the sea at the southern end of the Marina. Although the present Neo-Gothic structure dates from 1896, San Thome stands on the site of two earlier churches (the first possibly erected by Nestorian Christians from Persia during the

THE ICE HOUSE

Over the years, Chennai has seen its fair share of world-shaping moments, but few can have been met with the wonder and unanimous approval that greeted the arrival of an American clipper in the early 1830s. Its cargo, rolled in pine sawdust and steered through the surf in small *masula* boats, had never been seen in peninsular India before, and one can only imagine the amazement of the local coolies when they first felt the weight and burning cold of melting **ice** on their shoulders.

In a little over four months, the ship, the *Tuscany*, had sailed halfway around the world with its precious load, harvested from frozen ponds around Boston. Little technology was required to gather the ice: grappling hooks, lengths of blocks and tackle, a few horse-drawn sleds and one hundred Irish labourers. The real breakthrough that made the trade possible was the discovery, by one Frederic Nathaniel Jarvis, that fresh pine sawdust would insulate ice, even from high tropical temperatures. A few years earlier, his friend, Frederick Tudor Boston, had tried to transport $10,000 dollars worth of New English ice to Martinique in the Caribbean, only to watch the entire cargo melt en route. However, Jarvis's bright idea enabled Boston's Tudor Ice Company to export 180 tons of ice to Calcutta in 1833. From that initial shipment enough profit was generated to build warehouses in Bombay and Madras, and thereafter the trade continued to boom for nearly forty years, until the invention of steam-powered ice-making machines, which put the company out of business.

Overlooking Chennai's sun-scorched Marina Beach, the building erected by the Tudor Ice Company in the 1840s to store their stock still stands as an evocative reminder of this brief, but extraordinary, episode in the city's mercantile history. It was sold by Boston to a rich lawyer when the bottom fell out of the trade, and it was with him that the famous Indian philosopher, **Vivekananda** stayed after his return from the States in 1897, when crowds would gather on the steps outside to hear the sage speak. In memory of this event – and in spite of the fact it now serves as a hostel for the adjacent teacher training college – the local municipality have rechristened the building "Vivekananda House", but to everyone else in Chennai, the stalwart old pile, with its peeling yellow-painted walls and distinctive twin circular tiered facade, is still known simply as **"The Ice House"**.

tenth century) built over the tomb of St Thomas; his relics are kept inside. Behind the church, a small **museum** houses stones inscribed in Tamil, Sanskrit (twelfth-century Chola) and early Portuguese, and also a map of India dated 1519.

The **Kapalishvara**, less than 1km west of the San Thome Cathedral, is the most famous temple in Chennai, the principal shrine being dedicated to Shiva. Seventh-century Tamil poet-saints sang its praises, but the present structure probably dates from the sixteenth century. Until then, the temple is thought to have occupied a site on the shore; sea erosion or demolition at the hands of the Portuguese led it to be rebuilt inland. The huge (40m) *gopura* towering above the main east entrance, plastered in stucco figures, is comparatively recent (1906). Surrounding an assortment of busy shrines, where priests offer blessings for devotees and non-Hindus alike, the courtyard features an old tree where a small shrine to Shiva's consort, Parvati, shows her in the form of a peahen (*mayil*) worshipping a *lingam*. This commemorates the legend that she was momentarily distracted from concentrating on her lord by the enchanting dance of a peacock. Shiva, miffed at this dereliction of wifely duty, cursed her, whereupon she turned into a peahen. To expiate the sin, Parvati took off to a place called Kapalinagar, and embarked upon rigorous austerities. To commemorate her success, the town was named Mayilapore or **Mylapore**. The oldest artefacts in the Kapalishvara temple are the movable bronze images of deities and the 63 Shaivite Nayanmar poet-saints, two of whom came from Mylapore. Unusually, the main shrine faces west, towards a space dominated by an eighteenth-century water-lily tank, that appears vast in this cramped suburban district.

Important **festivals** held at Kapalishvara include Tai Pusham (Jan/Feb), when the bronze images of Shiva and Parvati are pulled around the temple tank in a decorated boat to the accompaniment of music. Brahmotsava (March/April) celebrates the marriage of Shiva and Parvati; on the eighth day, in the afternoon, all 63 bronze images of the Nayanmar saints are clothed, garlanded and taken out in palanquins along the streets to meet the bejewelled images of Shiva and Parvati. Vasantha (May/June), the summer festival, is marked by concerts.

In the busy **market streets** that surround the temple, amid stalls selling pots and pans, flowers, religious paraphernalia and vegetables, glittering shops spill over with gold wedding-jewellery. Exquisite saris are unfolded for scrutiny in silk emporia; the finest quality comes from Kanchi and is delicately embroidered with gold and silver thread. Saris of this distinction can add as much as Rs30,000 to the cost of a wedding.

A little further west, before you come to TTK Rd, the **Luz Church**, on Luz Church Rd, is thought to be the earliest Christian building in Chennai, built by the Portuguese in the sixteenth century. Its founding is associated with a miracle: Portuguese sailors in difficulties at sea were once guided to land and safety by a light which, when they tried to find its source, disappeared. The church, dedicated to Our Lady of Light, was erected where the light left them.

Little Mount

St Thomas, who Indians believed first brought Christianity to the subcontinent in the first century AD, is said to have sought refuge from persecution in a group of caves on the **Little Mount**, 8km south of the city centre (bus #18 from Anna Salai), now 200m off the road between the Maraimalai Adigal Bridge and the Residence of the Governor of Tamil Nadu. Entrance to the caves is beside steps leading to a statue of Our Lady of Good Health. Inside, next to a small natural window in the rock, are impressions of what are believed to be St Thomas's handprints, made when he made his escape through this tiny opening.

Behind the new circular church of Our Lady of Good Health, together with brightly painted replicas of the Pietà and Holy Sepulchre, is a natural **spring**. Tradition has it that this was created when Thomas struck the rock, so the crowds that came to hear him preach could quench their thirst; samples of its holy water are on sale.

St Thomas Mount

Tradition has it that St Thomas was speared to death (or struck by a hunter's stray arrow), while praying before a stone cross on **St Thomas Mount**, 11km south of the city centre, close to the airport (take a suburban train to Guindy train station, and walk from there). **Our Lady of Expectation Church** (1523) is reached by 134 granite steps marked at intervals with the fourteen stations of the Cross. At the top of the steps, a huge old banyan tree provides shade for devotees who come to fast, pray and sing. Inside the church, St Thomas's cross is said to have bled in 1558; above the altar which marks the spot of the apostle's death, a painting of the Madonna and Child is credited to St Luke. A memento stall stands nearby and cool drinks are available in the adjacent Holy Apostle's Convent.

The Theosophical Society Headquarters

The **Theosophical Society** (buses #23C or #5 from George Town/Anna Salai) was established in New York in 1875 by American Civil War veteran Colonel Henry S.

Olcott, a failed farmer and journalist, and the eccentric Russian aristocrat Madame Helena Petrovna Blavatsky, who claimed occult powers and telepathic links with "Mahatmas" in Tibet. Based on a fundamental belief in the equality and truth of all religions, the society in fact propagated a modern form of Hinduism, praising all things

THE RELUCTANT GURU

For a spiritual organization based on principles of inclusiveness and harmony, the Theosophical Society has suffered some acrimonious schisms over the years, particularly after the deaths of its founders Olcott and Blavatsky, when its most prominent personalities clashed in an unseemly power struggle. The most infamous rift of all, though, was one between the Society's mandarins and the young man they identified in 1905 as the "Buddha to Be".

Jiddu Krishnamurti, a Telegu-speaking *brahmin* boy brought to Adyar by his father after his mother died, was first "discovered" in 1911 by Charles Webster Leadbeater, a leading light in the Theosophical Society who claimed clairvoyant powers. Among the central tenets of the movement was a belief that Lord Krishna and Christ were about to be reborn as a "World Teacher", and from the moment Leadbeater saw the ten-year-old Krishnamurti playing football on the beach at Adyar he knew he'd found the "Enlightened One". Jiddu, however, did not initially look the part. Wild, malnourished and sickly, with "crooked teeth . . . and a vacant, almost moronic expression", he seemed more like a street kid than a messiah in the making.

Informed that the "Vehicle" had been identified, **Annie Besant** – the then President of the Theosophical Society – was quick to take the boy under her wing. Over the coming years, Krishnamurti, with the support of the TS and its benefactors, was to receive the best education that money could buy, with places at famous colleges in England and California. Spiritual instruction, meanwhile, came from Leadbeater's own guru, a mystical Buddhist lama who lived in a remote Tibetan ravine and delivered his teachings on the "astral plane".

Not surprisingly, Krishnamurti's father resented Besant's adoption of his son and initiated custody proceedings to prevent the TS from taking him abroad. The High Court of Madras found in Krishnamurti senior's favour, but its decision was overturned after Besant took the case to London (in spite of allegations of "unnatural practices" levelled against Leadbeater). By the time the legal battle had run its course, however, Krishnamurti was legally an adult and already teaching. He'd also matured into an exceedingly handsome, suave young man, with a trademark sweep of jet black hair and a taste for fashionable clothes.

While his teachings were being received with growing enthusiasm, both within India and the US, the fledgling guru was showing definite signs of resenting the role thrust upon him by the Theosophists. Soon, this found expression in criticism of the ritual, mysticism and self-aggrandizing "wise-men" that had become features of the Society's new leadership, some of whom then began to turn against their charismatic detractor, claiming he had been "possessed by black forces". The conflict came to a head when Krishnamurti, addressing a Theosophy camp in the US, formally renounced his position as head for the OSE (Order of the Star in the East), originally formed to promote his teachings. He resigned from the TS soon afterwards, with the famous pronouncement that "Truth is a pathless land . . . you cannot approach it by any path whatsoever, by any religion, by any sect".

For the rest of his life, Krishnamurti – or K as he preferred to be known — wandered the world as a individual, lecturing, writing and setting up educational institutions where young people could, as he said, "flower as human beings, without fear, without confusion, with great integrity". When he died in 1986, aged ninety-one, he was one of the most famous philosophers of his generation, but always resisted the label of guru; "mediators . . .", he said, "must inevitably step down the Truth, and hence betray it."

Indian and shunning Christian missionaries – so its two founders were greeted enthusiastically when they transferred their operations to Madras in 1882, establishing their headquarters near Elliot's Beach in Adyar. Even after Madame Blavatsky's psychic powers were proved to be bogus, the society continued to attract Hindus and Western visitors, and its buildings still stand today, sheltering several shrines and an excellent **library** of books on religion and philosophy (Mon–Sat 8.30–10am & 2–4pm). The collection, begun by Olcott in 1886, comprises 165,000 volumes and nearly 200,000 palm-leaf manuscripts, from all over the world, a selection of which is housed in an exhibition room on the ground floor. This includes eight hundred-year-old scroll pictures of the Buddha, a seventeenth-century treatise on embalming bodies from London, rare Tibetan xylagraphs written on bark paper, exquisite illuminated Korans, a giant copy of Martin Luther's *Biblia* printed in Nuremburg three hundred years ago and a Bible in seven languages that's the size of a thumb nail.

The 270 acres of woodland and gardens surrounding the Society's headquarters are a serene place to sit and restore spirits, away from the noise and heat of the city streets. In the middle of the grounds, a vast four-hundred-year-old **banyan tree**, said to be the second largest in the world, provides shade for up to three thousand people at a time. J Krishnamurthi and Maria Montessori have both given talks under its tangle of pillar-like root stems, whose growth Theosophists see as symbolizing the spread of the Society itself.

The Enfield factory

India's most stylish homemade motorcycle, the **Enfield Bullet**, is manufactured at a plant on the outskirts of Chennai, 18km north of Anna Salai (bus #1 from LIC Building or Parry's Corner). With its elegant tear-drop tank and thumping 350cc single-cylinder engine, the Bullet has become a contemporary classic — in spite of its propensity to leak oil and break down with a frequency unknown in the industry since Enfields were made in England. Bike enthusiasts should definitely brave the long haul across town to see the **factory**, which is as much a period piece as the machines it turns out. Guided tours (Mon–Fri 9.30am–5.30pm; ☎044/543 3000), which last around one and a half hours and are free, have to be arranged in advance by telephoning the Enfield's Marketing General Manager, Mr K. Muralidharan. You can do this yourself, or through the tourist office on Anna Salai.

Guindy National Park

South of Elliot Beach Rd, not far from Guindy train station, the peaceful **Guindy National Park** is home to a healthy community of **black buck**, **chital** (spotted deer), mongooses and monkeys. However, it's rather neglected, and many visitors leave disappointed, without spotting any animals. One section is fenced off as a **Snake Park** (daily 9am–5.30pm; Rs2; camera Rs5; video Rs100), but its reptilian residents are neither unusual nor plentiful. Dotted along the north side of the park are three large memorials to Kamaraj, Gandhi and Rajaji.

MGR Film City

The only one of Chennai's movie studios that actively encourages visitors is **MGR Film City** (daily 8am–8pm; Rs25, plus Rs50 for still camera permits), on the southern outskirts near Guindy National Park. You can travel to and from Film City by **bus** (#1 from the LIC Building on Anna Salai, #5C from Parry's Corner, or #23C from Egmore Station), and plenty of auto-rickshaws hang around outside the main gates. A sprawling campus of decaying film sets, it offers little of interest for foreign visitors unless there happens to be an outdoor shoot in progress. At other times, action is confined to a small amusement park, and a group of disused sets dominated by a giant concrete shark's mouth, where bus parties of posing local tourists take advantage of the site's best photo opportunity. Inexpensive meals and cold drinks are available at the busy crew canteen, next to the crossroads in the middle of the campus.

Accommodation

Finding a **place to stay** in Chennai can be a problem, as hotels are often full. Demand has pushed prices up, so only a couple of places offer anything for less than Rs100. Standards in the less expensive places are not high; in contrast Chennai's topnotch hotels are truly palatial.

OF MOVIE STARS AND MINISTERS

Bollywood may be better known, but the film studios of Chennai churn out more movies than any other city in the world – on average, around 900 each year. Featuring the usual Indian *masala* mix of fast action, wide-eyed melodrama, romance (without kisses), punch-ups, shoot-outs and, of course, pelvic-grinding song and dance sequences with as many costume changes as camera angles, they cater for the largely illiterate rural population of Tamil Nadu, although the biggest blockbusters also get dubbed into Hindi and exported north.

One notable difference between the Chennai movie industry and its counterpart in Mumbai (see p.108) is the influence of politics on Tamil films – an overlap that dates from the earliest days of regional cinema, when stories, stock themes and characters were derived from traditional folk ballads about low-caste heroes vanquishing high-caste villains. Already familiar to millions, such Robin Hood-style stereotypes were perfect propaganda vehicles for the nascent Tamil nationalist movement, the Dravida Munnetra Kazhagam, or **DMK**. It is no coincidence that the party's founding father, **C.N. Annadurai**, was a top screenplay and script writer. Like prominent Tamil Congress leaders and movie-makers of the 1930s and 1940s, he and his colleagues used both popular film genres of the time – "mythologicals" (movie versions of the Hindu epics) and "socials" (dramas set around caste conflicts) – to convey their political ideas to the masses. Audiences were actively encouraged by party workers to boo the villains and cheer each time the proletarian hero, or DMK icons and colours (red and black), appeared on the screen. From this tradition were born the fan clubs, or *rasigar manrams*, that played such a key role in mobilizing support for the nationalist parties in elections.

The most influential fan club of all time was the one set up to support the superstar actor Marudur Gopalamenon Ramchandran, known to millions simply as "**MGR**". By carefully cultivating a political image which mirrored the folk-hero roles he played in films, the maverick matinee idol generated fanatical grass-roots support in the state, especially among women, and rose to become chief minister in 1977. His eleven-year rule is still regarded by liberals as a dark age in the state's history (chronic corruption, police brutality, political purges and rising organized crime were all rife during the period), but even the fact that his bungled economic policies penalized precisely the rural poor who voted for him never dented MGR's mass appeal. When he suffered a paralytic stroke in October 1984, twenty-two people cut off limbs, toes and fingers as offerings to pray for his recovery, while more than a hundred followers attempted to burn themselves to death. For the next three years he was barely able to speak, let alone govern effectively, yet the party faithful and fan club members still did not lose faith in his leadership. His funeral in 1987 was attended by two million mourners, more than followed Mahatma Gandhi's cortege in 1948, and 31 grief-stricken devotees committed ritual suicide. Even today, MGR's statue, sporting trademark sunglasses and lamb's-wool hat, is revered at tens of thousands of wayside shrines across Tamil Nadu.

The main concentration of mid-range and inexpensive hotels is in **Egmore**, around the train station. Head for the ones listed below first; if they're full, a bit of hunting around should turn up a reasonable fallback. Other popular areas include **Anna Salai**, which tends to be more expensive, and **Triplicane**, a largely Muslim area boasting some of the city's best budget guesthouses (among them *Broadlands*). The bulk of the top hotels are in the south of the city, along Nunggambakam, Dr Radha Krishnan Salai and Cathedral roads; several offer courtesy buses to and from the airport. Note that if you're arriving late at night, it pays to book a room well in advance (most of the places listed below accept telephone reservations). Finding a room, particularly one in a reasonably priced mid-range place, in the small hours of the morning after a long flight or train ride can be an ordeal.

Due to frequent shortages, visitors should use **water** as sparingly as possible.

MGR's political protégé, and eventual successor, was a teenage screen starlet called **Jayalalitha**, a convent-educated daughter of a *brahmin*, whom he spotted at a school dance and, despite an age difference of more than thirty years, recruited to be both his leading lady and mistress. The couple would star opposite each other in 25 hit films, and when MGR eventually moved into politics, Jayalalitha followed him, becoming leader of the **AIADMK** (the party MGR set up after being expelled from the DMK in 1972) after a much publicized power struggle with his widow. Larger than life in voluminous silver ponchos and heavy gold jewellery, the now portly *Puratchi Thalavi* ("Revolutionary Leader") took her personality cult to extremes brazen even by Indian standards. On her forty-sixth birthday in 1994, Rs50,000 of public money was spent on giant cardboard cut-outs depicting her in academic and religious robes, while 46 of her more fervent admirers rolled bare-chested along the length of Anna Salai. Jayalalitha's spell as chief minister, however, was brought to an ignominious end at the 1996 elections, after allegations of fraud and corruption on an appropriately monumental scale.

The intermingling of Tamil politics and cinema is now so established in the state that it's almost inconceivable for anyone to attain high office without some kind of movie credentials. Distinguished among Chennai's huge roadside hoardings by his MGR-style shades and yellow shawl, the current chief minister, Mr **M. Karunanidhi**, is another former screenwriter, while the wavy-haired megastar of the 1980s, **Rajnikanth**, ended years of speculation recently when he threw his lot in with Congress (I) party. As a type-cast villain rather than eternal do-gooder, his screen image differs wildly from MGR's (one commentator recently wrote that "Rajnikanth has 'drunk and raped' his way to superstardom"), but if he manages, as expected, to galvanize his fan club, the complexion of Tamil politics could be totally transformed for the first time in decades.

Working as an extra

You can rub shoulders with today's Tamil movie stars by appearing as an extra in a film at one of the studios on the outskirts of Chennai. Scouts regularly trawl the tourist spots downtown (notably the *Maharaja Restaurant* around the corner from *Broadlands Hotel* in Triplicane; see p.387) for foreigners to spice up crowd and party scenes. People with long blond hair stand a better chance of getting picked, but being in the right place at the right time is more important. If you're really keen, though, do the rounds of the studios yourself. The biggest are: MGR Film City, down in Adyar near Guindy National Park (see p.381; ☎044/235 2132); AVM, on the western outskirts at 35 NS Krishnan (Arcot) Rd, Vadapalani (☎044/493 6700); and nearby Prasad (☎044/483 3715) and Vijaya (☎044/483 8787). If someone does approach you with an offer of work as a movie extra, be sure to check their credentials (scouts always carry laminated cards from the studio with their photos on; you can also ask to see their business card), and the conditions of the job (Rs300 per day, meals and transport to and from your hotel are standard). For obvious reasons, it's also advisable to refuse any work offered to one person only, especially if you're female.

Egmore

Chandra Towers, 9 Gandhi Irwin Rd (☎044/823 3344, fax 825 1703). The station district's plushest hotel has all the comforts you'd expect, including central a/c, foreign exchange and a rooftop restaurant. ⑧.

Dayal De Lodge, 486 Pantheon Rd (☎044/825 1725). Old-fashioned town house set back from the main road. No frills, but clean enough, and quiet except during periodic siren blasts from the rifle range opposite. It's a 10min walk from the station, so jump in an auto if you're weighed down. ③.

Impala Continental, 12 Gandhi Irwin Rd (☎044/825 0484). Run-of-the-mill lodge with impersonal but clean en-suite rooms. Good value, so often full. ③–⑤.

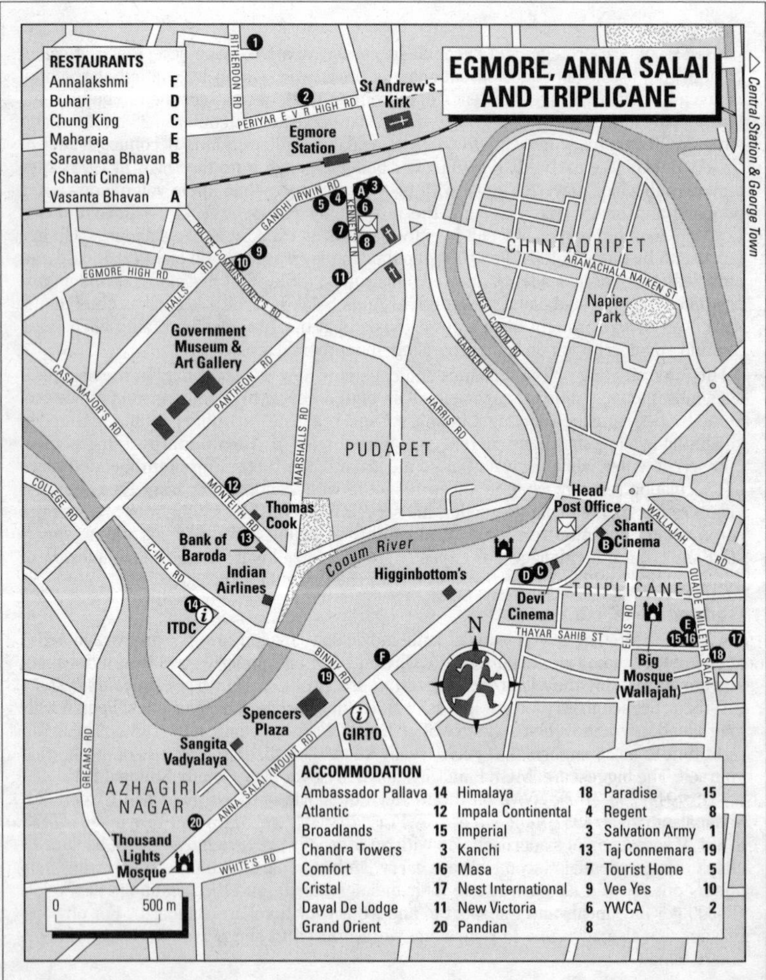

Imperial, 6 Gandhi Irwin Rd (☎044/825 0376). Large, efficient hotel set in its own enclosed courtyard, but sorely in need of a facelift. Assorted rooms include a/c suites. Restaurant, bar and travel services. ⑤–⑥.

Masa, 15/1 Kennet's Lane(☎044/825 2966). Variously priced rooms in a very clean, modern building, close to the station. Polite staff; good value. ④–⑤.

Nest International, 31 Gandhi Irwin Rd (☎044/828 0113, fax 824 0599). Upscale, business-orientated place that's the smartest option in the area after the *Chandra Towers*. Ethnic cotton-print decor and most mod cons. ⑦.

New Victoria, 3 Kennet's Lane (☎044/825 3638). Newish hotel and upscale for the area; all rooms a/c with hot shower and some with balconies. ⑦–⑧.

Pandian, 9 Kennet's Lane (☎044/825 2901, fax 825 8459). Pleasant, clean and modern mid-scale place within walking distance of Egmore station. Ask for a room on the Church Park side of the building for green views. Some a/c. ⑥.

Regent, 8 Kennet's Lane (☎044/825 3347). Quiet, respectable lodge with slightly grubbier rooms than you'd expect at this price, but spotless bathrooms. Fine for a night. ④.

Salvation Army Red Shield Guest House, 15 Ritherdon Rd (☎044/532 1821). Tucked away in a leafy suburban backstreet behind the station, this old-established Sally Army place has six- to eleven-bed dorms (Rs50), three plain doubles (Rs200), and very helpful, friendly management. A very dependable shoestring option. ①–③.

Southern Railway Retiring Rooms, First Floor, Egmore Station (turn right out of the main exit). Dorm beds for Rs40, and spacious, if run down, doubles (some "Deluxe a/c"), presided over by a stern matron in a regulation blue sari. The latter are excellent value, so they tend to fill up quickly. ①–④.

Tourist Home, 21 Gandhi Irwin Rd (☎044/825 0079). Deservedly popular hotel directly opposite the train station: fresher and better ventilated than many. Rooms (some a/c) with showers, telephones, clean sheets and towels. Good value and often full. ④–⑤.

Vee Yes, 35 Gandhi Irwin Rd (☎044/825 7801). Average small hotel, a 5min walk from the station; badly ventilated but clean enough. Carpeted, a/c rooms with hot showers. ③–⑤.

YWCA International Guest House, 1086 Periyar EVR High Rd (☎044/532 4234, fax 532 4263). Attractive hotel in quiet gardens behind Egmore station. Spotless, spacious rooms, safe deposit and a good restaurant. One of the best-value places in the city, so book ahead. ⑤–⑥.

Anna Salai and Triplicane

Ambassador Pallava, 53 Montieth Rd (☎044/855 4476, fax 855 4482). Colossal, opulent four-star, close to Anna Salai, with great views from its upper storeys, and all the facilities of an international five-star, including pool and health club. Rooms start at US$117 (Rs4500). ⑨.

Atlantic, 2 Montieth Rd (☎044/855 3914, fax 855 3239). Huge block hotel near the government museum that's a favourite with Tamil movie directors (who often use the "Deluxe" rooms as sets). The regular rooms are on the dowdy side, but large, with balconies and views. ⑥.

Broadlands, 16 Vallabha Agraham St, off Quaide Milleth Salai (☎044/854 5573). A whitewashed old house, which has all crumbling stucco and stained glass features, ranged around a leafy courtyard; the kind of budget travellers' enclave you either love or loathe. It has a large roof terrace and clean rooms, a few with shower, balcony and views of the mosque. Inexpensive left luggage facility is available, but a reprehensible "No Indians" policy. ④.

Comfort, 22 Vallabha Agraham St (☎044/858 7661). Don't be fooled by the deceptively shiny marble exterior. This place should be avoided: grotty rooms and vastly inflated prices. ⑤.

Cristal, 34 CNK Rd, off Quaide Milleth Salai (☎044/858 5605). Immaculately tiled en-suite rooms in a modern building. A relative newcomer, and if standards are maintained, easily the best budget deal in the district, although lacking the old-world character of Broadlands. ②–③.

Grand Orient, 693 Anna Salai (☎044/852 4111, fax 852 3412). Very swish, recently refurbished place on the main drag, with modern decor, central a/c and a multi-cuisine restaurant. ⑧.

Himalaya, 54 Quaide Milleth Salai (☎044/854 7522). Clean, spacious rooms and efficient service. TV, table and chair, hot shower and balcony in all rooms; some a/c. ⑤.

Kanchi, 28 C-in-C Rd (☎044/827 1100, fax 827 2928). Very good-value skyscraper hotel with superb views from its spacious non- and a/c rooms, two restaurants (one rooftop) and bar. ⑥.

Paradise, 17/1 Vallabha Agraham St, Triplicane (☎044/854 1542). Next door to Broadlands, and a dependable choice if you're after an inexpensive room with an attached shower-toilet. Clean and central. ②–③

Taj Connemara, Binny Rd (☎044/852 0123; fax 852 3361). Dating from the British era, this white-washed Art Deco five-star hotel, is situated near Anna Salai but is a world away from the traffic. It's a Chennai institution, patronized by the city's high society, visiting diplomats and international cricket teams. The best rooms are the big, characterful old ones, with dressing room and a verandah overlooking the pool. ⑨.

Outside the centre

Karpakam, 19 South Mada St, Mylapore (☎044/494 2987). Very ordinary mid-scale place whose only outstanding feature is its location overlooking the Kapalishvara temple; it's also on the right side of the city for the airport, 12km away. ⑤.

Maris, 9 Cathedral Rd (☎044/827 0541, fax 825 4847). Spruce, efficient 1970s concrete block hotel right next to the Sheraton, but a fraction of the price. At Rs750, their a/c rooms are a particularly good deal for the area. ⑥.

New Woodlands Hotel, 72–75 Dr Radha Krishnan Salai Rd(☎044/827 3111). Clean, spacious rooms with hot showers. Forex desk, billiards room and pool. ⑥.

Ranjith, 9 Nungambakkam High Rd (☎044/827 0521). Spotless en-suite rooms (some a/c) with satellite TV. Veg and non-veg restaurants, bar and travel agent. ⑥.

Savera, 69 Dr Radha Krishnan Salai Rd (☎044/827 4700, fax 827 3475). Slightly older than the competition, but boasting all mod-cons, including a pool, bar and rooftop restaurant with great views. ⑧.

Shelter, 19–21 Venkatesa Agraharam St, Mylapore (☎044/4995 1919, fax 493 5646). Spanking new, centrally air-conditioned luxury hotel that's a stone's throw from the Kapalishvara temple, and better value than most upscale places at this price. ⑧.

Sornam International, 7 Stringer St (☎044/535 3060). The best of a generally ropy bunch around the Central Station. Clean and respectable enough, but only worth considering if you can't face an auto ride across town. Vegetarian only. ④.

Trident, 1/24 GST Rd (☎044/234 4747, fax 234 6699). Comfortable five-star hotel in lovely gardens with swimming pool. Near the airport (3km), but long (albeit complimentary) drive into town (12km). Good restaurants, one of which serves Thai cuisine. ⑨.

Welcomgroup Chola Sheraton, Cathedral Rd (☎044/044/828 0101, fax 827 8779). Palatial five-star in the city centre, with all the trimmings, and a hefty US$190 per night room tariff. ⑨.

Welcomgroup Park Sheraton, 132 TTK Rd (☎044/499 4101, fax 499 7101). Last word in American-style executive luxury, with bow-tied valets and in-room fax machines. Three excellent restaurants, 24hr coffee shop and other five-star facilities. The best choice for business travellers. ⑨.

Eating

Compared with Delhi and Mumbai, Chennai suffers from a surprising dearth of quality **places to eat**. This may in part be because its indigenous fast-food restaurants and "meals" (*thalis*) joints, in particular the legendary *Saravanaa* chain, serve superb South Indian food for a fraction of the cost of a coffee at one of the five-stars. That said, a minor splurge at *Annalakshmi* on Anna Salai or the *Park Sheraton* on TTK Rd is well worth considering, while Raj-ophiles shouldn't miss high tea at the *Verandah* in the *Taj Connemara*.

Amaravati, corner of Cathedral/TKK Rd. One among a complex of four good regional speciality restaurants, south of the downtown area. This one does excellent Andhran food, including particularly tasty *biryanis*.

Annalakshmi, 804 Anna Salai (☎044/855 0296). Topnotch Indian vegetarian cuisine served in appropriately sumptuous, a/c surroundings on Chennai's main drag. Profits go to organizations sponsored by the Rishikesh-based guru Shivanjali, and is served by his devotees, whose mothers do the cooking. Extremely popular with the city's affluent set, so book ahead. Most main dishes around Rs200, with a Rs100 per person cover charge.

Buhari, 83 Anna Salai. Idiosyncratic 1950s-style dining hall overlooking the main street. For some reason, Russian chicken dishes are the house speciality ("à la Moscow, Kiev or Leningrad"), but they also offer a full *tandoori* menu, cold beers and freshly baked cakes.

Chung King, Anna Salai, down an alley next to Buhari. Genuine cuisine prepared by pukka Chinese chef.

Copper Chimney, 74 Cathedral Rd (☎044/827 5770). Franchise of the famous Mumbai restaurant. Quality tandoori cuisine, opulent decor and a/c comfort. The meat-eater's equivalent of Annalakshmi. Count on Rs200–250 per head.

Geetham, Kanchi hotel, 28 C-in-C Rd. Circular glass-sided restaurant on rooftop of nine-storey tower block. The multi-cuisine menu is surprisingly inexpensive, and the views superb. Open 11am–noon & 7–10pm only.

Hot Breads, opposite Hotel Maris, Cathedral Rd. Wholewheat breads, baguettes, fresh quiches and an impressive range of cakes, biscuits and pastries. Decent espresso coffee, too. Eat in or take away.

Maharajah, 307 Quaide Milleth Salai. Simple vegetarian restaurant, popular with budget travellers staying at Broadlands, around the corner. Excellent-value set meals and a good range of cheap and filling snacks (try their great *uttapams* or huge paper *dosas*); also ice-creams, *lassis* and good coffee. Open till midnight.

Saravanaa Bhavan, Thanigai Murugan Rathinavel Hall, 77 Usman Rd, T Nagar. This famous South Indian fast food chain is an institution among the Chennai middle class, with branches opposite the bus stand in George Town, and in the forecourt of the Shanti cinema (at the top of Anna Salai). Try their delicious *rawa idlys*, rounded off with a cup of *badam* milk, bubbling with pistachios and cardamom in large vats outside.

Señor Pepés, First Floor, above Hot Breads, Cathedral Rd. Swish new a/c Tex-Mex joint, serving a predictable menu of fajitas, enchiladas, tortillas, burritos etc, and so-so pasta dishes (dubbed "Euro-Mex"). Main courses Rs90–130.

Taj Connemara, Binny Rd. The ideal venue for a posh Sunday morning breakfast: crisp newspapers and fresh coffee served in silver pots. The blow-out lunch-time buffets (Rs400) are also recommended, and they serve Chennai's best à la carte Italian food in the evening (also around Rs400 per head). Even if you can't afford a meal here, drop in for afternoon tea, when Mr Andrews, resident pianist for almost as long as the hotel's been open, tinkles evocative colonial-era tunes in the corner.

Vasanta Bhavan, 20 Gandhi Irwin Rd. Easily the best "meals" joint among many around Egmore station, with ranks of attentive waiters and delicious pure veg food. It's busy, spotlessly clean and cheap, and their coffee's delicious.

Welcomgroup Chola Sheraton, 10 Cathedral Rd (☎044/828 0101). Upmarket hotel with two good restaurants; the *Peshawari* serves lavish (and expensive) northwestern frontier food, while the excellent rooftop *Sagari* specializes in Chinese dishes.

Welcomgroup Park Sheraton, 132 TTK Rd (☎044/499 4101, fax 499 7101). More – extremely good – upmarket hotel restaurants. The *Residency* serves Indian, Western and Chinese, the *Khyber* is a meaty poolside barbecue, but best of all is the *Dakshin*, one of the country's top South Indian restaurants. It offers an excellent choice of unusual dishes from the four southern states, including seafood in marinated spices, Karnataka mutton *biryani* and piping-hot *idlyappam* and *appam* made on the spot. There is live Carnatic music and costs around Rs500 per head, with beer.

Woodlands Drive-In, *New Woodlands Hotel*, 72–75 Dr Radha Krishnan Salai Rd (☎044/827 3111). Pure veg tiffin joint, in garden setting, popular with young people on scooters and families in cars. Transport, however, is not compulsory. Best for breakfast.

Listings

Bookstores Higginbothams on Anna Salai is Chennai's oldest bookshop, with a vast assortment of titles at rupee rates. Its main competitor, Bookpoint, at 160 Anna Salai, has a more up-to-date selection of fiction, and handy free publicity newsletters with reviews of the latest Indian releases. Serious bookworms, however, head for the hole-in-the-wall Giggles, in the *Taj Connemara Hotel,* where, stacked in precariously high piles, you'll find a matchless stock of novels, academic tomes on the region and coffee-table books. Unlike other bookstores in the city, this one will take credit cards and post purchases abroad for you at nominal charges. Giggles & Scribbles, Wellingdon Estate, 24 C-in-C Rd (Mon–Sat 9.30am–7.30pm) is a larger branch, set back 50m from the road, selling rare reprints of historical books on India and Indian music cassettes, and with an efficient mail-order system. Karnatic Music Book Centre, 14 Sripuram First St, Royapettah, is an excellent bookshop for Carnatic classical music and Indian dance fanatics, with mail-order service. Finally, the Theosophical Society's bookshop (Mon–Fri 8–11am & 2–5pm, Sat 8–11am & 2–4pm), at the entrance to the campus in Adyar, is the best place in Chennai to pick up literature on yoga, meditation and religion.

Cinemas such as the *Abhirami* and *Lakshmi* along Anna Salai show English-language films, but for the full-on Tamil film experience, take in a show at the *Shanti*, off the top of Anna Salai, which boasts the city's biggest screen and a digital stereo sound system. Nearby, the equally massive *Devi* hosts the latest Bollywood blockbusters.

Consulates Canadian, 3rd Floor Dhun Bldg, 827 Anna Salai, (☎044/852 9828); French, Kothari Building, 114 Nungambakkam High Rd (☎044/472131); German, 22 C-in-C Rd (☎044/827 1747; 9am–noon); Indonesian, 5 North Leith Castle Rd, San Thome (☎044/245 1095); Dutch, 738 Anna Salai (☎044/811566); Norwegian, Royal Parry House, 43 Moore St (☎044/517950; 10am–5pm); Sri Lankan, 9-D Nawab Habibullah Rd (☎044/827 0831); Swedish, 6 Cathedral Rd (☎044/827 5792; 9.30am–1pm); UK, 24 Anderson Rd, Nungambakkam (☎044/827 3136); USA, 220 Anna Salai (☎044/827 3040; Mon–Fri 8am–5.15pm).

Cultural institutions Alliance Française, 3/4-A College Rd, Nungabakkam (☎044/827 2650); British Council, 737 Anna Salai (☎044/826 9402; Mon–Fri 10am–5pm); Max Mueller Bhavan, 13 Khadar Nawaz Khan Rd (☎044/826 1314).

Hospitals The best-equipped private hospital in Chennai is the Apollo, 21/22 Greams Rd (☎044/827 7447). For an ambulance, try ☎102, but it's usually quicker to jump in a taxi.

Left luggage Counters at Egmore and Central train stations store bags for Rs2–4 per day; they usually require proof of train-booking. Some hotels also guard luggage at a daily rate.

Music stores Musee Musical, 67 Anna Salai (☎044/849380), stocks sitars, percussion, flutes and the usual shoddy selection of Hoffner/Gibson-copy guitars. For the best range of concert quality Indian instruments, including *vinas*, check out Saptaswara Music Store, on Raipetha Rd, Mylapore (☎044/499 3274). Music World, on the first floor of Spencer Plaza, has the best selection of audio cassettes and CDs in the city.

Opticians Eye tests, glasses and contact lenses are available at Lawrence and Mayo, 68 Anna Salai.

Pharmacy Lalitha's Medical and General Store, 11 Gandhi Irwin Rd; Spencer & Co, Spencer Plaza, Anna Salai (Mon–Sat 8am–7pm; ☎044/826 3611).

Photographic equipment Dozens of stores around town offer film and developing services on modern machines, but the only Kodak-approved Q-Lab in the city (recommended for transparency processing) is Image Park, GEE Plaza, 1 Craft Rd, Numgambakkam (☎044/827 6383). Reliance Opticals, at 136 Anna Salai stocks Fuji Provia and Sensia II. For camera repair, your best bet is Camera Crafts, 325/8A Quaide Milleth High Rd, Triplicane, near the *Broadlands Hotel*. Delhi Photo Stores, in an arcade directly behind the big Konica shop on Wallajah Rd, is crammed with spare parts and other useful Indian-made bits and bobs.

Tax clearance To get a tax clearance certificate (see Basics, pp.11-12) take exchange documents and passport to 121 Uttamar Gandhi Rd, and allow for 3–4hr of tedious form-filling.

Travel agents Reliable travel agents include American Express, G-17 Spencer Plaza, 768/769 Anna Salai (☎044/852 3592); Diana World Travels, 45 Monteith Rd (☎044/826 1716); PL Worldways, G-11 Ground Floor, Spencer Plaza (☎044/852 1192); Surya Travels, F-14 First Floor,

THE CHENNAI FESTIVAL AND THE SABHAS

The **sabhas** of Chennai – the city's arts societies and venues, of which the most illustrious is the Chennai Music Academy – stage regular public performances of Carnatic classical music and Bharatanatyam dance, where ambitious artists have to undergo the scrutiny of an often fanatical audience and a less-than-generous bevy of newspaper critics, whose reviews can make or break a career.

Musicians are expected to interpret correctly the subtleties of any given composition, *raga* or *tala*. The sets of notes that make up a *raga* occupy a place midway between melody and scale; they must be played imaginatively in improvisation, but in strict sequences and with correct emphasis. The worst crime, the sign of an amateur, is to slip accidentally into a different *raga* that might share the same scale. *Tala*, the rhythmic cycle and bedrock of the music, will often be demonstrated by someone on stage, and consists of a series of claps and waves; unlike in North India, this element is overt in the South and the audience delights in clapping along to keep the often-complex time signatures. The pleasure is heightened during percussion improvisations on the barrel-shaped *mridangam* drum or *ghatam* clay pot that accompany many performances.

During the second half of December and early January, the two- to three-week **Chennai Festival** stages up to five hundred events in an orgy of classical music and dance recitals, in which many of India's greatest artistes – from both North and South – can be seen at work.

Female vocalists to look out for include M.S. Subbulakshmi, Mani Krishnaswamy, Charumathi Ramachandran, Sudha Raghunathan and Bombay Jayashree; duos such as the Bombay and Hyderabad Sisters are also popular. Top-ranking **male singers**, K.V. Narayanaswamy, Thanjavur M. Thiagarajan, B. Rajam Iyer and younger artists like Thrissur Ramachandran and T.N. Seshagopalan should not be missed. Among the best of the **instrumentalists** are Balachandar, Kalyana Krishna Bhavatar, E. Gayatri and Rama Varma on the gentle melodic *vina*, a stringed instrument unique to the South; Ramani on flute; violinists such as T.N. Krishnan, D. Ananda Raman; and N. Ravikiran on *gottuvadyam*, a rare member of the *vina* family, laid flat on the floor and played much like a slide guitar. Carnatic music's answer to John Coltrane is Kadri Gopalnath, whose soaring saxophone and flamboyant dress have made him one of the most distinctive figures on the circuit. Former child prodigy, U. Sriniwas, is the electric mandolin maestro. Cassettes and CDs of all the above artistes are available at Music World in Spencer Plaza. For addresses of good musical instrument shops in the city, see "Listings" opposite.

The predominant **dance** style is Bharatanatyam, as performed by stars such as Alarmail Valli, and the Dhananjayans. Dance dramas are also staged by the *Kalakshetra Academy*, a school of dance and music set in a beautiful hundred-acre compound near the sea in Tiruvanmiyur, on the southern outskirts of the city.

Outside the festival, to find out about **performances of music and dance**, ask at the government tourist office on Anna Salai, or consult the listings pages of local papers such as the *Hindu*. You may also like to pay a visit to the **Sangita Vadyalaya**, behind the HDF Bank on Anna Salai (Mon–Fri 9.15am–5.45pm), which displays an impressive array of Indian musical instruments. The centre, recently shifted to this new ground-floor building in the centre of town, was set up to preserve and restore antique pieces, but resident artisans also revive rare instruments which are no longer commonly played. You can try your hand at a few of them yourself, and experiment with an amazing horde of old percussion pieces.

Spencer Plaza (☎044/855 0285); Thomas Cook, Chebroos Centre, Monteith Rd, Egmore (☎044/827 3092).

Yoga Chennai may seem like an insalubrious place to study yoga, but some of South India's most renowned schools are based here. The following offer short courses: Adyar Yoga Research Institute, 15 III Main Rd, Kasturba Nagar, Adyar, near the Theosophical Society Headquarters;

Bharatiya Vidya Bhavan, East Mada Street, Mylapore; Prof T. Krishnamacharya's Yoga Mandiram, 103 St Mary's Rd (☎044/499 7602).

Onwards from Chennai

Transport connections between Chennai and the rest of India are summarized on p.392. If you're short of time, consider employing one of the **travel agents** on p.388 to book your plane, train or bus ticket for you. This doesn't apply to boat tickets for the Andaman Islands, which have to be booked in person.

By plane

Chennai's domestic airport stands adjacent to the international terminal, 16km southwest of the centre at **Meenambakkam**. The easiest way to get there is by taxi or autorickshaw, but if you're not too weighed down with luggage you can save money by jumping on a suburban train to **Trisulam station**, 500m from the airport.

Indian Airlines flies from Meenambakkam to 21 destinations around the country. In addition, Jet Airways operates services to Bangalore, Coimbatore, Delhi, Hyderabad, Mumbai, Pune and Thiruvananthapuram, Sahara flies daily to Delhi and Air India has domestic departures for Mumbai and Delhi. A full summary of flights appears on p.498.

AIRLINE OFFICES IN CHENNAI

Airline offices (most Mon–Fri 10am–5am, Sat 10am–1pm) include:

Air India, 19 Marshalls Rd (☎044/855 4477, airport ☎044/234 7400)

Air France, Thaper House, 43–44 Monteith Rd (☎044/855 4899)

Air Lanka, Nagabrahma Towers, 76 Cathedral Rd (☎044/826 1535)

British Airways, Khaleeli Centre, Monteith Rd (☎044/855 4680)

Gulf Air, 52 Montieth Rd (☎044/855 3091)

Indian Airlines, 19 Marshalls Rd (open round the clock, but for bookings daily 8am–5pm; ☎044/855 3039, fax 855 5208)

Jet Airlines, Thaper House, 43–44 Monteith Rd (☎044/855 5353)

Lufthansa, 167 Anna Salai (☎044/852 5095); KLM, *Hotel Connemara*, Binny Rd (☎044/852 0123)

Malaysia Airlines, Karumuttu Centre, 498 Anna Salai (☎044/434 9632)

Qantas, Eldorado Building, 112 Nungambakkam High Rd (☎044/827 8680)

Sahara, Lokesh Towers, 18 Kodambakkam High Rd (☎044/828 3180)

Singapore Airlines, 108 Dr Radhakrishnan Salai (☎044/852 2871)

Swissair, 191 Anna Salai (☎044/852 2541)

Thai International, GSA, Malavikas Centre, 144 Kodambakkam High Rd, Nugambakkam (☎044/822 6149).

For **American**, **Air Canada**, **Biman**, **Philippine**, **Royal Jordanian** and **TWA**, contact **Jetair**, Apex Plaza, 3 MG Rd (☎044/826 2409).

By boat

Boats leave Chennai every week to ten days for **Port Blair**, capital of the **Andaman Islands**. However, getting a ticket and the relevant permit can be a rigmarole, compounded by the absence of a regular schedule. The first thing you'll need to do is head up to the Chennai Port Trust, next to the Directorate of Shipping on Rajaji (North

Beach) Rd, George Town, where a small hut houses the Andaman Administration Office. A chalk board on the wall advertises details of the next sailing, but before you buy a ticket (from the hatch around the corner, at the front of the main building), you'll need to take a form from here to the Foreigners' Registration Office (Mon–Fri 9.30am–5pm), a twenty-minute auto-rickshaw ride southwest across town on Haddow's Rd (between the UK High Commission and French Consulate). Hand your form and photos in before lunch and you should be able to pick up the permit later that same day. When you've got it, you can return to the Port Trust to buy your ticket.

The three- to four-day crossing gets mixed reviews from travellers. Conditions, especially in the rock-bottom bunk-class (Rs1000), can be hot and squalid, so go for the most expensive ticket you can afford. Cabins fares (per bed) range from Rs2250 for B-Class (four- to six-berth), to Rs2900 for A-Class (two-berth), or Rs3500 for Deluxe two berth. Meals are available on board, but they're very basic, so take along a good supply of fresh fruit, nuts and biscuits.

By bus

Most long-distance **buses** leave from the **Thiruvallur,** aka **Express Bus Stand**, on Esplanade Rd, near Parry's Corner, George Town. It's a well-organized place with a computerized **reservations** hall on the first floor (7am–9pm; ☎044/534 1835–6) where you can make advance bookings for all State Express Transport Corporation (SETC) services, as well as interstate buses to neighbouring Andhra, Kerala and Karnataka. A full run-down of these, giving frequency and journey times, appears in Travel Details on p.498.

If you're heading to Mamallapuram, Pondicherry or Chidambaram via the fast new coastal highway, you'll have to jump on an unreserved bus from the much more chaotic **Broadway Bus Stand**, on the opposite side of Prakasam Rd. Lacking platforms or signs in English, this place is total anarchy – a nightmare of pot holes and high-beam air horns. Foreigners are dragged through the melee by gangs of rapacious slum kids who grab your sleeve when you arrive and, for a few rupees, will tug you towards your bus.

The fastest services to **Mamallampuram** are #188, #188A and anything marked "East Coast Express" (every 30min; less than 2hr); #19A, #19C, #119 and #119A take a little longer; #108B (via the airport and Chengalpattu) takes at least 3hr, and is only convenient if you're travelling direct to Mamallapuram from the airport.

In theory, you can pick up most buses at Parry's Corner, Anna Salai and Adyar, but the struggle to hail the right one, get through the crowds and find a seat is best avoided.

By train

Trains to Tiruchirapalli (Trichy), Thanjavur, Pudukottai, Rameshwaram, Kodaikanal Rd, Madurai, and most other destinations in south Tamil Nadu leave from **Egmore Station**. Many of these services, however, have been disrupted over the past couple of years by upgrading work being carried out on the line between Trichy and Dindigul (the stop before Kodaikanal Rd), so check departure times carefully when you book. All other trains leave from **Central**. Left of the main building, on the first floor of the Moore Market Complex, the efficient **tourist reservation counter** (Mon–Sat 8am–8pm, Sun 8am–2pm) sells tickets for trains from either station. The booking office at Egmore, up the stairs left of the main entrance (same hours), also handles bookings for both stations, but has no tourist counter. If you're arriving in Chennai by plane, note that Southern Railways also has a reservation counter (daily 10am–5pm) outside the domestic terminal at the airport.

RECOMMENDED TRAINS FROM CHENNAI

Destination	Name	Number	From	Departs	Total time
Bangalore	*Shatabdi Exp**	#2007	Central	6am**	4hr 45min
	Bangalore Mail	#6007	Central	10.10pm	7hr 15min
Bhubaneshwar	*Coromandel Exp*	#2843	Central	9.05am	20hr 10min
	Howrah Mail	#6004	Central	10.30pm	23hr 45min
Calcutta	*Coromandel Exp*	#2842	Central	9.05am	28hr 15min
	Howrah Mail	#6004	Central	10.30pm	32hr 25min
Coimbatore	*Shatabdi Exp**	#2023	Central	3.10pm	6hr 50min
	Kovai Exp	#2675	Central	6.15am	7hr 35min
Delhi	*Tamil Nadu Exp*	#2621	Central	10pm	33hr
	Grand Trunk Exp	#2615	Central	11pm	36hr 45min
Hyderabad	*Charminar Exp*	#2759	Central	6.10pm	14hr 15min
Kochi/Ernakulam	*Alleppey Exp*	#6041	Central	7.35pm	13hr
	Trivandrum Mail	#6319	Central	6.55pm	12hr
	Kodaikanal Pandyan Exp	#6717	Egmore	7.30pm	10hr
Kanyakumari	*Kanyakumari Exp*	#6721	Central	1pm	17hr 15min
Madurai	*Madurai Exp*	#6717	Egmore	7.30pm	11hr 20min
Mettuppalayam (for **Ooty**)	*Nilgiri Exp*	#6605	Central	8.15pm	12hr 15min
Mumbai	*Mumbai Exp*	#6012	Central	11.45am	27hr 20min
	Chennai Exp	#1064	Central	6.40am	24hr 15min
Mysore	*Shatabdi Exp**	#2007	Central	6am**	4hr 45min
	Mysore Exp	#6222	Central	10.30pm	11hr 20min
Rameshwaram	*Sethu Exp*	#6701	Egmore	8.25pm	18hr 10min
Thanjavur	*Cholan Exp*	#6153	Egmore	8am	9hr 15min
	Sethu Exp	#6701	Egmore	8.25pm	9hr 30min
Tirupathi	*Saptagiri Exp*	#6057	Central	6.25am	3hr
Thiruvananthapuram	*Trivandrum Mail*	#6319	Egmore	6.55pm	17hr
Varanasi	*Ganga Kaveri Exp***	#6039	Central	5.30pm	38hr 30min

*a/c only
**Mon & Sat only

CHAPTER SIX

TAMIL NADU

When Indians refer to "the South", it's usually **TAMIL NADU** they're talking about. While Karnataka and Andhra Pradesh are essentially cultural transition zones buffering the Hindi-speaking north, and Kerala and Goa maintain their own distinctively syncretic identities, the peninsula's Tamil-speaking state is India's Dravidian Hindu heartland. Traditionally protected by distance and the military might of the southern Deccan kingdoms, the region has, over the centuries, been less exposed to northern influences than its neighbours. As a result, the three powerful dynasties dominating the South – the Cholas, the Pallavas and the Pandyans – were able, over a period of more than a thousand years, to develop their own unique religious and political institutions, largely unmolested by marauding Muslims. The most visible legacy of this protracted cultural flowering is a crop of astounding temples, whose gigantic gateway towers, or *gopuras*, still soar above just about every town large enough to merit a train station. It is the image of these colossal wedge-shaped pyramids, presiding over canopies of dense palm forest, or against patchworks of vibrant green paddy fields, which Edward Lear described as "stupendous and beyond belief", and which linger longest in the memory of most modern travellers.

The great Tamil temples are merely the largest landmarks in a vast network of **sacred sites** – shrines, bathing places, holy trees, rocks and rivers – interconnected by a web of ancient pilgrims' routes. Tamil Nadu harbours 274 of India's holiest Shiva temples, and 108 others which are dedicated to Vishnu; in addition, five shrines devoted to the five Vedic elements (earth, wind, fire, water and ether) are to be found here, along with eight to the planets, as well as other places revered by Christians and Muslims. Scattered from the pale orange crags and forests of the Western Ghats, across the fertile deltas of the **Vagai** and **Kaveri** rivers to the Coromandel Coast on the Bay of Bengal, these sites were celebrated in the hymns of the Tamil saints, between one and two thousand years ago. It is an extraordinary fact that the same songs are still widely sung and understood today in the region, little changed since they were first composed.

The Tamils' living connection with their ancient Dravidian past has given rise to a strong **nationalist movement**. With a few fleeting lapses, one or other of the pro-Dravidian parties has been in power here since the 1950s, spreading their anti-Brahmin, anti-Hindi proletarian message to the masses principally through the medium of movies. Indeed, since Independence, the majority of Tamil Nadu's political leaders have been drawn from the state's prolific **cinema** industry. Indians from elsewhere in the country love to caricature their southern cousins as "reactionary rice growers" led

ACCOMMODATION PRICE CODES

All **accommodation prices** in this book have been coded using the symbols below. The prices given are for a double room, except in the case of categories ① and ② where the price can refer to dorm accommodation per bed. All taxes are included. For more details, see p.34.

① up to Rs100	④ Rs300–400	⑦ Rs900–1500
② Rs100–200	⑤ Rs400–600	⑧ Rs1500–2500
③ Rs200–300	⑥ Rs600–900	⑨ Rs2500 and upwards

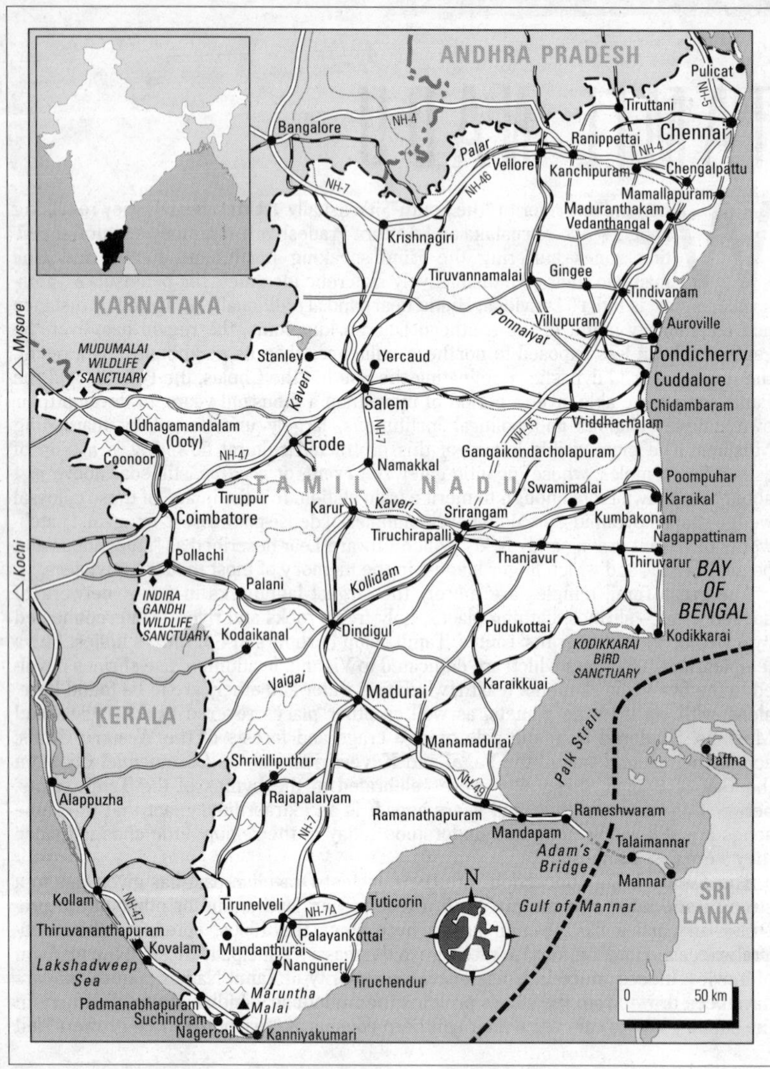

by "fanatical film stars". While such stereotypes should be taken with a pinch of salt, it is undeniable that the Tamil way of life, which has evolved along an unbroken path since prehistoric times, sets it apart from the rest of the subcontinent. This remains, after all, one of the last, if not the only, places in the world where a Classical culture has survived into the present – "India's Holy Land", described by Marco Polo as "the most splendid province in the world".

Where to go

Despite its seafront fort, grand mansions and excellence as a centre for the performing arts, the state capital **Chennai** (formerly **Madras**) – large enough to warrant a separate chapter in this guide – is probably its least appealing destination; a scruffy, dusty, noisy city with faint echoes of the Raj. Much the best place to start a **temple tour** is nearby **Mamallapuram**, a seaside village that, quite apart from some exquisite Pallava rock-cut architecture (fifth–ninth centuries), boasts a long stretch of beach. Inland, the pilgrimage city of **Kanchipuram** is filled with reminders of an illustrious past under successive dynastic rulers, while further down the coast is one of India's rare French colonial possessions, **Pondicherry**, where Auroville has found a new role as a "New Age" focal point. The road south from Pondicherry puts you back on the temple trail, leading to the tenth-century **Chola kingdom** and the extraordinary architecture of **Chidambaram**, **Gangaikondacholapuram**, **Kumbakonam** and **Darasuram**. For the best Chola bronzes, however, and a glimpse of the magnificent paintings that flourished under Maratha rajas in the eighteenth century, travellers should head for **Thanjavur**. Chola capital for four centuries, the city boasts almost a hundred temples and was the birthplace of **Bharatanatyam** dance, famous throughout India.

In the very centre of Tamil Nadu, **Tiruchirapalli**, a commercial town just northwest of Thanjavur, held some interest for the Cholas, but reached its heyday under later dynasties, when the temple complex in neighbouring **Srirangam** became one of South India's largest. Among its patrons were the Nayaks of **Madurai**, whose erstwhile capital further south, bustling with pilgrims, priests, peddlers, tailors and tourists, is an unforgettable destination.

Rameshwaram, on the long spit of land reaching towards Sri Lanka, and **Kanniyakumari**, at India's southern tip (the auspicious meeting point of the Bay of Bengal, the Indian Ocean and the Arabian Sea) are both important pilgrimage centres, with the added attraction of welcome cool breezes and vistas over the sea.

While Tamil Nadu's temples are undeniably its major attraction, it would take months to see them all, and there are plenty of other distractions for even the most ardent architecture buff. In the west of the state, where the hill stations of **Kodaikanal** and **Ootacamund (Ooty)** are the premier attractions, verdant hills offer mountain views, and a network of trails winds through forests and tea and coffee plantations. **Mudumalai Wildlife Sanctuary**, a vast spread of deciduous forest dominated by teak, offers a relaxing stopover on the route to or from Mysore, even though its protected forest area, like that of Tamil Nadu's other major national park, closer to Kodaikanal in the Palani hills, the **Anamalai sanctuary**, has been closed to visitors for a couple of years. To get close to any real wildlife, you'll have to head for the coast, where areas of wetland provide perfect resting places for migratory birds, whose numbers soar during the winter monsoon at **Vedanthangal**, near Chennai, and **Point Calimere**.

Temperatures in Tamil Nadu, which usually hover around 30°C, peak in May and June when they often soar above 40°, and the overpowering heat makes all but sitting in a shaded café exhausting. The state is barely affected by the southwest monsoon that pounds much of India from June to September: it receives most of its **rain** between October and January. Cooler, rainy days bring their own problems; widescale flooding can disrupt road and rail links and imbue everything with an all-pervasive dampness.

Accommodation prospects are good; all but the smallest towns and villages have something for every budget. Most hotels have their own dining halls which, together with local restaurants, sometimes serve sumptuous *thalis*, tinged with tamarind and presented on banana leaves. **Indigenous dishes** are almost exclusively vegetarian; for North Indian or Western alternatives, head for the larger hotels or more upmarket city restaurants.

Some history

Since the fourth millennium BC, Tamil Nadu has been shaped by its majority **Dravidian** population, of uncertain origins and physically quite different from North Indians. Their language developed separately, as did their social organization; the difference between high-caste *brahmins* and low-caste workers has always been more pronounced here than in the north – caste divisions that continue to dominate the state's political life. The influence of the powerful *janapadas*, established in the north by the fourth and third centuries BC, extended as far south as the Deccan, but they made few incursions into **Dravidadesa** (Tamil country). Incorporating what are now Kerala and Tamil Nadu, it was ruled by three dynasties: the **Cheras**, who held sway over much of the Malabar Coast (Kerala), the **Pandyas** in the far south, and the **Cholas**, whose realm stretched along the Coromandel Coast in the east. Indo-Roman trade in spices, precious stones and metals flourished at the start of the Christian era, when **St Thomas** arrived in the South, but dwindled when trade links began with southeast Asia.

The prosperity of the early kingdoms having faded by the fourth century AD, the way was clear for the **Pallavas**, who emerged in the sixth century as leaders of a kingdom centred around **Kanchipuram**. By the seventh century the successors of the first Pallava king, Simhavishnu, were engaged in battles with the southern Pandyas and the forces of the Chalukyas, based further west in Karnataka. However, the centuries of Pallava dominion are not marked simply by battles and territorial expansion; this was also an era of social development. **Brahmins** became the dominant community, responsible for lands and riches donated to temples. The emergence of *bhakti*, devotional worship, placed temples firmly at the centre of religious life (see p.585), and the inspirational *sangam* literature of poet-saints fostered a tradition of dance and music that has become Tamil Nadu's cultural hallmark.

The **Vijayanagars**, who gained a firm footing in Hampi (Karnataka) in the fourteenth century, resisted Muslim incursions from the north and spread to cover most of South India by the sixteenth century, heralding a new phase of architectural development by building new temples, expanding older ones and introducing colossal *gopuras*, or gateway towers. In Madurai Vijayanagar governors, Nayaks, set up an independent kingdom whose impact spread as far as Tiruchirapalli. For a short period (1740–48) the Marathas, a strong force further north, took power in Madurai, Thanjavur and Tiruchirapalli, but they made little impact on the South's development.

Much more significant was the arrival of **Europeans**. First came the Portuguese, who landed in Kerala and monopolized Indian trade for about a century before they were joined by the British, Dutch and French. Though mostly on cordial terms with the Indians, the Western powers soon found themselves engaged in territorial disputes. The most marked were between the French, based in **Pondicherry**, and the British, whose stronghold since 1640 had been Fort St George in **Madras**. After battles at sea and on land, the French were confined to Pondicherry, while British ambitions reached their apex in the eighteenth century, when the East India Company occupied Bengal (1757) and consolidated its bases in Bombay and Madras.

As well as rebellions against colonial rule, Tamil Nadu also saw anti-*brahmin* protests, in particular those led by the Justice Party in the 1920s and 1930s. Independence in 1947 signalled the need to reorganize state boundaries, and by 1956 areas had been demarcated on a linguistic basis. Andhra Pradesh and Kerala were formed, along with Mysore state (later Karnataka) and **Madras Presidency**, a slightly smaller area than that governed from Madras by the British, where Tamil was the predominant language. In 1965 Madras Presidency became Tamil Nadu, the latter part of its name coming from the Chola agrarian administrative units known as *nadus*.

Since Independence, Tamil Nadu's industrial sector has mushroomed. Initially the state was led by Congress, but in 1967 the **DMK** (Dravida Munnetra Kazhagam), championing the lower castes and reasserting Tamil identity, won a landslide victory. Anti-

Hindi and anti-centre, the DMK flourished until the film star **"MGR"** (M.G. Ramachandran) broke away to form the **All India Anna Dravida Munnetra Kazhagam** (AIADMK) and won an easy victory in the 1977 elections. Virtually deified by his fans-turned-supporters, MGR remained successful until his death in 1988, when the Tamil government fell back into the hands of the DMK. Soon afterwards, the AIADMK was reinstated, led by **Sri Jayalalitha Jayaram**, an ex-film star and dancer once on close terms with MGR (see box on p.383). In 1996, the AIADMK, in alliance with Congress, was routed conclusively by the DMK, and Jayalalitha, increasingly plagued by corruption scandals, lost her seat.

THE NORTHEAST

Phased by the fierce heat and air pollution of the capital, Chennai (Madras), most visitors escape as fast as they can, heading down the Coromandel Coast to India's stone-carving capital, **Mamallapuram**, whose ancient monuments include the famous Shore temple and a batch of extraordinary rock sculpture. En route, it's well worth jumping off the bus at the artists' village of **Cholamandal**, just beyond the city limits, and at **Dakshina Chitra**, a superb new folk museum 30km south of Chennai, where traditional buildings from across South India have been beautifully reconstructed. Further inland, **Kanchipuram** is an important pilgrimage and silk-sari-weaving town. From Kanchipuram you can loop west towards the Andhran border, taking in the fourteenth-century fort at **Vellore** on the way to **Tiruvannamalai**, a wonderfully atmospheric temple town clustered at the base of the sacred mountain, Arunachala. The sprawling ruins of **Gingee** stand midway between here are the coast, where you can breakfast on baguettes and espresso coffee in the former French colony of **Pondicherry**. A short way north, **Auroville**, the utopian settlement founded by followers of the Shri Aurobindo Ghose's spiritual successor, "The Mother", provides a New Age foil to the hedonistic ways of its neighbour.

Both Mamallapuram and Pondicherry are well connected to Chennai by nail-bitingly fast bus services, running along a smooth new coastal highway that was recently completed with World Bank funding. You can also get to Pondy by train, but this involves a change at the junction town of **Villupuram**, from where services are slow and relatively infrequent.

Mamallapuram (Mahabalipuram)

Scattered around the base of a colossal mound of boulders on the Bay of Bengal, **MAMALLAPURAM** (aka Mahabalipuram), 58km south of Chennai, is dominated less by the sea, as you might expect, than by the smooth volcanic rocks surrounding it. From dawn till dusk, the rhythms of chisels chipping granite resound through its sandy lanes – evidence of a stone-carving tradition that has endured since this was a major port of the Pallava dynasty, between the fifth and ninth centuries. Little is known about life in the ancient city, and it is only possible to speculate about the purpose of much of the boulder sculpture, which includes one of India's most photographed monuments, the **Shore Temple**. It does appear, however, that the friezes and shrines were not made for worship at all, but rather as a showcase for the talents of local artists. Due in no small part to the maritime activities of the Pallavas, their style of art and architecture had wide-ranging influence, spreading from South India as far north as Ellora, as well as to southeast Asia. This international cultural importance was recognized in 1995 when Mamallapuram was granted World Heritage Site status by UNESCO.

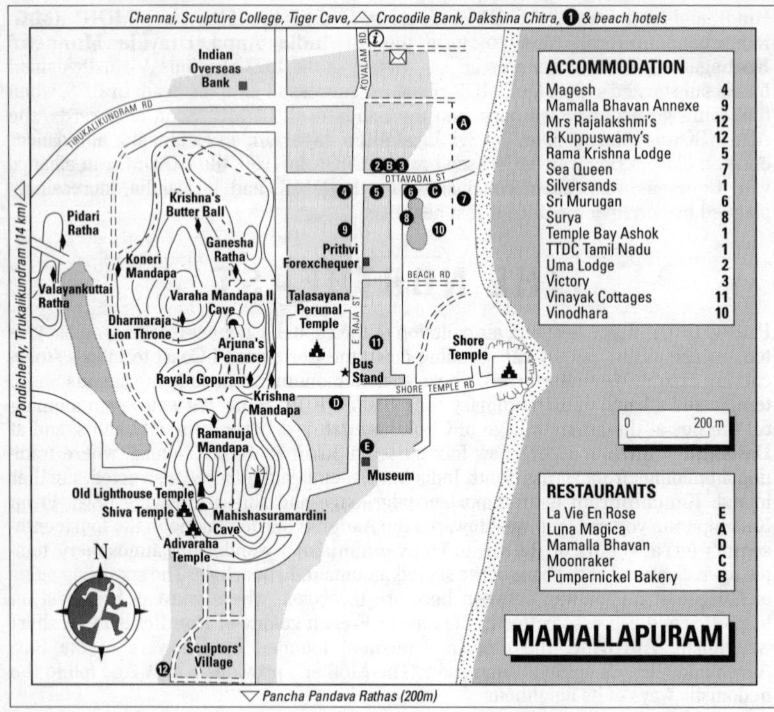

Given the coexistence of so many stunning archeological remains with a long white-sand **beach**, it was inevitable this would become a major travellers' hangout. Over the past two decades, however, mass tourism has made a real mess of Mamallapuram. Piles of plastic rubbish, persistent postcard and trinket sellers and the sheer volume of visitors, especially on weekends, can sour the experience of the monuments, while the beach itself, trawled by hawkers and used as a public toilet, is certainly no place to swim and sunbathe. Even the Shore temple, now protected from the salt spray by a wall of fir trees and stone blocks, is a shadow of the exotic spectacle it used to be when the waves lapped its base. That said, the atmosphere generated by the stone-carvers' workshops and ancient rock-art backdrop is unique in India, and worth at least a couple of days if you're heading to or from Chennai (many people actually prefer to stay here and travel into the city for the day to book tickets or pick up mail).

Arrival and information

Numerous daily **buses** ply to and from **Chennai**, along three different routes. The most direct is via Kovalam (aka Covelong), on the recently upgraded coastal highway; aim for a #188/#188A (every 30min) or an *East Coast Express* (hourly), which stops en route to Pondicherry and takes a little under two hours. Buses #19c and #115 run via Thirupperur, and take around half an hour longer, but the slowest is #108b, which takes three hours to get here via Chengalpattu/Chennai airport – only worth considering if you're arriving by plane. In addition, Mamallapuram is served by about a dozen buses to **Kanchipuram** (2hr 30min), and nine express buses run south to **Pondicherry** (#188a/b/d/k, or the faster *East Coast Express*; 2hr). The **bus stand** is in the centre of the village.

The nearest **train station**, at Chengalpattu (Chingleput), 29km northeast on the bus route to Kanchipuram, is on the main north–south line, but not really a convenient access point. A **taxi** from Chennai costs around Rs500 (or Rs450 from the airport); bookable through the tourist office and the pre-paid taxi booth at Chennai airport.

The **Government of Tamil Nadu Tourist Office** (Mon–Sat 9.45am–5.45pm; ☎04133/42232) is one of the first buildings you see in the village; on your left as you arrive from Chennai, it's a good place to find out about local festivals, and it keeps a comprehensive list of bus times posted.

Unless you're staying at one of the upscale hotels, there are only two official places to **change money** in the village: the Indian Overseas Bank, on TK Kunda (Tirukalikundram) Rd, or the more efficient Prithvi Forexchequer, 55 E Raja St, (☎04133/42875).

Getting around

Mamallapuram itself is little more than a few sandy roads. By far the best way to get to the important sites, if you're up to it, is by **bicycle**, which you can rent from shops on E Raja St (Kovalam Rd), opposite the entrance to the *Temple Bay Ashok Beach Resort*, or MK Cycle Centre, 28 Ottavadai St, for around Rs20 per day. **Scooters** and Enfield **motorcycles** are also available for Rs150–300 a day, from Poornima Travels, next to *Moonraker* restaurant, or Metro Tours, 137 E Raja St (☎04133/42456).

The Monuments

Mamallapuram's monuments divide into four categories: open-air **bas-reliefs**, structured **temples**, man-made **caves** and **rathas** ("chariots", carved in situ from single boulders, to resemble temples or the chariots used in temple processions). The famous bas-reliefs, **Arjuna's Penance** and the **Krishna Mandapa**, adorn massive rocks near the centre of the village, while the beautiful **Shore temple** presides over the beach-front. Sixteen man-made caves, in different stages of completion, are scattered through the area, but the most complete of the nine *rathas* are in a group, named after the five Pandava brothers of the *Mahabharata*.

The Krishna Mandapa and Arjuna's Penance

A little to the west of the village centre, the enormous bas-relief known as the **Krishna Mandapa** shows Krishna raising Mount Govardhana aloft in one hand. The sculptor's original intention must have been for the rock above Krishna to represent the mountain, but the seventeenth-century Vijayanagar addition of a columned *mandapa* (or entrance hall), prevents a clear view of the carving. Krishna is also depicted seated milking a cow and standing playing the flute. Other figures are *gopas* and *gopis*, the cowboys and girls of his pastoral youth. Lions sit to the left, one with a human face, and above them a bull.

Another bas-relief, **Arjuna's Penance** – also referred to as the "Descent of the Ganges" – is a few metres north, opposite the modern Talasayana Perumal temple. The surface of this rock erupts with detailed carving, most notably the endearing and naturalistic renditions of animals. A family of elephants dominates the right side, with tiny offspring asleep beneath a great tusker. Further still to the right, separate from the great rock, is a free-standing sculpture of an adult monkey grooming its young.

On the left-hand side, Arjuna, one of the Pandava brothers and a consummate archer, is shown standing on one leg. He is looking at the midday sun through a prism formed by his hands, meditating on Shiva, who is nearby represented by a statue, fashioned by Arjuna himself. The *Shiva Purana* tells that Arjuna made the journey to a forest on the banks of the Ganges to do penance, in the hope that Shiva would part with his favourite weapon, the *pashupatashastra*, a magic staff or arrow. Shiva eventually materialized in the guise of Kirata, a wild forest-dweller, and picked a fight with Arjuna over a boar they both claimed to have shot. Arjuna only realized he was dealing with the deity after his attempts to drub the wild man proved futile; narrowly escaping death at the playful hand of Shiva, he was finally rewarded with the weapon. Not far away, mimicking Arjuna's devout pose, an emaciated (presumably ascetic) cat stands on its hind legs, surrounded by mice.

To the right of Arjuna, a natural cleft represents the **Ganges**, complete with *nagas* – water spirits in the form of cobras. Near the bottom, a fault in the rock that broke a *naga* received a quick-fix of cement in the 1920s. Evidence of a cistern and channels remain at the top, which at one time must have carried water to flow down the cleft, simulating the great river. It's not known if there was some ritual purpose to all this, or whether it was simply an elaborate spectacle to impress visitors. You may see sudden movements among the carved animals: lazing goats often join the permanent features.

A little way north of Arjuna's Penance, precipitously balanced on the top of a ridge, is a massive, natural, almost spherical boulder called **Krishna's Butter Ball**. Picnickers and goats often rest in its perilous-looking shade.

Ganesha Ratha and Varaha cave

Just north of Arjuna's Penance a path leads west to a single monolith, the **Ganesha Ratha**. Its image of Ganesh dates from this century; some say it was installed at the instigation of England's King George V. An interesting sculpture at one end, of a protecting demon with a tricorn headdress, is reminiscent of the Indus Valley civilization's 4000-year-old horned figure known as the "proto-Shiva".

Behind Arjuna's Penance, southwest of the Ganesha Ratha, is the **Varaha Mandapa II cave**, whose entrance hall has two pillars with horned lion bases and a cell flanked by two *dvarpalas* (guardians). One of four **panels** shows the boar incarnation of Vishnu, who stands with one foot resting on the *naga* snake-king as he lifts a diminutive Prithvi – the earth – from the primordial ocean. Another is of Gajalakshmi, the goddess Lakshmi seated on a lotus being bathed by a pair of elephants. Trivikrama, the dwarf *brahmin* who becomes huge and bestrides the world in three steps to defeat the demon king Bali, is shown in another panel, and finally a four-armed Durga is depicted in another.

For more background on the temples of Tamil Nadu, see Contexts, p.585.

The Shore temple

East of the village, a distinctive silhouette above the crashing ocean, Mamallapuram's **Shore temple** dates from the early eighth century and is considered to be the earliest stone-built temple in South India. The design of its two finely carved towers was profoundly influential as it was exported across South India and eventually to southeast Asia; today, due to the combined forces of wind, salt and sand, much of the detailed carving has eroded, giving the whole a soft, rounded appearance.

The taller of the towers is raised above a cell that faces out to sea – don't be surprised to see mischievous monkeys crouching inside. Approached from the west through two low-walled enclosures lined with small Nandi (bull) figures, the temple comprises two

HANS GEORGE ROTH / CORBIS

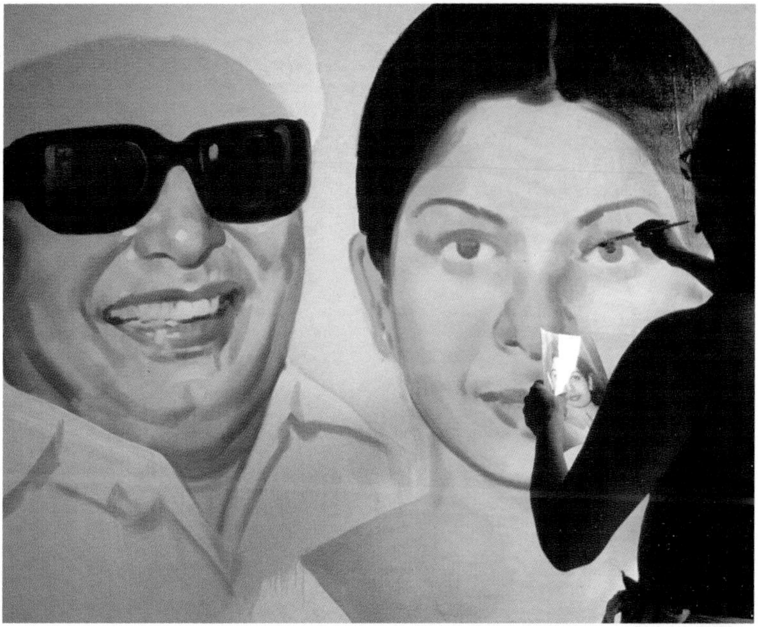

Film poster, Chennai (TN)

ROBERT HOLMES / CORBIS

Fort St George, Chennai (TN)

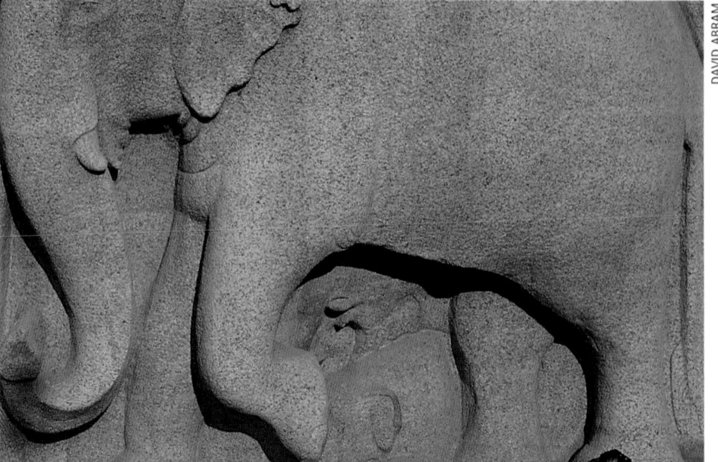
DAVID ABRAM

Goats relaxing at Arjuna's Penance, Mamallapuram (TN)

STEVE DAVEY / LA BELLE AURORE

Charminar, Hyderabad (AP)

SIMON REDDY / TRAVEL INK

Carved wood deities, Madurai (TN)

R. A. ACHARYA /IMAGES OF INDIA, DPA

Nilgiri Blue Mountain Railway, Ooty (TN)

ASHVIN MEHTA / IMAGES OF INDIA, DPA

Temple detail, Mamallapuram (TN)

STEVE DAVEY / LA BELLE AURORE

Elephant procession (Ker)

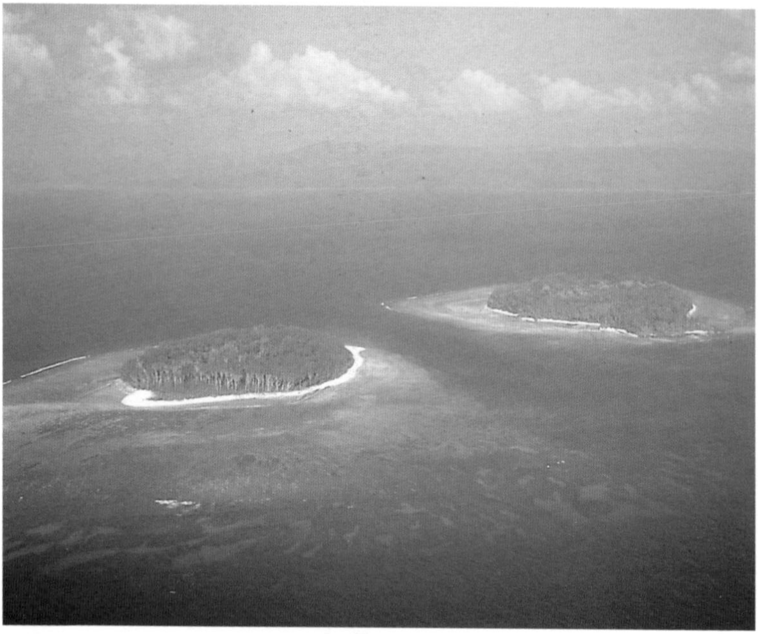

ASHVIN MEHTA / IMAGES OF INDIA

Andaman Islands

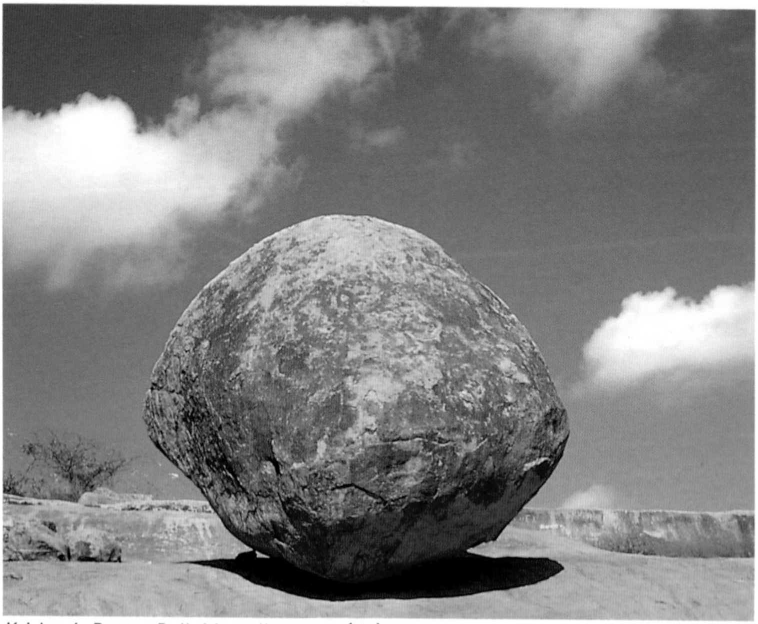

Krishna's Butter Ball, Mamallapuram (TN)

lingam shrines (one facing east, the other west), and a third shrine between them housing an image of the reclining Vishnu. Recent excavations, revealing a tank containing a structured stone column thought to have been a lantern, and a large Varaha (boar incarnation of Vishnu) aligned with the Vishnu shrine, suggest that the area was sacred long before the Pallavas chose it as a temple site.

The Lighthouses and the Mahishasuramardini cave

At the highest point in an area of steep paths, unfinished temples, ruins, scampering monkeys and massive rocks, south of Arjuna's Penance, the **New Lighthouse** affords fine views east to the Shore Temple, and west across paddy fields and flat lands littered with rocks. Next to it, the **Olakanesvara** ("flame-eyed" Shiva), or **Old Lighthouse temple**, used as a lighthouse until the beginning of the twentieth century, dates from the Rajasimha period (674–800 AD) and contains no image.

Nestling between the two lighthouses is the **Mahishasuramardini cave**, whose central image portrays Shiva and Parvati with the child Murugan seated on Parvati's lap. Shiva's right foot rests on the back of the bull Nandi, and Parvati sits casually, leaning on her left hand. On the left wall, beyond an empty cell, a panel depicts Vishnu reclining on the serpent, his attitude of repose contrasted with the weapon-brandishing demons, Madhu and Kaithaba. Other figures seek Vishnu's permission to chase them.

Opposite, in one of the most celebrated sculptures in Indian art, a carved panel shows the eight-armed goddess **Durga** as Mahishasuramardini, the "crusher" of the buffalo demon **Mahishasura**. The story goes that Mahishasura became so powerful that he took possession of heaven, causing great misery to its inhabitants. To deal with such a dangerous foe, Vishnu and Shiva hit upon the idea of combining all the gods' powers into a single entity. This done, fiery jets appeared, from which emerged the terrifying "mother of the universe", Durga. In the ensuing battle, Durga caught Mahishasura with a noose, and he changed into a lion; she beheaded the lion, and he transformed into a human wielding a sword; she fired off a flight of arrows, only to see him turn into a huge trumpeting elephant; and she cut off his trunk, whereupon the buffalo returned. Now furious, Durga partook of her favourite beverage – blood, "the supreme wine". Climbing on top of the buffalo, she kicked him about the neck and stabbed him with her trident. The impact of her foot forced him halfway out of his own mouth, only to be beheaded by his own sword, at which point he fell. The panel shows Durga riding a lion, in the midst of the struggle. Accompanied by dwarf *ganas*, she wields a bow and other weapons; Mahishasura equipped with a club, can be seen to the right, in flight with fellow demons.

The tiny **Archaeological Survey of India Museum** (daily 9am–1pm & 2–5pm; free) on W Raja St, near the lighthouse, has a collection of Pallava sculpture found in and around Mamallapuram.

Pancha Pandava Rathas

In a sandy compound 1.5km south of the village centre stands the stunning group of monoliths known for no historical reason as the **Pancha Pandava Rathas**, the five chariots of the Pandavas. Dating from the period of Narasimhavarman I (*c*.630–70 AD), and consisting of five separate free-standing sculptures that imitate structured temples plus some beautifully carved life-size animals; they were carved either from a single gigantic sloping boulder or from as many as three distinct rocks.

The "architecture" of the *rathas* reflects the variety of styles employed in temple building of the time, and stands almost as a model for much subsequent development in the **Dravida**, or southern, style. The Arjuna, Bhima and Dharmaraja *rathas* show strong affinities with the Dravidian temples at Pattadakal in Karnataka. Carving was always executed from top to bottom, enabling the artists to work on the upper parts with no fear of damaging anything below. Any unfinished elements there may be are always in the lower areas.

Intriguingly, it is thought that the *rathas* were never used for worship. A Hindu temple is only complete when the essential pot-shaped finial, the *kalasha*, is put in place – which would have presented a physical impossibility for the artisans, as the *kalasha* would have had to have been sculpted first. *Kalashas* can be seen next to two of the *rathas* (Dharmaraja and Arjuna), but as part of the base, as if they were perhaps to be put in place at a later date.

The southernmost and tallest of the *rathas*, named after the eldest of the Pandavas, is the pyramidal **Dharmaraja**. Set on a square base, the upper part comprises a series of diminishing storeys, each with a row of pavilions. Four corner blocks, each with two panels and standing figures, are broken up by two pillars and pilasters supported by squatting lions. Figures on the panels include Ardhanarishvara (Shiva and female consort in one figure), Brahma, the king Narasimhavarman I and Harihara (Shiva and Vishnu combined). The central tier includes sculptures of Shiva Gangadhara, holding a rosary with the adoring river goddess Ganga by his side and one of the earliest representations in Tamil Nadu of the dancing Shiva, Nataraja, who became all-important in the region. Alongside, the **Bhima** *ratha*, the largest of the group, is the least complete, with tooling marks all over its surface. Devoid of carved figures, the upper storeys, as in the Dharmaraja, feature false windows and repeated pavilion-shaped ornamentation. Its oblong base is very rare for a shrine.

The Arjuna and Draupadi *rathas* share a base. Behind the **Arjuna,** the most complete of the entire group and very similar to the Dharmaraja, stands a superb unfinished sculpture of Shiva's bull Nandi. **Draupadi** is unique in terms of rock-cut architecture, with a roof that appears to be based on a straw thatched hut (a design later copied at Chidambaram; see p.427). There's an image of Durga inside, but the figure of her lion vehicle outside is aligned side-on and not facing the image, a convincing reason to suppose this was not a real temple. To the west, close to a life-size carving of an elephant, the *ratha* named after the twin brothers **Nakula** and **Sahadeva** is, unusually, apsidal-ended. The elephant may be a visual pun on this, as the Sanskrit technical name for a curved ended building is *gajaprstika*, "elephant's backside".

The road out to the *rathas* resounds with incessant chiselling from sculptors' workshops. Much of their work is excellent, and well worth a browse – the sculptors produce statues for temples all over the world and are used to shipping large-scale pieces. Some of the artists are horrifyingly young; children often do the donkey work on large pieces, which are then completed by master craftsmen.

Accommodation

With more than twenty years' experience of tourism, Mamallapuram is not short of **accommodation**. The bulk of cheap and mid-range lodges are within the village, some distance from the beach, which is the preserve of the more expensive places. Large hotels of varying standards sit side by side along a six-kilometre stretch of coast. Without a bike, getting to these can prove a bit of a hassle; it's easy enough to take a rickshaw out there from the village, but not in the other direction. However, the walk back into Mamallapuram, either along the beach or the Kovalam Rd (to which they are all connected by long driveways) is pleasant – if you're not carrying luggage.

Long-term lodgings can be arranged in the sculptors' village behind the workshops on the way to the Pancha Pandava *rathas*. The two oldest established guesthouses are *R. Kuppuswamy's* and *Mrs Rajalakshmi's*, next door. They're both pretty basic, with thatched roofs and common shower-toilets in the yard, but have serviceable fans and are clean and homely. At around Rs350 per week, they're also just about the cheapest places to stay in the area.

In the village

Magesh, E Raja St (☎04133/42201). Basic, clean rooms in a small roadside lodge at the centre of the village. No restaurant. ①–③.

Mamalla Bhavan Annexe, E Raja St (☎04133/42260, fax 42160). Brisk, efficient and modern hotel on the main drag through the village, with spotless (mostly a/c) rooms overlooking a courtyard. Non-a/c rooms have mosquito nets. There's BBC World Service on the TV, and a very good restaurant. ④–⑤.

Rama Krishna Lodge, 8 Ottavadai St (☎04133/42331 or 42431). Clean, well-maintained rooms in the heart of the tourist enclave, all with bathroom but no a/c, set round a courtyard filled with pot plants. The newest ones are on the top storey, and have sea views. There's a backup generator, too, and often vacancies when everywhere else is full, because of its size. ③.

Sea Queen, 29A Ottavadai St (☎04133/42326). Small, but very neat budget rooms close to the beach. Those on the upper storey have sea views. One of the best cheapies. ②.

Sri Murugan Guest House, Ottavadai St (☎04133/42772). New, good-value place next door to the *Ramakrishna Lodge*. Small and peaceful, with courteous service: one of the nicest options in the area. ③.

Surya, off Ottavadai St (☎04133/42239). Lakeside hotel that gets very mixed reviews, set in a leafy compound. Simple rooms (some a/c), although the bathrooms are on the shabby side; mosquito nets are available and, considering the proximity of the lake, essential. ③.

Uma Lodge, 15 Ottavadai St (☎04133/42322). Run-of-the-mill lodge just off the main street, with rudimentary, but fair-sized rooms (avoid the ones on the top floor because of restaurant noise). ①–③.

Victory, 5 Ottavadai St (☎04133/42179). A small, European-run guesthouse with comfortable rooms and its own back-garden restaurant. ③.

Vinayak Cottages, 68 E Raja St (☎04133/42445). Four spacious, thatched cottages set in a leafy garden; a stone's throw from the bus stand. Offers Western toilets, and has tables outside. Good value. ③.

Vinodhara, Cross St (☎04133/42694). A large new place, immaculately tiled, cool rooms catch the sea breezes, and you can see the Shore temple from the top floor. Easily the best value mid-price hotel in the village. ④.

On the beach

Golden Sun, 3km from town, 59 Kovalam Rd (☎04133/42245, fax 498 2669). Not as smart as the *Ideal*, but the garden compound's attractive; the sea-facing rooms are the best value. Health club and pool. ⑥.

Ideal Beach Resort, 4km from town, Kovalam Rd (☎04133/42240, fax 42243). Very appealing cottages a little way before the Tiger Cave. Fine pool, inexpensive restaurant and friendly Sri Lankan management. Popular with overland tour groups, so book well ahead in season. ⑧.

Mamalla Beach Resort, 2.5km from town, Kovalam Rd (☎04133/42375, fax 42160). One of the less luxurious complexes along the beach road, with reasonable rates. ⑥–⑦.

Silversands, Kovalam Rd (☎04133/42228, fax 42280). India's first self-styled "Beach Resort" has definitely seen better days, but renovation work promises to improve standards. Even so, the rooms, which have circular mozzie nets and "sitouts", are still comfortable and very good value (except the priciest one, which has its own indoor pool). In addition there is a great new main pool, with wet bar. ⑥–⑧.

Taj Fisherman's Cove, Covelong Beach, 30min drive north from Mamallapuram (☎04133/44304). Four-star hotel, with bar and restaurants. Rooms in main building overlook a beachside garden, while circular cottages stand at the ocean's edge. ⑨.

Temple Bay Ashok (ITDC) Beach Resort, Kovalam Rd (☎04133/42251, fax 42257). Despite its great location – on the beach near the village, with views of the Shore temple – this place is somewhat overpriced and is geared towards conference bookings. Basic cottages on the beach all have sea-facing balconies; there are huge rooms in the main building, a swimming pool and restaurant. ⑧.

TTDC Hotel Tamil Nadu Beach Resort, Kovalam Rd (☎04133/42235, fax 42268). A predictably shabby state-run place made up of huge split-level cottages (some non-a/c) with sea-facing "sitouts", very large pool and multi-cuisine restaurant. ⑤.

TTDC Hotel Tamil Nadu Unit II Camping Site, Kovalam Rd (☎04133/42287). Just behind the beach, adjacent to the village tank. The site is slightly run-down, but has cheap dorm (Rs50 per bed), as well as new a/c rooms, and standard non-a/c – those facing the sea are more expensive. ③–⑤.

Eating

Mamallapuram is crammed with small restaurants, most of them specializing in **seafood** – tiger prawns, pomfret, tuna, shark and lobster – all of which can be mouth-wateringly succulent and relatively inexpensive. Prices are higher at the **beach hotels**, but the atmosphere and often the food are usually worth it. Wherever you eat, avoid a nasty shock at the end of your meal by establishing exactly how much your fish, or lobster, is going to cost in advance, as the price quoted is often just the cost per kilo.

Golden Palette, *Mamalla Bhavan Annexe*, E Raja St. Blissfully cool a/c café with tinted windows, serving the best veg food in the village (Rs50 *thalis* at lunchtime, North Indian *tandoori* in the evenings) and wonderful ice-cream sundaes. Worth popping in just for a coffee to beat the heat.

Ideal Beach Resort, 4km from town, Kovalam Rd. Sri Lankan, Chinese, Indian and Western dishes served on an open poolside terrace at this upscale resort complex. Most main dishes around Rs120.

La Vie En Rose, next to the sculpture museum, E Raja St. The usual Westerner-orientated menu, plus a few unusual French-style salads, pasta dishes (their spaghetti's great) and chicken specialties. Get a balcony seat overlooking the stone-carvers' workshops and lighthouse. Closes in the summer.

Luna Magica, beyond Ottavadai St. Slap on the beach, this is the place to splash out on topnotch seafood, particularly tiger prawns and lobster, which are kept alive in a tank. The big specimens cost a hefty Rs600-800, but are as tasty as you'll find anywhere, served in a rich tomato, butter and garlic sauce. They also do passable sangria, made with Chennai sweet red wine, and cold beer, and offer plenty of less expensive dishes for budget travellers.

Mamalla Bhavan, opposite the bus stand, Shore Temple Rd. The best no-frills pure-veg "leaf meals" joint for miles, and invariably packed. Equally good for *iddli-wada* breakfasts, evening *dosas* and other snacks. *Thalis* cost Rs20.

Moonraker, Ottavadai St. Cool jazz and blues sounds, and slick service, ensure this place is filled year round with foreign tourists. The food's not bad, either, and inexpensive; sharkfish and fresh calamari are a speciality, but their curd-fruit-and-muesli breakfasts are delicious, too.

Pumpernickel Bakery, 15 Ottavadai St. Popular Nepali-run place, above the *Uma Lodge*, serving delicious German-bakery-style breads, cakes, cheesy pasta dishes, Chinese food and strong beer up on the roof terrace. Closed May–Nov.

Around Mamallapuram

The sandy hinterland and flat estuarine paddy fields around Mamallapuram harbour a handful of sights well worth making forays from the coast to see. A short way north along the main highway, the **Government College of Sculpture** and elaborately carved **Tiger Cave** can easily be reached by bicycle, but to get to the **Crocodile Bank**, where rare reptiles from across South Asia are bred for release into the wild, or **Dakshina Chitra**, a museum devoted to South Indian architecture and crafts, you'll need to jump on and off buses or rent a moped for the day. Further north still, the **Cholamandal Artists' Village** is a showcase for less traditional arts that's best visited en route to or from Chennai. Finally, a good target for a day-trip inland is the hilltop temple at **Tirukalikundram**, west of Mamallapuram across a swathe of unspoilt farmland.

Government College of Sculpture

A visit to the **Government College of Sculpture**, 2km from Mamallapuram on the Kovalam (Covelong) Rd (☎04133/42261), gives a fascinating insight into the processes of sculpture training. You can watch anything from preliminary drawing, with its strict rules regarding proportion and iconography, through to the execution of sculpture, both in wood and stone, in the classical Hindu tradition. Contact the college office to make an appointment.

Tiger Cave

Set amid groves close to the sea, 5km north from Mamallapuram on the Kovalam (Covelong) Rd, the extraordinary **Tiger Cave** contains a shrine to Durga, approached by a flight of steps that passes two subsidiary cells. Following the line of an irregularly shaped rock, the cave is remarkable for the elaborate exterior, which features multiple lion heads surrounding the entrance to the main cell.

Crocodile Bank

The **Crocodile Bank** (daily 8am–5.30pm; Rs10, plus Rs10 for cameras) at Vadanemmeli, 14km north of town on the road to Chennai, was set up in 1976 by the American zoologist Romulus Whittaker, to protect and breed indigenous crocodiles. The bank has been so successful (fifteen crocs to five thousand in the first fifteen years) that its remit now extends to saving endangered species, such as turtles and lizards, from around the world.

Low-walled enclosures in its garden compound house hundreds of inscrutable crocodiles, soaking in ponds or sunning themselves on the banks. Breeds include the fish-eating, knobbly-nosed gharial and the world's largest species, the saltwater *crocodylus porosus*, which can grow to 8m in length. You can watch feeding time at about 4.30pm each Wednesday. The temptation to take photos is tempered by the sight of those hungry saurians clambering over each other to chomp the chopped flesh, within inches of the top of the wall.

Another important field of work is conducted with the collaboration of local Irula people, whose traditional expertise is with snakes. Cobras are brought to the bank for **venom collection**, to be used in the treatment of snakebites. Elsewhere, snakes are repeatedly "milked" until they die, but here at the bank only a limited amount is taken from each snake, enabling them to return to the wild. Coastal route buses #117 and #118 stop at the entrance.

Dakshina Chitra

Occupying a patch of sun-baked sand dunes midway between Chennai and Mamallapuram, **Dakshina Chitra** (daily except Tues 10am—6pm; Rs50), literally "Vision of the South", is one of India's best conceived folk museums, devoted to the rich architectural and artistic heritage of Kerala, Karnataka, Andhra Pradesh and Tamil Nadu. Apart from giving you the chance to look around some immaculately restored old buildings, the museum, set up by the Chennai Craft Foundation with support from local government and American sponsors, exposes visitors to many disappearing traditions of the region which you might otherwise not be aware of, from tribal fertility cults and *Ayyannar* field deities to pottery and leather shadow puppets.

The visit kicks off with a short introductory video, followed by a guided tour of the campus, where a selection of traditional buildings from across peninsular India have been painstakingly reconstructed using original materials. These include an airy Tamil *brahmins*' dwelling, a Chettinad merchant's mansion filled with Burmese furniture and Chinese laquerware, a Syrian Christian home from the backwaters of Kerala, with a fragrant jackwood interior, and a north Keralan house that has separate rooms for the women – a unique feature reflecting the area's strongly matrilineal society. Exhibitions attached to the various structures convey the environmental and cultural diversity of the south, most graphically expressed in a wonderful textile collection featuring antique silk and cotton saris from various castes and regions. Other highlights include a pottery demonstration, where you can try your hand at throwing clay on a Tamil wheel, and a memorable slapstick shadow puppet (*tolu bommalaatam*) display.

Cholamandal Artists' Village

Tucked away on the scruffy southern edge of Chennai, the **Cholamandal Artists' Village** (daily 10am–7pm; admission free) was established in the mid-1960s to encourage contemporary Indian art. In a country whose visual culture is so comprehensively dominated by convention, fostering innovation and artistic experimentation proved no easy feat, but despite an initially hostile response from the Madrasi establishment (who allegedly regarded the tropical storm that destroyed the artists' first settlement as an act of nemesis), the village has prospered. Today, Cholamandal's thirty-strong community has several studios and a large gallery filled with paintings, sketches, sculpture and metalwork, and a shop selling work produced here. For those with more than a passing interest in the village, there's also a small **guesthouse** (☎044/492 6092; ②).

Tirukalikundram

The village of **TIRUKALIKUNDRAM**, 16km east on the road to Kanchipuram, is locally famous for its hilltop Shiva temple, where a pair of white Egyptian vultures (*Neophron percnopterus*), believed to be reincarnated saints on their way between Varanasi and Rameshwaram, used to swoop down at noon to be fed by the priests. No one knew how long these visits had been going on, nor why, when in 1994, the vultures suddenly stopped coming. Their absence, however, was taken as a bad omen, and sure enough, that year massive cyclones ravaged the Tamil Nadu coast.

Four hundred hot stone steps need to be scaled to reach the top, but don't let that – nor the effort required to disabuse various individuals, including the priests, of the impression that you need their multifarious services and paid company – deter you. Once on the hilltop, the views are sublime, especially at sunset. Visits to Tirukalikundram are made more worthwhile if you take the time to explore the vast **Vijayanagar temple** at its heart, which harbours a collection of conches said to manifest themselves each year in the large tank on the edge of town.

Regular **buses** run to Tirukalikundram from Mamallapuram, en route to Kanchipuram, but it's more fun to rent a moped or motorcycle for the trip (see p.399). You could conceivably peddle out here, too (the route is flat all the way), but start out early in the day to avoid the worst of the heat.

Kanchipuram

Ask any Tamil what **KANCHIPURAM** (aka Kanchi) is famous for, and they'll probably say silk saris, shrines and saints – in that order. A dynastic capital throughout the medieval era, it remains one of the seven holiest cities in the subcontinent, sacred to both Shaivites and Vaishnavites, and among the few surviving centres of goddess worship in the South. Year round, pilgrims pour through for a quick *puja* stop on the Tirupati tour circuit and, if they can afford it, a spot of shopping in the sari emporia. For non-Hindu visitors, however, Kanchipuram holds less appeal. Although the temples are undeniably impressive, the city itself is unremittingly hot, dusty and congested, with only basic accommodation and amenities. You'll enjoy its attractions a whole lot more if you come here on a **day-trip** from Chennai or Mamallapuram, a two-hour bus ride east.

Arrival and information

Flanked on the south by the Vegavathi River, Kanchipuram lies 70km southwest of Chennai, and about the same distance from the coast. **Buses** from Chennai (1hr 30min–2hr), Mamallapuram (2hr–2hr 30min), and Chengalpattu (1hr) stop at the potholed and chaotic stand in the centre on Raja St. The sleepy **train station** in the northeast sees only five daily passenger services from Chengalpattu (one of them, #161, originating in Chennai) and two from Anakkonam.

As most of the main roads are wide and traffic rarely unmanageable, the best way **get around** Kanchi is by **bicycle** – available for minimal rates (Rs1.50/hour) at stalls west and northeast of the bus stand. The town's vegetable markets, hotels, restaurants and bazaars are concentrated in the centre of town, near the bus stand.

Note that unless you have used dollars and are happy to chance the black market, there is nowhere in the town to **change money**; the nearest official foreign exchange places are in Chennai and Mamallapuram.

The City and temples

Established by the **Pallava** kings in the fourth century AD, Kanchipuram served as their capital for five hundred years, and continued to flourish throughout the Chola, Pandya and Vijayanagar eras. Under the Pallavas, it was an important scholastic forum, and a meeting point for Jain, Buddhist and Hindu cultures. Its **temples** dramatically reflect this enduring political prominence, spanning the years from the peak of Pallava construction to the seventeenth century, when the ornamentation of the *gopuras* and pillared halls was at its most elaborate (for more on Tamil Nadu's temples, see Contexts, p.585). All can be easily reached by foot, bike or rickshaw, and all close between noon and 4pm. You'll be offered a panoply of services – from sanctuary priests,

shoe bearers, guides, women giving out food for fish in the temple tanks, and well-trained temple elephants that bless you with their trunks – so go prepared with a pocketful of change. Always animated, the temples really come alive during major festivals such as the **Car Festival** (May) and **Navaratri** (Oct/Nov).

Ekambareshvara temple

Kanchipuram's largest temple and most important Shiva shrine, the **Ekambareshvara temple** – also known as Ekambaranatha – is easily identified by its colossal white-washed *gopuras*, which rise to almost 60m, on the north side of town. The main temple contains some Pallava work, but was mostly constructed between the sixteenth and seventeenth centuries, and stands within a vast walled enclosure beside some smaller shrines and a large fish-filled water tank.

The entrance is through a high-arched passageway beneath an elaborate *gopura* in the south wall, it leads to an open courtyard and a majestic "thousand-pillared hall" (*kalyan mandapa*), whose slightly decaying grey stone columns are modelled as nubile maidens, animals and deities. This hall faces the tank in the north and the sanctuary in the west that protects the emblem of Shiva (here in his form as **Kameshvara**, Lord of Desire), an "earth" *lingam* that is one of five *lingam* in Tamil Nadu that represent the elements. Legend connects it with the goddess **Kamakshi** (Shiva's consort, "Wanton-Eyed"), who angered Shiva by playfully covering his eyes and plunging the world into darkness. Shiva reprimanded her by sending her to fashion a *lingam* from the earth in his honour; once it was completed, Kamakshi found she could not move it. Local myths tell of a great flood that swept over Kanchipuram and destroyed the temples, but did not move the *lingam*, to which Kamakshi clung so fiercely that marks of her breasts and bangles were imprinted upon it.

Behind the sanctum, accessible from the covered hallway around it, an eerie bare hall lies beneath a profusely carved *gopura*, and in the courtyard a venerable **mango tree** represents the tree under which Shiva and Kamakshi were married. This union is celebrated during a festival each April, when many couples are married in the *kalyan mandapa*. Believed to symbolize the four Vedas, the four branches of the tree are supposed to yield different-tasting fruit, collected by the temple priests and given to women who come here to petition for fertility. For Rs50 you can perform a special problem-solving *puja*: walk three times around the tree to sort out financial difficulties or to find a husband for your daughter. Finally, don't miss the temple's other "thousand-pillared *mandapa*", beneath the *gopura* on the west wall, which houses the extraordinary "**Pictorial Depication of Historical Episodes in Sound and Light by Electronic Meriods**" (sic), a collection of bizarre gizmos elucidating the basic tenets of Hinduism. One involves thrusting your head into a contraption to hear electronically triggered excerpts from the *Vedas*.

The somewhat neglected twelfth-century **Jvaraheshvari temple**, in leafy gardens to the south, is the only Chola (tenth–twelfth centuries) structure in Kanchipuram not to have been modified and overshadowed by later buildings. Unlike the Pallava constructions, it is built of hard grey stone and its sculpted pyramidal roof is an early form of the *gopuras* used extensively by the Pandyas.

Kailasanatha temple

The **Kailasanatha temple**, the oldest structure in Kanchipuram and the finest example of Pallava architecture in South India, is situated among several low-roofed houses just over 1km west of the town centre. Built by the Pallava king Rajasimha early in the eighth century, its intimate size and simple carving distinguish it from the town's later temples. Usually quieter than its neighbours, the shrine becomes the focus of vigorous celebrations during the Mahashivratri festival each March. Like the contemporaneous Shore temple at Mamallapuram, it is built of soft sandstone, but its sheltered position has spared it from wind and sand erosion, and it remains remarkably intact, despite some rather clumsy recent renovation work.

Topped with a modest pyramidal spire, the small temple stands within a rectangular courtyard, enclosed by a wall inlaid with tiny meditation chambers and sculpted with images of Shiva, Parvati and their sons, as well as rearing mythical lions (*yalis*). On the south side of the spire Shiva is depicted as a begging ascetic (Bhikshatana); on the north he's in the pose of the dance of destruction (Samhara-Tandava). Walls in the dim interior bear traces of frescoes, and the ceilings are etched with religious verses written in Pali. The sanctum, inaccessible to non-Hindus, shelters a sturdy sixteen-sided black *lingam,* guarded by elephant-headed Ganesh and Shiva's other son, Skanda, the god of war, with whom the king Rajasimha was closely associated. Double walls were built round the sanctuary to support the weighty tower above; the passage between them is used as a circumambulatory path as part of the ritual worship of Shiva.

Vaikuntha Perumal temple

Built shortly after the Kailasanatha temple at the end of the eighth century, the smaller **Vaikuntha Perumal temple**, a few hundred metres south of the train station, is dedicated to Vishnu. Its lofty carved *vimana* (towered sanctuary) crowns three shrines containing images of Vishnu, stacked one on top of the other. Unusual scenes carved in the walls enclosing the temple yard depict events central to Pallava history, among them coronations, court gatherings and battles with the Chalukyas who ruled the regions to the northwest. The temple's pillared entrance hall was added by Vijayanagar rulers five centuries later, and is very different in style, with far more ornate sculpting.

Kamakshi Amman temple

Built during Pallava supremacy and modified in the fourteenth and seventeenth centuries, the **Kamakshi Amman temple**, northeast of the bus stand, combines several styles, with an ancient central shrine, gates from the Vijayanagar period and high *gopuras* set above the gateways much later. The *gopuras* and the *vimanas* are a dazzling sight, painted a riot of gold, pink and blue. To the right of the central shrine, inaccessible to non-Hindus, a raised *mandapa* is now an art gallery, housing many pictures of the recent **Acharyas** (see following account on Sankaramandam).

This is one of India's three holiest shrines to Shakti, Shiva's cosmic energy depicted in female form, usually as his consort. The goddess Kamakshi, a local form of Parvati, shown with a sugar-cane bow and arrows of flowers, is honoured as having lured Shiva to Kanchipuram, where they were married, and thus having forged the connection between the local community and the god. In February or March, deities are wheeled to the temple in huge wooden "cars", decked with robed statues and swaying plantain leaves. During the rest of the year, the "cars" are kept on Gandhi Rd.

Varadarajaperumal temple

The Vaishnavite **Varadarajaperumal temple** stands within a huge walled complex in the far southeast of town, guarded by high gates topped with *gopuras*. The inner sanctuary boasts superb carving and well-preserved paintings, but non-Hindus only have access to the outer courtyards and the elaborate sixteenth-century pillared hall close to the Western entrance gate. The outer columns of this *mandapa* are sculpted as lions and warriors on rearing horses, to celebrate the military vigour of the Vijayanagars, who believed their prowess was inspired by the power of Shakti.

Sankaramandam

Kanchipuram is the seat of a line of holy men bearing the title **Acharya**, whose line of saints dates back, according to different versions as far as 1300–482 BC, to the saint Adi

Sankaracharya. The sixty-eighth Acharya, the highly revered Shri Chandrasekharendra Sarasvati Swami, died in January 1994 at the age of 101. Buried in the sitting position, as is the custom for great Hindu sages, his mortal remains are enshrined in a *samadhi* at the **Sankaramandam**, a *math* (monastery for Hindu renouncers) down the road from the Ekambareshvara temple. The present incumbent, the sixty-ninth Acharya, has his quarters on the opposite side of a marble meditation hall to the shrine, and gives *darshan* to the public during the morning and early evening, when the *math*'s two huge elephants are given offerings. Lined with old photographs from the life of the former swami, with young *brahmin* students chanting Sanskrit verses in the background, it's a typically Tamil blend of simple sanctity and garish modern glitz.

Accommodation and eating

There's not a great choice of **accommodation** in Kanchipuram, but the hotels are sufficient for a short stay, and all except the *Tamil Nadu Hotel* are in the centre. The less expensive lodges offer minimal comfort, while the pricier places, if not exactly elaborate, are clean and comfortable and generally serve good South Indian dishes in their own **restaurants**. The most highly rated place to eat in town, however, is **Saravana Bhavan** on Gandhi Rd, an offshoot of the famous Chennai chain of pure veg restaurants, which offers superb Rs30 "meals" at lunchtime, and a long list of South Indian snacks the rest of the day. They open at 6am for breakfast, and there's a cool a/c annexe inside. It's also marginally less like bedlam than the other main meals joints in the centre, which tend to get swamped by shaven-headed pilgrims from Tirupati.

Baboo Surya, 85 E Raja Veethi St (☎/fax 04112/22555). Kanchee's top hotel: large and modern, with immaculate a/c and non-a/c rooms, glass elevator and a good veg/*tandoori* restaurant. Ask for a room with a "temple view". ⑤.

Jaybala International, 504 Gandhi Rd (☎04112/24348). Slightly more old-fashioned than the *Baboo Surya*, but with huge rooms and some lower tariffs. They also offer excellent-value single occupancy rates, and *Saravana Bhavan* (see above) is on the doorstep. Some a/c. ④–⑦.

Raja's Lodge, 20 Nellukkara St (☎04112/22603). Very cheap and very basic, with small, stuffy rooms. ①.

Sri Krishna Lodge, next to the *Sri Kusal Lodge*, Nellukkara St (☎04112/22831). Another cheap and basic rooms option, this time with attached bathrooms. ①–②.

Sri Kusal Lodge, 68C Nellukkara St (☎04112/22356). Newish, marble-lined lodge; the best of the bunch, though the rooms open onto an airless corridor. ②–③.

Sri Rama Lodge, 21 Nellukkara St (☎04112/22435). Good, fairly clean budget lodge with attached bathrooms and some a/c rooms. Best bet if *Sri Kusal* is booked. ②–④.

Sri Vela Lodge, Railway Station Rd (☎04112/21504). Another run-of-the-mill lodge, which offers larger than average rooms, with attached shower-toilets and fans, but is still airless. Busy meals restaurant downstairs. ②.

TTDC Tamil Nadu, Railway Station Rd (☎04112/22553). State-run hotel near the train station. The rooms are large enough, if a little on the shabby side, but their dingy restaurant is a dead loss. ④–⑤.

Vellore

Unless you are a connoisseur of military architecture, or have succumbed to a tropical disease, you're unlikely to find much inspiration in **VELLORE**, 150km west of Chennai. The limited charms of its sixteenth-century Hindu fort, whose blue-grey granite ramparts form an incongruous backdrop to the fast-moving traffic dominating the centre, are less memorable than the mayhem of its main streets, which are more jammed than average because of the presence in the middle of town of the **CMC Hospital**, one of South India's foremost medical centres. Patients and their relatives travel here for treatment from all over India, giving Vellore a more upbeat feel than you'd expect for a city of its size, but the only foreign visitors that spend a night here tend to be those breaking the long haul between Bangalore and Chennai.

The approach to the **fort** (daily 7am–8pm; free) is from the east, over a modern bridge that straddles a wide moat, once filled with crocodiles. Locals assert the giant four-sided structure, with its impressive crenellated walls, was built in the late sixteenth century by Chinna Bomma Reddi, viceroy of the Aravidu kings of Chandragiri. Over time, his reign gave way to the Vijayanagar dynasty, but the fort held off attacks until it fell to the Muslim Adi Shahis of Bijapur in the seventeenth century. Later the Marathas ousted their Muslim enemies, only to be overthrown in turn by Daud Khan of Delhi in the early 1700s. British officers took control in 1768, and remained overlords until Independence.

Close to the northern wall, the magnificent *kalyan mandapa* (thousand-pillared hall) in the outer courtyard of the **Jalakanteshvara temple** boasts a vitality and richness of carving matched only at Srirangam (see p.448). The outer pillars depict rearing steeds, mythical dragons and warriors, while the central columns support sculptures of *yalis*, mythical lions prominent in much earlier Pallava temples. The temple shrine is dedicated to Shiva, represented by a *lingam*. Although it was never pillaged, the presence of Muslim and European troops during successive occupations was considered a desecration, and worship was suspended until 1981 when a new Nataraja bronze was installed.

A **cemetery** to the right of the fort entrance holds the graves of the British soldiers who died during a swiftly defeated mutiny in 1806, when *sepoys* rose in protest against demands for them to shave their beards and adopt a common dress code. Nearby, a small **archeological museum** (daily except Fri 10am–1pm & 2–4.30pm) houses fragments of sculpture, hero stones and inscriptions found on the site. The only other buildings of interest, Tipu Sultan's palace, lie within the confines of the Police Cadet College and are off-limits to casual visitors.

Practicalities

Regular **buses**, from the two adjacent bus stands just east of the fort's entrance, connect Vellore with Chennai (every 30min; 3–4hr), Kanchipuram (every 30min; 2hr 30min) and Bangalore (10 daily; 5–6hr). Buses to and from Tiruvannamalai (every 15min; 2hr), however, work from a smaller stand at the southeast corner of the fort, ten minutes' walk down Town Hall Rd. The nearest main-line **train station** lies 3km north of the city at **Katpadi Junction**, where you can pick up direct services to and from Chennai (2hr–2hr 30min), Bangalore (4hr 15min) and beyond. Trains on the metre-gauge line between Vellore and Tirupathi, Tiruvannamalai and Pondicherry pull in to the **Cantonment Station**, 2km south of the bus stand.

Finding **accommodation** in Vellore can be a problem, as most rooms tend to be booked out by people visiting relatives in the hospital. There are, however, dozens of modest lodges in the narrow road opposite the CMC Hospital. Three reliable options in the area include: *VDM Lodge*, at 13/1 Beri Bakkali St (☎0416/24008; ②–③), whose cosy "deluxe" rooms on the fifth floor have great views and air coolers; the large and well-run *Gayathri*, on 22 Babu Rao St (☎0416/27714; ②), and, in a similar mould, the *Solai*, a couple of doors down the same street (☎0416/22876 or 22606; ②), which has a few a/c rooms. If you're on a tight budget, try the *Mayura*, 85 Babu Rao St (☎0416/25488; ①), whose small rooms need a lick of paint, but are clean, cheap and within walking distance of the bus stand; alternatively, the *New Sri Balaji* at 75 Babu Rao St (☎0416/26951; ②), is a dependable fallback. The top hotel in the town centre is the *Prince Manor*, on Katpadi Rd next to the hospital (☎0416/27726 or 22926; ⑤); it's a comfortable three-star with a choice of spacious a/c and non-a/c rooms, and two restaurants. Offering similar standards, but 1.5km north of town on New Katpadi Rd, is the more modern, business-orientated *River View* (☎0416/25568), which is nowhere near the river, but perfectly pleasant, cool and quiet, with a choice of quality in-house restaurants.

For **eating** options in the town centre, you've the usual string of simple veg "meals" joints along Ida Scudder St, opposite the hospital, of which the *Anand* is about the brightest. Further down the street, past the hospital and on the first floor of the *Susil Hotel* (look for the giant neon hoarding), is an excellent little Chinese restaurant, *Chinatown*, which serves tasty, mild chicken and vegetable dishes in a dark, blissfully cool a/c dining room. Their chicken in lemon sauce is delicious, and they have plenty of vegetarian and North Indian options on the menu, priced at around Rs40-70, as well as piping hot *naans* and *parathas* from the *tandoor*. A greater choice of North Indian dishes, most of them chicken-based, is offered at the *Prince Manor*'s fourth-floor a/c restaurant, where you can stretch your legs on a roof terrace between courses. Downstairs, on the ground floor, is Vellore's only "deluxe" South Indian vegetarian; it's your usual marble-lined *udipi* canteen, but has a/c and a colour TV blaring Tamil movies, and is not as chaotic at lunchtime as the competition on Ida Scudder St.

Vedanthangal

One of India's most spectacular bird sanctuaries lies roughly 1km east of the village of **VEDANTHANGAL**, a cluster of squat, brown houses set in a patchwork of paddy fields 30km from the east coast and 86km southwest of Chennai. It's a tiny, relaxed place, bisected by one road and with just two *chai* stalls.

The **sanctuary** (daily, dawn–dusk) a low-lying area less than half a kilometre square, is at its fullest between December and February, when it is totally flooded. The rains of the northeast monsoon, sweeping through in October or November, bring indigenous water birds ready to nest and settle until the dry season (usually April), when they leave for wetter areas. Abundant trees on mounds above water-level provide perfect nesting spots, alive by January with fledglings. Visitors can watch the avian action from a path at the water's edge, or from a watchtower (fitted out with strong binoculars). Try to come at sunset, when the birds return from feeding. Common Indian species to look out for are openbill storks, spoonbills, pelicans, black cormorants and **herons** of several types. You may also see ibises, grey pelicans, migrant cuckoos, sandpipers, egrets, which paddle in the rice fields, and tiny, darting bee-eaters. Some migrant birds pass through and rest on their way between more permanent sites; swallows, terns and redshanks are common, while peregrine falcons, pigeons and doves are less regularly spotted.

Practicalities

Getting to Vedanthangal can present a few problems. The nearest town is Maduranthakam, 8km east, on NH45 between Chengalpattu and Tindivanam. Head here to wait for the hourly buses to the sanctuary, or catch one of the four daily services from Chengalpattu. Taxis make the journey from Maduranthakam for Rs200–250, but cannot be booked from Vedanthangal.

Vedanthangal's only accommodation is the two-roomed **forest lodge** (①) near the bus stand, school and *chai* stall. Rooms, spacious and comfortable with attached bath, have to be booked through the Wildlife Warden, 50 4th Main Gandhi Nagar, Adyar,

Chennai (☎044/413947); if you turn up on spec, it may well be full, especially in December and January. They'll prepare food if given enough notice.

Tiruvannamalai

Synonymous with the fifth Hindu element of fire, **TIRUVANNAMALAI**, 100km south of Kanchipuram, ranks, along with Madurai, Kanchi, Chidambaram and Trichy, as one of the five holiest towns in Tamil Nadu. Its name, meaning "Red Mountain", derives from the spectacular extinct volcano, **Arunachala**, which rises behind it, and which glows an unearthly crimson colour at dawn. This awesome natural backdrop, combined with the presence in the centre of town of the colossal Arunchaleshvara temple, make Tiruvannamalai one of the region's most memorable destinations. Well off the tourist trail, it is a perfect place to get to grips with life in small-town Tamil Nadu, while the countless shrines, sacred tanks, *ashrams* and paved pilgrim paths scattered around the sacred mountain (not to mention the legions of dreadlocked *babas* who line up for alms outside the main sites) will keep anyone interested in Hinduism absorbed for weeks.

Mythology identifies Arunachala as the place where Shiva asserted his power over Brahma and Vishnu by manifesting himself as a *lingam* of fire, or **agnilingam**. The two lesser gods had been disputing their respective strengths when Shiva pulled this primordial pyro-stunt, challenging his adversaries to locate the top and bottom of his blazing column. They couldn't (although Vishnu is said to have faked finding the head) and collapsed on their knees in a gesture of supreme submission. The event is commemorated each year at the rising of the full moon in November/December, when the **Deepam ceremony**, bringing to an end the ten-day **Karttigai festival**, culminates with the illumination of gallons of camphor in the temple courtyard. This acts as a signal for *brahmins* stationed on the summit of Arunachala to light a vast vat of ghee and paraffin, which blazes for days and can be seen from a radius of more than 20km. It represents the fulfilment of Shiva's promise to reappear each year to vanquish the forces of darkness and ignorance with fire-light. The massive *agnilingam* attracts tens of thousands of pilgrims, who rush from the temple below to the summit in time to fuel the inferno with their own offerings. The whole event, best enjoyed from the relative safety of a rooftop in town, is one of the great spectacles of sacred India. The latest incarnation of a prehistoric fire-worshipping cult, it has probably been performed here in some form or another, without interruption, for four thousand years.

The alleged regenerative and healing powers of the sacred Red Mountain also explain why the famous twentieth-century saint **Shri Ramana Maharishi** chose this as the site for his twenty-three-year meditation retreat, in a cave on the side of the hill. Shri Ramana's subsequent teachings formed the basis of a worldwide movement, and his former ashram on the edge of Tiruvannamalai attracts a stream of Western devotees. A crop of other smaller ashrams have mushroomed alongside it, some of them more authentic than others, and the ranks of white-cotton-clad foreigners floating between them have become a defining feature of the area south of town over the past five or six years.

Arrival and information

Tiruvannamalai is served by regular buses from Vellore (every 15min; 2hr), and by less frequent services from Pondicherry (4–5 daily; 2hr). Coming from the coast, it's easiest to make your way from Tindivanam, picking up one of the numerous buses to

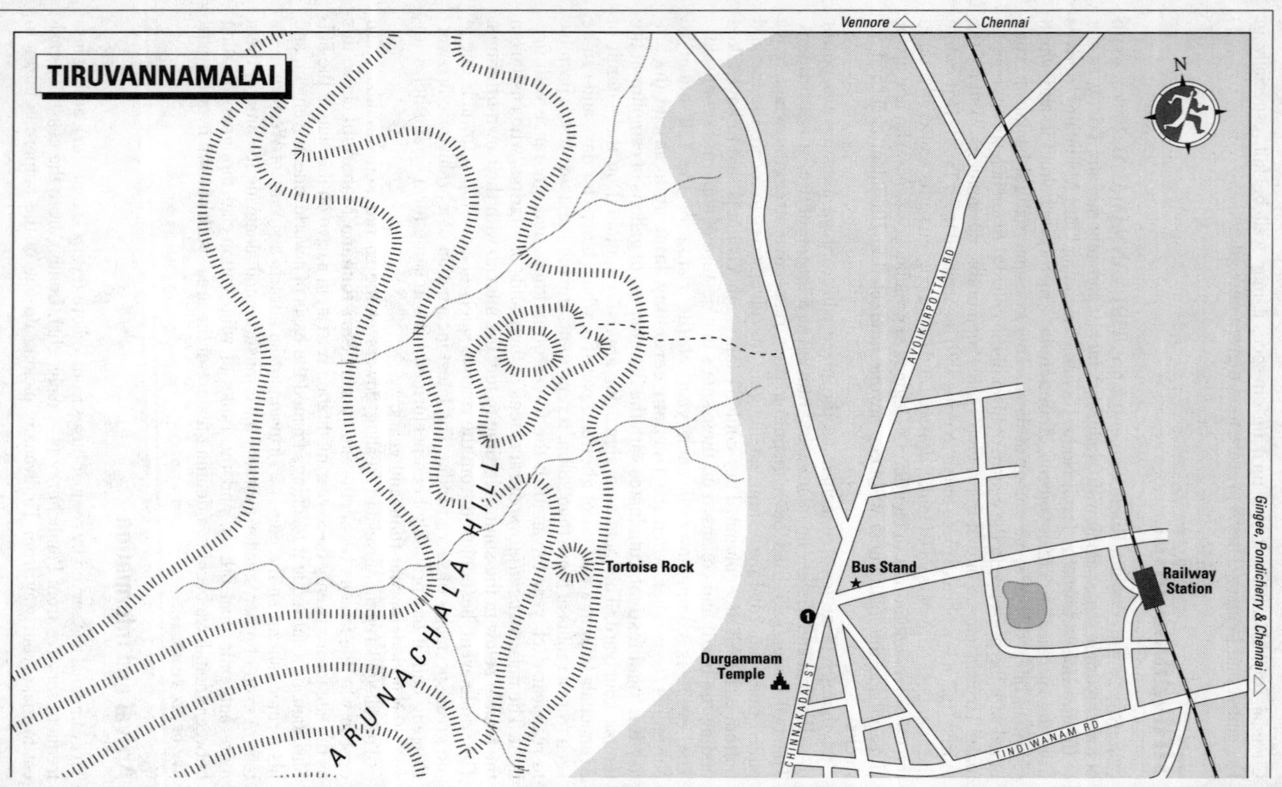
TIRUVANNAMALAI
N
Vennore
Chennai
AVOIKURPOTTAI RD
ARUNACHALA HILL
Tortoise Rock
Bus Stand
Railway Station
Gingee, Pondicherry & Chennai
1
Durgammam Temple
CHINNAKADAI ST
TINDIWANAM RD

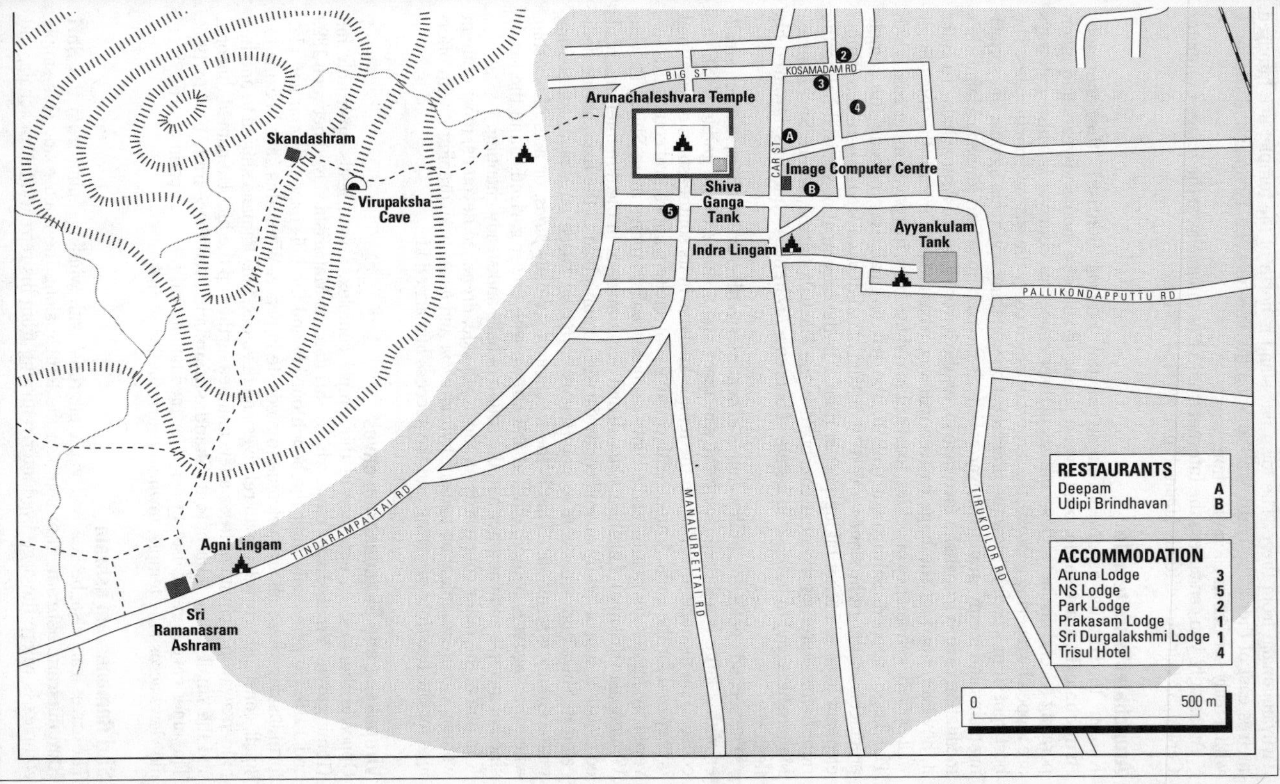
BIG ST
KOSAMADAM RD
Arunachaleshvara Temple
Skandashram
Virupaksha Cave
CAR ST
Image Computer Centre
Shiva Ganga Tank
Indra Lingam
Ayyankulam Tank
PALLIKONDAPPUTTU RD
TINDARAMPATTAI RD
Agni Lingam
Sri Ramanasram Ashram
MANALURPETTAI RD
TIRUKOILOR RD
RESTAURANTS
Deepam A
Udipi Brindhavan B
ACCOMMODATION
Aruna Lodge 3
NS Lodge 5
Park Lodge 2
Prakasam Lodge 1
Sri Durgalakshmi Lodge 1
Trisul Hotel 4
0
500 m

Tiruvannamalai from there. The town bus stand is north of the temple; five hundred metres east of there, the **train station** is on the line between Tirupati and Madurai, with a daily service in each direction.

Amazingly, you can access the Internet from Tiruvannamalai, at the Image Computer Centre, 52 Car Street (daily 10am–10pm; ☎04174/27128).

Arunchaleshvara temple

Known to Hindus as the "Temple of the Eternal Sunrise", the enormous **Arunchaleshvara temple**, built over a period of almost a thousand years and incorporating several distinct styles, consists of three concentric courtyards whose gateways are topped by tapering *gopuras*, the largest of which cover the east and north gates. The best spot from which to view the precinct, a breathtaking spectacle against the sprawling plains and lumpy, granite Shevaroy Hills, is the path up to Shri Ramana Maharishi's meditation cave, Virupaksha (see below), on the lower slopes of Arunachala. To enter it, however, head for the huge eastern gateway, which leads through the thick outer wall carved with images of deities, local saints and teachers, to a paved inner courtyard. The large stepped Shivaganga tank to the left originally lay outside the temple precincts; on the right stands a vast "thousand-pillared" *mandapa*, where the temple elephant lives when not taking part in rituals. In the basement of a raised hall to the right before entering the next courtyard is the Parthala *lingam*, where Shri Ramana Maharishi is said to have sat in a state of Supreme Awareness while ants devoured his flesh.

The second enclosure, built a couple of centuries earlier, in the 1200s, is much smaller, with a large Nandi bull facing the sanctuary and a shrine to the goddess (Shiva's consort) on its northern edge. In the temple kitchens in its southeastern corner, food is prepared for the gods. A nineteenth-century roof shelters the central courtyard, surveyed by numerous deities etched into its outer walls, among them Shiva, Parvati, Venugopala (Krishna), Lakshmi, Ganesh and Subrahmanya. In the dim interior, arcaded cloisters supported by magnificently carved columns lead to the main shrine dedicated to Shiva and accessible to non-Hindus: a *lingam* raised on a platform bearing tenth-century inscriptions. This is the location of six daily *pujas*, or acts of worship, when the *lingam* is bathed, clothed and strewn with flower garlands amid the heady smell of incense and camphor and the sound of bells and steady chanting.

In one of the outer courtyards on the north side, drenched devotees, most of them women, circumambulate an ancient hybrid *neem* and *bodhi* tree, draping it with offerings for the health of offspring and the success of married life.

Virupaksha and Skandashram caves

Opposite the western entrance of the temple complex, a path leads up a holy hill (15min) to the **Virupaksha cave**, where Shri Ramana Maharishi stayed between 1899 and 1916. He personally built the bench outside and the hill-shaped *lingam* and platform inside, where all are welcome to meditate in peace. When this cave became too small, constantly crowded with relatives and devotees, Shri Ramana shifted to another, hidden away in a clump of trees a few minutes further up the hill. He named this one, and the small house built onto it, **Skandashram**, and lived there from 1916 to 1922. The inner cave here is also set aside for meditation, and the front patio affords splendid views across the temple, town and surrounding plains.

Shri Ramanasram ashram

The caves can also be reached via a pilgrims' path winding uphill from the **Shri Ramanasram ashram**, 2km south of the temple along the main road. This simple complex is where the sage lived after returning from his retreat on Arunachala, and where his body is today enshrined (Hindus customarily bury saints in the sitting position rather than cremate their bodies). The *samadhi* has become a popular place for Shri Ramana's devotees on pilgrimage, but interested visitors are welcome to stay in the dorms here. There's also an excellent bookshop stocking a huge range of titles on the life and teachings of the guru, as well as quality postcards, calendars and religious images.

Accommodation and eating

For such an important pilgrimage place, Tiruvannamalai has surprisingly few decent **hotels**. If your budget can stretch to it, stay at the two-star *Trisul*, a couple of minutes' walk from the main temple entrance (☎04175/22219; ⑤–⑥), which has huge, immaculately clean rooms (some of them with a/c), courteous staff and a good restaurant. Its only drawback is that it gets booked for long periods by Westerners studying at one or other of the *ashrams*. The next best option, and excellent value for money, is *NS Lodge*, facing the temple's south entrance at 47 Thiruvoodal St (☎04175/25388; ③). Its rooms are neat and clean, and all have TVs (which pick up BBC Worldwide) and attached shower-toilets; there's also a great view of the temple towers from the roof. Moving down the scale, pick of the budget lodges is the recently opened *Sri Durgalakshmi*, just west of the bus stand at 73 Chinnakadai St (☎04174/26041; ②). If it's full, try the shabbier *Prakasam* next door (☎04175/26041; ①), owned by the same family. Otherwise, the most reliable options are both further into town towards the temple: *Aruna Lodge*, 200m northeast of the main temple entrance at 82 Kosamadam Rd (☎04175/323291; ①), looks grubby from the outside, but has reasonably clean rooms with a common balcony overlooking the bazaar and sacred precinct, and the *Park Lodge* (☎04175/22471; ②), a little further along the same road at number 26, which is marginally more comfortable, with a busy veg canteen on the ground floor.

For **food**, you've a choice of a dozen or so typical South Indian "meals" joints, of which the *Udipi Brindhavan Hotel*, just off the bottom of Car St, is the most traditional (though not hygienic, it has to be said). Delicious hot *ghee chappatis* are served here all afternoon, as well as all the usual rice specialties. The other commendable *udipi* restaurant in town is the *Deepam Restaurant*, also on Car St opposite the temple's east entrance, which boasts a newer, cooler "Deluxe" wing next door (same name), where you can order ice-creams and milkshakes; both branches serve excellent *parottas* for

PRADAKSHANA

During the annual Karttigai festival, Hindu pilgrims are supposed to perform an auspicious circumambulation of Arunachala, known as the **Pradakshana** (*pra* signifies the removal of all sins, *da* the fulfilment of desires, *kshi* freedom from the cycle of rebirth and *na* spiritual liberation). Along the way, offerings are made at a string of shrines, tanks, temples, *lingams*, pillared meditation halls, sacred rocks, springs, trees and caves related to the Tiruvannamalai legends. Although hectic during the festival, the paved path linking them all together is quiet for most of the year and makes a wonderful day hike, affording fine views of the town and its environs.

An even more inspiring prospect is the **ascent of Arunachala** itself, which can be completed in two to three hours if you're fit and can cope with the heat (if you can't, don't attempt this hike). The path is less easy to follow than the Pradakshana, and you may feel like employing one of the guides who offer their services at the trailhead, just above the Shri Ramanasram ashram. At the summit, where you can see remnants of the annual Deepam blaze, sits Swami Narayana, a renunciate who has been performing an austerity of silence here for more than twelve years.

under Rs10. If you feel like a change from South Indian, head for the *Trisul*, whose posh ground-floor restaurant serves a North Indian buffet for around Rs100, as well as a full *tandoori* menu.

Gingee

An epic landscape of huge boulder hills, interspersed by lush splashes of rice paddy and banana plantations, stretches east of Tiruvannamalai towards the coast. The scenery peaks at **GINGEE** (pronounced "*Shinjee*"), 37km east of the Red Mountain along the Pondicherry highway, where the ruins of Tamil Nadu's most spectacular **fort** sprawl over a vast swathe of sun-scorched granite. If this were anywhere except India, you wouldn't be able to move for interpretative panels and Walkman posts, but here the miles of crumbling ramparts and temple masonry have been left to the mercy of the weeds and tropical weather. Only on weekends, when bus parties pour around the most accessible monuments, does the site receive more than a trickle of visitors. Come here in the week, and you'll have the place to yourself, save for the odd troupe of monkeys and inquisitive tree squirrels.

Dissected by the main Tiruvannamalai–Pondicherry road, Gingee fort comprises three separate citadels, crowning the summits of three dramatic hills: Krishnagiri to the north, Rajagiri to the west and Chandrayandurg to the southeast. Connecting them to form an enormous triangle, 1.5km from north to south, are twenty-metre-thick walls, punctuated by bastions and gateways giving access to the protected zones at the heart of the complex. It's hard to imagine such defences ever being overrun, but they were, on numerous occasions following the fort's foundations by the Vijayanagars in the fifteenth century. The Muslim Adil Shahis from Bijapur, Shivaji's Maharatas and the Moghuls all conquered Gingee, using it to consolidate the vulnerable southern reaches of their respective empires. The French also took it in 1750, but were ousted by the British after a bloody five-week siege eleven years later.

A network of raised, paved paths links the site's principal landmarks. From the road, head south to the main **east gate**, where a snaking passage emerges after no less than four changes of direction, inside the **palace** enclave. Of the many structures unearthed by archeologists here, the most distinctive is the square seven-storey **Kalyana Mahal tower**, focal point of the former governor's residence; featuring an ingenious hydraulic system that carried water to the uppermost levels, it is crowned by a tapering pyramidal tower. Continue west through a gateway, and you'll pick up the path to **Rajagiri**, Gingee's loftiest citadel; at 165 metres above the surrounding plain, it's a very stiff climb in the heat, but the views are well worth the effort.

The other ruins worth exploring lie a short way beyond the east gate. Typifiying Gingee's position at the interface between the warring powers of North and South India, the **mosque of Sadat Ullah Khan I**, built in the early years of the eighteenth century, stands a stone's throw from the sixteenth-century **Venkatarama temple**, dedicated to an aspect of Vishnu known as 'Lord of the Venkata Hills'. A dilapidated seven-storey *gopura* caps the east entrance, its passageway carved with scenes from the *Ramayana*.

Practicalities

Gingee is easily accessible by **bus** from Tiruvannamalai 37km west and Pondicherry 68km southeast. You can either alight at the site itself, 2km west of **Gingee** town, or, if you intend to spend the night there, dump your bags at the hotel and continue to the ruins by auto-rickshaw. The only **accommodation** to speak of (and the only dependable place to leave luggage while you visit the fort), is the *Shivasand Hotel*, on MG Road, opposite the main bus stand (☎04145/22218; ③–⑤), whose *Vasantham* South

Indian restaurant is Gingee's classiest place to eat. Auto-rickshaws charge Rs75 for the return trip from the town centre to the fort; you'll have to settle an additional fee for waiting time. Note that there are no refreshments, not even drinking water, available at the site, so take your own, or wander 500m back down the road towards town to the small roadside *chai* stall in the village.

Pondicherry and around

First impressions of **PONDICHERRY**, the former capital of French India, can be unpromising. Instead of the leafy boulevards and *pétanque* pitches you might expect, its messy outer suburbs and bus stand are as cluttered and chaotic as any other typically Tamil town. Closer to the seafront, however, the atmosphere grows tangibly more Gallic, as the bazaars give way to rows of houses whose shuttered windows and colour-washed facades wouldn't look out of place in Montpellier. For anyone familiar with the British colonial imprint, it can induce culture shock to see richly ornamented Catholic churches, French road names and policemen in de Gaulle-style kepis, not to mention hearing French spoken in the street.

Known to Greek and Roman geographers as "Poduke", Pondicherry was an important staging post on the second-century maritime trade route between Rome and the Far East (a Roman amphitheatre has been unearthed at nearby Arikamedu). When the Roman empire declined, the Pallavas and Cholas took control, followed by a succession of colonial powers, from the Portuguese in the sixteenth century to the French, Danes and British, who exchanged the enclave several times after the various battles and treaties of the Carnatic Wars in the early eighteenth century. Pondicherry's heyday, however, dates from the arrival of **Dupleix**, who accepted the governorship in 1742 and immediately set about rebuilding a town decimated by its former British occupants. It was he who instituted the street plan of a central grid encircled by a broad oblong boulevard, bisected north to south by a canal dividing the "Ville Blanche", to the east, from the "Ville Noire", to the west.

Although relinquished by the French in 1954 – when the town became the headquarters of the **Union Territory of Pondicherry**, administering the three other former colonial enclaves scattered across South India – Pondicherry's split personality still prevails. West of the canal stretches a bustling Indian market town, while to the east, towards the sea, the streets are emptier, cleaner and decidedly European. The seaside promenade, **Goubert Salai** (formerly Beach Rd), has the forlorn look of an out-of-season French resort, complete with its own white Hôtel de Ville. Tanned sun-worshippers share space with grave Europeans in white Indian costume, busy about their spiritual quest. It was here that **Shri Aurobindo Ghose** (1872–1950), a leading figure in the freedom struggle in Bengal, was given shelter after it became unwise to live close to the British in Calcutta. His **ashram** attracts thousands of devotees from all around the world, most particularly from Bengal.

Ten kilometres north, the utopian experiment-in-living **Auroville** was inspired by Aurobindo's disciple, the charismatic Mirra Alfassa, a Parisian painter, musician and mystic better known as "The Mother". Today this slightly surreal place is populated by numbers of expats and visited by long-stay Europeans eager to find inner peace.

More dissolute visitors find solace in the fact that Pondicherry levies no tax on alcohol. **Beer** is extremely cheap.

Arrival and information

The **STC bus stand**, arrival point for some long-distance services from Chennai, Madurai and Bangalore, lies on the west edge of town. Most services, however, including

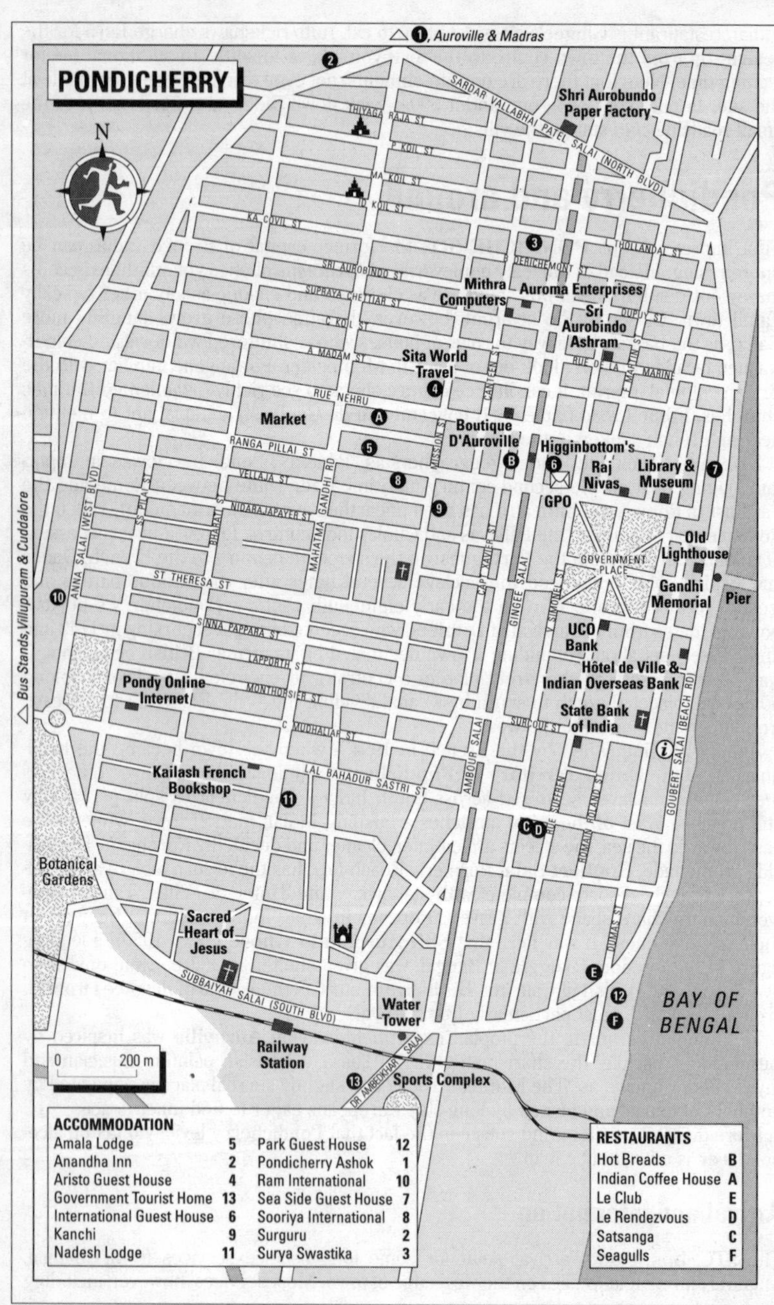

ACCOMMODATION			
Amala Lodge	5	Park Guest House	12
Anandha Inn	2	Pondicherry Ashok	1
Aristo Guest House	4	Ram International	10
Government Tourist Home	13	Sea Side Guest House	7
International Guest House	6	Sooriya International	8
Kanchi	9	Surguru	2
Nadesh Lodge	11	Surya Swastika	3

RESTAURANTS	
Hot Breads	B
Indian Coffee House	A
Le Club	E
Le Rendezvous	D
Satsanga	C
Seagulls	F

those from Mamallapuram via the new "ECR" (East Coast Rd), pull into another, busier bus stand, 500m further west; for a summary of routes, see the "Travel Details" on p.498. Pondicherry's **train station** is south of the centre, five minutes' walk from the sea; on a branch line, it's connected by four daily trains to the main line at Villupuram (departures 5.10am, 7.50am, 4.15pm & 9.45pm; 2hr). The first of these services, train #46, continues on to Chennai.

The friendly and helpful staff at the tiny **Pondicherry Tourism Development Corporation** office on Goubert Salai (daily 8.45am–1pm & 2–5pm; ☎0413/339497), can give you their leaflet and city map, book you onto their **city tour** (half-day 2–5.30pm; Rs40) and arrange **car rental** (Rs1000 per day, including fuel). Recommended places to **change money** include: the Indian Overseas Bank, in the Hôtel de Ville; Sita World Travels, 124 Mission St; the State Bank of India on Surcouf St; and UCO Bank, rue Mahe de Labourdonnais. The **GPO** is on Ranga Pillai St (Mon–Sat 10am–7.30pm).

The cheapest **Internet access** in Pondicherry is offered by Mithra Computers, at 55 Canteen St, one block east of Mission St in the northeast of town (daily 7am–9.30pm). A slightly more expensive, but correspondingly more comfortable option is the a/c Pondy On Line, 125 Candappa St (Mon–Sat 9.30am–12.30pm & 4–9pm).

Pondicherry is well served with both auto- and cycle-rickshaws, but for **getting around** most tourists rent a **bicycle** from one of the many stalls dotted around town. If you're staying at the *Park Guest House*, use one of theirs (they're all immaculately maintained). At the time of writing, the tourist office (see above) were also planning to offer good-quality cycles for rent. For trips further afield (to Auroville, for example), you may want to rent a **moped** or **scooter**. Of the rental firms operating in town, Auroma Enterprises, 9 Sri Aurobindo St (☎0413/36179) is the cheapest and has the best reputation, with new Honda Kinetics for Rs100/day. You'll have to pay a Rs500 deposit and leave your passport as security.

The Town

Pondicherry's beachside promenade, **Goubert Salai**, is a favourite place for a stroll, with cafés and bars to idle in and cooling breezes blowing in off the sea. There's little to do, other than watch the world go by, but the Hôtel de Ville, today housing the municipal offices, is still an impressive spectacle, and a four-metre-high Gandhi memorial, surrounded by ancient columns, dominates the northern end. Nearby, on the land side, a French memorial commemorates French Indians who lost their lives in World War I.

Just north of the Hôtel de Ville, a couple of streets back from the promenade, is the leafy old French-provincial-style square now named **Government Place**. A fountain stands at the centre, and among its paths and lawns are a number of sculptures carved in nearby Gingee. On its northern side, guarded by policemen in red képis, the impressive, gleaming white **Raj Nivas**, official home to the present lieutenant governor of Pondicherry Territory, was built late in the eighteenth century for Joseph Francis Dupleix, who became governor of French India. Unfortunately, the home of Ananda Ranga Pillai (1709–61), *dubash*, or close adviser of Dupleix – once one of the highlights of a visit to Pondicherry – is now closed to the public.

When this book was researched, the **Pondicherry Museum** (daily except Mon 10am–5pm) was about to reopen at new premises on Ranga Pillai St, opposite Government Place. While the location may have improved, the archeological collection – comprising Neolithic and 2000-year-old remains from Arikamedu, a few Pallava (sixth–eighth centuries) and Buddhist (tenth-century) stone sculptures, bronzes, weapons and paintings – should remain unchanged. Alongside these are displayed a bizarre assembly of French salon furniture and bric-a-brac from local houses, including a velvet S-shaped "conversation seat".

The **Sri Aurobindo Ashram** on rue de la Marine (daily 8am–noon & 2–6pm; no children under 3; photography with permission) is one of the best-known and wealthiest ashrams in India. Founded in 1926 by the Bengali philosopher-guru, Aurobindo Ghose, and his chief disciple, personal manager and mouthpiece, "The Mother", it serves as the headquarters of the Sri Aurobindo Society, or SAS, which today owns most of the valuable property and real estate in Pondicherry, and wields what many consider to be a disproportionate influence over the town. A beautifully maintained small rockery, cactus and flower garden greets you as you enter the compound. The **samadhi**, or mausoleum, of Sri Aurobindo and "The Mother" is covered daily with flowers and usually surrounded by supplicating devotees with their hands and heads placed on the tomb. Inside the main building, an incongruous and very bourgeois-looking Western-style room complete with three-piece suite, is where "The Mother" and Sri Aurobindo chilled out. Make sure not to tread on the Persian carpet on the floor, as devotees prostrate here also. A bookshop in the next room sells tracts, and frequent cultural programmes are presented in the building opposite.

In the southwest of town, near the train station, you can hardly miss the huge cream and brown **Sacred Heart of Jesus**, one of Pondicherry's finest Catholic churches, built by French missionaries in the 1700s. Nearby, the shady **Botanical Gardens** established in 1826, offer many quiet paths to wander (daily 8.45am–5.45pm). The French planted nine hundred species here, experimenting to see how they would do in Indian conditions; one, the *khaya senegalensis*, has grown to a height of 25m. You can also see an extraordinary fossilized tree, found about 25km away in Tiravakarai.

Accommodation

Pondicherry's **basic lodges** are concentrated around the main market area, Ranga Pillai St and rue Nehru. Guesthouses belonging to the **Sri Aurobindo Ashram** offer fantastic value for money, but come with a lot of baggage apart from your own (regulations, curfews and overpowering "philosophy of life" notices). Although supposedly open to all, they are not keen on advertising, or on attracting misguided individuals indulging in "spiritual tourism".

Inexpensive

Amala Lodge, 92 Ranga Pillai St (☎0413/338910). A cute, leafy little budget place off MG Rd, hemmed in by "Job Typing" offices. The rooms are large for the price, though most have common toilets, and they'll only take foreign backpackers. ①.

Aristo Guest House, 124 Mission St (☎0413/336728, fax 330057). Hard to find (look for the blue and white 'Sita World Travels' sign). Only nine budget rooms, ranged around a raised courtyard. Could be cleaner, but fine for a short stay. ②.

Government Tourist Home, Dr Ambedkhar Salai, Uppalam (☎0413/36376). Charmless, neon-lit concrete block at the bottom end of town and within earshot of the rail line, but an unbelievable bargain (doubles only Rs30). All rooms with attached shower-toilets and there are two ultra-cheap a/c rooms. ①.

International Guest House, Gingee Salai, near the GPO (☎0413/336699). The largest Aurobindo establishment, which has dozens of very large rooms, some a/c. ①–④.

Kanchi, 223 Mission St (☎0413/335544). A 1960s hotel that's seen better days. The rooms are huge, with green tiles and attached bathrooms, and the dearer ones have balconies. There's a meals canteen on the ground floor. Good value. ②.

Nadesh Lodge, 539 Mahatma Gandhi Rd, near Small Market Clock Tower (☎0413/339221). A popular backpackers' lodge, in a bustling neighbourhood bazaar, with twenty simple rooms fronting an elongated courtyard. In-house camera-repair-*wallah*, small library and walls of pot plants. ①.

Park Guest House, at the south end of Goubert Salai (☎0413/334412). Very comfortable, spotless rooms, slap on the seafront, with new mozzie nets and sitouts overlooking a well-watered garden.

Cycle rental, laundry and cafeteria. By far the best choice in town, if you can handle the churlish reception. ③.

Sea Side Guest House, 14 Goubert Salai (☎0413/326494). The most characterful Aurobindo guesthouse, in an old converted mansion on the promenade. Often full as there are only eight rooms (two are a/c), some of them palatial. ②–④.

Surya Swastika, 11 Iswaran (ID) Koil St (☎0413/343092). Traditional Tamil guesthouse in a quiet corner of town, with nine basic rooms around a central courtyard that doubles as a pilgrims' canteen at lunchtime. Incredibly cheap (Rs70 for a double room), and cleaner than most of the bazaar lodges. ①.

Moderate to expensive

Anandha Inn, Sardar Vallabhai Patel Salai (☎0413/330711, fax 331241). Pondy's swishest hotel. seventy luxurious rooms, two restaurants and a pastry shop, in a gleaming white building. Good value at this price. ⑦.

Pondicherry Ashok, Chinnakalapet, 12km from Pondicherry on the old coastal road to Mamallapuram, near Auroville (☎0413/65160, fax 65140). Twenty comfortable rooms in a quiet, breezy location on the seashore. Children's park, restaurant, barbecue and bar. Generous discounts for stays of three days or more. ⑦.

Ram International, 398 Anna Salai (☎0413/337230, fax 337238). Very good-value, efficient, modern place on the western edge of town. Advance booking recommended. ⑤.

Sooriya International, 55 Ranga Pillai St (☎0413/338910). Very large, immaculate rooms in new, central hotel. An ostentatious exterior, but reasonable tariffs. ⑥.

Surguru, next door to the *Anandha Inn*, 104 Sardar Vallabhai Patel Salai (North Blvd), (☎339022, fax 334377). Best value among Pondy's mid-price hotels. Spruce, spacious rooms, brisk service and most mod cons, including an excellent veg restaurant (see Eating). ⑤–⑥.

Eating

If you've been on the road for a while and are hankering for healthy salads, fresh coffee, crusty bread, cakes and real pastry, you'll be spoilt for choice in Pondicherry. Unlike the traveller-oriented German-bakery-style places elsewhere in the country, the Western restaurants here cater for a predominantly expatriate clientele, with discerning palettes and fat French-franc pay cheques. Pick of the bunch has to be the sophisticated *Le Club*, but you can eat well for a lot less at the more atmospheric *Satsanga*. **Beer** is available just about everywhere except the SAS-owned establishments.

Anugraha, *Hotel Surguru*, 104 Sardar Vallabhai Patel Salai (North Blvd). Widely rated as the best lunch-time "meals" restaurant in town (Rs30 for the full works), but they also serve superb *dosa-iddli* breakfasts and coffee, and a full *tandoori* menu in the evening. The only downside is the dingy basement location.

Hot Breads, 42 Ambour Salai. Crusty croissants, fresh baguettes, and delicious savoury pastry snacks, served in a squeaky clean French boulangerie-café and the espresso's a dream.

Indian Coffee House, rue Nehru. Not their cleanest branch, but the coffee is good, and the waiters are as picturesque as usual in ice-cream-wafer hats.

Le Club, 33 Dumas St. Beyond the pocket of most travellers, not to mention locals, but far and away the town's top restaurant. The predominantly French menu features their famous *coq au vin, steak au poivre*, plenty of seafood options and a full wine list, rounded off with cognac at Rs200 a shot. Count on Rs300 per head (if you forgo the shorts).

Le Rendezvous, 30 rue Suffren. Filling seafood sizzlers and *tandoori* brochettes are specialties of this popular ex-pat-orientated restaurant. They also serve fresh croissants and espresso for breakfast, either indoors or up on the more romantic rooftop, with jazz sounds and chilled beer in discreet ceramic jugs. Most main dishes Rs70–120.

Satsanga, Lal Bahadur Sastri St. If you only eat once in Pondy, it should be here. Served on the colonnaded verandah of an old colonial mansion, the menu (devised by the French patron) is carefully prepared and exactly the kind of thing you dream about elsewhere in India: organic salads with fresh herbs, tsatsiki and garlic bread, sauté potatoes, tagliatelle à la carbonara, and mouthwatering pizzas washed down with chilled Kingfisher beer. Check their *plat du jour* for fresh fish dishes. Around Rs250 per head for three courses with drinks.

Seagulls Restaurant and Bar, 19 Dumas St. Reasonably priced, open-air rooftop restaurant in breezy spot right next to the sea, new pier and cargo harbour. Huge menu, with veg dishes, meat, seafood, Indian, Chinese and even some Italian (pizza, risotto, spaghetti). Inexpensive.

Auroville

The most New Age place anywhere in India must surely be **AUROVILLE**, the planned "City of Dawn", 10km north of Pondicherry, just outside the Union Territory in Tamil Nadu. Founded in 1968, Auroville was inspired by "The Mother", the spiritual successor of Sri Aurobindo. Around 1350 people live in communes (two-thirds of them are non-Indians), with such names as Fertile, Certitude, Sincerity, Revelation and Transformation, in what it is hoped will eventually be an ideal city for a population of 50,000. Architecturally experimental buildings, combining modern Western and traditional Indian elements, are set in a rural landscape of narrow lanes, deep red earth and lush greenery. Income is derived from agriculture, handicrafts, alternative technology, educational and development projects and *Aurolec*, a computer software company.

Although the avowed aim is to live in harmony, a life made meaningful through hard physical work backed up by spiritual discipline, the place has had its ups and downs, not least of which have been the **disputes** between the community and the Sri Aurobindo Society (SAS) over ownership since the death of "The Mother" in 1973. Rejecting the Aurovillians' calls for self-determination, the SAS cut off funds to the community, forcing them to become financially self-sufficient. The power struggle intensified in the mid-1970s, erupting into full-blown violence on a couple of occasions before the police were called in. At one stage, the war of attrition got so tough that some Western countries had to provide aid to the Aurovillians. Eventually, however, the High Court ruled in their favour, and in 1988, the Auroville Foundations Act was passed, placing responsibility for the administration of the settlement in the hands of a seven-member council, with representatives from the state government, the SAS and Auroville itself.

One of the accusations levelled at the settlers around this time was that, although Auroville was supposedly an egalitarian community, most of the Indians involved were being relegated to the status of labourers. Aurovillians countered these attacks by pointing to the numerous ways they had worked to improve the lives of low-caste Tamils in the surrounding villages, many of whom had been given full-time jobs manufacturing textiles, software and eco-friendly unbaked bricks. The site also has a school for local Tamil children, started by a retired policeman from Essex, England.

Considering how little there is to see here, Auroville attracts a disproportionately large number of day-trippers – much to the chagrin of its inhabitants, who rightly point out that you can only get a sense of what the settlement is all about if you stay a while. Interested visitors are welcomed as paying guests in most of the communes, where you can work alongside permanent residents (see "Practicalities" opposite).

The Matri Mandir

The various conflicts of the past two decades have inevitably spawned divisions among the Aurovillians themselves. While some still treat the teachings of "The Mother" with the same uncritical devotion as the Pondicherry ashramites, others have strayed from the orthodoxy. One thing, however, unites the whole community: the **Matri Mandir**, or "dwelling place of The Mother", a gigantic, almost spherical, hi-tech meditation centre at the heart of the site.

Begun in 1970, the space-age structure was conceived as "a symbol of the Divine's answer to man's inspiration for perfection. Union with the Divine manifesting in a progressive unity". Earth from 126 countries was symbolically placed in an urn, now kept in a concrete cone from which a speaker can address an audience of 3000 without amplification. Due to the lack of funds resulting from the split with the SAS, the complex remains largely unfinished, its bare concrete casing covered in rusting scaffolds. Only the **Inner Room** at its very centre has been completed. In accordance with the instructions of "The Mother", this is open to all (daily 4–5pm; arrive at least one hour in advance), although the Aurovillians' reluctance to admit outsiders is palpable. After a long wait for tickets to be issued, accompanied by strict instructions on how to behave while inside, visitors are ushered in silence to the Matri Mandir's ramped entrance for a fleeting glimpse of the 70cm crystal ball that forms its focal point, made by the Swiss optics company, Karl Zeiss, and believed to be the largest of its kind in the world. Contrary to the intentions of the architects, the whole experience can leave a bad taste in your mouth; the Aurovillians clearly hate having to herd day-trippers through what most of them regard as the soul of their community. However, you'll get a different response if you express more than a passing interest; your original entry ticket allows you to return later for an hour of silent meditation, and if you are keen to come back after this, you may be granted permission for a visit out of normal hours. Only then, Aurovillians claim, will you appreciate the real significance of the place.

Practicalities

Auroville lies 10km north of Pondicherry on the main Chennai road; you can also get there via the new coastal highway, turning off at the village of Chinna Mudaliarchavadi. **Bus** services are frequent along both routes but – as Auroville is so spread out, covering some fifty or so square kilometres – it's best to come with your own transport, at the very least a bike. Most people rent a scooter or **motorcycle** from Pondicherry and ride up. Alternatively, book onto Tamil Nadu Tourism's daily **tour** from Pondicherry (depart 2pm, return 5.30pm; Rs40).

For a pre-visit primer, call in at the **visitor centre** (daily 9.30am–5.30pm), bang in the middle of the site near the Bharat Niwas, which holds a permanent exhibition on the history and philosophies of the settlement. You can also pick up some inexpensive literature on Auroville in the adjacent bookshop and check out a notice board for details of **activities** in which visitors may participate (these typically include yoga, reiki and Vipassana meditation, costing around Rs50 per session). In addition, there's a handicrafts outlet and a pleasant little veg café serving snacks and drinks.

The information desk at the visitor centre is also the place to enquire about **paying guest accommodation** in Auroville's thirty or so communes. Officially there's no lower limit on the time you have to stay, but visitors are encouraged to stick around for at least a week, helping out on communal projects; tariffs are in the range Rs100–400 per day, depending on levels of comfort. Alternatively, you can arrange to stay in one of four **guesthouses**, offering simple non-a/c rooms from US$5–15 (payable in rupees). Beds in these, and in the communes, tend to be in short supply during the two peak periods of December to March and July to August, when it is advisable to book well in advance by fax (0413/62274), email *guests@auroville.org.in*, or in writing (c/o Auroville Guest Programmes, Auroville 605 101, Tamil Nadu). Otherwise, the only rooms in the area are just outside Auroville. In the village of Chinna Mudaliarchavadi, the *Palm Beach Cottage Centre* (①) is nothing of the kind (the sea is fifteen minutes' walk away), but has passably clean rooms with shared toilets and a small garden, where meals are served. Nearby, the *Cottage Guest House* (②) offers a little more comfort in thatched huts or a recently built block boasting en-suite rooms. For **food**, you won't do better than the simple, filling veg meals served in the visitor centre café, already mentioned.

CENTRAL TAMIL NADU: THE CHOLA HEARTLAND

"To be on the banks of the Cauvery listening to the strains of Carnatic music is to have a taste of eternal bliss."

Tamil proverb

Continuing south from Pondicherry along the Coromandel Coast, you enter the flat landscape of the **Kaveri** (aka Cauvery) **Delta**, a watery world of canals, dams, dykes and rivulets that has been intensively farmed since ancient times. Only a hundred miles in diameter, it forms the rice-bowl core of Tamil Nadu, crossed by more than thirty major rivers and countless streams. The largest of them, the **Kaveri River**, known in Tamil as *Ponni*, "The Lady of Gold" (a form of the Mother Goddess), is revered as a conduit of liquid *shakti*, the primordial female energy that nurtures the millions of farmers who live on her banks and tributaries. Three bumper crops each year are coaxed from the giant patchwork of paddy, which Colonel Fullarton in his *View of English Interests in India* (1785) described as " …teeming with an industrious race expert in agriculture. Such are the natural benefits it enjoys that no spot on the globe is superior in productions for the use of man." Amid the stifling heat of mid-July, on the eighteenth day of the solar month Adi, villagers have for hundreds, possibly thousands, of years gathered in vast numbers to mark the rising of the river. During the festival, money, cloth, jewellery, food, tools and household utensils are thrown into the river as offerings, so that the goddess will have all she needs for the coming year.

This mighty delta formed the very heartland of the **Chola** empire, which reached its apogee between the ninth and thirteenth centuries, an era often compared to Classical Greece and Renaissance Italy, both for its cultural richness and the sheer scale and profusion of its architectural creations. Much as the Cholas originally intended, every visitor immediately stands in awe of their huge temples, not only in cities such as **Chidambaram**, **Kumbakonam** and **Thanjavur**, but also out in the countryside at places like **Gangaikondacholapuram**, where the temple is all that remains of a once-great city.

Exploring the area for a few days will bring you into contact with the more delicate side of Cholan artistic expression, such as the magnificent **bronzes** of Thanjavur, and the incantatory **saints' hymns** of the *Sangam* and *Tevaram*, bodies of oral poetry that emerged in the delta more than a thousand years ago. Its composers were wandering poets who travelled the length and breadth of the south, singing, dancing and spreading a new devotional brand of Hinduism known as **bhakti**. Phrased in a classical Tamil of a richness rarely equalled since, their verses praise the beauty of the delta's natural landscape and recall the significance of the countless shrines and other sacred sites strewn across it (more than half of the 274 holy Shaivite places in Tamil Nadu are found here). Considering many were not set down in Sanskrit until centuries after they were composed, it is a miracle that the hymns have survived at all. But today, they form the basis of a thriving oral tradition, sung in temples, *maths* (religious institutions), pilgrims' buses and homes wherever Tamil is the lingua franca. The poems have also provided the raw material for many a hit mythological movie, and you'll hear modern versions of the better-known ones, jazzed up with electric guitars and synthesizers, blaring out of audio-cassette stores.

Nowhere else in the world has a classical civilization survived the twentieth century, and the knowledge that the ancient culture of the Cholas endures here alongside their awesome monuments lends a unique resonance to any journey across the Kaveri Delta.

Chidambaram

CHIDAMBARAM, 58km south of Pondicherry, is so steeped in myth that its history is hard to unravel. As the site of the *tandava*, the cosmic dance of Shiva as **Nataraja,** King of the Dance, it is one of the holiest sites in South India. A visit to the **Sabhanayaka Nataraja temple** affords a fascinating glimpse into ancient Tamil religious practice and belief. The legendary king **Hiranyavarman** is said to have made a pilgrimage here from Kashmir, seeking to rid himself of leprosy by bathing in the temple's Shivaganga tank. In thanks for a successful cure, he enlarged the temple. He also brought 3000 *brahmins,* of the Dikshitar caste, whose descendants are to this day the ritual specialists of the temple, distinguishable by topknots of hair at the front of their heads.

Few of the fifty *maths*, or monasteries, that once stood here remain, but the temple itself is still a hive of activity and hosts numerous **festivals**. The two most important are ten-day affairs, building up to spectacular finales: on the ninth day of each, temple chariots process through the four Car streets (**"car festival"**), while on the tenth, **abhishekham**, the principal deities in the *raja sabha* (thousand-pillared hall) are anointed. For exact dates (one is in May/June, the other in Dec/Jan), contact any TTDC tourist office and plan well ahead, as they are very popular. Other local festivals include fire-walking and *kavadi* folk dance (dancing with decorated wooden frames on the head) at the Thillaiamman Kali (April/May) and Keelatheru Mariamman (July/Aug) temples.

The town also has a hectic market, and a large student population, which is based at Annamalai University, a centre of Tamil studies, to the east. Among the simple thatched huts in the local flat, sparsely populated countryside, which becomes very dry and dusty in summer, the only solid-looking structures are small roadside temples. Many honour Aiyannar, the village deity who protects borders, and are accompanied by *kudirais*, brightly painted terracotta or wooden figures of horses.

Arrival and information

The town revolves around the Sabhanayaka Nataraja temple and the busy market area that surrounds it, along North, East, South and West Car streets. Though little more than a country halt, the **train station**, 2km southeast of the centre, has good connections both north and south, boasts retiring rooms and on platform 1 a **post office** (Mon–Sat 9am–1pm & 1.30–5pm). Buses from Chennai, Thanjavur, Mamallapuram, and Madurai pull in at the **bus stand**, also in the southeast, but nearer the centre, about 1km from the temple.

Staff at the TTDC **tourist office**, next to the *TTDC Tamil Nadu Hotel* on Railway Feeder Rd, are charming and helpful, but only have a small pamphlet to give to visitors. None of the **banks** in Chidambaram changes money.

Sabhanayaka Nataraja temple

For South India's Shaivites, the **Sabhanayaka Nataraja temple** (daily 4am–noon & 4.30–10pm), where Shiva is enthroned as Lord of the Cosmic Dance, Nataraja, is the holiest of holies. Its huge *gopuras*, whose lights are used as landmarks by sailors far out to sea in the Bay of Bengal, soar above a fifty-five-acre complex, divided by four concentric walls. The oldest parts now standing were built under the Cholas, who adopted Nataraja as their chosen deity and crowned several kings here. The rectangular outermost wall, of little interest in itself, affords entry on all four sides, so if you have the time the best way to tackle the complex is to work slowly inwards from the third enclosure in clockwise circles. **Guides** are readily available but tend to shepherd visitors towards the central shrine too quickly. Frequent **ceremonies** take place at the innermost sanctum, the most popular being at 5pm. On Friday nights before the temple closes, during a particularly elaborate *puja*, Nataraja is carried on a palanquin accompanied by music and attendants carrying flaming torches and tridents. At other times, you'll hear ancient devotional hymns from the *Tevaram*.

The third enclosure

Four gigantic *gopura* towers rise out of the irregular third wall, each with a granite base and a brick-built superstructure of diminishing storeys covered in a profusion of carved figures. The western *gopura* is the most popular entrance, as well as being the most elaborately carved and probably the earliest (*c*.1150 AD). Turning north (left) from here, you come to the colonnaded **Shivaganga tank**, the site of seven natural springs. From the broken pillar at the tank's edge, all four *gopuras* are visible.

Facing the tank, on the left side, is the **Shivakamasundari temple**, devoted to Parvati, consort of Shiva. Step inside to see the Nayak (sixteenth-century) ceiling paintings arranged in cartoon-like frames in muted reds and yellows. On the right as you enter, the story of the leper king Hiranyavarman is illustrated, and at the back, frames form a map of the temple complex. Next door, in the northwest corner, a shrine to Subrahmanya, the son of Shiva, is adorned with paintings illustrating stories from the *Skanda Purana*. Beyond this, in front of the northern *gopura*, stands a small shrine to the Navagraha (nine planets).

In the northeast corner, the largest building in the complex, the **Raja Sabha** (fourteenth–fifteenth century) is also known as "the thousand-pillared hall"; tradition holds that there are only nine hundred and ninety-nine actual pillars, the thousandth being Shiva's leg. During festivals the deities Nataraja and Shivakamasundari are brought here and mounted on a dais for the anointing ceremony, *abhishekha*.

The importance of **dance** at Chidambaram is underlined by the reliefs of dancing figures inside the east *gopura* demonstrating 108 *karanas* (a similar set is to be found in the west *gopura*). A *karana* (or *adavu*, in Tamil) is a specific point in a phase of movement prescribed by the extraordinarily comprehensive Sanskrit treatise on the performing arts, the *Natya Shastra* (*c*.200 BC–200 AD) – the basis of all Indian classical dance, music and theatre. A caption from the *Natya Shastra* surmounts each *karana* niche. Four other niches are filled with images of patrons and *stahapatis* – the sculptors and designers responsible for the iconography and positioning of deities.

A pavilion at the south *gopura* houses an image of Nandi, Shiva's bull. Although not accessible from here, the central Nataraja shrine faces south; as with all Shiva temples, Nandi sits opposite the god. In the southwest corner, a shrine contains one of the largest images in India of the elephant-headed son of Shiva, Ganapati (Ganesh). If you stand inside the entrance (*mandapa*), with your back to Ganapati, you'll see at the base of the two pillars nearest the shrine, carvings of the two important devotees of Nataraja at Chidambaram (see box opposite). To the right is the sage Patanjali, with a snake's body, and on the left Vyaghrapada, with a human body and tiger's feet.

The second enclosure

To get into the square second enclosure, head for its **western entrance** (just north of the west *gopura* in the third wall), which leads into a circumambulatory passageway. Once beyond this second wall it's easy to become disorientated, as the roofed inner enclosures see little light and are supported by a maze of colonnades. The atmosphere is immediately more charged, reaching its peak at the very centre.

On the north side, the **Mulasthana** houses the *svayambhulingam* worshipped by Patanjali and Vyaghrapada. The **Deva Sabha**, or "hall of the gods", on the east, shelters as many as a hundred bronze images used in processions and is a meeting place for members of the three hundred Dikshitar *brahmin* families who own and maintain the temple. Beyond it lies the other, eastern entrance to the second enclosure.

The **Nritta Sabha**, or "dance hall", stands on the site where Shiva outdanced Kali (see box below), now the southwest corner of the second enclosure. Probably the oldest surviving structure of the two inner areas, its raised platform was fashioned in stone to resemble a wooden temple chariot, or *ratha*. Before they were inexplicably concreted over in the mid-1950s, the east and west sides of the base were each adorned with a wheel and a horse; all that can be seen now are fragments.

THE DANCE COMPETITION BETWEEN SHIVA AND KALI

The thousand-headed cosmic serpent, **Adisesha**, upon whose coiled body Vishnu reclines in the primordial ocean, once expressed a wish to see Shiva's famed dance. Having arranged time off from his normal duties with Vishnu, Adisesha prayed to Shiva, who was so impressed by the serpent's entreaties that he promised to dance in the forest of Tillai (the site of Chidambaram). Adisesha was reborn as the human sage **Patanjali** (represented as half-man, half-snake) and made straight for Tillai. There he met another sage who shared his wish to see Shiva dance, **Vyaghrapada** – "Tiger Feet", who had been granted the claws of a tiger to help him climb trees and pluck the best flowers to offer Shiva. Together, they worshipped a *svayambhulingam*, a *shivalingam* that had "self-manifested" in the forest, now housed in the Mulasthana shrine of Sabhanayaka temple. However, the guardian of the forest, who turned out to be the goddess **Kali**, refused to allow Shiva to dance when he arrived. In response, he challenged her to a **dance competition** for possession of the forest. Kali agreed but, perhaps due to modesty, could not match a pose of Shiva's which involved raising the right foot above the head. Defeated, Kali was forced to move off a little way north, where a temple now stands in her honour.

The innermost enclosure

Passing through the southern entrance (marked by a gold flagstaff) to the **innermost enclosure** brings you immediately into a hallway, which leads west to the nearby **Govindaraja shrine**, dedicated to Vishnu – a surprise in this most Shaivite of environments. Govindaraja is attended by non-Dikshitar *brahmins*, who, it is said, don't always get along with the Dikshitars. From outside the shrine, non-Hindus can see through to the most sacred part of the temple, the **Kanaka Sabha** and the **Chit Sabha**, adjoining raised structures, roofed with copper and gold plate and linked by a hallway. Two huge bells and extremely loud *nagaswarams* (double-reed wind instruments), *tavils* (drums) and *nattuvangams* (cymbals) call worshippers for ceremonies. The only entrance – closed to non-Hindus – is up five silver-plated steps into the Chit Sabha, guarded by the devotees Vyaghrapada and Patanjali and lit by an arc of flickering oil lamps.

The Chit Sabha houses bronze images of Nataraja and his consort Shivakamasundari. Behind and to the left of Nataraja, a curtain, sacred to Shiva and strung with rows of leaves from the bilva tree, demarcates the most potent area of all. Within it lies the **Akashalingam**, known as the Rahasya, or "secret", of Chidambaram: made of the most subtle of the elements, Ether (*akasha*) – from which air, fire, water and earth are born – the *lingam* is invisible. This is said to signify that God is nowhere, only in the human heart.

A crystal *lingam*, said to have emanated from the light of the crescent moon on Shiva's brow, and a small ruby Nataraja are worshipped in the Kanaka Sabha. They are ritually bathed in the flames of the priests' camphor fire or oil lamps six times a day. This inner area is where you're most likely to hear **oduvars**, hereditary singers from the middle, non-*brahmin* castes, intoning verses of ancient Tamil poetry. The songs with which they regail the deities at *puja* time, drawn from compilations such the *Tevaram* or earlier *Sangam*, are more than a thousand years old

Accommodation and eating

To cope with the influx of tourists and pilgrims, Chidambaram abounds in budget **accommodation**, but there are few upper-bracket options beyond the *Saradharam* hotel, near the bus stand, and the *Aksha Plaza*, a brand-new place (nearing completion when this book was researched) on South Car Street between the bus stand and temple. There are plenty of basic, wholesome "meals" places on and around the Car streets: *Shri Ganesa Bhavan*, on West Car St, gets the locals' vote, but for quality, inexpensive South Indian food you can't beat the *Pallavi*, at the *Saradharam* hotel, which is packed at lunchtimes for its good-value *thalis*. The *Annu Pallai* behind it is an equally commendable, though somewhat dingy, non-veg alternative. There's also a small *Indian Coffee House*, on Venugopal Pillai St, that's a pleasant breakfast venue or place to peruse the papers.

Akshaya, 17/18 E Car St (☎04144/20591). Pleasant mid-range hotel, backing onto the temple wall, with thirty rooms (three a/c: non-a/c is better value) and helpful staff. ③–④.

Mansoor Lodge, 91 East Car St (☎04144/21072). Walls are on the grubby side, but otherwise a good cheapy: spotless, tiled floors and clean bathrooms. Watch out for the "Speed Breakers" on the corridors, though. ②.

Railway Retiring Rooms, ask at the Station Master's Office, platform 1. The best deal in town – huge clean rooms, though the bathrooms are a little dilapidated. ①.

Raja Rajan, 162 West Car St (☎04144/22690). Neat and clean rooms close to the temple, with tiled bathrooms and low tariffs. Good value. ②.

Sabanayagam, 22 East Sannathi, off E Car St (☎04144/20896). Despite a flashy exterior, this is a run-of-the-mill budget place. Ask for a room with a window, preferably on the second floor overlooking the temple entrance. There's a good veg restaurant downstairs. Some a/c. ②–③.

Saradharam, 19 Venugopal Pillai St, opposite the bus stand (☎04144/21336, fax 22656). Until the *Aksha Plaza* opens, Chidambaram's poshest hotel. Large, clean and well-kept rooms (some a/c) in modern buildings, with two decent restaurants, a small garden, bar, laundry and foreign exchange. ⑤–⑦.

TTDC Hotel Tamil Nadu, Railway Feeder Rd, located between the train station and bus stand (☎04144/20056). Friendly, but some rooms are woefully neglected: check the bedding is clean, and if the a/c works. Also dorm beds (①–⑤).

Gangaikondacholapuram

Devised as the centrepiece of a city built by the Chola king Rajendra I (1014–42) to celebrate his conquests, the magnificent **Brihadishwara temple** stands in the tiny village of **GANGAIKONDACHOLAPURAM**, in Trichy District, 35km north of Kumbakonam. The tongue-twisting name means "the town of the Chola who took the Ganges". Under Rajendra I, the Chola empire did indeed stretch as far as the great river of the north, an unprecedented achievement for a southern dynasty. Aside from the temple and the rubble remains of Rajendra's palace, 2km east at Tamalikaimedu, nothing of the city remains. Nonetheless, this is among the most extraordinary archeological sites of South India, outshone only by Thanjavur, and devoid of visitors most of the time, which gives it a memorably forlorn feel.

Hourly **buses** run here from Kumbakonam, and it is also served by some between Trichy and Chidambaram. Be sure not to get stuck here between noon and 4pm when the temple is closed. Parts of the interior are extremely dark, and a torch is useful. Facilities are minimal; there's little more than a few cool drinks stands.

Brihadishwara temple

The **Brihadishwara temple** (daily 6am–noon & 4–8pm) is enclosed by a rectangular wall; visitors enter through a gateway to the north, separated from the main road by a car park. From here you arrive at a well-maintained, grassy courtyard, flanked by a closed hallway (*mandapa*). Over the sanctuary, to the right, a massive pyramidal tower (*vimana*) rises 55m in nine diminishing storeys. Though smaller than the one at Thanjavur, the tower's graceful curve gives it an impressive refinement.

Turning left (east) inside the courtyard you pass a small shrine to the goddess **Durga**, containing an image of Mahishasuramardini (see p.401). Just beyond, steps climb from a large seated lion, known as Simha-kinaru and made from plastered brickwork, to a well. King Rajendra is said to have had Ganges water placed in it to be used for the ritual anointing of the *lingam* in the main temple.

Set into the east wall, the remains of a *gopura* entranceway lead directly to a large water tank. Directly in front, before the eastern entrance to the temple, stands a small altar for offerings and a huge Nandi bull. Two flights of steps on the north and south ascend to a porch, the *mukhamandapa*, where a large pair of guardian deities flank the entrance to the long pillared *mahamandapa* hallway. Here you're likely to meet the ASI caretakers, who are worth taking as guides, especially if you'd like to climb up onto the roof for views of the vicinity and of the tower. Access is from within the temple, up steep steps. Immediately inside, on either side of the doorway, sculptures of Shiva in his various benevolent (*anugraha*) manifestations include him blessing Vishnu, Devi, Ravana and the saint Chandesha (see p.435). In the northeast corner an unusual square, stone block features carvings of the nine planets (*navagraha*). A number of **Chola bronzes** (see p.588) stand on the platform; the figure of Karttikeya, the war god, carrying a club and a shield, is thought to have had particular significance.

The base of the main temple sanctuary is decorated with lions and scrollwork. Above this decoration, running from the southern to the northern entrance of the *ardhamandapa*, a series of sculpted figures in plastered niches portray different images of Shiva. The most famous is at the northern entrance, showing Shiva and Parvati garlanding the saint Chandesha, who here is sometimes identified as Rajendra I. For more on the temples of Tamil Nadu, see Contexts, p.585.

Two minutes' walk east along the main road (turn right from the car park), the tiny **Archeological Museum** (daily except Fri 10am–1pm & 2–5.45pm) contains Chola odds and ends, discovered locally. The finds include terracotta lamps, coins, weapons, tiles, bronze, bangle pieces, palm-leaf manuscripts and an old Chinese pot.

Kumbakonam and around

Sandwiched between the Kaveri (Cauvery) and Arasalar Rivers, **KUMBAKONAM**, 74km southwest of Chidambaram and 38km northeast of Thanjavur, is believed by Hindus to be the place where the water pot (*kumba*) of *amrita*, the ambrosial beverage of immortality, was washed up by a great deluge from atop sacred Mount Meru in the Himalaya. Shiva, who happened to be passing in the guise of a wild forest-dwelling hunter, for some reason fired an arrow at the pot, causing it to break. From the shards, he made the *lingam* that is now enshrined in the **Kumbareshwara temple**, whose *gopuras* tower over the town, along with those of some seventeen other major shrines. A former capital of the Cholas, who are said to have kept a high-security treasury here, Kumbakonam is today the chief commercial centre for the

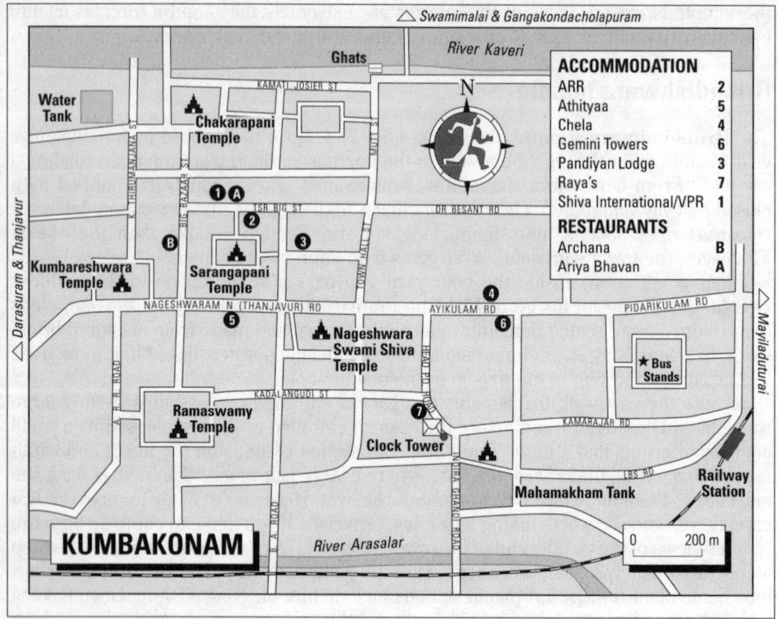

Thanjavur region. The main bazaar, **Big St**, is especially renowned for its quality costume jewellery.

The main reason to stop in Kumbakonam is to admire the exquisite sculpture of the **Nageshwara Swami Shiva temple**, which contains the most refined Chola stone carving still in situ. The town also lies within easy reach of the magnificent Darasuram and Gangaikondacholapuram temples, both spectacular ancient monuments that see very few visitors. In addition, the village of Swamimalai, only a bike ride away, is the state's principal centre for traditional **bronze-casting**.

Arrival and information

Kumbakonam's small **train station**, in the southeast, 2km from the main bazaar, is well served by trains both north and south, and has a left luggage office (24hr) and decent **retiring rooms** (①). The hectic **Moffussil** (local) and **Aringannar** (long-distance) bus stands are opposite each other in the southeast of town, between the train station and the Mahamakham tank. All the timetables are in Tamil, but there's a 24-hour enquiry office. Buses leave for Gangaikondacholapuram hourly, and Thanjavur every few minutes, many via Darasuram. Frequent services run to Chennai, and several daily to Bangalore and Pondicherry.

The Town

Surmounted by a multicoloured *gopura*, the eastern entrance of Kumbakonam's seventeenth-century **Kumbareshwara temple**, home of the famous *lingam* from where the town derived its name, is approached via a covered market selling a huge assortment of cooking pots, a local speciality, as well as the usual glass bangles and trinkets. As you enter, you pass the temple elephant, Manganal, with painted forehead and necklace of bells. Beyond the flagstaff, a *mandapa* houses a fine collection of silver *vahanas* (vehicles of the deities, used in festivals), and *pancha loham* (compound of silver, gold, brass, iron and tin) figures of the sixty-three Nayanmar poet-saints (see p.550).

The principal and largest of the Vishnu temples in Kumbakonam is the thirteenth-century **Sarangapani temple**, entered through a ten-storey pyramidal *gopura* gate, more than 45 metres high. The **central shrine** dates from the late Chola period with many later accretions. Its entrance, within the innermost court, is guarded by huge *dvarpalas*, identical to Vishnu whom they protect. Between them are carved stone *jali* screens, each different, and in front of them stands the sacred, square *homam* fireplace. During the day, pinpoints of light from ceiling windows penetrate the darkness around the sanctum, designed to resemble a chariot with reliefs of horses, elephants and wheels. A painted cupboard contains a mirror for Vishnu to see himself when he leaves the sanctum sanctorum.

The small **Nageshwara Swami Shiva temple**, in the centre of town, is Kumbakonam's oldest temple, founded in 886 and completed a few years into the reign of Parantaka I (907–*c*.940). First impressions are unpromising, as much of the original building has been hemmed in by later, Disney-coloured accretions, but beyond the main courtyard, occupied by a large columned *mandapa*, a small *gopura*-topped gateway leads to an inner enclosure where the earliest Chola shrine stands. Framed in the main niches around its sanctum wall are a series of exquisite stone figures, regarded as the finest surviving pieces of **ancient sculpture** in South India. With their languid stance and mesmeric, half-smiling facial expressions, these modest-sized masterpieces far outshine the more monumental art of Thanjavur and Gangaikondacholapuram. The figures show Dakshinamurti (Shiva as a teacher, on the south wall), Durga and a three-headed Brahma (north wall) and Ardanari, half-man, half-woman (west wall). Joining them are near-life-size voluptuous maidens believed to be queens or princesses of King Aditya's court.

The most famous and revered of many sacred **water tanks** in Kumbakonam, the **Mahamakham tank** in the southeast of town, is said to have filled with ambrosia (*amrit*) collected from the pot broken by Shiva. Every twelve years, when Jupiter passes the constellation of Leo, it is believed that water from the Ganges and eight other holy rivers flows into the tank, thus according it the status of *tirtha*, or sacred river crossing. At this auspicious time, as many as four million pilgrims come here for an absolving bathe. On the last occasion, on February 18, 1992, the former chief minister of Tamil Nadu, Jayalalitha Jayaraman (see box on p.383), numbered among them. Her visit, billed by the spin-doctors as coinciding with her birthday, had been advertised throughout the state by giant roadside hoardings and headlines imploring Hindus to "Come, have a holy dip on the auspicious day." However, the publicity stunt backfired tragically. As Jayalalitha was being showered with sacred water in a specially reserved corner of the tank, the crowds pressed forward to get a closer look, provoking a *lathi* charge from her police bodyguard. In the ensuing stampede, 48 pilgrims were crushed to death. Newspaper reports over the following weeks ascribed the accident to "collapsing walls" and "general mayhem".

Accommodation

Kumbakonam is not a major tourist location, and has limited **accommodation**, with only one upper-range hotel, the *Sterling Swamimalai*, 10km southeast of town on the outskirts of Swamimalai village (see p.436). The good news for budget travellers is that most of the inexpensive places are clean and well maintained.

ARR, 21 TSR Big St (☎0435/421234). Fifty large, clean rooms (some a/c), on five floors, all with windows, and TVs on request. Bland, but comfortable enough. ②–⑤.

Athityaa, Nageshwaram N (Thanjavur) Rd (☎0435/421794, fax 431019). This place has gone downhill in the past couple of years, and is a bit grubby for the price, although the rooms are spacious – ask for one on the west side, facing the temple. ⑤.

Chela, 9 Ayikulam Rd (☎0435/430336, fax 431592). Another large, mid-range place, between the bus stand and centre, distinguished by its horrendous mock-Classical facade. Soap and fresh towels, and TVs, are offered as standard. They also have a bar and backup generator. ④–⑤.

Gemini Towers, 18 Ayikulam Rd (☎0435/423559). Across the road from the *Chela*. A grand name for a very run-of-the-mill budget lodge, but their rooms are clean and good value. ②.

Pandiyan Lodge, 52 Sarangapani E Rd (☎0435/430397). The single rooms in this small, modern lodge have windows, but the dingier doubles open onto corridors. ①.

Raya's, 28–29 Head Post Office Rd (☎0435/432170, fax 422479). A central, well-maintained hotel whose rooms are a little small for the price, but clean, comfortable, and near the sights. The saucy "Royal Suite" has mirrors on all four walls and ceiling. ④–⑥.

Shiva International/VPR Lodge, 101/3 TSR Big St (☎0435/424013). After the temple *gopuras*, these huge, co-owned adjacent lodges are the largest buildings in the town. *VPR Lodge* offers rock-bottom rates for cleanish rooms and a prison-block atmosphere; *Shiva International* is altogether more pleasant, with very spacious, airy doubles. Their standard non-a/c is a bargain (ask for #301, which has great views on three sides). ①–②.

Eating

There's nothing very exciting about **eating out** in Kumbakonam, and most visitors stick to their hotel restaurant. For a change of scene, though, a few places stand out.

Archana, Big Bazaar St. Right in the thick of the market. Popular among shoppers for its good-value South Indian "meals", and particularly recommended for women, with a large female clientele most evenings, although it can get hot and stuffy inside.

Ariya Bavan, TSR Big St. Convenient if you're staying in *VPR/Shiva* two doors down, and a dependable all-rounder, serving the usual South Indian menu, with tasty *biryani* and piping hot *chapfatis*.

Arogya, Ground floor of the *Athityaa*, Nageshwaram N (Thanjavur) Rd. By general consent, the best veg restaurant in town. No surprises on the menu, but their lunchtime "unlimited meals" (Rs30) are excellent, and they serve North Indian *tandoor* in the evenings. No alcohol.

Around Kumbakonam: Darasuram and Swamimalai

The delta lands **around Kumbakonam** are scattered with evocative vestiges of the Cholas' golden age, but the most spectacular has to be the crumbling Airavateshwara temple at **Darasuram**, 6km southwest. Across the fields to the north, the bronze casters of **Swamimalai** constitute a direct, living link with the culture that raised this extraordinary edifice, using traditional "lost wax" techniques, unchanged since the time when Darasuram was a thriving medieval town, to create graceful Hindu deities.

You can combine the two sights in an easy half-day trip from Kumbakonam. The route is flat enough to cycle, although you should keep your wits about you when pedalling the main Thanjavur highway, which sees heavy traffic. To reach Swamimalai from Darasuram, return to the main road from the temple and ask directions in the bazaar. Swamimalai is only 3km north, but travelling between the two involves several turnings, so expect to have to ask a local to wave you in the right direction at regular intervals. From Kumbakonam, the route is more straightforward; cross the Kaveri at the top of Town Hall Rd (north of the centre), turn left and follow the main road west through a ribbon of villages.

Darasuram

The **Airavateshwara temple**, built by King Rajaraja II (*c*.1146–73), stands in the village of **DARASURAM**, 6km southwest of Kumbakonam. This superb, if little-visited Chola monument ranks alongside those at Thanjavur and Gangaikondacholapuram;

but while they are grandiose, emphasizing heroism and conquest, it is far smaller, exquisite in proportion and detail and said to have been decorated with *nitya-vinoda*, "perpetual entertainment", in mind. Shiva is here known as Airavateshwara, because he was worshipped at this temple by Airavata, the white elephant of the king of the gods, Indra.

The entrance is through a large *gopura* gateway, 1m below ground level, in the main wall, which is topped with small reclining bull figures. Inside, the main building is set in a spacious courtyard. Next to the inner sanctuary, fronted by an open porch, the steps of the closed *mandapa* feature elegant, curled balustrades decorated with elephants and *makaras* (mythical crocodiles with floriate tails). At the corners, rearing horses and wheels make the whole into a chariot. Elsewhere, clever sculptural puns include the head of an elephant merging with that of a bull.

Fine Chola black basalt images in wall-niches in the *mandapa* and the inner shrine include Nagaraja, the snake-king, with a hood of cobras, and Dakshinamurti, the "south-facing" Shiva as teacher, expounding under a banyan tree. One rare image shows Shiva as Sharabha, part man, beast and bird, destroying the man-lion incarnation of Vishnu, Narasimha – indicative of the animosity between the Shaivite and Vaishnavite cults.

Outside, a unique series of somewhat gruesome panels, hard to see without climbing onto the base, form a band along the top of the basement of the closed *mandapa* and the sanctum sanctorum. They illustrate scenes from Sekkilar's *Periya Purana*, one of the great works of Tamil literature. The poem tells the stories of the Tamil Shaivite saints, the Nayanmars, and was commissioned by King Kulottunga II, after the poet criticized him for a preoccupation with erotic, albeit religious, literature. Sekkilar is said to have composed it in the Raja Sabha at Chidambaram; when it was completed the king sat every day for a year to hear him recite it.

Each panel illustrates the lengths to which the saints were prepared to go to demonstrate devotion to Shiva. The boy Chandesha, for example, whose job it was to tend the village cows, discovered one day that they were involuntarily producing milk. He decided to bathe a *lingam* with the milk as part of his daily worship. Appalled by this apparent waste, the villagers complained to his father, who went to the field, cursed the boy, and kicked the *lingam* over. At this affront to Shiva, Chandesha cut off his father's leg with an axe; he is shown at the feet of Shiva and Parvati, who have garlanded him. Another panel shows a man who frequently gave food to Shiva devotees. When his wife was reluctant to welcome and wash the feet of a mendicant who had previously been their servant, he cut off her hands. Elsewhere, a Pallava queen has her nose cut off for inadvertently smelling a flower, rendering it useless as an offering to Shiva. The last panel shows the saint **Sundara** who, by singing a hymn to Shiva, rescued a child who had been swallowed by a crocodile.

Swamimalai

SWAMIMALAI, 8km west of Kumbakonam, is revered as one of the six sacred abodes of Lord Murugan, Shiva's son, whom Hindu mythology records became his father's religious teacher (*swami*) on a hill (*malai*) here. The site of this epic role reversal now hosts one of the Tamils' holiest shrines, the **Swaminatha temple**, crowning the hilltop of the centre of the village. Of more interest to non-Hindus, however, are the hereditary **bronze-casters**' workshops dotted around the bazaar and the outlying hamlets.

Known as **sthapathis**, Swamimalai's casters still employ the "lost wax" process (*madhuchchishtavidhana* in Sanskrit) perfected by the Cholas to make the most sought-after temple idols in South India. Their finished products are displayed in numerous showrooms along the main street, from where they are exported worldwide, but it can be more memorable to watch the *sthapathis* in action, fashioning the original figures from beeswax and breaking open the moulds to expose the mystical finished metalwork inside. One of most welcoming workshops lies 2km south of the village, sheltered under a coconut coppice along the main road to Darasuram (look out for it on the right if you're coming from this direction). At any one time, you can see most stages of the manufacturing process, and they keep a modest selection of souvenir pieces for sale. For more on Tamil bronze-casting, see p.588.

The nearby hamlet of **Thimmakkudy**, 2km back towards Kumbakonam, is the site of the area's swishest **hotel**, the *Sterling Swamimalai*, (☎0435/420044, fax 421705; ⑨), a beautifully restored nineteenth-century *brahmins'* mansion kitted out with mod cons, such as fans and fridges. They also have an in-house yoga teacher and Ayurvedic massage room, and lay on a lively culture show in the evenings.

Thanjavur

One of busiest commercial towns of the Kaveri Delta, **THANJAVUR** (aka Tanjore), 55km east of Tiruchirapalli and 35km southwest of Kumbakonam, is often overlooked by travellers. However, its history and treasures – among them the breathtaking **Brihadishwara temple**, Tamil Nadu's most awesome Chola monument – give it a crucial significance to South Indian culture. The home of the world's finest Chola bronze collection, it holds enough of interest to keep any visitors who stay here enthralled for at least a couple of days, and is the most obvious base for trips to nearby Gangaikondcholapuram, Darasuram and Swamimalai.

Thanjavur is roughly split in two by the east–west **Grand Anicut Canal**. The **old town**, north of the canal and once entirely enclosed by a fortified wall, was between the ninth and the end of the thirteenth centuries chosen as the capital of their extensive empire by all the Chola kings save one. None of their secular buildings survives, but you can still see as many as ninety temples, of which the Brihadishwara most eloquently epitomizes the power and patronage of Rajaraja I (985–1014), whose military campaigns spread Hinduism to the Maldives, Sri Lanka and Java. Under the Cholas, as well as the later Nayaks and Marathas, literature, painting, sculpture, Carnatic classical music and Bharatanatyam dance all thrived here. Quite apart from its own intrinsic interest, the Nayak **Royal Palace compound** houses an important library and museums including a famous collection of bronzes.

Of major local **festivals,** the most lavish celebrations at the Brihadishwara temple are associated with the birthday of King Rajaraja, in October. An eight-day celebration of **Carnatic classical music** is also held each January at the Panchanateshwara temple at **Thiruvaiyaru**, 13km away, to honour the great Carnatic composer-saint, Thyagaraja.

Arrival and information

Buses from Chennai, Pondicherry, Madurai and Tiruchirapalli pull in at the long-distance Thiruvalluvar (aka STC) stand, opposite the city bus stand, in the south of the old town. Other services from Tiruchirapalli, and those to local destinations such as Kumbakonam, stop at the new bus stand, inconveniently located 4km southwest of the centre, in the middle of nowhere. Rickshaws into town from here cost Rs40–50, or you can jump on one of the private services that shuttle to and from the centre.

The **train station**, just south of the centre, has a new computerized system (Mon–Sat 8am–2pm & 3–5pm, Sun 8am–2pm), for booking trains to Chennai Tiruchirapalli and Rameshwaram. There are also several fast passenger services daily to Thiruvarur, Nagappattinam and Nagore. The red and cream station itself has an antiquated air, with its decorated columns in the main hall and sculptures of dancers and musicians. Luggage can be left in the parcel office.

The **GPO** and most of the hotels and restaurants lie on or around **Gandhiji Rd** (aka Railway Station Rd), which crosses the canal and leads to the train station in the south. The **TTDC Tourist Office**, opposite the post office (Mon–Fri 10am–5.45pm; ☎04362/33017) is a good source of local information; there's a smaller, less efficient branch in the compound of the *TTDC Tamil Nadu* hotel on Gandhiji Rd (daily 8am–4pm).

You can **change money** at Canara Bank on South Main St, and, with a bit of gentle persuasion, the *Parishutham Hotel* – useful out of banking hours, although the rates are not always favourable. The Government **hospital** is on Hospital Rd, and there are plenty of pharmacies on Gandhiji Rd.

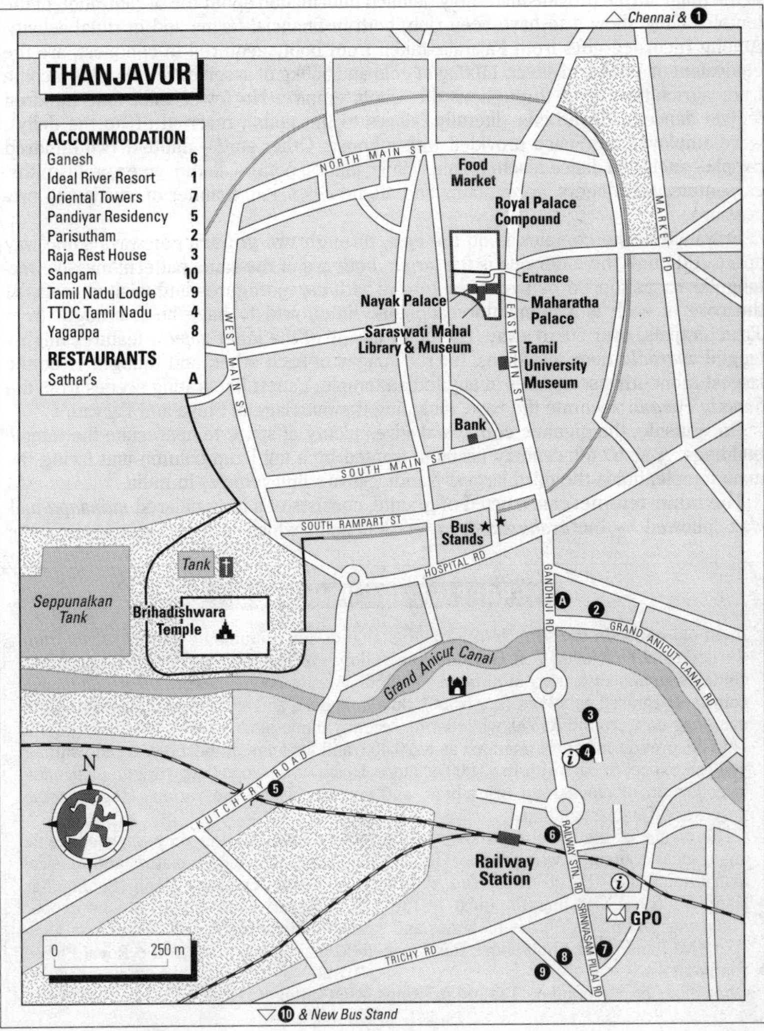

For **Internet access**, head for Gemini Soft, on the first floor of the *Oriental Towers* hotel, Srinivasam Palai Rd (☎04362/34459); as you pass through the main gate, take the white external staircase on your left.

Brihadishwara temple

Thanjavur's skyline is dominated by the huge tower of the **Brihadishwara temple**, which for all its size lacks the grandiose excesses of later periods. The site has no great significance; the temple was constructed as much to reflect the power of its patron, King Rajaraja I, as to facilitate the worship of Shiva. Profuse **inscriptions** on the base of the main shrine provide incredibly detailed information about the organization of the temple. They show it to have been rich, both in financial terms and in ritual activity. Among recorded **gifts** from Rajaraja, taken from booty acquired in conquest, are the equivalent of 1320kg of silver, 1100kg of gold and 550kg of assorted jewels, plus income from agricultural land throughout the Chola empire. No fewer than four hundred female dancers, **devadasis** (literally "slaves to the gods", married off to the deity), were employed, and each provided with a house. Other staff – another two hundred people – included dance teachers, musicians, tailors, potters, laundrymen, goldsmiths, carpenters, astrologers, accountants and attendants for all manner of rituals and processions.

Entrance to the complex is on the east, through two **gopura** gateways some way apart. Although the outer one is the larger, both are of the same pattern: massive rectangular bases topped by pyramidal towers with carved figures and vaulted roofs. At the core of each is a monolithic sandstone lintel, said to have been brought from Tiruchirapalli, over 50km away. The outer facade of the inner *gopura* features mighty fanged *dvarpala* door guardians, mirror images of each other, and thought to be the largest monolithic sculptures in any Indian temple. Panels illustrating scenes from the *Skanda Purana* decorate the base, including the marriage of Shiva and Parvati.

Once inside, the gigantic **courtyard** gives plenty of space to appreciate the temple buildings. A sixteenth-century pavilion, fronted by a tall lamp column and facing the main temple, holds the third largest Nandi (Shiva's bull-vehicle) in India.

The **main temple**, constructed of granite, consists of a long pillared *mandapa* hallway, followed by the *ardhamandapa*, or "half-hall", which in turn leads to the inner

SHOPPING IN THANJAVUR

In an old house in the suburb of Karanthattangudi, ten minutes by auto-rickshaw from the centre of Thanjavur, V. R. Govindarajan's shop at 31 Kuthirakkatti St (☎04362/30282) contains an amazing array of **antiques**, including brass pots, betel nut boxes, oil lamps, coins and Tanjore paintings (see p.590). Small, modern and simple examples of Tanjore paintings cost around Rs500, while large, recently made pictures with twenty-four-carat gold decoration may cost as much as Rs20,000, and for a fine hundred-year-old painting you can expect to part with Rs80,000 or more. Upstairs, seven artists work amid a chaotic collection of clocks and bric-a-brac, and you can watch the various stages in the process of Tanjore painting.

The owner of the small craft shop in the *Parishutham* hotel is very knowledgeable about local craftsmen who produce Tanjore paintings, copper "art plates" and musical instruments like the classical *vina*. A branch of the government chain, Poompuhar Handicrafts, on Gandhiji Rd (next to the *TTDC Tamil Nadu Hotel*), stocks copper Thanjavur "art plates", brass oil lamps and sandalwood carvings, and there's also a co-operative handicrafts shop above the Sangeeta Mahal concert hall in the Royal Palace compound.

For more background on Tanjore paintings, see Contexts, p.590.

sanctum, the *garbha griha*. The plinth of the central shrine measures 46 square metres; above it, the pyramidal *vimana* tower (at just under 61m high, the largest and tallest in India when it was built in 1010) rises in thirteen diminishing storeys, the apex being exactly one third of the size of the base. Such a design is quite different from later temples, where the *vimanas* become smaller as the *gopura* entranceways increasingly dominate – a desire to protect the sanctum sanctorum from the polluting gaze of outsiders.

The long pillared *mandapa* from the Vijayanagar period (sixteenth century) has been roughly adjoined to the *ardhamandapa*; you can see the mouldings do not match. Inside, the walls are decorated with eighteenth-century Maratha portraits. The *vimana* is an example of a "structured monolith", a stage removed from the earlier rock-cut architecture of the Pallavas, whereby blocks of stone are assembled and then carved. The profusion of carvings, aside from the inscriptions, include *dvarpala* door guardians, Shiva, Vishnu, Durga, Ganapati (Ganesh), Bhu-devi (the female goddess Earth) and Lakshmi, arranged on three sides in two rows.

As the stone that surmounts the *vimana* is said to weigh eighty tons, there is considerable speculation as to how it got up there; the most popular theory is that it was hauled up a six-and-a-half-kilometre-long ramp. Others have suggested the use of a method comparable to the Sumer ziggurat style of building, whereby logs were placed in gaps in the masonry and the stone raised by leverage. The simplest answer, of course, is that perhaps it's not a single stone at all.

The black *shivalingam,* over 3.5m high, in the **inner sanctum** is called Adavallan, "the one who can dance well" – a reference to Shiva as Nataraja, the King of the Dance, who resides at Chidambaram and was the *ishtadevata*, chosen deity, of the king. The *lingam* is not always on view, but during *puja* ceremonies (8 & 11am, noon & 7.30pm), to the accompaniment of clanging bells, a curtain is pulled revealing the god to the devotees.

Surrounding the *garbha griha*, an **ambulatory passage** contains some of South India's greatest art treasures: a frieze of beautiful **frescoes** dating from the reign of Rajaraja I. Unfortunately, the passage was recently closed to the public to protect the paintings, which were only recovered in the 1930s, having remained hidden for nearly one thousand years behind layers of inferior murals from the seventeenth century. Featuring uncannily lifelike portraits of the royals, deities, celestials and dancing girls – naked save for their jewellery and ornate hairstyles – the frieze is a swirl of rich pigments made from lapis lazuli, yellow and red ochre, lime, and lamp soot. In the upper ambulatory, also kept under lock and key, a sculpted series of reliefs showing the 108 classical dance poses predates the famous sets at Chidambaram (see p.428).

Outside, the walls of the courtyard are lined with **colonnaded passageways** – the one along the northern wall is said to be the longest in India. The one on the west, behind the temple, contains 108 *linga* from Varanasi and (heavily graffitied) panels from the Maratha period. At the centre stands a small shrine to Varuna (the Vedic god, associated with water and the sea), next to an image of the goddess Durga, usually kept clothed.

Other **shrines** in the enclosure include one behind the main temple to a devotee-saint, Karuvurar, supposedly able to cure barrenness. To the northwest, a seventeenth-century temple to Subrahmanya (a son of Shiva) has a base finely decorated with sculptures of dancers and musicians. Close to the figure of Nandi is a thirteenth-century Devi shrine; in the northeast corner, a *mandapa* houses images of Nataraja, his consort and a devotee, and is also used for decorating icons prior to processions. A **path** leads from between the two *gopuras* the length of the main wall where, behind the temple, the manicured lawn lined with benches is a haven of quiet. The temple water tank lies just beyond, next to the northwest corner.

In the southwest corner of the courtyard, the small **Archeological Museum** (daily 9am–1pm & 4–8pm) houses an interesting collection of sculpture, including an extremely tubby, damaged Ganesh, before-and-after photos detailing restoration work to the temple in the 1940s and displays about the Cholas. You can also buy the excellent ASI booklet *Chola Temples*, which gives detailed accounts of Brihadishwara and the temples at Gangaikondacholapuram and Darasuram. For more on Tamil Nadu's temples, see Contexts, p.585.

The Royal Palace Compound

The **Royal Palace Compound**, where members of the erstwhile royal family still reside, is on E Main St (a continuation of Gandhiji Rd), 2km northeast of Brihadishwara Temple. Dotted around the compound are several reminders of Thanjavur's past under the Nayaks and the Marathas, including an exhibition of oriental manuscripts and a superlative museum of **Chola bronzes**. The dusty and run-down **Tamil University Museum** contains coins and musical instruments, while near the entrance to the complex, the rambling **Royal Museum** (daily 9am–6pm; Rs1) houses a modest collection of costumes, portraits, musical instruments, weapons, manuscripts and courtly accessories.

The palace buildings have been in a sorry state for years; hopes were raised for their preservation when the responsibility for maintenance passed in 1993 to the Indian National Trust for Cultural Heritage (INTACH), but almost immediately some suffered extensive damage in storms. The Sarja Madi, "seven-storey" bell tower, built by Serfoji II in 1800, is closed to the public due to its unsafe condition.

Work on the palace began in the mid-sixteenth century under Sevappa Nayak, the founder of the Nayak kingdom of Thanjavur; additions were made by the Marathas from the end of the seventeenth century onwards. Remodelled by Shaji II in 1684, the **Durbar Hall**, or hall of audience, houses a throne canopy decorated with the mirrored glass distinctive to Thanjavur. Although damaged, the ceiling and walls are elaborately painted. Five domes are striped red, green and yellow, and on the walls, friezes of leaf and pineapple designs, and trumpeting angels in a night sky show European influence.

Niches in the walls hold sculptures of deities, and figures including the Shiva devotee Patanjali (see box on p.429), with a snake winding around his leg, and an Englishman said to be in the unlikely position of learning classical dance from a young woman, to whom he is presenting a gift. Visible on the left wall, as you face the throne, are traces of a Nayak mural of deer in a forest. Next to this, two holes in the floor, once entrances to a secret passageway, are allegedly home to cobras and not recommended for exploration. Some of the later paintings portray the entertainers who as recently as the 1960s revelled in the now overgrown square outside – fighters, circus performers and wrestlers.

The **courtyard** outside the Durbar Hall was the setting for one of the more poignant moments in Thanjavur's turbulent history when, in 1683, the last of the Nayak kings gave himself up to the king of Madurai, whose forces were swarming through the city after a long siege. Legend has it that the attackers gained the upper hand after the Raja of Madurai's chief guru-magician filled the Kaveri with rotten pumpkins, casting a spell to ensure that whoever drunk its water would defect to their side. Finding himself deserted by his troops, the Nayak king is said to have donned his ceremonial gem-studded robes, pinned his bushy eyebrows back with gold wires and marched to his death intoning Vishnavite verses. As he did so, a massive explosion behind him signalled the destruction of the palace harem, along with all its inhabitants, whose honourable deaths the king had ensured by packing the ground floor with gunpowder.

Saraswati Mahal Library and Museum

The **Saraswati Mahal Library**, one of the most important oriental manuscript collections in India, is closed to the public, but used by scholars from all over the world. Over eighty percent of its 44,000 manuscripts are in Sanskrit, many on palm-leafs, and some very rare or even unique. The Tamil works include treatises on medicine and commentaries on works from the Sangam period, the earliest literature of the South.

A small **museum** (daily except Wed 10am–1pm & 1.30–5.30pm) displays a bizarre array of books and pictures from the collection. Among the palm-leaf manuscripts is a calligrapher's tour-de-force, in the form of a visual mantra, where each letter in the inscription "Shiva" comprises the god's name repeated in microscopically small handwriting. Most of the Maratha manuscripts, produced from the end of the seventeenth century, are on paper; they include a superbly illustrated edition of the *Mahabharata*. Sadists will be delighted to see that the library managed to hang onto its copy of the explicitly illustrated **Punishments in China**, published in 1804. Next to it, full rein is given to the imagination of French artist, **Charles Le Brun** (1619–90), in a series of pictures on the subject of physiognomy. Animals such as the horse, bullock, wolf, bear, rabbit and camel are drawn with painstaking care above a series of human faces which bear an uncanny, if unlikely, resemblance to them. You can buy postcards of this scientific study and exhibits from the other palace museums in the **shop** next door.

Nayak Durbar Hall Art Museum and Rajaraja Cholan Museum

A magnificent collection of **Chola bronzes** – the finest of them from the Tiruvengadu hoard unearthed in the 1950s – fills the **Nayak Durbar Hall Art Museum** (daily 9am–1pm & 3–6pm; Rs3), a high-ceilinged audience hall with massive pillars, dating from 1600. The elegance of the figures and delicacy of detail are unsurpassed. A tenth-century statue of Kannappa Nayannar (#174), a hunter-devotee, shows minutiae right down to his embroidered clothing, fingernails and the fine lines on his fingers. The oldest bronze, four cases left of the main doorway (#58) shows Vinadhra Dakshinamurti ("south-facing Shiva") who, with a deer on one left hand, would have originally been playing the *vina* – the musical instrument has long since gone. However, the undisputed masterpiece of the collection shows Shiva as Lord of the Animals (#86), sensuously depicted in a skimpy loin cloth, with a turban made of snakes. Next to him stands an equally stunning Parvati, his consort (# 87), but the cream of the female figures, a seated, half-reclining Parvati (#97), is displayed on the opposite side of the hall.

A special feature on **Chola Bronzes** appears in Contexts, p.588.

The **Rajaraja Cholan Museum** (same hours) houses Chola stone sculpture and small objects excavated at Gangaikondacholapuram (see p.431) such as tiny marbles, games boards, bangles and terracotta pieces. Two illuminated maps show the remarkable extent of the Chola empire under the great kings Rajaraja I and his son, Rajendra I. Towering over these buildings is the Nayak-period **arsenal**, cunningly designed to resemble a temple *gopura*, with fine views of Thanjavur from the top.

Accommodation

Most of Thanjavur's **hotels**, which as a rule charge higher rates than you'd pay elsewhere in the state, are concentrated in the area between the train station and bus stands; a flurry of building activity in the run-up to the 1995 World Tamil Conference has led to a proliferation of upper-range options, many of them south of the centre, but there's very little choice at the bottom of the market. If you're travelling on a tight budget, this may be somewhere to consider treating yourself to an upgrade.

Ganesh, 314 Srinivasam Pillai Rd, Railady (☎04362/31113). A stone's throw from the train station and currently the best budget option, at just over Rs200 for a double. The rooms are not overly large, but they're clean, and there's a good veg restaurant downstairs. Some rooms are a/c. ③–⑤.

Ideal River Resort, Vennar Bank, Palli Agrharam (☎04362/34533, fax 34933). Luxurious chalet-rooms in a self-contained campus slap on the riverside, 12km towards Kumbakonam. A very pleasant location, but too far from the city without your own transport. Popular with tour groups. ⑤–⑥.

Oriental Towers, 2889 Srinivasam Pillai Rd (☎04362/31467). Huge, all mod-cons hotel-cum-shopping complex, with small swimming pool on the fourth floor and luxurious rooms. Although it is good value at this price, it's not as slick as the other four- and five-star hotels. ⑧.

Pandiyar Residency, 14 Kutchery Rd (☎04362/30574). A newish hotel across the canal from the Brihadishwara temple, next to a busy flyover; it's gone rapidly downhill, and the rooms are small for the price, but the a/c deluxe have temple views. ④–⑤.

Parisutham, 55 Grand Anicut Canal Rd (☎04362/31801, fax 30318). The town's most luxurious hotel boasts spacious centrally a/c rooms overlooking a large, palm-fringed pool (residents only), a swish multi-cuisine restaurant (see Eating, below), craft shop, foreign exchange, travel agent, and superb service, making this highly recommended, though at US$100 for a double, it's not cheap. ⑨.

Railway Retiring Rooms, contact Matron on the first floor of the train station. Six big, clean double rooms opening out onto a large communal verandah, overlooking station approach. Great value, as ever, though invariably booked up. ①.

Raja Rest House, down a lane next to the *TTDC Tamil Nadu*, off Gandhiji Rd (☎04362/30515). Basic rooms ranged around a huge open courtyard, situated between the bus and train stations. This is where most backpackers end up, but it's become a bit of a dive, and has dirty rooms and surly staff. ②.

Sangam, Trichy Rd (☎04362/34151 or 34026, fax 36695). Thanjavur's newest luxury hotel is 2km southwest of the centre. International four-star standards, with excellent restaurant, new pool and beautiful Tanjore paintings (the one in the lobby is worth a trip here in itself). ⑦.

Tamil Nadu Lodge, off Trichy Rd, 33 Mary's Corner (☎04362/31088). The best of a pretty rotten rock-bottom bunch. It's basic, acceptably clean and all the rooms have windows. ②.

TTDC Tamil Nadu, off Gandhiji Rd, 10min from the bus and railway stands (☎04362/21024). Once the raja's guesthouse, now a typically shoddy state-run hotel, with more character, however, than modern alternatives. Large, comfortable carpeted rooms (some with a/c), set around a leafy enclosed garden. ④–⑤.

Yagappa, off Trichy Rd (☎04362/30421 or 33548). Offering spacious, well-appointed rooms with sitouts, large, tiled bathrooms and friendly staff; there's also a bar and restaurant. Reception features intriguing furniture made from coffee roots. A good-value option. ③–④.

Eating and drinking

For **food**, there's the usual crop of meals canteens dotted around town, the best of which are *Annantha Bhavan* and the *Sri Venkantan*, both on Gandhiji Rd near the textile stores. The *Sangam* hotel's swish *Thillana* restaurant is a lot pricier, but worth it for the live Carnatic music. Of Thanjavur's dingy bars, *King's* in the *Yagappa* hotel, is the best choice for a quiet beer.

Annam, *Pandiyar Residency*, 14 Kutchery Rd (☎04362/30574). Small, inexpensive and impeccably clean veg restaurant that's recommended for its cut-above-the-competition lunchtime *thalis* (Rs25), and evening South Indian snacks (especially the delicious cashew *uttapams*). A relaxing option for women travellers.

King's, *Yagappa*, Trichy Rd. Seven kinds of beer are served in the usual dimly lit room, or on the "lawn" – read: "sandy back yard" – where decor includes stuffed lizard and plastic flowers in fish tanks. They also serve tasty chicken and *pakora* plate snacks.

Sathar's, Gandhiji Rd. This is the town's most popular non-veg restaurant, and a pretty safe place to eat chicken (because of the constant turnover); seating is downstairs or on a covered terrace. Dishes are around Rs60–80. There's a mostly male clientele.

Thillana, *Sangam*, Trichy Rd. Swish multi-cuisine restaurant that's renowned for its superb lunchtime South Indian *thalis* (11am–3pm; Rs75). Evenings feature an extensive à la carte menu (their *chettinad* specialties are superb). Worth a splurge just for the live Carnatic music (*veena*, flute and vocals on alternate days). Count on Rs250–300 per head.

MOVING ON FROM THANJAVUR

Travelling to **Trichy**, it's best to catch a **bus** (from the less crowded new bus stand, 4km southwest of the centre), rather than the train, as most services from Thanjavur junction are slower passenger ones that frequently run late. The same applies to buses for **Kumbakonam**. For most other destinations, you're better off going by **train**. The best services for **Chennai** are the *Cholan Express* (#6154; depart 9.15am; 9hr 45min), which goes via **Chidambaram** (2hr 50min), and the overnight *Sethu Express* (#6702; depart 10.45pm; 10hr 30min). In the opposite direction, the latter train (as #6701) runs as far as **Rameshwaram** (depart 5.50am; 8hr 30min). For **Madurai**, you have to travel to Trichy and pick up a train from there.

Thiruvarur

Often bypassed by visitors travelling between Thanjavur and the coast, **THIRUVARUR**, 55km east of Thanjavur, is famed as the birthplace of the musical saint Thyagaraja, to whom the town's huge temple is dedicated. According to Hindu myth, the first temple was built on this spot after Shiva and Parvati, at rest in a garden at the foot of Mt Kailash, were disturbed by a handful of bilva leaves scattered over them by a playful monkey. Shiva, delighted, blessed the beast, who was reincarnated as the kindly King Muchukunda of the Manu dynasty. The king built many temples but later got involved in a fight with the demon Vala, who was finally killed by the god Indra. Muchukunda was offering *pujas* in thanks for his salvation when Shiva appeared and instructed him to build a temple at Thiruvarur. Today, the **Thyagarajaswamy temple**, on the north side of town, dating mainly from the fourteenth and fifteenth centuries, measures nearly three hundred metres by more than two hundred metres. Its three successive enclosed courtyards contain a number of shrines, including one to Thyagaraja with an unusual line of the nine *navagralias* (planet deities) peering in at the saint's image. The inner sanctum houses a bronze *lingam* crowned with a seven-headed cobra, its outer walls and ceilings brightly painted with vivid images of Shiva and accompanying deities.

In March the town hosts the **Arulmigu Thyagarajaswamy car festival**, when for ten days animated crowds pull, push and wish the great temple car (the largest in Tamil Nadu) and its smaller companions well on their laborious path around the surrounding streets – worth stopping for.

Practicalities

Frequent **buses** and **trains** arrive in Thiruvarur from Thanjavur and Nagappattinam; there are also a few train services from Mayiladuturai in the north. The train station and bus stand are five minutes' walk apart in the south of town. To reach the temple, cross the bridge just north of the bus stand, and carry straight on for ten minutes or so. It's not difficult to find **accommodation**, even during the car festival. Several adequate lodges (all ①) are situated close to the bus stand on Thanjavur Rd: try the *President* (☎04366/22748) or *Sekar* (☎04366/22525), which is next to the post office. If you're not on a rock-bottom budget, the best option by far, though, is the *Royal Park Hotel*, just over 1km out of the centre on Bye-Pass Road (☎04366/21020, fax 21024; ③–⑤), which has a choice of a/c and non-a/c rooms, and two decent **restaurants**.

Nagapattinam and around

NAGAPATTINAM, 170km south of Pondicherry and 90km east of Thanjavur at the mouth of the Kaveri, was the key port of the Chola empire. Nowadays unprepossessing, it warrants little more than an overnight stop on the way to the pilgrimage sites of **Nagur** and **Velankanni**, where devotees of all faiths testify to the region's tradition of religious tolerance. In the flat **Kaveri Delta**, paddy fields stretch as far as the eye can see, broken up by tamarind, palmyra and coconut trees, and occasional fields of maize. Roads pick their way through a tangle of rivers, which most of the year are more sand than water. In December, however, destructive **cyclonic storms** render the area extremely dangerous, when the already poor roads become veritable rivers with potholes of depths best left unplumbed. The surrounding villages, clusters of thatched huts with long sloping roofs, are largely Muslim, but the nearer you get to Nagappattinam the more red flags and hammer-and-sickle symbols you see. Here too are tight-knit, impoverished fishing communities that frequently come under suspicion of harbouring Tamils who arrive under cover of night from Sri Lanka.

Nagur

In the village of **NAGUR**, 10km north of Nagappattinam, the five-hundred-year-old **dargah** of the Muslim saint Hazrat Mian Sahib comprises five golden-domed mosques set in a warren of paths, open courtyards and hallways teeming with pilgrims. Elaborately embossed silver steps decorate the shrines, while the paths and walls are covered in white tiles with patterned friezes. At the back of the mosques, people bathe in the large **Pirkulam tank** in the hope of being granted good health. In a little shelter at the water's edge, barbers busily shave the heads of children and adults who dispense with their hair as a form of penance. Stalls throughout the complex sell the blue, black or gold hats, similar to Nehru caps, worn by many male visitors, colourful Mecca and Koranic verse pictures and *bhartia* – little baskets of sugar – joss and *shambrani* incense for offerings.

Nagappattinam is connected by **train** to Thanjavur and Chennai, and frequent **buses** from Nagur and Velankanni (both 20min), Chennai, Thanjavur and Trichy call at the Thiruvalluvar bus stand. The only decent **accommodation** in the village is at the *Tamil Nadu Hotel*, Thonitthurai Salai, near the train station (☎04365/22389; ③–⑤). The rooms, some of them a/c, lack charm, but staff are friendly and the basic restaurant is a little more attractive than the "meals" places elsewhere.

Velankanni

At **VELANKANNI**, 11km south of Nagappattinam, a strong atmosphere of devotion pervades the white, spired Roman Catholic church of **Our Lady of Good Health**, the Lourdes of South India. Families hold lighted candles, which are up to one metre tall, in front of the altar, while officials wave their carrier bags of offerings in front of the image of the Virgin. Rows of display cases in the **museum** (daily 9am–6pm) contain silver and gold models of parts of the body – arms, legs, feet, livers, hearts – and of objects such as cars, cows, stethoscopes and houses. Each is accompanied by a testimonial and photograph of the person whom Our Lady has helped. Also on show is a case of various gold jewellery stated to have been stolen on November 20, 1987 and recovered by police "with miraculous help of Our Lady" on November 20, 1988, as well as hundreds of notes, in Tamil and English, thanking her for enabling couples to have children (especially the male variety) and students to pass their exams. Next door to the museum a shop sells plastic finger rings, postcards and novelty picture key-rings that flash between images of Our Lord and Our Lady. Close by are several simple "meals" **restaurants**.

Kodikkarai (Point Calimere)

On a small knob of land jutting out into the sea, 65km south of Nagappattinam and 80km southeast of Thanjavur, **KODIKKARAI BIRD SANCTUARY** plays host to around 250 species in an area of swampland, known as "the great swamp", and dry evergreen forest. On the way to the sanctuary, you pass through fifty thousand acres of salt marshes around **Vedaranyam**, the nearest town, 11km north. Vast salt fields, traditionally the mainstay of the local economy, line the road, the salt drying in thatched mounds. During the struggle for independence this was an important site for demonstrations in sympathy with Gandhi's famous salt protest. Over the last few years, however, salt has been pushed into second place by prawn cultivation, which brings a good income, but has necessitated widespread forest clearance and has reduced the numbers of birds visiting Kodikkarai.

The **best time** to visit the sanctuary is between November and February, when migratory birds come, mostly from Iran, Russia and Poland, to spend the winter. The rarest species include black bittern, barheaded goose, ruddy shelduck, Indian black-crested baza and eastern steppe eagle. During December and January the swamps host spotted billed pelicans and around ten thousand flamingos, who live on tiny shrimps (the source of the lurid pink colouring of their plumage), and whose numbers have dropped from the 30,000 that wintered here in the days before prawn production took off. The deep forest is also the home of one of the most colourful birds in the world, the Indian pitta (*pitta brachyura*).

Prodigiously well-informed local **guides**, equipped with powerful binoculars, can take you to key wildlife haunts. The Forest Department works with the Mumbai Natural History Society to ring birds and trace their migrating patterns, and occasionally the MNHS organizes **field trips** around the area.

From the jetty, you might be lucky enough to spot a school of **dolphins**. To do so, however, you need to seek permission from the Navy Command – Kodikkarai is only 40km across the Palk Strait from Jaffna, and from the grounds of the *Rest House* (see below) the navy monitors all seaborne activity between Sri Lanka and the Indian coast.

Practicalities

Kodikkarai can only be reached (by regular bus) via Vedaranyam, connected by **bus** to Nagappattinam, Thanjavur, Trichy, Chennai and Ramanathapuram (for Rameshwaram). Chennai buses can be booked in advance in a house next door to Shitharthan Medical Stores on Vedaranyam's E Main St (over the road from the bus stand). The nearest **train station** is 30km away at Tiruthuraipondi.

The only **accommodation** in the area, the Forest Department's exceptionally inexpensive *Poonarai Rest House* (reserve through DFO, W Main St, Thanjavur, ☎281/1846, or the wildlife warden in Nagappattinam; ①), has ten plain, spacious rooms, each with chairs, desk, fan, bedding, bath and balcony. Apart from in January, when the rest house is invariably full, it's usually possible to turn up without a reservation. **Food** is limited to a couple of *chai* shops outside the gate, although staff will bring it in if asked. If you need to eat in **Vedaranyam** turn left out of the bus stand, and again at a T-junction, into the main bazaar, Melai St. The best place is the simple *Karaivani*, on the left-hand side, which serves veg "leaf" meals.

Tiruchirapalli and around

TIRUCHIRAPALLI – more commonly referred to as **Trichy** – stands in the plains between the Shevaroy and Palani hills, just under 100km north of Madurai. Dominated by the dramatic Rock Fort, it's a sprawling commercial centre with a modern feel; the town itself holds little attraction, but pilgrims flock through en route to the spectacular **Ranganathaswamy temple** in **Srirangam**, 6km north.

The precise date of Trichy's foundation is uncertain, but though little early architecture remains, it is clear that between 200 and 1000 AD control of the city passed between the Pallavas and Pandyas. The Chola kings who gained supremacy in the eleventh century embarked upon ambitious building projects, reaching a zenith with the Ranganathaswamy temple. In the twelfth century, the Cholas were ousted by the Vijayanagar kings of Hampi, who stood proudly against invading Muslims until they were eventually overcome in 1565 by the Sultans of the Deccan. Less than fifty years later the Nayaks of Madurai came to power, constructing the fort and firmly establishing Trichy as a trading city. After almost a century of struggle against the French and British, who both sought lands in southeast Tamil Nadu, the town came under British control until it was declared part of Tamil Nadu state in 1947.

Arrival and information

Trichy's **airport**, 6km south of the centre, has flights to Chennai (daily except Mon; 50min). The journey into town, by taxi (Rs70–90) or bus (#7, #28, #59, #63, #122 or #K1) takes less than half an hour; for enquiries and bookings go to Indian Airlines, in the *Ramyas*, 4A Dindigul Rd (☎0431/462233). There are also two weekly flights from **Colombo** on Air Lanka, which is based in the *Femina*, 14C Williams Rd (☎0431/460844).

Trichy's main train station, **Trichy Junction** – which has given its name to the southern district of town – provides frequent rail links with Chennai, Madurai and the east coast. From here you're within easy reach of most hotels, restaurants and banks, as well as the **bus stands**. State transport and Thiruvalluvar buses run frequently to major towns such as Madurai. During the day, Thiruvalluvar buses depart from the central bus stand, and only go from their own stand, next to the train station, after 6pm. The efficient local service (#1) is the most convenient way of getting to the Rock Fort and Srirangam. **Rickshaws** are also widely available.

The **tourist office** (Mon–Fri 10am–5.45pm; ☎0431/460136), stocked with maps and information, is opposite the state bus stand in Trichy Junction just outside the *TTDC Tamil Nadu*. **Banks** for foreign exchange include the State Bank of India on Dindigul Rd. Outside bank hours, you can change money at the forex dealer in the Jenney Plaza Building, a mall just beyond *Jenney's Residency*.

Email can be sent and received (for Rs10) at Darshan Internet Point, Dindigul Rd (☎0431/411705).

The Town

Although Trichy conducts most of its business in **Trichy Junction**, the southern district, the main sights are at least 4km north. The **bazaars** immediately north heave

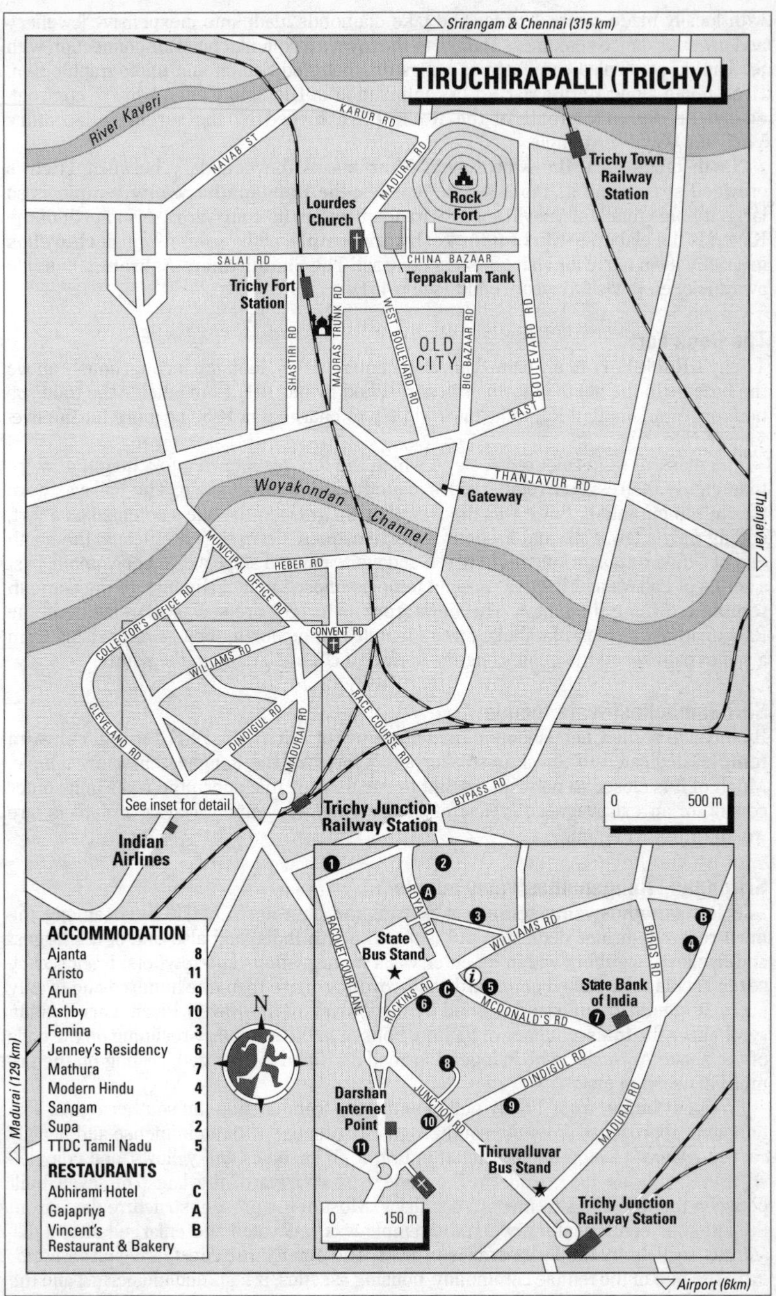
TIRUCHIRAPALLI (TRICHY)
Srirangam & Chennai (315 km)
River Kaveri
KARUR RD
NAVAB ST
MADURA RD
Rock Fort
Trichy Town Railway Station
Lourdes Church
SALAI RD
CHINA BAZAAR
Teppakulam Tank
Trichy Fort Station
SHASTIRI RD
MADRAS TRUNK RD
WEST BOULEVARD RD
OLD CITY
BIG BAZAAR RD
EAST BOULEVARD RD
THANJAVUR RD
Gateway
Woyakondan Channel
Thanjavur
MUNICIPAL OFFICE RD
HEBER RD
COLLECTOR'S OFFICE RD
CONVENT RD
WILLIAMS RD
CLEVELAND RD
DINDIGUL RD
MADURAI RD
RACE COURSE RD
BYPASS RD
See inset for detail
Trichy Junction Railway Station
0 500 m
Indian Airlines
ACCOMMODATION
Ajanta 8
Aristo 11
Arun 9
Ashby 10
Femina 3
Jenney's Residency 6
Mathura 7
Modern Hindu 4
Sangam 1
Supa 2
TTDC Tamil Nadu 5
RESTAURANTS
Abhirami Hotel C
Gajapriya A
Vincent's Restaurant & Bakery B
N
Madurai (129 km)
ROYAL RD
RACQUET COURT LANE
State Bus Stand
WILLIAMS RD
BIRDS RD
ROCKINS RD
MCDONALD'S RD
State Bank of India
DINDIGUL RD
JUNCTION RD
MADURAI RD
Darshan Internet Point
Thiruvalluvar Bus Stand
Trichy Junction Railway Station
0 150 m
Airport (6km)

with locally made cigars, textiles and fake diamonds made into inexpensive jewellery and used for dance costumes. Thanks to the town's frequent, cheap air connection with Sri Lanka, you'll also come across boxes of smuggled Scotch and photographic film. Head north along Big Bazaar Rd (a continuation of Dindigul Rd) and you're confronted by the dramatic profile of the **Rock Fort**, topped by the seventeenth-century Vinayaka (Ganesh) temple.

North of the fort, the wide Kaveri River marks the boundary between Trichy's crowded streets and its more serene temples; the **Ranganathaswamy temple** is so large it holds much of the village of Srirangam within its courtyards. Also north of the Kaveri is the elaborate **Shri Jambukeshwara temple**, while several British **churches** in Trichy town make for an interesting contrast. The **Shantivanam Ashram**, a bus ride away, is open to visitors year round (see p.451).

The Rock Fort

Trichy's **Rock Fort** (daily 6am–8pm; Rs1, camera Rs10), looming incongruously above the bazaars in the north of town, is best reached by bus (#1) from outside the train station, or from Dindigul Rd; rickshaws will try to charge you Rs50 or more for the five-minute ride.

The massive sand-coloured rock on which the fort rests towers to a height of more than eighty metres, its irregular sides smoothed by wind and rain. The Pallavas were the first to cut into it, but it was the Nayaks who grasped the site's potential as a fort, adding only a few walls and bastions as fortifications. From the entrance, at the north end of China Bazaar, a long flight of red and white painted steps cuts steeply uphill, past a series of Pallava and Pandya rock-cut temples (closed to non-Hindus), to the **Ganesh temple** crowning the hilltop. The views from its terrace are spectacular, taking in the Ranganathaswamy and Jambukeshwara temples to the north, their *gopuras* rising from a sea of palms, and the cubic concrete sprawl of central Trichy to the south.

Shri Jambukeshwara temple

By the side of the Chennai-bound road north out of Trichy, the **Shri Jambukeshwara temple**, dedicated to Shiva, is smaller and later than the Ranganathaswamy temple. Much of it is closed to non-Hindus, but the sculptures that adorn the walls in its outer courts, of an extravagance typical of the seventeenth-century Nayak architects, are worth the short detour.

Srirangam: Ranganathaswamy temple

The **Ranganathaswamy temple** at **Srirangam**, 6km north of Trichy, is among the most revered shrines dedicated to Vishnu in South India, and also one of the largest and liveliest, engulfing within its outer walls homes, shops and markets. Enclosed by seven rectangular walled courtyards and covering more than one-hundred-and-twenty acres, it stands on an island defined by a tributary of the Kaveri River. This location symbolizes the transcendence of Vishnu, housed in the sanctuary reclining on the coils of the snake Adisesha, who in legend formed an island for the god, resting on the primordial ocean of chaos.

Frequent **buses** from Trichy pull in and leave from outside the southern gate. The temple is approached from the south. A gateway topped with an immense and heavily carved *gopura*, plastered and painted in bright pinks, blues and yellows, and completed as recently as 1987, leads to the outermost courtyard, the latest of seven built between the fifth and seventeenth centuries. Most of the present structure dates from the late fourteenth century, when the temple was renovated and enlarged after a disastrous sacking by the Delhi armies in 1313. The outer three courtyards, or *prakaras*, form the hub of the temple community, housing ascetics, priests and musicians, and the streets are lined with food stalls and shops selling souvenirs, ritual offerings and fresh flower garlands to be presented to Vishnu in the inner sanctuary.

At the fourth wall, the entrance to the temple proper, visitors remove footwear before passing through a high gateway, topped by a magnificent *gopura* and lined with small shrines to teachers, hymn-singers and sages. In earlier days, this fourth *prakara* would have formed the outermost limit of the temple, and was the closest members of the lowest castes could get to the sanctuary. It contains some of the finest and oldest buildings of the complex, including a temple to the goddess **Ranganayaki** in the northwest corner where devotees worship before approaching Vishnu's shrine. On the east side of the *prakara*, the heavily carved "thousand pillared hall" (*kalyan mandapa*) was constructed in the late Chola period. During the month of Margali (Dec/Jan) Tamil hymns are recited from its southern steps as part of the Vaikuntha Ekadasi festival.

The pillars of the outstanding **Sheshagiriraya Mandapa**, south of the *kalyan mandapa*, are decorated with rearing steeds and hunters armed with spears. These are splendid examples of **Vijayanagar** style, which depicts chivalry defending the temple against Muslim invaders, and represents the triumph of good over evil. On the southern side of the *prakara*, the Venugopala shrine, dedicated to Krishna, probably dates from the Nayak period (late sixteenth century).

To the right of the gateway into the fourth courtyard, a small museum (daily 10am–noon & 3–5pm) contains a modest collection of stone and bronze sculptures, and some delicate ivory plaques. For a small fee you can climb to the roof of the fourth wall and take in the view over the temple rooftops and *gopuras*, which increase in size from the centre outwards. The central tower, crowning the holy sanctuary, is coated in gold and carved with images of Vishnu's incarnations, on each of its four sides.

Inside the gate to the third courtyard – the final section of the temple open to non-Hindus – is a pillared hall, the **Garuda Mandapa**, carved throughout in typical Nayak style. Maidens, courtly donors and Nayak rulers feature on the pillars that surround the central shrine to Garuda, the man-eagle vehicle of Vishnu. Other buildings in the third courtyard include the vast kitchens, which emanate delicious smells as *dosas* and *vadas* are prepared for the deity, while devotees ritually bathe in the tanks of the moon and the sun in the northeast and southeast corners.

The dimly lit innermost courtyard, the most sacred part of the temple, shelters the image of Vishnu in his aspect of Ranganatha, reclining on the serpent Adisesha. The shrine is usually entered from the south, but for one day each year, during the **Vaikuntha Ekadasi festival**, the north portal is opened; those who pass through this "doorway to heaven" can anticipate great merit. Most of the temple's daily festivals take place in this enclosure, beginning each morning with *vina*-playing and hymn-singing as Vishnu is awakened in the presence of a cow and an elephant, and ending just after 9pm with similar ceremonies.

For more on Ranganathaswamy and Tamil Nadu's other great temples, see Contexts, p.585.

Accommodation

Trichy has no shortage of **hotels** to accommodate the thousands of pilgrims that visit the town. Most offer good value for money, keeping tariffs below the Rs200 mark to avoid incurring luxury taxes. Dozens of characterless lodges, as well as some more comfortable upmarket hotels, cluster around the bus stand. Traffic noise can be a real problem in this area, so ask for a room on the rear side of any hotel you check into.

Ajanta, Junction Rd (☎0431/415504). A huge, 86-room complex centred on its own Vinayagar shrine, and with an opulent Tirupati deity in reception. Popular with middle-class pilgrims; plain, clean rooms (the singles are particularly good value). Some a/c. ③.

Aristo, 2 Dindigul Rd (☎0431/415858). A jaded offbeat 1960s hotel, set back from the road in its own quiet compound. The bargain standard rooms have a fair amount of superficial grime, but are huge for the price, and open onto a deep common verandah. Cosier "cottages" are the honeymooners' alternative: pebble-strewn verandahs, whacky colour schemes and mouldy bathrooms. ②–④.

Arun, 24 Dindigul Rd (☎0431/415021). A dependable budget option, whose "ordinary" rooms are spacious and clean, and much the best deal ("deluxe" buys you different colour wallpaper and Western toilet). ②–④

Ashby, 17A Junction Rd (☎0431/460652). This old-fashioned Raj-era place (formerly owned by Marks and Spencer) is most foreign tourists' first choice. The rooms are large and impeccably clean, and there's a relaxing covered courtyard that doubles as a so-so restaurant (best avoided after breakfast). The drawbacks are infernal traffic noise from 4am, and less than helpful staff. ③–⑤.

Femina, 14C Williams Rd (☎0431/414501, fax 460615). Well-maintained place east of the state bus stand. Rooms and suites, some with balconies looking to the Rock Fort. Plush restaurants, 24hr coffee bar. ⑤–⑦.

Jenney's Residency, 3/14 McDonald's Rd (☎0431/414414, fax 460615). Along with the *Sangam*, Trichy's swishest hotel. It features a "Wild West" bar, and two good restaurants – including an upmarket Chinese place – cocktail bar and swimming pool (open to non-residents for Rs100). ⑥–⑦.

Mathura, 9-C Rockins Rd (☎0431/414737). Large, modern hotel opposite the bus stand. One of the best budget deals in the area. ②–③.

Modern Hindu, Dindigul Rd (☎0431/460758). Best of the rock-bottom lodges: an old fashioned place, with basic but clean rooms (those on the top floor open on to a large common verandah and shady wall of trees). Single occupancy rates available. ②.

Ramyas, 13 D/2 Williams Rd (☎0431/415128, fax 462750). The "standard" rooms in this business-orientated hotel are overpriced, but their more spacious "executive" options are worth the extra. Restaurant, bar, laundry and foreign exchange. ⑤.

Sangam, Collector's Office Rd (☎0431/464700). Trichy's top hotel boasts all the facilities of an international four-star, including an excellent pool (open to non-residents for Rs100, and shadier and less plagued by staring staff than the one at *Jenney's Residency*). ⑧.

Supa, 5 Royal Rd (☎0431/460055). A mansion home of a famous 1940s Tamil singer that's somehow become a dilapidated budget lodge run by elderly staff, with huge double and triple rooms, and rank bathroomless singles. A bit grimy, but cheap, and with a certain melancholic charm. ①–②.

TTDC Tamil Nadu, McDonald's Rd (☎0431/460383). One of their better hotels, and just far enough from the bus stand to escape the din. Best value are the non-a/c doubles, though even these are dowdier than most of the competition. ②–④.

Eating

To eat well in Trichy, you won't have to stray far from the bus stand, where the town's most popular "meals" joint, the *Abhirami*, does a roaring trade. For more atmosphere, stroll up Dindigul Rd to *Vincent's*, where you can eat al fresco.

Abhirami, 10 Rockins Rd, opposite the bus stand. Trichy's most famous South Indian restaurant serves up unbeatable value lunchtime "meals" (Rs20), and the standard range of snacks the rest of the day. They also have a "Fast Food" counter where you can get *dosas* and *uttapams* at any time. It opens at 6.30am for piping hot *wada-pongal* breakfasts.

Gajapriya, on the ground floor of the *Gajapriya Hotel*, Royal Rd. Non-veg North Indian and noodle dishes are specialties of this small, but blissfully cool and clean a/c restaurant. A good place to chill out over coffee, and there's a separate "family" room for women.

Vincent's Bakery, up Dindigul Rd, opposite the Petrol Pump. More than a dozen varieties of freshly baked cakes (including solidly old-fashioned British fruit slab), and melt-in-the-mouth coconut biscuits, to take away or eat on a terrace. They also serve flaky savouries and their own brand of not-too-sweet bottled fruit juices.

Vincent's Restaurant, next door to the bakery, Dindigul Rd. Relaxing "oriental" theme restaurant, set back from the road in its own terrace, with mock pagodas, concrete bamboo and a multi-cuisine menu that includes tasty chicken *tikka* and other *tandoori* dishes. No alcohol; opens at 5pm.

Around Tiruchirapalli: Shantivanam Ashram

Situated on the banks of the Kaveri, the **Shantivanam** (Sanskrit for "Forest of Peace") **Ashram** is in the small village of **THANNEEPALLI**, about forty minutes by bus on the route to Kullithalai, northwest of Trichy. The programme here is based on a fusion of Christianity and Hinduism, and is the work of the Benedictine monk, Bede Griffiths, who died in 1993 at an advanced age. In the ashram's chapel, lines from the *Bhagavad Gita* and *om* symbols share space with crosses and biblical verses. Visitors can participate in as much or as little of the programme as they wish, staying in dorms or private rooms, and sharing meals, in exchange for a donation and chores. The ashram is usually full during Christian celebrations.

THE FAR SOUTH

The **far south** of Tamil Nadu comprises a great amphitheatre of the Vaigai plains, enfolded in the west by the bare brown Alagar Hills, arching south from the edge of the Kaveri Delta to the tip of peninsular India. Studded with massive outcrops of pink and pale brown granite, the region is rich in ancient myths, where evil elephants were turned into stone boulders by Shiva, and rivers were formed to quench the thirst of giant pot-bellied dwarfs. Many of these stories probably pre-date the earliest traces of human settlement, but most were set down when this was the heartland of the mighty **Pandyans**, the southernmost of South India's three great warring dynasties. Their former capital, **Madurai**, is today the state's second city and, as the site of the famous Meenakshi-Sundareshwarar temple, the region's spiritual tap root, often dubbed "The Varanasi of the South". Further east, **Rameshwaram**, occupying a narrow spit that fractures into dozens of islets as it nears the war-torn north coast of neighbouring Sri Lanka, is equally sacred to Hindus. It forms the eastern point of a sacred triangle whose apex, at **Kanniyakumari**, combines the heady intensity of an age-old pilgrimage place with all the gimcrackery you'd expect from India's own Land's End.

Madurai

"(Madurai is) a city gay with flags, waving over homes and shops selling food and drinks; the streets are broad rivers of people, folk of every race, buying and selling in the bazaars, or singing to the music of wandering bands and musicians…(around the temple), amid the perfume of ghee and incense, (are stalls) selling sweet cakes, garlands of flowers, scented powder and betel paan…(while nearby are) men making bangles of conch shells, goldsmiths, cloth dealers, tailors making up clothes, coppersmiths, flower sellers, vendors of sandalwood, painters and weavers."

The Garland of Madurai, traditional Tamil poem, second century AD

One of the oldest cities in south Asia, **MADURAI**, on the banks of the Vaigai River, has been an important centre of worship and commerce for as long as there has been civilization in South India. Megasthenes, the Greek ambassador who came here in 302 BC, wrote of its splendour and its queen, Pandai, "a daughter of Herakles", while the Roman geographer Strabo complained at how the city's silk, pearls and spices were draining the imperial coffers of Rome. It was this lucrative trade, meticulously detailed in an Alexandrian mariner's manual dating from the first century AD, *The Periplus of the Erythraean Sea*, that enabled the **Pandyan** dynasty to erect the mighty

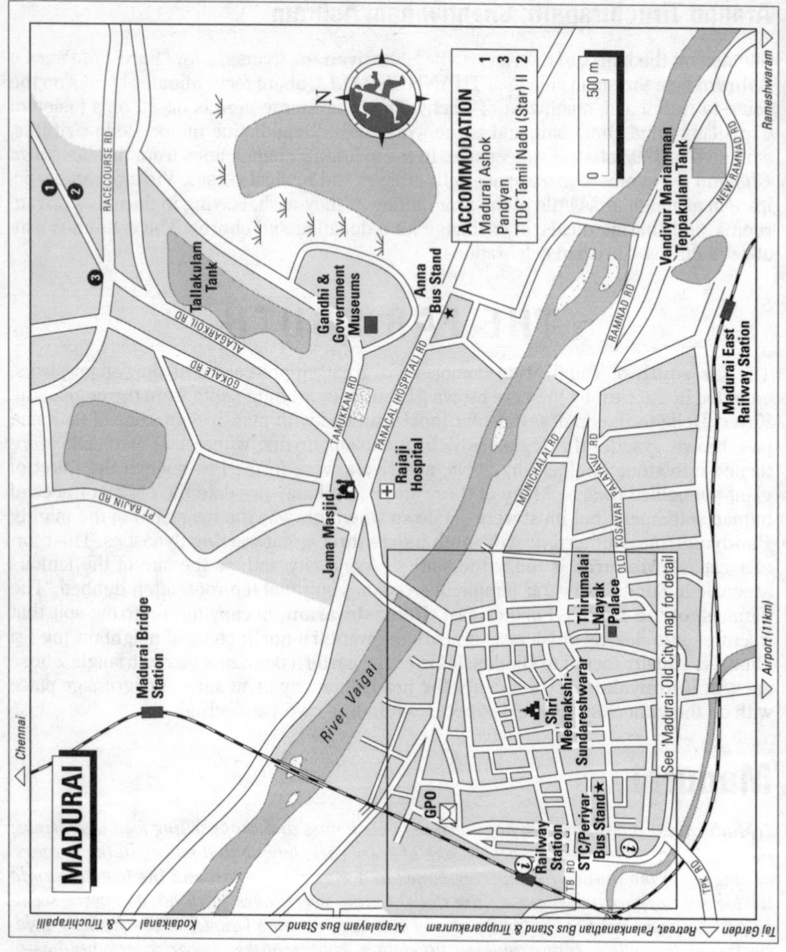

Meenakshi-Sundareshwarar temple. Although today surrounded by a sea of modern concrete cubes, the massive *gopuras* of this vast complex, writhing with multi-coloured mythological figures and crowned by golden finials, remain the greatest man-made spectacle of the south. Any day of the week no fewer than 15,000 people pass through its gates, increasing to 25,000 on Friday (sacred to the goddess Meenakshi), while the temple's ritual life spills out into the streets in an almost ceaseless round of festivals and processions. The chance to experience sacred ceremonies that have persisted largely unchanged since the time of the ancient Egyptians is one that few travellers pass up.

Madurai is the subject of an extraordinary number of myths. Its origins stem from a *sthala* (a holy site where legendary events have taken place) where Indra, the king of the gods, bathed in a holy tank and worshipped Shiva. Hearing of this, the Pandyan king Kulashekhara built a temple on the site and installed a *shivalingam*, around which the city grew. The name Madurai is popularly derived from the Tamil word *madhuram*, meaning "sweetness"; according to legend, Shiva shook his matted locks over the city, coating it with a fine sprinkling of *amrita*, the nectar of immortality.

Madurai's urban and suburban sprawl creates traffic jams to rival India's very worst. Chaos on the narrow, potholed streets is exacerbated by political demonstrations and religious processions, wandering cows, demanding right of way with a peremptory nudge of the haunch, and put-upon pedestrians forced onto the road by ever-increasing numbers of street traders. Open-air kitchens extend from *chai*-shops, where competing *paratha-wallahs* literally drum up custom for their fresh breads with a tattoo of spoon-on-skillet signals. Given the traffic problems, it's just as well that Madurai, with its profusion of markets and intriguing corners, is an absorbing city to walk around.

Some history

Although invariably interwoven with myth, the traceable history and fame of Madurai stretches back well over 2000 years. Numerous natural **caves** in local hills and boulders, often modified by the addition of simple rock-cut beds, were used both in prehistoric times and by ascetics, such as the Ajivikas and Jains, who practised withdrawal and penance.

Madurai appears to have been the capital of the Pandyan empire without interruption for at least a thousand years. It became a major commercial city, trading with Greece, Rome and China; *yavanas* (a generic term for foreigners), frequent visitors to Pandyan seaports, were employed as palace guards and policemen; the Tamil epics describe them walking around town with their eyes and mouths wide open with amazement, much as foreign tourists still do when they first arrive. Long a seat of Tamil culture, Madurai under the Pandyas is credited with being the site of three literary **sangams**, "literary academies", said to have lasted 10,000 years and supported some 8000 poets; despite this fanciful reckoning, the most recent of these academies does have a historical basis. The "Sangam period" is generally taken to mean the first three to four centuries of the Christian era.

The Pandyas' capital fell in the tenth century, when the **Chola** King Parantaka took the city; they briefly regained power in the thirteenth century, but early in the 1300s the notorious **Malik Kafur**, the Delhi Sultanate's "favourite slave", made an unprovoked attack during a plunder-and-desecration tour of the south, and destroyed much of the city. Forewarned of the raid, the Pandya king, Sundara, fled with his immediate family and treasure, leaving his uncle and rival, Vikrama Pandya, to repel Kafur. Nevertheless, the latter returned to Delhi with booty said to consist of "six hundred and twelve elephants, ninety-six thousand *mans* of gold, several boxes of jewels and pearls and twenty thousand horses".

Shortly after this raid Madurai became an independent Sultanate; in 1364, it joined the Hindu **Vijayanagar** empire, ruled from Vijayanagar/Hampi (see p.248) and administered by governors, the **Nayaks**. In 1565, the Nayaks asserted their own independence. Under their supervision and patronage, Madurai enjoyed a renaissance, being rebuilt on the pattern of a lotus centring on the Meenakshi temple. Part of the palace of the most illustrious of the Nayaks, **Thirumalai** (1623–55), survives today.

The city remained under Nayak control until the mid-eighteenth century when the **British** gradually took over. A hundred years later the British de-fortified Madurai, filling its moat to create the four Veli streets that today mark the boundary of the old city.

Arrival and information

Madurai's small **airport**, 11km south of the city, is served by flights to and from Chennai, Mumbai and Thiruvananthapuram. Theoretically you should be able to get information at the **Government of Tamil Nadu Tourist Information Centre** booth by the exit, but it's not always open to meet flights. Very simple snack meals ("bread-omelette") are served at the **restaurant** (daily 9am–5pm). There's also a bookshop and a branch of Indian Bank, but they can't change money. **Taxis** into the city charge a fixed rate of around Rs200. Airport buses leave hourly either from near the exit or to the left, near the staff canteen.

Arriving in Madurai by **bus**, you come in at one of five stands, all served by long-distance and city buses. The largest is the **STC bus stand** (Chennai, Kerala, Bangalore, Karnataka and Andhra Pradesh) on West Veli St in the west of the old city, close to the train station and most accommodation. Next door to this is the **Periyar bus stand**, which takes the overflow and most local services. **Arapalayam bus stand** (some services within the state, including Kodaikanal and Coimbatore, and Kerala) is in the northwest, close to the south bank of the river, about 2km from the train station. **Palankanathan bus stand** (also written as Pazhanganatham, for south Tamil Nadu and south Kerala) is in the southwest, 5km from the centre, and **Anna bus stand** (points north, such as the Chola cities, and Rameshwaram) is 5km out in the northeast, north of the Vaigai. Wherever you arrive, the easiest way to get to a hotel is by auto-rickshaw, although from West Veli St it's feasible to reach most of the budget places on the west side of town by cycle-rickshaw.

Madurai's clean and well-maintained **train station** is just west of the centre off West Veli St. You can leave your luggage at the cloakroom (24hr) next to the **reservations office** in the main hall, where you'll also find a branch of the **Tourism Department Information Centre** (daily 6.30am–8.30pm). There's a good veg **canteen** on platform 1, and, unusually, a **pre-paid auto-rickshaw booth** outside the main entrance, open to coincide with train arrivals.

Information

The **Tourist Dept Main Office** is on West Veli St (Mon–Fri 10am–5.45pm, sometimes Sat 10am–1pm; ☎0452/34757), but its staff are less helpful than those at the train station office (see above), which is the best place for general information about Madurai and surrounding areas. They have details of **car rental**, however, and will also arrange, with a little notice, **city tours** with one of the Government-approved **guides**, who can usually be found at the southern entrance to the temple. Find out their names first at the tourist office as they're a much better bet than the other guys hanging around; the latter, however well-meaning, may be ill-informed and more than likely will want to get you into a shop double-quick. Official guided city tours, for one to four visitors, cost around Rs250 for a half-day, and Rs350 for up to eight hours. The fee for a temple tour is negotiable.

Madurai's **head post office** is at the corner of Scott Rd and North Veli St. For postal services, enter on the Scott Rd side (Mon–Sat 8am–7.30pm, Sun & hols 9am–4.30pm; speedpost 10am–7pm); for **poste restante** (Mon–Sat 9.30am–5.30pm), go to the Philatelic Bureau on the southwest corner of the building, and remember to take along your passport.

Internet access is offered at a string of small offices on West Perumal Maistry St, which all charge Rs100 per hour; try the *Supreme* hotel at No. 110, or ABC at No. 55.

The best place in Madurai to **change money** is VKC Forex Services, opposite the head post office, 168 North Veli St, (Mon–Sat 9am–6.30pm), which offer more or less the same rates as the State Bank of India, 6 West Veli St. *Mastercard* and *Visa* are accepted at the *Andhra Bank* on West Chitrai St, but no currency or travellers' cheques. If you get caught out by a public holiday or need to change money in the night, head for the *Supreme* hotel, whose 24hr forex desk is open to non-visitors.

Bike rental at low rates is available at SV, West Tower St, near the west entrance to the temple, or the stall on West Veli St, opposite the *TTDC Tamil Nadu* hotel.

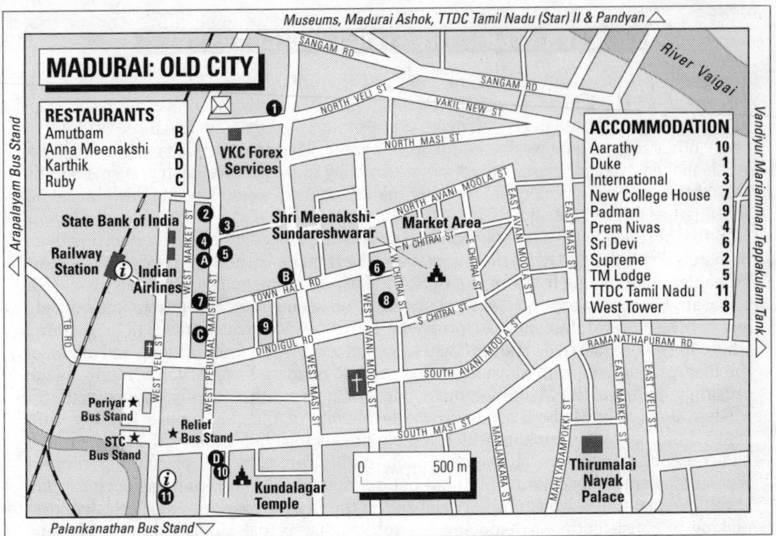

The City

Although considerably enlarged and extended over the years, the overall layout of Madurai's **old city**, south of the Vaigai River, has remained largely unchanged since the first centuries AD. It comprises a series of concentric squares, centred on the massive Shri Meenakshi-Sundareshwarar temple and aligned with the cardinal points. The intention of the ancient architects was clearly to follow the dimensions of an auspicious *mandala*, or sacred diagram, set down in canonical texts known as the *Vastu Shastras*. These provided the blueprints for the now lost cities of the Vedic age, 3000 years ago, and were believed to represent the laws governing the universe; they are also abstract depictions of the Hindu creator god, Brahma, in the form of the primeval being, Parusha. Whereas rectangular grid plans symbolize temporal or royal power, squares are used by Hindus to indicate the Absolute, which is why the streets boxed around Madurai's temple, each named after the different Tamil months, are of even lengths. The reason many of the city's mass rituals involve circuits of these streets in a strictly clockwise direction is because circumambulation of a powerful shrine, such as the Meenakshi temple, is believed to activate the sacred properties of the giant *mandala*.

North of the river, Madurai becomes markedly more mundane and irregular. You're only likely to cross the Vaigai to reach the city's more expensive hotels, the Gandhi Museum and the Anna bus stand.

Shri Meenakshi-Sundareshwarar temple

Enclosed by a roughly rectangular six-metre-high wall, in the manner of a fortified palace, the **Meenakshi-Sundareshwarar temple** (daily 5am–12.30pm & 4–9.30pm) is one of the largest temple complexes in India. Much of it was constructed during the Nayak period between the sixteenth and eighteenth centuries, but certain parts are very much older. The principal shrines (closed to non-Hindus) are those to Sundareshwarar

MEENAKSHI, THE FISH-EYED GODDESS

The goddess Meenakshi of Madurai emerged from the flames of a sacrificial fire as a three-year-old child, in answer to the Pandyan king Malayadvaja's prayer for a son. The king, not only surprised to see a female, was also horrified that she had three breasts. In every other respect, she was beautiful, as her name, **Meenakshi** ("fish-eyed"), suggests – fish-shaped eyes are classic images of desirability in Indian love poetry. Dispelling his concern, a mysterious voice told the king that Meenakshi would lose the third breast on meeting her future husband.

In the absence of a son, the adult Meenakshi succeeded her father as Pandyan monarch. With the aim of world domination, she then embarked on a series of successful battles, culminating in the defeat of Shiva's armies at the god's Himalayan abode, Mt Kailasah. Shiva then appeared at the battlefield; on seeing him, Meenakshi immediately lost her third breast. Fulfilling the prophecy, Shiva and Meenakshi travelled to Madurai, where they were married. The two then assumed a dual role, firstly as king and queen of the Pandya kingdom, with Shiva assuming the title Sundara Pandya, and secondly as the presiding deities of the Madurai temple, into which they subsequently disappeared.

Their **shrines** in Madurai are today the focal point of a hugely popular **fertility cult**, centred on the gods' coupling, which temple priests maintain ensures the preservation and regeneration of the Universe. Each night, the pair are placed together in Sundareshwarar's bedchamber, but not before Meenakshi's nose ring has been carefully removed so that it won't cut her husband in the heat of passion. Their celestial lovemaking is consistently earth-moving enough to ensure that Sundareshwarar remains completely faithful to his consort (exceptional for the notoriously promiscuous Shiva). Nevertheless, this fidelity is never taken for granted, and has to be ritually tested each year when the beautiful goddess Cellattamman is brought to Sundareshwarar "to have her powers renewed". After she is spurned, she flies into a fury that can only be placated with the sacrifice of a buffalo – one among the dozens of arcane ceremonies that make up Madurai's round of temple rituals.

(Shiva) and his consort Meenakshi (a form of Parvati); unusually, the goddess takes precedence and is always worshipped first.

For the first-time visitor, confronted with a confusing maze of shrines, sculptures and colonnades, and unaware of the logic employed in their arrangement, it's very easy to get disorientated. However, if you're not in a hurry, this should not deter you. Quite apart from the estimated thirty-three million sculptures to arrest your attention, the life of the temple is absolutely absorbing, and many visitors find themselves drawn back at several different times of the day. Be it the endless round of *puja* ceremonies, loud *nagaswaram* and *tavil* music, weddings, *brahmin* boys under religious instruction in the *Vedas*, the prostrations of countless devotees, the busy glittering market stalls inside the east entrance, or, best of all, a festival procession, something is always going on to make this quite simply one of the most compelling places in Tamil Nadu.

Approximately fifty priests work in the temple, and live in houses close to the north entrance. They are easily identified – each wears a white *dhoti* (*veshti* in Tamil) tied between the legs; on top of this, around the waist, is a second, coloured cloth, usually of silk. Folded into the cloth, a small bag contains holy white ash. The bare-chested priests invariably carry a small towel over the shoulder. Most wear earrings and necklaces including *rudraksha* beads, sacred to Shiva. As Shaivite priests, they place three horizontal stripes of white ash on the forehead, arms, shoulders and chest and a red powder dot, sacred to the goddess, above the bridge of the nose. The majority wear their long hair tied into a knot, with the forehead shaved. Inside the temple they also carry brass trays holding offerings of camphor and ash.

Madurai takes the **gopura**, so prominent in other southern temples, to its ultimate extreme. The entire complex has no fewer than twelve such towers; set into the outer walls, the four largest rise to a height of around forty-six metres, and are visible for miles outside the city. Each is covered with a profusion of gaily painted stucco gods and demons, with the occasional live monkey scampering and chattering among the divine images. After a referendum in the 1950s, the *gopuras*, which had become mono-chrome and dilapidated, were repainted in the vivid kingfisher greens, blues and bright reds you can see today; they have to be completely redone every ten years or so (the last repaint was in the mid-1990s). It is sometimes possible, for a small fee, to climb the southern and tallest tower, to enjoy superb views over the town.

The most popular **entrance** is on the east side, where the *gopura* gateway has reopened after a period of closure following the inauspicious suicide of a temple employee who leapt from the top. You can also enter nearby through a towerless gate which is directly in line with the Meenakshi shrine deep inside. In the **Ashta Shakti Mandapa** ("Eight Goddesses Hallway"), a sparkling market sells *puja* offerings and souvenirs, from fat garlands of flowers to rough-hewn sky-blue plaster deities. Sculpted pillars illustrate different aspects of the goddess Shakti, and Shiva's 64 miracles at Madurai. Behind this hall, to the south, are stables for elephants and camels.

If you continue straight on from here, cross East Ati St, and go through the seven-storey **Chitrai gopura**, you enter a passageway leading to the eastern end of the **Pottamarai Kulam** (Tank of Golden Lotuses), where Indra bathed before worshipping the *shivalingam*. From the east side of the tank you can see the glistening gold of the Meenakshi and Sundareshwarar *vimana* towers. Steps lead down to the water from the surrounding colonnades, and in the centre stands a brass lamp column. People bathe here, prior to entering the inner shrines, or just sit, gossip and rest on the steps.

The ceiling paintings in the corridors are modern, but Nayak murals around the tank illustrate scenes from the *Gurur Vilayadal Puranam* which describes Shiva's Madurai miracles. Of the two figures located halfway towards the Meenakshi shrine on the north side, one is the eighth-century king Kulashekhara Pandyan, said to have founded the temple; opposite him is a wealthy merchant patron.

On the west side of the tank is the entrance to the **Meenakshi shrine** (closed to non-Hindus), popularly known as **Amman Koyil**, literally the "mother temple". The immovable green stone image of the goddess is contained within two further enclosures that form two ambulatories. Facing Meenakshi, just past the first entrance and in front of the sanctum sanctorum, stands Shiva's bull-vehicle, Nandi. At around 9pm, the movable images of the god and goddess are carried to the **bedchamber**. Here the final *puja* ceremony of the day, the **lalipuja**, is performed, when for thirty minutes or so the priests sing lullabies (*lali*), before closing the temple for the night.

The corridor outside Meenakshi's shrine is known as the **Kilikkutu Mandapa** or Parrot Cage Hallway. Parrots used to be kept just south of the shrine as offerings to Meenakshi; a practice discontinued in the mid-1980s, as the birds suffered due to "lack of maintenance". Sundareshwarar and Meenakshi are brought every Friday (6–7pm) to the sixteenth-century **Oonjal Mandapa** further along, where they are placed on a swing (*oonjal*) and serenaded by members of a special caste, the Oduvars. The black and gold, almost fairground-like decoration of the *mandapa* dates from 1985.

Across the corridor, the small **Rani Mangammal Mandapa**, next to the tank, has a detailed eighteenth-century ceiling painting of the marriage of Meenakshi and Sundareshwarar, surrounded by lions and elephants against a blue background. Sculptures in the hallway portray characters such as the warring monkey kings from the *Ramayana*, the brothers Sugriva (Sukreeva) and Bali (Vahli), and the indomitable Pandava prince, Bhima, from the *Mahabharata*, who was so strong that he uprooted a tree to use as a club.

Walking back north, past the Meenakshi shrine, through a towered entrance, leads you to the area of the Sundareshwarar shrine. Just inside, the huge monolithic figure of Ganesh, **Mukkuruni Vinayaka**, is said to have been found during the excavation of the Mariamman Teppakulam tank (see below). Chubby Ganesh is well known for his love of sweets, and during his annual **Vinayaka Chathurti festival** (Sept), a special *prasad* (gift offering of food) is concocted from ingredients including 300 kilos of rice, 10 kilos of sugar and 110 coconuts.

Around a corner, a small image of the monkey god **Hanuman**, covered with *ghee* and red powder, stands on a pillar. Devotees take a little with their finger for a *tillak*, to mark the forehead. A figure of Nandi and two gold-plated copper flagstaffs face the entrance to the **Sundareshwarar shrine** (closed to non-Hindus). From here, outsiders can just about see the *shivalingam* beyond a blue and red neon Tamil *om* sign.

Causing a certain amount of fun, north of the flagstaffs are figures of Shiva and Kali in the throes of their dance competition (see box on p.429). A stall nearby sells tiny **butter balls** from a bowl of water, which visitors throw at the god and goddess "to cool them down". If you leave through the gateway here, on the east, you'll find in the northeast corner the fifteenth-century **Ayirakkal Mandapa** (thousand-pillared hall), now transformed into the temple's **Art Museum**. In some ways it is a great shame, as screens have been erected and dusty educational displays replace a clear view of this gigantic hall. However, there's a fine, if rather dishevelled, collection of wood, copper, bronze and stone sculpture, an old nine-metre-high teak temple door and general miscellanea.

For more on the temples of Tamil Nadu, see Contexts, p.585.

Vandiyur Mariamman Teppakulam tank and the floating festival

At one time, the huge **Vandiyur Mariamman Teppakulam** tank in the southeast of town (bus #4 or #4A; 15min) was full with a constant supply of water, flowing via underground channels from the Vaigai. Nowadays, thanks to a number of accidents, it is only filled during the spectacular Teppa **floating festival** (Jan/Feb), when pilgrims take boats out to the goddess shrine in the centre. Before their marriage ceremony, Shiva and Meenakshi are brought in procession to the tank, where they are floated on a raft decorated with lights, which devotees pull by ropes three times, encircling the shrine. The boat trip is believed to be the overture to a seduction that reaches its passionate conclusion later that night in the temple. This traditionally makes the Teppa the most auspicious time of year to get married.

During the rest of the year the tank and the central shrine remain empty. Accessible by steps, the tank is most often used as an impromptu cricket green, and the shade of the nearby trees makes a popular gathering place. Tradition states that the huge image of Ganesh, Mukkuruni Vinayaka, in the Meenakshi temple, was uncovered here when the area was originally excavated to provide bricks for the Thirumalai Nayak palace.

Thirumalai Nayak palace

Roughly a quarter survives of the seventeenth-century **Thirumalai Nayak palace** (daily 9am–1pm & 2–5pm; Rs1), 1.5km southeast of the Meenakshi temple. Much of it was dismantled by Thirumalai's grandson, Chockkanatha Nayak, and used for a new palace at Tiruchirapalli. What remains was renovated in 1858 by the Governor of Chennai, Lord Napier, and again in 1971 for the Tamil World Conference. The palace originally consisted of two residential sections, plus a theatre, private temple, harem, royal bandstand, armoury and gardens.

The surviving building, the **Swargavilasa** ("Heavenly Pavilion"), is a rectangular courtyard, flanked by eighteen-metre-tall colonnades. As well as occasional live performances of music and dance, the Tourism Department arranges a nightly **Sound and Light Show** (in English 6.45–7.30pm; Rs2–5), which relates the story of the Tamil epic, *Shilipaddikaram*, and the history of the Nayaks. Some find the spectacle edifying, and others soporific – especially when the quality of the tape is poor. In an adjoining hall, the palace **museum** (same hours as the palace) includes Pandyan, Jain and Buddhist

TEMPLE FESTIVALS AT MADURAI

Date	Name	No. of days	Date	Name	No. of days
Jan/Feb	**Teppa**	12	July/Aug	**Ati Mulaikkottu**	10
Feb/March	**Machi Mantala**	10	Aug/Sept	**Avani Mula**	12
March/April	**Kotaivasanta**	9	Sept/Oct	**Navaratri**	9
April/May	**Chittirai**	12	Oct/Nov	**Kolatta**	6
May/June	**Vasanta**	10	Nov/Dec	**Tirukkarttikai**	10
June/July	**Unchal**	10	Dec/Jan	**Ennai Kappu**	9

The date of each of the Madurai temple's annual festivals varies each year; check with a tourist office when you plan your visit. The principal and most exciting component of most of them is the **procession** (*purappatu*, or "setting forth"), held on the morning and evening of every day. Each procession is accompanied by officiating *brahmins*, temple employees bearing royal insignia, umbrellas, silver staffs and, at night, flaming torches. The entourage is invariably preceded by the penetrating orchestra of *tavil* (barrel drum), hand cymbals and the distinctive *nagaswaram* (double-reed oboe-like wind instrument), for which the Madurai area is particularly famous.

Processions circumambulate clockwise inside the temple, and many leave its precincts, starting from the east entrance, passing along the Chitrai, Avani Moola or Masi streets and, on special occasions such as the floating festival (days 10 and 11 of the Teppa ceremonies), leave the centre of the city altogether. Locals and visiting pilgrims crowd the streets for *darshan*, a view of the deities. The evening processions, weaving through the starlit night, are undoubtedly the most atmospheric.

Icons from the temple, special movable images, are taken out, lavishly clothed in silk and ornaments of rubies, sapphires, pearls, silver and gold. When the festival celebrates both Meenakshi and Sundareshwarar, the contingent is usually led by Vinayaka (Ganesh, son of Shiva), as the "remover of obstacles", followed in succession by Subrahmanya (another son of Shiva), Sundareshwarar (a multiple image of the marriage of Shiva), Meenakshi and Chandeshwarar (another form of Shiva). On some occasions, the deities are enshrined by simple canopies, but on others they ride on silver or gold vehicles (*vahanas*) such as horses, elephants or, most auspiciously, huge silver bulls.

At the Avani Mula festival, the coronation of Shiva is celebrated and his Maduran miracles are enacted in a series of plays (*lilas*). During the greatest festival of all, **Chittirai**, more plays are staged, telling the story of Meenakshi. The eighth day sees the goddess crowned as queen of the Pandyas, and, on the tenth, her marriage to Shiva draws as many as fifty thousand people to the temple. Out in the streets the next morning, mayhem ensues when the most elaborate transport is brought into use for procession. The god and goddess travel in fifteen-metre-high **chariots**, with giant wooden wheels, hauled through the streets by hundreds of devotees, all tugging on long ropes. Rising from a wooden platform, the massive pyramidal bamboo superstructures are decorated in colourful appliqué and fronted by a row of rearing wooden horses.

The god and goddess are taken to the banks of the Vaigai River, to meet Meenakshi's brother who, in southern mythology, is Lord Kallalagar (Vishnu). The icon of Vishnu is brought from the forested hilltop temple at Alagarkovil, 20km northeast of Madurai. Vishnu travelled to Madurai to give his sister away at the wedding, only to find on reaching the river that the ceremony had already occurred. Because of this, to appease the deity, the festivities always take place on the northern bank of the river.

sculpture, terracottas and an eighteenth-century print showing the palace in a dilapidated state.

All that remains of the **Rangavilasa**, the palace where Thirumalai's brother Muthialu lived, are just ten pillars, wedged in a tiny back street. Take Old Kudiralayam St, right of the palace as you face it, pass the Archaeological Department Office and turn right into Mahal Vadam Pokki St. The third turning on the left (opposite the New India Textile Shop) is the unmarked Ten Pillars South Lane. One pillar contains a **shivalingam** which is worshipped by passers-by.

Tamukkam palace: the Gandhi and Government museums

Across the Vaigai, 5km northeast of the centre near the Central Telegraph Office, stands **Tamukkam** (bus #2, #3, #4, or #26; 20min), the seventeenth-century multi-pillared and arched palace of Queen Rani Mangammal. Built to accommodate such regal entertainment as elephant fights, Tamukkam was taken over by the British, used as a courthouse and collector's office, and in 1955 became home to the Gandhi and Government museums.

Madurai's **Gandhi Memorial Museum** (daily 10am–1pm & 2–5.30pm; free), far better organized than most of the species, charts the history of India since the landing of the first Europeans, viewed in terms of the freedom struggle. Generally the perspective is national, but where appropriate, reference is made to the role played by Tamils. Wholeheartedly critical of the British, it states its case clearly and simply, quoting the Englishman John Sullivan: "We have denied to the people of the country all that could raise them in society, all that could elevate them as men; we have insulted their caste; we have abrogated their laws of inheritance; we have seized the possessions of their native princes and confiscated the estates of their nobles; we have unsettled the country by our exactions, and collected the revenue by means of torture." One chilling artefact, kept in a room painted black, is the bloodstained *dhoti* the Mahatma was wearing when he was assassinated. Next door to the museum, the **Gandhi Memorial Museum Library** (daily except Wed 10am–1pm & 2–5.30pm) houses a reference collection, open to all, of 15,000 books, periodicals, letters and microfilms of material by and about Gandhi.

Opposite, the small **Government Museum** (daily except Fri 9am–5pm; closed 2nd Sat each month; free) displays stone and bronze sculptures, musical instruments, paintings (including examples of Tanjore and Kangra styles) and folk art such as painted terracotta animals, festival costumes and hobby horses. There's also a fine collection of shadow puppets, said to have originated in the Thanjavur area and probably exported to southeast Asia during the Chola period. A small house in which **Gandhi** once lived stands in a garden within the compound. Beside it, a number of unfinished latrines may have been intended as an exhibit, or a public amenity. It's rather hard to tell.

Kochadai Aiyannar temple

The village of **Kochadai**, a northwestern suburb of Madurai, has a beautifully maintained temple dedicated to **Aiyannar**, the Tamil village deity and guardian of the borders. Travelling in Tamil Nadu, you often see such shrines from the road, but it may not always be possible, or appropriate, to investigate them. Here, however, they are accustomed to visitors. Flanked by two huge garish *dvarpalas* (doorkeepers), the entrance opens directly onto two gigantic horses with riders and furious-looking armed attendants. The shrine on the left houses the god Rama and his brother Lakshmana and, facing the entrance, is the shrine to Aiyannar. To the right, the *alamaram* tree, also a shrine, apparently houses a **cobra**, fed with eggs and milk. According to the priests he only comes out during full moon. During a big **festival** in the Tamil month of Panguni (March/April), Aiyannar is taken around the village to the accompaniment of music and fireworks.

Kochadai is served by frequent buses (#68 or #54) en route to Solavandan.

SHOPPING AND MARKETS IN MADURAI

Old Madurai is crowded with **textile and tailors' shops**, particularly in West Veli, Avani Moola and Chitrai streets and Town Hall Rd. Take up the offers you're bound to receive to go into the shops near the temple, where locally produced textiles are generally good value, and tailors pride themselves on turning out faithful copies of favourite clothes in a matter of hours. Many shops in the immediate vicinity also offer an incentive by allowing visitors to climb up to their roofs for views over the Meenakshi complex. South Avani Moola St is packed with **jewellery**, particularly gold shops, while at 10 North Avani Moola St, you can plan for the future at the Life & Lucky Number Numerology Centre.

Madurai is also a great place to pick up South Indian **crafts**. Among the best outlets are All India Handicrafts Emporium, 39–41 Town Hall Rd; Co-optex, West Tower St, and Pandiyan Co-op Supermarket, Palace Rd, for hand-woven textiles; and Surabhi, West Veli St, for Keralan handicrafts. For souvenirs such as sandalwood, temple models, carved boxes and oil lamps head for Poompuhar, 12 West Veli St (%0452/25517), or Tamilnad Gandhi Smarak Nidhi Khadi Gramodyog Bhavan, West Veli St, opposite the train station, which sells crafts, oil lamps, Meenakshi sculptures and khadi cloth and shirts.

The old purpose-built, wooden-pillared fruit and vegetable market, between North Chitrai and Avani Moola streets, provides a slice of Madurai life that can't have changed for centuries; beyond it, on the first floor of the concrete building at the back, the **flower market** (24hr) is a riot of colour and fragrance. Weighing scales spill with tiny white petals, and plump pink garlands hang in rows. Varieties such as orange, yellow or white marigolds (*samandi*), pink jasmine (*arelli*), tiny purple spherical vanameli and holy tulsi plants come from hill areas such as Kodaikanal and Kumily. These are bought in bulk and distributed for use in temples, or to wear in the hair; some are made into elaborate wedding garlands (*kalyanam mala*). The very friendly traders will show you each and every flower, and if you've got a camera will more than likely expect to be recorded for posterity. It's a nice idea to offer to send them a copy of any photograph you take.

Accommodation

Madurai has a wide range of **accommodation**, from rock-bottom lodges to good, clean mid-range places that cater for the flocks of pilgrims and tourists. There's a cluster of hotels on **West Perumal Maistry St**. Upmarket options lie a few kilometres out of the town centre, north of the Vaigai River.

Inexpensive

Duke, 6 N Veli St, close to the junction with W Masi St (☎0452/741154). A modern hotel, a 10min walk from the train station. Their larger-than-average non-a/c options are the best value; ask for one on the "open side", with a window. ③.

International, 46 W Perumal Maistry St (☎0452/741553). This one's a basic but clean lodge and a dependable low-budget option. ③.

New College House, 2 Town Hall Rd (☎0452/742971). Huge maze of a place with more than 200 basic rooms, and one of the town's best "meals" canteens on the ground floor (see Eating). Likely to have vacancies when everywhere else is full. ②–③.

Railway Retiring Rooms, First floor, stairway on platform 1 (turn right from the main entrance hall). There are huge, cleanish rooms (some a/c) situated in the main station building. Often booked. ①–③.

Sri Devi, 20 W Avani Moola St (☎0452/747431). Very good-value non-a/c doubles right next to the temple. For a romantic splurge, splash out on their "deluxe" a/c rooftop room (⑥), which has matchless views over the western *gopura*. No restaurant, but room service will send out for food. ②.

TM Lodge, 50 W Perumal Maistry St (☎0452/651682). Immaculately clean, with spotless attached bathrooms; the top-floor rooms are the airiest. It's the best of the budget bunch on this street. ②–③.

West Tower, 60 W Chitrai St (☎0452/746908). One of the few hotels close to the temple, with good views from the rooftop (but not from the rooms). Clean and good value. Some a/c. ②–④.

Moderate

Aarathy, 9 Perumalkoil, W Mada St (☎0452/731571). Great location, overlooking the Kundalagar temple near the STC bus stand. All rooms with TV, some with a/c and balcony, and a busy open-air restaurant that is especially popular when the temple elephant, Mahalakshmi, is led through each morning. This place is only hampered by occasionally surly staff. Usually full of foreigners, so book ahead. ④–⑤.

Madurai Ashok, Alagarkoil Rd (☎0452/537531, fax 537530). Plush hotel on the outskirts, with 24hr room service, bar, currency exchange, craft shops and a pleasant swimming pool. ⑦–⑧.

Padman, 1 Perumal Tank W St (☎0452/740702, fax 743629). The views from the front-side rooms of this modern hotel, overlooking the ruined Perumal tank, are worth paying extra for. Clean, comfortable and central. Rooftop restaurant. ④.

Pandyan, Alagarkoil Rd, Race Course (☎0452/537090, fax 533424). A comfortable, centrally a/c hotel north of the river, with a good restaurant, bar, exchange facilities, travel agency, bookstores and several craft shops. Nice garden, too. ⑦–⑧.

Prem Nivas, 102 W Perumal Maistry St (☎0452/742532, fax 743618). From the outside this place looks a lot swankier than it is, but their spacious rooms rank among the best mid-price deals in the city. ③–④.

Supreme, 110 W Perumal Maistry St (☎0452/743151, fax 742637). A large, swish and central hotel, offering a rooftop restaurant, 24-hr forex desk, Internet facilities and travel counter. A "duplex" gives views of Yanna Malai hill range and railway line. ④–⑤.

Taj Garden Retreat, Pasumalai Hills (☎0452/601020). This choice is Madurai's most exclusive hotel; a refurbished colonial house in the hills overlooking the city, 6km out. There are three kinds of rooms: "Standard" (US$110); "Old World", in the period block (US$132); and "Deluxe" modern cottages with the best views (US$150). Facilities include gourmet restaurant, pool, bar and tennis court. ⑨.

TTDC Hotel Tamil Nadu I, W Veli St (☎0452/737471, fax 627945). A dingy, overpriced government hotel, that's best avoided. ④–⑤.

TTDC Tamil Nadu II (Star), Alagarkoil Rd (☎0452/537461, fax 533203). The posher of Madurai's two government hotels, north of the river, 5km from the centre. Good-sized rooms (some a/c) and restaurant, though service can be sloppy. ⑤.

Eating

As with accommodation, the range of places to eat in Madurai is gratifyingly wide, and standards are generally high, whether you're eating at one of the numerous utilitarian-looking "meals" places around the temple, or in an upscale hotel. When the afternoon heat gets too much, head for one of the **juice bars** dotted around the centre, where you can order freshly squeezed pomegranate, pineapple, carrot or orange juice for around Rs20 per glass. To make the most of Madurai's exotic skyline, though, you'll have to seek out a **rooftop restaurant** – another of the modern city's specialties. Rock-bottom-budget travellers should try the street-side stalls at the bottom of West Perumal Maistry St, where old ladies dish up filling leaf plates of freshly steamed *iddli* and spicy fish *masala* for Rs10 per portion.

Aarthy, *Aarthy Hotel*, 9 Perumalkoil, W Mada St. Tasty tiffin (*dosas, iddlis* and hot *wada sambar*), served on low tables in a hotel forecourt, where the temple elephant turns up at 6am and 6pm. For more filling, surprisingly inexpensive main meals, step into their blissfully cool a/c annexe.

Amutbam, 30 Town Hall Rd. A huge menu featuring everything from full-on chicken sizzlers to Western-style snacks, via the usual range of noodles, North Indian and veg dishes. Ask for a table in their a/c compartment, where you can chill out for an extra Rs2 per head.

Anna Meenakshi, opposite *TM Lodge*, W Perumal Maistry St. An upmarket branch of *New College House's* more traditional canteen, serving top tiffin to a discerning, strictly vegetarian clientele. This one's smaller and brighter, with shiny marble tables and an ornate bell-metal lamp in the doorway. Arguably the most hygienic, best-value food in the centre. Opens 6am–9.30pm ("rice meals" are served 10.30am–4pm).

Apollo 96, *Supreme Hotel*, 110 W Perumal Maistry St. Boasting 75,000 flashing diodes and a punchy sound system, South India's most hi-tech bar looks like the set from a low-budget 1970s sci-fi movie. Beers cost Rs75. Closes at 11pm sharp. It's altogether a surreal experience.

Karthik, W Perumal Maistry St (around the corner from the *Aarthy*, near the Relief bus stand). Run-of-the-mill from the outside, but this pure veg tiffin joint is famous for its delicious *iddli*-fry-masala – mini *iddlis* turned in a spicy chilli paste. Eat in or ask for a "parcel".

New College House, 2 Town Hall Rd. Huge meals-cum-tiffin hall in old-style hotel. Lunchtime, when huge piles of pure veg food is served on banana leaves to long rows of locals, is a real deep-south experience; and the coffee's pure Coorg.

Ruby, W Perumal Maistry St. Ignore the "Alcohol Strictly Prohibited" note on the menu card: this is essentially an unlicensed bar, periodically raided by the police but a popular meeting place for foreign travellers. Cold beers are served a leafy courtyard or more claustrophobic compartments indoors, and they do hot snacks, including a fiery "Chicken 65", noodles and *biryani*.

Supreme, *Supreme Hotel*, 110 W Perumal Maistry St. Arguably Madurai's best and breeziest rooftop restaurant, with sweeping views of the city and temple, and an eclectic multi-cuisine menu; ideal venue for a sundowner. Open 4pm–midnight.

Around Madurai: Tirupparakunram

Stretching west towards the blue haze of the Alagar Hills, the Vaigai plains **around Madurai** are broken by colossal outcrops of granite, some of them weathered into weird forms like petrified monsters. Each occupies a place in the mythological landscape of the Pandyan heartland. To the northeast of the city, the "Elephant Hill" is said to have been created by Shiva to punish a rampaging pachyderm. The holiest rock hereabouts, however, looms over the southwest fringes of the city, where the Muslim conquerors of the early fourteenth century consolidated their fleeting colonization of the far south by founding a capital at the foot of an ancient Hindu site. Referred to by Islamic historians as **"City of Ma'bar"**, the orderly grid-planned town served as the headquarters of the **Madurai Sultanate**, whose origins remain obscure, but which endured for eight generations until the army of the mighty Hindu Vijayanagar empire swept south to mop up the remnants of Muslim rule left after Malik Kafir's bloody sack of 1311. The last sultan, **Sikander Shah**, allegedly died defending the town, and his tomb crowns the top of the 365-metre-monolith, known to Muslim pilgrims throughout India as **Sikandermalai**, "Hill of Sikander" (see below).

For Hindus, however, the sheer-sided rock at **TIRUPPARAKUNRAM**, 8km southwest of Madurai (buses #4A & 32 from the STC bus stand), is revered as **Skandermalai**, one of the six abodes of Shiva's son and the Tamils' favourite god, Lord Murugan. Identified by mythology as the site of Murugan's marriage to Indra's daughter, Deivani, it is one of the most sacred shrines in Tamil Nadu. At the auspicious time of Murugan's wedding anniversary in early February, thousands of newly-weds come here to be blessed, and in the summer, the god's birthday is celebrated with displays of fire-walking and body-piercing, along with other acts of ostentatious masochism, such as devotees dragging ox carts along with chains fastened to the flesh of their shoulders.

Outside festival time, however, Tirupparakunram is a peaceful spot offering a welcome respite from the frenzy of Madurai. Its **temple**, built around an eighth-century shrine cut into the rock 35m above the town's rooftops, comprises a series of huge terraces and halls, interconnected by stone staircases. At ground level, the main colonnaded *mandapa*, adorned with brightly painted horses and *yalis*, served as a field hospital for British soldiers in the 1760s, when the temple was badly vandalized (one local priest allegedly burned himself to death in protest at the British vandalism). Perhaps as a consequence of this, non-Hindus are not always allowed to visit the upper levels (if you're refused entry, ask at the temple office), but it is definitely worth making the climb to see the ancient rock-carvings in, around and below the walls of the central

MOVING ON FROM MADURAI

By plane

Indian Airlines flies daily to Chennai and four times each week to Mumbai (Mon, Weds, Fri & Sun). Their a/c office at 7a W Veli St, near the post office (☎0452/37234), is efficient and helpful. To get to the airport, catch a taxi for around Rs200. Indian Airlines also lays on a bus to meet flights, but don't bank on it.

By bus

At the last count, five different stations operated long-distance buses from Madurai (see Arrival and Information, p.453); if you're unsure which one you need, ask at the tourist office in the train station, and ignore the hustlers hanging around the STC bus stand. From the STC bus stand, numerous government buses leave day and night to Chennai (11hr). Destinations in Karnataka include Bangalore, for which there are 19 TTC (first 6am, last 10.15pm) and two KSRTC (7.45am & 10.30pm) buses. Night services also leave here for Mysore (depart 4pm; 10hr). For Kerala there are three JJTC and two PRC buses a day to Ernakulam/Kochi (10hr), via Kottayam. There are no direct services to Ooty, but buses to Coimbatore (6hr) leave from the Arapalayam stand, 3km west of the centre, every 30min during the day. Kodaikanal (4hr) is well served with departures every 15mins or so. You can also get buses to Kumily (for Periyar Wildlife Sanctuary) every 30min, and one a day to Palakaad (9hr). The Anna stand, 3km northeast of the temple, offers regular buses to destinations north such as Thanjavur, Tiruchirapalli and Kumbakonam, and Rameshwaram (every 30min; 4hr). Long-distance buses from Palankanathan stand, in the southwest, 5km from the centre of town, include regular services to both Kanniyakumari (every 30min; 6hr) and Thiruvananthapuram.

By train

Madurai is on the main line and well connected to most major towns and cities in South India. However, at the time of writing the stretch between here and Trichy was closed for conversion work, severely disrupting services to and from Chennai. To make reservations, you have to join the queues in the main forecourt at the train station. For timetable details, ask at the Tourism Department Information Centre, right of the ticket counters.

It is possible to reach the railhead for Kodaikanal by train, but the journey is much faster by bus. From Madurai, a line also runs southwest towards Kollam in Kerala, crossing the Ghats via Shengottai on one of India's most impressive mountain rail routes. Travelling it in the day time involves a change of train: first catch the *Madurai–Tuticorin Fast Passenger* (#729) at 8.05am to Virudunagar Junction, which arrives at 8.45am to connect with the west-bound *Chennai–Quillon Mail* (#6105), arriving in Kollam around seven-and-a-half hours later at 4.20pm. From there, regular services continue south to Thiruvananthapuram. For Ooty, catch any train to Coimbatore (see below), where you should spend the night in order to pick the early morning *Nilgiri Express* to Mettapalayam, departure point for the Blue Mountain Railway (see below).

The daily express trains below are recommended as the fastest or most convenient from Madurai, although, as stated above, conversion work on the line may affect many main-line services; check the current situation when you book your ticket.

To	Name	Number	Departs	Duration
Bangalore	*Madurai–Bangalore Express*	#6731	8pm	12hr
Chennai	*Vaigai Express*	#2636	5.20am	9hr 40min
	Pandyan Express	#6718	7.35pm	11hr 15min
Coimbatore (Ooty)	*Madurai–Coimbatore Fast Passenger*	#778	2.30pm	5hr 20min
Kanniyakumari	*Madurai–Kanniyakumari Express*	#6721	12.30am	5hr 45min
Rameshwaram	*Coimbatore–Rameshwaram Express*	#6115	6am	4hr 50min
Trichy	*Vaigai Express*	#2636	5.20am	2hr 45min

shrine, where Murugan's vehicle (*vahana*) the peacock, features prominently; these are some of the best surviving examples of Pallava rock art in the South.

Crowning the windswept summit of the hill, amid gnarled old umbrella trees that cling to the bare rock, the **Dargah of Sikander Shah** is the region's holiest Muslim shrine. The ruler whose heroic death on this spot failed to save his capital from the Viyayanagar reconquest is today revered as a saint, and his tomb complex – known as Skandermalai to Muslim pilgrims – made up of a domed mosque and covered colonnade dating from the fifteenth century, attracts pilgrims from across the country. Sikander's reputation for piety, however, doesn't square with the account of the Madurai Sultanate featured in the chronicles of Shams Siraj of Delhi, in which Sikander is accused of having succumbed to the decadence of neighbouring Madurai:

"He began to perform acts of indecency in public... when he held court in the audience hall he wore women's ornaments on his wrists and ankles, and his neck and fingers were adorned with feminine decorations. His indecent acts with pederasts were performed openly... (and) the people of Ma'bar were utterly and completely weary and out of patience with him and his behaviour."

Given the paucity of other historical sources relating to this brief period of Muslim supremacy in South India, it is hard to know which version of the story – Sikander as valiant sage or as sybaritic sultan – is the more apocryphal, but the **views** of Madurai and the surrounding plains from the tomb are unambiguously impressive.

Rameshwaram and around

The sacred island of **RAMESHWARAM**, 163km southeast of Madurai and less than 20km from Sri Lanka across the Gulf of Mannar is, along with Madurai, South India's most important pilgrimage site. Hindus tend to be followers of either Vishnu or Shiva, but Rameshwaram brings them together, being where the god Rama, an incarnation of Vishnu, worshipped Shiva in the *Ramayana*. The **Ramalingeshwara temple** complex, with its magnificent pillared walkways, is the most famous on the island, but there are several other small temples of interest, such as the **Gandhamadana Parvatam**, sheltering Rama's footprints, and the **Nambunayagi Amman Kali temple**, frequented for its curative properties. **Dhanushkodi**, "Rama's bow", at the eastern end of the peninsula, is where Rama is said to have bathed, and the boulders that pepper the sea between here and Sri Lanka, known as "Adam's Bridge", are the stepping stones used by Hanuman in his search for Rama's wife, Sita, after her abduction by Ravana, the demon king of Lanka.

Rameshwaram is always crowded with day-trippers, and ragged mendicants who camp outside the Ramalingeshwara and the **Ujainimahamariamman**, the small goddess shore temple. An important part of their pilgrimage is to bathe in the main temple's sacred tanks and in the sea; the narrow strip of beach is shared by groups of bathers, relaxing cows and mantra-reciting *swamis* sitting next to sand *linga*. As well as fishing – prawns and lobsters for packaging and export to Japan – shells are a big source of income in the coastal villages.

The heavy military presence along the approach roads to Rameshwaram remind you of the proximity of the **war in Sri Lanka**, a short boat ride east across the Palk Strait. As the crow flies, Jaffna, the epicentre of the protracted and bloody conflict between the Tamil Tigers and the Sri Lankan army, is actually a lot closer to Rameshwaram than Madurai, and the strait has long served as a key supply line for the separatists – a trade covertly tolerated by the state's pro-Tamil DMK government. However, after the Tigers assassinated Rajiv Gandhi in 1991 for supporting the Sri Lankan government, it looked temporarily as if the war might spread to the mainland (the coast around Rameshwaram supports a huge population of Tamil refugees), and the Indian army was

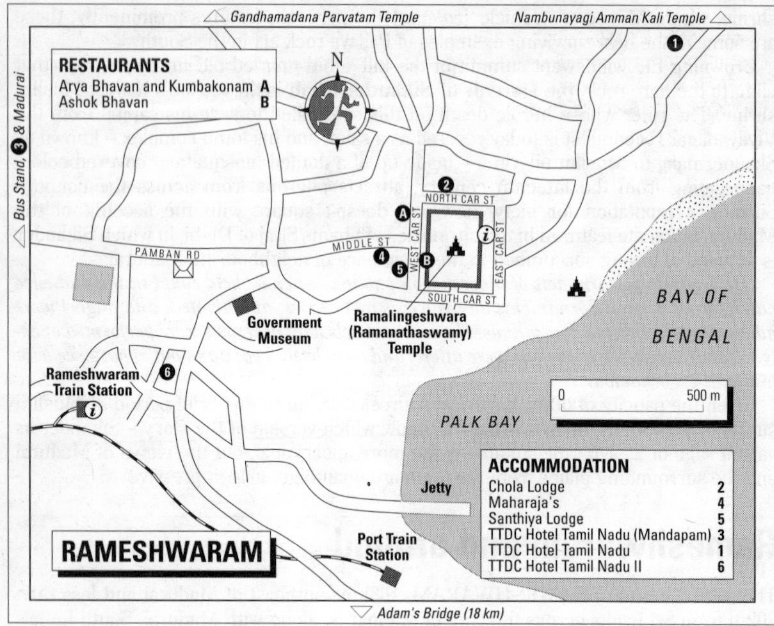

drafted in to keep the peace. More recently, **caste conflicts** in the town of **Ramanathapuram** (Ramnad), opposite Rameshwaram, have claimed many lives; rioting and 24-hour curfews in the winter of 1998 closed the NH49 to tourist traffic. That said, once you've crossed the bridge over the Pamban Channel, the oppressive atmosphere of the mainland gives way to Rameshwaram's infectious devotional intensity.

Arrival and information

NH49, the main road from Madurai, connects Rameshwaram with Mandapam on the mainland via the impressive two-kilometre-long Indira Gandhi bridge, originally built by the British in 1914 as a rail link, and reopened in 1988 by Rajiv Gandhi for road traffic. Armed guards at checkposts at either end keep a watchful eye on travellers. **Buses** from Madurai (via Ramnad), Trichy, Thanjavur, Kanniyakumari and Chennai pull in at the bus stand, 2km west of the centre. The **train station**, 1km southwest of the centre, is the end of the line for trains from Chennai, Coimbatore, Thanjavur, Madurai and Ramnad, and boasts decent **retiring rooms**, a veg restaurant and a left luggage office (5.30am–10pm). There are two daily express trains to and from Chennai, and one (the *Rameshwaram–Coimbatore Express* #6116) for Coimbatore, via Madurai. Buses run every half hour to Madurai (4hr) and four times daily to Kunniyakumari (9–10hr). Travel agents around the temple run faster and more comfortable **minibuses** around South India.

Red and white city buses run every ten minutes from the bus stand to the main temple; otherwise, **local transport** consists of unmetered cycle- and auto-rickshaws that gather outside the bus stand. Jeeps are available for rent near the train station, and bicycles can be rented from shops in the four Car streets around the temple. There is no **ferry service** to and from Sri Lanka, due to the troubles there.

The tiny TTDC **tourist office**, 14 East Car St (Mon–Fri 10am–5pm; ☎04573/21371), gives out information about guides, accommodation and boat trips. TTDC also have a counter at the train station (☎04573/21373), which opens to coincide with the arrival of trains, and a small booth at the bus stand (daily except holidays 10am–5.45pm). The **post office** is on Pamban Rd.

Ramalingeshwara temple

The core of the **Ramalingeshwara** (or Ramanathaswamy) **temple** was built by the Cholas in the twelfth century to house two much-venerated **shivalinga** associated with the *Ramayana.* After rescuing his wife Sita from the clutches of Ravana, Rama was advised to atone for the killing of the demon king – a *brahmin* – by worshipping Shiva. Rama's monkey lieutenant, Hanuman, was despatched to the Himalaya to fetch a *shivalingam*, but when he failed to return by the appointed day, Sita fashioned a *lingam* from sand (the *Ramanathalingam*) so the ceremony could proceed. Hanuman eventually showed up with his *lingam* and in order to assuage the monkey's guilt Rama decreed that in future, of the two, Hanuman's should be worshipped first. The *linga* are now housed in the inner section of the Ramalingeshwara, not usually open to non-Hindus. Much of what can be visited dates from the 1600s, when the temple received generous endowments from the Sethupathi rajas of Ramanathapuram (see p.468).

High walls enclose the temple, forming a rectangle with huge pyramidal *gopura* entrances on each side. The gateways lead to a spacious closed ambulatory, flanked to either side by continuous platforms with massive pillars set on their edges. These **corridors** are the most famous attribute of the temple, their extreme length – 205m, with 1212 pillars on the north and south sides – giving a remarkable impression of receding perspective. Delicate scrollwork and brackets of pendant lotuses supported by *yalis*, mythical lion-like beasts, adorn the pillars.

Before entering the inner sections, pilgrims are expected to bathe in water from each of the twenty-two **tirthas** (tanks) in the temple; hence the groups of dripping-wet pilgrims, most of them fully clothed, making their way from one tank to the next to be doused in a bucket of water by a temple attendant. Each tank is said to have special benefits: the Rama Vimosana Tirtha provides relief from debt, the Sukreeva Tirtha gives "complete wisdom" and the attainment of *Surya Loka*, the realm of the Sun, and the Draupadi Tirtha ensures long life for women and "the love of their spouses".

Monday is Rama's auspicious day, when the Padilingam *puja* takes place. **Festivals** of particular importance at the temple include **Mahashivaratri** (10 days during Feb/March), **Brahmotsavam** (10 days during March/April) and **Thirukalyanam** (July/Aug), celebrating the marriage of Shiva to Parvati.

Minor temples

The **Gandhamadana Parvatam** (daily 6–11am & 3.30–6.30pm), on a hill 2km north of Rameshwaram town centre, is a venerable shrine housing Rama's footprints. On some days, ceremonies are conducted here after the 5.30am *puja* at the Ramalingeshwara temple, encouraging pilgrims to climb the hill to continue their devotions. From the roof, fine views extend over the surrounding country and on clear nights you can see the lights of Jaffna.

Three kilometres east of town towards the old fishing village of Dhanushkodi, the small **Nambunayagi Amman Kali temple**, set in a quiet sandy grove 200m off the main road, attracts people in search of cures for illnesses. Inside a banyan tree next to it is a shrine dedicated to the spirit Retatalai, "the two-headed". A pair of wooden sandals with spikes, said to belong to the spirit, is left in the shrine and locals say they can hear them clip-clopping at night when Retatalai chooses to wander. Pieces of cloth are tied to the branches of the tree to mark thanks for such boons as pregnancy after barrenness and the healing of family feuds. The bus terminates at Dhanushkodi, from where you can walk along the ever-narrowing spit of sand until the sea finally closes in and the island peters out, tantalizingly short of Sri Lanka.

Accommodation

Apart from the TTDC hotels, **accommodation** in Rameshwaram is restricted to basic lodges, mostly in the Car streets around the temple. The temple authorities have a range of rooms for pilgrims; ask at the Devasthanam Office, East Car St (☎04573/21292).

Chola Lodge, N Car St (☎04573/21307). A basic place in the quietest of the Car streets. ②.

Maharaja's, 7 Middle St (☎04573/21271). Good clean rooms located next to the temple's west gate, two with a/c and TV. There are temple views from balconies. No restaurant here, although management will bring food in. ③–⑤.

Railway Retiring Rooms, Six large double and three triple rooms, generally cleaner (and quieter) than town lodges for the same price, plus a dorm. ①.

Santhiya Lodge, 1 W Car St (☎21329). Shabby, but very cheap. ①.

TTDC Hotel Tamil Nadu, near the beach (☎04573/21277). The best place in Rameshwaram, in a pleasant location and with bar and restaurant. There're comfortable, sea-facing rooms, some a/c; also cheaper dorm and hostel beds. However, it's often full, so book in advance from another TTDC hotel or office. ③–④.

TTDC Hotel Tamil Nadu II, near the train station on Railway Feeder Rd (☎04573/20171). New hotel, cheaper than the above, but in a far less attractive location and decidedly grubby. ②.

TTDC Hotel Tamil Nadu (Mandapam). This place is 13km away, close to the mainland side of the Indira Gandhi bridge (☎04573/41512). It consists of twelve drab double cottages on the beach, in a bay harbouring fishing boats and is primarily used by tour groups, so it's quite likely to be full. ③.

Eating

Eating in Rameshwaram is more about survival than delighting the taste buds. Most places serve up fairly unexciting "meals".

Arya Bhavan and **Kumbakonam**, W Car St. These places are both run by the same family and dish up standard veg "meals".

Ashok Bhavan, W Car St. Offers regional varieties of *thalis*.

TTDC Hotel Tamil Nadu, near the beach. Gigantic, noisy, high-ceiling glasshouse near the sea, serving good South Indian snacks and "meals"; many items on the menu are unavailable, however.

Around Rameshwaram: Ramanathapuram (Ramnad)

RAMANATHAPURAM (aka Ramnad) offers a possible break on the bus or train between Madurai (120km northwest) and Rameshwaram (36km east). It's worth stopping here to see the neglected but atmospheric **Ramalinga Vilas**, palace of the Sethupati rajas, who by tradition were guardians of the mythical Sethu bridge built by Rama to cross to Lanka. **Caste conflicts** in the winter of 1998, however, during which riots resulted in the deaths of more than a dozen people and closed the bazaar for weeks amid extended curfews, meant this town was off-limits to tourists; check beforehand to ensure it's not in the midst of another flare-up.

The entrance to the **palace** (daily except Fri 9am–1pm & 2–5pm; Rs2), 2km from the bus stand, takes you into the big and dusty **Durbar Hall**, whose central aisle is hung with oil portraits of the rajas of the last few hundred years. Ceilings and walls throughout the building are decorated with early eighteenth-century murals depicting subjects such as business meetings with the English and battles with the Maratha king Sarabhoji, as well as scenes from the epics. One battle scene shows soldiers fighting with boomerangs, and there's a real Indian boomerang on display. Also on show are palm-leaf manuscripts, a Ravi Varma painting with appliquéd brocade and sculptures of Vishnu from the eighth and thirteenth centuries. From the **throne room**, a secret passageway once gave an escape route to a local temple. The raja's throne, supported on carved elephant legs, is decorated with a coat of arms, given by the British, featuring a lion and unicorn. As further proof of the royal family's compliance with the foreign power, the raja, at the end of the eighteenth century, allowed them to use the bedchambers upstairs – decorated with erotic murals – as a meeting hall. This cosy relationship did not find unanimous approval among his subjects. Influential local landowners showed their contempt for the British by responding to tax demands with bags of stones and, in 1798 and 1801, rebellions took place, sometimes dubbed the "South Indian War of Independence". In 1803, at the request of the British, the Ramnad raja was obliged to accept the lesser rank of *zamindar* (feudatory chieftain).

On the roof is a stone bed on which the raja would lounge in the evenings to enjoy panoramic views of the town and surrounding country. The buildings immediately below were royal guesthouses, in one of which a descendant of the rajas now resides.

Tirunelveli and around

Separated by the only perennial river in the far south, the Tambraparni, **TIRUNELVELI** and its modern counterpart, **PALAYANKOTTAI**, together form the largest conurbation in the densely populated red-soil region south of Madurai. Aside from the huge **Nellaiyappa temple**, built by the Pandyas in the thirteenth century with a towering pyramidal *gopura*, situated 2km west of the river, neither holds much of specific interest. However, you may want to use Tirunelveli as a base for day-trips to nearby **Thiruppudaimarudur**, 25km west, whose old riverside temple is famed for its wood-carvings, or further west to **Kuttalam**, in the foothills of the Ghats, where a series of dramatic waterfalls attract streams of day-trippers. An hour or so east on the Coromandel Coast, the traditional Tamil pilgrimage town of **Tiruchendur** has the region's most spectacular shore temple, dominating an appropriately impressive sweep of surf-lashed beach. The sea between the Coromandel and Sri Lanka is rich enough to support a string of fishing settlements, but the most lucrative harvest yielded by the Gulf of Mannar are the pearls gathered by divers from the port of **Tuticorin**, an hour north of Tiruchendur, where the Portuguese founded one of their first colonies in India.

Tirunelveli's **bus stand**, in the town centre just across the river from Palayankottai, has services to and from Madurai (3hr), Nagercoil (1hr 30min), Tuticorin (1hr), Tiruchendur (1hr) and Kollam (5hr). For Kuttalam, you have to head to Tenkasi (1hr) and change onto a local bus. **Trains** from Chennai, Madurai, Nagercoil and Kollam pull in at the main-line station, five minutes' walk west on the opposite side of Madurai Rd.

Most of the **accommodation** in town is lined up outside the bus stand, on Madurai Rd. Pick of the bunch is the *Sri Jankiran* (☎0462/331941; ④), which has some a/c rooms, a cosy **restaurant** and roof terrace. Next door, the *Barani* (☎0462/333234; ③) is marginally cheaper, but dependably clean, as is the *Aryaas* (☎0462/339001; ③), a short walk further down the road.

Thiruppudaimarudur

THIRUPPUDAIMARUDUR, a small riverside village 25km west of Tirunelveli, is the site of a temple renowned throughout the region for its splendid medieval wood-carvings and murals. The best preserved of these line the interior of the temple's east tower, which you can scale via flights of precariously steep wooden steps. Pillars and brackets propping up a succession of ceilings have been sumptuously decorated, while the walls (which you'll need a flashlight to see clearly) are covered with vibrant paintings, depicting scenes from the *Ramayana*, Vishnu's various incarnations and mythical battles.

Buses to Thiruppudaimarudur leave more or less hourly from Tirunelveli, and take fifty minutes. The village doesn't have any hotels or guesthouses.

Kuttalam (Courtalam)

An image familiar to collectors of exotic prints and engravings in Victorian Britain was that of the great waterfalls at **KUTTALAM (Courtalam)**, 136km northwest of Kanniyakumari, where the Chittar River plunges down a sheer cliff on the very edge of the Western Ghats. A couple of centuries ago, when the famous Raj-era artist, Thomas Daniells, came to sketch the falls, this was still a remote spot, overgrown with vegetation and frequented only by wandering *sadhus* and the odd party of sickly Brits. A hydro project upstream has somewhat diminished the falls' splendour, and the barrage of film music and hoardings in the modern concrete village that has sprung up at their foot does little to enhance the overall atmosphere, but it is still worth coming here for an invigorating bathe. Bussing in from all over the state, thousands of Tamils do just that each day, especially between July and late September, when water levels are at their highest. From late January until May, the falls can dry up completely.

In all, nine major cascades are dotted around Kuttalam, but only one, known for obvious reasons as **Main Falls**, is located in the village proper. This is where the largest crowds congregate – the "ladies" to the left, fully dressed in soaking saris; old folk and kids to the right; and men, in regulation voluminious underpants, taking the full force of the central flow. It's worth pointing out that few foreigners come to Kuttalam, so expect to create a bit of a stir if you strip off; for a little more privacy, try jumping onto one of the minibuses that run throughout the day to smaller waterfalls around Kuttalam.

To reach Kuttalam by bus, you first have to head for **Tenkasi**, which is well connected to Tirunelveli (2hr) and Madurai (3hr), from where local buses run the final twenty minutes to the falls. The only **accommodation** to speak of when you get here is the government-run *Hotel Tamil Nadu* (04633/22423; ②–④) which offers a range of uniformly shabby rooms; if they are full, ask at the Town Panchayat (no phone; ②), the local council building in the centre of the village, where simple accommodation is sometimes available.

Tuticorin

TUTICORIN, 51km east of Tirunelveli on the NH7 or 130km northeast of Kanniyakumari, developed as a flourishing Portuguese colony in the sixteenth century and later expanded under the Dutch and British. Eclipsed by Madras in the late 1700s, it is nowadays the state's second port and would be an entirely forgettable, gritty Tamil town were it not for the prodigious quantities of **pearl**-bearing saltwater molluscs, *Pinctada martensi*, that grow in the shark-infested shallows offshore. These are harvested for a short period of around one month each year (normally in March–April) by divers equipped with little more than antiquated face masks. The pearls they collect are said to rank among the finest in the world, on a par with those found in the Persian Gulf, which is presumably why you won't easily find any for sale in the bazaar; all but a tiny proportion are exported.

Tuticorin is largely industrial and not a particularly appealing place to stay, but if you find yourself in need of a hotel, head for the *Jony International* (☎0461/328350; ⑤) or the less expensive *Sugam* (☎0461/328172; ③), both dependable options on VE Road, a short rickshaw ride from the centre of town.

Tiruchendur

TIRUCHENDUR means "beautiful holy town" in Tamil, and for once the epithet fits, thanks to the awesome presence on its shoreline of the mighty **Subramanya temple**. The shrine – one of the six sacred abodes of the Tamils' favourite god, **Lord Murugan** (Shiva's son, Subramanya), here in the form of the Ascetic ("renouncer of the transitory and illusory") – presides over a spectacular sandy beach, with breakers crashing in off the Gulf of Mannar. Corrosive salt winds have taken their toll on the original building erected by the Pallavas in the ninth century, and large sections of what you see today are modern, dating from 1941. However, references to the deity inside occur in some of the Tamils' oldest scriptures, while archeological digs conducted in the 1890s on the banks of the Tambraparni River nearby yielded evidence of a three-thousand-year-old religious cult focused on a spear-wielding deity very similar to Murugan. More extraordinary still were the prehistoric mouth locks that came to light at the same time, identical to those worn by more fervent devotees at Murugan festivals in Tamil Nadu today.

The Subramanya temple is approached via a long colonnaded walkway, running 700m through a packed sacred precinct lined with shops selling *puja* paraphernalia and pilgrims' souvenirs. Non-Hindus are permitted to enter the central shrine on payment of a small donation. The deity inside is among the most revered in South India, attracting crowds of more than a million during the temple's annual festival, just before the monsoon, when 108 different herbs and auspicious preparations are offered to the god, symbolizing the renewal of the earth. The ritual is accompanied by the chanting of some of the oldest Sanskrit verses surviving in India. In his 1995 travelogue *The Smile of Murugan*, the British historian Michael Wood speculates that these may even predate human speech; scholars have shown their nearest analogue is birdsong, lending credence to the theory that ritual came before verbal language in human evolution.

Tiruchendur is well connected by bus to Tirunelveli (1hr), Madurai's Palankanathan bus stand (4hr), Tuticorin (40min) and Nagercoil (2hr), and there are four daily trains to and from Tirunelveli. Aside from a handful of spartan pilgrims' hostels in the sacred precinct, the only **accommodation** in the town is TN Tourism's typically lacklustre *Hotel Tamil Nadu* (☎04638/44268; ③–⑤), whose inexpensive **restaurant** serves veg and non-veg food.

Kanniyakumari

KANNIYAKUMARI, at the southernmost extremity of India, is almost as compelling for Hindus as Rameshwaram. It is significant not only for its association with a virgin goddess, Kanya Devi, but also as the meeting point of the Bay of Bengal, Indian Ocean and Arabian Sea. Watching the sun rise and set is the big attraction, especially on full moon day in April, when it's possible to see both the setting sun and rising moon on the same horizon. Although Kanniyakumari is in the state of Tamil Nadu, most foreign visitors arrive on day-trips from Thiruvananthapuram (Trivandrum), the capital of Kerala, 86km northwest. While the place is of enduring appeal to pilgrims, others may find it bereft of atmosphere, with nature's power to engender wonder in the human spirit obliterated by ugly buildings and hawkers selling shells and trinkets.

Arrival and local transport

Trains from Thiruvananthapuram, Mumbai, Bangalore – and even Jammu, at 86hr the longest rail journey in India – stop at the **train station** in the north of town, 2km from the seafront. **From Madurai**, the best train service is the #6721 *Tuticorin Express*, which leaves Madurai Junction at 12.30am, and arrives at 6.15am the following morning, just in time for sunrise. You can leave **luggage** in the generator room behind the ticket office for Rs5 per item.

The new and well-organized Thiruvalluvar **bus stand**, west of town, is served by regular buses from Thiruvananthapuram (hourly; 2hr), Kovalam (every 2–3hr; 1hr 30min), Madurai (13 daily; 6hr), Rameshwaram (4 daily; 9–10hr; change at Madurai during the rainy season in Nov and Dec) and Chennai (11 daily; 14–16 hr). Auto-rickshaws and taxis provide **local transport**.

The Town

The seashore **Kumari Amman temple** (daily 4.30–11.30am & 5.30–8.30pm) is dedicated to the virgin goddess **Kanya Devi**, who may originally have been the local guardian deity of the shoreline, but was later absorbed into the figure of Devi, or Parvati, consort of Shiva. One version of Kanya Devi's story relates how she did penance to win the hand of Shiva. The god was all in favour and set out from Suchindram for the wedding, due to take place at midnight. The celestial *devas*, however, wanted Kanya Devi to remain a virgin, so that she could retain her full quota of

shakti, or divine power, and hatched a plot. Narada the sage assumed the form of a cock and crowed; on hearing this, Shiva, thinking that it was dawn and that he had missed the auspicious time for the ceremony, went home. The image of Kanya Devi inside the temple wears a diamond nose stud of such brilliance that it's said to be visible from the sea. Male visitors must be shirtless and wear a *dhoti* before entering the temple; non-Hindus are not allowed in the inner sanctum. It is especially auspicious for pilgrims to wash at the bathing *ghat* here.

Resembling a pre-war British cinema, the **Gandhi Mandapam** (daily 6.30am–12.30pm & 3–7.30pm), 300m northwest of the Kumari Amman temple, was actually conceived as a modern imitation of an Orissan temple, designed so that the sun strikes the auspicious spot where the ashes of Mahatma Gandhi were laid, prior to their immersion in the sea, at noon on his birthday, October 2.

Possibly the original sacred focus of Kanniyakumari are two rocks, about sixy metres apart, half-submerged in the sea five hundred metres off the coast, which came to be known as the Pitru and Matru *tirthas*. In 1892 they attracted the attention of the Hindu reformer Vivekananda (1862–1902), who swam out to the rocks to meditate on the syncretistic teachings of his recently dead guru, Ramakrishna Paramahamsa. Incorporating elements of architecture from around the country, the 1970 **Vivekananda Memorial** (daily except Tues 7–11am & 2–5pm), reached by the Poompuhar ferry service from the jetty on the east side of town (every 30min; same hours), houses a statue of the saint. The footprints of Kanya Devi can also be seen here, at the spot where she performed her penance.

For more on the life and teachings of Vivekananda, visit the **Wandering Monk museum (Vivekananda Puram)**, just north of the tourist office at the bottom of town (daily 8am–noon & 4–8pm; admission free), where a sequence of 41 panels (in English, Tamil and Hindi) recounts the *swami*'s odyssey around the subcontinent at the end of the nineteenth century. Born in Calcutta, Vivekananda received a Western education, which he subsequently rejected – largely as a result of a "defiling encounter" with the West during a visit to the Parliament of Religions in Chicago. Based on the Vedic scriptures (in spite of the fact Vivekananda never mastered Sanskrit), he countered the traditional Hindu dogma that the universe is a delusion beyond the sole reality of Brahma with a pro-active ethos based on social work and reform – a kind of early Indian *engagement* without Jean-Paul Sartre's baggy suits and strong coffee.

Accommodation

As Kanniyakumari is a "must see" for Indian tourists and pilgrims, **hotels** can fill up early. However, recent developments have raised standards, and relieved the pressure on space.

Kerala House, Seafront (☎04652/71257). A large colonial-era building, converted into a rest house for Keralan civil servants. The cavernous doubles (two of them are a/c) have dressing rooms and bathrooms, and some rooms have sea views. Book in advance through the Political Department of the State Secretariat in Thiruvananthapuram. ③–④.

Lakshmi Tourist Home, E Car St (☎04652/71333). The rooms are smart, some are sea-facing and have swish a/c. There's an excellent non-veg restaurant. ③–⑦.

Maadhini, E Car St (☎04652/71787, fax 716570). Large, newly built hotel right on the seafront above the fishing village. It has fine sea views, comfortably furnished rooms and one of the best restaurants in town. A good mid-range choice. ③–⑥.

Manickam Tourist Home, N Car St (☎04652/71387). Spacious, modern a/c and non-a/c rooms, some with sea views. Faces the sunrise and the Vivekananda rock. Good value. ③–⑤.

Samudra, Sannathi St (☎04652/71162). Smart new hotel near the temple entrance, with well-furnished deluxe rooms facing the sunrise. Facilities include satellite TV and veg restaurant. ④–⑥.

TTDC Hotel Tamil Nadu, Seafront (☎04652/71257). Offering cottages (some are a/c) and clean rooms (a/c on the first floor), most with sea view. There are cheaper and very basic "mini" doubles at the back and a youth hostel dorm. Good square meals are served in functional surroundings. ①–⑤.

Eating

Aside from the usual "meals" places and hotel dining rooms, there are a few popular veg and non-veg **restaurants** in the centre of town, most of them attached to one or other of the hotels.

Archana, *Maadhini Hotel*, E Car St. An extensive veg and non-veg multi-cuisine menu served inside a well-ventilated dining hall, or al fresco on a sea-facing terrace (evenings only). They also serve the town's best selection of ice-cream.

Saravana, Sannathi St. Arguably Kanniyakumari's best "meals" restaurant, serving all the usual snacks, cold drinks and huge Tamil *thalis* at lunchtime to hoards of hungry pilgrims. Their coffee is good, too.

Around Kanniyakumari: Suchindram and Maruntha Malai

Construction of the **Stanunathaswami temple** at **SUCHINDRAM**, 12km northwest of Kanniyakumari, extended over a period of at least six hundred years. Parts date back as far as the ninth or tenth century, others are from the fifteenth, and a huge seven-storey pyramidal *gopura* was erected during the sixteenth. Its oldest and most remarkable feature, however, are a series of beautifully preserved **epigraphs** carved on a huge boulder in the main *mandapa*. Some are in the ancient Pali language, dating from the third century BC when this was the most southerly outpost of the Mauryan empire. Later inscriptions in classical Tamil are the first known references to the three traditional dynasties of the South, the Cholas, the Pandyas and the Pallavas. Although its main sanctuary houses a *shivalingam*, the temple is jointly dedicated to Brahma, Vishnu and Shiva. Its proudest boasts, aside from the epigraphs and some remarkably extravagant stone sculpture, are **musical pillars**, which emit a chime when struck, and an extraordinarily tall, three-metre-high figure of Hanuman. A special *puja* takes place at sunset (around 6pm) every Friday, with music and a procession. The temple is open to non-Hindus and all castes, although male visitors must remove their shirts before entering.

As you head along the NH47 towards Kerala, the spectacular crags of the Travancore Hills encroach upon the flats of viridescent rice paddy lining the coastal strip, completely dominating the landscape to Thiruvananthapuram. The most prominent peak in the area is the pyramidal **Maruntha Malai** (aka "Maruval Malai"), 13km from Kanniyakumari, renowned among Tamils as "Medicine Mountain". During the monsoon, its steep green slopes sprout a profusion of medicinal herbs. Local healers must have been aware of this fact for thousands of years because the hill crops up time and again in Hindu mythology, most famously in the *Ramayana*. According to the epic, Hanuman dropped a piece of Mt Kailash at this spot on his way back from the Himalaya, where he had been dispatched to look for herbs for Rama, who had been wounded by a poisoned arrow during the battle with the evil demon Ravana's army in Lanka. Instead of picking the plants, however, Hanuman ripped up the whole mountain to keep them fresh. Today, the Maruntha Malai remains an important source of curative herbs, used in the preparation of Ayurvedic medicines. It's also home to a scattering of *sadhus* who, when they aren't away wandering, live in a string of caves that dot the pilgrim path to the *shivalingam* crowning the summit. Taking around six hours, the **hike** to it is especially popular with pilgrims who have walked to Kanniyakumari in fulfilment of a vow, but should not be attempted without a guide as the route is hard to follow; the best place to find a guide is in the village of **Pothayadi**, near the trailhead.

The Ghats

Sixty or more million years ago, what we know today as peninsular India was a separate land mass drifting northeast across the ocean towards central Asia. Current geological thinking has it that this mass must originally have broken off the African continent along a fault line that is today discernible as a north–south ridge of volcanic mountains, stretching 1400km down the west coast of India, known as the **Western Ghats**. The range rises to a height of around 2500m, making it India's second highest mountain chain after the Himalaya.

Forming a natural barrier between the Tamil plains and coastal Kerala and Karnataka, the *ghats* (literally "steps") soak up the bulk of the southwest monsoon, which drains east to the Bay of Bengal via the mighty Kaveri and Krishna river systems. The massive amount of rain that falls here between June and October (around two and a half metres) allows for an incredible **biodiversity**. Nearly one third of all of India's flowering plants can be found in the dense evergreen and mixed deciduous forests cloaking the *ghats*, while the woodland undergrowth supports the subcontinent's richest array of wildlife, from jungle civets, muntjac and the rare *tahr* antelope, to *gaur* (Indian bison), herds of wild Asian elephant and tigers.

It was this abundance of game, and the cooler temperatures of the range's high valleys and grasslands, that first attracted the sun-sick British, who were quick to see the economic potential of the temperate climate, fecund soil and plentiful rainfall. As the forests were felled to make way for tea plantations, and the region's many tribal groups – among them the Todas – were forced deeper into the mountains, permanent **hill stations** were established. Today, as in the days of the Raj, these continue to provide welcome escapes from the fierce summer heat for the fortunate middle-class Tamils, and foreign tourists, who can afford the break.

Much the best known of the hill resorts – in fact better known, and more visited, than it deserves – is **Udhagamandalam** (formerly Ootacamund, still often "Ooty"), in the **Nilgiris** (from *nila-giri*, "blue mountains"). The ride up to Ooty, on the **miniature railway** via Coonoor, is fun, and the views breathtaking, but in general, unless you have the means to stay in the best hotels, the town itself comes as a rude shock. The other main hill station, founded by American missionaries, is **Kodaikanal**, further south near Madurai.

Accessed via the hill stations, the forest areas lining the state border harbour Tamil Nadu's principal wildlife sanctuaries, **Annamalai** and **Mudumalai**, which, along with Wayanad in Kerala, and Nagarhole and Bandipur in Karnataka, form the vast **Nilgiri Biosphere Reserve**, the country's most extensive tract of protected forest. Road building, illegal felling, hydro projects and overgrazing have gradually whittled away at this huge wilderness area over the past two decades. In recent years a more pressing threat has arisen in the form of the infamous sandalwood smuggler, **Veerapan** (see p.490), whose kidnappings of forest wardens and government officials have led to the parks being indefinitely closed to the public. However, as the main route between Mysore and the cities of the Tamil plains wriggles through the Nilgiris, you may well find yourself pausing for a night or two along the way, if only to enjoy the cold air and serene landscape of the tea terraces. Whichever direction you're travelling in, a stopover at the dull textile city of **Coimbatore** is hard to avoid.

The **best time to visit** the *ghats* is between late November and early March. At other times, either the weather is too cloudy and wet, or the hill stations are swarming with hoards of summer tourists. Winter is also the optimum period for **trekking** in the Nilgiris, which allows you to visit some of the region's most unspoilt forest areas, traditional homeland of the Todas.

Coimbatore

Visitors tend only to use the busy industrial city of **COIMBATORE** as a stopover on the way to Ooty, 90km northwest. Once you've climbed up to your hotel rooftop to admire the blue, cloud-capped haze of the Nilgiris in the west, there's little to do here other than kill time wandering through the nuts-and-bolts bazaars, lined with lookalike textile showrooms, "General Traders" and shops selling motor parts.

Coimbatore earned its reputation as the "Manchester of South India" in the 1930s, when the nearby **Pykara Falls** hydro-electricity project was built to provide cheap power for its huge textile mills and spin-off industries. Since then, the city has never looked back, and if you've arrived here from more traditional corners of Karnataka or the deep south you'll find it distinctly prosperous, modern and orderly: new office buildings and business hotels dominate the skyline, while in the street, trousers far outnumber *lunghis* and virtually every man sports a pen in his shirt pocket.

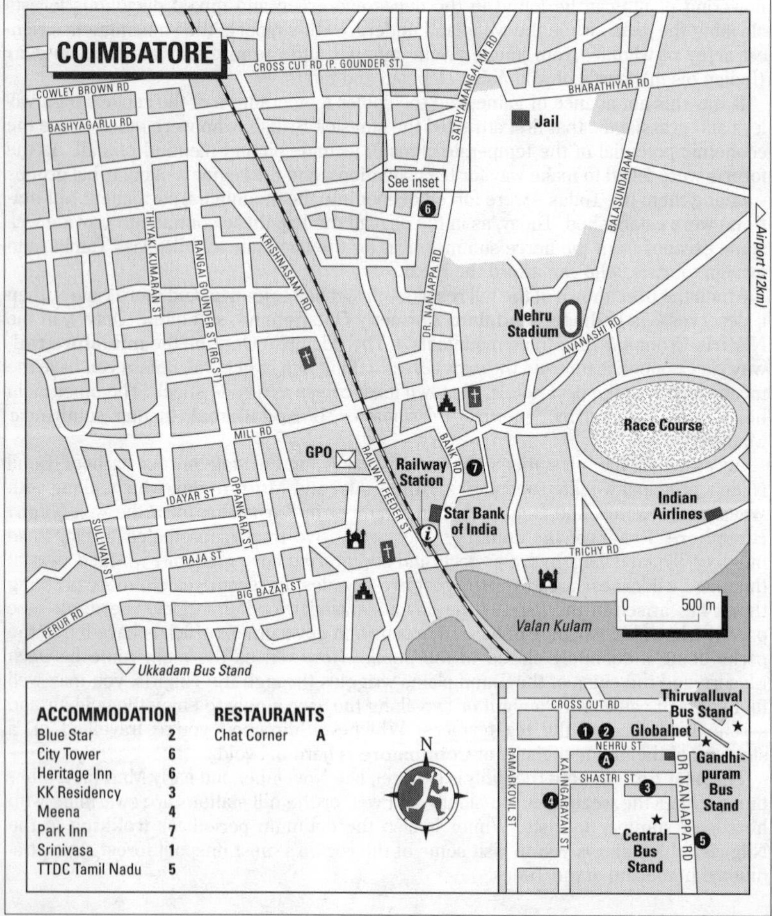

THE COIMBATORE BOMB BLASTS

Coimbatore is known throughout the South for its industry, but since February 14, 1998, the city has also been synonymous with the kind of boom more often generated by Semtex than textile sales. During a pre-election rally by the Hindu fundamentalist BJP, due to be addressed by party chief and home affairs minister, L.K. Advani, a bomb hidden in a handcart full of fruit exploded without warning, killing 52 people. Advani, whose arrival at the rally ground was delayed by Indian Airlines, had what his *swami* aides construed as a providential escape, but over the next six hours, fourteen more blasts shook Coimbatore's major landmarks, including the train station, Central bus stand and, most cynically of all, the Medical College Hospital.

Altogether, three hundred were seriously wounded, and sixty people killed. Suspicion immediately fell on Coimbatore's Muslim minority, and more specifically **Al-Umma**, an Islamic extremist group based in the Kotaimedu district of the city. Eighteen Muslims had died in a bout of communal blood-letting the previous November, and this attack was seen as a reprisal. Eight men (one of them related to Al-Umma's leader, S.A. Basha) were subsequently arrested and charged in connection with the bomb blasts, but communal tension remains high in Coimbatore.

Arrival, information and moving on

Coimbatore's two main **bus stands**, Central and Thiruvalluvar, are close together towards the north of the city centre; the busy town bus stand is sandwiched in between. From Central bus stand, on Dr Nanjappa Rd, buses leave for Ooty every fifteen minutes. Buses to Bangalore and Mysore can be booked in advance at the **reservation office** (9am–noon & 1–8pm). There are also frequent services to and from Madurai, Chennai and Tiruchirapalli (Trichy). A third stand, Ukkadam bus stand, serves local towns and destinations in northern Kerala, such as Pollachi, Palghat, Munnar, Trissur and Kannur; it's 4km from the others, in the southwest of the city next to the lake.

The **train station**, 2km south of two central bus stands, is well connected to major southern destinations. To catch the Nilgiri Blue Mountain Railway to **Ooty** (see box on p.483), join the #6005 *Nilgiri Express* from **Chennai**, which leaves Coimbatore at 5.30am (1hr), and change onto the narrow-gauge steam railway at **Mettupalayam**, from where a train departs at 7.30am. The other connection leaves Coimbatore at 10.50am, to meet up with the 1.15pm from Mettupalayam. If you're catching the early service, try to stay near the train station, or arrange transport the night before, as auto-rickshaws are few and far between at this early hour of the morning. Alternatively, jump on a bus to Mettupalayam from the Central bus stand before 6am, which will get you to the head of the narrow-gauge line in time for the 7.30am departure.

Coming from **Ooty**, you'll get into Mettupalayam at either 12.45pm or 6.30pm, leaving you plenty of time to grab something to eat and catch onward trains from Coimbatore to Chennai and Madurai (if you intend to do this, reserve tickets in advance at Ooty). Of the overnight services to **Chennai**, the *Cheran Express* #2674 (daily 11.05pm; 9hr) is marginally quicker than the *Nilgiri Express* #6606 (daily 8.40pm; 9hr 35min), but nowhere near as smart and fast as the swish #2024 *Shatabdi Express*, (daily 7.25am; 6hr 35min). The daily #6115 *Rameshwaram Express* leaves at 11.25pm for **Rameshwaram** via **Madurai** (arrive 6am). For Kochi, catch the daily #6865 *Tiruchchi Express* (daily depart 12.45am; 5hr 30min). The best train for **Mangalore** is the #6627 *West Coast Express* (daily depart 7.55pm; 9hr).

From Coimbatore **airport**, 12km northeast and served by buses to and from the town bus stand (taxis charge around Rs175), Indian Airlines and Jet Airways fly to Mumbai (daily) and Chennai (Tues, Thurs & Sat), Kozhikode (one or two daily) and

Bangalore (three weekly). Indian Airlines' office is 2km northeast of the train station on Trichy Rd (☎0422/399833 or 399821); Jet Airways is 4km along the same road (☎0422/212036).

You can **change money** at the State Bank of India and Bank of Baroda, near the train station or, more quickly and efficiently, at TT Travels, #102 A-Block Raheja Centre, Avanashi Rd (☎0422/212854), a five-minute rickshaw ride northeast of the train station; the latter is the only one open on Sundays (daily 9.30am–5.30pm). **Internet** booths are springing up all over Coimbatore, where you can send and receive **email** for around Rs30. Two of the most convenient places are: Globalnet, on the first floor of the *Krishna Towers*, on the corner of Nehru Street and Dr Nanjappa Rd, just north of the bus stands; and the STD place directly opposite the *Blue Star* hotel.

Accommodation and eating

Most of Coimbatore's **accommodation** is concentrated around the bus stands. The cheapest places line Nehru St and Shastri St, but, whatever you do, avoid the rock-bottom places facing the bus stand itself, which are plagued with traffic noise from around 4am onwards.

As for **eating**, your best bets are the bigger hotels such as the *City Tower*, whose excellent rooftop restaurant, *Cloud 9*, serves a topnotch multi-cuisine menu to a predominantly business clientele. The *Malabar*, on the first floor of the *KK Residency*, is a less pricey option, popular with visitors from across the Ghats for its quality non-veg Keralan cuisine. For vegetarian South Indian food, however, you won't do better than the ultra-modern *Chat Corner*, opposite the *Blue Star* hotel on Nehru St, which has a squeaky clean "meals" restaurant, open-air terrace and excellent little juice bar. The food here is superb, and only marginally pricier than average.

Blue Star, 369 Nehru St (☎0422/230635). Impeccably clean rooms, all with balconies, quiet fans and bathrooms, in a modern multistorey building five minutes' walk from the bus stands. The best mid-price place in this area. ③–④.

City Tower, Sivaswamy Rd, just off Dr Nanjappa Rd, a two-minute walk south of the Central bus stand (☎0422/230681, fax 230103). A smart upscale hotel situated in the city centre with modern interiors (heavy on leatherette and vinyls); the "Executive" rooms are more spacious. Some rooms are a/c. ⑥–⑦.

Heritage Inn, next to *City Tower*, 38 Sivaswamy Rd (☎0422/231451, fax 233223). Coimbatore's top hotel featuring sixty-three centrally a/c rooms, a couple of quality restaurants and foreign exchange. Credit cards accepted. ⑧.

KK Residency, 7 Shastri St (☎0422/232433). Large tower-block hotel around the corner from the main bus stands. Very clean with a couple of good restaurants downstairs. ④.

Meena, 109 Kalingarayan St (☎0422/235420). Tucked away off the main drag, but handy for the bus stand. The rooms are clean, with attached shower-toilets and small balconies. A good budget choice. ②.

Park Inn, 21 Geetha Hall Rd (☎0422/301284, fax 301291). Business-orientated hotel that's the smartest option around the train station. Immaculate, quiet and good value. Room rates include breakfast. ⑤.

Srinivasa, 365 Nehru St, next door to *Blue Star* (☎0422/230116). Near the bus stands and the cleanest of the cheap lodges in this area, which isn't saying much. ①.

TTDC Tamil Nadu, Dr Nanjappa Rd (☎0422/236311). Opposite Central bus stand. Convenient, clean and reliable. Better than most in the chain, and often booked, so phone ahead. ④–⑤.

Coonoor and Kotagiri

COONOOR, a scruffy bazaar and tea planters' town on the Nilgiri Blue Mountain Railway (see box on p.483), lies at the head of the Hulikal ravine, 27km north of

Mettupalayam and 19km south of Ooty, at an altitude of 1858m, on the southeastern side of the Dodabetta mountains. Often considered to be second best to its more famous neighbour, Coonoor has avoided Ooty's over-commercialization, and can make a pleasant place for a short stop. In addition to an atmospheric little hill market specializing in leaf tea and fragrant essential oils, its outlying hills and valleys, carpeted with spongy green tea bushes and stands of eucalyptus and silver oak, offer some of the most beautiful scenery in the Nilgiris, immortalized in many a Hindi movie dance sequence. Cinema fans from across the South flock here to visit key locations from their favourite blockbusters, among them **Lamb's Nose** and **Dolphin's Nose**, former British picknicking spots with paved pathways and dramatic views of the Mettupalayam plains.

Visible from miles away as tiny orange or red dots amid the green vegetation, **tea-pickers** work the slopes around Coonoor, carrying wicker baskets of fresh leaves and bamboo rods that they use like rulers to ensure that each plant is evenly plucked. Once the leaves reach the factory, they're processed within a day, producing seven grades of tea. **Orange Pekoe** is the best and most expensive; the seventh and lowest grade, a dry dust of stalks and leaf swept up at the end of the process will be sold on to make instant tea. To visit a tea or coffee plantation, contact UPASI (United Planters' Association of Southern India), "Glenview", Coonoor.

Coonoor loosely divides into two sections, with the bus stand (regular services to Mettupalayam, Coimbatore and elsewhere in the Nilgiris), train station and market huddled together in **Lower Coonoor**. In Upper Coonoor, **Sim's Park** is a fine botanical garden on the slopes of a ravine, with hundreds of rose varieties (daily 8am–6.30pm; Rs5). The only other conventional tourist attractions are a couple of **viewpoints. Lamb's Rock** (5km), where an old British path winds up through some dense woodland to a vantage point-cum-picnic place overlooking the ravine and plains to Mettupalayan, can be reached by rickshaw, taxi or bus (see below). **Dolphin's Nose**, 9km away, has featured in a couple of hit Bollywood movies recently and draws streams of day-trippers from Ooty, although its spectacular views – onto St Catherine's Falls on one side and Coonoor and Kotagiri streams, tributaries of the Bhavani, on the other – more than compensate. Buses run out here from Coonoor every two hours; it's a good idea to catch the first one at 7am, which gets you to Dolphin's Nose before the mist starts to build up, and walk the 9km back into town via Lamb's Rock – an enjoyable amble that takes you through tea estates and dense forest.

The only other major settlement hereabouts, **KOTAGIRI**, lies a winding one-hour bus ride from Coonoor, at an altitude of just under 2000m. High on the cloudy hilltops, it's even more given over to tea planting than Coonoor, and as a result has little to recommend it as a tourist destination. The one reason you might want to venture up here is to shop at the **Women's Co-operative** off Ramchand Square, which stocks the region's best selection of locally made handicrafts, including traditional red and black **Toda embroidery** (see box on p.484). Hand-woven woollen shawls are the most expensive items on offer, but they also keep smaller souvenir items such as spectacle cases and wallets, all at very fair fixed prices. Income from the shop is used to fund women's development projects in the area, principally among the Todas; they've an interesting frieze of photos on the wall showing where the money goes.

Kotagiri is connected to Coonoor (every 15min; 1hr) and Mettupalayam (every 30min; 2hr) by regular and reliable **bus** services. You can also get here from Ooty, 28km west (hourly; 2hr), via one of the highest motorable roads in the Nilgiris. **Accommodation** in the town is in short supply, limited to a couple of flea-infested lodges in the bazaar; it's a better idea to stay somewhere else and travel here for the day.

YOGA IN COONOOR

You can maximize the beneficial effects of Coonoor's mountain air with a short yoga course at the *YWCA*. Yoga therapist Dr A.R. ("Raj") Hirudhayaraj, co-warden of the hostel, offers introductory tuition in the basic *asanas* (postures), *pranayama* (breathing exercises), dietary prescriptions and meditation techniques of Hatha Yoga. He's also a qualified herbalist and a mine of information on Tamil culture in general. Lessons cost Rs150 per hour, or Rs2100 for a seven-day course, comprising two hours of teaching each day. Bookings can be made in advance by telephone (☎0423/33426), or on spec at the *YWCA*.

Practicalities

When it comes to finding somewhere to **stay** or **eat**, there's not a lot of choice in Coonoor, and it's not a good idea to leave it too late in the day to be looking for a room. By and large the hotels are dotted around Upper Coonoor, within 3km of the station; you'll need an auto-rickshaw to find most of them. As ever, ignore any rickshaw *wallahs* who tell you the hotel you want to go to is "full" or "closed". The correct fare from the bus stand to Bedford Circle/*YWCA* is Rs20–25.

If you're staying at the *YWCA,* or one of the upmarket hotels, your best bet is to eat there. In the bazaar, the only commendable **restaurants** are *Hotel Tamizhamgam* (pronounced "Tamirangum"), on Mount Rd near the bus stand, which is Coonor's most popular vegetarian meals-cum-*tiffin* joint. For good-value non-veg North Indian *tandoori* and Chinese food, try the *Greenland* hotel, up the road.

The Travancore Bank, on Church Rd in Upper Ooty, near Bedford Circle, **changes currency**, but not always travellers' cheques. Otherwise, the nearest place is the State Bank of India in Ooty (see p.483).

ACCOMMODATION

Blue Hills, Mount Rd (☎0423/30103). Clean doubles with soulless Formica furnishing are offered here, in a dilapidated concrete eyesore, 1km from the bus stand. Ramshackle surroundings, but the non-veg restaurant is good. ④.

La Barrier Inn, Coonoor Club Rd (☎0423/32561). Located way up above the bazaar, with views of surrounding hills (and cricket nets). The rooms are spotless and very large. This is a comfortable mid-range option. ⑤.

Riga, Appleby Rd (☎0423/34405). An ugly tower block 2km out of the centre in Wellington. Plush enough, and the views are good, but tariffs are inflated. ⑦.

Sri Lakshmi Tourist Home, Kamrajpuram, Rockby (☎0423/21022). Uninspiring, basic lodge at the top of town that doubles as a brothel. Only worth considering if everywhere else is full. ②–③.

Taj Garden Retreat, Hampton Manor (☎0423/20021). Old colonial-era hotel with cottage accommodation, lawns and views. Luxurious, but is way overpriced, especially for foreigners, who pay thirty percent more. The restaurant serves spectacular lunchtime buffets. ⑨.

Venlan (Ritz), Ritz Rd, Bedford (☎0423/20484). Recently refurbished this luxury hotel is in a great location on the outskirts. Very spacious with carpeted rooms, deep balconies and fine views. Much better value than the Taj Garden Retreat. ⑦.

Vivek, Figure of Eight Rd, nr Bedford Circle (☎0423/30658 or 32318). Best-value budget hotel after the YWCA. Clean rooms (some with tiny balconies overlooking tea terraces), but beware of "Monkey Menace". Catch a town bus to Bedford Circle and walk from there. ②–③.

YWCA Guest House, Wyoming, near the hospital (☎0423/20326). A characterful Victorian-era house on a bluff overlooking town, with flower garden, tea terraces and fine views from relaxing verandahs. There are five double rooms, two singles and a dorm, and superb home-cooked meals at very reasonable rates (Rs60 non-veg; Rs40 veg). This is among the most congenial budget hotels in South India. No alcohol. ④.

Udhagamandalam (Ootacamund)

When John Sullivan, the British *burra-sahib* credited with "discovering" **UDHAGAMANDALAM** – still more commonly referred to by its anglicized name, **Ootacamund** – first clambered into this corner of the Nilgiris through the Hulikal ravine in the early nineteenth century, the territory was the traditional homeland of the pastoralist **Toda** hill-tribe, who lived in almost total isolation from the cities of the surrounding plains and Deccan Plateau lands. Realizing the agricultural potential of the area, Sullivan acquired tracts of land for Rs1 per acre from the Todas, and set about planting flax, barley and hemp, as well as potatoes, soft fruit and, most significantly of all, **tea**, which all flourished in the mild climate. Within twenty years, the former East India Company clerk had made himself a fortune, while the town he and his business cronies founded, complete with artificial lake, churches and stone houses that wouldn't have looked out of place in Surrey or the Scottish Highlands, had become the most popular hill retreat in peninsular India, known fondly by the *burra-* and *memsahibs* of the south as **"Ooty"**, the "Queen of Hill Stations".

Of the Todas, little further note was made beyond a couple of anthropological monographs, references to their *munds*, or settlements, in the *Madras Gazette*, and the financial transactions that deprived them of the traditional lands. Christianized by missionaries and uprooted by tea planters and forest clearance, they retreated with their buffalo into the surrounding hills and wooded valleys where, in spite of hugely diminished numbers, they continued to preserve a more-or-less traditional way of life (see p.484).

By a stroke of delicious irony, the Todas outlived the colonists whose cash crops originally displaced them – but only just. Until the mid-1970s "Snooty Ooty", as the notoriously snobby town became known, was home to some of the subcontinent's last British inhabitants who chose to "stay on", living out their final days on tiny pensions that only here would allow them to keep a lifestyle to which they had become accustomed. Over the past two decades, travellers have continued to be attracted by Ooty's cool climate and peaceful green hills, forest and grassland. However, if you come in the hope of finding quaint vestiges of the Raj, you're likely to be disappointed; what with indiscriminate development and a deluge of holidaymakers, they're few and far between.

The **best time to come** is between January and March, avoiding the high-season crowds (April–June & Sept–Oct). In May, the summer festival brings huge numbers of people and a barrage of amplified noise – worlds away from the peaceful retreat envisaged by the *sahibs*. From June to September, and during November, it'll be raining and misty, which appeals to some. From October or November to February it can get really cold.

Arrival, information and local transport

Most visitors arrive in Ooty either by bus from Mysore in Karnataka (the more scenic, if steeper, route goes via Masinagudi), or on the **miniature mountain railway** from Coonoor and Mettupalayam. The bus and train stations are fairly close together, at the western end of the big bazaar and racecourse. **Local transport** consists of auto-rickshaws and taxis, which meet incoming trains and gather outside the bus stand and also on Commercial Rd around Charing Cross. You can **rent bikes** but the steep hills make cycling very hard work.

The **TTDC tourist office** (Mon–Sat 10am–5.45pm; ☎0423/43977) in Super Market Building, Charing Cross, is eager to help, but information is not always reliable. You can book tours here, among them the Ooty, Pykara and Mudumalai tour (daily 9am–7.30pm; Rs150), which calls at Pykara dam, falls and boathouse and Mudumalai Wildlife Sanctuary, making a very long day, and the Ooty and Coonoor tour (daily 9am–6pm; Rs80), which goes to Sim's Park, the botanical gardens, the lake, Dodabetta Peak, Lamb's Rock and Dolphin's Nose.

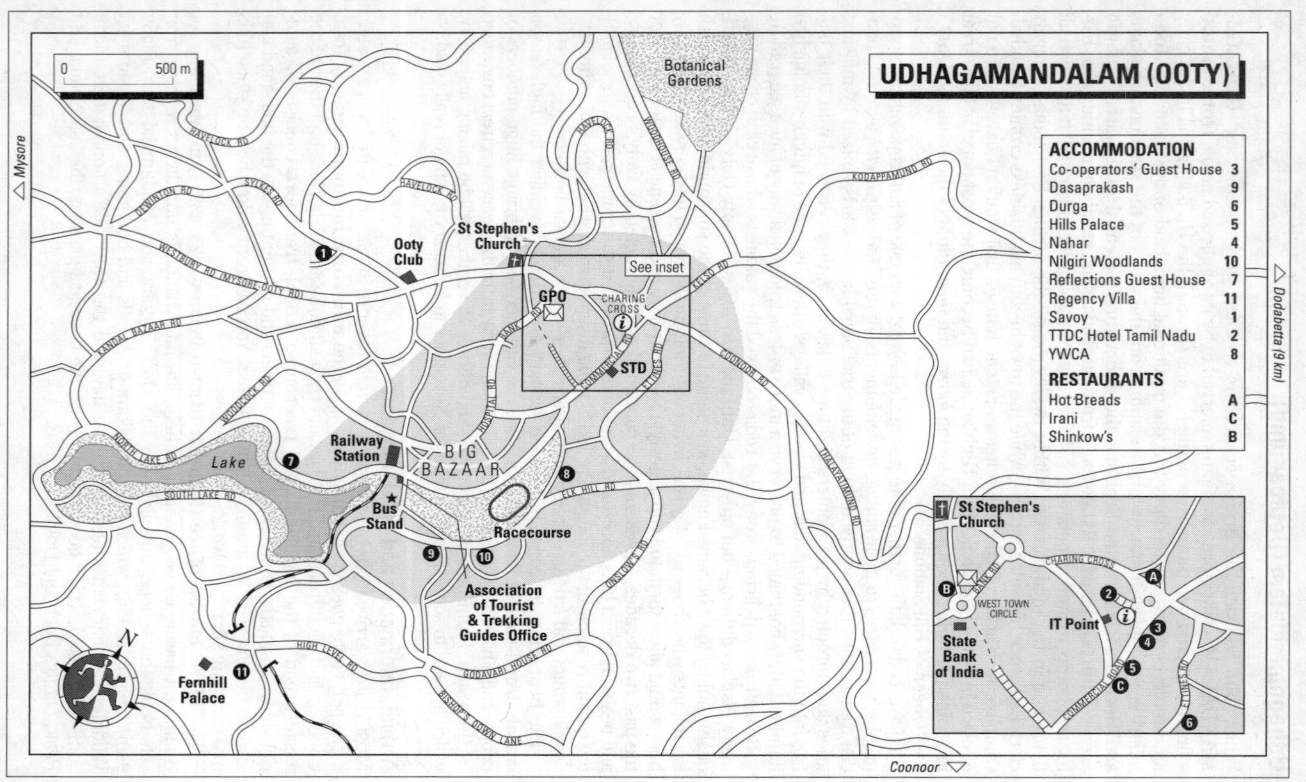
UDHAGAMANDALAM (OOTY)
ACCOMMODATION
Co-operators' Guest House 3
Dasaprakash 9
Durga 6
Hills Palace 5
Nahar 4
Nilgiri Woodlands 10
Reflections Guest House 7
Regency Villa 11
Savoy 1
TTDC Hotel Tamil Nadu 2
YWCA 8
RESTAURANTS
Hot Breads A
Irani C
Shinkow's B
Dodabetta (9 km)
Coonoor
Mysore
0
500 m
Botanical Gardens
St Stephen's Church
Ooty Club
GPO
STD
See inset
CHARING CROSS
Railway Station
Bus Stand
BIG BAZAAR
Racecourse
Association of Tourist & Trekking Guides Office
Fernhill Palace
Lake
IT Point
State Bank of India
WEST TOWN CIRCLE
HAVELOCK RD
DEWINTON RD
SYLKES RD
WESTBURY RD (MYSORE-OOTY RD)
KANDAL BAZAAR RD
WOODCOCK RD
NORTH LAKE RD
SOUTH LAKE RD
WOODHOUSE RD
KODAPPAMUND RD
KELSO RD
BANK RD
HOSPITAL RD
COMMERCIAL RD
ETTINES RD
COONOOR RD
THALAYATIMUND RD
ELK HILL RD
ONSLOW'S RD
HIGH LEVEL RD
GODAVARI HOUSE RD
BISHOP'S DOWN LANE
N

Ooty's **post office**, northwest of Charing Cross at West Town Circle, off Spencers Rd and near St Stephen's Church, has a poste restante counter (enquiries and stamps Mon–Fri 9am–5pm; parcels Mon–Fri 9am–3pm & Sat 9am–2pm). For **email**, go to IT Point, near the Anglo Indian School, on the road between Charing Cross and Commercial Rd.

The only **bank** in Ooty that changes travellers' cheques and currency is the very *pukka* State Bank of India, on West Town Circle. Service is painfully slow, but while you're waiting, check out the photos in the hallway connecting the old and new blocks, dating from the era when this was the "Imperial Bank of India": stalwart, stiff-backed *burra-sahibs* pose with pipes, wives and mandatory Scottish terriers in front of the old bank building.

The Town

Ooty sprawls over a large area of winding roads and steep climbs. The obvious focal point is **Charing Cross**, a busy junction on dusty **Commercial Rd**, the main, relatively flat, shopping street that runs south to the big bazaar and municipal vegetable market. Goods on sale range from fat plastic bags of cardamom and Orange Pekoe tea to presentation packs of essential oils (among them citronella, which is a highly effective natural mosquito repellent). A little way northeast of Charing Cross, the **Botanical Gardens** (daily 8am–6.30pm; Rs5, camera Rs5, video Rs25), laid out in 1847 by gardeners from London's Kew Gardens, consist of forty acres of immaculate lawns, lily ponds and beds, with more than a thousand varieties of shrubs, flowers and trees. There's a refreshment stand, and shops outside sell candy floss, peanuts and snacks.

Northwest of Charing Cross, the small Gothic-style **St Stephen's Church** was one of Ooty's first colonial structures, built in the 1820s on the site of a Toda temple; timber for its bowed teak roof was taken from Tipu Sultan's palace at Srirangapatnam and hauled up here by elephant. The area around the church gives

THE NILGIRI BLUE MOUNTAIN RAILWAY

The famous narrow-gauge **Nilgiri Blue Mountain Railway** climbs up from Mettupalayam on the plains, via Hillgrove (17km) and Coonoor (27km) to Udhagamandalam, a journey of 46km passing through sixteen tunnels, eleven stations and nineteen bridges. It's a slow haul of four and a half hours or more – sometimes the train moves little faster than walking pace, and always takes much longer than the bus – but the **views** are absolutely magnificent, especially along the steepest sections in the Hulikal ravine.

The line was built between 1890 and 1908, paid for by the tea planters and other British inhabitants of the Nilgiris. It differs from India's two comparable narrow-gauge lines, to Darjeeling and Shimla, for its use of the so-called **Swiss rack system**, by means of which the tiny locomotives are able to climb gradients of up to 1 in 12.5. Special bars were set between the track rails to form a ladder, which cogs of teeth, connected to the train's driving wheels, engage like a zipper mechanism. Because of this novel design, only the original locomotives can still run the steepest stretches of line, which is why the section between Mettupalayam and Coonoor has remained one of South Asia's last functioning **steam routes**. The chuffing and whistle screeches of the tiny train, echoing across the valleys as it pushes its blue and cream carriages up to Coonoor (where a diesel locomotive takes over) rank among the most romantic sounds of South India, conjuring up the determined gentility of the Raj era even more strongly than Ooty's faded colonial monuments. Even if you don't count yourself as a train spotter, a boneshaking ride on the Nilgiri Blue Mountain Railway should be a priority when crossing the Nilgiris between southern Karnataka and the Tamil plains.

Timetable details for the line appear in the account of Coimbatore (see p.477), and in the Moving On from Ooty box on p.489.

THE TODAS AND THE THREAT TO THE NILGIRIS

Until the arrival of the British, the **Todas** of the Nilgiri Hills maintained their own language and customs in villages (*munds*) of wagon-shaped huts of bamboo, thatch and reeds. Today the Toda tribal community still exists, albeit in depleted numbers. Some wear traditional costume; plain white waist-cloths under thick white woven shawls (*puthikuzhi*) striped with red and black. Once, all adult women had their upper body tattooed and their hair oiled and curled into long ringlets at the front; feminine beauty is judged by the narrowness of the feet and facial hair is admired. Men keep their hair and beards long.

Toda culture centres around the **buffalo**, which is held sacred; the only product they use is its milk, consuming it in vast quantities. Toda temples are dairies, off-limits to everyone save the officiating priests. The community is divided into fourteen patriarchal clans, though its polyandrous social system is fast breaking down. "Marriages" were arranged at birth with partners from another clan; at the age of fifteen the female moved in with the husband's family and automatically became the wife of his younger brothers too. She could also seek further partners from other families, with the permission of her principal partner, who would generally assume the paternal role for any resultant offspring.

Traditionally, the Todas lived in interdependence with four other tribal groups, based on a barter system under which their main responsibility was to supply the others with dairy products. Of these, the **Irulus**, Vishnu-worshipping tool-makers and ritual specialists who are regarded by the Todas as caste inferiors, are today the most numerous, with a population of around seven thousand. Fears of caste pollution also determine relations between the Todas and the **Kotas**, ironsmiths and potters who provide music for rituals. The jungle-dwelling **Kurumbas**, known for their aptitude in magic, gathered honey and wood, while the **Badagas**, who arrived in the fourteenth century after being displaced by the Muslim invasions, kept the others supplied with grain and beans.

At present there are about seventeen hundred Todas, of whom a quarter are Christian. Due to high infant mortality and the introduction of life-threatening diseases by the British, their population had dwindled to little more than six hundred by the 1940s. This alarming situation was dramatically reversed though, largely through the efforts of an exceptional Toda woman, **Evam Piljain-Wiedemann**, who trained as a nurse in England, and succeeded in winning the confidence of other Todas to take advantage of a mobile medical clinic. She continues to work to secure rights for the Todas, and to protect the natural environment.

some idea of what the hill station must have looked like in the days of the Raj; on the way up to it you'll pass **Spencer**'s store on Church Hill, opened in 1909, which still serves from old wooden counters. Nearby, in the same compound as the post office, gowned lawyers buzz around the red-brick **Civil Court**, a quasi-Gothic structure with leaded diamond-shaped windows, corrugated-iron roofs and a clock tower capped with a weather vane. Over the next hill (west), the most snooty of Ooty institutions, the **Club**, dates from 1830. Originally the house of Sir William Rumbold, it became a club in 1843 and expanded thereafter. Its one claim to fame is that the rules for snooker were first set down here (although the members of Jabalpur Club in Madhya Pradesh are supposed to have originated the game in the first place). Entry is strictly restricted to members and their guests or members of affiliated clubs. Further along Mysore Rd, the modest **Government Museum** (daily except Fri & second Sat of month 9am–1pm & 2–5pm) houses a few paltry tribal objects, sculptures and crafts.

West of the train station and racecourse (races mid-April to mid-June), the **Lake**, constructed in the early 1800s, is one of Ooty's main tourist attractions, despite being

Blame for the threat to the survival of the Nilgiris cannot simply be laid at the door of colonial exploitation, though the story does begin with the arrival of the British in 1821. Despite the British penchant for hunting (panther, tiger and deer) and fishing, they were aware, within the vision of the time, of protecting the natural landscape. The most destructive period came after Independence. From 1952, a series of "five-year plans" towards "development" were implemented. Widespread planting of exotic trees, principally eucalyptus, wattle and pine, provided a generous income for the government, but has had far-reaching effects on local ecology. A new synthetic fibre industry, established in the foothills, requires huge amounts of pulp to make fibre. Despite local fears and protests, including a *satyagraha*-style public fast, more and more acreage is cleared in order to feed factories.

Traditional *shola* forest, once destroyed, takes thousands of years to replace, and newly planted eucalyptus draws water from miles around. For the first time in its history, this once swampy region suffers from **water shortages**. The Todas can no longer get enough thatching grass to build houses and temples, and their traditional homes are being replaced by concrete. Nothing grows under eucalyptus and pine, and the sacred buffalo have nowhere to graze. Many Todas have been forced to sell their stock, and barely enough are left to perform the ceremonies at the heart of Toda life.

Visiting the Todas

In recent years, the Todas have become something of a tourist curiosity, particularly among the groups of well-heeled foreigners passing through the Nilgiris, and numerous trekking agencies and guides offering day-trips, or longer treks, to their settlements from Ooty. Although nothing on the scale of Thailand's Hill Tribe tourist circuit, the experience has to be a hollow one, consisting of a brief visit, and possibly a meal, followed up with the inevitable photo session. That said, the Todas in the more commonly visited villages do little to discourage foreigners from coming; on the contrary, they seem only too happy to pose in traditional costume for the pre-arranged fee handed over to them by the tour leaders.

A recommended **guide** for trips to Toda settlements around Ooty is R. Seniappan (aka "Sinni"), contactable through the official guides' office on the corner between the bus stand and train station. He has been running tours into the area for years, is highly knowledgeable about local customs and etiquette and enjoys cordial relations with Toda people in the villages visited. Count on around Rs250 per day for his fee, and additional costs for meals and transport. You'll probably learn just as much, however, if not more, about the Todas' way of life by reading Anthony Walker's definitive anthropological study, *The Todas of South India: A New Approach*, researched in the 1970s.

heavily polluted (most of the town's raw sewage gets dumped here – worth bearing in mind if you're tempted to venture out on it). Honeymoon couples in particular go boating (8am–6pm; rowing, paddle and motor Rs3–120) and horse-riding (short rides Rs30–75, or Rs100 per hour).

Fernhill Palace, not far from the southeast end of the lake and once the summer residence of the Maharaja of Mysore, is owned by a large hotel chain who recently closed it for renovation. It's an extraordinary pile, built in the fullest expression of Ooty's characteristic Swiss-chalet style, with carved wooden bargeboards and ornamental cast-iron balustrades. Among the compound of firs, cedars and monkey puzzle trees, a bizarre church-like building was erected as an indoor badminton court. Just down the road from Fernhill, a lane with a mouldering, indecipherable sign board leads to the former **Palace Hotel**, the Nizam of Hyderabad's old hill mansion. The Andhran millionaire sold it a few years back, but one of his wives (a former Miss Turkey) sued him, claiming it was hers. As the case limps slowly through the Indian courts, the building lapses into what looks like terminal dereliction, inhabited by monkeys and squatters.

TREKKING IN THE NILGIRIS

The best way to appreciate the Nilgiri Hills is to get well away from the towns by **trekking**, which gains you access to the most unspoilt and dramatic parts of the range, where settlements, let alone visitors, are few and far between. Unfortunately, the activities of the renowned bandit and sandalwood smuggler, **Veerapan** (see box on p.490), at large in the thick forests along the Tamil border, recently forced the Forest Department to ban trekking in the less accessible areas. In fact, at the time of writing no permits had been issued since March 1998. The stand-off between Veerapan and the authorities cannot last forever, but pending the bandit's long-promised surrender, the following guidelines apply only to a handful of shorter routes around Ooty, and to a time in the future when the situation returns to normal.

The **landscape** of the upper Nilgiris is astonishingly diverse. Treks in the **west** of the region (best Dec–May) take you across former Toda territory: largely uninhabited grassland and natural *shola* forest where wild flowers include rhododendron and orchids. Other areas comprise man-made forest of eucalyptus, wattle and pine – strangely reminiscent of Australia (from where much of the vegetation was originally introduced). On the far western edge of the escarpment, forming the western border of Mukurti Sanctuary, thousand-metre drops plummet to the heavy evergreen rainforest of Kerala.

The lower areas in the **north** and **east** are completely different; a dry, rough, rocky terrain with patches of dense thorny scrub, populated by diverse wildlife, including *sambar*, sloth bear and some *gaur* (Indian bison). Trekking in this area is possible all year round, but the intense heat between March and May is not conducive to long walks.

Animals indigenous to the Nilgiris include the rare Nilgiri *tahr* (see p.326) and *sambar* (deer), wild dog, elephant, and even panther and tiger. The bird population is small: grey jungle fowl, hawks and harriers. At higher altitudes, bright daytime sunshine with temperatures of around 20°C is followed by a dramatic cooling to freezing point at night; warm clothing is essential.

Trekking practicalities

Unlike most areas of the Indian Himalaya, trekking in the environmentally sensitive (and Veerapan-plagued) Nilgiris can involve lots of forward planning and, above all, bureaucracy. **Permits** have to be obtained, at least one week to ten days in advance, from the Forest Department for just about any itinerary that wanders off-road. However, it can be difficult to establish which office you need to apply to for which route, and even harder to gain the requisite forms, never mind the signatures and stamps. As a rule of thumb, the Deputy Forest Officer (North Division), at Udhagamandalam Forest Department, behind the police station (Mon–Fri 10am–5.30pm; ☎0423/43968), issues permits for the northern and eastern Nilgiris, while the DFO (South Division), in the same building (same hours; ☎0423/44083), is the man to see if you want to head south beyond Avalanchi and Parson's Valley (18km west). Just to confuse matters, there's also the Wildlife Warden's Office, five minutes' down Coonoor Rd from Charing Cross, on the first floor of the Mahalingam Petrol Company (look for the green building behind the petrol pump on the right as you head out of town), who deals with the Upper Bhavani area and Mudumalai.

As stated above, the Forest Department officially ceased issuing trekking passes when the "Veerapan problem" forced the closure of the nearby national parks. However, you may be able to obtain permission for some routes if you employ a **guide** to help you through the paperwork; without one, you'll also find it hard to arrange **accommodation** and **food** along your chosen route. Most trekking groups stay in Forest Department and Electricity Rest Houses or bungalows, with the odd night in local village temple *choultries*, homes or schools – all of which a Tamil-speaking guide will be able to sort out a lot more easily than you. In addition, cooking equipment and provisions have to be bought or ordered along the way; and then, of course, there's the route to follow (no simple matter given the total absence of marked paths and reliable topo maps).

Official guides, distinguished by their blue shirts, can be contacted in Ooty through their office opposite the bus stand. One of the most knowledgeable and dependable is R. Seniappan (aka "Sinni"); if he's not around, ask for "Sherif" or "Carlton". All three charge fixed rates of between Rs200–250 per day depending on the length and nature of the trek. Before you leave, be sure to check the cost of accommodation and meals, and whether you'll be expected to pay for transport by jeep to the trailhead. Note, too, that it's standard practice for punters to feed their guides and porters while trekking, and to tip at the end of the route if things have gone well. Finally, remember to allow plenty of time for the processing of **passes**.

If you'd rather, you can book an **all-in package** – saving you the hassle of arranging your own permits – with guides, food, accommodation and transport covered in a single price. Contact one of the following **agencies**, who are all reliable and experienced (although not necessarily the cheapest) operators in the Nilgiri area:

Clipper Holidays, Suite 406, Regency Enclave, 4 Margath Rd, off Brigade Rd, Bangalore (☎080/221 0454, fax 559 9833; *cliphol@clipper.wiprobt.ems.vsnl.net.in*). A highly professional, and admirably eco-conscious, outfit run by conservationist Ranjan Abraham.

Jungle Tours & Travel, Masinagudi, near the entrance to Madumalai Wildlife Sanctuary (☎0423/56336). Check out this place if you're staying in Madumalai – its packages are a notch cheaper than those offered in the resort hotels.

Nilgiri Trekking Association (NTA), Kavitha Nilayam, 31-D Bank Rd, Udhagamandalam (☎042341887, fax 42883). A relatively inexpensive option, and good source of general information on the area, although their Nilgiri treks are infrequent these days.

Ozone, 55th Main, 12th Block, Kumara Park West, Bangalore (☎/fax 080/331 0441; *nomads@giasbga.vsnl.net.in*). Typically dynamic Bangalorean agent, offering a range of outdoor activities in the Nilgiri area.

Routes

When this book went to press, trekking **routes** in the Nilgiris were severely limited by the permit restrictions, but you can be pretty confident of obtaining a pass to hike in the **Mukurthi** area, on the fringes of the Mukurthi National Park, around 32km west of Ooty via Pykhara village. Although access to the core area of the reserve is not allowed, you can still cross the rolling high pastureland along the Kerala border, roamed by herds of elephant and Nilgiri *tahr*, and take in sweeping views of conical Mukurthi Peak (2467m), an extinct volcano known to the Todas as "Gateway to the World of the Dead". When the current access restrictions are eased, it should also be possible to explore the virgin tropical forest lining **Silent Valley**, for which you'll need at least three days.

The other most popular trekking area currently open to tourists is around **Avalanchi**, a high region of windswept grassland southwest of Ooty. The rest house in the village serves as an ideal base for round day-hikes to reservoirs and mountains in the area, or (if permits are issued) you can head northwest, skirting the Keralan border towards Mukurthi Peak.

Also open at present is a network of trails starting at **Parson's Valley**, another area of open grassland, 18km west, from where you can hike to the Portmund Dam via Mukurthi Peak (one day). A paved road runs to the valley from Ooty (17km), for which you don't need a permit; alternatively, catch a bus (four daily). In the other direction, a rewarding route from **Dodabetta** (see p.489), the region's second highest peak, takes you northwards via Ebanad village to the edge of the Mudumalai wildlife sanctuary – a four-day round trip from Ooty. This is probably the most adventurous option currently open to tourists, passing through a string of Toda villages and some truly isolated country, but don't attempt it without a guide.

Trekking tips

To minimize your impact on this ecologically vulnerable area while trekking, try to observe the following **"golden green rules"** (you may need to impress some of them upon your porters or guides): pack out all rubbish; never burn plastics; purify your own water rather than use bottled water; never use toothpaste or any kind of detergent (even biodegradable ones) in streams, rivers or lakes (wash up with metal scourers); cook with kerosene or multi-fuel stoves, not on wood fires; where you are unable to use a toilet, bury your faeces and carefully burn the paper after you (better still use water).

Accommodation

Ooty is a lot more expensive than many places in India; during April and May prices mentioned below can double. It also gets very crowded, so you may have to hunt around to find what you want. The best by far are the grand old Raj-era places; otherwise, the choice is largely down to average hotels at above-average prices. In winter (Nov–Feb), when it can get pretty cold, most hotels provide heating at extra cost.

Co-operators Guest House, Charing Cross (☎0423/44046). A cranky old banker's budget place with fairly clean rooms, although the walls are a bit grubby, and turquoise and pink "sitouts". Very cheap for Ooty, and central. ②.

Dasaprakash, south of racecourse, near the bus stand (☎0423/42434). This option's a solid, old-style Indian hotel, clean and reasonably quiet, overlooking the racecourse. Their cheapest ("Deluxe") rooms are a bit gloomy, but the "First Class" doubles are fine. There are two veg restaurants and a travel agent. ④–⑤.

Durga, Ettines Rd (☎0423/43837). This is the best deal among the many mid-range places around Charing Cross. It's clean, comfortable and central. ④–⑤.

Hills Palace, Commercial Rd, Charing Cross (☎0423/42239, fax 43430). Spanking new place that's just below the main bazaar, but secluded, quiet and spotlessly clean inside. ⑤.

Nahar, Commercial Rd, Charing Cross (☎0423/42173, fax 45173). One of Ooty's poshest hotels, offering spacious, well-furnished rooms in the centre (the best rooms are in the modern building at the back). Two veg restaurants (see Eating below). ⑤.

Nilgiri Woodlands, Racecourse Rd, 1km from bus stand and train station (☎0423/42551, fax 42530). Arrange to be collected from the station. It's a Raj-era building, with wood-panelled lobby, hunting trophies and bare, clean rooms. Their "cottages" are worth the extra. Good restaurant (see Eating below). ④–⑥.

Reflections Guest House, North Lake Rd (☎0423/43834). Homely, relaxing guesthouse by the lake, five minutes' walk from the train station, with rooms opening onto a small terrace. Easily the best budget option in Ooty. ②.

Regency Villa, Fernhill (☎0423/43097). The Maharaja of Mysore's former guesthouse, now a rather run-down, atmospheric old hotel. If you're here for faded traces of the Raj, this is the place. The palatial suites in the main block are locked in a time warp, with frayed nineteenth-century furniture, original bathtubs, and old sepia photos of the Ooty hunt. By contrast, the second- and third-rate rooms, in separate blocks, are cheerless and not at all good value. Even if you can't afford to stay here, come out for a nose around and coffee on the lawn. ④–⑦.

Savoy, 77 Sylkes Rd (☎0423/44142). Long-established pukka hotel, now run by the Taj group. It has manicured lawns, immaculate and chintzy old-world cottages with working fireplaces, wood and brass fittings – but at US$154 per night, it's ridiculously expensive, especially for foreigners (who pay an inflated dollar rate). ⑨.

TTDC Hotel Tamil Nadu, Wenlock Rd (☎0423/44370, fax 44369). Reached via steps by the tourist office. A large, characterless complex in the centre, but good-value restaurant, bar and billiards rooms. ③–⑤.

YWCA "Anandagiri", Ettines Rd (☎0423/42218). Charming 1920s building, set amid four and a half acres of grounds near the racecourse. Seven types of recently refurbished, immaculate rooms and chalets, all with hot water and bathrooms. Excellent value, but book ahead. ③–⑥.

Eating

Many of the mid-range hotels serve up good South Indian food, but Ooty has yet to offer a gourmet restaurant. The *Regency Villa*, however, is well worth checking out for its colonial ambience.

Chandan, *Nahar Hotel*, Commercial Rd, Charing Cross (☎0423/42173). Carefully prepared North Indian specialities (their *paneer kofta* is particularly good), and a small selection of *tandoori* vegetarian dishes, served inside a posh restaurant or on a lawnside terrace. They also do a full range of *lassis* and milkshakes.

Dasaprakash, *Hotel Dasaprakash*, south of the racecourse (☎0423/42434). Congenial tiffin café, serving tasty *dosas*, special *uttapams* and (hygienic) Bombay snacks (*bhel puri*, *pani puri* and spicy *pao bhaji*; see p.104).

Hot Breads, Charing Cross. French-established franchise selling the usual range of quality pastries, breads and savouries from a bakery outlet downstairs, as well as pizzas and other tasty snacks in a wood-lined first-floor café; their South India espresso is superb.

Irani, Commercial Rd. A gloomy old-style Persian joint run by Ba'hais. Uncompromisingly non-veg (the menu's heavy on mutton and liver), but an atmospheric coffee stop, and a popular hangout for both men and women.

Nilgiri Woodlands, Racecourse Rd, 1km from bus stand and train station (☎0423/42551). The speciality is beefsteak, but the inexpensive *thalis* are good too. Checked tablecloths and cane chairs give it the look of a village hall. No alcohol.

Shinkows, 42 Commissioners Rd (☎0423/42811). Good-value, authentic Chinese place serving up huge portions at low prices, but on the spicy side.

Around Ooty: Dodabetta

Regular local bus services to outlying villages and plantations allow you to reach the less developed regions **around Ooty**. The most popular destination for a day-trip is the Nilgiris' second highest mountain, **Dodabetta** (2638m), 10km east along the Kotagiri road. Sheltering Coonor from the southwest monsoon (and, conversely, Ooty from the reach of the northwest monsoon of October and November), the peak is the region's most prominent landmark. It's also easily accessible by road: buses run every couple of hours from Ooty (10am–3.30pm) to the summit, where a viewing platform and telescope make the most of a stunning panorama. To enjoy it, however, you'll have to get here before the daily deluge of bus parties.

For details of other possible day-trips from Ooty, notably to **Avalanchi** and **Mukuthi**, see Trekking in the Nilgiris on p.486.

MOVING ON FROM OOTY

Ooty **train station** has a reservation counter (10am–noon & 3.30–4.30pm) and a booking office (6.30am–7pm), where you can buy tickets for the Nilgiri Blue Mountain Railway, as well as onwards services to most other destinations in the South. From Ooty, four trains run along the narrow-gauge line to Coonoor each day, with two (depart 9.15am and 3pm) continuing down the Mettapalayam, on the main broad-gauge network. If you are heading to Chennai, take the second service, which meets up in Mettupayalam with the fast #6606 *Nilgiri Express* (depart 7.25pm; 10hr 30min).

You can also book **buses** in advance, at the reservation offices for both state buses (daily 9am–12.30pm & 1.30–5.30pm) and the local company, Cheran Transport (daily 9am–1pm & 1.30–5.30pm), at the bus stand. Towns served include Bangalore and Mysore (buses to both pass through Mudumalai), Kodaikanal, Thanjavur, Thiruvananthapuram and Kanniyakumari, as well as Kotagiri, Coonoor and Coimbatore nearer to hand. **Private buses** to Mysore, Bangalore and Kodaikanal can be booked at hotels, or agents in Charing Cross; even when advertised as "super-deluxe", many turn out to be cramped minibuses.

Mudumalai Wildlife Sanctuary

Set 1140m up in the Nilgiri Hills, **MUDUMALAI WILDLIFE SANCTUARY** is one of the most accessible in the South, covering 322 square kilometres of deciduous forest, split by the main road from Ooty (64km) to Mysore (97km). Unfortunately, the park has been **closed** to visitors for the past couple of seasons amid fears that the sandalwood smuggler, **Veerapan** may abduct tourists or Forest Department wardens (see box on p.490). You can, however, still stop here en route to or from Mysore to sample the peace and fresh air of the Nilgiri forest after the bus parties of day-trippers from Ooty have all gone home.

Coming from Ooty, the approach to Mudumalai is spectacular, twisting and turning down 36 hairpin bends, through wooded hills and past waterfalls (in season). Monkeys dart and play in the trees, and you may glimpse a tethered elephant from the camp at **Kargudi**, where wild elephants are tamed for work in the timber industry. Mudumalai has one of the largest populations of elephants in India, along with wild dogs, *gaur* (Indian bison), common and Nilgiri langur and bonnet macaques (monkeys), jackal, hyena and sloth bear – even a few tigers and panthers.

Practicalities

Until the Forest Department relax restrictions on trekking in the remote woodland areas around the Mudumalai, you can only reach the park by road. The fastest and most spectacular route, via Sighur Ghat, is not negotiable by large vehicles, but private minibuses and a regular Cheran Transport bus service run to Masinagudi (1hr) from Ooty. Travelling on the longer, less steep route via Gudalur, standard buses to Mysore and Bangalore from Ooty take 2hr 30min to reach **Theppakkadu**, which is connected to Masinagudi, 8km away, by bus and jeep. You can also walk this route, but should beware of animals, especially wild elephant.

At **Theppakkadu**, the main access point to the sanctuary, the big event of the day now that the van tours of the park have been suspended is an **Elephant Camp show** (daily 6pm; Rs20) – fine if you're into seeing put-upon pachyderms performing *puja* or playing soccer to a Boney M accompaniment.

SANDALWOOD SMUGGLING

The delicate scent of **sandalwood** – *chandan* in Hindi – is one of the quintessential fragrances of South India, particularly around Mysore in Karnataka, where specialist craftsmen carve combs, beads, elephants and gods and use its oil to make incense and soap. Mashed into a paste, the valuable heartwood of the tree is regarded as a powerful antiseptic capable of curing migraine and skin ailments. Vaishnavites (devotees of the god Vishnu) also smear their foreheads with sandalwood powder before performing *puja*, a practice recorded in the two-thousand-year old epic, the *Ramayana*, as well as the poetry of the sage Kalidasa, dating from the third century BC.

Sandalwood may be integral to traditional Indian culture, but it is fast becoming a rare commodity due to demand from foreign markets, which has forced the price skywards in recent years (a kilo of sandal oil currently fetches around US$14,000). The largest importer is the US perfume industry, which uses vast quantities of the oil as a base and fixative, followed by the Gulf states, where sandalwood (along with myrrh, jasmine and amber) ranks among the few fragrances permitted by Islamic law.

The vast bulk of India's sandalwood comes from mixed, dry deciduous forests of the southern Deccan Plateau, around Bangalore, where trees – if allowed to grow for at least thirty years – reach an average height of twenty metres. Extraction and oil pressing are strictly controlled by the Indian government, in accordance with a law passed by the Sultan of Mysore in 1792, who declared that no individual other than himself could own a sandalwood tree, even if it grew on private land. This law is still enforced, although these days, foresters receive seventy percent of the sale value if they can prove they have grown and protected the wood.

In spite of having the law on their side, the Indian government has been failing miserably in its attempts to control sandalwood stocks and trade over the past decade or so, thanks largely to the activities of the notorious smuggler **Veerapan**, whose cartel handles an estimated three-quarters of Karnataka's total export, amounting to billions of rupees of lost revenue each year. South India's most infamous brigand began his career at the age of fourteen, when he poached his first elephant. Two thousand pachyderm carcasses later, he jacked in ivory smuggling for the sandalwood racket, and, apart from a

ACCOMMODATION

Standards of **accommodation** in Mudumalai are generally high, with most of the hotels in gorgeous, peaceful settings. The best of them are up to 5km off the main road from Masinagudi in **Bokkapuram**, although two budget options overlook the main road. Book in advance, and arrange for your hosts to pick you up from the bus stop – taxis or jeeps are rare in the village. Most places expect guests for full board, as Masinagudi only has a few simple restaurants.

Bamboo Banks Guest House, 2km from the main road, Masinagudi (☎0423/56222). Two rooms, and four cottages, situated in a very attractive setting. Excellent food served outdoors. ⑥.

Chitral Walk (Jungle Trails), near Valaitotam village, 7km southeast of Masinagudi (☎0423/56256). The most remote and atmospheric option, it's well off the beaten track and offers better value for money than the competition. ⑥.

Dreamland, next to the Masinagudi crossroads (☎0423/56127). Until the Kargudi rest house re-opens, this is the cheapest option within reach of the park. Unremarkable, but clean and secure. ③.

Forest Hills, Bokkapuram (☎0423/56216). This is a comfortable mid-range guesthouse in a pleasant forest setting, with large rooms and hospitable management. ⑤–⑥.

Jungle Hut, 5km from the road, Bokkapuram, Masinagudi (☎/fax 0423/56240). The park's most expensive option: twelve comfortable cottages, and a swimming pool, at premium rates. ⑦.

Jungle Retreat, Bokkapuram (☎0423/56470). Swish rooms and pricey camping space (Rs200 per tent) at the newest of this area's purpose-built complexes. ⑥–⑦.

Mountania Resthouse, Masinagudi (☎0423/56337). This place offers good-value cabins in Masinagudi's only roadside lodge. ⑤.

brief period of imprisonment in 1986 (when he managed to escape), has been on the run ever since.

Moving continually between sixty camps in the dense jungle lining the Karnataka–Tamil Nadu border, Veerapan and his men, with their regulation green army fatigues and swaggering moustaches, keep one step ahead of the heat to manage their lucrative operation over a massive area. Because of the sums his smuggling generates, the bandit can afford to pay local villagers Rs30 per day to cut and transport wood – more than double what the Forest Service pays for the same work. This, combined with rumours of extravagant gifts to poor people and temples, have earned him a near mythical Robin Hood status across a 6000 square kilometre swathe of forest, despite the policy of systematic and violent intimidation which he employs to discourage informers and punish those who cross him.

Veerapan's treatment of Forest Service and government officials who fall into his clutches has been brutal over the years, with regular murders, kidnappings and incidents of torture to enhance his already fearsome reputation. The worst atrocity to date, however, was in April 1993, when 21 policemen were lured into an ambush and killed by landmines. The Indian government responded swiftly by launching the largest manhunt in history; six hundred border security troops were flown in for the operation, but somehow Veerapan still managed to slip through the net, and today remains at large with a million-rupee "dead-or-alive" bounty on his head.

Veerapan and his band are the reason why the government has closed huge tracts of protected forest in the Western Ghats to tourists, among them are all the region's major wildlife reserves. The only hope for resolution is that the arch smuggler, following the example of equally notorious Indian bandits such as Phoolan Devi (India's "Bandit Queen") and Malkhan Singh from the Chambal Valley in Uttar Pradesh, will surrender. Negotiations have been taking place for years, but at the time of writing were stalled by a hostage crisis: six officials were being held, in spite of renewed pleas by Phoolan Devi (now an MP) that Veerapan give himself up. If, and when, he does, he'll no doubt lead the same scandalously comfortable life in prison enjoyed by other famous bandits before him – perks agreed upon as terms of a justice-dodging surrender with kudos-seeking local politicians and police chiefs.

TTDC Hotel Tamil Nadu, Theppakkadu (☎0423/56249). Functional, clean four-bed rooms and dorms. Meals are by arrangement and there's a seven-night maximum stay. Book at the TTDC office in Ooty, but you may be lucky on spec if they're not full. ①–⑤.

Kodaikanal

Perched on top of the Palani range, around 120km northwest of Madurai, **KODAIKANAL**, also known as **Kodai**, owes its perennial popularity to the hilltop position of the town, which, at an altitude of over 2000m, affords breathtaking views over the blue-green reaches of the Vagai plain. Raj-era houses and flower-filled gardens add atmosphere, while short walks out of the centre lead to rocky outcrops, waterfalls and dense *shola* forest. With the wildlife sanctuaries and forest areas of the *ghats* now officially closed to visitors, Kodai's outstandingly scenic hinterland also offers South India's best **trekking** terrain. Even if you're not tempted by the prospect of the open trail and cool air, the jaw-dropping **bus ride** up here from the plains makes the detour into this easternnmost spur of the *ghats* an essential one.

Kodaikanal's history, with an absence of wars, battles for leadership and princely dominion, is uneventful, and the only monuments to its past are the neat British bungalows that overlook the lake and Law's Ghat Rd on the eastern edge of town. The British first moved here in 1845, to be joined later by members of the American Mission

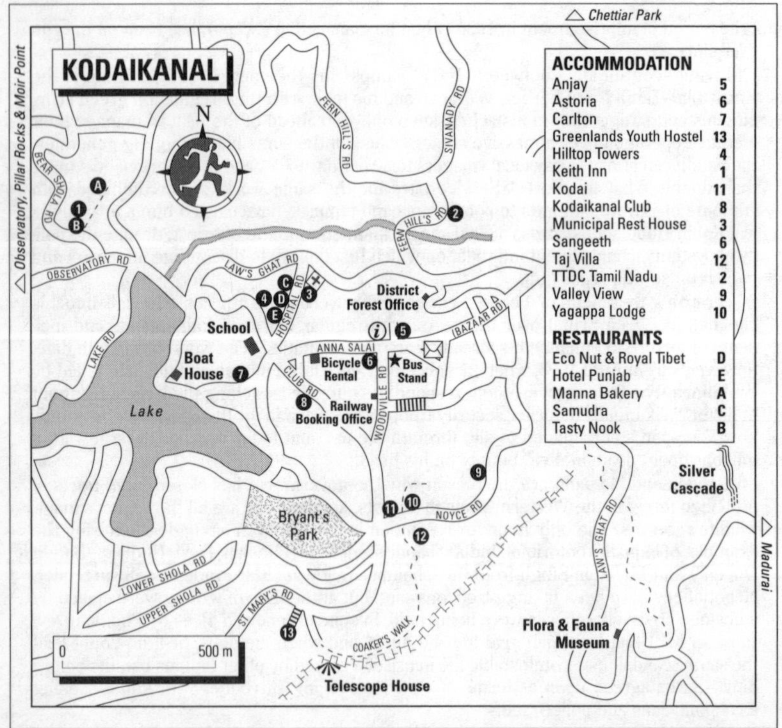

who set up schools for European children. One remains as Kodai International School; despite the name, it has an almost exclusively Indian student population. The school lays a strong emphasis on music, particularly guitar playing, and occasionally holds workshops, and concerts on the green just east of the lake.

After a while in the plains of South India a retreat to Kodai's cool heights is more than welcome. However, in the height of summer (June–Aug), when temperatures compete with those in the lowlands, it's not worth the trip – nor is it a good idea to come during the monsoon (Oct–Dec), when the town is shrouded in mists and drenched by heavy downpours. In late February and early March the nights are chilly; the busiest tourist season therefore, is from April to June, when prices soar.

Arrival, information and getting around

The **buses** from Madurai and Dindigul that climb the spectacular road up the steep hillside to Kodai from the plains below pull in at the stand in the centre of town. Unless you're coming from as far as Chennai or Tiruchirapalli, buses are much more convenient than trains: the nearest **railhead**, Kodaikanal Road – also connected to Dindigul (30min) and Madurai (50min) – is three hours away by bus. Note, too, that **the road from Palani** is by far the most spectacular approach, although the least travelled (except during the monsoons when the other is invariably blocked). If you plan to spend a few days in Kodai, it's worth visiting Palani, an atmospheric destination in itself (see p.496), as a day-trip, just to travel this route.

Tickets for onward rail journeys from Kodaikanal Road can be booked at an office (Mon–Sat 9am–1pm & 1.30–5pm, Sun 1.30–5pm) above the *Hilltop Inn* restaurant next to the *Hilltop Towers* hotel on Club Rd, or at King Tours and Travels on Woodville Rd, which will also reserve buses and planes within South India. The **tourist office** (daily 10am–5.30pm), on the main road, Anna Salai (Bazaar Rd), offers little except unclear sketch maps of the area.

Taxis line Anna Salai in the centre of town, offering sightseeing at high but fixed rates. Most tourists, however, prefer to amble around at their own pace. Compact and hilly as it is, Kodaikanal is best explored on foot, or by **bicycle**, which you could rent from a stall on Anna Salai for Rs15–20 per day (those on offer at the lakeside are much more expensive); it may be fun to freewheel downhill, but most journeys will involve a hefty uphill push too.

If you need to **change money**, head for the State Bank of India on Anna Salai.

The Town

Kodai's focal point is its **lake**, sprawling like a giant amoeba over a full 48 acres just west of the town centre. This is a popular place for strolls, or bike rides along the five-kilometre path that fringes the water's edge, and pedal- or rowboats can be rented on the eastern shore (Rs10–30 for 30min). Lakeside horse-riding is also an option with prices varying from Rs20 for a guided ride to Rs100 per hour on your own. Shops, restaurants and hotels are concentrated in a rather congested area of brick, wood and corrugated-iron buildings east and downhill from the lake. To the south is **Byrant's Park**, with tiered flowerbeds on a backdrop of pine, eucalyptus, rhododendron and wattle, which stretches southwards to Shola Rd, less than 1km from the point where the hill drops abruptly to the plains. A path, known as **Coaker's Walk**, skirts the hill, winding from the *Taj Villa* to *Greenland's Youth Hostel* (10min), offering remarkable views that on a clear day stretch as far as Madurai.

One of Kodai's most popular natural attractions is **Pillar Rocks**, 7km south of town, a series of granite cliffs rising more than one hundred metres above the hillside. To get there, follow the westbound Observatory Rd from the northernmost point of the lake (a steep climb) until you come to a crossroads. The southbound road passes the gentle **Fairy Falls** on the way to Pillar Rocks. Observatory Rd continues west to the

Astrophysical Observatory, perched at Kodai's highest point (2347m). Visitors cannot go in, but a small **museum** (daily 10am–noon & 2–5pm; Fri only outside peak season) displays assorted instruments. Closer to the north shore of the lake, **Bear Shola Falls** are at their strongest early in the year, just after the monsoon.

East of the town centre, about 3km south down Law's Ghat Rd (towards the plains), the **Flora and Fauna Museum** (daily except Sun 10am–noon & 3–5pm; Rs1) has a far from inviting collection of stuffed animals. However, the orchid house is spectacular, and well worth a look on the way to **Silver Cascade** waterfalls a further 2km along.

HIKES IN THE PALANI HILLS

Kodai has become something of a low-key trekking centre in recent years. As you wander around town, **guides** continually approach you offering their services on day hikes to local view points and beauty spots, or for longer trips involving night halts in villages. Scrutinize their recommendation books for comments by other tourists, and before you employ anyone, go for a coffee to discuss the possible routes, costs and nature of the walks they're offering. While most are relatively straightforward, some tackle unstable paths and steep climbs for which you'll need sturdy footwear. You should also clarify accommodation and food arrangements, transport costs and also their fees, in advance.

Generally, simple meals and tiffin are available at villages along the routes of longer hikes, so you don't need to carry much more than a sleeping bag, water, emergency food supplies and warm clothes for the evening. **Maps** of the area tend to be hopelessly inaccurate, but the one featured in the booklet *Beauty In Wilderness* (Rs10), available from the DFO (District Forest Office) near the *Hotel Tamil Nadu* (☎04542/40287), gives you a rough idea of distances, if not the lie of the land. While at the DFO, get permission to stay in the **Forest Rest Houses**, which provide rudimentary accommodation for around Rs25–50 per night; most have fireplaces, but bear in mind that any wood you might burn contributes to the overall **deforestation** of the Palanis. Local environmental groups are concerned about the potential long-term impact of trekking on the economy and ecology of the range, and as a result encourage walkers to pack out rubbish, bury their faeces where toilets are not available and use purification tablets rather than bottled water.

If you'd prefer to hike without a guide, the following route is worth considering; most of it follows forest roads, and there are settlements at regular intervals, many of them connected to Kodai by daily bus services. You don't get to explore the wild tops of the range, but the views and countryside throughout are beautiful, with patches of indigenous *shola* forest accessible at various points.

First head out of town on the **Pillar Rocks** road towards Berijam; if you can hitch a ride, you'll avoid the horn beeping that otherwise accompanies your progress as far as the end of the road at **Moir Point**. **Berijam** (23km), where a picturesque lake surrounded by dense pine and acacia forest, is little more than an outpost for forest wardens. From here, however, you can follow quiet back-country roads, taking local herders' and wood gatherers' paths that cut between the bends, to **Kavunji**, which is served by six daily buses to Kodai – handy if you're short of time. This sleepy Palani village is the home of a small NGO which promotes children's health projects, run by S.A. Iruthyaraj (look for the house with a white chicken painted on the wall), who is highly knowledgeable about local *shola* forests and off-track routes in the area. Further along the trail at **Polur** (8km) are some spectacular **waterfalls**. The locals say it is impossible to get close to them, but you can, by scrambling down the hillside via a muddy overgrown cattle path – and it's well worth it for the refreshing shower.

For more information on environmentally friendly trekking in the Kodai area, contact the **Palani Hills Conservation Council (PHCC)**, Amarville House, Lower Shola Rd, Kodaikanal 62410 (☎04542/40711). This excellent environmental organization also welcomes foreign volunteer workers to help with their various campaigns and grass-roots projects in the Palanis.

Chettiar Park, on the very northwest edge of town, around 3km from the lake at the end of a winding uphill road, flourishes with trees and flowers all year round, and every twelve years is flushed with a haze of pale-blue **Kurinji blossoms** (the next flowering will be in 2006). These unusual flowers are associated with the god Murugan, the Tamil form of Karttikeya (Shiva's second son), and god of Kurinji, one of five ancient divisions of the Tamil country. A temple in his honour stands just outside the park.

Accommodation

Kodaikanal's inexpensive **lodges** are grouped at the lower end of Anna Salai. Many are dim and pokey, however, so hunt around. Always ask whether blankets and hot water are provided. **Mid-range hotels** are usually good value, especially if you get a room with a view, but hike their prices drastically during high season (April–June). For its stunning location alone, *Greenland's Youth Hostel* offers unbeatable value for money at the bottom of the range.

INEXPENSIVE

Anjay, Anna Salai, near the bus stand (☎04542/41089). Simple budget lodge slap in the centre, it has smarter rooms than you'd expect from the outside, but does suffer from traffic noise. If they're full, check out the equally good-value *Jaya* behind. ②–③.

Greenland's Youth Hostel, St Mary's Rd (☎04542/41099). Attractive old stone house offering unrivalled views from its deep verandahs, simple rooms and a cheap bunk-bed dorm. One of the best budget places in South India. Book ahead. ①–③.

Keith Inn, off Bear Shola Rd (☎04542/40723). There are rooms for under Rs200 per night in an old red-tiled bungalow, or larger, airier rooms in a posher modern block. It's a good budget choice, although its views have been obscured by the adjacent hotel. ②–③.

Municipal Rest House, Hospital Rd (☎04542/42718). Basic, but surprisingly spacious rooms with coir carpets and attached shower-toilets; the rooms open onto a long corridor. Rock-bottom rates. ②.

Yagappa Lodge, Noyce Rd (☎04542/41235 or 42116). Small budget lodge in old buildings ranged around a courtyard. Good views; the best budget deal after *Greenland's Youth Hostel*, but you'll have to haggle. ③.

MODERATE TO EXPENSIVE

Astoria, Anna Salai (☎04542/40524). Well-kept hotel opposite the bus stand, with homely rooms and a good, mid-priced restaurant. No views, but comfortable enough. ④–⑤.

Carlton, off Lake Rd (☎04542/40071). The most luxurious hotel in Kodaikanal. Spacious, tastefully renovated and well-maintained colonial house overlooking the lake, with a bar and comfortable lounge. Cottages within the grounds are available at higher prices; all rates include meals. ⑨.

Hilltop Towers, Club Rd (☎04542/40413). Modern, swish rooms and good service, very near the lake and school. ⑤.

Kodai, Noyce Rd (☎04542/41301, fax 42108). Large campus of fifty incongruous but very comfortable chalets situated at the top of the hill, with good views of the town, and a quality restaurant. ⑥.

Kodaikanal Club, Club Rd (☎04542/41341). Sixteen spacious doubles, with wicker furniture and "sitouts", based in an old colonial club near the lake. Gentile and understated; very stylish. Rates include temporary membership. Book ahead. ⑥.

Sangeeth, Anna Salai (☎04542/40456). Reasonably sized, comfortable rooms with bath. Centrally located, but with no views over the plains. ③–④.

Taj Villa, Coaker's Walk off Noyce Rd (☎04542/40940). Comfortable hotel with more character than most in pleasant gardens and superb views. All rooms have attached bathrooms, but you'll have to get hot water by the bucket. A touch overpriced. ③–⑥.

TTDC Tamil Nadu, Fern Hill's Rd (☎04542/41336). Large, government-run hotel northwest of town. Standard rooms with TVs, a deluxe cottage and a cheap dorm. ①–⑥.

Valley View, Noyce Rd (☎04542/40181, fax 40189). Swish modern place at the top of town overlooking the bazaar. ⑥.

Eating

If you choose not to eat in any of the **hotel restaurants**, head for the food stalls along **Hospital Rd** just west of the bus stand. Menus include Indian, Chinese, Western and Tibetan dishes, and some cater specifically for vegetarians. Look out, too, for the **bakeries**, with their wonderful, fresh, warm bread and cakes each morning.

Carlton, *Carlton Hotel*, off Lake Rd. Splash out on a buffet spread (Rs300) at Kodai's top hotel, rounded off with a *chota* peg of IMFL scotch in the bar.

Eco Nut, J's Heritage Complex, Hospital Rd. One of South India's few bona fide Western-style wholefood shops and a great place to stock up on trekking supplies: muesli, homemade jams, breads, pickles and muffins, high-calorie "nutri-balls" and delicious (real) cheese from Auroville.

Manna Bakery, off Bear Shola Rd. The fried breakfasts, pizzas and home-baked brown bread and cakes served in this eccentric, self-consciously eco-friendly café-restaurant are great, but some might find the bare concrete dining hall dingy.

Hotel Punjab, Hospital Rd. Top North Indian cuisine and reasonably priced *tandoori* specialities. Try their great butter chicken and hot *naan*.

Royal Tibet, Hospital Rd. The better of the town's two Tibetan joints, with dishes ranging from thick homemade bread to particularly tasty *momos* and noodles, and some Indian and Chinese options.

Samudra, Hospital Rd. Moderately priced seafood specialties, trucked in weekly by freezer lorry from Kochi and served in an attractive rafia and fishing-net filled dining room. Try their *tandoori* pomfret or filling "fish fry" budget option; for a splurge, the tiger prawns are the thing, but they do plenty of chicken dishes too, which are steeped in tasty Chinese sauces.

Tasty Nook, Bear Shola Rd. Tiny, laidback budget travellers' café, co-owned by an Italian ex-pat, specializing in passably authentic pizzas, pasta and sizzlers.

Palani

Few sacred sites in South India enjoy as dramatic a location as **PALANI**, just over 100km northwest of Madurai. Crowning a smooth-sided, perfectly dome-shaped outcrop of granite, the town's principal shrine overlooks a vast lake, **Vyapuri**, enfolded by the pale yellow crags of the Palani Hills, rising sheer to the south. During the monsoons, the torturous road that scales the mountains from here provides the only dependable access to Kodaikanal. At other times, relatively few travellers are aware of its existence, but the views outstrip those from the busier southern approach to the hill station, while Palani itself, a busy little Tamil pilgrimage town, warrants at least a day-trip or stopover between Kodai and Ooty.

Praised for over two thousand years in the songs of the wandering Tamil saints, Palani's red and white striped **Malaikovil temple** attracts thousands of Hindu pilgrims each day. Each visitor is expected to perform two important rituals: the first involves an auspicious circuit of the base of the hill, via a two-kilometre-long sandy path known as the **Giri-Veedhi**, which is punctuated with shrines and stone-carved peacocks (Murugan's *vahana*, or vehicle); the second is an ascent of the sacred walkway via its 659 steps, illuminated from dusk onwards with tiny camphor lamps left by the devotees (and interrupted by more prosaic billboards advertising the names of the temple's corporate sponsors), to the hilltop shrine itself. During Palani's main festival in April/May, thousands of devotees – mostly male and clad in black *dhotis* – pour up the winding flight to worship the image, said to be formed from an aggregate of poisonous minerals, that, if mixed with coconut milk, fruits and flowers, produces medicinal herbs. Some carry pails of milk on yokes as offerings for Lord Murugan, while the more fervent among them perform austerities (cheek piercing with metal leaf-shaped skewers is a favourite). Those unable to climb the steps can ascend in a carriage pulled slowly up the steep incline by electric winch (Rs1) but it can take a lot of queuing to get on. From the summit, the **views** across the Vyapuri lake and Vaigai plain, with the *ghats* looming behind, are unforgettable.

Apart from the numerous simple *choultries* – pilgrims' hostels owned by various caste associations from all over South India – Palani has two proper **hotels**: a small new unit of *TTDC Tamil Nadu*, West Giri St, opposite the winch station (☎04545/41156; ④) and the smart new *Subam Hotel*, 7 North Giri St near the main temple entrance (☎04545/42672; ③?⑤). **Buses to Palani** from Kodaikanal (every 1hr 30min; 3hr) are often full, so it's wise to reserve. The town is also well connected by train and bus to Coimbatore, via Pollachi (for the Indira Gandhi Wildlife Sanctuary), and Madurai, and a private "deluxe" service passes through each morning en route to Ooty.

Indira Gandhi (Anamalai) Wildlife Sanctuary

Anamalai Wildlife Sanctuary, officially renamed the **Indira Gandhi Wildlife Sanctuary**, is a 958-square-kilometre tract of forest on the southern reaches of the Cardamom Hills, southwest of the busy junction town of **Pollachi**. Vegetation ranges from dry deciduous to tropical evergreen, and the sanctuary is home to lion-tailed **macaques** (black-maned monkeys), wild elephants, crocodiles, *sambar*, spotted and barking deer, as well as fifteen elusive **tigers** at the last count.

The Indira Gandhi Wildlife Sanctuary has been at the centre of several water and land rights disputes over the past few years, mostly between local tribal people and the government, which have been developing major hydro and irrigation projects in the area. Access to visitors was always strictly limited, but in 1998, the park was closed altogether, ostensibly for the same reasons the Forest Department have shut the other wildlife sanctuaries in Tamil Nadu. Until the "Veerapan problem" (see box on p.490) is resolved, the Indira Gandhi Wildlife Sanctuary will remain out of bounds, which can, in the long run, only benefit its fragile population of predators.

travel details

Note that no individual route appears more than once in this chart; for any specific journey, check against where you want to get to as well as where you're coming from. Bear in mind, also, that there is only room here for a general summary; see the Moving On sections in specific cities for more details.

Trains

Chennai to: Chengalpattu (10 daily*; 1hr 10min); Chidambaram (5 daily*; 5hr 30min); Coimbatore (10 daily; 8–9hr); Dindigul (6 daily*; 6hr 30min–12hr); Kanniyakumari (1 daily; 19hr 30min); Kochi (3 daily; 13–14hr); Kodaikanal Road (3 daily*; 10–13hr); Kumbakonam (3 daily*; 7hr 20min); Madurai (6 daily*; 7hr 40min–14hr); Rameshwaram (2–3 daily*; 14hr 30min–24hr); Salem (10 daily; 4–5hr); Thanjavur (3 daily*; 8–9hr); Tiruchirapalli (11 daily*; 5hr 30min–11hr).

* Trains from Egmore; all others from Central.

Chidambaram to: Chengalpattu (5 daily; 4hr 30min); Kodaikanal Road (1 daily; 7hr 10min); Kumbakonam (4 daily; 1hr 40min); Rameshwaram (1 daily; 11hr); Thanjavur (4 daily; 2hr 30min–3hr); Tiruchirapalli (4 daily; 4hr); Tirupati (2 daily; 5–6hr); Tiruvannamalai (2 daily; 4hr 50min).

Coimbatore to: Bangalore (1 daily; 9hr 30min); Delhi (1–2 daily; 35–43hr); Hyderabad (1 daily; 20hr 50min); Kanniyakumari (2 daily; 12hr 35min–14hr); Kochi (8 daily; 6hr–6hr 30min); Mumbai (1–2 daily; 9hr 50min–11hr); Rameshwaram (1 daily; 12hr 20min); Salem (4 daily; 3hr); Thiruvananthapuram (4 daily; 9hr 50min–11hr); Tiruchirapalli (1 daily; 5hr).

Kanniyakumari to: Delhi (Fri only; 58hr); Kochi (2–3 daily; 7hr 30min–9hr); Mumbai (1 daily; 48hr); Salem (1 daily; 15hr); Thiruvananthapuram (2–3 daily; 2hr–2hr 30min).

Madurai to: Bangalore (1 daily; 12hr 50min); Chengalpattu (6 daily; 10hr–12hr 40min); Chidambaram (2 daily; 8hr–9hr 30min); Coimbatore (3 daily; 5hr 50min–7hr); Kodaikanal Road (6 daily; 40min–1hr); Rameshwaram (3 daily; 6hr 15min–7hr); Thanjavur (2 daily; 4hr

35min–6hr); Tiruchirapalli (8 daily; 2hr 20min–4hr); Tirupati (1 daily; 18hr 20min); Tiruvannamalai (1 daily; 12hr 20min); Vellore (1 daily; 14hr 30min).

Tiruchirapalli to: Chengalpattu (9 daily; 6hr 30min–9hr 20min); Kodaikanal Road (5 daily; 2hr 40min); Thanjavur (4 daily; 1hr 40min).

Buses

Chennai to: Chengalpattu (60 daily; 1hr 30min–2hr); Chidambaram (20 daily; 5–7hr); Coimbatore (9 daily; 11–13hr); Dindigul (10 daily; 9–10hr); Kanchipuram (46 daily; 1hr 30min–2hr); Kanniyakumari (9 daily; 15–17hr); Kodaikanal Road (1 daily; 14–15hr); Kumbakonam (17 daily; 7–8hr); Madurai (37 daily; 10hr); Mamallapuram (80 daily; 2–3hr); Pondicherry (70 daily; 4–5hr); Rameshwaram (1 daily; 14hr); Salem (20 daily; 5–7hr); Thanjavur (18 daily; 8hr 30min); Tindivanam (40 daily; 3–4hr); Tiruchirapalli (46 daily; 8–9hr); Tiruvannamalai (23 daily; 4–6hr); Udhagamandalam (Ooty) (3 daily; 14hr); Vedanthangal (3 daily; 2–3hr); Vellore (30 daily; 4hr).

Chidambaram to: Chengalpattu (20 daily; 4hr 30min–5hr); Kumbakonam (58 daily; 2hr 30min); Thanjavur (21 daily; 4hr); Tiruchirapalli (9 daily; 5hr); Tiruvannamalai (5 daily; 3hr 30min); Vellore (5 daily; 4hr 30min).

Coimbatore to: Bangalore (2 daily; 8–9hr); Kanniyakumari (3 daily; 14hr); Kodaikanal Road (2 daily; 6hr); Rameshwaram (2 daily; 14hr); Salem (40 daily; 3–4hr); Thiruvananthapuram (2 daily; 12hr); Tiruchirapalli (11 daily; 6hr).

Kanchipuram to: Tiruvannamalai (8 daily; 3hr); Vellore (20 daily; 2hr 30min).

Kanniyakumari to: Chennai (11 daily; 14–16hr); Kovalam (10 daily; 1hr 30 min); Madurai (every 30min; 6hr); Rameshwaram (4 daily; 9–10hr); Thiruvananthapuram (20 daily; 2hr).

Madurai to: Bangalore (17 daily; 8–9hr); Chengalpattu (37 daily; 9hr); Chidambaram (5 daily; 7–8hr); Coimbatore (55 daily; 10hr); Kochi (4 daily; 10hr); Kodaikanal Road (11 daily; 4hr); Pondicherry (2 daily; 9–10hr); Rameshwaram (26 daily; 4hr); Thanjavur (36 daily; 4–5hr); Thiruvananthapuram (18 daily; 7hr); Tiruchirapalli (60 daily; 2hr 30min–3hr); Tirupati (6 daily; 15hr).

Pondicherry to: Bangalore (4 daily; 8hr); Kanchipuram (8 daily; 3hr); Mamallapuram (9 daily; 3hr); Thanjavur (4 daily; 5hr); Tiruchirapalli (4 daily; 6hr); Tiruvannamalai (4–5 daily; 2hr).

Tiruchirapalli to: Chengalpattu (46 daily; 7–8hr); Kanchipuram (2 daily; 6–7hr); Kodaikanal Road (1 daily; 5hr); Thanjavur (60–70 daily; 1hr–1hr 30min); Tiruvannamalai (2 daily; 4–5hr).

Flights

Chennai to: Coimbatore (2–3 daily; 1hr 15min); Madurai (3 weekly; 50min); Tiruchirapalli (3 weekly; 45min).

Coimbatore to: Bangalore (6 weekly; 50min); Mumbai (1–3 daily; 1hr 40min–2hr 10min).

CHAPTER SEVEN

ANDHRA PRADESH

Although **ANDHRA PRADESH** is the largest state in South India and occupies a great swathe of land, stretching for over 1200km along the coast from Orissa to Tamil Nadu and reaching far inland from the fertile deltas of the Godavari and Krishna rivers to the semi-arid Deccan Plateau, it's not a place that receives many tourists. Most foreign travellers pass through en route to its more attractive neighbours, which is understandable as places of interest are few and far between. However, the sights that Andhra Pradesh does have to offer are absorbing and well enough connected to warrant at least a few stops on a longer tour of South India.

The state capital, **Hyderabad**, is a run-down but undoubtedly atmospheric city dating from the late sixteenth century. Its endless bazaars, eclectic Salar Jung museum and the mighty **Golconda Fort** nearby make it an enticing place to spend a day or two. By contrast, its modern twin, commercial **Secunderabad**, excels only in characterlessness. **Warangal**, 150km northeast of Hyderabad, has both Muslim and Hindu remains from the twelfth and thirteenth centuries, while the region's Buddhist legacy – particularly its superb sculpture – is preserved in museums at sites such as **Nagarjunakonda** (south of Hyderabad) and **Amaravati**, the ancient Satavahana capital. In the east, the big cities of **Vishakapatnam** and **Vijayawada** have little to recommend them, though the latter makes a convenient access point for Amaravati. However, the temple town of **Tirupati** in the far southeast – best reached from Chennai in Tamil Nadu – is one of India's great Hindu phenomena, a fascinating and impossibly crowded pilgrimage site, said to be more popular even than Mecca. In the southwest of the state, the small town of **Puttaparthy** attracts a more international pilgrim crowd, drawn here by the prospect of *darshan* from spiritual leader Sai Baba.

Although modern industries have grown up around the capital, and shipbuilding, iron and steel are important on the coast, most people in Andhra Pradesh remain poor. Away from the Godavari and Krishna deltas, where the soil is rich enough to grow rice and sugar cane, the land is in places impossible to cultivate.

Some history

Earliest accounts of the region, dating back to the time of **Ashoka** (third century BC), refer to a people known as the Andhras. The **Satavahana dynasty** (second century BC–second century AD), also known as the Andras, came to control much of central and southern India from their second capital at Amaravati on the Krishna. They enjoyed extensive international trade with both eastern Asia and Europe, and were

ACCOMMODATION PRICE CODES

All **accommodation prices** in this book have been coded using the symbols below. The prices given are for a double room, except in the case of categories ① and ② where the price can refer to dorm accommodation per bed. All taxes are included. For more details, see p.34.

① up to Rs100	④ Rs300–400	⑦ Rs900–1500
② Rs100–200	⑤ Rs400–600	⑧ Rs1500–2500
③ Rs200–300	⑥ Rs600–900	⑨ Rs2500 and upwards

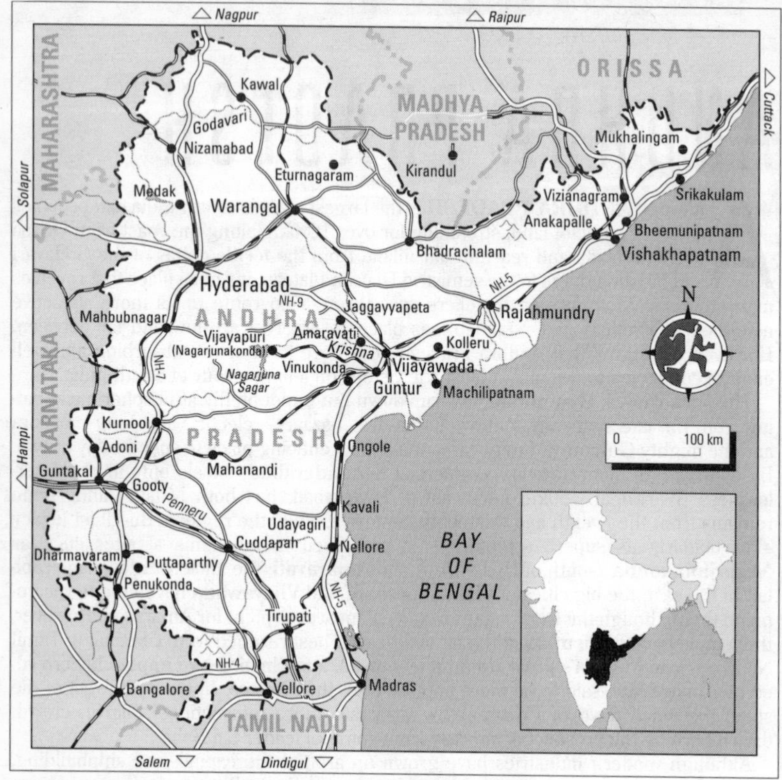

great patrons of Buddhism. Subsequently, the Pallavas from Tamil Nadu, the Chalukyas from Karnataka, and the Cholas all held sway. By the thirteenth century, the Kakatiyas of Warangal were under constant threat from Muslim incursions, while later on, after the fall of their city at Hampi, the Hindu Vijayanagars transferred operations to Chandragiri near Tirupati.

The next significant development was in the mid-sixteenth century, with the rise of the Muslim **Qutb Shahi dynasty**. In 1687, the son of the Moghul emperor Aurangzeb seized Golconda. Five years after Aurangzeb died in 1707, the Viceroy of Hyderabad declared independence and established the Asaf Jahi dynasty of **Nizams**. In return for allying with the British against Tipu Sultan of Mysore, the Nizam dynasty was allowed to retain a certain degree of autonomy even after the British had come to dominate all India.

During the struggle for Independence, harmony between Hindus and Muslims in Andhra Pradesh disintegrated. **Partition** brought matters to a climax, as the Nizam desired to join other Muslims in the soon-to-be created state of **Pakistan**. In 1949 the capital erupted in riots, the army was brought in and Hyderabad state was admitted to the Indian Union. Andhra Pradesh state was created in 1956 from Telegu-speaking regions (although Urdu is widely spoken in Hyderabad) that had previously formed part of the Madras Presidency on the east coast and the princely state of Hyderabad to the west. Today almost ninety percent of the population is Hindu, with Muslims largely concentrated in the capital.

Hyderabad/Secunderabad

A melting-pot of Muslim and Hindu cultures, the capital of Andhra Pradesh comprises the twin cities of **HYDERABAD** and **SECUNDERABAD**, with a combined population of around six million. Secunderabad, of little interest to visitors, is the modern administrative city founded by the British, whereas Hyderabad, the old city, with its seething **bazaars**, **Muslim monuments** and **Salar Jung Museum** has heaps of charm. Despite this, Hyderabad has been in decline since Independence. While 45 percent of the population inhabit the old city, a mere 25 percent of the city's budget is spent on it, exacerbating a tension that is never far from the surface. In recent years, the area has

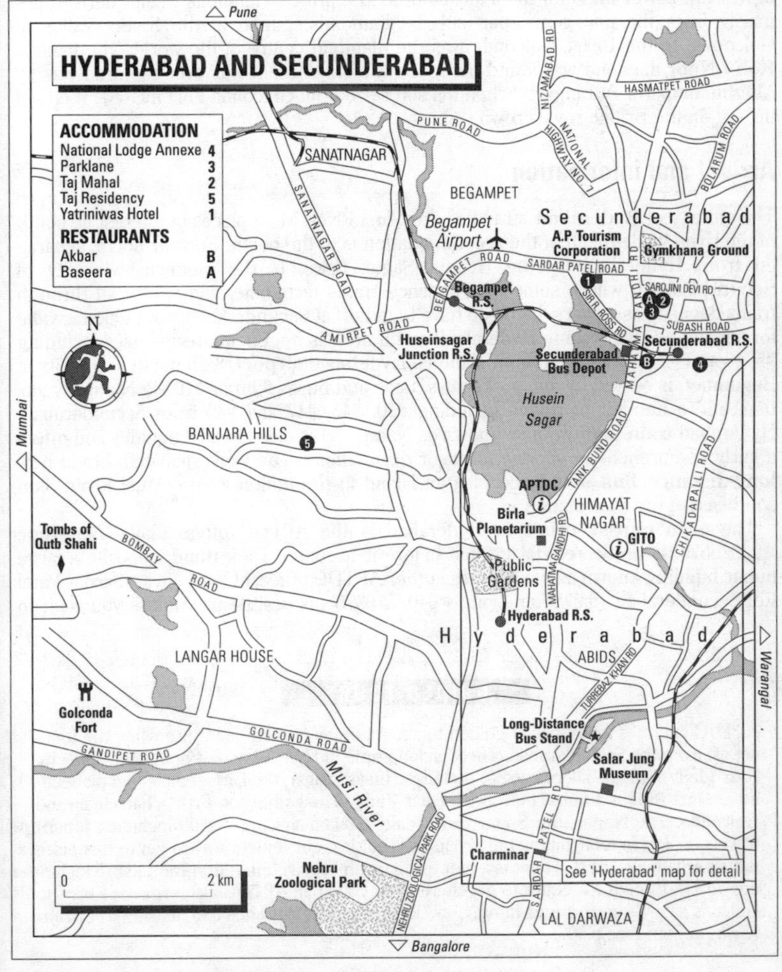

received a new lease of life from the computer industry, and Hyderabad is now at the forefront of software training, rivalling Bangalore as the South's hi-tech capital.

Hyderabad was founded in 1591 by **Muhammad Quli Shah** (1562–1612), beside the Musi River, 8km east of Golconda, the fortress capital of the Golconda empire which by now was suffering from overcrowding and a serious lack of water. Unusually, this new city was laid out on a grid system, with huge arches and stone buildings that included Hyderabad's most famous monument, **Charminar**. At first it was a city without walls; these were only added in 1740, as defence against the Marathas. Legend has it that a secret tunnel linked the spectacular **Golconda Fort** with the city, dotted with dome-shaped structures at suitable intervals to provide the unfortunate messengers who had to use it with the opportunity to come up for fresh air.

For the 300 years of Muslim reign, there was harmony between the predominantly Hindu population and the minority Muslims. Hyderabad was the most important focus of Muslim power in South India at this time; the princes' fabulous wealth derived primarily from the fine gems, particularly diamonds, mined in the Kistna Valley at Golconda. In the 1600s, Golconda was the diamond centre of the world. The famous **Koh-i-Noor** diamond was found here, and the only time it was ever captured was by Moghul emperor Aurangzeb, when his son seized the Golconda Fort in 1687. It ended up, cut, in the British royal crown.

Arrival and information

The old city of **Hyderabad** straddles the Musi River. Most places of interest lie south of the river, while much of the accommodation is to the north. Further north, separated from Hyderabad by the Husain Sagar Lake, is the modern twin city of **Secunderabad**, where some long-distance trains terminate, and where all through trains deposit passengers. If you do have to get off at Secunderabad, your ticket is valid for any connecting train to Hyderabad; and if none is imminent, many buses including #5, #8 and #20 ply between both stations. Hyderabad **airport**, 8km north of the city at Begumpet, is served by auto-rickshaws, taxis and buses #9m or #10 via Nampally station, and a number of routes including #10, #45, #47 and #49 from Secunderabad. Hyderabad **train station** (also known as Nampally) is close to all amenities and offers a fairly comprehensive service to major destinations. The well-organized, brand new **long-distance bus stand** occupies an island in the middle of the Musi River, 3km southeast of the train station.

The main **tourist office** in Hyderabad is the APTDC office (daily 7am–7pm; ☎040/557531) on Secretariat Rd just before it becomes Tank Bund, opposite a large public building known as the BRK; the other APTDC office, at Yatri Nivas, Sardar Patel Rd, Secunderabad (daily 7am–7pm; ☎040/516375), is of little use unless you want to

GUIDED TOURS

APTDC operates a number of guided tours. All times quoted below are when the tours set off from the Secunderabad office; pick-up time in Hyderabad is 45min later. The **city tour** (daily 7.45am–5.30pm; Rs90) includes Husain Sagar, the Birla temple and planetarium, Qutb Shahi tombs (not Fri), Salar Jung Museum (not Fri), Charminar and Golconda. The **Nagarjuna Sagar tour** (daily 6.30am–9.30pm; Rs190 including lunch) travels 360km in total, and is rather rushed, but is a convenient way to get to this fascinating area (see p.511). There is a tour to **Tirupati** (Fri 3.30pm–Mon 7am; Rs675 including hotel), though it's better to get there from Chennai. APTDC also organizes trips to Golconda Fort's **sound and light** show (Rs45, includes entrance fee), leaving from Yatri Niwas at 5pm (see p.507).

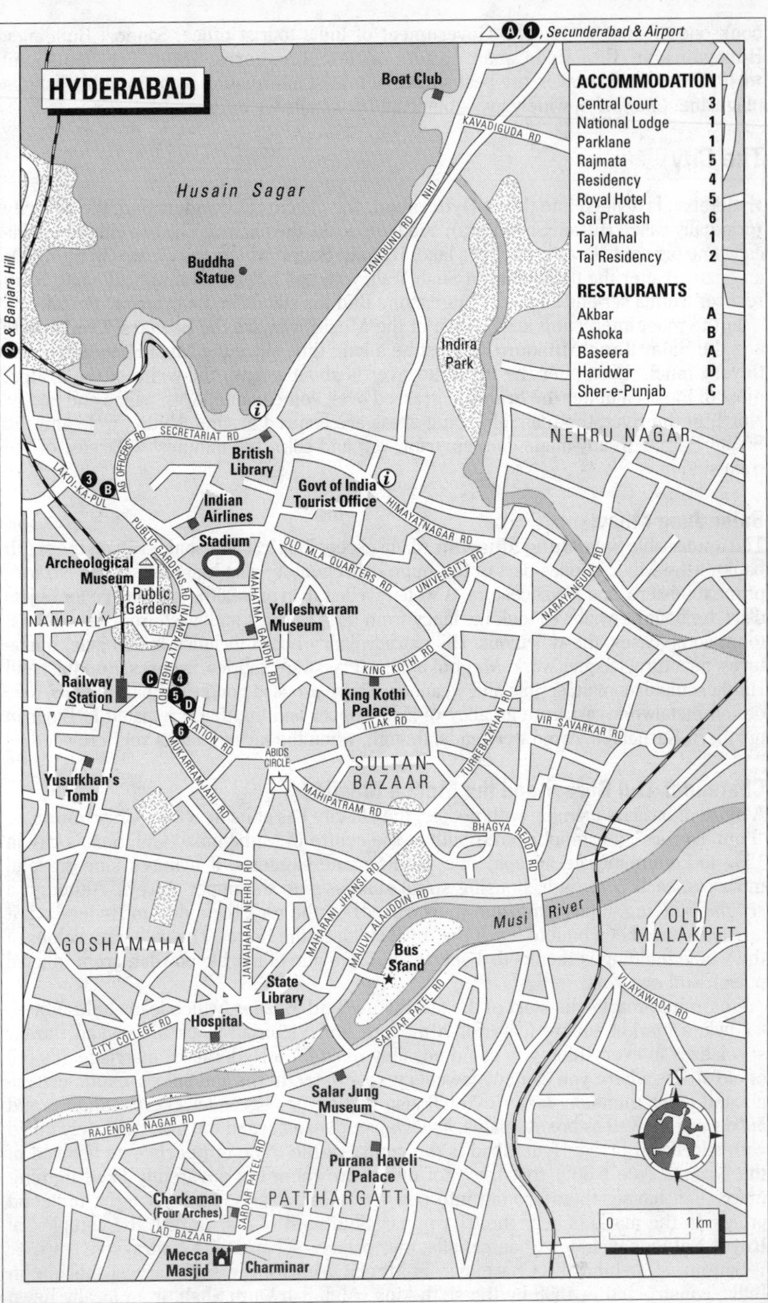
HYDERABAD
A, 1, Secunderabad & Airport
2 & Banjara Hill
ACCOMMODATION
Central Court 3
National Lodge 1
Parklane 1
Rajmata 5
Residency 4
Royal Hotel 5
Sai Prakash 6
Taj Mahal 1
Taj Residency 2
RESTAURANTS
Akbar A
Ashoka B
Baseera A
Haridwar D
Sher-e-Punjab C
Boat Club
KAVADIGUDA RD
Husain Sagar
Buddha Statue
TANKBUND RD NH7
Indira Park
NEHRU NAGAR
SECRETARIAT RD
British Library
Govt of India Tourist Office
HIMAYATNAGAR RD
LAKDI-KA-PUL
AG OFFICERS' RD
Indian Airlines
PUBLIC GARDENS RD
Stadium
OLD MLA QUARTERS RD
UNIVERSITY RD
NARAYANGUDA RD
Archeological Museum
Public Gardens
NAMPALLY
NAMPALLY HIGH RD
MAHATMA GANDHI RD
Yelleshwaram Museum
KING KOTHI RD
King Kothi Palace
Railway Station
STATION RD
TILAK RD
TURREBAZKHAN RD
VIR SAVARKAR RD
MUKARRAMJAHI RD
ABIDS CIRCLE
SULTAN BAZAAR
Yusufkhan's Tomb
MAHIPATRAM RD
BHAGYA REDDI RD
MAHARANI JHANSI RD
MAULVI ALAUDDIN RD
Musi River
OLD MALAKPET
GOSHAMAHAL
JAWAHARAL NEHRU RD
Bus Sfand
State Library
VIJAYAWADA RD
Hospital
CITY COLLEGE RD
SARDAR PATEL RD
Salar Jung Museum
RAJENDRA NAGAR RD
N
Purana Haveli Palace
Charkaman (Four Arches)
SARDAR PATEL RD
PATTHARGATTI
0 1 km
LAD BAZAAR
Mecca Masjid
Charminar

book one of their tours. The Government of India tourist office, Sandozi Buildings, Himayatnagar Rd, Hyderabad, offers a few brochures (Mon–Fri 9am–5pm; ☎040/7630037). However, the best source of tourist information is the monthly listings magazine, *Channel 6*, widely available from bookstalls for Rs10.

The City

Hyderabad is divided into three: **Hyderabad**, the old city; **Secunderabad**, the new city (originally called Husain Shah Pura); and **Golconda**, the old fort. The two cities are basically one big sprawl, separated by a lake, **Husain Sagar**, which was created in the 1500s and named after the noble Husain Shah Wali, who had helped Ibrahim Quli Qutb Shah recover from a serious illness. A huge stone Buddha stands in the centre of the lake.

In the most interesting area, south of the Musi River, are the **bazaars**, **Charminar** and the **Salar Jung Museum**. It must be a long time since the Musi River amounted to very much. Even after the rains the river is about a tenth the width of the bridge; most of the area under the bridge is grassed over, some planted with palms and paddy. North of the river, the main shopping areas are centred around Abids Circle and the Sultan Bazaar (ready-made clothes, fruit, veg and silk), ten minutes' walk east of the train station.

Salar Jung Museum

The unmissable **Salar Jung Museum** (daily except Fri 10.30am–5pm; Rs5), on the south bank of the Musi, houses part of the huge collection of Salar Jung, one of the Nizam's prime ministers, and his ancestors. A well-travelled man of wealth, with an eye for objets d'art, he bought whatever took his fancy from both the east and west, from the sublime to, in some cases, the ridiculous. His extraordinary hoard includes Indian jade, miniatures, furniture, lacquer work, Moghul opaque glassware, fabrics, bronzes, Buddhist and Hindu sculpture, manuscripts and weapons. There are also good examples of *bidri*, decorated metalwork cast from an alloy of zinc, copper and tin, that originated in Bidar in northern Karnataka. Avoid weekends, though, when the museum gets very crowded.

Charminar, Lad Bazaar and the Mecca Masjid

A maze of bazaars teeming with people, the old city has at its heart the **Charminar**, or "Four Towers", a triumphal arch built at the centre of Muhammad Quli Shah's city in 1591 to commemorate an epidemic. As its name suggests, it features four graceful minarets, each 56m high, housing spiral staircases to the upper storeys. Although a secular building, it has a mosque (now closed) on the roof; the oldest in Hyderabad, it is said to have been built to teach the royal children the Koran. The yellowish colour of the whole building is thanks to a special stucco made of marble powder, *gram* (a local pulse), and egg yolk.

Charminar marks the start of the fascinating **Lad Bazaar**, which leads to Mahboob Chowk, a market square featuring a mosque and Victorian clock tower. Lad Bazaar specializes in everything you could possibly need for a Hyderabadi marriage; it's full of old stores where you can buy jewellery, rosewater, herbs and spices, exotic materials and more mundane *lunghis*. You'll also find silver filigree jewellery, antiques and *bidri* ware, as well as boxes, plates, *hookah*-paraphernalia and the like, delicately inlaid with silver and brass. Hyderabad is the centre of the trade in **pearls** – so beloved of the Nizams (see p.500) that they not only wore them but apparently liked nothing more than having them ground into powder to eat. Pearls can be bought, for good prices, in the markets near the Charminar. Southeast of Lad Bazaar, the complex of **Royal Palaces** includes Chaumahalla, four palaces set around a central courtyard.

Southwest, behind the Charminar, is **Mecca Masjid**, the sixth largest mosque in India, constructed in 1598 by the sixth king, Abdullah Qutb Shah, from locally hewn blocks of black granite and small red bricks from Mecca, which are slotted over the central arch. The mosque itself can hold 3000 worshippers with up to 10,000 in the courtyard; on the left of the courtyard are the tombs of the Nizams. Outside the mosque is a stall where they will change your torn, cut rupee bills at good rates.

The **Charkaman**, or "Four Arches", north of Charminar, were built in 1594 and once led to the parade ground of royal palaces to the south (now long gone). The surrounding narrow streets spill over with interesting small shops; through **Doulat-Khan-e-Ali** – the western arch, which originally led to the palace – stores sell lustrous brocade and antique saris. The arch itself is said to have been once hung with rich gold tapestries.

North of the river

Just north of the train station, set in Hyderabad's tranquil public gardens, the **archeological museum** (daily except Fri 10.30am–5pm; Rs0.50) displays a modest but well-labelled collection of bronzes, prehistoric tools, copper inscription plates, weapons, household utensils and even an Egyptian mummy. There's a gallery of modern art in the new extension, too. The **Birla Venkateshwara temple** (daily 7am–noon & 3–9pm), on Kalabahad ("black mountain") Hill, north of the Public Gardens, is open to all, irrespective of caste, creed or nationality. Constructed in Rajasthani white marble in 1976 by the Birla Trust, it was set up by the wealthy industrialist Birla family. Although the temple itself is not of great interest, the views are spectacular. Nearby, and also built by the Birla Trust, is the **planetarium** (shows are in English: Mon–Sat 11.30am, 4pm & 6pm; Sun & hols 11.30am, 3.45pm & 6pm; Rs10).

Husain Sagar

Husain Sagar, the large expanse of water separating Hyderabad from Secunderabad, lends a welcome air of tranquillity to the busy conurbation. People come here to stroll along Tank Bund, the road that runs around the eastern side of the lake, and to relax in the small parks dotted along the water's edge. The parks contain numerous statues of prominent local figures over the last several centuries, and come alive with ice-cream and snack stalls, particular as sunset approaches and people gather to witness its natural splendour across the lake.

In the centre of the lake, stands an enormous, modern stone statue of the Buddha Purnima or "Teacher Buddha", which was eventually erected onto its plinth by a salvage company in 1992, after spending a couple of years underwater. It had sunk at the first disastrous attempt to transport it there by barge in 1990, a tragedy that caused the deaths of eight people in an inauspicious effort to place the huge figure, which had taken five years to build, measuring 55ft high and weighing 350 tons. Boats regularly chug out to the statue from Lumbini Park, just off Secretariat Rd, every hour from 9am to 6pm, the half-hour round trip costing Rs10.

Golconda Fort and the tombs of the Qutb Shahi Kings

Golconda Fort 122m above the plain of Hyderabad and 11km west of old Hyderabad, was the capital of the seven Qutb Shahi kings from 1518 until the end of the sixteenth century, when the court moved to Hyderabad. Well preserved and set in lush green scrubland, it is one of the most impressive forts in India. Large portions of its battlements are draped in grasses, lending it a soft, natural air. Its outer wall reached 18m, and the citadel boasted 87 semicircular bastions and eight mighty gates, four of which are still in use, complete with gruesome elephant-proof spikes.

To get **to the fort**, bus #119 runs from Nampally, and both the #66G direct bus from Charminar and #80D from the train station in Secunderabad stop outside the main entrance. **For the tombs**, take #123 and #142S from Charminar. From Secunderabad the #5, #5S, #5R all go to Mehdipattanam, where you should hop onto #123. Or, take an auto-rickshaw and agree a waiting fee in advance. Set aside a day to explore the

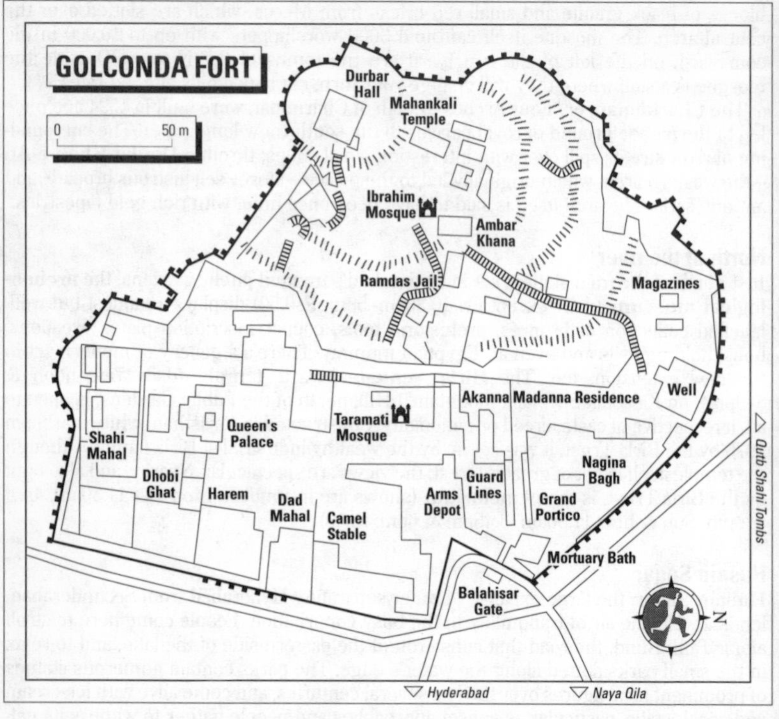

fort, which covers an area of around forty square kilometres; it's well worth hiring one of the many guides who gather at the entrance, or at least buying one of the handy little pamphlets, including map, sold by vendors.

Entering the **fort** (daily 9am–5pm; Rs2, free on Fri) by the Balahisar gate, you come into the grand portico, where guards clap their hands to show off the fort's acoustics; the claps can be clearly heard as far as the Durbar hall. To the right is the **mortuary bath**, where the bodies of deceased nobles were ritually bathed prior to burial. If you follow the arrowed anti-clockwise route, you pass along a straight, walled path before coming to the two-storey residence of ministers Akkana and Madanna, and start the proper ascent to the Durbar hall. Halfway along the steps, which pass assorted water channels and wells that supplied the fort's water system, you come to a small, dark cell named after the court cashier **Ramdas**, who during his incarceration here, produced the clumsy carvings and paintings that litter the gloomy room. Nearing the top, you come across the small, pretty mosque of Ibrahim Qutb Shah; beyond this, set beneath two huge granite stones, is an even smaller temple dedicated to Durga in her manifestation as Mahakali.

The steps are crowned by the three-storey **Durbar hall** of the Qutb Shahs**.** The lower level of the hall has vaulted bays and the rooftop pavilion gave the monarchs uninterrupted views over their domain. Their accompaniment was the lilting strains of court musicians, as opposed to the cacophony of incessant clapping heard today from far below.

The ruins of the **Queen's palace**, in the southern end of the fort, stand in a courtyard centred on an original copper fountain that used to be filled with rosewater. The Queen's palace was once elaborately decorated with multiple domes. Traces of the "necklace" design on one of the arches can still be seen at the top of which a lotus bud sits below an opening flower with a cavity at its centre that once contained a diamond. Petals and creeper leaves are dotted with tiny holes that formerly gleamed with rubies and diamonds; parrots, long gone, had rubies for their eyes. Today visitors can only speculate how splendid it must all have looked, especially at night, when flaming torches illuminated the glittering decorations. At the entrance to the palace itself, four chambers provided protection from intruders. Passing through two rooms, the second of which is overgrown, you come to the **Shahi Mahal**, the royal bedroom. Originally, it had a domed roof and niches on the walls that once sheltered candles or oil lamps, and it is said that the servants used silver ladders to get up there to light them. Golconda Fort's **sound and light** show (spoken in English; March–Oct Wed, Sat & Sun 7pm; Nov–Feb 6.30pm; Rs20) is suitably theatrical.

There are 82 **Qutb Shahi tombs** (daily except Fri 9am–4.30pm) about 1km north of the outer wall. Set in peaceful gardens, they commemorate commanders, relatives of the kings, dancers, singers and royal doctors, as well as all but two of the Qutb Shahi kings. Faded today, they were once brightly coloured in turquoise and green; they all have an onion dome on a block, with a decorative arcade. You can reach them by road or, more pleasantly, by picking your way across the quiet grassy verges and fields below the fort's battlements.

THE QUTB SHAHI DYNASTY

Quli, destined to become the first king of the Qutb Shahi dynasty, came from Persia with his uncle to sell horses to the Bahmani kingdom at Gulbarga and Bijapur. After a spell as a popular governor, he was titled **Quli Qutb Shah** by the Bahmani ruler Mamu Shbahmani who had appointed him. By 1518 the power of the Bahmanis was waning and Quli Qutb Shah raised an army and established independence for his state, ruling for twenty-five years and making Golconda his dynastic capital. When he was in his nineties, his eldest son Jamshed – who had briefly succeeded to the throne – conspired to have his father beheaded while praying in the mosque and his brothers exiled. However, an outraged people prevented Jamshed's coup by forcibly deposing him. Quli Qutb Shah preferred, thereafter, one of his younger sons, Ibrahim, to inherit his throne.

Ibrahim Quli Qutb Shah returned from exile to take over the kingdom at the age of eighteen. He was a learned man who wrote poetry in both Urdu and Telugu and he oversaw the construction of many of Golconda's most important buildings, including the stone fort. His reign saw the dynasty reach the height of its power, despite occasional conflicts with the neighbouring states of Bijapur and Ahmadnagar. These three kingdoms later formed an alliance to defeat the powerful Vijayanagars in 1565.

The reigns of Ibrahim's only son, **Muhammed Quli Qutb Shah** (1580–1612), and grandson, **Muhammed Qutb Shah** (1612–26), both cultured men, saw the expansion of Golconda and foundation of Hyderabad after a bridge had been built over the Musi River in 1578. Despite the growing threat from the Moghuls to the north, these were peaceful times and prosperous trade was established with the European merchants on the coast. Trade was established, including diamonds, and rumour has it that a mine still exists in the fort, its exact location known only to the government.

Increasing pressure came from the Moghuls during the long reign of **Abdullah Qutb Shah** (1626–72), and the dynasty finally ended with the surrender of his son, **Abdul Hasan Qutb Shah** in 1687 to the forces of Aurangzeb. This followed an eight-month battle, which, as the story goes, only ended when Aurangzeb bribed a doorman to allow his troops in to secure victory.

Accommodation

The area in front of Hyderabad **train station** (Nampally) has the cheapest accommodation, but you're unlikely to find anything basic for less than Rs150. The real **bargains** are more in the mid- to upper-range hotels, which offer better facilities for lower rates than in other big cities. About 2km north of Secunderabad train station, decent places mid-range line **Sarojini Devi Rd**, near the Gymkhana Ground.

HYDERABAD ADDRESSES

Hyderabadis appear to have a deep mistrust of logical, consistent road-naming, mapping and addresses. One road merges into another, some addresses refer to nothing more specific than a locality, and others identify themselves as being opposite buildings that no longer exist. Just as confusing are those that have very specific addresses consisting of a string of hyphenated numbers referring to house and plot numbers, incomprehensible to anybody other than town surveyors. All this is somewhat ironic in a city that is home to one of the major sections of the Survey of India.

Hyderabad

Central Court, Lakdi-ka-Pul (☎040/233262; fax 232737). Smallish, new hotel, 2km from railway, with standards as good as many twice the price. Comfortable rooms with satellite TV and 24hr room service. Travel desk, coffee shop and restaurant. ⑥.

Rajmata, Nampally High Rd, opposite train station (☎040/3201000). Set back from the road near the various *Royal* lodges. Next door to the *Lakshmi* restaurant. Largish, clean non-a/c rooms. ④.

The Residency, Nampally High Rd (☎040/204060). Swish, modern hotel beautifully presented in plush surroundings; the most upmarket option near the station. The restaurant serves good veg food. ⑦.

Royal Hotel, opposite train station, Nampally High Rd (☎040/3201020). Decent, basic lodge with clean bathrooms (common or attached). Singles available. ①–②.

Sai Prakash, Station Rd (☎040/511726). Near railway, 2km from bus stand. Modern hotel, complete with capsule lift. Comfortable, carpeted rooms (all with satellite TV) set around atrium. High standards (non-a/c in particular), and very popular. Good restaurants and bar. ⑤.

Taj Residency, Rd No. 1, Banjara Hills (☎040/3399999). Taj Group hotel overlooking a lake, 4km from the centre of Hyderabad. All the usual facilities including swimming pool, a good restaurant and a coffee shop. ⑧–⑨.

Secunderabad

National Lodge Annexe, opposite Secunderabad train station (☎040/7705572). No-frills lodge; but the best of the bunch for awkwardly timed trains. To the left of the older *National* as you come out from the station. ②.

Parklane, 115 Park Lane, Secunderabad (☎040/840466). Large rooms (ordinary and deluxe), with views onto other buildings, very clean bathrooms, satellite TV, restaurant and friendly staff. ④–⑥.

Taj Mahal, 88 Sarojini Devi Rd, Secunderabad (☎040/812105). Old-fashioned hotel with character, built in 1949, but bears no detectable relation to the Taj Mahal. Rooms are clean, comfortable and spacious, although a bit dark. Veg restaurant with snacks and spicy Andhra meals. No bar. ③–④.

Eating

In addition to the hotel restaurants, plenty of "meals" places around town specialize in **Hyderabadi cuisine**, such as authentic *biryanis*, or the famously chilli-hot Andhra cuisine that often tends to have a sweeter to taste and to feature fruit blended into the spicy sauces.

Akbar, 1-7-190 MG Rd, Secunderabad. Hyderabadi cuisine at moderate prices.
Ashoka, 6-1-70 Lakdi-ka-Pul. Hotel with a/c *Saptagiri* cafeteria serving good-value South Indian snacks and some North Indian dishes.
Baseera, 9-1-167/168 Sarojini Devi Rd, Secunderabad. There are two restaurants within *Baseera*: the simply furnished *Daawat* serves veg South Indian snacks, breakfasts and North Indian food in the evenings. The posher *Mehfill* is heavy on Mughlai meat dishes with a few Chinese and Western choices thrown in. It also has a bar.
Haridwar, next to *The Residency*, Nampally High Rd. Excellent, tasty stand-up *dosas*, *vadai* and other snacks.
Sai Prakash, Station Rd. Two options to choose from here: the *Woodlands* serves good-value veg South Indian snacks and North Indian dishes. *Rich'n'Famous* is much posher and pricier, with comfy chairs and imaginative daily specials including crab, prawns and specialties from both Hyderabad and further afield.
Sher-e-Punjab, corner of Nampally High Rd and station entrance. Basic basement restaurant with good tasty North Indian food at cheap rates.
Taj Residency, Rd No. 1, Banjara Hills. The *Dakhni* restaurant inside the hotel serves excellent, pricey, authentic South Indian cuisine and Hyderabadi specialties.
Touch of Class, *Central Court*, Lakdi-ka-Pul. This place offers dining on good Hyderabadi non-veg plus some veg options and barbecue kebabs on a small patio; also Mughlai, Western and Chinese food. Lunch is a buffet, evenings are à la carte.

Listings

Airlines Air India, 5–9–193 HACA Bhavan (☎040/232747), opposite Public Garden Saitabad; Indian Airlines, opposite Assembly Saitabad (☎040/599333; general flight information ☎140; pre-recorded flight info ☎142;); Jet Airways, 6–3–1109/1 GF Nav Bharat Chambers, Raj Bhavan Rd (☎040/230978).
Banks and exchange For a state capital, most Indian banks in Hyderabad are surprisingly ill-equipped to carry out foreign exchange transactions. To change money, it's best to head for an agency such as Thomas Cook (☎040/231988) on AG Office Rd, or L.K.P. Merchant Financing on Public Gardens Rd, only ten minutes' walk north of Nampally station (both open Mon–Sat 9.30am–5.30pm).
Bookstores Higginbothams, 1 Lal Bahadur Stadium, Hyderabad; Gangarams, 62 DSD Rd, near *Garden Restaurant* in Secunderabad; and Kalaujal, Hill Fort Rd, opposite the Public Gardens, which specializes in art books. Both shops offer a wide selection of literature, non-fiction titles and reference books.
Car rental Air Travels in Banjora Hills (☎040/3355088) provides a 24hr service, with or without driver. Hertz is based at the *Hotel Viceroy*, Tank Bund (☎040/241175).
Crafts Utkalika (Government of Orissa handicrafts), House no. 60-1-67, between the Ravindra Bharati building and *Hotel Ashoka*, sells silver filigree jewellery, handloom cloth, *ikhat* tie-dye, Jagannath papier-mâché figures and buffalo-bone carvings. Cheneta Bhavan is a modern shopping complex a little south of the train station, stuffed with handloom cloth shops from various states, including Tamil Nadu, Uttar Pradesh, Rajasthan, Madhya Pradesh and Andhra Pradesh. For silks and saris, try Meena Bazaar, Pochampally Silks and Sarees, and Pooja Sarees, all on Tilak Rd.
Email Internet access is available at Modern Xerox (☎040/4603894; daily 9am–10pm), near the Ek-minar mosque, behind Nampally station, for Rs60 per half-hour.
Hospitals The government-run Gandhi Hospital is in Secunderabad (☎040/770 2222). The private CDR Hospital is in Himayatnagar (☎040/596100). As usual, there are plenty of English-speaking doctors in both.
Library The British Library, Secretariat Rd (Tues–Sat 10am–6pm; ☎040/230774) has a wide selection of books and recent British newspapers. You must be a member or a British citizen to get in.
Pharmacies Apollo Pharmacy (☎040/231380) and Health Pharmacy (☎040/210618) are both 24hr.
Police by the train station in Nampally, Hyderabad, or, call ☎040/230191.
Travel agents General agents for airline and private-bus tickets include: Alam Tours and Travels, 5-9-189/104 1st floor, Lenaine Estate, next to SBH Gunfoundry, Abids Rd (☎040/203761); Kamat Travels, in the *Hotel Sai Prakash* complex (☎040/4612096); Travel Corporation, 102 Regency House, 680 Somajiguda, Greenlands Rd (☎040/212722); all are in Hyderabad.

MOVING ON FROM HYDERABAD AND SECUNDERABAD

Daily **train** services from **Hyderabad train station (Nampally)** include: the *Charminar Express* #2760 to Chennai (7pm; 14hr); the *Hyderabad–Cochin Express* #7030 (11.30am; 27hr); the *Andhra Pradesh Express* #2723 (6.40am; 26hr) and *Secunderabad Rajdhani Express* #2437 to Delhi (7.20pm; 21hr 10min); the *Hyderabad–Mumbai Express* #7032 (8.40pm; 17hr); the *East Coast Express* #7046 to Calcutta (7am; 33hr) via Vijayawada (6hr), Vishakapatnam (13hr 30min) and Bhubaneshnar (23hr); and the *Rayasaleema Express* #7429 to Tirupati (4.45pm; 15hr). All northeast-bound services call at Warangal and most at Vijayawada. **From Secunderabad**, there are many through trains in all directions. Useful services include the *Secunderabad–Bangalore Express* #7685 (7.30pm; 13hr), and the *Kacheguda–Mandad Express* #7664 to Aurangabad (6pm; 13hr).

The **railways reservations office** (Mon–Sat 8am–2pm & 2.30–8pm, Sun 8am–2pm) is to the left as you enter the station. Counter #213 (next to enquiry counter) is supposedly for tourist reservations, but it's also used for group bookings and lost tickets. Foreign visitors can make bookings at the Chief Reservation inspector's office on platform 1 (daily 9am–5pm). All trains from Secunderabad can be booked from Hyderabad.

From the Central bus stand, **regular bus services** run to Amaravati (2 daily; 7hr), Bangalore (12 daily; 13hr), Bidar (19 daily; 3hr 30min), Chennai (1 daily; 16hr), Mumbai (8 daily; 17hr), Tirupati (7 daily; 12hr), Vijayawada (every 15 min daily; 6hr). Also various **deluxe and video coaches** depart for Bangalore, Chennai, Mumbai and other major destinations, from outside Nampally station where you will find a cluster of private agencies.

There are up to three daily flights to Bangalore (1hr; Indian Airlines, NEPC), at least five to Mumbai (1hr 15min; Indian Airlines, Jet), two daily to Delhi (2hr; Indian Airlines), two or three to Chennai (1hr; Indian Airlines), and one daily except Mon to Calcutta, via Bhubaneshwar on three of those days (1hr 55min; Indian Airlines). Air India (☎040/232747) also has flights to Mumbai, and a new service twice weekly direct to Singapore (2hr 30min).

Around Hyderabad

Heading north from Hyderabad towards the borders of Maharashtra and Madhya Pradesh, the landscape becomes greener and more hilly. There is little to detain visitors here except the small town of **Warangal**, conveniently situated on the main railway line as it loops across to the east, which warrants a stop to visit the nearby medieval fort and Shiva temple. Heading south from the capital, flat farmland stretches for miles into the centre of the state, where the Nagarjuna Sagar dam has created a major lake, with the important Buddhist site of **Nagarjunakonda**, now an island, in its midst.

Warangal

WARANGAL – "one stone" – 150km northeast of Hyderabad, was the Hindu capital of the Kakatiyan empire in the twelfth and thirteenth centuries. Like other Deccan cities, it changed hands many times between the Hindus and the Muslims – something that is reflected in its architecture and the remains you see today.

Warangal's **fort**, 4km south, is famous for its two circles of fortifications: the outer made of earth with a moat, and the inner of stone. Four roads into the centre meet at the ruined temple of **Svayambhu**, built in 1162 and dedicated to Shiva. At its southern, free-standing gateway, another Shiva temple, from the fourteenth century, is in much better shape; inside, the remains of an enormous *lingam* came originally from the Svayambhu shrine. Also inside the citadel is the **Shirab Khan**, or audience hall, an early eleventh-century building very similar to Mandu's Hindola Mahal.

The largely basalt Chalukyan-style "thousand-pillared" **Shiva temple**, just off the main road, beside the slopes of Hanamkonda Hill (6km north), was constructed by King Rudra Deva in 1163. A low-roofed building, on several stepped stages, it features superb carvings and three shrines to Vishnu, Shiva and Surya. They lead off the *mandapa* whose numerous finely carved columns give the temple its name. In front, a polished Nandi bull was carved out of a single stone. A Bhadrakali temple stands at the top of the hill.

Practicalities

If you make an early start, it's just about possible to visit Warangal in a day-trip from Hyderabad. Frequent buses and trains run to the site (2–3hr). Warangal's **bus stand** and **train station** are opposite each other, served by local buses and auto-rickshaws. The easiest way to cover the site is to **rent a bicycle** from one of the stalls on Station Rd (Rs2 per hr). As you follow Station Rd from the station, turn left for the fort just beyond the post office, under the railway bridge and left again at the next main road. For Hanamkonda turn right at the next main junction after the post office, left at the next major crossroads, and right at the end on to the Hanamkonda main road. The temple and hill are on the left.

Accommodation is limited; the *Hotel Ashok* on Main Rd, Hanamkonda, 6km from the train station and bus stand(☎08712/85491; ③–⑤), has a/c rooms, a restaurant and bar, while basic lodges near the train station on Station Rd include the *Vijaya* (☎08712/25851; ①), which is the closest and best value, and *Venkateshwara* (☎08712/26455; ①). The slightly posher *Hotel Ratna* (☎08712/60645; ③–④) is further down on MG Rd.

Nagarjunakonda

NAGARJUNAKONDA, or "Nagarjuna's Hill", 166km south of Hyderabad and 175km west of Vijayawada, is all that now remains of the vast area, rich in archeological sites, submerged when the huge Nagarjuna Sagar Dam was built across the Krishna River in 1960. Ancient settlements in the valley were first discovered in 1926; extensive excavations carried out between 1954 and 1960 uncovered more than one hundred sites dating from the early Stone Age to late medieval times. Nagarjunakonda was once the summit of a hill, where a fort towered 200m above the valley floor; now it's just a small oblong island near the middle of Nagarjuna Sagar Lake, accessible by boat from the mainland. Several Buddhist monuments have been reconstructed, in an operation reminiscent of that at Abu Simbel in Egypt, and a **museum** exhibits the more remarkable ruins of the valley. **VIJAYAPURI**, the village on the shore of the lake, overlooks the colossal dam itself, which stretches for almost 2km. Torrents of water flushed through its 26 flood-gates produce electricity for the whole region, and irrigate an area of almost 800 square kilometres. Many villages had to be relocated to higher ground when the valley was flooded.

The island and the museum

Boats arrive on the northeastern edge of Nagarjunakonda island, unloading passengers at what remains of one of the gates of the fort, built in the fourteenth century and considerably renovated by the Vijayanagar kings in the mid-sixteenth century. Low, damaged stone walls skirting the island mark the edge of the fort, and you can see ground-level remains of the Hindu temples that served its inhabitants.

Well-kept gardens lie between the jetty and the museum, beyond which nine Buddhist monuments from various sites in the valley have been rebuilt. West of the jetty, there's a reconstructed bathing *ghat*, built entirely of limestone during the reigns of the Ikshvaku kings (third century AD). A series of levels and steps leads to the water's edge; boards etched into some of its slabs were probably used for dice games.

The **maha-chaitya**, or *stupa*, constructed at the command of King Chamtula's sister in the third century AD, is the earliest Buddhist structure in the area. It was raised over relics of the Buddha – said to include a tooth – and has been reassembled in the southwest of the island. Nearby, a towering **statue** of the Buddha stands draped in robes beside a ground plan of a monastery that enshrines a smaller **stupa.** Other *stupas* stand nearby; the brick walls of the *svastika chaitya* have been arranged in the shape of swastikas, common emblems in early Buddhist iconography.

In the **museum** (daily except Fri 9am–5pm), **Buddhist sculptures** include large stone friezes decorated with scenes from the Buddha's life: his birth; his mother's vision of an elephant and a lotus blossom; his renunciation, and his subversion of evil as he meditated and realized enlightenment under the *bodhi* tree. Twelve statues of standing Buddhas – one of which reaches 3m – show the Buddha in various postures of teaching or meditation. Many pillars are undamaged, profusely carved with Buddha images, bowing devotees, elephants and lotus medallions.

Earlier artefacts include stone tools and pots from the Neolithic age (third millennium BC), and metal axe heads and knives (first millennium BC). Among later finds are several inscribed pillars from Ikshvaku times, recording in Prakrit or Sanskrit the installation of Buddhist monasteries and statues. The final phase of art at Nagarjunakonda is represented by sculptures: a thirteenth-century *tirthankara* (Jain saint), a seventeenth-century Ganesh and Nandi, and a set of eighteenth-century statues of Shiva and Shakti, his female consort. Also on display is a model showing the excavated sites in the valley.

Practicalities

Organized **APTDC tours** from Hyderabad to Nagarjunakonda (see box on p.502), taking in the sites and museum, the nearby Ethiopothala waterfalls and an engraved third-century Buddhist monolith known as the Pylon, can be a bit rushed: if you want to spend more time in the area you can take a bus from the Central bus stand in Hyderabad (4hr; all the regular Macherla services stop at Vijayapuri) or Vijayawada (6hr; a direct service runs daily at 11am and frequent services leave from Guntur). It can be quicker to change at Macherla.

Accommodation at Vijayapuri is limited, and you need to decide in advance where you are going to stay to know where to get off the bus, as there are two distinct settlements 6km apart on either side of the dam. For easy access to the sites it is better to stay near the jetty on the right bank of the dam. Ask the bus to leave you at the launch station. The drab-looking concrete *Nagarjuna Motel Complex* (☎08642/78188; ②) has adequate rooms and some a/c. Five hundred metres away in the village, the *Golden Lodge* (☎08642/78148; ①) is much more basic. Both APTDC places are on the other side of the dam approaching the lake from the direction of Hyderabad. The APTDC *Vijay Vihar Complex* (☎08680 /76633; ③), which has spacious rooms with balconies and a good restaurant, is 2km further up the hill from the APTDC project house(☎08680/76540; ②) in the left bank village. However, if you want to stay in these more comfortable surroundings, there is a frequent shuttle bus to the right bank and it is a pleasant walk to the dam and lake shore.

Tickets for **boats** to the island (daily 9am & 1.30pm; 45min; Rs 20) are on sale 25 minutes before departure. Each boat leaves the island ninety minutes after it arrives, which allows reasonable time to see the museum and walk briskly round the monuments, but if you want to take your time and soak up the pleasant atmosphere without the crowds from the boat, take the morning boat and return in the afternoon. A cafeteria on the island serves drinks and occasionally biscuits, but only opens when the boat is in, so take provisions.

Eastern Andhra Pradesh

Perhaps India's least visited area, eastern Andhra Pradesh is sandwiched between the Bay of Bengal in the east and the red soil and high peaks of the Eastern Ghats in the north. Its one architectural attraction is the ancient Buddhist site of **Amaravati**, near the city of **Vijayawada**, whose sprinkling of historic temples is far overshadowed by impersonal, modern buildings. Some 350km north, the major port of **Vishakapatnam** is not as grim as it first seems, but it's not a place to linger. For anyone with a strong desire to explore, however, pockets of natural beauty along the coast and in the hills of eastern Andhra Pradesh can offer rich reward. In this sleepy landscape, little affected by modernization, bullocks amble between swaying palms and the rice fields are viridescent against rusty sands. However, unless you have the patience to endure the excruciatingly slow public transport system, your own vehicle is essential.

Vijayawada

Almost 450km north of Chennai, a third of the way to Calcutta, **VIJAYAWADA** is a bustling commercial centre on the banks of the Krishna delta, hemmed in by bare granite outcrops 90km from the coast. This unattractive city is seldom visited by tourists, but it does, however, make the obvious stop-off point for visits to the third-century Buddhist site at **Amaravati**, 60km west.

A handful of temples in Vijayawada merit a quick look. The most important, raised on the low Indrakila Hill in the east, is dedicated to the city's patron goddess **Kanaka Durga** (also known as Vijaya), goddess of riches, power and benevolence. Though it is believed to be thousands of years old, what you see today, with the exception of a few pillared halls and intricate carvings, is largely renovated (and freshly whitewashed). Across the river, roughly 3km out of town, there's an ancient, unmodified cave temple at **Undavalli**, a tiny rural village set off the main road, easily reached on any Guntur-bound bus, or the local #13 service. The temple is cut out of the granite hillside in typical Pallava style: simple, solid and bold. Each of its five levels contains a deep low-roofed hall, with small rock-cut shrines to Vishnu, Shiva and Parvati, and pillared verandahs guarded by sturdy grey statues of gods, saints and lions. Views from the porches take in a sublime patchwork of rivulets, paddy fields and banana plantations.

Practicalities

Vijayawada's **train station**, on the main Chennai–Calcutta line, is in the centre of town. Buses arriving from Vishakapatnam, Guntur, Amaravati, Hyderabad and as far afield as Chennai pull into the **bus stand** further east, where specific ticket offices cater for each service, and a **tourist office**, has details on local hotels and sights.

Vijayawada is a major business centre, with a good selection of mid-range **hotels**, all less than 2km from the train station and bus stand. Most have reasonably priced restaurants serving Andhra *thalis* and Western food. Budget options include *Monika Lodge* (☎0866/571334; ②), just off Elluru Rd about 500m from the bus stand: very simple, and slightly grubby. Two better-value places, both on Hanumanpet, which links the train station to Elluru Rd, are the *Hotel Narayana Swamy* (☎0866/571221; ③) and the *Sri Ram* (☎0866/579377; ③) with simple clean rooms. The smartest option is the modern *Hotel Swarna Palace* (☎0866/577222; ⑥) on Elluru Rd at the junction with Hanumanpet. The rooms are comfortably furnished, and have satellite TV; the fourth-floor restaurant provides large portions of Indian, Chinese and continental food with city views and something of a disco atmosphere. The *Raj Towers* (☎0866/571311; ④–⑤), also on Elluru Rd, is a tall modern building with good mid-range rooms.

Guntur

Another sprawling and bustling commercial city 30km southwest of Vijayawada, **GUNTUR** has no merits of its own but makes an even more convenient jumping-off point for Amaravati than Vijayawada, especially if coming from the area of Nagarjuna Sagar. There are buses every ten to fifteen minutes to Vijayawada (45min–1hr), and every half hour to Amaravati from the old bus stand (adjacent to the main bus stand). If you decide to spend the night here, there are some perfectly adequate lodges right opposite the bus stands. *Annapurna Lodge* (☎0863/356493; ②) has decent-sized clean rooms and some a/c; *Padmasri Lodge* (☎0863/223813; ②) also has a/c and cheaper singles.

Amaravati

AMARAVATI, a small village on the banks of the Krishna River 30km west of Vijayawada, is the site of a Buddhist settlement, formerly known as Chintapalli, where a *stupa* larger than those at Sanchi was erected over relics of the Buddha in the third century BC, during the reign of Ashoka. The *stupa* no longer stands, but its great size is evident from the large mound that formed its base. It was originally surrounded by grey stone railings with a gateway at each of the cardinal points, one of which has been reconstructed in an open courtyard. Its decoration, meticulously carved and perfectly preserved, shows the themes represented on all such Buddhist monuments: the Buddha's birth, renunciation and life as an emaciated ascetic, enlightenment under the *bodhi* tree (see p.568), his first sermon in the Deer Park, and *parinirvana*, or death. Several foundation stones of monastic quarters remain on the site.

Exhibits at the small but fascinating **museum** (daily except Fri 10am–5pm) range in date from the third century BC to the twelfth century AD. They include statues of the Buddha, with lotus symbols on his feet, a head of tightly curled hair, and long ear lobes, all traditional indications of an enlightened teacher. Earlier stone carvings represent the Buddha through such symbols as the *chakra* (wheel of *dharma*), a throne, a *stupa*, a flaming pillar or a *bodhi* tree – all being worshipped. The lotus motif, a central symbol in early Buddhism, is connected with a dream the Buddha's mother had shortly after conception, and has always been a Buddhist symbol of essential purity: it appears repeatedly on railings and pillars. Later sculptures include limestone statues of the goddess Tara and *bodhisattva* Padmapani, both installed at the site in medieval times when the community had adopted Mahayana teachings in place of the earlier Hinayana doctrines. What you see here are some of the finer pieces excavated from the site – other remains have been taken to the Madras Government Museum and the British Museum in London.

Practicalities

Theoretically **buses** run hourly from Vijaywada to Amaravati but the service seems to be unreliable, so it's best to take a bus to Guntur (every 15min; 45min–1hr), where you can pick up a connection to Amaravati (1hr–1hr 30min). Buses return to Guntur every half-hour, and during the monsoon **boats** gather at the jetty in Amaravati and follow the Krishna River all the way to Vijayawada. Organized tours run from the APTDC *Krishnaveni Motel*, next to the main bridge, on the south bank of the Krishna in Vijiyawada, to Amaravati and back for Rs50 when the river is high enough. The excavated site and museum are roughly 1km from the bus stand. Tri-shaws – miniature carts attached to tricycles and brightly painted with chubby film stars – take tourists to the site and the river bank, where there are several drink stalls. There is an excellent little APTDC *Tourism Guest House* (☎08645/65332; ②) on the banks of the Krishna beside the attractive Sri Amareshwara Swamy temple at the far end of the main street. Some rooms have a river view and there's an inexpensive dorm and canteen.

Vishakapatnam and around

One of India's most rapidly growing industrial cities, and its fourth largest port, **VISHAKAPATNAM** (aka Vizag), 350km north of Vijayawada, is a big unpleasant city choked with the smells and dirt of a busy shipbuilding industry, an oil plant and a steel factory. Such is its sprawl that it has overtaken and polluted much of the neighbouring town of Waltair, once a health resort. Although there's little to warrant a stop at Vishakapatnam, the district of Waltair with its uncrowded treelined roads and attractive seafront make for a pleasant stroll. If you head that way, you can visit the modest collection of art and sculpture at the Visakha museum, (Tues–Sun 4–8pm; Rs1.50) on Beach Rd near the *Hotel Park*. The beach around here is far enough from the port for the sea to be reasonably clean, though the best beach for swimming is at Kalshagiri further north, reached by regular buses from the RTC complex.

Various traces of older civilizations lie within a day's journey of the city. At **Bheemunipatnam**, 30km north, you can see the remains of a Dutch fort and a peculiar cemetery where slate-grey pyramidal tombs are abandoned to nature. **Borra**, 70km inland on a minor road that winds through the Eastern Ghats and the Araku forests, boasts a set of eerie limestone caves whose darkness is pierced with age-old stalactites and stalagmites (daily 10am–12.30pm & 2–5pm; Rs10). You'll need a car to get to **Mukhalingam**, 100km north of Bheemunipatnam, where three Shaivite temples, built between the sixth and twelfth centuries, rest in low hills. Their elaborate carvings and well-preserved towering *shikharas* display slight local variations to the otherwise standard Orissan style. There's nowhere to stay in Mukhalingam.

Practicalities

Vishakapatnam's **train station**, on the Chennai–Calcutta coastal route, is in the old town, towards the port. The ride to Delhi takes a tedious two days. The **bus stand**, known as RTC Complex, is in a newer area, 3km from the coast. There's an **airport**, 12km west of town, with daily connections to Hyderabad and Mumbai, and several weekly to Calcutta and Bhubaneshwar. Bus #38 runs from the airport to the centre. Irregular **ships** make the three-day crossing from here to Port Blair on the Andaman Islands.

The **tourist office** (Mon–Sat 10.30am–5pm; ☎0891/546446) at the Vuda complex, Siripuram, is difficult to find and only of use if you want to book a tour: city tour (daily 8.30am–6pm; Rs65) or Borra caves (daily 7am–9pm; Rs165 including lunch); this can be done more easily in any case at the APTDC booth in the RTC complex. The Andhra Bank near the RTC complex will **change money**.

If you arrive late by bus, head for the well-maintained **retiring rooms** (①) in the bus stand. Otherwise, most **hotels** are in the old town, near the train station: turn right out of the station and walk for a few minutes. The best is *Hotel Karanths*, 33-1-55 Patel Marg (☎0891/502048; ②–④), whose spotless rooms have balconies, pressed sheets, colour TV and attached bathrooms. The downstairs restaurant serves unbeatable *thalis* and tiffin at low prices. Next door, *Dakshayani* (☎0891/561798; ①) offers simple grotty rooms, some with private bathrooms. Round the corner in Bowdara Rd, the *Sri Ganesh Hotel* (☎0891/563274; ②) is a better budget option with simple clean rooms. Vishakapatnam's nicest upmarket hotel, the *Park* on Beach Rd (☎0891/554488; ⑧), has luxurious rooms, a swimming pool, a bar, restaurant, and access to the beach. Adjacent to the *Park* is the smart *Palm Beach* (☎0891/554026; ⑥), which also offers full amenities.

Southern Andhra Pradesh

The further south you travel from the fertile lands watered by the great Krishna and Godavari rivers, the less hospitable the terrain becomes, especially in the rocky southwest of the state. For Hindus, the main attraction in southern Andhra Pradesh is the tenth-century **Shri Venkateshvara temple**, outside **Tirupati**, the most popular Vishnu shrine in India, where millions of pilgrims come each year to receive *darshan*. **Puttaparthy**, the home town of the spiritual leader Sai Baba, is the only other place in the region to attract significant numbers of visitors, mostly devotees of the guru from many parts of India and the world. Both Tirupati and Puttaparthy are closer to Bangalore and Chennai than to other points in Andhra Pradesh, and for many tourists, constitute their only foray into the state.

Tirupati

Set in a stunning position, surrounded by wooded hills capped by a ring of vertical red rocks, the **Shri Venkateshvara temple** at Tirumala, an enervating drive 700m up in the Venkata hills, 11km from **TIRUPATI** and 170km northwest of Chennai, is said to be the richest and most popular place of pilgrimage in the world, drawing more devotees than either Rome or Mecca. Apart from the main temple, other shrines like the **Ganesh temple** at the foot of the hill and the **Tiruchanur Padmavati temple** are also firmly on the pilgrim trail and so the whole area around Tirumala Hill provides a fascinating insight into contemporary Hinduism practised on a large scale. If you are not particularly keen on waiting in line for hours at a time, choose the day of your visit with care; avoid weekends, public and school holidays, and particularly special festivals, at which times you are likely to meet at least 10,000 other visitors.

Arrival and information

The best way of **getting to Tirupati** is by train from Chennai; the trip can be done in a day if you get the earliest of the three daily services (3hr 30min). From Hyderabad it takes sixteen hours. An information counter at the **train station** is accessible from the entrance hall and platform 1, where there's a 24-hour left-luggage office and a self-service veg refreshment room. Stands sell English copies of TKT Viraraghava Charya's *History of Tirupati*, and there's a Vivekananda religious bookshop next door. Tirupati's APSRTC Central **bus station** – also with 24-hour left luggage – is about 1km from the train station. Frequent express services run from Chennai (4hr), but the train is far more comfortable. However, if you're travelling south and want to avoid Chennai, there are three buses daily to Mamallapuram (7hr) via Kanchipuram (5hr). Local transport is provided by beautifully decorated **cycle-rickshaws**, with silver backs, colourfully painted, some with coverings of appliquéd cloth.

To avoid waiting in line for a bus to Tirumala and the Venkateshvara temple, try and catch one of the earliest services before 7am (though bear in mind that on Fridays there's no special *darshan* until 10am). An easier option is to take a **taxi**, best organized through the APTDC **tourist counter** at the train station; avoid the unlicensed taxis outside the station as they could be stopped by the Tirumala police. The tourist office also run a tour (9.45am–5.30pm; Rs70 not including entrance tickets) which takes in Chandragiri fort (except Fri) and a number of temples, but does not include the Venkateshvara temple owing to the long queues. The only other tourist office, also APTDC, is two blocks behind the station (☎08574/25602) but it makes more sense to stick with the one inside.

Govindarajaswamy temple

Just a five-minute walk from the train station, the one temple in Tirupati itself definitely worth a visit is Govindarajaswamy, whose modern grey *gopura* is clearly visible from many points in town. Begun by the Nayaks in the sixteenth century, it is an interesting complex with large open courtyards decorated with lion sculptures and some ornately carved wooden roofing. The temple's inner sanctum is open to non-Hindus and contains a splendid large black reclining Vishnu, coated in bronze armour and bedecked in flowers. The *sanadarsanan* (daily 9.30am–12.30pm; Rs5) will let you in to glimpse the deity, and participate in fire blessings at the main and subsidiary shrines.

Tucked away at the back of the complex, just inside the south *gopura*, there is also the Venkateshvara Museum of Temple Arts. Set in a colonnaded compound, the single hall displays photographs, models and diagrams of buildings and various ritual objects.

Tiruchanur Padmavati temple

Between Tirupati and Tirumala Hill, the **Tiruchanur Padmavati temple** is another popular pilgrimage halt. A gold *vimana* tower with lions at each corner surmounts the sanctuary, which contains a black stone image of goddess Lakshmi with one silver eye. At the front step, water sprays wash the feet of the devotees. A Rs5 ticket allows you to jump the line to enter the sanctuary. If you'd like to donate a sari to the goddess, you may do so, on payment of Rs1200. Cameras are prohibited.

Tirumala Hill, the Venkateshvara temple and Kapilateertham

There's good reason for the small shrine to Ganesh at the foot of **Tirumala Hill**. The journey up is hair-raising and it's worth saying a quick prayer when embarking on it. Overtaking is strictly forbidden, but drivers do anyway; virtually every bend is labelled "blind" and every instruction to drive slowly is blithely ignored. The fearless sit on the left for the best views; the most devout, of course, climb the hill by foot. When you get to the top, you will see barbers busying themselves giving pilgrims tonsures as part of their devotions. Non-Hindus are permitted to enter the inner sanctum, but for everyone, *darshan*, a view of the god, is the briefest of brief experiences. Temple funds support a university, hospital, orphanages and schools at Tirupati as well as providing cheap, and in some cases free, accommodation for pilgrims.

The **Venkateshvara temple**, dedicated to **Vishnu** and started in the tenth century, has been recently renovated to provide facilities for the thousands of pilgrims who visit daily; a rabbit warren of passages and waiting rooms wind their way around the complex in which pilgrims interminably shuffle towards the inner sanctum. Unless your visit is intended to be particularly rigorous, on reaching the temple you should follow the signs for the special *darshan* that costs Rs50 (usually 6–10am and noon–9pm). This will reduce the time it takes to get inside by hours, if not days. You have to sign a declaration of faith in Lord Venkateshvara and give your passport number. There is a seated waiting area.

Once inside, you'll see the somewhat incongruous sight of *brahmins* sitting at video monitors, observing the goings-on in the inner sanctum; the constant to-ing and fro-ing includes temple attendants bringing in supplies, truckloads of oil and other comestibles, and huge cooking pots being carried across the courtyard. You may also catch deities being hauled past on palanquins to the accompaniment of *nagesvaram* (a South Indian oboe-like double-reed wind instrument) and *tavil* drum, complete with an armed guard. At the entrance is a colonnade, lined with life-sized statues of royal patrons, in copper or stone. The *gopura* gateway leading to the inner courtyard is decorated with sheets of embossed silver; a gold *stambha* (flagstaff) stands outside the inner shrine next to a gold upturned lotus on a plinth. Outside, opposite the temple, is a small museum, the **Hall of Antiquities** (daily 8am–8pm). Your special *darshan* ticket entitles you to enter the museum via a shorter queue opposite the exit and to pick up two free *laddu* sweets. **Kapilateertham**, a temple at the bottom of the hill, has a gaily painted little Hindu pleasure garden at the entrance; after the rains, a powerful waterfall crashes into a large tank surrounded by colonnades, and everyone piles in for a bath, with typically good-natured pilgrim bedlam ensuing.

Chandragiri Fort

In the sixteenth century, **Chandragiri**, 11km southwest of Tirupati, became the third capital of the Vijayanagars, whose power had declined following the fall of the city of Vijayanagar (Hampi) in Karnataka. It was here that the British negotiated the acquisition of the land to establish Fort St George, the earliest settlement at what is now Chennai. The original fort, thought to date from *c*.1000 AD, was taken over by Haider Ali in 1782, followed by the British in 1792. A small **museum** of sculpture, weapons and memorabilia (daily except Fri 10am–5pm; Rs2) is housed in the main building, the Indo-Saracenic Raja Mahal. Another building, the **Rani Mahal**, stands close by, while behind that is a hill with two free-standing boulders that was used as a place of public execution during Vijayanagar times. A small temple from the Krishna Deva Raya period and a freshwater tank stand at the top of the hill behind the Raja Mahal.

Accommodation and eating

Unless you're a pilgrim seeking accommodation in the *dharamshalas* near the temple, all the decent places to stay are in Tirupati, near the railway and bus stand. The *Bhima* chain are probably the best-maintained hotels in town. **Eating** is recommended in the bigger hotels, although there are, of course, cheap "meals" places in town and near the temple.

Bhimas Deluxe, 34–38 G Car St, near train station (☎08574/25521). Decent, comfortable rooms (all a/c). *Maya* veg restaurant serves South Indian snacks in the morning, and North Indian plus some Chinese dishes in the evenings. Very reasonable prices. ⑥.

Bhimas Paradise, Renigunta Rd (☎08574/25747). Spotless, functional rooms (pristine leatherette but no carpet), some a/c, and tiny balconies. satellite TV, pool, garden, 24hr coffee shop. The restaurant, *Bharani*, is clean and dark, serving veg South Indian snacks, *thalis* and North Indian dishes. ⑤–⑥.

Indira Rest House, Tiruchanur Rd (☎08574/231125), a few minutes' walk behind the railway lines from the bus stand. Basic no-nonsense lodge. ②.

Mayura, 209 TP Area (☎08574/25251). Well-maintained hotel with some a/c rooms, satellite TV, exchange and travel desk. *Surya* restaurant serves South Indian breakfast and North Indian evening meals. ⑤–⑥.

Mini Bhimas, Railway Station Rd (☎08574/25930). No-frills bottom of the range lodge. ②.

Raghunadha, 191 Railway Station Rd (☎08574/23130). Good simple clean lodge; one of the better cheap places. ②–③.

Vishnu Priya, opposite Central bus stand (☎08574/25070). Dilapidated rooms (some a/c with TV) with views over the bus stand. Veg food, and travel desk. US$ travellers' cheques accepted. ④–⑤.

Puttaparthy

Deep in the southwest of the state, amid the arid rocky hills bordering Karnataka, a thriving community has grown up around the once insignificant village of **PUTTAPARTHY**, birthplace of spiritual leader Sai Baba, whose followers believe him to be the new incarnation of God. Indeed, you will not be in the town long before being greeted by the oft-heard salutation of "Sai Ram". Centring on **Prasanthi Nilayam**, the ashram where Sai Baba resides from July to March, the town has schools, a university, a hospital and sports centre which offer up-to-date, free services to all. There's even a small airport. The **ashram** itself is a huge complex with room for thousands, canteens, shops, a museum and library, and a vast assembly hall where Sai Baba gives *darshan* twice daily (6.40am & 3pm). Queues start more than an hour before the appointed time, and a lottery decides who gets to sit near the front.

The **museum** (daily 10am–noon), situated up a small hill to the left after entering the main gates, is undoubtedly the most interesting place for the casual visitor. The ground floor contains a detailed, fascinating display on the **major faiths** with illustrations and quotations from their sacred texts, punctuated by Sai Baba's comments. These are invariably intended to point out the underlying unity of the different belief systems. The first floor has more colourful exhibits, focusing on various places of worship and one dedicated to Sai Baba's predecessor, the Shirdi Sai Baba (see box below). Finally, the third floor displays bring the animistic tribal religions of Africa into the universal fold, as well as the beliefs and philosophy of the ancient Greeks. It is noteworthy that the divinity of Socrates is accorded special emphasis.

Practicalities

Puttaparthy is most accessible from Bangalore in Karnataka (see p.182), from where seven daily **buses** (4hr) run to the stand outside the ashram entrance. The town is also connected to Hyderabad (3 daily; 10hr) and Chennai (1 nightly; 11hr). Regular buses make the 42-kilometre run to **Dharmavaram**, the nearest **railhead**, which has good services north and south. There are also two **flights** a week from Mumbai and Chennai.

Most visitors **stay** at the ashram in large bare sheds or smaller rooms if available. Except in the case of families, accommodation is strictly segregated by sex, as are meals and *darshan*. Overt socializing is discouraged and there is a strict policy of lights-out at 9pm. Costs are minimal, and though you can't book in advance, you can enquire about availability at the secretary's office (☎08555/87583). Space is only usually a problem around the time of Sai Baba's birthday in late November. If you do want to stay, you have to register by filling out forms and surrendering your passport at the office before being allocated a bed by the Public Relations Officer. Your passport is returned after

SHRI SATYA SAI BABA

Born **Satyanarayana Raju** on November 23, 1926 in Puttaparthy, then an obscure village in the Madras Presidency, Satya is reported to have shown prodigious talents and unusual purity and compassion from an early age. His apparently supernatural abilities initially caused some concern to his family, who took him to Vedic doctors and eventually to be exorcised. Having been pronounced to be possessed by the divine rather than the diabolical, at the age of fourteen, he calmly announced that he was the new incarnation of **Sai Baba**, a saint from Shirdi in Maharashtra who died eight years before Satya was born.

Gradually his fame spread, and a large following grew. In 1950 the **ashram** was inaugurated and a decade later Sai Baba was attracting international attention; today he has millions of devotees worldwide, a considerable number of whom turn out for his birthday celebrations in Puttaparthy, when he delivers a message to his devotees. His smiling, diminutive, saffron-clad figure is seen on posters, framed photos and murals all over South India. Though his **miraculous powers** reportedly include the ability to materialize *vibhuti* – sacred ash – with curative properties, Sai Baba claims this to be an unimportant activity, aimed at those firmly entrenched in materialism, and emphasizes instead his message of **universal love**. Indeed, he prefers the ash to be seen as a representation of the final condition of worldly things and the desire to give them up in search of the divine. Whatever your feelings about the divinity of Sai Baba, the atmosphere around the ashram is undeniably peaceful, and the growth of such a vibrant community in this once-forgotten backwater is no small miracle in itself.

attending the first orientation session. Outside the ashram, many of the basic lodges are rather overpriced. However, the *Sai Ganesh Guest House* near the police station (☎08555/87079; ②) is friendly and a good cheap option. The new, great-value *Sri Sai Sadam* is at the far end of the main street (☎08555/87507; ③–④); all rooms have fridge, TV and balcony with views of the countryside or the ashram, and there's a meditation room and rooftop restaurant. At the top end, the all a/c *Sai Towers*, near the ashram entrance (☎0855/87270; ⑦) charges a lot for its smallish rooms, but has a good restaurant downstairs. Even non-residents can **eat** in the ashram canteen, and there are simple snack stalls along the main street.

travel details

Note that no individual route appears more than once in this chart; for any specific journey, check against where you want to get to as well as where you're coming from. Bear in mind, also, that there is only room here for a general summary; see the Moving On sections in specific cities for more details.

Trains

Hyderabad/Secunderabad to: Bangalore (3 daily; 11hr 25min–15hr 50min); Calcutta (2 daily; 27hr–33hr 15min); Chennai (2 daily; 14hr); Delhi (3–4 daily; 21hr 10min–32hr 50min); Mumbai (3 daily; 14–17hr); Tirupati (2 daily; 12hr 15min–15hr); Vijayawada (7 daily; 6–7hr); Vishakhapatnam (5 daily; 11hr 30min–14hr); Warangal (7 daily; 2hr–2hr 50min).

Tirupati to: Chennai (5 daily; 3–5hr); Tiruchirappalli (1 daily; 14hr 10min); Varanasi (1 daily; 36hr); Vijayawada (3 daily; 7hr 40min–8hr 45min).

Vijayawada to: Calcutta (10 daily; 21hr 30min–27hr); Chennai (14 daily; 6hr 30min–8hr); Delhi (5–6 daily; 24– 34hr); Vishakhapatnam (12 daily; 7–8hr).

Vishakhapatnam to: Bhubaneshwar (10 daily; 7hr–8hr 30min); Calcutta (10 daily; 14–19hr); Chennai (12 daily; 13hr 30min–16hr); Delhi (1–2 daily; 29hr–36hr 30min).

Buses

Hyderabad to: Amaravati (2 daily; 7hr); Bangalore (12 daily; 13hr); Bidar (19 daily; 3hr 30min); Chennai (1 daily; 16hr); Mumbai (8 daily; 17hr); Puttaparthy (3 daily; 10hr); Tirupati (7 daily; 12hr); Vijayawada (daily every 15min; 6hr); Vijayapuri (10 daily; 4hr); Warangal (35 daily; 3hr).

Tirupati to: Chennai (half-hourly; 4hr); Kanchipuram (3 daily; 5hr); Mamallapuram (3 daily; 7hr); Puttaparthy (1 daily; 10hr).

Vijayawada to: Amaravati (hourly; 2hr); Guntur (every 15min; 1hr–1hr 30 min).

Flights

Hyderabad to: Bangalore (3–4 daily; 1hr); Calcutta (1–3 daily; 2hr–3hr 10min); Chennai (3–4 daily; 1hr–1hr 45min); Delhi (2 daily; 2hr); Mumbai (5–7 daily; 1hr 15min); Vishakhapatnam (6 weekly; 1hr).

Puttaparthy to: Chennai (2 weekly; 55min); Mumbai (2 weekly; 1hr 20min).

Vishakhapatnam to: Calcutta (3 weekly; 1hr 20min); Chennai (3 weekly; 1hr 5min); Mumbai (4 weekly; 3hr 30min).

CHAPTER EIGHT

THE ANDAMAN ISLANDS

India's most remote state, the **ANDAMAN ISLANDS**, lies over 1000km off the east coast in the middle of the Bay of Bengal, connected to the mainland by flights and ferries from Calcutta, Chennai and Vishakapatnam. Thickly covered by deep green tropical forest, the archipelago supports a profusion of wildlife, including some extremely rare species of bird, but the principal attraction for tourists lies offshore, around the pristine reefs ringing most of the islands. Filled with colourful fish and kaleidoscopic corals, the crystal-clear waters of the Andaman Sea feature among the world's richest and least spoilt marine reserves – perfect for snorkelling and scuba diving.

For administrative purposes, the Andamans are grouped with the **Nicobar Islands**, 200km further south but, as yet, strictly off-limits to foreigners. Approximately two hundred islands make up the Andaman group and nineteen the Nicobar. They are islands of varying size, the summits of a submarine mountain range stretching 755km from the Arakan Yoma chain in Burma to the fringes of Sumatra in the south. All but the most remote of these are populated in parts by **indigenous tribes** whose numbers have been slashed dramatically as a result of nineteenth-century European settlement and, more recently, rampant **deforestation**. Today felling is supposed to be restricted, and 86 percent of the islands' forest is officially "protected". Nevertheless, *padauk* and teak are still extensively used for building materials, furniture and tourist knick-knacks, and those areas of woodland that are still open to the lumberjacks are being stripped of valuable foreign-currency-earning timber ahead of the all-out ban on extraction, expected in the next few years.

Foreign tourists are only permitted to visit certain parts of the **Andaman** group, separated by the deep Ten Degree Channel from the **Nicobar Islands**. The point of arrival for boats and planes is **South Andaman**, where the predominantly Tamil and Bengali community in the small but busy capital, **Port Blair**, accounts for almost half the total population. **Permits** obtainable on the mainland or on arrival are granted for a stay of one month. The most beautiful beaches and coral reefs are found on outlying islands. A healthy get-up-and-go spirit is essential if you plan to explore these, as connections and transport can be erratic, frequently uncomfortable and severely limited, especially on the smaller islands. Once away from the settlements, you enter a Coca-Cola-free zone where you'll need your own camping supplies and equipment. It's also worth pointing out that a surprising number of travellers fall sick in the Andamans. The dense tree cover, marshy swamps and high rainfall combine to provide the perfect breeding ground for mosquitoes, and **malaria** is endemic in even the most remote settlements.

ACCOMMODATION PRICE CODES

All **accommodation prices** in this book have been coded using the symbols below. The prices given are for a double room, except in the case of categories ① and ② where the price can refer to dorm accommodation per bed. All taxes are included. For more details, see p.34.

① up to Rs100
② Rs100–200
③ Rs200–300
④ Rs300–400
⑤ Rs400–600
⑥ Rs600–900
⑦ Rs900–1500
⑧ Rs1500–2500
⑨ Rs2500 and upwards

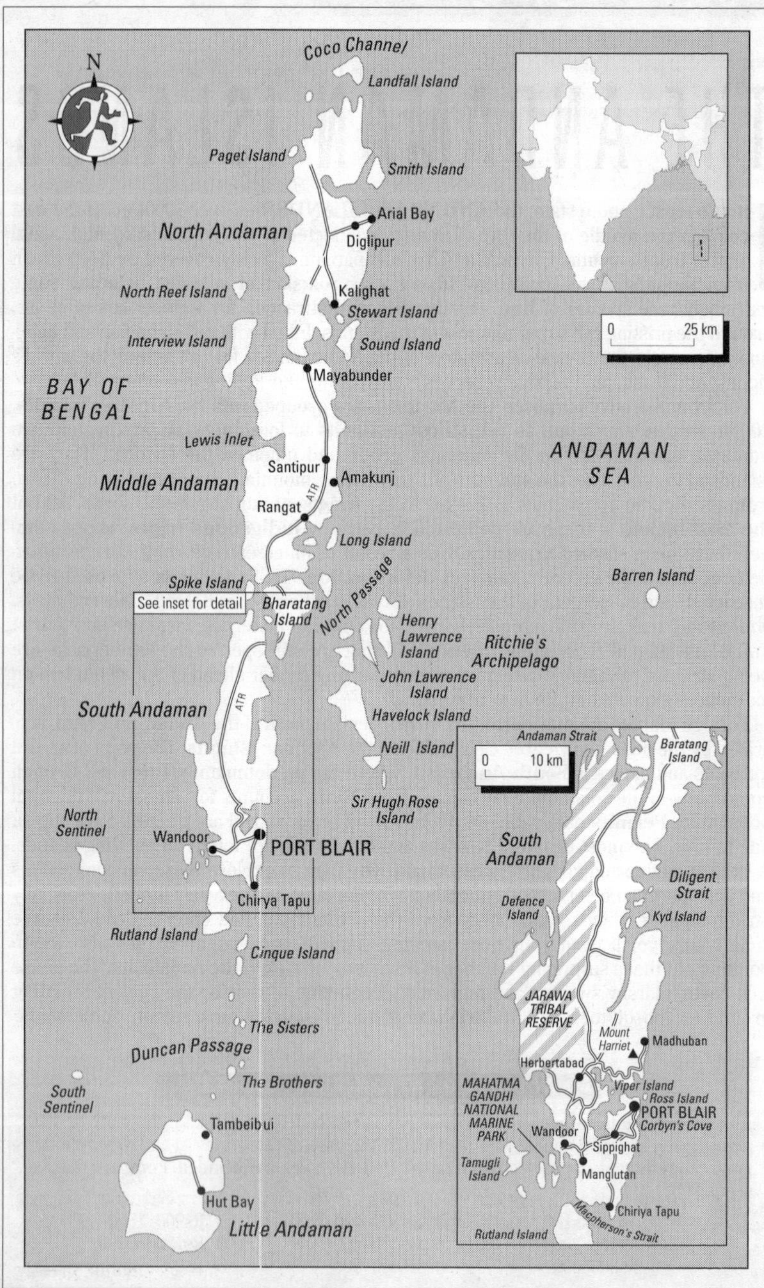

N
Coco Channel
Landfall Island
Paget Island
Smith Island
Arial Bay
North Andaman
Diglipur
North Reef Island
Kalighat
Stewart Island
Interview Island
Sound Island
Mayabunder
BAY OF BENGAL
Lewis Inlet
Santipur
Amakunj
Middle Andaman
Rangat
ATR
Long Island
Spike Island
North Passage
See inset for detail
Bharatang Island
Henry Lawrence Island
Ritchie's Archipelago
John Lawrence Island
South Andaman
Havelock Island
Neill Island
Sir Hugh Rose Island
North Sentinel
Wandoor
PORT BLAIR
Chirya Tapu
Rutland Island
Cinque Island
The Sisters
Duncan Passage
The Brothers
South Sentinel
Tambeibui
Hut Bay
Little Andaman
ANDAMAN SEA
Barren Island
0 25 km
Andaman Strait
Baratang Island
0 10 km
South Andaman
Diligent Strait
Defence Island
Kyd Island
JARAWA TRIBAL RESERVE
Mount Harriet
Madhuban
Herbertabad
MAHATMA GANDHI NATIONAL MARINE PARK
Viper Island
Ross Island
PORT BLAIR
Corbyn's Cove
Wandoor
Sippighat
Tamugli Island
Manglutan
Chiriya Tapu
Rutland Island
Macpherson's Strait

The **climate** remains tropical throughout the year, with temperatures from 24° to 35°C. By far the best time to visit is between November and May. From mid-May to October, heavy rains flush the islands, often bringing violent cyclones that leave west coast beaches strewn with fallen trees, while in November and December less severe rains arrive with the northeast monsoon. Despite being so far east, the islands run on Indian time, so the sun rises at 4.30am and darkness falls soon after 5pm.

Some history

The earliest mention of the Andaman and Nicobar Islands is found in **Ptolemy**'s geographical treatises (second century AD). Other records from the Chinese Buddhist monk I'Tsing (seventh century AD) and Arabian travellers who passed by in the ninth century depict the inhabitants as fierce and cannibalistic. **Marco Polo** arrived in the thirteenth century and could offer no more favourable description of the natives: "The people are without a king and are idolaters no better than wild beasts. All the men of the island of Angamanian have heads like dogs… they are a most cruel generation, and eat everybody they catch…" It is unlikely, however, that the Andamanese were cannibals, as the most vivid reports of their ferocity were propagated by Malay pirates who held sway over the surrounding seas, and needed to keep looters well away from trade ships that passed between India, China and the Far East.

During the eighteenth and nineteenth centuries **European missionaries** and trading companies turned their attention to the islands with a view to colonization. A string of unsuccessful attempts to convert the Nicobaris to Christianity was made by the French, Dutch and Danish, all of whom were forced to abandon their plans in the face of hideous diseases and a severe lack of food and water. Though the missionaries themselves seldom met with any hostility, several fleets of trading ships that tried to dock on the islands were captured, and their crews murdered, by Nicobari people.

In 1777 the British Lieutenant Blair chose the South Andaman harbour now known as **Port Blair** as the site for a **penal colony**, based on the deportation of criminals that had proved successful in Sumatra, Singapore and Penang. Both this scheme, and an attempt to settle the Nicobar Islands in 1867, were thwarted by adverse conditions. However, the third go at colonization was more successful, and in 1858 Port Blair finally did become a penal settlement, where political activists who had fuelled the Mutiny in 1857 were made to clear land and build their own prison. Out of 773 prisoners, 292 died, escaped or were hanged in the first two months. Many also lost their lives in attacks by Andamanese tribes who objected to forest clearance, but the settlement continued to fill with people from mainland India, and by 1864 the number of convicts had grown to 3000. In 1896 work began on a jail made up of hundreds of tiny solitary cells, which was used to confine political prisoners until 1945. The prison still stands and is one of Port Blair's few "tourist attractions".

In 1919 the British government in India decided to close down the penal settlement, but it was subsequently used to incarcerate a new generation of freedom fighters from India, Malabar and Burma. During World War II the islands were occupied by the **Japanese**, who tortured and murdered hundreds of indigenous islanders suspected of collaborating with the British, and bombed the homes of the Jarawa tribes. British forces moved back in 1945, and at last abolished the penal settlement.

After Partition, refugees, mostly low-caste Hindus from Bangladesh and Bengal, were given land in Port Blair and North Andaman, where the forest was clear-felled to make room for rice paddy, cocoa plantations and new industries. Since 1951 the population has increased by more than ten times, further swollen by repatriated Tamils from Sri Lanka, thousands of Bihari labourers, ex-servicemen given land grants, economic migrants from poorer Indian states and the legions of government employees packed off here on two-year "punishment postings". This replanted population greatly outnumbers the Andamans' indigenous people, who currently comprise around half of one percent of the total. Contact between the two societies is limited, and is not always friendly. In addition, there exists within Port Blair a clear divide between the relatively recent incomers and the so-called "**pre-42s**" – descendants of the released convicts and freedom fighters whose families settled here before the major influx from the mainland. This small but influential minority, based at the exclusive Browning Club in the capital, has been calling for curbs on immigration and new property rules to slow down the rate of settlement. While doubtless motivated by self-interest, their demands nevertheless reflect growing concern for the future of the Andamans, where rapid and largely unplanned development has wrought havoc on the natural environment, not to mention on the indigenous population.

With the days of the timber-extraction cash cow now numbered, the hope is that **tourism** will replace tree felling as the main source of revenue. However, the extra numbers envisaged are certain to overtax an already inadequate infrastructure, aggravating seasonal water shortages and sewage disposal problems. Given India's track record with tourism development, it's hard to be optimistic. Perhaps the greatest threat

NATIVE PEOPLE OF THE ANDAMAN AND NICOBAR ISLANDS

Quite where the indigenous population of the Andaman and Nicobar Islands originally came from is a puzzle that has preoccupied anthropologists since Radcliffe-Brown conducted his famous field work among the Andamanese at the beginning of this century. Asian-looking groups such as the Shompen (see below) may have migrated here from the east and north when the islands were connected to Burma, or the sea was sufficiently shallow to allow transport by canoe, but this doesn't explain the origins of the black populations, whose appearance suggests African roots. Wherever they came from, the survival of the islands' first inhabitants has been threatened by traders and colonizers, who introduced disease and destroyed their territories by widespread felling. Thousands also died from addiction to alcohol and opium, which the Chinese, Japanese and British exchanged for valuable shells. Of perhaps 5000 aborigines in 1858, from six of the twelve native tribal groups, only five percent remain.

On the Nicobar Islands, the distinctly Southeast Asian **Nicobaris**, who claim descent from a Burmese prince and were identified as *lojenke* (naked people) by I'Tsing, have integrated to some extent with recent settlers, following widespread conversion by Christian missionaries. While they continue to live in small communities of huts raised on stilts, most have adopted modern agricultural methods, raising pigs and cultivating fruit and vegetable gardens rather than hunting. One of the largest communities of Nicobaris is at John Richardson Bay, near the town of Hut Bay on Little Andaman. The **Shompen** of Great Nicobar, on the other hand, have not assimilated, and fewer than two hundred survive, living predominantly on the coast, where they barter in honey, cane and nuts with the Nicobaris.

The indigenous inhabitants of the Andamans, divided into *eramtaga* (those living in the jungle) and *ar-yuato* (those living on the coast), traditionally subsisted on fish, turtles, turtle eggs, pigs, fruits, honey and roots. Although they comprised the largest group when the islands were first colonized, fewer than twenty **Great Andamanese** remain, settled on Strait Island, north of South Andaman. In the 1860s the Rev H. Corbyn set up a "home" for them to learn English on Ross Island, insisting that they wear clothes and attend reading and writing classes. Five children and three adults from Corbyn's school were taken as curiosities to Calcutta in 1864, where they were shown around the sights. The whole experience, however, proved more fascinating for the crowds who'd come to ogle the "monkey men" than for the Andamanese themselves; one of the organizers of the trip ruefully remarked of them " ... [they] never evinced astonishment or admiration at anything which they beheld, however wonderful in its novelty we might suppose it would appear to them." From the foreign settlers the Andamanese tragically contracted looming on the horizon is the plan to extend the airport runway, which will allow long-haul flights from Southeast Asia to land here. If only a trickle of the tourist traffic flooding between Bangkok and India is diverted through the Andamans, the impact on this culturally and ecologically fragile region could be catastrophic.

Getting to the Andaman Islands

Port Blair, on South Andaman, is served by Indian Airlines **flights** from Calcutta (Tues, Thurs, Sat & Sun; 2hr) and Chennai (Mon, Weds & Fri; 2hr); tickets are expensive though, and difficult to acquire (see p.390). At the time of writing, Jet was also hopeful of obtaining permission to fly to the islands, which may alleviate the overwhelming demand for seats.

It's also possible to get to Port Blair by **ship**. Schedules are notoriously erratic, but, in principle, sailings leave Calcutta and Chennai every one or two weeks, and Vishakapatnam once every month or so (see Travel Details, p.541). Although far cheaper than flying, the crossings are long (3–4 days), uncomfortable and often delayed by bad conditions and bureaucracy.

diseases such as syphilis, measles, mumps and influenza, and fell prey to opium addiction. Within three years almost the entire population had died.

The **Jarawas**, who shifted from their original homes when land was cleared to build Port Blair, now live on the remote western coasts of Middle and South Andaman, hemmed in by the Andaman Trunk Rd which since the 1970s has cut them off from hunting grounds and freshwater supplies. Some contact with the Indian government used to be made through gift-exchanges at each full moon, when consignments of coconuts, bananas and red cloth were taken to a friendly band of Jarawas on a boat, but the initiative was recently cancelled. Over the past two decades, encroachments on their land by loggers, road-builders and Bengali settlers have met with fierce resistance. Dozens, possibly hundreds, of people have died in skirmishes. Most recently a party of Burmese were caught poaching on Jarawa land; of the eleven men involved, six limped out with horrific injuries, two were found dead, and the other three were never seen again. Most of the incidents have occurred on or near the Andaman Trunk Rd, which is why armed escorts board the buses at several points during the journey north from Port Blair to Mayabunder.

Aside from a couple of violent encounters with nineteenth-century seamen (seventy were massacred on first contact in 1867), relations with the **Onge**, who call themselves the **Gaubolambe**, have been relatively peaceful. Distinguished by their white-clay and ochre body paint, they continue to live in communal shelters (*bera*) and construct temporary thatched huts (*korale*) on Little Andaman. The remaining population of around one hundred retain their traditional way of life on two small reserves. The Indian government has erected wood and tin huts in both, dispatched a teacher to instruct them in Hindi and encouraged coconut cultivation, but to little avail. Contact with outsiders is limited to an occasional trip into town to purchase liquor, and visits from rare parties of anthropologists. The reserves are strictly off-limits to foreigners, but you can learn about the Onges' traditional hunting practices, beliefs and rituals in the wonderful ethnography *Above the Forest* by Vishvajit Pandya.

The most elusive tribe of all, the **Sentinelese**, live on North Sentinel Island west of South Andaman. Some contact was made with them in 1990, after a team put together by the local administration had left gifts on the beaches every month for two years, but subsequent visits have invariably ended in a hail of arrows. Since the early 1990s, the AAJVS, the government department charged with tribal welfare, has effectively given up trying to contact the Sentinelese, who are estimated to number around eighty. Flying in or out of Port Blair, you pass above their island, ringed by a spectacular coral reef, and it is reassuring to think that the people sitting at the bottom of the plumes of smoke drifting from the forest canopy have for so long resisted contact with the outside world.

Tourists arriving by plane can pick up the **permit** necessary to visit the islands on arrival at Port Blair airport; passengers travelling on a ship should obtain one at a Foreigners' Registration office before leaving India. For full details on obtaining permits from Chennai refer to p.390.

Scuba diving in the Andaman Islands

The seas around the Andaman and Nicobar Islands are some of the world's most unspoiled. Marine life is abundant, with an estimated 750 species of fish existing on one reef alone. Parrot, trigger and angel fish live alongside manta rays, reef sharks and loggerhead turtles. Many species of fish and coral are unique to the area. Fascinating life-systems exist in ash beds and cooled lava based around the volcanic island of Barren Island (see p.540).

For a quick taste of marine life, you could start by **snorkelling**; most hotels can supply masks and snorkels, though some equipment is in dire need of replacement. The only way to get really close, however, and venture out into deeper waters, is to **scuba dive** (see below). The experience of weaving in and out of coral beds, coming eye to eye with fish or swimming with dolphins and barracudas is unforgettable.

At present, the islands have only two **dive centres**, both are based in the Port Blair area, thoroughly reputable and PADI-registered, but far from cheap. **Samudra** (☎01392/33159 or 32937, fax 32038), whose dive base occupies a former Japanese bunker at the *Sinclair Bay View Hotel* (see p.530), charges around Rs2200 for local dives and Rs3500 for trips to Wandoor and beyond. For a hefty Rs15,000, you can also do a three- or four-day PADI open-water course. Samudra's rates are comparable with those offered by the German-run **Port Blair Underwater** (☎01392/85389, fax 040/339 2718), in the *Peerless Resort* at Corbyn's Bay. When booking dives with either, check which sites they use: Cinque Island offers arguably the best diving in the area, and it is worth shelling out a little extra to visit it as it is otherwise difficult to reach.

Underwater in the Andamans, it is not uncommon to come across schools of reef sharks, which rarely turn hostile, but one thing to watch out for and avoid is the **black-and-white sea snake**. Though the snakes seldom attack – and, since their fangs are at the back of their mouths, would find it difficult to get a grip on any human – their bite is twenty times more deadly than that of the cobra.

Increased tourism inevitably puts pressure on the delicate marine eco-system, and poorly funded wildlife organizations can do little to prevent damage from insensitive visitors. You can ensure your presence in the sea around the reefs does not harm the coral by observing the following **Green Coral Code** while diving or snorkelling:

- Never touch, or walk on, living coral or it will die.
- Try to keep your feet away from reefs while wearing fins; the sudden sweep of water caused by a flipper kick can be enough to destroy coral.
- Always control the speed of your descent while diving; enormous damage can be caused by divers landing hard on a coral bed.
- Never break off pieces of coral from a reef, and remember that it is illegal to export dead coral from the islands, even fragments you may have found on a beach.

SOUTH ANDAMAN

South Andaman is today the most heavily populated of the Andaman Islands – particularly around the capital, **Port Blair** – thanks in part to the drastic thinning of tree cover to make way for settlement. Foreign tourists can only visit its southern reaches – including the beaches at **Corbyn's Cove** and **Chirya Tapu**, and the fine reefs on the western shores at **Wandoor**, 35km southwest of Port Blair.

With your own transport it's easy to find your way along the narrow bumpy roads that connect small villages, weaving through forests and coconut fields, and skirting the swamps and rocky outcrops that form the coastline.

Port Blair

PORT BLAIR, a characterless cluster of tin-roofed buildings tumbling towards the sea in the north, east and west and petering into fields and forests in the south, merits only a short stay. There's little to see here – just the **Cellular Jail** and a few small **museums** – but as the point of arrival for the islands, and the only place with a bank, tourist offices and hotels, it can't be avoided. If you plan to head off to more remote islands, this is also the best place to stock up on supplies and buy necessary equipment.

The Town

Port Blair's only firm reminder of its gloomy past, the sturdy brick **Cellular Jail** (Mon–Sat 9am–noon & 2–7pm), overlooks the sea from a small rise in the northeast of town. Built between 1896 and 1905, its tiny solitary cells were quite different and far worse than the dormitories in other prison blocks erected earlier. Only three of the seven wings that originally radiated from the central tower now remain. Visitors can peer into the cells (3 x 3.5m), and imagine the grim conditions under which the prisoners existed. Cells were dirty and ill ventilated, drinking water was limited to two glasses per day, and the convicts were expected to wash in the rain as they worked clearing forests and building prison quarters. Food, brought from the mainland, was stored in vats where the rice and pulses became infested with worms; more than half the prison population died long before their twenty years' detention was up. Protests against conditions led to hunger strikes in 1932, 1933 and 1937, resulting in yet more deaths, and frequent executions took place at the gallows that still stand in squat wooden shelters in the courtyards, in full view of the cells. The **sound and light show** (in English Wed, Sat & Sun 7.15pm; in Hindi daily 6pm; not during the rainy season of May–Sept & Nov; Rs10) outlines the history of the prison, and a small **museum** by the entrance gate (same hours as the jail) exhibits lists of convicts, photographs and grim torture devices.

South of the jail near the Water Sports Complex, you can see tanks full of fish and coral from the islands' reefs at the **Aquarium** (daily 9am–1.30pm & 2–5.30pm; free). In the Haddo area in the west side of town, exhibits in the **Anthropological Museum** (Mon–Sat 9am–noon & 1–4pm; free), devoted to the Andaman and Nicobar tribes, include weapons, tools and also rare photographs of the region's indigenous people taken in the 1960s. Among the most striking of these is a sequence featuring the Sentinelese, taken on April 26, 1967, when a party of Indian officials made the first contact with the tribe. After scaring the aborigines, the visitors marched into one of their hunting camps and made off with the bows, arrows and other artefacts now displayed in the museum. The anthropologist charged with documenting the expedition noted afterwards that "the whole atmosphere was that of conquering hordes over-running conquered territory."

Further west along MG Rd opposite T&N Tourism's *Teal House* hotel, the **Samudrika Naval Maritime Museum** (Tues–Sun 9am–noon & 2–5.30pm; Rs10) is an excellent primer if you're heading off to more remote islands, with a superlative shell collection and informative displays on various aspects of local marine biology. One exhibit features a cross-section of the different corals you can expect to see on the Andamans' reefs, followed up with a run-down of the various threats these fragile animals face, from mangrove depletion and parasitic starfish to clumsy snorkellers.

Wildlife lovers are advised to steer clear of the grim little **zoo** (Tues–Sun 8am–5pm; Rs1), further down MG Rd, whose only redeeming feature is that it has successfully bred rare crocodiles and monkeys for release into the wild. The adjoining **Forest Museum** is an equally dismal spectacle, feebly attempting to justify the Indian Forest Service's wholesale destruction of the Andamans' forests with a series of lacklustre photographs of extraction methods. However, if you really want to confront the grim reality of the local timber industry, press on north to **Chatham Sawmill** (daily

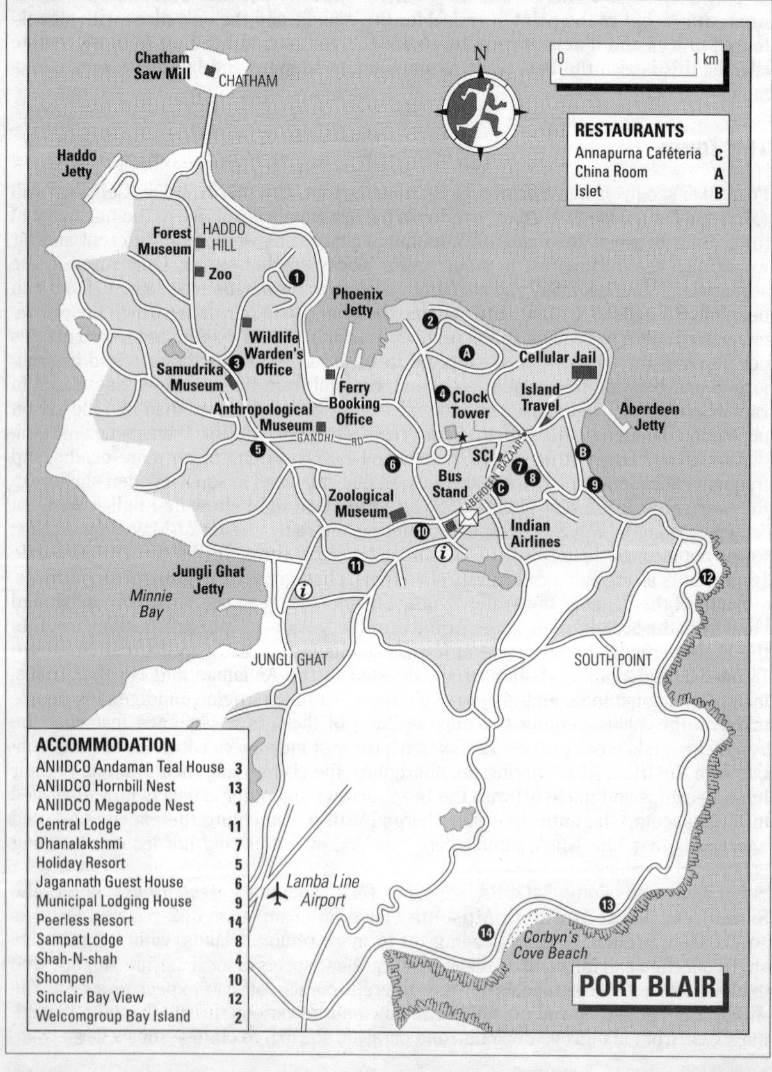

7am–2.30pm), at the end of the peninsula marking the northernmost edge of Port Blair. One of the oldest and largest wood-processing plants in Asia, it seasons and mills rare hardwoods taken from various islands – a sad testimony to the continued abuse of international guidelines on tropical timber production; photography is prohibited.

Arrival and information

Port Blair has two jetties: **boats** from the mainland moor at **Haddo Jetty**, north of the arrival point for inter-island ferries. **Phoenix Jetty**, is 1km further south around the bay. The Marine Department at Phoenix Jetty has the latest information on boats and ferries, but you can also check the shipping news column of the local newspaper, the *Daily Telegrams*, for details of forthcoming departures. Advice on booking ferry tickets appears in the box on p.533.

The ramshackle **airport** is 4km south of town at Lamba Line. Entry **permits** are issued to foreigners from the counter in the corner of the arrivals hall while the baggage is being transferred. **Taxis** are on hand for the Rs50 trip into town, but if you've pre-booked a room at either the *Sinclair Bay View*, the *Welcomgroup Bay Island* or any Andaman Tourism (ANIIDCO) hotel, you should find a shuttle bus waiting outside.

A counter at the airport has leaflets listing accommodation and sights around South Andaman Island, but the main **A&N tourist office** (Mon–Sat 10am–5pm; ☎03192/32694) is situated in a modern building, diagonally opposite Indian Airlines on the southern edge of the town. Unless you want to book accommodation in an ANIIDCO hotel or a seat on one of their tours (such as to Wandoor, see p.534), it's hard to think of a reason to go there; they don't keep transport timetables or any useful information about the rest of the archipelago. North of the centre on Junglighat Main Rd, the **India Government Tourist Office** (Mon–Fri ☎01392/33006) is little better.

Road names are not used much in Port Blair, with most establishments addressing themselves simply by their local area. The name of the busiest and most central area is **Aberdeen Bazaar**, where you'll find the superintendent of police (for permit extensions), the SCI office for onward bookings by sea (☎01392/33347) and the State Bank of India (Mon–Fri 9am–1pm, Sat 9–11am). Some hotels will change travellers' cheques, but you'll get faster service and better rates at Island Travels (Mon–Sat 2–5pm) just up the road from the clock tower in Aberdeen Bazaar, opposite *Sampat Lodge*, which has a licence to change money.

Local transport and tours

Walking is tiring and time-consuming in hilly Port Blair – even taking into account the minimal amount of sightseeing the place offers – making transport essential. Yellow-top **taxis** gather opposite the bus stand. They all have meters, but negotiating the price before leaving is usual practice. Expect to pay Rs50 for a trip from the centre of town to Corbyn's Cove. No rickshaws, auto- or otherwise, operate on the island.

Local **buses** run infrequently from the bus stand in central Port Blair to Wandoor and Chirya Tapu, and can be used for day-trips, though it's best to rely on your own transport to get around South Andaman. **Bicycles** can be rented from Aberdeen Bazaar, at Rs4–5 per hour, but the roads to the coasts are most easily covered on a **Vespa** or **motorcycle**, both available for rent at TSG Travels (Mon–Sat 9am–5pm; ☎01392/20894) on Babu Lane in the centre of town at Rs120–200 per day. Around the corner in the narrow lane behind the main bazaar, Ankur Travels has four newish 50cc Scooties, great value at Rs200 per day. Neither place asks to see a licence, but you'll be expected to leave a deposit of around Rs1000, and sometimes your passport. The petrol pump is on the crossroads west of the bus stand, and there's another on the road towards the airport. Fill up before you leave town, as gas is hard to come by elsewhere.

Cramming the island's few interesting sights together with a string of dull destinations, most of the ANIIDCO **tours** are a complete waste of time; you're better off renting a scooter or taxi and taking in the jail and museums at your own pace. However, more worthwhile are their **harbour cruises** (daily 3–4.30pm; Rs20) that depart from Phoenix Jetty for fleeting visits to the floating docks and **Viper Island** (see p.531), and the day-trips to **Wandoor** and the **Mahatma Gandhi marine reserve** (see p.534).

Accommodation

Port Blair boasts a fair selection of places to stay. Concentrated mainly in the centre of town, the bottom-range **accommodation** can be as dour as any port town on the mainland; assume if a lodge isn't listed below, it's not worth looking at, let alone sleeping in. More comfortable hotels occupy correspondingly more salubrious locations on the outskirts. Wherever you intend to stay, it's definitely worth booking ahead during peak season.

ANIIDCO Andaman Teal House, Haddo (☎03192/32642). High on the hill above the port this place offers great views, spacious and pleasant rooms, and is very good value, although can be inconvenient without your own transport. ③.

ANIIDCO Hornbill Nest, 1km from Corbyn's Cove (☎03192/20018). Clean, roomy cottages on a hillside by the coast. Great location, catching the sea breezes, but transport to and from town is a problem unless you rent a scooter. ③.

ANIIDCO Megapode Nest, Haddo Hill (☎03192/33659, fax 32702). A&N Tourism's upscale option has 25 comfortable rooms, and pricier self-contained "cottages", ranged around a central lawn, with good views, and a quality restaurant. ⑥–⑦.

Central Lodge, Middle Point (☎03192/33632). Ramshackle wooden building situated in a secluded top corner of town. A rock-bottom option, offering basic rooms or garden space for hammocks. ①.

Dhanalakshmi, Aberdeen Bazaar, Port Blair (☎03192/33952). Friendly, clean and very central. The rooms are all en suite and tiled, but can get stuffy (you have to keep the front windows closed because of traffic noise, and the back ones shut to keep out the mosquitoes). ④.

Holiday Resort, Premnagar, located a fifteen-minute walk from the centre (☎03192/30516).This is the best mid-price deal in the town centre; it's clean and spacious, with some a/c. ③–⑥.

Jagannath Guest House, Moulana Azad Rd (☎03192/32148). One of the best-value basic lodges: clean, central and convenient for the jetty. The front-side rooms are the nicest, though are marginally more expensive. No telephone bookings taken. ②.

Municipal Lodging House, opposite Municipal Swimming Pool (☎03192/34919). Port Blair's best budget deal: clean rooms with good beds, fans, bathrooms, balconies and sea views, but it's often booked up with Bengali tourists and inter-island travellers. ①.

Peerless Resort, Corbyn's Cove (☎03192/21463). Perfect setting amid gardens of palms, jasmine and bougainvillaea, opposite a white sandy beach. Balconied a/c rooms, cottages, a bar and a medium-priced restaurant where the evening buffet doesn't always match up to what is served in simpler places elsewhere. Ideal for families. ⑨.

Sampat Lodge, Aberdeen Bazaar (☎03192/30752). Cellular-Jail-size rooms with common bathrooms. Only worth considering as a fallback. ②.

Shah-N-Shah, Mohanpura, near the bus stand (☎03192/33696). Despite being set at the grotty port end of town near the boat jetty, this is a comfortable, lively place to stay, with en-suite rooms and sociable terrace. ②–③.

Sinclair Bay View, on the coast road to Corbyn's Cove (☎03192/21159). Clifftop hotel offering spotless carpeted rooms, balconies, en-suite bathrooms, dramatic views, bar and restaurant, in-house diving school and airport shuttle bus. ⑦.

Welcomgroup Bay Island, Marine Hill, Port Blair (☎03192/20881). Port Blair's swishest hotel; elegant, airy and finished with polished dark wood. All rooms have carpets and balconies overlooking Phoenix Jetty (the less expensive ones are a little cramped); quality restaurant, gardens and open-air sea-water swimming pool, though tariffs are decidedly steep at US$120 per double. ⑨.

Eating

Between them, Port Blair's restaurants offer dishes from North and South India, Burmese specialties and a wide variety of seafood. For rock-bottom budget travellers, there are roadside stalls selling plates of grilled fish at less than Rs20, in addition to the usual crop of cheap but run-of-the-mill "meals" cafés in the main bazaar: of these, the *Majestic*, *Gagan* and *Milan* on AB Rd are the best, but you should steer clear of the *Dhanalakshmi*'s notoriously dreadful canteen.

In Port Blair, as throughout the Andamans, attitudes to **alcohol** lag somewhat behind the mainland, and you'll be lucky to find a cold beer outside the upscale hotels. For the usual range of IMFLs, you'll have to join the drunken scrum at the seedy state liquor shop, tucked away down the alley running alongside the *Shah-N-Shah* hotel.

Annapurna Cafeteria, Aberdeen Bazaar, towards the post office. Far and away Port Blair's best South Indian joint, serving the usual range of huge crispy *dosas*, North Indian and Chinese plate meals, delicious coffee and wonderful *pongal* at breakfast. The lunchtime *thalis* are also great.

China Room, on the hill above the Phoenix Jetty (☎03192/30759). The most tourist-orientated restaurant in town, run by a Burmese-Punjabi couple whose roots are vividly reflected in the chilli-and-ginger-rich cuisine. Particularly recommended for seafood (try the mouth-watering prawn in lemon and cashew nut sauce). Reserve a table in advance, and expect cordial but slow service.

Islet, below the Cellular Jail. A safe option for non-veg North Indian tandoori, especially chicken, although they offer a good selection of vegetarian dishes, too. Snappy service and good views of the bay from the window seats.

Mandalay, *Welcomgroup Bay Island*, Marine Hill, Port Blair (☎03192/20881). Ridiculously overpriced (even the staff suggest you order drinks elsewhere), but many visitors feel the breezy verandah and bay views well worth the extra. Count on around Rs200 per head.

Waves, *Peerless Resort*, Corbyn's Cove. Pricey, but very congenial al fresco hotel restaurant under a shady palm grove, and one of the few places in town you can order a beer with your meal. Most dishes around Rs80.

Around Port Blair

At some point, you're almost certain to find yourself killing time in Port Blair, waiting for boats to show up or tickets to go on sale. Rather than wasting days in town, it's worth exploring the coast of South Andaman which, although far more densely populated than other islands in the archipelago, holds a handful of easily accessible beauty spots and historic sites. Among the latter, the ruined colonial monuments on **Viper** and **Ross islands** can be reached on daily harbour cruises or regular ferries from the capital. For **beaches**, head southeast to **Corbyn's Cove**, or cross South Andaman to reach more secluded **Chirya Tapu**, both accessible in easy day-trips if you rent a moped or taxi. By far the most rewarding way to spend a day out of town, however, is to catch the tourist boat from **Wandoor** to **Jolly Buoy** or **Red Skin Islands** in the **Mahatma Gandhi Marine Reserve**, which boasts some of the Andamans' best snorkelling.

Viper and Ross islands

First stop on the harbour cruise from Port Blair (daily 3–5pm; Rs20) is generally **Viper Island**, named not after the many snakes that doubtless inhabit its tangled tropical undergrowth, but a nineteenth-century merchant vessel that ran aground on it during the early years of the colony. Lying a short way off Haddo Wharf, it served as an isolation zone for the main prison, where escapees and convicts (including hunger strikers) were sent to be punished. Whipping posts and crumbling walls, reached from the jetty via a winding brick path, remain as relics of a torture area, while occupying the site's most prominent position are the original gallows.

No less eerie are the decaying colonial remains on **Ross Island**, at the entrance to Port Blair harbour, where the British sited their first penal settlement in the Andamans. Originally cleared by convicts wearing iron fetters (most of them sent here in the wake of the 1857 Mutiny, or First War of Independence), Ross witnessed some of the most brutal excesses of British colonial history, and was the source of the prison's infamy as "**Kalapani**", or Black Water. Of the many convicts transported here, distinguished by their branded foreheads, the majority perished from disease or torture before the clearance of the island was completed in 1860. Thereafter, it served briefly as the site of Revd Henry Corbyn's "**Andaman Home**" – a prison camp created with the intention of "civilizing" the local tribespeople – before becoming the headquarters of the revamped penal colony, complete with theatre hall, tennis courts, swimming pool, hospitals and grand residential bungalows. Rather ambitiously dubbed "the Paris of the East", the settlement typified the stiff-upper-lipped spirit of the Raj at its most cruel: while the *burra-* and *memsahibs* dressed for dinner and sang hymns in church, convicts languished in the most appalling conditions less than a mile away. In the end, the entry of the Japanese into World War II, hot on the heels of a massive earthquake in 1941, forced the British to evacuate, and in the coming years most of the buildings were dismantled by the new overlords, who themselves founded a POW camp here.

Little more than the hilltop Anglican church, with its weed-infested graveyard, has survived the onslaught of tropical creepers and vines, and the island makes a peaceful

MOVING ON FROM PORT BLAIR

Port Blair is the departure point for all flights and ferry crossings to the **Indian mainland**; it is also the hub of the Andamans' inter-island bus and ferry network. Unfortunately, booking tickets (especially back to Chennai, Calcutta or Vishakapatnam) can be time-consuming, and many travellers are obliged to come back here well before their permit expires to make reservations, heading off to more pleasant parts to kill their remaining days afterwards.

To the mainland

If you've travelled to the Andamans **by ship**, you'll know what a rough ride the sixty-hour crossing can be in bunk class, and how difficult tickets are to come by (see pp.390–1). It's also a good idea to talk to fellow travellers about current conditions, which vary from year to year and vessel to vessel. The one factor you can be sure about is that the ship offers the cheapest route back. The downside is that schedules can be erratic, and accurate information about them difficult to obtain — annoying when you only have a one-month permit. Basically, the only sure way of finding out when the next ship is leaving, and whether or not passages on it are available, is to join the "queue" outside the SCI office (☎03192/33347), opposite the *Dhanalakshmi* hotel in Aberdeen Bazaar. This is the point of sale for crossings to **Calcutta**; for **Chennai** and **Vishakapatnam**, you'll have to head down to Phoenix Jetty. In theory, tickets are supposed to go on sale a week in advance of departure, but don't bank on it. Bear in mind, too, if you're reading this a couple of days' journey away from the capital, and with only a week or less left on your permit, that the local police can get heavy with foreigners who outstay their allotted time.

Returning to the mainland by **plane** in only two hours instead of sixty can save lots of time and hassle, but at US$200 one-way, air tickets to **Chennai** and **Calcutta** are far from cheap, and are often hard to obtain; in peak season, such as Diwali, they're like gold dust. That said, it's amazing how polite persistence at the Indian Airlines reservation office (Mon–Sat 9am–1pm & 2–4pm), around the corner from the GPO can pay off. The reason for this is that the staff are frequently not sure how many seats will be available until the freight has been weighed in the previous day; if the holds are not filled, they can fly with a larger number of passengers (the runway is too short for Indian Airlines' old 737s to take off with a full payload). If, after badgering the main office, you still can't get on a break from Port Blair. To get here, jump on one of the regular launches from Phoenix Jetty (daily except Wed; departing 8.30am, 10am, 12.30pm, 2pm and returning 8.45am, 10.15am, 12.40pm, 2.10pm; Rs15).

Corbyn's Cove and Chirya Tapu

The best beach within easy reach of the capital lies 10km southeast at **Corbyn's Cove**, a small arc of smooth white sand backed by a swaying curtain of palms. There's a large hotel here (see p.530), but the water isn't particularly clear, and bear in mind that lying around scantily clothed will bring you considerable attention from crowds of local workers.

For more isolation, rent a moped or take a taxi 30km south to **Chirya Tapu** ("Bird Island"), at the tip of South Andaman. The motorable track running beyond this small fishing village leads through thick jungle overhung with twisting creepers to a large bay, where swamps give way to shell-strewn beaches. Other than at lunchtime, when it often receives a deluge of bus parties, the beach offers plenty of peace and quiet, forest walks on the woodcutters' trails winding inland from it and easy access to an inshore reef. However, the water here is nowhere near as clear as at some spots in the archipelago, and serious snorkellers and divers may be tempted to try for a boat out to volcanic

flight, it may be worth trying through Ankur Travel (☎03192/21723), next to the Laxmi Narayan temple by the clock tower in Aberdeen Bazaar, who claim to have an "arrangement" with Indian Airlines, though expect to pay extra for the privilege.

On the day of your flight, be sure to check in at least ninety minutes before the scheduled departure time (security formalities can be protracted), and expect to have to "click" your camera to prove it is just that. Note, too, that Indian law strictly forbids the removal of coral from the Andamans. Get caught with any in your luggage and you'll lose your flight, and probably have to pay a hefty bribe to the police.

Travellers intending to catch onward **trains** from their port of arrival on the mainland should note that Port Blair has a computerized Southern Railways reservation office near the Secretariat (Mon–Sat 8.30am–1pm & 2–4pm).

Inter-island services

Buses connect Port Blair with most major settlements on South and Middle Andaman, mainly via the Andaman Trunk Rd. From the crowded, disorganized bus stand at the bottom of town, three daily government services run as far as **Mayabunder** (9hr 30min–12hr), the furthest point north reachable in a day from the capital, from where you have to catch a boat across the straits to **Kalighat** on North Andaman in order to press on north to **Diglipur** and **Ariel Bay**. If you're planning to head as far north as possible without stopping at other islands en route, aim to catch Geetanjali Travels' "super-fast" video coach (ear plugs essential), which leaves from the road outside the bus stand daily at 6am (book through any of the agents' stalls advertising this service in the bazaar).

Most of the islands open to foreign tourists, including **Neill**, **Havelock**, **Middle** and **North Andaman**, are also accessible by **boat** from Phoenix Jetty. Details of forthcoming departures are posted in the shipping news columns of the local newspapers, but the most reliable source of information is the office on the first floor of the Harbour Authority building, Phoenix Jetty, where you can also book tickets in advance. The journeys themselves can be a lot longer and more uncomfortable than you might expect. From 9am onwards, the heat on board the old boats is intense, with only corrugated plastic sheets for shade, while the benches are highly uncomfortable and the toilets generally dismal. You should take adequate supplies of food and water with you; only biscuits and simple snacks are sold on the boats. More details of boat services to destinations outside the capital appear in the relevant accounts.

Cinque Island (see p.540), a couple of hours further south. Groups from the big hotels in Port Blair use inflatables with outboard motors to reach Cinque, but it is also possible to charter your own fishing boat here; ask around the bar in the village; and expect to pay around Rs3000 per boat for the return trip.

Wandoor and the Mahatma Gandhi National Marine Park

Much the most popular excursion from Port Blair is the boat ride from **Wandoor**, 30km southwest, to one or other of the fifteen islets comprising the **Mahatma Gandhi National Marine Park**. Although set up purely for tourists, the trip is worth doing, gaining you access to one of the richest coral reefs in the region. Boats depart from Wandoor at 10am (daily except Mon; Rs75, plus Rs10 entry permit to the park); you can get there on A&N Tourism's **tour** (bookable through the ANIIDCO tourist office in Port Blair) or by local bus, but it is more fun to rent a moped and ride down to meet the boat yourself.

The long white beach at **Wandoor** is littered with the dry, twisted trunks of trees torn up and flung down by annual cyclones, and fringed not with palms, but by dense forest teeming with birdlife. You should only snorkel here at high tide. From the jetty, the boats chug through broad creeks lined with dense mangrove swamps and pristine forest to either **Red Skin Island** or, more commonly, **Jolly Buoy**. The latter, an idyllic deserted island, boasts an immaculate shell-sand beach, ringed by a bank of superb coral. The catch is that the boat only stops for around an hour, which isn't nearly enough time to explore the shore and reef. While snorkelling off the edges of the reef, however, beware of **strong currents**.

NORTH OF PORT BLAIR

Printed on the permit card you receive on arrival in the Andamans is a list of all the other islands you're allowed to visit in the archipelago; the majority of them are north of Port Blair. Given the great distances involved, not to mention the often erratic connections between them (and the time limit imposed by the one-month permit), it definitely pays to know where to head for as soon as you arrive rather than drift off on the first promising ferry out of Phoenix Jetty. The best way of doing this is to talk to fellow travellers arriving back in the capital. The following accounts will give you a good idea of what to expect upcountry, but new islands are opened up to tourists each year and these may well offer the kind of wilderness experience you're here for.

Having travelled all the way to the Andamans, it is surprising how many visitors make a beeline for the two only developed islands in the group, **Neill** and **Havelock**, both within easy reach of Port Blair. To get further north, where tourism of any kind has thus far had very little impact, you can take a ferry from Havelock to ramshackle **Rangat**, at the south end of **Middle Andaman**, or bypass the whole east coast by catching a bus from Port Blair direct to **Mayabunder**, the main market town for the central and north Andamans. Either way, you'll be lucky not to be marooned from time to time in some truly grim little settlements, interspersed with a few long hard slogs up the infamous **Andaman Trunk Rd** (or "ATR").

On Middle and North Andaman, and their satellite islands, **accommodation** is scarce, to say the least. Aside from a handful of new ANIIDCO hotels (bookable in advance in Port Blair), the only places to stay are APWD rest houses set aside for government officials and engineers, where you may (or may not) be granted a room if one is free. Settlements such as Rangat, Mayabunder and Diglipur, in the far north, also have very rudimentary lodges. To escape the settled areas you have to be prepared to rough it, travelling on inshore fishing dugouts, sleeping on beaches and cooking your own food. The rewards, however, are great. Backed by dense forest filled with colourful birds and insects, the beaches, bays and reefs of the outer Andamans teem with wildlife, from gargantuan crabs, pythons and turtles, to dolphins, sharks, giant rays and the occasional primeval-looking dugong.

Essential **kit** for off-track wanderings includes a sturdy mosquito net, mats to sleep on (or a hammock), a large plastic container for water, some strong antiseptic for cuts and bites (sand flies are a real problem on many of the beaches) and, most important of all, **water purification** tablets or a water purifier since bottled water is virtually non-existent. Wherever you end up, preserve the goodwill of local people by packing your rubbish out – carrying it in your backpack – or burning it, and being sensitive to scruples about dress and nudity, especially in areas settled by conservative Bengali or Tamil Hindus.

Neill

Tiny, triangular-shaped **Neill** is the most southerly inhabited island of **Ritchie's Archipelago**, a couple of hours' ferry ride northeast of Port Blair. The source of much of the capital's fresh fruit and vegetables, its fertile centre, ringed by a curtain of stately tropical trees, comprises vivid patches of green paddy dotted with small farmsteads and banana plantations. The beaches are mediocre by the Andamans' standards, but worth a day or two en route to or from Havelock.

Boats leave Port Blair four times each week for Neill (Mon, Tues, Thurs & Fri; depart 6.30am), continuing on to Havelock and Rangat. From the jetty, a two-minute walk brings you to the ANIIDCO *Yatri Niwas* (aka *Hornbill's Nest*; ☎003192/82630; ④–⑤), a dozen or so clean, carpeted rooms with sitouts, ranged around a central courtyard and restaurant. This is the only **accommodation** on the island, so book ahead before you leave Port Blair.

Neill boasts three **beaches** all of them within easy cycling distance of the small bazaar, just up the lane from the hotel (you can rent **cycles** from one or other of the stall-holders at Rs20–30 per day). **Neill Kendra**, a gently curving bay of white sand, straddles the jetty, scattered with picturesque wooden fishing boasts. A more secluded option, **Lakshmangar**, lies 2km north: head right at the hotel and follow the road for around twenty minutes until it dwindles into a surfaced track, then turn right. Wrapped around the headland, the beach is a broad spur of white shell sand with shallow water offering good snorkelling. Exposed to the open sea and thus prone to higher tides, **Sitapur** beach, 6km south at the tip of the island, is less appealing, but the ride across Neil's central paddy land is pleasant.

Havelock

Havelock is the largest island in Ritchie's Archipelago, and the most intensively cultivated, settled like many in the region by Bengali refugees after Partition. Thanks to its regular ferry connection with the capital, it is also visited in greater numbers than anywhere else in the Andamans. In peak season, as many as three hundred tourists may be holed up here, and at such times Havelock's much photographed Radhnagar beach, often touted as the most beautiful in India, can feel overwhelmed. Party-lovers from Goa have also turned up over the past few winters, complete with rave gear and full-on sound systems, so the writing may well be on the wall for Havelock. On the plus side, the boat journey here from Neill, skirting a string of uninhabited islets with shadowy views of Middle Andaman to the west, is wonderful, and wildlife – both on land and in the sea – remains abundant despite intensive settlement and deforestation.

Havelock's main **jetty** is on the north side of the island, adjoining the village known as **Havelock #1**. If you've booked a room at the ANIICDO *Dolphin Yatri Niwas*, 5km south along the east coast (see below), you'll be whisked away in the hotel minibus. Otherwise, rent a **moped** (Rs150 per day) or **cycle** (Rs50 per day) for a few days and head straight inland through the bazaar, turning right at the first T-junction you come to towards **Radhnagar** (aka **#7 beach**), 12km southwest. An intermittent bus service also covers the route, but you could find yourself waiting all day for it and miss out on a room.

After a picturesque ride past a string of thatched villages hemmed in by banana groves and paddy fields, the road drops down through some spectacular woodland to a kilometre-long arc of perfect white sand, backed by stands of giant *mowhar* trees. The water is a sublime turquoise colour, and although the coral is sparse, marine life here is diverse and plentiful, especially among the rocks around the corner from the main beach (to get there on foot, backtrack along the road and follow the path through the woods and over the bluff). During the season, Radhnagar has two **places to stay**: ANIIDCO's basic *Tent Camp* (no phone), rows of old canvas tents and a toilet block, and the luxurious *Jungle Camp* (☎/fax 03192/32838; ⑧), run by a friendly Swiss-Andaman family, which offers beautiful wood and thatch cottages in a clearing behind the beach. For the past few years, the same family has rented bare wood shelters to budget travellers (①–②), but plans are afoot to pull these down.

As the nesting site for a colony of olive ridley **turtles**, Radhnagar is strictly protected by the Forest Department, whose wardens ensure tourists do not light fires or sleep on the beach. Other accommodation options on Havelock are limited to the aforementioned *Dolphin Yatri Niwas* (☎03192/21238; ④–⑥), a cluster of well-furnished bungalows in a green enclosure right on the water's edge, 5km south of Havelock #1. A long but secluded sandy beach stretches away on both sides, broken by fallen tree trunks, and the canopy overhead is alive with giant moths and flying foxes. The hotel also has an adjoining *Tent Camp* (②). If this is full, the only other option is the less salubrious *MS Lodge* (no phone; ②–③), on the mangrove-lined outskirts of Havelock #1. In high season, the demand for rooms far outstrips supply, so be sure to book ahead. Both of the ANIIDCO places, and the *Jungle Camp*, have **restaurants**, but you can eat more cheaply at the unnamed "meals" café just north of the jetty end, which serves up hot *iddlyappams* and spicy rice plates throughout the day.

Long Island

Just off the southeast coast of Middle Andaman, **Long Island** is dominated by an unsightly plywood mill, but don't let this put you off. Served by only two boats per week from the capital (usually Wed & Sat), and two daily lumber launches from Rangat, it sees far fewer visitors than either Neill or Havelock, but boasts a couple of excellent beaches, at **Marg Bay** and **Lalaji Bay**, both most easily reached by chartering a fisherman's dingy from the jetty. The latter beach is earmarked as the site of a new ANIIDCO *Yatri Niwas*; check at the tourist office in Port Blair to see if it's opened yet. Otherwise, you could try your luck at the APWD Rest House (②), or camp. This is a good island to head for if you want to sidestep the hordes at Havelock, but don't have time to tackle the long trip north.

Middle Andaman

For most travellers, **Middle Andaman** is a charmless rite of passage to be endured en route to or from the north. The sinuous Andaman Trunk Rd, hemmed in by walls of towering forest, winds through miles of jungle, crossing the strait that separates the island from its neighbour, Baratang Island, by means of rusting flat-bottomed ferry. The island's frontier feeling is heightened by the presence on the buses of armed guards, and the knowledge that the impenetrable forests west of the ATR are the **Jarawa Tribal Reserve**. Until recently, friendly groups of Jarawa (see p.525) have emerged at Baratang jetty to accept gifts of coconuts, cloth and bananas from the Indian government, but, by and large, the only contact between them and the settlers since has been violent, with at least a dozen of deaths on both sides since 1996.

Rangat and around

At the southeast corner of Middle Andaman, **RANGAT** consists of little more than two rows of insanitary *chai* shops and general stores divided by the ATR, which in the monsoon degenerates into a fly-infested mud slick, churned at regular intervals by overladen buses. However, as a major staging post on the journey north, it's impossible to avoid; just don't get stranded here if you can help it.

Daily **ferries** to and from Port Blair (9hr) dock at **Rangat Bay** (aka **Nimbutala**), 8km east; some stop at Havelock Island (4 weekly) and Long Island (twice weekly), and there are also two daily lumber boats to Long Island. In addition, the village is served by three daily **buses** to Port Blair (8hr–9hr 30min) as well as Geetanjali Travel's express bus (7hr 30min), which passes through around lunchtime en route from Mayabunder. The APWD *Rest House* (☎01392/74237; ②), pleasantly situated up a winding hill from the bazaar with views across the valley, is the best **place to stay** and eat, providing good, filling fish *thalis*. There are also a couple of very grim lodges in the bazaar, of which the *Hare Krishna* (①) is preferable to the *Chandra Mohan* (☎01392/74219; ①). Next door to the latter is the market's best **restaurant**, the *Hotel Vijay*, whose amiable proprietor serves up copious *thalis* and, if the boat is in, crab curry, along with the usual range of soft drinks and mineral water.

If you do get stuck here, rather than staying put in Rangat jump on a bus heading north, or find a jeep to take you to **Amakunj beach**, 8km along the road to Mayabunder. On the right of the road just beyond the helipad, a Forest Department signboard saying "Sand Collection Point" marks the start of a track running the remaining 500m to the sea. The beach has little shade to speak of, but the snorkelling is good and, best of all, there's a new and very comfortable ANIIDCO *Yatri Niwas* (no phone; ③–⑤) **hotel** on the roadside, which is invariably empty.

Mayabunder

Nearly three hours further north by road, perched on a long promontory right at the top of the island and surrounded by mangrove swamps, is **Mayabunder**, springboard for the remote northern Andaman Islands. The village, which is home to a large minority of former Burmese **Karen** tribal people who were originally brought here as cheap logging labour by the British, is more spread out and more appealing than Rangat, but again there is little to hold your interest for long. The APWD Rest House (☎01392/73211; ①), occupying a prime spot above the jetty, is large and very comfortable, with a pleasant garden and gazebo overlooking the sea, and a dining room serving good set meals. The only other **accommodation** is offered by the dilapidated and cockroach-infested *Lakshminarayan Lodge* (①), five minutes' walk into town from the rest house, which should be avoided at all costs (wooden walls, nocturnal noise and no running water).

MOVING ON FROM MAYABUNDER

Until the last stretch of the Andaman Trunk Rd is completed and a bridge across the narrow strait to North Andaman Island constructed just west of Mayabunder, the shortest crossing is the ferry ride to **Kalighat** (2 daily; 2hr 30min). The first departure of the day leaves at 9.30am, on a boat that's hopelessly small and cramped, so come prepared for hours of relentless sun (or torrential rain in the monsoons). That said, the journey is very memorable, especially towards its latter stages when the mangrove-lined sides of the creek close in as you approach Kalighat. Once a week, the Port Blair ferry also calls here en route to **Diglipur**, but you'll find it less hassle, and a lot quicker, to catch the bus as this boat stops at several off-limits islands en route.

Heading in the opposite direction, **buses to Port Blair** are regular but it is advisable to book ahead, with tickets for the first of five daily government departures (at 6am) going on sale from 3pm the previous day at the bus stand, 2km from the jetty near the bazaar. Of the private services, the fastest and most comfortable is the one operated by Geetanjali Travels, which links up with the arrival of the first ferry from Kalighat, leaving the jetty at 7.30am (you can buy tickets on the bus). The trip takes between 9hr 30min and 12hr, depending on how long you have to wait at the various ferry crossings along the way. There are also four or five additional services to **Rangat**, the first at 8.30am from the bus stand.

Details of transport to **Interview Island** and **Karmateng beach** appear in the relevant accounts.

Interview Island

Mayabunder is the jumping-off place for **Interview Island**, a windswept nature sanctuary off the remote northwest coast of Middle Andaman. Only opened to tourists in 1997, it's large and mainly flat, and completely uninhabited save for a handful of unfortunate forest wardens, coast guards and policemen, posted here to ward off poachers. As foreigners aren't permitted to spend the night on the island, few tourists ever make it to Interview, but those that do are rarely disappointed. If you've come to the Andamans to watch **wildlife**, this should be top of your list.

The only way to reach Interview is to charter a private fishing dingy from Mayabunder jetty. Arrange one the day before and leave at first light. Approaching the island, you'll be struck by its wild appearance, particularly noticeable on the northwest where the monsoon storms have wrecked the shoreline forest. If you can, however, get your boatman to pull up on to the **beach** at the southern tip of the island, which has a perennial freshwater pool inside a low cave; legend has it that the well, a nesting site for white-bellied **swifts**, has no bottom. At the forest post, where you have to sign an entry ledger, ask the wardens about the movements of Interview's feral **elephants**, descendants of trained elephants deserted here by a Calcutta-based logging company after its timber operation failed in the 1950s. When food (or potential mates) are scarce, the elephants take to the sea and swim to other islands (sometimes, it is said, all the way to Mayabunder).

NORTH ANDAMAN

Shrouded in dense jungle, **North Andaman** is the least populated of the region's large islands, crossed by a single road linking its scattered Bengali settlements. Timber extraction is proceeding apace here, despite the decision by the Island Development

Authority to phase out logging by the year 2000, but the total absence of motorable roads into northern and western areas has ensured blanket protection for a vast stretch of convoluted coastline, running from Austin Strait in the southeast to the northern tip, Cape Price. Even if it were physically possible to reach this region, you wouldn't be allowed to, but it's reassuring to know at least one extensive wilderness survives in the Andamans. That said, the imminent completion of the ATR's final section, which will connect the far north to Mayabunder, may herald the start of a new settlement influx, with the same disastrous consequences for the environment seen elsewhere.

Kalighat

Until the new road is finished, **KALIGHAT**, where the river becomes unnavigable and the ferryboat from Mayabunder turns around, serves as the main entry point to North Andaman. A cluttered little bazaar unfolds from the top of the slipway, hemmed in by dense mangrove swamps, and when you arrive you should hope a bus is standing here to take you to Diglipur. If there isn't, head for one of the village's dismal little *chai* stalls and dig in for a wait, or turn right to see if there's a room in the three-roomed **Government Rest House** (no phone; ②) on the hill overlooking the end of the street. The *chowkidar* in this quaint wooden house is friendly, but refuses to cook for tourists so you'll have to chance the *chai* stalls for a meal.

The one worthwhile place to visit in this area is **Radhnagar**, 10km out of town and served by hourly buses, where there's a beautiful sandy beach backed by unspoilt forest where camping is feasible. Try to rent a **cycle** from one of the stalls in Kalighat though, as the beach is 2km outside Radhnagar bazaar, providing the nearest source of fresh water.

In principle, four **buses** per day run north from Kalighat to **Diglipur** (at 12.30pm, 1pm, 3pm & 4pm); they're crammed full, but the trip takes only 45 minutes. Heading south, the **boat** leaves at 5am for Mayabunder. If you're continuing on to **Port Blair**, buy a through bus ticket for Geetanjali Travels' express video coach (Rs100) at P.V.L. Sharma's grocery store, in the bazaar; this service is timed to leave just after the boat arrives from Kalighat.

Diglipur and Arial Bay

Known in the British era as Port Cornwallis, **DIGLIPUR**, North Andaman's largest settlement, is another disappointing market where you're only likely to pause long enough to pick up a local bus further north to the coast. On the hill above the bus stand, the APWD **Rest House** (☎01392/72203; ①) offers the village's only accommodation, but the *chowkidar*'s less than welcoming and you're better off pressing on 9km to **ARIAL BAY**, where a smaller but much more congenial APWD **Rest House** (no phone; ①) stands on a hillock overlooking the settlement's small bazaar. Better still, continue 1km further to **Kalipur**, served by hourly buses, where ANIIDCO recently opened what must rank among the region's biggest white elephant. Occupying a perfect spot on a hilltop, with superb views inland, the *Yatri Niwas* (aka *Turtle Resort*; no phone; ③–⑤), an unfeasibly large concrete hotel for such a remote location, has spacious, clean rooms with fans and a restaurant (residents only).

The staff at the hotel claim it's possible to walk from here to **Saddle Peak**, at 737m the highest mountain in the Andamans, which rises dramatically to the south, swathed in lush jungle. Permission to make the three- to four-hour climb must be obtained from the Range Officer at Arial Bay, but don't attempt the hike without a guide and plenty of drinking water. The majority of tourists who find their way up here, however, do so in order to explore the various islands dotted around the gulf north of Arial Bay. None is officially open to foreigners, but local dinghy owners will ferry you across to them for a small fee.

The best **place to eat** for miles around is the *Mohan Restaurant*, at the far end of the bazaar in Arial Bay, which serves cold drinks and huge portions of fresh local seafood to a surreal backdrop of lurid cherubs and a poster of the racehorse Red Rum.

From Arial Bay the **boat** that has made its way up with long layovers at Rangat and Mayabunder usually returns direct (weekly; 13–14hr) to Port Blair, often overnight.

OTHER ISLANDS

The remaining islands open to foreign tourists in the Andaman group are all hard to get to and, with the exception of **Little Andaman** — where a vestigial population of Onge tribespeople have survived a massive influx of Indian Tamils and native Nicobars – uninhabited. Two hours' boat ride south of Chirya Tapu on South Andaman, **Cinque Island** offers superlative diving, outshone only by distant **Barren Island**, whose volcanic sand beds teem with marine life.

Cinque and Barren islands

Cinque Island actually comprises two islets, joined by a spectacular sand isthmus, with shallow water either side that covers it completely at high tide. The main incentive to come here is the superlative diving and snorkelling around the reefs. However, heaps of dead coral on the beach attest to damage recently wrought by the Indian navy during the construction of the swish air-conditioned "cottages" overlooking the beach. Rumour has it that these were built for the visit of a Thai VIP in 1996, but local government officials now use them as bolt holes from Port Blair.

Although there are no **ferries** to Cinque, it is possible to arrange dinghies from Chirya Tāpu village on South Andaman (see p.533). The two dive centres in Port Blair also regularly come here with clients. Currently, your permit only allows you to spend the day on the island; overnights stays are prohibited.

The most intriguing island open to tourists in the Andaman group has to be **Barren Island**, twenty hours' sea voyage east of Port Blair. India's only active **volcano**, the arid brown mountain blew its top in May 1991 after lying dormant for 188 years, and has done so on two occasions since between 1994 and 1995. The only living creatures on Cinque are a herd of **goats**, released in 1891 by the British to provide sustenance for any shipwrecked sailors. There are no ferries to the island, but diving expeditions regularly make the trip as the seas around Barren are the richest in the region.

Little Andaman

Little Andaman is the furthest point south in the archipelago you can travel to on a standard one-month tourist permit. Located eight hours by sea from Port Blair, most of the island has been set aside as a tribal reserve for the **Onge** (see p.525) and is thus off-limits. The only areas you're allowed to visit lie on either side of the main settlement, Hut Bay. The northern part of this stretch has been mercilessly clear-felled, leaving a stark wasteland flanking the main road, while the coast to the south boasts few beaches to compare with those further north in the Andamans. Given the discomfort involved in getting here (the boat journey can be hideous experience), it's not hard to see why so few travellers bother.

Those that do rarely venture far out of **Hut Bay**, a scruffy agglomeration of *chai* shacks, hardware and provision stores ranged along Little Andaman's single surfaced road. The only remarkable feature of this insalubrious, unwelcoming place is an extraordinarily high incidence of cerebral **malaria** – another reason not to come here. Unfortunately, the late afternoon arrival time of the ferry means that unless you're kitted out to camp and have enough provisions, you'll have to spend at least a night in town (see below). As soon as you can, though, head south down the coast, beyond the Christian Nicobari settlements around **John Richardson Bay** (3km), to the island's only accessible **beaches**; be prepared for sand flies and long walks to water sources, and try not to wander into the Onges' reserve, which begins at the lighthouse.

Practicalities

Boats leave Port Blair for Little Andaman around twice a week; the service to aim for is the one that continues south to Car Nicobar, capital of the Nicobar Islands, as the ferry is larger and marginally more comfortable. Both arrive at the main jetty (specially enlarged for the full-on logging operation still under way here), 3km plod from the bazaar, where you'll find the island's only **accommodation**. Before leaving Port Blair, it's worth making a reservation for the APWD **Rest House** (no phone; ②) enquire at the APWD *Rest House* at Port Blair, 1km north of the shops behind the **hospital**, which has clean and spacious en suite rooms. Otherwise your only option is the bleak and nameless **lodge** (no phone; ①) in the bazaar, whose rooms wouldn't look out of place in the Cellular Jail. If you find yourself having to sleep here, take your mattress and mosquito net onto the roof as constant power cuts render the fans useless.

travel details

Note that no individual route appears more than once in this chart; for any specific journey, check against where you want to get to as well as where you're coming from. Bear in mind, also, that there is only room here for a general summary; see the Moving On sections in specific accounts for more details.

Planes

Port Blair to: Calcutta (4 weekly; 2hr); Chennai (3 weekly; 2hr).

Boats

Port Blair to: Chennai (1 every 1 or 2 weeks; 60hr); Calcutta (1 every 1 or 2 weeks; 60 hr); Vishakapatnam (1 monthly; 60hr); Neill Island (4 weekly; 3hr); Havelock Island (4 weekly; 4hr); Long Island (2 weekly; 7hr 30min); Arial Bay (1 weekly; 24hr); Little Andaman (2 weekly; 7–8hr).

Buses

Port Blair to: Mayabunder (3 daily; 9hr 30min–12hr).

Those that do venture [illegible] Mayabunder [illegible] generally quite [illegible] Andaman's [illegible] [illegible] into the [illegible] [illegible] beyond the [illegible] [illegible] walks [illegible] [illegible]

[illegible]

[illegible] for Little Andaman around [illegible] in the [illegible] capital of the Nicobar Islands [illegible] larger and [illegible] port [illegible] under way [illegible] It's worth making a reservation for the APWD Rest House [illegible] the APWD [illegible] has [illegible] and [illegible] rooms. Otherwise your only option is [illegible] in the [illegible] If you find yourself having to sleep here, [illegible] the East [illegible]

[illegible]

Note that [illegible]

Boats

Port Blair [illegible]

Flights

Port Blair to [illegible]

Planes

Port Blair to [illegible] (weekly; 2hr).

PART THREE

THE CONTEXTS

A BRIEF HISTORY OF SOUTH INDIA

South India – the vast triangular-shaped peninsula beyond the Narmada River – is separated from the north by the Vindhya Range, a barren band of sheer-sided table mountains. For many centuries, this geographical obstacle discouraged the movement of peoples between the two regions. The South thus remained largely isolated from the changes imported by successive waves of invaders who swept across the Gangetic plains from the northwest.

Tracing the progress of these newcomers, written histories of the subcontinent have tended to focus on the impact of North upon South. Influences did traverse the Vindhyas and Deccan Plateau, but they invariably did so slowly, by a process of gradual assimilation rather than conquest, enabling the societies of the peninsula to develop in their own way. Moreoever, some of India's most defining cultural traits and traditions originated in the deep Dravidian south, from where they spread northwards.

PREHISTORY

By comparison with the extraordinary wealth of archeological finds in northwestern India, evidence of **prehistoric settlement** in the South is scant. Yet one of the oldest human artefacts ever unearthed in Asia was discovered at Pallavaram, near Chennai (Madras). In 1863, British archeologist Bruce Foote found an oval-shaped hand-axe, flaked on both faces to produce a clean cutting edge, that he surmised must have originated in the Lower Paleolithic era. Since this initial discovery, similar tools have come to light as far south as the Kaveri River delta, indicating that the region was inhabited by **nomadic hunter-gatherers** at the same time as similar groups emerged in the distant north, between 400,000 and 10,000 years ago.

The first archeologist to establish a sequence for the various stone implements discovered in the South was Mortimer Wheeler, whose work on the Coromandel Coast near Pondicherry in 1945 showed that metal was introduced comparatively late to the region. Fixing the date-spans of upper strata with the Roman coins he found in them, Wheeler showed how copper made its first appearance midway through the second millennium BC, by which time rudimentary **agriculture** and the **domestication of animals** were widespread along open, coastal areas and river deltas.

It has never been proven, but new technologies, including metal, were probably imported into South India from the northwest, where sophisticated urban civilizations of the Indus Valley – the region straddling the present-day India–Pakistan border – were already well established by 3000 BC. Recent paleobotanical studies have shown that a sharp rise in rainfall occurred around this time, which probably explains why agriculture was able to flourish and cities emerge. The inhabitants of **Harappa** and **Mohenjo Daro**, large urban centres that reached their peaks between 2300 and 1800 BC, were certainly expert water managers. Amid the ruins of their well-organized cities, remnants of elaborate sewerage and irrigation systems have been found, along with scales and weights, metal jewellery, weapons, precious stones, seals and delicate pottery. Huge communal granaries stored the surplus grain that underpinned a flourishing foreign trade, and the existence of palaces and spacious houses show that this was a highly stratified society, with its own script and formalized religion.

After the sensational rediscovery of the Harappan ruins in the 1920s, it was long assumed that invasions from the northwest brought about the eventual demise of the Indus Valley civilizations, but it now seems more likely prolonged drought caused the decline. The same climatic changes may also explain how **metal** technology and knowledge of **rice cultivation** first found their way south: as rainfall decreased, the corresponding drop in agricultural output impoverished the once-thriving cities of the Indus Valley, forcing its inhabitants to flee south in search of more fertile land.

THE DRAVIDIANS

Some historians have advanced this migration theory to account for the origins of the so-called **Dravidians**, who are believed to have colonized the South around the same time as the Indus Valley civilization went into decline in the second millennium BC. However, the most compelling evidence that the Dravidians originated in the northwest is linguistic. Kanad, Telegu, Malayalam and Tamil – the principal modern languages of South India – have a completely different root to the main languages of the north, which derive from the so-called Indo-Aryan group, and are based principally on Sanskrit. Over the years, some wild comparisons have been made between Dravidian and other Asian tongues (most notably Japanese), but the only surviving Asian language with definite Dravidian antecedents is Brahui, spoken by the transhumant people of the Baluchistan uplands on the Iran–Pakistan border. This fact suggests that the Dravidians almost certainly came from the Baluchi grasslands in the fourth or third millennium BC, via the Indus Valley, where they would have acquired the metalwork and farming techniques that subsequently allowed them to establish permanent settlements in the far south.

Although far less technologically advanced than the Indus Valley civilizations, the Dravidian tribes, based around fertile riverine lands that were separated by densely wooded hills and mountain ranges, forged a strong agrarian base and gradually evolved into distinct chiefdoms. Like the Harappans, their essentially agricultural economies were supplemented by trade in luxury goods such as shells, precious stones and pearls (the Old Testament records that King Solomon sent ships every three years to South India to buy silver, gold, ivory, monkeys and peacocks). This maritime trade expanded steadily over the centuries, enabling the region's chiefs to extend their rule inland and create larger settlements away from the coast.

THE ARYANS

For most of the twentieth century, archeologists believed the dramatic demise of the Indus Valley cities, between 1800 and 1700 BC, was precipitated by the arrival of invaders from the northwest. Recent carbon-dating techniques, however, have shown that the decline occurred between two and three centuries before the first appearance on the northern plains of a fairer-skinned nomadic people, who called themselves the *Aryas*, or **Aryans**.

The precise route of this migration remains a moot point among historians. Some argue that the newcomers travelled southeast through Persia, while others claim they came via Afghanistan. There is, however, a general consensus that they originated in a region around the Caucasus Mountains, and were part of an ancient diaspora that spread as far as western Europe (their language, an antiquated form of Sanskrit, has astonishingly close affinities with Latin, Greek and Celtic).

The main historical source for this era is the **Rig Veda**, a vast body of 1028 hymns, epic chants, spells, songs and instructions for religious rituals equal in length to the *Iliad* and *Odyssey* combined. Phrased in 10,600 elaborate metered verses, this laboriously sophisticated work includes sections composed between 1400 and 1500 BC, transmitted orally and only set down in writing in the modern era. The Aryans' sacred scriptures contain a wealth of detail about their daily life, philosophical ideas and religious practices. Frequent references to Agni, the "God of Fire", and Indra, "the Fort Breaker", are indicative of violent encounters with the dark-skinned indigenous inhabitants of northern Indian, known as *Dasa* or *Dasyas*, whom the warrior bands swept aside in their slow expansion eastwards over the middle of the second millennium BC. These conquests were facilitated by the Aryans' use of horse-drawn, spoke-wheeled **chariots**, an incomparably fast and effective way of crossing the dry plains.

By the dawn of the **Iron Age** early in the first millennium BC, the dominion of the Aryans, by now a loose confederacy of tribes who fought each other as much as their indigenous enemies, stretched south as far as the Vindhya Range and the rich soils of the Deccan Plateau. Beyond lay the wild unexplored territory of **Dakshinapatha**, "the Way South", blocked by dense forests and ravine-scarred hills.

SANSKRITIZATION OF THE SOUTH

The *Rig Veda* records the reluctance of the Ayrans to press south along this route, but it is clear some of their priests (*brahmins*) and wandering ascetics (*rishis*) did, probably in search of patronage. Along with their sacred verses, Vedic philosophies and knowledge of iron, they took with them concepts of racial discrimination derived from centuries of war with the Dyasas, who by this time seem to have become a sub-class below the three existing grades in Aryan society: priests (*brahmins*), warriors (*kshatriyas*) and artisans (*vaishyas*). A product of the transition from nomadic to settled society, the **caste** system – based on notions of **varna**, or colour, and ritual pollution – seemed to have found favour among the tribal chiefs of southern India, who deployed the new ideas and scriptures of the *brahmins* to legitimize their rule.

The transmission of cultural influences from north to south was slow, but pervasive. By the sixth century BC, brahmanical philosophies formed the religious bedrock of the many petty chiefdoms and larger principalities that had proliferated in the South, where village culture had by now firmly taken root under the tutelage of the *brahmins* – a way of life that would remain largely intact in the region for another two thousand years.

THE MAURYAN ERA

In the Gangetic basin, meanwhile, small tribal kingdoms (*janapadas*) were beginning to merge with others to form larger confederacies (*mahajanapadas*) governed by single rulers from fortified capitals. Two new reforming religious movements were also gaining ground in the north. The first, **Buddhism** (see p.568), arose from the teachings of a young prince from the Nepalese foothills, Siddharta, or **Gautama Buddha** (563–483 BC). In addition, **Jainism**, founded by the prophet **Mahavira** (599–527 BC) around the same time, began to attract followers, most notably among the ruling elite of a dynasty that was destined to become the most powerful in the subcontinent.

Stepping into the vacuum left by the departure of **Alexander the Great** from the northwest, the **Mauryans**, who ruled the region southeast of the Ganges, usurped the throne of their arch-adversaries, the Nandas, in 320 BC to make their king, **Chandragupta Maurya**, the first *de facto* emperor of India, with an empire that stretched from the Punjab to Karnataka. A strict Jain, he eventually renounced his throne and starved himself to death on a hilltop at Sravanabelgola (still an important South Indian pilgrimage centre), thereby achieving the status of a saint.

From their capital at Pataliputra (in Bihar, near present-day Patna), the Mauryans ruled over a vast swathe of the subcontinent, greatly enlarged during the reign of Chandragupta's grandson, **Ashoka**, who defeated the mighty Kalingas on the east coast (modern Orissa). It was the bloody aftermath of that battle, in which 100,000 people were killed and 150,000 abducted, that the emperor embraced Buddhism and the path of non-violence. Edicts proclaiming the tenets of the new imperial faith were erected throughout the empire, and missionaries and ambassadors dispatched to spread the message of "right conduct", or *dhamma*, abroad. No such edicts, however, have so far come to light further south than the goldfields around Mysore, and it seems likely that most of the Deccan and peninsular India, including all of modern Andhra Pradesh, Kerala and Tamil Nadu, remained outside Mauryan influence.

The Mauryans may never have conquered the far south, but their way of life and system of government strongly influenced developments in the region. Through trade and interaction with Jain and Buddhist monk-missionaries, concepts of statehood gradually filtered south, encouraging the dominant powers in the peninsula to expand their realms.

DRAVIDADESA: THE EARLY KINGDOMS

Inscribed on the eight rock-cut edicts that Ashoka raised on the frontiers of his empire in the third century BC are verses expressing goodwill towards his "undefeated neighbours" (*avijita*). The list includes the earliest known references to the three ancient ruling clans who dominated the far south in the final centuries of the first millennium BC: the **Cholas** of the Coromandel region and Kaveri basin; the **Pandyas**, whose capital was at Madurai; and the **Cheras**, from southwest Kerala. Collectively, the kingdoms of these three dynasties comprised a domain known to northerners as **Dravidadesa**, "Land of the Tamils".

A wealth of historical detail relating to the early kingdoms of the South has survived, most of it in a remarkable body of classical Tamil poetry known as the **Sangam**, composed between the first and third centuries AD in the literary academies (*sangam*) of Madurai. The texts, which were only rediscovered in the nineteenth century, refer to an era when the indigenous Dravidian culture of the deep south was being transformed by Sanskritic influences from the north. Nevertheless, they vividly demonstrate that some of the most distinctive characteristics of Indian civilization – including *yoga*, *tantra*, the cult of the god Murugan and goddess worship – were almost certainly indigenous to the South, and widespread well before the Aryan came to dominate the region completely.

The Sangam also records the stormy political relations between the three dynasties, who were frequently at war with each other, or with the rulers of neighbouring Sri Lanka. Ultimately, however, all three seem to have succumbed to an enigmatic fourth dynasty, the **Kalabhras**, about whom the Sangam poems say very little other than that they were "bad kings" (*kaliarasar*). Buddhist texts from a later period suggest the Kalabhras were originally hill tribes who swept down from the Deccan to harass the inhabitants of the river valleys and coastal areas, and later took up Jainism and Buddhism, deposing the Dravidian kings and persecuting the *brahmins*.

THE EXPANSION OF TRADE

The cultural flowering of the Sangam era in the South, during the first two centuries AD, was stimulated by a rapid growth in **maritime trade** throughout the region. As well as Arab merchants, the ports of the Malabar and Coromandel coasts now began to welcome **Roman** ships. After a century of relentless civil war, peace had returned to Rome, bringing with it renewed demand in the imperial capital for luxury goods such as pearls, spices, perfumes, precious stones and silk. When Augustus conquered Egypt to open up the Red Sea, and Hippalus discovered that the monsoon winds would blow a ship from there across the Arabian Sea in around a fortnight, the means to supply this appetite for exotic oriental merchandise was within the Romans' grasp.

A vivid picture of the boom that ensued has survived in an extraordinary mariners' manual entitled the *Periplus of the Erythraean Sea*, written by an anonymous Alexandrian merchant-adventurer. Featuring meticulous descriptions of the trade, ports and capital cities of the far south, it reveals that the region was an entrepôt for valuable foreign goods – notably Chinese silk and oil from the Gangetic basin – and that the Coromandel was gradually eclipsing the Malabar as peninsular India's principal trade platform.

This fact has been borne out by Mortimer Wheeler's discovery of the Romans' main trading post at **Arikamedu**, just south of modern Pondicherry in Tamil Nadu, where large brick buildings, water reservoirs, baths and a huge number of artefacts – including shards of pre-Christian ceramics from Arezzo and hoards of coins – suggest it was largely the lust for Roman gold that fuelled the ancient trade in the South. Indeed, the Roman chronicler, Strabo, famously complained that the Indian merchants were threatening to completely empty the treasuries of Rome of gold coins. Prodigious quantities of these have been unearthed in recent times, especially in the area around the ancient port of **Muziris**, near present-day Kannur in northern Kerala.

THE SATAVAHANAS

Coupled with the advances in knowledge of state administration made by the Mauryans, the vast trade wealth pouring into South India around the turn of the millennium enabled the region's rulers to create larger and more organized kingdoms, backed by well-equipped armies. Conditions were ripe for the rise of a major power, and this came in the first century BC with the advent of the **Satavahanas**, an obscure tribal dynasty from the Deccan who, in the space of a hundred years, assumed the imperial mantle of the Mauryans. By the time Ptolemy was writing his *Geography*, midway through the second century AD, the empire, based in **Pratisthana** (near modern Paithan in Maharashtra), comprised thirty fortified cities and stretched from coast to coast. Administered by a network of noblemen, it was upheld by semi-autonomous military garrisons, with an army said by the Roman chronicler Pliny to consist of 30,000 cavalry and 9000 war elephants.

Thanks to their control of the region's lucrative foreign trade, the Satavahanas (or Andhras as they are referred to in some ancient texts) were also prolific patrons of the arts, responsible for the greatest monuments in India at that time, notably the famous ornamental gateways (*toranas*) of the Buddhist *stupa* at **Sanchi** (in Madhya Pradesh), and many of the most accomplished rock-cut caves of the northwest Deccan. However, the crowning glory of Andhran art was to be the Great Stupa complex at **Amaravati**, in Andhra Pradesh (see p.514), whose exquisite bas-reliefs (now housed in the Government Museum, Chennai; see p.376) are considered by many scholars to be the finest ancient Indian sculpture.

THE EARLY MIDDLE AGES: 600–1200 AD

The history of the early middle ages in South India, from the time of the Satavahanas' demise to the arrival of the Muslims, hinges on the rise and fall of a mosaic of **regional dynasties**. These invariably fought each other to gain supremacy for short periods, and then found their rule usurped by one or other of their adversarial neighbours. Not until the sword of Islam descended on the Deccan in the thirteenth century did the peninsula succumb to a single overlord.

Various theories have been advanced to explain this, but the most convincing is that the warring kingdoms were generally too small to exert control over large territories for long. Bringing rebellious chiefdoms to heel meant costly military expeditions, which would inevitably render the ruler's own region vulnerable to attack.

Despite this, the on-going power balance miligtated against the rise of an empire and the long-term political stability it afforded allowed for the development of distinct regional cultures. The wealth of historic monuments scattered across South India today graphically exemplify the differences between these cultures, and the way in which they interacted over the centuries.

CHALUKYAS, PALLAVAS AND CHOLAS

Foremost among the states of the southern Deccan were the **Chalukyas**, who had been underlings of the Kadamabas (Hindu rulers of the region that later became Goa) until **Pulakeshin I** broke away and founded a capital at Vatapi (**Badami**; see p.250). Here, atop a rocky escarpment overlooking a lake, the king and his descendants erected a series of magnificent stone temples. From simple rock-cut excavations, these evolved into more sophisticated free-standing structures, embellished with elaborate iconographic sculpture, that were among the first buildings in the region to fuse indigenous architectural styles with those of northern India.

The Chalukyas' conspicuous wealth inevitably attracted the attentions of their covetous neighbours. After fending off two invasions, they eventually succumbed in 753 AD to the **Rashtrakutas**, whose domain extended most of the way across the Deccan.

The Chalukyas' southern enemies, the **Pallavas**, emerged after defeating the Kalabhras, the "bad kings" who originally routed the region's three early dynasties. Originally Buddhists, they converted to brahmanism sometime in the fifth century and thereafter carved out a kingdom that would spread from the mouth of the Krishna River to the edge of the Kaveri basin in the south. From the outset, the Pallavas seem to have been keen seafarers, trading with Greeks, Satavahanas and Romans, whose coins have all been found amid the ruins of ancient **Mamallapuram** (see p.397), just south of Chennai. The extraordinary crop of stone temples, open-air bas-reliefs and finely carved caves dotted around this fishing and stone-carving village recall the era when it ranked among the busiest ports in Asia.

The majority of Mamallapuram's monuments were begun in the mid-seventh century, during the reign of Narasimha Varman I (aka *Mamalla*, "the Great Wrestler"), and completed over the following two generations. Of them all, the best known is the **Shore temple**, overlooking the beach and thought to be the first shrine built of loose stone blocks in the subcontinent. Surmounted by a steep pyramidal tower (*vimana*), it closely resembles the better preserved Kailasanatha temple in the Pallavas' former capital, **Kanchipuram**, where, in the mid-seventh century, the Chinese pilgrim, Hsiuen-tsang, reported seeing one hundred Buddhist monasteries as well as eighty major Hindu temples.

The Shore temple at Mamallapuram provided the main architectural inspiration for the **Cholas**, an offshoot of the ancient dynasty of the same name who asserted their independence from the Pallavas in 897 AD, when the latter had their hands full fighting off the Rastrakutas. During their two-hundred-and-fifty-year rule, the Cholas expanded out of their royal capital, **Thanjavur**, in the Kaveri basin, defeating both the Pandyas and Cheras, and later conquering Sri Lanka, the Maldives and the Andamans, in addition to enclaves in Java and Sumatra, which they captured in order to control trade with Southeast Asia.

Combined with the huge sums in plunder yielded by their military campaigns, the Cholas' trade monopoly financed an awesome building spree. The dynasty's most visionary ruler was **Rajaraja I** (985–1014), who erected the colossal Brihadishwara temple, in its day the largest in India. Decorating the walls of the shrine, beneath its soaring tower, exquisite frescoes recall the opulence and sophistication of the Chola court, where keen patronage of the arts – most famously bronze-casting, but also Carnatic music, sculpture, dance and literature – produced works that have never been surpassed since.

BHAKTI AND THE TAMIL POETS

From the eighth century onwards, the devotional form of Hinduism known as **bhakti**, which blossomed in Tamil Nadu, spread north into the rest of India to become, as it still is, the dominant strain of Hinduism throughout the country. It was essentially a popular movement, whose emphasis that each individual devotee could form a personalized, emotionally charged relationship with a chosen god (*ishtadevata*) revolutionized Hindu practice by offering a religious path and goal open to all castes.

The great champions of *bhakti* were the **poet-saints** of Tamil Nadu, often said to have "sung" the religions of Jainism and Buddhism out of South India. Although in practice a variety of deities was worshipped, the movement had two strands: the **Nayanmars**, devoted to Shiva, and the **Alvars**, centred on Vishnu. Collections of their poetry, the greatest literary legacy of South India, remain popular today, and the poets themselves are almost deified, featuring in carvings in many temples.

The four most prominent of the 63 Nayanmar poet-saints were **Campantar**, who converted the king of Madurai from Jainism and had a great cult centre at Chidambaram; **Cuntarar**, a *brahmin* who had two low-caste wives; **Appar**, himself a convert from Jainism; and **Manikkavachakar**, whose mystical poems are still sung in homes and temples throughout Tamil Nadu. The Vaishnavite movement centred on Srirangam (near Trichy), its poets including men and women of all social classes. The most celebrated Alvar was **Nammalvar**, a *shudra* who spent his life in fasting and meditation. **Antal**, the most popular female Alvar, is said to have married Vishnu's statue at Srirangam, and was thereafter regarded as an incarnation of Vishnu's consort, Shri.

All the poems tell of the ecstatic response to intense experiences of divine favour, an emotion frequently described in terms of conjugal love, and expressed in verses of great tenderness and beauty. They stress selfless love between man and god, claiming that such love alone can lead to everlasting union with the divine. Devotees travelled the South, singing, dancing and challenging opponents to public debates.

Among the most significant consequences of the *bhakti* revolution in Hinduism was the emergence of **temple cities**. By stressing the importance of the individual's devotion to a particular god or goddess, *bhakti* inspired a massive upsurge in popular worship and, inevitably, a proliferation of shrines to accommodate worshippers. This process went hand in hand with the assimilation of important regional deities into the Hindu pantheon. Thus, trees, rocks, caves or bodies of water held sacred in a given place began to be "legitimized" through identification with Shiva or Vishnu. Notable examples include the deities of Chidambaram and Madurai, two of South India's most important religious centres, whose importance was firmly established well before the Sanskritization that associated them with Shiva in the sixth century.

In time, the same happened to lesser local gods and village deities, until innumerable cult centres across the South became bound in a complex web of interconnections. The institution of **pilgrimage**, linking local and distant deities, emerged for the first time as an essential element of Hinduism during the era of the Tamil saints, and has remained an important unifying force in India ever since. It is no coincidence that some of the most defining texts of the *bhakti* movement are the *Mahatmyas*, oral chants intoned by *brahmins* that elucidate the significance of individual temples and their relationship to other shrines.

MUSLIM INCURSIONS

At the start of the eleventh century, a new player appeared on the political map of northern India. **Mahmud**, a Turkish chieftain who had established a powerful kingdom at Ghazni, near Kabul in Afghanistan, made seventeen plundering raids into the plains of India between 1000 and 1027 AD. His was the first of many Muslim incursions from the northwest that would, after two hundred years of constant infighting and wars with local rulers, lead to the creation of an Islamic empire based in Delhi.

Founded in 1206 AD, the **Delhi Sultanate** made little impact on the South during its formative years. In 1309, however, the redoubtable Sultan **Allauddin Khilji**, set his sights southwards. Having heard rumours of the treasures stored in the great Tamil temples (Rajaraja had not long before donated 880kg of gold to the Brihadishwara temple), he took advantage of the Cholas' decline to mount a raid. It is recorded that his general, the ruthless military genius and former Hindu slave, **Malik Kafur**, returned with a thousand camels bearing booty, including the famous Kohinoor diamond.

This, however, was merely a prelude to the Sultanate's second expedition of 1310–1311, in the course of which Allauddin's army pressed into the deep south itself. Raiding towns and desecrating the splendid Chola temples of the Kaveri Delta, it reached Madurai on April 10, 1311 and mercilessly sacked the Pandyas' capital, massacring the few of its inhabitants who had not fled. Forewarned of Kafur's approach, many temples had hidden or buried their treasures. Some, like the eighty priceless Chola bronzes that came to light in Chidambaram in the 1960s, were rediscovered; others remain lost.

Aside from the wholesale destruction of art treasures, the main legacy of Allauddin's plunder was the creation of a short-lived **Muslim Sultanate** at Tirupparakunram (see p.463), near Madurai. Overlooking the town from the top of a huge sandstone outcrop, the tomb of its eighth and last Sultan, **Sikander Shah**, remains one of the far south's few bona fide Muslim shrines.

THE DECCAN SULTANATES

The Delhi Sultanates possessed sufficient military strength to subdue most of India, but time and again showed themselves incapable of consolidating their territorial gains with strong administrations. In the end, the despot **Muhamed Tuqluq**'s incessant wars, together with his crackpot plan to relocate the capital from Delhi to Daulatabad, 1000km south on the Deccan, saw the Sultanates' reign degenerate into one of terror and profligacy. Forced by drought, famine and the threat of Moghul invasion to abandon Daulatabad and return to Delhi, Tuqluq struggled until his death to hold onto power. By the mid-fourteenth century, his succesor, **Feroz Shah**, had completely lost control of the Deccan.

In the wake of the Daulatabad debacle, one of Tuqluq's former generals, **Zafar Shah**, aka **Bahman Shah**, saw his chance to found his own dynasty, which he located at a safe distance south of the old capital, at **Gulbarga** (in present-day northern Karnataka). The **Bahmanis'** rule lasted around two hundred years, and was as bloody as the old Delhi Sultanate's; Zafar Shah's son, Muhammed Shah (1358–73) is said to slaughtered half a million people in his wars with neighbouring states, which included the Vijayanagars, who founded their empire at around the same time (see p.552).

In the fifteenth century AD, the Bahmanis shifted their capital further northeast to **Bidar**, constructing a massive fortress that still survives. Under the careful stewardship of **Mahmud Gawan**, a talented prime minister who served several successive sultans, the dynasty flourished, but went into a dramatic decline after his death. The ensuing power struggle saw the governors of the four largest districts in the kingdom – Bijapur, Ahmadnagar, Bidar and Golconda – declare independence, with Bijapur eventually emerging as the major power by the sixteenth century. Their rule, however, was bedevilled by conflict with both Vijayanagar and the Portuguese; they lost the port of Goa to the latter in 1510.

The power balance between the Deccan kingdoms was decisively turned in the Muslims' favour after 1565 when, following years of fighting each other, the sultanates formed a pact to wage war on their common Hindu enemies, the Vijayanagars. At the battle of Talikota that year, the alliance crushed the Hindu army and set about the most destructive sack of a city the subcontinent had ever seen.

Within twenty-one years, however, the Deccan sultanates had succumbed completely to the might of the Moghuls.

VIJAYANAGAR: 1346–1565

To the north of the Bahmanis' territory, the Krishna River formed the border with the mighty Hindu kingdom of **Vijayanagar**, which emerged in the south in response to the threat of Muslim invasions. Its founders were two brothers from Andhra Pradesh, **Harihara** and **Bukka**, who were allegedly captured by Tuqluq during his sack of Kampili in 1327 AD and taken as prisoners to Delhi, where they converted to Islam before being dispatched as governors to their native town to restore order after an uprising. Legend has it that the sage Vidyaranya then reconverted the brothers to Hinduism and encouraged them to defect (although some Indian historians have disputed this, claiming Harihara and Bukka were actually offshoots of the Hoysalas).

Whatever its roots, the dynasty the brothers founded on the banks of the Tungabadhra River (at modern-day Hampi; see p.248) quickly flourished. Following a series of short wars with the Hoysalas, Madurai and the Gajapatis of eastern Indian, the rulers of the southern kingdoms pragmatically threw in their lot with the ambitious newcomers, realizing their best chance of protection from marauding Muslims lay in a strong Hindu front to the north. This proved to be the case. At a time when the influence of Turkish, Persian and Afghan culture on northern India was most marked, the South, insulated by Vijayanagar, remained outside the sway of Islam – a fact that accounts perhaps better than anything else for the striking cultural differences that still exist between the north and the south of the subcontinent.

Vijayanagar's golden period was during the reign of **Krishna Deva Raya** (1509–29), before its monopoly over the trade in spices and Arabian horses had been undermined by the Portuguese and other European powers. While the Bijapuris were a constant and costly source of irritation, the king's well-organized administration, together with his control of some thirty or so rich ports, ensured a steady flow of wealth.

The dynastic capital, Vijayanagar ("City of Victory") became, for an all too brief period, among the most splendid in the world. Travellers such as Domingo Paes, who spent from 1522 to 1524 there, marvelled at the opulence of its royal court, the richness of its bazaars and the sumptuousness of its festivals. Krishna Deva Raya's rule was also the period when the South acquired some of its most impressive **temple towers** (*gopuras*), erected by the king to foster loyalty among *brahmins* and inhabitants of distant regions over which Vijayanagar's hold was precarious.

After Krishna Deva Raya's death in 1529, internal struggles and conflicts with the Portuguese weakened the empire. However, it was the Vijayanagar old foe, the Bijapuris, who eventually brought their glorious rule to an abrupt and bloody end. Having benefited from the Deccan Sultanates' constant feuding for more than a century, the Vijayanagars made a fatal mistake when they desecrated mosques during campaigns in the 1550s. This finally galvanized the sultans to set aside their differences and march on Vijayanagar. The armies met at Talikota in 1565. At first, the battle seemed to be going the Hindus' way, but suddenly turned against them when two of their Muslim generals defected. The Vijayanagar regent, Rama Raya, was captured and beheaded, while his brother, Tirumala, fled with what was left of the army, leaving the capital defenceless.

The ensuing sack lasted six months and reduced Asia's most illustrious city to rubble. Predictably, the Deccan sultans squabbled over the spoils and spent the next century fighting each other, leaving the region vulnerable to invasion by the Moghuls.

THE PORTUGUESE

Around the same time as Vijayanagar was enjoying its period of greatest prosperity, the harbinger of a new regional power appeared on the horizon of the Arabian Sea. Driven by the lust for "Christians and Spices", Vasco da Gama's arrival on the Malabar Coast in 1498 (see box on p.554) blazed a trail that would, after only fifteen years, result in the creation of Europe's first bona fide colony in the East.

Formerly a Vijayanagar port, **Goa** had been taken by the Bahmanis, whom the Portuguese, under **Admiral Alfonso Albuquerque**, expelled in 1510. Thereafter, despite repeated attempts by the Muslims to regain their possession, the colony expanded at a breathless pace. At the height of its power, the city was the linchpin of a trade network extending from the Philippines to the north Atlantic, with cathedrals to rival Rome's and a population that at one time was greater even than Lisbon's.

Yet despite enjoying an early monopoly on maritime trade in Asia, ruthlessly enforced by

THE QUINCENTENNIAL CONTROVERSY

On May 18, 1498, three Portuguese *caravelas* dropped anchor off the coast of northern Kerala at a beach called Kappad, having sailed from Lisbon via the Cape of Good Hope in a little over ten months. Five hundred years later, to the day, groups of angry protesters gathered on the same beach to burn effigies of the explorer who stepped ashore, **Vasco da Gama**. By rounding the tip of Africa and opening up a maritime route to the spice markets of western India, da Gama would change the pattern of world history, for which he has been feted as a national hero ever since by the Portuguese public. Among the educated classes of India, however, he is reviled as a pirate and looter, who committed acts of appalling barbarism out of greed for "black gold" – the pepper of the Malabar Coast.

While the ramifications of da Gama's voyages remain a subject of heated debate, the essential facts of his three expeditions to India have survived, thanks to the diaries of Alvaro Velho, one of da Gama's soldiers. These describe in detail how the small fleet of five ships set sail from Lisbon in July 1497, with an aura of messianic resolve as the sacred symbol of Christ billowed in their sails. Their route took them around the islands of Cabo Verde (Cape Verde) and four thousand miles southeast to round the Cape of Good Hope at the beginning of November.

At Malindi, da Gama was granted the services of an expert navigator, an Arab sea captain called **Ibn' Masjid**, who piloted the three remaining *caravelas* across the Indian Ocean to Calicut. However, news of atrocities committed by the Portuguese en route had preceded their arrival, and the local *zamorin*, Mana Vikrama, briefly imprisoned da Gama before he was allowed to fill his holds with pepper and leave – an insult the proud Portuguese admiral would never forget.

Four years later he returned to Calicut, this time bent on revenge. In addition to what he perceived as his own "contumely treatment" at the hands of the Hindu ruler, he intended to avenge the murder of 53 Portuguese killed during a previous expedition in 1500. As a prelude to the onslaught, da Gama waylaid a Muslim ship en route from Mecca and burned alive all 700 of its passengers and crew. Then he set about bombarding the city. While the cannonade decimated Calicut's temples and houses, da Gama ordered the crews of a dozen or so trade ships anchored in the harbour to be rounded up. Before killing them, he had the prisoners' hands, ears and noses hacked off and the pieces sent ashore piled in a small boat.

This horrific act set the precedent, and genocide became a hallmark of early Portuguese colonialism in Asia, as the Europeans extended their trade links up the South Indian coast to Goa. And so it was with some astonishment that, five centuries later, Goan nationalist politicians and journalists greeted Portugal's invitation to participate in the festivities marking the quincentennial of Vasco da Gama's voyage. Quite apart from those original atrocities, Goan freedom fighters, who had struggled to oust the Portuguese, found it particularly absurd that they should now be expected to celebrate the start of their rule. An organization called **Deshpremi Samiti** was duly formed to campaign against the celebrations, stirring up acrimonious debate in the Goan press. While some maintained the quincentennial glorified colonial oppression, pro-Portuguese Goans advocated a "forgive-and-forget" approach (epitomized by comments in the *Navhind Times* by former MP Erasmo Sequeira, who wrote that "... whatever [Vasco da Gama] was, he was. It is historians who must involve themselves in critical appreciation. The rest of us can just enjoy the celebrations."

The controversy eventually came to a head with the Kerala Tourism Development Corporation's announcement that they were intending to stage a full-blown re-enactment of da Gama's landing, complete with wooden replicas of the three caravelas and tourists acting the parts of Portuguese mariners. The plans provoked large protest marches in Goa, and the Delhi government was forced to issue a statement saying India would not under any circumstances participate in the so-called "celebrations" of 1498.

In the event, the anniversary passed off peacefully, though clearly the raking over of da Gama's unsavoury conduct did little to enhance relations between India and its first colonizer. Significantly however, the controversy did serve to fix in Indian minds a parallel between the exploitation of colonial times and the activities of today's multinationals, who use current trade agreements to open up emerging markets in India. It is no coincidence that alongside the effigies of Vasco da Gama being burned on Kappad beach were others of Coca Cola and Pepsi bottles.

their insurmountable naval supremacy, the Portuguese were unable to sustain an early lead over their European rivals. Repeated outbreaks of disease depleted the population of Goa, while the defeat in 1565 of Vijayanagar, which by that time accounted for a significant portion of the city's trade, had a disastrous effect on the whole Portuguese economy. Unable to maintain control of the sea lanes, Portugal gradually saw its trade empire whittled away, first by the Dutch, and later by the French and British. Goa actually survived as a Portuguese colony until 1961, but was effectively a spent force by the end of the seventeenth century.

THE MOGHUL EMPIRE

Descendents of Timur and Genghis Khan's Mongols from Samarkhand in Central Asia, the **Moghuls** staked their claim to North India with Babur's defeat of the Delhi Sultan, Ibrahim Lodi, in 1526. Through the revolutionary deployment of small arms and mobile artillery, the invaders routed an army ten times their size. The victory inaugurated an empire that would, by the time of its demise two hundred years later, become the largest and most powerful since Ashoka's, eighteen centuries earlier. Keen patrons of the arts as well as fearsome military strategists, successive emperors blended Persian and Indian culture to create some of the subcontinent's greatest treasures, including the Red Fort in Delhi and the Taj Mahal in Agra.

AURANGZEB AND THE MARATHAS

The Moghuls' influence, however, had little impact on the South until the reign of **Shah Jehan** (1627–58), when the northernmost of the Deccan Sultanates, Ahmadnagar, was annexed. A hundred years after their sack of Vijayanagar, Bijapur and Golconda also succumbed, this time to the last of the Great Moghuls, **Aurangzeb** (1658–1707).

The most expansionist ruler of the dynasty, Aurangzeb was also a devout Sunni, notorious for his rough treatment of Hindus, and for reinstating the much-hated *jizya* tax on non-Muslims that his great-grandfather, Akbar, had repealed. Aurangzeb's arch-adversaries in the Deccan region were a confederacy of low-caste Hindu warriors called the **Marathas**. Unlike the Moghuls, they attacked not with large, formal armies, but by mounting guerrilla-style raids, retreating to the safety of impregnable fortresses perched on the top of table mountains.

Under their most audacious and gifted leader, **Shivaji**, whom Aurangzeb named "The Mountain Rat", the Marathas managed on numerous occasions to outwit the Moghul's superior forces, and over time held sway over a large chunk of western India. The year of Shivaji's death in 1680, Aurangzeb's son, Akbar, slipped south from Delhi to form an alliance with his opposite number, with whose help he hoped to overthrow his father. But the plot ended in a heavy defeat for the usurper and his Hindu allies. Soon afterwards, Aurangzeb moved his court from Delhi to Aurangabad in order personally to supervise the subjugation of the Marathas. It was from there, too, that he mounted the victorious campaigns against Bijapur and Golconda which would extend Moghul rule to its eventual highwater mark.

Aurangzeb may have pushed the empire's boundaries further south than any of his predecessors, but his policies ultimately brought about the dynasty's downfall. To win over the nobles of his new acquisitions in the Deccan, the emperor demanded lower taxes from them, which left an administrative shortfall that he subsequently made up for by over-taxing his farmers. This duly provoked **peasant uprisings**, made more deadly by the proliferation of small arms at that time, which Aurangzeb's cumbersome, elephant-based army was ill suited to quell. In addition, the burden on the shattered Deccan states of reprovisioning an army whose annual losses were calculated at 100,000 men and around 300,000 animals was enormous. In 1702–3, famine and pestilence wiped out an estimated two million people in the region.

After the last Great Moghul's death in 1707, half a century of gradual decay was presided over by a succession of eight incompetent emperors. The final blow to the Moghul dynasty came in 1779, when the Persian Nadir Shah raided Delhi and made off with a vast loot that included the Peacock Throne itself. "The streets," wrote one eyewitness, "were strewn with corpses like a garden with weeds. The city was reduced to ashes and looked like a burnt plain."

DUTCH, BRITISH AND FRENCH

The Portuguese domination of the Indian Ocean was complete by the time Babur descended on

Delhi, and neither he nor his Moghul successors felt in the least threatened by the presence of foreign powers on their coastal borders. In fact, they welcomed the traders as providers of silver and gold which they could use to mint money. In the course of the seventeenth and eighteenth centuries, however, the European powers would become a force to be reckoned with, eventually replacing the Moghuls as India's rulers.

The first challengers of the Portuguese trade supremacy were the **Dutch**, whose cheaper and more manoeuvrable *fluyt* ships easily outsailed the more old-fashioned, ungainly *caravelas* from Lisbon. Determined not to allow Asia to be carved up by the proselytizing Roman Catholics, the Protestant Dutch East India Company – founded in 1602, only a couple of decades after Holland's victorious war of independence over Spain – systematically took control of the international spice trade, relieving the Portuguese of the strategically essential Molaccas in 1641, Ceylon in 1663 and their chief ports on the Malabar Coast soon after.

Although established two years before its Dutch counterpart, the **English** East India Company lagged behind initially, operating on a more modest scale with a fleet of smaller, privately run ships. Following the example of the Dutch, they set up a string of trading posts, or **factories**, around the coast, where goods – mostly **textiles** – could be stored awaiting annual shipment. Its first headquarters (from 1612), in Surat, Gujarat, was relocated to Bombay (Mumbai) in 1674 – the company had acquired the headquarters for a pittance from Charles II after he gained possession of it as a dowry gift on his marriage to the Portuguese Infanta, Catherine of Braganza. By the mid-seventeenth century, the British possessed 27 such outposts, the largest being **Fort St George** on the Coromandel Coast – the forerunner of Madras (modern Chennai). Over time, as the nature of the textile trade in India changed, the factories evolved from mere warehouses into large financial centres whose influence spread far inland. Gradually, communities of weavers settled around them, while growing numbers of recruits arrived to staff ever-expanding administrations and the military apparatus required to protect them.

The greatest threat to Britain's early Indian colonies was not local rulers, but rival Europeans. In the case of Fort St George, the **French** – whose own East India Company, started in 1664, was based further south on the Coromandel Coast at **Pondicherry** – were to prove the most troublesome. Initially, agreements between the two rival companies forestalled any armed encounters. But with the outbreak of the War of the Austrian Succession in 1740, Britain and France found themselves members of opposing coalitions in a conflict which, although rooted in central Europe, proved a turning point in the history of South Asia.

The first clash between France and Britain came in 1746 when the French governor of Pondicherry the wily diplomat **Joseph François Dupleix**, captured Fort St George with the help of a French fleet commanded by **Admiral La Bourdonnais**. Among those imprisoned during the short French occupation (the fort was handed back two years later) was a young East India Company clerk whose humiliation at the hands of the French is often used to explain his sudden career change from pen-pushing to soldiering. Considered one of the founders of the British Raj, **Robert Clive** cut his military teeth in the politically unstable Carnatic region around Madras.

Dupleix had long since learned that the best way to extend French influence, and trade, was to forge alliances with whichever local ruler looked likely to emerge victorious from the furious in-fighting that wracked the South during the break-up of the Moghul empire. In this way, the British and the French were drawn into the conflicts of regional rulers, often facing each other from opposite ends of a battlefield.

In one such encounter, where the European powers pitched in to support rival sons of the Nawab of **Arcot** in 1751, Clive, then only 26 years old, distinguished himself by holding a breached and sprawling fortress for fifty days with only two hundred men against a vastly superior force of 15,000 French and their Indian allies. The first great triumph of British arms in the history of India, this feat made Clive a hero, a reputation he consolidated soon afterwards by marching through the monsoons to intervene decisively at the siege of **Trichinopoly**. The French lost half their army in this second battle, and saw their protégé, Chandra Sahib, captured and killed. Dupleix's reputation never recovered; he was recalled two years later and died destitute.

The British went on to defeat the French again at Wandiwash in 1760, and finally took Pondicherry after an eight-month siege, effectively bringing to an end the French bid for power in India. For Robert Clive, the Carnatic war was but a local skirmish compared to the significance of his later achievements in Bengal, where his victory at **Plassey** in 1757 laid the foundations of a British rule that would last for two hundred years. It did, however, teach him and his compatriots lessons that would serve them well in the future: not least of all, how effective a relatively small number of highly disciplined troops could be against a far larger undisciplined army.

HAIDER ALI AND TIPU SULTAN OF MYSORE

After the heavy defeats in the Carnatic, the French were certainly down, but they were not yet quite out, thanks to the one remaining thorn in the side of British territorial ambitions: **Haider Ali**. A former general of the Maharaja of Mysore, Haider Ali had usurped his master's throne in 1761 and within a short time ruled over virtually the entire South. The secret of his dramatic success lay in his readiness to learn from the Europeans, in particular the French, whose military tactics he emulated, and who provided him with officers to train his infantry. Between 1767 and 1769, he fought a series of battles with the British, whom he had always, unlike other Indian rulers, regarded as a threat to India as a whole, and whom he eventually coerced into a highly favourable treaty after threatening to attack Madras.

Held back by corrupt officials in both Madras and Calcutta, the British failed to provide a robust response, but rallied during the governorship of **Warren Hastings**. In 1778, they were once again at war with the French, and fending off Marathas in the west, which Haider Ali took as his cue to launch a major offensive. Assisted by the French, who landed troops by sea to join the battle, Haider again forced the British to sue for peace.

This was far from the most honourable period in the imperial history of France and Britain. During their various marches and skirmishes across the Carnatic, temples were regularly desecrated and massacres were commonplace; in all, a million Tamils were killed. On one occasion, four hundred wounded Hindu women were raped by rioting British soldiers, while in the Kaveri region, the French general, Lally, fired *brahmin* priests from his cannons for refusing to tell him where their temple treasure was hidden.

After Haider's death in 1782, his son, **Tipu Sultan**, aka "the Tiger of Mysore" carried on his father's campaigns, but did so with diminished support from the French, who had by this time begun to wind down their Indian operations. In the end, Tipu Sultan was let down badly by his father's former allies. In 1799, they failed to dispatch troops to reinforce him when an army, led by Lord Wellesley and his brother Arthur (later the Duke of Wellington, of Waterloo fame) marched on **Srirangapatnam**. Tipu Sultan died defending a breach in his capital's walls (a story that later inspired Wilkie Collins's novel, *The Moonstone*), and Mysore was returned to the old Hindu dynasty Haider Ali had deposed. After more than a century of continual conflict between the European powers and their various allies, the struggle for control of India was finally won by the British.

BRITISH RULE IN THE SOUTH

Following their victory at Srirangapatnam, the British, under Hastings' successor, **Lord Cornwallis**, annexed the coastal areas and interior plains that had been under Tipu Sultan's sway, settling down to a period of relatively trouble-free rule. Stretching from the Telegu-speaking region of present-day Andhra Pradesh to the Malabar Coast, the **Madras Presidency** was a notoriously "hands-off" regime, with vast administrative districts on which colonial officers could make very little impact. Life basically continued as it had before the advent of the British Raj. Unlike in the north, where the economic changes brought about by the Industrial Revolution in England had a huge impact, the South's output was geared towards domestic consumption; when the Lancashire mills forced the bottom out of the cotton industry in Bengal, the weavers of Madras were largely unaffected.

Nevertheless, resentment at British rule was not confined to the northern plains, where the so-called **Indian Mutiny** (redubbed "the First War of Independence" by nationalist politicians) broke out in Lucknow in 1857. **Uprisings** also occurred in forest regions of Andhra Pradesh, and the Mopilah Muslims of the Malabar mounted small insurrections. Generally, however, opposition to the British came not from low-caste or tribal populations, but ironically from members of the English-speaking, university-educated elite in Madras, where the nineteenth century saw the emergence of a nascent **nationalist movement**. Based at the Theosophical Society's headquarters in Adyar, Annie Besant's Home Rule League openly objected to the colonial regime, while publications such as *The Hindu* spread the nationalist message among the literate classes.

THE SOUTH SINCE INDEPENDENCE

Independence passed off relatively peacefully in South India in 1947, as the north succumbed to the horrors of Partition. With the exception of the Nizam of Hyderabad – who tried to retain his dominions and had to be ousted by the new Indian army – the Princely States – namely Cochin, Travancore and Mysore – acceded gracefully to the Indian Union. Although deprived of their privy purses and most of their land, many of the former rulers used their privileged backgrounds to secure powerful roles in their new states, becoming members of parliament or industrialists.

The dissolution of British rule also generated an upsurge in regional sentiments. In the South, calls to restructure state boundaries along linguistic lines gained pace, culminating in the 1956 **State Reorganization Act**, when the region was divided into four main states: the Kanada-speaking area became Mysore (later changed to Karnataka; the Telegu zone made up Andhra Pradesh; the former Tamil region of the Madras Presidency became Madras (subsequently renamed Tamil Nadu); and Kerala was created from the Malayalam-speaking Malabar coastal zone. Goa, meanwhile, remained under Portuguese control until 1961, when India's first Prime Minister, **Jawaharlal Nehru**, lost his patience with the Portuguese dictator Salazar and sent in the troops.

From the start, Nehru vociferously opposed the creation of language-based states, predicting such a move would lead to fragmentation, schisms and regionalism. The political upheavals of the past fifty years have proved him right. With the rise in popularity of the pro-Dravidian **DMK** in Tamil Nadu and the **Telegu Desam** in Andhra Pradesh, the South's political scene has been completely dominated by **regional parties** in one guise or another, reflecting widespread mistrust of central government rule from Delhi. This has been most vehemently expressed in resistance to the imposition of Hindi – the most widely spoken language in northern India – as the medium of education and law. As these parties gained larger shares of the vote, state-specific issues and calls for greater regional autonomy have increasingly dominated the political agendas of all four states.

CASTE CONFLICT

The period since independence has also seen a marked rise in caste conflicts. Caste has always been more firmly rooted in South Indian society than the more Muslim-influenced north, but political legislation passed over the previous two decades to encourage greater participation in government and education of low, tribal and "Other Backward Castes" (OBCs) has somewhat deepened these age-old social divisions. Adopted in 1950, the Constitution of India paved the way for laws to combat caste discrimination, with clauses obliging the states to implement policies of "positive discrimination". "Untouchables" and OBCs were given **quotas** in educational institutions, parliament, regional assemblies and state sector jobs.

The Mandal Commission was set up in 1979 to look at the impact of quotas. Its final report showed that although backward castes made up 52 percent of the population, they still only held 12.5 percent of government jobs (and 4.7 percent of the higher administrative positions). Mandal came out strongly in favour of positive discrimination, and in August 1990 Prime Minister **V.P. Singh** announced that his party would implement the recommendations of the commission. Cynics accused him of trying to poach the Muslim and low-caste vote blocks from the opposition Congress Party, but the ensuing backlash was a strong contributory factor in the downfall of V.P. Singh's Janata Dal coalition in the elections of 1991.

The issue of quotas remains a contentious one in the South. "Affirmative action" policies, as quotas have been euphemistically dubbed, have certainly increased the level of scheduled caste participation in government, but they have had some negative effects too. Inevitably, sought-after university places and public sector jobs are often granted to unqualified people instead of better qualified members of higher castes, creating sectarian resentment that has increasingly spilled into violence. In Rajasthan and Uttar Pradesh, students have committed suicide in protest at quotas, and violent clashes between *brahmins* and low-caste farmers have led to whole districts of Tamil Nadu being placed under martial law.

The other harmful repercussion of positive discrimination has been the **politicization** of caste. In order to be elected or to form power-wielding coalitions, Indian politicians these days have to galvanize **vote banks** – blocs of support from specific caste or ethnic groups. In return, these vote banks look to their leaders to advance their agendas in government, a process that all too often results in national or state interests being subordinated to the demands of minority groups.

With the expansion of the quota system under Prime Minister **Narasimha Rao** in 1994 to include disadvantaged Muslims and other "ethnic" minorities, state and national politics have become increasingly dominated not only by caste, but by **communal issues** – precisely the kind of sectarianism that the Mandal report and India's resolutely secular Constitution sought to eradicate.

The South has traditionally been spared the kind of communal conflict that has so often plagued the north – most recently in the aftermath of the Babri Masjid disaster, when the destruction of a mosque in Ayodhya, Uttar Pradesh, by Hindu extremists sparked off bouts of Hindu–Muslim bloodletting. Over the past five years, however, the steady rise of communal parties, such as the far right pro-Hindu BJP, has been accompanied by violent confrontations between Hindus and Muslims, particularly in Tamil Nadu. The spiralling violence came to a head on February 14, 1998, when fifteen bombs exploded in crowded districts of Coimbatore, killing sixty people (see p.476). The Home Affairs Minister and BJP leader at that time, L.K. Advani, was due to address a rally in the city, which the Islamic extremist organization, **Al-Umma** decided to use as a pretext to settle communal scores for earlier attacks on Muslims in the region.

RAJIV GANDHI AND WAR IN SRI LANKA

The highest profile victim of communal violence in India since the assassination of Mahatma Gandhi by Hindu extremists in 1948 was **Rajiv Gandhi**, son of Indira, and a former Prime Minister, who was killed while electioneering in Tamil Nadu on May 21, 1991. The killing was a reprisal for Rajiv's intervention in the war of neighbouring Sri Lanka – a conflict that has dominated foreign policy in the South over the past fifteen years and made a lasting impression on the coastal regions of Tamil Nadu.

The ongoing ethnic conflict between the majority (Buddhist) Sinhala and minority Tamil populations of Sri Lanka escalated into full-scale war in 1987. With the help of various foreign powers, the Sinhala President, Jayawardene, mounted an invasion of the Tamil guerrillas' stronghold on the Jaffna peninsula, in the north of the island. Jayawardene was furious when it transpired that Rajiv's Indian government had air-dropped supplies for the beleaguered Tamil freedom fighters. The two countries signed a peace accord in July 1987, part of which permitted the Indian army to intervene and disarm the Tamils. But in the event, India became bogged down in a messy war with high casualties on both sides. Tamil refugees, meanwhile, poured in their millions across the Palk Straits to settle in camps around Rameshwaram, Tamil Nadu, where they remain, awaiting the end of a war that looks set to rumble on for some years to come.

India was only able to extricate itself after the defeat of Rajiv Gandhi in the 1989 elections, after which, in March 1990, the new government withdrew all troops from the island. It was during the campaign for the following elections, in May 1991, that Rajiv and sixteen others were killed by a female suicide bomber. Seven years later, an Indian court convicted 26 people for the assassination. They were all Sri Lankan militants or Indian allies of the Liberation Tigers of Tamil Eelam (LTTE) conspirators. The assassination had been a revenge attack for Rajiv's enforcement of the 1987 peace accord, which resulted in Indian troops being sent to fight Tamil separatist guerrillas.

THE GREEN REVOLUTION

Among the major **changes to rural life** in South India since Independence have been those brought about by the so-called **Green Revolution**. From the 1960s, encouraged by Western governments and aid donors, India introduced modern farming techniques to intensify wheat and rice production. Based on the use of new high-yield varieties of seed, together with chemical fertilizers, the new methods led to a dramatic increase in agricultural output (India survived a severe drought in 1988 and even managed to contribute grain to famine-stricken farmers in the African Sahel at around the same time). Their longer-term impact, however, remains under scrutiny.

One of the major drawbacks of the Green Revolution has been a growing disparity between the wealthy land-owning farmers and their landless share-cropping tenants. Unable to afford the expensive seeds and accompanying chemicals, poor farmers and the families have been forced, by mounting debts, to leave the countryside in search of waged employment. The majority end up living on the streets, or in the vast slum encampments that have sprung up on the edges of all South Indian cities over the past two decades.

Recent global economic trends have also been felt in the South Indian countryside. The General Agreement on Tariffs and Trade, or **GATT**, is potentially the most significant of these. Signed in 1994, the treaty aims to promote free trade by defending foreign investors from economic protectionism. While popular with the business community, however, GATT and other policies like it have proved controversial in a country as sensitive to its colonial history as India (particularly one brought up on the Gandhian ideals of *svadeshi*, or small-scale, non-polluting self-reliance).

A component of the treaty that has come in for particular criticism in India is its promotion of **genetic patenting**. This enables the large multinationals who manufacture seed used by South Indians to patent their products, making it illegal for farmers to replant them. No matter that the seeds may have originated in developing countries such as India, where generations of peasant farmers have painstakingly experimented to create pest- and drought-resistant strains. If a company can prove that it has modified the seed in any way, it is entitled by GATT to patent it.

The issue prompted indignation in India, but little more than that until it transpired the expensive seeds didn't even produce the promised increased yields – their one redeeming feature in the eyes of small farmers. In 1993, on the anniversary of Gandhi's birthday, half a million farmers issued "Quit India" notices to the US company Cargill, whose genetically modified sunflower seeds had been used by many farmers in northern Karnataka. Angry protesters succeeded in dismantling the company's plant in Bangalore within half an hour. The police, most of whom had family in the countryside, did not offer any significant resistance.

The **Seed Satyagraha,** as this grassroots farmers' movement became known, makes explicit the connection with the anticolonial struggle by using the name chosen by Gandhi for his campaign of non-violent civil disobedience, or *satyagraha*. Replacing the spinning wheel with a seed as the movement's symbol, it has been seen by many as a second freedom struggle and its ideas have spread from Karnataka through Andhra Pradesh, Tamil Nadu and Kerala in recent years.

To a great extent, the survival into the next millennium of the traditional South Indian way of life will depend on how effectively the region responds to the challenges of economic globalization. Industrial and technological developments such as Bangalore's software centre, "Silicon Valley" (see p.184), may represent a bright future for India's urban, educated middle classes, but its benefits have little impact on the region's rural poor.

THE RELIGIONS OF INDIA

The south of India has long been regarded as a bastion of Hindu values and boasts many of the finest and oldest temples in the country. Hinduism permeates every aspect of life, from commonplace daily chores to education and politics. The vast pantheon of Hindu deities is manifest everywhere – not only in temples, but in shops, rickshaws and even on *bidi* packets and matchboxes. Muslims are the other most prominent religious group; they have formed an integral part of Indian society since the twelfth century, although their numbers are lower in much of the South outside Kerala. Though Jains and Buddhists are now a tiny fraction of the population, their impact is still felt, and they have many magnificent temples in South India. Both these ancient faiths, like the more recently established Sikh community, were formed in reaction to the caste laws and ritual observances of Hinduism. There are also small communities of Zoroastrians, descended from Iranians, Christians, who have been here since the first century, and Jews (see p.332).

Hindu practices, such as caste distinction, have crept into most religions, and many of the **festivals** – see Basics, p.60-61 – that mark each year with music, dance and feasting, are shared by all communities. Each has its own **pilgrimage** sites, **heroes**, **legends** and even culinary specialities, mingling in a unique diversity that is the very pulse of society.

HINDUISM

Contemporary **Hinduism** – the religion of over 85 percent of South Indians – is the product of several thousand years of evolution and assimilation. It has neither founder nor prophet, no single creed and no single prescribed practice or doctrine; it takes in hundreds of gods, goddesses, beliefs and practices, and widely variant cults and philosophies. Some are recognized by only two or three villages; others are popular right across the subcontinent. Hindus (from the Persian word for Indians) call their beliefs and practices *dharma*, which embraces natural and moral law to define a way of living in harmony with a natural order, while achieving personal goals and meeting the requirements of society.

EARLY DEVELOPMENTS

The foundations of Hinduism were laid down by the **Aryans**, seminomads who entered northwest India during the second millennium BC, and mixed with the indigenous Dravidian population (see p.546). With them they brought a belief in gods associated with the elements, including **Agni**, the god of fire and sacrifice, **Surya**, the sun god, and **Indra**, the chief god. Most of these deities faded in later times, but Indra is still regarded as the father of the gods, and Surya was widely worshipped until the medieval period.

Aryan beliefs were set out in the **Vedas**, scriptures "heard" (*shruti*) by "seers" (*rishis*). Transmitted orally for centuries, they were finally written, in Sanskrit, between 1000 BC and 500 AD. The earliest were the *Samhitas*, or hymns; later came the *Brahmanas*, sacrificial texts, and *Aranyakas*, or "forest treatises".

The earliest and most important *Samhita*, the **Rig Veda**, contains hymns to deities and *devas* (divine powers), and is supplemented by other books detailing rituals and prayers for ceremonial use. The **Brahmanas** stress correct ritual performance, drawing heavily on concepts of **purity and pollution** that persist today and concentrating on sacrificial rites. Pedantic attention to ritual soon supplanted the importance of the *devas*, and they were further undermined by a search for a single cosmic power thought to be their source, eventually conceived of as **Brahma**, the absolute creator, personified from earlier mentions of Brahman, an impersonal principle of cosmic unity.

The **Aranyakas** focused on this all-powerful godhead, and reached their final stage in the **Upanishads**, which describe in beautiful and emotive verse the mystic experience of unity of the soul (*atman*) with Brahma, ideally attained through asceticism, renunciation of worldly values and meditation. In the *Upanishads* the concepts of **samsara**, a cyclic round of death and rebirth characterized by suffering and perpetuated by desire, and **moksha**, liberation from *samsara*, became firmly rooted. Fundamental aspects of the Hindu world view, both are accepted by all but a handful of Hindus today, along with the belief in **karma**, the belief that one's present position in society is determined by the effect of one's previous actions in this and past lives.

HINDU SOCIETY

The stratification of Hindu society is rooted in the **Dharma Shashtras** and **Dharma Shutras**, scriptures written from "memory" (*smriti*) at the same time as the *Vedas*. These defined four hierarchical classes, or **varnas**, each assigned specific religious and social duties known as **varnashradharma**, and established Aryans as the highest social class. In descending order the *varnas* are: **brahmins** (priests and teachers), **kshatryas** (rulers and warriors), **vaishyas** (merchants and cultivators) and **shudras** (menials). The first three classes, known as "twice-born", are distinguished by a sacred thread worn from the time of initiation, and are granted full access to religious texts and rituals. Below all four categories, groups whose jobs involve contact with dirt or death (such as undertakers, leather workers and cleaners) were classified as **Untouchables**. Though discrimination against Untouchables is now a criminal offence, in part thanks to the campaigns of Gandhi – he renamed Untouchables *Harijans*, "Children of God" – the lowest stratum of society has by no means disappeared.

Within the four *varnas*, social status is further defined by **jati**, classifying each individual by family and precise occupation (for example, a *vaishya* may be a jewellery-seller, cloth merchant, cowherd or farmer). A person's *jati* determines his **caste**, and lays restrictions on all aspects of life from food consumption, religious obligations and contact with other castes, to the choice of marriage partners. In general, Hindus marry members of the same *jati* – marrying someone of a different *varna* often results in ostracism from both family and caste, leaving the couple stranded in a society where caste affiliation takes primacy over all other aspects of individual identity. There are almost three thousand *jatis*; the divisions and restrictions they have enforced have become, time and time again, the substance of reform movements and the target of critics.

A Hindu has three aims in life: **dharma**, fulfilling one's duty to family and caste and acquiring religious merit (*punya*) through right living; **artha**, the lawful making of wealth; and **karma**, desire and satisfaction. These goals are linked with the four traditional stages in life. The first is as a child and student, devoted to learning from parents and guru. Next comes the stage of householder, expected to provide for a family and raise sons. That accomplished, he or she may then take up a life of celibacy and retreat into the forest to meditate alone, and finally renounce all possessions to become a homeless ascetic, hoping to achieve the ultimate goal of *moksha*. The small number of Hindus, including some women, who follow this ideal life assume the final stage as **sannyasis**, saffron-clad **sadhus** who wander throughout India, begging for food, and retreat to isolated caves, forests and hills to meditate. They're a common feature in most Indian towns, and many stay for long periods in particular temples. Not all have raised families: some assume the life of a *sadhu* at an early age as *chellas*, pupils, of an older *sadhu*.

THE POPULAR DEITIES

Alongside the *Dharma Shashtras* and *Dharma Shutras*, the most important works of the *smriti* tradition, thought to have been completed by the fourth century AD at the latest, were the ***Puranas***, long mythological stories focused on the Vedic gods and their heroic actions, and Hinduism's two great epics, the ***Mahabharata*** and the ***Ramayana***. Through these texts, the main gods and goddesses became firmly embedded in the religion. Alongside **Brahma**, the creator, **Vishnu** was acknowledged as the preserver, and **Shiva** ("auspicious, benign"), referred to in the *Rig Veda* as Rudra, was recognized for his destructive powers. The three are often depicted in a trinity, *tri-murti*, but in time Brahma's importance declined, and Shiva and Vishnu became the most popular deities. Nearly all Hindus belong to sects that actively worship Shiva or Vishnu in one form or another (see box on p.564).

Other gods and goddesses who came alive in the mythology of the *Puranas* – each depicted in human or semi-human form and accompanied by an animal "**vehicle**" – are still venerated across South India. River goddesses, ancestors, guardians of particular places and protectors against disease and natural disaster are as central to village life as the major deities.

PHILOSOPHICAL TRENDS

The complications presented by Hinduism's view of deities, *samsara*, *atman* (the human soul) and *moksha* naturally encouraged philosophical debate, and led eventually to the formation of six schools of thought, known as the **Darshanas**. Each presented a different exposition of the true nature of *moksha* and how to attain it.

Foremost among these was the **Advaita Vedanta** school of **Shankara** (*c.*788–850 AD), who interpreted Hinduism as pure monotheism verging on monism (the belief that all is one: in this case, one with God). Drawing on Upanishadic writings, he claimed that they identified the essence of the human soul with that of God (*tat tvam asi*, "that thou art"), and that all else – the phenomenal world and all *devas* – is an illusion (*maya*) created by God. Shankara is revered as saint-philosopher at the twelve **jyotirlinga**, the sacred Shaivite sites associated with the unbounded *lingam* of light, which as a manifestation of Shiva once persuaded both Brahma and Vishnu to acknowledge Shiva's supremacy.

Another important *Darshana* centred around the age-old practice of **yoga** (literally "the action of yoking [to] another"), elucidated by **Patanjali** (second century BC) in his *Yoga Sutras*. Interpreting yoga as the yoking of mind and body, or the yoking of the mind with God, Patanjali detailed various practices, which used in combination may lead to an understanding of the fundamental **unity** of all things. The most common form of yoga known in the West is *hatha-yoga*, whereby the body and its vital energies is brought under control through physical positions and breathing methods, with results said to range from attaining a calm mind to being able to fly through the air, enter other bodies or become invisible. Other practices include *mantra-yoga*, the recitation of formulas and meditation on mystical diagrams (*man-*

THE MAHABHARATA

Eight times as long as the *Iliad* and *Odyssey* combined, the **Mahabharata** is the most popular of all Hindu texts. Written around 400 AD, it tells of a feuding *kshatrya* family in upper India (Bharata) during the fourth millennium BC. Like all good epics, the *Mahabharata* recounts a gripping tale, using its characters to illustrate moral values. In essence it attempts to elucidate the position of the warrior castes, the *kshatryas*, and demonstrate that religious fulfilment is as accessible for them as it is for *brahmins*.

The chief character is **Arjuna**, a superb archer, who with his four brothers – Yudhishtra, Bhima, Nakula and Sahadeva – represents the **Pandava** clan, upholders of righteousness and supreme fighters. Arjuna won his wife **Draupadi** in an archery contest, but wishing to avoid jealousy she agreed to be the shared wife of all five brothers. The Pandava clan is resented by their cousins, the evil **Kauravas**, led by Duryodhana, the eldest son of Dhrtarashtra, ruler of the Kuru kingdom.

When Dhrtarashtra handed his kingdom over to the Pandavas, the Kauravas were far from happy. Duryodhana challenged Yudhishtra (known for his brawn but not his brain) to a gambling contest. The dice game was rigged; Yudhishtra gambled away not only his possessions, but also his kingdom and his shared wife. The Kauravas offered to return the kingdom to the Pandavas if they could spend thirteen years in exile, together with their wife, without being recognized. Despite much scheming, the Pandavas succeeded, but on return found that the Kauravas would not fulfil their side of the bargain.

Thus ensued the great battle of the *Mahabharata*, told in the sixth book, the **Bhagavad Gita** – immensely popular as an independent story. Vishnu descends to earth as **Krishna**, and steps into battle as Arjuna's charioteer. The *Bhagavad Gita* details the fantastic struggle of the fighting cousins, using magical weapons and brute force. Arjuna is in a dilemma, unable to justify the killing of his own kin in pursuit of a rightful kingdom for himself and his brothers. Krishna consoles him, reminding him that his principal duty, his *varnashradharma*, is as a warrior. What is more, Krishna points out, each man's soul, or *atman*, is eternal, and transmigrates from body to body, so Arjuna need not grieve the death of his cousins. Krishna convinces Arjuna that by fulfilling his *dharma* he not only upholds law and order by saving the kingdom from the grasp of unrighteous rulers, he also serves God in the spirit of devotion (*bhakti*), and thus guarantees himself eternal union with the divine in the blissful state of *moksha*.

The Pandavas finally win the battle, and Yudhishtra is crowned king. Eventually Arjuna's grandson, Pariksit, inherits the throne, and the Pandavas trek to Mt Meru, the mythical centre of the universe and the abode of the gods, where Arjuna finds Krishna's promised *moksha*.

dalas), *bhakti-yoga* (devotion), *jnana-yoga* (knowledge) and *raja*, or royal, *yoga* the highest form of yoga when the mind is absorbed in God.

PRACTICE

The primary concern of most Hindus is to reduce bad karma and acquire merit (*punya*), by honest and charitable living within the restrictions imposed by caste and worship, in the hope of attaining a higher status of rebirth. Strict rules address purity and pollution, the most obvious of them requiring high-caste Hindus to limit their contact with potentially polluting lower castes. All bodily excretions are polluting (hence the strange looks Westerners receive when they blow their noses and return the handkerchief to their pocket). Above all else, **water** is the agent of purification, used in ablutions before prayer, and revered in all rivers, especially Ganga (the Ganges).

In most Hindu homes, a chosen deity is worshipped daily in a shrine room, and scriptures are read. Outside the home, worship takes place in temples, and consists of **puja**, or devotion to God – sometimes a simple act of prayer, but more commonly a complex process when the god's image is circumambulated, offered flowers, rice, sugar and incense, and anointed with water, milk or sandalwood paste (which is usually done on behalf of the devotee by the temple priest, the *pujari*). The aim in *puja* is to take **darshan** – glimpse the god – and thus receive his or her blessing. Whether devotees simply worship the deity in prayer, or make requests – for a healthy crop, a son, good

THE RAMAYANA

Rama is the seventh of Vishnu's ten incarnations and the story of his life unfolds in the epic **Ramayana**. Although possibly based on a historic figure, Rama is seen rather more as a representation of the qualities of Vishnu. Rama was the oldest of four sons born to Dasaratha, King of Ayodhya, by his three wives and was heir to the throne. At the time of the coronation one of the king's wives, Kaikeya, seized the moment to ask for the two favours he had previously promised her in a moment of rash appreciation. Her first request was that her oldest son Bharata be anointed king instead of the rightful Rama. Her second request was that Rama be banished to the forest for fourteen years.

Rama in an exemplary show of filial piety accepted his father's unfortunate request and left the city together with his wife **Sita** and brother **Laksmana**. From their place of exile they continued their long battle against the demon forces led by **Ravana**, the evil king of Lanka. One day Ravana's sister Suparnakhi spotted Rama in the woods and immediately fell in love with him. Being a faithful and ideal husband Rama rebuffed her advances; Suparnakhi as a result tried to kill Sita, seeing her as the obstacle to Rama's heart. Laksmana intervened and cut off her nose and ears in retaliation. Suparnakhi fled to her brother, who mobilized fourteen giants to dispose of Rama. Rama destroyed them single-handedly and then similarly killed 14,000 warriors. Ravana was furious but heeded his advisers who suggested they should no more fight Rama but just kidnap his beloved, hinting that he would then quickly die of a broken heart. Sita was thus captured and flown by chariot to one of Ravana's palaces on the island of Lanka.

Determined to find Sita, a distraught Rama enlisted the help of **Hanuman**, lord of the monkeys. Rama and Laksmana then start their search for Sita, which leads to the discovery that she is being held on the island of Lanka. Hanuman leaps across the strait and makes his way surreptitiously into Ravana's palace where he hears the evil king trying to persuade Sita to marry him instead of the squeaky clean Rama – offering her the choice of consummation or consumption – become my bride or "My cooks shall mince thy limbs with steel and serve thee for my morning meal." Hanuman reports back to Rama who gathers an army and prepares to attack. This time the monkeys form a bridge across the straits allowing the army to cross and after much fighting Sita is rescued and reunited with the victorious Rama.

During the long journey back to Ayodhya Sita's honour was brought into question. To verify her innocence she asks Laksmana to build a funeral pyre. She prays to **Agni** before stepping into the flames and asks for protection before walking through them. Agni walks her through the fire to a delighted Rama. They march into Ayodhya guided by a trail of lights put there by the local people and this enlightened homecoming has long since been celebrated as **Divali** – the festival of lights. Soon after, Rama is finally crowned as rightful king, his younger brother gladly stepping down.

HINDU GODS AND GODDESSES

VISHNU

The chief function of **Vishnu**, "pervader", is to keep the world in order, preserving, restoring and protecting. With four arms holding a conch, discus, lotus and mace, Vishnu is blue-skinned, and often shaded by a serpent, or resting on its coils, afloat on an ocean. He is usually seen alongside his half-man-half-eagle vehicle, Garuda.

Vaishnavites, often distinguishable by two vertical lines on their foreheads, recognize Vishnu as supreme lord, and hold that he has manifested himself on earth nine times. These incarnations, or *avatars*, have been as fish (Matsya), tortoise (Kurma), boar (Varaha), man-lion (Narsingh), dwarf (Vamana), axe-wielding *brahmin* (Parasuram), Rama, Krishna and Balaram (though some say that the Buddha is the ninth *avatar*). Vishnu's future descent to earth as Kalki, the saviour who will come to restore purity and destroy the wicked, is eagerly awaited.

The most important *avatars* are Krishna and Rama. **Krishna** is the hero of the *Bhagavad Gita*, in which he proposes three routes to salvation (*moksha*): selfless action (*karmayoga*), knowledge (*jnana*) and devotion to god (*bhakti*), and explains that *moksha* is attainable in this life, even without asceticism and renunciation. This appealed to all castes, as it denied the necessity of ritual and officiating *brahmin* priests, and evolved into the popular *bhakti* cult that legitimized love of God as a means to *moksha*, and also found expression in emotional songs of the quest for union with God. Through *bhakti*, Krishna's role was extended, and he assumed different faces: most popularly he is the playful cowherd who seduces and dances with cowgirls (*gopis*), giving each the illusion that she is his only lover. He is also pictured as a small, chubby, mischievous baby, known for his butter-stealing exploits, who inspires tender motherly love in women. Like Vishnu, Krishna is blue, and is often shown dancing and playing the flute.

Rama is the chief character in the *Ramayana*. Born a prince in Ayodhya, he was denied succession to the throne by one of his father's wives, and was exiled for fourteen years, together with his wife Sita. The *Ramayana* details his exploits during these years, and his defeat of the demon king of Lanka, Ravana. When Rama was reinstated as king in Ayodhya, he put Sita through "trial by fire" to prove that she had remained pure while in the clasps of Ravana. Sita passed the trial unharmed, and is held up as the paradigm of women – faithful, pure and honest.

Vishnu is worshipped especially in the form of Lord Venkateshvara at Tirumala in Andhra Pradesh and the huge popularity of this pilgrimage centre is largely due to his role as the granter of wishes, leading many thousands to his shrine daily to pray for favours.

SHIVA

Shaivism, the cult of **Shiva**, was also inspired by *bhakti*, requiring selfless love from devotees in a quest for divine communion, but Shiva has never been incarnate on earth. He is presented in many different aspects, such as **Nataraja**, Lord of the Dance, **Mahadev**, Great God, and **Maheshvar**, Divine Lord, source of all knowledge. Though he does have several terrible forms, his role extends beyond that of destroyer, and he is revered as the source of the whole universe.

Shiva is often depicted with four or five faces, holding a trident, draped with serpents, and bearing a third eye in his forehead. In temples, he is identified with the *lingam*, or phallic symbol, resting in the *yoni*, a representation of female sexuality. Whether as statue or *lingam*, Shiva is guarded by his bull-vehicle, Nandi, and often accompanied by a consort, who also assumes various forms and is looked upon as the vital energy, *shakti*, that empowers him. Their erotic exploits were a favourite sculptural subject between the ninth and twelfth centuries.

While Shiva is the object of popular devotion all over India, as the terrible **Bhairav** he is also the god of the Shaivite **ascetics**, who renounce family and caste ties and perform extreme meditative and yogic practices. Many, though not all, smoke *ganja*, Shiva's favourite herb; all see renunciation and realization of God as the key to *moksha*. Some ascetic practices enter the realm of **tantrism**, in which confrontation with all that's impure, such as alcohol, death and sex, is used to merge the sacred and the profane, and bring about the profound realization that Shiva is omnipresent.

GANESH

Chubby and smiling, elephant-headed **Ganesh**, the first son of Shiva and Parvati, is invoked before every undertaking (except funerals). Seated on a throne or lotus, his image is often placed above temple gateways, in shops and in houses. In his four arms he holds a conch, discus, bowl of sweets (or club) and a water lily, and he's always attended by his vehicle, a rat. Credited with writing the *Mahabharata* as it was dictated by the sage Vyasa, Ganesh is regarded by many as the god of learning, the lord of success, prosperity and peace. In the South he is often known as Vinayaka and as such there is a huge festival in his honour in late monsoon.

MURUGAN

Pictured as a triumphant youth, bedecked with flowers, images of this son of Shiva are particularly common in Tamil Nadu and other parts of the South. He provides protection and is thus a popular family deity. It is possible that he derives from a pre-Aryan fertility god.

AYAPPA

Another son of Shiva, this time from a peculiar mythological union with Vishnu (see box on p.320), **Ayappa** is also associated with the role of protection, and his shrine in northern Kerala is a huge magnet to pilgrims, making the black-clad, mostly male, devotees a familiar sight. The common depiction of Ayappa riding a tiger with an entourage of leopards denotes his victory over evil.

DURGA

Durga, the fiercest of the female deities, is an aspect of Shiva's more conservative consort, Parvati (also known as Uma), who is remarkable only for her beauty and fidelity. In whatever form, Shiva's consort is *shakti*, the fundamental energy that spurs him into action. Among Durga's many aspects, each a terrifying goddess eager to slay demons, are Chamunda, Kali and Muktakeshi, but in all her forms she is Mahadevi (Great Goddess). Statues show her with ten arms, holding the head of a demon, a spear, and other weapons; she tramples demons underfoot, or dances upon Shiva's body. A garland of skulls drapes her neck, and her tongue hangs from her mouth, dripping with blood – a particularly gruesome sight on pictures of Kali. Durga is much venerated in Bengal; in all her temples, animal sacrifices are a crucial element of worship, to satisfy her thirst for blood and deter her ruthless anger.

LAKSHMI

The comely goddess **Lakshmi**, usually shown sitting or standing on a lotus flower, and sometimes called Padma (lotus), is the embodiment of loveliness, grace and charm, and the goddess of prosperity and wealth. Vishnu's consort, she appears in different aspects alongside each of his *avatars*; the most important are Sita, wife of Rama, and Radha, Krishna's favourite *gopi*. In many temples she is shown as one with Vishnu, in the form of Lakshmi Narayan.

KARTTIKEYA

Though some legends claim that his mother was Ganga, or even Agni, **Karttikeya** is popularly believed to be the second son of Shiva and Parvati. Primarily a god of war, he was popular among the northern Guptas, who worshipped him as Skanda, and the southern Chalukyas, for whom he was Subrahmanya. Usually shown with six faces, and standing upright with bow and arrow, Karttikeya is commonly petitioned by those wishing for male offspring.

HANUMAN

India's great monkey god **Hanuman** features in the *Ramayana* as Rama's chief aide in the fight against the demon king of Lanka. Depicted as a giant monkey clasping a mace, Hanuman is the deity of acrobats and wrestlers, but is also seen as Rama and Sita's greatest devotee, and an author of Sanskrit grammar. As his representatives, monkeys find sanctuary in temples all over India.

SARASWATI

The most beautiful Hindu goddess, **Saraswati**, the wife of Brahma – with her flawless milk-white complexion – sits or stands on a water lily or peacock, playing a lute, *sitar* or *vina*. Associated with the Saraswati River, mentioned in the *Rig Veda*, she is seen as a goddess of purification and fertility, but is also revered as the inventor of writing, the queen of eloquence and goddess of music.

SANI

Closely linked with the planet Saturn, **Sani** is feared for his destructive powers. His image, a black statue with protruding blood-red tongue, is often found on street corners; strings of green chillies and lemon are hung in shops and houses each Saturday (*Saniwar*) to ward off his evil influences.

KHAMDENU

Mention must also be made here of the **sacred cow**, Khamdenu, who receives devotion through the respect shown to all cows, left to amble through streets and temples all over India. The origin of the cow's sanctity is uncertain; some myths record that Brahma created cows at the same time as *brahmins*, to provide *ghee* (clarified butter) for use in priestly ceremonies. To this day cow dung and urine are used to purify houses (in fact the urine keeps insects at bay), and the killing or harming of cows by any Hindu is a grave offence. The cow is often referred to as mother of the gods, and each part of its body is significant: its horns symbolize the gods, its face the sun and moon, its shoulders Agni (god of fire) and its legs the Himalaya.

results in exams, a vigorous monsoon or a cure for illness – they leave the temple with *prasad*, an offering of food or flowers taken from the holy sanctuary by the *pujaris*.

Communal worship and get-togethers en route to pilgrimage sites are celebrated with *kirtan* or *bhajan*, singing of hymns, perhaps verses in praise of Krishna taken from the *Bhagavad Purana*, or repetitive cries of "Jay Shankar!" (Praise to Shiva). Temple ceremonies are conducted in Sanskrit by *pujaris* who tend the image in daily rituals that symbolically wake, bathe, feed and dress the god, and finish each day by preparing the god for sleep. The most elaborate is the evening ritual, **arthi**, when lamps are lit, blessed in the sanctuary, and passed around devotees amid the clanging of drums, gongs and cymbals. In many villages, shrines to *devatas*, village deities who function as protectors and may bring disaster if neglected, are more important than temples.

Each of the great stages in life – birth, initiation (when boys of the three twice-born *varnas* are invested with a sacred thread, and a mantra is whispered into their ear by their guru), marriage, death and cremation – is cause for fervent prayer, energetic celebration and feasting. The most significant event in a Hindu's life is **marriage**, which symbolizes ritual purity, and for women is so important that it takes the place of initiation. Feasting, dancing and singing among the bride and groom's families, usually lasting for a week or more before and after the marriage, are the order of the day all over India. The actual marriage is consecrated when the couple walk seven times round a sacred fire, accompanied by sacred verses read by an officiating *brahmin*. Despite efforts to reduce the importance of a **dowry**, a valuable gift from the bride's family to the groom, dowries are still demanded, and among wealthier families may include televisions, videos and cars, in addition to the more common items of jewellery and money. Burning of wives whose dowry is below expectations is still known to occur.

Life transitions are by no means the only cause for celebration among Hindus, whose year is marked by **festivals** devoted to deities, re-enacting mythological stories and commemorating sacred sites. The grandest festivals are held at places made holy by association with gods, goddesses, miracles and great teachers, or at rivers and mountains; throughout the year these are important **pilgrimage** sites, visited by devotees eager to receive *darshan*, glimpse the world of the gods, and attain merit. The journey, or *yatra*, to a pilgrimage site is every bit as significant as reaching the sacred location, and bands of Hindus (particularly *sadhus*) often walk from site to site. Modern transport, however, has made things easier, and every state lays on pilgrimage tours, when buses full of chanting families roar from one temple to another, filling up with religious souvenirs as they go.

South India has many important sites. The Venkateshvara temple atop Tirumala Hill in Andhra Pradesh claims to draw more pilgrims than any other holy place in the world. At Kanniyakumari, the southern tip of India, the waters of the Indian Ocean, the Bay of Bengal and the Arabian Sea are thought to merge. Pilgrimages here are often combined with visits to the great temples of **Tamil Nadu**, where Shaivite and Vaishnavite saints established cults and India's largest temples were constructed. Madurai, Thanjavur, Chidambaram and Srirangam are major pilgrimage centres, representing the pinnacle of the architectural development that began at Mamallapuram. Their festivals often involve the tugging of deities on vast wooden chariots through the streets, lively and noisy affairs that make for an unforgettable experience. As well as specific temples sacred to particular gods, historical sites, such as the former Vijayanagar capital at **Hampi**, remain magnets for pilgrims. More than a common ideology, it is this sacred geography, entwined with popular mythology, that unites hundreds of millions of Hindus, who have also been brought together in nationalistic struggles, particularly in response to Christian missionaries and Muslim and British domination.

ISLAM

Indian society may be dominated by Hindus, but **Muslims** – some ten percent of the population – form a significant presence in almost every town, city and village. The percentage is lower in most southern states, the exception being Kerala, where nearly a quarter of the populace are Muslims, and are concentrated in fishing and trading communities along the coast, especially the northern stretch. The only major southern city with a distinctly Islamic flavour is Hyderabad in Andhra Pradesh.

The belief in only one god, Allah, the condemnation of idol worship and the observance of strict dietary laws and specific festivals set Muslims apart from their Hindu neighbours, with whom they have co-existed for centuries. Such differences have often led to communal fighting, most notably during Partition in 1947, and more recently after the destruction of the Babri Masjid in Ayodhya, although southern India avoided the worst excesses.

Islam, "submission to God", was founded by **Muhammad** (570–632 AD), who was regarded as the last in a succession of prophets, and who transmitted God's final and perfected revelation to mankind through the writings of the divinely revealed "recitation", the **Koran** (Quran). The true beginning of Islam is dated at 622 AD, when Muhammad and his followers, exiled from Mecca, made the *hijra*, or migration, north to Yathrib, later known as Medina, "City of the Prophet". The *hijra* marks the start of the Islamic lunar calendar; the Gregorian year 1995 is for Muslims 1416 AH (*Anno Hijra*).

From Medina, Muhammad ordered raids on caravans heading for Mecca, and led his community in battles against the Meccans, inspired by *jihad*, or "striving" on behalf of God and Islam. This concept of holy war was the driving force behind the incredible expansion of Islam – by 713 Muslims had settled as far west as Spain, and on the banks of the Indus in the east. When **Mecca** was peacefully surrendered to Muhammad in 630, he cleared the sacred shrine, the Ka'ba, of idols, and proclaimed it the pilgrimage centre of Islam.

The Koran, the authoritative scripture of Islam, contains the basics of Islamic belief: that there is one god, Allah (though he is attributed with 99 names), and his prophet is Muhammad.

Muhammad was succeeded as leader of the *umma*, the Islamic community, by Abu Bakr, the prophet's representative, or Caliph, the first in a line of Caliphs who led the orthodox community until the eleventh century AD. However, a schism soon emerged when the third Caliph, Uthman, was assassinated by followers of Ali, Muhammad's son-in-law, in 656 AD. This new sect, calling themselves **Shi'as**, "partisans" of Ali, looked to Ali and his successors, infallible *Imams*, as leaders of the *umma* until 878 AD, and thereafter replaced their religious authority with a body of scholars, the *ulema*.

By the second century after the *hijra* (ninth century AD), orthodox, or **Sunni**, Islam had assumed the form in which it endures today. A collection of traditions about the prophet, **Hadith**, became the source for ascertaining the **Sunna**, customs, of Muhammad. From the Koran and the Sunna, seven major **items of belief** were laid down: the belief in God, in angels as his messengers, in prophets (including Jesus and Moses), in the Koran, in the doctrine of predestination by God, in the Day of Judgement, and in the bodily resurrection of all people on this day. Religious practice was also standardized under the Muslim law, **Sharia**, in the **Five Pillars of Islam**. The first "pillar" is the confession of faith, *shahada*, that "There is no god but God, and Muhammad is his messenger." The other four are prayer (*salat*) five times daily, almsgiving (*zakat*), fasting (*saum*), especially during the month of Ramadan, and, if possible, pilgrimage (*hajj*) to Mecca, the ultimate goal of every practising Muslim.

The first Muslims to settle in India were traders who arrived on the south coast in the seventh century, probably in search of timber for shipbuilding. Later, in 711, Muslims entered Sind, in the northwest, to take action against Hindu pirates, and dislodged the Hindu government. Their presence, however, was short-lived. Much more significant was the invasion of north India, first under **Mahmud of Ghazni**, who in the spirit of *jihad*, engaged in a war against infidels and idolaters, then under the Turkish **Sultanates** from the twelfth century on. It was the powerful **Moghuls** (see p.553) who succeeded them and pushed Islam deep into India, although the southern tip remained unconquered.

Many Muslims who settled in India intermarried with Hindus, Buddhists and Jains, and the community spread. A further factor in its growth was missionary activity by **Sufis**, who emphasized abstinence and self-denial in service to God, and stressed the attainment of inner knowledge of God through meditation and mystical experience. In India, Sufi teachings spread among Shaivites and Vaishnavites, who shared their passion for personal closeness to God. Their use of music (particularly *qawwali* singing) and dance, shunned by orthodox Muslims, appealed to Hindus, for whom *kirtan* (singing) played an important role in religious practice. One *qawwali*, relating the life of the Sufi saint Waris Ali Shah, draws parallels between his early life and the childhood of Krishna – an outrage for orthodox Muslims, but attractive to Hindus. Sufi shrines, or *dargars*, all over India bridge the gap between Islam and Hinduism.

Muslims are enjoined to pray five times daily, following a routine of utterances and positions. They may do this at home or in a **mosque**; the latter are always full at noon on Friday, for communal prayer. (Only the Druze, an esoteric sect based in Mumbai, hold communal prayers on Thursdays.) Characterized by bulbous domes and high minarets, from which a *muezzin* calls the faithful to prayer, mosques always contain a *mihrab*, or niche indicating the direction of prayer (to Mecca), a *mimbar* or pulpit, from which the Friday sermon is read, a source of water for ablutions, and a balcony for women. Firm reminders of Muslim dominance, mosques all over India display a bold linear grandeur quite different to the delicacy of Hindu temples. In South India this is most evident in Hyderabad.

The position of **women** in Islam is a subject of great debate. It is customary for women to be veiled, and in strictly orthodox communities most wear a *burqa*, usually black, that covers them from head to toe. In larger cities, however, many women do not cover their head. Like other Indian women, Muslim women take second place to men in public, but in the home, where they are often shielded from men's eyes in an inner courtyard, they wield great influence. In theory education is equally available to boys and girls, but girls tend to forgo learning soon after sixteen, encouraged instead to assume the traditional role of wife and mother. Contrary to popular belief, polygamy is not widespread; while it does occur, and Muhammad himself had several wives, many Muslims prefer monogamy, and several sects actually stress it as the duty of Muslims. In marriage, women *receive* a dowry (Hindu women must provide one) as financial security.

BUDDHISM

For several centuries, **Buddhism** dominated India, with adherents in almost every part of the subcontinent. However, having reached its height in the fifth century, it was all but eclipsed by the time of the Muslim conquest. Today Buddhists are a tiny fraction of the population, but superb monuments are firm reminders of the prior importance of the faith, and essential elements in India's cultural legacy.

The founder of Buddhism, **Siddhartha Gautama**, known as the **Buddha**, "the awakened one", was born into a wealthy *kshatrya* family in Lumbini, north of the Gangetic plain in present-day Nepal, around 566 BC. Brought up in luxury as a prince and a Hindu, he married at an early age, and renounced family life when he was thirty. Unsatisfied with the explanations of worldly suffering proposed by Hindu gurus, and convinced that asceticism did not lead to spiritual realization, Siddhartha spent years in meditation, wandering through the ancient kingdom, or *janapada*, of Magadha. His enlightenment (*bodhi*) is said to have taken place under a *bodhi* tree in **Bodhgaya** (Bihar), after a night of contemplation during which he resisted the worldly temptations set before him by the demon, Mara. Soon afterwards he gave his first sermon in **Sarnath**, now a major pilgrimage centre. For the rest of his life he taught, expounding **Dharma**, the true nature of the world, human life and spiritual attainment. Before his death (*c*.486 BC) in Kushinagara (UP), he had established the **sangha**, a community of monks and nuns, who continued his teachings.

The Buddha's view of life incorporated the Hindu concepts of *samsara* and karma, but remodelled the ultimate goal of religion, calling it **nirvana**, "no wind". Indefinable in worldly terms, since it is by nature free from conditioning, *nirvana* represents a clarity of mind, pure understanding and unimaginable bliss. Its attainment signals an end to rebirth, but no communion of a "soul" with God; neither has independent existence. The most important concept outlined by the Buddha was that all things, subject to change and dependence, are characterized by **impermanence**, and there is **no self**, no permanent ego, so **attachment** to anything (possessions, emotions, spiritual attainment and *devas*) must be renounced before impermanence can be grasped, and *nirvana* realized.

Disregarding caste and priestly dominance in ritual, the Buddha formulated a teaching open to all. His followers took refuge in the three jewels: *Buddha*, *Dharma*, and *Sangha*. The teachings became known as **Theravada**, or "Doctrine of the Elders". By the first century BC the ***Tripitaka***, or "Three Baskets" (a Pali canon in three sections), had set out the basis for early Buddhist practice, proposing *dana*, selfless giving, and *sila*, precepts which aim at avoiding harm to oneself and others, as the most important guidelines for all Buddhists, and the essential code of practice for the lay community.

Carried out with good intentions, *dana* and *sila* maximize the acquisition of good karma, and minimize material attachment, thus making the individual open to the more religiously oriented teachings, the **Four Noble Truths**. The first of these states that all is suffering (*dukkha*), not because every action is necessarily unpleasurable, but because nothing in the phenomenal world is permanent or reliable. The second truth states that *dukkha* arises through attachment, the third refers to *nirvana*, the cessation of suffering, and the fourth details the path to *nirvana*. Known as the **Eightfold Path** – right understanding, thought, speech, action, livelihood, effort, mindfulness and concentration – it aims at reducing attachment and ego and increasing awareness, until all four truths are thoroughly comprehended, and *nirvana* is achieved. Even this should not be clung to – those who experience it are advised by the Buddha to use their understanding to help others to achieve realization.

The Sanskrit word ***bhavana***, referred to in the West as **meditation**, translates literally as "bringing into being". Traditionally meditation is divided into two categories: **Samatha**, or calm, which stills and controls the mind, and **Vipassana**, or insight, during which thought processes and the noble truths are investigated, leading ultimately to a knowledge of reality. Both methods are taught in Buddhist centres across India.

At first, Buddhist iconography represented the Buddha by symbols such as a footprint, *bodhi* tree, parasol or vase. These can be seen on *stupas* (domed monuments containing relics of the Buddha) built throughout India from the time of the Buddhist emperor Ashoka (see p.547), and in ancient Buddhist caves, which served as meditation retreats and *viharas* (monasteries). Though the finest examples are to be found in the North, there are interesting sites in the South, such as the *stupas* at Amaravati and Nagarjunakonda in Andhra Pradesh and caves at Aihole and Badami in Karnataka.

This artistic development coincided with an increase in the devotional side of Buddhism, and a recognition of ***bodhisattvas*** – those bound for enlightenment who delayed self-absorption in *nirvana* to become teachers, spurred by selfless compassion and altruism.

The importance of the *bodhisattva* ideal grew as a new school, the **Mahayana**, or "Great Vehicle", emerged. By the twelfth century it had become fully established and, somewhat disparagingly, renamed the old school **Hinayana**, or "Lesser Vehicle". Mahayanists proposed emptiness (*sunyata*) as the fundamental nature of all things, taking to extremes the belief that nothing has independent existence. The **wisdom** necessary to understand *sunyata*, and the **skilful means** required to put wisdom into action in daily life and teaching, and interpret emptiness in a positive sense, became the most important qualities of Mahayana Buddhism. Before long *bodhisattvas* were joined in both scripture and art by female consorts who embodied wisdom.

Hinayana Buddhism survives today in Sri Lanka, Burma, Thailand, Laos and Cambodia. Mahayana Buddhism spread from India to China, Japan, Korea and Vietnam, where it incorporated local gods and spirits into a family of *bodhisattvas*. In many places further evolution saw the adoption of magical methods, esoteric teachings and the full use of sense experience to bring about spiritual transformation, resulting in a separate school known as **Mantrayana** or **Vajrayana** based on texts called *tantras*. Mantrayana encouraged meditation on *mandalas* (symbolic diagrams representing the cosmos and internal spiritual attainment), sexual imagery and sometimes sexual practice, in which the female principle of wisdom could be united with skilful means.

Buddhism was introduced to **Tibet** in the seventh century, and integrated to a certain extent with the indigenous **Bön** cult, before emerging as a faith considered to incorporate all three vehicles – Hinayana, Mahayana and Vajrayana. Practised largely in Ladakh, along with parts of Himachal Pradesh, Sikkim and Bihar, Tibetan Buddhism worships historical Buddha, known as Shakyamuni, alongside other Buddhas and a host of *bodhisattvas* and protector deities. Elaborate rituals and ceremonies incorporating music and dance mark important dates in the Buddhist calendar. There is a heavy emphasis on teachers, *lamas* (similar to gurus), and reincarnated teachers, known as *tulkus*. The **Dalai Lama**, the head of Tibetan Buddhism, is the fourteenth in a succession of incarnate *bodhisattvas*, the representative of Avalokitesvara (the *bodhisattva* of compassion), and the leader of the exiled Tibetan community whose headquarters are in Dharamsala, Haryana and Punjab.

For Buddhist monks and nuns, and some members of the lay community, meditation is an integral part of religious life. Most lay Buddhists concentrate on *dana* and *sila*, and on auspicious days, such as *Vesak* (marking the Buddha's birth, enlightenment and death), make **pilgrimages** to Bodh Gaya, Sarnath, Lumbini and Kushinagar. After laying offerings before Buddha statues, devotees gather in silent meditation, or join in chants taken from early Buddhist texts. *Uposathas*, full moon days, are marked by continual chanting through the night when temples are lit by glimmering butter lamps, often set afloat on lotus ponds, among the flowers that represent the essential beauty and purity to be found in each person in the thick of the confusing "mud" of daily life.

Among Tibetan communities, devotees hang prayer flags, turn prayer wheels, and set stones carved with *mantras* (religious verses) in rivers, thus sending the word of the Buddha with wind and water to all corners of the earth. Prayers and chanting are often accompanied by horns, drums and cymbals.

JAINISM

Though the **Jain** population in India is small – accounting for less than one percent of the population – it has been tremendously influential for at least 2500 years. A large proportion of Jains live in Gujarat, and all over India they are commonly occupied as merchants and traders. Similarities to Hindu worship, and a shared respect for nature and non-violence, have contributed to the decline of the Jain community through conversion to Hinduism, but there is no antagonism between the two sects.

Focusing on the practice of **ahimsa** (non-violence), Jains follow a rigorous discipline to avoid harm to all **jivas**, or "souls", which exist in animals and humans, and in plants, water, fire, earth and air. They assert that every *jiva* is pure, omniscient and capable of achieving liberation, or *moksha*, from existence in this universe. However, *jivas* are obscured by **karma**, a form of subtle matter that clings to the soul, is born of action, and binds the *jiva* to physical existence. For the most orthodox Jain, the only way to dissociate karma from the *jiva*, and thereby escape the wheel of death and rebirth, is to follow the path of asceticism and meditation, rejecting passion, wrong view, attachment, carelessness and impure action.

The Jain doctrine is based upon the teachings of **Mahavira**, or "Great Hero", the last in a succession of 24 **tirthankaras** ("crossing-makers") said to appear on earth every 300 million years. Mahavira (*c*.599–527 BC) was born as Vardhamana Jnatrputra into a *kshatrya* family near modern Patna, in northeast India. Like the Buddha, Mahavira rejected family life at the age of thirty, and spent years wandering as an ascetic, renouncing all possessions in an attempt to conquer attachment to worldly values. Firmly opposed to sacrificial rites and caste distinctions, after gaining complete understanding and detachment, he began teaching others, not about Vedic gods and divine heroes, but about the true nature of the world, and the means required for release, *moksha*, from an endless cycle of rebirth.

His teachings were written down in the first millennium BC, and Jainism prospered throughout India, under the patronage of kings such as Chandragupta Maurya (third century BC). Not long after, there was a schism, in part based on linguistic and geographical divisions, but mostly due to differences in monastic practice. On the one hand the **Digambaras** ("sky-clad") believed that nudity was an essential part of world renunciation, and that women are incapable of achieving liberation from worldly existence. The ("white-clad") **Svetambaras**, however, disregarded the extremes of nudity, incorporated nuns into monastic communities and even acknowledged a female *tirthankara*. Today the two sects worship at different temples, but the number of naked Digambaras is minimal. Many Svetambara monks and nuns wear white masks to avoid breathing in insects, and carry a "fly-whisk", sometimes used to brush their path; none will use public transport, and they often spend days or weeks walking barefoot to a pilgrimage site. Practising Jain householders vow to avoid injury, falsehood, theft (extended to fair trade), infidelity and worldly attachment.

Jain **temples** are wonderfully ornate, with pillars, brackets and spires carved by *silavats* into voluptuous maidens, musicians, saints and even Hindu deities; the swastika symbol commonly set into the marble floors is central to Jainism, representing the four states of rebirth as gods, humans, "hell beings" or animals and plants. Worship in temples consists of prayer and *puja* before images of the *tirthankaras*; the devotee circumambulates the image, chants sacred verses and makes offerings of flowers, sandalwood paste, rice, sweets and incense. It's common to fast four times a month on *parvan* (holy) days, the eighth and fourteenth days of the moon's waxing and waning periods. While reducing attachment to the body, this emulates the fast to death (while in meditation), or *sallekhana*, accepted by Jain mendicants as a final rejection of attachment, and a relatively harmless way to end worldly life.

To enter a monastic community, lay Jains must pass through eleven *pratimas*, starting with right views, the profession of vows, fasting and continence, and culminating in renunciation of family life. Once a monk or nun, a Jain aims to clarify understanding through meditational practices, hoping to extinguish passions and sever the ties of karma and attachment, entering fourteen spiritual stages, *gunasthanas*, to emerge as a fully enlightened, omniscient being. Whether pursuing a monastic or lay lifestyle, however, Jains recognize the rarity of enlightenment, and religious practice is, for the most part, aimed at achieving a state of rebirth more conducive to spiritual attainment.

Pilgrimage sites are known as **tirthas**, but this does not refer to the literal meaning of "river crossing", sacred to Hindus because of the purificatory nature of water. Although one of the foremost Svetambara *tirthas*, Shatrunjaya, where over nine hundred temples crown a single hill, is in Gujarat, an important Digambara *tirtha* is **Sravanabelagola** in Karnataka, where an eighteen-metre-high image of Bahubali (recognized as the first human to attain liberation), at the summit of a hill, is anointed in the huge *abhisheka* festival every twelve years.

In an incredibly complicated process of philosophical analysis known as **Anekanatavada** (many-sidedness), Jainism approaches all questions of existence, permanence and change from seven different viewpoints, maintaining that things can be looked at in an infinite number of valid ways. Thus it claims to remove the intellectual basis for violence, avoiding the potentially damaging result of holding a one-sided view. In this respect Jainism accepts other religious philosophies, and it has adopted, with a little reinterpretation, several Hindu festivals and practices.

SIKHISM

Sikhism, India's youngest religion, remains dominant in the Punjab, while its adherents have spread throughout northern India, and several communities have grown up in Britain, America and Canada.

Guru Nanak (1469–1539) was the movement's founder. Born into an orthodox Hindu *kshatrya* family in Talwandi, a small village west of Lahore (in present-day Pakistan), he was among many sixteenth-century poet-philosophers, sometimes referred to as Sants, who formed emotional cults, drawing elements from both Hinduism and Islam. Nanak declared "God is neither Hindu nor Muslim and the path which I follow is God's"; he regarded God as *Sat*, or truth, who makes himself known through gurus. Though he condemned ancestor worship, astrology, caste distinction, sex discrimination, auspicious days and the rituals of *brahmins*, Nanak did not attack Islam or Hinduism – he simply regarded the many deities as names for one supreme God, and encouraged his followers to shift religious emphasis from ritual to meditation.

In common with Hindus, Nanak believed in a cyclic process of death and rebirth (*samsara*), but he asserted that liberation (*moksha*) was attainable in this life by all women and men, regardless of caste, and religious practice can and should be integrated into everyday practical living. He contested that all people are characterized by *humai*, a sense of self-reliance that obscures an understanding of dependence on God, encourages attachment to temporal values (*maya*), and consequently results in successive rebirths. For Sikhs, the only way to achieve release from human existence is to conquer *humai*, and become centred on God (*gurmukh*). The only people believed to have realized the ultimate truth embodied by God are the Sikh gurus.

Guru Nanak, who died in 1539, was succeeded by a disciple, Lehna, known as **Guru Angad** ("limb"), who continued to lead the community of Sikhs ("disciples"), the **Sikh Panth**, and wrote his own and Nanak's hymns in a new script, **Gurumukhi**, which is today the script of written Punjabi.

After Guru Angad's death in 1552, eight successive gurus acted as leaders for the Sikh Panth, each introducing new elements into the faith and asserting it as a separate and powerful religious movement. Guru Ram Das (1552–74) founded the sacred city of **Amritsar**; his successor, Guru Arjan, compiled the gurus' hymns in a book called the **Adi Granth**, and became Sikhism's first martyr when he was executed at the hands of Jahangir.

The last leader, **Guru Gobind Singh**, was largely responsible for moulding the community as it exists today. In 1699 he founded the **Khalsa Brotherhood**, requiring members to renounce tobacco, *halal* meat and sexual relations with Muslims, and to adopt the **five Ks**: *kesh* (unshorn hair), *kangha* (comb), *kirpan* (sword), *kara* (steel wristlet) and *kachch* (short trousers). This code, assumed at initiation, together with the replacement of caste names with Singh ("lion") for men and Kaur ("princess") for women, and the wearing of turbans by men, created a distinct cultural identity. Guru Gobind Singh compiled a standardized version of the *Adi Granth*, which contains the hymns of the first nine gurus as well as poems written by Hindus and Muslims, and installed it as his successor, naming it **Guru Granth Sahib**. This became the Sikh's spiritual guide, while political authority rested with the Khalsa, or *sangat*.

Demands for a separate Sikh state – Khalistan – and fighting in the eighteenth century, and later after Independence, have burdened Sikhs with a reputation as military activists, but Sikhs regard their religion as one devoted to egalitarianism, democracy and social awareness. Though to die fighting for the cause of religious freedom is considered to lead to liberation, the use of force is officially sanctioned only when other methods have failed.

The main duties of a Sikh are *nam japna*, *kirt karni* and *vand chakna*; keeping God's name in mind, earning honest means and giving to charity. Serving the community (*seva*) is a display of obedience to God, and the ideal life is uncontaminated by the **five evil impulses**: lust, covetousness, attachment, anger and pride.

Sikh **worship** takes place in a **gurudwara** ("door to the guru") or in the home, providing a copy of the *Adi Granth* is present. There are no priests, and no fixed time for worship, but congregations often meet in the mornings and evenings, and always on the eleventh day (*ekadashi*) of each lunar month, and on the first day of the year (*sangrand*). During *kirtan*, or hymn singing, a feature of every Sikh service, verses from the *Adi Granth* or *Janam Sakhis*, stories of Guru Nanak's life, are sung to rhythmic clapping. The communal meal, *langar*, following prayers and singing, reinforces the practice laid down by Guru Nanak that openly flouted caste and religious differences.

Gurudwaras – often schools, clinics or hostels as well as houses of prayer – are generally modelled on the Moghul style of Shah Jahan, considered a congenial blend of Hindu and Muslim architecture; usually whitewashed, and surmounted by a dome, they are always distinguishable by the *nishan sahib*, a yellow flag introduced by Guru Hargobind (1606–44). As in Islam, God is never depicted in pictorial form. Instead, the representative symbol *Il Oankar* is etched into a canopy that shades the *Adi Granth*, which always stands in the main prayer room. In some *gurudwaras* a picture of a guru is hung close to the *Adi Granth*, but it's often difficult to distinguish between the different teachers: artistically they are depicted as almost identical, a tradition that unites the ten gurus as vehicles for god's words, or *mahalas*, and not divine beings.

Important occasions for Sikhs, in addition to naming of children, weddings and funerals, are **Gurpurbs**, anniversaries of the birth and death of the ten gurus, when the *Adi Granth* is read continuously from beginning to end.

ZOROASTRIANISM

Of all India's religious communities, Western visitors are least likely to come across – or recognize – **Zoroastrians**, who have no distinctive dress and few houses of worship. Most live in Mumbai, where they are known as **Parsis** (Persians) and are active in business, education, and politics, such as the Tata family, leading industrialists who until recently had a virtual monopoly on Indian truck-building, and control many major chemical factories. Zoroastrian numbers (roughly 90,000) are rapidly dwindling, due to a falling birth rate and absorption into wider communities.

The religion's founder, **Zarathustra** (Zoroaster), who lived in Iran in 6000 BC (according to

Zoroastrians), or between 1700 and 1400 BC, was the first religious prophet to expound a dualistic philosophy, based on the opposing powers of good and evil. For him, the absolute, wholly good and wise god, **Ahura Mazda**, together with his holy spirit and six emanations present in earth, water, the sky, animals, plants and fire, is constantly at odds with an evil power, **Angra Mainyu**, who is aided by **daevas**, or evil spirits.

Mankind, whose task on earth is to further good, faces judgement after death, and depending on the proportion of good and bad words, thoughts and actions, will find a place in heaven or suffer the torments of hell. Zarathustra looked forward to a day of judgement, when a saviour, **Saoshyant**, miraculously born of a seed of the prophet and a virgin maiden, will appear on earth, restoring Ahura Mazda's perfect realm and expelling all impure souls and spirits to hell.

The first Zoroastrians to enter India arrived on the Gujarati coast in the tenth century, soon after the Arabian conquest of Iran, and by the seventeenth century most had settled in Bombay. Zoroastrian practice is based on the responsibility of every man and woman to choose between good and evil and to respect God's creations. Five daily prayers, usually hymns (*gathas*), uttered by Zarathustra and standardized in the main Zoroastrian text, the **Avesta**, are said in the home or in a temple, before a fire, which symbolizes the realm of truth, righteousness and order. For this reason, Zoroastrians are often, incorrectly, called "fire-worshippers". **No Ruz**, or "New Day", which celebrates the creation of fire and the ultimate triumph of good over evil, is the most popular Zoroastrian festival.

Members of other faiths may not enter Zoroastrian temples, but one custom that is evident to outsiders is the method of disposing of the dead. A body is laid on a high open rooftop (or isolated hill) known as *dakhma* (often referred to as a "tower of silence" see p.93), for the flesh to be eaten by vultures, and the bones cleansed by the sun and wind. Recently, some Zoroastrians, by necessity, have adopted more common methods of cremation or burial; in order not to bring impurity to fire or earth, they only use electric crematoria, and shroud coffins in concrete before laying them in the ground.

CHRISTIANITY

Christianity in India is a largely indigenized and fluid mix of established Church denominations and alternative experiments, such as the ashrams that practise a synthesis of Hindu and Christian elements. There are currently just under two and a half million Christians in India, who celebrate a long and colourful past. The **Apostle Thomas** ("Doubting Thomas") is said to have arrived in Kerala, in 54 AD, to convert itinerant Jewish traders living in the flourishing port of Muziris, just after the death of Jesus. There are many tales of miracles by Mar Thoma, as St Thomas is called in Malayalam. One legend tells of how he approached a group of Hindu *brahmins* of Palur (now Malabar) who were trying to appease the gods by throwing water into the air; if the gods accepted the offerings, the droplets would hang above them. St Thomas also threw water in the air, which miraculously remained suspended, leading most of the *brahmins* to convert to Christianity. It is customarily believed in the South, that St Thomas was martyred on December 21, 72 AD at Mylapore in Madras (which comes from the Syriac, "*madrasa*" meaning "monastery"). The tomb has since been a major place of pilgrimage and in recognition of this, in the late nineteenth century the Portuguese built the Gothic San Thome Cathedral on the site. By oral tradition, this is the **oldest denomination in the world**, but documentary evidence of Christian activity in the subcontinent can only be traced to the sixth century, when immigrant Syrian communities were granted settlement rights by royal charter.

The history of **foreign domination** from the sixteenth century in India is closely affiliated to the spread of Christianity across the subcontinent. **St Francis Xavier** arrived in the Portuguese trading colony of Goa in 1552 to convert and establish missions to reach out to the Hindu 'untouchables'; his tomb and alleged relics are retained in the Basilica of Bom Jesus in Old Goa. In 1559, the bloody and brutal Inquisition in Goa by Portuguese Jesuit missionaries, at the behest of their king, marked the height of a campaign to "cleanse" the small colony of Hindu and Muslim religious practice. At first, the **British** took the attitude that the subcontinent was a heathen and polytheistic civilization waiting to be proselytized. Later, the

British were less zealous in their conversion efforts and content to provide social welfare and build very English-looking churches in their cantonments.

As Christianity, based on the equality and brotherhood expounded by its founder Jesus Christ, is intended to be free of caste stigmas, it is attractive to those seeking social advancement and consequently pockets of **converts** have been made among tribal peoples and untouchables. There have recently been attacks on the Christian communities in some areas by alleged Hindu extremists, which Christian organizations believe to be part of a systematic anti-Christian campaign. After an international outcry, the government said that it would be taking measures **to protect** the rights of the minority religions to worship in peace.

The strong sense of state history and culture has distinctly influenced the presence of Christianity in India. The St Thomas Christians of the South congregate in small white churches, decorated with colourful pictures and statues of figures from the New Testament. This is visibly different from the great twin-steepled churches of Goa and Madras, with their heavy gold interiors and candlelit shrines to the Virgin Mary. Christians in Goa and Kerala number nearly a third and a fifth of the population respectively. While most in Goa follow the **Catholicism** of their Portuguese forbeares, Kerala is home to an array of sects from Catholic through Syrian and Malankara **Orthodox** to the Church of South India, modelled on **Anglicanism**.

In Tamil Nadu, Christian **festivals** are highly structured along "caste" ranks and in the same way as their Hindu brethren, Christians there never eat beef or pork as it is considered polluting. By contrast in Goa, Christians eat beef and pork as a feature of their Portuguese heritage. In many churches you will often see devotees offering the Hindu *arati*-plate of coconut, sweets and rice, and the women will wear a tilak dot on their forehead. In the same way that Hindus and Muslims consider the **pilgrimage** to be an integral part of life's journey, Indian Christians also have numerous sites of devotion such as St Jude's shrine in Jhansi and the temple of Mother Mary in Mathura, both in Uttar Pradesh, but these sites feature mostly in the north. Christians carry plates of food to the graves of their ancestors to honour their dead, on the anniversary of their death, in much the same manner as Hindus do. At **Christmas** time you cannot fail to notice the brightly coloured paper stars and small nativity scenes glowing and flashing outside schools, houses, shops and churches in Christian areas of South India.

SOCIETY AND PEOPLE

This great and ancient nation was once the fountain of human light, the apex of human civilisation, the exemplar of courage and humanity, the perfection of good government and settled society, the mother of all religions, the teacher of all wisdom and philosophy.
Shri Aurobindo (1907)

Indian society at the turn of the millennium has changed, but the institutions that go into its making run deep, and their foundations can be traced back hundreds, even thousands, of years. Indians pride themselves on their antique civilization with some justification. Sanskrit, the classical language that provides the foundations of Hindu thought, goes back to rituals of the Vedic age, and the fire and nature worship of migrant Aryans who had crossed through the Caucasus and Persia with their cattle in search of new pastures before entering northern India. The Dravidians of southern India were also migrants, but they pre-dated the Aryans by several hundred years. Although the two cultures – Aryan and Dravidian – mingled to a certain extent, Dravidian culture eventually came to be centred in the far south, where, thousands of years later it continues to flourish. Today, India's colourful tapestry of people is nowhere better exemplified than in the South, with its myriad cultures, languages and religions.

Visitors to India soon notice the sharp contrast between the North and the South, especially in terms of people, language and culture. But the differences are not as deep as they first appear. The south has played a vital role in the religious history of the country, with reformers like Shankara, who travelled throughout India in the ninth century, bringing about sweeping reforms by utilizing Buddhist models to establish a revitalized Hindu monastic order that is still in use today. Later, in the thirteenth century, in the face of a Muslim onslaught on Hindu institutions, South Indian **Vaishnavas** (worshippers of Vishnu and his incarnations) played an important role in the development of Krishna worship by establishing centres in Krishna's mythological homeland of Braj, to the south of Delhi. Ever since, Vaishnavism has been at the heart of South Indian Hindu life.

LANGUAGE AND LITERATURE

The Aryan–Dravidian divide is most pronounced when it comes to **language**. The official language of India, and the dominant language of the north and centre of the country, is of course **Hindi**, and most northern and central languages, like Marathi (the language of Mumbai), are related in some way to it. However, the main **Dravidian** languages are distinctly different from those of the north, and outside cities like Mumbai and Hyderabad Hindi is of little use in most parts of southern India. Instead, you'll hear Tamil (in Tamil Nadu) Telugu (in Andhra Pradesh), Kannada (in Karnataka) and Malayalam (in Kerala), each of which developed in comparative isolation from the languages of the north. With the growth of Dravidian pride since Independence, the South fiercely resisted the national government's efforts to push Hindi as the official language of independent India. In fact, this resistance to Hindi, especially in Tamil Nadu and the far south, has been intense enough to spark occasional riots, especially in the early 1970s.

DRAVIDIAN LANGUAGES AND LITERATURE

The rich will make temples for Shiva,
What shall I, a poor man, do?
My legs are pillars, the body the shrine,
The head a cupola of gold.
Listen, O lord of the meeting rivers,
Things standing shall fall, but the moving shall stay forever.
Basavanna (Kannada poet, *c.*10th century AD)

The art of writing developed much faster in the south of India than it had in the north, and in the sixth and seventh centuries. **Dravidian scripts** abandoned the box-like characters of the northern Brahmi script for a more florid and rounded style, partly due to the fact that writing was done on the palmyra and talipot palm leaves found easily in the South but not in the North: a hard stylus was held partly rigid while the leaf was turned to create the letters. This same script was to be adopted for other languages of Southeast Asia, such as those of Thailand, Cambodia and Burma (Myanmar). Although sharing many similarities, each of the main Dravidian languages has its own particular script, however.

Of South India's main languages, **Tamil** boasts a literary tradition that goes back to pre-Pallava times, prior to the sixth century. According to popular belief, three literary academies or **Sangam** met at Madurai, the earliest of which was attended by the gods and is no longer in existence. The Second Sangam is supposed to have been responsible for the **Tolkappiyam** – a treatise on Tamil grammar – but on close examination this would seem to have appeared later than the **Ettutogai**, the "Eight Anthologies" ascribed to the Third Sangam. Although in archaic Tamil, and barely readable by ordinary Tamils today, the Eight Anthologies, consisting of over 2000 poems composed by around two hundred authors, and the **Pattuppattu**, or "Ten Songs", represent the greatest works of ancient Tamil literature. Even from this early stage, literature was subject to the Tamil love of classification, and the poems were divided into two main categories: *agam* (internal), dealing with love, and *puram* (external), laudatory poems in praise of the kings.

Although the Aryan influence on Tamil culture was already evident in Sangam literature, the influence of northern civilization grew, and, in the sixth century, Hindu, Buddhist and Jain practices were widespread in the far south. Sanskrit left an indelible impression on Tamil literature, and the epic style of Sanskrit was emulated by long narrative poems such as **Shilappadigaram** (The Jewelled Anklet). Unlike the Sanskrit epics, however, Tamil poems such as the *Shilappadigaram* deal with the lives of ordinary people – in this case the hapless couple, Kovalan and Kannagi – and provide an invaluable insight into everyday life of the time. Shortly after the *Shilappadigaram* was written, Sattan, a poet from Madurai, composed the **Manimegalai**, a sort of anthology to the *Shilappadigaram*, but with a philosophical bent and a Buddhist message. The **Shivaga Shidamani**, another great early Tamil epic, was written by the Jain author Tiruttakkadevar and emulates Sanskrit court poetry, but concerns itself with the fantastic heroics of Shivaga (aka Jivaka) who eventually embraces the faith and becomes a monk.

Perhaps the greatest of all Tamil epics is Kamban's **Ramayanam**, composed in the ninth century – not just a translation from the Sanskrit *Ramayana* but a reinterpretation, with additional story lines, and, on occasion, markedly different interpretations of the main characters. Rama is not always shown as heroic, while Ravana, the demon king, occasionally is. During this period, inspired by the *Bhagavad Purana*, Vaishnavism became a predominant force in Tamil literature, promoting the new-found hero and man-god, Krishna.

In terms of antiquity, **Kannada**, the language of Karnataka, comes second only to Tamil amongst the Dravidian languages, with its earliest literature dating back to the ninth century AD and evidence from inscriptions that traces the language back to the fifth century. The golden age of Kannada literature was between the tenth and the twelfth centuries, when the poet-saints of the **Virashaiva** sect composed their **Vacanas** or "sayings". Also known as the **Lingayatas**, or "those who wear the *linga*", the Virashaiva poets dedicated their lives to the god Shiva. Although the sect, distinguished by the *lingam* encased in a small stone casket and worn around the neck, is still in existence, and *vacanas* are still composed, the four greatest poet-saints – **Basvanna**, **Dasimayya**, **Allama** and **Mahadeviyakka** – all flourished in the early medieval period. Basvanna, the most illustrious of all, epitomized the spirit of Virashaiva, with an uncompromising view of life and society and a single-minded devotion to the pursuit of truth through homage to Shiva. Basvanna and the Virashaivas rejected caste and believed the true path was open to all; they believed in the equality of women and the right of widows to remarry. They also rejected the highly structured poetic devices of classical Sanskrit poetry and composed simple free verse with a direct and universal philosophical wisdom which has caused some to refer to their work as the **Kannada Upanishads**.

The Lingayatas also composed their *vacanas* in **Telugu**, the language of Andhra Pradesh and parts of northern Tamil Nadu and southeast Karnataka. Although Telugu literature dates back to the twelfth century, its literary tradition did not develop as strongly as those of Tamil and Kannada until the sixteenth century, when it was adopted at the court of the Vijayanagar empire at Hampi (see p.248). Telugu-speaking *brahmins* – most dedicated Vaishnavas (devotees of the god Vishnu and his incarnations) – were attracted to the court of King Krishna Deva

Raya, who was also an accomplished composer of Sanskrit and Telugu verse. After the fall of Vijayanagar, the cultural centre shifted to the court of Tanjore, where despite its location in the heart of Tamil country, Telugu continued to enjoy its privileged status, partly due to the high calibre of religious poets who travelled to Tanjore and the surrounding country. In its heyday Tanjore was home to the merging of devotional literature with theatre, music and dance – nowhere better seen than in the work of the saint, poet and songwriter Tyagaraja (1767–1847), another Telugu-speaking *brahmin*, who was to leave an indelible impression on Carnatic music (see box on p.602).

Finally, **Malayalam**, the language of coastal Kerala and spoken by over thirty million people, is a relatively new language, dating back to around the thirteenth century, with its roots in the Tamil language and heavily influenced by Sanskrit.

Of the several **non-Dravidian languages** of South India, **Dakhani**, "the language of the Deccan" is the most important, as it was the first form of **Urdu**, the Muslim language of the north, and has a literary tradition that dates back to the fourteenth century. Urdu (literally "camp" in Turkish) was an amalgamation of the languages (mainly Persian) introduced by central Asian Muslims, and local Hindi-based languages – especially Khari Boli, the most common form of Hindi today. For some time around the nineteenth to mid-twentieth centuries, due to shared grammar, and, for most part, a shared vocabulary, the two languages were regarded as the same thing – Hindustani. However, over the last fifty years there has been a politically motivated tendency to separate the two languages, weeding out Urdu (and Persian) words from Hindi. Today, although spoken in pockets throughout much of India, including Hyderabad and Bijapur, Urdu is seen as a Muslim language.

Konkani was only recognized as the official language of Goa in 1992, after a long campaign. For a long time it was considered a dialect of Marathi, and even today the number of schools teaching Konkani are few. Goa in any case has a confusing mixture of languages, with Portuguese still in evidence, alongside **English**, Marathi and Konkani – as well as the Hindi spoken by the increasing number of migrant workers here that have been brought in to service the tourist industry. **Marathi**, the language of Mumbai, is also spoken along the cultural fault line that runs through northern Karnataka around Hubli.

THE PEOPLE

South India's different ethnic groups live in close proximity, with surprisingly little conflict, except for the occasional – mostly politically motivated – confrontation. Aryan civilization may have reached here relatively late, but South India stands firmly at the heart of Hindu culture, with lavish temples and a history of reformers who have played a major role in Hindu religious life throughout the subcontinent. Although predominantly Hindu, South India also has a rich Muslim heritage and a Christian history that is older than that of Britain, tracing its roots back to the Apostle Thomas. The once influential Keralan Jews are now a pitifully small community, but the influence of their community, originally attracted here from both the Arab world and Europe by the rich pickings of the Malabar Coast and its spice belts, can still be felt. There are few traces of Buddhism left in South India, but the tiny Jain community still plays an influential role and has some of its most important shrines dotted around the southern Deccan and the Malabar Coast. The Nilgiris are home to proud warrior races and tribes who shelter in the highlands – most notable of which are the Todas (see box on p.484) – while deep within the forests of the Western Ghats, small groups of hunter-gatherers continue to shun the modern world. Away from the mainland, the Andaman and Nicobar Islands support a fragile eco-system that is home to tribal groups vulnerable to the outside world.

Dravidian society embraced Hinduism wholeheartedly, and because the far south of India was not touched by the Muslim influence in the same way as the north, the temples and centres of Hindu learning were allowed to develop long, continuous traditions. Today's Dravidian Hindu societies have also developed along this continuum. A prime example is the **Namboodri** sect of *brahmins* from Kerala, which continues to nurture ancient hereditary privileges according to a lineage that can be traced back to the reformer and philosopher Shankara in the eleventh century. Communities usually lived in close interaction with each other, and this is also the case for the Namboodris, who in the past maintained a complex relationship with the **Nayar** community, one step down in the social hierarchy. The Nayars, a martial race, dominated Kerala until the nineteenth century, but, with demobilization of Nayar armies, lost its power-base and saw much of its social organization go through radical change. The Nayars once had a fearful reputation for dominating and even enslaving lower caste groups. One casualty of Nayar society was its curious matrilineal households known as *taravads*, home to joint families, which, during the Nayar heyday, could include up to around forty members. The matrilineal system has now gone but traces remain throughout Keralan society and can be seen today in the role and equality of women.

There are large pockets of **Muslims** all over the South, especially in the central Deccan, where some of the earliest Indian Muslim kingdoms flourished from the fourteenth century onwards. The spread of Islam in the Deccan was partly aided by groups of **sufis**, who were easily able to adapt to Indian ways – although not all groups of sufis were benign. Some took to the task of spreading the word with zeal and with the occasional use of force. Seven percent of Andhra Pradesh's population is Muslim, and sufi shrines are to be found throughout the Deccan. The Muslims of the Malabar Coast and especially Kerala owe their roots, not to migration from central Asia, but to the long history of trade and interaction with the Arab world. These Muslims of the **Moplah** community have nurtured a unique heritage alongside their Hindu and Christian neighbours. Returning expatriate workers from the Gulf have helped more recently to inject a new wealth into the Moplah community and provide a facelift to towns like Kozhikode.

Ever since the Apostle Thomas landed at the Roman trading port of Muziris near Thrissur in Kerala (see p.316), **Christianity** has flourished along the Malabar Coast, aided by magnanimous Hindu rulers. Christianity spread by attracting indigenous congregations, but there was some migration to the coast as well, especially in the Syrian Christian community of Kerala. Christianity here was affected by its environment, and it retained Indian customs, with congregations bringing their social beliefs and habits to church. The Syrian Christians, especially, developed a social hierarchy that had overtones of the Hindu caste system.

Right-wing Hindu groups have tried in recent years to pressurize non-Hindu communities by staging marches and protests. A march against a mosque near Chikmaglur in central Karnataka in 1998, by the Vishwa Hindu Parishad, failed to gather local support, but the attacks on Christian communities have created far more alarm. Following harrowing attacks on Christians elsewhere in India, the Christians of Bangalore brought the city to a standstill through peaceful protest in November 1998, and a couple of months later major riots broke out in Mangalore, leaving several Christians injured. However, despite these developments, South Indian communities are still for the most part able to live in comparative harmony, and most confrontations are instigated by right-wing groups from outside the region.

CUSTOMS

According to ancient custom, the life of a high-class Hindu man progressed through four distinct stages – *brahmachari* (celibate) following his initiation or "thread ceremony", *grhastha* (householder), *vanaprashta* (forest dweller) following middle age and after his children have grown up, and finally, *sannyasin* (a renunciate). However, in practice, few follow this course in life and the *vanaprashta* is no more. In general, life is, however, meant to progress along ordered lines from initiation (for high caste Hindus) through education, career and marriage.

Marriage, which is the single most important act in Indian life, attracts close and distant family from all over the country who come to witness not just the union of man and wife but a reaffirmation of the group's social standing. Traditionally, Hindu marriage customs bind caste groups together, sometimes through inter-caste marriage, where one caste traditionally marries another such as the case of Namboodris marrying Nayars. Today, with increasing modernization and mobility, marriage can transcend old caste barriers to a certain extent, and base itself, like anywhere else on earth, on wealth and social standing. But caste does invariably play a role in Hindu society – despite a wealthy alliance, the family will disapprove of a high caste person marrying someone from a caste well below them. Most Indian marriages traditionally involve the parents, who negotiate or even insist on the match; love marriages are increasingly common, especially in urban areas, but still tend to depend on parental consent and collusion.

Today one of the greatest burdens on the Indian family is the institution of the **dowry** given by the bride's family to the groom. The practice, prevalent among Christians as well as Hindus, is as common among the middle classes as it is amongst the poor, but for the latter it can represent years of saving. Dowries are often undeclared, and they contribute to the illegal or "black" economy so important to everyday Indian commercial activity, but the government seems helpless to stop the practice.

Indian society frowns upon **divorce**, but with increasing modernization, especially among the middle classes, it has become more common. Hindu law does not recognize divorce, and the procedure is relatively complicated, but for Muslims, both men and women, it is in principle straightforward and does not involve drawn-out litigation.

For Hindus, **death** is an essential process in an endless cycle of rebirth in the grand illusion (*maya*) until the individual attains enlightenment and freedom (*moksha*) from *samskara* (transmigration). Hindus cremate their dead except for young children, whom they bury. The eldest son is entrusted to light the funeral pyre and the ashes are scattered usually on a river. Rites after death can be lengthy and complicated according to each Hindu community, and the role of the *purohit* (priest) is indispensable. **Widows** traditionally wear white, and, according to ancient Hindu belief, are considered to be outside society.

SUPERSTITION

Indians are extremely **superstitious**, and will rarely take a major decision without consulting some form of oracle or visiting a shrine. Indeed, approaching the gods for a boon is part and parcel of Hindu life, and the fundamental reason for many to visit a temple. Roadside **fortune-tellers** are common, and utilize various simple methods of telling the future. These include parrots that are trained to pick the right answer and palmists. Many Indians dabble with palmistry but usually on a very elementary level.

The most hallowed form of Indian futurology is the ancient art of **astrology**, based on the science of astronomy that goes back to the Vedic period. Contact with the Greeks around the second century BC led to great progress in Indian astronomy, when the signs of the zodiac were introduced. However, thanks to the achievements of Indian mathematicians, Indian astronomy made huge advances that were in turn passed back to the west through contacts with Arab traders. With the naked eye, Indian astronomers were able to discern the seven planets or *graha*: Surya or Ravi (the Sun), Chandra or Soma (the Moon), Budha (Mercury), Shukra (Venus), Mangala (Mars), Brihaspati (Jupiter) and Shani (Saturn). In addition to these, Indian astrologers use two more *grahas* – Rahu and Ketu, respectively the ascending and descending nodes of the moon. The *jyotish* (astrologer) plays an important role in Hindu life, providing exact calculations for auspicious events such as marriages. Much like the Chinese art of feng shui, **Vastu**, the art of balancing energies in the design of buildings and interiors, is making a comeback and is currently popular with the urban middle classes in organizing the layout of their homes.

India is the only country where the worship of the **mother goddess** is still widely practised. The tradition goes back to the pre-Aryan Indus Valley civilization, and manifests itself in different forms throughout the country. Equated with the primordial feminine energy or **shakti**, the mother goddess stands at the heart of fertility cults and is found in practically every pastoral community. In South India most villages have their own association with the mother goddess or **amma**. The goddess dwells in a stone, or a shrine, a tree, or at the water's edge, and is commonly depicted as the ferocious and unpredictable **Kali**.

Gods are treated as an extension of society, and visiting a **temple** to ask a favour in exchange of a gift helps to reaffirm the relationship. After the ceremony, blessed food is passed back in the form of *prasad* (offerings) to the devotee reaffirming the devotee's relationship to the god.

CASTE AND KINSHIP

The divisions of Hindu society, commonly referred to as "**caste**", run deep. The migrating **Aryans** already had a class system in place before reaching the subcontinent, their nobility was known as the *kshatra* and the ordinary tribesman as the *vish*. However, their contact with darker-skinned people known as the **Dasas** caused them concern about racial purity, resulting in a division of society based on **varna** – literally "colour" – a unique institution of **racism** that has lasted over three thousand years. The non-Aryans who lived on the fringe of Aryan society were considered inferior, as were those of mixed blood. Meanwhile, the priests, who had developed ever more complex rituals to service the needs of a developing society, gave themselves more and more privileges, and when the four-fold system of *varna* was put in place, they gave themselves the highest position. The resulting division of the four classes was, from top to bottom – **brahmana** (priest, *brahmin*), **kshatriya** (warrior), **vaishya** (peasant) and **shudra** (serf). While the three top varnas (*brahmana*, *kshatriya* and *vaishya*) were considered "**twice born**" – once born in their native place and then again born at initiation as an Aryan – the aboriginal Dasas were not considered Aryan at all and did not have the privilege of initiation. They were, however, accommodated at the bottom strata of society as *shudras*. Children, widows and ascetics remained outside the *varna* system.

When, at the end of the Vedic age new ideas threatened the absolute power of the priesthood, and religions such as Buddhism and Jainism preached equality, the priesthood responded with the manuscript **Manu-smriti** (the words of Manu, the original man, remembered). Composed by a succession of *brahmin* authors sometime around the third century BC, *Manu-smriti* laid out the *varna* system in detail and defined the role and tasks of each *varna*, as well as the strict interaction between each group. The moral grounds laid out for the system of division was that one should perform every task well and with pride rather than to try and take on someone else's tasks. This argument, combined with **karma** (the result of one's deeds), and the concept of rebirth which developed from the late Vedic period onwards, proposes that you are what you are born. Through good deeds you may have the fortune of being reborn at a higher level in the next life.

These ethics are also carried through to the **Bhagavad Gita**, where Aryan beliefs are protected against reformers and non-believers by singing the virtues of each of the four divisions – wisdom for the *brahmin*, valour for the *kshatriya*, industry for the *vaishya* and service for the *shudra*. Interaction between the divisions had become clearly defined. *Manu-smriti*, which continues to act as the foundation of **Hindu law**, lays down the rules of purity – for example, a *shudra*'s shadow may never cross a *brahmin* and if it does the *brahmin* will have to perform a ritual to purify himself. Certain groups were considered too menial to be included at all and are therefore looked on as "untouchable".

The four-fold division – *varna* – is often but erroneously referred to as "**caste**", a word which actually relates to **jati**, the subdivisions within society. While *varna* refers to the four classes of Hindu society, *jati* refers to numerous social groupings within Hindu society. When the Portuguese first came to India in the sixteenth century, they came across these divisions and referred to them as "castas" (tribes, clans or families), a term which led to the word "caste". The *jati* refers to its *varna* and slots into the hierarchy but is more flexible. Whereas *varna* is fixed from birth to death, *jati* can change through the **social mobility** of whole groups or subgroups. The key to the social hierarchy of any particular caste is its interaction with other castes – a relation that fixes its position. Some castes may have a tendency to be upwardly mobile, in which case they try and assume ethics, manners and ways of the caste group they would like to be. Their tenure at this new rung in the hierarchy depends solely on whether the other castes are willing to accept their new position.

Castes have distinctive patterns of intra-caste relationships within themselves while at the same time interacting with other castes along strict rules of behaviour. While *varna* has its roots in theology, caste is able to adapt itself to its environment and each region has its own social groupings which are unable to directly relate to distant castes. For example, a northern *brahmin* caste say from Bengal will not relate to a southern *brahmin* caste from Kerala. Although castes maintain their place in society through both interaction and segregation, there is an element of fraternity, especially with castes close to each other in the hierarchy. One curious institution of inter-caste relationships is illustrated by the Namboodri *brahmins* of Kerala, where the men traditionally marry down a step to Nayar women who come from the dominant non-*brahmin* secular caste.

THE LEFT HAND VERSUS THE RIGHT

Literature suggests that caste came late to Tamil country, in about the ninth century. As Tamil society was fundamentally agrarian, there were few families who could claim to be *kshatriyas* (warriors) and so most of the population was divided between *brahmins*, *shudras* and untouchables. The largest group among the Tamils, the *shudras*, divided itself into a further two groups, the **left-handed** and the **right-handed** castes – the **Idangai** and the **Valangai**. The left and right hands allude to which hand was considered pure by either group (in most of Hindu India, the right hand is the pure hand while the left is menial). These two seemingly innocuous divisions have been at odds with each other ever since their inception, leading to bitter conflict and rivalry. The left-hand group includes craftsmen, weavers, some cultivators, cowherds and leather workers; the right-hand one includes traders, most cultivators, some weavers, musicians, barbers, washermen, potters and labourers. Few have been able to explain the division or the bitter animosity between the two caste groups.

SOUTH INDIA TODAY

South India **today** presents a conflicting yet mesmerizing mix of the old and the new. The pressures on modern Indian society are tremendous, as the country enters a global market. Some critics of modernization fear the destruction of age-old tradition and Indian civilization through increasing globalization. But traditions run deep and so far at least have been able to survive.

POPULATION, LITERACY AND EDUCATION

One of India's greatest burdens is its massive **population**, which has grown almost threefold since Independence in 1947 to around a billion people today. There is no comprehensive programme of population control, unlike China, and existing control programmes have proved incapable of stemming the population explosion. However, some of South India's states have shown that where there is literacy, growth can be brought down to a minimum and in a state like Kerala, which enjoys nearly 100 percent literacy, the population has been brought down to almost zero growth.

Kerala, ironically, is one of India's most densely populated states, with a population of around 31 million and a landmass of 39,000 square kilometres. Population in some of the other southern states, like Tamil Nadu (56 million; 130,000 sq km), Andhra Pradesh (66 million; 275,000 sq km) and Karnataka (50 million; 192,000 sq km), is higher, but these states are far larger than Kerala. By comparison, the Andaman and Nicobar Islands have a population of under 200,000. Goa is one of the smallest of the mainland states, with an overall area of 3800 square kilometres and a population of around 1.17 million.

Although India's **literacy** rate has been creeping up from under twenty percent at Independence to just over fifty percent today, some states, such as Bihar in the north of the country, have less than forty percent literacy. South India, however, has the highest literacy rates in the country: Tamil Nadu 63.5 percent, Karnataka 55.5 percent, Goa 77 percent, Andaman and Nicobar 74 percent and Lakshwadeep 82 percent. Andhra Pradesh's literacy figures are the lowest of those in the South, with a mere 45 percent literacy, while, at the other end of the scale, Kerala's literacy rate is 95 percent, and some districts boast 100 percent literacy.

While women, in general, have fewer opportunities for **education** than men, Kerala is an exception, and women there have equal access to literacy. During the nineteenth century, with the abolition of hereditary slavery and the rise in influence of Christian missionaries, the Nayar ruling elite lost much of its domination and took to education as a means for ensuring a healthy future. By the late nineteenth century, Kerala had a wide network of village schools, and Christian missionary schools played an important role in providing education to women.

Education is usually bilingual, and English is still commonly taught despite a growing trend to eradicate it as the basis of learning. Besides village schools, government schools and missionary schools, India has a network of private schools – many modelled directly on the English public school system – for the middle classes. Here education is usually primarily in English. India has over two hundred universities and a large variety of other higher education options, including government colleges where education is cheap, missionary colleges renowned for their quality, and technical institutions such as the five IITs (Indian Institutes of Technology), including one in Chennai. A huge number of Indian students sit for one of several government examinations every year, the most prestigious of which is the IAS (Indian Administrative Service), which supplies the upper echelons of the civil administration and IFS (Indian Foreign Service).

COMMERCE AND NEW TECHNOLOGY

The software boom has catapulted cities like Bangalore and Hyderabad into the forefront of **new technology**, and the effect has rubbed off on several other South Indian cities as well. Traditional trading cities such as Chennai (Madras) are prospering, and the region as a whole looks much more prosperous than parts of northern India, which are more dependent on traditional industries.

The software industry relies on two essential ingredients – cheap labour and brainpower. Cheap labour means that Bangalore- and Hyderabad-based companies are able to provide international data input at very competitive rates and have managed to secure lucrative international contracts, for example with US medical records and British Airways flight ticketing. The difference in time zones also helps, as when the US goes to sleep, the Indian data houses are busy keying away. But data entry is not the sole cause of the boom; software engineers in India are a dime a dozen and Indian software has a growing international reputation for its reliability.

The **Internet** has also been very successful in connecting the new cyber-aware culture, and cybercafés are cropping up all over the South, many of them out of necessity, as a lot of software and computer professionals cannot afford their own machines and rely on these places for access. Cities like Bangalore, renowned for its high-tech industries, and Chennai, a traditional trading city, continue to be at the forefront of **commerce**, but, with added contacts in the Middle East and especially the Gulf, expatriate workers have brought new wealth to towns like Thiruvananthapuram and Kozhikode in Kerala. With a high level of unemployment, Keralans, especially, are willing to travel, and in a state that lacks heavy industry, ample manpower and brainpower are helping to underwrite growth. Rice, sugar, cotton, tea and coffee still provide a backbone to the South-Indian economy and the spice trade thrives, but there is also shipbuilding at Vishakapatnam, heavy engineering at Bangalore and large industrial belts around Chennai. Karnataka and Andhra Pradesh both have huge hydroelectric projects and a rich supply of forest produce – though these activities have had a predictably debilitating effect on the environment and have caused the displacement of millions of people.

POLITICS

Indian **democracy** balances administration and political power between the Government of India, commonly known as the "central government" and the state governments. Political power at the centre is modelled in part on the British parliamentary system, and organized into the Lok Sabha (the House of Commons) and a representative, appointed body, the Rajya Sabha (the House of Lords). The Lok Sabha, which has 544 voted members of parliament, holds elections, according to the Indian constitution, once every five years. However, due to intense fragmentation within the political system, elections now tend to come around once a year. Today, in a country with myriad political views and with everyone a budding politician, few parties can command a majority, and this results in a series of tenuous coalitions. In 1999 the **BJP** (Bharatiya Janata Dal) government saw its coalition of thirteen parties fall apart when **Jayalalitha**, the Tamil politician, walked out with her fifteen MPs.

Since Independence, when the **Congress Party** led the way, Indian politics has lacked a clear vision of the future, and even the Congress Party has become very fragmented. The main core, the Congress Party (I) (after "Indira") obsessively regards the Gandhi family as the only hope for the future, and has turned to Sonia Gandhi, Rajiv's Italian widow, to take the party back to government; Priyanka, Rajiv's daughter, is also being feted as a possible leader of the future. The rival **BJP** meanwhile has encouraged the concept of **Hindutva** (the Hindu reign) to create schisms within a country made up of numerous communities and religions, thus alienating the Muslim and Christian communities. South India has thankfully been spared much of this conflict, but there have been occasional confrontations, such as the anti-Christian riots of Mangalore in early 1999.

Each **state government** in South India – except for Lakshadweep, the Andaman and Nicobar Islands, and Pondicherry, which are governed centrally – has its own legislative assembly, and with the gradual demise of the Congress Party in the 1960s party politics here have gained an increasingly regional flavour, especially in Tamil Nadu, where the **Dravida** movement provided a focus. The **DMK** (Dravida Munetra Kazhagam) took power here in 1967, when it abandoned its separatist stance and joined the political mainstream. After its leader Annadurai's death, the party split, with a splinter group forming the **AIADMK** (All India Anna DMK), and the DMK and AIADMK have since alternated in power in Tamil Nadu – though they have not managed to make much impact nationally, except when the AIADMK, led by the ex-actress **Jayalalitha**, walked out of the national coalition with the BJP in 1999, causing elections. Jayalalitha and her predecessor in the AIADMK, M.G. Ramachandran (known affectionately as "**MGR**"), illustrate the rise of the celebrity as politician in India (see box on p.382). MGR, once a great hero of Tamil cinema, turned out to be a dynamic politician, but his successor Jayalalitha was a despotic chief minister. After sponsoring a ridiculously lavish wedding in 1996, she lost the elections and her seat and faced several criminal charges relating to her misuse of power and wealth. She has since managed to bounce back, with a minority in both local and central government.

In contrast, **Keralan politics** has over the past few decades been a tussle between the Congress party and the **CPI (M)** (Communist Party of India-Marxists), the first democratically elected communist government in the world. The seesaw battle started with the first elected assembly in 1957, since when Kerala on occasion has come under President's Rule – a form of government imposed by the centre when the political process of a state is deemed unstable – but the CPI (M) remain in power today.

Of the other states, inter-caste rivalries have been an important factor in **Karnataka** politics, where a weakened Congress faces up to the coalition of the **Janata Dal** (the People's Party). The Congress had a good power-base in **Andhra Pradesh** until 1983, when it was trounced by the **Telugu Desam** led by another popular film star, N.T. Rama Rao. But the Congress fought back and with it Andhra produced a prime minister – P.V. Narasimha Rao. Politics in **Goa** lies under the shadow of its big neighbour Maharashtra; the Maharashtrawada Gomantak Party was in power here between 1963 and 1979. The Congress has always played a part in Goan politics but has not been able to hold onto power.

SACRED ART AND ARCHITECTURE

It is often said that South India is the most religious place on earth, and if the region's vast storehouse of sacred art and architecture is anything to go by, this is probably true. For thousands of years, successive chieftains, emperors, *nawabs* and *nizams* – whether Hindu, Buddhist, Jain or Muslim – have assigned huge sums of money and human resources towards raising religious structures, as much to symbolize the power of their earthly rule as the superhuman power of the gods and natural forces. Some, like the towering temple *gopuras* of Tamil Nadu or the gigantic Golgumbaz tomb at Bijapur, were conceived on an awesome scale; others, such as the rock-cut shrines of the Pallava period in Mamallapuram or the meticulously crafted architecture of the Hoysalas in Karnataka, were more intimate. Yet the South's religious monuments have one thing in common: nearly all of them testify to the Indians' enduring love of elaboration. Even the most austere Muslim Sultans of the Deccan couldn't resist decorating their tombs and mosques with exquisite geometric shapes, while the attention to fine detail demonstrated by the sculptors of the Cholas is astonishing juxtaposed with the sheer size of the buildings.

Another common feature of South Indian religious art and architecture is the extent to which the various mediums have, over the centuries, been governed by **convention**. In the same way as ritual follows precise rules passed through generations, buildings and their decor conform to the most exacting specifications, set down in ancient canonical texts. This is particularly true of **iconography** – the complex language of symbols used to represent gods, goddesses and saints, in their many and diverse forms. Even nowadays, the stone-carvers of Mamallapuram spend years learning how to render the exact size and lines of their subjects. Without such exactitude, an icon or religious building is deemed to be devoid of its essential power. If the porportions are incorrect, the all-important sequence of auspicious numbers through which the magical power of the gods become manifest is disrupted, and the essential order of the universe compromised.

Such rigorous adherence to tradition would seem to leave little scope for innovation, but somehow South Indian artists have devised an amazing variety of **regional styles**. One of the most absorbing aspects of travelling around the peninsula is comparing these. After a while, you'll begin to be able to differentiate between them and, in the process, gain a more vivid sense of the people and period that created them. The following notes are intended as a primer; for more indepth explorations, hunt out some of the titles listed under "The Arts and Architecture" in Books on p.618.

STUPAS

Among the very earliest sacred structures built in India were hemispherical mounds known as **stupas**, which have been central to Buddhist worship since the sixth century BC, when the Buddha himself modelled the first prototype. Asked by one of his disciples for a symbol to help disseminate his teachings after his death, the Master took his begging bowl, teaching staff and a length of cloth – his only worldly possessions – and arranged them into the form of a *stupa*, using the cloth as a base, the upturned bowl as the dome and the stick as the projecting finial, or spire.

Originally, *stupas* were simple burial mounds of compacted earth and stone containing relics of the Buddha and his followers. As the religion spread, however, the basic components multiplied and became imbued with **symbolic significance**. The main dome, or *anda* – representing the sacred mountain, or "diving axis" linking heaven and earth – grew larger, while the wooden railings, or *vedikas*, surrounding it were replaced by massive stone ones. A raised ambulatory terrace, or *medhi*, was added to the vertical sides of the drum, along with two flights of stairs and four ceremonial entrances, carefully aligned with the cardinal points. Finally, crowing the tip of the *stupa*, the single spike evolved into a three-tiered umbrella, or *chhattra*, representing the Three Jewels of Buddhism: the Buddha, the Law and the community of monks, or *Sangham*.

The *chhattra*, usually enclosed within a low square stone railing, or *harmika* (a throwback to the days when sacred *bodhi* trees were surrounded by fences) formed the topmost point of the axis, directly above the reliquary in the heart of the *stupa*. Ranging from bits of bone wrapped in cloth, to fine caskets of precious metals, crystal and carved stone, the reliquaries were the "seeds" and their protective mounds the "egg". Excavations on the estimated eighty-four thousand *stupas* scattered around the subcontinent have shown that the solid interiors were also sometimes built as elaborate **mandalas** – symbolic patterns that exerted a beneficial influence over the *stupa* and those who walked around it. The ritual of **circumambulation**, or *pradakshina*, which enabled the worshipper to tap into a magical force-field and be transported from the mundane to the divine realms, was always carried out in a clockwise direction from the east, in imitation of the sun's passage across the heavens.

In South India, the **Satavahana** (or Andhra) dynasty, who ruled a vast tract of the country towards the end of the first millennium (see History, p.548), erected *stupas* across the region, among them the Great Stupa at **Amaravati** in Andhra Pradesh (see p.514). Little of this once-impressive monument remains in situ, but you can admire some of the outstanding sculpture that decorated its ornamental gateways (*toranas*) in the Government Museum at Chennai (see p.376). To see a *stupa* in action, however, you have to follow in the footsteps of the emperor Ashoka's missionaries southwards to Sri Lanka, where, as *dagobas*, *stupas* are still revered as repositories of sacred energy.

TEMPLES

To make sense of Hindu **temples**, you need to be able to identify their common features. Many of these conventions are recorded in the **Shilpa Shastras** – Sanskrit manuals that set out, in meticulous detail, ancient building specifications and their symbolic significance.

Unlike Christian churches or Muslim mosques, temples are not simply places of worship, but are objects of worship in themselves – recreations of the "Divine-Cosmic-Creator-Being" or the particular deity enshrined within them. For a Hindu, to move through a temple is akin to entering the very body of the God and to be glimpsed in the shrine-room during the moment of *darshan*, or ritual viewing of the deity, is the culmination of an act of worship. In South India, this concept also finds expression in the technical terms used in the *Shastras* to designate different parts of the structure: the foot, shin, torso, neck, head and so forth.

THE TEMPLES OF TAMIL NADU

No Indian state is more dominated by its **temples** than Tamil Nadu, whose huge temple towers dominate most towns and villages. The majority were built in honour of Shiva, Vishnu and their consorts; all are characterized not only by their design and sculptures, but by constant activity – devotion, dancing, singing, *pujas*, festivals and feasts. Each is tended by *brahmin* priests, recognizable by their *dhotis* (loincloths), a sacred thread draped over the right shoulder and marks on the forehead. One to three horizontal (usually white) lines distinguish Shaivites; vertical lines (yellow or red), often converging into a near-V shape, are common among Vaishnavites.

Dravida, the temple architecture of Tamil Nadu, first took form in the **Pallava** port of **Mamallapuram**. A step up from the cave retreats of Hindu and Jain ascetics, the earliest Pallava monuments were **mandapas**, shrines cut into rock-faces and fronted by columns. The magnificent **bas-relief** at Mamallapuram, **Arjuna's Penance**, shows the fluid carving of the Pallavas at its most exquisite. This sculptural skill was transferred to freestanding temples, **rathas**, carved out of single rocks and incorporating the essential elements of Hindu temples: the dim inner sanctuary, the *garbhagriha*, capped with a modest tapering spire featuring repetitive architectural motifs. In turn, the Shore temple was built with three shrines, topped by a *vimana* similar to the towering roofs of the *rathas*; statues of Nandi, Shiva's bull, later to receive pride of place, surmount its low walls. In the finest structural Pallava temple, the Kailasanatha temple at **Kanchipuram**, the sanctuary, again crowned with a pyramidal *vimana*, stands within a courtyard enclosed by high walls. The projecting and recessing bays of the walls, carved with images of Shiva, his consort and ghoulish mythical lions, *yalis*, were the prototype for later styles.

Pallava themes were developed in Karnataka by the Chalukyas and Rashtrakutas, but it was the Shaivite **Cholas** who spearheaded Tamil Nadu's next architectural phase, in the tenth century. In **Thanjavur**, Rajaraja I created the Brihadeshwara temple principally as a status symbol. Its proportions far exceed any attempted by the Pallavas. Set within a vast walled courtyard, the sanctuary, fronted by a small pillared hall (*mandapa*), stands beneath a sculpted *vimana* that soars over sixty metres high. Most sculptures once again feature Shiva, but the *gopuras*, or towers, each side of the eastern gateway to the courtyard, were a new innovation, as were the lions carved into the base of the sanctuary walls, and the pavilion erected over Nandi in front of the sanctuary. The second great Chola temple was built in **Gangaikondacholapuram** by Rajendra I. Instead of a mighty *vimana*, he introduced new elements, adding subsidiary shrines and placing an extended *mandapa* in front of the central sanctuary, its pillars writhing with dancers and deities.

By the time of the thirteenth-century **Vijayanagar** kings, the temple was central to city life, the focus for civic meetings, education, dance and theatre. The Vijayanagars extended earlier structures, adding enclosing walls around a series of *prakaras*, or courtyards, and erecting free-standing *mandapas* for use as meeting halls, elephant stables, stages for music and dance, and ceremonial marriage halls. Raised on superbly decorated columns, these *mandapas* became known as **thousand-pillared halls** (*kalyan mandapas*). **Tanks** were added, doubling as water stores and washing areas, and used for festivals when deities were set afloat in boats surrounded by glimmering oil lamps.

Under the Vijayanagars, the *gopuras* were enlarged and set at the cardinal points over the high gateways to each *prakara*, to become the dominant feature. Rectangular in plan, and embellished with images of animals and local saints or rulers as well as deities, *gopuras* are periodically repainted in pinks, blues, whites and yellows, a sharp and joyous contrast with the earthy browns and greys of halls and sanctuaries below. **Madurai** is *the* place to check out Vijayanagar architecture, and experience the timeless temple rituals. Dimly lit halls and sun-drenched courtyards hum with murmured prayers, and regularly come alive for festivals in which Shiva and his "fish-eyed" consort (see p.564) are hauled through town on mighty wooden chariots tugged by hordes of devotees. Outside Tiruchirapalli, the temple at **Srirangam** was extended by the Vijayanagar Nayaks to become South India's largest. Unlike that in Madurai, it incorporates earlier Chola foundations. The ornamentation, with pillars formed into rearing horses, is superb.

HOYSALA TEMPLES

The Hoysala dynasty ruled southwestern Karnataka between the eleventh and thirteenth centuries. From the twelfth century, after the accession of King Vishnu Vardhana, they built a series of distinctive temples centred primarily at three sites: **Belur** (see p.213) and **Halebid** (see p.211) close to modern Hassan, and **Somnathpur** (see p.208), near Mysore.

At first sight, and from a distance, Hoysala temples appear to be modest structures, compact and even squat. On closer inspection, however, their profusion of fabulously detailed and sensuous sculpture, covering every inch of the exterior, is astonishing. Detractors are prone to class Hoysala art as decadent and overly fussy, but anyone with an eye for craftsmanship is likely to marvel at these jewels of Karnatakan art.

The intricacy of the carvings was made possible by the material used in construction: a soft **steatite soapstone** that on oxidization hardens to a glassy, highly polished surface. The level of detail, similar to that seen in sandalwood and ivory work, became increasingly freer and fluid as the style developed, and reached its highest point at Somnathpur. Beautiful bracket figures, often delicate portrayals of voluptuous female subjects, were placed under the eaves, fixed by pegs top and bottom. A later addition (except possibly in the Somnathpur temple), these serve no structural function.

Another technique more usually associated with wood is the unusual treatment of the massive stone pillars: lathe-turned, they resemble those of the wooden temples of Kerala. They were probably turned on a horizontal plane, pinned at each end, and rotated with the use of a rope. It may be no coincidence that, to this day, wood-turning is still a local speciality. Only the central shaft of each pillar seems to have been turned; in the base and capitals, a less precise, presumably handworked imitation of turning is evident.

The architectural style of the Hoysala temples is commonly referred to as *vesara*, or "hybrid" (literally "mule"), rather than belonging to either the northern, *nagari*, or southern, Dravidian styles. However, they show great affinity with *nagari* temples of western India, and represent another fruit of contact, like music, painting and literature, facilitated by the trade routes between the North and the South. All Hoysala temples share a star-shaped plan, built on high plinths (*jagati*) that follow the shape of the sanctuaries and *mandapas* to provide a raised surrounding platform. Such northern features may have been introduced by the designer and artists of the earliest temple at Belur, who were imported by Vishnu Vardhana from further north in Andhra Pradesh. Also characteristic of the Hoysala style is the use of ashlar masonry, without mortar. Some pieces of stones are joined by pegs of iron or bronze, or mortice and tenon joints. Ceilings inside the *mandapas* are made up of corbelled domes, looking similar to those of the Jain temples of Rajasthan and Gujarat; in the Hoysala style they are only visible from inside.

KERALAN TEMPLES

As you'd expect from one of India's most culturally distinct regions, Kerala's temples are quite unlike those elsewhere in the South. Their most striking features – to accommodate the torrential downpours – are the sloping tiled roofs that crown the sanctuaries, colonnades and gateways. In addition, the innermost shrines are invariably circular, or apsidal ended – perhaps in imitation of earlier indigenous styles.

In the corner of the spacious temple courtyards (which are often very broad to make room for the annual elephant processions), stands a covered hall with beautiful lathe-turned pillars and wooden panels, where performances of Kathakali and other forms of ritualized theatre are held (see p.610). In some older temples, **murals** also adorn the inner faces of the high enclosing walls (see p.589).

Keralan temples are generally closed to non-Hindus, but many make exceptions during festivals, when drum bands, tuskers and ritual dances comprise some of the most compelling spectacles in all of South India (see "Trissur Puram", p.347).

GOAN TEMPLES

Stick to the former Portuguese heartland of Goa, and you'd be forgiven for thinking the state was exclusively Christian. It isn't, of course, as the innumerable brightly painted Hindu temples hidden amid the lush woodland and areca groves of the more outlying areas confirm. The oldest-established and best-known lie well away from the coastal resorts, but are worth hunting out if you've an eye for quirky religious buildings.

Goa's first stone temples date from the rule of the Kadamba dynasty, between the fifth and fifteenth century AD. From the few fragments of sculpture and masonry unearthed at the ruins of their old capital, it is clear that these were as skilfully constructed as the famous monuments of the neighbouring Deccan region. However, only one, the richly carved Mahadeva temple at **Tamdi Surla** in east Goa, has survived. The rest were systematically destroyed, first by Muslim invaders, and later by the Portuguese.

Goan temples incorporate the main elements of Hindu architecture, but boast some unusual features of their own – some necessitated by the local climate, or the availability of building materials, others the result of outside influences. The impact of European/Portuguese styles (inevitable given the fact that the majority of Goan temples were built during the colonial era, but ironic considering the Portuguese destroyed the originals) is most evident on the exterior of the buildings. Unlike conventional Hindu temple towers, which are curvilinear, Goan *shikharas*, taking their cue from St Cajetan's church in Old Goa (see p.135), consist of octagonal drums crowned by tapering copper domes. Hidden inside the top of these is generally a pot of holy water called a **poornakalash**, drawn from a sacred Hindu river or spring. The sloping roofs of the *mandapas*, with their projecting eves and terracotta tiles are also distinctively Latin, while the glazed ceramic Chinese dragons often perched above them, originally imported from Macau, add to the colonial feel. Embellished with Baroque-style balustrades and pilasters, Islamic arches and the occasional bulbous Moghul dome, the sides of larger temples also epitomize Goan architecture's flair for fusion.

Always worth looking out for inside the main assembly halls are **wood-carvings** and panels of **sculpture** depicting mythological narratives, and the opulently embossed solid silver **doorways** around the entrance to the shrines, flanked by a pair of guardians, or **dvarpalas**. The most distinctively Goan feature of all, however, has to be the **lamp tower**, or *deepmal*, an addition introduced by the Marathas, who ruled much of Goa during the seventeenth and eighteenth centuries. Also known as *deep stambhas*, literally "pillars of light", these five- to seven-storey whitewashed pagodas generally stand opposite the main entrance. Their many ledges and windows hold tiny oil lamps that are illuminated during the *devta*'s weekly promenade, when the temple priests carry the god or goddess around the courtyard on their shoulders in a silver sedan chair known as a **palkhi**.

Near the *deepmal* you'll often come across a ornamental plant pot called a **tulsi vrindavan**. The straggly sacred shrub growing inside it, *tulsi*, represents a former mistress of Vishnu whom his jealous consort Lakshmi turned into a plant after a fit of jealous pique.

HINDU SCULPTURE

Hindu sculpture has traditionally been an integral part of temple architecture. Masons and stone-carvers often laboured for decades, even a whole lifetime, on the same site, settled in camps with their families, in much the same style as modern construction workers live around what they are building in India today. Each grade of artisan – from the men who cut the stone blocks or etched bands of decorative friezes, to the master-artists who fashioned the main idols – was a member of a **guild** that functioned along the same lines as caste, determining marriages and social relations. Guilds also controlled the handing down of tools, specialist knowledge and techniques to successive generations, through years of rigorous apprenticeship.

Another role of the guilds was to apply the rules of iconography set in the *Shilpa Shastras*, still followed today. Measurement always begins with the proportions of the artist's own hand and the image's resultant face-length as the basic unit. Then follows a scheme which is allied to the equally scientific rules applied to classical music, and specifically *tala* or rhythm. Human figures total eight face-lengths, eight being the most basic of rhythmic measures. Figures of deities are *nava-tala*, nine face-lengths.

Like their counterparts in medieval Europe, South Indian sculptors remained largely anonymous. Even though the most talented artists may have been known to their peers – in some rare cases earning renown in kingdoms at opposite ends of the subcontinent – their names have become lost over time. An explanation often advanced for this is the *Shastras*' insistence that the personality of an individual artist must be suppressed in order for divine inspiration to flow freely. For this reason, only a tiny number of stone sculptures in India bear inscriptions that preserve the identity of their creators.

With the entry of Indian religious sculpture into the international art market, the old conventions of anonymity are beginning to break down. A handful of sculptors at South India's stone-carving capital, **Mamallapuram** in Tamil Nadu (see p.397), have become well known, as the demand for pieces to adorn temples and shrines in the homes of expatriate Indians has increased. However, age-old guidelines governing iconographic sculpture are still applied here as rigorously as they have been for more than a thousand years, which makes it somewhat difficult to differentiate between the work of masters and less experienced apprentices.

You can watch sculptors in action, and buy their work, at innumerable workshops around Mamallapuram, while the Government Sculpture College nearby welcomes visitors, offering you the chance to see how students learn to measure out the proportions of the sculpture with their hands, and memorize the extraordinary body of iconographic lore that must be fully internalized before they graduate.

CHOLA BRONZES

Originally sacred temple objects, **Chola bronzes** are another art form from Tamil Nadu that has become highly collectable (even if their price tags are considerably higher than stone sculptures). The most memorable bronze icons are the **Natarajas**, or dancing Shivas. The image of Shiva, standing on one leg, encircled by flames, with wild locks caught in mid-motion, has become almost as recognizably Indian as the Taj Mahal, and few Indian millionaires would feel their sitting rooms would be complete without one.

The principal icons of a temple are usually stationary and made of stone. Frequently, however, ceremonies require an image of the god to be led in procession outside the inner sanctum, and even through the streets. According to the canonical texts known as *Agamas*, these moving images should be made of metal. Indian bronzes are made by the **cire perdu** ("lost-wax") process, known as *madhuchchistavidhana* in

Sanskrit. Three layers of clay mixed with burned grain husks, salt and ground cotton are applied to a figure crafted in bees' wax, with a stem left protruding at each end. When that is heated, the wax melts and flows out, creating a hollow mould into which molten metal—a rich five-metal alloy (*panchaloha*) of copper, silver, gold, brass and lead—can be poured through the stems. After the metal has cooled, the clay shell is destroyed, and the stems filed off, leaving a unique completed figure, which the caster-artist, or *sthapathi*, remodels to remove blemishes and add delicate detail.

Knowledge of bronze-casting in India goes back at least as far as the Indus Valley civilization (2500–1500 BC), and the famous **"Dancing Girl"** from Mohenjo Daro. The earliest produced in the South were made by the Andhras, whose techniques were continued by the Pallavas, the immediate antecedents of the Cholas. The few surviving **Pallava** bronzes show a sophisticated handling of the form; figures are characterized by broad shoulders, thick-set features and an overall simplicity that suggests all the detail was completed at the wax stage. The finest bronzes of all, however, are from the **Chola** period, from the late ninth to early eleventh centuries. As the Cholas were predominantly Shaivite, Nataraja, Shiva and his consort Parvati (frequently in a family group with son Skanda) and the sixty-three Nayanmar poet-saints are the most popular subjects. Chola bronzes display more detail than their predecessors. Human figures are invariably slim-waisted and elegant, with the male form robust and muscular and the female graceful and delicate.

As with stone sculpture, the design, iconography and proportions of each figure are governed by the strict rules laid down in the *Shilpa Shastras*, which draw no real distinction between art, science and religion.

Those bronzes produced by the few artists practising today invariably follow the Chola model; the chief centre is now **Swamimalai**, 8km west of Kumbakonam (see p.435). Original Chola bronzes are kept in many Tamil temples, but as temple interiors are often dark it's not always possible to see them properly. Important **public collections** include the Nayak Durbar Hall Art Museum at Thanjavur, the Government State Museum at Chennai and the National Museum, New Delhi.

MURALS

Fragments of paint indicate that murals adorned the walls and ceilings of India's oldest rock-cut prayer halls, dating from the third century BC. Only a couple of hundred years later, the art form reached its peak in the sumptuous Satavahana paintings at Ajanta, in the northwest Deccan, where the walls of huge caves were covered in the most exquisite images, rendered in muted reds, greens and blues. For the most part, these show religious scenes – episodes from the life of the Buddha (*jatakas*) – but they also encorporate pictures of courtly life, battles and a host of secular detail. However, remnants of ancient murals in the far south are scant, limited to a few patches at **Badami** in Karnataka (see p.258), and the Kailasanatha temple at **Kanchipuram** (see p.406).

Not until the resurgence of the Tamil Cholas in the ninth and tenth centuries did mural painting flourish again in the region. The finest examples – showing in the most sensuous detail vignettes from life at the royal court of Rajaraja I – are those decorating the interior of the main sanctum of the Brihadishwara temple at **Thanjavur** (see p.436). Sadly, these are closed to the public, but you can still enjoy the wonderful ceiling paintings of the Nayak rulers at the Shivakamasundari temple in **Chidambaram** (see p.427), which illustrate Shaivite myths and legends.

KERALAN MURALS

One of the best-kept secrets of South Indian art has to be the quality and unique style of the murals at Mattancherry Palace in old Kochi (see below), along with those in as many as sixty other locations in Kerala. Most are on the walls of functioning temples, not marketable, transportable or indeed even seen by many non-Hindus. Few date from before the sixteenth century, depriving them of the aura of extreme antiquity. Their origins may go back to the seventh century, however, and are probably influenced by the Pallava style of Tamil Nadu; unfortunately only traces in one tenth-century cave temple survive from the earliest period. The traveller Castaneda, who accompanied Vasco da Gama on the first Portuguese landing in India, described how he strayed into a temple, supposing it to be a church, and saw "monstrous looking images with two inch fangs" painted on the walls, causing one of the party to fall to his knees exclaiming, "if this be the devil, I worship God."

Technically classified as *fresco-secco*, Keralan murals employ vegetable and mineral colours, predominantly ochre reds and yellows, white and blue-green, and are coated with a protective sheen of pine resin and oil. Their ingenious design, strongly influenced by the canonical text, *Shilparatna*, incorporates intense detail with clarity and dynamism in the portrayal of human (and celestial) figures; subtle facial expressions are captured with the simplest of lines, while narrative elements are always bold and arresting. In common with all great Indian art, they share a complex iconography and symbolism. Non-Hindus can see fine examples in **Kochi**, **Padmanabhapuram** (see p.298), **Ettumanur** (see p.317) and **Kayamkulam** (see p.306). Visitors interested in how they are made should head for the Mural Painting Institute at **Guruvayur** (see p.353). A paperback book, *Murals of Kerala*, by M.G. Shashi Bhooshan (Kerala Government Department of Public Relations) serves as an excellent introduction to the field.

TANJORE (THANJAVUR) PAINTING

The name **Tanjore painting** is given to a distinctive form of southern picture-making that came to prominence in the eighteenth century, encouraged by the Maratha Raja of Thanjavur, Serfoji. The term "painting", however, is misleading, and inadequate to describe work of the Tanjore school. It is distinctive because – aside from a painted image – details such as clothing, ornaments, and any (typically Baroque) architectural elements are raised in low plaster relief from the surface, which is then decorated by the sumptuous addition of glass pieces, pearls, semiprecious or precious stones and elaborate gold leaf work. Other variations include pictures on mica, ivory and glass.

Figures are delineated with simple outlines; unmixed primary colours are used in a strict symbolic code, similar to that found in the make-up used in the classical dramas of Kerala, where each colour indicates qualities of character. Other schools of painting normally show Krishna with blue-black skin; in the Tanjore style, he is white.

Traditionally, most depicted Vaishnavite deities, with the most popular single image probably being that of **Balakrishna**, the chubby baby Krishna. In the tenth-century Sanskrit *Bhagavata Purana*, Balakrishna was portrayed as a rascal who delighted in stealing and consuming milk, butter balls and curd. Despite his naughtiness, all women who came into contact with him were seized with an overflowing of maternal affection, to the extent that their breasts spontaneously oozed milk. Thanks to such stories, Krishna as a child became the chosen deity par excellence of mothers and grandmothers. Tanjore paintings typically show him eating, accompanied by adoring women.

Although Tanjore painting went into decline after the nineteenth century, in recent years there has been new demand for domestic, rather than temple, shrines. High-quality work is produced in Thanjavur (see p.57), Kumbakonam (see p.431) and Tiruchirapalli (see p.446).

KALAM EZHUTTU

The tradition of *kalam ezhuttu* (pronounced "kalam-erroo-too") – detailed and beautiful ritual drawings in coloured powder, of deities and geometric patterns (*mandalas*) – is very much alive all over **Kerala**, although few visitors to the region even know of its existence. The designs usually cover an area of around thirty square metres, often outdoors and under a *pandal* – a temporary shelter made from bamboo and palm fronds. Each colour, made from rice flour, turmeric, ground leaves and burnt paddy husk, is painstakingly applied using the thumb and forefinger as a funnel. Three communities produce *kalams*; two come from the temple servant (*amblavasi*) castes, whose rituals are associated with the god Ayappa (see p.320) or the goddess Bhagavati; the third, the *pullavans*, specialize in serpent worship. Iconographic designs emerge gradually from the initial grid lines and turn into startling figures, many of terrible aspect, with wide eyes and fangs. Noses and breasts are raised, giving the whole a three-dimensional effect. As part of the ritual, the significant moment when the powder is added for the iris or pupil, "opening" the eyes, may well be marked by the accompaniment of *chenda* drums and *elatalam* hand-cymbals.

Witnessing the often day-long ritual is an unforgettable experience. The effort expended by the artist is made all the more remarkable by the inevitable destruction of the picture shortly after its completion; this truly ephemeral art cannot be divorced from its ritual context. In some cases, the image is destroyed by a fierce-looking *vellichapad* ("light-bringer"), a village oracle who can be recognized by shoulder-length hair, red *dhoti*, heavy brass anklets and the hooked sword he brandishes either while jumping up and down on the spot (a common sight), or marching purposefully about to control the spectators. At the end of the ritual, the powder, invested with divine power, is thrown over the onlookers. *Kalam ezhuttu* rituals are not widely advertised, but check at tourist offices.

THE ARCHITECTURE OF ISLAM

South India may be best known for its Hindu monuments, but the southern **Deccan** region, encompassed by the modern states of Karnataka and western Andhra Pradesh, is littered with wonderful Muslim **mosques** and **tombs**, dating from an era when this was the buffer zone between the ancient Indian cultures of the Dravidian south and the dynasties who succeeded the Delhi Sultans (see "History" p.551).

The buildings that survive from this era illustrate the extraordinary cross-fertilization that took place between indigenous art forms and Islamic styles from distant Central Asia. Thus, some of the oldest Muslim constructions at **Bidar** (see p.270) and **Gulbarga** (see p.268), look Afghan, whereas the later masterpieces of the Bahmani dynasty, such as the Ibrahim Rauza at **Bijapur** (see p.263), incorporate motifs that wouldn't have looked out of place on a temple. This fusion occurred both because of a certain stylistic tolerance on the part of later Muslim rulers in southern India, and because the craftsmen they employed were often Hindus to whom lotus flowers and fancy floral scrollwork came more easily to hand than Persian geometric patterns.

The most famous Muslim monument in the South is the **Golgumbaz** at **Bijapur** – India's largest domed structure – but enough superb buildings stand in the same town, and in the other old capitals of the former Deccan Sultans, dotted along the northern border of Karnataka between Bijapur and Hyderabad, to keep enthusiasts of Islamic architecture occupied for weeks.

WILDLIFE

A fast-growing population and the rapid spread of industries have inflicted pressures on the rural landscape of South India, but the region still supports a wealth of distinct flora and fauna. Although many species have been hunted out over the past fifty years, enough survive to make a trip into the countryside well worthwhile. Walking on less frequented beaches or through the rice fields of the coastal plain, you'll encounter dozens of exotic birds, while the hill country of the interior supports an amazing variety of plants and trees. The majority of the peninsula's larger mammals keep to the dense woodland of the Western Ghat mountains, where a string of contiguous reserves affords them some protection from the hunters and loggers that have wrought such havoc in India's fragile forest regions over the past few decades.

FLORA

Something like 3500 species of flowering plants have been identified in South India, as well as countless lower orders of grasses, ferns and brackens. The greatest floristic diversity occurs in the Western Ghats, where it is not uncommon to find one hundred or more different types of trees in an area of one hectare. Many were introduced by the Portuguese from Europe, South America, Southeast Asia and Australia, but there are also a vast number of indigenous varieties which thrive in the moist climate.

Along the coast, the rice **paddy** and **coconut** plantations predominate, forming a near-continuous band of lush foliage. Spiky **spinifex** also helps bind the shifting sand dunes behind the miles of sandy beaches lining both the Malabar and Coromandel coasts, while **causerina** bushes form striking splashes of pink and crimson during the winter months.

In towns and villages, you'll encounter dozens of beautiful **flowering trees** that are common in tropical parts of India but unfamiliar to most Europeans and North Americans. The Indian **labernum**, or cassia, throws out masses of yellow flowers and long seed pods in late February before the monsoons. This is also the period when mango and Indian **coral trees** are in full bloom; both produce bundles of stunning red flowers.

Among the most distinctive trees that grow in both coastal and hill areas is the stately **banyan**, which propagates by sending out shoots from its lower branches. The largest specimens grow over an area of two hundred metres. The banyan is also revered by Hindus, and you'll often find small shrines at the foot of mature trees. The same is true of the *peepal*, which has distinctive spatula-shaped leaves. Temple courtyards often enclose large *peepals*, usually with strips of auspicious red cloth hanging from their lower branches.

Tree lovers and botanists should not miss an opportunity to visit the Western Ghats, which harbour a bewildering wealth of flora, from flowering trees and plants, to ferns and fungi. **Shola** forests, lush patches of moist evergreen woodland that carpet the deeper mountain valleys, exhibit some of the greatest biodiversity. Sheltered by a leafy canopy, which may rise to a height of twenty metres or more, buttressed roots and giant trunks tower above a luxuriant undergrowth of brambles, creepers, and bracken, interspersed by brakes of bamboo. Common tree species include the **kadam**, **sisso** or **martel**, **kharanj** and **teak**, while rarer **sandalwood** thrives on the higher, drier plateaulands south of Mysore - homeland of the infamous smuggler and bandit, Veerapan (see p.490). There are dozens of representatives of the *Ficus*, or fig, family too, as well innumerable (and ecologically destructive) eucalyptus and rubber trees, planted as cash crops by the Forest Department.

MAMMALS

During a field expedition to Goa in the 1970s, the eminent Indian naturalist, Salim Ali, complained the only animal he spotted was a lone leopard cat dead at the roadside. For although peninsula India boasts more than fifty species of wild mammals, visitors who stick to populated coastal areas are unlikely to spot anything more inspiring than a monkey or tree squirrel. Most of the larger animals have been hunted to the point of extinction; the few that remain roam the dense woodland lining the Western Ghats, in the sparsely populated forest zones of the **Nilgiri Biosphere Reserve**.

The largest Indian land mammal is, of course, the Asian **elephant**, stockier and with much smaller ears than its African cousin, though no less venerable. Travelling around Kerala and Tamil Nadu, you'll regularly see elephants in temples and festivals, but for a glimpse of one in the wild you'll have to venture into the mountains where, in spite of the huge reduction of their natural habitat, around six and a half thousand still survive. Among the best places for sightings are Periyar in Kerala (see p.317) and Nagarhole in Karnataka (see p.207). In the era when it was a maharaja's hunting reserve, the latter became infamous as the place where the British hunter, G.P. Sanderson, devised the brutal *khedda* system for trapping elephants: herds were driven into lethal stockades and captured, or killed. Between 1890 and 1971, 1536 were allegedly caught in this way, while 225 of them died – a figure that probably only represents the tip of the ice berg. Today, wild elephants, which are included under the Endangered Species Protection Act, are under increasing pressure from villagers: each adult animal eats roughly two hundred kilos of vegetation and drinks one hundred litres of water a day, and their search for sustenance inevitably brings them into conflict with neighbouring rural communities.

Across India, local villagers displaced by wildlife reserves have often been responsible for the poaching that has reduced **tiger** populations to such fragile levels. These days in South India sightings are very rare indeed; however, several kinds of big cat survive. Among the most adaptive and beautiful is the leopard or **panther** (*Panthera panthus*). Prowling the thick forests of the Ghats, these elusive cats prey on monkeys and deer, and occasionally take domestic cattle and dogs from the fringes of villages. Their distinctive black spots make them notoriously difficult to see amongst the tropical foliage, although their mating call (reminiscent of a saw on wood) regularly pierces the night air in remote areas. The **leopard cat** (*Felis bengalensis*) is a miniature version of its namesake, and more common. Sporting a bushy tail and round spots on soft buff or grey fur, it is about the same size as a domestic cat and lives around villages, picking off chickens, birds and small mammals. Another cat with a penchant for poultry, and one which villagers occasionally keep as a pet if they can capture one, is the docile Indian civet (*Viverricual indica*), recognizable by its lithe body, striped tail, short legs and long pointed muzzle.

Wild cats share their territory with a range of other mammals unique to the subcontinent. One you've a reasonable chance of seeing is the **gaur**, or Indian bison (*Bos gaurus*). These primeval-looking beasts, with their distinctive sleek black skin and knee-length white "socks", forage around bamboo thickets and shady woods. The bulls are particularly impressive, growing to an awesome height of two metres, with heavy curved horns and prominent humps.

With its long fur and white V-shaped bib, the scruffy **sloth bear** (*Melursus ursinus*) – whose Tamil name (*bhalu*) inspired that of Rudyard Kipling's character in *The Jungle Book* – ranks among the weirder-looking inhabitants of the region's forests. Sadly, it's also very rare, thanks to its predilection for raiding sugar-cane plantations, which has brought it, like the elephant, into direct conflict with man. Sloth bears can occasionally be seen shuffling along woodland trails, but you're more likely to come across evidence of their foraging activities: trashed termite mounds and chewed-up ants' nests. The same is true of both the portly Indian **porcupine** (*Hystrix indica),* or *sal,* which you see a lot less often than the mounds of earth it digs up to get at insects and cashew or teak seedlings, and the **pangolin** (*Manis crassicaudata*), or *tiryo*: a kind of armour-plated anteater whose hard grey overlapping scales protect it from predators.

Full-moon nights and the twilight hours of dusk and dawn are the times to look out for nocturnal animals such as the **slender loris** (*Loris tardigradus*). This shy creature – a distant cousin of the lemur, with bulging round eyes, furry body and pencil-thin limbs – grows to around twenty centimetres in length. It moves as if in slow motion, except when an insect flits to within striking distance, and is a favourite pet of forest people. The **mongoose** *(Herpestes edwardsi)* is another animal sometimes kept as a pet. Rudyard Kipling's "Rikitikitavi" keeps dwellings free of scorpions, mice, rats and other vermin. It will also readily take on snakes, which is why you often see it writhing in a cloud of dust with king cobras during performances by snake charmers.

Late evening is also the best time for spotting **bats**. South India boasts four species, including the fulvous fruit bat (*Rousettus leshenaulti*), or *vagul* – so-called because it gives off a scent resembling fermenting fruit juice – Dormer's bat (*Pipistrellus dormeri*), the very rare rufous horseshoe bat and the Malay fox vampire (*Magaderma spasma*), which feeds off the blood of live cattle. **Flying foxes** (*Pteropus gigantus*), the largest of India's bats, are also present in healthy numbers. With a wingspan of more than one metre, they fly in cacophonous groups to feed in fruit orchards, sometimes falling foul of electricity cables on the way: frazzled flying foxes dangling from live cables are a common sight in the interior.

Other species to look out for in forest areas are the Indian **giant squirrel** (*Ratufa indica*), or *shenkaro*, which has a coat of black fur and red-orange lower parts. Two and a half times larger than its European cousins, it lives in the canopy, leaping up to twenty metres between branches. The much smaller three-striped squirrel (*Funambulus palmarum*), or *khadi khar*, recognizable by the three black markings down its back, is also found in woodland. However, the five-striped palm squirrel (*Funambulus pennanti*) is a common sight all over the state, especially in municipal parks and villages.

Forest clearings and areas of open grassland are grazed by four species of deer. Widely regarded as the most beautiful is the **cheetal** (*Axis axis*), or spotted axis deer, which congregates in large groups around water holes and salt licks, occasionally wandering into villages to seek shelter from its predators. The plainer buff-coloured **sambar** (*Cervus unicolor*) is also well represented, despite succumbing to diseases spread by domestic cattle during the 1970s and 1980s. Two types of deer you're less likely to come across, but which also inhabit the border forests, are the **barking deer** (*Muntiacus muntjak*), whose call closely resembles that of a domestic dog, and the timid **mouse deer** (*Tragulus meminna*), a speckled-grey member of the *Tragulidae* family that is India's smallest deer, growing to a mere thirty centimetres in height. Both of these are highly secretive and nocturnal; they are also the preferred snack of Goa's smaller predators: the **striped hyena** (*Hyaena hyaena*), **jackal** (*Canis aureus*), or *colo*, and **wild dog** (*Cuon alpinus*), which hunt in packs.

Long-beaked **dolphins** are regular visitors to the shallow waters of South India's more secluded bays and beaches. They are traditionally regarded as a pest by local villagers, who believe they eat scarce stocks of fish. However, this long-standing antipathy is gradually eroding as local people realize the tourist-pulling potential of the dolphins: Palolem beach, in Goa (see p.172), is a dependable dolphin-spotting location

Finally, no rundown of South Indian mammals would be complete without some mention of **monkeys**. The most ubiquitous species is the mangy pink-bottomed **macaque** (*Macaca mulatta*), or *makad*, which hangs out anywhere scraps may be scavenged or snatched from unwary humans: temples and picnic spots are good places to watch them in action. The black-faced Hanuman **langur**, by contrast, is less audacious, retreating to the trees if threatened. It is much larger than the macaque, with pale grey fur and long limbs and tail. In forest areas, the langur's distinctive call is an effective early-warning system against big cats and other predators, which is why you often come across herds of cheetal grazing under trees inhabited by large colonies of them.

REPTILES

Reptiles are well represented in the region, with more than forty species of snakes, lizards, turtles and crocodiles recorded. The best places to spot them are not the interior forests, where dense foliage makes observation difficult, but open cultivated areas: paddy fields and village ponds provide abundant fresh water, nesting sites and prey (frogs, insects and small birds) to feed on.

Your house or hotel room, however, is where you are most likely to come across tropical India's most common reptile, the **gecko** (*Hemidactylus*), which clings to walls and ceilings with its widely

THE INDIAN TIGER: SURVIVAL OR EXTINCTION?

Feared, adored, immortalized in myth and used to endorse everything from breakfast cereals to petrochemicals, few animals command such universal fascination as the **tiger**. Only in India, however, can this rare and enigmatic big cat still be glimpsed in the wild, stalking through the teak forests and terai grass to which it is uniquely adapted. A solitary predator at the apex of the food chain, it has no natural enemies save one.

As recently as the turn of the century, up to 40,000 tigers still roamed the subcontinent, even though *shikar* (tiger-hunting) had long been the "sport of kings". An ancient dictum held it auspicious for a ruler to notch up a tally of 109 dead tigers, and *nawabs*, maharajas and Moghul emperors all indulged their prerogative to devastating effect. But it was the trigger-happy British who brought tiger-hunting to its most gratuitous excesses. Photographs of pith-helmeted, bare-kneed *burra-sahibs* posing behind mountains of striped carcasses became a hackneyed image of the Raj. Even Prince Philip, who has since become president of the Worldwide Fund for Nature, couldn't resist bagging one during a royal visit in 1960.

In the years following Independence, demographic pressures nudged the Indian tiger perilously close to extinction. As the human population increased in rural districts, more and more forest was cleared for farming – thereby depriving large carnivores of their main source of game and of the cover they needed to hunt. Forced to turn on farm cattle as an alternative, tigers were drawn into direct conflict with humans; some animals, out of sheer desperation, even turned man-eater and attacked human settlements.

Poaching has taken an even greater toll. The black market has always paid high prices for live animals – a whole tiger can fetch up to $50,000 – and for the various body parts believed to hold magical or medicinal properties. The meat is used to ward off snakes, the brain to cure acne, the nose to promote the birth of a son and the fat of the kidney – applied liberally to the afflicted organ – as an antidote to male impotence.

By the time an all-India moratorium on tiger-shooting was declared in the 1972 Wildlife Protection Act, numbers had plummeted to below two thousand. A dramatic response geared to fire public imagination came the following year, with the inauguration of Project Tiger. At the personal behest of Indira Gandhi, nine areas of pristine forest were set aside for the last remaining tigers. Displaced farming communities were resettled and compensated, and armed rangers employed to discourage poachers. Demand for tiger parts did not end with Project Tiger, however, and the poachers remained in business, aided by organized smuggling rings. In August 1993, undercover investigators found a four-hundred-kilo haul of tiger bones, together with forty fresh carcasses, with a team of Tibetan smugglers in Delhi which had promised to supply a further thousand kilos on demand. Unfortunately, such exposure is rare, and perpetrators are most likely to get off with bail, free to return to their trade. Well-organized guerrilla groups operate out of remote national parks, where inadequate numbers of poorly armed and poorly paid wardens offer little more than token resistance, particularly as increased use of poison is making it more and more difficult to track poachers. Project Tiger officials are understandably reluctant to jeopardize lucrative tourist traffic by admitting that sightings are getting rarer, but the prognosis looks very gloomy indeed.

Today, even though there are twenty-three Project Tiger sites in India, numbers continue to fall. Official figures optimistically claim a population of up to four thousand and growth of nearly three percent, but independent evidence is more pessimistic, putting the figure at more like two- to two-and-a-half thousand. The population rise indicated by counts based on pug marks – thought to be like human fingerprints, unique to each individual – that gave such encouragement in the early 1990s has been declared inaccurate.

Poorly equipped park wardens are still fighting a losing battle against the failure of bureaucratic and legal systems to face the seriousness of the situation. It was estimated in 1996 that one tiger was being poached every eighteen hours and the situation is believed to be as depressing today. The most pessimistic experts even claim that at the present rate of destruction, India's most exotic animal could face extinction early on in the new millennium.

splayed toes. Deceptively static most of the time, these small yellow-brown lizards will dash at lightning speed for cracks and holes if you try to catch one, or if an unwary mosquito, fly or cockroach scuttles within striking distance. The much rarer chameleon is even more elusive, mainly because its constantly changing camouflage makes it virtually impossible to spot. They'll have no problem seeing you, though: independently moving eyes allow them to pinpoint approaching predators, while prey is slurped up with their fast-moving forty-centimetre-long tongues. The other main lizard to look out for is the **Bengal monitor**. This giant brown speckled reptile looks like a refugee from *Jurassic Park*, growing to well over a metre in length. It used to be a common sight in coastal areas, where they basked on roads and rocks. However, monitors are often killed and eaten by villagers, and have become increasingly rare. Among the few places you can be sure of sighting one is South Andaman, in the Andaman archipelago.

The monsoon period is when you're most likely to encounter **turtles**. Two varieties paddle around village ponds and wells while water is plentiful: the flap-shell (*Lissemys punctata*) and black-pond (*Melanochelys trijuga*) turtles, neither of which are endangered. Numbers of marine turtles (*Lepidochelys olivacea*), by contrast, have plummeted over the past few decades because villagers raid their nests when they crawl onto the beach to lay their eggs. This amazing natural spectacle occurs each year at a number of beaches in the region, notably Morgim in north Goa and Havelock Island in the Andamans (see p.535). Local coastguards and scientists from the Institute of Oceanography in Goa monitor the migration, patrolling the beaches to deter poachers, but the annual egg binge remains a highlight of the local gastronomic calendar, eagerly awaited by fisher families, who sell the illegal harvest in local markets. Only in Orissa, in eastern India, where a special wildlife sanctuary has been set up to protect them, have the sea turtles (also known as olive ridleys) survived the seasonal slaughter to reproduce in healthy numbers.

An equally rare sight nowadays is the **crocodile**. Populations have dropped almost to the point of extinction, although the Cambarjua Canal near Old Goa, and more remote stretches of the Mandovi and Zuari estuaries, support vestigial colonies of saltwater crocs, which bask on mud flats and river rocks. Dubbed "salties", they occasionally take calves and goats, and will snap at the odd human if given half a chance. The more ominously named mugger crocodile, however, is harmless, inhabiting unfrequented freshwater streams and riversides. You can see all of India's indigenous crocodiles at the wonderful Crocodile Bank near Mamallapuram (see p.397).

SNAKES

Twenty-three species of snake are found in South India, ranging from the gigantic **Indian python** (*Python molurus*, or *har* in Konkani) – a forest-dwelling constrictor that grows up to four metres in length – to the innocuous worm snake (*Typhlops braminus*), or *sulva*, which is tiny, completely blind and often mistaken for an earthworm.

The eight poisonous snakes present in the region include India's four most deadly species: the cobra, the krait, the Russel's viper and saw-scaled viper. Though these are relatively common in coastal and cultivated areas, even the most aggressive snake will slither off at the first sign of an approaching human. Nevertheless, ten thousand Indians die from snake bites each year, and if you regularly cut across paddy fields or plan to do any hiking, it makes sense to familiarize yourself with the following four or five species just in case; their bites nearly always prove fatal if not treated immediately with anti-venin serum – available at most clinics and hospitals.

Present in most parts of the state and an important character in Hindu mythology, the Indian **cobra** (*naja naja*), or *naga*, is the most common of the venomous species. Wheat-brown or grey in colour, it is famed for the "hood" it unfurls when confronted and whose rear side usually bears the snake's characteristic spectacle markings. Its big brother, the king cobra *(Naja hannah*), or *Raj naga*, is much less often encountered. Inhabiting the remote forest regions along the Karnatakan border, this beautiful brown, yellow and black snake, which grows to a length of four metres or more, is very rare, although the itinerant snake charmers that perform in markets occasionally keep one. Defanged, they rear up and "dance" when provoked by the handler, or are set against mongooses in ferocious (and often fatal) fights. The king cobra is also the only snake in the world known to make its own nest.

Distinguished by their steel-blue colour and faint white cross markings, **kraits** (*Bungarus coerulus*), are twice as deadly as the Indian cobra: even the bite of a newly hatched youngster is lethal. **Russel's viper** (*Viperi russeli*), is another one to watch out for. Distinguished by the three bands of elliptical markings that extend down its brown body, the Russel hisses at its victims before darting at them and burying its centimetre-long fangs into their flesh. The other common poisonous snake in South India is the **saw-scaled viper** (*Echis carinatus*). Grey with an arrow-shaped mark on its triangular head, it hangs around in the cracks between stone walls, feeding on scorpions, lizards, frogs, rodents and smaller snakes. They also hiss when threatened, producing the sound by rubbing together serrated scales located on the side of their head. Finally, **sea snakes** (*Enhdrina schistosa*), are common in coastal areas and potentially lethal (with a bite said to be twenty times more venomous than a cobra's), although rarely encountered by swimmers as they lurk only in deep water off the shore.

Harmless snakes are far more numerous than their killer cousins and frequently more attractive. The beautiful **golden tree snake** (*Chrysopelea ormata*) for example, sports an exquisitely intricate geometric pattern of red, yellow and black markings, while the **green whip snake** (*Dryhopis nasutus*), or *sarpatol*, is stunning parakeet green with a whip-like tail extending more than a metre behind it. The ubiquitous **Indian rat snake**, often mistaken for a cobra, also has beautiful markings, although it leaves behind it a foul stench of decomposing flesh. Other common nonpoisonous snakes include the wolf snake (*Lycodon aulicus*), or *kaidya*, the Russel sand boa (*Eryx conicus*), or *malun*, the kukri snake (*Oligodon taeniolatus*), or *pasko*, the cat snake (*Boiga trigonata*), or *manjra*, and the keelbacks (*Natrix*).

BIRDS

You don't have to be an aficionado to enjoy South India's abundant birdlife. Travelling around the region, you can see breathtaking birds regularly flash between the branches of trees or appear on overhead wires at the roadside.

Thanks to the internationally popular brand of Goan beer, the **kingfisher** has become that state's unofficial mascot: it's not hard to see why the brewers chose it as their logo. Three common species of kingfisher frequently crop up amid the paddy fields and wetlands of the coastal plains, where they feed on small fish and tadpoles. With its enormous bill and pale green-blue wing feathers, the stork-billed kingfisher (*Perargopis capensis*) is the largest and most distinctive member of the family, although the white-breasted kingfisher (*Halcyon smyrnensis*) – which has iridescent turquoise plumage and a coral-red bill – and the common, or small blue, kingfisher (*Alcedo althis*) are more alluring.

Other common and brightly coloured species include the grass-green, blue and yellow **bee-eaters** (*Merops*), the stunning **golden oriole** (*Oriolus oriolus*), and the **Indian roller** (*Coracias bengalensis*), famous for its brilliant blue, flight feathers and exuberant aerobatic mating displays. **Hoopoes** (*Upupa epops*), recognizable by their elegant black-and-white tipped crests, fawn plumage and distinctive "*hoo...po...po*" call, also flit around fields and villages, as do **purple sunbirds** (*Nectarina asiatica*) and several kinds of **bulbuls**, **babblers** and **drongos** (*Dicrurus*), including the fork-tailed black drongo (*Dicrurus adsimilis*) – a winter visitor that can often be seen perched on telegraph wires. If you're lucky, you may also catch a glimpse of the **paradise flycatcher** (*Tersiphone paradisi*), which is widespread and among the region's most exquisite birds, with a thick black crest and long silver, tail streamers.

Paddy fields, ponds and saline mudflats are teeming with water birds. The most ubiquitous of these is the snowy white **cattle egret** (*Bubulcus ibis*), which can usually be seen wherever there are cows and buffalo, feeding off the grubs, insects and other parasites that live on them. The large egret (*Ardea alba*) is also pure white, although lankier and with a long yellow bill, while the third member of this family, the little egret (*Egretta garzetta*), sports a short black bill and, during the mating season, two long tail feathers. Look out too for the mud-brown **paddy bird**, India's most common heron. Distinguished by its pale green legs, speckled breast and hunched posture, it stands motionless for hours in water waiting for fish or frogs to feed on.

The hunting technique of the beautiful **white-bellied fish eagle** (*Haliaetus leucogaster*), by contrast, is truly spectacular. Cruising twenty to thirty metres above the surface of the water, this black and white osprey stoops at high speed to snatch its prey – usually sea snakes and mackerel – from the waves with its fierce yellow talons. More common birds of prey such as the **brahminy kite**

(*Haliastur indus*) – recognizable by its white breast and chestnut head markings – and the **pariah kite** (*Milvus migrans govinda*) – a dark-brown buzzard with a fork tail – are widespread around towns and fishing villages, where they vie with raucous gangs of house **crows** (*Corvus splendens*) and **white-eyed jackdaws** (*Corvus monedulal*) for scraps. Gigantic pink-headed **king vultures** (*Sarcogyps clavus*) and the **white-backed vulture** (*Gyps bengalensis*), which has a white ruff around its bare neck and head, also show up whenever there are carcasses to pick clean.

Other birds of prey to keep an eye open for, especially around open farmland, are the **white-eyed buzzard** (*Butastur teesa*), the **honey buzzard** (*Pernis ptilorhyncus*), the **black-winged kite** (*Elanus caeruleus*) – famous for its blood-red eyes – and **shikra** (*Accipiter badius*), which closely resembles the European sparrowhawk.

FOREST BIRDS

The region's forests may have lost many of their larger animals, but they still offer exciting possibilities for bird-watchers. One species every enthusiast hopes to glimpse while in the woods is the magnificent **hornbill**, of which three species have been spotted: the grey hornbill (*Tockus birostris*), with its blue-brown plumage and long curved beak, is the most common, although the Indian pied hornbill (*Anthracoceros malabaricus*), distinguished by its white wing and tail tips and the pale patch on its face, often flies into villages in search of fruit and lizards. The magnificent great pied hornbill (*Buceors bicornis*), however, is more elusive, limited to the densest forest areas where it may occasionally be spotted flitting through the canopy. Growing to 130 centimetres in length, it has a black-and-white striped body and wings, and a huge yellow beak with a long curved casque on top.

Several species of **woodpecker** also inhabit the interior forests, among them two types of goldenback woodpecker: the lesser goldenback (*Dinopium bengalensis*), is the more colourful of the pair, with a crimson crown and bright splashes of yellow across its back. The Cotigao sanctuary in south Goa (see p.176) is one of the last remaining strongholds of the Indian great black woodpecker, which has completely disappeared from the more heavily deforested hill areas further north. In spite of its bright red head and white rump, this shy bird is more often heard than seen, making loud drumming noises on tree trunks between December and March.

A bird whose call is a regular feature of the Western Ghat forests, particularly in teak areas, is the wild ancestor of the domestic chicken – the **jungle fowl**. The more common variety is the secretive but vibrantly coloured, red junglefowl (*Gallus gallus*), which sports golden neck feathers and a metallic black tail. Its larger cousin, the grey or sommerat's jungle fowl (*Galolus sommeratii*), has darker plumage scattered with yellow spots and streaks. Both inhabit clearings, and are most often seen scavenging for food on the verges of forest roads.

WILDLIFE VIEWING

Although you can expect to come across many of the species listed above on the edge of towns and villages, a spell in one or other of South India's nature reserves offers the best chance of **viewing wild animals**. Administered by poorly funded government bodies, they're a far cry indeed from the well-organized and well-maintained national parks you may be used to at home. Information can be frustratingly hard to come by and the staff manning them can be less than helpful.

That said, at the larger, more easily accessible wildlife reserves – such as Periyar and Mudumalai – a reasonable infrastructure exists to transport visitors around, whether by jeep, minibus, coach or, in the case of the former, boat. Don't, however, expect to see much if you stick to these standard excursion vehicles laid on by the park authorities. Most of the rarer animals wisely keep well away from noisy groups of trippers. Wherever possible, try to organize **walking safaris** with a reliable, approved guide in the forest, while bearing in mind that not all guides may be as knowledgable and experienced as they claim, and that an untrained, unconfident guide may actually lead you into life-endangering situations; before parting with any money, ask to see recommendation books.

Accommodation is generally available at all but the most remote sanctuaries and reserves, although it may not always be very comfortable. Larger parks tend to have a batch of luxurious, Western-style resort campuses for tour groups. In all cases, you'll find reviews of the accommodation on offer in the descriptions of individual parks featured in the Guide section of this book, along with full details of how to travel to, from and around the site. Our accounts will also advise you on the best times of year to visit in each case, and indicate the kind of wildlife present.

Finally, it's worth stating the bad news that for the past few years, some of the main parks in the Nilgiri Biosphere region – notably Mudumalai, Anamalai, Bandipur and Nagarhole – have been **closed** because of the threat of abduction or violence from the sandalwood smuggler **Veerapan** (see p.490). This is particularly annoying for travellers making their way between Mysore in Karnataka and Ooty in Tamil Nadu. If you intend to stop off at any of the parks in this area, check before you set off that they're open.

SOUTH INDIAN WILDLIFE SANCTUARIES AND NATIONAL PARKS

The South Indian states covered in this book harbour a total of 96 separate wildlife sanctuaries and national parks – if you include the various protected islets of the Andaman and Nicobar Islands, and the many minor reserves dotted around the region. What follows is a selection (listed in alphabetical order) of those we found most rewarding, both in terms of their wildlife and the natural environment. Bear in mind that, at the time this book went to press, those in the Western Ghats were closed pending the surrender or capture of the sandalwood smuggler Veerapan (see p.490). Before heading into the countryside, therefore, check with the local tourist office to ensure the park you hope to visit is currently accessible.

Cotigao Wildlife Sanctuary (Goa). Tucked away in the extreme south of Goa, near Palolem beach, its extensive mixed deciduous forest and hilly backdrop make up for a relative paucity of wildlife. Best time: November to March. See p.176.

Eravikulam National Park (Kerala). 17km northeast of Munnar in the lap of the Western Ghats. Famous for its thriving population of Nilgiri *tahr*, a rare antelope that lives only here, on the high rolling grasslands. See them on the hard hike up Anamudi, South India's biggest mountain. Best time: January to April. See p.326.

Indira Gandhi (Anamalai) Wildlife Sanctuary (Tamil Nadu). On the southernmost reaches of the Cardamom Hills, this park is more remote than Mudumalai, and consequently less visited, but encompasses some beautiful mountain scenery as well as abundant fauna. Best time: January to March. See p.497.

Kodikkarai (Point Calimere) (Tamil Nadu). On a promontory jutting into Palk Bay, some 250 species of birds, mostly migrants, descend on a swathe of mixed swampland and dry deciduous forest in the wake of the monsoon. Best time: November to February. See p.445.

Mahatma Gandhi National Marine Park (Andaman Islands). The islets in this reserve, encircled by vivid coral reefs, rise out of crystal-clear water that teems with tropical fish, turtles and other marine life. Can be reached by daily excursion boats, via bus links, from the capital Port Blair. Best time: January to March. See p.534.

Mudumalai Wildlife Sanctuary (Tamil Nadu). Set 1140m up in the Nilgiri Hills, Mudumalai is one of the most easily reached reserves in the South. It offers a full range of accommodation and trails and gives access to huge areas of protected forest. Best time: January to March. See p.489.

Periyar Wildlife Sanctuary (Kerala). A former Maharaja's hunting reserve, centred on an artificial lake high in the Cardamom Hills. Occasional tiger sightings, but you're much more likely to spot an elephant. Well placed for trips into the mountains and tea plantations, with good accommodation, including remote observation tower which you have to trek to. Best time: October to March. See p.317.

Vadanemmeli Crocodile Bank (Tamil Nadu). Endangered species of indigenous crocodiles, lizards and turtles are bred here, 15km north of Mamallapuram, for release into the wild. Local Irula tribes people collect venom from poisonous snakes to make serum. Open year round. See p.405.

Vedanthaangal Bird Sanctuary (Tamil Nadu). A wonderful mixed heronry, 86km southwest of Chennai, where you can sight 250 species of migrant wetland birds, blown in by the northwest monsoon. Best time: December and February. See p.412.

MUSIC

One who is an expert in playing the veena, well versed in shruti and other forms of musical sound, and has a deep understanding of tala, will attain enlightenment with ease.

Tyagaraja (1767–1847)

Travelling through India it's difficult to get away from the cacophony of sounds which emanate from every corner: street noise mingles with popular tunes from Bollywood movies screeching from crude roadside sound systems, and strains of religious song drift along from temples and roadside shrines. Robust festival music incorporating energetic ensembles of drums and the plaintiff notes of a *sehnai* (oboe) accompanying a wedding, are also some of the most evocative sounds of the subcontinent. Whether religious, film, popular, folk or classical, music plays a significant role in the life of South India.

Apart from South Indian popular music, only a small proportion of music from the region actually reaches foreign shores. Only the cream of musicians, those who are also able to adapt to an international stage, are heard outside their traditional milieu. Unfortunately few travellers in South India make the effort to enjoy the music in its original context. *Qawwali* (sufi religious song), essentially North Indian but present in pockets of South India, for example, has been extremely successful as performance music in the West but few travellers ever get to hear the music within the setting of a *sufi* shrine in India. Those who do, witness music fired by devotional inspiration, as dynamic as it can get.

Indian music outside India is most successful when it fuses with other contemporary forms; strictly traditional music is left to the aficionados. Most Indian musicians, content with maintaining their traditions, are unable to bridge the gap but a few do so very successfully. U Srinivas, the exciting mandolin player, is currently enjoying great success in the West partly because of his fusion work, although his traditional music, steeped in South Indian classical conventions, enjoys less universal appeal. South Indian music has a remarkable ability to absorb new instruments into a traditional system: instruments such as the ***ghatam*** (clay pot used for percussion), are played alongside the violin, saxophone and mandolin to great impact, at home and abroad.

Due to the intense climatic conditions of the subcontinent, performances of South Indian classical music are seasonal, **high season** is from November to February when the atmosphere is more congenial to public performances. During the peak of the season – around the end of December – major cities such as Chennai host several multi-day music festivals known as "**conferences**" designed to promote up-and-coming musicians as well as attracting the musical elite. Chennai, with over thirty major musical associations (called *sabahs*), sometimes holds as many as fifteen conferences simultaneously. Conferences are advertised in the local press and music magazines such as *Shruti*, and season tickets (priced around Rs700 for a two-week conference) allow you to pick and choose from an extensive range of performances.

The South Indian music **audience** does not conform to Western norms and, although essentially attentive, tolerates a certain amount of comings-and-goings. Immersed in their art, the performers seem unfazed by the movement and will even greet people they know. Many musicians perform better with a vocally appreciative audience and, especially in the north, a certain degree of positive audience participation goes a long way to ensure a successful and memorable performance.

Except for modern Indian pop which lends easily from the West, most Indian music can be divided into two distinctive regional umbrellas – **Hindustani music**, the classical music of the northern half of the country and **Carnatic music**, the classical music system of much of South India. Popular preconceptions of all Indian music as represented by the exotic sounds of a **sitar** (long-necked lute) and accompanying **tabla** (hand drums) are no longer relevant in the South as these are essentially North Indian instruments. North and South Indian music, despite a few similarities, are essentially different. These differences are based on the historical development of the subcontinent, especially during the medieval period, which left a marked delineation between the languages and cultures of the two regions. The Muslim influx into India from Central Asia from the tenth century onwards, led to an amalgamation of indigenous and Muslim influences, while the music of the far south retained an older Dravidian culture.

The north–south linguistic and musical divide, however, cuts through some southern states such as Karnataka where the northern enclave is predominantly Marathi-speaking, and in musical terms, similar to North India. Although Telugu, one of the key languages in Carnatic music originates from Andhra Pradesh, northern tradition prevails in the large pockets of Muslim culture, particularly around Hyderabad. The further south you travel though, the more noticably the northern Hindu-Muslim amalgam gives way to Dravidian culture and the Carnatic classical system.

When you examine the two classical systems, however, they reveal some marked similitude as well. Both rely heavily on **raga** (musical mode) and **tala** (time cycle) and share key features, but differ in detail.

CLASSICAL MUSIC

Although classical music has a minority following, the structures it's built on provide the foundations of much traditional pop music today. Sometimes referred to by modern musicologists as the "**great tradition**", classical music refers back to ancient treatises and has developed through the centuries within a complex relationship with the "**little traditions**" of regional folk and other popular music. There are clear borrowings on both sides, with several classical modes bearing names alluding to places as well as to the seasons, while light classical genres such as the northern *thumri*, a love song, rely heavily on classical structures while displaying folk roots.

The concept of the "great tradition" refers to music with a strong **textual** and **theoretic base**. In India this base is the *shastrya sangeet*, or, the music of the *shastras* (Sanskrit treatises), which the two music systems refer back to with varying degrees of success. Dramatic changes have occurred since the early treatises, and in some cases, such as the fifth-century manuscript, the *Natyashastra* (the *shastrya* of dramaturgy), essentially a treatise on drama, the manuscript bears little resemblance to modern-day musical practice and only appears as accompaniment. Several later treatises, in particular Sarngadeva's thirteenth-century manuscript, *Sangeeta-ratnakara* (the treasures of music), has more bearing on modern classical music theory with structures described, which are faintly recognizable in musical practice today. It is also worth mentioning that a body of *shastrya* scholarship emerged from the Deccan in south-central India, from the fourth century onwards, which provided a common theoretical base for both southern and northern Indian systems.

While theorists may debate the influence of these treatises, these manuscripts play a dimishing role today as traditional music relies more on the **guru-shishya paramapara** (the tradition of guru and disciple), for its perpetuation. Musical knowledge is transferred orally between teacher and disciple. Indian music is only written with the aim of being committed to memory – the music is never traditionally read in performance and there is no practical system of notation.

Ever since the *Sangeeta-ratnakara*, Indian musicologists have tried to explain the classical systems in terms of families of musical modes or **ragas**. While the Carnatic system classifies *ragas* into a system of **melakartas**, or families, the Hindustani system generally recognizes the work of the theoretician, V.N. Bhatkande, who, after considering various treatises, published a system based on ten basic *ragas* as melodic types or *thats*. *Melakarta ragas* come with all seven notes but each of these *ragas* spawns a next generation of *janya ragas* that may have fewer or more convoluted sequences of notes. While *raga* grouping is incidental to Hindustani music, the *melakartas* play a far more important role in Carnatic music, and several composers have taken the scheme into account in their compositions.

In the Hindustani system, each *raga* comes with its own female counterpart; the *raga Bhairav*, for example, has strong contrasts between flattened and plain notes, and its female counterpart, the *ragini Bhairavi*, is perhaps the most flexible and evocative of all Indian *ragas*. Some treatises went even further and besides the **raga–ragini** groupings, extended the families by adding sons (*putras*). Despite general acceptance of the male–female relationship within the musical system, the term "*ragini*" is rarely used in practice. In the Hindustani system, in particular, *ragas* (and *raginis*) are assembled into times of day as well as seasons. Both *Bhairav* and *Bhairavi* are morning *ragas*, and, in general, towards the extremities of the day's cycle, *ragas* appear to be more dissonant while afternoon and early evening *ragas* are more balanced. The best of the seasonal *ragas* are rain *ragas* such as *Megh*, a pentatonic *raga*. While the North and South Indian *ragas* bear some resemblance in terms of structure, there remain marked differences, and some Hindustani *ragas* remain peculiar to the north, while the Carnatic system of the South has its own particular *ragas*. There is, however, increasing migration of musical practice between the North and South today with the result that certain Carnatic *ragas* such as *Hamsadhwani* are now firmly part of the Hindustani system. Similarly, elements of Hindustani music have been creeping into the repertoire of South Indian virtuosi and a sprinkling of northern melodies such as *thumris* and *bhajans* (religious songs) are almost part and parcel of a Carnatic performance.

The Carnatic and Hindustani music systems also differ in their approach to **performance**. The Hindustani system encourages far more improvisation through methodical development of a *raga*, whereas Carnatic music, though retaining improvisation, places a greater importance on the actual composition. For instance, in Carnatic performance the *alap* (a free-form introduction to the *raga* developed in set stages) forms the major part of the *dhrupad* performance leading up to the composition accompanied by rhythm; the *alapana* is a much shorter introduction with the emphasis on the following song. These differences are based on the historical development and role of the music: Hindustani music was heavily influenced by the Moghul court, and Carnatic music developed within a strong religious framework which was often retained by the Hindu courts of the far south. Moghul courts, especially that of Akbar (1556–1605), helped develop the Hindustani *raga* by patronizing musicians who were to inspire traditions that continue today.

Despite the fact that religious music in South India can be traced back to seventh-century **Tamil hymns**, modern Carnatic music owes much of its roots to the **Vijayanagar** court of the fourteenth to sixteenth centuries. Its proximity to the Muslim strongholds of the Deccan opened up Vijayanagar to a certain degree of cross-cultural synthesis between the predominantly Hindu Carnatic and the Muslim Hindustani worlds. The Muslim kingdoms actually represented a small minority governing a large Hindu population. The fall of the Vijayanagar empire in the late sixteenth century

THE TRILOGY

Carnatic music is dominated by the work of a trilogy of composers: **Shyama Shastri** (1762–1827), **Muttuswami Dikshitar** (1775–1835) and the saintly **Tyagaraja** (1767–1847). All three played essential roles in the lively musical atmosphere of **Tanjore**, though none was actually patronized by the court itself. Most Carnatic lineages trace their roots back to one of these composers, and while Shyama Shastri and Muttuswami Dikshitar's successors were known (Shastri's successor was his own son, Subbaraya, another prolific composer), Tyagaraja did not leave direct successors in the same way. Tyagaraja's direct disciples were his devotees. While most Vaishnavas were followers of Krishna, Tyagaraja devoted his life to Rama (another incarnation of Vishnu) from an early age and spent much of his life travelling and visiting temples. The devotion to Rama, the hero of the great Hindu epic the *Ramayana*, is significant as it emphasizes *dasyabhava* (devotional love) and provides an alternative to the sensual approach of Krishna worship. In comparison, Krishna worship places an emphasis on *madhuryabhava* (sexual love), epitomized by the recurrent theme, expressed in music and dance, of Krishna and his dalliance with the *gopis* (cow-girls). Tyagaraja was and still is the foremost champion of Rama worship and went on to leave a remarkable legacy in both religious and music terms. His compositions, which form the core of the Carnatic music heritage, brought together two major streams – the Vaishnava devotional song (*kirtana*) and the great tradition of high court music. Tyagaraja was able to marry the two forms but also developed a large repertoire of simple devotional songs in keeping with his lifestyle of an unaffected itinerant musician. In comparison with Tyagaraja, Muttuswami Dikshitar who spent some time in the north, in Banaras (Varanasi), was also an exponent of instrumental music and especially the *veena*. Unlike Shastri and Tyagaraja who composed in their native tongue of Telugu, Dikshitar composed his songs in Sanskrit.

caused a shift in the fulcrum of Carnatic music to the Cauvery (Kaveri) Delta and the Hindu kingdoms further south, particularly to **Tanjore**. It was the shift to the Hindu heartlands of the far south at this time which caused the differences between the Hindustani and the Carnatic systems to become more pronounced and allowed each to develop in its own particular ways.

The predominant tongue of Carnatic music was and still is, **Telugu**, the language of the central Deccan, and at one time the language of both the Vijayanagar court and that of Tanjore. In the seventeenth century, **Vaishnavas** (devotees of the god Vishnu and his incarnations), such as the *brahmin* Kshetrayya, developed large repertoires of *bhajans* and *padams* (types of devotional songs), some of which seeped into temple dance music. Kshetrayya found patronage at the court of Tanjore and composed several elegies in favour of his royal patron. A giant amongst Carnatic composers and songwriters, **Tyagaraja** (1767–1847) was another Telugu-speaking *brahmin*. Tyagaraja, whose compositions form the core of the Carnatic music heritage, travelled south to Tanjore and, despite living the itinerant life of a devotee, was able to combine the devotional song with the art of music encouraged by the court. With the decline of the court of Tanjore, towards the end of the eighteenth century, a group of musicians sought patronage at the court of **Travancore**, centred on Trivandrum (Thiruvananthapuram), in Kerala. The ruler of Travancore, Swati Tirunal (1829–47) was an accomplished musician himself. Thiruvananthapuram continues today to play an important role in Carnatic music and hosts large music conferences patronized by the descendants of the ruling family. The emergence of a substantial middle-class patronage in **Madras** (Chennai), however, shifted the focus of the Carnatic music world.

THE CARNATIC RECITAL

A Carnatic performance may be entirely unrehearsed, and in some cases musicians may never have played together before. The music is so structured, however, that musicians can anticipate what is expected from a performance – although they prefer to practice with accompanists they are used to.

A typical **ensemble** consists of a singer, backing vocals, a *mridangam* (double membrane barrel drum), a violinist and a *ghatam* (clay pot) player. Traditionally, the *ghatam* accompanies the violinist, and the *mridangam* accompanies the singer. The singer will also rely on one or two *tanburas* (long-necked, plucked lutes used as drones) for resonance, to provide the tonic (the bass note) and an essential reference with which to anchor the voice. Occasionally a singer may resort to mechanical means in place of the *tanburas* with a small electric *shruti* box (an electronic drone box providing the bass note). Changes in Carnatic music mean that the voice is often replaced by instruments at centre stage, and not just the traditional *veena* but instruments such as the violin, which, until recently, were only used as instruments of accompaniment. This is true of the *ghatam*, which with the immense popularity of Vikku Vinayakaram, has had tremendous success abroad.

A Carnatic recital traditionally starts off with a piece called a **varnam** – a simple composition designed as a warm-up allowing the vocalist to show his or her dexterity. The large repertoire of compositions used in performance, including the work of the great masters, means there is no single set procedure for a recital. A popular form that lies at the heart of many Carnatic recitals, is the "**ragam, tanam, palavi**" which allows the performer to explore the *raga* to the full. The *ragam, tanam, palavi* is nearly always introduced by an *alapana* after which the accompanist, usually a violinist, takes over in the same vein. In the next section – the *tanam* – the performer develops the *raga*, accompanied by the *mridangam* and *ghatam*, and followed by the violin. The next part of the performance, the *palavi*, is the most involved, the performer permutes and combines segments of the central *palavi* composition in a movement known as *neraval*. In the final movement, the *tani avartam*, the performer allows the percussionists scope to improvise with alternating solos and interplay between the *mridangam* and *ghatam*. Other compositions popular on the Carnatic stage include **kirtana**, long religious compositions such as those composed by Tyagaraja, and **kriti**. Far more musically flexible than a *kirtana*, the *kriti* combines composition with extemporaneous musical form and, although not essentially religious in nature, has also been a favourite medium for religious composers like Tyagaraja, and another composer saint, Purandara Dasa.

Before the demise of court patronage, owing to the loss of power and wealth and the emergence of modern India, accompanists in the north were drawn traditionally from sub-caste and other **hereditary groups** that were considered inferior. From the middle of the twentieth century, however, classical music became increasingly patronized by sections of the **middle classes** resulting in a shift in attitudes, and the removal of old taboos and superstitions. One taboo concerns the handling of leather, such as that used on *tabla* heads – previously only lower castes handled leather. Increasingly, musicians came from middle-class homes although, the **gharana** (literally "house" or school of music) system of the north continues to thrive. The *gharanas* remain the crucible of musical style, and attitudes are passed on between the guru (*ustad* in the Urdu language) (teacher) and his or her *shishya* or *chela* (*shagird* in Urdu) (student), and thus protected from generation to generation. In the north, especially among the Muslim musicians, long considered some of the finest, the *gharana* system favoured the actual family and the art was, and still is in many cases, protected as part of the family tradition. In the South, the equivalent of the *gharana* is the **gurukulam**, which also involved a direct relationship between master and pupil, but due to the development of modern music education the influence of this institution is now on the wane.

Though some theoreticians try and place classical music in an ancient mould, evidence suggests that the great tradition of Indian music continues to grow, absorbing local, lesser traditions and even foreign imports. The *maqaam*, for example, a musical mode from the Middle East introduced by Muslim culture into the subcontinent, appears in certain *ragas* and is still an important part of the *qawwali* (sufi devotional song) repertoire. Absorption of outside influences is more visible when it comes to **musical instruments**. Carnatic music has absorbed several key instruments from the West including the violin, mandolin and even the saxophone. Some instruments have only become popular over the last fifty years: the *tabla* and *sarangi*, were, until recently, seen as accompanying instruments of a lower social standing.

THE INSTRUMENTS

In Carnatic music the traditional purpose of the ensemble was in support of the song. Virtuosity in Carnatic grew from within the ensemble where each instrument in turn was given the freedom to **improvise**. Today, however, some Carnatic instrumentalists are more renowned than vocalists, particularly outside South India and abroad, whereas the song still tends to rule supreme within the heartland.

Besides the voice, the most hallowed of all instruments in South India is the **veena**, a long-necked lute that pre-dates the *sitar*. The *veena* comes in various shapes and sizes, from the fretted long-necked lute to the **bin**, a minimalist stick zither with two large gourds balanced towards either end. Unlike the common South Indian *veena* (the **saraswati veena**), the **gottuvadhyam**, also known as the **chitra veena**, comes without frets but, like the *saraswati veena*, has impressive ornamentation, including carved dragon heads. The *veena* – an indigenous instrument steeped in antiquity and mentioned in the *shastras* – has been at the forefront of solo instrumental performance for quite some time, although in recent years several other accompanying instruments have progressed to centre stage.

The internationally recognizable *sitar* – predominantly played in North India – is a uniquely Indian instrument, although its roots lie with the Persian *shetar*, a simpler instrument but also a plucked stick zither with a long neck. Another import into the subcontinent was the northern **sarod**, derived from the Afghan *rabab*, a fretless lute with a wooden sound box. The *sarod* developed its main sound chamber from a wooden finger board to a metal strip, which allows the finger nail to slide along the string between notes. Metal strings (instead of gut) and sympathetic strings, which are not struck but vibrate to add to the resonance and charm of the instrument, are commonly used.

The **sarangi**, a bowed instrument with folk roots, is popular as an accompanying instrument for vocalists in the Hindustani tradition. The *sarangi* graduated as a main performance instrument in the mid-twentieth century. *Sarangi* players are few and far between and the harmonium, a hand organ introduced by the Portuguese, is now far more common as the accompaniment. The **violin**, introduced as early as the eighteenth century to Carnatic music, plays the same role as that of the *sarangi* and has also enjoyed recent success centre-stage. In Carnatic tradition, the violinist squats on the floor and rests the end of the violin on his or her foot. The Carnatic violin is played in a robust manner and without the delicate timbre often present in Western violin technique.

Amongst the drums, the **tabla** is far the most successful and adaptable, but in the South, the **mridangam**, the large barrel drum, reigns supreme. The northern equivalent of the *mridangam*, know both as **pakhawaj** and *mridangam*, enjoys a repertoire similar to that of a *tabla*. The **ghatam**, a clay pot played with fingers against the surface while the mouth of the pot is rested against a naked belly to modulate sound depth, is another part of the exciting Carnatic rhythm section and has enjoyed considerable success abroad. Some of the curious rhythm instruments which occasionally appear on the Carnatic stage include a tambourine known as a **kanjira** and a **morsing**, a Jew's harp. The **nagaswaram**, a shawm used in ceremonial music, now appears as a concert instrument, while outdoor drums from South India include the **tavil** and the **maddalam**, a hand-beaten drum used in the accompaniment of Kathakali dance. The **damaru**, an hourglass drum popular in religious ceremony (and also with monkey dancers), is struck quickly so as the striker – a string with a hardened knot at the end – strikes both sides of the drum simultaneously. Snake charmers, traditionally use a **pungi** (also known as a *been*), a flute with a gourd sound box. The snake charmer moves his head, and the snake, incapable of picking up sound, follows the charmer's every movement thereby appearing to dance.

CEREMONIAL AND PROCESSIONAL MUSIC

The **procession**, whether religious in nature or as accompaniment to a wedding party, is designed to be loud and intrusive so as to announce the occasion and to attract as much attention as possible. Shawms (similar to a large clarinet) such as the penetrating *nagasvaram* accompanied by the *tavil* (a large double-membrane drum beaten with hands and sticks) are used not only on stage during temple ceremonies, but also with processional troupes, known in Tamil as *periya melam* or "great ensemble". The pleasing if loud sound of a *nagasvaram* has meant that the instrument, having adopted a standard Carnatic repertoire, has been accepted in recent years onto the indoor concert platform. The North Indian equivalent of the *nagasvaram* is the *sehnai* (oboe) which, as an essential part of a *naubat* procession, was introduced to India from the Middle East in the Middle Ages. The *naubat* (literally "time" in Urdu) ensemble also features large kettledrums known as *naqqara*, and was used in Muslim courts to mark the times of day as well as to perform at ceremonial functions. *Naubat* processions are now rarely seen on the streets but the tradition still continues at some of the larger sufi shrines. The *sehnai*, like the South Indian *nagasvaram*, migrated onto centre stage with musicians such as Bismillah Khan, considered one of the finest classical musicians in present-day Hindustani music. The *sehnai* is also popular during weddings where, in emulation of earlier court traditions, the ensemble is often positioned in a chamber above the gate.

The most memorable, the most cacophonic and the most raucous of all processional music, however, has to be the **tinsel bands** that accompany weddings. Consisting of part-time musicians with limited training, the bands are kitted out to look like toy soldiers: they beat marching drums and cymbals, blow trumpets and trombones, and play popular tunes drawn, on the whole, from Bollywood film songs – barely recognizable above the din. Other forms of processional and ceremonial music include the army's **pipe bands** – a Scottish tradition introduced during the days of the British Raj but still nurtured by the Indian armed forces.

STUDYING CLASSICAL MUSIC

Studying India's classical music systems in India is one of the best ways of getting to know the culture and the people. It is not to be undertaken lightly, however, as it involves serious dedication and long-term commitment. For those prepared to devote substantial time and effort there are several well-established institutions such as the **Madras Music Academy**, in Chennai and the **Kerala Kalamandalam** in Cheruthuruthy, Kerala (see p.354).

The most influential source of information on Carnatic music, is the magazine *Sruti*, published in Chennai (see box overleaf for their Web site). For those with access to the **Internet**, the box overleaf lists several excellent Web sites, focusing on Carnatic music.

CARNATIC MUSIC ON THE INTERNET

The Carnatic Cafe
http://www.geocities.com/Vienna/5908/
An excellent site with information about concerts, recordings available and links to other Carnatic sites.

Carnatic Music Online
www.geocities.com/Vienna/Strasse/5926/
Large, informative, if somewhat dense site with a strong academic leaning.
www.carnaticmusic.com/
Fantastic site with history, news, reviews, audiogallery and an extensive noticeboard.

Carnatic Music @ SKULE
http://www.ecf.utoronto.ca/~iyer/
A growing site hosted by students of the Engineering Computing Facility at the University of Toronto. It contains a large collection of live, streamable audio files in RealAudio and MP3 formats.

Carnatic Webring
www.carnatic.com/webring/
Brilliant site and a must if you want to link in to music on the Web, it also has a large number of good links.

Kala Arts Quarterly
http://www.geocities.com/Vienna/Choir/4687/
Well-designed online magazine which covers visual and performing arts, with a special focus on Carnatic music events in North America.

Khazana
www.khazana.com
A cornucopia of arts and curios, which has a large, amusing and informative section on Carnatic music.

Music India Online
http://bharath.com/music/
Extensive site with a wide coverage of both Hindustani and Carnatic music as well as a whole lot more plus sound bites.

The Music Magazine
www.themusicmagazine.com
Smart new online magazine from Bangalore covering a wide range from popular music, Bollywood, Hindustani and Carnatic music, to the Spice Girls and Tchaikovsky. Informative, it offers reviews, listings, interviews and articles – although at times it can lack focus.

Sruti
www.sruti.com/
Online version of the reputable Carnatic music magazine, with in-depth features.

DANCE AND POPULAR MUSIC

The standard Carnatic ensemble is little changed, except for its repertoire, for accompanying dance forms such as Bharatanatyam but the ensemble used for **Kathakali** is far more ceremonial. Apart from the *maddalam*, a hand-beaten drum, the kathakali ensemble also includes **cenda**, cylindrical drums held vertically and beaten with sticks. The drummers are an integral part of the performance, and place emphasis on the steps and *mudras* (hand gestures) of the dancers. Two singers accompanied by a gong stand to the right of the stage, and relate the story in verse as the dancers unfold the action utilizing gestures, *mudras* and facial expressions to full effect.

Particularly prevalent in South India, Vaishnavism places its main emphasis on devotion; devotional song such as the **bhajan** is an important vehicle of worship. Though the *bhajan* can be heard on stage sung by virtuosi, the main form of *bhajan* is as a chorus. **Qawwali** music is less choral and more performance orientated, with an emphasis on the performer attaining *haal*, or a state of spiritual ecstasy. The Vaishnava **kirtan** also has a similar aim.

Although Chennai has an indigenous film industry, it cannot compete with the immense popularity of **Bollywood songs**. Bollywood has the ability to borrow from almost everywhere, and the process is not just one of imitation but also interpretation. Large, heavily choreographed dance scenes are popular and were originally inspired by Hollywood song and dance extravaganzas of the 1930s. Although Bollywood has changed with the times the industry continues to produce fantasies along a similar vein, and with phenomenal popularity, not just within the country but as far afield as Israel, Turkey, Morocco and even Peru.

India has a small but lively **contemporary music** scene centred on cosmopolitan cities such as Mumbai and Bangalore. Bands like Dhoom try to fuse contemporary ideas with traditional themes. Old-fashioned jazz-cum-dance bands can be found in some nightclubs and bars in the cities. These bands, which often feature crooners, have traditionally drawn heavily from the musically talented Goanese and Anglo-Indian (Eurasian).

CARNATIC DISCOGRAPHY

Vocalists to look out for include **M.S. Subbalakshmi** – a living legend – now in her eighties but still considered the doyen of Carnatic music. Other remarkable female vocalists include the **Bombay Sisters**. **Yesudas**, a Christian yet a worshipper of Krishna, has a wonderful voice and is currently enjoying great popularity. **P. Unni Krishnan** is another young, talented and much-lauded vocalist. Other eminent vocalists include the **Hyderabad Brothers** and **Dr Balamurali Krishna**. **Jon Higgins**, a Canadian singer, took the Carnatic world by storm in the seventies but tragically died young. Among famous instrumentalists, the mandolin player **U. Srinivas** has been the find of the decade and has worked in fusion (*Dream*, with Michael Brook (Realworld)). **T.R. Mahalingam** was a giant among flautists and left a legacy of good recordings. The two brothers **Dr L. Subramaniam** and **L. Shankar** are violin legends as are **Lalgudi Jayaraman** and **Kunnakudi Vaidyanathan.** L. Shankar got heavily involved with fusion, especially during and after his work with **Shakti**, which originally featured the guitarist John McLaughlin as well as the *tabla* maestro Zakir Hussein. Other instrumentalists well worth seeking out are **T.H. Vikku Vinayakaram** (*ghatam*), **Kadri Gopalnath** (saxophone), **Dr S. Balachandar** (*veena*), **Dr N. Ramani** (flute) and **Dr Namagiripettai Krishnan** (*nagaswaram*). **T.H. Vikku Vinayakaram** was extremely successful in promoting the *ghatam* on the international stage and has been involved with several fusion projects.

The best, and the bulk, of Carnatic music is available on **cassette**, with a small selection on CD. Labels to look out for are Magnasound, Shankar, EMI (India), and Music Today. The following list is by no means exhaustive and is divided into Classical (vocal), Classical (instrumental), Jugalbandi (a fusion of Carnatic and Hindustani music), and Fusion (East meets West).

CLASSICAL (VOCAL)

M. Balamurali Krishna: *Vocal Genius* (All India Radio Realease; T Series)

M. Balamurali Krishna: *Live at Bombays Nehru Center December 1994* (with Zakir Hussain, *tabla*; Mysore Nagarajan, violin; T.H. Vikku Vinayakaram, *ghatam*) (Moment)

Bombay Sisters: *Evergreen Melodies* (Pyramid)

Bombay Sisters: *Carnatic Vocal* (with A. Kanyakumari, violin; Govinda Rajan, *ghatam*; Srimushnam V. Raja Rao, *mridangam*) (EMI India)

Jon B. Higgins: *Vocal* (with V. Thyagrajan, violin; T. Ranganathan, *mridangam*; V. Nagarajan, kanjira) (EMI India)

Hyderabad Brothers: *Scintillating Ragas* (with Peri Sriramamurthy, violin; T.K. Murthy, *mridangam*; E.M. Subramaniam, *ghatam*) (OMI Music Inc)

Dr Semmangudi Srinivasa Iyer: *The Doyen of Carnatic Music* (with L. Subramaniam, violin; Guruvayoor Dorai, *mridangam*; and V.R. Krishnan, vocal support) (Oriental)

M. S. Subbulakshmi: *The Golden Collection* - (2CD set; EMI India (Golden))

M.S. Subbulakshmi: *Greatest Classics* (Shankar)

P. Unnikrishnan: *Unnikrishnan* (with M.A. Sundareswaran, violin; A. Eswaran, *mridangam*; Vaikkom Gopalakrishnan, *ghatam*) (AVM)

P. Unnikrishnan: *Mellifluous Melodies* (Vani)

K.J. Yesudas: *Gayatri Mantra – Music For Meditation* (Oriental)

K.J. Yesudas: *Hymns From The Rig Veda* (Oriental)

K.J. Yesudas: *Arathi* (Shankar)

CLASSICAL (INSTRUMENTAL)

S. Balachander: *Vina Virtuoso* (with R. Ramesh, *mridangam*; S.B.S. Raman, *tanpura*) (World Music Library/King Records)

Kadri Gopalnath: *Jugulbandi Classical Confluence* (with Narasinhalu Wadvati, *clarionet*; M.R. Sairam, *mridangam*; K. Datatreya, *tabla*) (OMI Music Inc)

Kadri Gopalnath: *Shadows* (with V.V. Ravi, violin; K.V. Prasad, *mridangam*; T.H. Subash, *ghatam*; R. Raman, *morsing*; S.N. Subramanian, *tanpura*) (Inreco Pyramid)

Lalgudi Jayaraman: *Quintessence of Indian Classical Music* (Kaveri)

Lalgudi Jayaraman: *Violin Virtuoso* (with G.V.R. Krishnan, violin, and Karaikudi R. Mani, *mridangam*) (Oriental)

T.R. Mahalingam: *Divine Sounds of the Bamboo Flute Vol 1 & 2* (with Dwaram Mangathayaru, *violin* Karaikudi R Mani; *mrindangam*, Gurumurthy, *ghatam*) (Oriental)

T.R. Mahalingam: *Carnatic Flute* (EMI India)

Namagiripettai Krishnan: *Enchanting Nadaswaram Recital* (with *nadaswaram*: K. Murugan Thavil: K. Arumugam & Manikandan *sruthi box*: K. Thangavelu Thalam: K. Mani) (Pyramid)

N Ramani: *Lotus Signatures* (with Trichy Sankaran, *mridangam*; Nagai Muralidaran, *violin*; V. Nagarajan, *kanjira*; E.M. Subramaniam, *ghatam*; A. Kannan, *morsing*) (Music of the World)

N Ramani: *New Dimensions on the Flute* (with V. Ravi, violin; Srimushnam Rajarao, *mridangam*; E.M. Subramaniam, *ghatam*) (OMI Music Inc)

continued overleaf

CARNATIC DISCOGRAPHY (continued)

RARE GEMS OF SOUTH INDIAN MUSIC: Namagiripettai: *Krishnan, nagaswaram*, U. Srinivas mandolin; T.N. Krishnan, violin; S. Balachander, *veena*; N. Ramani, flute and Kadri Gopalnath, saxophone (Oriental)

L. Shankar: *Soul Searcher* (with V. Lakshminarayana, T.H. Vikku Vinayakaram, Zakir Hussain) (Axiom)

U. Srinivas: *Double Mandolin* (with Guruvayur, *mridangam*; G. Harishankar, *ganjeera*; E.M. Subranmaniam, *ghatam*) (OMI Music Inc)

U. Srinivas: *Mandolin Ecstasy* (with Sikkil Bhaskaran, violin; Tanjore Upendran, *mridangam*; and Palghat Sundaram, *ghatam*) (Oriental)

U. Srinivas: *Dawn Raga* (Womad)

U. Srinivas: *The Magical Fingers of Mandolin* (with Delhi P. Sunder Rajan, violin; K.V. Prasad, *mridangam*; and E.M. Subramaniam, *ghatam*) (Oriental)

L. Subramaniam: *Distant Visions* (with K. Gopinath, *mridangam*; K.M. Rajah, *ganjira*) (Audiorec C)

L. Subramaniam: *Pacific Rendezvous* (with K. Gopinath, *mridangam*) (Manu)

Kunnakkudi R. Vaidyanathan: *Gems of Kunnakudi* (with Darasuram M Ganapathy, *mridangam*; T. Dakshinamurthy, *ganjira*; Trichy Kumar, *ghatam*; M. Raja Raman, *morsing*) (Silver Disc)

Kunnakkudi R. Vaidyanathan: *Violin & Thavil* (with Valayapatti A. R. Subramaniam, *thavil*) (Vani)

L. Vaidyanathan: *The Violin Trio* (with L. Subramaniam & L. Shankar on violins; Palghat T.S. Mani Iyer, *mridangam*) (EMI India)

T.H. Vikku Vinayakaram: *Percussion Music of Madras* (with the Tala Vadya Ensemble) (JVC Japan)

T.H. Vikku Vinayakaram: *Thala Vadya Katcheri* (OMI Music Inc)

JUGALBANDI

A mix of North and South Indian music

Lalgudi Jayaraman: *South Meets North* (with Amjad Ali Khan, *sarod*) (EMI India)

M. Balamurali Krishna: *Jugalbandi – Live at Royal Festival Hall, London, October 1994* (with Bhimsen Joshi, vocal; Shashikant Muley, *tabla*; T.H. Vikku Vinayakram, *ghatam*; Muthukrishna Balachander, *mridangam*; Tulsidas Borkar, harmonium, etc.) (Navras)

L. Subramaniam: *Live in Geneva – Jugalbandi* (with Bismillah Khan, *shenai*) (Audiorec C)

FUSION

East meets West

L. Vaidyanathan: *Nirvana Music of the Soul* (Music Today)

L. Vaidyanathan: *Musical Yatra* (TIPS Club)

T.H. Vinayakaram: *Generations* (T Series) (*Prayer, Tidal Waves, African Safari, Four in Five, Sounds of Clay* (Laya Mishra Guru Murthy, violin; A.K. Palanivel, *thavil*; T.H. Shubash *chandran, konnakkol*; V. Selva Ganesh, drums)

T.H. Vinayakaram: *Together* (with T.H. Vinayakram, *ghatam*; with Selva Ganesh, *kanjira* and percussion; Uma Shankar, *ghatam*. Guitar & keyboard: Rikhi Ray, *morsing*: Ganesh, *mridangam*: Ramakrishna (OMI Music Inc)

John McLaughlin: *Natural Elements* (with L. Shankar, violin, viola and vocals; Zakir Hussain, *tabla*; T.H. Vikku Vinayakaram, *ghatam*) (Sony Records)

John McLaughlin: *A Handful of Beauty* (with L. Shankar, violin; Zakir Hussain, tabla; T.H. Vikku Vinayakaram, *ghatam* and *mridangam*) (Sony Records)

John McLaughlin: *Shakti* (with L. Shankar, Zakir Hussain, R. Raghvan, T.S. Vinayakram) (Columbia/Legacy/CBS)

L. Shankar: *Soul Seacher* (with Zakir Hussain, *tabla*; T.H. Vikku Vinayakaram, *ghatam*; Peter Gabriel, vocals and keyboards Caroline and Ganam Rao (Polygram)

L. Shankar: *Song for Everyone* (with Jan Garbarek, Zakir Hussain, Trilok Gurtu) (BMG/ECM)

U. Srinivas: *Dream* (with Michael Brook, Nigel Kennedy, Caroline Levelle, Jane Siberry, Sikkil R Bhaskaran, Nana Vasconcelos) (Realworld)

L. Subramaniam: *Live in Moscow with the Kirov Symphony Orchestra* (Pan Classics)

L. Subramaniam: *Conversations* (with Stephane Grappeli, Frank Bennett, Frank Morgan) (Pan Classics)

L. Subramaniam: *Spanish Wave* (with Alla Rakha, Kevin Brandon, Gary Chang, Guruvayoor Dorai, Emil Richards) (Pan Classics)

DANCE

Among the most magical experiences a visitor to South India can have is to witness one of the dance forms that play such an important part in the cultural life of the region. India's most prevalent classical dance style, Bharatanatyam, originated in the South and still fills concert halls in Tamil towns, while other types of ritualized theatre, such as Kathakali, Kuttiyattam and Teyyam, remain integral to temple worship in Kerala. If you're lucky enough to catch an authentic performance in situ, you'll never forget it. The stamina of the performers and the spectacle of an audience sitting up all night to see the finale of a dance drama at dawn is remarkable to Western eyes.

THE NATYA SHASTRA

All forms of Indian dance share certain broad characteristics and can be traced back to principles enshrined in the **Natya Shastra**, a Sanskrit treatise on dramaturgy dating from the first century BC. The text covers every aspect of the origin and function of **Natya**, the art of dance-drama, which combines music, stylized speech, dance and spectacle, and characterizes theatre throughout South Asia.

The spread of this art form occurred during the centuries of cultural expansion from the second BC to the eighth AD, when South Indian kings sent trade missions, court dancers, priests and conquering armies all over the region. Even in countries that later embraced Buddhism or Islam, dances continue to show evidence of Indian forms, and Hindu gods and goddesses still feature, mixed with indigenous heroes and deities.

Indian dance is divided into two temperaments: **tanava**, which represents the fearful male energy of Shiva, and **lasya**, representing the grace of his wife Parvati. Dances can fall into one or other category (Kathakali is *tanava* and Bharatanatyam, *lasya*), or combine the two elements. Equally, they include in differing degrees the three main components of classical dance: **nritta**, pure dance in which the music is reflected by decorative movements of the body; **natya**, which is the dramatic element of the dance and includes the portrayal of character; and **nritya**, the interpretive element, in which mood is portrayed through hand and facial gestures and the position of the feet and legs.

The term **abinaya** describes the resources at the disposal of a performer in communicating the meaning of a dance; they include costume and make-up, speech and intonation, psychological understanding and, perhaps the most distinctive and complex element, the language of gestures. Stylized gestures are prescribed for every part of the body - there are seven movements for the eyebrows, six for the nose and six for the cheeks, for example - and they can take a performer years of intensive training to perfect.

Once complete control of the body has been mastered, a performer will have a repertoire of several thousand meanings. In combination with other movements a single hand gesture, with the fingers extended and the thumb bent for example, can be used to express heat, rain, a crowd of men, the night, a forest, a flight of birds or a house. Similarly, up to three characters can be played by a single performer by alternating facial expressions.

Despite frequent feats of technical brilliance, performers are rarely judged by their skill in executing a particular dance, but by their success in communicating certain specific emotions, or **bhava**, to the audience. This can only be measured by the quality of **rasa**, a mood or sentiment, one for each of the nine *bhava*, which the audience experiences during a performance.

BHARATANATYAM

The best-known Indian classical dance style, **Bharatanatyam**, is a graceful, gestural form performed by women. A popular subject for temple sculptures throughout South India (especially Tamil Nadu), it originated in the dances of the **devadasis**, temple dancing girls who originally performed as part of their devotional duties in the great Tamil shrines. Usually "donated" to a temple by their parents, the young girls were formally "wedded" to the deity and spent the rest of their lives dancing or singing as part of their devotional duties. Later, however, the *devadasis* system became debased, and the dancers, who formerly enjoyed high status in Hindu society, became prostitutes controlled by the *brahmins*, whom male visitors to the temple would pay for sexual services.

In the latter half of the nineteenth century, four brothers set themselves the task of saving the dance from extinction and pieced together a reconstruction of the form through study of the *Natya Shastra*, the images on temple friezes and through information gleaned from former *devadasis*. Although the dance today is largely based on their findings, this was only the first step in its revival, as Bharatanatyam continued to be confined to the temples and was danced almost exclusively by men – the only way, as the brothers saw it, of preventing its moral decline. Not until the 1930s, when **Rukmini Devi**, a member of the Theosophical Society, introduced the form to a wider middle-class audience, did Bharatanatyam began to achieve popularity as a secular art form.

As ward of the nineteenth-century British rebel **Annie Besant**, Devi had greater exposure to foreign arts than many women of her generation. She developed an interest in Western dance while accompanying her husband, George Arundale, former principal of the Theosophical Society's school in Adyar, Chennai, on lecture tours and had studied under Pavlova, among others. In 1929, however, after witnessing a performance of the dance she later named "Bharatanatyan", she dedicated her life to its revival. The dance school she founded at Adyar is now known as Kalakshetra and continues to develop some of the world's most accomplished exponents.

In her determination to make the art form socially respectable, Devi eliminated all erotic elements and was known to be rigid and authoritarian in her views about how Bharatanatyam should be danced. Many ex-pupils have gone on to develop their own interpretations of the style, but the form continues to be seen as an essentially spiritual art. Its theme is invariably romantic love, with the dancer seen as a devotee separated from the object of her devotion. In this way, she dramatizes the idea of **sringara bhakti**, or worship through love.

As with other classical dance forms, training is rigorous. Performers are encouraged to dissolve their identity in the dance and become instruments for the expression of divine presence. The order in which the phases of the dance are performed and practised is considered to be the one best suited to this goal. A recital usually lasts about two hours and consists of the following phases: *alarippu, jatiswaram, sabdam, varnam, padams javalis, tillana* and *mangalam*.

All performances are preceded by a *namaskaram*, a salutation to the gods, offered by the stage, musicians and audience; a floral offering is made to a statue of the presiding deity, which stands at the right of the stage. The pivotal part of the performance is **varnam**, which the preceding three phases build up to through *nritta* (pure dance based on rhythm), adding melody and then lyrics. In *varnam*, every aspect of the dancer's art is exercised through two sections, the first slow, alternating *abinhaya* with rhythmic syllables, and the second twice the pace of the first, alternating *abinhaya* with melodic syllables. In the following two phases the emphasis is on the expression of mood through mime, and in the penultimate phase, the *tillana*, the dancer reverts again to the pure rhythm which began the dance. A *mangalam*, or short prayer, marks the end of a performance.

KATHAKALI

Here is the tradition of the trance dancers, here is the absolute demand of the subjugation of body to spirit, here is the realization of the cosmic transformation of human into divine.

Mrinalini Sarabhai, classical dancer

The image of a Kathakali actor in a magnificent costume with extraordinary make-up and a huge gold crown has become Kerala's trademark, seen on anything from matchboxes to TV adverts for detergents. Traditional performances, of which there are still many, usually take place on open ground outside a temple, beginning at 10pm and lasting until dawn, illuminated solely by the flickers of a large brass oil lamp centre stage. Virtually nothing about Kathakali is naturalistic, because it depicts the world of gods and demons. Both male and female roles are played by men.

Standing at the back of the stage, two musicians play driving rhythms, one on a bronze gong, the other on heavy bell-metal cymbals; they also sing the dialogue. Actors appear and disappear from behind a handheld curtain and never utter a sound, save the odd strange cry. Learning the elaborate hand gestures, facial expressions and choreographed movements, as articulate and precise as any sign language, requires rigorous training that can begin at the age of eight and last ten years. At least two more drummers stand left of the stage; one plays the upright **chenda** with slender curved sticks, the other plays the **maddalam**, a horizontal barrel-shaped hand drum. When a female character is "speaking", the chenda is replaced by the hourglass-shaped *ettaka*, a "talking drum" on which melodies can be played. The drummers keep their eyes on the actors, whose every gesture is reinforced by their sound, from the gentlest embrace to the gory disembowelling of an enemy.

Although it bears the unmistakable influences of Kutiyattam and indigenous folk rituals, Kathakali, literally "story-play", is thought to have crystallized into a distinct theatre form during the seventeenth century. The plays are based on three major sources: the *Mahabharata*, *Ramayana* and the *Bhagavata Purana*. While the stories are ostensibly of god-heroes such as Rama and Krishna, the most popular characters are those that give the most scope to the actors – the villainous, fanged, red-and-black-faced *katti* ("knife") anti-heroes. These types, such as the kings Ravana and Duryodhana, are dominated by lust, greed, envy and violence. David Bolland's handy paperback *Guide to Kathakali*, widely available in Kerala, gives invaluable scene-by-scene summaries of the most popular plays and explains in simple language a lot more besides.

When attending a performance, arrive early to get your bearings before it gets dark, even though the first play will not begin much before 10pm. Members of the audience are welcome to visit the dressing room before and during the performance, to watch the **masks** and **make-up** being applied. The colour and design of these, which specialist artists take several hours to apply, signify the personality of each character. The principal characters fall into the seven following types.

Pacca ("green" and "pure") characters, painted bright green, are the noble heroes, including gods such as Rama and Krishna.

Katti ("knife") are evil and clever characters such as Ravana. Often the most popular with the audience, they have green faces to signify their noble birth, with upturned moustaches and white mushroom knobs on the tips of their noses.

Chokannatadi ("red beard") characters are power-drunk and vicious, and have black faces from the nostrils upwards, with blood-red beards.

Velupputadi ("white beard") represents Hanuman, monkey son of the wind god and personal servant of Rama. He always wears a grey beard and furry coat, and has a black and red face and green nose.

Karupputadi ("black beard") is a hunter or forest-dweller and carries a sword, bow and quiver. He has a coal-black face with a white flower on his nose.

Kari ("black") characters, the ogresses and witches of the drama, have black faces, marked with white patterns, and huge breasts.

Minnukku ("softly shaded") characters are women, *brahmins* and sages. The women have pale yellow faces sprinkled with mica and the men wear orange *dhotis*.

Once the make-up is finished, the performers are helped into their costumes – elaborate wide skirts tied to the waist, towering head-dresses and long silver talons fitted to the left hand. Women, *brahmins* and sages are the only characters with a different style of dress: men wear orange, and the women wear saris and cover their heads. The transformation is completed with a final prayer before the performance begins.

Visitors new to Kathakali will undoubtedly get bored during such long programmes, parts of which are very slow indeed. If you're at a village performance, you may not always find accommodation, so you can't leave during the night. Be prepared to sit on the ground for hours, and bring some warm clothes. Half the fun is staying up all night to witness, just as the dawn light appears, the gruesome disembowelling of a villain or a demon *asura*.

KUCHIPUDI

Kuchipudi, which originated in Andhra Pradesh, was only accorded the status of Classical Dance Form by the Sangeet Natak Academi in New Delhi in 1958. Before this – although considered to follow the **Natya Shastra** more closely than any other form – it was seen essentially as a folk idiom, a means of presenting scenes from mythology and the Hindu epics to relatively unsophisticated audiences.

Similar in form to Bharatanatyam, it also shares a history of decline and regeneration. Its present form is thought to date back to the seventeenth century when a local man capsized his boat while on the way to his wedding and prayed that his life might be saved. On finding his prayers answered, he wrote, in his new incarnation as **Siddhappa Yogi**, a dance drama in praise of Krishna and gathered a troupe of *brahmin* men to perform it. When presented at court in 1675, it so impressed the resident *nawab* that he granted the village of Kuchipudi to the artists so that they might pass on their art to future generations. Taking its name from the village, the dance has been practised by the same fifteen *brahmin* families ever since.

Traditionally performed only by groups of men, Kuchipudi requires seven years of rigorous training, with parallel education in music, Sanskrit, the ancient scriptures and mythology. Since the turn of the century, however, there has been an increase in the numbers of women dancing, as well as solo performances.

Like Bharatanatyam, Kuchipudi follows a fixed sequence of phases and uses similar techniques and costume, but it is distinguished by the importance of dialogue and song, and differs from other forms in that the dancers sing for themselves, usually in Telugu. Humour and spectacle are other important elements that distinguish it from the more restrained mood of Bharatanatyam: the highlight of most performances is a scene in which one dancer carries a pot of water on her head while balancing on the edge of a brass plate.

MOHINIYATTAM

A semiclassical form from Kerala, **Mohiniyattam** has its origins, like Bharatanatyam, in the temple dances of the *devadasis*. It, too, was revived through the efforts of enthusiastic individuals, first in the nineteenth century by Swati Thirunal, the king of Travancore, and again in the 1930s, after a period of disrepute, by the poet Vallathol.

Mohiniyattam ("the dance of the enchantress") takes its name from the mythological maiden **Mohini**, who evoked desire and had the ability to steal the heart of the onlooker. Usually a solo dance performed by women, it is dominated by the mood of **lasya**, with graceful movements distinguished by a rhythmic swaying of the body from side to side. The central theme is one of love and devotion to god, with Vishnu or Krishna appearing most frequently as the heroes. The mark of a successful performance is if the dancer successfully communicates her dreams and ambitions to the audience.

Dancers of Mohiniyattam wear realistic make-up and the white, gold-bordered Kasavu sari of Kerala. The music which accompanies the dancer is classical Carnatic with lyrics in Malayalam.

KUTIYATTAM

Three families of the Chakyar caste and a few outsiders perform the Sanskrit drama **Kutiyattam**, the oldest continually performed theatre form in the world. Until recently it was only performed inside temples and then only in front of the uppermost castes. Visually it is very similar to its offspring, Kathakali, but its atmosphere is infinitely more archaic. The actors, eloquent in sign language and symbolic movement, speak in the bizarre, compelling intonation of the local *brahmins*' Vedic chant, unchanged since 1500 BC.

A single act of a Kutiyattam play can require ten full nights; the entire play forty. A great actor, in full command of the subtleties of gestural expression, can take half an hour to do such a simple thing as murder a demon, berate the audience or simply describe a leaf falling to the ground. Unlike Kathakali, Kutiyattam includes comic characters and plays. The ubiquitous Vidushaka, narrator and clown, is something of a court jester, and traditionally has held the right to criticize openly the highest in the land without fear of retribution.

TEYYAM

In northern Kerala, a wide range of ritual "performances", loosely known as Teyyam, are extremely localized, even to particular families. They might include *bhuta* (spirit or hero worship), trance dances, the enactment of legendary events and oracular pronouncements. Performers are usually from low castes, but during the ritual, a *brahmin* will honour the deities they represent, so the status of each individual is reversed.

Although Teyyam can nowadays be seen in government-organized cultural festivals, the powerful effect is best experienced in the courtyard of a house or temple, in a village setting. Some figures, with painted faces and bodies, are genuinely terrifying; costumes include metres-high headgear, sometimes doubling as a mask, and clothes of leaves and bark.

The only place you can be sure of seeing Teyyam is at **Parassinikadavu**, a small village 20km north of Kunnur, in the far north of Kerala, where the head priest of the local temple dances each day. This is an extraordinary spectacle that shouldn't be missed if you're in the area. For more typical village Teyyam, you have to be in the right place at the right time. First, head for Kannur and ask the local tourist officer to point you in the right direction; after a few days' of waiting around, someone will hear you're looking for Teyyam and take you back to their village if a performance is planned – an experience anyone with more than a passing interest in ritual theatre and costume should definitely not miss.

Vicki Maggs

FINDING DANCE

Dance recitals take place throughout the winter, building up to fever pitch during April and May before pausing for the monsoon (June, July & Aug). Finding them requires a little perseverance, and a certain amount of luck, but it's well worth the effort.

Bharatanatyam is performed at concert halls in most major cities and towns in the South. In addition, it is always well represented at the annual dance festivals held at Mamallapuram (see p.397), Hampi (see p.284 and Tiruvananthapuram (see p.278). Wherever you are, it is always worth enquiring at tourist offices, and if you are in **Chennai**, check out the Listings pages of the regional press, such as *The Hindu*, for details of forthcoming events.

In **Kerala**, buy a copy of the Malayalam daily paper *Mathrabhumi* and ask someone to read the listings for you. Temple festivals, where most of the action takes place, are invariably announced. Tourist Kathakali is staged in Kochi (see p.336) but to find authentic performances, contact performing arts schools such as Thiruvananthapuram's Margi (see p.282) and Cheruthuruthy's Kerala Kalamandalam. Kutiyattam artists work at both, as well as at Natana Kairali at Irinjalakuda (see p.350). A good source of information on more obscure Keralan rituals, festivals and dance forms is the privately run Tourist Desk at Main Boat Jetty, Ernakulam (see p.334).

BOOKS

Appropriately for a part of the world with a written history dating back nearly two and a half thousand years, South India has spawned an extraordinary wealth of books. What follows is merely a selection of those that have proved most useful or enjoyable during the preparation of this guide. Most are available in the UK and US, and frequently in India too, where they tend to be much cheaper.

Where separate editions exist in the UK and USA, publishers are detailed below in the form "UK publisher; US publisher", unless the publisher is the same in both countries. Where books are published in India only, this follows the publisher's name.

O/p signifies out-of-print but still a recommended book (which you may well be able to pick up on the Internet via *www.amazon.com* or *www.amazon.co.uk*).

HISTORY

A.L. Basham *The Wonder that was India* (South Asia Books, India). Scholarly survey of Indian history, society, music, art and literature from 400 BC to the coming of the Muslims. Volume II, by **S.A. Rizvi**, brings it up to the arrival of the British. An undergraduate set text on Indian history courses the world over.

Larry Collins and Dominique Lapierre *Freedom at Midnight* (HarperCollins). Readable, if shallow, account of Independence, highly sympathetic to the British and, particularly, to Mountbatten, who was the authors' main source of information.

Patrick French *Liberty or Death* (HarperCollins). The definitive account of the last years of the British Raj. Material from hitherto unreleased intelligence files shows how Churchill's "florid incompetence" and Atlee's "feeble incomprehension" contributed to the debacle that was Partition, which French concludes was doomed through "confusion, human frailty and neglect". All in all, a damning indictment of Britain's role, that debunks many myths; it also shows up *Freedom at Midnight* as fundamentally flawed.

Richard Hall *Empires of the Monsoon* (HarperCollins). An impeccably researched account of early colonial expansion into the Arabian Sea and Indian Ocean, which traces the web of trade connections binding Europe, Africa and the subcontinent. It features a particularly vivid account of Vasco da Gama's expeditions, in all its brutality, and the subsequent conquest of Goa.

Gordon Johnson *Cultural Atlas of India* (Andromeda). A lavishly illustrated general introduction to the religions, societies, arts and sciences of the subcontinent, written by top scholars and presented in accessible coffee-table format. Colour maps and boxes bring a particularly strong history section to life.

Bhermann Kulke & Dietmar Rothermund *A History of India* (Routledge). Among the few complete histories of India to give adequate coverage to the South (one of the authors' specialist subjects), from the Mesolithic era (100,000 BC) to the war in Sri Lanka.

Amaurg de Riencourt *The Soul of India* (Honeyglen). A wide-ranging exploration of India's past, from the Indus Valley civilization to Indira's death. The focus is squarely philosophical, which makes it hard going in places, but this is one of the most erudite reference books in print.

Romila Thapar *History of India* Volume I (Penguin/Viking). Concise paperback account of early Indian history, ending with the Delhi Sultanate. **Percival Spear's** *History of India* Volume II covers the period from the Moghul era to the death of Gandhi. Among the most readable offerings of its kind, and the most easily available.

Gillian Tindall *City of Gold* (Penguin, India). Definitive, if rather dry biography of Mumbai (Bombay), from colonial trading post to modern metropolis.

SOCIETY

Gita Mehta *Karma Cola: Marketing the Mystic East* (Minerva/Fawcett Books). Satirical look at the psychedelic 1970s freak scene in India, with some hilarious anecdotes, and many a wry observation on the whackier excesses of spiritual tourism. Her latest book, *Snakes and Ladders* (Vintage/Fawcett Books), is a brilliant overview of contemporary urban India in the form of a pot-pourri of essays, travelogues and interviews. It covers issues from Bollywood and the sex industry, to caste, gender, ecology and the contradiction between Indian poverty and the country's multi-million-dollar arms and business sector.

V.S. Naipaul *India: A Wounded Civilisation* (Penguin). This bleak political travelogue, researched and written during and shortly after the Emergency, gained Naipaul, an Indian Trinidadian, a reputation as one of India's harshest critics. Two decades later, he returned to see what had happened to the country his parents left. The result, *A Million Mutinies Now*, is an altogether more sympathetic and rounded portrait – a superbly crafted mosaic of individual lives from around the subcontinent, including a memorable portrait of a staunchly traditional Tamil *brahmin*. One of the best books on India ever written.

Ramesh Thakur *The Government and Politics of India* (Macmillan). For the most part, this critical overview of contemporary Indian government and politics is as dry as its title suggests, but there are no more succinct, comprehensive treatments of the subject in print. Includes strong essays on caste and the quota controversy, the police force, regionalism and why religion has dominated politics over the past two decades.

Mark Tully *No Full Stops in India* (Penguin/Viking). Crystallizing a lifetime's experience as the BBC's man in India, Tully's thesis – that Indians should seek inspiration for their future in their own great traditions rather than those of the West – provoked widespread scorn from the country's westernized elite. Yet this remains among the best-informed critiques on India of its generation. Most of the ten essays in it refer to the North, but the issues tackled are equally relevant to the South.

Various *India* (Granta). To commemorate the fiftieth anniversary of Indian Independence, Granta published this mixed bag of new fiction, comment, poetry, reportage and memoirs from an impressive cast of Indian and foreign contributors. Among its many highlights are notes from the diary of V.S. Naipaul and Sebastião Salgado's photographic essay on Mumbai.

TRAVEL

William Dalrymple *The Age of Kali* (HarperCollins). Though not quite in the same league as *City of Djinns*, Dalrymple's latest offering – a collection of stylish essays from ten years of journalistic assignments – is rich with insights drawn from encounters and interviews with a vast range of personalities. Madurai's Meenakshi temple and the extraordinary history of the *Nizam* of Hyderabad comprise the South India content. Published in India as *In the Court of the Fish-Eyed Goddess*.

Alexander Frazer *Chasing the Monsoon* (Penguin). Frazer's wet-season jaunt down the west coast and across the Ganges plains took him through an India of muddy puddles and grey skies: an evocative account of the country as few visitors see it, and now something of a classic of the genre.

Geoffrey Moorhouse *Om* (Sceptre). Not Moorhouse's best, but nevertheless an absorbing account of his 1992 journey to South India's key spiritual centres, following the death of his daughter, with typically well-informed asides on history, politics, contemporary culture and religion.

Dervla Murphy *On a Shoestring to Coorg* (Flamingo/Overlook Press). Murphy stays with her young daughter in the little-visited tropical mountains of Coorg, Karnataka. Arguably the most famous modern Indian travelogue, and a manifesto for single-parent budget travel.

François Pryard *Voyage to the East Indies, the Maldives, the Moluccas and Brazil* (Hakluyt Society, India). Albert Gray's translation of the famous French chronicler's travelogue includes a vivid first-hand description of the Portuguese colony during its decadent heyday. Goa was Pryard's first port of call after being shipwrecked in the Maldives in 1608.

Jeremy Seal *The Snake Bite Survivor's Club* (Picador). Includes three chapters on snake-obsessed corners of India by someone whose fascination only just outweighs his phobia. The best of them describes a visit to a snake-venom extraction centre near Chennai.

Tahir Singh *Sorcerer's Apprentice* (Weidenfeld & Nicolson). A journey through the weird underworld of occult India. Travelling as apprentice to a master conjurer and illusionist, Singh encounters hangmen, baby renters, skeleton dealers, *sadhus* and charlatans. If it were set anywhere else in the world, this would be an unbelievable story.

Michael Wood *The Smile of Murugan* (Viking). A supremely well-crafted and affectionate portrait of Tamil Nadu and its people in the mid-1990s, centred on a video-bus pilgrimage tour of the state's key sacred sites. Indispensable if you plan to explore the deep southeast.

FICTION

Clive James *The Silver Castle* (Picador/Random House). A delightful story of a street urchin's rise from the roadside slums of outer Mumbai to the bright lights of Bollywood. James succeeds in balancing his witty celebration of the Hindi film world with an earnest attempt to dissect the ironies of the Maharashtran capital.

Rohinton Mistry *A Fine Balance* (Faber/Vintage). Two friends seek promotion from their low-caste rural lives to the glitz of the big smoke. A compelling and savage triumph-of-the-human-spirit novel exposing the evils of the caste system and of Indira Gandhi's brutal policies during the Emergency Years. Mistry's *Such a Long Journey* (Faber/Vintage) is a highly acclaimed account of a Mumbai Parsi's struggle to maintain personal integrity in the face of betrayals and disappointment.

R.K. Narayan *Gods, Demons and Others* (Minerva/University of Chicago Press). Many of Narayan's beautifully crafted books, full of subtly drawn characters and good-natured humour, are set in the fictional South Indian territory of Malgudi. This one tells classic Indian folktales and popular myths through the voice of a village storyteller.

Arundhati Roy *The God of Small Things* (Flamingo/HarperCollins). Haunting Booker Prize-winning novel about a well-to-do South Indian family caught between the snobberies of high-caste tradition, a colonial past and the diverse personal histories of its members. Seen through the eyes of two children, the assortment of scenes from Keralan life are as memorable as the characters themselves, while the comical and finally tragic turn of events says as much about Indian history as the refrain that became the novel's catchphrase: "things can change in a day."(See also box on p.314).

Salman Rushdie *The Moor's Last Sigh* (Jonathan Cape/Pantheon). Set in Kerala and Mumbai, Rushdie's follow-up to *The Satanic Verses*, a characteristically lurid and spleen-ridden evocation of the Maharashtran capital's paradoxes, caused a stir in India, and was the subject of a defamation case brought by Shiv Sena leader Bal Thackeray.

Manohar Shetty (ed) *Ferry Crossing: Short Stories From Around Goa* (Penguin, India). This long-awaited anthology of Goan fiction, compiled by a local poet, comprises broadly themed short stories woven around the local landscape and people. Translated from Konkani, Marathi, and Portuguese, none are what you might call world-class, but they offer fresh perspectives on Goan life, particularly the impact of modernization on villages.

William Sutcliffe *Are You Experienced?* (Penguin). Hilarious easy-read sending up a "typical" backpacker trip around India.

BIOGRAPHY AND AUTOBIOGRAPHY

Charles Allen *Plain Tales from the Raj* (Abacus). First-hand accounts from erstwhile *sahibs* and *memsahibs* of everyday British India, organized thematically ("The Club", "The Barracks", "The Hot Weather" and so on).

James Cameron *An Indian Summer* (Penguin). Affectionate and humorous description of the veteran British journalist's visit to India in 1972, and his marriage to an Indian woman. An enduring classic.

M.K. Gandhi *Experiments with Truth* (Penguin/Dover). Gandhi's fascinating records of his life, including the spiritual and moral quests, changing relationship with the British Government in India, and gradual emergence into the fore of politics.

Robert Harvey *Clive: The Life and Death of a British Emperor* (Sceptre). The most recent biography of the man often dubbed the "founding father" of the British empire. Although more famous for his role in the battle of Plassey, he pulled off some extraordinary military feats during a formative early spell in the Carnatic, based in Madras, which are recounted here in an accessible, lively style.

WOMEN

Chantal Boulanger *Saris: An Illustrated Guide to the Indian Art of Draping* (Shakti Press

International). The fruit of six years' fieldwork by a French anthropologist, this astonishingly comprehensive book catalogues the numerous styles of sari tying, and their sociocultural significance. Check out their site *www.devi.net* on the Internet.

Elizabeth Bumiller *May You Be the Mother of a Hundred Sons* (Fawcett Books/Penguin India). Lucid exploration of the Indian woman's lot, drawn from dozens of first-hand encounters, by an American journalist. Subjects tackled include dowries, arranged marriages, *sati*, magazines, and film stars.

Sashi Deshpande *The Binding Vine* (Virago). Disturbing story of one woman's struggle for independence, and her eventual acceptance of the position of servitude traditionally assumed by an Indian wife.

Anees Jung *The Night of the New Moon* (Penguin UK/India). Revealing and poetic stories woven around interviews with Muslim women from all sectors of Indian society. Jung's *Unveiling India* is a compelling account of the life of a Muslim woman who has chosen to break free from orthodoxy.

Vrinda Nabar *Caste as Woman* (Penguin India). Conceived as an Indian counterpart to Greer's *The Female Eunuch*, this is a wry study of the pressures brought to bear during the various stages of womanhood. Drawing on scripture and popular culture, Nabar looks at issues of identity and cultural conditioning.

Viramma, Josiane Racine & Jean-Luc Racine *Viramma: Life of an Untouchable* (Verso). Unique autobiography of an untouchable woman told in her own words (transcribed by French anthropologists), over a fifteen-year period, offering frank, often humorous insights into life in rural Tamil Nadu, the universe and everything.

DEVELOPMENT AND THE ENVIRONMENT

Julia Cleves Mosse India: *Paths to Development* (Oxfam). Concise analysis of the economic, environmental and political changes affecting India, focusing on the lives of ordinary poor people and the exemplary ways some have succeeded in shaping their own future. The best country brief on the market; only available through Oxfam.

Jeremy Seabrook *Notes from Another India* (Pluto Press). Life histories and interviews – compiled over a year's travelling and skilfully contextualized. They reveal the everyday problems faced by Indians from a variety of backgrounds, and how grassroots groups have tried combat them. One of the soundest, and most engaging, overviews of Indian development issues ever written.

Paul Sinath *Everybody Loves a Good Drought* (Review). A classic report on India's poorest districts, telling the stories of individual villages that are usually lost in a maze of development statistics.

WILDLIFE

Salim Ali, Dillon and Ripley *The Handbook of the Birds of India and Pakistan* (OUP, UK). Covers all of South Asia's birds in a single volume, with plates and maps: the definitive work, although hard to come by.

Claude Alvares (ed.) *Fish Curry and Rice: A Citizens' Report on the Goan Environment* (Ecoforum, India). A comprehensive overview of Goan green issues, giving a region-by-region rundown of the state's natural habitats, followed by articles outlining the principal threats to the environment from tourism, transport policy, changes in local farming practices and a host of other eco-evils.

P.V. Bole and Yogini Vaghini *Field Guide to the Common Trees of India* (OUP, UK/US). A handy-sized, indispensable tome for serious tree-spotters.

Bikram Grewal *Birds of India, Bangladesh, Nepal, Pakistan and Sri Lanka* (Odyssey). Five hundred species are detailed in this glossy and practical field guide – most with excellent colour photographs. Based on Salim Ali & Co's authoritative work, and the best of the bunch available in UK and US high-street bookshops.

Insight Guides *Indian Wildlife* (APA Publications, UK). An excellent all-round introduction to India's wildlife, with scores of superb colour photographs, features on different animals and habitats and a thorough bibliography. Recommended.

S. Prater *The Book of Indian Animals* (OUP /Bombay Natural History Society, India). The most comprehensive single-volume reference book on the subject, although only available in India.

Romulus Whitaker *Common Indian Snakes* (Macmillan, UK). A detailed illustrated guide to the subcontinent's snakes, with all the main species included.

Martin Woodcock *Handguide to the Birds of the Indian Subcontinent* (Collins, UK). For years the market leader, although now superseded by Grewal's guide. Available in light-weight, pocket-sized paperback form, and very user-friendly, with nearly every species illustrated (some in black and white).

THE ARTS AND ARCHITECTURE

Roy Craven *Indian Art* (Thames & Hudson). Concise general introduction to Indian art, from Harappan seals to Moghul miniatures, with lots of illustrations.

Mohan Khokar *Traditions of Indian Classical Dance* (Clarion Books, India). Detailing the religious and social roots of Indian dance, this lavishly illustrated book, with sections on regional traditions, is an excellent introduction to the subject.

George Michell *The Hindu Temple* (University of Chicago Press). The definitive primer, introducing Hindu temples, their significance, and architectural development.

Bonnie C. Wade *Music in India: The Classical Traditions* (Manmohar, India). A scrupulous catalogue of Indian music, outlining the most commonly used instruments, with illustrations and musical scores.

RELIGION

Dorf Hartsuiker *Sadhus: Holy Men of India* (Inner Traditions International). The weird world of India's itinerant ascetics exposed in glossy colour photographs and erudite but accessible text.

Roger Hudson *Travels through Sacred India* (o/p). Knowledgeable and accessible introduction to religious India, with a gazetteer of holy places, listings of ashrams and lively essays on temples, *sadhus*, gurus and sacred sites. Hudson derives much of his material from personal encounters, which brings the subjects to life. Includes sections on all India's main faiths, and an excellent bibliography.

GLOSSARY

ACHARYA religious teacher.

ADIVASI official term for tribal person.

AGARBATI incense.

AHIMSA non-violence.

AMRITA nectar of immortality.

ANDA literally "egg": the spherical part of a stupa.

ANICUT irrigation dam.

ANKUSHA elephant goad.

ANNA coin, no longer minted (16 annas to one rupee).

APSARA heavenly nymph.

ARAK liquor distilled from rice or coconut.

ARATA evening temple *puja* of lights.

ASANA yogic seating posture; small mat used in prayer and meditation.

ASHRAM centre for spiritual learning and religious practice.

ASURA demon.

ATMAN soul.

AVATAR reincarnation of Vishnu on earth, in human or animal form.

AYURVEDA ancient system of medicine employing herbs, minerals and massage.

BABA respectful term for a *sadhu*.

BAGH garden, park.

BAKSHEESH tip, donation.

BANDH general strike.

BANDHANI tie-and-dye.

BANIYA another term for a *vaishya*; a money lender.

BANYAN vast fig tree, used traditionally as a meeting place, or shade for teaching and meditating. Also, in South India, a cotton vest.

BASTEE slum area.

BASTI Jain temple.

BAZAAR commercial centre of town; market.

BEGUM Muslim princess; Muslim women of high status.

> Note that many **religious** terms are explained in detail in the section which begins on p.560; and **musical** instruments and other terms on p.600 onwards.

BETEL leaf chewed in *paan*, with the nut of the areca tree: loosely applies to the nut.

BHAJAN song.

BHAKTI religious devotion expressed in a personalized or emotional relationship with the deity.

BHANG pounded marijuana, often mixed in *lassis*.

BHAWAN (also *bhavan*) palace or residence.

BHUMI earth, or earth goddess.

BHUMIKA storey.

BIDI tobacco rolled in a leaf; the "poor man's puff".

BIDRI inlaid metalwork as produced in Bidar.

BINDU seed, or the red dot (also *bindi*) worn by women on their foreheads as decoration.

BIRADIRI summer house, pavilion.

BODHI enlightenment.

BODHI TREE/BO TREE *peepal* tree, associated with the Buddha's enlightenment (*Ficus religiosa*).

BODHISATTVA Buddhist saint.

BRAHMIN a member of the highest caste group; priest.

BUNDH (also *bandh*) general strike.

BURKHA body-covering shawl worn by orthodox Muslim women.

BURRA-SAHIB colonial official, boss or a man of great importance.

CANTONMENT area of town occupied by military quarters.

CASTE social status acquired at birth.

CELLA chamber in temple, often housing the image of a deity.

CENOTAPH ornate tomb.

CHAAT snack.

CHADDAR large head-cover or shawl.

CHAITYA Buddhist temple.

CHAKRA discus; focus of power; energy point in the body; wheel, often representing the cycle of death and rebirth.

CHANDAN sandalwood paste.

CHANDRA moon.

CHAPPAL sandals or flip-flops (thongs).

CHARAS hashish.

CHARBAGH garden divided into quadrants (Moghul style).

CHARPOI string bed with wooden frame.

CHAUMUKH image of four faces placed back to back.

CHAURI fly whisk, regal symbol.

CHELA pupil.

CHERUVU lake.

CHHATRI tomb; domed temple pavilion.

CHILLUM cylindrical clay or wood pipe for smoking *charas* or *ganja*.

CHITAL spotted deer.

CHOLI short, tight-fitting blouse worn with a sari.

CHOR robber.

CHOULTRY quarters for pilgrims adjoining South Indian temples.

CHOWGAN green in the centre of a town or village.

CHOWK crossroads or courtyard.

CHOWKIDAR watchman/caretaker.

COOLIE porter/labourer.

CRORE ten million.

CUPOLA small delicate dome.

DACOIT bandit.

DALIT "oppressed", "out-caste". The term, introduced by Dr Ambedkar, is preferred by so-called "untouchables" as a description of their social position.

DANDA staff, or stick.

DARGAH sufi shrine.

DARSHAN vision of a deity or saint; receiving religious teachings.

DARWAZA gateway; door.

DAWAN servant.

DEG cauldron for food offerings, often found in *dargahs*.

DEVA god.

DEVADASI temple dancer.

DEVI goddess.

DHABA food hall selling local dishes.

DHAM important religious site, or a theological college.

DHARAMSHALA rest house for pilgrims.

DHARMA sense of religious and social duty (Hindu); the law of nature, teachings, truth (Buddhist).

DHOBI laundry.

DHOLAK double-ended drum.

DHOLI sedan chair carried by bearers to hilltop temples.

DHOOP thick pliable block of strong incense.

DHOTI white ankle-length cloth worn by males, tied around the waist, and sometimes hitched up through the legs.

DHURRIE woollen rug.

DIGAMBARA literally "sky-clad": a Jain sect, known for the habit of nudity among monks, though this is no longer commonplace.

DIKPALAS guardians of the four directions.

DIWAN (*dewan*) chief minister.

DIWAN-I-AM public audience hall.

DIWAN-I-KHAS hall of private audience.

DOWRY payment or gift offered in marriage.

DRAVIDIAN of the southern culture.

DUKKA tank and fountain in courtyard of mosque.

DUPATTA veil worn by Muslim women with *salwar kamise*.

DURBAR court building; government meeting.

DVARPALA guardian image placed at sanctuary door.

EVE-TEASING sexual harassment of women, either physical or verbal.

FAKIR ascetic Muslim mendicant.

FENI Goan spirit, distilled from coconut or cashew fruits.

FINIAL capping motif on temple pinnacle.

GADA mace (the weapon).

GADI throne.

GANDHARVAS Indra's heavenly musicians.

GANJ market.

GANJA marijuana buds.

GARBHA GRIHA temple sanctuary, literally "womb-chamber".

GARH fort.

GARI vehicle, or car.

GAUR Indian bison.

GHAT mountain, landing platform, or steps leading to water.

GHAZAL melancholy Urdu songs.

GHEE clarified butter.

GIRI hill.

GODOWN warehouse.

GOMPA Tibetan, or Ladakhi, Buddhist

monastery.

GOONDA ruffian.

GOPI young cattle-tending maidens who feature as Krishna's playmates and lovers in popular mythology.

GOPURA towered temple gateway, common in South India.

GUMBAD dome on mosque or tomb.

GURU teacher of religion, music, dance, astrology etc.

GURUDWARA Sikh place of worship.

HAJ Muslim pilgrimage to Mecca.

HAJJI Muslim engaged upon, or who has performed, the *haj*.

HAMMAM sunken hot bath, Persian-style.

HARIJAN title – "Children of God" – given to "untouchables" by Gandhi.

HARTAL one-day strike.

HAVELI elaborately decorated (normally wooden) mansion.

HIJRA eunuch or transvestite.

HINAYANA literally "lesser vehicle": the name given to the original school of Buddhism by later sects.

HOOKAH water pipe for smoking strong tobacco or marijuana.

HOWDAH bulky elephant saddle, sometimes made of pure silver, and often shaded by a canopy.

IDGAH area laid aside in the west of town for prayers during the Muslim festival Id-ul-Zuhara.

IMAM Muslim leader or teacher.

IMAMBARA tomb of a Shi'ite saint.

INDO-SARACENIC overblown Raj-era architecture that combines Muslim, Hindu, Jain and Western elements.

IMFL Indian-made foreign liquor.

INAM *baksheesh* in Tamil.

ISHWARA God; Shiva.

IWAN the main (often central) arch in a mosque.

JAGHIDAR landowner.

JALI lattice work in stone, or a pierced screen.

JANGHA the body of a temple.

JATAKAS popular tales about the Buddha's life and teachings.

JATI sub-caste, determined by family and occupation.

JAWAN soldier.

JHUTA soiled by lips: food or drink polluted by touch.

-JI suffix added to names as a term of respect.

JIHAD striving by Muslims, through battle, to spread their faith.

JINA another term for the Jain *tirthankaras*.

JOHAR old practice of self-immolation by women in times of war.

JYOTIRLINGA twelve sites sacred by association with Shiva's unbounded *lingam* of light.

KABUTAR KHANA pigeon coop.

KAILASA or **KAILASH** Shiva's mountain abode.

KALAM school of painting.

KALASHA pot-like capping stone characteristic of South Indian temples.

KAMA satisfaction.

KAMISE women's knee-length shirt, worn with *salwar* trousers.

KARAN *wallah* in Tamil.

KARMA weight of good and bad actions that determine status of rebirth.

KATCHA the opposite of pukka, unacceptable.

KATHAKALI traditional Keralan dance/drama.

KAVAD small decorated box that unfolds to serve as a travelling temple.

KHADI home-spun cotton; Gandhi's symbol of Indian self-sufficiency.

KHAN honorific Muslim title.

KHOL black eye-liner, also known as *surma*.

KHUD valley side.

KIRTAN hymn-singing.

KOT fort.

KOTHI residence.

KOTLA citadel.

KOVIL term for a Tamil Nadu temple.

KSHATRYA the warrior and ruling caste.

KUMKUM red mark on a Hindu woman's forehead (widows are not supposed to wear it).

KUND tank, lake, reservoir.

KURTA men's long shirt worn over baggy pyjamas.

LAKH one hundred thousand.

LAMA Tibetan Buddhist monk and teacher.

LATHI heavy stick used by police.
LINGAM phallic symbol in places of worship representing the god Shiva.
LIWAN cloisters in a mosque.
LOKA realm or world, eg *devaloka*, world of the gods.
LUNGHI male garment; long wrap-around cloth, like a *dhoti*, but usually coloured.
MADRASA Islamic school.
MAHADEVA literally "Great God", a common epithet for Shiva.
MAHAL palace; mansion.
MAHARAJA (*Maharana, Maharao*) king.
MAHARANI queen.
MAHATMA great soul.
MAHAYANA literally "great vehicle": a Buddhist school that has spread throughout Southeast Asia.
MAHOUT elephant driver or keeper.
MAIDAN large open space or field.
MAKARA crocodile-like animal featuring on temple doorways, and symbolizing the River Ganges. Also the vehicle of Varuna, the Vedic god of the sea.
MALA necklace, garland or rosary.
MANDALA religious diagram.
MANDAPA hall, often with many pillars, used for various purposes: eg *kalyan(a) mandapa* for wedding ceremonies and *nata mandapa* for dance performances.
MANDI market.
MANDIR temple.
MANTRA sacred verse or word.
MAQBARA Muslim tomb.
MARG road.
MASJID mosque.
MATAJI female *sadhu*.
MATH Hindu or Jain monastery.
MAUND old unit of weight (roughly 20kg).
MAYUR peacock.
MEDHI terrace.
MELA festival.
MEMSAHIB respectful address to European woman.
MIHRAB niche in the wall of a mosque indicating the direction of prayer (to Mecca). In India the *mihrab* is in the west wall.
MIMBAR pulpit in a mosque from which the Friday sermon is read.
MINARET high slender tower, characteristic of mosques.
MITHUNA sexual union, or amorous couples in Hindu and Buddhist figurative art.
MOKSHA blissful state of freedom from rebirth aspired to by Hindus and Jains.
MOR peacock.
MUDRA hand gesture used in Vedic rituals, featuring in Hindu, Buddhist and Jain art and dance, and symbolizing teachings and life stages of the Buddha.
MUEZZIN man behind the voice calling Muslims to prayer from a mosque.
MULLAH Muslim teacher and scholar.
MUND village.
MUNDA male garment like *lunghi*.
MUTT Hindu or Jain monastery.
NADI river.
NAGA mythical serpent.
NALA stream gorge in the mountains.
NATAK dance.
NATYA drama.
NAUTCH performance by dancing girls.
NAWAB Muslim landowner or prince.
NILGAI blue bull.
NIRVANA Buddhist equivalent of *moksha*.
NIWAS building or house.
NIZAM title of Hyderabad rulers.
NULLAH stream gorge in the mountains.
OM (aka *AUM*) symbol denoting the origin of all things, and ultimate divine essence, used in meditation by Hindus and Buddhists.
PAAN betel nut, lime, calcium and aniseed wrapped in a leaf and chewed as a digestive. Mildly addictive.
PADA foot, or base, also a poetic metre.
PADMA lotus; another name for the goddess Lakshmi.
PAGODA multistoreyed Buddhist monument.
PAISE small unit of currency (100 paisa = 1 rupee).
PALANQUIN enclosed sedan chair, shouldered by four men.
PALI original language of early Buddhist texts.
PALLI old mosque or church in Kerala.
PANCHAYAT village council.
PANDA pilgrims' priest.

PARIKRAMA ritual circumambulation around a temple, shrine or mountain.

PARSI Zoroastrian.

PIR Muslim holy man.

POLE fortified gate.

PRADAKSHINA PATHA processional path circling a monument or sanctuary.

PRAKARA enclosure or courtyard in a South Indian temple.

PRANAYAMA breath control, used in meditation.

PRASAD food blessed in temple sanctuaries and shared among devotees.

PRAYAG auspicious confluence of two or more rivers.

PUJA worship.

PUJARI priest.

PUKKA correct and acceptable, in the very English sense of "proper".

PUNYA religious merit.

PURDAH seclusion of Muslim women inside the home, and the general term for wearing a veil.

PURNIMA full moon.

PUROHIT priest.

QABR Muslim grave.

QAWWALI devotional singing popular among sufis.

QILA fort.

RAGA or **RAAG** series of notes forming the basis of a melody.

RAJ rule; monarchy; in particular the period of British imperial rule 1857–1947.

RAJA king.

RAKSHASA demon (demoness: *rakshasi*).

RANGOLI geometrical pattern of rice powder laid before houses and temples.

RATH processional temple chariot of South India.

RAWAL chief priest (Hindu).

RISHI "seer"; philosophical sage or poet.

RUDRAKSHA beads used to make Shiva rosaries.

SADHU Hindu holy man with no caste or family ties.

SAGAR lake.

SAHIB respectful title for gentlemen; general term of address for European men.

SALABHANJIKA wood nymph.

SALWAR KAMISE long shirt and baggy ankle-hugging trousers worn by Muslim women.

SAMADHI final enlightenment; a site of death or burial of a saint.

SAMSARA cyclic process of death and rebirth.

SANGAM sacred confluence of two or more rivers, or an academy.

SANGEET music

SANNYASIN homeless, possessionless ascetic (Hindu).

SARAI resting place for caravans and travellers who once followed the trade routes through Asia.

SARI usual dress for Indian women: a length of cloth wound around the waist and draped over one shoulder.

SAROVAR pond or lake.

SATI one who sacrifices her life on her husband's funeral pyre in emulation of Shiva's wife. No longer a common practice, and officially illegal.

SATSANG teaching given by a religious figurehead.

SATYAGRAHA literally "grasping truth": Gandhi's campaign of non-violent protest.

SCHEDULED CASTES official name for "untouchables".

SEPOY an Indian soldier in European service.

SETH merchant or businessman.

SEVA voluntary service in a temple or community.

SHAIVITE Hindu recognizing Shiva as the supreme god.

SHANKHA conch, symbol of Vishnu.

SHASTRA treatise.

SHIKAR hunting.

SHIKHARA temple tower or spire.

SHISHYA pupil.

SHLOKA verse from a Sanskrit text.

SHRI respectful prefix; another name for Lakshmi.

SHUDRA the lowest of the four castes or *varnas;* servant.

SINGHA lion.

SOMA medicinal herb with hallucinogenic properties used in early Vedic and Zoroastrian rituals.

STAMBHA pillar, or flagstaff.

STHALA site sacred for its association with legendary events.

STUPA large hemispherical mound, representing the Buddha's presence, and often protecting relics of the Buddha or a Buddhist saint.

SURMA black eyeliner, also known as *kohl*.

SURYA the sun, or sun god.

SUTRA (*sutta*) literally "thread": verse in Sanskrit and Pali texts.

SVETAMBARA "white-clad" sect of Jainism, that accepts nuns and shuns nudity.

SWAMI title for a holy man.

SWARAJ "self-rule"; synonym for independence, coined by Gandhi.

TALA rhythmic cycle in classical music; in sculpture a *tala* signifies one face-length; in architecture a storey.

TALUKA district.

TANDAVA vigorous, male form of dance; the dance of Shiva Nataraja.

TANDOOR clay oven.

TAPAS literally "heat": physical and mental austerities.

TEMPO three-wheeled taxi.

THALI combination of vegetarian dishes, chutneys, pickles, rice and bread served, especially in South India, as a single meal; the metal plate on which a meal is served.

THERAVADA "Doctrine of the Elders": the original name for early Buddhism, which persists today in Sri Lanka and Thailand.

TIFFIN light meal.

TIFFIN CARRIER stainless steel set of tins used for carrying meals.

TIKA devotional powder-mark Hindus wear on forehead, usually after *puja*.

TILAK red dot smeared on the forehead during worship, and often used cosmetically.

TIRTHA river crossing considered sacred by Hindus, or the transition from the mundane world to heaven; a place of pilgrimage for Jains.

TIRTHANKARA "ford-maker" or "crossing-maker": an enlightened Jain teacher who is deified – 24 appear every 300 million years.

TOLA the weight of a silver rupee: 180 grains, or approximately 11.6g.

TONGA two-wheeled horse-drawn cart.

TOPI cap.

TORANA arch, or free-standing gateway of two pillars linked by an elaborate arch.

TRIMURTI the Hindu trinity.

TRISHULA Shiva's trident.

TUK fortified enclosure of Jain shrines or temples.

TULKU reincarnated teacher of Tibetan Buddhism.

UNTOUCHABLES members of the lowest strata of society, considered polluting to all higher castes.

URS Muslim saint's day festival.

VAHANA the "vehicle" of a deity; the bull Nandi is Shiva's *vahana*.

VAISHYA member of the merchant and trading caste group.

VARNA literally "colour": one of four hierarchical social categories – *brahmins*, *kshatryas*, *vaishyas* and *shudras*.

VEDAS sacred texts of early Hinduism.

VEDIKA railing around a *stupa*.

VIHARA Buddhist or Jain monastery.

VILASA hall or palace.

VIMANA tower over temple sanctuary.

WADA mansion or palace.

WALLAH suffix implying occupation, eg *dhobi-wallah*, rickshaw *wallah*.

WAZIR chief minister to the king.

YAGNA Vedic sacrificial ritual.

YAKSHA pre-Vedic folklore figure connected with fertility and incorporated into later Hindu iconography.

YAKSHI female *yaksha*.

YALI mythical lion.

YANTRA cosmological pictogram, or model used in an observatory.

YATRA pilgrimage.

YATRI pilgrim.

YOGI *sadhu* or priestly figure possessing occult powers gained through the practice of yoga (female: *yogini*).

YONI symbol of the female sexual organ, set around the base of the *lingam* in temple shrines.

YUGA aeon: the present age is the last in a cycle of four *yugas*, *kali-yuga*, a "black age" of degeneration and spiritual decline.

ZAMINDAR landowner.

ZENANA women's quarters; segregated area for women in a mosque.

USEFUL WORDS AND PHRASES

India has eighteen main languages, over thirty major dialects and around seven hundred other minor languages and dialects. Most Indians are, at least, bilingual, using their own language at home and a mixture of languages at work. Despite efforts to adopt an Indian language (Hindi) as the official language of the country, the South has maintained much of its cultural-linguistic independence by rejecting the northern "imposition" and emphasizing the role of its own vernaculars. This is especially true of Tamil Nadu, where the influence of Hindi has been politically opposed. **Tamil** is the most dominant of the South Indian group of Dravidian languages, and is considered as India's second classical language after Sanskrit. Tamil developed over three distinct phases, with modern Tamil split into a written form and a spoken form. The other Dravidian language closest to Tamil is **Malayalam**, the language of Kerala, which grew out of Tamil but with strong Sanskrit influences. **Telugu**, the language of Andhra Pradesh, is South India's second most spoken language and plays an important role in Dravidian culture as the medium of the great poet-saints and composers of Carnatic music. **Kannada**, the language of most of Karnataka, is the next most spoken Dravidian language, spoken by over thirty million people. Goa has a mixture of languages including Marathi, **Hindi** and its local idiom, **Konkani**. Although Hindi, the language of Delhi and much of the north and centre of the country, is widely spoken and understood everywhere, you won't find it in the far south where you will either have to rely on English or the vernacular language. **Urdu**, the Muslim language of the north and spoken in parts of the Deccan including Andhra Pradesh and Karnataka, is closely related to Hindi except in its higher, literary form, where it differs from Hindi's Sanskritic vocabulary in its predominance of Persian and Arabic words. Despite efforts to impose Hindi as the national language, **English** is widely spoken and is the only language commonly understood throughout the country; it remains the official language of the courts as well as much of commerce and government. English is used by many middle-class Indians as their first language and some communities, like the Anglo-Indians, rarely speak any other.

Most Indian languages use distinct parts of the mouth creating sounds unfamiliar to the native English speaker. One area of pronunciation that is remarkably different is the Indian use of the retroflex where the tongue is struck firmly against the top of the palate creating a hard resonant sound. The retroflex is especially noticeable in "Ts", "Ds" and "Rs" but also used with "Ns" and "Ls" and is more noticeable in Dravidian languages. One curious form of communication, particularly in South India, is the shake of the head. The head loosely rolling from side to side, is a sign of agreement rather than disagreement. This is opposed to a firmer shake of the head which is usually taken to be "no".

TAMIL

Basic Words

Yes	*Aamaam*	What is this/that?	*Idhu/adhu ennaanga*
No	*Illai*	Very good	*Romba nallayirukkudhu*
Goodbye (will return again)	*Varavaanga*	Not bad	*Paravaayillai*
Please	*Koncham dhayavuseydhu*	Come (inviting someone in)	*Vaanaga*
Thanks	*Nauri*	Stop	*Neruthu*
Thank you very much	*Romba nanringa*	These	*Evaikal*
Excuse me	*Enga*	Big	*Pareya*
Pardon	*Mannikkavum*	Small	*Sarreya*
This	*Idhu*	Much	*Athekam*
That	*Adhu*	Little	*Kuvrairu*

Time

Today	*Enrru*	Evening	*Maalai*
Tomorrow	*Naalai*	Monday	*Thengal*
Yesterday	*Neerru*	Tuesday	*Chavvaay*
Day	*Pakal/kezhamai*	Wednesday	*Buthan*
Night	*Eravu*	Thursday	*Veyaacha*
Early morning	*Athekaalai*	Friday	*Valle*
Morning	*Kaalai*	Saturday	*Chane*
Afternoon	*Matiyam*	Sunday	*Gnaayetrru/Kezhama*

USEFUL WORDS AND PHRASES (continued)

TAMIL

Communicating

I don't understand	*Enakku puriyavillaiye*	Could you speak slowly?	*Koncham methuvaa pesuveengalaa*
I understand	*Enakku puriyudhu*		
I don't know Tamil	*Enakku thamizh theriyaathunga*	Could you speak loudly	*Koncham balamaa pesunga*
Do you know someone who knows English?	*Inge aangilam therinchavanga yaaraavadhu irukkiraangalaa?*	What does he say?	*Avar enna sollugiraar*

Food and shopping

I am hungry	*Enakku pasikkudhul*	Tea	*Teyneer*
am thirsty	*Enakku dhaga maayirukkudhu*	Milk	*Paal*
		Sugar	*Sakkaray*
How much is it?	*Athanudaiya vilai enna?*	Water	*Neer*
		Rice	*Arese*
I want only coffee	*Enakku kapi maththi-ram than vendum*	Cooked Rice	*Satham*
		Vegetables	*Kaaykarikal*
Please show me	*Koncham kanpikkireengalaa*	Cooked vegetables	*Kane*
		Curd/yoghurt	*Thayer*
Coffee	*Kaapi*	Coconut	*Thaenkaay*

Directions

Far	*Turam*	Where is the bus stand?	*Bas staandu enge irukkiradhu?*
Near	*Arukkil*		
Where is… ?	*Enge irukkuthunga?*	Where is the train station?	*Tireyn staashan enge irukkuthunga?*
From here is it near?	*Athu ingeyirundhu pakkam thaane?*	Where is the restroom?	*Kakkoos enge irukkudhu*
How far is it from here?	*Athu ingeyirundhu evvalavu dhoora-mayirukkunga?*	Where is the enquiries (information) office?	*Visaranai enge irukki radhu?*
Where can I get an auto?	*Enga auto enga kidaikunga?*	Where is… road?	*... theru enge irukkiradhu?*
What is the charge to get there?	*Empaa, anga povad hukku evvalavu?*	Post office	*Anja lagam*
Where is the bank?	*Vangi enge irukkuthunga?*	Temple	*Kohvil*

Numbers

1	*onru*	16	*pathenaaru*
2	*eranndu*	17	*pathnaezshu*
3	*mundru*	18	*pathenayttu*
4	*naangu*	19	*pathenthonbathu*
5	*iyendhu*	20	*erapathu*
6	*aaru*	30	*muppathu*
7	*aezshu*	40	*naarpathu*
8	*ayttu*	50	*iymbathu*
9	*nbathu*	60	*arupathu*
10	*patthu*	70	*azhupathu*
11	*pathenonrru*	80	*aennapathu*
12	*panereynndu*	90	*thonnoorru*
13	*pathemoonrru*	100	*noorru*
14	*pathenaangu*	1000	*aayeram*
15	*pathenainthu*	100,000	*latcham*

MALAYALAM

Basic Words

Yes	*Aanaate*	Coffee	*Kaappi*
No	*Alla*	Tea	*Chaaya*
Hello	*Namaste*	Milk	*Paalu*
Please	*Dayavuchetu*	Sugar	*Panchasara*
Thank you	*Nanni*	Medicine	*Marunnu*
Excuse me	*Ksamikkuu*	Water	*Vellam*
How much is it?	*Etra?*	Vegetables	*Pachakkari*
I don't understand	*Enikka arriyilla*	Fish	*Meen*
Do you speak English?	*Ninal englisha sam-saarikkumo?*	Curd	*Tairu*
		Rice	*Ari*
My name is...	*Ente pero...*	Banana	*Eyttappalam*
Where is... ?	*Eviteyaannaa?*	Coconut	*Teynna*
How much is it?	*Etra?*		

Numbers

1	*onnu*	20	*irupatu*
2	*randu*	21	*irupattonnu*
3	*muunu*	22	*irupatti-randu*
4	*naalu*	30	*muppatu*
5	*anchu*	31	*muppati-yonnu*
6	*aaru*	40	*nalpatu*
7	*eylu*	50	*anpatu*
8	*ettu*	60	*arupatu*
9	*ombatu*	70	*elapatu*
10	*pattu*	80	*enpatu*
11	*pationnu*	90	*tonnuru*
12	*pantrantu*	100	*nuura*
13	*pati-muunu*	1000	*aayiram*
14–18	*pati-...*	100,000	*laksham*
19	*pattonpattu*		

TELUGU

Basic Words

Yes	*Awunu*	Big	*Pedda*
No	*Kaadu*	Small	*Tsinna*
Goodbye	*Namaskaram*	Today	*Iroju*
Please	*Dayatesi*	Day	*Pagalu*
Thank you	*Dhanyawadalu*	Night	*Raatri*
Excuse me	*Ksamiynchannddi*	Coffee	*Kaafii*
How much is it?	*Enta?*	Tea	*Tti*
What is your name?	*Ni peru eymitti?*	Milk	*Palu*
My name is...	*Naa peru...*	Sugar	*Chakkera*
I don't understand	*Naadu artham kaawattamleydu*	Salt	*Uppu*
		Water	*Nillu*
Do you speak English?	*Miku angalam vaacha?*	Rice	*Biyyamu*
		Fish	*Chepa*
Where is... ?	*Ekkada undi?*	Vegetables	*Kuragayalu*
How far is... ?	*... Enta duram?*		

Numbers

1	*okatti*	4	*naalugu*
2	*renddu*	5	*aaydu*
3	*muddu*	6	*aaru*

USEFUL WORDS AND PHRASES (continued)

TELUGU

Numbers (continued)

7	*eyddu*	40	*nalapay*
8	*enimidi*	50	*yaabay*
9	*tommidi*	60	*aruvay*
10	*padi*	70	*debbay*
11	*pada-kondu*	80	*enabay*
12	*pad-rendu*	90	*tombay*
13 – 19	*pad-…*	100	*nuru/wanda*
20	*iruvay*	200	*renddu-wanda*
21	*iruvay-okatti*	1000	*veyi*
30	*muppay*	100,000	*laksha*
31	*muppay-okati*		

KANNADA

Basic Words

Yes	*Havdu*	Day	*Hagalu*
No	*Illa*	Night	*Raatri*
Hello	*Namaskara*	Today	*Ivattu*
Please	*Dayavittu*	Coffee	*Kaafi*
Thank you	*Vandanegallu*	Tea	*Tea*
Excuse me	*Kshamisi*	Milk	*Haalu*
Stop	*Nillisu*	Sugar	*Sakkare*
How much is it?	*Eshttu?*	Water	*Neeru*
What is your name?	*Nimma hesaru eynu?*	Rice	*Akki*
My name is…	*Nanna hesaru…*	Vegetables	*Tarakari*
Where is… ?	*Ellide?*	Fish	*Massali*
I don't understand	*Nanage artha aagalla*	Coconut water	*Yella-neeru*
Do you speak English?	*Neevu english mataaddtiiraa?*		

Numbers

1	*ondu*	20	*ippattu*
2	*eradu*	21	*ippattondu*
3	*mooru*	30	*muvattu*
4	*naalku*	31	*muvattondu*
5	*aydu*	40	*naalvattu*
6	*aaru*	50	*aivattu*
7	*eylu*	60	*aravattu*
8	*entu*	70	*eppattu*
9	*ombhattu*	80	*embattu*
10	*hattu*	90	*tombattu*
11	*hannondu*	99	*tombattombattu*
12	*hanneradu*	100	*nooru*
13	*hadi- mooru*	1000	*ondu saavira*
14 – 18	*hadi-…*	100,000	*laksha*
19	*hattombhattu*		

KONKANI

Basic Words

Yes	*Hoee*	Please	*Upkar kor*
No	*Na*	Thank you	*Dio borem korunc*
Hello	*Paypadta*	Excuse me	*Upkar korkhi*
Goodbye	*Miochay*	How much?	*Kitlay?*

How much does it cost?	*Kitlay poisha lakthele?*	Tea	*Chai*
I don't want it	*Mhaka naka tem*	Milk	*Dudh*
I don't understand	*Mhaka kay samzona na*	Sugar	*Shakhar*
		No sugar	*Shakhar naka*
Where is… ?	*Khoy aasa?*	Rice	*Tandul*
Beach	*Prayia*	Water	*Oodak*
Road	*Rosto*	Coconut	*Nal*
Coffee	*Kaafi*	Tender coconut	*Adzar*

Numbers

1	*ek*	10	*dha*
2	*dohn*	20	*vees*
3	*teen*	30	*tees*
4	*char*	40	*cha-ees*
5	*paanch*	50	*po-nas*
6	*soh*	100	*chem-bor*
7	*saht*	1000	*ek-azaar*
8	*ahrt*	100,000	*laakh*
9	*nou*		

HINDI/URDU

(Not spoken in Tamil Nadu, Kerala, Karnataka (except in the northeast) or much of Andhra Pradesh)

Basic Words and phrases

Greetings (said with palms together at chest height as in prayer – not used for Muslims)	*Namaste*	Bad	*Kharaab*
		My name is…	*Mera nam… hai*
		What is your name? (formal)	*Aapka naam kya hai?*
		What is your name? (familiar)	*Yumhara naam kya hai?*
Greetings (to a Muslim)	*Aslaam alequm*	I don't understand	*Samaj nahin aayaa*
in reply	*U ale qum aslaam*	It is OK	*Thiik hai*
We will meet again (goodbye)	*Phir milenge*	How much?	*Kitna?*
		Where is the… ?	*… Kahaan hai?*
Goodbye (to a Muslim)	*Khudaa Haafiz* (may god bless you)	How far?	*Kitnaa duur?*
		Stop	*Ruko*
How are you? (formal)	*Aap kaise hain*	Wait	*Thero*
How are you? (familiar)	*Kya hal hai*	Medicine	*Dawaaii*
Brother (a common address to a stranger)	*Bhaaii / bhaayaa*	Pain	*Dard*
		Stomach	*Pet*
Sister	*Didi*	Eye	*Aankh*
Sir (Sahib)	*Saaheb*	Nose	*Naakh*
Yes	*Haan*	Ear	*Kaan*
OK/good	*Achhaa*	Back	*Piit*
No	*Nahiin*	Foot	*Paao*
How much	*Kitna*		

Numbers

1	*ek*	8	*aatth*
2	*do*	9	*now*
3	*tin*	10	*das*
4	*char*	100	*saw*
5	*paanch*	1000	*hazaar*
6	*chey*	100,000	*laakh*
7	*saat*		

INDEX

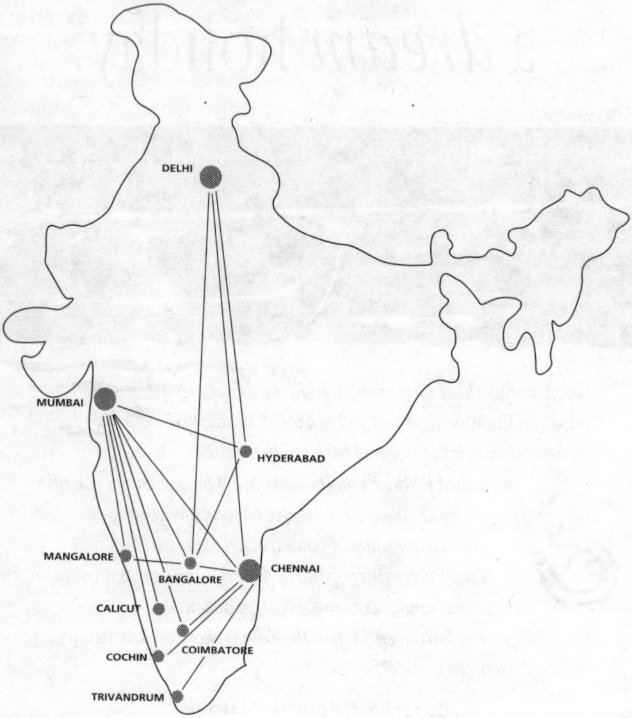

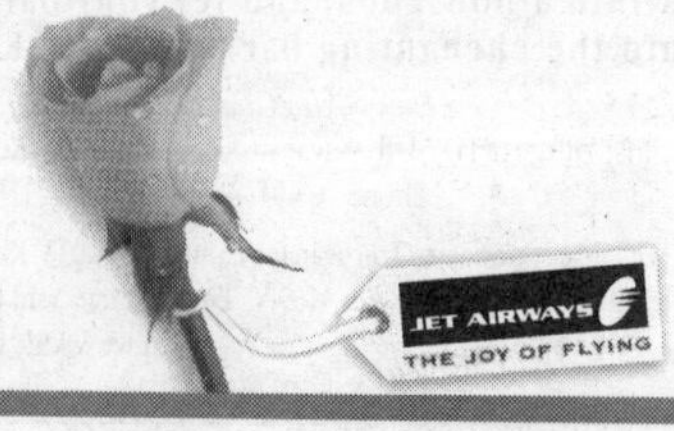

NUTSHELLS

European Union Law

Titles in the Nutshell Series

A Level Law
Company Law
Constitutional and Administrative Law
Consumer Law
Contract Law
Criminal Law
Employment Law
English Legal System
Environmental Law
Equity and Trusts
European Union Law
Evidence
Family Law
Human Rights
Intellectual Property Law
International Law
Land Law
Medical Law
Tort

Titles in the Nutcase Series

Constitutional and Administrative Law
Contract Law
Criminal Law
Employment Law
Equity and Trusts
European Union Law
Evidence
Family Law
Human Rights
International Law
Land Law
Medical Law
Tort

NUT**SHELLS**

European Union Law

SEVENTH EDITION

by
MIKE CUTHBERT, LLM, BSc (ECON), BA (Law)
formerly Senior Tutor in Law
University of Northampton

SWEET & MAXWELL

First edition – 1994
Second edition – 1997
Third edition – 2000
Fourth edition – 2003
Fifth edition – 2006
Sixth edition – 2009

Published in 2012 by Sweet & Maxwell
part of Thomson Reuters (Professional) UK Limited
(Registered in England and Wales, Company No. 1679046.
Registered Office and address for service:
Aldgate House, 33 Aldgate High Street, London EC3N 1DL)

For further information on our products and services, visit
www.sweetandmaxwell.co.uk

Typeset by YHT Ltd
Printed in Great Britain by
Ashford Colour Press, Gosport, Hants

No natural forests were destroyed to make this product;
only farmed timber was used and re-planted

A CIP catalogue record for this book is available from the British Library.

ISBN: 978-0-414-02296-6

Contents

Using this Book

Welcome to our new look **NUTSHELLS** revision series. We have revamped and improved the existing design and layout and added new features, according to student feedback.

NEW DETAILED TABLE OF CONTENTS for easy navigation.

Contents

REDESIGNED TABLES OF CASES AND LEGISLATION for easy reference.

Table of Cases

DEFINITION CHECKPOINTS, EXPLANATION OF KEY CASES AND LEGISLATION HIGHLIGHTERS to highlight important information.

... REMEDIES

...terim injunctions

DEFINITION CHECKPOINT

Although an application for summary judgme... IPR proprietor, an interim injunction can ofte... remedy to an IP rightholder. This and the fac... disputes do not progress beyond the interim... by the old terminology—"interlocutory s... injunctions are particularly important in IP...

standard guidance as to when an int... ... American Cyanamid v Eth...

...struction under oat... ...warded in interim proceedings. ...this remedy can be ordered against an... that the patent is inextricably entwined.

KEY CASE

KIRIN-AMGEN INC V TRANSKARYOTIC THEARAPIES...
In *Kirin-Amgen Inc v Transkaryotic Thearap...* cells carrying small amounts of patented prote... delivery up.

(c) Court order for a party to reveal relev... Procedure Rules (rule 31) such an ord... example, the name and addre... ...th the tradition...

... on July 22, 2004, ... some of which are discussed... ...0(1) was inserted by the Patent Act ... ...nventions. Alongside the addition to the ... to the Patent Rules.

LEGISLATION HIGHLIGHTER

The Patent Rules 2007 (No. 3291), Patent (... and Patents (Compulsory Licensing an... Certificate) Regulations 2007 (No. 3293)... patent system.

...ING A PATENT

DIAGRAMS, FLOWCHARTS AND OTHER DIAGRAMMATIC representation to clarify and condense complex and important information and break up the text.

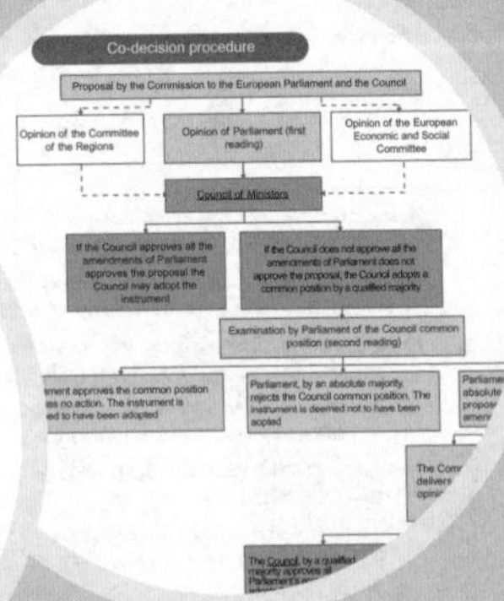

... EU LAW ...
...are the players and wh... their roles?

Role of European Commission as INITIATOR

COR European Parliament ECOSOC

First Reading

COUNCIL OF MINISTERS

...ouncil Approves Council Does Not Approve

Adopts Common P...

END OF CHAPTER REVISION CHECKLISTS outlining what you should now know and understand.

END OF CHAPTER QUESTION AND ANSWER SECTION with advice on relating knowledge to examination performance, how to approach the question, how to structure the answer, the pitfalls (and how to avoid them!) and how to get the best marks.

HANDY HINTS AND USEFUL WEBSITES—revision and examination tips and advice relating to the subject features at the end of the book, along with a list of useful websites.

NEW COLOUR CODING throughout to help distinguish cases and legislation from the narrative. At the first mention, cases are highlighted in colour and italicised and legislation is highlighted in colour and emboldened.

...ses (*Ocular Science v Aspe...*
interface with a socket would also b...
See also *Dyson Ltd v Qualtex Ltd* (2004,...

(iii) "Must match" designs are excluded, *i.e.* ...
"features of shape or configuration which are...
ance of another article of which the article...
to form an integral part" (**CDPA 1988**, s.21...
features which need to be made in a certain...
will be excluded (e.g. see *Mark Wilkinson Fur...*
(1998). See also *Dyson Ltd v Qualtex Ltd* (200...
also be excluded under "must match".

(iv) Surface decoration (**CDPA 1988**, s.213(...
subsist in surface decoration such as a pair...
of an article (*Mark Wilkinson Furniture*...

...fit" and "must match" e...

Table of Cases

Table of United Kingdom Legislation

Table of European Legislation

Conventions and Treaties

Regulations

Directives

Introduction

1

The study of European law does cause anxiety for some students because it seems to be so different from the common law approach that they are familiar with from their other studies of English law. However, as a member of the European Union the United Kingdom is bound to follow EU law and its courts must provide a remedy for those who seek to enforce it or claim rights under it.

An understanding of European law is considered so important that the professional legal bodies representing solicitors and barristers in the UK have made it a compulsory subject for all those students who wish to qualify as a legal professional. This is in recognition that not only businesses but also individuals are affected by European law in their everyday lives as employees or consumers.

To support your understanding of European law this book attempts to provide an overview of the key definitions, cases and principles that have been developed since the 1950s. The chapters contain a short introduction plus a list of the key points that you should familiarise yourself with. Key points and cases are boxed to show the importance they have for the topic.

All this is preparation for you to understand European law better and to help you prepare for examinations or assessments. Each chapter has a question that can be used to test yourself with a list of main points that you should include in your answer.

The most recent EU Treaty is the **Treaty of Lisbon** and this is explained and analysed in the appropriate chapters of this book. The outcome of the **Treaty of Lisbon** is two separate documents—the **Treaty on European Union (TEU)** and the **Treaty on the Functioning of the EU (TFEU)**. This is to some extent a compromise because of the failure to ratify a constitutional treaty in 2008 and it means that there is not the single document that was envisaged when the reform process started in 2001.

The European Union Institutions

2

INTRODUCTION

When the **TEU** came into force on November 1, 1993 it became legally correct to refer to the European Community (EC). The word "economic" was dropped to reflect the fact that there has been a change of emphasis towards non-economic provisions such as citizenship. It also became usual to refer to the European Union at the expense of the European Community. There were originally three Communities, with the European Coal & Steel Community (ECSC) being established in 1952 and the EC together with EURATOM coming in 1957. However, the ECSC had a fixed life of 50 years so it ceased to exist in 2002. The policy areas of coal and steel have been subsumed into the EC Treaty. Thus we now have two Communities, but the European Community is the most important pillar of the EU and the **EC Treaty,** as amended by the **TEU** and **TFEU,** still dominates. This will be observed in this book, as you will see repeated reference to the **EC Treaty**. (Chapter 12 looks at the **TEU** and its subsequent amendment by the Treaty of Amsterdam, the Treaty of Nice and more importantly the **Treaty of Lisbon** in more detail see p.124.)

In 1952 the first of the European Communities was established in the form of the European Coal and Steel Community (ECSC). Although this had followed on from other bodies established by an international agreement, such as the Council of Europe (1949), the development of this Community was characterised by a clear transfer of rights to special institutions. These rights had been previously seen as sovereign to national governments. In 1957 the European Economic Community (now simply the European Community under the **TEU**) and EURATOM were established. Initially the three European Communities had different institutions and in the case of the Commission a different name in the sense that for the purposes of the ECSC it was called the High Authority. The Merger Treaty of 1965 that made the institutions common to all three Communities changed all this. The Three Pillars of the **TEU** were replaced by the **Treaty of Lisbon** in 2009 to reflect the failure of the implementation of the Convention on the Future of the European Union proposals in the Constitutional Treaty. This is discussed in more detail in Ch.12. Although we now have a European Union it is still common to refer to the European Community as it is built upon the dominance of the European Community Treaty.

EUROPEAN PARLIAMENT

It is Pt 6 of the **Lisbon Treaty** which lays out the "Institutional Provisions". The first institution dealt with is the European Parliament (EP), although it was initially referred to as the European Assembly. Perhaps, given the democratic underpinning that is now explicitly stated in art.10 **TEU**, we now assume this to be essential for the EU, but the original Parliament was not democratically elected nor did it fulfil any of the functions we might identify as the characteristics of a parliament, of any tradition. The membership was originally nominated by the governments of the Member States (MS) to exercise advisory and supervisory powers. However, its place as the first institution in Pt 6 may have more significance for the "vision" of Europe shared by the authors of the Treaty. The current discussions between those who see the Community as having a purely economic function as against those with a wider political "federal" viewpoint have their philosophical base in the Treaty. The original Parliament was very weak because the establishment and success of the EC depended upon a strong role for the governments of the MS and thus the Council of Ministers. However, having recognised the need for a "democratic" institution in the Treaty it was possible to strengthen its powers and thus its role over time. This is what happened and is happening with regard to the European Parliament.

The **Lisbon Treaty** did not come into effect until after the 2009 elections to the EP so those elections took place on the old allocation of EP seats. Article 14(2) **TEU** states that there shall be a maximum of 750 MEPs with a minimum threshold of 6 and a maximum of 96 seats for any MS. This allocation is based on the relative size of population for each MS and is shown in Table 2.1 below. When the **Treaty of Lisbon** did come into force an Inter-Governmental Conference was held on June 23, 2010 to allow the additional MEPs to take up their seats with all the MEPs coming up for election in 2014. Therefore there will be an adjustment to the number of MEPs between now and 2014. The allocation of MEPs to MS no longer appears in the Treaties as art.14(2) **TEU** allows the Council by unanimity, on the initiative and consent of the EP, to decide on the composition of the EP. Direct elections specified under art.14(3) **TEU** have taken place every five years since 1979.

The original delegates, nominated by Member States, have been replaced by directly elected Members of the European Parliament (MEPs) who represent their constituents. All elections to the European Parliament are based on the principle of proportional representation, unlike under the

Table 2.1 Number of Representatives by Member State 2009–2014

Belgium	22
Bulgaria	18
Czech Republic	22
Denmark	13
Germany	96
Estonia	6
Greece	22
Spain	54
France	74
Ireland	12
Italy	73
Cyprus	6
Latvia	9
Lithuania	12
Luxembourg	6
Hungary	22
Malta	6
Netherlands	26
Austria	19
Poland	51
Portugal	22
Romania	33
Slovenia	8
Slovakia	13
Finland	13
Sweden	20
United Kingdom	73

Source: Inter-Governmental Conference June 23, 2010

normal British principle of "first past the post". This led to the novel introduction on the British mainland of the results of the 1999 European Parliamentary elections being based on a "list" system rather than the traditional "one MEP—one constituency" of previous elections in Britain. Since the introduction of direct elections in 1979 it is obvious that the character of the European Parliament has changed. This is reflected not only in the procedures that the MEPs have adopted for themselves where they have become more professional, but also in the demands they have made to increase their role and powers within the Community. MEPs basically want to have the role of a "parliament". Although this concept varies between the Member States, the common characteristic is the role in the legislative process and the accountability of the "government" to the MEPs. There is no "government" in the national sense within the EU, thus the emphasis has been on the involvement in the legislative process and the approval of the EU budget. The Single European Act (SEA) recognised this and introduced the cooperation procedure as one of the legislative procedures. The **TEU** took this a step further with the co-decision procedure and the subsequent Treaty of Amsterdam and **Treaty of Nice** have consolidated this development. The failed Constitutional Treaty 2004, discussed in Ch.10, was intended to take this further but this has now been achieved by the **Treaty of Lisbon**. Article 14(1) **TEU** states that the EP shall exercise jointly with the Council the legislative and budgetary functions of the EU.

DECISION-MAKING PROCEDURES

The role of the European Parliament has increased with the **Treaty of Lisbon** and it now participates as an equal with the Council in the legislative and budgetary process associated with art.288 **TFEU**. Article 225 **TFEU** gives the EP the authority to request the Commission to submit any appropriate proposal on matters that it considers that the Union should act. Previously this was something only the Council of Ministers could do (see art.241 **TFEU**). Requests have to be made to the European Commission because under the Treaty they are given the role of initiator and producer of draft proposals.

As a result of increasing the powers of the European Parliament the Community's decision-making procedures became very complex, but the **Treaty of Lisbon** has simplified this dramatically by concentrating on what was called the Co-decision, but is now referred to as the "ordinary legislative procedure" (art.289 **TFEU**). There are other decision-making procedures, which vary with the area of legislation under consideration.

Consultation: This is the original procedure with a single Parliamentary reading that was laid down by the **EC Treaty** in 1957. The voting in the Council of Ministers has to be unanimous.

The Ordinary Legislative Procedure (previously the Co-decision): (Article 294 **TFEU**) This is the most important procedure with regard to legislation. The Co-decision procedure was introduced by the **TEU** in 1993 and extensively developed by the **Treaty of Amsterdam** and the **Treaty of Nice**. Under this procedure the Parliament is given the power to prevent legislation being

HOW IS EU LAW MADE?
Who are the players and what are their roles?

Role of European Commission as INITIATOR

COR European Parliament ESC
First Reading

COUNCIL OF MINISTERS

Council Approves

Council Does Not Approve
Adopts Common Position

European Parliament
Second Reading

European Parliament
Proposes Amendments

Conciliation Committee
IF NO AGREEMENT THE MEASURE FALLS

adopted. Generally qualified majority voting (qmv) is required in the Council except on two issues where unanimity applies. (See Ch.3 below, p.27). Examples of policy areas now under the co-decision procedures include: transport policy; development aid; Trans-European Networks; employment policy; public health; and equal opportunities.

Assent: The **SEA** originally introduced this procedure, but its scope has been increased by the **TEU**. It applies in the case of international agreements, Treaty decisions and accession of new members. It means that the European Parliament must agree for the proposal to be implemented. An example is art.49 **TEU** which states that the EP must consent to any new MS.

Budget: This is covered by a procedure in arts 313–319 **TFEU**, which gives equal authority to the European Parliament in relation to budgetary matters. See the EP and the Union's Annual Budget below, p.10.

However, whatever weight is given to the views of the European Parliament, the right to be consulted must be respected. Failure to follow this procedural requirement may lead to the measure being declared invalid. This happened in the cases of Case 138/79 *Roquette v Council* and Case 139/79 *Maizena v Council*, both reported in 1980.

The European Parliament has certain characteristics similar to national parliaments. There are a number of standing committees that mirror the major policy areas of the Community. These committees carry out investigations and hear evidence from experts and interested parties, including the Commission. They also issue reports. In addition parliamentary questions are an important element of control over the Commission. Under art.230 **TFEU** the Commission must reply orally or in writing to questions put to it by MEPs. In fact the Council and foreign ministers also take part in this process. It is common practice now for the President of the Council of Ministers to make a statement at the commencement of their Presidency outlining their objectives and to report to the Parliament at the end of their term on the outcomes.

Ordinary Legislative Procedure

Proposal by the Commission to the European Parliament and the Council

Opinion of the Committee of the Regions

Opinion of Parliament (first reading)

Opinion of the European Economic and Social Committee

Council of Ministers

If the Council approves all the amendments of Parliament approves the proposal the Council may adopt the instrument

If the Council does not approve all the amendments of Parliament does not approve the proposal, the Council adopts a common position by a qualified majority

Examination by Parliament of the Council common position (second reading)

Parliament approves the common position of takes no action. The instrument is deemed to have been adopted

Parliament, by an absolute majority, rejects the Council common position. The instrument is deemed not to have been adopted

Parliament, by an absolute majority, proposes amendments

The Commission delivers a positive opinion

The Commission delivers a negative opinion

The Council, by a qualified majority approves all Parliament's amendments and adopts the instrument

The Council does not approve all Parliament's amendments. By mutual agreement, the presidents of the Council and of Parliament convene a meeting of the Conciliation Commitee. The Commission participates in its work

The Council unanimously approves all Parliament's amendments and adopts the instrument.

The Conciliation Committee reaches an agreement. Parliament, by an absolute majority, and the Council, by a qualified majority, adopt the instrument. If either of these two institutions fails to approve the instrument, it is deemed not to have been adopted

The Conciliation Committee does not reach an agreement. The instrument is deemed not to have been adopted

KEY CASE

Case 138/79 Roquette v Council and Case 139/79 Maizena v Council

The Council had sent a proposal to the EP for a measure it wished to enter into force on July 1, 1979. There was a delay in the EP due to the opinion of the Parliamentary Agriculture Committee being rejected in the plenary session. The EP offered to have a special meeting to approve the measure but the Council ignored this and adopted the measure on June 25, 1979. In its judgment the ECJ stated that the requirement of consultation implies that the Parliament has expressed its opinion. This had not happened so the Court declared the measure void.

European Ombudsman

As with national parliaments, those who are affected by particular policies or proposals can complain to their representative. The **TEU** allows for such petitions to be made to their MEP but in addition there is the provision in art.228 **TEFU** for the appointment by the EP of an Ombudsman to deal with complaints from any citizen of the Union, including those undertakings with a registered office in a Member State. The complaints can deal with any instances of maladministration. This encompasses the activities of all Community institutions and bodies, excluding the ECJ and General Court when acting in their judicial role.

European Parliament and the Commission

The original treaties of the then EC made the European Commission responsible to the European Parliament but now the EP has to approve the appointment of first the President of the Commission and the other Commissioners (art.17(7) **TEU**). Once appointed by the Member States and the EP the 27 Commissioners can only be removed by the EP passing a censure motion by a two-thirds majority vote and an absolute majority of its members under art.234 **TFEU**. Such a motion successfully passed would force the resignation of the whole Commission. Although threatened on occasion this has never happened, however, in order to avoid the motion of censure the Commission can resign, as it did on March 16, 1999 when the Commission headed by President Santer resigned at a time of accusations of fraud against particular Commissioners (See "Commissioners" below, p.14). Edith Cresson, one of the Commissioners accused, was found by the European Court of Justice in July 2006 to have been in breach of her obligations when holding that office by appointing her dental surgeon to positions that he was not qualified or experienced to hold (*Commission v Cresson* Case C-432/04).

European Parliament and the Community Budget

The right of the European Parliament to make changes to the budget in the past depended on the distinction between expenditure which is "compulsory" and other expenditure which is "non-compulsory". Compulsory expenditure covered that expenditure which is committed under Treaty provisions or Community legislation, e.g. the **Common Agricultural Policy**. Parliament could only propose modifications to this category of expenditure, thus giving the Council the final say in such matters. However, non-compulsory expenditure which included all expenditure which is not the inevitable consequences of Community legislation, could be amended by the majority of MEPs voting in favour of such proposals. This expenditure includes the Union's social policy, regional and industrial policies, and accounts for about 43 per cent of the total budget. For this type of expenditure it was the European Parliament that had the final control. Therefore, although the Parliament did have some powers of approval as far as the budget was concerned, these were weak with regard to compulsory expenditure, which is the vast majority of the total budget.

In 1975 the European Parliament was given increased powers in relation to the Union's budget by a conciliation procedure. The aim of these powers was to give the Parliament more effective participation in the budgetary process, by seeking agreement between the Parliament and the Council of Ministers. If the Parliament refused to pass the budget as presented to it by the Council, a number of important consequences followed. First, the budget could not be implemented, which had implications for the expenditure level of the Community which is limited to one-twelfth of the previous year's budget per month (see art.315 **TFEU**). Second, a "conciliation committee", consisting of the Council and representatives of the European Parliament was established to try to resolve the disagreement. The European Commission assisted the work of this committee.

Ultimately the Parliament could reject the budget outright by a two-thirds vote cast by a majority of its members. Although it may reject it, the Parliament could not increase the total amount of the budget beyond the maximum rate of increase set by the Commission, unless the alteration was agreed by the Council. In 1988, in an attempt to improve the budgetary procedure, an Institutional Agreement was entered into by the Council, Commission and the European Parliament. While recognising the varying competencies of the institutions in the budgetary field, it fixed new rules for co-operation between the institutions. The **Treaty of Lisbon** treats the budget like any other piece of legislation so the difference in types of expenditure has been removed. The current procedure is in art.314 **TFEU** with the Commission submitting a draft budget to both the EP and the Council. The Council then adopts its position and this is forwarded to the EP, which can either approve it or propose amendments. If the Council does not approve the EP's amendments then a Conciliation Committee is convened with equal membership from both institutions. As can be seen this is the same as the "ordinary legislative procedure" so the Commission can take initiatives in order to reconcile the two views. If there is no agreement then the budget is not adopted and the restrictions on expenditure under art.315 **TFEU** would apply. This review of the budgetary powers of the EP illustrates the increased authority that has been given to the EP by successive treaties.

The Council or the Council of Ministers

Article 13 **TEU** refers to the Council but previously this institution was referred to as the Council of Ministers which is a more accurate description. It is specifically covered in art.16 **TEU** and arts 204–243 **TFEU**. This is the main political institution of the EU. Its membership is made up of one representative of each of the 27 Member States. Although the main representative is the foreign minister of each Member State, the actual minister varies with the main business of the meeting. Thus if the **Common Agricultural Policy** is being discussed it will be the agricultural ministers who will attend and so on. In all there are nine different Council configurations. The presidency of the Council used to be held in rotation by each Member State for a period of six months although attempts have been made to introduce "Team Presidencies". The **Treaty of Lisbon** introduced greater authority to the position of the High Representative for Foreign Affairs and Security Policy (see below) and this person chairs the foreign ministers when they meet as the Foreign Affairs Council, but with this exception the representative of the Member State holding the Presidency will always chair the meetings during this period. This has been criticised on the grounds that the period is too short for individual ministers to acquire expertise in the role. There has been an attempt to resolve some of these problems by having greater coordination between the past, current and future Presidencies. This is often referred to as the "troika format".

Voting Procedures However, the main discussion and action involving the Council of Ministers has centred on its voting procedures. There are two voting procedures for the Council; unanimous and qualified majority voting (qmv). Some areas of policy specified in the Treaties require unanimity and these include taxation and asylum and immigration. Where unanimity is required it does provide a "veto" on the part of any MS (see below) but it was felt that this slowed down the development of the Union and so the **Treaty of**

Nice reduced quite drastically the number of such policy areas. In the first **EC Treaty** it was envisaged that the Council would move, after the transitional period, to majority voting except for those specific matters identified by the Treaty as requiring unanimity. This was not to be a simple majority but a qualified one (qmv) on the basis of art.238 **TFEU**. Protocol 36 on Transitional Provisions provides the details of the allocation of votes to each Member State depending roughly upon the size of its population but with a minimum of three votes for the smallest country, Malta. The "big four" of France, Germany, Italy and the UK have 29 votes. On any issue before the Council it requires a combination of the larger and smaller Member States to accumulate the necessary votes to adopt the measure. This seeks to ensure that no interest group in the Council can dominate the voting and encourages a compromise in the sense that the measure must be acceptable to a range of Member States. The necessary voting majority at present is 255 or 73.9 per cent in favour of the measure. In preparation for enlargement in 2004 the **Treaty of Nice** introduced the possibility of a member of the Council requesting that such a majority vote also constitutes 62 per cent of the total population of the EU. This is retained in art.3(3) of the protocol and if the figure of 62 per cent is not met the act in question will not be adopted. (See Ch.12—"The TEU and Beyond", p.124.)

"Veto" The intention of the Treaty was hindered by the events of 1966 that led to the Luxembourg Accord or Compromise, which was instituted to obtain the co-operation of the French government in the working of the EC. This recognition of a "veto" in the sense that unanimity was required on particular issues not specified as requiring them under the Treaty, slowed down the actions of the Council in that it could not proceed faster than its slowest participating government. The governments of Denmark, Ireland, the UK, Greece, Portugal and Spain who joined in the 1970s and 1980s assumed that they did so with a power of veto on issues they considered important to them. Although they were politically shocked on occasions when they were thwarted in their attempts to exercise it, it was not until the **SEA** that attempts were made to speed up the decision-making process of the Council. For example, art.100(a) (now repealed) provided the legal base for adopting the measures necessary for the establishment and functioning of the internal market, and was passed to meet the target date of January 1, 1993 for completing this objective. Although academic debate still continues on whether the veto still exists, it is important to recognise the political nature of the Council. If the President of the Council is aware of the political implications of calling for a vote where a minority of the Council have strong objections, it is likely that such a vote will be postponed for further discussion.

The European Union Act 2011

There is a mechanism under the "Simplified revision procedure" of art.48(6) **TEU** which allows for changes to the Treaties which in effect amount to a transfer of powers or competences from the MS without the need for a formal treaty amendment procedure. Any MS, the EP or the Commission may submit to the European Council such proposals as long as they do not increase the competences conferred on the Union by the Treaties. However, they do affect how decisions are made and this raised concerns with the UK government. Specifically, the UK government thought that this simplified revision procedure could be used to permit qualified majority voting in place of unanimity. The **TEU** and **TFEU** are large documents and there are within them certain articles which are referred to a "passerelles" or "rachet clauses". These can be used to transfer competences from the MS to the EU and thus be subject to qmv. The **2011 European Union Act** provides the possibility of a positive referendum vote having to take place in the UK before the UK can agree to such action.

Democratic Control

As the European Parliament, as indicated above, has gained more authority in the legislative process it has been at the reduction of that held by the Council. Some politicians see the control of national parliaments over their government ministers as being the democratic control element of the Community. Such politicians see the European Parliament as a weak alternative and do not welcome changes to the relationship with the Council which they feel weakens the status of the Member State governments. In the UK the analogy is of the Westminster Parliament becoming like a county or local council in relation to the European Parliament. The **Constitutional Treaty 2004** would have given more authority to national parliaments than they have at present but that Treaty has not been ratified. However, art.12 **TEU** and Protocol 1 to the **TFEU** do give a greater role to national parliaments in a number of ways. The communications between national parliaments and EU institutions is to be improved with draft Union legislative acts to be sent to them in good time for them to submit their opinions. This also has links with the principle of subsidiary (Protocol 2) which emphasises that some decisions may be more appropriate at national rather than EU level.

However, given the important role of the Council of Ministers is it realistic to expect the national government ministers to play a significant role in developing EU policy as against making decisions to adopt such policies or legislation? If you look at any British minister who may be involved in a meeting of the Council of Ministers, he is in charge of a government department and takes part in debates and answers questions in the House of Commons or in exceptional cases the House of Lords. As an MP there are constituent problems and interests to deal with. How much time is there for EC matters? Obviously there has to be some time because it is part of the minister's job, but a great deal of the work of the Council of Ministers is undertaken by the Committee of Permanent Representatives or COREPER.

Committee of Permanent Representatives (COREPER)

Article 240 **TFEU** identifies the key role of this group of diplomats who represent the views or interests of their particular government. They liaise with the various government ministries and bring these views to the discussions which take place in Brussels. The idea is that when the Council of Ministers meets much of the preliminary discussion has taken place and the Ministers can concentrate on those issues which may require a political compromise or are politically sensitive. Thus the Council's agenda will have "A" items, which have already been agreed in principle and "B" items where further discussion by the ministers is necessary to get agreement.

European Commission

The European Commissioners are sometimes described as a kind of European civil servant. However, this is too simplistic as civil servants are merely expected to carry out the wishes of their political masters. Although the European Commission acts as the executive of the EU by implementing the policies decided by the Council and the European Parliament, they must make proposals as to what those policies should be. Such proposals made by the Commissions are not always welcomed by the Council in the sense that they take a European stance against the perceived interests of the individual Member States. Much of the impetus for the legislation for the completion of the internal market came from the Commission as well as the move towards a "federal Europe". There are also examples where the authority of the EU has been extended to the embarrassment of some Member States, e.g. the directives dealing with beaches or water purity.

Commissioners There are 27 Commissioners in total, with one being nominated by each Member State. It is usual for Commissioners to have held high political office in their national governments, although once appointed they are required to act independently in the best interests of the EU and not for any individual country (art.17(3) **TEU**). From January 7, 1995 the term of office was extended to five years, to synchronise with the term of the European Parliament. Commissioners can be re-appointed. The Maastricht Treaty required that Parliament had to approve the appointment of the Commission and be consulted by the Member States before the President was nominated. This was strengthened by the **Treaty of Amsterdam,** which required the EP to approve the appointment of the President of the

Commission. The President-elect of the Commission was then consulted by the Member States before they nominated the remaining Commissioners. Although the Commission acts as a collegiate body, each Commissioner is allocated a portfolio from the directorate-generals covering all Community policies. The problems in the Santer Commission in 1999 led to the strengthening of importance of the position of the President of the Commission so that he could reshuffle the allocation of the responsibilities of the Commissioners and with the approval of the rest of the Commission he could ask for an individual Commissioner to resign. The current position has consolidated this relationship in art.17 **TEU** whereby the European Council, after taking into account the elections to the EP, propose to the EP a candidate for the position of President of the Commission. This person has to be approved by the EP otherwise the European Council must nominate another candidate. The person appointed to be President of the Commission then plays a role in the selection of the other Commissions put forward by the MS. These Commissioners must also be approved by the EP before they can be appointed by the European Council acting by qualified voting. The President allocates the portfolios of the Commissioners and a member of the Commission shall resign if the President so requests.

Duties of the Commission Article 17 **TEU** and arts 244–250 **TFEU** deal with the European Commission. It is art.17 **TEU** that shows the wide range of duties imposed on the Commission. The Commission initiate policies by making proposals, but they also act as the executive arm of the Community once a proposal has been adopted by an administrative act under art.288 **TFEU**. They are the "guardians of the Treaty". This covers not only questions concerning the relationship between the institutions, but more specifically the Enforcement Action under art.258 **TFEU** and Competition Policy of the EC. Both of these topics are dealt with in Ch.8, p.85. The Commission is responsible to the EP and art.234 **TFEU** facilitates the EP passing a motion of censure to remove the whole Commission as a body, as mentioned above. There is also the possibility of the European Court of Justice under art.247 **TFEU** compulsorily retiring a Commissioner who can no longer perform their duties or is guilty of serious misconduct.

High Representative of the Union for Foreign Affairs and Security Policy This new post was created by the **Treaty of Lisbon** when it came into force on December 1, 2009. The **Treaty of Amsterdam** had introduced such a post, held by Javier Solana in 1999, but the role has been widened and given more prestige. The first incumbent is Baroness Catherine Ashton who has been appointed for a five year period. In addition to chairing the Foreign Affairs Council, she has to develop the European External Action Service

(EEAS) to provide a coordinated and consistent policy reflecting the Union's external action.

European Court of Justice

The European Court of Justice is the final main institution of the EU and fulfils the judicial role necessary to ensure that Community law is observed. In fact art.19 **TEU** is very short and states:

> "The Court of Justice of the EU shall include the Court of Justice, the General Court and specialised courts. It shall ensure that in the interpretation and application of the Treaties the law is observed. Member States shall provide remedies sufficient to ensure effective legal protection in the fields of Union law".

This is achieved via specific direct and indirect actions, which are discussed in the chapters dealing with Preliminary References and Judicial Review (Ch.6, p.60). However, the important points to note at this stage are the membership and procedures of the Court of Justice (ECJ) and the General Court. The main influences in the early formative years of the Court were the German but more predominantly the French legal tradition. This is shown in the fact that the working language of the Court is French, but more importantly in the office of Advocates-Generals.

Judges There are 27 judges in the ECJ with each Member State providing one judge. Appointed for a term of six years, the judges elect their own President of the Court who serves in that post for three years. Like all posts within the Court it is possible for the period in office to be renewed. Although this fixed but renewable term of office is not found in English courts, the attributes the judges should have are the same. Article 253 **TFEU** specifies, "they should be independent and qualified for the highest judicial office within their respective countries". However, an important difference is that whereas English judges are selected from barristers, and to a lesser extent solicitors, judges in some Member States are chosen from a much wider field, including academic lawyers. Thus when the judges in the European Court deliberate they are bringing together a variety of legal backgrounds which would not be found in an English court.

Advocates-Generals The post of Advocate-General is derived from the French legal system and is unknown in English law. There are eight Advocates-Generals appointed to the Court. They have the same backgrounds as judges, the same term of office and perhaps most importantly the same status. Therefore Advocates-Generals should not be seen as inferior to judges, as the precedent within the Court for both depends upon the date of appointment and not the designated office. Advocates-Generals are given a specific role under art.252 **TFEU** which states that "it should be the duty of the Advocate-General, acting with complete impartiality and independence, to make, in open court, reasoned submissions on cases brought before the Court of Justice, in order to assist the Court in the performance of" its tasks.

Judgments Unlike in senior English courts where a full judgment is given, including dissenting views, only one judgment is ever given by the ECJ. All the judges must agree to the one judgment, which is why they can appear so terse and lacking in any real discussion of the Law. They do not contain the obiter dicta as well as the ratio decidendi found in the common law tradition. Hence the importance of the Advocate-General is that she hears and reads all the evidence as a judge would do but she gives her opinion to the court as to what the judgment should be before the judges themselves reach their decision. In her opinion the Advocate-General can range over the case law of the court or if appropriate the jurisprudence of the Member States. In this way some insight is given as to the direction European Union Law may take in the future.

Workload The workload of the ECJ has increased tremendously since the Court was established in 1957. To help the court deal with cases, the judges sit in Chambers with three or five judges, but always with an odd number so that there can be a clear decision in the case. If the case before the Court concerns a Member State or the EU institutions the Grand Chamber of 13 judges may sit in judgment. In 1989 the General Court (formerly the Court of First Instance (CFI)) was set up to assist the ECJ by taking a specific jurisdiction with the safeguard of appeal to the ECJ itself. The ECJ has a general jurisdiction with regard to Union Law only fettered by the types of action specified in the Treaty. There are a number of direct actions available that include judicial review (art.263 **TFEU**) and actions against a Member State for failure to fulfil an obligation (arts 258 and 259 **TFEU**). In addition there is the special procedure for preliminary references under art.267 **TFEU**.

Procedures Whenever a case is brought to the ECJ, whether as a direct action which is heard in its entirety only by the Court or a request for a preliminary reference from a Member State under art.267 **TFEU**, it is processed by the Court Registry to ensure that the progress of the case can be recorded. This is especially important with preliminary references where the "file" of written documentation sent by the national court dominates the whole procedure. The procedure is that on receipt by the Registrar, the President of the Court will assign the case to one of the Chambers and nominate one of the judges to act as "rapporteur". The First Advocate-General will at the same time designate the Advocate-General for the case. The role of the judge rapporteur is that although all the papers will go to every judge hearing the case, only he will have studied them closely in order to produce a preliminary report. This report, together with any views expressed by the Advocate-General, will help the court decide what the relevant issues are. It may be decided that the Grand Chamber should hear the case, as normally happens with cases between the Member States or Community institutions. These early stages covering the written proceedings and the preparatory inquiry are held in private. Where oral proceedings follow, as with direct actions, these are held in open court in Luxembourg. The next stage is for the Advocate-General to deliver his opinion to the court and sometime after this the court will deliver its judgment. In order to speed up the procedure for preliminary references the ECJ may decide not to require the Advocate-General to deliver an opinion where no new point of law is concerned. In 2009 52 per cent of the judgments of the ECJ were delivered without an opinion being given.

The future The President of the ECJ presented to the Justice Ministers of the Member States a number of proposals and ideas on the future of the judicial system of the EU. Principally he thought that the judicial system would be affected by an increase in the volume of cases due to the Economic Monetary Union (EMU), the full implementation of the **Treaty of Amsterdam** and the enlargement of the EU in 2004. There was also the Due Report in 2001 which looked at the future of the EU court structure. The increase to 27 Member States, the widening policy areas where the EU has competence, the potential for cases arising from aspects of criminal and family law and the implementation of the **Treaty of Lisbon** have all contributed to a greater workload of both the ECJ and the General Court. The ECJ wants to avoid the situation where case congestion leads to growing delays by simplifying procedures and filtering appeals from the General Court. The Court was also concerned with the increase in the number of judges associated with enlargement and a loss of its collegiate function. The development of specialist courts such as the Civil Service Tribunal has taken some of the workload off the General Court in particular, but the possibility of a large volume of cases from the European Chemical Agency (ECHA) could further increase the workload and thus increase delays.

The General Court

The General Court was originally established under the **SEA** as the Court of First Instance (CFI) and came into operation in 1989. The General Court is attached to the ECJ and has a wide jurisdiction with a possible appeal to the

ECJ itself on a point of law. The Treaties use the word "attach" quite deliberately. The General Court is not a separate institution. It shares not only the building in Luxembourg with the ECJ but other facilities such as the library. It appoints its own Registrar but other administrative services are shared.

The General Court is based on art.19 **TEU** and art.256 **TFEU**. There are 27 judges appointed to the court, one from each Member State. Although there are no Advocates-General specifically appointed to the General Court the need for such a role to be fulfilled is recognised. Where an Advocate-General is required in a particular case, one of the judges is requested to carry out this role. This will not happen in every case before the General Court. The court may sit in chambers of three or five judges in order to hear cases brought before it.

Like the judges appointed to the ECJ, those appointed to the General Court have a six-year term of office, which is renewable. The criteria for selection as a judge in the General Court is not so high as for the ECJ. In the ECJ prospective judges must possess the ability for appointment to high judicial office. Article 254 **TFEU** states that for the General Court judges are to be chosen "from persons whose independence is beyond doubt and who possess the ability required for appointment to judicial office".

Jurisdiction The initial jurisdiction of the General Court reflected one of the problems encountered by the ECJ. These were those cases that required a long examination of questions of fact. These are very time consuming and involve sifting through a great deal of evidence. There were three categories of cases that formed the original jurisdiction of the General Court:

(1) Staff cases, where employees of the European Union have a dispute with regard to their employment;
(2) cases brought under the **European Coal and Steel Community Treaty** concerned with production and prices; and
(3) most importantly, competition cases brought under either art.230 EC (ex 173 EC) or art.232 EC (ex 175 EC).

If these cases also contain a claim for damages, the General Court can hear that claim as part of the action. Appeals from the General Court are to the ECJ and have to be brought within two months. The appeal will only be heard on points of law and not of fact. The three grounds of appeal mirror the grounds of annulment under art.263 **TFEU**, namely lack of competence; breach of procedure; or infringement of Community law by the General Court.

In September 1993 there was the first major increase in the jurisdiction of the General Court since its creation in 1989. The Council of Ministers extended the jurisdiction to cover all direct actions brought by private parties against the Community institutions. One of the main purposes for the extension of the jurisdiction was to permit the ECJ to reduce still further delays in hearing cases by cutting the court's case load. However, the ECJ will take on the role as the appeal court for all the cases transferred to the General Court—all cases heard by the General Court at first instance may be appealed to the ECJ on a point of law. The General Court has been recognised as a success and the **Treaty of Nice** allowed for the Court to hear references for preliminary ruling under art.276 **TFEU** after 2004. To allow for this increase in workload cases brought by staff members of the EU are now dealt with by the European Union Civil Service Tribunal with an appeal to the General Court. With the ending of the **European Coal and Steel Community Treaty** it may be thought that the General Court would be able to accommodate the additional workload associated with the enlargement of the EU. However, even with the increase in the number of judges in the General Court it still struggles to cope with the increased number of cases within a reasonable period. Suggestions have been made to appoint Advocate-Generals specifically to the General Court or to establish another specialist tribunal dealing with intellectual property cases but these have so far been rejected due to budget restraints.

Court of Auditors

There has been such a Court since the EU was established although it is not a court in the traditional sense as it has no judicial capacity but has an auditing/accountancy role. In the **Maastricht Treaty** in 1992 it was upgraded to the status of an EU institution due to the need to monitor the large budgets now controlled by the Union. The **TFEU** still has a Court of Auditors but with less prestige.

Articles 285–287 **TFEU** detail the appointment and role of the Court. The duty of the Court of Auditors is to carry out audits of all revenue and expenditure of the Union and the bodies set up by the Union. It must provide the Parliament and the Council with a statement that transactions have been legally made and that the accounts produced are accurate. At the end of the financial year the Court of Auditors has to draw up an annual report that is presented to the other Community institutions for their observations. These and the report are then published in the Official Journal. For a number of years now the Court of Auditors have not been able to sign off the Union's accounts due to errors or possible fraud.

There are 27 members of the Court of Auditors each serving for a six-year period that is renewable. The members of the Court elect their own President, who serves for a period of three years.

It is the Council, after consulting the Parliament, which appoints the members of the Court of Auditors. Apart from the end of their period in office or death, the Court of Justice can terminate the office of a member at the request of the Court of Auditors if he no longer fulfils the obligations of his office.

The audits carried out by the Court of Auditors can be carried out on the spot in the other institutions of the Union and the Member States. Where it takes place in the Member States they liaise with the national audit bodies, who may take part in the audit. All the EU institutions and national audit bodies must forward to the Court of Auditors any document or information it requests to carry out its task.

Advisory Institutions

There are also advisory bodies with the power to give opinions either in situations where they have been consulted by the Council or Commission or in cases where they consider it appropriate (see art.300 **TFEU**).

The European Economic and Social Committee was established by the original **EC Treaty** in 1957. A new one, the Committee of the Regions, was established by the **TEU** in 1992.

European Economic and Social Committee (EESC)

This is an advisory committee appointed under arts 301–304 **TFEU**. It consists of representatives of the various sections of economic and social life of the Community. Although the opinions of the Committee are not binding they do appear to have influence. The Commission has a very good working relationship with the Economic and Social Council Committee. The relationship with the Council has not been so well developed although attempts have been made in recent years to improve this. Since 1987 it has become a regular practice for the person holding the office of President of the Council to address the Committee on matters discussed at the European Council. This has spread to ministers from the member state holding the Presidency to address meetings of the Committee.

Although advisory, the Commission or Council consults the Committee when it considers it appropriate in addition to those instances where it is obligatory under some articles of the Treaty for the Council or the Commission to consult the Committee. An example of this is art.91 **TFEU** which deals with international transport within the Union and the common rules established to implement the policy.

The total number of members of the Economic and Social Committee cannot exceed 350. These are allocated to the different Member States to reflect their size, with the large countries such as France, Italy, Germany and the UK having 24 each, down to six for Luxembourg and five for Malta. The Committee reflects three particular groups of people. The Employers Group which is made up of representatives of employers organisations and chambers of commerce; the Workers Group which represent trade unions; and a group of "Other Interests" which includes small businesses, family, environmental and similar representatives. Within these groups can be found the representatives of the various categories of economic and social activity specified in art.300 **TFEU**.

Committee of the Regions

This Committee consists of representatives of regional and local bodies and cannot exceed a total of 350 members. The number of members allocated from each Member State for the Committee of the Regions is the same as for the EESC. The numbers are given in Table 2.2 below.

The individual Member States propose their members who are appointed by the Council for five years, which is renewable. The members have a duty to act independently, in the general interest of the Union. In view of the expansion of the Community's Structural Funds and the creation of a Cohesion Fund to redress the imbalance of prosperity within the Community, it is likely that this Committee will make an important contribution to the Union's decision-making.

Institutional Reforms

Apart from the European Parliament, the main institutions have remained largely unchanged since the Treaty of Rome, yet the membership and policies of the EU have been greatly enlarged. This has caused the present main institutions to creak and struggle to meet the expectations placed upon them. Reports have been produced since the mid-1970s calling for reforms to be made. The Council of Ministers and the European Parliament have both funded enquiries into the state of the institutions and made recommendations. The European Parliament also produced a draft Union Treaty that specified the reforms it considered necessary. It is interesting to note the reforms called for and what actually appeared in the **SEA** and the **TEU**, both of which amended the **EC Treaty**. The main omission was that although reforms associated with the European Commission were identified, they were not included. Apart from voting procedures in the Council and the "co-operation" and "co-decision" procedures, the main success was the setting up of the General Court to supplement the European Court of Justice. Why has there been this delay? It is often due to the individual perspective of the relationship between the institutions held by the governments of the Member States. After all it is these governments who must agree to such reforms in the Council of Ministers and obtain the ratification of the amendment in their national parliaments. The expansion in the number of Member States renewed the pressure for institutional reform and the **Treaty of Amsterdam**, but more importantly the **Treaty of Nice**, brought about some

Table 2.2 Committee of the Regions, Number of Representatives by Member States

Belgium	12
Bulgaria	12
Czech Republic	12
Denmark	9
Germany	24
Estonia	7
Greece	12
Spain	21
France	24
Ireland	9
Italy	24
Cyprus	6
Latvia	7
Lithuania	9
Luxembourg	6
Hungary	12
Malta	5
Netherlands	12
Austria	12
Poland	21
Portugal	12
Romania	15
Slovenia	7
Slovakia	9
Finland	9
Sweden	12
United Kingdom	24

Source: Art.263 EC

reforms but not perhaps those thought necessary by some. However, at the Nice Inter-Governmental Conference (IGC) a declaration was made that has led to the establishment of the European Convention on the Future of Europe. This Convention had the remit to consider fundamental questions about the institutions needed by an enlarged EU and they presented a draft Constitutional Treaty that was signed by the heads of government in 2004. The problems of ratification in summer 2005 meant that this Treaty was not brought into law. Due to the failure to get a positive referendum vote in France and the Netherlands a "period of reflection" was taken to discuss future action. It was decided that the best way forward was for an amending treaty to be agreed instead of the "constitutional treaty" that had such a negative reception. The subsequent **Treaty of Lisbon** was ratified on December 1, 2009 and that is why we now have two treaties—the **Treaty on European Union** (**TEU**) and the **Treaty on the Functioning of the European Union** (**TFEU**). (See Ch.12—"TEU and Beyond", p.124.)

"True Europeans"

Although the European Commissioners see themselves as the true Europeans as they have to take an independent European view on policy, the European Court sees itself as having a very pro-European Union role. Perhaps the strongest example is the way the Court developed the principle of "Direct Effect" in the very early stages of the EU. It may also take the form of guarding its own position within the context of a unique international community as with the Laying-up Fund case in Opinion 1/76 or the recent European Economic Area case; or recognising the exclusive Community competence, and thus European Commission role, in international negotiations in the ERTA case. The final example is the ECJ decisions allowing the European Parliament to bring an action under art.263 **TFEU** in certain circumstances, even though at that time the Parliament was not listed as a privileged applicant under the article.

European Council

In 1974 the Heads of Government from the Member States began to meet to deal with some of the problems of political deadlock in the Council of Ministers. It was not formally recognised as an institution of the EU until art.2 of the **SEA** stated that it should meet at least twice a year although this is now generally four times. Article 15 **TEU** states that "the European Council shall provide the Union with the necessary impetus for its development and shall define the general political guidelines thereof". Thus, although it has no role in the formal legislative process of the Community, the European Council does play a very important part in deciding the future political direction of the Community. The **TEU** in the **Treaty of Lisbon** also introduced the formal role of the President of the European Council. Before this change the political head of the MS which held the Presidency of the Council of Ministers would take on this role but this was sometimes difficult to combine with the busy role of the prime minister or president of a MS and it also failed to provide for continuity. The appointment of a full time President of the European Council is intended to overcome these problems and to provide more focus for the role of the MS within the EU. Article 15 **TEU** provides for the European Council to elect by qmv a person to have this role for two and a half years, renewable once. They cannot hold any national office and chair meetings of the European Council and drive forward its work. The ex-Prime Minister of Belgium, Herman Van Rompuy was unanimously appointed to this new office when the **Treaty of Lisbon** came into force on December 1, 2009.

Revision Checklist

You should now know and understand:

- **the role, functions & memberships of the European Parliament**
- **the decision making process within the European Union**
- **the relationship between the European Parliament and the Council of Ministers and the Commission**
- **the role, function and membership of the Council of Ministers**
- **the role of the Committee of Permanent Representatives (COREPER)**
- **the role, function and membership of the European Court of Justice**
- **the role, function and membership of the General Court**
- **the role, function and membership of the European Economic and Social Committee and the Committee of the Regions**
- **the role, function and membership of the European Council**

QUESTION AND ANSWER

The Question

Critically review the powers of the European Parliament in the light of recent treaty amendments.

Advice and the Answer

Points you should cover in your answer to this essay question: Introduction—The EP is the only democratic institution in the EU as it is directly elected since 1979. At that time there was the role in budget approval and the consultation procedure.

Recent treaties should be identified with the **Treaty of Lisbon** being the most important in the form of the **TEU** and the **TFEU**. The role played by the **Maastricht**, **Amsterdam** and **Nice Treaties** with the recognition that the **SEA** in 1986 did introduce the cooperation procedure. The recent developments have been on two fronts, namely the involvement in the legislative procedure and the appointment of the Commission.

In relation to the legislative procedure the co-decision procedure (art.294 **TFEU**), now called the ordinary legislative procedure, has been the most significant development as it gives the EP the right to stop EU legislation being passed unless it is content. Introduced in the **TEU** the policy areas covered by the co-decision procedure have been extended by all subsequent treaties including **Amsterdam**, **Nice** and now **Lisbon**.

With regard to the appointment of the Commission the EP has to agree to the nominated candidate for the role of President of the Commission otherwise the Council has to come forward with another candidate. Subsequently the EP has to approve the appointment on the remaining members of the Commission.

Conclusion—The momentum from the previous treaties and the failed Constitution Treaty has been maintained by the **Treaty of Lisbon**. This reflects the greater powers that had to be given to the EP in response to what has been identified as the "democratic deficit" in the EU. This strategy is likely to be followed in the future to give more powers to the EP.

Sources of Union Law

3

INTRODUCTION

For the study of any legal system the sources of law are important and this applies to the European Union. However, some of the terminology is different and that sometimes causes problems for students. It is important to understand the supremacy of the Treaties as a source of law and this is not easy from a UK perspective where there is no single document like a written constitution that the student would look to as being of greater importance than others and where international law is viewed as being a different type of law outside the scope of the courts.

PRIMARY AND SECONDARY SOURCES OF UNION LAW

The European Union is founded upon treaties. The transfer of sovereignty or powers from the Member States to the institutions of the Union is limited to specific policies and specific procedures to be found in the treaties. Thus the main treaties establishing the European Union (but originally called the European Economic Community), EURATOM, the **TEU** (or **Maastricht Treaty**), subsequently amended by the **Treaties of Amsterdam** and **Nice** and now the **Treaty of Lisbon** are the primary source of Union law. Wherever there is any doubt about the validity or authority of a particular measure, the lawyer should always go back to the source document, which invariably is one of the treaties. This is obviously in recognition of the international law aspect of the Union. All other sources of Union law are secondary or derived in that they originate from powers conferred on particular institutions by the treaties.

Treaties

The main treaties, listed above, set down the aims and objectives of the Union and provide a framework for legislation. The most important Treaty is the Treaty of Lisbon which is divided into two parts—the **TEU** and the **TFEU**. These treaties have greatly extended the original Treaty of Rome signed in

1957 which formed the then European Economic Community. There are other treaties in the sense that there has to be one whenever new members join the Union, together with an Act of Accession for that particular member. In addition there have been important amendments to the original Treaty such as the **Merger Treaty** (1965) and the **SEA** (1986). However, these amend and do not replace the original Treaty. It is usual for a "consolidation edition" of the **EU Treaty** to be produced to make for ease of reference.

Administrative Acts under article 289 TFEU

TREATY HIGHLIGHTER

Article 288 **TFEU** has been greatly amended by previous treaties such as the **SEA** and the **TEU**, principally to recognise the increasing role of the European Parliament. Under the article "the institutions shall adopt regulations, directives, decisions, recommendations and opinions". Recommendations and opinions are not legally binding and therefore will not be considered in detail. The **Constitutional Treaty 2004** would have simplified this by having two categories: European Laws (the current Regulations) and European Framework Laws (currently Directives) but this treaty was never ratified. Therefore under the **Treaty of Lisbon** the appropriate terms remain Regulations and Directives.

Regulations

Regulations are the most important derived source of Union law in that they are the chosen form when legislating for the whole Union, without going through any national channels. It is defined as "having general application, binding in its entirety and directly applicable in all member States". In the Joined Cases 16 & 17/62 *Producteurs de Fruits v Council* the Court stated that "a regulation, being essentially of a legislative nature, is applicable not to a limited number of persons, defined or identifiable, but to categories of persons viewed abstractly and in their entirety". The confusion over the term "directly applicable" is discussed with the principle of direct effect in the next chapter (see p.36).

Directives

"Directives shall be binding, as to the result to be achieved, upon each Member State to which it is addressed, but shall leave to the national authorities the choice of form and methods".

This shows that directives lay down an objective and then leave it to the individual Member State to decide how best to achieve it. In the UK this may take the form of an Act of Parliament, as with the **Consumer Protection Act 1987** or by one of the other methods available such as a statutory instrument. It may be that in a given situation, a Member State feels that it already has domestic legislation that meets most of the objectives set and will therefore merely introduce domestic legislation on the remainder. This does carry the hidden danger that they are mistaken and subsequent action in the national courts (Case 8/81 *Ursula Becker v Finanzamt*), or by the Commission under art.258 **TFEU** is necessary to enforce the obligation under the directive.

Although the form may differ between Member States, allowing for national traditions, the obligation on the Member State remains the same. Every directive specifies a time period, which is usually two years, by which time the Member State should have achieved the result required. If it has not done so, an individual may seek to enforce in their national courts any rights given to them under the directive by the principle of direct effect (Case 148/78 *Tullio Ratti v Ministero Pubblico*).

Decisions

Decisions are addressed to specific Member States, individuals or companies and are binding in their entirety upon those to whom they are addressed. They are most commonly used where the Commission has reached the conclusion that an undertaking is acting contrary to the competition policy of the Union under art.101 or 102 **TFEU**.

Publication and notification

Under art.296 **TFEU** regulations, directives and decisions must state the reasons on which they are based. In the preamble to such measures the justification or authority for them is based upon a Treaty article. They must be published in the Official Journal (art.297 **TFEU**). The regulation or directive will come into force on the date specified in them or if no date is given on the twentieth day following their publication. Decisions are notified to whom they are addressed and take effect upon notification.

All Union acts are numbered together with the year they were enacted. For example, a directive would appear as **Council Directive 64/221**, recording that it was the 221st directive of 1964. Regulations have the year at the end, i.e. **Council Regulation 4064/89**.

The Ordinary Legislative Procedure under article 294 TFEU

There are different procedures which apply to different areas of legislation as explained in art.289 **TFEU** but the ordinary legislative procedure is the main one. It used to be referred to as the Co-decision Procedure although this term never appeared in the **Maastricht Treaty** which introduced it. The scope of the procedure was limited initially but it gradually developed to apply to many of the areas which established the internal market. The scope of the procedure was reviewed in 1996 and, in recognition of its success, the areas of policy requiring the co-decision procedure to be used were increased by both the **Treaty of Amsterdam** and the **Treaty of Nice**.

Under the Ordinary Legislative Procedure the Commission sends a copy of their proposal to the Council and the European Parliament. The Parliament gives the proposal a "first reading". The Council then adopts a common position, giving its reasons for doing so to the European Parliament who then gives the proposal a "second reading". At this stage the Parliament has three months in which to accept the Council's common position, in which case it is adopted by the Council as legislation, or to reject it. If it does neither the Council's common position is accepted anyway. In the case of a rejection by an absolute majority of Parliament, a Conciliation Committee composed of an equal number of representatives of the Council and Parliament is convened. The Commission also takes part in the work of this Committee, as it may alter its proposal at any time before it is adopted. The Committee has six weeks in which to approve a joint text, which if accepted by an absolute majority of Parliament and a qualified majority in the Council becomes adopted. Failure to agree such a joint text means that the proposal will fall unless within six weeks a qualified majority of the Council confirm their common position, in which case it will be adopted. Even in these circumstances the proposal can still be defeated if within six weeks the Parliament rejects the text of the common position by an absolute majority of its members. The periods of three months and six weeks referred to above can be extended by a maximum of one month and two weeks respectively by agreement by the Council and the Parliament.

GENERAL PRINCIPLES OF UNION LAW

These are an important source of Union law in that they provide a useful tool for interpretation and allow Union law to be challenged on the basis that it is contrary to a general principle of EU law. They may also support a claim for damages under art.244 **TFEU**. Every legal jurisdiction has its own general principles, which are principles which command common assent, such as the right to natural justice. The ECJ has justified its action by referring to three articles in the Treaty. Article 19 **TEU** states that the Court shall ensure that in the interpretation and application of the Treaty the law is observed. Second, in art.263 **TFEU** the grounds for annulment include "infringement of the Treaty, or of any rule of law relating to its application". In both of these references "law" must refer to something outside the Treaty itself. Lastly, art.340(2) **TFEU**, which is concerned with non-contractual liability, expressly provides that the liability of the Union is based on the "general principles common to the laws of the Member States".

The ECJ has derived general principles of Union law from the Treaties and from the legal systems of the Member States. For example, art.7 EC (now repealed) which prohibited discrimination based on nationality was used by the ECJ as the foundation for a general principle which forbids arbitrary discrimination on any ground. Article 6 **TEU** contains a strong statement in relation to fundamental rights of citizens of the EU. When looking at the legal systems of the Member States the ECJ is not looking for a principle to be common to all of them before it may be adopted. It is sufficient if it is generally accepted. Whatever the factual origin of the principle, it is applied by the ECJ as a general principle of Community law. The most important examples of general principles are as follows.

Proportionality

A public authority may not impose obligations on a citizen except to the extent to which they are strictly necessary in the public interest to attain the purpose of the measure. If the burdens imposed are clearly out of proportion to the object in view, the measure will be annulled if challenged in the courts. This principle, derived from German law, is important in economic law where levies or charges are involved. In the *Skimmed-Milk Powder* case (Case 114/76) the Commission needed to reduce a surplus of skimmed-milk powder in the Union by requiring animal feed producers to incorporate it into their products in place of soya. Unfortunately this also meant that the price of the feed would be increased by three fold. The ECJ declared the regulation concerned was invalid, partly because it discriminated against some farmers and partly because it was against the principle of proportionality. The requirement placed on the producers was not necessary in order to diminish the surplus.

Protection of Legitimate Expectations

This is another principle derived from German law, whereby Union measures must not violate the legitimate expectations of those concerned, unless there is an overriding matter of public interest. In Case 78/74 *Deuka v EVGF*, the ECJ interpreted a Commission regulation setting the denaturing premiums for common wheat so as to protect the legitimate expectations of the processors.

Non-Discrimination

As was mentioned above this was derived from the Treaty arts 7 (now repealed) and 157 **TFEU**. However, the ECJ has gone beyond these specific provisions to hold that there is a general principle of non-discrimination (see

Deuka v EVGF above). In Case 20/71 *Sabbatini v European Parliament*, Sabbatini, who was employed by the European Parliament, successfully used the principle against her employer's staff regulations when she lost an expatriation allowance on her marriage. In Case 130/75 *Prais v Council* the principle was extended to discrimination on the grounds of religion.

Protection of Fundamental Rights

In Case 29/69 *Stauder v Ulm* the ECJ recognised that the protection of such rights was inspired by the constitutional traditions common to all the Member States. The protection of fundamental rights was therefore enshrined in the general principles of Union law and thus protected by the ECJ. Stauder had been required to give his name when he applied for cheap butter under a Community scheme. Case 11/70 *Internationale Handelsgesellschaft* took the recognition of this principle a step further as the German courts were unhappy with the Union's protection of fundamental rights in contrast with that provided by the German basic law.

KEY CASE

CASE 11/70 INTERNATIONALE HANDELSGESELLSCHAFT

In this case the attempt to control the common agriculture policy led to the introduction of a system whereby exports were permitted only if the exporter first obtained an export licence. To obtain a licence a deposit had to be paid which would be forfeited if the level of exports did not happen. The applicants complained that this was contrary to fundamental rights protected by the German constitution. The ECJ held that the matter had to be approached from Community law and not German law but came to the conclusion that no fundamental right had been violated.

(See also Case 44/79 *Hauer v Land Rheinland-Pfalz*.) There was a similar discussion in Italy in Case 33/84 *Fragd v Amministrazione delle Finanze dello Stato*. Article 6 **TEU** now gives specific recognition of this general principle. There is a Charter of Fundamental Rights of the EU and by art.6 **TEU** this now has legal force and "shall have the same legal value as the Treaties". However, by Protocol 30 the Charter does not extend to Poland and the UK unless those Member States have specifically extended the rights in their national laws.

Procedural Rights

The main procedural rights are the right to be heard and the right to due process.

(a) Right to be Heard

Based on English law this principle requires that a person whose interests are perceptively affected by a decision taken by a public authority must be give the opportunity to make his point of view known (Case 17/74 *Transocean Marine Paint v Commission*).

(b) Right to Due Process

This right follows on from the duty of those exercising authority to give reasons for a decision. In Case 222/84 *Johnston v Chief Constable of the Royal Ulster Constabulary* a certificate issued by the Secretary of State for Northern Ireland sought to provide exclusive evidence that the derogation from Community obligations under **Directive 76/207** was on the grounds of national security. Mrs Johnston claimed that she had been subject to sex discrimination by her employer, contrary to Union law. The ECJ held that the action of the Secretary of State was contrary to the requirement of judicial control, recognised as a general principle by the Member States.

JUDGMENTS OF THE EUROPEAN COURT OF JUSTICE AND THE GENERAL COURT

Although these courts do not follow the system of binding precedent found in common law jurisdictions such as England, they do accept the importance of certainty as a principle of law. Therefore the judgments of previous cases before these courts do affect future cases. After all the ECJ is the final arbiter of Union law. They are thus a source of Union law when an individual is seeking to identify what the law is. For example, there have been certain cases which appear to have no obvious connection with either the Treaty or legislative act, but which have been used by the Court of Justice to develop the principle of direct effect.

Methods of interpretation

When called upon to identify what the law is the ECJ has to interpret the treaties, administrative acts and other such generic sources of law. To assist in this process the ECJ has evolved a number of methods of interpretation, which other courts can utilise when dealing with questions of Union law. The methods used by the ECJ have been influenced by the traditions of the Member States, notably France and Germany. However, there are special problems facing the Court, including the linguistic one that there are nine official versions of a text. This principle of linguistic equality has affected the Court as it has developed a particular "Community way" of interpretation.

The main "tools" of interpretation used by the Court are:

(a) teleological, which requires the judge to look to the purpose or object of the text before him;
(b) the contextual approach, which involves the court placing the provision within its context and interpreting it in relation to other provisions of Union law;
(c) historical interpretation, which requires an attempt to ascertain the subjective intention of the author by looking at documentation available to the court;
(d) literal interpretation, which is familiar to any judge, but with Union law once its literal meaning has been identified it is then necessary to apply the teleological or contextual approach.

The Court appears to favour the first two methods of interpretation, teleological and contextual, as they assist in the development of the Union towards the objectives listed in the first part of the **Lisbon Treaty**.

Revision Checklist

You should now know and understand:

- **the importance of the Treaties as the primary source of EU law**
- **the types of administrative acts under art.288 TFEU**
- **the definition of a Regulation, a Directive and a Decision**
- **the requirements of the Ordinary Legislative Procedure in art.294 TFEU**
- **the use of General Principles as a source of EU law and the important role they play**
- **the meaning of general principles such as—Proportionality, Protection of legitimate expectations, Non-discrimination, Protection of fundamental rights and Procedural rights**
- **the main "tools" of interpretation used by the ECJ Court**

QUESTION AND ANSWER

The Question

What general principles of law have been developed in the EU? How do they assist the individual?

Advice and the Answer

Introduction—all legal systems have developed general principles of law to incorporate into law fundamental principles which may be taken for granted. Sometimes they may appear formally as with the principle of equality and non-discrimination found in the Union treaties. The European Court of Justice has developed many principles which have been derived from the law of the Member States or from other sources to provide general principles of Community law.

Examples of the main general principles should then be reviewed including:

Protection of fundamental rights—Case 29/69 *Stauder v Ulm*
Non-discrimination—Case 20/71 *Sabbatini v European Parliament*
Proportionality—the *Skimmed-Milk Powder* Case 114/76
Protection of legitimate expectations—Case 78/74 *Deuka v EVGF*
Right to be heard—Case 17/74 *Transocean Marine Paint v Commission*

The assistance that is provided for the individual is that they can provide rights which the courts will recognise when deciding questions of Union law. For example if the action is under art.263 **TFEU** the breach of a general principle could be a ground for declaring a Community measure such as a Decision void. If the matter is before a national court, which can not declare a Union law void, the general principle may influence the enforcement of the Union law or make the national court use the preliminary ruling procedure under art.267 **TFEU** to clarify the law.

EU and National Law

4

SUPREMACY OF UNION LAW

INTRODUCTION

In the UK the legislation passed by Parliament has been given greater importance than any other source of law. However, the EU is based on principles of international law and gives greater priority to the international agreements or treaties entered into by sovereign countries. How European law has dealt with the issues arising from this relationship is the subject of this chapter.

The relationship between Union and national law was established in the case of *Costa v ENEL*, one of the earliest cases to come before the European Court of Justice.

KEY CASE

Case 6/64 Costa v ENEL

In Case 6/64 *Costa v ENEL* an action was brought in Italy against the nationalised National Electricity Board (ENEL) over a bill of 1,950 lire which then amounted to less than €1. Mr Costa claimed that he was not obliged to pay the bill as the nationalisation legislation had infringed Italian and EC law. A reference was made for a preliminary ruling by the Italian court under art.267 **TFEU**. The Italian government argued that such a reference was "absolutely inadmissible" because the national court had to apply national law.

The ECJ rejected that argument in a passage that has been repeated on many subsequent occasions.

> "By contrast with ordinary international treaties, the EEC Treaty has created its own legal system which ... became an integral part of the legal systems of the Member States and which their courts are bound to apply. By creating a Community of unlimited

duration, having its own institutions, its own personality, its own legal capacity ... and real powers stemming from a limitation of sovereignty or a transfer of powers from the States to the Community, the Member States have limited their sovereign rights, albeit within limited fields, and thus created a body of law which binds both their nationals and themselves ... It follows ... that the law stemming from the Treaty, an independent source of law, could not, because of its special and original nature, be overridden by domestic legal provisions, however framed, without being deprived of its character as Community law and without the legal basis of the Community itself being called into question."

Union Law Prevails

Thus on the basis of a case involving very little money the principle was established that where there is conflict between Union law and national law it is Union law which is to prevail. If it was otherwise "the obligations under the Treaty could be called into question" by any subsequent national legislation the government of a Member State passed through its legislature. *Costa v ENEL* developed this basic principle that had been set down in Case 26/62 *Van Gend en Loos v Nederlanse Tariefcommissie* one year earlier.

Although the Treaties do not expressly mention the principle of supremacy, a number of provisions require it. For the ECJ the position is unequivocal. By creating the Union the Member States consented to transfer to it certain of their powers and to restrict their sovereign rights. The ECJ case-law is directed at the national courts who apply the law in the cases which come before them and apply effective remedies. Thus we have the statement in Case 92/78 *Simmenthal v Commission* that the provisions of Union law "are an integral part of, and take precedence in, the legal order applicable in the territory of each of the Member States".

Full recognition was given in the UK to the principle of supremacy in Case 213/89 *R. v Secretary of State for Transport, Ex p. Factortame Ltd.*

KEY CASE

R. v Secretary of State for Transport, Ex p. Factortame

A number of cases were brought by Factortame as a result of the government passing the **Merchant Shipping Act 1988** and the **Merchant Shipping (Registration of Fishing Vessels) Regulations 1988.** This legislation had been passed following criticism that a number of UK registered fishing boats were in fact operated by Spanish fishermen. This legislation required a nationality link for registration of vessels so that ownership would remain in British hands. The ECJ, in response to a request for a preliminary reference under art.267 **TFEU**, restated the relationship between national and Community law. Lord Bridge in his judgment in the House of Lords stated: "If the supremacy within the EC of Community law over the national law of the Member States was not always inherent in the **EEC Treaty** it was certainly well established in the jurisprudence of the Court of Justice long before the UK joined the Community. Thus, whatever limitation of its sovereignty Parliament accepted when it enacted the European Communities Act 1972 was entirely voluntary". Therefore, Union law will prevail over inconsistent UK legislation, even where that legislation has been enacted by Parliament subsequent to the entry into force of the Union rule.

In *Equal Opportunities Commission v Secretary of State for Employment* [1995] 1 A.C. 1 the House of Lords held that the **Employment Protection (Consolidation) Act 1978** requirements regarding qualifying periods of employment were contrary to European law.

Incorporation of Union law into National Law

When a State joins the European Union it is obliged to reconcile its constitution with Union membership. It does this by making provision for the application of Union law within its territory and for the supremacy of Union law over national law. How the State will achieve this will depend upon its conception of international law, as there are two possibilities: namely monist and dualist.

DEFINITION CHECKPOINT

Monist Approach

The monist conception is that international law and national law are both part of one legal structure, even though they operate in different spheres. In such countries there is no reason why the national courts should not apply international law, provided that the appropriate constitutional procedures have been gone through to receive them into the national system. In cases where there is a conflict with national law, monist countries usually recognise the supremacy of treaty provisions, as for example happens in France and the Netherlands.

DEFINITION CHECKPOINT

Dualist Approach

The dualist conception is that international law and national law are two fundamentally different structures. Therefore in such countries national courts can never apply international treaties unless domestic legislation makes this possible. The UK is a dualist country and therefore the **European Communities Act 1972** was specifically enacted to make provision for UK membership of the Community. Lord Denning made clear in *McWhirter v Attorney-General* [1972] C.M.L.R. 882 that without this Act the **EC Treaty** and Community legislation would have been binding on the UK in international law but would have had no effect internally. Sections 2 and 3 of the **European Communities Act 1972** achieve this purpose.

DIRECT EFFECT

This important principle was created by the ECJ and follows on from the principle of supremacy of Union law. It is a novel concept and can appear complex in the way it applies to particular Union provisions. If a legal provision is said to be directly effective, it means that it grants individual rights that must be upheld by the national courts. There are two initial requirements that have to be satisfied as the provision must be part of the legal order and its terms must be appropriate to confer rights on individuals. There is thus a close link between supremacy of Union law and direct effect as they both flow from the nature of the Union. In the important case of Case 26/62 *Van Gend en Loos v Nederlanse Tariefcommissie*, Van Gend imported chemicals from Germany. In 1959 a Dutch law was passed which imposed a duty on some imported chemicals. This was contrary to art.30 **TFEU** which required Member States to refrain from introducing new duties or raising existing ones on imports between the States. Van Gend objected to paying the duty and a reference was made under art.67 **TFEU** to the ECJ to ascertain whether the duty on the chemicals was prohibited.

The conclusion reached by the ECJ was that:

> "the Community constitutes a new legal order of international law for the benefit of which the states have limited their sovereign rights, albeit within limited fields, and the subjects of which comprise not only the Member States but also their nationals. Independently of the legislation of the Member States,

Community law therefore not only imposes obligations on individuals but is also intended to confer upon them rights which become part of their legal heritage".

Direct Effect and Member States

The judgment in *Van Gend* was not the one that the Member States argued for. As far as they were concerned if there was a breach of a Union obligation the Treaty provided for action to be taken by the Commission under art.258 **TFEU**, or by another Member State under art.259 **TFEU**. These procedures have the advantage for the Member State that they take a long time to come before the ECJ and, until the **Maastricht Treaty**, did not carry any real sanction. The statements in *Van Gend*, clearly giving the individual who is affected by Union law the equipment to take action in his national courts, ensure that the Member States observe their obligations.

Conditions for Direct Effect

The principle of direct effect is a very powerful one and the ECJ has taken the view that it has to be limited by being interpreted restrictively. The judgment in *Van Gend* pointed out that art.25 EC (ex 12 EC) was ideally adapted to have direct effect on the legal relations between the Member States and their subjects. The Court did this by establishing what are now recognised as the conditions which must apply if direct effect is to be enforced.

The conditions which must apply if direct effect is to be enforced are:

1. the provision must be clear and unambiguous;
2. it must be unconditional; and
3. its operation must not be dependent on further action being taken by Union or national authorities.

The principle of direct effect has been applied to all the legally binding sources of Union law. Whether or not a provision has direct effect is a question of interpretation of Union law. In this way the ECJ seeks to ensure uniformity throughout the European Union.

Direct effect of Treaty provisions

The ECJ established in *Van Gend en Loos* that Treaty articles that impose on Member States an obligation to abstain from something, such as levying duties under art.30 **TFEU** have direct effect. In Case 57/67 *Firma Alfons Lutticke GmbH v Hauptzollamt* a preliminary reference was made asking if art.110 **TFEU**, which deals with taxation, had direct effect. The Court used the familiar phrases when it stated, "The first paragraph of Article 110 TFEU contains a prohibition against discrimination, constituting a clear and unconditional obligation". There being no discretion left to Member States, it concluded that art.110 **TFEU** produced direct effects and creates individual rights of which national courts must take account. See also Case 43/75 *Defrenne v Sabena (No.2)*.

Direct effect of Regulations

Under art.288 **TFEU** regulations have general application and are binding in their entirety and directly applicable in all Member States. The term used in the article is "directly applicable" and not "direct effect", although as the ECJ often use the terms inconsistently there is often confusion as to the difference in meaning. Direct applicability is not the same as direct effect, as the conditions or test mentioned above still has to be satisfied if direct effect is to be applied. Direct applicability means that the national courts must apply a regulation whenever their contents grants rights to individuals or impose obligations on them. In the *Politi* judgment (Case 43/71 *Politi v Ministry for Finance of the Italian Republic*) the Court held that "by reason of their nature and their function in the system of the sources of Community law, regulations have direct effect and are, as such, capable of creating individual rights which national courts must protect". The resulting enforcement of his rights by the individual is the same whether the regulation is said to be directly applicable or directly effective.

In Case 93/71 *Orsolina Leonesio v Ministero dell'agricoltura e foreste* an Italian farmer claimed a subsidy for slaughtering a cow under Community regulations. The Italian government refused on the basis that under the Italian Constitution national legislation had to be enacted before they could do so. The ECJ held that regulations become part of the national legal system and the direct applicability under art.288 **TFEU** cannot be hindered by national practices. There are instances where regulations do require further legislation, such as in the form of directives. In these circumstances the condition that the provision must not be dependent on further action being taken cannot be satisfied.

Direct effect of Decisions

In Case 9/70 *Franz Grad v Finanzamt Traunstein* the ECJ held that Decisions could have vertical direct effect:

> "the provisions according to which decisions are binding in their entirety on those to whom they are addressed enables the question to be put whether the obligation created by the decisions can only be invoked by the Community institutions against the addressee or whether such a right may possibly be exercised

by all those who have an interest in the fulfilment of this obligation".

The answer given by the Court was that all those with an interest should have the right.

Direct effect of Directives

In contrast to the direct applicability of regulations, art.288 **TFEU** states that directives are addressed to Member States and are binding as to the result to be achieved. The Member States have argued that this wording means that directives cannot be directly effective because they cannot satisfy the conditions. This view was supported by the Conseil d'Etat in *Minister of the Interior v Cohn-Bendit* [1980] 1 C.M.L.R. 543. If the choice is left to the Member States as to the form and method to achieve the obligation, they must require further action in the form of domestic legislation required. The ECJ has not accepted this argument. The effectiveness (l'effet utile) of a directive would be weakened if the nationals of a Member State that had failed to implement a directive, or had implemented it wrongly, were denied the rights contained in the directive by the national court. This was stated in *Grad*, which although concerned with a Community Decision, developed the principle that was closely repeated in Case 41/74 *Yvonne Van Duyn v Home Office* that did involve a directive. (See now Case 91/92 *Paola Faccini Dori v Recreb Srl.*)

The principle in *Van Duyn* was **Directive 64/221** concerning restriction on the admission and movement of aliens that required interpretation. Miss Van Duyn, a Dutch national, sought a declaration that the UK government was wrong to deny her admission to take up employment with the Church of Scientology, a sect which the government considered undesirable. On a preliminary reference under art.267 **TFEU**, the ECJ held that the Directive was directly effective because it "imposes on a Member State a precise obligation which does not require the adoption of any further measure on the part of either the Union institutions or of the member States and which leaves them, in relation to its implementation, no discretionary powers". Thus the conditions for direct effect were satisfied, although on the facts of the case it agreed that the UK government could exclude her.

In Case 148/78 Criminal proceedings against Tullio Ratti the ECJ took the opportunity to refine its arguments for direct effect of directives. "A Member State which has not adopted the implementing measures required by a directive in the prescribed period may not rely, as against individuals, on its own failure to perform the obligations which the directive entails". If it was the government that had not fulfilled its obligations arising from the Directive, it is against the government that rights arising from the Directive can be enforced. In Case 81/83 *Ursula Becker v Finanzamt Munster-Innenstadt*, a German credit broker successfully claimed the benefit of a provision of the sixth VAT Directive against the German VAT authorities as they had failed to implement the Directive. In the important case of Case 271/91 *Marshall v Southampton and South West Hampshire AHA* the UK government had failed to properly implement the **Equal Treatment Directive 76/207**, which was held to be directly effective.

DEFINITION CHECKPOINT

Vertical and horizontal direct effect

The articles of the Treaty and regulations have been held by the ECJ as being capable of giving both horizontal and vertical direct effect. Vertical effect means that an individual can invoke the obligation arising from the provision against the Member State before a national court. Horizontal effect means that an individual can invoke the obligation arising from the provision against another individual before the national court. It was also made clear in the Marshall judgment that there was no question of a directive having horizontal direct effect.

Mrs Marshall was employed by the Southampton Area Health Authority when she was dismissed because she had reached the age of 62, the Authority's retirement age for females. The ECJ accepted that this was contrary to **Equal Treatment Directive 76/207**. As the Area Health Authority was an "emanation of the State", Mrs Marshall succeeded in her action. This is also illustrated by Case 188/89 *Foster v British Gas* where the employer was the pre-privatised Gas Board. In contrast Mrs Duke, who was employed by a public company, GEC Reliance Ltd, did not succeed because she was requesting horizontal effect to enforce the Directive against another individual, albeit a company. The principle is therefore, that unless the individual is able to show that there is some relationship with the State the principle of direct effect will not apply even if all three conditions mentioned above can be fulfilled (see *Webb v EMO Air Cargo (UK) Ltd* [1993] 1 W.L.R. 49).

In a number of cases Advocates-Generals have called on the Court to abolish the distinction between vertical and horizontal direct effect of directives. In Case 91/92 *Faccini Dori v Recreb Srl* (1995) the ECJ refused to follow this path. In this case the Court found that the relevant provisions of the directive were unconditional and sufficiently precise, but stated that if the Community wished to enact obligations between individuals with immediate effect it could do so by adopting regulations. See the comments of the Advocate-General in Case C- 104/09 *Roca Álvarez v Sesa Start España ETT SA* at para.55.

Every Directive involves a time-scale for implementation. This period, normally two years, is to give the government of the Member State time to formulate and pass the appropriate domestic measure. Until this period has elapsed the Directive cannot, as was confirmed in *Ratti*, have direct effect. Ratti ran a business in Italy selling solvents and varnishes. The Union had adopted two Directives specifying the labelling and packaging of these products. Italy had not implemented the Directives but Ratti had complied with them with regard to his products. Unfortunately for him, the domestic legislation in Italy set other requirements that he had breached and he was prosecuted before the Italian court. A preliminary reference was made to the ECJ which held that as the time for the implementation of one of the Directives had passed it was directly effective thus providing Ratti with a defence. The other Directive still had time to be implemented and therefore could not be directly effective until that time had expired.

In Case 208/90 *Emmott v Minister for Social Welfare*, Mrs Emmott brought an action against the Irish Minister for Social Welfare on the basis that she received less benefit than a man would have done in equivalent circumstances. **Directive** 79/7 should have been implemented by 1984 but was not implemented in Ireland until 1988. Mrs Emmott's action in 1987 followed a previous case before the ECJ where it had declared that the Directive had direct effect. The vertical relationship between herself and the Irish government satisfied the case law of the Court. The Irish government, however, claimed that her action was statute barred because it had not been brought within the three months required by Irish law for judicial review. The Court held that Union law precludes the competent national authorities from relying on national procedural rules relating to time limits to stop an action by one of its citizens seeking to enforce a right that Member State has failed to transpose into its domestic legal system. The time limit does not run until the date when the national implementing legislation is correctly adopted.

Von Colson principle

If a Community act cannot satisfy the three conditions for direct effect, the individual cannot seek to have any right arising from it enforced in the national courts. This is what happened in the *Von Colson* and *Harz* cases.

KEY CASE

CASE 14/83 VON COLSON AND KAMANN V LAND NORDRHEIN-WESTFALEN AND CASE 79/83 HARZ V DEUTSCHE TRADAX GMBH

Case 14/83 *Von Colson and Kamann v Land Nordrhein-Westfalen* and Case 79/83 *Harz v Deutsche Tradax GmbH*—when women sought remedies in the German courts for unlawful discrimination. They claimed that this was contrary to the **Equal Treatment Directive 1976**. On a preliminary reference the ECJ was asked whether art.6 of the Directive had direct effect. The Court did not restrict itself to the question whether there was vertical or horizontal direct effect. Instead it used art.4(3) **TEU** which requires Member States to "take all appropriate measures to ensure fulfilment of their Community obligations". Therefore even if the principle of direct effect does not apply, the courts in the Member States are required to interpret national legislation specifically passed to implement the Union act to comply with Community law.

In *Litster v Forth Dry Dock & Engineering Co Ltd* [1990] 1 A.C. 546, the House of Lords interpreted the **Transfer of Undertakings (Protection of Employment) Regulation 1981** in such a way as to give effect to the **Directive 77/187**. This was because it was for the purpose of implementing the Directive that the domestic Regulation had been introduced. In this way the House of Lords was using the *Von Colson* principle to give effect not only to the Directive but also the subsequent interpretation by the ECJ of the Directive in *Case 101/87 Bork International v Forening af Arbejdsledere I Danmark*.

In Case 106/89 *Marleasing SA v La Comercial Internacional de Alimentacion SA*, the *Von Colson* principle was taken a stage further when the ECJ held that the principle could be applied even if the necessary national legislation had not been introduced to comply with the Directive. However, the ECJ has limited the *Von Colson* principle with regard to criminal prosecutions, if this would make the accused guilty where he would otherwise have been acquitted (see Case 80/86 *Officer van Justitie v Koplinghuis Nijmegen* and Case 168/95 *Criminal proceedings against Luciano Arcaro*).

In the case of *Mangold v Helm* (C-144/04) a 56 year old entered into an eight month fixed term contract of employment with Helm, a German Lawyer. He subsequently challenged the contract on the grounds that it was contrary to **Directive 2000/78/EC**. The Directive was not due to be transposed into national law until December 2003 at the earliest so the German government argued that it could not have legal effect until that date. The ECJ enforced the Directive not by direct effect but by stating that the Directive was fulfilling the general principle of EU law relating to non-discrimination.

Direct effect and claims for damages

In Case 479/93 *Francovich v Italian State* the ECJ extended the impact of the law regarding directives. "Community law lays down a principle according to which a Member State is liable to make good damage to individuals caused by a breach of Community law for which it is responsible". Under a Council Directive aimed at protecting employees in the event of the insolvency of their employers, Member States were required to ensure that payment of employees' outstanding claims arising from the employment relationship and relating to pay was guaranteed. Unfortunately, the Italian government had not set up any Italian system to act as a guarantor in these circumstances, hence his claim against them. His insolvent employers owed Mr Francovich six million lire. As he was unable to enforce a judgment against them, he brought an action against the Italian government for compensation. The ECJ held that damages are available against the State for failure to implement EU directives, if three conditions are met. These were redefined in the case of C-46/93 *Brasserie du Pecheur SA v Germany* and case C-48/93 *R. v Secretary of State for Transport, Ex p. Factortame Ltd* which were held together by the ECJ. (See below.)

Limits for damages Case 271/91 *Marshall v Southampton and South West Hampshire AHA* followed a successful action by Mrs Marshall against her employer under the **Equal Treatment Directive**. Under UK enacting legislation there was a limit imposed on the compensation payable for sex discrimination and no interest was allowed on this sum. The ECJ in this second case rejected the UK government's argument that limits on compensation were matters for national law. Article 6 of the Directive was directly effective and therefore such compensation had to be "adequate" to make good the loss sustained by the individual as a result of the wrongful discrimination. In computing the amount of compensation, interest should be included from the date of the discrimination.

In the Cases 46/93 and 48/93 *Brasserie du Pecheur* and *Factortame (No.4)* judgment the ECJ stated that the principles in *Francovich* applied whether it was an act or omission by the organ of the state that had caused the breach. If the three conditions were met the national court could award exemplary damages if such damages could be awarded in similar claims founded on domestic law. National legislation, which generally limited the damage for which reparation could be granted, was not compatible with Union Law.

DEFINITION CHECKPOINT

The conditions for imposing state liability are:

1. The rule of Union law infringed must be intended to confer rights on individuals;
2. the breach must be sufficiently serious to justify imposing state liability; and
3. there must be a causal link between the breach of the obligation imposed on the state and the damage actually suffered by the applicant.

These three conditions are a development of those stated in *Francovich*. The decisive test for finding that a breach of community law was sufficiently serious was whether the member state or the Community institution had manifestly and gravely disregarded the limits on its discretion (see Lord Bingham's judgment in *R. v Secretary of State for the Home Department, Ex p. Gallagher* [1996] 2 C.M.L.R. 951). The case of C-453/99 *Courage Ltd v Crehan* illustrates how the Francovich principle has developed. Here an individual sought to bring an action against another individual as they had suffered damage as a result of a breach of EU competition law. The ECJ confirmed that as no national remedy was available an action may be brought under the Francovich principle against a Member State but also against private individuals or bodies that caused the damage through a breach of Union law.

Revision Checklist

You should now know and understand:

- **the relationship between Union and national law**
- **the supremacy of EU law**
- **the difference between a monist and a dualist system of law**
- **the meaning of "direct effect" and the conditions required to enforce it**
- **direct effect of Treaty articles**
- **direct effect of Regulations, Directives and Decisions**
- **the difference between vertical and horizontal direct effect**
- **the development and application of indirect effect**

- **the development and application of the principle of State liability**
- **the conditions required for State liability to be imposed**

QUESTION AND ANSWER

The Question

Critically review the requirements for direct effect of Community law.

Advice and the Answer

Introduction—the principle of direct effect has been developed by the ECJ in its early judgments in the 1960s such as *Costa v ENEL* and *Van Gend en Loos v Nederlanse Tariefcommissie*. The benefit this provides to the individual is that they can use the principle to enforce Community rights in their national courts but within the test set by the Court.

The requirements are that the provision must be clear and unambiguous, it must be unconditional and its operation must not be dependent on further action being taken by Community or national authorities.

The initial application of the principle was to Treaty provisions (*Van Gend en Loos*) but it has also been applied to Regulations (*Politi v Ministry for Finance of the Italian Republic*) and Decisions (*Franz Grad v Finanzamt Traunstein*).

The main issue has been whether the test can be applied to Directives given the definition of these measures under art.288 **TFEU**. In the case of *Van Duyn v Home Office* it was decided that Directives could have direct effect if the test is satisfied and there is a situation of "vertical direct effect" involving an emanation of the State. If there was no relationship with the State, for example where the employer was a private company, then the individual could not enforce the Community right.

This failure to use direct effect has led the court to introduce indirect effect but many see this as an artificial solution which could be removed if the distinction between vertical and horizontal direct effect was removed. This is something the ECJ has been reluctant to do.

Preliminary References

5

INTRODUCTION

In English law it is not unknown for senior judges to provide guidance by answering specific questions, as demonstrated by the "appeal by case stated" procedure. However the system of preliminary references is much more important and has had a much greater impact on our law. The intention was to provide a procedure that would allow for consistency of interpretation and application of EU law in the Member States but has been used effectively by the ECJ to create principles like supremacy and direct effect. In this way the influence of European law and the impact on the individual has been extended.

Under the system of preliminary references a court in any Member State may make a reference to the ECJ in order to ascertain its view with regard to the interpretation or validity. The case in the Member States is suspended while the question(s) are despatched for consideration by the ECJ. When the Court has given its judgment the answers are sent back to the national courts which, having had the Community law clarified for them, apply it to the case before them in the normal way. The period that it takes for this process to take place is around 18 months, although every effort is made by the ECJ to reduce this timescale.

Objectives of preliminary references

As was shown in Ch.4 above, p.36 the principle was established whereby Union law must override national law in the event of a conflict. To do otherwise would allow a Member State to avoid the application of Union law which they considered disadvantageous by the simple expedient of passing conflicting legislation for their national courts to apply. As Union law does have this superiority over national law it is important that such law should have the same meaning and effect in all Member States. This requires that there should be a single court, the ECJ, whose jurisdiction extends over the whole European Union. Also, if Union law is under certain circumstances to be directly effective, the ECJ must have the final say with regard to its validity and interpretation. Thus the objectives of the preliminary reference procedure under art.267 **TFEU** is to provide for a definitive judgment regarding the interpretation and validity of Union law.

Matters for referral under article 267 TFEU

There are two parts to art.267(1) **TFEU** and both are important as they state that the EU Courts have the ability to give preliminary rulings on:

(a) the interpretation of the Treaty; and
(b) the validity and interpretation of acts of the institutions, bodies, offices or agencies of the Union.

There is an obvious distinction in that there is only the possibility of seeking interpretation of the Treaty as its validity cannot be challenged. This is what one would expect when the Treaty is seen as the primary source of Community law. The "acts of the institutions" refers to the European Parliament, Council and Commission making legally binding acts defined in art.288 **TFEU** such as Regulations and Directives.

Direct effect and art.267 TFEU references There are two important points to make which show that the list above is not exhaustive. First, as was shown in the last chapter, the principle of direct effect has had an important influence on the development of Union law. The ECJ has used the procedure for preliminary rulings to look at the effectiveness of Community provisions, as well as the supremacy of Community law. The majority of the most important cases on Union law have been brought before the Court by the art.267 **TFEU** procedure. Although the Court would argue that it is merely exercising its authority as interpreter of Union law, it is in reality going much further than what would normally be regarded as interpretation. This is sometimes referred to as the judicial activism of the ECJ.

The result is that there are really three issues which may be referred to the Court for a ruling: interpretation, effect and, for certain provisions, validity. Questions of fact and of national law may not be referred, nor may the Court rule on the application of the law to the particular facts of the case. However, the boundary between interpretation and application is sometime uncertain, and although the ECJ may cross it the national court receiving the ruling can decide for itself.

The second point is that wherever possible the Court has taken a liberal view with regard to the "acts" of the institutions it is called upon to consider. It is not restricted to art.288 **TFEU**. For example, although agreements with non-Member States are clearly not part of the Treaty they are negotiated by the Commission and concluded by the Council under procedures and powers to be found in art.218 **TFEU** of the Treaty. Thus in Case 181/73 *R & V*

Haegeman v Belgium the Court seized upon this ground for regarding the Association Agreement between the Community and Greece as a Community act and therefore covered by art.267(1)(b) **TFEU**. Having done this the Court then went on to interpret the Agreement itself! The view of the Court is that since such international agreements are part of Community law and binding on the Member States, it is clearly desirable that they should receive uniform interpretation throughout the Union. Obviously the ruling of the Court is not binding on the other party, i.e. Greece in the *Haegeman* case as they were not members of the Union at that time.

General principles of Community law may not form the subject matter of a reference as they are neither part of the Treaty nor are they Community acts. However, as was illustrated above, the art.267 **TFEU** procedure has been used with regard to them by the simple expedient of using a suitable Treaty provision or Community act to provide a peg on which to hang the general principle. The latter can then be interpreted in the course of the reference. Which courts are covered by art.267 **TFEU**?

Article 267(2) and 267(3) **TFEU** both refer to courts and tribunals. There are two requirements that these must fulfil. First, the body requesting the reference must be a court or tribunal and, second, they must be of a Member State. This second requirement is straightforward but the first has produced some clear statements from the Court.

Court or tribunal? For the ECJ it does not matter what the body is called or whether it is recognised as a court or tribunal under national law. The key question of the Court is whether it performs a judicial function. What constitutes a "judicial function" is not always easy to clarify but, generally, a body is regarded as judicial if it has power to give binding determinations of the legal rights and obligations of individuals. In Case 61/65 *Vaassen v Beamtenfonds Mijnbedrij* a reference was made by an "arbitration tribunal", which settled disputes regarding the pension fund for the Dutch mining industry. The fund had been set up privately with representatives of both employers and employees and was approved by the ministers responsible for both the mines and social security. Members of the tribunal were appointed by the minister and any pension dispute had to go before it and be subject to its adversary procedure. The Court of Justice concluded that this tribunal came within art.367 **TFEU** because it was a judicial body representing the power of the State and settling as a matter of law disputes concerning the application of the pension scheme. In contrast, the ECJ refused to give a ruling in Case 138/80 *Borker, Re* on a reference from the Paris Chambre des Avocats on the ground that it was not exercising a judicial function. In Cases 69/96–79/96 *Garofalo v Ministera della Sanita* the ECJ specified a number of factors to be taken into account in order to determine whether a body is a "court or tribunal".The conclusion from this is that all administrative tribunals established in the UK by statute would be recognised as having a right under art.267 **TFEU** to make a reference. However, if they were merely domestic tribunals the ECJ would have to decide whether the element of acting for the state, the adversarial procedure and possible recourse to the national courts were -sufficient for it to be within the art.367 **TFEU** procedure.

Preliminary references and national law

Where a court or tribunal has a right to make a reference under art.267 **TFEU**, it cannot be deprived of that right by national law. The Court stated this rule in the *Rheinmuhlen* cases which were heard in the German Tax Courts. The lower court hearing the case wished to make a reference to the ECJ as a number of questions had been raised which required interpretation. This was despite a ruling having been given to it by the higher Federal Tax Court. In the end both German courts made a reference. The Federal Tax Court asked whether art.267 **TFEU** gives lower courts an unfettered right to refer, or whether it is subject to national provisions under which lower courts are bound by the judgments of superior courts. The response of the ECJ was unequivocal. The power of a lower court to make a reference cannot be abrogated by a provision of national law. Lower courts must be free to make a reference if it considers that the superior court's ruling could lead it to give judgment contrary to Community law (see Chadwick L.J. in *Trent Taverns Ltd v Sykes* [1999] EU.L.R. 492).

The practical situation is that national law cannot take away the right given by art.267(2) **TFEU**, but this does not prevent the lower court's order for a reference being quashed on appeal. In *R. v Plymouth Justices, Ex p. Rogers* [1982] Q.B. 863, Lord Lane C.J. stated that magistrates had the jurisdiction to make a reference but that they should consider whether a higher court might be in a better position to assess the need for a reference and to formulate the questions to be sent to the Court. A counter argument has been put in that if a reference seems likely to be made at some stage in the proceedings, time may actually be saved if this is done as soon as possible, for an appeal within the domestic system may thereby be obviated.

Article 267(2) TFEU

The word "may" appears in this article, giving those courts and tribunals concerned a discretion as to whether or not to make a reference to the ECJ. There are two requisites which have to be fulfilled before art.267(2) **TFEU** comes into operation.

1. An appropriate question of Community law must be raised before the court. In fact the "question" can be raised by either the parties to the

action or the court itself, as is allowed for under the procedural rules in England (Civil Procedure Rules (CPR) Pt 68).

2. A decision on that question must be necessary to enable the court to give judgment. It should be noted that it is not the reference which is necessary but a decision on the question. The Treaty makes it clear that this is for the national court to decide and the ECJ will not question the necessity of the decision or whether Community law is even applicable to the case. Lord Denning in *Bulmer v Bollinger* [1974] 3 W.L.R 202 said that "necessary" meant that the outcome of the case must be dependent on the decision. "If the Community point is decided one way, judgment for one party must be the result; if it decided in another way, judgment must be given for the other party". This is perhaps too restrictive an interpretation. A better suggestion is that "necessary" should be interpreted to mean that the point could be decisive. To assist in this process it is better if the facts of the case are fully ascertained before a reference is made. This will help because it may result in the national court deciding that the case can be settled on a point of national law and a reference would not be required. However, it should be remembered that under Civil Procedure Rules (CPR) Part 68 a reference may be made at any stage in the proceedings. In Case 157/92 *Pretore di Genova v Banchero* the ECJ said that the national court must define the factual and legal framework in which the questions arise before making a preliminary reference.

Previous judgments of the ECJ to preliminary references

It may be that the question for interpretation or validity specified in art.267(1) **TFEU** has already come before the ECJ and it has provided an answer. In such circumstances the point may be regarded as settled and the authority of the previous ruling would remove the need to make a reference. However, it should be remembered that the ECJ does not have the same judicial tradition towards precedent as English courts, and that if the national court wishes to exercise the right under art.267 **TFEU** it cannot be fettered.

Article 267(3) TFEU

This article appears to lay down an obligation to make a reference where the court or tribunal of a Member State is one "against whose decision there is no judicial remedy under national law". What courts are included? There are two propositions, an Abstract Theory and a Concrete Theory.

The literal reading of art.267(3) **TFEU** would seem to favour the Abstract Theory. Certainly Lord Denning was of the opinion in *Bulmer v Bollinger* that only the House of Lords came with the scope of this article. However, the ECJ appears to favour the Concrete Theory when it suggests that art.267(3) **TFEU** refers to the highest court in the case rather than the highest court in the Member State (*Costa v ENEL*). The case of *Chiron Corp v Murex Diagnostics* [1994] F.S.R. 202 discussed these issues in relation to the Court of Appeal and the House of Lords.

DEFINITION CHECKPOINT

Abstract theory
Only those courts whose decisions are never subject to appeal are within the scope of this provision. For example, in the UK the House of Lords would obviously be the only court in this category.

Concrete theory
The important question is whether the court's decision in the case in question is subject to appeal. An example of this would be the case of *Costa v ENEL*, where the sum involved in the case meant that there could be no appeal from the lower court within the Italian court system.

Obligation to refer

As early as Case 28/62 *Da Costa en Schaake v Netherlands Inland Revenue Administration* the ECJ had stated that if the Court had already pronounced on a question of interpretation it might deprive the obligation to refer of its purpose and empty it of its substance. The important ECJ judgment in Case 283/81 *CILFIT v Ministry of Health* put the obligation on art.267(3) **TFEU** courts to make a reference in a clearer position. In this case the Court said that the obligation to refer was based on co-operation between the national courts and the ECJ. The purpose of this co-operation was to prevent divergences in judicial decisions on question of Community law, i.e. uniformity. It may be that the correct application of Community law was so obvious that there was no scope for reasonable doubt about the answers to any questions raised. This reflects the principle of *acte clair*.

Acte Clair

This principle has its origins in French law, where the ordinary courts were required to request a ruling from the Ministry of Foreign Affairs on a question of treaty interpretation unless the point was regarded as clear. Thus, in relation to preliminary references under art.267(3) **TFEU**, the courts might consider that the state of Community law is sufficiently clear to be applied without the need for a reference to be made. This would assist in the workload of the ECJ and perhaps is overdue in that the national courts affected by the principle are those which contain experienced and well qualified judges. However, the ECJ did give a warning to those who wished to apply the principle of *acte clair*. They should remember that although the matter may be obvious to them, is it equally obvious to the courts in other Member States and the ECJ itself? The Court specifically mentioned three particular difficulties:

1. Community legislation is drafted in several languages and that the different language versions are all equally authentic. Any interpretation therefore involves the comparison of different language versions.
2. Community law uses terminology which is peculiar to itself and some legal concepts do not necessarily have the same meaning in Community law or in the various Member States.
3. Every provision of Community law must be placed in its context and interpreted in the light of provisions of Community law as a whole (see Interpretation above, p.33).

KEY CASE

CASE 283/81 CILFIT V MINISTRY OF HEALTH
This case involved a number of textile firms in Italy (CILFIT) challenging an EC levy on wool imported from outside the EC, as required by an EC Regulation dealing with animal products. The Italian Ministry of Health argued that there was no need to make a preliminary reference to the ECJ as it was obvious that wool was an animal product. The Italian court decided to make a reference anyway and the judgment of the ECJ has proved to be of great importance.

The Court said that art.234(3) EC (ex 177(3) EC) does place an obligation to refer on the court unless it was established (a) that the question raised is irrelevant or (b) has already been interpreted or (c) that the correct application of Community law is so obvious as to leave no scope for any reasonable doubt.

However, the national court still remains entirely at liberty to make a reference if it wishes. In the UK the House of Lords has adopted the approach recommended by the ECJ in *CILFIT*.

Guidelines and procedures used in the English courts

As was stated above the national courts cannot be fettered by national rules when it comes to exercising their rights to make a preliminary reference.

Having accepted this principle a number of guidelines have been given to help the court or tribunal decide whether or when to make a reference.

KEY CASE

BULMER V BOLLINGER [1974]

Lord Denning in *Bulmer v Bollinger* [1974] was the first senior judge to provide some guidance for lower courts. He said that the following facts should be taken into account:

(a) the facts should be decided first, so that the question of whether it was "necessary" could be settled;
(b) the reference to Luxembourg will cause delay and therefore add to the costs of the parties, so the lower court should deal with the case and leave it to an appeal court to decide whether or not to make a reference;
(c) the difficulty or importance of the question;
(d) the wishes of the parties should be taken into account, although it was the court's decision whether to make a reference or not; and
(e) the need to avoid overloading the ECJ.

These guidelines are still used by the English Courts, although other judges have clarified them. See MacPherson J. in *R. v HM Treasury, Ex p. Daily Mail & General Trust Plc* [1989] 1 All E.R. 328, Kerr L.J. in *R. v The Pharmaceutical Society of Great Britain, Ex p. the Association of Pharmaceutical Importers* [1987] 3 C.M.L.R. 951 and Bingham M.R. in *The Stock Exchange* case (1993).

Civil Procedure Rules (CPR) Part 68

Once a court or tribunal has decided to make a reference the procedure for it to be made in England is provided by the Civil Procedure Rules Pt 68. Although this rule applies specifically to the High Court and the Court of Appeal similar provisions are applicable in the other courts for which no special provision has been made. The court frames the questions it wishes answered and the Senior Master sends a copy to the Registrar of the European Court. There is sometimes a delay where the reference is being made by the High Court, to allow for any appeal against the reference to be made to the Court of Appeal. While a reply is awaited from the ECJ the proceedings in the national court are stayed.

Effects of a preliminary ruling

The national court or tribunal, which made the reference, may actually decide the case on other grounds, but if it does apply Community law it is bound by the ruling of the ECJ. As far as other courts are concerned they may accept the interpretation in the ruling which makes it unnecessary for them to make their own reference on the same point of Union law, but they can still make a separate reference if they wish. In the case of C-487/07 *L'Oreal SA & Others v Bellure NV & Others* a trade mark was involved in a dispute which came before the Court of Appeal (Civil Division). The judge, Jacob L.J. made a reference under art.267 **TFEU** but was of the opposite view to that of the ECJ when he received their judgment. He said that "My duty as a national judge is to follow EU law interpreted by the ECJ ... As I have said I do not agree with or welcome this conclusion—it amounts to a pointless monopoly. But my duty is to apply it".

Refusal of a preliminary reference

The ECJ recognises that the preliminary reference procedure has an important contribution to make towards the co-operation it seeks to develop with national courts. It is very rare for the ECJ to refuse a reference if the court or tribunal making it comes within art.267 **TFEU**. However, in the *Foglia v Novello* cases (Cases 104/79 and 244/80 respectively) the Court refused a reference because it felt that there was an absence of any real legal dispute between the parties. It was felt that this case would herald a restrictive approach by the ECJ but this has not happened. In Case 150/88 *Parfumerie-Fabrik v Provide* the ECJ confirmed that it would not lightly infer an absence of a genuine dispute between the parties. In Case 83/91 *Meilicke v ADV/ORGA FA Meyer* the Court ruled that "the spirit of cooperation which must prevail in preliminary ruling proceedings requires the national court to have regard to the function entrusted to the Court of Justice, which is to contribute to the administration of justice in member states and not give opinions on general or hypothetical questions". In the recent judgement in Case 318/00 *Bacardi-Martini v Newcastle United FC* the ECJ said that it had to apply special vigilance when a reference came in from one Member State seeking to question the compatibility of legislation in another Member State with EU law. In that case the Court refused to deal with the reference about TV advertising of alcohol under French law.

Preliminary rulings on validity

In Case 314/85 *Foto-Frost v Hauptzollamt Lubeck Ost* the ECJ held that national courts were entitled to find that acts adopted by the institutions of the Community were valid, but they had no power in normal proceedings to declare such acts invalid. This is to stop them placing in jeopardy the unity of the Community legal order and would detract from the fundamental requirement of legal certainty. The only exception to this would possibly be in interlocutory proceedings. If a national court suspects that an act may be invalid a reference must be made.

Revision checklist

You should now know and understand:

- **objectives of the system of preliminary references**
- **what can be the subject of a reference under art.267(1) TFEU**
- **the development of the principle of Direct Effect and the system of preliminary references**
- **the definitions used to determine whether the reference is from a "court or tribunal"**
- **the relationship between preliminary references and national law**
- **the discretion under art.234(2)EC compared with the "duty" under art.267(3) TFEU**
- **the principle of *acte clair***
- **the guidelines produced to assist judges when deciding to make a reference**
- **the effects of a preliminary ruling**
- **the refusal of a preliminary reference**
- **the situation where the preliminary rulings is about validity**

QUESTION AND ANSWER

The Question

What guidelines are provided for national judges considering making a preliminary reference under art.267 TFEU?

Advice and the Answer

Introduction—The preliminary reference procedure allows courts or tribunals in Member States to ask the ECJ or the General Court questions on Union law as defined by art.267(1) **TFEU**. The article itself provides some guidance in art.234(1) and (2) **TFEU** in relation to those courts that may or shall make a reference but case law has also provided some guidance.

A court in a Member State cannot be stopped from making a reference (*Rheinmuhlen* cases) but guidance is permitted. For courts which are not the final court in the case Denning has provided some guidance in *Bulmer v Bollinger* [1974], he was the first senior judge to provide some guidance for lower courts. He said that the following should be taken into account:

(a) the facts should be decided first, so that the question of whether it was "necessary" could be settled;
(b) the reference to Luxembourg will cause delay and therefore add to the costs of the parties, so the lower court should deal with the case and leave it to an appeal court to decide whether or not to make a reference;
(c) the difficulty or importance of the question;
(d) the wishes of the parties should be taken into account, although it was the court's decision whether to make a reference or not, and
(e) the need to avoid overloading the ECJ.

These guidelines have been expanded by subsequent senior judges including Lord Bingham in the Stock Exchange case (1993).

With regard to those courts which come within art.267(3) **TFEU** such as the Supreme Court, the ECJ itself has provided some guidelines when it accepted the principle of *acte clair* for Union law. In the case of (C283/81) *CILTFIT v Ministry of Health* the ECJ raised some circumstances where it might be better for a court to make a reference rather than to decide the law themselves.

Judicial Remedies and Review

6

INTRODUCTION

Although the indirect action associated with a request for a preliminary reference is important, there are a number of direct actions specified in the Treaties. These actions cover a range of actions that can be brought by the European Commission, a Member State or other specified person but they are restrictively interpreted by the ECJ. This means that they are not used as much as perhaps the authors of the Treaties envisaged. This chapter reviews these types of actions and the interpretation given to them by the ECJ.

ENFORCEMENT ACTIONS BY THE EUROPEAN COMMISSION

In Case 6/64 *Costa v ENEL* the Court of Justice stressed the point that the Community was a new legal order which required Community law to be obeyed. If this did not happen the "legal basis of the Union itself would be called into question". There needs to be, therefore, a mechanism for forcing the Member States to fulfil their obligations under the Treaty. As was stated in Ch.3 above, p.27, the European Commission have been given the general duty under art.17 **TEU** to "ensure that the provisions of this Treaty and the measures taken by the institutions pursuant thereto are applied". The Commission has been given this power under art.258 **TFEU**. The art.258 **TFEU** procedure can be initiated whenever the Commission considers that a Member State has failed to fulfil an obligation under the Treaty. This would include breach of administrative acts, general principles of Union law or international agreements. The breach may take the form of either an act or an omission such as the non-implementation of EC law or the retention of national laws which conflict with EC law. One of the problems for the Commission is that they receive many complaints that Member States are failing to fulfil their obligations. They come from individuals, companies, trade unions, pressure groups, MEPs and even from other governments. Member States have a legal duty to co-operate with the Commission investigations into alleged breaches by them (Case 45/93 *Commission v Spain*).

There are two stages to the procedure; an administrative stage and a judicial stage. The administrative stage is where the Director-General responsible for the policy of the Union will write to the Member State informing it that the Commission has formed the view that there is a breach of an obligation under the Treaty. Obviously there has been some investigation by the Director-General's office before this happens. The Member State then has an opportunity to answer the allegations or rectify the position. This is a very delicate stage because no government likes to be considered in breach of a treaty obligation. If, after receiving a reply from the Member State, the Commission considers that the Member State has been in breach it may deliver a reasoned opinion.

Reasoned opinion

The reasoned opinion is a very important document because it will form the basis of the legal proceedings under art.258 **TFEU** if the Commission decides to go on to that stage. At this stage the reasoned opinion is considered confidential and is not legally binding and cannot be challenged (Case 4/69 *Alfons Lutticke GmbH v E.C. Commission No.1*). It has two purposes:

1. It must set out the reasons of facts and law for which the Commission considers that the Member State concerned has failed to fulfil its obligations; and
2. It must inform the State of the measures which the Commission considers necessary to bring the failure to an end.

The Treaty does not specify the time-scale in which this must take place, but a reasonable time must be given by the Commission. The delivery of the reasoned opinion marks the end of the administrative stage.

The Commission has discretion as to whether to take the procedure on to the next stage. Advocate-General Roemer in Case 26/69 *Commission v France* suggested a number of situations in which the Commission might be justified in not initiating the enforcement procedure. These included the possibility that an amicable settlement could be achieved if formal proceedings were delayed, or where the effects of the violation were only minor, or where there is a possibility that the Union provision in question might be altered in the near future. Other situations that have been put forward are where the breach is the isolated act of an official or where action might inflame a politically sensitive situation. It is interesting to note that no action has been brought against the violation of Union law by national courts, even in situations like the *Cohn-Bendit* judgment in 1978. This is perhaps due to the fear that such an action might be seen as undermining the independence of the judiciary (see *Syndicat General de Fabricants de Semoules de France*

[1970] C.M.L.R 395). However in Case 224/01 *Kobler v Austria*, the Austrian Administrative court refused to make a preliminary reference and declared that the calculation of a university professor's pay was compatible with Union law. In its judgement the ECJ said that a breach of Union law by a national court may make the state liable in damages if the breach was "manifest and sufficiently serious". This would seem to open the possibility of an enforcement action if the breach persisted.

Interim measures

An application for interim relief can be made to the ECJ at any time once the administrative stage of the art.258 **TFEU** procedure has been completed. Article 279 **TFEU**: "The Court of Justice may in any cases brought before it prescribe any necessary interim measures". In such situations the European Commission must show that a prima facie case is made out and that the urgency of the situation requires action by the Court.

Judicial stage

If the Member State has not rectified its breach and the time period has elapsed, the Commission may bring the matter before the ECJ. This would indicate that the Commission has discretion at this stage. However, the duty under art.17 **TEU** mentioned above must be remembered. The duty requires the Commission to take appropriate action to ensure that the breach is rectified. Every attempt will be made to reach an amicable settlement.

The Court will consider whether the violation specified in the reasoned opinion has taken place. The Commission cannot raise new violations at the judicial stage. However, the Commission can continue with the action even if the Member State has terminated its infringement during the judicial stage, as happened in Case 7/61 *Commission v Italy (Pork Imports case)*. The Member States put forward many reasons for their failure, some of them quite ingenious. These have included the inability of the national government to get the required legislation through their national parliaments or where trade union pressure prevented the Member State (Case 128/78 *Commission v UK*).

ENFORCEMENT ACTIONS BY A MEMBER STATE

Generally the governments of Member States are prepared to leave breaches of Community obligations by other Member States to the Commission to seek enforcement under art.258 **TFEU**. It is only in exceptional situations that a Member State will take on the responsibility itself, but if it does it has the procedure under art.259 **TFEU** to follow. The applicant Member State has to report the breach to the Commission, which will give the defaulting Member State an opportunity to make representations and carry out its own investigations. If the Commission has not issued a reasoned opinion within three months, the Member State complaining of the breach may bring the matter before the ECJ. It may be that a Member State wants to make a particular political point and for that reason brings the action under art.259 **TFEU** rather than leaving it to the Commission's procedure (Case 141/78 *France v UK*).

Remedy under article 260 TFEU

Whether the action against a Member State is brought under art.258 or art.259 **TFEU**, the remedy provided is that of art.260 **TFEU**. Originally the remedy was only a declaration by the Court that the Member State was in default and that it should take the necessary steps to comply with the judgment of the Court. On some occasions this meant that if the Member State continued with the breach the whole procedure had to be started again. However, this was changed by the **Maastricht Treaty** on European Union with regards to actions under art.258 **TFEU**. Now if the Commission considers that the Member State has continued with the breach, it may issue a reasoned opinion after allowing the Member State to make their observations. The reasoned opinion must specify the points where the Member State has not complied with the Court's judgment and give a time limit for compliance to be achieved. If this does not happen the Commission may bring the matter before the Court again, but this time specifying an appropriate lump sum or penalty to be paid by the Member State. If the Court considers that the Member State has not complied with its judgment, it may impose a lump sum or penalty. In January 1997 the Commission agreed a procedure so that it could recommend to the Court the appropriate fine based on a daily fine multiplied by the gravity and the time duration of the breach. The first case brought before the ECJ on the basis of this procedure was Case 387/97 *Commission v Hellenic Republic*.

KEY CASE

Case 387/97 Commission v Greece

In 1987 the Commission received a complaint drawing its attention to uncontrolled waste disposal in the river Kouroupitos, 200 metres from the sea, by several municipalities in the prefecture of Chania (Crete). The waste came from military bases, hospitals and industry in the area. By its judgment in 1992 the Court of Justice held that Greece had failed to take the necessary measures for toxic and dangerous waste to be disposed of in the area of Chania while ensuring that human health and the environment were protected, as required by two Community directives of 1975 and 1978 which Greece should have applied from 1981.

Since the Commission was not notified of any measures to comply with that judgment it decided at the end of 1995 to initiate a fresh procedure using the possibilities introduced by the **TEU** of a fine being imposed.

In its judgment the ECJ decided that Greece was still in breach of its obligations and held that a periodic penalty payment was the most appropriate means of ensuring that Community law was applied uniformly and effectively and of inducing Greece to comply with its obligations.

The Court then fixed the amount of the fine. The basic criteria to be considered are, in principle, the duration of the infringement, its degree of seriousness and the ability of the Member State concerned to pay. In applying those criteria, the Court imposed a penalty payment of 20,000 euros for each day of delay in complying with the 1992 judgment.

In the recent case of Case C-304/02 *Commission v French Republic*, France was ordered to pay a lump sum of 20,000,000 euros and a penalty payment of 57,761,250 euros for each six-month period that it continued not to comply with its obligations. Thus the penalty payment is not an alternative to the lump sum payment but can be imposed together if the ECJ considers it appropriate.

There are a number of "mays" in the art.260 **TFEU** and there was some doubt as to what would happen when the Commission or the Court decided to exercise the new powers given to them. In 1996 the first fines were imposed and the ECJ has noted "that the use of fines has led to a more uniform, complete and simultaneous application of Community law rules in all Member States". However, there continues to be a discretion exercised by the Commission, illustrated by its decision in November 2002 not to take France back to the Court to be fined for the breach associated with the BSE issue surrounding the export of beef from the UK to France.

Action for annulment under article 263 TFEU

The action under art.263 **TFEU** is a direct challenge upon the validity of a Union act. There are five grounds on which the challenge can be based, the sole purpose of which is to get the act annulled. In any annulment proceedings the ECJ has no other option but to annul or not to annul. It cannot replace the act or amend it. The exception to this is where the Court can declare a regulation void but decide that the particular effects accomplished by it shall remain valid even if only temporarily. This provides time for the Commission or Council to rectify the situation.

Which Acts can be challenged?

The amended art.263 **TFEU** gives the Court the authority to review the legality of all those acts specified in art.288 **TFEU** which are intended to be legally binding. Therefore opinions and recommendations are not covered as they are not legally binding. The acts covered include those of the Council, the Commission, the European Parliament and the European Central Bank. However, there is some flexibility.

The most important requirement in any action under this article is that the measure being challenged should be legally binding. Thus in Case 22/70 *EC Commission v EC Council* (the ERTA case) the Commission had started actions under art.263 **TFEU** for the annulment of the Council's discussions resulting in a common position. The Commission disagreed with the procedure adopted by the Council for the negotiations for the European Road Transport Agreement because they felt that this was now a matter for the Community and not the individual Member States. The main point of the case concerned who had competence with regard to external agreements on this policy area. The ECJ held that "it would be inconsistent with the objectives [of the Article] to interpret the conditions under which an action is admissible so restrictively as to limit the availability of this procedure merely to the categories of measures referred to by art.288 **TFEU**". The Court's judgment in ERTA was followed in the more recent Case 294/83 *Les Verts v Parliament* where a French political grouping sought the annulment of two measures adopted by the European Parliament.

Privileged applicants

Under art.263(2) **TFEU** the European Parliament, the Member States, the Council or the Commission can challenge any legally binding act. They do not have to show any specific locus standi. The European Parliament had made a number of attempts to be accepted by the Court as being within this same category of privileged applicants on the basis that its status had become more important since direct elections. In Case 70/88 *European Parliament v Council* (the Chernobyl case) the ECJ held that Parliament had the right to seek annulment of acts adopted by the Council and the Commission where the purpose of the proceedings was to protect the Parliament's prerogatives. The **Treaty of Nice** finally included the EP as a fully privileged applicant. Under the provisions of the **TEU**, the article had been amended to allow for actions by both the Court of Auditors and the ECB for "the purpose of protecting their prerogatives". The case brought by Les Verts against the Parliament mentioned above would now come under art.263(2) **TFEU**.

Non-privileged applicants

This category of applicant includes all those listed in art.263(4) **TFEU**, namely any natural or legal person. The ability of these individuals to challenge Community acts are severely restricted, in contrast to the "privileged applicants".

TREATY HIGHLIGHTER

Article 263(4) **TFEU** Non-privileged applicants may only bring proceedings against three types of act, namely:

- (a) a decision addressed to the applicant;
- (b) a decision in the form of a regulatory act which is of direct and individual concern to the applicant;
- (c) a decision addressed to another person which is of direct and individual concern to the applicant.

This shows that if a decision is addressed to an individual, as would happen, e.g. in competition policy cases, he may challenge it before the Court under this procedure. There is no mention of directives in the list, but it has been argued before the ECJ that directives are decisions addressed to the Member States. Therefore they could come within (c) above. The main points which need to be resolved are to clarify what amounts to a "decision in the form of a regulatory act" and "direct and individual concern".

A decision in the form of a regulatory act

The title of the particular Union act is not decisive, therefore because it is called a "regulation" it will not automatically bar the action. It is the content and not the form that is important. A regulation under art.249 EC (ex 189 EC) is essentially of a legislative nature and is applicable to a number of persons viewed abstractly and in their entirety. In the *Fruit & Vegetables* case the Court held that "a measure which is applicable to objectively determined situations and which involves immediate legal consequences in all Member States for categories of persons viewed in a general and abstract manner cannot be considered as constituting a decision".

A regulation does not lose its character as a regulation simply because it may be possible to ascertain the number or even the identity of the persons to which it applies at any given time (see Case 6/68 *Zuckerfabrik Watenstedt v Council* and Case 789/79 *Calpak SpA v Commission*). In Case 25/62 *Plaumann & Co v EEC Commission* the ECJ stated that "it follows from Articles 249 EC and 254 EC (ex 189 and 191 EC) that decisions are characterised by the limited number of persons to whom they are addressed".

If the ECJ concludes that the act is a true regulation then it cannot be challenged under art.230 EC, but the individual may seek a remedy within their national courts.

Direct and individual concern

The inclusion of this phrase in the article has severely restricted the possibilities for it to be used by an individual who is seeking to challenge a decision not addressed to them.

Direct concern This is interpreted by the Court to mean that the addressee is left no latitude of discretion so that the decision affects the applicant without the addressee being required to take any decision himself. In the *Toepfer* case mentioned below the applicant was directly concerned because the decision was addressed to the German government, who could not alter its application. When the Japanese companies challenged the Community rules on ball bearings the action was admissible because the national implementing measures were purely automatic (see *Japanese Ball-Bearing* cases, e.g. Cases 113/77 and 119–121/77).

In the Chinese Mushrooms case (Case 62/70 *Werner A. Bock v EC Commission*) the fact that the German authorities had already made up their mind to reject the applicant's request when they had authorisation to do so from the Commission, made the matter of direct concern to the applicant.

The notion of direct concern has some similarities with that of direct effect. In both cases the government of the Member State has no discretion and the act is of legal relevance to individuals who need not be the addressee of the decision.

Individual concern Plaumann, an importer of clementines, instituted proceedings against a decision addressed to the German government by the Commission, refusing them permission to suspend the collection of import duties on the fruit. Plaumann claimed that as he was required to pay the duty he was "individually concerned". The ECJ disagreed when it held,

> "Persons other than those to whom a decision is addressed may only claim to be individually concerned if that decision affects them by reason of certain attributes which are peculiar to them or by reason of circumstances in which they are differentiated from

> all other persons and by virtue of these factors distinguishes them individually just as in the case of the person addressed".

As any importer would be affected in the same way as Plaumann, he was not distinguished sufficiently to put him in the same category as the German government who received the decision.

However, in the first *Toepfer* case a decision addressed to the German government was considered to be of individual concern to the applicant. In this case the number of importers involved was in the past and therefore fixed as no new names could be added to the list. The Court said that the facts "differentiates the said importers ... from all other persons and distinguishes them individually just as in the case of the person addressed" (see also Case 100/74 *CAM SA v EC Commission* (the CAM case)).

It would appear from the case law of the Court that a natural or legal person can only claim to be individually concerned when he disputes an act concerning a period in the past and which affects an identifiable group of persons, to which the applicant belongs.

Despite statements in *Plaumann* that art.263 **TFEU** should not be interpreted too restrictively; the number of successful actions by private individuals where the decision is not addressed to them is very small. It was thought that perhaps the ECJ was in the process of changing this view (see Case 358/89 *Extramet Industrie v Council*) but recent judgments have reaffirmed the *Plaumann* judgment. In Case 50/00 *Union de Pequenos Agricultores v EC Council* Advocate-General Jacobs suggested that where an individual would have no other possible remedy, it was only just that their action should be heard under art.263 **TFEU**. This was followed by the Court of First Instance in Case 177/01 *Jégo-Quéré et Cie SA v Commission* also supporting reform.

KEY CASE

CASE C-263/02 P COMMISSION V JÉGO-QUÉRÉ & CIE SA

The fishing company Jégo-Quéré & Cie, established in France, was involved in fishing mainly for whiting, to the south of Ireland. It used nets which were prohibited by a Commission regulation of 2001, the aim of which was to renew hake stocks. It brought an action before the General Court of the European Communities for annulment of two of the provisions of that regulation. The General Court held the action to be admissible and in doing this adopted a new definition of individual concern. The Commission appealed to the ECJ on the basis that the General Court had applied the wrong test.

The ECJ reaffirmed its restrictive interpretation of art.263 **TFEU** in the *Plaumann* case and said that it was for national courts to provide a remedy. This could be achieved by the claimant indirectly challenging a regulation in an action before their national court or having raised the question of validity to ask that court to make a reference using the preliminary reference procedure under art.267 **TFEU**.

The ECJ set aside the judgment of the Court of First Instance and declared the application for annulment by Jégo Quéré & Cie to be inadmissible.

However, the Court of Justice reiterated in the judgment in *Union de Pequenos Agricultores* that the *Plaumann* test should apply and it was for the national courts to provide a remedy if the individual did not satisfy the test for an action under art.263 **TFEU**. However, if the individual can satisfy the test for locus standi they still have to prove one of the five grounds specified in the second paragraph of the article if the measure is to be annulled.

Grounds for annulment

The grounds for illegality must have been present at the time the decision was taken. There are five such grounds, although they have gradually lost their individual importance. The case law of the Court would seem to indicate that the ECJ is not concerned with the specific ground of illegality. The most common grounds pleaded are "infringement of this Treaty or of any rule of law relating to its application".

1. Lack of Competence—The institutions of the Community have no general powers and may only act where the Treaty expressly attributes competence to them. This idea is similar to that of ultra vires in English law.
2. Infringement of an essential Procedural requirement—For the purposes of annulment of an act three procedural requirements have been identified as essential. These are (a) that the required advice must have been sought, e.g. from the European Parliament; (b) the acts must be reasoned; and (c) the acts must have been published (see Case 139/79 *Maizena GmbH v EC Council* and Case 138/79 *SA Roquette Frere v EC Council* where the opinion of the European Parliament was not received before the Council acted. The result was that the measure was annulled).
3. Infringement of this Treaty—This is the most important ground as virtually any error by a Community institution can be viewed as a violation of the Treaty. Therefore this ground is the most widely used and is one which has been the most often successful.

4. Infringement of any rule of law relating to the application of this Treaty—The ECJ has stated that this includes all rules of Community law other than those found in the Treaty. It therefore includes all the general principles of Community law.
5. Misuse of Powers—Derived from French administrative law this ground covers those situations where a power is used for a purpose other than that for which it was granted, i.e. an improper purpose. Unlike the other grounds of invalidity, which are objective in character, the misuse of powers is subjective. It is therefore difficult to prove.

Time limits

Under art.263(5) **TFEU** proceedings must be instituted "within two months of the publication of the measure, or of its notification to the plaintiff, or, in the absence thereof, of the day on which it came to the knowledge of the latter, as the case may be."

Effect of the annulment

The remedy for actions under art.263 **TFEU** is stated in art.264 **TFEU**:

> "If the action is well founded, the Court of Justice shall declare the act concerned to be void. However, the Court shall, if it considers this necessary, state which of the effects of the act which it has declared void shall be considered as definitive".

Thus the measure will be declared erga omnes, as if it never existed. Under art.233 **TFEU** the institution whose act has been declared void must take the necessary measures to comply with the judgment of the Court. If the successful applicant has suffered financial loss he may seek damages under art.340(2) **TFEU**.

Action for failure to act

This action, which is often called the appeal against inaction, is founded upon art.265 **TFEU**. Although it is rarely used, its potential use is against the Council or Commission and the European Parliament. As with art.263 **TFEU** mentioned above there are the two classes of applicant, the privileged and the non-privileged. The article requires that the defaulting institution must first be called upon to act. If after two months the institution concerned has not defined its position, the action may be brought after a further two months. The remedy for the action is contained in art.266 **TFEU**, i.e. the institution should act.

The ECJ has concluded that the obvious similarities between art.263 and 265 **TFEU** mean that the two articles are concerned essentially with the same remedy. This is referred to as the "unity principle". Therefore an individual cannot use one against the other. For example in the first *Lutticke* case the applicant invoked art.265 **TFEU** and called upon the Commission to initiate proceedings against the German government under art.258 **TFEU**. When they replied that there was no violation of art.110 **TFEU** by Germany, Lutticke brought an action under art.263 **TFEU** to have the reply annulled. The Court said that neither action was admissible as the Commission's reply was not a reviewable act and that by sending it they had acted so art.265 **TFEU** did not apply. Also in Case 289/97 *Eridania SpA v Azienda Agricola San Luca di Rumagnoli Viannj*, the applicant failed under art.263 **TFEU** because he was not directly and individually concerned. He asked for the acts to be repealed and when after two months they had not been he brought an action under art.265 **TFEU**. The Court refused to consider art.265 **TFEU** because it would have allowed the applicant to circumvent the conditions of art.263 **TFEU**.

Plea of illegality

The plea of illegality under art.277 **TFEU** is designed to prevent the application of an illegal act from being used as a legal basis for further action. It specifically refers to the fact that it applies when the time period mentioned in art.263(5) **TFEU** would otherwise bar an action. The article refers to "any party" being able to plead illegality, which would include both privileged and non-privileged applicants discussed above. Thus art.277 **TFEU** does not give a right of action in itself, but can be pleaded in other actions, such as annulment or failure to act or those for damages under art.340(2) **TFEU**.

The article refers specifically to "any proceedings in which an act of general application adopted by an institution, body, office or agency of the Union is at issue", so under the definitions in art.288 **TFEU** this would mean a regulation. However, as with art.263 **TFEU** above, the Court is concerned with the substance rather than the form. Article 277 **TFEU** is very rarely used because it can only be pleaded in actions before the ECJ or the General Court, which have very narrow locus standi for non-privileged applicants. It is not necessary to use the plea in domestic proceedings as under art.267(1)(b) **TFEU** the validity of a Union Act, including regulations, can be raised.

Remedies available before the national courts

A request for a preliminary ruling on the validity of a Union act can be brought by national courts when they have to apply a Union act whose validity is doubted. This is done under the procedure of art.267(1)(b) **TFEU**. It obviates the situation where national courts would otherwise be obliged to apply invalid rules of Community law. However, the ECJ refused in Case 188/92 *TWD Textilwerke Deggendorf GmbH v Germany* to declare on the validity of a

Commission decision because the applicants had been informed by the German government of their rights of challenge under art.263 **TFEU**.

As was held by the Court in Case 479/93 *Francovich v Italian Republic* it is also possible to obtain damages in the national courts (see Ch.4 above, p.36).

Damages under article 340 TFEU

Article 268 **TFEU** gives the ECJ exclusive jurisdiction to hear cases relating to compensation for tortious damage under art.340(2) **TFEU**. The contractual liability of the Community is governed by the law applicable to the contract in question.

The Court is instructed to decide cases of tortious liability in accordance with the general principles common to the laws of the Member States. In this way it is intended to make good any damage caused by Union institutions or by its servants in the performance of their duties. Unfortunately, the Court has adopted a very restrictive approach towards the tortious liability of the Community, although there have been some successes (see Case 145/83 *Adams v Commission*). Liability under art.340(2) **TFEU** can extend to liability in respect of legislation. Case 5/71 *Zuckerfrabrik Schoppenstedt v Council* developed certain guidelines for such situations. The court said that the non-contractual liability of the Union presupposes at the very least the unlawful nature of the act alleged to be the cause of the damage. No non-contractual liability will arise involving measures of economic policy unless a sufficiently flagrant violation of a superior rule of law for the protection of the individual has occurred. Having set this principle the court had to decide whether such a violation had actually occurred in this case.

Analysing this sentence "a superior rule of law for the protection of individuals" includes any general principle of Community law. This would include such examples as equality or proportionality. The requirement that there should be a "sufficiently flagrant" or serious violation has been narrowly construed by the court. In the joined Cases 83 and 94/76 and 4, 15 and 40/77 of *Bayerische HNL Vermehrungsbetriebe GmbH v Council and Commission* the court stated that no liability would be incurred by the Union institutions unless the institution concerned had manifestly and gravely disregarded the limits on the exercise of its power. In subsequent cases the court's view has been that the breach must be both serious and inexcusable. See C- 46 and C-48/93 *Brasserie du Pecheur* & *Factortame* joined cases.

Limitation period

Actions under art.340(2) **TFEU** are subject to a limitation period of five years.

Revision Checklist

You should now know and understand:

- **the procedure for enforcement actions under arts 258, 259 and 260 TFEU**
- **the calculation of fines and penalties under art.263 TFEU**
- **the action for annulment under art.263 TFEU**
- **the problems for non-privileged applicants**
- **the meaning of direct and individual concern**
- **the grounds for annulment**
- **the action for failure to act under art.265 TFEU**
- **the plea of illegality**
- **remedies available before the national courts**

QUESTION AND ANSWER

The Question

How and in what circumstances may an individual use art.263 **TFEU** to challenge a measure of EU law?

Advice and the Answer

Introduction—The ability to bring an action before the ECJ or the General Court for judicial review has been severely restricted by the ECJ's interpretation of art.263 **TFEU** as far as non-privileged applicants are concerned. Only the Community institutions as privileged applicants are able to challenge any Community act.

Individuals can only challenge a Union act in certain circumstances. If a Decision is addressed to them, as may happen under competition law, they may challenge it. However if it is not addressed to them but is a decision addressed to someone else (*Werner A. Bock v EC Commission*) or in the form of a regulation (*CAM SA v EC Commission*) it has to be of direct and individual concern to the applicant if they are going to be able to challenge it.

This is where the ECJ has been very restrictive in its interpretation (*Union de Pequenos Agricultores v EC Council*) and held that the case of *Plaumann & Co v EEC Commission* provided the best interpretation that should be followed.

The challenge under art.263 **TFEU** must be brought within the time limit of two months and even if the challenge is heard by the Court the individual still has to prove one of the grounds specified in art.263(2) **TFEU** if they are to succeed.

Free Movement of Goods

7

INTRODUCTION

To many the term "common market" is used to describe what the European Union is all about. The association with trade and the free movement of goods is what promoted the ideas to the forefront of the development of the Union in the 1950s and encouraged the UK to apply for membership in the 1960s. However, although the Union has developed other priorities the free movement of goods is still a fundamental principle. This chapter reviews the law on this topic.

An essential element of the common market is the series of freedoms which constitute the "foundations of the Union". Of these freedoms the most important is the free movement of goods which also includes agricultural products.

The Treaty does not provide a definition of the concept "common market", but art.28(1) **TFEU** states that:

> "The Union shall comprise a customs union which shall cover all trade in goods and which shall involve the prohibition between Members States of customs duties on imports and exports and of all charges having equivalent effect, and the adoption of a common customs tariff in their relations with third countries."

The latter differentiates between a customs union and a free trade area, such as NAFTA, which has no common customs tariff and is therefore limited to free movement of products originating in states belonging to the trade area.

The customs union was completed on June 30, 1968 for the original Member States. It was given effect by two essential measures:

1. abolition of customs duties between Member States, and
2. full application of the common customs tariff.

In order to create a single internal market of the whole Union it was necessary to remove the economic frontiers and legal obstacles to transnational trade. In theory the operation was based on the twin principles of free circulation of goods and non-discrimination between domestic and foreign products of the Member States. In that sense exports and imports as between Member States has become only a matter of domestic accounting as far as individual Member States are concerned. In fact the Commission now collects the information on trade. In practice the ECJ initially insisted on the enforcement of both principles, but seems now to be content to enforce the principle of free circulation which was given a broad meaning. On the question of non-discrimination the ECJ seems more concerned with cases involving internal trading between the Member States.

Thus the Treaty envisages the Community based on a Customs Union. This concept rests upon arts 28 and 110 **TFEU**.

Article 28 **TFEU**—enumerates the elements necessary to achieve a customs union.

Article 110 **TFEU**—prohibits internal taxation on imports having an equivalent effect to customs duties.

DEFINITION CHECKPOINT

Free circulation

Goods benefiting from the right to free circulation are the products originating from Member States as well as products coming from non-Member States which are in free circulation in that Member State.

"Products coming from a third country shall be considered to be in free circulation in a Member State if the import formalities have been complied with and any customs duties or charges having equivalent effect which are payable have been levied in that Member State" art.29 **TFEU**.

Elimination of duties between Member States

This was a formidable task because it was not merely a question of clearing up the jungle of national customs laws but basically of overcoming the idea of Member States being sovereign economic units. To ensure an immediate effect art.30 **TFEU** prohibits the increase of existing customs duties and the imposition of new duties on imports and exports or any charges having an equivalent effect (see *Van Gend en Loos*).

Charges having equivalent effect

While the illegality of customs duties, export taxes and levies is a straightforward proposition "charges having an equivalent effect" prohibited by art.30 **TFEU** have posed a continuous problem as they are often subtle in execution. Although they are not defined by the Treaty, the ECJ defined these charges as

> " ... duties whatever their description or techniques imposed unilaterally, which apply specifically to a product imported by a Member State, but not to a similar national product and which by altering the price, have the same effect upon the free movement of goods as a customs duty" (Case 24/68 *Commission v Italy*).

Examples

(a) A statistical levy on imported goods—Case 7/68 *EC Commission v Italy.*
(b) A tax on cardboard egg containers charged to egg importer for the benefit of a national organisation set up for the promotion of production of paper and cellulose in Italy (Case 94/74 *Industria Gomma v Ente Nazionale per la Cellulose*).

Both (a) and (b) are prohibited by the Treaty.

(c) Charging 0.50 per cent ad valorem duty for administrative services in respect of goods imported from other MS. Italy was found to be guilty of a failure to fulfil an obligation under the Treaty.
(d) More plausible charges such as for phyto-sanitary inspection of fruit or veterinary and public health inspection of meat are also prohibited unless authorised by the Community and applied accordingly.

It is not the test that is disapproved of but the charge for the test. It would appear from the case law of the Court that a charge levied for a service rendered to the importer and which is not too general and uncertain would be permissible. This principle has, however, been given the narrowest possible scope. The ECJ has held that where an inspection service is imposed in the general interest, e.g. for health or safety purposes or quality control, this cannot be regarded as a service rendered to the importer or exporter to justify the imposition of a charge.

Article 110 TFEU

Similar to customs duties and equivalent charges are internal taxes which if imposed upon goods coming from a fellow Member State would discriminate against such goods. Such taxes are prohibited by art.110 **TFEU** if they are in excess of taxes imposed upon similar domestic products. For example, a German importer of powdered milk was able to resist the demand for a payment in lieu of a turnover tax from which a similar national product was exempted (see also *Commission v France* and *Commission v Greece*).

Elimination of quantitative restriction

Having abolished customs duties the Treaty purports to eliminate quotas by prohibiting quantitative restrictions on imports (art.34 **TFEU**) and exports (art.35 **TFEU**). Quantitative restrictions have been interpreted by the ECJ "as any measure which amounts to a total or partial restraint on imports, exports or goods in transit" (see Case 2/73 *Riseria Luigi Geddo v Ente Nazionale Risi*).

There are still problems with Member States acting independently to manipulate trade for domestic reasons. In law they can no longer resort to protectionist measures either to regulate the influx of foreign goods as a matter of national policy or to respond to pressures from industries incapable of coping with foreign competition. There were many examples initially but it is now rare for countries to resort to quotas, e.g. UK potatoes, French sheep meat. However, covert quota systems might operate by means of an import licence requirement. A licensing system might in itself amount to a quantitative restriction or, alternatively, a measure of equivalent effect to a quantitative restriction. Even if the granting of the licence was a pure formality the requirement of such a licence to import would amount to a breach of art.34 **TFEU**.

To offer States guidance as to the meaning and scope of "measures having equivalent effect" to quantitative restrictions the Commission passed **Directive 70/50**. Although this Directive was concerned with the transitional period of the Community and therefore no longer binding, it does offer a non-binding guideline as to the measures to be considered as having equivalent effect.

There are "measures equivalent to quantitative restrictions" prohibited but not defined by the Treaty. To the surprise of Member States, both the Commission and the ECJ have been very generous in their interpretation of this term, to include not merely overtly protective measures or measures applicable only to imports (i.e. distinctly applicable measures), but measures applicable to imports and domestic goods alike (indistinctly applicable measures), often introduced for the best of motives. Such measures range from regulatory measures designed to enforce minimum standards, e.g. of size, weight, quality, price or content, to tests and inspections or certification requirements to ensure that goods conform to these standards, to any activity capable of influencing the behaviour of traders such as promoting goods by reason of their national origin (Case 113/80 *Commission v Ireland* (the Buy Irish Campaign Case).

Dassonville formula

In 1974 the ECJ had the opportunity in *Dassonville* (the Scotch whisky case) to provide its own definition of measures having equivalent effect to quantitative restrictions. This definition, known as the *Dassonville* formula, has since been applied consistently. According to the formula:

> "All trading rules enacted by Member States which are capable of hindering, directly or indirectly, actually or potentially, intra-Community trade are to considered as measures having effect equivalent to quantitative restrictions."

Thus it is not necessary to show actual effect on trade between Member States as long as the measure is capable of such effects.

The measure in issue in *Dassonville* was a requirement, under Belgian law, that imported goods should carry a certificate of origin issued by the State in which the goods were manufactured. Dassonville imported a consignment of Scotch whisky from France. Since the sellers were unable to supply the required certificate he attached a homemade certificate of origin to the goods and appeared before the Belgian court on a forgery charge. In his defence, he claimed that the Belgian regulation was contrary to EC law. On a reference from the Belgian court under art.267 **TFEU**, the ECJ, applying the above formula, found that the measure was capable of breaching art.34 **TFEU**.

KEY CASE

Case 120/78 Rewe-Zentral AG v Bundesmonopolverwaltung fur Branntwein

The ECJ took another decisive step in the case of *Cassis de Dijon* (Case 120/78 *Rewe-Zentral AG v Bundesmonopolverwaltung für Branntwein*). This made a distinction between distinctly and indistinctly applicable measures. The question before the ECJ concerned the legality under EC law of a German law laying down a minimum alcohol level of 25 per cent for certain spirits, which included cassis, a blackcurrant-flavoured liqueur. German cassis complied with this minimum, but French cassis, with an alcohol content of 15–20 per cent did not. Thus although the German regulation was indistinctly applicable, the result of the measure was effectively to ban French cassis from the German market. A number of German importers contested the measure, and the German court referred a number of questions to the ECJ under art.267 **TFEU**.

The ECJ applied the *Dassonville* formula above but added:

> "Obstacles to movement within the Community resulting from disparities between the national laws relating to the marketing of the products in question must be accepted in so far as those provisions may be recognised as being necessary in order to satisfy mandatory requirements relating in particular to the effectiveness of fiscal supervision, the protection of public health, the fairness of commercial transactions and the defence of the consumer."

This has subsequently been called the first Cassis principle, i.e. that certain measures will not breach art.34 **TFEU** if they are necessary to satisfy mandatory requirements even though they may come within the *Dassonville* formula because they are indistinctly applicable. If the measure is distinctly applicable it will normally breach art.34 **TFEU** but may be justified under art.36 **TFEU**.

Thus in the *Cassis* case the ECJ found that the German law was in breach of art.34 **TFEU**. Although the measure was allegedly enacted in the interests of public health (to prevent increased consumption resulting from lowering the alcoholic content of cassis) and the fairness of commercial transactions (to avoid giving the weak imported cassis an unfair advantage over its stronger, hence more expensive German rival), the measure was not necessary to achieve these ends. Other means, such as labelling, which would have been less of a hindrance to trade, could have been used to achieve the same ends.

The ECJ established another important principle in the *Cassis* case ("the second Cassis principle"). "There was no valid reason why, provided that goods have been lawfully produced and marketed in one of the Member States, they should not be introduced into any other Member State." This gives rise to a presumption that goods which have been lawfully marketed in another Member State will comply with the "mandatory requirements" of the importing State. This can be rebutted by evidence that further measures are necessary to protect the interest concerned. However, the burden of proving that a measure is necessary is a heavy one and the presumption will be very hard to rebut.

Price controls, resulting in the fixing of profit margins, may be regarded as a measure having an equivalent effect to quantitative restrictions on imports if they place imported goods at a disadvantage in relation to identical national products/goods, e.g. a Dutch licensed victualler, prosecuted for selling liquor at prices below the minimum fixed by the national law, successfully raised a defence that the prosecution was contrary to art.34 **TFEU**.

KEY CASE

Case 267/91 Criminal Proceedings against Keck

In Case 267/91 *Criminal Proceedings against Keck*, a case concerned with resale at a loss, the Court was anxious to discourage excessive use of art.34 **TFEU** with regard to "certain selling arrangements" which are non-discriminatory. Such arrangements apply to all affected traders in the territory of the Member State and affect all traders in the same manner in law and in fact. In doing so they fall outside of the scope of art.34 **TFEU**.

The Court applied *Keck* in Case 391/92 *Commission v Greece*, a case involving the sale of processed milk for infants. Although the national legislation might restrict the volume of sales the legislation satisfied the conditions laid down in *Keck* and consequently did not breach art.34 **TFEU**. The recent judgment in Case 322/01 *Deutscher Apothekerverband* involving the prohibition of the sale of medicines on the internet by German law illustrates the application of *Keck* to modern situations. The prohibition was found to be contrary to art.34 **TFEU**, although there may be an argument for derogation under art.36 **TFEU**.

Derogation under article 36 TFEU

Article 36 **TFEU** allows Member States to legitimately limit the freedom of movement of goods and thus derogate from principles comprised in arts 34 and 35 **TFEU**. Although the grounds in art.36 **TFEU** appear extensive they have been narrowly construed by the Court. They must not constitute a means of arbitrary discrimination or a disguised restriction on trade between Member States.

The grounds for derogation are "public morality, public policy and public security; the protection of health and life of humans, animals or plants; the protection of national treasures possessing artistic, historic or archaeological value; or the protection of industrial and commercial property".

"Public morality, policy and security"

These terms express "peculiar national values" and it is difficult to envisage a uniform Community application of a diversity of values. The ECJ recognised its limitations in dealing with public policy and decreed that a certain margin of appreciation may be left to national authorities. However, it does not follow that these matters are reserved to the exclusive jurisdiction of Member States, but permits national law to derogate from the principle of free movement of goods to the extent that such derogation is and continues to be justified under art.36 **TFEU**.

Public morality Examples—compare pornographic material freely available in another Member State in *R. v Henn*, *R. v Darby* [1980] 2 All E.R. 166 with *Conegate Ltd v Customs & Excise Commissioners* [1987] Q.B. 254 which involved the seizure of a number of inflatable rubber love dolls imported from Germany.

Public policy This ground, potentially wide, has been strictly construed, and has only succeeded as a basis for derogation under art.36 **TFEU** on few occasions. One example is *R v Thompson and Others* (Case C-7/78) where the UK government prosecuted Thompson and others for importing gold coins to be melted down. The "oyblic policy" at issue was the protection of the national coinage and the right to mint coinage.

Public security This ground was successfully invoked in Case 72/83 *Campus Oil Ltd v Minister for Industry and Energy* to justify an Irish order requiring importers of petroleum oils to buy up to 35 per cent of their requirements of petroleum products from the Irish National Petroleum Company at prices fixed by the minister. The Irish government argued that it was justified on public security grounds, to maintain a viable refinery that would meet essential needs in times of crisis. This was accepted by the ECJ.

Protection of public health

The cases reveal devices used by Member States to raise revenue or to discriminate against imported products. The health protection plea seems to have been argued rather tenuously and it was the commercial aspect which characterised those cases. However, it is possible to envisage a legitimate and compelling use in some cases such as those involving health precautions against rabies or humanitarian considerations in the transport of livestock.

There have been a number of attempts to derogate from the Treaty under this heading, e.g. *Commission v UK (Re UHT Milk)*, *Commission v UK (Re Imports of Poultry Meat)* and Case 42/82 *Commission v France (Re Italian Table Wines)*.

If a charge is levied for the inspection it may be considered as a charge having equivalent effect. If it is not prohibited by the Treaty and not seen as a way of raising revenue but actually seen to assist the flow of goods it may be acceptable.

Protection of industrial and commercial property

This includes patents, copyright and trademarks. Faced with the problem of such rights being used in order to frustrate the Community competition policy or to impede the free movement of goods the ECJ distinguished between the existence of rights and their use. Only a legitimate use, i.e. one that is compatible with the rules on competition and the free movement of goods is justified.

In the opinion of the Court:

> "... in as much as it provides an exception to one of the fundamental principles of the Common Market, art.36 **TFEU** in fact admits exceptions to the free movement of goods only to the extent to which such exceptions are justified for the purpose of safeguarding rights which constitute the specific subject matter of that property" (Case 119/75 *Terrapin (Overseas) Ltd v Terranova Industrie* (see also Competition Policy in the next chapter)).

Revision Checklist

You should now know and understand:

- **the meaning of the "common market" and a customs union**
- **the meaning of a quantitative restriction**
- **the meaning of "measures having equivalent effect"**
- **the *Dassonville* formula**
- **the impact of the *Cassis de Dijon* case**
- **the derogations under art.30 EC**

QUESTION AND ANSWER

The Question

Arthur Rose Ltd imported a consignment of plastic tulips into the UK from the Netherlands and was required to have each flower individually tested to ensure that it conformed to a new test for imported plastic products. The company wishes to challenge this requirement on the ground that it is incompatible with European Union law. Advise Arthur.

Advice and the Answer

Introduction—this problem question concerns the free movement of goods. The EU is based upon a customs union (art.28 **TFEU**) which requires a common external tariff and the removal of all barriers to intra-Community trade. As these tulips are being imported from another Member State (the Netherlands) these principles should apply here.

Article 34 **TFEU** states that all barriers to trade which amount to quantitative restrictions and all measures having equivalent effect are prohibited. (*Riseria Luigi Geddo v Ente Nazionale Risi.*) The ECJ has given the concept a wide interpretation by dividing it into measures which are indistinctly applicable and those which are distinctly applicable, the latter being those which only apply to imported goods.

The main case law on this can be found in the cases of *Dassonville* (1974) and *Cassis de Dijon* (1987). These cases developed the Dassonville formula which states that all trading rules enacted by Member States which are capable of hindering intra-community trade are to be considered to be as measures having an effect equivalent to quantitative restrictions. However, art.34 **TFEU** will not be breached if the requirements can satisfy a public interest such as the protection of public health. There is a presumption under the *Cassis de Dijon* second principle that goods lawfully marketed in one Member State will comply with the mandatory requirements of the importing Member State.

The advice to Arthur is that the requirements imposed by the UK for testing are applicable to imported goods only so the measure would be considered as a distinctly applicable one. As the goods are sold in the Netherlands the second principle from the *Cassis de Dijon* case would seem to apply. The best way for Arthur to proceed would be for him to bring an action in the national court and then ask for a request for a preliminary reference to be made by the court to the ECJ.

Competition Policy

8

INTRODUCTION

This chapter follows the discussion of the free movement of goods because it was felt that if trade restrictions by governments were to be removed they were not to be replaced by business creating their own barriers. This chapter reviews the law that has been developed to deal with anti-competitive activity by a few businesses working together or by one large business exercising what could be called monopolistic power.

ROLE OF COMPETITION IN THE EUROPEAN UNION

From its very beginning the European Community has always accorded great importance to competition. In art.3 **TEU**, where the principles or aims of the Union are listed, art.3(3) refers to a "highly competitive social market economy" and then in art.3(1)(b) **TFEU** it states that the Union shall have exclusive competence in the "establishing of the competition rules necessary for the functioning of the internal market".

This emphasis on competition has two advantages. For the European Commission competition is the best stimulant of economic activity as it guarantees the widest possible freedom of action to all. Second, it prevents the introduction within the internal market of any new obstacles to trade by individuals, undertakings or Member States now that old barriers have been removed. A strong competition policy can be used to fulfil the objectives of the Community, such as economic integration.

The Treaty does not define the concept of "competition", but it does refer to certain measures which interfere with competition and which are therefore prohibited, subject to exemptions granted by the Commission.

There are two dimensions to competition policy within a Member State; that of the national laws of the Member State and imposed upon that a system of Union law. The European Union rules are administered and enforced by the national authorities, subject to the special role of the Commission in the field of competition policy. Good communications between the

Commission and the national authorities are important to ensure uniformity and to avoid the danger of concurrent national and Union action. If the Commission takes action under the Union's competition rules, it has priority over any subsequent action taken in the national courts.

Article 101 TFEU and restrictive practices

Article 101 **TFEU** complements art.102 **TFEU** as they both seek to secure fair competition by curbing restraints on trade. The procedure for the application of these two articles is set out in **Regulation 1/2003**, which replaced **Regulation 17/62**. Article 101 **TFEU** is concerned with the effect on trade of various restrictive practices involving two or more undertakings, while art.102 **TEU** is primarily concerned with monopolist situations. Both are concerned with the abuse rather than the existence of economic power. The European Union claims extra-territorial jurisdiction in that even if the undertaking is established outside the EU the competition policy will still apply if its actions will affect trade between the Member States.

TREATY HIGHLIGHTER

ARTICLE 101 TFEU

1. The following shall be prohibited as incompatible with the common market: all agreements between undertakings, decisions by associations of undertakings and concerted practices which may affect trade between Member States and which have as their object or effect the prevention restrictions or distortion of competition within the common market, and in particular those which:

- **(a)** directly or indirectly fix purchase or selling prices or any other trading conditions;
- **(b)** limit or control production, markets, technical development, or investment;
- **(c)** share markets or sources of supply;
- **(d)** apply dissimilar conditions to equivalent transactions with other trading parties, thereby placing them at a competitive disadvantage; and
- **(e)** make the conclusion of contracts subject to acceptance by the other parties of supplementary obligations which, by their nature or according to commercial usage, have no connection with the subject of such contracts.

2. Any agreements or decisions prohibited pursuant to this article shall be automatically void.

3. The provisions of para.1 may, however, be declared inapplicable in the case of:

- any agreement or category of agreements between undertakings;
- any decision or category of decisions by associations of undertakings; or
- any concerted practice or category of concerted practices;

which contributes to improving the production or distribution of goods or to promoting technical or economic progress, while allowing consumers a fair share of the resulting benefit, and which does not;

(a) impose on the undertakings concerned restrictions which are not indispensable to the attainment of these objects; and
(b) afford such undertakings the possibility of eliminating competition in respect of a substantial part of the products in question.

Agreements and Concerted Practices There are clearly three parts to art.101 **TFEU**. Article 101(1) **TFEU** is concerned with agreements between undertakings and decisions by associations of undertakings. However, it goes further by the use of the term "concerted practices". This refers to behaviour and includes any "gentleman's agreement" which has not been put into writing. The Court defined concerted practices in Case 48/69 *ICI v Commission* (the *Dyestuffs* case) as "a form of co-ordination between enterprises that has not yet reached the point where there is a contract in the true sense of the word but which, in practice consciously substitutes a practical co-operation for the risks of competition". It may be that the similarity of actions by undertakings is coincidental, in which case they are not prohibited. It is only where they are planned as a result of some collusion or concentration that they are prohibited. The Commission does have problems in proving such arrangements where the evidence may be circumstantial. However, the onus may be on the undertakings to prove that they had not entered into such an arrangement (*Dyestuffs*). Article 101 **TFEU** is not concerned with agreements between undertakings belonging to the same concern, such as a parent company and its subsidiaries. A business must have economic independence in order to qualify as an undertaking within art.101 **TFEU** (see Joined Cases 159/91 and 160/91 *Poucet v AGF*).

Whatever behaviour or agreement is involved the prohibition under this article will not apply unless it has as its object or effect the prevention, restrictions or distortion of competition within the "common market". This can arise when any kind of action by an undertaking directly affects the market and is detrimental to production or sales to purchasers or consumers because it limits freedom of choice. The ECJ has refined the meaning of distortion of competition by adding the phrase "to an appreciable extent". In this way the Court has shown that it is not really concerned with small affects by applying the de minimus rule. It is necessary under the guidelines from the Court to take into account the nature and quantity of the product covered by the agreement, the position and importance of the parties on the market for the products concerned, the isolated nature of the disputed agreement, the severity of the clauses limiting trade between Member States and the opportunities for commercial competition in the same product. The term "within the Union" does not necessarily refer to competition in several Member States or even all. If there is an adverse effect on competition in one single Member State it may be considered as taking place within the Union and prohibited by the article. There is also listed (a) to (e) examples of such behaviour or agreements.

Exemption Article 101(2) **TFEU** states quite clearly that anything prohibited by art.101(1) **TFEU** is automatically void. However, art.101(3) **TFEU** provides for the possibility of exemption. Exemption in individual cases may only be granted once the Commission has been notified of the agreement concerned and the four conditions of art.101(3) **TFEU** fulfilled. The exemption may not enter into force on a date earlier than the date of notification. They are issued for a specified period and can have conditions or obligations attached to them. They can be renewed but also revoked, sometimes with retroactive effect. As a result of the timescale needed for the Commission to deal with individual claims for exemption, a number of block exemptions have been issued in the form of regulations. These cover such commercial activities as exclusive purchasing agreements, exclusive agency agreements, patent licensing and research, and development agreements. If the undertakings can ensure that the clauses of the agreement are within that specified by the block exemption they will not risk being fined and do not need to notify the Commission of the agreement. The Commission also publishes notices, which are not binding, specifying agreements which in its view do not fall within art.101(1) **TFEU**.

Negative clearance and comfort letters—now Guidance Letters

If an undertaking wishes to obtain official confirmation that an agreement is outside those prohibited by art.101(1) **TFEU**, it could seek negative clearance under **Regulation 17/62**. However, the Commission was spending a disproportionate amount of time in dealing with applications for negative clearance and applications for exemption under art.101(3) **TFEU**. When **Regulation 1/2003** replaced **Regulation 17/62** this situation was changed fundamentally. Under **Regulation 1/2003** it was no longer necessary for the undertaking to notify the Commission in order to obtain negative clearance. The Regulation puts the burden on the undertaking to decide if it offends art.101 **TFEU**. To ease this workload and to speed up its decision-making processes, the Commission began to issue "comfort letters". These provided a quick and informal way of providing assurance for the parties concerned. A comfort letter is a communication from the Commission to the effect that, in its opinion, the agreement either does not infringe art.101(1) **TFEU** or that if it does infringe the article it is of a type that qualifies for exemption. The letter generally concludes with the statement that the Commission considers the "file closed". Such letters have been held by the Court to be outside the framework of **Regulation 17/62** (now **Regulation 1/2003**) as they are only administrative letters and as such are not legally binding on national courts (see the *Perfumes* cases, Case 99/79 *SA Lancôme v Etos BV*). Also the Commission can reopen the file at any time. What the Commission can now do is to issue non-legally enforceable "guidance letters" under **Regulation 1/2003.**

All agreements or practices covered by art.81(1) EC (ex 85(1) EC) must be notified to the Commission as failure to do so, for any reason, may result in heavy fines being imposed by the Commission (see below, p.91).

Article 102 TFEU and the abuse of a dominant position

TREATY HIGHLIGHTER

ARTICLE 102 TFEU

Any abuse by one or more undertakings of a dominant position within the common market or in a substantial part of it shall be prohibited as incompatible with the common market in so far as it may affect trade between Member States. Such abuse may, in particular, consist in:

- (a) directly or indirectly imposing unfair purchase or selling prices or unfair trading conditions;
- (b) limiting production, markets or technical development to the prejudice of consumers;
- (c) applying dissimilar conditions to equivalent transactions with other trading parties, thereby placing them at a competitive disadvantage; and

> (d) making the conclusion of contracts subject to acceptance by the other parties of supplementary obligations which, by their nature or according to commercial usage, have no connection with the subject of such contracts.

There are three essential ingredients to this article. There must be a dominant position; an abuse of that position and that abuse must affect trade between the Member States.

Dominant Position What is meant by dominance? The Court stated in Case 27/76 *United Brands v Commission* that it is "a position of economic strength enjoyed by an undertaking which enables it to prevent effective competition being maintained on the relevant market by giving it the power to behave to an appreciable extent independently of its competitors, customers and ultimately of its consumers". The Commission added in Case 62/86 *AKZO Chemie BV v Commission* "The power to exclude effective competition is not ... in all cases coterminous with independence from competitive factors but may also involve the ability to eliminate or seriously weaken existing competitors or to prevent potential competitors from entering the market". The existence of a dominant position is a question of fact determined by the relevant market factors. There has to be a relevant market for art.102 **TFEU** to operate, but this is not always easy to define. For example, in *United Brands* the Commission made a detailed analysis and concluded that the relevant market was the banana market, of which United Brands had a substantial share. The company argued that it was the fresh fruit market which was relevant, of which they had a much smaller share. The ECJ held that the banana market was in fact a distinct market because the characteristics of the consumers meant that the product was not interchangeable. In Case 6/72 *Europemballage and Continental Can v Commission* the problem of product substitution and the inability on the part of the Commission to define the relevant market led to the annulment of the Commission's Decision (see also Case 333/94 *Tetra-Pak International v Commission*).

With regard to the territory of the relevant market there is no fixed geographical definition. It could be a worldwide market or a narrowly localised market. The important point is that the abuse of the dominant position must take effect in the common market or a substantial part of it (Case 68/78 *Liptons Cash Registers v Hugin*).

If there is an abuse of a dominant position under art.102 **TFEU** there is no exemption.

Enforcement of competition policy

The recent cases of C-95/04 *British Airways Plc v Commission* (extra commission payments for travel agents), T-340/03 *France Telecom SA v Commission* (predatory pricing) and T-201/04 *Microsoft Corp v Commission* (refusal to supply) demonstrate the vigilance of the Commission in policing arts 101 and 102 **TFEU**. The European Commission has a central role in enforcing the Community's competition policy through Directorate-General 4 (DG4), the department responsible. To fulfil its tasks the Commission enjoys substantial powers, subject to strict procedural requirements under **Regulation 1/2003** and a general duty of confidentiality. A breach of these duties can result in the annulment of the Commission's Decision by the General Court and possibly a successful action for damages (Case 145/83 *Adams v Commission*).

Investigative powers

If the Commission is to undertake market analysis to enable it to make a Decision it needs powers of investigation.

(a) The Commission can request all information that is necessary to enable it to carry out its task from governments, competent authorities in the Member State such as the Office of Fair Trading in the UK, undertakings and associations of undertakings.

(b) The Commission may conduct general enquiries into whole sectors of the economy if economic trends suggest that competition in the common market is being restricted or distorted.

(c) The Commission may undertake all necessary on-the-spot investigations including entering premises, examining and copying business records and conducting oral examinations.

Before undertaking such investigations the officials of the Commission are required to produce written authorisation in the form of a Decision specifying the subject matter and purpose of the investigations (see Case 136/79 *National Panasonic v Commission* and Case 46/87 *Hoechst v Commission*). The undertakings are required to comply with the legitimate demands from the Commission. If they fail to do so or give false information they may be fined, as information cannot be withheld even if it is self-incriminating. In Case 155/79 *AM & S v Commission*, the ECJ stated that it was possible to claim privilege for correspondence between a client and an independent lawyer, but not where the lawyer is employed "in-house".

Fines and penalties

The Commission has power under **Regulation 1/2003** to impose fines for breaches of arts 101 and 102 **TFEU**. These can be up to one million euros or 10 per cent of the undertaking's global turnover, whichever is the greater. The largest fine imposed to date has been that imposed by the Commission against those in the Vitamins Cartel in 2001 where a fine of over 855 million euros was imposed. In 2002 The European Commission imposed fines totalling 478 million euros on four companies which operated a long-running cartel on the market for plasterboard, a product which is widely used in the building industry and by DIY practitioners. Substantial fines have also been imposed on the US firm Microsoft.

None of the fine is paid to the party injured by the anti-competitive activity. Such victims must seek a remedy in their national courts. The size of the fine will depend on factors such as the nature and duration of the infringement, the economic importance of the undertakings and whether the parties have already infringed the Community's competition policy. To provide more transparency in the calculation of fines the European Commission adopted a number of guidelines in 1997.

Interim measures

Although not specifically granted under **Regulation 1/2003**, the ECJ has held that interim measures can be granted provided they were:

(1) indispensable,
(2) urgent, and
(3) necessary to avoid serious or irreparable damage to the party seeking the action or where there is a situation which is intolerable to the public interest (see Case 792/79 *Camera Care v Commission*).

Competition law and property rights

The ECJ has recognised that there has to be some protection given to owners of intellectual property rights such as patents or trademarks. If this were absent the incentive to advance technological developments would be removed. This is why art.36 **TFEU** provides derogation from art.34 **TFEU**, as discussed above. The Court has managed to balance these rights, confirmed in art.345 **TFEU** with the need not to impair competition. The specific subject matter of the right has been identified and protected but its exercise may be restricted or limited by the Treaty (see Joined Cases 56/64 and 58/64 *Consten and Grundig v Commission* and Case 24/67 *Parke Davis v Centrafarm*). For example, the owner of a patent is entitled to his "reward" of a higher price when the goods are first put on the market. He cannot control their price or distribution by refusing parallel imports as this may affect trade between Member States.

However, the ECJ decision in Case 355/96 *Silhouette International v Hartlauer Hendelsgesellschaft* seemed to take a more restrictive view when interpreting the **Trade Mark Directive 89/104**. Silhouette was allowed to exercise its trademark rights to prevent the importation of its sunglasses from outside the EEA, where they had been sold at a lower price. The ECJ had decided that Silhouette's trademark rights had not been exhausted when they had sold the sunglasses to a retailer in Bulgaria and therefore outside the EEA. In the later case of Case 173/98 *Sebago Inc and Ancienne Maison Dubois et Fils SA v GB-UNIC SA* the ECJ confirmed its interpretation of the Directive, but did raise the possibility for the importer to show that the owner of the trademark had consented to the exhaustion of their rights. In the English case of *Zino Davidoff SA v A & G Imports Ltd* [2002] Ch. 109, where the facts concerned the importation of luxury perfumes, the trademark owner was held to have consented. The essential function of a trademark is to guarantee to consumers the real origin of goods or services, as the ECJ recently stated in the *Arsenal* case (Case 206/01 *Arsenal Football Club Plc v Reed*).

Anti-competitive behaviour by governments

Public undertakings and similar bodies are in principle subject to the same rules on competition as private undertakings (art.106 **TFEU**). However, they are exempted to the extent necessary to perform the particular tasks assigned to them. The Commission supervises such undertakings to ensure that the development of trade between the Member States is not affected.

With regard to state aids, art.107 **TFEU** prohibits any aid that distorts or threatens to distort competition by favouring certain undertakings or the production of certain goods. However, art.107(2) **TFEU** states that certain aid is always permissible, e.g. if it has a social character, and art.107(3) **TFEU** that other aids maybe permissible, e.g. for areas with high unemployment. There is a procedure laid down by art.108 **TFEU** by which the Commission can allow or prevent such aids.

EU merger policy

The Commission originally sought to deal with the impact of mergers on Community competition policy by using art.101 **TFEU** (Case 730/79 *Philip Morris v Commission*) and art.102 **TFEU** (Case C-6/72 *Continental Can*). In September 1990 **Council Regulation 4064/89**, known as the Merger Regulation, came into force. This regulation applied to mergers involving enterprises with an aggregate worldwide turnover of more than five billion euros and where the aggregate Community turnover of each of at least two of the enterprises concerned is more than 250 million euros. Even when these thresholds are not met the merger may still be covered by art.1(3) of **Regulation 1310/97** where other turnover thresholds are specified. Such mergers are subject to examination by the European Commission, unless they are primarily within one Member State (see the *Aérospatiale–Alenia–de Haviland* case (Case IV/M53)). **Regulation 1310/97** amended **Regulation 4064/89** to facilitate greater procedural harmony in the assessment of different types of mergers.

Under art.2(3) of the Regulation there is a two-stage test of compatibility. The initial consideration is whether the concentration "creates or strengthens a dominant position within the common market or a substantial part of it". If this is satisfied, the Commission is required to assess whether the merger will significantly impede effective competition within the Community. The Commission will then either clear the merger, allowing it to take place, or stop it from taking place. This is not an easy task as is evidenced by the recent decisions by the General Court that annulled Commission decisions because the Court was not satisfied with the economic analysis of the anti-competition effects produced by the Commission. These were the cases of *Tetra Laval BV* (T-5/02) and Case T-77/02 *Schneider Electric SA v Commission*. Schneider subsequently brought a successful claim in damages against the Commission under art.340 TFEU in the case of T-352/03 *Schneider SA v Commission*.

The new **Merger Regulation 139/2004** is the latest attempt by the Commission to improve the speed and efficiency of the control of "concentrations". This Regulation recognises that national controls may be more efficient if the EU is to compete in the global market. It provides for a "one-stop shop" so that clearance or refusal can be given quickly. The turnover thresholds under the new Regulation remain the same.

Remedies in the national courts

The courts of the Member States can apply arts 101 and 102 **TFEU** as they are directly effective. If the court applies the rule of reason devised by the ECJ to decide if the agreement is contrary to art.101(1) **TFEU** and comes to the conclusion that it does, it can only declare it void under art.101(2) **TFEU**. Only the Commission can grant exemption under art.101(3) **TFEU** and impose fines under **Regulation 1/2003**. The national court should grant the same remedies as would be available in similar actions under national law, including interlocutory proceedings. However, in *Garden Cottage Foods Ltd v Milk Marketing Board* [1984] A.C. 130, the House of Lords left it unclear as to whether a breach of art.101 **TFEU** could give rise to a remedy in damages. In the subsequent case of C-453/99 *Courage Ltd v Crehan* the right for an individual to claim damages before a national court for breaches of arts 101 and 102 **TFEU** EC was recognised by the ECJ.

Revision Checklist

You should now know and understand:

- the role of competition policy in the EC
- the control of restrictive practices under art.101 **TFEU**
- the control of abuse of a dominant position under art.102 **TFEU**
- the role and powers of the European Commission in policing the competition policy
- the possibilities for exemption and negative clearance for businesses
- the enforcement of competition policy and **Regulation 1/2003**
- fines and penalties that can be imposed
- anti-competitive behaviour by governments
- the EU merger policy
- the remedies in the national courts

QUESTION AND ANSWER

The Question

What powers are given to the European Commission with regard to the enforcement of EU competition policy?

Advice and the Answer

Introduction—the European Commission has been given extensive powers with regard to competition policy (art.101 **TFEU**) as they are seen to be the guardians of the Treaties (see art.17 **TEU**). The Treaties take the maintenance of competition very seriously and cover anti-competitive behaviour of undertakings or businesses (arts 101 & 102 **TFEU**) but also the governments of Member States (art 106 **TFEU**).

It is **Regulation 1/2003**, which replaced **Regulation 17/62**, which gives the Commission its investigative powers. These include the ability to undertake market analysis to enable it to make a Decision; it can request all information that is necessary to enable it to carry out its task from governments, competent authorities in the Member State, undertakings and associations of undertakings. It can conduct general enquiries into whole sectors of the economy if economic trends suggest that competition in the common market is being restricted or distorted. Finally, where necessary, the Commission may undertake all necessary on-the-spot investigations including entering premises, examining and copying business records and conducting oral examinations.

Only the European Commission can grant an exemption to undertakings where a breach of art.101(3) **TFEU** is concerned or can give approval to a Member State acting contrary to the principle of competition in special circumstances. The Commission can also impose fines of one million euros or 10 per cent of the undertaking's global turnover whichever is the greater if there has been a breach of the competition rules. This demonstrates their authority in this area of policy. The Commission works closely with the national competition authorities but ultimately it is the Commission's responsibility to enforce the competition policy of the EC.

Free Movement of Workers

9

INTRODUCTION

The EU seeks to promote comprehensive economic integration and these provisions apply to all workers of the Member States, regardless of occupation. Since a common market requires the removal of all obstacles to the free movement of the factors of production, the free movement of workers in the Union may be seen as simply a prerequisite to the achievement of an economic objective. This chapter reviews the main points associated with the free movement of workers and their families.

The Treaties do not purport to establish an absolute freedom of migration in a general sense, but confine themselves to this economic activity. Eventually the object is to create a "common market in manpower", which would serve the purpose of moving labour to areas which reveal shortage of manpower and to solve the problem of unemployment in overpopulated areas. Whether such a simplistic view can still be held in the light of future enlargement is an important question.

However this policy does not only have economic implications. There are also social consequences. The Preamble of **Regulation 1612/68** (now amended by **Directive 2004/38**) stated:

> "The freedom of movement constitutes a fundamental right of workers and their families; mobility of labour within the Community must be one of the means by which the worker is guaranteed the possibility of improving his living and working conditions and promoting his social advancement, while helping to satisfy the requirements of the economy of the Member States".

The freedom of movement of workers is mainly based on the principle of non-discrimination on the ground of nationality, while the freedom of non-wage earners to move within the Community is, generally speaking, expressed by the right of establishment and the right to provide service. For the non-economically active three Directives were adopted in 1990 giving rights to those of independent means (**Directive 90/364**) and retired persons who did not satisfy **Directive 1251/70** (**Directive 90/365**). In addition there was **Directive 90/366** which provided rights to students undertaking a vocational course at a university in another Member State whereby they can reside in the host Member State for the duration of their course. This Directive was later annulled by the Court (Case 295/90 *European Parliament v Council*) on the grounds that the legal base claimed by the Council was wrong so that the Parliament was merely consulted and the co-operation procedure was not utilised. However, the Directive remained in force until it was replaced by **Directive 93/96**. For all these directives there is one common factor, which is that the individual who is seeking to enforce a right under them is not economically dependent upon the benefits system of the host Member State. These directives are no longer in force because they have been superseded by a new **Directive 2004/38** and more importantly by the development of the rights of "citizens of the EU". To try to show that the EU was not just for businesses and in an attempt to strengthen the links between the EU and its citizens, the concept of citizen of the EU was introduced in the **Treaty of Amsterdam**. It is now stated in art.20 **TFEU** that every person holding the nationality of a Member State is a citizen of the Union. Importantly in the context of the free movement of workers is art.21 **TFEU** which states that every EU citizen has the right to move and reside freely within the territory of the Member States subject to any limitations and conditions laid down in the Treaties or by measures adopted to give them effect. The most important one of these conditions is that the citizen should not be a burden upon the welfare of the Member State. This condition has been tempered by ECJ judgments such as Case C-138/02 *Collins* where jobs seekers allowance was allowed to be claimed and Case C-209/03 *Bidar* where a subsidised student loan could be obtained.

Directive 2004/38, which came into force in May 2006, consolidates several provisions that affect the worker. It is known as the Citizens Free Movement Rights Directive and it repeals **Directive 68/360**, arts 10 and 11 of **Regulation 1612/68** and **Directive 64/221**.

Directives concerned determine the scope and detailed rules for exercise of rights conferred directly by the Treaty. No exit or entry visas are required from EC nationals, only an identity card or a passport.

Concept of "worker"

Article 45 **TFEU** refers to "freedom of movement for workers" and art.1 of **Regulation 1612/68** on Freedom of Movement for Workers within the Community referred to the right to "take up an activity as an employed person", but neither give definitions. The Court has said that the words must be given their ordinary meaning and not interpreted restrictively. However, the concept only covers pursuit of effective and genuine activities. Provided that he pursues this effective and genuine activity the motives of the individual are not to be taken into account. In Case 66/85 *Lawrie-Blum v Land Baden-Württemberg* the ECJ suggested that the essential characteristics of a worker are of someone who performs services for another during a certain period of time and under the direction of another in return for remuneration. In the *Levin* case (Case 53/81) the Court held that those who worked part-time were included provided the work was "real" work and not nominal or minimal (see Case 139/85 *Kempf v Staatssecretaris van Justitie*).

Regulation 1408/71 defines a worker as anyone who is insured either compulsorily or voluntarily within the framework of a social security system of a Member State organised for the benefit of salaried employees.

The definition of "worker" in the Community sense rarely causes difficulty because if an economically active claimant under art.45 **TFEU** is not a worker, he is probably self-employed in which case art.49 or 56 **TFEU** would apply. The ECJ has held that arts 45, 49 and 56 **TFEU** are based on the same principles as far as entry, residence and non-discrimination on the grounds of nationality are concerned and so categorisation under art.45, as opposed to art.49 or 50 **TFEU** will rarely be crucial. This is even more so since the increase in the rights of the EU citizen mentioned above and detailed in arts 18 to 25 **TFEU**.

Removal of restrictions

The Council issued **Directive 68/360** on the abolition of restrictions on movements and residence for workers of the Member State and their families. Both art.45 **TFEU** and the Directive have been held by the ECJ to be directly effective, giving individuals' rights that the courts in the Member States must protect and enforce. **Directive 2004/38** has replaced **Directive 68/360**.

Article 45(3) **TFEU** envisages the free movement of workers for pursuit of accepting employment but makes no mention of a right to move freely in search of employment. **Directive 68/360** made no reference to this point either, but it has been generously interpreted by the Court. In Case 48/75 *Procureur du Roi v Royer* the Court held that art.3 of the Directive included the right of workers to enter the territory of a Member State and reside there for the purposes intended by the Treaty, in particular to look for or pursue an activity as an employed person. In the *Levin* case this right was limited to three months on the proviso that the individual could support themselves without recourse to public assistance. Also in Case 292/89 *R. v Immigration Appeal Tribunal, Ex p. Antonissen* the Court held that immigrants seeking employment had the right to enter another Member State and stay there for a sufficient period of time to find out about the job market opportunities and to find a job. In the UK six months is allowed for a "worker" to find a job although generally at least three months are given by Member States.

Right of residence

A worker's right to a residence permit is implied once he has secured a job but if he finds no job or if he loses it voluntarily he cannot expect to be entitled to a residence permit. Thus a British subject continuously unemployed was not entitled to a renewal of his residence permit in the Netherlands—*Williams v Dutch Secretary of State* (1977).

The right of residence means the right to stay indefinitely in the host country. A worker cannot be expelled except in cases justifiable under derogation from the freedom of movement (see Limitations below, p.103). The residence permit is issued for a period of five years but it is renewable. The permit is merely proof of the right granted by the Treaty that exists independently of the document.

Directive 2004/38

Articles 16–18 of this Directive replace **Regulation 1251/70**. As a corollary to the freedom of movement protected by **Regulation 1612/68** and **Directive 68/360, Regulation 1251/70** (now **Directive 2004/38**) gave the worker the right to remain in the territory of a Member State after having been employed there. This right applies to the retired and the incapacitated worker. A worker acquires a right of residence on retirement provided that he has reached the age laid down in that Member State for entitlement to an old-age pension, and has resided continuously in that Member State for more than three years the last year of which he has been employed. If the incapacity of the worker is due to an industrial accident or disease entitling him to the payment of a pension, he can remain in the Member State regardless of the length of his previous residence. If the incapacity did not arise from employment he is entitled to remain if he has resided in the Member State for at least two years.

Worker's dependants

The principle of non-discrimination must be extended to his or her dependants; otherwise the practical implementation becomes meaningless. This non-discrimination as regards dependants must not be limited to the right to reside in another Member State, together with the worker. It must encompass the whole treatment afforded to national dependants, including education, training, welfare and housing.

Under art.2 of **Directive 2004/38** family members include not only the spouse but also a partner in a registered partnership.

In principle members of the family have rights analogous to the rights of the person primarily concerned, i.e. entry, residence and exit, together with social security rights. Family rights terminate with the primary rights of the worker and also when a dependant ceases to be a member of the family, e.g. divorced spouse or a married child).

Directive 2004/38 would now cover this situation and so the individual would no longer be dependent upon the law in any one Member State.

KEY CASE

CASE 59/85 NETHERLANDS STATE V REED

In Case 59/85 *Netherlands State v Reed* the ECJ held that the term "spouse" included cohabitee. Reed was a UK national who went to live in the Netherlands with her partner W. She applied for a residence permit but this was rejected because she did not have a full-time job. She appealed this decision as under the law of the Netherlands a Dutch national would have had the right to live with her unmarried partner. This decision was based upon non-discrimination on the part of the State authorities. The Dutch did not discriminate between a spouse and a cohabitee when dealing with their own nationals and therefore they could not do so in Reed's case.

The death of the holder of primary rights will not deprive members of his family of their right to remain in the country. If not already acquired the workers survivors will do so if:

(a) resided continuously in the host country for two years preceding his death; or
(b) the worker died from an occupational disease or an industrial accident; or
(c) the surviving spouse was a national of the host country and lost that nationality on marriage to him.

Freedom of movement could nevertheless be illusory if by moving from one Member State to another the worker would lose the rights acquired under social security regulations, notably with regards to the pension rights of the worker and his dependants. The divorce or annulment of marriage or civil partnership may not affect the right of residence of a non-EU national (see *Baumbast and R* [2004]).

The Treaty has therefore provided for the adoption of a system ensuring that:

(a) all periods are taken into account under the laws of the several countries where the beneficiary has worked will be added together for calculating the amount of his benefits; and
(b) that those benefits will be paid to the beneficiary in whichever Member State he resides.

Overall, therefore, the freedom of movement for the worker means applying the same treatment to the migrant worker and dependants as to the nationals of the Member State of residence.

LEGISLATION HIGHLIGHTER

Obstacles to the Free Movement of Workers

1. Discrimination based on nationality.
2. Incompatibility of the various social security systems.
3. Recognition of educational/professional qualifications.

Therefore any discrimination based on nationality between workers of the Member States as regards employment, remuneration and other labour conditions must be abolished. The workers' rights include:

(a) to accept offers of employment actually made;
(b) to move freely within the territory of a Member State for this purpose;
(c) to enter into and reside in a Member State for the purpose of employment in accordance with the provisions governing the employment of nationals of that Member State laid down by law, regulation or administrative action; and
(d) to remain in the territory of a Member State after having been employed in that state.

Public service employment

The principle of non-discrimination does not apply to employment in the public service art.45(4) states, which means that public authorities may refuse to hire non-nationals, but they have to justify such exclusion (Case 137/80 *Commission v Belgium*). The Court has held that the exemption provided by art.45(4) **TFEU** does not apply to all employment in the public sector as this is too wide an interpretation. Article 45(4) **TFEU** applies to those activities in the public service which were connected with the exercise of discretion or official authority involving the national interest. However, once a worker from another Member State is employed in the public service, he must be treated in the same way as the nationals, since exception only concerns access to the post (Case 152/73 *Sotgiu v Deutsche Bundespost*).

Limitations to the free movement of workers

The limitations specified in art.45(3) **TFEU** are on the grounds of Public Policy, Public Security or Public Health. National authorities applying these provisions upon a Community national must justify their action. They cannot impose restrictions upon a Community national unless "his presence or conduct constitutes a genuine and sufficiently serious threat to public policy"—see Case 36/75 *Roland Rutili v Ministre de l'interieur*. This cannot be applied to a group, but only to individual members of the group (see Case 41/74 *Van Duyn v Home Office*). On the basis of the UK government's view of the Church of Scientology, the Court held in *Van Duyn* that the UK's action was justified. The question was asked "Was it discriminatory in that a UK national could have taken up the post Van Duyn had accepted?" The Court response was:

> " ... a Member State for reasons of public policy, can where it deems necessary, refuse a national of another Member State the benefit of the principle of freedom of movement of workers in a case where such a national proposes to take up a particular offer of employment even though the Member State does not place a similar restriction on its own nationals".

It follows from the case law of the Court that Member States have not relinquished all control over Community nationals as regulations governing the registration of aliens and criminal sanctions in this respect are compatible with their Treaty obligations unless they are so rigorous as to be tantamount to a denial of the freedom of movement over and above the cases covered by the derogation provisions.

Public Policy provides a Member State with discretion but only within the limits allowed for by the Treaty, which are narrowly interpreted by the ECJ. Criminal conviction does not automatically justify deportation (see Case 67/74 *Bonsignore v Stadt Köln*). In Case 30/77 *R. v Bouchereau* a conviction for drug offences was regarded as a sufficient ground for deportation.

Revision Checklist

You should now know and understand:

- **the definition of "a worker"**
- **the Treaty provisions—arts 45,46 & 48 TFEU**
- **the protection provided by Regulation 1612/68 and Directive 68/360, Directive 2004/38**
- **the special rules for public service employment**
- **the limitations to the free movement of workers**
- **the derogation provisions**

QUESTION AND ANSWER

The Question

Advise Thomas, a German national on the following circumstances:

(a) having been employed as a part-time computer programmer in the UK for the past 16 months Thomas receives a letter from the UK authorities stating that he has 28 days in which to find full-time employment or else he must leave the country as he is unable to support himself;

(b) as a result of the economic situation in the UK Thomas decides to go to France. However, he is refused entry at Calais because he is a prominent member of the Animal Life Front, a group dedicated to the idea of protecting animals from slaughter for food products. It appears that the French authorities are afraid that his presence will cause violent demonstrations by France's farming lobby;

(c) Thomas is ultimately offered a full-time post in Spain. The Spanish authorities issue him with a residence permit but stipulate that his American wife can only visit him for a maximum period of four weeks every three months.

Advice and the Answer

Introduction—this problem question involves the rights given to an individual to move freely within the EU as a worker. Article 45 **TFEU** gives an individual who is a worker in one Member State the freedom to move to another Member State to accept offers of employment actually made. There is no definition of worker in the Treaty but subsequent secondary legislation and case law has provided such a definition (*Lawrie-Blum* case).

(a) It was held in *Levin* (1982) that the term worker and the associated rights applied to those who worked part-time as well as full-time provided that the work was "real" work and not minimal or minimal (*Kempf* (1986)). It would seem that the UK authorities are acting contrary to Community law. However, it is recognised that it is important that someone claiming the right of free movement should not become a burden on the social security system of the host Member State.

(b) Article 45 **TFEU** allows for derogation whereby the Member State does not have to fulfil their obligations under the Treaties. This includes the public policy ground but this has been interpreted very restrictively by the ECJ (*Van Duyn* case (1975)) and cannot be determined by the Member State without regard to EC policy (*Rutili* (1976)). Article 3(1) of **Directive 64/221** states that where this ground is used it must be based exclusively on the personal conduct of the individual. Would this include membership of the Animal Life Front? Also under art.6 of the Directive Thomas is entitled to know the ground for the refusal and this will help him prepare for any legal action.

(c) Article 10(1) of **Regulation 1612/68** defines those who may install themselves with the worker in the host Member State and this includes the worker's spouse, irrespective of her nationality. So Thomas's wife should be able to live with him all the time he is exercising his rights as a worker in Spain.

The Freedom of Establishment and the Freedom to Provide Services

FREEDOM OF ESTABLISHMENT

INTRODUCTION

As the initial emphasis of the EU was to exploit economic activity there was a need to facilitate the freedom of movement of professionals and companies. This chapter reviews the law as it applies to those exercising these freedoms.

Articles 49–55 TFEU

The right of establishment, necessary to exercise a profession or to render a service, is not confined to individuals. It is available to companies and bodies corporate which are treated like individuals. The immigration rules are broadly like those that apply to "workers", but the full enjoyment of "the right of establishment" depends upon the recognition of professional qualifications and this, in turn, depends upon the progress of harmonisation of national laws in this field.

There is no definition of the group of persons entitled to the right of establishment. In distinction from "workers" (who are salaried) art.49 **TFEU** contemplates a group of people who, in principle, pursue activities as self-employed persons or set up and manage undertakings within the meaning of art.54 **TFEU**.

Such persons belong, as a rule, to recognised professions whose status and membership is regulated by law. Hence the need of harmonising the national rules and regulations to facilitate their mobility within the Community and, in the first place, to remove restrictions on the ground of nationality and other peculiar national grounds (see Case 213/89 *R. v Secretary of State for Transport, Ex p. Factortame*).

To carry out its mandate the Council adopted in 1962 two General Programmes for the:

(i) Abolition of Restrictions on Freedom to provide Services; and
(ii) on Freedom of Establishments;

and in subsequent years has embarked on extensive legislation in these fields. However, as the Commission recorded in its White Paper on completing the internal market, the results as of 1987 were still unsatisfactory. Therefore the Commission recommended action in specific areas including a more efficient policing and enforcement system, resulting in measures to suspend the enforcement of any national legislation which manifestly infringes Community law.

Independently of this harmonisation policy, the ECJ was able to remove some of the restrictions in accordance with the principle of non-discrimination. Thus it has held that a Dutch national resident in Belgium with the appropriate qualifications to practice law could not be debarred from his professional activity on the ground that, according to Belgian law, a lawyer must be a Belgian national (Case 2/74 *Reyners v Belgian State*). Similarly the Court ruled in the case of a Belgian lawyer (Case 71/76 *Thieffry v Conseil de l'Ordre des Avocats á la Cour de Paris*) and a British architect qualified to practise in France (Case 11/77 *Patrick v Ministère des Affaires Culturelles*), a Dutch motor insurance claims investigator in Italy (Case 90/76 *Van Ameyde v UCI*).

The principle of non-discrimination on the ground of nationality was further extended when the Court held that residential qualification of a properly qualified person was not a legitimate condition of his exercising the profession.

However, conviction for the illegal exercise of the veterinary profession was upheld in the case of a person qualified in Italy who, having become naturalised in France, attempted to practise on his own without first obtaining the requisite French qualifications. Such a bar was considered justified pending the implementation of the harmonising directives (Case 136/78 *Ministère Public v Auer*) but no longer after. In the recent Case 55/94 *Reinhard Gebhard v Consiglio dell'Ordine degli Avvocati e Procuratori di Milano*, the ECJ brought the rules relating to establishment into line with those relating to services.

In the absence of a Treaty definition of the class of persons entitled to the right of establishment was, and is likely to be, confronted with fringe "professions" including sports activities (Case 36/74 *Walgrave and Koch v Association Union Cycliste Internationale*). So far the Court has held that such activities may come under the non-discrimination principle if they entail "economic activities". Amateur activities seem unaffected by Community rules. In Case 415/93 *Bosman* the ECJ held that arts 45 and 56 **TFEU** can in certain circumstances impose obligations on individual football clubs and associations not to impose restrictions on the free movement of footballers.

FREEDOM TO PROVIDE SERVICES

Articles 56–62 TFEU

According to art.56 **TFEU** services mean "services for remuneration in particular activities of an industrial and commercial character, craftsmanship and exercise of a profession". However, the provision of services is often connected with the exercise of a profession and in this respect inseparable from the right of establishment. The difference between the provision of services and that of establishment is that the latter is associated with actually setting up in another Member State whereas the former involves only a transient visit to provide the services. **Directive 2006/123** covers both the right to provide services and the right of establishment.

Right to receive services

Although arts 56 and 57 **TFEU** provide for the removal of restrictions on the freedom to provide services on the basis of **Directive 73/148**, they have been interpreted by the European Court of Justice to embrace the freedom to receive services. In Joined Cases 286/82 and 26/83 *Luisi v Ministero del Tesoro*, following the Commission's view in Case 118/75 *Criminal Proceedings against Watson and Belman*, the Court held that there was a freedom for the recipient of services to go to another Member State, without restriction, in order to receive a service there. Although the case involved the transfer of money out of Italy in breach of Italian currency law for the purpose of tourism and medical treatment, the principle in the judgment included persons travelling for the purpose of education. The right of residence exists during the period for which the service is provided. Any breach of this freedom would be prima facie a breach of arts 56 and 57 **TFEU** (see *R. v Secretary of State for the Home Department, Ex p. Flynn* [1997] 3 C.M.L.R. 888). **Directive 2004/38** deals specifically with the situation where a student moves to another Member State to undertake a vocational course.

The student, spouse and dependent children have the right to remain for the duration of the course. In every case the student must assure the relevant national authority that he has sufficient resources to avoid becoming a burden on the social assistance system of the host Member State during the period of residence. In *Watts v Bedford Primary Care Trust* (2003) the right to go to another Member State to receive medical treatment at the expense of the NHS was upheld.

Vocational training

The Court has given a wide definition to the meaning of vocational education. In Case 29/83 *Gravier v City of Liège* the Court held it to include all forms of teaching which prepares for and leads directly to a particular profession or which provides the necessary skills for such a profession. In these circumstances a student may claim equal access and on the same basis as nationals of the Member State. This was confirmed in Case 24/86 *Blaizot v University of Liège*, where the course involved was a university veterinary studies course.

Derogation

As with all the freedoms arising from the Treaty there are exceptions where the Member State may derogate from their obligation under the Treaty. These are specifically those in arts 52 and 62 **TFEU**, which allow for derogation on the grounds of public policy, public security and public health. The public policy provision has been interpreted strictly by the European Court to ensure that its scope is not unilaterally determined by a Member State without control by the European Community institutions (*Van Duyn*). In Case 36/75 *Rutili v Ministre de l'Interieur* the Court held that restrictions on the movement of an EU national on the grounds of public policy could only be accepted where the behaviour of the individual constitutes a genuine and sufficiently serious threat to public policy.

Directive 2004/38

Article 27(2) of **Directive 2004/38** states that any exclusion on the grounds of public policy or public security must be based exclusively on the personal conduct of the individual. In *Van Duyn* the Court held that although past association with an organisation does not count as personal conduct, present association does and the activities in question must constitute a genuine and sufficiently serious threat to public policy affecting one of the fundamental interests of society. In this case the Court allowed the UK to apply a stricter standard on an EC national than the one it applied to its own nationals because the UK deemed that it was necessary. In *Bonsignore* it was accepted that the concept of personal conduct expresses the requirement that a deportation order may only be made for breaches of the peace and public security that might be committed by the individual concerned.

Under art.30 of **Directive 2004/38** the individual is entitled to know on which ground, i.e. public policy or public security, the decision is based, unless this information contravenes state security. This allows the individual to prepare his defence. If a Member State fails to comply with art.6 it may lead to the quashing of a deportation order (*R. v Secretary of State for the Home Office, Ex p. Dannemberg* [1984] Q.B. 766). Article 8 of the Directive requires that the individual is entitled to the same legal remedies in relation to a decision on entry as any other national. For example in the UK an immigrant normally has a right of appeal against immigration decisions to a person called an adjudicator and then to the Immigration Appeal Tribunal. Such appeals cover issues of fact, law and the exercise of discretion, so the merits of the decision would be fully reviewed.

Mutual recognition

The European Community principle of equal treatment is not always sufficient to ensure that the immigrant is able to practice his profession in another Member State. There is no directly applicable provision in the EU Treaty requiring Member States to recognise qualifications acquired in another Member State or obliging them to allow immigrants to practice a profession without the appropriate qualifications (Case 136/78 *Ministère Public v Auer*).

In order to make the right of establishment effective the Union embarked on a harmonising process in which the rules governing the formation and exercise of the medical profession took the lead. Article 53 **TFEU** requires the European Parliament and the Council to adopt directives on the mutual recognition of diplomas, certificates and other evidence of formal qualifications. Without a relevant directive the migrant is likely to find that Union law is of limited assistance to him. The Commission had attempted to remedy the situation by promoting separate directives for each profession, such as medicine, dentistry, veterinary medicine, midwifery and the exercise of the profession of architect. The objective of these directives has been to make it easier for a person practising a profession in one Member State to practice that profession in another Member State.

However, in order to avoid legislating piecemeal the Mutual Recognition **Directive 89/48** was adopted. Like all directives on establishment **Directive 89/48** benefits Community citizens with regard to qualifications awarded in a Member State. **Directive 2005/36** replaced this earlier Directive and retained the essential content as a way forward. Under this Directive recognition is to be given to diplomas as defined by art.1. There must be three essential characteristics for such "diplomas"; it must be awarded by a competent authority in a Member State following the successful completion of a course lasting at least three years at a university or equivalent institution plus professional training. Finally, such a "diploma" must qualify the holder for the pursuit of a regulated profession in a Member State. Article 3 of the Directive provides the basic rule that if a Member State requires a "diploma" as a condition for exercising a regulated profession, it must accept a "diploma" obtained in another Member State.

Lawyers

The Commission had attempted to deal with various professional bodies by promoting separate directives for each. The objective of these directives has been to make it easier for a person practising a profession in one Member State to practice that profession in another Member State. However, the important difference between these professions and lawyers is that although the principles of medicine or dentistry are much the same in every Member State, those of law differ. It is therefore hardly surprising that the progress on facilitating the free movement of lawyers has been very slow.

Directive 77/249 (the Services Directive) was specifically aimed at lawyers but it is only concerned with the provision of services and not the right of establishment, which was dealt with by the Lawyer's Establishment **Directive 98/5**. It makes provision for lawyers to carry out their profession in another Member State on a temporary basis. "Lawyer" under this Directive is defined by a list of terms to reflect the diversity in the European Community. The function of the list is to indicate those practitioners who are able to benefit from the rights conferred by the Directive and the activities to which it applies. Thus anyone who is recognised as a "lawyer" for the purpose of the Directive can perform the work of a lawyer in another Member State but only on a temporary basis. While he is performing this work he must use the title of his home country, as it would appear in that country. In this capacity the foreign lawyer can do all the work of a local lawyer, unless the national law of the Member State reserves certain activities for its national lawyers and on the proviso that he represents a client in court work in conjunction with a local lawyer. In the UK such foreign lawyers cannot undertake probate or conveyance work, which is reserved for UK lawyers. The Lawyers' Establishment **Directive 98/5** confers rights on lawyers qualified in one Member State to practice in another.

The **Mutual Recognition Directive 2005/36** discussed above applies to the legal profession. The profession of a lawyer is in the list of regulated professions. Article 3 of the Directive provides the basic rule that if a Member State requires a "diploma" as a condition for exercising a regulated profession, it must accept a "diploma" obtained in another Member State. In contrast to the situation where a lawyer is providing a "service" of a temporary nature, when he is exercising the right of establishment the lawyer is entitled to use the professional designation of the Member State in which he practices. Thus a French avocat who establishes himself and practices in the UK can call himself a solicitor.

The Directive recognises that professional training does vary between

Member States and allows the Member State where the individual wishes to practice to set certain conditions. This may involve an adaptation period during which supervision by a qualified practitioner is required of the foreign national or an aptitude test of professional knowledge. In England the test for foreign lawyers wishing to practice as solicitors is called the Qualified Lawyers Transfer Test. Having successfully passed this test the normal rules concerning registration and admission to the appropriate professional body will apply. In Case 313/01 *Morgenbesser* [2004] the Italian Bar refused to recognise as equivalent university study by the student in France as that undertaken by an Italian law student. The ECJ agreed with the Italian Bar.

Companies

The **EC Treaty** identified two rights for companies, namely establishment and provision of services and these are now embedded within the **Treaty of Lisbon**. Under art.49 **TFEU** companies have the right to establish themselves in another Member State by setting up agencies, branches or subsidiaries. Having so established themselves, the companies have the right not to be discriminated against and must be treated under the same conditions as those laid down by the Member State for its own nationals. The same rule applies to companies as it does to individuals, who must be nationals of a Member State if they are to benefit from the freedom specified in the Treaty. Article 54(1) **TFEU** specifies that as far as companies are concerned they must be formed in accordance with the law of a Member State and have their registered office, central administration or principal place of business within the Community. The Court of Justice held in Case 79/85 *Segers* that to allow a Member State in which a company carried on its business to treat that company in a different manner solely because its registered office was in another Member State would render art.54 **TFEU** valueless. This was confirmed by the ECJ in Case 212/97 *Centros Ltd*, which involved an attempt by the Danish Trade and Companies Board to refuse to register a company set up, but not trading, in England.

KEY CASE

Case 212/97 Centros Ltd

In this case B, a Danish national, came to the UK to register her company, Centros, in May 1992. Under UK company law there is no specified paid up capital for a company whereas in Denmark it has to be a minimum of 200,000 Danish Krona. Subsequently B requested the Danish Trade & Companies Board to register a branch of Centros in

Denmark. They refused as the Danish requirements regarding capital had not been met.

The ECJ held that this was contrary to arts 49 & 54 **TFEU** as a company formed in accordance with the legal requirements of one Member State (the UK) had to be recognised as such by the government of another Member State (namely Denmark).

Just as there is a requirement that workers and the self-employed should receive remuneration in order to satisfy the Treaty, so companies which are non-profit making do not come within the definition of art.54(1) **TFEU.** The remuneration requirement is repeated in art.56 **TFEU** dealing with the right to provide services. This provision deals with a company established in one Member State providing service of an industrial, commercial or professional nature in another Member State. The main difference with services is that in contrast to establishment the company is entering another Member State only temporarily to pursue this activity.

Article 293 EC, now repealed by the **Lisbon Treaty** required the Member States to negotiate conventions with each other in order to secure uniformity of recognition of business practices across the Community. The article specifically mentioned the mutual recognition of companies within the meaning of art.48(2) EC. As a result of this requirement a Convention on the Mutual Recognition of Companies and Bodies Corporate was signed in 1968 by the six founder members of the European Community. However, it is not in force as it was not ratified by the Member State. Given this failure but recognising the importance of company law, the policy of the EU has been to move forward on the basis of directives dealing with specific matters. The fact that over 13 directives have been proposed reflects the extensive programme of harmonisation of company law embarked upon by the European Union. Although not all of these directives have been adopted, those which have cover such technical matters as company capital, company accounts, appointment of auditors and disclosure of information. These are important because companies established or providing services in different Member States facing the need to adjust to different regulatory regimes may lead to duplication of accounting, licensing and other requirements. This would act as a disincentive to penetrating other national markets. It may also reduce the opportunities for benefiting from economies of scale.

Another way of seeking to reduce the problems for companies operating in more than one Member State is to establish EC corporate structures. **Regulation 2173/85** took the first step in this development with the establishment of European Economic Interest Groupings (EEIGs). These EEIGs permit companies and others to co-operate within the Community on a cross-border basis, and thus provide a vehicle for joint ventures. EEIGs have the mixed characteristics of companies and partnership. They are not separate in the sense that the companies are still liable for the debts of the EEIG but they do have a separate legal capacity. Such Groups have to be registered, which in the UK is a requirement to register with the Registrar of Companies. An EEIG cannot have more than 500 employees or offer any share participation to the public. Obviously there are certain limitations with EEIGs but they do provide a flexible vehicle for economic activity.

The ultimate aim of the Community is to have a new company formation which will have legal capacity throughout the Community. This is the European Company or Societas Europaea (SE), which is established by registration with the European Court in Luxembourg under a distinctive European Community company statute. Even though registration is with the Court, the SE could be domiciled in a particular Member State. The role of the SE is to facilitate cross-border co-operation by means of large-scale mergers and associations. It can be seen that this is perhaps the natural extension from the EEIG, which facilitates such ventures, but on a smaller scale. There have been some criticisms of the establishment of SEs, which led to delay in the adoption of the necessary Community legislation. However, the proposal was given a new impetus at the Nice IGC and in October 2001 the Council adopted the **Regulation and Directive on the SE** which came into force in October 2004.

Revision Checklist

You should now know and understand:

- **the right of establishment and freedom to provide services under arts 49–54 TFEU**
- **the impact on individual professionals, companies and bodies corporate**
- **the importance of the principle of non-discrimination**
- **the right to receive services as interpreted by the ECJ**
- **the application of the rules to vocational training**
- **the impact of the Mutual Recognition Directive**
- **the right as applied to lawyers and companies**
- **the role and possibilities for the European Company or Societas Europaea**

QUESTION AND ANSWER

The Question

How has EU law addressed the issue of the right of establishment?

Advice and the Answer

Introduction—The EC is founded on certain economic principles which promote economic activity by individuals and companies. The Treaty protects this right and is supplemented by various administrative measures as the Community attempt to deal with the problems experienced by professionals and companies in exercising their business activities.

Initially the EC attempted to harmonise rules associated with particular sectors but this proved to be very slow due to the difficulties of dealing with established professional groups and traditions.

The ECJ played its part in developing the case law associated with the right of establishment. For example where it held that a Dutch national resident in Belgium with the appropriate qualifications to practice law could not be debarred from his professional activity on the ground that, according to Belgian law, a lawyer must be a Belgian national (*Reyners v Belgian State*). Similarly the Court ruled in the case of a Belgian lawyer (*Thieffry v Conseil de l'Ordre des Avocats a la Cour de Paris*) and a British architect qualified to practise in France (*Patrick v Ministere des Affaires Culturelles*).

As with all freedoms granted under the Treaties there are circumstances where the Member State can seek the power of derogation. However, these must be proportionate and must not be used to provide a barrier to the right of establishment. The idea of mutual recognition of qualifications gained in one Member State to be recognised in another Member State has been applied to professional qualifications and to degrees (*Ministere Public v Auer*). It has also been used to ensure that companies lawfully registered in one Member State are recognised in another (*Centros Ltd* case).

EU law has addressed the issue of the right of establishment by building upon the base provided by the Treaties in arts.49–54 **TFEU**, introducing the specific legislation to deal with specific professions, such as the **Lawyers' Establishment Directive 98/5**, and the case law of the ECJ.

Sex Discrimination

INTRODUCTION

The **EU Treaty** has always been concerned with discrimination and the ECJ has said that one of the fundamental human rights is non-discrimination. The initial impact was on the area of sex discrimination and equal pay. The types of discrimination have been extended but sex discrimination remains the focal point of anti-discrimination legislation. This chapter reviews the law on sex discrimination.

The Treaty rule

In art.3 **TEU** reference is made to the underlying principles of the Union and the principle of equality. This indicates the special status given by Community law to the principle of equality. The specific article dealing with equality in employment is art.157 **TFEU**. Article 3(3) **TEU** states that the Union's aims include "It shall combat social exclusion and discrimination, and shall promote social justice and protection, equality between men and women, solidarity between the generations and protection of the rights of the child".

Pay is defined in art.157(2) **TFEU** as the ordinary basic or minimum wage or salary and any other consideration, whether in cash or in kind, which the worker receives, directly or indirectly, in respect of his employment from his employer.

The term "consideration" should not be interpreted too restrictively as it has been held by the ECJ to include other benefits such as favourable rates for family travel for railway employees (Case 12/81 *Garland v BREL*). As long as the "pay" has been (1) received by the employee in respect of his employment and (2) received from the employer, it will come within the meaning of the article. Thus it includes pensions paid under a contracted-out private occupational scheme (Case 262/88 *Barber v Guardian Royal Exchange Assurance Group*). (See also Case 7/93 *Beune.*)

In Case 43/75 *Defrenne v Sabena* the Court of European Justice held that the article has direct effect, the Court has identified a right which can be enforced by the individual employee in the courts of the Member State. Madame Defrenne had been employed by the Belgian airline Sabena as an air hostess. She complained of being paid a lower salary than her male colleagues although the work they did was the same. In an art.267 **TFEU** reference the Belgian court asked if art.157 **TFEU** could be relied upon before national courts. In its judgment the court said that discrimination on the grounds of sex could be indirect and disguised discrimination or direct and overt discrimination. The latter type of discrimination was more easily identified and could be based solely upon the criteria of equal work and equal pay referred to in art.157 **TFEU**. In such cases art.157 **TFEU** was directly effective and gave use to individual rights which national courts must protect. It was necessary for additional measures to be taken with regard to indirect discrimination. This was achieved initially by the **Equal Pay Directive 75/117** which supplements art.157 **TFEU** and this has now been replaced by **Directive 2006/54** (see below).

KEY CASE

CASE 129/79 MACARTHYS LTD V WENDY SMITH

Article 157 **TFEU** requires that men and women should receive equal pay for equal work. In Case 129/79 *Macarthys Ltd v Wendy Smith* the Court held that a requirement of contemporaneity of employment is not to be read into the article. Smith was paid £50 per week whereas her male predecessor had received £60. Under UK legislation the requirement was for the male and female workers to be doing the same job at the same time if a comparison was to be made. However, the Court of Justice held that the only issue was whether or not the work was "equal" and it did not matter whether or not the man and woman whose work and pay were to be compared were employed at the same time in the undertaking or not.

In Case 127/92 *Enderby v Frenchay HA* the Court held that the burden of proof, which is normally on the claimant, might shift to the employer where that is necessary to avoid depriving workers who appear to be victims of discrimination of any effective means of enforcing the principle of equal pay.

KEY CASE

CASE 170/84 BILKA-KAUFHAUS GMBH V WEBER VON HARZ

In Case 170/84 *Bilka-Kaufhaus GmbH v Weber von Harz*, Weber was a female part-time worker who was seeking to challenge her employer's occupational pension scheme. Although the scheme was noncontributory for full-time employees with the employer paying all the contributions, this was not the case with part-timers. Under the scheme, only part-time employees who had been employed by the company for at least 15 out of a total of 20 years could qualify. The Court held that the benefit constituted consideration paid by the employer to the employee in respect of her employment and thus came within art.157 **TFEU**. Also in this case the Court provided guidelines to assist in identifying what might constitute objective justification for such differences in pay. The onus is on the employer to prove that the difference in treatment corresponded to a genuine need of the enterprise.

In Case 171/88 *Rinner-Kuhn* art.141 EC (ex 119 EC) was also held by the Court to be applicable to a statutory social security benefit. This case also included a part-time employee who was employed as a cleaner. She challenged the German legislation which permitted employers to exclude workers who worked less than ten hours per week from entitlement to sick pay. Despite statements in Case 192/85 *Newstead v Department of Transport* that social security schemes were outside the scope of art.157 **TFEU**, the Court held that sick pay fell within the article. Therefore the German legislation was contrary to art.157 **TFEU**. In an action brought by the Equal Opportunities Commission in 1994, the House of Lords held that the qualifying periods of employment in the UK's **Employment Protection (Consolidation) Act 1978** were contrary to EU law. This was because they differentiated unfairly between part-time and full-time employees.

In *Barber* a group of male employees challenged their employer's contracted-out pension scheme. The employer's scheme was a substitute for the statutory scheme and was payable at different ages for men and women. The Court held that since the worker received these benefits from his employer as a result of his employment, the fact that the benefits were payable at different ages for men and women resulted in a difference in pay. Following this case it would appear that the only social security pension schemes provided for workers which fall outside the scope of art.157 **TFEU** are those which provide for workers in general, as a matter of social policy.

Following the *Barber* and *Bilka-Kaufhause* cases there have been a number of important developments. In Case 200/91 *Coloroll Pension Trustees Ltd v Russell* it was held that art.157 **TFEU** applied to occupational pension schemes and confirmed that survivors' and dependents' benefits constitute pay under the article. In Case 57/93 *Vroege v NCIV Institut voor Volkshuisvesting BV* and Case 128/93 *Fisscher v Stichting Bedrijfspensioenfonds voor de Detailhandel* the exclusion of married women and part-time workers from occupational schemes was also contrary to art.141 EC (ex 119 EC).

However, in Case 249/96 *Grant v South-West Trains Ltd* the ECJ rejected the claim by a female employee with a female partner for rail benefits to which heterosexual couples were entitled. The ECJ stated that references to "sex discrimination" was not a reference to gender orientation. This was confirmed by Case 264/97 *D v Council* where the Court said that it was "unfit" as a judicial institution to bring about a positive change which was properly to be enacted by legislation. However, in *Chief Constable of West Yorkshire Police v A* [2004] UKHL 21 the Court of Appeal held that the **Equal Treatment Directive** covered discrimination against a transsexual. In Case 117/01 *KB v NHS Pensions Agency* the ECJ held that British legislation that prevented post operative transsexuals from marrying in their acquired gender could be a breach of EU "sex" discrimination law.

LEGISLATION HIGHLIGHTER

Directives

The basic role of the **EU Treaty** has been developed and refined by a number of directives. The Directives listed below illustrate how the EU has developed its policy by gradually widening the rights for EU citizens.

Directive 75/117 on equal pay for men and women has now been replaced by **Directive 2006/54** but was important in establishing a number of principles. Article 1 of this Directive provided for the elimination of all discrimination on the grounds of sex with regard to all aspects and conditions of remuneration. This Directive defined the scope of art.157 **TFEU** and introduced the principle of equal pay for work of equal value. Thus this directive met the points raised by the ECJ in *Defrenne* as to why art.157 **TFEU** could not apply to indirect discrimination. The UK government implemented this Directive by means of the **Sex Discrimination Act 1975** but not to the satisfaction of the Commission who brought proceedings under art.258 **TFEU** (see *Commission v UK*). This resulted in the **Equal Pay (Amendment) Regulations 1983** which empowered a panel of independent experts to prepare a report on whether or not any work was of equal value to that of a man in the same employment (see Case 96/80 *Jenkins v Kingsgate (Clothing Productions) Ltd*).

Directive 76/207 on equal treatment for men and women as regards access to employment, vocational training and promotion, and working conditions. The principle of "equal treatment" is defined as meaning "that there shall be no discrimination whatsoever on grounds of sex either directly or indirectly by reference in particular to material or family status". The important case of Case 152/84 *Marshall v Southampton and South West Hampshire AHA* was brought under this Directive. The Court in this case held that the Directive was directly effective as the employer was an emanation of the State (see Ch.4 above, p.36). In the subsequent Case 271/91 *Marshall v Southampton & South West Hampshire AHA No.2*, Mrs Marshall successfully challenged the UK legislation which limited the compensation paid to those individuals who had been discriminated against on the grounds of sex. This Directive has been amended by **Directive 2002/73** which attempts to bring EU sex discrimination law into line with the other forms of discrimination.

Directive 79/7 on equal treatment in occupational and social security schemes. This Directive applies to the working population both employed, and self-employed, and includes those whose work has been interrupted by illness, accident or involuntary unemployment (Case 208/90 *Emmott v Minister for Social Welfare*). There are exemptions to the principle of equal treatment, e.g. the determination of pensionable age for the granting of retirement pensions. This Directive has made little impact upon the various forms of indirect discrimination (see Joined Cases 63/91 and 64/91 *Jackson and Cresswell v Chief Adjudication Officer*).

Directive 86/378 on equal treatment in occupational social security schemes. As "occupational pensions" are to be considered as "pay" under the *Barber* judgment, the importance of this Directive has been reduced.

Directive 86/613 on equal treatment in self-employed occupations. This Directive extends the application of **Directive 76/207** to the self-employed.

Directive 92/85 provides a uniform level of social protection for pregnant workers and those who have recently given birth. Under art.10 of this Directive a pregnant worker, whether full-time or part-time, may not be dismissed. The new **Equal Treatment Directive 2002/73** has links with the less favourable treatment principle with regard to pregnancy. The Directive defines direct discrimination as where one person is treated less favourably on grounds of sex than another is, has been or would be treated in a comparable situation.

Directive 2006/54 is termed the Recast Directive because it recast the existing legislation on equal pay, equal treatment, and occupational social security and is principally concerned with providing remedies for those who feel that they have suffered discrimination.

Application of the sex discrimination rules

In response to the *Barber* case and its implications for employers and pension funds, a Protocol was annexed to the **TEU** to limit its impact. It states that:

> "For the purpose of Article 157 TFEU ... benefits under occupational social security schemes shall not be considered as remunerations if and in so far as they are attributable to periods of employment prior to May 17, 1990, except in the case of workers or those claiming under them who have before that date initiated legal proceedings or introduced an equivalent claim under the applicable national law."

In addition the Protocol on Social Policy added by art.6 of the Agreement attached to it, purports to permit a Member State to maintain or adopt measures discriminating in favour of women in certain circumstances. The precise meaning of this is unclear, especially as the UK explicitly excludes itself from this Protocol. In Case 177/88 *Dekker* the ECJ held that refusal to employ a woman because she was pregnant was per se direct discrimination on grounds of sex under art.2(1) of the **Equal Treatment Directive**. As pregnancy was something which could only happen to a woman, refusal to employ because of Dekker's pregnancy was direct discrimination. Similarly in Case 179/88 *Handels-og Kontorfunktionaerernes Forbund v Dansk Arbejdsgiverforening* (the *Hertz* case) the dismissal of a woman because of her pregnancy was ruled by the Court to be direct discrimination. If there had been another reason for the dismissal, such as absence from work through illness originating in pregnancy this would not be direct discrimination. In Case 32/93 *Webb v EMO Air Cargo (UK) Ltd* the ECJ reaffirmed that dismissal for reasons of pregnancy is illegal. Case 147/02 *Alabaster v Woolwich Plc* said that pay awards made while the woman was pregnant had to be taken into account when determining her pay.

Revision Checklist

You should now know and understand:

- **the principle of equality as found in the Treaties**
- **the impact of art.157 TFEU**
- **the Directives that have developed the law of sex discrimination, especially the Equal Treatment Directive**
- **the application of the sex discrimination rules**

QUESTION AND ANSWER

The Question

Review the development of EU law on sex discrimination.

Advice and the Answer

Introduction—one of the fundamental principles of the EU is that of equality. Since the **Treaty of Rome** in 1957 a key aspect of this has been art.157 **TFEU** which deals with equal pay. However, as the *Defrenne v Sabena* case demonstrated this article is limited in the way it can deal with indirect discrimination in modern society. This has led the EU to introduce a range of legislation to deal with these more subtle areas of discrimination on the grounds of sex.

The main example of the secondary legislation is the **Directive 2006/54** on equal treatment for men and women as regards access to employment, vocational training and promotion, and working conditions. The principle of "equal treatment" is defined as meaning "that there shall be no discrimination whatsoever on grounds of sex either directly or indirectly by reference in particular to material or family status". The important case of Case 271/91 *Marshall v Southampton and South West Hampshire AHA* was brought under this Directive.

Other legislation has developed the principle of equal pay, such as **Directive 75/117** (now **Directive 2006/54**) on equal pay for men and women. Article 1 of this Directive provides for the elimination of all discrimination on the grounds of sex with regard to all aspects and conditions of remuneration. This Directive defined the scope of art.157 **TFEU** and introduced the principle of equal pay for work of equal value. Thus this directive met the points raised by the ECJ in *Defrenne* as to why art.157 **TFEU** could not apply to indirect discrimination (*Jenkins v Kingsgate (Clothing Productions) Ltd*).

The latest piece of legislation is **Directive 2006/54**, which is termed the Recast Directive because it recast the existing legislation on equal pay, equal treatment, and occupational social security and is principally concerned with providing remedies for those who feel that they have suffered discrimination. As well as these examples there have also been legislation dealing with the rights of pregnant employees as demonstrated in the case of *Webb v EMO Air Cargo (UK) Ltd*.

The Maastricht Treaty on European Union and Beyond

12

INTRODUCTION

As the Treaties are the primary source of European law it is important to recognise the incremental changes that have taken place since the 1950s. This chapter provides a review of the most significant changes since the **TEU** and the attempts in recent years to provide a Constitutional Treaty.

The **TEU** was signed in Maastricht on February 7, 1992 and came into force on November 1, 1993. This was later than anticipated by art.52 **TEU** (ex R(2)) due to delays in ratification caused by referendum in Ireland, France and Denmark, and legal action in the UK and Germany. For the first time it became legally correct to refer to the European Community since this is the new name under art.8 **TEU** (ex G(1)) for the European Economic Community. The word economic has been dropped to reflect the fact that there has been a change of emphasis towards non-economic provisions such as citizenship.

The **TEU** was the result of two regulation conferences, one on political union and the other relating to economic and monetary union. The **TEU** articles were numbered alphabetically to avoid confusion with the founding treaties which it amended. The result was that the treaties of the Community were lengthy documents and quite complex. The **Treaty of Amsterdam** has resolved this by completely renumbering the EC and EU treaties, which is why both the old and new article numbers are given in this book so as to avoid confusion.

Treaty of Amsterdam

The original **TEU** signed at Maastricht was to be reconsidered at an intergovernmental conference (IGC) in 1996/1997. At the IGC held in Amsterdam in 1997 the governments of the Member States negotiated about the changes to the **TEU**. The **Treaty of Amsterdam** came into effect on May 1, 1999. The main pressures on the negotiations were:

1. As indicated above, some Member States experienced problems in ratifying the **Maastricht Treaty** due to the feeling that the EU was not relevant or accountable to ordinary people. The **Treaty of Amsterdam**

attempts to deal with this by emphasising employment within the Union (see art.2 **TEU** and Title VIII EC). Reference is also made to sustainable development with regard to protecting the environment.

2. Applications had been received from ten former central and eastern European states plus Turkey and Cyprus for membership of the Union. This potential enlargement of the Union could not be accomplished within the present institutional structure.

The changes to the institutions are dealt with in Ch.2 above, p.2, but there are some others which will not come into operation until there has been enlargement to 29 Member States. In relation to the European Parliament the number of MEPs had been fixed at 700 regardless of the number of states, although this has now been increased to 732 by the **Treaty of Nice**. Therefore, there will need to be some reallocation of seats to accommodate new members of the Union. The European Commission was also to be affected by making it one Commissioner per Member State, thus removing the extra Commissioner enjoyed by the UK, Germany, France, Italy and Spain. As far as the Council of Ministers was concerned there was to be more emphasis on qualified majority voting (qmv).

Main points from the amended TEU

Acquis Communautaire art.2 **TEU** (ex art.B) explicitly refers to acquis communautaire, a principle which had been previously associated with the accession of new Member States. There is no formal definition of the term but it goes beyond the formal acceptance of Community law to include rules which have no binding force. These would include recommendations and opinions of the Council and Commission, resolutions of the Council and common agreements of the Member States. Some writers believe that the term has more of a political than a legal meaning. Perhaps the development of the Community into the fields of co-operation in foreign policy, Justice and Home Affairs measures has brought about the need to ensure that Member States work closely together. How it will work in practice will become clearer as the Community acts on these policies.

Subsidiarity

Article 5 EC (ex 3(b) EC) now states that:

> "... the Community shall take action, in accordance with the principle of subsidiarity, only if and in so far as the objectives of the proposed action cannot be sufficiently achieved by the Member States and can therefore by reason of the scale or

effects of the proposed action, be better achieved by the Community".

This article follows the statements in the Preamble that:

> "... the process of creating an ever closer union among the peoples of Europe in which decisions are taken as closely as possible to the citizens in accordance with the principle of subsidiarity".

As it is the European Commission which makes proposals, it would appear that the onus is on it to justify its action at Community level rather than leaving it to the Member States. This could perhaps lend to a challenge in the European Court of Justice on the grounds that the proposed Community measure offends against the principle of subsidiarity. The **Treaty of Amsterdam** has a Protocol on the application of the Principles of Subsidiarity and Proportionality. This builds upon the guidelines developed in recent years and gives them the force of law. The Protocol cites three criteria for judging whether the conditions have been fulfilled:

1. Does the action have transnational aspects that cannot be satisfactorily regulated by the Member States?
2. Would action by the Member States or lack of action conflict with the requirements of the Treaty?
3. Would action at Community level produce clear benefits?

Amendments to the EC Treaty

1. Change in name. The term economic is dropped, as the Community is now to be known as the European Community (art.8 **TEU**). This change acknowledges the reality of today when Community competence is no longer restricted to the economic domain. The areas of activity in the amended art.5 EC (ex 3 EC) show extension to citizenship, social cohesion and social development, and the environment.
2. Article 1 **TEU** states that the Union is "founded on" the Communities, supplemented by the policies and forms of co-operation established by the **TEU**. Unlike the European Community under art.281 EC (ex 210 EC), the new Union does not have legal personality. Article 5 **TEU** (ex E **TEU**) makes it clear that the Union operates under or through the institutions of the Community. However, the objectives of the Union are wider than those of the EC, notably in the fields of foreign and security policy and justice and home affairs.

3. Article 6 (2) **TEU** (ex F(2) **TEU**) requires the Union to respect fundamental rights, both as guaranteed by the European Convention on Human Rights and Fundamental Freedoms and as they result from the constitutional traditions common to the Member States. This article repeats much of the language used by the ECJ in its case law relating to the protection of fundamental rights as a general principle of Community law.

4. Article 7 **TEU** (ex F(1) **TEU**) requires the Union to respect the national identities of its Member States. This idea complements the principle of subsidiarity (art.5 EC) but also includes the cultural heritage of the Member States. It also recognises that the system of government found in all Member States is based on the principles of democracy.

   The **Treaty of Amsterdam** includes a Protocol that encourages closer ties with the national parliaments of Member States. There is to be a six-week interval between the tabling of any legislative proposal and appearance on the Council agenda. This will give national parliaments an opportunity to hold a debate and thus contribute to wider discussion of legislative proposals.

5. The European Community is to conduct its activities on the basis of "an open market economy with free competition".

Citizenship of the Union

The **TEU** contained five new articles 17–21 EC (ex 8 to 8(d) EC), concerning citizenship of the Union. Although citizenship of the Union is established, the rights conferred and the duties imposed are those that flow from the **EC Treaty**. This is because the main impact is by the amendments the **TEU** makes to the **EC Treaty** and not as an independent Treaty. These do not materially affect the existing rights of economically active persons (see free movement of workers and the right of establishment above, pp.97–105).

Citizenship of the Union is mandatory for all nationals of the Member States; there is no provision for opting out. However, the **Treaty of Amsterdam** has amended the **EC Treaty** to reflect the point that citizenship of the European Union will complement and not replace national citizenship. All Union citizens residing in a Member State of which they are not a national have the right to vote and stand as candidates in both municipal elections and elections to the European Parliament in that State.

If the Union citizen is in a third country where the Member State of which he is a national is not represented, he is entitled to protection by the diplomatic authorities of any Member State, on the same conditions as that State's own nationals. There is also the right to petition the EP and to apply to the Ombudsman who was appointed by the Parliament in 1996 under arts 21 EC (ex 8(d) EC), 194 EC (ex 138(d)) and 195 EC (ex 138(e)). The Ombudsman has wide-ranging powers of inquiry and can request documents and evidence from Community institutions. He is empowered to act as a conciliator between citizens and the Community administration and can, if appropriate, refer a case to the EP. Every citizen of the Union has the right to write to the EU institutions, including the Ombudsman, in their own language and to receive a reply in their own language, which is assumed to be one of the 12 official languages. (There are now 23 official languages following recent enlargements.)

Three pillars

The **TEU** makes the point that the Community is built on three pillars, like a temple. The first pillar is the European Community as it now exists, the second refers to home affairs and justice, and the third to a common foreign and security policy. It should be noted that these two latter areas of policy are intergovernmental bodies and are not covered by the voting procedures in the Council of Ministers or as binding on Member States as other areas of **EC Treaty** policy. However, with the Treaty requirement for Member States to work together within a common position the decisions of these intergovernmental bodies are important. The European Commission is associated with the work of these bodies and the European Parliament is kept informed.

The home affairs and justice policy includes policies on asylum, drugs, refugees and terrorism. It is claimed that with the completion of the internal market and the removal of border controls, there has to be common European Community approach to these problems. The co-operation on justice and home affairs introduced by the **Maastricht Treaty** is to be incorporated into the Community by the creation of an "area for freedom, security and justice" by the **Treaty of Amsterdam**. This will be achieved over a period of five years, although under specific protocols the UK, Ireland and Demark are excluded from this development. The object is to make it easier for European citizens and nationals of non-member countries to move freely, while at the same time building up effective co-operation on border controls, asylum and immigration matters and the fight against international crime. This has been achieved by the incorporation of the Schengen Convention 1990 into the **EC Treaty**. Thus only police and judicial co-operation will remain under the third pillar, but to which the **Treaty of Amsterdam** now adds "preventing and combating of racism and xenophobia".

A common foreign and security policy (CFSP) was in its infancy in the original **TEU** and the Commission and the Council wished to establish the machinery for "joint action". The reality of the post-Yugoslavia disintegration showed that this needed amendment, with the aim of providing an effective and coherent external policy. The **Treaty of Amsterdam** introduced more efficient decision-making based on qualified majority voting and the safeguard of "constructive abstention". This is designed to improve the ability of the EU to defend its interest on the international stage. The post of High Representative for the common foreign and security policy has been created to resolve some of the problems with the CFSP by providing continuity. Lastly, the common commercial policy is also extended to include services and intellectual property rights in the new art.133 EC. This will help in negotiations within the World Trade Organisation.

Treaty of Nice

The IGC at Nice in 2000 led to the **Treaty of Nice** being approved in February 2001. Although there were problems in ratification in Ireland these were resolved. The Irish government held a referendum in June 2001, as required by the Irish constitution, but this resulted in a "no" majority. However, in October 2002 another referendum provided a positive response to the **Treaty of Nice**. Therefore all Member States had ratified the Treaty by the end of October 2002.

The main emphasis of the **Treaty of Nice** was to prepare the way for the enlargement of the EU. In 2004 the number of Member States increased to 25 and in 2007 increased to 27. As the result of the political reluctance to grapple with the problem, the institutions have remained largely the same since the time when there were only six Member States, but the impending enlargement concentrated the minds of those heads of government meeting at Nice.

The main implications for the EU institutions arising from the **Treaty of Nice** are:

1. The European Parliament—as a result of the decision to cap the number of MEPs to 732 on enlargement of the existing Member States, with the exception of Germany and Luxembourg, have had the number of elected representatives reduced.
2. The Council of Ministers—from January 1 the system of decision by qualified majority voting will be modified. This will mean that in future a qualified majority will be secured when the number of votes in favour is close to the present threshold of 71 per cent and the majority of Member States vote in favour. In addition a Member State may ask for verification that the qualified majority comprises at least 62 per cent of the total population of the EU. If this is not the case the measure will not be adopted. The policy areas requiring qualified majority voting were also extended.
3. Co-decision procedure—in order for the EU to become more democratic those policy areas that were now to be subject to qualified majority voting in the Council would also give more authority to the European Parliament by making them subject to the co-decision procedure.

4. The Commission—from 2005 onwards the Commission will consist of one Commissioner per Member State. When there are 27 Member States the number of Commissioners will not be one per State, but will be on a rotation system based on the principle of equality. The EU has 27 Member States now and although this should mean that there should be some rotation at the appointment of the next Commission in 2014 there has been some opposition to this, especially from the smaller Member States. The President of the Commission has also been given greater authority to organise the internal administration of the Commission and can request a Commissioner to resign if he has the support of the remainder of the Commissioners to do so.
5. The Court of Justice—with the increasing case load and resulting delays for cases to be heard the impending enlargement would only make this worse, even with the increased number of judges. Therefore, to ease the workload of the Court of Justice the Court of First Instance is allowed to receive requests for preliminary rulings in certain specific areas. For the latter's workload to be reduced there will be a number of specialist chambers or panels to take over the jurisdiction for staff cases and possibly some aspects of intellectual property.
6. Closer co-operation—some believed that this will lead to a two-speed Community but the **Treaty of Amsterdam** allowed for the possibility for a number of Member States to establish a closer co-operation between themselves but within the framework of the Treaty. The **Treaty of Nice** has extended this within the second pillar of common foreign and security policy. A minimum of eight Member States is needed to form a closer co-operation. The veto mechanism to stop this closer co-operation has been abolished as each Member State now has the right to refer the matter to the European Council. If the matter comes within the EC pillar of the EU the European Parliament must give its assent to the development.

Convention on the future of Europe

At Nice there was a "Declaration on the Future of the Union", which was followed up in December 2001 by the Laeken Declaration. The result was that the European Council decided to convene a Convention on the Future of Europe. The task of this Convention was to consider the key issues arising from the EU's future development and to try to identify the various possible responses. The membership of the Convention was drawn from the EU institutions and the national parliaments and governments. The Convention presented a draft Constitutional Treaty that was signed by the heads of government in October 2004 but it has not come into force because all Member States did not ratify it. Although some Member States did ratify the

Treaty by Parliamentary procedure the referendums in France and the Netherlands in May 2005 rejected the Treaty. The Treaty has become academic even though it included some important developments in respect to the appointment of a full-time President of the Council and more involvement of national parliaments, which were seen by some commentators as ways of dealing with the "democratic deficit" suffered by the EU. An attempt to resurrect some parts of the **Constitutional Treaty** was made in the **Reform Treaty,** which was an amending treaty and did not replace the previous Treaties. This attempt has too foundered on a referendum held in June 2008 by the Irish government, as required by the Irish Constitution. Some attempts have been made to put pressure on Ireland to hold another referendum to pass the Treaty, as it did in 2002 for the **Nice Treaty**. However, this does seem to be politically impossible until after the next general election in Ireland and would be opposed by some even then.

The Lisbon Treaty

The **Constitutional Treaty** did not become law because it was never ratified by all the Member States. However, the necessary ratification by each Member State was scuppered when referenda in France and the Netherlands voted against it. A "period of reflection" was established so that each Member State could carry out a broad debate. The subsequent **Treaty of Lisbon** was not going to be subject to the need for referenda in Member States, with the exception of Ireland where such a popular vote is required under their constitution. In June 2008 the Irish Republic had voted against ratifying the **Treaty of Lisbon**. This was not the only Member State which had encountered delays in the ratification of the Treaty as Germany, the Czech Republic and Poland all had problems. Although Poland did ratify the Treaty if the goals of the **Treaty of Lisbon** were to be achieved ratification had to be accomplished in all 27 Member States.

In December 2008 the concerns of the Irish people were set out by the Irish Prime Minister to the European Council which agreed that provided the **Treaty of Lisbon** did come into force these concerns would be met. On October 2, 2009 the Irish people voted by 67.1 per cent to 32.9 per cent in favour of ratifying the **Treaty of Lisbon.** The German Constitutional Court gave a ruling in June 2009 that the **Treaty of Lisbon** complied with the German Constitution but some aspects of the "accompanying laws" would require further national legislation. This was achieved by September 2009 allowing Germany to ratify the Treaty. At the European Council meeting at the end of October 2009 the concerns of the President of the Czech Republic were settled by agreement for action to be taken at the conclusion of the next **Accession Treaty** by way of protocols annexed to it. To satisfy the Czech President's concern these protocols will contain the statement that "competences not conferred upon the Union in the Treaties remain with the Member States" and also add the Czech Republic to Poland and the UK as countries exempt from the Charter of Fundamental Rights.

On December 1, 2009 the **Treaty of Lisbon** finally came into force and the challenge that the European Union had set itself in the Laeken Declaration had finally been achieved.

Revision Checklist

You should now know and understand:

- the main changes brought about by the **Treaty of Lisbon** with the two elements of the **TEU** and the **TFEU**
- the issues developed by the **Treaty of Amsterdam** and why they were considered important
- the three pillars of the **Maastricht Treaty**
- the main points of the **Treaty of Nice**
- the background to the Convention on the future of Europe
- the problems with the proposed **Constitutional Treaty** resulting in it not being ratified
- the **Reform Treaty** and the difficulties it is encountering

The European Convention on Human Rights

13

INTRODUCTION

For many there is confusion when the term European law is used in so many different ways. Sometimes the law being described has nothing directly to do with the European Union. The main example of this is in relation to human rights. Although all the Member States are signatories of the European Convention on Human Rights this is a separate organisation based upon the Council of Europe. This chapter attempts to deal with this confusion by explaining the key elements of the European Convention.

There is always confusion about the relationship between the EU and the European Law dealing with human rights. The media often compound the problem by referring to the European Court without recording the fact that they are referring to the court adjudicating on this convention and not the European Court of Justice of the EU. This chapter is intended to clarify the distinction.

Following the atrocities of the Second World War, there was an impetus for an agreement directed at protecting the individual rights of people in Europe. The European Convention on Human Rights was drafted in 1949 and was influenced by the UN Declaration of Human Rights adopted in 1948. It has been extended by a number of protocols since then. All the Member States of the EU are parties to the Convention.

The UK was a signatory to the Convention in 1950 and it came into force in 1953. The Convention is binding in international law. However, some legal systems treat international law differently from national or domestic law, i.e. depending upon whether a Dualist or Monist approach is taken (see Ch.4, p.36). Thus the UK, as a dualist system, had to specifically legislate with the **Human Rights Act 1998** to make the Convention available in UK courts.

Human rights machinery

The original human rights machinery consisted of the Commission of Human Rights, which received and examined complaints about the infringement of human rights, and the European Court of Human Rights, which adjudicated on cases which were referred to it by the Commission. There is also the

Committee of Ministers of the Council of Europe, which consists of the Foreign Ministers of the High Contracting Parties.

The increasing case-load prompted a reform of the Convention supervisory machinery. The outcome of the debate was the decision to abolish the Commission and create a single full-time Court. This Court is composed of 41 judges, which is equivalent to the number of Contracting States. The judges are elected by the Parliamentary Assembly of the Council of Europe for a term of six years, with half retiring every three years. The judges sit on the Court in their individual capacity and do not represent any State. Committees of three judges sit to carry out the filtering work formerly carried out by the Commission. The Court sits in chambers of seven judges, although in exceptional circumstances it may sit as a Grand Chamber consisting of 17. Where the Court finds that there has been a breach of the Convention, it has the power to order the offending State to make just compensation. If changes are necessary to domestic legislation, the offending state is free to determine what these should be in order to comply with its obligations under the Convention.

RIGHT OF INDIVIDUAL PETITION

Although initially the purpose of the Convention was directed at preventing large scale infringements of human rights by States which were party to it, the right of individual petition became effective on July 5, 1955. The UK recognised the right of individual petition in 1966. It is this right of individual petition that has given rise to the bulk of the cases coming before the Commission. This change of emphasis has led to the Convention being seen as a bulwark against specific infringements of human rights rather than large-scale violations.

Applications can be admitted from individual persons, non-governmental organisations or groups of individuals provided that the alleged violation concerns them directly. The application can only be brought against a Contracting Party to the Convention, i.e. a government or its agents. They cannot be brought against private individuals or bodies whose acts do not entail the responsibility of a Contracting Party.

As a "dualist" system the Convention did not become part of domestic law within the UK when the UK signed the Convention. However, as with other international treaty obligations, the Convention was applicable in the interpretation of statute law. This is based on the generally recognised principle of construction that Parliament does not intend to legislate contrary to the UK's international obligations. The House of Lords has indicated that where the law is either unclear or ambiguous, or concerns an issue not yet ruled on, the courts ought to consider the implications of the Convention (*Derbyshire CC v Times Newspapers Ltd* [1992] 3 W.L.R. 28). However, this situation has been superseded by the **Human Rights Act 1998.**

LEGISLATION HIGHLIGHTER

Human Rights Act 1998

The aim of introducing the **Human Rights Act 1998** (HRA) is to make more directly accessible the rights which the British people already enjoy under the European Convention on Human Rights. The Act will thus obviate the need to take human rights issues to Strasbourg.

Section 2 of the **HRA** requires courts and tribunals to take into account the "Strasbourg jurisprudence", i.e. previous decisions of the European Human Rights Court or the European Commission on Human Rights before its abolition. However, it is not just the courts and tribunals that will be affected, as the Act requires a whole new culture to be developed by public authorities and government bodies. Section 3(1) states that "so far as it is possible to do so, primary legislation must be read and given effect in a way which is compatible with the Convention rights". It is no wonder that the implementation date for the Act has been put back to allow public bodies, government departments and the courts to review their procedures and train their staff.

Section 8(1) gives the courts wide powers, including the award of damages to injured parties:

> "In relation to any act (or proposed act) of a public authority which the court finds is (or would be) unlawful, it may grant such relief or remedy, or make such order, within its powers as it considers just and appropriate".

The Convention and the EU

In 1976 the Commission ruled out the necessity of accession by the Community to the Convention, but it did call for a joint declaration by the three political institutions affirming their commitment to fundamental rights. This Joint Declaration was made in 1977. However, in 1979 the Commission did formally propose accession to the Council and subsequently the European Parliament made statements supporting this development. However, the ECJ in its Opinion No.2/94 stated that as Community law stood the EC had no competence to accede to the Convention. In its Opinion the ECJ pointed out that although the original treaties made no specific mention of fundamental rights, the Court had in its judgments upheld the protection by way of general principles of Community law. Specific mention has also been made of the Convention in the Preamble to both the **SEA** and the **TEU**. This has been repeated in the **Treaty of Amsterdam** which amends **art.6 TEU** so as to reaffirm the principle of respect for human rights and fundamental freedoms. There is also the Charter of Fundamental Rights of the European Union, agreed at the Nice IGC, but which does not at present have legal force. It reaffirms the commitment of the EU to the principles of the European Convention and other international obligations that affect the freedom of the individual. The unratified **Constitutional Treaty 2004** included the Charter and so would have made it legally binding. However, the ECJ began to take the Charter into account in appropriate situations as illustrated by the case below.

KEY CASE

Bosphorous Airways v Ireland (2005)

In the European Court of Human Rights case of *Bosphorous Airways v Ireland* (2005) the Turkish airline brought an action because the Irish authorities had seized its plane. An action had been brought under EU law but the ECJ had found that the Irish authorities were applying a directly applicable law, **Regulation 990/93**. Having failed in the ECJ the airline brought this action before the ECHR claiming that the impounding of their aircraft was contrary to the European Convention on Human Rights. The ECHR held that the protection of fundamental rights by EC law was generally equivalent to that of the Convention system. Therefore there was a presumption that by enforcing the Regulation Ireland did not depart from the Convention as the Irish court was bound by the EU law. However, the ECHR left open the possibility that in circumstances where the Member State was exercising discretion when applying EU law they may be infringing the Convention. This would seem to put the onus on the Member State to consider its action in the light of the Convention when exercising any discretion it has under EU law.

The Treaty of Lisbon

Article 6 **TEU** specifically states that the EU will accede to the European Convention on Human Rights. The original European Convention was drafted on the basis that only individual states would accede, but Protocol 14 to the ECHR contains a provision which would allow an organisation like the EU to accede. Negotiations are on-going and there are some difficulties that have arisen. All 47 existing parties to the ECHR have to agree to the EU acceding and there is some concern amongst non-EU parties that the EU with its present 27 Member States will nominate the proceedings of the Convention.

Revision Checklist

You should now know and understand:

- **the background to the European Convention of Human Rights**
- **the human rights machinery**
- **the right of the individual to petition**
- **the Human Rights Act 1998**
- **the Charter of Fundamental Rights**
- **the relationship between EC law and the case law of the ECHR**
- **the relationship between the ECJ and the ECHR**

Handy Hints and Useful Websites

HANDY HINTS

When you have to answer a question on European law you should approach it on the same basis as any other legal question. In the introduction you should set the context of your answer by demonstrating that you understand the relevance or importance of the topic.

- **For example if the question is on the "democratic deficit" of the EU you should explain what you understand the term to mean and the importance it has for the EU which is said to be based on democratic principles.**
- **You can then go on in the next paragraphs to review the main institutions of the EU and examine their democratic credentials. The European Parliament has been directly elected since 1979 but the Council of Ministers is not. The accountability of the Council is towards the national parliaments. Is this a form of indirect democratic control?**
- **The European Commission has been given a great deal of authority by the Treaties but it is appointed and not elected.**
- **The European Council is now recognised as a formal EU institution but these heads of government represent their Member States. They have been democratically elected but not for this role.**
- **In the final paragraph you can bring the main points of your answer together by looking at what has been done to deal with this deficit such as giving more authority and influence to the European Parliament by the greater use of the ordinary legislative procedure which is an extension of the co-decision procedure introduced by the Maastricht Treaty and the European Parliament's involvement in the appointment of the Commission.**

USEFUL WEBSITES

Some very good web sites for EU materials are:

The main site is http://europa.eu where you will find useful information on the history and enlargement of the EU but perhaps more importantly the Treaties and other documents like Regulations and Directives. It also provides links to the main institutions.

The European Court of Justice website http://curia.eu is where there is information about the cases reported in the Press Releases, law reports from the Court of Justice and the General Court, information about the personnel and jurisdictions of the courts. It is also possible to access the cases via http://www.bailii.org/ which is the web site for the British and Irish Legal Information Institute.

The European Commission website can be accessed via www.europa.eu or you can go direct via http://ec.europa.eu/index_en.htm. Here you will find information about the individual policies of the Commission as well as background information on the Commissioners and proposals for future policies. You might find it useful to look at the specific web sites for particular policy areas such as competition: http://ec.europa.eu/competition/index_en.html.

The European Parliament has a useful site which is getting better at providing information about debates and the involvement of the EP in passing legislation. It also provides details about the working of the EP and the individual MEPs: http://www.europarl.europa.eu.

The Council of the EU provides information about the Council of Ministers and the European Council—http://europa.eu/about-eu/institutions-bodies/council-eu/index_en.htm.

For a viewpoint from the British Government plus other resources the Britain in the European Union web pages of the Foreign and Commonwealth Office are generally good—http://www.fco.gov.uk/en/global-issues/european-union/.

A valuable resource is the website for the European Union Committees of the House of Lords. There are a number of Committees covering various areas of EU policy but a good general one is the European Union Committee on Law and Institutions—http://www.parliament.uk/parliamentary_committees/lords_s_comm_e.cfm.

Index

This index has been prepared using Sweet and Maxwell's Legal Taxonomy. Main index entries conform to keywords provided by the Legal Taxonomy except where references to specific documents or non-standard terms (denoted by quotation marks) have been included. These keywords provide a means of identifying similar concepts in other Sweet & Maxwell publications and online services to which keywords from the Legal Taxonomy have been applied. Readers may find some minor differences between terms used in the text and those which appear in the index.
Suggestions to **taxonomy@sweetandmaxwell.co.uk**.

(*all references are to page number*)